THE ARAB-ISRAELI CONFLICT

Volume I: Readings

The Arab-Israeli Conflict

Volume I: Readings

EDITED BY

JOHN NORTON MOORE

SPONSORED BY THE

American Society of International Law

Princeton University Press
Princeton, New Jersey

Acknowledgments

THE PRINCIPAL PURPOSE of this reader on the Arab-Israeli conflict is to promote greater understanding of one of the most persistent and explosive challenges to world order of our time. It has been reassuring to see the enthusiasm from all quarters with which the project has been greeted. The very enthusiasm of the response, however, makes it impossible to thank adequately all who assisted in the preparation of the reader. Among the special debts which stand out, I should particularly like to thank the authors and publishers who made this project possible by generously giving permission to reprint their work and the American Society of International Law under whose auspices the reader has been published. A list of contributors and a list of individual permissions appear in the back of each volume.

In selecting readings and documents for inclusion, every effort has been made to achieve balance on the issues and presentation of the principal viewpoints. To facilitate this balance and to ensure inclusion of as wide as possible a range of materials, a draft table of contents and introduction were circulated to the members of the American Society of International Law Panel on the Role of International Law in Civil Wars as well as a number of other scholars and statesmen familiar with the issues. Responses to these drafts were most helpful and were in large part responsible for the growth of the reader from two to three volumes. I regret that even in three volumes it was not possible to include all of the many excellent suggestions. I am particularly grateful for the suggestions of Professor M. Cherif Bassiouni of De Paul University College of Law, Dr. Yehuda Z. Blum, Senior Lecturer in International Law at the Hebrew University of Jerusalem, Stephen M. Boyd, the Assistant Legal Adviser for Near Eastern and South Asian Affairs of the Department of State, Professor John Claydon of the Queens University Faculty of Law, Professor Irwin Cotler of the Osgoode Hall Law School, His Excellency Dr. Abdullah El-Erian, Ambassador of the United Arab Republic to France and formerly Deputy Permanent Representative of the United Arab Republic to the United Nations, Professor Roger Fisher of the Harvard Law School, Burhan W. Hammad, the Deputy Permanent Observer of the League of Arab States to the United Nations, Dr. Rosalyn Higgins of the Royal Institute of International Affairs, Professor Majid Khadduri of The

Johns Hopkins School of Advanced International Studies, Professor W. T. Mallison, Jr., of George Washington University National Law Center, Professor Rouhollah K. Ramazani of the University of Virginia Department of Government and Foreign Affairs, Professor Michael Reisman of the Yale Law School, Stephen M. Schwebel, Executive Vice President of the American Society of International Law, Dr. Amos Shapira, Senior Lecturer in Law at the Tel Aviv University, Professor Julius Stone of the University of Sydney Faculty of Law, and Dr. Yaacov S. Zemach, Lecturer in Law at the Hebrew University of Jerusalem.

A very special debt is owed the American Society of International Law for its commitment to scholarly integrity and the free interchange of ideas, which continues to serve as an inspiration. I should especially like to thank Stephen M. Schwebel, the Executive Vice President of the Society, for his early encouragement and continuing assistance. The members of the Society's Civil War Panel have also assisted with helpful suggestions throughout the project. The members of the Panel are: Thomas Ehrlich, Dean of the Stanford Law School, Richard A. Falk, Milbank Professor of International Law and Practice at Princeton University and past Chairman of the Panel, Tom J. Farer, Professor of Law at Rutgers University, Edwin Brown Firmage, Professor of Law at the University of Utah, Wolfgang Friedmann, Professor of Law at Columbia University and Chairman of the Panel, G. W. Haight of the New York Bar, Eliot D. Hawkins of the New York Bar, Brunson MacChesney, Professor of Law at Northwestern University and former President of the American Society of International Law, Myres S. McDougal, Sterling Professor of Law at Yale and former President of the American Society of International Law, John Norton Moore, Professor of Law and Director of the Graduate Program at the University of Virginia School of Law and Rapporteur of the Panel, Stephen M. Schwebel, Executive Vice President of the American Society of International Law and Professor of International Law at the School of Advanced International Studies of The Johns Hopkins University, Louis B. Sohn, Bemis Professor of International Law at Harvard and formerly Counselor on International Law of the Department of State, Howard J. Taubenfeld, Professor of Law at Southern Methodist University, Lawrence R. Velvel, Professor of Law at the Catholic University of America, and Burns H. Weston, Professor of Law at the University of Iowa.

John E. Claydon, now Assistant Professor of International Law at Queens University, helped greatly in compiling the reader while he was my research assistant at the University of Virginia, and I am much indebted to him. Mr. Stephen M. Dichter, Mrs. Karen M. Yates and Mr. Frederick S. Tipson also helped in innumerable ways as research assistants. Sir John Wheeler-Bennett aided in obtaining from the British Museum photostats of a draft of the Balfour Declaration and the original letter to Lord Rothschild, which have contributed a touch of historical excitement to the project. Finally, I wish to thank Sanford G. Thatcher, Social Science Editor of the Princeton University Press, for his continuing assistance throughout the project.

The selection of readings and documents in these volumes does not imply endorsement of any article or position by the American Society of International Law. Nor does assistance in the preparation of the reader or authorship by a government official imply official endorsement either of the reader or of the viewpoint expressed by the author. The final responsibility for the reader and any errors and infelicities are my own.

JOHN NORTON MOORE*

* This volume was completed for the American Society of International Law in the editor's capacity as Professor of International Law at the University of Virginia School of Law. The views expressed do not necessarily represent the views of the United States Government or any Department or Agency thereof.

Contents

Volume One

Volume Two

Volume Three

DOCUMENTS RELATING TO THE
ARAB-ISRAELI CONFLICT

II. Establishment of the State of Israel and the 1948 War: 1947-1949

III. From Armistice to War: 1949-1956

D. *The Status of Jerusalem*

THE ARAB-ISRAELI CONFLICT

Volume I: Readings

Introduction

INTERNATIONAL LAW AND THE CONTINUING
MIDDLE EAST CRISIS

THIS IS an introduction to Volumes One and Two in a three-volume compilation of readings and documents on the Arab-Israeli conflict published under the auspices of the American Society of International Law. Volumes One and Two bring together a selection of readings on the principal issues and alternatives for their settlement. Volume Three brings together the principal documents relating to the conflict. The American Society of International Law is an association of American and foreign international legal scholars and practitioners from more than ninety countries. It is not affiliated with any government or ideology other than a commitment to the settlement of international disputes on the basis of law and justice and the free exchange of ideas to that end.

A principal purpose of this compilation is to promote wider understanding of one of the most persistent and explosive international problems of our time. United States Assistant Secretary of State Joseph J. Sisco has warned that "the Middle East . . . holds greater . . . risks for world peace than any other area in the world." The warning should be heeded. The Arab-Israeli conflict is one that has defied solution since the commencement of the British Mandate for Palestine in 1922, and since the termination of that Mandate in 1948 it has precipitated three wars—once in 1948, again in 1956, and still again in 1967. Yet in the aftermath of the third Arab-Israeli War of June 1967 the conflict has become even more volatile. The main factors responsible for this increased volatility have been a more active Soviet and American involvement, particularly an increased sophistication of weapons systems on both sides, the growth of the Palestine liberation organizations, the joining of New Arab states in the conflict, the destabilizing effect of the withdrawal of the United Nations Emergency Force, and the territorial dislocations of the Six-Day War. Events during the past five years, including the Egyptian "war of attrition" against Israeli positions in the Suez Canal area, Israeli bombing raids against Egypt, the introduction in an operational capacity of Soviet military personnel into Egypt and their confused withdrawal two years later, the internal

conflict in Jordan in which Syria militarily intervened on behalf of Palestinian insurgents and the United States considered counterintervention,
the hijackings of commercial aircraft in international flight by the Popular Front for the Liberation of Palestine, and the continued pattern of
terrorist attack and Israeli response, have underscored the crisis proportions of the Middle Eastern threat.

The Arab-Israeli conflict, like all major world-order disputes, has its
own unique background and issues. Efforts at containment and conciliation of the conflict will have a better chance for success to the extent
that they are informed on these issues. Sometimes, of course, apparent
issues may conceal more fundamental disagreement. But usually there
is at least a sufficient relation between what the parties claim and their
perceptions about the dispute to make an understanding of competing
claims useful in efforts at settlement. An understanding of opposing
arguments is also useful in shedding parochial identifications and in
recognizing reasonable and unreasonable contentions in one's own and
opposing positions. In appraising complex issues of world order there
is no escape from the necessity for in-depth familiarity with the circumstances of the conflict and the competing claims of the belligerents.

A second purpose of this compilation is to facilitate access to a range
of scholarly readings in the international legal literatures and to demonstrate the utility of an international legal perspective in the analysis
and settlement of major world-order disputes. Although each world-
order dispute is unique, each is subject to appraisal against a common
backdrop of international norms and institutions for the management
of conflict. A substantial body of international law, representing centuries of thought and development from at least St. Thomas Aquinas
to the United Nations, is specialized to the mitigation and appraisal of
international conflict. The international legal literature which builds
on this tradition is a rich source of normative analysis and suggestion
for alternative policies. As such, an international legal perspective
should consistently be taken into account in decisions relating to major
issues of world order. One difficulty in encouraging greater consideration of an international legal perspective, however, has been the
general unfamiliarity with and difficulty of access to the relevant
literature. By providing convenient access to the best of the legal literature and the relevant legal documents it is hoped that this compilation will in some modest measure increase the role of international law
in decisions relating to the issues of world order it develops.

It is also hoped that this compilation will serve as a catalyst for further development of a range of important international legal problems raised by the Arab-Israeli conflict. Among other issues in need of development are the principle of self-determination, the law of reprisal in settings of continued belligerency, the legal effects of cease-fire and armistice agreements, the meaning of "no acquisition of territory by war" and its interrelation with the Charter principle permitting defense against an armed attack, the identification and utilization of international straits and waterways, the constitutional nature of and most effective structure for United Nations peacekeeping forces, the constitutional authority of the General Assembly, Security Council, and Secretary-General in recommending, guaranteeing, and enforcing plans for settlement, the structure of international fact-finding machinery, criteria for appraisal of the obligation to pursue peaceful settlement of international disputes, and the perennial problem of distinguishing lawful from unlawful coercion. Many of the readings brought together in these volumes make substantial contributions to the theory of international law in one or more of these areas.

A Brief Historical Overview of the Arab-Israeli Conflict[1]

The Arab-Israeli conflict has been one of the most persistent world-order disputes of the contemporary international system. There have been three Arab-Israeli wars in the past twenty-three years, and until the cease-fire of August 7, 1970, the level of hostilities at Suez was such as to suggest a description of it as "the fourth Arab-Israeli War."[2] Accordingly, it may be helpful in assimilating the range of readings in this volume to set out briefly a historical overview of the conflict. The reader should be careful, however, not to uncritically accept a historical framework as the only or even the most important framework for appraisal. The United Nations Charter embodies the judgment that unilateral coercion against the territorial integrity or political inde-

---

[1] For an excellent summary of the history of the Arab-Israeli conflict through July 1967 and an introduction to the United Nations role in the conflict, see LOUIS B. SOHN, CASES ON UNITED NATIONS LAW 416-74, 527-634 (2nd rev. edn., 1967). This introductory overview draws heavily on Professor Sohn's work.

[2] The level of continuing hostilities has been such that some observers on both sides view the conflict as one war. Whether it is viewed as one, three, or four wars, the essential points about the conflict are that there have been three to four outbreaks of relatively more intense coercion during its history and that claims to continuing belligerency should be subjected to appraisal under the United Nations Charter and other applicable legal regimes.

pendence of any state may not be used even to redress circumstances which are perceived by the belligerents as major wrongs. Instead, major unilateral coercion may be lawfully employed only in defense and only "until the Security Council has taken measures necessary to maintain international peace and security." Similarly, the Charter focus on fundamental human rights and self-determination of peoples is most meaningfully a focus on present rather than past circumstances.

The latter part of the nineteenth and early part of the twentieth century witnessed a dramatic growth in both Arab and Jewish nationalism. Arab nationalism sought independent Arab states free from Turkish and later British and French control. Jewish nationalism sought a homeland for the Jews. Both were destined to collide over the territory of Palestine. During World War I Great Britain made a series of ambiguous and, by some interpretations, contradictory promises to both Arabs and Jews in support of their national aspirations. In the Balfour Declaration, a letter of November 2, 1917, from Lord Balfour, the British Foreign Secretary, to Lord Rothschild, the British government announced that it viewed "with favour the establishment in Palestine of a national home for the Jewish people. . . ." It went on to say, however, ". . . it being clearly understood that nothing shall be done which may prejudice the civil and religious rights of existing non-Jewish communities in Palestine. . . ." The British militarily occupied Palestine during 1917-18, and by an agreement between the Allied Powers Palestine was placed under British Mandate. The complementary terms of the Balfour Declaration were incorporated in the British Mandate for Palestine, which was confirmed by the Council of the League of Nations on July 24, 1922. At the commencement of the Mandate there were approximately 486,000 Moslems, 84,000 Jews, and 71,000 Christians in Palestine.[3]

---

[3] The Report of the United Nations Special Committee on Palestine provides perhaps the most detailed figures. It states that in 1922 there were 486,177 Moslems, 83,790 Jews, 71,464 Christians, and 7,616 others in Palestine. See the *Report to the General Assembly of the United Nations Special Committee on Palestine*, 2 U.N. GAOR, Supp. 11, at 11, U.N. DOC. A/364 (Sept. 3, 1947). Some other sources give a slightly higher figure for Moslems or Arabs in Palestine at the commencement of the Mandate. Professor Quincy Wright maintains that the 1922 population of Palestine consisted of "600,000 Moslems, 73,000 Christians and 84,000 Jews." Wright, "The Middle East Crisis," in THE MIDDLE EAST: PROSPECT FOR PEACE, BACKGROUND PAPERS AND PROCEEDINGS OF THE THIRTEENTH HAMMARSKJÖLD FORUM 1, 4 (The Association of the Bar of the City of New York, 1969). See also L. SOHN, CASES ON UNITED NATIONS LAW 417 (2nd rev. edn., 1967).

The ambiguity of the Balfour Declaration and League Mandate and the factual setting to which they were applied led to increasing strife between Arab and Jewish communities in Palestine, each of which interpreted the ambiguities to support its vision of the future of Palestine. Jews interpreted the mandatory obligation as leading toward a Jewish state. Arabs, on the other hand, interpreted the obligation as creating only a Jewish National Home within Palestine. These differences and resentment of continued Jewish immigration and settlement in Palestine provoked Arab riots in Palestine in 1920-21, 1929, 1933, and 1936-38. A Royal Commission chaired by Lord Peel was appointed in 1936 in response to the Arab revolt earlier that year. Its report in 1937 contended that the Arab desire for national independence and their opposition to the establishment of a Jewish National Home in Palestine were the principal causes of the rioting. Finding the Arab and Jewish positions irreconcilable under the terms of the Mandate, it recommended the partition of Palestine into separate Arab and Jewish states. The Peel Commission plan was opposed by the Arabs, and although the Jewish Agency approved the fundament of partition, it opposed the particulars of the Peel plan. With the opposition of both Arabs and Jews, the plan was not adopted.

Following the failure of the Peel plan and a London Conference of 1939 called to work out agreement between the parties, the British Government adopted a more restrictive policy toward Jewish immigration and announced its policy to be the creation of an independent Palestine State within ten years. The Jewish community opposed this shift in British policy, which had been announced in a White Paper of May 17, 1939, particularly in view of events in Germany, which lent a special urgency to efforts for the establishment of a Jewish National Home.

The assumption of power by the Nazi Party in Germany in 1933 and the subsequent genocide of European Jews during World War II prompted Jews to immigrate to Palestine in ever greater numbers, particularly after the end of the war in 1945. As Jewish immigration accelerated following the war, conflicts between the Arab and Jewish communities and the Jewish community and restrictive British immigration policy gave rise to increased terrorism and civil strife. During this postwar period, several additional British proposals for a compromise plan were rejected by both sides.

By April 2, 1947, the British Government had had enough of the situation and requested the General Assembly "to make recommendations, under Article 10 of the Charter, concerning the future government of Palestine. . . ." The General Assembly considered the British request at a Special Session of the Assembly held in 1947. During the session the General Committee of the Assembly refused to include on the agenda a request by five Arab states that the Assembly also consider "the termination of the Mandate over Palestine and the declaration of its independence." Subsequently, the General Assembly appointed a Special Committee on Palestine to investigate and report to the Assembly. The Assembly also called on all governments and peoples to refrain from the use of force pending action by the General Assembly on the report of the Special Committee.

In August 1947 the majority of the United Nations Special Committee on Palestine recommended a plan of partition with economic union. The plan was to partition Palestine into an Arab state, a Jewish state, and an international trusteeship for the City of Jerusalem, with some degree of economic and other union between the successor states and Jerusalem. The Special Committee plan was approved by the General Assembly with only minor changes. The vote on November 29, 1947, was 33 to 13 with 10 abstentions. Although the Jewish Agency accepted the plan, it was rejected by the Arab states, which denied the authority of the General Assembly to partition Palestine. An Arab-supported draft resolution to refer the legality of the partition plan to the International Court of Justice was rejected by the General Assembly *Ad Hoc* Committee on the Palestinian Question.

After General Assembly approval of the partition plan, disorder and terrorism in Palestine grew rapidly. Despite this accelerated collapse of order, the Security Council refused to take action on the recommendations of the General Assembly concerning implementation of the plan. On March 5, 1948, however, the Security Council appealed "to all governments and peoples . . . to take all possible action to prevent or reduce such disorders as are now occurring in Palestine," and on April 1 the Council called upon "the Arab and Jewish armed groups in Palestine to cease acts of violence immediately." Subsequently, on April 17, the Council called upon "all persons and organizations in Palestine and especially upon the Arab Higher Committee and the Jewish Agency" to cease military activities immediately. On April 23 the Security Council established a Truce Commission for Palestine, and in

May the General Assembly adopted a resolution authorizing the appointment of a United Nations Mediator in Palestine. Count Folke Bernadotte of Sweden, then Vice-President of the International Red Cross, was appointed on May 20 as the United Nations Mediator.

The Palestine Mandate was terminated at midnight on May 14, 1948. The Jewish community immediately proclaimed the State of Israel within the territorial boundaries of the partition plan, and the new state was quickly recognized by a number of states, including the United States and the Soviet Union. Almost immediately Egypt, Syria, Transjordan, Lebanon, and other Arab states intervened, in the words of a cablegram of May 15 from the Secretary-General of the League of Arab States to the United Nations Secretary-General, "to restore law and order and to prevent disturbances prevailing in Palestine from spreading into their territories and to check further bloodshed." The first Arab-Israeli War had begun. A Security Council call for a four-week cease-fire produced a short-lived truce which went into effect on June 11, 1948. The Arab states rejected a Security Council appeal for an extension of the cease-fire, and, following the resumption of hostilities, Israel secured substantially greater territory than it was initially allotted under the 1947 partition plan. A Security Council Resolution of July 15, 1948, determined that "the situation in Palestine constitutes a threat to the peace" and ordered the governments concerned "to desist from further military action." Both sides complied with the resolution, and an uneasy cease-fire began on July 18, 1948. Following negotiations on the Island of Rhodes with respect to the settlement with Egypt and Jordan and in no-man's land at the front itself with respect to the settlement with Syria and Lebanon, armistice agreements went into force between Israel and Egypt, Lebanon, Jordan and Syria in February, March, April, and July of 1949 respectively. The Armistice Agreements were concluded through the mediation of Dr. Ralph J. Bunche, who had been appointed Count Bernadotte's successor after the Count was assassinated by Jewish terrorists in the summer of 1948. Under the terms of the Armistice Agreements a United Nations Truce Supervision Organization was to observe and maintain the Armistice arrangements. Though little noticed, UNTS observers continued to function in the Syrian and Suez sectors even after the withdrawal in 1967 of the United Nations Emergency Force. On May 11, 1949, Israel was admitted to membership in the United Nations.

One of the tragic consequences of the 1948 war was the displacement of a large number of refugees. It has been estimated that there were approximately 726,000 Arab refugees who fled from Israel during the first Arab-Israeli War.[4] In December of 1948 the General Assembly established a Conciliation Commission for Palestine which was charged with assisting the parties to achieve a final settlement, with preparing a proposal for an international regime for the Jerusalem area under effective United Nations control, and with facilitating the repatriation, resettlement and economic and social rehabilitation of refugees. The Resolution which created the Conciliation Commission provided with respect to the refugees that "the refugees wishing to return to their homes and live at peace with their neighbors should be permitted to do so at the earliest practicable date, and . . . compensation should be paid for the property of those choosing not to return and for loss of or damage to property which, under principles of international law or in equity, should be made good by the Governments or authorities responsible. . . ."[5] In December 1949 the United Nations Relief and Works Agency (UNRWA) was created to assist in carrying out a relief and works program. UNRWA subsequently assumed responsibility for the refugee assistance programs. Although there have been a number of proposals made by Israel and the Arab states toward solution of the refugee problem, to date it has not been solved. Rather, each successive war, particularly the Six-Day War, has increased the number of refugees. According to the Annual Report of UNRWA, on the eve of the Six-Day War there were 1,344,576 refugees registered with UNRWA and living in the Gaza Strip, Jordan, Lebanon, and Syria.[6] It has been estimated that the Six-Day War created approximately 234,000 new Arab refugees as well as again displacing a substantial number of the earlier refugees.[7]

[4] See Holborn, *The Palestine Arab Refugee Problem*, 23 INT'L JOURNAL 82, 88 (1968).
[5] G.A. Res. 194 (111), U.N. DOC. A/810 at 21 (1948).
[6] See Holborn, *The Palestine Arab Refugee Problem*, 23 INT'L JOURNAL 82, 88 n.9 (1968). Any estimate of the number of refugees is fraught with dangers, including a threshold problem of who is a Palestinian refugee. See *ibid.* at 88-90.
[7] According to a 1967 Report of the Commissioner-General of UNRWA, approximately 100,000 persons who were not previously registered as UNRWA refugees fled from the West Bank to the East Bank, over 99,000 nonregistered persons living in Syria moved northwards and eastwards from the area occupied by Israel, and approximately 35,000 persons moved from the Sinai Peninsula to the United Arab Republic in the months immediately following the June War. In addition, over 116,000 UNRWA-registered refugees were displaced from these areas. See the *Report of the Commissioner-General of the United Nations*

Although Israel regarded the Armistice Agreements of 1949 as creating an obligation to effect transition to a permanent peace, the Arab states did not regard the agreements as a final peace terminating the state of belligerency with Israel. One consequence of this continuing state of belligerency was the imposition by Egypt of restrictions on passage through the Suez Canal of Israeli ships and cargo bound for Israel. In response to these restrictions and the claim to maintain continuing belligerency, on September 1, 1951, the Security Council called upon Egypt to terminate restrictions on the passage of goods through the Suez Canal to Israeli ports and considered that, "since the Armistice regime . . . is of a permanent character, neither party can reasonably assert that it is actively a belligerent. . . ."[8]

Though marred by numerous violations, the Armistice regime prevented major hostilities until 1956. In July 1956 Egypt nationalized the Suez Canal Company. After Egypt rejected the proposals of a London Conference of Canal Users, France and Britain informed the Security Council that the Egyptian action constituted a threat to peace and security. France and Britain were principally concerned with Egyptian nationalization and management of the Canal. Israel was primarily concerned with stepped-up *fedayeen* raids from Gaza and Sinai, intensified raids from Jordan, Egyptian harassment of Israeli shipping in the Strait of Tiran, and a tripartite military alliance concluded on October 23 between Egypt, Syria, and Jordan. On October 29 Israeli armor invaded the Sinai and raced to the Canal and the Southern tip of Sinai at Sharm El-Sheikh. The Israeli strike was supported by a delayed joint French–British airborne attack on the Canal area allegedly to restore the security of the area.

Because of the negative votes of France and Great Britain, both permanent members of the Council, the Security Council was unable to reach agreement on a resolution calling for an immediate cease-fire in this second Arab-Israeli War. This inability to reach agreement because of the negative vote of a permanent member set the stage for a subsequent Council vote on October 31 to summon the first Emergency Special Session of the General Assembly under the machinery of the Uniting for Peace Resolution. Subsequently, the Assembly adopted a

---

Relief and Works Agency for Palestine Refugees in the Near East, 1 July 1966 – 30 June 1967, 22 U.N. GAOR, Supp. 13, at 11-14, U.N. DOC. A/6713 (1967).

[8] 6 U.N. SCOR, 558th meeting, at 2-3, U.N. DOC. 5/2322 (1951).

series of resolutions calling for a cease-fire and return to armistice lines and creating a United Nations Emergency Force in the Middle East (UNEF). Under the combined pressure of the United Nations, the United States, and the Soviet Union, Britain, France, and Israel agreed to a cease-fire and on the arrival of UNEF French and British troops began withdrawing. French and British withdrawal was completed by December 22, 1956. Israeli withdrawal, particularly from Gaza and the strategic Sharm El-Sheikh area which dominated the Strait of Tiran, was slower. After receiving assurance in an *aide-mémoire* of February 11, 1957, that the United States viewed the Gulf of Aqaba and the Strait giving access thereto as international waterways and that it would be prepared "to join with others to secure general recognition of this right," Israeli forces withdrew on March 8, leaving the area in the control of UNEF forces. Since Israel had refused permission for the stationing of UNEF forces on Israeli territory, UNEF forces were stationed solely on Egyptian territory.

Though disturbed by repeated violations and in later years by a pattern of repeated Arab fedayeen raids from the territory of neighboring Arab states followed by larger-scale Israeli reprisal raids, the 1956 cease-fire and UNEF presence contributed to preventing the outbreak of major hostilities for over ten years. In May and June of 1967, however, an escalating series of threats and counterthreats culminating in the withdrawal of UNEF at Egyptian request, Egyptian reimposition of the blockade against Israeli shipping in the Strait of Tiran, and massing of Egyptian forces in Sinai led to the third or "Six-Day" Arab-Israeli War. On June 5, 1967, the Israeli air force attacked Egyptian military airfields. The war quickly enlarged to include Syrian, Jordanian, and other Arab forces, but within six days Israel had occupied large areas of territory including the Gaza Strip, the Sinai, the Golan Heights, East Jerusalem, and the West Bank of Jordan.

For a variety of reasons, including the threat of a Soviet veto, the Security Council was unable to act prior to the Six-Day War. But after the outbreak of fighting the Security Council passed a series of four resolutions from June 6 through June 12 calling for a cease-fire. Shortly thereafter a cease-fire went into effect. During 1967 the General Assembly and the Security Council also passed several resolutions concerning humanitarian assistance to civilians and prisoners of war and calling on Israel not to take unilateral measures to alter the status of the City of Jerusalem. The Security Council later reemphasized, in both 1968 and 1969, its call to Israel not to take measures to change the status of the City of Jerusalem.

After prolonged diplomatic effort, on November 22, 1967, the Security Council unanimously adopted Resolution 242 affirming a package basis for settlement of the Arab-Israeli conflict. The Resolution affirmed "that the fulfillment of Charter principles requires the establishment of a just and lasting peace" which should include "[w]ithdrawal of Israel armed forces from territories occupied in the recent conflict" and "[t]ermination of all claims or states of belligerency and respect for and acknowledgement of the sovereignty, territorial integrity and political independence of every State in the area and their right to live in peace within secure and recognized boundaries free from threats or acts of force." The Resolution also affirmed the necessity "for guaranteeing freedom of navigation through international waterways in the area," "for achieving a just settlement of the refugee problem," and "for guaranteeing the territorial inviolability and political independence of every State in the area, through measures including the establishment of demilitarized zones" and requested "the Secretary-General to designate a Special Representative to . . . maintain contacts with the States concerned in order to promote agreement and assist efforts to achieve a peaceful and accepted settlement in accordance with . . . this resolution." Pursuant to Resolution 242, Secretary-General U Thant appointed Dr. Gunnar Jarring, Swedish Ambassador to the Soviet Union, as his Special Representative. Initial efforts of Dr. Jarring, and subsequent bilateral Soviet–United States and four-power British–French–Soviet–United States talks, failed to produce an agreement within the framework of Resolution 242 acceptable to both Arabs and Israelis.

In the years following the passage of Resolution 242 the cease-fire steadily deteriorated. One incident which illustrated the trend was the Israeli raid on December 28, 1968, on the Beirut International Airport. The precisely executed commando raid resulted in the destruction of thirteen Arab commercial aircraft of an estimated value of approximately $44 million but did not cause loss of life. Israel announced that the raid was in retaliation for an attack two days earlier by members of the Popular Front for the Liberation of Palestine upon an El Al passenger plane in Athens, in which an Israeli passenger had been killed when the airplane was machine-gunned as it was preparing to take off. On December 31 the Security Council unanimously adopted a resolution condemning Israel for the Beirut raid.

Fearing that prolonged Israeli occupation of the territories seized in the Six-Day War would lead to legitimation of the *de facto* borders, President Gamal Abdel Nasser of Egypt announced in the spring of 1969 that the cease-fire with Israel was no longer valid, and thereupon Egyptian armed forces began a "war of attrition" against Israeli defenses along the Suez Canal. Heavy artillery exchanges along the Canal led to an acceleration of air activity, and during January and February of 1970 the Israelis conducted deep penetration bombing raids against targets in Egypt. In response to the raids a secret trip by Nasser to Moscow led to the introduction on Egyptian territory of Soviet SA-3 ground-to-air missiles. During the spring of 1970 the situation deteriorated further with the introduction of Soviet military advisers into Egypt in an operational capacity, an intensification of the war along the Suez Canal, and a rise in the pattern of Palestinian guerrilla raids on Israeli settlements launched from within Jordan and Lebanon and Israeli responses against the guerrilla encampments within those countries.

In June of 1970 United States Secretary of State William P. Rogers negotiated an "at least" 90-day standstill cease-fire between Israel, Egypt, and Jordan, which went into effect on August 7. Under the terms of the agreement between Israel and Egypt, both sides were to "stop all incursions and all firing, on the ground and in the air, across the cease-fire line," and to "refrain from changing the military status quo within zones extending 50 kilometers to the east and the west of the cease-fire line." In order to verify observance, each side was permitted to "rely on its own national means, including reconnaissance aircraft, which will be free to operate without interference up to 10 kilometers from the cease-fire line on its own side of that line."[9] Ambassador Jarring then invited them to take part in discussions opening in New York on August 25. On September 6 Israel informed Dr. Jarring that, because of Egyptian violation of the standstill cease-fire by continuing construction and emplacement of Soviet anti-aircraft mis-

---

[9] Cease-Fire-Standstill Agreement Between Israel and the United Arab Republic Effective August 7, 1970, obtained from the United States Department of State. See also 63 DEP'T. STATE BULLETIN 178-79 (1970).

siles in the Suez cease-fire zone, Israel was suspending participation in the talks until the missiles installed in violation of the cease-fire were withdrawn. For its part, Egypt charged Israel with violations of the cease-fire in the form of overflights west of the Canal into the Egyptian sector of the cease-fire zone.

The Rogers initiative for an "at least" 90-day standstill cease-fire was followed by a rash of hijackings and attacks on commercial aircraft by the Popular Front for the Liberation of Palestine, which opposed the cease-fire. Jordanian acceptance of the Rogers initiative and the hijackings by the Popular Front in turn triggered a series of major clashes between Palestine Liberation Organization forces in Jordan and the army of King Hussein, culminating in an abortive Syrian intervention on behalf of the Palestinian guerrillas and a threatened United States counterintervention. Although the level of external intervention in Jordan quickly receded, military clashes have periodically recurred between Jordanian troops and Palestinian guerrilla forces, and the Jordan–Syria border has remained tense.

President Nasser died on September 28, 1970. He was succeeded as President of the United Arab Republic by Anwar el-Sadat. On November 4, 1970, the General Assembly passed a resolution requesting an additional three-month extension of the cease-fire. Subsequently, on December 30, 1970, Abba Eban, the Foreign Minister of Israel, informed Ambassador Jarring that in view of "present political and military conditions" Israel was willing to resume talks. During January and February of 1971 an exchange of views between Egypt, Israel, and Jordan through Ambassador Jarring seemed to narrow the gap between them only slightly. The most significant exchange was occasioned by an *aide mémoire* of February 8 from Ambassador Jarring to Israel and the United Arab Republic. The replies of the United Arab Republic on February 15 and Israel on February 26 indicated substantial continuing disagreement over the interpretation of Resolution 242, particularly whether it required territorial withdrawal from all the occupied territories or a negotiated withdrawal to "secure and recognized boundaries." The United Arab Republic reply, however, did for the first time indicate willingness to enter into a peace agreement with Israel if other differences could be resolved.

Diplomatic efforts since the Jarring initiatives of January and February 1971 have focused on United States efforts to promote "proximity talks" and to negotiate an interim settlement centering on a reopened Suez Canal. Although by August 1972 no such settlement had been reached, the Rogers-initiated cease-fire had survived its second anniversary.

The Principal Issues in the Conflict

The legal and political issues raised by the continuing Arab-Israeli conflict are as diverse as might be expected from the prolonged history of the conflict. The principal issues, however, are grouped around five major clusters of problems. First, the establishment of the State of Israel, the human rights of Arab and Jewish refugees of the repeated conflicts, and, closely related, the claim to self-determination of the Palestinian people. Second, freedom of navigation through waterways in the area, including the Strait of Tiran, the Gulf of Aqaba, and the Suez Canal. Third, the status of the City of Jerusalem and protection of and access to the Holy Places. Fourth, issues relating to the lawfulness of resort to coercion and the consequences of such resort. Among others, these issues include the legal effect of an armistice regime, the legality under the United Nations Charter of a continuing state of belligerency, the lawfulness of the belligerents' use of force in each of the Arab-Israeli wars, the extent of the legal duty for surrounding states to prevent fedayeen raids against Israel launched from their territory, the legality of Israeli raids and other actions against guerrilla bases in neighboring Arab states, the meaning of no acquisition of territory by war and the interrelation with the Charter principle proscribing aggressive coercion and permitting defense against an armed attack, and the scope and applicability of the Geneva Conventions of 1949 for the humanitarian protection of civilians and prisoners of war. Finally, the Arab-Israeli conflict raises a series of issues concerning the authority and structure of the United Nations. These issues include, among others, the authority of the General Assembly and the Security Council to recommend and enforce settlement of international disputes (such as the General Assembly recommendation concerning partition of Palestine and the more recent Security Council Resolution 242), the structure of and basis for United Nations peacekeeping in the light of the UNEF withdrawal, the danger of a credibility gap with respect to United Nations fact-finding and the need to depoliticize such proceedings, and the perennial problem of increasing the effectiveness of the United Nations as an agency for promoting justice and managing international conflict.

Appraisal of the Issues in the Conflict

The readings selected for this volume are, in general, careful and scholarly. Nevertheless, it should not be assumed that merely because an argument is made it has merit. A careful comparison of the opposing arguments is usually the safest guide to appraisal. Perhaps more importantly, not all of the legal issues raised are of equal importance in analyzing the conflict. Development of a hierarchy of issues is a critical task in appraisal.[10] In weighing individual selections it is also useful to keep in mind the principal elements of choice which account for different conclusions. They are: first, a differing emphasis on the descriptive (roughly, what the law is) and prescriptive (roughly, what the author believes the law ought to be) intellectual tasks; second, in carrying out the descriptive task, differing fact selection, rule selection (and interpretation), and application of the rule (or principle or standard) to the facts; and third, in carrying out the prescriptive task, differing goal selection and varying assessment of the impact of alternative actions on postulated goals. Most disagreement about "the facts" of world-order disputes is less disagreement about whether a particular event occurred than it is selection from a complex context those events which support the world-view of the writer. Accordingly, the reader should ask why the author selected the events he did and what criteria the author used consciously or unconsciously to determine which of the "facts" were most relevant. Similarly, in most scholarly dialogue it is important to ask why a particular legal rule or principle is selected as determinative in a particular context as well as whether the rule is authoritative. In this regard it is particularly important to keep in mind that Article 103 of the United Nations Charter provides: "[i]n the event of a conflict between the obligations of the Members of the United Nations under the present Charter and their obligations under any other international agreement, their obligations under the present Charter shall prevail." Thus, since all of the states parties to the Arab-Israeli conflict are bound by the Charter, the obligations of the Charter are the most important source of legal rights and duties in appraising the conflict.

Arrangement of Volumes One and Two

Volumes One and Two have been organized around the five principal sets of legal and political issues in the conflict. In addition, a brief in-

10 And, of course, legal issues are not the only considerations relevant for appraisal.

troductory section on the relevance of international law and a concluding section on settlement alternatives have been added. The section on
settlement is particularly useful in demonstrating that a range of positive solutions is available if the parties can be persuaded to undertake
meaningful negotiations.

Volume One begins with a section on the relevance of international
law which examines the role played by international law in the Arab-
Israeli conflict and some of the ways in which an international legal
perspective can contribute to the management of international conflict.
Volume One then moves to an analysis of underlying issues in the conflict, taking up in turn Arab and Jewish nationalism and the rights of
refugees, freedom of navigation through the Strait of Tiran, the Gulf
of Aqaba, and the Suez Canal, and the status of Jerusalem and the Holy
Places. The section on Arab and Jewish nationalism and the rights of
refugees includes articles on both the self-determination and refugee
issues. Although a separate focus on these issues would have been at
least equally plausible, they were combined because articles concerning
one also frequently concern the other and because from a Palestinian
perspective these issues are frequently viewed as congruent. Territorial issues, particularly Israeli withdrawal from the occupied
territories and the establishment of "secure and recognized boundaries," are certainly major issues in the conflict, but for the most
part they are dealt with in articles concerning the aftermath of the Six-
Day War and contemporary efforts at settlement. As such, they have
been left to Volume Two.

Volume Two begins with a section on the Six-Day War and continued hostilities, which examines in turn the background and setting
of recent hostilities, legal issues concerning the use of force and its consequences, and the applicability and implementation of the Geneva
Conventions for the protection of civilians and prisoners of war. Following this is a section on the role of the United Nations, which surveys the general historical and constitutional aspects of the United Nations role in the Arab-Israeli conflict and discusses issues raised by the
withdrawal of the United Nations Emergency Force prior to the Six-
Day War as well as the implications of the withdrawal for the future
of United Nations peacekeeping. Volume Two then concludes with an
extensive section on settlement. This final section includes a variety of
private perspectives on settlement in addition to some of the more
complete statements of governmental positions.

In selecting and organizing articles in the reader, it has not always been possible to neatly divide the articles according to the organizational framework of the reader. When minor overlap between sections has occurred, it has been felt preferable to accept this rather than to edit the articles too severely, which might result in a strained presentation of the author's major points. In general, editing has been resorted to only where necessary to delete obviously repetitious or extraneous materials or to meet overall page limitations for publication. Consequently, most selections have been printed in full. Where editing has been necessary, the usual scholarly conventions have been followed, and every effort has been made to avoid weakening or bolstering the arguments of any proponent by the editorial process. For the reader who would like to refer to the unedited version, citations to the original publication are included in the list of permissions in the back of each volume.

One of the many educational aspects of editing *The Arab-Israeli Conflict* has been the opportunity to review the voluminous scholarly literature on the subject. Unfortunately, the literature is so extensive that it could not be included even in a three-volume reader. Inevitably, then, it has been necessary to make hard judgments about which articles among those available should be included and which excluded. Regrettably, some essays which merited republication could not be included because of lack of space.[11] In making these selections, a cardinal principle has been to make as balanced a presentation on each issue and on the conflict as a whole as the range of the existing scholarly writing would permit. An effort has also been made to include the leading articles as well as a representative sample of the major positions. For reference to additional materials on the conflict, Volume Three includes a bibliography prepared by Mrs. Helen Philos, the Librarian of the American Society of International Law.

JOHN NORTON MOORE

11 For example, space limitations prevented the inclusion of Dr. Rosalyn Higgins's definitive study of the creation and withdrawal of the United Nations Emergency Force. See I R. HIGGINS, UNITED NATIONS PEACEKEEPING 1946-1967: DOCUMENTS AND COMMENTARY, 221-78, 335-415 (1969). Similarly, it was not possible to include a section on "Utilization of the Jordan Waters" which had been initially planned. For an excellent statement of the Jordan waters controversy, see K. Boals, "Jordan Waters Conflict," INT'L CONCILIATION, #553, May 1965, pp. 3-66.

I. THE RELEVANCE OF INTERNATIONAL LAW

Law, Lawyers, and the Conduct of American Foreign Relations

RICHARD A. FALK

Recent commentary on the role of law in international affairs has frequently degenerated into a debate between legalists and anti-legalists. The legalists argue that world peace depends upon enlarging the scope and range of legal rules, the growth of habitual respect for law, and the creation of international institutions capable of interpreting and enforcing the law.[1] The anti-legalists argue that the expectations of the legalists are naive and misleading in a world of independent sovereign states, and that the best prospects for peace depend upon the maintenance of balance between the capabilities and commitments of antago-nistic countries and ideologies. This balance must be grounded in a diplomatic equilibrium in which no state has any rational prospect of achieving significant expansion by conquest. As the world changes, the legalists, by and large, would alter and reform the legal rules, whereas the anti-legalists would concentrate upon making political readjust-ments to preserve the balance.[2] After an investigation of the arguments made by both sides in the debate, this essay will focus on three particu-lar facets of the general problem posed by the assumed dichotomy between law and politics: (A) Lawyers as Foreign Policy Planners; (B) Adherence to Law and the Conduct of Foreign Policy; (C) Law and the Future of World Order. The discussion attempts to shift the focus of the present debate to an intermediate position that makes a more

† Milbank Professor of International Law, Princeton University; Fellow, Center for Advanced Study in the Behavioral Sciences 1968-69; B.S. Econ. 1952, University of Pennsylvania; LL.B. 1955, Yale Law School; S.J.D. 1962, Harvard Law School.

1. Judith Shklar, in her excellent book on the subject, defines legalism as "the ethical attitude that holds moral conduct to be a matter of rule following, and moral relationships to consist of duties and rights determined by rules." J. SHKLAR, LEGALISM: AN ESSAY ON LAW, MORALS, POLITICS 1 (1964).

2. The conflicting positions of the legalists and antilegalists have recently been set forth with clarity and insight by Louis Henkin. L. HENKIN, HOW NATIONS BEHAVE; LAW AND FOREIGN POLICY 245-71 (1968).

precise and realistic estimate of the contributions, limitations, and potentialities of law and lawyers to the foreign policy-making process of the United States.

The polarity of the opposing positions was clearly visible at the 1963 Annual Meeting of the American Society of International Law. On that occasion Dean Acheson dismissed the importance of law in matters of high sovereign concern in as unqualified a manner as we have heard in recent years from a person of high stature. Mr. Acheson told the large assembly of international lawyers, no doubt attracted partly by the lustre of his presence, that international law is of no significance in the resolution of important issues of foreign policy. His words were characteristically astringent:

> I must conclude that the propriety of the Cuban quarantine is not a legal issue. The power, position, and prestige of the United States had been challenged by another state; and law simply does not deal with such questions of ultimate power—power that comes close to the sources of sovereignty.[3]

Mr. Acheson's remarks were highly provocative. He shared the platform with Abram Chayes, then Legal Adviser to the Secretary of State, who appeared to be proud of the role that law had played in moderating and shaping the execution of the decision to interdict the placement of Soviet missiles on Cuban territory.[4] But what is more, Mr. Acheson was himself an eminent international lawyer, who had returned to the practice of law after leaving the government in 1952. Perhaps the immediate adverse reaction to his comments was magnified by a subconscious feeling among the members of the audience that they had borne witness to a betrayal of their vocation. To justify their feeling it is not difficult to show that many governmental decisions on matters of war and peace are shaped in beneficial ways by a sophisticated handling of international law.[5] Moreover, there are many practical drawbacks to a position that encourages all governments to insist on the legitimacy of sovereign prerogative on occasions of their own choosing.

But, perhaps the anti-legalist position was disputed too mechanically and without sufficient consideration of the way in which legal arguments can be and have been used. In the 1960's a series of controversial

---

3. Acheson, Remarks, Proceedings American Society of International Law 13, 14 (1963).
4. See Chayes, Law and the Quarantine of Cuba, 41 FOREIGN AFF. 550 (1963); Chayes, The Legal Case for U.S. Action on Cuba, 47 DEP'T. STATE BULL. 763 (1962). See also Meeker, Defensive Quarantine and the Law, 57 AM. J. INT'L L. 515 (1963).
5. See HENKIN, supra note 2.

American foreign policy undertakings drew heavily upon legal rhetoric and argumentation to defend their validity, especially in reaction against domestic critics in the United States. We find, for instance, the Legal Adviser to the State Department, Mr. Leonard D. Meeker, going to considerable lengths to demonstrate a legal basis for the American military occupation of the Dominican Republic in April of 1965. Mr. Meeker suggested that his approach to international law "would properly be described as practical idealism." In his thinking "fundamentalist views on the nature of international legal obligations are not very useful as a means to achieving practical and just solutions of difficult political, economic, and social problems." Mr. Meeker went on to say that

> [i]t does not seem to me that law and other human institutions should be treated as abstract imperatives which must be followed for the sake of obeisance to some supernatural power or for the sake of some supposed symmetry that is enjoined upon the human race by external forces. Rather, it seems to me that law and other institutions of society should be seen as deliberate and hopefully rational efforts to order the lives of human communities—from small to great—in such a way as to permit realization by all members of a community of the full range of whatever creative powers they may possess.[6]

The cosmic vision expressed by these sentiments is widely shared, but arouses suspicion when used to validate what appeared to most impartial observers as a blatant violation of one of the basic norms of modern international law: the prohibition of unilateral recourse to force except in a situation of self-defense. However one might interpret the Dominican turbulence at the time of the American military involvement, it was not a situation in which the United States could purport to be acting in collective self-defense to protect the Dominican Republic against external attack.[7] Rather, the intervention in Dominican affairs bears an obvious, if odious, resemblance to the Soviet intervention in Czechoslovakia in August 1968. The strength of the comparison is heightened by the reliance of both principal governments upon a regional or collective endorsement to veil the unilateral nature of their use of military power to interfere with the domestic

6. Meeker, *The Dominican Situation on the Perspective of International Law*, 53 DEP'T. STATE BULL. 60 (1965).
7. This interpretation that the United States did not act in self-defense is strongly supported even in a conservative account of the Dominican intervention. *See* J. MARTIN, OVERTAKEN BY EVENTS (1966).

politics of a foreign country.[8] Certainly the Soviet claim to maintain the integrity of governments in the socialist community has a hollowness comparable to the State Department's "practical idealism" when it is used to justify suppressing Czech domestic developments that appear to be merely antithetical to Soviet interests.

This excursion into the dark domains of interventionalist diplomacy adds a dimension to the debate between the legalists and the anti-legalists. The anti-legalists are entitled to complain when a government dresses rationalizations of policy in legal language. In such circumstances, law is less a fig leaf than a see-through garment. Consequently, there is a strong impulse to strip away the legalistic pretension; better see policy as naked power than disguise the choice by enshrouding it in a gauzy film of legalism. Such a call for directness, perhaps an element of Mr. Acheson's remarks, is evident in some more recent comments on the role of law and lawyers in the making of foreign policy.

Mr. Henry Kissinger, the now influential Assistant to President Nixon on National Security Affairs, has often inveighed against what he regards as the detrimental effects of legalism on the formulation of American foreign policy. In his widely studied article on settling the Vietnam war, Kissinger argued that these legalistic tendencies of the Government inhibited the commencement of negotiations with the North Vietnamese. He suggested that ours is "a government which equates commitments with legally enforceable obligations," and that our preoccupation with this equation prevented us from even discerning signals sent by North Vietnam's government indicating its willingness to take satisfactory action in exchange for a bombing halt provided that its action did not have to be based on a formal commitment. Kissinger also contended that "the legalistic phrasing" of Washington's demands "obscured their real merit," in effect arguing that the language of law was inappropriate to the setting and had an undesirable impact upon diplomacy.[9] The repetition of this point several times in Mr. Kissinger's article makes it clear how strongly he feels that talking like a lawyer may keep the policy-maker from perceiving and resolving "the real issues."

This point of view becomes even more pronounced in a general

---

8. *Cf.* the principal Soviet legal argument (the so-called Brezhnev Doctrine) for occupying Czechoslovakia as formulated in an article translated from Pravda and published under the title *Sovereignty and International Duties of Socialist Countries.* N.Y. Times, Sept. 27, 1968, at 27, col. 1.
9. Kissinger, *The Viet Nam Negotiations,* 47 FOREIGN AFF. 211, 222-23 (1969).

essay that Kissinger wrote on foreign policy just before he took office.[10] In this essay Kissinger contended that "we have historically shied away" from an inquiry "into the essence of our national interest and into the premises of our foreign policy" because of an insistence on casting our political interests in the form of legal responsibilities: "It is part of American folklore that, while other nations have interests, we have responsibilities; while other nations are concerned with equilibrium, we are concerned with the legal requirements of peace."[11] The rejection of law by Mr. Kissinger was particularly significant because he reoriented his entire analysis of foreign policy in the direction of world order: "The greatest need of the contemporary international system is an agreed concept of order."[12] And at the close of his essay he implied that unless we "ask the right questions"—that is, those that bear on interests—"we will never be able to contribute to building a stable and creative world order . . . ."[13] It seems fair to suggest that Mr. Kissinger regards law and legal rhetoric as an encumbrance rather than as a resource in the construction of a stronger system of world order.

Presumably in the background of this analysis lies John Foster Dulles's frantic search for treaties of alliance in the 1950's, as if a treaty, however fragile its political basis, could give assurance of the ability and willingness of governments around the world to contain Communism. In the foreground, of course, lies the defense of the United States involvement in the Vietnam war by an appeal to treaty commitments and by a claim that a world legal order is thereby sustained.[14] The pseudo-legalist ideology of Dean Rusk and Walt Rostow is the work of non-lawyers, who have frequently been more guilty than

---

10. Kissinger, *Central Issues of American Foreign Policy*, in AGENDA FOR THE NATION 585 (K. Gordon ed. 1968).
11. *Id.* 610.
12. *Id.* 588.
13. *Id.* 614.
14. Even Mr. Kissinger, despite his concern for the formalism and legalism of American foreign policy, writes as follows about "commitments" in the context of the Vietnam war:
   Much of the bitter debate in the United States about the war has been conducted in terms of 1961 and 1962. Unquestionably, the failure at that time to analyze adequately the geopolitical importance of Viet Nam contributed to the current dilemma. But the commitment of 500,000 Americans has settled the issue of the importance of Viet Nam. For what is involved now is confidence in American promises. However fashionable it is to ridicule the terms "credibility" or "prestige," they are not empty phrases; other nations can gear their actions to ours only if they can count on our steadiness. The collapse of the American effort in Viet Nam would not mollify many critics; most of them would simply add the charge of unreliability to the accusation of bad judgment. Those whose safety or national goals depend on American commitments could only be dismayed. In many parts of the world—the Middle East, Europe, Latin America, even Japan—stability depends on confidence in American promises.
Kissinger, *supra* note 9, at 218-19. Mr. Kissinger uses commitment in two different senses and is somewhat vague about the causal link between American "commitments" and specific behavior.

lawyers of rigid application of legal rules and the rhetorical use of the language of the law. In fact, Dean Acheson is just one of many attorneys who have served in the State Department; such lawyers tend to be exemplary exponents of the pragmatic traditions of the common law and are themselves anti-legalist in their philosophy. What is disturbing about the simpler statements of the anti-legalist position is its double confusion: first, an inaccurate and simplistic presentation of the legal tradition and, second, a false depiction of the relationship between "a characteristic legalism"[15] and certain recent extravagances in American foreign policy.

The comments of Mr. Kissinger, among others, suggest how important it is to enter the debate between legalists and anti-legalists and to examine some particular aspects of the controversy in order to achieve a more realistic and constructive analysis of the proper role for lawyers in foreign policy-making on behalf of the United States Government.[16]

A. Lawyers as Foreign Policy Planners

Henry Kissinger characterizes "the sort of analysis at which [Americans] excel" in the conduct of foreign relations as "the pragmatic, legal dissection of individual cases."[17] The same point is made more negatively by Zbigniew Brzezinski, the foreign policy specialist and former government adviser, who writes:

Coming from a society traditionally suspicious of conceptual thought (where a "problem-solving" approach is held in esteem and concepts are denigrated as "intellectual cubbyholes"), shaped by a legal and pragmatic tradition that stresses the case method and the importance of precedents, the understandable

---

15. Law functions within a structure of shared assumptions; its starting point is the acceptance, by all parties, of the legitimacy of the legal structure and of the values it embodies.

Everyone understands that this shared value commitment and belief in the adjudication of conflict does not exist in more than a fragmentary manner in international society. Nevertheless, the legal habit of mind has sometimes led the United States to discount these difficulties, even to assume for itself and its own policies an international legitimacy which other states were unwilling to concede. Along with this has gone a trust in formal arrangements and alliances which the social and political realities have not at all times justified.
N.Y. Times, Jan. 6, 1969, at 46, col. 1 (editorial). The intellectual underpinnings of this analysis are explicitly attributed to the celebrated critiques of American foreign policy made more than a decade ago by Kennan and Morgenthau. G. KENNAN, REALITIES OF AMERICAN FOREIGN POLICY (1954); G. KENNAN, AMERICAN DIPLOMACY, 1900-1950 (1952); H. MORGENTHAU, POLITICS AMONG NATIONS (4th ed. 1967); H. MORGENTHAU, IN DEFENSE OF NATIONAL INTEREST (1951).
16. For fuller development along these lines, see R. FALK, THE STATUS OF LAW IN INTERNATIONAL SOCIETY (1969).
17. Kissinger, supra note 9, at 221.

conditioned reflex of the policy-maker is to universalize from the success of specific policies, formulated and applied in the "pre-global" age of American foreign policy.[18]

Kissinger and Brzezinski are associating the case method, which is the main emphasis of the lawyer's professional training, with an inductive and pragmatic approach to foreign policy. And Brzezinski also emphasizes this approach as the distinctive character of the common law as a legal system. Both authors find this strain expressed in the dominant philosophical traditions of the United States, themselves continuations and outgrowths of British empiricism that emphasize problem-solving and pragmatic criteria of judgment. This kind of inductive orientation toward governmental policy-making contrasts with the more conceptual, deductive traditions associated with Continental jurisprudence and philosophy.[19] Each tradition has its distinctive strengths and weaknesses, biases and predispositions that have distinct impacts, depending on a country's particular historical setting.

What is important to appreciate, however, is that a particular legal style is derived from a wider tradition of thought prevailing within a particular society; it is a product of many influences and not attributable in any very illuminating way to a particular experience of vocational training in the law. Thus it is not surprising that ideological predispositions might take precedence over the problem-solving mentality for lawyers (e.g., John Foster Dulles) and non-lawyers (e.g., Dean Rusk, Walt Rostow) in the service of government. And whatever it is that is properly associated with the pragmatic approach of the common law is not at all identical with the legalistic patterns of justification invoked by some lawyers in the course of carrying out their governmental functions.

A parallel tradition of piety and self-sacrifice has its roots in the religious origins of the United States and can be seen clearly in the Puritan heritage. This religiosity seeks to disguise self-interested mo-

---

18. Brzezinski, *Purpose and Planning in Foreign Policy*, THE PUBLIC INTEREST, Winter 1969, at 52, 54-55. Kissinger also argues for a better conceptual framework for foreign policy in the essay cited in note 10, *supra*.

19. Brzezinski's statement about the legal tradition contains an odd mixture of misconceptions. The case method is a technique of analysis and pedagogy rather than a widely accepted system of adjudication. (Arbitration would be closer to the ad hoc "problem-solving" that Brzezinski first refers to.) The very importance of precedent is a demonstration that each case is not seen as a discrete problem in the American legal system. Universalizing from the numerous cases which form a line of precedent will quickly bring the thoughtful student of the law to the intellectual cubbyholes of conceptual thought. The difference from Continental systems lies in how we reach that plane of conceptual discussion rather than in taking the extreme nominalist position that generalized concepts have no value at all. The Restatement is the end rather than the beginning.

tives, aspires to act for the common good, and is interested in setting a moral example of unselfish sacrifice for the other governments of the world that, according to this outlook, follow a much more self-centered course of action in foreign affairs.[20] The ideas underlying the doctrine of the separation of church and state, together with the progressive secularization of American society, have stimulated a search for non-religious modes of expression by those entrusted with the task of making and justifying American foreign policy. Law and lawyers have often fulfilled this social need, providing a kind of idealistic discourse that represents partly a genuine reformist tradition and partly a hypocritical disguise for acquisitive behavior. Calvinism has

20. Those who support the role of the United States in the Vietnam War often emphasize the *absence* of any selfish American interests in Vietnam. We want no territory or foreign bases, and we have no economic holdings or ambitions. Although the denial of any selfish interest may not be altogether convincing, its frequent repetition by high officials is a powerful illustration of the point made in the text. The United States substitutes the rightness of its cause for the selfish pursuit of interests, and feels no compunctions about unleashing its destructive might upon a poor and rather backward Asian country. When interests are pursued then costs tend to be assessed and the enterprise confined by some concept of net worth. But when supposedly selfless principles underlie the commitment then no assessment can be made, and no cost is too high. The American effort to end the Vietnam war indicates that some sense of "worth" finally took precedence over the moralistic insistence that the United States was acting to show that aggression doesn't pay, or that collective self-defense works, or that we are a government that upholds its commitments; since no moral contention was very convincing there was a tendency to shift from one to another in a desperate struggle to plug the dike erected against the mounting tide of domestic and international opposition to the war. But up until President Johnson's speech of March 31, 1968, no government official moved the debate about the war off the terrain of selfless promotion of moral and legal principles the value of which could not be weighed against the adverse effects of its continuation. Within the American elite it has been the pragmatic counter-tradition that has broken with the moralism and legalism of the Rusk-Rostow position. The formulations of Arthur Schlesinger, McGeorge Bundy, and Henry Kissinger are characteristic of this pragmatic (opportunistic?) reevaluation of American policy in Vietnam. Bundy's Address at DePauw University in October 12, 1968, is one of the best examples of this break with moralism. Mr. Bundy says:

Until the present burden of Vietnam is at least partly lifted from our society, it will not be easy—it may not even be possible—to move forward effectively with other great national tasks. This has not always been my view, but . . . it seems to me wholly clear now that at its current level of effort and cost the war cannot be allowed to continue for long. Its penalities upon us all are much too great. (Mimeographed text, p. 2)

Lest he be understood as a sudden convert to matters of principle, Mr. Bundy makes plain that his change of position on Vietnam was a matter of pure expediency:

I remind you also, if you stand on the other side, that my argument against escalation and against an indefinite continuation of our present course has been based not on moral outrage or political hostility to the objective, but rather on the simple and practical ground that escalation will not work and that continuation of our present course is unacceptable.

Mr. Schlesinger expresses the same theme when he writes: "The tragedy of Vietnam is the tragedy of the catastrophic overextension and misapplication of valid principles. The original insights of collective security and liberal evangelism were generous and wise." *Vietnam and the End of the Age of Superpowers*, HARPERS, March 1966, at 41-49. My overriding contention, one that will be developed in later stages of the article, is that neither moralism-legalism of the Rusk-Rostow variety nor expediency of the Bundy-Schlesinger variety provide America with an adequate basis for policy and choice in world aflairs.

contributed the zealously held notions of personal salvation and a vigilant, omnipotent god, and this combination has led to a confusion between what is beneficial for oneself and for the general welfare. Socially this confusion is compounded by the suggestively similar ideas of *laissez faire*, the "invisible hand" of Adam Smith, and Social Darwinism that are all embodied in American intellectual traditions. The world views of Woodrow Wilson after World War I exemplified these confusions—the idealistic gropings for the grand design conjoined to a search for American leadership and preeminence in world affairs.

In conclusion, then, the inductive particularism of the common law is neither confined to law, nor is it espoused by all American lawyers. The "case" approach reflects a broader kind of philosophical tradition associated with British empiricism and the whole struggle against Thomistic and Cartesian modes of thought and organization evolved out of Catholic dogma and Continental traditions of speculation.[21] Similarly, the legalism that is found in American diplomacy often represents displaced religious and moral sentiments that derive from the whole spiritual foundation of the Republic in colonial times. Legalism in formulation and approach is a way of maintaining the pristine integrity of a moral system in a pluralistic society; the emphatic piety remains resonant even when the rhetorical appeal has been shifted to more secular grounds. It seems no accident that Woodrow Wilson and John Foster Dulles, our two most eminent legalists, were both men of deep, central, religious conviction who devoted themselves to careers in the vortex of secularism. It seems that the espousal of legalism has little, if anything, directly to do with membership in the legal profession. Law may be a foil for suppressed religious concerns; equally lawyers may be problem-solvers with neither the virtues nor the vices of statesmen of more grandiose visions who would build a new world order for our time.

B. *Adherence to Law and the Conduct of Foreign Policy*

The value of a law-oriented foreign policy is obscured by the character of the legalist-anti-legalist debate. The acceptance of a framework for legal restraint in the external relations of the country seems at least as much related to the promotion of national welfare as does adherence to law in domestic affairs. A discretionary basis for foreign policy in

---

21. Such particularism is also associated with the importance of "town meetings" in early America and the rise of a congregationalist tradition in ecclesiastical affairs.

the nuclear age seems to increase the risks of self-destructive warfare. The scale of violence is now so large that it becomes less and less tenable to entrust decisions affecting the interests and welfare of the world community to the particular appraisals of policy made by small numbers of executive officials at the national level.[22] The problems of the world—peace, welfare, dignity—increasingly presuppose some form of supranational control to protect the general interest. The prospects for building governmental structures at the world level remain poor, and so in the interest of preventing disastrous breakdowns, the restriction of national freedom of choice could function as one formidable source of restraint upon the ruinous tendencies of our present international society. The norms of international law, impartially interpreted and applied, are a forceful source of restraint upon the self-seeking proclivities of sovereign states. The real difficulty with Mr. Acheson's views about the conduct of diplomacy in a situation of crisis is a prudential one, namely, that to affirm the discretionary basis of foreign policy in the nuclear age is to invite eventual disaster, even if, or perhaps especially if, the effective discretion to act is vested only in the governments of the major powers.

Mr. Kissinger contends that our dedication to "principle" makes it hard for us to articulate a truly vital interest which we would defend against a challenge we thought was "legal."[23] We deny that force is being used by the United States to uphold or enhance America's power and prestige, much less its wealth. American policy-makers normally rely upon a selfless explanation for action taken abroad. Thus we tend to justify our foreign policy decisions by turning to principles of universal appeal, such as the need to resist "aggression." According to Kissinger, these patterns of generalized justification lead to an indefinite multiplication of commitments. He counsels, instead, a hard-headed appraisal of vital interests as a strategy for bringing our "commitments" into better correlation with our "interests" and "capabilities." In such a reorientation it may be necessary to undertake some "illegal" courses of action and to refrain from joining many "legal" causes.

Why is international law a better source of national self-restraint than the kind of interest calculus that Mr. Kissinger proposes? Clearly

---

22. Garrett Hardin makes this argument in vivid and generic terms through an interpretation of the experience with over-grazing of community commons. Hardin, *The Tragedy of the Commons*, 162 SCIENCE 1243 (1968).

23. Kissinger, *supra* note 10, at 611.

law has little to offer as a basis for guidance and restraint if it is manipulated in a self-serving and post-facto fashion or becomes assimilated into the tradition of formulating pious self-avowals in legal rhetoric.[24] At the same time, international law provides the potential basis for guiding the action of all governments within an agreed framework. It has relatively stable principles that are not easily altered by shifts in governmental conception of the national interest or by miscalculations as to the intermeshing of definitions of national interests by adversary governments. Kissinger's views seem overly dependent on the wisdom and prudence of the particular group in control of a government.

Self-determination of rights and duties—a self-help system—is severely biased by self-serving interpretations of what is reasonable, interpretations which are marked by hostility, distrust, self-seeking, and wide cultural diversity. In this situation the position and traditions of the United States make its adherence to international law particularly important. The great power of the United States relative to every other country, including the Soviet Union, make its acceptance of restraint particularly significant. Secondly, there is little incentive or likelihood that other principal states could take advantage of American adherence to international law. Technological developments much more than territorial expansion are the key to changes in relative power in the present world. As a result, the legal order presents neither obstacles nor temptations to the potential expansionist state. Thirdly, the rules and expectations embodied in international law are sufficiently permissive to allow a government to take whatever action is needed to uphold its territorial integrity and political independence. Fourthly, the United States needs to set certain examples of self-limitation in the interest of inducing reciprocal restraints by other states. Such reciprocity seems an essential part of any program designed to cope with the spread of weapons of mass destruction to more and more countries in the years ahead. Fifthly, there is a genuine American

---

24. The following passage is a striking illustration of this tradition:
In the period of primarily American responsibility for peace since 1945, we have used our force prudently, cautiously, and for limited and defensive ends. We have used force in conformity with international law, in order to enforce it. When we had a monopoly of nuclear weapons, we did not seek to impose our will on the rest of the world. Nor have we even overthrown the regime of Castro in Cuba.
E. ROSTOW, LAW, POWER, AND THE PURSUIT OF PEACE 11 (1968).

Mr. Rostow seems to be confusing adherence to law with certain decisions to refrain from using all the power at the disposal of a national government. But surely some lesser uses of power may not be compatible with the sovereign status of other countries, nor with the legal prohibitions on non-defensive uses of national force against foreign countries.

tradition of respect for law and concern for justice that could play a part in seeking to strengthen the quality of world order. For all these reasons it is important to bring impartial legal perspectives to bear early in the formation of policy.

As in domestic law it is possible, and necessary to distinguish between an *ex parte* manipulation of law and its impartial and autonomous application. The present bureaucratic structure is ill-suited to serve the latter objective. The Legal Adviser is a subordinate officer of the Secretary of State. His role is often couched in terms that require him to be an adversary litigator with the Government as his "client." While his advice on legal matters may be enlightened, and he may try to avoid violence, he still is a subordinate State Department official essentially advocating an adversary position in the Government. This status and arrangement seem too haphazard, except in relation to the routine affairs of international life that are rarely considered by the political officers of government.

The President needs to receive legal advice at the Cabinet level from an Attorney General for International Affairs. The conception of official duty for this proposed post should stress the obligations of impartiality, the search for objective criteria of guidance, and the importance of participating at all stages of the formation and application of foreign policy. Such an Attorney General should be assisted by official panels of experts on various dimensions of international life who have access to all governmental information and are obliged to deliver expert opinions. The Attorney General for International Affairs should be regarded as a non-political appointee, subject to removal from office only for cause. He should sit as an *ex officio* member of the National Security Council and command a budget sufficient to enable careful, rapid staff work on all legal questions.

C. *Law and the Future of World Order*

Images of world order may be developed from both legal and nonlegal traditions of thought about international affairs. Unfortunately, the images drawn from traditions of legal thought have tended to be models of domestic legal systems generalized to apply to the whole of international society. These models are static, tend to ignore the enormous difficulties of moving from the present decentralized structure of international society to a highly centralized structure, and appear artificial and unrealistic if offered as either a prediction of or a prescription for the future.

On the other hand, the images of world order deriving from non-legal traditions of thought tend to be models of interaction that are only marginally different from the existing structure of power and behavior in international society. Mr. Kissinger's notions about world order appear to be little more than an updating of Metternich's ideas for securing a stable and dynamic equilibrium in international society. The chief buttresses of the non-legal model are alliances, an assessment of the correlation between capabilities and commitments, and a hierarchial ordering of interests vital to the country. The achievement of such world order depends upon an acceptance of the international status quo for an indefinite period, or at least a perceived unwillingness on the part of all major governments to secure major gains through force of arms. The difficulty with this diplomatist image of world order is that it seems to accept decentralized procedures as adequate for the maintenance of minimum order and welfare in international society.

There is presently an intellectual vacuum that needs to be filled with more adequate images of world order, responsive to the history and traditions of a world of sovereign states and to the emerging functional problems that cannot be handled, in many cases, by the national governments of even the most powerful states. The control of oceanic and atmospheric pollution, the regulation of weather modification and other uses of space, the beneficial use of data collection relevant to many phases of human existence, the regulation of the multi-national corporation, problems of resource conservation and exploration, and the moderation of the effects of shifts in the supply of and demand for food suggest the urgency of evolving functional bodies that have a transnational center of authority and control. The maintenance of world order may depend on the design and acceptance of a scheme of overlapping, interlocking, and organizationally disparate functional institutions that ignore the confines of national boundaries and elude the control of national governments. Such a network may come to play an increasingly vital role as problems of armed violence across boundaries are subordinated to the differential opportunities for and hazards of various strategies of technological exploitation. The deployment of fast-breeder nuclear reactors, capable of converting arid land into an agro-industrial complex may become more significant than the deployment of missles with nuclear warheads. Failures to take adequate precautions to prevent damage from radioactive waste may pose greater problems than the danger of war and surprise attack. The proposals for order and control should be responsive to the problems emerging from the international environment.

Moderate population projections predict a world population by the first decade of the twenty-first century that will be almost double what it is today.[25] These increases will be concentrated in the poorer parts of the world which have no prospect of adequately feeding or caring for their populations. The problem is not only preventing famine, but also securing health, education, housing, and a life of some opportunity for most people in the world.[26] Population expansion vastly increases the difficulty of making reasonable progress along all these other lines, and also causes more than proportionate increases in garbage, pollution, and resource depletion. Increasing population densities also raise the propensity of social groups toward disease, riot, distress, and desperate politics. In such environments, strategies of internal and external change that rely on violence are much more likely.

Thus, like the Polish army of the thirties, supposedly buttressed by the working of the balance of power and by impressive treaty systems, we are a knight errant facing the future in gallant ignorance, equipped with ideas whose time has passed. Non-legal approaches to world order characteristically ignore the international dimension of the problems of pollution, population, and poverty. Legal approaches to world order equally ignore the problems of adapting to the new technological environment. Only in relation to nuclear war is the case for drastic change in our attitude toward world order sufficiently understood.

There are several suggestions that follow from this discussion: (1) the outline of a new kind of transnational functionalist world order should be put in explicit and coherent form; (2) international lawyers should begin to define ecological, demographic, and technological developments as within the province of their professional concern; (3) the idea of a world order emphasizing the problems of war and peace should be rejected in favor of a broader conception that is equally concerned with the protection and promotion of dignity, safety, and security for individuals and groups. Power and the mechanisms for restraining its use are no longer adequate foci of concern in our ever-more interdependent and overcrowded world of shared danger and opportunity.

25. Projections of population growth and their conservative interpretation are to be found in Notestein, *Population Growth and Its Control*, in OVERCOMING WORLD HUNGER 9, 16-17 (C. Hardin ed. 1969).

26. For some discussion of projected population growth and its global consequences, see P. EHRLICH, THE POPULATION BOMB (1968); G. MYRDAL, THE ASIAN DRAMA (3 vols. 1968); W. PADDOCK & P. PADDOCK, FAMINE—1975! (1967).

Conclusion

The purpose of this article is to redefine the debate on legalism in terms that are more responsive to the international needs of the day.[27] Such an endeavor requires some clarification of what is truly characteristic and distinctive about the legal tradition, especially as it presents itself in our national setting. Only on this basis is it possible to assess the claims advanced for and against law in relation to the conduct of foreign policy. Above all, it is essential to distinguish between the intellectual traditions of an American lawyer and the ideological orientations of American statesmen, who may or may not be lawyers but who use legal rhetoric to express moral preferences which often spring from other and wider sources.

The rejection of legalism does not make the case for anti-legalism. The argument for a common framework of restraint that has some objective standing independent of the judgment of government officials seems overwhelmingly persuasive in the nuclear age when the margin of fatal miscalculation is so small and the prospect of mutually contradictory selection of facts and claims is so great. The search for objectivity in such an atmosphere deserves priority, and the techniques and vocation of the lawyer are admirably suited for the task, especially if the search is removed from governmental pressures by giving national legal advisers greater independence than they now enjoy. In the American context serious consideration should be given to the creation of a Cabinet post of Attorney General for International Affairs. Such efforts at the national level should be accompanied by parallel and complementary efforts to create procedures for the settling of disputes on the international level, whether within specialized agencies, regional or global institutions.

Both the traditional legalist and anti-legalist notions of world order have been slow to adapt to a new set of international concerns that are becoming problems of the first magnitude. We must work for a system of world order which will not only diminish the probability of large-scale and sustained violence, but will also meet the threats that arise from over-population, pollution, technological innovation, and resource depletion. We need, in other words, a redefinition of the task of

27. My argument should not be read to imply that international lawyers are by and large either legalists or anti-legalists. On the contrary, the academic mainstream of contemporary international legal studies exhibits my search for an intermediate statement of the link between law and politics. The legalist/anti-legalist discussion enjoys prominence mainly in discussions of the proper framework of restraint for the conduct of U.S. foreign policy.

global planning. That work should include a new, common effort by both legalists and non-legalists. No single disciplinary perspective is adequate in either its analysis of the problems of world order or the design of strategies for their solution. The argument for inter-disciplinary collaboration is both convincing and urgent, as is the case for forging a new synthetic concern for world order that engages specialists in many areas, including law, political science, economics, sociology, ecology, systems design, and the computer sciences.

The primary task is to keep the existing system under some degree of reasonable control during a period of transition to some more centralized system. The task is urgent. Cumulative and symbiotic developments in population growth, resource supply, pollution of oceans and space, and the technology of destruction suggest that only a few decades, at most, remain before the risks and costs of maintaining the existing system of world order will become unendurable.

The Law Works: Suez (I)

LOUIS HENKIN

IN CONTEMPORARY INTERNATIONAL RELATIONS "Suez" has come to suggest a military action, probably in violation of international law, a turning point in the use of force between nations and in the history of the influence of major European powers in the Middle East and beyond. Those climactic events in the fall of 1956 have swallowed up the early acts in the drama, events in which international law fared far better.

The nationalization of the Suez Canal is an instance where law helped deter, at least delay, important measures in the face of powerful pressures and with major interests at stake.[1]

On July 26, 1956, Egypt's President Nasser announced the nationalization of the Universal Company of the Suez Maritime Canal, seized its property, and expelled its officials.* The decree of nationalization provided that compensation would be paid to the Company's shareholders. The governments of France, the United Kingdom, and the United States—representing shareholders in the Company, users of the Canal, parties to the treaty governing its status—protested this "arbitrary and unilateral seizure."[2] During the next months there were proposals, conferences, negotiations, but none produced any agreement between the erstwhile owners and users of the Canal and the government of Egypt. A resolution of the United Nations Security Council setting forth six principles was adopted with Egyptian acquiescence, although Egypt's formal acceptance of them was later withdrawn.[3]

---

* It is generally accepted that Nasser acted in angry response to a decision by the United States not to help finance the construction of the Aswan Dam. There are reasons to believe, however, that the idea of nationalizing the Canal did not come to him suddenly at that time, and that anger at Western powers merely precipitated what was already in contemplation for some later time.

[1] For one story of the events, see T. Robertson, *Crisis: The Inside Story of the Suez Conspiracy* (1965) [hereinafter cited as Robertson].

[2] Tripartite statement of August 2, 1956, 35 *Dep't. State Bull.* 262 (1956).

[3] 11 U.N. SCOR, Oct.–Dec. Supp., at 47-48, U.N. Doc. S/3675 (1956). For the Egyptian acceptance see U.N. GAOR, Annexes, Agenda Item No. 5 (Emer. Sess. I), at 13-14, U.N. Doc. A/3287 (1956).

Nationalization of the Canal Under International Law

Although my principal concern here is with the influence of law in determining the reactions to the nationalization of the Canal, it is interesting to examine, too, how law influenced President Nasser's action itself. For that purpose one must consider the legal issues which that action involved, and they can perhaps best be deduced from the objections to the nationalization which were raised later.

The issues here were not the issues common to controversies over nationalization. Ordinarily, governments do not question the right of any government to expropriate alien properties in its territory; the controversy is usually as to whether the compensation for the taking satisfies the requirements of international law. At Suez, the governments owning the shares in the Suez Canal Company did not object to the compensation as inadequate, although they did have doubts as to Nasser's ability to pay.* Rather, they objected to the nationalization, as a whole, as a violation of international law and treaty.

The argument against the lawfulness of the nationalization was made by the three Western powers in a joint memorandum:

> But the present action involves far more than a simple act of nationalisation. It involves the arbitrary and unilateral seizure by one nation of an international agency which has the responsibility to maintain and to operate the Suez Canal so that all the signatories to, and beneficiaries of, the Treaty of 1888 can effectively enjoy the use of an international waterway upon which the economy, commerce, and security of much of the world depends.[4]

The argument, then, was that Egypt could not undertake nationalization because the Canal was an international waterway and the Company had "international character," as Egypt had repeatedly recognized in the various agreements it had negotiated with the Company. The government of Egypt purported to nationalize the ownership of the Canal, but ownership in this unique body of international character cannot be dissociated from the question of control of the Canal and its operation as an international waterway.[5] It was also argued that in

---

* To have argued the adequacy of compensation might have implied acceptance of Egypt's right to nationalize upon acceptable compensation.

[4] Dep't. of State, Pub. No. 6392, The Suez Canal Problem 35 (1956).

[5] But see R. Delson, "Nationalization of the Suez Canal Company: Issues of Public and Private International Law," 57 Colum. L. Rev. 755, 772-75 (1957).

the package of arrangements, including the Treaty of 1888 and the concessions to the Company, Egypt had expressly or by implication agreed not to terminate the concession (and therefore not to nationalize the Company) before 1968.[6]

The objections made later (and those not made) show clearly that President Nasser had legal advice and tailored his actions, his statements, and his later arguments in its light. He was careful to satisfy the accepted requirement of international law by providing for compensation for the stock of the Company at its full value on the Paris Bourse. He was careful to separate the question of ownership of shares in the Company from the question of control and use of the Canal: he nationalized ownership of an Egyptian company organized under Egyptian law and enjoying a concession under Egyptian law; he reaffirmed Egypt's treaty obligations to permit free use of the Canal.[7] To nationalize an Egyptian company raised no problem under international law; to nationalize its ownership in no way implied interference with the freedom of use protected by treaty. That Egypt had given a concession until 1968 would not prevent the nationalization, although it may be a factor in determining compensation.

The skeptic may suggest that law did not influence Nasser in any fundamental way: it did not deter him from seizing the Canal; at most, he attended to the law only as to the way in which he acted and in what he said. Of course if nationalizing the Canal was in fact lawful, there is no reason in law why he should be deterred. In fact, however, the law molded his action in important ways. For Nasser to undertake adequate compensation was neither easy nor inevitable; there have been numerous nationalizations before and since that did not offer adequate compensation.* For Nasser to guarantee continued freedom

---

* *E.g.*, the Cuban nationalization of properties owned by United States nationals. Compare *Banco Nacional de Cuba* v. *Sabbatino*, 376 U.S. 398, 401-403, nn. 3, 4 (1964).

That Nasser was careful to provide effective compensation would support the argument of the capital-exporting nations that international law requires it; and, since he had to pay, Nasser himself might to that extent be less eager to support those who claim that they can nationalize without paying.

[6] Q. Wright, "Intervention, 1956," 51 *Am. J. Int'l L.* 257, 261 (1957). There were, in addition, subsidiary arguments suggesting that the nationalization was impermissible under international law because it did not have a public purpose but was solely an act of retaliation against the United States, which had withdrawn an offer of aid to build the Aswan Dam. For a discussion of motives see S. Strange, "Suez and After," 11 *Yearbook of World Affairs* 76, 77 (1957). Compare Robertson, p. 65.

[7] Republic of Egypt, Ministry for Foreign Affairs, *White Paper on the Nationalization of the Suez Maritime Canal Company* 9, 15-35 (1956).

of passage was also not inevitable; the temptation to assert "My canal is my own"[8] might also have been great. Of course, Nasser was making a bold move and failure to compensate or to assure freedom of movement would have made strong reaction even more likely—but fear of such reactions, we know, is often why governments observe law.

Lawyers have disagreed as to whether the nationalization violated any norm or agreement and, if so, how serious the violation was.[9] President Nasser might have been told by his lawyers that his action would pass legal muster. Even if he had some doubts about his case, he clearly sought to reduce any illegalities there might have been; obviously, he was not prepared to give up the whole idea.*

The Response of the "Victims"

International law had different relevance to the decisions of the principal victims of Nasser's action. The Suez Canal was vital for European powers dependent on the oil of the Middle East. In 1955 almost 15,000 vessels had gone through the Canal, three-quarters of them belonging to NATO countries, one-third of them British.[10] From the

---

* If Nasser's lawyers told him that his action could be deemed a violation of law, he might still have decided to do it. A later report by a reputed confidant of President Nasser tells that he had two policy papers prepared, one setting forth the reasons in support of nationalization, the other anticipating the probable reactions of the Western powers. (See *N.Y. Times*, Oct. 9, 1966 § 1, p. 21.) The advantages must have loomed large: he could slap at the Western powers, and enhance his prestige at home and abroad. The Canal would be an important weapon in his hands and a source of income he sorely needed for major domestic development programs and ambitious international designs. The probable costs of his action, on the other hand, did not seem high. The legal case against him was not clear and nationalization of a company redolent of colonialism would be widely accepted if not applauded. Nor did he need to fear judgment, judicial or political. (He made it clear that while he was prepared to submit some questions for adjudication his authority to nationalize was not one of them.) In the U.N. Security Council, he could count on the Soviet veto; in the General Assembly, he had at least enough support to prevent a two-thirds vote necessary for action against him. The only danger he ran was that some powers might attempt to seize the Canal. But the use of force was illegal and was no longer "done." The Soviet Union would afford some protection, and even the United States would not wish to risk action which might throw the Arab states wholly into the Soviet camp. (The report cited above alleges that Nasser's intelligence estimates indicated Great Britain was militarily unprepared, and he expected that if Great Britain could not act promptly, it was increasingly less likely to act later.)

8 To paraphrase Ezekiel 29:3.

9 Compare R. Delson, cited 762-75, with T. Huang, "Some International and Legal Aspects of the Suez Canal Questions," 51 *Am. J. Int'l L.* 277, 278-86 (1957).

10 A. Eden, *Full Circle: The Memoirs of Anthony Eden* 474 (1960) [hereinafter cited as Eden].

viewpoint of Great Britain, in particular, President Nasser's action called for prompt and effective response.* Habits of empire, indeed, called for force, and a generation earlier it would have been invoked promptly and without hesitation. There were voices in the British government urging force now.

Their arguments might have seemed overwhelming. Great Britain had "protected" Egypt for decades. Only recently (1954) it had generously given up its remaining authority and perquisites.[11] Nasser's move was an intolerable affront. It was a violation, at least in spirit, of important international agreements. Most important, it was essential that the Canal run, and Nasser could not run it. In any event it was unthinkable that this "lifeline of empire" should be in the control of another government, and one less than wholly friendly and responsible. Efforts to restore international control by negotiation were futile, for Nasser was a difficult man and he held all the cards. It was important, moreover, to deal firmly with him, for he was an upstart and a troublemaker and, unless put in his place promptly, he would continue to trouble British interests in the Middle East, French interests in Algeria, and the Western position in Asia and Africa generally. A quick and limited military action would restore the Canal and assure its future operations. President Nasser would be humbled and might have to go. Stability would be restored.

The advantages of action were clear. The cost would not be high.† There need be few casualties and little damage to property. The act would be quickly done, and the *fait accompli* could not easily be undone. British relations with Nasser and with the Arab countries that supported him were not very good and could not seriously worsen; some of Nasser's neighbors, moreover, might be pleased to see him humbled. The matter would probably be brought to the United Nations, but Great Britain could survive that readily. The Soviet Union might attack the action in the Security Council, but there would be no

* Although there is even less evidence as to the motivations of French policy, one may guess that the attitudes of France were not too different from those of Great Britain except that its interests in the Canal were not as great. France, no doubt, deeply resented Nasser's support of "rebellion" in Algeria.

† The other "costs," *e.g.*, "world opinion," the effect on order and stability and on the influence of law, if considered, were probably too intangible and too indeterminate to be given much weight.

11 The treaty between Egypt and the United Kingdom was signed Oct. 19, 1954. 210 U.N.T.S. 3, 24. The Egyptian government terminated it by a decree of Jan. 1, 1957, effective retroactively to Oct. 31, 1956. U.N.T.S. 366.

adverse action in the face of unanimous Western opposition (even apart from any veto). Legal justification for the action could be found in the fact that it was strictly limited to achieve the obviously necessary purpose of protecting an international waterway against unlawful seizure and the interruption of its operations. Politically—even in the General Assembly—the action would command substantial sympathy and some support, since many nations were shocked by Nasser's highhanded action and most believed that he could not keep the Canal operating. And Great Britain could be very conciliatory, disclaim any selfish interests, indicate willingness to negotiate with any Egyptian government, promise to withdraw promptly upon the assurance of international control, offer something to Egypt, give the United Nations some new authority in the operation and protection of the Canal. In the end, the United Nations would do nothing or very little and might even help assure an international status for the Canal (which even the Soviet Union basically favored).

I do not know whether any policy paper along these lines was ever written or how the counsels of government divided. We do know that Great Britain (and the other governments) did not at the time respond with force and for several months engaged in various diplomatic efforts to achieve an acceptable status for the Canal. Later, Prime Minister Eden wrote that from the beginning the British government had determined that

> our essential interests in this area must be safeguarded, if necessary by military action, and that the needful preparations must be made. Failure to keep the Canal international would inevitably lead to the loss one by one of all our interests and assets in the Middle East, and even if Her Majesty's Government had to act alone they could not stop short of using force to protect their position.[12]

Eden then tells us that the British did not act for two reasons:

> The first answer is political. As signatories of the Charter of the United Nations, we were bound first to seek redress by peaceful means. Though we were conscious of the Soviet veto and of the weakness of the United Nations as an executive body, we knew that we must at some time take the issue to the Security Council. We

12 Eden, pp. 474-75.

might even be able to prod them into action. To accept this did not mean abandoning the use of force as a last resort.[13]

The second reason given by Eden for British failure to react with force was that Great Britain was militarily unprepared to take effective action.

One cannot, of course, weigh the two reasons given to determine how much each contributed to the decision. The skeptic about law may suggest that the military reason was wholly sufficient to explain what happened. (There is evidence that Great Britain began immediately to improve its military posture in the area.) But military preparedness is often a matter of degree, and Britain obviously had some military forces in the area. One cannot disentangle, either, the "political" reason given by Eden into its legal component and others. Important, no doubt, was opposition by the United States to any military action; but that too reflected, in part, the influence of the U.N. Charter. Eden did expressly assert that Great Britain (and France presumably) were deterred in some measure by Charter obligations and were motivated, at least, to postpone action which might be deemed unlawful until lawful efforts proved inadequate to safeguard their interests.

The importance of the law's achievement should not be underestimated. Violations that are not committed immediately often do not occur at all. Lawful alternatives can develop. (In the present case, some progress was being made at the end of October, when the situation exploded.[14]) Inertia and other forces set in. Even the sad aftermath at Suez does not wholly contradict this. The British and French invoked military force after Israeli troops swept into Sinai; indeed, it is now accepted that the three nations acted in concert. But one can only speculate whether if other developments had not pressed Israel to action, the British and French would have attempted to seize the Canal (even if negotiations had not produced a satisfactory solution). Perhaps having failed to act promptly and decisively, the political fac-

---

[13] Eden, pp. 478-79. In fact, lawyers told him that force would be illegal even as a last resort. In the House of Lords, on September 12, 1956, Lord McNair, one of Great Britain's leading international lawyers, said that he was "puzzled by the massing and display of armed force in the Eastern Mediterranean." He went on to remind the government that the law was no longer what it had been fifty years earlier, and concluded that "so far as the events in the present controversy up to date are known to us, I am unable to see the legal justification of the threat or use of armed force by Great Britain against Egypt in order to impose a solution of this dispute." 199 Parl. Deb., H.L. (5th ser.) 659-62 (1956).

[14] See n. 3 above.

tors which earlier deterred military action—including the influence of law—might have become even stronger and prevailed. Indeed it is difficult to imagine that having failed to react immediately, the British and French could have taken military action later, when the shock and the tension had ebbed, the Canal was running, and some kind of compromise had been offered by Nasser and approved in the United Nations.[15] Perhaps they later recognized that nationalization of the Canal gave no plausible legal justification for the use of force, whereas acting in Israel's wake afforded at least some colorable justification. If so, one might say, the use of force occurred later only because, for reasons mostly independent of the nationalization of the Canal, Israel was prepared to attack Egypt.

One cannot deal confidently with the might-have-beens of history. One need not claim more than the evidence supports. One can say with some confidence that in regard to the nationalization of the Suez Canal, law helped at least to postpone the use of force and give diplomacy an opportunity.

[15] This, it is said, was President Nasser's expectation too. See *N.Y. Times*, Oct. 9, 1966 § 1, p. 21.

The Law Fails But Is Vindicated: Suez (II)

LOUIS HENKIN

AT SUEZ AND AT SINAI, in the autumn of 1956, international law failed in its primary purpose: to maintain order by deterring violation of agreed norms. But law was later vindicated, its authority reaffirmed, and the violations largely undone.

Major hostilities in the area began on October 29, when Israeli forces moved into the Sinai Peninsula. These hostilities had a background and context—in Arab opposition to the creation of the state of Israel, the war of 1948, the armistice agreements of 1949, continued Arab hostility (including periodic border incidents thereafter), the closing to Israeli shipping of the Suez Canal and the Gulf of Aqaba.

The outbreak of hostilities had its immediate cause. Since 1955, Israel had been subjected to hit-and-run guerrilla raids by armed "Fedayeen" operating from Egypt and other Arab countries with the knowledge and support of the Arab governments.[1] Such raids took place again on October 20 and 24, 1956, and several Israelis were killed. On October 23, Egypt, Jordan, and Syria announced a unified command of their military forces. On October 27 Israel began mobilizing. On October 29 its forces crossed the armistice lines into the Sinai Peninsula and routed the Egyptian forces.

In consequence of the Israeli attack (and its success), the governments of France and the United Kingdom, on October 29, issued an ultimatum calling on both sides, within twelve hours, to cease hostilities and to withdraw their forces to a distance ten miles from the Suez Canal. They asked the Egyptian government to agree that Anglo-French forces should move temporarily into the area to protect the Canal. Israel accepted the ultimatum, but Egypt did not.[2] British and French airborne forces landed at key points around the Canal.[3]

The United States and the Soviet Union both condemned the resort to force, the latter even threatening military intervention. After efforts to deal with the situation in the Security Council were frustrated by veto, the General Assembly adopted resolutions calling for cease-fire and withdrawal of forces, and establishing a United Nations Emer-

[1] Robertson, pp. 10-11, 19-21.   [2] Id. at 171-72.
[3] Id. at 238.

gency Force to supervise and secure the cessation of hostilities.[4] Eventually all British, French, and Israeli forces were withdrawn from Egyptian soil.

The Attack at Sinai Under International Law

It was Israel that initiated major military action in the area, on October 29. Was this in violation of international law? If so, why did international law fail to inhibit Israel?

The members of the United Nations, and most writers, have taken the view that the action of Israel was a violation of Article 2(4) of the U.N. Charter.[5] There was clearly a use of force against the territorial integrity and political independence of Egypt. The only question is whether Israel's action was within the exception permitted by Article 51 for self-defense against armed attack. The argument for Israel would recite that Egypt had insisted that there was still a state of war with Israel (which it invoked to justify its denial of the Suez Canal to Israeli vessels); that this state of war, plus repeated Arab threats to destroy Israel, the recent announcement of a joint Egyptian-Jordanian-Syrian High Command, and the recurrent "Fedayeen" raids were part of a single, recurring armed attack that began in and had continued since 1948. The denial of the Suez Canal to Israel in violation of the Treaty of 1888, of the armistice agreements, and of an express resolution of the Security Council would be cited as additional evidence of the continued aggression.[6] And Israel's action was not a disproportionate response since only destruction of the "Fedayeen" bases and their equipment could assure its security.[7] There also are those who might justify Israel with the argument that the Charter did not outlaw the use of force in "anticipatory self-defense" or to protect vital interests,[8] but the government of Israel eschewed such broad readings of the Charter.

[4] G.A. Res. 997 and 1000 (Emer. Sess. I), U.N. GAOR, Supp. 1, at 2, U.N. Doc. A/3354 (1956).

[5] For opposing views compare those of A. Goodhart and Q. Wright, "Some Legal Aspects of the Suez Situation," in *Tensions in the Middle East* 243 (C. Thayer ed., 1958).

[6] Article I of the Treaty of Constantinople provides: "The Suez Maritime Canal shall always be free and open, in time of war as in time of peace, to every vessel of commerce or of war, without distinction of flag." For the Security Council resolution calling on Egypt to remove its restriction, see 6 U.N. SCOR, 558th meeting, 2-3 (1951). A brief statement of the Israeli position appears in Israel Office of Information, *The Gulf of Akaba* (1957).

[7] Robertson, p. 159.   [8] See Chapter XVI, pp. 231-36.

Israel's situation was unique and its arguments were not implausible. Still, Israel's lawyers, one may guess, recognized that the contemplated action might be viewed as a violation of the Charter. And there are many reasons why one might have expected Israel to obey this international law. Although Israel is a new nation, it draws on long roots of law and law observance. It has well-developed legal institutions and many lawyers trained in Western legal traditions. As a small country surrounded by enemies, Israel also needs the protection of international law, particularly of the United Nations Charter. It owes its existence, in substantial measure, to the United Nations organization and is concerned for the support of the majority of its members. It has had a strong legal and political case against renewed Arab attacks (which it continues to expect) and does not wish to jeopardize its case by unlawful and unwise action.

If nevertheless Israel disregarded the probable law, there must have been much on the other balance. There was domestic pressure on the government to "do something" about the "Fedayeen" raids. There were, principally, Israel's security needs as it saw them. The cost of inaction loomed high, with increasing Arab armament and aggressiveness and harassing border attacks that took lives and interrupted the life of a struggling country; unless something was done, the Arabs might be emboldened to strike harder, or to goad Israel into striking, at a time of *their* choosing. The Sinai action, then, would, at the very least, dramatize the situation as intolerable. If successful, it would put an end to border attacks and the danger of all-out attack for some time thereafter. It might permit capture of important equipment. It could provide a buffer on Egyptian territory against further Egyptian attacks. It could open the Gulf of Aqaba to Israel. If it truly succeeded— and if Anglo-French cooperation helped seize control of the Canal—it might finally open the Suez Canal to Israeli shipping. And it might even topple Nasser, cause instability and disarray in Egypt and additional humiliation to all the Arabs, thus further reducing the threat of Arab attacks for a long time and perhaps even leading to a true peace in the area.

The gains to be anticipated were substantial. On the other hand, the cost of the action and of the possible violation of international law did not seem very high. Israel had confidence in its military prowess and disdain for Egypt's army and the other Arab military forces; Anglo-

French military support, we now know, was promised.[9] Off the battle-field, Israel had little to suffer in response from the Arabs; there were no relations with them and their hostility was already acute. In the United Nations, there might be some criticism, but Israel had a politi-cally sympathetic position even if not an undeniable legal case. Israel had been making friends in Africa and Asia and had some sympathy in Latin America; Nasser had lost friends and sympathy by the seizure of the Canal (even if he also had gained prestige in some quarters).[10] Israel could, of course, count on British-French political support. So-viet hostility could be expected but it would not matter; the United States, in the face of British and French support and just before a na-tional election in which a large "Jewish vote" was at stake, might chas-tise mildly but would not urge or permit strong action.

The Anglo-French Action Under International Law

On October 30, British and French forces landed around the Canal. If the decision was carefully considered, the governments must have been aware that most lawyers would consider the action a violation of Article 2(4) of the United Nations Charter.[11] The action at Suez was clearly a use of force against the territorial integrity and political in-dependence of Egypt. Nor could that use of force be justified within the exception of Article 51. On its face, at least, that provision permits unilateral force only to defend oneself or another member if an armed attack occurs; the British-French attack could hardly fall within that exception.[12]

Whatever the lawyers said, the governments did not claim that the

[9] Robertson discusses the Anglo-French commitment of aid to Israel at 157-74. This has been confirmed in a book by one close to the events and decisions, Anthony Nutting, *No End of a Lesson, the Story of Suez* (1967).

[10] Compare Robertson, pp. 85 and 127, for differing attitudes toward Egypt.

[11] Compare Lord McNair's admonitions in the House of Lords, Chapter XIII, n. 13, above, though these were not addressed to the use of force in the context of an Israeli attack. See also, *e.g.*, Q. Wright, "Intervention, 1956," 51 *Am. J. Int'l L.* 257, 272-74.

[12] Later, indeed, especially after and in the light of Suez, some British and Common-wealth writers did argue that self-defense against armed attack was not the only unilateral force permitted by the Charter, that the Charter does not bar necessary force to protect vital interests against injustice or against violations of international law. See, *e.g.*, J. Stone, cited above, Chapter X, n. 28; J. Stone, *Aggression and World Order* (1958); D. Bowett, *Self-Defense in International Law* (1958) 182-99; J. Brierly, *The Law of Nations* (6th ed., H. Waldock, 1963) 413-32. But in 1956 the British and French Foreign Offices must have known this was not the accepted view, or the view that would probably prevail in this case. And indeed this was not the view espoused by these governments.

use of force was justified because Nasser's nationalization of the Canal had violated international law or had jeopardized their vital interests. After the passage of months and intervening negotiations with some prospect of success, that justification would have appeared ludicrous. Their ultimatum, and the arguments later made in support of it, principally asserted a right to act as "volunteer policeman," to use force to separate Israel and Egypt in order to protect the Canal—akin to the right, in some municipal systems, for a private citizen to intervene to put down a breach of the peace if the police failed to do so.[13] Accepting the *bona fides* of the justification, the ultimatum offered a novel interpretation of the Charter. Note that it was a narrow exception to Article 2, tailored to the circumstances, not likely to recur often, and not subject to the dangers of some broader theory which would have permitted force at any time in support of vital interests as each nation saw them. Still, the United Kingdom and France might have expected that it was not a theory that would be acceptable to most nations. One may even wonder whether these countries would be prepared to promote this proposition as a general principle of law.

Why did the law fail to deter them? Again, one can only speculate. France and the United Kingdom played important roles in the creation of the United Nations and the drafting of its Charter. They had no doubt taken seriously their undertaking to eschew unilateral force. Both were generally law-abiding countries with an interest in law observance and developed institutions to take account of law. In both countries there were domestic forces, including powerful opposition parties, that might condemn such violations of the Charter.[14] On the other hand, perhaps, although the Charter had been influential in the decision not to respond to the nationalization by immediate use of force, its influence was not yet strong enough to rule out force altogether. There were long traditions, old habits, established institutions involving reliance on military power, in particular to support interests of empire and trade in Asia and Africa. Perhaps neither France nor Great Britain had yet fully recognized that the day of white force against independent nations on the non-white continents was over.

---

[13] *Restatement (Second) of the Law of Torts* §§ 116, 119 (c) (1965).

[14] See the sharply critical speech delivered on September 12, 1956, by the British Leader of the Opposition, Hugh Gaitskell, 558 Parl. Deb., H.C. (5th ser.) 15-32 (1956). On November 3, Gaitskell demanded the resignation of the government because it had flouted the call for a cease-fire by the United Nations General Assembly, *id.* at 1858-62.

There was, of course, the calculation of cost and advantage. No doubt the principal motivation of the Anglo-French action was to take the Canal from Egypt. If their action on the heels of Israel's victories also toppled President Nasser, so much the better. As regards the Canal, they had refrained from prompt military action because of American insistence and to see what political pressure could achieve. But President Nasser had not given way, and indeed his action had brought him new prestige and new confidence. Diplomatic efforts, including those in the United Nations, had produced some concessions to the international character of the Canal but would still leave Egypt with more control than was desirable or safe. Most of the reasons for moving against the Canal—the great advantages and the low cost—remained persuasive. Perhaps it would be difficult, especially after the intervening delay and the diplomatic efforts, to act in admitted response to the nationalization, but Israel's problems, interests, and plans gave a new and better opportunity. Now force could be used not in response to Nasser's nationalization but for the purpose of protecting the Canal against destruction due to Israeli-Egyptian hostilities. In this context the costs of the action might be even lower. Militarily, Egypt, defeated by Israel, could do little to frustrate the operation. Politically, the United Kingdom and France could "ride out" whatever the defeated President Nasser and his friends, even the Soviet Union, could attempt. In the Security Council, the Soviet Union could muster few votes against the united opposition of all the Western powers and their friends; in any event they could veto action in the Security Council, as indeed they did after Israel marched.[15] In the Assembly, there might be criticism, particularly from the Asian-African bloc, but especially if Nasser was humbled or even replaced, the United Kingdom and France could be very conciliatory. They could stress the limited and temporary nature of their action, their concern for the international waterway so essential to world trade, their readiness to withdraw after settling the Canal question with a new Egyptian government, and perhaps even their contribution to relieving another world sore spot by bringing a measure of peace also between the Arabs and Israel. In such circumstances even those most concerned for the Charter and for international law might accept the justification claimed for the action or treat it as a small violation—in any event, one best quickly forgotten after the situation was restored.

[15] 11 U.N. SCOR, 749th meeting, 30 (1956).

Such might have been the position paper written in the Foreign Office or the Quai d'Orsay, taking into account the views of the lawyers. And the policy might have succeeded in some measure if the military operation had been more successful. In the end, these calculations, even more than those of Israel, went awry, partly because they did not anticipate the strong threat of intervention by the Soviet Union, largely because of erroneous assumptions as to what the United States would say and do. Israel, in fact, despite all that happened later in the United Nations and the eventual withdrawal of its forces, did not miscalculate badly. If it did not succeed in getting passage through the Canal or toppling Nasser, it dealt a severe blow to his prestige and that of the Egyptian army, dramatized an intolerable situation, halted the "Fedayeen" raids, obtained access to the Gulf of Aqaba, and succeeded in bringing into the area a United Nations force as a buffer against attack and further raids. The British and French, on the other hand, suffered deep humiliation and mortal injury to their aspirations to maintain big-power status, important damage to their relations with the Arabs, and the end of any hope of restoring some international control over the Suez Canal.

The Law Vindicated

Suez is an instance of the law's failure: it did not deter violations. Suez is also an instance of the law's vindication: the violations were judged and condemned, the unlawful acts largely undone, the law of the Charter reaffirmed and established. The law was applied by the General Assembly, a highly political body. The members were no doubt moved by a variety of motives, among which the authority of the Charter and of the United Nations itself were not insignificant.

It is pertinent to ask, in particular, whether international law played any role in the major determinants in the drama, in the attitudes of Russia and the United States. In political terms one can explain their attitudes without mention of international law. The Soviet Union was delighted with events that diverted attention and political pressure from its military action against the rebellion in Hungary. The Soviet Union also seized an opportunity to pursue the policy it had already initiated of wooing the Arabs and trying to replace Western influence with their own. Condemnation of Israel, even more of Britain and France, suited that policy. Russia could gain great kudos with the Arabs even if French and British forces were not in fact withdrawn.

That in part under threat of Soviet military intervention the Western powers had to withdraw gave the Soviet Union a new standing as friend of the Arabs.

It was exactly this political gain for the Soviet Union which Secretary of State Dulles sought to avoid or minimize, and which largely determined the policy of the United States.[16] Dulles strove to maintain Arab friendship and to prevent an Arab-Soviet alignment. Perhaps Dulles also feared that the Soviet Union might indeed send troops to aid Egypt and obtain a military toehold in the Middle East.* The position of the United States, on the side of Soviet Union and against its principal allies, can be explained, then, as an effort to keep Russia out of the Middle East and to keep the Arabs from aligning themselves firmly on Russia's side. But many are persuaded that the United States, at least, was substantially influenced by its view of the law. It saw the attacks on Egypt as violations of the Charter, which, if tolerated, would damage the principles against the use of force and the future of the United Nations as an influence for peace and security. American spokesmen, including Secretary Dulles and President Eisenhower, repeatedly invoked the Charter and expressed sorrow that they felt obliged to vindicate the law even against their country's best friends.[17] Others in the United States, including lawyers sympathetic to Israel, felt that it would be a serious blow to the United Nations and the law against force if the attacks were not disowned and condemned. (It is another question whether, even as a matter of good law, the United States should not have pressed for United Nations action, which, while requiring the withdrawal of the attacking forces, would have achieved some settlement between Israel and Egypt and perhaps imposed some international control over the Canal.[18])

That Russia, too, cared about the law of the Charter is a possibility that few in the West would even consider. Still, it may well be that the law against external force is in the Soviet interest to maintain. The So-

---

* Domestic opposition to this policy in the United States was not effective against President Eisenhower's tremendous popularity; perhaps it was decided that the Republican party could not command "the Jewish vote" in any event.

[16] For a critical discussion of United States policy at Suez see essays by A. Wolfers, E. Hula, and H. Morgenthau in *Alliance Policy in the Cold War* (A. Wolfers ed., 1959).

[17] See, *e.g.*, 35 *Dep't of State Bull.* 745 (1956).

[18] See L. Henkin, "The United Nations and Its Supporters: A Self-Examination," 78 *Pol. Sci. Q.* 504, 519-20 (1963). See also B. Cohen, *The United Nations; Constitutional Developments, Growth, and Possibilities* 43-66 (1961).

viet Union may have begun to recognize by 1956 that war is too dangerous, that external aggression could not succeed, that the world community will no longer tolerate it, that Soviet interests do not require it, indeed that dynamic communism must use indirect, more subtle methods, and that outlawing war would improve the climate for internal "wars of liberation."[19] The Soviet Union, then, it is plausible to suggest, also was partly concerned to vindicate the law against unilateral, external force.

I conclude that, at Suez, after helping to induce Great Britain and France not to react immediately with force to Nasser's nationalization of the Canal, the law failed to deter them from collusion with Israel in important violations of the Charter of the United Nations. But the transgressors were called to order, and members of the United Nations, including at least the United States, were motivated, in some measure, by concern to uphold the principles of the Charter and the effective authority of the United Nations organization for maintaining peace and security.

In turn, the actions in the Suez-Sinai drama had their effect on international law.* The position of the United States and the Soviet Union, supported by the overwhelming majority of members in the United Nations, reaffirmed the norm of Article 2(4), and did so against major powers. Rejected too, in effect, were arguments that the Charter took a broad view of "armed attack" which justified self-defense, that it permitted anticipatory self-defense, national "police action," or the use of force to protect vital interests against injustice. The facts of the case indeed demonstrated that what each nation believes is necessary (or important, or conducive) to its survival (or security, or national interest) is a very uncertain affair. What may at one moment seem essential may prove hardly so at the next; within the same government there will be many views as to whether a particular action is essential to survival, or only possibly convenient to some immediate interest; those outside will often see the situation quite differently. Suez enhanced the authority of the United Nations, showing its particular effectiveness when the United States and the Soviet Union joined to lead it; and it is credible,

---

* By nullifying all efforts to establish some permanent international control for the Canal, the Suez-Sinai affair helped confirm the right of a nation to exercise eminent domain within its territory, even as to property which had some international character, and even in the face of undertakings not to do so.

[19] See *Hearings*, cited above, Chapter VIII, n. 26.

as claimed, that the United States, perhaps others, felt compelled to act as it did because of the existence of the United Nations and the influence of its members. Suez helped confirm that, despite provocation, external unilateral force against another nation was not acceptable international behavior, at least by big powers against small, at least by Western nations against Asian or African states.* It remained to be seen whether the principle could also withstand other forces—opposition to colonialism or racial oppression, the rising influence of Communist China, the declining influence of India, new instabilities, new configurations of power and influence in and out of the United Nations, the sad example of the Kashmir war of 1965, and, most seriously, the spreading hostilities in Vietnam.

* Later Israel-Arab hostilities, in June, 1967, do not vitiate these conclusions. See pp. 160-62, above.

II. UNDERLYING ISSUES

A. *Arab and Jewish Nationalism and the Rights of Refugees*

The Recognition of the Jewish People in International Law[1]

NATHAN FEINBERG

I. *Humanitarian Interventions*

EVERY student of international law who deals with the history and problems of humanitarian intervention knows how considerable is the part played by intervention on behalf of the Jews.[2] Nor is this surprising. The history of the Jewish people is so permeated by persecution and oppression, that the need for extending to Jews some measure of protection has never yet ceased. This tragic situation was succinctly summarized by Jean Jaurès when he described the Jews as "the world's great victim of spoliation."

Towards the end of the Eighteenth Century, Edmund Burke, speaking in the House of Commons, summed up the situation of the Jews in the following terms:

> "Having no fixed settlement in any part of the world, no kingdom nor country in which they have a Government, a community and a system of laws, they are thrown upon the benevolence of nations and claim protection and civility from their weakness as well as from their utility.... From the east to the west, from one end of the world to the other, they are scattered and connected.... Their abandoned state and their defenceless situation calls most forcibly for the protection of civilized nations. If Dutchmen are injured and attacked, the Dutch have a nation, a Government and armies to redress or revenge their cause. If Britons are injured, Britons have armies and laws, the laws of nations ... to fly to for protection and justice. But the Jews have no such power and no such friend to depend on. Humanity then must become their protector and ally."[3]

[1] This article was written before the creation of the Jewish State and the international resolutions which preceded it. It does not deal, therefore, with the various questions arising thereout and bearing on the present subject.

[2] In this article the term "intervention" is used not in its extensive sense including all forms of representation and action, and even forcible interference by foreign Powers, but in its more limited meaning and milder form, usually known as "intercession."

[3] *The Parliamentary History of England from the earliest period to the year 1803* (London, 1814), Vol. XXII, cols. 223-224.

See also *British and Foreign State Papers* where the following sentence occurs in a dis-

The record of humanitarian interventions on behalf of the Jews is, indeed, a very long one. Some of them were made at international conferences, and congresses, while others involved the use of normal diplomatic channels; some were intended to ameliorate the situation of the Jews alone, while others aimed at the weal of a wider class, in which the Jews were included.[4]

As early as 1648, the Peace Congress of Westphalia dealt with the question of the Jews of the Netherlands and took steps to secure for the Jews of that country the right to settle and trade in Spain and Portugal. Rather more than a century later, in 1774, England and Holland interceded with the Empress Maria Theresa, and succeeded in preventing the expulsion of the Jews of Bohemia and Moravia.

From the beginning of the Nineteenth Century until the outbreak of the First World War there was scarcely a single important international congress or conference at which the state of the Jews in one country or another was not under consideration either directly or indirectly. Thus, the Congress of Vienna endeavoured to ameliorate the civil state of the Jews in the German Confederated States; it also forbade Holland to alter those articles in its Constitution which secured to members of all faiths freedom of religion and equality before the law. At the Congress of Aix-la-Chapelle consideration was given to the Memorandum of the Reverend Lewis Way, an English Clergyman, who advocated a "reform of the civil and political legislation concerning the Jewish Nation." A special protocol was signed in which the Congress recognized the justice of the general tendency and the worthiness of the object of his proposals, and in which it declared that the Jewish problem was one "which should equally occupy the statesman and the friend of humanity." The London Conference of 1830 required Greece, upon its liberation from Turkey, to recognize the freedom of worship and perfect equality of all the subjects of the new State, and hence of the Jews as well. The Conference of Constanti-

---

patch sent by the British Government to Bucharest in 1867: "The peculiar position of the Jews places them under the protection of the civilised world." (Vol. 62, p. 705.)

[4] Regarding interventions on behalf of the Jews, see more particularly Lucien Wolf, *Notes on the Diplomatic History of the Jewish Question, with Texts of Treaty Stipulations and other Official Documents*, London, 1919; Cyrus Adler and Aaron M. Margalith, *With Firmness in the Right, American Diplomatic Action Affecting Jews, 1840-1945*, New York, 1946; Max J. Kohler, *Jewish Rights at International Congresses*, Reprint from the American Jewish Year Book 5678, Philadelphia, 1917; N. Leven, *Cinquante Ans d'Histoire, l'Alliance Israélite Universelle (1860-1910)*, tome premier, Paris, 1911.

nople, held in 1856, dealt with the state of the minorities in Moldavia and Wallachia; and the Paris Congress of the same year took note of the Firman of the Sultan known as the *Hatti-Humayoun*, which confirmed the equal rights and privileges of all Christian Communities and other non-Mohammedan subjects of the Sultan, including the Jews. The Berlin Congress of 1878 demanded that civil and political rights be granted to the Jews of Bulgaria, Serbia, Montenegro and Roumania, and this, in spite of the determined opposition of the Russian representative Prince Gortchakow, who wanted to restrict Jewish rights to freedom of religion alone. The Conferences of Madrid in 1880 and of Algeciras in 1906 considered the situation of the Jews of Morocco. The Peace Conference of Bucharest in 1913 dealt, at the suggestion of the United States of America, with the state of the minority populations of those areas which were to be transferred from one State to another as a result of the Balkan Wars.

Quite apart from these international gatherings, however, interventions on behalf of the Jews were made from time to time. Thus, in 1840, Great Britain, the United States and Austria intervened against the Damascus Blood Libel. In 1867 the United States intervened on behalf of the Jews of Serbia, and in 1897 against the persecution of the Jews in Persia. From 1878 onwards repeated protests were made by the signatories to the Treaty of Berlin against the violation of the Treaty by the Roumanian Government. In order to evade the fulfilment of the express obligations imposed on her by Article 44 of that Treaty, Roumania had proclaimed all the Jews in her territory as aliens and made their naturalization dependent upon separate parliamentary approval in each individual case. The extent to which such approval was given may be seen from the fact that out of a total Jewish population of 250,000, only some 400 Jews were granted Roumanian citizenship during the thirty-six years which elapsed between the Congress of Berlin and the First World War. So critical had the situation of the Jews in Roumania become that even the United States, which was not a signatory to the Treaty of Berlin, was led to intervene on their behalf. "This Government cannot be a tacit party to such an international wrong," wrote John Hay, Secretary of State, in his famous note of July 17th, 1902; "it is constrained to protest against the treatment to which the Jews of Roumania are subjected, not alone because it has unimpeachable ground to remonstrate against the resultant injury to itself, but in the name of humanity. The United States may not authoritatively appeal to the stipulations of the Treaty of Berlin to which it was not and can not become a signatory, but it does earnestly appeal to the principles consigned therein, because they are the principles of international law and eternal justice. . . ."[5]

It may be of interest to mention in this connection that for a period of more than seventy years protection was extended to the Jews of Palestine by the British Consulate at Jerusalem, from the time it was opened in 1839 until the outbreak of the First World War. This duty was imposed on the Consulate in a special instruction given by Lord Palmerston, then Foreign Secretary, "to afford protection to the Jew generally."[6]

So much for interventions on humanitarian grounds, which aimed at protecting Jews in foreign countries where security of life and elementary human rights were refused to them. There were also, however, "interventions by right," that is to say, interventions the purpose of which was to protect the citizens of the intervening State itself from any deprivation of rights by foreign Governments by way of racial discrimination.

The first interventions of this kind appear to have been those of the Grand Dukes of Lithuania, Sigismund the First and Sigismund August. Towards the middle of the Sixteenth Century they interceded with the Muscovite Grand Duke, later Tzar of Muscovy Ivan the Terrible, to obtain freedom of travel and trade for Lithuanian Jews in his dominions and to secure the liberation of a number of Jewish merchants of Lithuania who had been detained in Muscovy. At approximately the same time, the Turkish Sultan Suleiman the Magnificent intervened on behalf of certain Marranos (forced Jewish converts) in Ancona who had been condemned to the stake and most of whom were Turkish subjects. In his ultimatum of 1556 to the Pope, the Sultan demanded the immediate liberation of his subjects, and threatened retaliation on the Christians resident in his Empire if his demand was not fully satisfied.

The most important of these "interventions by right" were undoubtedly the interventions of the United States against the expulsion of its Jewish nationals from Tzarist Russia on the sole ground of their being Jews. The American Government stressed that it was not prepared un-

---

[5] Adler and Margalith, *op.cit.*, pp. 125-126.

[6] Albert M. Hyamson, *The British Consulate in Jerusalem in Relation to the Jews in Palestine, 1838-1914* (London, 1939), part I, p. 2.

der any conditions to acquiesce in the application of a religious test to citizens of the United States and solemnly protested against any religious or racial discrimination being directed at American Jews "when availing themselves of the common privilege of civilized peoples to visit other friendly countries for business or travel."

Such protests were repeatedly made for more than thirty years; they ended only in 1911 with the abrogation of the Commercial Treaty with Russia. Incidentally, it is significant that in its notes to Tzarist Russia the United States Government did not neglect the opportunity of protesting against the persecution of the Jews of Russia itself. The reason given, and stressed as early as 1881, was "that an amelioration of the treatment of American citizens in Russia could only result from a very decided betterment of the condition of the native Hebrews."

The above instances do not exhaust the list of interventions, but they sufficiently demonstrate that over a period of a century and more international law was frequently concerned with the Jewish question and resorted to for the purpose of ameliorating the state of the Jews in various countries.

II. *Rights of Jews, not of the Jewish People*

The common element, and indeed the chief characteristic, of all interventions during the period preceding the First World War was that the Jewish question was not dealt with in its entirety, as a question concerning a nation or a people and requiring a political solution; consideration was given only to the state of the Jews in particular countries where and when they were deprived of their rights. These interventions had in common the further characteristic that they aimed at protecting only individual and not collective rights. The struggle for rights which the Jews pursued in their respective countries was carried on under the banner of the emancipation of the individual Jew, and aimed only at obtaining religious freedom and civil and political rights. For this reason such international support as was extended to Jews did not go beyond these objectives. The whole conception of the Jewish question in the age of emancipation was made clear by Clermont-Tonnerre when, on December 23rd, 1789, he said in the French Constituent Assembly: *Il faut refuser tout aux Juifs comme nation et tout leur accorder comme individus*, and this phrase is illustrative of the attitude of international law towards the Jewish question throughout the Nineteenth Century.

Moreover, during the period in question the Jews were merely the subject of negotiations. Nor could they possibly have been anything else, since they were treated only as a mass of dispersed persons, as fragments of a people which could not be provided with any international legal status.

This view of the Jewish question is to some extent reflected in the terminology used during the Nineteenth and at the commencement of the Twentieth Centuries in the exchange of notes and correspondence between States or Governments or diplomatic representatives abroad, as well as in the minutes of international conferences and in the texts of treaties. The terms generally used are: Jew, Israelite or, more rarely, Hebrew, thus clearly referring to individuals who belong to a certain section of the population and differ from the majority. No particular intention or distinction appears to have been attached to these terms which, in certain documents, are used quite indiscriminately. Nor are there any grounds for assuming that the term "Jew" was used chiefly in describing the Jews of Eastern Europe, and that "Israelite" was meant for those of Western Europe.

None of the documents just referred to contains a definition of the terms in question or suggests a criterion whereby a man is recognized as a Jew, an Israelite or a Hebrew. But it is clear that these terms were meant in the sense generally current at that period, namely, as indicating the faith of the persons so described and distinguishing them from followers of other religions. Indeed, many documents expressly refer to "persons of Jewish faith," "persons of Israelitish faith," and even "persons of Hebrew faith" or "persons professing Judaism." Occasionally we also find the expression "persons of Jewish origin," or "persons of Jewish ancestry."[7]

When it was desired to designate the Jews of a given State as a group, it was customary to use the term "race" and hardly ever "people."[8] Thus, for example, at the meeting of the Congress of Berlin in

[7] Mention may be made in this connection of the peculiar phrase used by the Austro-Hungarian Government at the time of the "incident" relating to the appointment, in 1885, of Mr. Anthony M. Keiley as Envoy Extraordinary and Minister Plenipotentiary of the United States of America at Vienna. The Austro-Hungarian Government objected to the appointment of Mr. Keiley because his wife was a Jewess, and argued "that a person of *proximate Semitic descent* would be excluded both by the social and diplomatic circles of Vienna" (Adler and Margalith, *op.cit.*, p. 336).

[8] Mr. Ch. E. Smith, United States Minister in Russia, reported in his dispatch of April 6th, 1891, to the American Secretary of State Blaine that he had suggested to the Russian Foreign Minister de Giers that an international conference should be called "to consider

1878 the senior French representative Waddington described the Jews of Roumania as "the Jewish race"; and in the terms of reference to the United States Mission which was sent to Poland in 1919 to inquire into the relations between the Jewish and non-Jewish elements in Poland, the Secretary of State Lansing used such expressions as "discrimination against the Jewish race" and "advantage to the Jewish race." It is unnecessary to remark that in such cases the term "race" is used not in its anthropological or biological sense, but as descriptive of a group of human beings who are associated and linked by common history, religion, culture, tradition and language.

The term "race" was usual in the negotiations conducted between Tzarist Russia and the United States with reference to the situation of the Jews in Russia, the Russian Government standing firmly by the claim that "the Russian Jews constitute a race separate and apart from the rest of the people," and that therefore the Jewish question in that country must be viewed as one of race and not of religion.

International documents employing the term "Jewish nation" are hardly to be found during the period in question. The most important of them is the protocol signed at Aix-la-Chapelle and already mentioned above.[9] Among the signatories were Metternich, Castlereagh, Hardenberg and Nesselrode; and it cannot be assumed that their intention was to describe a political unit, i.e., an aggregation of individuals united by political ties. This may have been a case of merely customary usage, for it was the practice not only in the Middle Ages but also in the Seventeenth and Eighteenth Centuries to describe the Jews as a "nation" in the wider sense of the term as used in those days. Thus, for example, the Declaration of the Estates General of the United Netherlands of 1657 speaks of the Jews of Holland as "the Jewish nation"; while even the famous Edict of Toleration issued by King Joseph II in 1782 describes the Jews of the Hapsburg Empire as "the Jewish

---

the conditions of the Israelites and the question of restoring Palestine to the hands of this people as the asylum and home of such of their race as might choose to go from other lands" (Adler and Margalith, op.cit., p. 225). It may be mentioned by the way that the expression "Jewish nation" is to be found in the Report of the Anglo-American Committee of Enquiry regarding European Jewry and Palestine (Cmd. 6808 [1946], p. 26).

9 In a dispatch sent by Viscount Palmerston, British Foreign Secretary, on August 11th, 1840, to Viscount Ponsonby, the British Ambassador at Constantinople, the following passage appears inter alia: "There exists at present among the Jews dispersed over Europe a strong notion that the time is approaching when their nation is to return to Palestine . . ." (Albert M. Hyamson, op.cit., part I, p. 33).

nation." It is, however, possible that the use of the term "Jewish nation" in the Protocol of Aix-la-Chapelle is largely due to the Memorandum of the Reverend Lewis Way, in which the Jewish question was dealt with not only from its political and social but also from its national aspect. Way himself used the term "Jewish nation" because he regarded the Exile of the Jews as only an intermediate stage in their history and advocated their restoration to Palestine.

III. *The change during the First World War*

It was felt necessary to offer this cursory survey of the humanitarian interventions on behalf of the Jews, because it is only in the light of these interventions that the fundamental, if not indeed revolutionary, change in the approach to the Jewish question during the First World War can be adequately appreciated. Thereafter the Jewish question was raised to the level of a question involving a nation as a whole, i.e., an entity entitled to separate national existence and to the organization of its life within the framework of the State.

This change came about as a consummation of the development which took place in the life of the Jews themselves during the second half of the Nineteenth Century, with the awakening of their national consciousness. Yet, fundamentally, it may be said to be the outcome of the principle of national self-determination which became the basis of the new world order—a principle which recognizes the inherent right of every nation to maintain its national existence and considers the national State to be the natural framework within which this object may be achieved. Indeed, from the moment that the Principal Allied and Associated Powers began to formulate their War Aims during the First World War, they steadily proclaimed that one of the principal purposes of the war was the liberation of oppressed and persecuted peoples and the achievement of freedom and independence by all nations, whether large or small.

It is clear that this principle could not fail to be applied to the Jewish people, which has continued to preserve its national identity since the destruction of the Jewish State, persevering in the hope of its redemption and keeping faith with its lost fatherland throughout its wanderings. It can hardly be denied that when the Jews were expelled from their country they departed *animo revertendi*. The hope of returning to their ancestral home and once again taking up the broken thread of their history has remained the mainspring of Jewish life, being manifested both in the religious garb of faith in the coming of the Messiah and in those practical efforts to return and settle in the land of their forefathers which were repeatedly made whenever the possibility arose.

During the second half of the Nineteenth Century the urge to return to Zion began to assume a modern form, which culminated in the convening by Theodor Herzl of the First Zionist Congress at Basle and the creation of the Zionist Organization in 1897.

The official United States publication entitled "Mandate for Palestine" characterizes Zionism in its broader aspect as a movement of return which "dates from the final destruction (135 A.D.) of the Jewish Kingdom and the resulting edict of Rome which denied to the Jews further access to Palestine."[10] Similarly, the British official monograph on "Zionism" prepared during the First World War recognizes Zionism as "the oldest national movement in history." It even speaks of the Zionism of the Bible, which "is far anterior to the Exile of Israel—even the first Exile. It dates back to the prehistoric days of Israel in Egypt; and Moses was the first Zionist."[11]

On November 2nd, 1917, the document known as the Balfour Declaration was issued. In this document the British Government declared its sympathy with "Jewish Zionist aspirations" in the following terms:

"His Majesty's Government view with favour the establishment in Palestine of a national home for the Jewish people, and will use their best endeavours to facilitate the achievement of this object, it being clearly understood that nothing shall be done which may prejudice the civil and religious rights of existing non-Jewish communities in Palestine, or the rights and political status enjoyed by Jews in any other country."

The Balfour Declaration, which was made public immediately upon issue, was endorsed by many of the Allied Powers, and also received full support from the United States. At the session held by the

10 *Mandate for Palestine*, prepared in the division of Near Eastern Affairs, Department of State (Washington 1927), p. 7.

11 *Zionism*, Handbooks prepared under the direction of the Historical Section of the Foreign Office, No. 162 (London, 1920), p. 2.

Supreme Council of the Peace Conference early in 1920 the Declaration was defined by Lord Curzon, then Foreign Secretary, as a "formal declaration." Lord Curzon went on to add that the Jews regarded it "in its entirety as the charter of their rights."[12]

In its judgment regarding the legal status of Eastern Greenland, the Permanent Court of International Justice laid down that an oral declaration made by a Minister for Foreign Affairs constitutes a valid obligation and "is binding upon the country to which the Minister belongs."[13] Even more binding, therefore, is a written declaration following upon negotiations with the prospective beneficiaries and issued as the considered decision of the Cabinet as a whole.

The Balfour Declaration, it is true, was given not to a State but to an entity which, in French terminology, is referred to as *collectivité non-étatique*. This, however, does not deprive the Declaration of its binding effect, for in accordance with contemporary international law, a "people" can also be the recipient and subject of international rights, as Article 80 of the Charter of the United Nations explicitly states.

The British Government itself never held the Balfour Declaration to be a mere assurance of benevolent attitude, but always regarded it as a binding promise and formal undertaking. In a letter to the Palestine Arab Delegation, dated March 1, 1922, the British Colonial Office stressed that "His Majesty's Government are bound by a pledge which is antecedent to the Covenant of the League of Nations, and they cannot allow a constitutional position to develop in a country for which they have accepted responsibility to the Principal Allied Powers, which may make it impracticable to carry into effect a solemn undertaking given by themselves and their Allies."[14] And a few months later, in the White Paper of June 1922, the British Government expressly declared that the Declaration "is not susceptible of change."[15] Similar

---

[12] David Lloyd George, *The Truth about the Peace Treaties* (London 1920), vol. II, pp. 1182 and 1188.

[13] *Publications of the Court*, Series A/B, Nr. 53, p. 71.

It may be observed that in Article 6 (a) of the Charter of the International Military Tribunal which tried the German Major War Criminals at Nuremberg, the crimes against peace, in addition to waging war in violation of international treaties and agreements, included the waging of war in violation of international assurances (see *Cmd.* 6964 [1946], p. 3). Indeed, the principle *pacta sunt servanda* was first formulated not with regard to treaties alone but also in respect of assurances. It was Cicero who raised the question: *pacta et promissa semperne servanda sint.*

[14] *Cmd.* 1700 (1922), p. 6.

[15] *Ibid.*, p. 19.

statements were made by members of the British Government and British statesmen on other occasions as well.[16]

The legal validity of the Balfour Declaration is also demonstrated by the Preamble to the Mandate for Palestine which states in its third recital regarding the Balfour Declaration that "recognition has thereby been given to the historical connection of the Jewish People with Palestine and to the grounds for reconstituting their National Home in that country." It is clear that recognition can be given only by a document which has legal validity and binding force.

In 1937, Mr. Ormsby Gore, then Colonial Secretary, was asked by the Permanent Mandates Commission whether the British Government still considered itself to be bound by the Balfour Declaration after the Royal Commission had stated that the Mandate had become unworkable. In his reply he stated that he certainly had no intention of conveying the impression that the Balfour Declaration was not still a binding obligation on both the League and the United Kingdom. "Obviously, like the Mandate, it was still a binding obligation, and would remain so until replaced by an independent Jewish State."[17]

[16] Georges Scelle compares the Balfour Declaration to the "Law of Guarantees" of the Italian Government enacted in 1871: "Bien qu'émanant d'un seul gouvernement, elle se présentait comme la constatation de la solidarité internationale, de l'utilité publique internationale en ce qui concerne la situation des Juifs dispersés parmi les Etats. Elle constatait la nécessité de donner une expression juridique à la solidarité spéciale de la communauté Juive, au sein de la solidarité générale de la communauté internationale" (Les caractéristiques juridiques internationales du Foyer National Juif, in Palestine, No. 8 [Mai, 1928], p. 103).

In Temperley's classic work on the Paris Peace Conference it is pointed out that "in spirit, if not in form, this [the Balfour] Declaration recorded an understanding between the Entente Powers and World Jewry" (H.W.V. Temperley, A History of the Peace Conference of Paris [London, 1924], vol. VI, p. 135).

The synallagmatic character of the Declaration is further stressed in the statement that it is beyond doubt that the Declaration "is in purpose a definite contract between the British Government and Jewry represented by the Zionists. . . . No time limit is set for the performance; completion alone appears to have been intended as a conclusion of the contract. It would thus seem to be an agreement incapable of being greatly varied except by consent" (Ibid., pp. 173-174).

In the course of the debate which took place in the House of Commons on May 23rd, 1939, Mr. Winston Churchill criticized the White Paper issued a few days earlier on the ground that it was "a breach and repudiation of the Balfour Declaration," "a violation of the pledge," "another Munich," adding that this was "but a one-sided denunciation, what is called in the jargon of the present time a unilateral denunciation of an engagement" (Parliamentary Debates, House of Commons, vol. 347, Nr. 108, col. 2183).

[17] Permanent Mandates Commission, Minutes of the Thirty-Second (Extraordinary) Session (Geneva, 1937), p. 182.

The British Government considered the Balfour Declaration from the very outset as the cornerstone of its future policy in Palestine. On two occasions, the British Government insisted that the Declaration should be incorporated in the text of the Mandate and was not prepared to give way to the objections raised. On the first occasion, in 1920, the opposition came from the representative of France on the Supreme Council, when Great Britain demanded that the text of the Mandate should "repeat the pledge in the precise form in which it had originally been given."[18] On the second occasion, the question came up during the drafting of the Anglo-American Convention of December 3, 1934, relating to the Palestine Mandate, when Great Britain adopted a similar attitude, based in this case on the interest taken in the United States "in the policy of establishing a national home for the Jewish People in Palestine and the warm support which it has received in that country."[19]

Eventually the Balfour Declaration was incorporated in the Preamble to the Mandate which, in its second recital, declares that the Principal Allied Powers had agreed "that the Mandatory Government should be responsible for putting into effect the Declaration originally made on November 2, 1917, by the Government of His Britannic Majesty, and adopted by the said Powers." In the third recital, as we have seen, it is stated that by his Declaration "recognition has . . . been given to the historical connection of the Jewish people with Palestine and to the grounds for reconstituting their national home in that country." It follows that, by virtue of the confirmation of the Mandate by the Council of the League of Nations, the existence of the Jewish people, its historical connection with Palestine and its right to reconstitute its National Home in that country were internationally recognized. And if we further refer to Article 4 of the Mandate, which provides for the establishment of an appropriate Jewish Agency as the representative of the Jews in all countries of the world, it will clearly appear how fundamental was the change which took place in the treatment of the Jewish question.

Before, however, considering the various aspects of the new status acquired by the Jewish people under the Palestine Mandate, brief reference should be made to the appearance of the Zionist Delegation before the Peace Conference in 1919-1920. This, indeed, is no mere epi-

[18] David Lloyd George, op.cit., vol. II, p. 1182.
[19] Mandate for Palestine, Department of State, p. 81.

sode in Jewish diplomatic history, but a fact which throws light, from the legal point of view, on the international status there and then granted to the Jewish people

IV. *The Zionist Organization at the Peace Conference*

The representatives of the Zionist Organization were invited to appear on February 27th, 1919, before the Supreme Council of the Peace Conference—the "Council of Ten"—and to submit the demands of the Jewish people in connection with Palestine. It was only natural that the Zionist Organization should have been the body invited to submit the historical claim of the Jewish people to Palestine, just as later the same body should have been recognized by the Mandate as the representative of the Jewish people.

As far back as 1896, Theodor Herzl had already stressed, in his book "The Jewish State," that the organization to be established as the organ of the Zionist movement would assume the functions of a *negotiorum gestor*, since "the Jewish people is prevented at present through the Diaspora from itself conducting its political transactions."

And indeed, during the twenty-two years which elapsed between its foundation and its appearance at the Peace Conference, the Zionist Organization was the spokesman of the Jewish people in all that concerned Palestine. Even before its efforts were rewarded by the Balfour Declaration, the Zionist Organization could point to considerable political achievements, including negotiations with the British Government in respect of two proposals which involved the recognition of Jewish aspirations towards self-government. One proposal, made in 1902, envisaged the establishment of a Jewish Colony at Al Arish, a territory in the Peninsula of Sinai. This project came to nought on account of difficulties in securing the necessary supply of water for irrigation. The second proposal related to the establishment under general British control of an autonomous Jewish Colony or settlement in East Africa (Uganda) with a Jewish official as the Chief of the local administration.[20] This plan was likewise abandoned, largely because of the oppo-

[20] It may be mentioned by the way that the terms of the proposed concession to be granted to the Jews in Uganda were drafted in the offices of Lloyd George, Roberts & Co.— a firm of solicitors headed by the man who, fourteen years later, was to play so important a part in the issue of the Balfour Declaration. The principal object of the enterprise was defined in the Draft Concession as "the settling of Jews under conditions favourable to their retention and encouragement of the Jewish National idea." Further on, it was stated

sition of the Zionist Organization to Jewish settlement in any country other than Palestine, even for a *Nachtasyl*. The Seventh Zionist Congress of 1905 rejected the proposal, while expressing its appreciation of the interest shown by the British Government in the solution of the Jewish question and uttering the hope that it would in the future give its support to the Zionist cause.

It is only from a purely formal aspect that we are here concerned with the appearance of the Zionist Delegation before the Supreme Council. In a note on the organization of the Peace Conference, prepared by the French Government in November 1918, consideration had already been given to the form of representation of "the States which are in the process of formation but not yet recognized . . . : the Yugoslavs, the Finns, the Ukrainians, the Lithuanians, the Esthonians, the Latvians, the Arabs, the Armenians and the Jews of Palestine."[21] The Jews are expressly listed among the peoples about to establish States of their own. It is true that the expression "Jews of Palestine" is used and not the unqualified term "Jews," but it is reasonable to assume that the reference was not to the Jews at the same time resident in Palestine, who then numbered about 60,000 in all, but to the Jewish people as a whole, and in particular to those Jews who saw their future in Palestine. This is clearly corroborated by the fact that the Peace Conference invited the Zionist Organization and not the representatives of Palestine Jewry.

The invitation to the Zionist Organization was sent under Article 1, paragraph 5, of the Rules of Procedure of the Peace Conference which provided that neutral Powers and States in process of formation would be heard, whether orally or in writing, upon the invitation of the five Principal Allied and Associated Powers, at meetings especially devoted to the examination of questions which concerned them directly.[22]

On previous occasions, too, the Jews had sent representatives to in-

---

that the laws and regulations should be adopted for the "well-being of the Jewish people." The territory was to have been called "New Palestine" and to have been given the right to adopt and use a special national flag of its own. The form of popular Government to be established was to have been Jewish in character and with a Jewish Governor to be appointed by His Majesty in Council. The original text of the draft is to be found in the Central Zionist Archives at Jerusalem.

21 David Hunter Miller, *My Diary at the Peace Conference with Documents* (New York, 1928), vol. II, pp. 11 ff.

22 *Ibid.*, vol. III, p. 355.

ternational conferences and congresses in order to plead in defence of their rights. The Congress of Vienna had been attended by representatives of the Jewish communities of Frankfort-on-the-Main as well as of the three main Hanseatic cities, Hamburg, Bremen and Luebeck, while representatives of the *Alliance Israélite Universelle* had been present at the Berlin Congress. The communications of those representatives, however, had been in the nature of petitions only. Similarly, the Committee of Jewish Delegations and other Jewish organizations, which in 1919 and 1920 appealed to the Peace Conference for the protection of Jewish minorities, had the status of petitioners only. If, on the other hand, the Zionist Organization as the representative of the Jewish people was granted a different status—one which, rudimentary though it may have been, was actually equivalent to that of the neutral States— this could only have been by reason of the fact that the Jewish people was recognized as a national State-forming entity, as a "State in formation."

V. *Recognition of Nations*

In addition to the recognition of States, of Governments, of insurgents and of belligerents, an entirely new concept was introduced into international law during the First World War, namely, that of the recognition of Nations. Thus, the Czechoslovaks and the Poles who had long aspired to national independence formed national Committees for the purpose of representing their respective liberation movements and serving as "trustees" for their future Governments; they also recruited from among their fellow-nationals, who were prisoners of war in the Allied countries, separate armed forces under their own flags and military jurisdictions.[23] So long as the peoples themselves had not revolted

23 In the first World War more than a million Jews fought in the ranks of the Allies. About the same number of Jewish soldiers served in the armies of the United Nations during the Second World War. In both wars, however, Zionists made strenuous efforts to secure for the Jews an opportunity of making their contribution to Allied victory not only as citizens of their respective countries, but also as members of the Jewish people, as distinct units under the Jewish flag.

In July 1917, during the darkest days of the war, the British Cabinet accepted the Zionist proposal to raise a Jewish Regiment within the framework of the British Army. Accordingly, all Jewish volunteers were distributed in four Battalions, known as the Thirty-Eighth, Thirty-Ninth, Fortieth and Forty-Second Royal Fusiliers. After the conquest of Transjordan they were permitted to be known as the Judaean Regiment, as a mark of appreciation for their achievements. The Menorah (seven-branched candlestick) with the word *Kadimah* (Forward) engraved at the base was the badge of the Jewish Battalions.

Upon the outbreak of the Second World War, the Jewish Agency took steps to secure the

and so long as effective authority had not been established by them anywhere within the territories of the future States, the Czechoslovaks and the Poles could clearly not have been recognized as belligerents, nor, *a fortiori*, could there be any recognition of a Czechoslovak or Polish State. It was at this point that the innovation came, peoples standing on the threshold of their political independence being recognized as nations. Recognition of a nation has been described as a step, not indeed equivalent to recognition of a new State, since there is no such State in existence as yet, but as a preliminary recognition, which means that the State about to be born is regarded as though it were already born: *nasciturus pro jam nato habetur*. And since that recognition is preliminary, it is also conditional.[24]

In his standard work on international law, the eminent French authority, Paul Fauchille, reaches the conclusion that the Balfour Declaration and the similar declarations of the other Allied and Associated Powers, "undoubtedly constituted the recognition of the Jewish people as a nation."[25] To the recognition of the Czechoslovaks and the Poles was thus added "the official recognition as a nation of yet another oppressed people."[26] True, neither the Balfour Declaration nor the Palestine Mandate speaks of a State but of a National Home. Without dwelling on the various interpretations which have been given to this new term in international law, it should be pointed out that no less an authority than the Palestine Royal Commission of 1936 reached the conclusion that, although there had been no intention of immediately establishing a Jewish State, "His Majesty's Government evidently realized that a Jewish State might in the course of time be established."[27] In his evidence before that Commission, Mr. Winston Churchill also stated that there was nothing in the phraseology of the Balfour Declaration to

---

approval of the British Government for the formation of a Jewish fighting force; but this was granted only after numerous disappointments and as a result of protracted negotiations lasting over a period of several years. Not before September, 1944, did the British Government agree to the establishment of a Jewish Brigade Group to take part in active operations. The Jewish flag was adopted as its colours, and its flash was the Shield of David in gold on a blue-and-white ground, with the initials of the equivalent for "Jewish Brigade Group" —*Hativa Yehudit Lohemet.*

[24] R. Erich, *La naissance et la reconnaissance des Etats*, Recueil de Cours de l'Académie de Droit International (Paris, 1926) tome 13, pp. 438, 479-480.

[25] Paul Fauchille, *Traité de Droit International Public* (Paris, 1921), tome 1, première partie, pp. 314-316.

[26] *Ibid.*

[27] *Cmd.* 5479 (1937), pp. 24 and 33.

prohibit or preclude the ultimate establishment of a Jewish State. Possibly of even greater bearing is the interpretation of the Balfour Declaration by Lord Curzon, in 1920, as Secretary for Foreign Affairs, when he stated at a meeting of the Supreme Council: "That Declaration contemplated, first, the creation of a national home for the Jews. . . . Secondly, it was of the highest importance to safeguard the rights of minorities; first the rights of the Arabs, and then of the Christian Communities. Provision was made for this in the second part of the Declaration."[28] This explicit statement that the Arabs are to be safeguarded as a minority clearly means that the Jews would become the majority in the country. Lord Curzon's interpretation is of particular importance as he took part throughout in the formulation of the Balfour Declaration and during its early stages even showed signs of opposition to the policy embodied in it. He clearly had no other desire than to clarify the true intentions of those who made the Declaration and the purpose for which it was made.

The Balfour Declaration may thus be regarded as involving the recognition of the Jewish people as a nation, similar to the recognition afforded to the Czechoslovaks and the Poles; which means that the Declaration granted that homeless people a right to independent existence in their own State. But the situation of the Jews was in no way the same as that of the Czechoslovak and Polish peoples. The latter were settled in their own countries and required nothing to achieve independence save the establishment of Governments which would take over the rule of the respective countries. At the time of the publication of the Balfour Declaration, however, the overwhelming majority of the Jewish people were absent from the country which was to be their National Home. And it was apparently this special circumstance which led to the term "people" being used instead of "nation." It may also be that for linguistic reasons the term "nation" was found inappropriate, since French and English, unlike the languages of Eastern Europe, often use "nation" as synonymous with "State," meaning a society under one Government. According to this terminology the Jews were considered to be members of the nations in whose midst they dwelt.[29]

However that may be, what we are here concerned with is the legal aspect of the question. If recognition of the Czechoslovaks and of the Poles as "nations" involved the right of peoples living in their own

[28] David Lloyd George, op.cit., vol. II, p. 1185.
[29] See Colonial No. 15, 1925, p. 26.

countries to constitute themselves into States and even offered a measure of advance recognition to such States, then the recognition of the
Jews as a "people" involved the grant to that people, absent as it was
from its home, of the right to return thereto, in order that in the course
of time it might achieve nationhood within the framework of a State
of its own.

VI. *The Special Circumstances Governing the Recognition of the Jewish People*

As we have seen, the Palestine Mandate recognized the Jews as a
people, the historical connection of that people with Palestine, and its
right to reconstitute its National Home in that country.

Insofar as the Mandate recognizes the existence of the Jewish people
and its connection with Palestine it confirms facts and is therefore
merely declaratory. But insofar as it grants the Jewish people the right
to return to Palestine and reconstitute there its National Home—thus
recognizing the Jewish people as a subject of international law—the
Mandate is constitutive of that right and is therefore law-making. It is
hardly necessary to add that the recognition of the Jewish people as a
subject of international law is confined to those rights and duties which
are provided for in the Palestine Mandate.

The right to the National Home is granted to the Jewish people as
a whole, and not to any part of it; it is granted not to Zionists or to
Jews who have settled in Palestine or who will settle there, but to all
Jews wherever they may be. When the Mandatory Power departed
from this fundamental principle in the White Paper of 1930, the then
Prime Minister, Ramsay MacDonald, felt bound to correct this misin-
terpretation. In his letter to Dr. Ch. Weizmann, President of the Jewish Agency, dated February 13th, 1931, which was stated to be the authoritative interpretation of the White Paper in question, MacDonald
expressly confirmed that "the undertaking of the Mandate is an undertaking to the Jewish people, and not only to the Jewish population of
Palestine."[30] In other words, as pointed out by Van Rees, Vice Chairman of the Permanent Mandates Commission, the Jewish people is virtually part of the population of Palestine.[31]

It was on the basis of the view that the undertaking of the Mandate,

[30] *Parliamentary Debates, House of Commons*, vol. 248, No. 58, col. 750.

[31] D.F.W. Van Rees, *Les Mandats Internationaux, Les Principes Généraux du Régime des Mandats* (Paris, 1928), p. 100.

was an undertaking to the Jewish people as a whole, that Article 80 of
the Charter of the United Nations provided that nothing shall be done
"to alter in any manner the rights whatsoever of any States or any peoples" in any of the mandated territories, as long as the mandates are
not replaced by trusteeship agreements. From the history of this Article it is known that the words "any peoples" were intended primarily
to refer to the Jewish people as far as its right to the National Home
was concerned.

It was also on the basis of the above view that, as early as 1917, when
the Balfour Declaration was drafted, it was thought necessary to remove any doubt as to the status of those Jews who would not settle in
Palestine. To this end the second part of the Declaration provided that
"nothing should be done which might prejudice . . . the rights and political status enjoyed by Jews in any other country."[32] Neither the
Czechoslovaks nor the Poles required any such provision, as no international rights were granted to members of those peoples who lived
outside the limits of the future States of Czechoslovakia and Poland.
Like Lithuanians, Latvians and Esthonians residing outside the limits
of their prospective States, both Czechoslovaks and Poles lent their aid
to the revival of their countries of national origin and greatly contributed to the setting up of the new States. Yet this was not an integral
part of the process and was not relevant from the legal point of view.
The building up of the National Home could not have been effected
without the collaboration and assistance of Jews throughout the world;
and it was for the purpose of representing them in all that concerned
the establishment of the National Home that the Jewish Agency was
created. Under these circumstances it was seen fit to secure that the
grant of the National Home, and the ensuing right of all Jews to take
part in the up-building of that home, did not in any way affect their
status and allegiance as citizens of the countries to which they
belonged.

It may be observed in this connection that neither the Mandate nor
any other international document contains a definition of the term
"Jewish people" or a criterion by which membership of the Jewish people could be ascertained. This is not accidental. The peculiar situation

---

[32] At first this provision could apply only to Great Britain, and to the other States which
endorsed the Balfour Declaration. As from the inclusion of the Declaration in the Palestine
Mandate, however, the provision became binding on all States members of the League of
Nations.

of the Jewish people, which is the outcome of its abnormal history, does not permit of a comprehensive legal formula which would be applicable to all Jews wherever they might be.[33]

"Generally we accept as Jews all who say they are Jews," declared the representative of the Jewish Agency before the United Nations Special Committee on Palestine; "all who come and say they are conscious of being Jews are accepted. . . ."[34]

VII. *Status of the Jewish Agency*

It was natural that the recognition of the right of the Jewish people to a National Home should be accompanied by the creation of a representative Jewish body with special rights and powers for the period of the establishment of the National Home. Accordingly, Article 4 of the Palestine Mandate provides for the establishment of an appropriate Jewish Agency, "recognized as a public body for the purpose of advising and co-operating with the Administration of Palestine in such economic, social and other matters as may affect the establishment of the Jewish National Home and the interests of the Jewish population in Palestine, and subject always to the control of the Administration, to assist and take part in the development of the country." Article 6 of the Mandate requires the Administration of Palestine to encourage, in co-operation with the Jewish Agency, close settlement by Jews on the

[33] "The term Jew has a fourfold meaning, according to whether it is defined on the basis of religion, nationality, origin or race." Arthur Ruppin, *The Jewish Fate and Future* (London, 1940), p. 3.

The constitution of the enlarged Jewish Agency, embodied in the agreement of August 14th, 1929, between Zionists and non-Zionists, refrained from defining the term "Jew," only "Zionist" and "non-Zionist" being defined. "Zionist means a person associated with the Agency in the capacity of a member and representative of the Zionist Organization. Non-Zionist means a person associated with the Agency otherwise than in the capacity of a member and representative of the Zionist Organization."

[34] In reply to the question: "Who is considered by the Jewish Agency as legally a Jew? Is it religion, or race, or what other criterion?", the representative of the Jewish Agency stated that "technically and in terms of Palestine legislation, the Jewish religion is essential." In this he was referring to the present organization of the Jewish Community in Palestine, under the Religious Communities (Organization) Ordinance, 1926. When the Chief Rabbi of Palestine was asked by a member of the United Nations Special Committee on Palestine: "Cannot those who, although they were once Jews, now believe in Christ as one of the Holy Trinity . . . still be regarded as Jews?" His Eminence replied: "A distinction must be drawn between a good Jew and one who is not a good Jew. The adoption of another faith does not make the Jew into a non-Jew from the Jewish religio-legal aspect. . . . In short, a Jew who has abandoned Judaism for another faith continues in a legal sense to be a Jew, but he is certainly not a good Jew—he is a renegade Jew."

land; while according to Article 11, paragraph 2, the Administration is authorized to "arrange with the Jewish Agency . . . to construct or operate, upon fair and equitable terms, any public works, services and utilities, and to develop any of the natural resources of the country, in so far as these matters are not directly undertaken by the Administration." In the second paragraph of Article 4 the Mandate recognizes the Zionist Organization as the Jewish Agency, "so long as its organization and constitution are in the opinion of the Mandatory appropriate," and requires it to take steps in consultation with the Mandatory "to secure the co-operation of all Jews who are willing to assist in the establishment of the Jewish National Home."

In 1929 the enlarged Jewish Agency was established, composed of both Zionists and non-Zionists. However, during the period in which the Zionist Organization was the Jewish Agency, it acted as the representative of the Jewish people and not of the Zionists only: "Nor does the Zionist Organization, in discharging its functions as the Jewish Agency for Palestine, regard its duty as being owed merely to its own supporters. It deems itself a trustee for the Jewish people as a whole."[35]

Although the Palestine Mandate required the Zionist Organization to secure the co-operation of non-Zionists in consultation with the British Government, the latter left it to the Zionist Organization itself to determine the form and method of participation of the non-Zionists in the Agency. When in 1923 the Zionist Organization notified the British Government of the first resolutions adopted regarding the proposed enlargement of the Jewish Agency, the Colonial Office replied that the matter was one which must be left to the discretion of the Zionist Organization.[36]

The British accredited representative to the Permanent Mandates Commission re-affirmed this attitude even more strongly in 1931. He drew attention to the limited extent to which the mandatory Power was entitled to interfere in the organization of the Jewish Agency.[37]

[35] *Memorandum on the Development of the Jewish National Home, 1925-1926*, submitted by the Zionist Organization to the Secretary-General of the League of Nations for the information of the Permanent Mandates Commission, 1926, pp. 31-32.

[36] *Memorandum submitted by the Zionist Organization to the Secretary-General of the League of Nations for the information of the Permanent Mandates Commission, 1924,* pp. 5-6.

[37] *Permanent Mandates Commission, Minutes of the Thirty-fourth Session, 1938,* p. 43. With the confirmation of the Constitution of the enlarged Jewish Agency, the British Government gave the Zionist Organization a binding promise that in the event of the dissolution of the enlarged Agency they "will, provided that they are satisfied that the organization

The Jewish Agency was recognized in the Palestine Mandate as a "public body," and as the result of the powers conferred upon it, the Agency was legally placed in a special position *vis-à-vis* the Administration of the country. As we have seen, however, the Zionist Organization had to act in connection with the enlargement of the Agency "in consultation with His Britannic Majesty's Government." Accordingly, the special position of the Jewish Agency appears to have extended beyond the boundaries of Palestine, as far as its relations with His Majesty's Government were concerned.[38] As to the powers vested in the Agency, although they relate only to advice and co-operation, their legal value as internationally recognized rights is thereby by no means diminished.

When the Permanent Court of International Justice was called upon to interpret Article 4 of the Mandate in connection with the Mavrommatis Palestine Concession, it expressed the opinion that "the Jewish Agency is in reality a public body, closely connected with the Palestine Administration."[39] Some of the judges went even further in their separate opinions. Thus, Judge Altamira pointed out that "the recognition of that organization as a true public body, with the rights conferred on it by Article 4 of the Mandate, implies that it must be accorded privileged or exceptional treatment."[40] Judge Caloyanni stated that "from the study of these texts [the English and French versions of the Palestine Mandate] it clearly appears that the Zionist Organization is so closely connected with the Palestine Administration that for purposes of developing the country as regards economic questions and as regards works of public utility, it appears to be unable to do without this Organization, unless it consented."[41]

As we have just seen, the functions of the Jewish Agency were lim-

---

and constitution of the Zionist Organization are at that time appropriate, recognize it as the Jewish Agency, and the Organization shall in that event be deemed to have reverted in all respects to the status which it possessed before the enlargement of the Agency." *Protokoll der Verhandlungen des XVI. Zionistenkongresses und der Konstituierenden Tagung des Council der Jewish Agency fuer Palaestina* (London, 1929), p. 73.

[38] In the Colonial Office letter dated June 3rd, 1922, the Zionist Organization was required to provide formal assurance that it "accepts the policy as set out in the enclosed statement and is prepared to conduct its own activities in conformity therewith." It is also stated in the letter that a special position is assigned to the Zionist Organization as "an agency authorized to co-operate with *His Majesty's Government*" (*Cmd.* 1700 [1922], p. 17).

[39] *Publications of the Court*, Series A, Nr. 2, p. 21.

[40] *Publications of the Court*, Series A, Nr. 11, p. 37.

[41] *Ibid.*, p. 50.

ited to advice and co-operation and did not embrace legislative or administrative authority. When the Mandate was being drafted the British Government had already found occasion to stress that the Jewish Agency did not "possess any share in the general administration of the country."[42] It later repeated this statement in the White Paper of 1930[43] and in various statements before the Permanent Mandates Commission.

In the course of its examination of the Annual Reports for Palestine, the Mandates Commission criticized the mandatory Power on a number of occasions on the ground that it did not fully implement Article 4 of the Mandate and that it did not enable the Jewish Agency, in its capacity of "official advisory body," to play the part "which, without any doubt, it had been intended to play by the authors" of the Mandate.[44]

It is not proposed to deal in this article with the relations between the Jewish Agency and the Palestine Administration during the twenty-five years of the mandatory regime, but one particular aspect of the question must here be discussed.

As early as 1922 the British Government stated, in its reply to Cardinal Gasparri, that the Order in Council providing for the administration of Palestine did not propose even to refer to the existence either of a Jewish Agency or of the Zionist Organization.[45] Nor was the Palestine Mandate as such incorporated in the municipal law of the country, although it was the duty of the Mandatory Power to do so in accordance with international law.[46] Moreover, the Palestine Courts have adopted the principle that "insofar as the Mandate is not incorporated into the Law of Palestine by Order in Council, its provisions have only the force of treaty obligations and cannot be enforced by the Courts."[47]

---

42 *Cmd.* 1700 (1922), pp. 7 and 18. See also *Cmd.* 1708 (1922), p. 4.

43 *Cmd.* 3692 (1930), p. 8.

44 See, in particular, *Permanent Mandates Commission, Minutes of the Seventeenth (Extraordinary) Session*, 1930, p. 39, and *Minutes of the Twentieth Session*, 1931, p. 85.

45 *Cmd.* 1708 (1922), p. 4.

46 In the advisory opinion of the Permanent Court of International Justice on the exchange of Greek and Turkish populations, it was laid down as a self-evident principle that "a State which has contracted valid international obligations is bound to make in its legislation such modifications as may be necessary to ensure the fulfilment of the obligations undertaken" (*Publications of the Court*, Series B, Nr. 10, p. 20).

47 See *inter alia* High Court case No. 55 of 1925, in *The Law Reports of Palestine, 1920-1933* (London, 1934), p. 51, and High Court case No. 19 of 1947 regarding the legality of the Land Transfer Regulations, 1940 (*Annotated Law Reports*, 1947, pp. 499 ff).

As a result, the legal position of the Jewish Agency is to this day so vague and unsatisfactory that it is even doubted whether the Agency may be considered as a juristic person with the right to own property, to sue and be sued in the Courts, etc.[48] Thus, when the Commissioner for Migration and Statistics was asked, in the course of the evidence he gave to the Royal Commission in 1936 on behalf of the Palestine Government, whether the Jewish Agency is regarded as "legally . . . a corporate body or anything of that sort," he did not hesitate to reply: "No, it is not a legal person in law."[49] Nor is this all. In the Memorandum which the Jewish Agency submitted in May 1930 to the British Government it was stated that—

"in recent months, when the Jewish Agency had pointed out to the Palestine Administration the rights and privileges of the Jewish Agency, and the obligations towards it of the Palestine Administration, it has on more than one occasion received the reply that the Mandate constitutes no part of the Law of Palestine, with the implication that legally the Administration of Palestine is under no obligation to recognize the Jewish Agency or its special position."[50]

[48] In 1926, however, the District Court of Jaffa gave judgment stating that the Zionist Organization was an agency recognized by the Mandatory as a "public body" and that although not registered with the Law of Palestine it is capable of bringing an action (*Collection of Judgments of the Courts of Palestine, 1919-1933* [Tel Aviv, 1935], vol. IV, pp. 1451-1452). To the best of our knowledge this is the only decision on the point.

In a Memorandum submitted by the Jewish Agency to the British Government in 1930, a special chapter was devoted to the position of the Jewish Agency. In this chapter the complaint was made that the British Government did not appreciate fully its obligation "to formulate the necessary provisions and to take the necessary measures to secure that the Administration of Palestine shall act in accordance with Article 4 of the Mandate." Consequently, "there has been no clear definition of the status and rights of the Jewish Agency" (*The Development of the Jewish National Home in Palestine*, Memorandum submitted to His Majesty's Government by the Jewish Agency for Palestine [London, 1930], pp. 70-71).

[49] *Palestine Royal Commission, Minutes of Evidence heard at Public Sessions*, London, 1937, p. 5. The Commissioner for Migration and Statistics also pointed out that the Jewish Agency was specifically mentioned in the Immigration Ordinance, and said: "I think this is probably the only Ordinance in which it has specific mention; but I cannot say that definitely." (*Ibid.*, p. 5). The Jewish Agency is also mentioned in the Concession granted to Pinhas Rutenberg for the generation and supply of electrical energy in the District of Jaffa, dated September 12, 1921 (*The Laws of Palestine* [London, 1934], vol. I, p. 653), and in the Road Transport (Amendment) Ordinance, 1941 (*The Palestine Gazette*, No. 1097, Supplement No. 1, p. 41).

[50] *The Development of the Jewish National Home*, Memorandum submitted to His Majesty's Government by the Jewish Agency for Palestine, 1930, p. 75.

It is submitted that the Jewish Agency should have been recognized as a juristic person, even though the Palestine Mandate had not been incorporated in the Palestine legislation. Support for this submission may be found in the advisory opinion of the Permanent Court of International Justice regarding the competence of the Courts in the Free City of Danzig, where the International Court recognized the right of Danzig railway officials, who had become Polish officials and were governed by Polish law, to avail themselves before the Danzig Courts of the Agreement concerning Officials (*Beamtenabkommen*) concluded between Poland and Danzig; and this, in spite of the fact that the Agreement had not been incorporated in Polish law.[51] According to this advisory opinion the intention of the contracting parties was the decisive factor. In respect of the Jewish Agency the intention of the Council of the League of Nations, which defined the terms of the Palestine Mandate, was undoubtedly to secure for the Jewish Agency a legal status within Palestine, irrespective of whether the Mandatory did or did not include the Mandate in the Palestine legislation.

It is because the Jewish Agency is the representative of the Jewish people in all matters affecting the establishment of the National Home that, as we are about to see, the proposal was made in 1937 to recognize the Agency as the nucleus of the Jewish Government. The Royal Commission, which recommended the establishment of a Jewish State in part of Palestine, proposed that a Treaty of Alliance should be negotiated by the Mandatory with the Zionist Organization and that such treaty should declare that, within as short a period as might be convenient, a sovereign independent Jewish State would be established.[52] In the course of the discussion of the Royal Commission's Report by the Permanent Mandates Commission, Mr. Ormsby Gore was asked whether the Zionist Organization could be given legal powers to negotiate treaties. He replied that although treaties could only be concluded with a Government, yet in view of the fact that there was no Jewish Government, it would be necessary to "create quite informally provisional bodies to enter into provisional agreements. . . . The negotiations would have to be conducted with such people as . . . in the Mandatory's opinion represented a nucleus of a provisional Government of the area eventually to become a State";[53] the suitable body for

---

[51] *Publications of the Court*, Series B, Nr. 15, pp. 17-18, 27.

[52] *Cmd.* 5479 (1937), p. 381.

[53] *Permanent Mandates Commission, Minutes of the Thirty-Second (Extraordinary) Session*, 1937, p. 43.

the purpose would be the Jewish Agency, the official body recognized under the Mandate as representing the Jews and, "though predominantly Zionist, it contained some non-Zionists as well."[54]

When the special session of the General Assembly of the United Nations was held in April-May 1947 in order to deal with the Palestine question, various Jewish organizations and bodies applied to be permitted to appear before the Assembly for the purpose of stating their views. At its meeting on the 5th of May, the General Assemby instructed the First Committee (Political and Security) to grant a hearing to the Jewish Agency, and left the decision regarding the other applications to the discretion of the Committee. Those who supported the hearing of the Jewish Agency based themselves among other considerations on the "legal status" of the Jewish Agency, on its "official character" and on the fact that it was a "public body" under the terms of the Mandate. As the First Committee had decided not to hear other Jewish Organizations, the Jewish Agency remained the only Jewish body which was given the right to appear before the Committee, to state its case, to reply to questions, and to express its opinion on the proposals discussed. The Jewish Agency was also the only Jewish body admitted to the *ad hoc* Committee on Palestine (set up by the second regular session of the United Nations General Assembly) and to the Partition sub-Committee of that *ad hoc* Committee.[55]

VIII. *Minority Rights*

From the formal legal point of view the grant of a minorities status to Jews in various European countries may not amount to the recognition of the Jews as a people. Even national minorities are only frag-

[54] *Ibid.*, p. 191. A measure of recognition of the Zionist Organization as the nucleus of a Jewish Government may also be found in the agreement signed in London on January 3rd, 1919, between Emir Feisal, representing and acting on behalf of the Arab Kingdom of Hedjaz, and Dr. Chaim Weizmann on behalf of the World Zionist Organization. This agreement, mindful of the racial kinship and ancient bonds existing between the Arabs and the Jewish people and realizing that the surest means of working out the consummation of their national aspirations was through the closest possible collaboration in the development of the Arab State and Palestine, set out to regulate the future relations between them. (For the full text of the Agreement see David Hunter Miller, *op.cit.*, vol. III, pp. 188-189.)

[55] Later, the Jewish Agency took part in the discussions relating to Palestine at the second special session of the General Assembly held in April-May 1948. It also participated in the deliberations of the Security Council on Palestine until July 1948, when a representative of the Jewish State was first invited to attend its meetings.

ments of a people with no legal connection between them, and their recognition as such is not in itself an admission of the legal existence of the people of whom they are part. Yet it is significant that, while the Jewish people was achieving its formal recognition, there was also an appreciable change in the scope and character of the rights provided for Jewish minorities under international law.

Faithful to the traditions of the international conferences and congresses of the Nineteenth Century, the Peace Conference of 1919-1920 dealt with the situation of the Jews in various countries with a view to protecting them against discrimination and persecution. It was this very object which greatly contributed to the inauguration of the system of international protection of minorities—a system which placed the minorities in the States of Eastern, Central and Southern Europe under the guarantee of the League of Nations.

While at previous conferences and congresses the Jews had appealed for religious freedom and civil and political rights, it was national rights that the Jewish minorities claimed at the Paris Conference. They were no longer satisfied with individual rights; they demanded collective rights. The spokesman of these minorities was the Committee of Jewish Delegations, a democratic body established in Paris at the beginning of 1919 and authorized to speak in the name of twelve million Jews. In its Memorandum of May 1919 the Committee asked the Peace Conference to grant the minorities of Eastern, Central and Southern Europe the right of organization and development as national minorities and to recognize them "as constituting distinct autonomous organizations, and as such having equally the right to establish, manage and control their schools and their religious, educational, charitable and social institutions." The Peace Conference, however, hesitated to describe the minorities as national; in the Minorities Treaties it used the expression "racial, religious or linguistic minorities"— a cautious substitute for the clear concept of national minorities. Nor was the Peace Conference prepared to go so far as to grant to the minorities collective rights and thus to recognize them as autonomous groups entitled to organize themselves on the basis of "personal autonomy." Nevertheless the rights granted to the minorities in respect of language, culture and social matters were not individual rights, but rights which by their very nature and effect could only be enjoyed collectively.

The Minorities Treaties were undoubtedly an important achievement inasmuch as they enlarged the rights of man and proclaimed the rights of national minorities. In spite of the vague formula used in these treaties, it cannot be denied that the purpose was, not only to protect individual rights, but also, as pointed out by the Permanent Court of International Justice, "to ensure for the minority elements suitable means for the preservation of their racial peculiarities, their traditions and their national characteristics."[56] Thus, in interpreting the Minorities Treaties, the Court did not hesitate to use the term "national."

Here, perhaps, it may be fitting to recall the remark which President Wilson made in a conversation with Jewish representatives during the Peace Conference to the effect that if national rights could be granted to the Jews alone, he would gladly assent, but since all minorities would have to be accorded such rights, including the Germans in Bohemia etc., the whole policy would be fraught with disturbances.[57]

It has been the intention in this article to stress the radical change that has come about in the approach to the Jewish question since the close of the First World War, and to outline the effects of the *de jure* recognition of the Jewish people as a State-forming entity.

Since then thirty years have passed. By successive interpretations culminating in the White Paper of 1939, a series of attempts have been made with the ultimate object of annulling the rights granted to the Jewish people under the Palestine Mandate. On February 25th, 1947, the Foreign Secretary of the State which had issued the Balfour Declaration said in the House of Commons, when dealing with the Palestine question, that he failed to understand how the Jews could demand the right of entry into the United Nations Organization, which is not founded on religious principles and where States and not religions are represented. This statement clearly ignores the basic change inaugurated by the Balfour Declaration and completely disregards the international recognition of the existence of the Jewish people and of its right to national life and statehood in Palestine.

---

[56] *Publications of the Court*, Series A/B, Nr. 64, p. 17.

It should be noted that the French text of the advisory opinion speaks of the minorities as *groupes sociaux* or *groupes minoritaires*. The corresponding expressions in the English version, "certain elements" and "minority elements," are more general and less precise.

[57] See Oscar J. Janowsky, *The Jews and Minority Rights, 1888-1919* (New York, 1933), p. 352; Max J. Kohler, *The Origin of the Minority Provisions of the Peace Treaty of 1919*, in *God in Freedom*, by Luigi Luzatti (New York, 1930), p. 785.

There is an old dictum which may be regarded as a canon of interpretation in Jewish matters, even though it is not to be found in treaties on international law. The dictum is etched in the long and turbulent history of the Jews, and its severity has even been enhanced in our own days: *Judæorum causae non ex æquitate sed rigore juris decidendae sunt.*

The Zionist–Israel Juridical Claims to Constitute "The Jewish People" Nationality Entity and to Confer Membership in It: Appraisal in Public International Law

W. T. MALLISON, JR.

[T]he connection between the Jewish people and the State of Israel constitutes an integral part of the law of nations. . . . The Balfour Declaration and the Palestine Mandate given by the League of Nations to Great Britain constituted an international recognition of the Jewish people. . . .

—The Eichmann Trial Judgment (1961)[1]

Most true is the saying, that all things are uncertain the moment men depart from law.

—Hugo Grotius
(writing in 1625)[2]

---

* Professor of Law, The George Washington University.

The writer expresses his appreciation to W. Theodore Pierson, Jr., Associate Editor of The George Washington Law Review, for assistance in this study which is part of a more comprehensive one concerning juridical problems arising from Zionist-Israel claims in public law.

The writer has served, from time to time, as consultant to the American Council for Judaism, a national organization of Americans of Jewish religious faith. The letterhead of its National Office states, in part: "The Council affirms that nationality and religion are separate and distinct; that no Jew or group of Jews can speak for all American Jews; that Israel is the 'homeland' of its own citizens only, and not of all Jews."

The analyses and conclusions in the present study are those of the writer alone.

1 The Attorney-General of the Government of Israel v. Adolf, the son of Karl Adolf Eichmann, Criminal Case No. 40/61, District Court of Jerusalem, Israel, Dec. 11-12, 1961, affirmed, Criminal Appeal No. 336/61 Supreme Court of Israel, May 29, 1962.

2 Grotius, De Jure Belli ac Pacis, 2 Classics of International Law, Prolegomena 17 (Scott ed., Kelsey transl. 1925).

I. THE CLARIFICATION OF VALUES:
ZIONIST NATIONALISM VERSUS
INDIVIDUAL FREEDOM

A. THE FUNDAMENTAL VALUES

The subject of this study is in the domain of public international law. It emphasizes the impact of diverse juridical doctrines and principles upon values. The task of public law, whether international or municipal, is conceived as providing an institutional framework in which the individual may achieve his fundamental values. These values[3] are:

(1) *Respect for the dignity of the individual*—negatively, this precludes discrimination based upon religion, race, and all other factors which are irrelevant to individual worth; positively, this includes recognition of the general merit of all people as human beings and the particular merit of each person as an individual.

(2) *Equality before the law and the sharing of governmental power*—this includes an opportunity for fair participation in the processes of government in the international, national, and local communities.

(3) *Enlightenment and information*—this includes freedom of inquiry and opinion, which are indispensable to rational decision-making.

(4) *Psychic and physical well-being*—negatively, this requires freedom from arbitrary burdens, restrictions, and punishments; positively, it includes the opportunity to develop individual abilities.

---

[3] The eight value categories reflect the work of Professors Lasswell and McDougal of the Yale University Law School. Their classic introductory study, Lasswell & McDougal, Legal Education and Public Policy: Professional Training in the Public Interest, 52 Yale L.J. 203 (1943), makes explicit the relevance of value clarification to juridical analysis. The eight categories appear substantially in McDougal & Leighton, The Rights of Man in the World Community: Constitutional Illusions Versus Rational Action, 14 Law & Contemp. Prob. 490, 491 (1949). Studies embodying value clarification include: McDougal & Associates, Studies in World Public Order (1960); McDougal, Perspectives for an International Law of Human Dignity, 53 Proc. Am. Soc. Int'l L. 107 (1959) (Address as President of the American Society of International Law); Lasswell & Kaplan, Power and Society (Yale Law School Studies No. 2, 1950). Other significant studies which do not include explicit value analysis but are, nevertheless, directly concerned with the impact of legal doctrines upon human values include: Rostow, The Sovereign Prerogative: The Supreme Court and the Quest for Law (1962); Freund, The Supreme Court of the United States: Its Business, Purposes, and Performance (1961).

(5) The opportunity to participate in *congenial and constructive inter-personal relationships.*

(6) *Goods and services* necessary to adequate standards of living.

(7) *Skills and "know-how"* necessary to achieve all values in a factual sense.

(8) Freedom to develop and apply *conceptions of morality and ethics*—this includes the freedom to worship God, or the freedom not to worship, depending upon individual choice.

A democratic conception of international and municipal law,[4] as opposed to totalitarian or authoritarian conceptions,[5] seeks to institutionalize the shaping and sharing of such values in a rational and peaceful context. At the minimum, such a democratic juridical conception must prohibit the coercion of individuals in their shaping and sharing of values where the coercion is exercised by public entities which are foreign to the individuals coerced.[6]

B. The Clarification of Word Symbols

Words without specified referents are highly ambiguous and are capable of having multiple and inconsistent meanings ascribed to them by writers and readers. In order to achieve clarity, it is desirable to set forth the general terms of reference which are connected with certain key word symbols which appear throughout the study.[7] It is recognized that these same word symbols are used by others with different terms of reference than those employed here.

Jew is used to refer to a voluntary adherent of the religion of Judaism. *Judaism* is used to refer to one of the monotheistic religions of universal moral values. The word "Jew" is used by the writer to refer to an adherent of Judaism in the same way that "Christian" refers to an adherent of Christianity.[8]

---

[4] Democratic conceptions of law are set forth in each of the studies cited in supra note 3 except the Lasswell and Kaplan one, which is a political science analysis.

[5] For a contemporary analysis of Soviet Russian conceptions, see Ramundo, The Socialist Theory of International Law (George Washington University Institute for Sino-Soviet Studies No. 1, 1964).

[6] Even in democratic municipal juridical systems, where individuals participate in governmental processes, they do not have effective means, as individuals, to protect themselves from foreign coercion. Consequently, they must seek governmental prohibition of such foreign coercion.

[7] Systematic analysis of the meaning of words appears in Ogden & Richards, The Meaning of Meaning (1936) and Morris, Signs, Language and Behavior (1946). See also Chafee, The Disorderly Conduct of Words, 41 Colum. L. Rev. 381 (1941). A useful introduction to word symbols employed in the present study appears in Sussman, "Jew," "Jewish People," and "Zionism," 20 Etc.: A Review of General Semantics 372 (1963).

[8] Professor Robert M. MacIver has written concerning the stated credo of the

In setting forth a religious conception of "Jew" and "Judaism" the writer is adopting a basic tenet of traditional and contemporary Judaism. In 1878 Rabbi Hermann Adler, then the Chief Rabbi in England, after stating that "Judaism has no political bearing whatever," continued:

> Ever since the conquest of Palestine by the Romans we have ceased to be a body politic. We are citizens of the country in which we dwell. We are simply Englishmen or Frenchmen or Germans, as the case may be, certainly holding particular theological tenets and practising special religious ordinances; but we stand in the same relation to our countrymen as any other religious sect, having the same stake in the national welfare and the same claim on the privileges and duties of citizens.[9]

The same religious concept of Judaism has been manifested in the United States. In 1883 Rabbi Isaac M. Wise, who had emigrated from Bavaria, wrote: "We, citizens of the United States who believe in Moses and the Prophets, are an integral element of this nation . . . with no earthly interests or aspirations different from those who believe in Jesus and his Apostles."[10]

In 1885 a group of Reform Rabbis met in Pittsburgh to enunciate basic principles of modern Judaism. Their Pittsburgh Platform included this statement:

> We consider ourselves no longer a nation but a religious community. And therefore expect neither a return to Palestine, nor a sacrificial worship under the administration of the sons of Aaron, nor the restoration of any of the laws concerning the Jewish state.[11]

American Jewish Committee that "A Jew in America can live a full and rich Jewish life as an integrated American":
> In the first place, what does it mean? Suppose we substitute another word in place of "Jewish"? We would then read, for example: "A Frenchman in America can live a full and rich French life as an integrated American." A Frenchman in America, a Pole, an Englishman, a Chinese? The statement would not be very meaningful and might easily be resented. But if we said instead: "a Roman Catholic, a Mohammedan, a Lutheran can live" and so forth, then the expression would be acceptable, since all religions have equal rights and none involves any limitations on American citizenship.

National Community Relations Advisory Council, Report on the Jewish Community Relations Agencies 39 (1951). A thoughtful appraisal appears in Lasky, An Analysis of the MacIver Report (American Council for Judaism, undated).

See the text accompanying note 304 infra.

[9] Quoted in Stein, The Balfour Declaration 75 (1961).

[10] Quoted in Berger, The Jewish Dilemma 239 (1946).

[11] Id. at 240. A contemporary conception of Judaism as a religion of universal moral values appears in American Council for Judaism, An Approach to an American Judaism (1953).

The sole element in the present writer's use of the word "Jew" is the religious one. Some individuals, while acknowledging the religious element, may regard Jewishness as involving another factor. The character of such an additional factor may be cultural, racial, or national depending upon the preferred values of the individual. Some individuals regard themselves, and may be regarded by others, as Jews because their parents were Jews. Jews, like Christians or Moslems, are fully entitled to regard their religious identification as derived from that of their parents. Similarly, a Jew who regards his identification as involving a common cultural heritage with other Jews should be entirely free to adopt such a view. It should not be necessary to emphasize the fact that there is no empirical basis upon which Jews can be deemed to be members of a single racial group.[12]

Zionist is employed to refer to a member or supporter of the modern political movement of Zionism, which was started as an organized political movement at the First Zionist Congress in Basle, Switzerland, in 1897.[13] Though many Zionists profess Judaism, there is no reason to limit an accurate functional conception of "Zionist" to those who claim to be Jews.[14] Prime Minister David Lloyd George[15] and Foreign Secretary Arthur Balfour,[16] who were members

---

[12] The distinction between racial conceptions in anthropology and non-scientific racist ideologies is demonstrated in Benedict, Race: Science and Politics (1945).

> Jews are people who acknowledge the Jewish religion. They are of all races, even Negro and Mongolian. European Jews are of many different biological types; physically they resemble the populations among whom they live. The so-called "Jewish type" is a generalized type common in the Near East in countries bordering on the Mediterranean. Wherever Jews are persecuted or discriminated against, they cling to their old ways and keep apart from the rest of the population and develop so-called "Jewish" traits. But these are not racial or "Jewish"; they disappear under conditions where assimilation is easy.

Id. at 177. See also Comas, Racial Myths 27-32 (UNESCO 1958).

[13] The Zionist Basle Program is examined in the text accompanying notes 59-63 infra.

[14] The distinction between "adherents of the Jewish faith" and "Zionism" was recognized in an Address by King Hussein of Jordan, Washington, D.C., April 15, 1964. Washington Post, April 16, 1964, p. 1, cols. 2-3.

[15] The compatibility between anti-Semitism and pro-Zionism is described by the authoritative Zionist historian of the Balfour Declaration with reference to Lloyd George. In some of his speeches there was "a streak of ordinary vulgar anti-Semitism," though he was also "sensitive to the Jewish mystique." Stein, supra note 8, at 143. Specific examples from his anti-Semitic speeches are provided by Stein. Id. at 143 & nn.20-21.

Stein describes the attitude of Field Marshal Smuts, another eminent political supporter of Zionism: "Smuts thought highly of Jews, but not so highly that he would not be glad to see some counterattraction provided for Jews who might otherwise be drawn to South Africa." Id. at 478.

[16] Stein describes a certain ambivalence in Balfour's attitude: "If Balfour became an ardent pro-Zionist it was not simply out of a sentimental tenderness for Jews." Id. at 163-64.

Balfour's introduction to a classic Zionist history of Zionism suggested that the

of the British Government which issued the Balfour Declaration, did not claim to be Jews. Yet, in view of their political support for Zionism, they should be regarded as Zionists.

Zionist Organization is used to refer to the political entity constituted by the First Zionist Congress.[17] It is an instrumentality designed to achieve the political objects of Zionism. Since the 1922 League of Nations Mandate for Palestine, the term "Zionist Organization" has been equivalent to the term "Jewish Agency."[18] Article 4 of the Mandate recognized the Zionist Organization as a Jewish Agency and as a "public body."

Anti-Zionist is employed to refer to an opponent of the Zionist movement. Anti-Zionists include those who are identified as Jews, such as Edwin Montagu,[19] a member of the same British Government which issued the Balfour Declaration and who insisted upon the inclusion of the safeguard clauses in it. Anti-Zionists also include democratically oriented individuals of other faiths who reject the juridical and secular separatism which Zionism attempts to impose upon Jews. From a democratic perspective, the term "anti-Zionist" is negative in form but positive in substance. In order to reject the political postulates of Zionism, an individual must have a set of political postulates and objectives inconsistent with Zionism. The most clearly inconsistent ones are those of democracy which are conceived as embracing the positive values of human dignity and individual freedom for all.[20] It should be recognized that some anti-

concerns of the anti-Zionists about political Zionism were baseless: "Everything which assimilates the . . . status of the Jews to that of other races ought to mitigate what remains of ancient antipathies . . . ." 1 Sokolow, History of Zionism xxxiii (1919), cited hereafter as "Sokolow."

[17] The Constitution of the World Zionist Organisation (as adopted by the Zionist General Council at its Session in Jerusalem, Israel, in December 1959-January 1960, in pursuance of the Resolution of the 24th Zionist Congress) demonstrates a high degree of centralized control over individual and group (such as the Zionist Organization of America) members. The writer, consequently, uses the term, "Zionist Organization," to refer to the World Zionist Organization, including its individual and group members, as a single public body. See the text accompanying note 246 infra.

[18] The Palestine Mandate, which established the equivalency, is examined in the text accompanying notes 210-22 infra.

[19] Stein, supra note 9, at 484, states, with reference to Montagu: "Thus, the question of a pro-Zionist declaration reached the War Cabinet at a time when the only Jew with direct access to the inner circle was an implacable anti-Zionist."

[20] See the studies cited in note 3 supra and Lasswell, Democratic Character (1951), in the compilation entitled The Political Writings of Harold D. Lasswell 463-525 (1951).

For a specific rejection of the postulates of Zionism see M. R. Cohen, The Faith of a Liberal, ch. 39, Zionism: Tribalism or Liberalism (1942); Berger, Judaism or Jewish Nationalism: The Alternative to Zionism (1957).

Concerning Zionist political activities in the United States, see Senate Committee on Foreign Relations, Report on Foreign Agents Registration Act, S. Rep. No. 875, 88th

Semites and other anti-democratic individuals may style themselves as anti-Zionists. The existence of such individuals, however, should not obfuscate the basic democratic character of many anti-Zionists.

Non-Zionist is a chameleon-like conception. Individuals who wish to support Zionism and the State of Israel financially, while attempting to disengage themselves from the juridical-political characteristics of Zionism and the State of Israel, may regard themselves as being "non-Zionists." Dr. Chaim Weizmann, the Zionist leader and first president of the State of Israel, has described non-Zionism in this way:

> [T]hose wealthy Jews who could not wholly divorce themselves from a feeling of responsibility toward their people, but at the same time could not identify themselves with the hopes of the masses, were prepared with a sort of left-handed generosity, on condition that their right hand did not know what their left hand was doing. To them the university-to-be in Jerusalem was philanthropy, which did not compromise them; to us it was nationalist renaissance. They would give—with disclaimers; we would accept—with reservations.[21]

One of the most confusing aspects of non-Zionism is that non-Zionists, unlike Zionists and anti-Zionists, often appear to have no clarified political values of their own.[22] Many anti-Zionists regard non-

---

Cong., 2d Sess. (Feb. 21, 1964). One of the nine cases studied by the Committee was Zionism. The cases were selected because of activities believed to be "inimical to the interests of the United States . . . ." Id. at 5. See Stevens, American Zionism and U. S. Foreign Policy, 1942-1947 (1962).

For uncritical approval of the postulates of Zionism, see Safran, The United States and Israel (1963); Halpern, The Idea of the Jewish State (1961).

[21] Trial and Error: The Autobiography of Chaim Weizmann 75 (1949). The Weizmann autobiography is cited hereafter as "Weizmann." It not only contains material of juridical significance but provides psychological insight into Zionist mentality. See generally Lasswell, Power and Personality (1948); Lasswell, Psychopathology and Politics (1930) in the compilation entitled The Political Writings of Harold D. Lasswell 1-282 (1951).

[22] Some regard the American Jewish Committee as a non-Zionist organization. See Appendix A for "An Exchange of Views" involving the American Jewish Committee. American Jewish Committee & Jewish Publication Society of America, 63 American Jewish Year Book 499 (1962) describes the American Jewish Committee as follows:

> Seeks to prevent infraction of the civil and religious rights of Jews in any part of the world and to secure equality of economic, social and educational opportunity through education and civic action. Seeks to broaden understanding of the basic nature of prejudice and to improve techniques for combating it. Promotes a philosophy of Jewish integration by projecting a balanced view with respect to full participation in American life and retention of Jewish identity.

The same source describes the anti-Zionist American Council for Judaism as follows:

> Seeks to advance the universal principles of a Judaism free of nationalism, and

Zionists as being among the practical supporters of Zionism. If this is an accurate appraisal, it must be added, nevertheless, that non-Zionists often conceal from themselves (and perhaps from others) the extent to which their support is employed for the political purposes of Zionism.

Israel is used to refer to the present Near Eastern State of Israel.[23] It and the Zionist Organization are employed as the two principal political instruments of Zionist nationalism. It is recognized, however, that the word "Israel" has a deeply significant theological meaning to Jews. Thus, one of the traditional religious ways of referring to Jews is to employ the term, "the Children of Israel." Nevertheless, since this study is a juridical one, the term "Israel" is not used in its religious sense.

The State of Israel is sometimes termed a "Jewish" state. Such a label must be rejected if "Judaism" is to be regarded as a religion of universal moral values, rather than a religion of nationalism or tribalism, and if a "Jew" is to be regarded as a voluntary adherent of Judaism. From a functional standpoint there should be no hesitation in describing Israel as a "Zionist" state. Since 1948, when the State of Israel was established, the basic political objectives of Zionism and the State of Israel have been the same.[24] This identity has been enunciated explicitly in claims advanced in public international law.[25] Where it is not made explicit, a continuing common political program may be presumed to be the result of coordinated political planning rather than of a long continuing series of coincidences.

Zionist-Israel sovereignty is used to refer to the integral relationship between the State of Israel and the Zionist Organization. The public law character of this relationship between the State of Israel and the Zionist Organization is recognized explicitly in the Israeli Status Law of 1952 and the ensuing Covenant between the Government of

---

the national, civic, cultural, and social integration into American institutions of Americans of Jewish faith.
Ibid.
Some regard the American Jewish Congress as pro-Zionist. It is described in the same source as follows:
Seeks to eliminate all forms of racial and religious bigotry; to advance civil rights, protect civil liberties, and defend religious freedom and separation of church and state; to promote the creative survival of the Jewish people; to help Israel develop in peace, freedom, and security.
Ibid.
[23] For official information concerning Israel, see the annual Israel Government Year-Book.
[24] See sec. III B. For official justification of Zionist political objectives see Israel Office of Information (New York), *Israel's Struggle for Peace* (1960).
[25] Ibid.

Israel and the Zionist Executive of 1954.[26] The Status Law did not create the relationship between State and Organization, but rather recognized it.[27] The Covenant spells out an allocation and coordination of governmental functions as between State and Organization in furthering the Zionist political objectives of both.

The Jewish people is the most ambiguous concatenation of word symbols employed in the present study. Although the term, "the Jewish people," does not appear in Holy Writ, it was given an almost exclusively religious meaning until the founding of Zionism. Its most usual use was as a synonym for "Jews," "Israelites," "the Children of Israel," and "the people of the Book." [28] The Zionist movement has captured the term for its own juridical-political purposes and, consequently, the writer uses "the Jewish people" to refer to the claimed constituency of Zionist nationalism. Even though the Zionists give a specific nationalistic meaning to the words, they have not rejected whatever political advantages accrue to them from the ambiguities of the words.[28a] Thus, they accept the support of those who have found humanitarian or religious meanings in "the Jewish people." [29]

C. POLITICAL ZIONISM

In a fundamental sense, political Zionism is the reaction of Jews to ghetto life and the consequent denial to them of an opportunity to participate meaningfully in the secular life of the states of their regular nationalities.[30] The existence of ghetto life in some states reflected anti-Semitism. Zionism postulated that anti-Semitism was fundamental and ineradicable. Upon this postulate, the Zionists base their juridical objectives: that "the Jewish people" be constituted as a nationality entity and that membership in it be conferred upon Jews.[31]

In order to understand the Zionist views, it is useful to quote from

---

[26] The Status Law and Covenant are examined in the text accompanying notes 236-46 infra.

[27] See Lasky, Between Truth and Repose 51 (1956). The Lasky study is subtitled: The World Zionist Organization, Its Agency for the State of Israel, The Means by Which It Raises Its Funds, and the Structure Through Which It Operates in the Diaspora: A Study in Organization.

[28] Sussman, supra note 7, at 373. See note 304 infra.

[28a] Sussman, supra note 7, at 374-75.

[29] Weizmann 75 and passim.

[30] The same conclusion is reached in Taylor, Prelude to Israel: An Analysis of Zionist Diplomacy, 1897-1947, v, vi (1959), cited hereafter as "Zionist Diplomacy."

[31] The juridical objectives of Zionist nationalism stated in the text are set forth and appraised in the balance of the present study.

the words of Dr. Theodor Herzl, the founder of political Zionism, in his classic Zionist statement entitled *The Jewish State*.[32]

> We naturally move to those places where we are not persecuted, and there our presence produces persecution. This is the case in every country, and will remain so, even in those highly civilized— for instance, France—till the Jewish question finds a solution on a political basis. The unfortunate Jews are now carrying Anti-Semitism into England; they have already introduced it into America.[33]

Herzl dealt with nationality status on the basis of Jewish identification as follows:

> But the distinctive nationality of Jews neither can, will, nor must be destroyed. It cannot be destroyed, because external enemies consolidate it. . . . Whole branches of Judaism may wither and fall, but the trunk remains.[34]

The desire for territory was summarized by Herzl as follows:

> The whole plan is in its essence perfectly simple, as it must necessarily be if it is to come within the comprehension of all.
> Let the sovereignty be granted us over a portion of the globe large enough to satisfy the rightful requirements of a nation; the rest we shall manage for ourselves.[35]

Herzl anticipated the opposition which Zionism would arouse among Jews:

> Perhaps we shall have to fight first of all against many an evil-disposed, narrow-hearted, short-sighted member of our own race.[36]

The most striking feature of Herzl's views is not that he stated a proposed political solution to the problem of anti-Semitism in 1896. Its deeper significance is that the juridical-political core of Zionism has not changed from Herzl's time to the present.[37] Today Zionist

---

[32] The book was published in German in 1896 as Der Judenstaat. The English translation from which the ensuing quotations in the text are taken is entitled The Jewish State: An Attempt at a Modern Solution of the Jewish Question (D'Avigdor and Israel Cohen transl. 1943).

[33] Id. at 19, 20.

[34] Id. at 24.

[35] Id. at 39.

[36] Id. at 108.

[37] Sec. III demonstrates the consistency through time of the juridical objectives of Zionism.

leaders stress the importance of saving Jews from the persecutions brought about by persistent anti-Semitism.[38] At the same time, they appear to be as afraid of religious freedom and secular integration as of persecution itself. Thus, Nahum Goldmann, the president of the World Zionist Organization, has stated: "The object of the Jewish State has been the preservation of the Jewish people, which was imperiled by emancipation and assimilation. . . ."[39] As recently as March 16, 1964, a Zionist Executive-Israeli Government Joint Communique referred to "the dangers of assimilation affecting Jewish communities. . . ."[40] Zionism continues to manifest defensiveness to the threat of democratic systems based upon individual rights. Recent commentary in the *Jerusalem Post* states: "Today, Zionist leaders do not speak for the majority of Jewry, though all but a tiny proportion of the nation [*i.e.*, "the Jewish people"] give their friendship and support to the State of Israel."[41]

D. CULTURAL ZIONISM

In addition to political Zionism, there also has been a movement known as "cultural" or "spiritual" Zionism. Achad Ha'am was the preeminent leader of this type of Zionism.[42] He accepted some of the aspects of political Zionism, provided that they were subordinated to the fundamental humanitarian principles of Judaism.[43] He participated in the negotiations leading to the issuance of the Balfour Declaration but attached an entirely different meaning to it than did

---

[38] See the Joint Israel-Zionist Communique of March 16, 1964, para. 1, in the text accompanying note 261 supra.

[39] Quoted in Zionist Diplomacy 2.

[40] Note 38 supra.

[41] March 16, 1964, p. 1, col. 1. The Jerusalem Post is regarded as a semi-official organ of the Israeli Government.

[42] 1 Esco Foundation for Palestine, Palestine: A Study of Jewish, Arab, and British Policies 18-22 (1947) contrasts the Zionism of Achad Ha'am with political Zionism. "Achad Ha'am" (also spelled Ahad Ha'am) was the pen name of Asher Ginsberg, whose work comprised a philosophy of Judaism. "Achad Ha'am" is translated as "One of the People."

The Esco work cited (comprising two volumes) is cited hereafter as "Esco, Study." The word "Esco" is an acrostic of Ethel S. Cohen, who with her husband, was a founder of the Esco Foundation for Palestine. The Esco Study is a scholarly one written by several contributing authors. Its authors include such Zionists as: Rose G. Jacobs, Avraham Schenker, and Benjamin Shwadran. It uses the word "Jewish" in the title and in the text passim in contexts where "Zionist" would be more accurate.

[43] Achad Ha'am, Ten Essays on Zionism and Judaism passim (Leon Simon transl. 1922). The translator's introduction states at 39:

It is not surprising that he went to the first Zionist Congress; but it is not surprising, either, that he came away disappointed. For he found that the similarity between his own ideal and that of the Zionist movement was only external.

the political Zionists.[44] He believed that "a national home" for some Jews in Palestine would be consistent with the nationalistic aspirations of the Arabs. He regarded Palestine as an opportunity for creative collaboration with the Arabs for the common benefit of all of the inhabitants of the country. He hoped that Palestine would become a center of Jewish religion and culture which would enrich Jews in other countries as well as those in Palestine.[45]

Achad Ha'am's central differences with the political Zionists concerned both the justification for the movement and its character. Whereas political Zionism thought of itself as the answer to negative and destructive anti-Semitism, Achad Ha'am regarded Zionism as an expression of the humanitarianism of Judaism and the creativity of Jews.[46] He valued individual rights and human dignity for all, including Arabs.[47] He believed that "a national home in Palestine" for some Jews did not conflict with the single nationality of other Jews. Thus, the humanitarian Zionism of Achad Ha'am was completely consistent with individual freedom for all, in Palestine and in other countries as well.

E. THE CONFLICT BETWEEN ZIONIST NATIONALISM AND INDIVIDUAL FREEDOM

Professor Morris Raphael Cohen, the distinguished American scholar, has stated the basic conflict between Zionist nationalism and individual freedom:

> Though most of the leaders of Zionism in America are sincerely and profoundly convinced of the compatibility of Zionism and Americanism, they are none the less profoundly mistaken. Nationalistic Zionism demands not complete individual liberty for the Jew, but group autonomy.[48]

Jews, with other individuals, have the opportunity to expand and perfect existing democratic systems which include religious free-

---

[44] Note 157 infra.

[45] Supra note 43; Esco Study 20.

[46] Esco Study 19.

[47] Professor Hans Kohn has described the last years of Achad Ha'am's life which were spent in Palestine at the start of the British Mandate. He died with the conviction that the ideals of cultural Zionism were being betrayed by the political Zionists. Kohn quotes one of Achad Ha'am's last letters which reflected his despair: "Is *this* the dream of a return to Zion which our people have dreamt for centuries: that we now come to Zion to stain its soil with innocent blood?" Kohn, Zion and the Jewish National Idea, 46 Menorah Journal 17, 39 (1958).

[48] M. R. Cohen, supra note 20, at 329.

dom and secular integration for all.[49] The significant juridical features of such democratic systems are individual rights and equality.[50] By contrast, Zionist nationalism seeks to limit the individual freedom of Jews, wherever they are, by attempting to constitute "the Jewish people" nationality entity and to confer membership in it. The irreconcilable value conflict between Zionist nationalism and individual freedom has not changed from the time of Achad Ha'am to the present. Professor Cohen provides accurate summary:

> The fact, however, is that the American ideal of freedom is just what the Zionists most fear. At bottom they have no confidence that with complete toleration and full freedom Judaism can hold its own in the open field.[51]

II. THE CENTRAL JURIDICAL ISSUES

The conflict of values considered in the previous section could be analyzed from the standpoint of any of several perspectives. For example, the religious or theological significance of the value conflict is highly important. The present study, however, is limited to public international law and excludes consideration of theological and other issues no matter how important they may be.

Two central issues are examined in the present study. The first is the juridical validity under public international law of the claim to *constitute*[52] "the Jewish people" nationality entity. The second issue is the juridical validity under public international law of the claim to *confer membership* in the same alleged nationality entity. The two issues are closely related and may appear at times to be simply different aspects of the same basic issue. When they are considered together, they may be referred to simply as "the Jewish people" nationality claims. They are the basic juridical claims of the Zionist-Israel sovereignty. Section III of this study will examine the formulation and implementation of these nationality claims and section IV

---

49 Secular integration does not impinge upon the retention of separate religious identification.

50 Obvious illustration is provided by the United States Constitution including its Bill of Rights.

51 M. R. Cohen, supra note 20, at 330.

52 The word "constitute" is used throughout the text to refer to creation or establishment in public law. In this sense, the creation of claimed nationality entities or public bodies is the outcome of the constitutive process in public law. Where such claimed entities or bodies are not so established in law, it is because of the failure to operate the constitutive process successfully. For an analysis of the constitutive process in a different public law context, see McDougal, Lasswell & Vlasic, Law and Public Order in Space 94-137, 1027-1092 (1963).

will appraise them under the applicable limitations of international law. A concluding appraisal will be made in section V.

"The Jewish people" nationality claims are used by the Zionists as the foundation for a second grouping of juridical claims such as the claims to constitute and employ public bodies to act in behalf of "the Jewish people." Thus, the State of Israel is claimed to be "the sovereign State of the Jewish people" rather than only the state of its regular nationals.[53] In the same way the Zionist Organization public body is claimed to represent and to act for "the Jewish people" rather than only Zionists.[54] These derivative claims, and others, are not examined in detail in the present study.

III. THE FORMULATION AND IMPLEMENTATION OF THE CLAIMS TO CONSTITUTE "THE JEWISH PEOPLE" NATIONALITY ENTITY AND TO CONFER MEMBERSHIP IN IT

A. "The Jewish People" Nationality Claims Advanced Prior to the Establishment of the State of Israel

1. The First Zionist Congress (Basle 1897)

Political Zionism, as opposed to the cultural concept of Zionism, has been important since the First Zionist Congress. In the period since the Balfour Declaration, however, it has become the dominant type of Zionism.[55]

The First Zionist Congress was called by Dr. Theodor Herzl to provide political and juridical implementation for his basic assumption of ineradicable anti-Semitism and the consequent necessity of a "Jewish" state.[56] In the opening address Herzl stated the object of the meeting: "We are here to lay the foundation stone of the house which is to shelter the Jewish nation." [57] The Congress then proceeded to constitute the Zionist Organization,[58] and concluded with the adoption of a statement of Zionist purpose known as the Basle Program. The key provision stated: "The aim of Zionism is to

---

[53] See, e.g., the excerpts from the Eichmann Trial Judgment in the text accompanying note 256 infra.

[54] See, e.g., the Status Law para. 2, reproduced in the text accompanying note 239 infra.

[55] Weizmann, ch. 18, The Balfour Declaration and subsequent chs.; Zionist Diplomacy passim, especially ch. 4, The Growth of Political Zionism; 2 Sokolow 83-99.

[56] Supra note 32; Zionist Diplomacy 3-6; 1 Sokolow 268-72; 1 Esco Study 40-42.

[57] 1 Esco Study 40.

[58] Id. at 42; Zionist Diplomacy 6.

create for the Jewish people a home in Palestine secured by public law." [59] Four means were formulated to obtain this objective: [60] (1) the promotion of Zionist (termed "Jewish") immigration to Palestine; (2) the "organization and binding together of the whole of Jewry" through appropriate means; (3) "strengthening and fostering of Jewish national sentiment and consciousness"; (4) taking steps toward "obtaining government consent" for the objectives of Zionism.

The means proposed were the same as those formulated in the previous year by Herzl in *The Jewish State*[61] except that the word "home" was substituted for the word "state." The change in terminology was designed to appease those Jews who had a sentimental, cultural, or religious attachment to Palestine, but who objected to the concept of Jewish nationality or a Jewish state.[62] At the same time, Herzl recognized that his political supporters would read it as meaning "Jewish State" in any event.[63] This calculated ambivalence concerning a central element of the Zionist political program aided Herzl in obtaining support for Zionism. Succeeding Zionist leaders have consistently used this technique of calculated ambiguity in terminology in order to enhance Zionist appeal among those opposed to Zionist nationality concepts.[64]

Herzl, as the first president of the Zionist Organization, started the practical implementation of the Zionist program. In October and November 1898, he met with Kaiser Wilhelm II, who was visiting the Ottoman Empire.[65] Herzl suggested the establishment of a land development company which would be operated under German protection by Zionists in Palestine.[66] At the first meeting, the Kaiser indicated interest and even enthusiasm,[67] but he rejected Herzl's proposal at the second meeting.[68]

Herzl next attempted to negotiate directly with the Sultan of Turkey. In May 1901, he proposed Zionist immigration to Palestine

---

[59] 1 Sokolow 268.
[60] The ensuing summary and quotations in the text are taken from 1 Sokolow 268-69 where the Basle Program is set forth.
[61] Supra note 32.
[62] Zionist Diplomacy 5.
[63] Id. at 6.
[64] The preeminent example remains "the Jewish people." See Weizmann passim; see Stein passim.
[65] 1 Esco Study 43; Zionist Diplomacy 6-7.
[66] 1 Esco Study 43; Zionist Diplomacy 7.
[67] See 1 Esco Study 43, which partially attributes the interest and enthusiasm to anti-Semitic motivations.
[68] Zionist Diplomacy 7. See also 1 Esco Study 43.

together with the enticing suggestion that generous financial assistance could be provided in developing the natural resources of the Ottoman Empire.[69] The Sultan rejected the idea of mass Zionist immigration to Palestine.[70]

In October 1902, the Zionist Executive entered into negotiations with the British Government to obtain portions of the Sinai Peninsula for immigration and settlement.[71] These negotiations broke down,[72] but in 1903 the British Government offered the Zionist Organization the opportunity to colonize a portion of Uganda.[73] Herzl favored the Uganda offer. No concrete action was taken upon it, however, and it was dropped after Herzl's death in 1904.[74] In view of the subsequent Zionist emphasis upon Palestine, the Uganda proposal may appear to be surprising. It is significant as an indication of the secular and political character of the Zionist movement. The search for territory elsewhere when the Palestine objective appeared to be frustrated reveals the lack of strong cultural and religious ties to Palestine. Only at a later stage, did the emotional attachment of the Zionist movement to Palestine become so great that no other territory would be considered.[75]

At the outset of the First World War, the Zionist record was one of failure and frustration in public international law. The Zionist Organization had been created, and diplomatic negotiations had been conducted with governments. Perhaps the mere conduct of such negotiations amounted to a measure of recognition for the Zionist Organization as an international public body. Nevertheless, the negotiations brought no practical political results for either the Organization or its claimed nationality entity of "the Jewish people."

2. The Balfour Declaration (1917)

a. Preliminary Description of the Basic Document

In 1904, Chaim Weizmann, a man of Russian origin, moved to England because of his conviction that the British Government was the most likely supporter of political Zionism.[76] During the decade

---

[69] 1 Esco Study 44; Zionist Diplomacy 7.
[70] 1 Esco Study 44 attributes humanitarian motives to the Sultan in allowing some Jewish refugees to settle while rejecting the "national aspects" of immigration.
[71] Zionist Diplomacy 7.
[72] Ibid.
[73] Ibid.; 1 Esco Study 48-49.
[74] Ibid.
[75] The time of this attachment was no later than the Balfour Declaration of Nov. 2, 1917.
[76] Weizmann 93.

before the First World War, Dr. Weizmann and other Zionist leaders contacted many influential persons in behalf of political Zionism.[77] Their chief purpose was to implement the Zionist Basle Program by obtaining public law assent from the British Government to the Zionist nationality claims. During the First World War, Dr. Weizmann became the principal Zionist negotiator for such a British public law declaration.[78] He habitually spoke and acted in behalf of the Zionist-claimed constituency of "the Jewish people." The British Government did not unequivocally curtail his claimed authority as spokesman for "the Jewish people" until anti-Zionist British Jews entered into the negotiations and made it clear that Dr. Weizmann lacked authority to speak for anti-Zionist Jews. The ensuing Balfour Declaration marked a "painful recession," [79] to use Dr. Weizmann's words, from the juridical objectives which the Zionists sought during the negotiations. The Zionists, nevertheless, have consistently claimed since the issuance of the Declaration that it provides juridical authority for their "Jewish people" nationality claims.

The Balfour Declaration was transmitted to the representatives of the Zionist Organization in a letter addressed to Lord Rothschild.[80] It is reproduced in full: [81]

> Foreign Office,
> November 2nd, 1917.

> Dear Lord Rothschild,
>   I have much pleasure in conveying to you, on behalf of His Majesty's Government, the following declaration of sympathy with Jewish Zionist aspirations which has been submitted to, and approved by, the Cabinet

---

[77] Id. at 93-145.

[78] Id. at 146-208; Stein, The Balfour Declaration passim (1961). The Stein book, written by a lawyer and Zionist, is the most complete history of the negotiations leading to the Balfour Declaration; it is cited hereafter as "Stein."

Stein, passim, shows that the negotiations covered three years. Stein 514 quotes Dr. Weizmann to the same effect.

[79] Weizmann 207.

[80] This was done to associate the Rothschild name with the Declaration. In addition Weizmann, though the chief Zionist negotiator, was President of the English Zionist Federation whereas Sokolow, "his senior in rank in the Zionist hierarchy," was a member of the Executive of the World Zionist Organization with headquarters in Germany. Stein 548.

The members of the Rothschild family were divided on Zionism as conceded by Dr. Weizmann. Weizmann 160-61. He refers to Lady Rothschild's "almost pathological anti-Zionism" and "her inplacable hostility to us." Id. at 161.

[81] The reproduction in the text, including its punctuation, is taken from the facsimile of the Balfour Declaration which appears as the frontispiece in Stein.

'His Majesty's Government view with favour the establishment in Palestine of a national home for the Jewish people, and will use their best endeavours to facilitate the achievement of this object, it being clearly understood that nothing shall be done which may prejudice the civil and religious rights of existing non-Jewish communities in Palestine, or the rights and political status enjoyed by Jews in any other country"

I should be grateful if you would bring this declaration to the knowledge of the Zionist Federation.

[S]   Yours
A W James Balfour

b. Preliminary Analysis of the Basic Agreement

Perhaps even more fundamental than analysis of the Balfour Declaration agreement is the issue of the juridical authority of the British Government to make a promise of political support in favor of Zionist nationalism.[82] Such a promise might be construed as derogating the existing rights of the population of Palestine. In the same way, it might be construed as derogating the single nationality status of Jews in other countries than Palestine. Without waiving this fundamental question of the juridical authority of the British Government, the balance of the analysis is based upon the assumption that the Balfour Declaration is a valid part of public international law. It has been so regarded by the League of Nations[83] and the United States,[84] which have agreed to it expressly. Even assuming the juridical validity of the Declaration, difficult interpretive problems concerning its scope and meaning remain to be considered.

In a typical situation involving the interpretation of a juridical undertaking or agreement the interpreter is required to interpret a text which all parties agree includes the basic undertaking or agree-

---

[82] It is clear that there was no explicit authority to do so in either the international law of peace or war. Hague Convention No. IV Respecting the Laws and Customs of War on Land, in addition to imposing explicit limitations upon belligerents, including those acting as military occupants, provides in its preamble:

> Until a more complete code of the laws of war has been issued, the High Contracting Parties deem it expedient to declare that, in cases not included in the Regulations adopted by them, *the inhabitants* and the belligerents remain under the protection and the rule of the principles of the law of nations, as they result from the usages established among civilized peoples, from the laws of humanity, and the dictates of the public conscience. . . . (Emphasis added.)

36 Stat. pt. 2, p. 2277 at 2279-80 (1910).

[83] League of Nations Mandate for Palestine, considered in the text at notes 210-22 infra.

[84] Anglo-American Convention on Palestine, considered in the text at notes 223-30 infra.

ment.[85] Interpretation of the Balfour Declaration is not such a typical situation. Neither the single paragraph of the Declaration quoted above nor the whole text of the Declaration includes the entire undertaking or agreement to be interpreted. The negotiating history of the Declaration demonstrates that Dr. Weizmann and the other Zionist negotiators promised to the British Government, whether expressly or impliedly, the political support of the alleged Zionist constituency of Jews in many states, in return for the political promise clause of the Declaration.[86] Since the Zionist promise was the *quid pro quo* without which the British promise would not have been made, it comprised an integral part of the Balfour Declaration

---

[85] Such a typical situation is envisioned in Harvard Research in International Law, Draft Convention on the Law of Treaties, 29 Am. J. Int'l L. Supp. 653, at 947 (1935), cited hereafter as "Harvard Research, Treaties."

[86] The primary authority for the textual statement is the negotiating context of conditions which is detailed in the ensuing pages.
One of the most explicit secondary authorities states:

> That it [the Balfour Declaration] is in purpose a definite contract between the British Government and Jewry represented by the Zionists is beyond question. In spirit it is a pledge that in return for services to be rendered by Jewry the British Government would 'use their best endeavours' to secure the execution of a certain definite policy in Palestine.

6 Temperley (ed.), A History of the Peace Conference of Paris 173-74 (1924).

Dr. Weizmann, after denying that "the Balfour Declaration [was] a *quid pro quo*, or rather payment in advance for Jewish service to the Empire," states: "The truth is that British statesmen were by no means anxious for such a *bargain*." (Emphasis added.) Weizmann 177. Dr. Weizmann countinues his narrative with a candid quotation from a letter he wrote to C. P. Scott, the pro-Zionist editor of the Manchester Guardian, that "England . . . would have in the Jews the best possible friends . . . ." Weizmann 178.

Leonard Stein also manifests ambivalence concerning the Zionist promise of "Jewish" political support to the British. He states: "It is, on the face of it, nonsensical to imagine that the Declaration was handed to him [Weizmann] as a kind of good conduct prize. We shall see later how closely the case for the Declaration was considered before being finally approved by the War Cabinet as a deliberate act of policy." Stein 120. "Zionist aspirations must be shown to accord with British strategic and political interests." Id. at 126. Stein, passim and especially at pages 309-556, indicates the Zionist offer of "Jewish" political support in return for a public law declaration. See also Zionist Diplomacy 23-24.

Stein also states: "Neither in this nor, indeed, in any later stage was there a bargain in the sense in which that word suggests an arm's-length negotiation on a *do ut des* basis. . . . What had happened was that events were now shaping in such a way as to provide a realistic basis for a closer understanding between the British Government and the Zionists—an understanding seen to correspond to the desires and interests of both." Stein 337. See generally 1 Esco Study 75-76.

Winston Churchill stated in an Address to the House of Commons, May 23, 1939: "It was in consequence of and on the basis of this pledge [the first or political promise clause of the Declaration] that we received important help in the War . . . ." Quoted in Jewish Agency for Palestine (compiled and annotated by Abraham Tulin), Book of Documents Submitted to the General Assembly of the United Nations Relating to the Establishment of the National Home for the Jewish People 3 (1947). This book, cited hereafter as "Jewish Agency Documents," contains Zionist juridical and political interpretations as well as juridical and political documents.

The Zionist promise of "Jewish" political support is clearly implied in the propaganda aspects of the Balfour Declaration considered in the text accompanying notes 194-95 infra.

agreement though not appearing in the text. Thus, the text of the Declaration together with the Zionist *quid pro quo* constitute the basic agreement which is to be interpreted in the present study. It is desirable for analytical purposes, however, to distinguish between this basic agreement which is being interpreted and the context of conditions (or negotiating history) which guide the interpreter in ascribing the most accurate possible meaning to the basic agreement.

Even a superficial reading of the Declaration indicates that its first clause, containing the words "best endeavours to facilitate" involves a political promise by the British Government, though one highly ambiguous in its terms.[87] The term "a national home," the "home in Palestine" of the Basle Program, was itself an ambiguous term in international law. The nominal beneficiary of the promise was the claimed Zionist constituency of "the Jewish people." The real beneficiaries of the British promise, however, were the Zionists themselves. Even though the phrase "the Jewish people" was used, it was clear that Weizmann and his fellow self-appointed representatives of "the Jewish people" had no authority to speak for members of the religious fellowship of Judaism. Weizmann admitted this fact ten years after the issuance of the Declaration:

> The Balfour Declaration of 1917 was built on air, and a foundation had to be laid for it through years of exacting work; every day and every hour of these last ten years, when opening the newspapers, I thought: Whence will the next blow come? I trembled lest the British Government would call me and ask: "Tell us, what is this Zionist Organisation? Where are they, your Zionists?" For these people think in terms different from ours. The Jews, they knew, were against us; we stood alone on a little island, a tiny group of Jews with a foreign past.[88]

Even if the term "the Jewish people" is given a juridical-political meaning, by its use in the Balfour Declaration, its scope was cut drastically by the second safeguard clause. Thus, the claimed constituency of "the Jewish people" was a fabrication.

The last two clauses of the Declaration are termed the safeguard clauses. The first safeguard was designed to protect the rights of the Palestinian Arabs, who then comprised the great majority of the

---

[87] All interpreters appear to agree that the first clause involves a political promise. There are diverse interpretations concerning its content and scope.

[88] Address by Dr. Weizmann at Czernowitz, Roumania, Dec. 12, 1917, in Goodman (ed.), Chaim Weizmann: Tribute in Honour of his Seventieth Birthday 199 (1945), cited hereafter as "Goodman (ed.), Weizmann."

Palestine population. Most of the Arabs were Moslems by religion, but a small group were Christians. The second safeguard was designed to protect the rights of Jews in any country other than Palestine from the incursions of Zionist nationalism. The common feature of these two safeguard clauses was that each was designed to protect existing rights in the event of conflict with the British Government's political promise made in the first clause. In contrast to the ambiguities of the first clause, the safeguard clauses were stated in unequivocal terms. In addition, they were given explicit priority over the first clause by the clarifying language that it was "clearly understood that nothing shall be done which may prejudice [such] rights."

c. The Zionist Interpretation

The Zionist interpretation of the Balfour Declaration is quite simple. The Declaration is regarded as providing juridical authority for "the Jewish people" nationality claims and for the Zionist national home enterprise in Palestine. The political promise clause has been extrapolated concerning the Palestine Arabs as if the first safeguard clause did not exist. In the same way, it has been extrapolated as to Jews in any other country than Palestine as if the second safeguard clause did not exist. The foregoing summary is supported by an extensive and detailed Zionist interpretation.[89]

The introductory paragraph in Mr. Balfour's letter of transmittal refers to the Balfour Declaration as one "of sympathy with Jewish Zionist aspirations." The last three words just quoted were given an authoritative Zionist interpretation by the Zionist Organization/Jewish Agency in 1947:

> The phrase "Jewish Zionist aspirations" in the first paragraph of the Document referred to the age-old hope of Jews the world over that Palestine shall be restored to its ancient role as the "Land of Israel". These aspirations were formulated as a concrete aim at the first World Zionist Congress at Basle, Switzerland, in 1897, under the leadership of Dr. Theodore Herzl. . . .[90]

The same Zionist interpretation then quotes Dr. Herzl concerning "a publicly secured" Zionist national home.[91] Thus, the Zionist interpretation of "Jewish Zionist aspirations" explicitly adopts

---

[89] In addition to the ensuing documentation, see Jewish Agency Documents passim.
[90] Jewish Agency Documents 1.
[91] Ibid.

the political Zionism of Herzl while implicitly rejecting the cultural Zionism of Achad Ha'am.

The Zionists have been unequivocal concerning the identity of the beneficiary of the grant clause of the Declaration. The beneficiary, in their view, is neither the Zionist Organization nor the Jews of Palestine but the claimed Zionist nationality entity of all Jews.[92] Dr. Weizmann has made this interpretation explicitly:

> The Zionist Organisation has taken the political steps necessary to obtain the recognition by the other nations of the Jewish right to a home in Palestine. But we have never wanted Palestine for the Zionists; we wanted Palestine for the Jews . . . . The Balfour Declaration is addressed to all Jewry.[93]

The words "national home for the Jewish people" have been interpreted by the Zionist Organization/Jewish Agency as authority to build "a Jewish State" in Palestine.

> The phrase "the establishment in Palestine of a National Home for the Jewish people" was intended and understood by all concerned to mean at the time of the Balfour Declaration that Palestine would ultimately become a "Jewish Commonwealth" or a "Jewish State", if only Jews came and settled there in sufficient numbers.[94]

This interpretation has been represented by Zionists as the intent of the Declaration. It is only the intent of the Zionists, however, because it is inconsistent with the safeguard clauses of the Declaration.

In 1948, Dr. Ernst Frankenstein, a Zionist legal writer, provided an interpretation in an article entitled "The Meaning of the Term 'National Home for the Jewish People.' "[95] After indicating that

---

[92] Id. at 2-4.

[93] Goodman (ed.), Weizmann 203.

[94] Jewish Agency Documents 5. The Zionist interpretation quoted in the text was made in 1947. Earlier Zionist interpretations were different. Mr. Stein states that "neither on the British nor on the Zionist side was there any disposition, at the time [of the issuance of the Declaration], to probe deeply into its meaning—still less was there any agreed interpretation." Stein 552.

Writing in 1919 in the author's introduction to his authoritative Zionist history of Zionism, Sokolow stated: "It has been said, and is still being obstinately repeated by anti-Zionists again and again, that Zionism aims at the creation of an independent 'Jewish State.' But this is wholly fallacious. The 'Jewish State' was never a part of the Zionist programme." 1 Sokolow xxiv-xxv.

The Zionist interpretation quoted in the text states that it was "understood by all concerned." Such an understanding cannot be attributed accurately to either Palestinian Arabs or anti-Zionists.

[95] Feinberg & Stoyanovsky (eds.), The Jewish Yearbook of International Law 1948, 27 (1949), cited hereafter as "Jewish Yb.I.L." The editors' introduction states: "The need for a periodical publication which would be devoted mainly to the study

"the National Home was to be a National Home for the *Jewish People* not merely for the Jews of Palestine," [96] Dr. Frankenstein concluded:

> Thus, as we have seen, the Jewish National Home may be defined as a scheme intended to give the Jewish people the opportunity to become, through immigration and settlement, a majority of the inhabitants of Palestine, and to make Palestine a Jewish State once again.[97]

Perhaps the most significant feature of the Zionist interpretation of the Declaration is the treatment accorded to the safeguard clauses. It was necessary for the Zionists to minimize these clauses, since it would be impossible to give them effect without narrowing the scope of the political promise clause. Therefore, these clauses are either ignored or considered briefly with a disclaimer of possible violation.[98]

The Zionist interpretation assumes that the Declaration is clear and unambiguous.[99] Despite the substantive changes made between the first and last drafts, Dr. Weizmann has declared: "[I]n spite of the phrasing the intent was clear." [100] After calling the penultimate draft (prepared after Edwin Montagu's attack upon the Zionist negotiating objectives) "a painful recession from what the Government itself was prepared to offer," [101] Weizmann said:

> The first [apparently the Zionist draft of July 18, 1917] declares that "Palestine should be reconstituted as the National Home of the Jewish people." The second [October 4 draft] speaks of "the establishment in Palestine of a National Home for the Jewish Race." The first adds only that the "Government will use its best endeavors to secure the achievement of this object and will discuss the neces-

---

of questions of international law affecting or of particular interest to the Jewish people has long been felt by all those who realized the *sui generis* character of those questions." Jewish Yb.I.L. v.

The present writer regards Jewish Yb.I.L. as *sui generis*. In addition to much Zionist juridical analysis and interpretation it contains a few studies of unquestioned objectivity. See, e.g., The Nationality of Denationalized Persons, Jewish Yb.I.L. 164 by the late Sir Hersch Lauterpacht who was a judge of the International Court of Justice and, earlier, Whewell Professor of International Law, Cambridge University. See also Lauterpacht, International Law and Human Rights (1950) which makes no religious discriminations among individuals.

[96] Frankenstein, Jewish Yb.I.L. 27, 39.

[97] Id. at 41.

[98] Id. at 29-30, 32-33; Akzin, The Palestine Mandate in Practice, 25 Iowa L.Rev. 32, 54-55 (1939).

[99] The intellectual inadequacies of such an assumption concerning the interpretive process are explained in Harvard Research, Treaties 937-39; 946-48.

[100] Weizmann 211.

[101] Id. at 207.

sary methods with the Zionist Organization"; the second introduced the subject of the "civic and religious rights of the existing non-Jewish communities" in such a fashion as to impute possible oppressive intentions to the Jews, and can be interpreted to mean such limitations on our work as completely to cripple it.[102]

Dr. Weizmann displayed commendable candor (writing in 1949) in recognizing the protective character of the phrasing and substance of the first safeguard clause as it appeared in the October 4 draft. In addition, he expressly recognized the compromise character of the October 4 draft: "Certain it was that Montagu's opposition . . . was responsible for the compromise formula which the War Cabinet submitted to us a few days later." [103] He also states: "[E]masculated as it was, [it] represented a tremendous event in exilic Jewish history—and that it was as bitter a pill to swallow for the Jewish assimilationists as the recession from the original, more forthright, formula was for us." [104] In 1949 Dr. Weizmann expressed doubt as to whether the "recession from the original, more forthright formula," should have been accepted or the Zionists should have been "intransigeant." [105] He recognized that: "[W]e did not dare to occasion further delay by pressing for the original formula . . . ." [106] Whatever his subsequent doubts, he did accept the Declaration with both safeguard clauses and with a substantial weakening of the political promise clause sought by the Zionists.[107] The Zionists did not have the political power to dictate the terms of the Declaration and had to accept the ultimate compromise document.

In spite of his contemporary concern, Dr. Weizmann subsequently developed a method of interpreting the Declaration which satisfied him: "It would mean exactly what we would make it mean—neither more nor less." [108]

---

[102] Ibid.
[103] Id. at 206.
[104] Id. at 207.
[105] Ibid.
[106] Ibid.
[107] Dr. Weizmann wrote:
  While the cabinet was in session, approving the final text, I was waiting outside, this time within call. Sykes brought the document out to me with the exclamation: "Dr. Weizmann, it's a boy!"
  Well—I did not like the boy at first. He was not the one I had expected. . . .
Id. at 208.
[108] Id. at 242. This was consistent with his general views: "Looking back, I incline to attach even less importance to written 'declarations' and 'statements' and 'instruments' than I did even in those days. Such instruments are at best frames which may or may not be filled in. They have virtually no importance unless and until they are supported by actual performance. . . ." Id. at 280.

d. *Interpretation in Context of Negotiation: The Balfour Declaration Compromise*

(1) International Law Criteria for the Interpretation of Agreements

It is obvious that an undertaking or agreement must exist before it can be interpreted. There are no particular words of art in international law which must be employed to describe an undertaking or agreement. The authoritative *Harvard Research in International Law* provides apt summary:

> Some international instruments are called "treaties" *eo nomine*, but a whole repertory exists from which names for instruments may be chosen. "Convention", "protocol", "agreement", "arrangement", "declaration", "act", "covenant", "statute"—all of these terms have been employed with reference to international instruments concluded in recent times, and the choice of one rather than another is in most cases, if not in all, without any significance in international law.[109]

In the *"Ihlen Declaration" Case*,[110] the Permanent Court of International Justice evaluated the juridical significance of an oral statement made by the Norwegian foreign minister in the context of Danish-Norwegian negotiations concerning their respective territorial interests in Eastern Greenland and Spitzbergen. Mr. Ihlen, the Norwegian foreign minister, stated orally to the Danish minister "that the Norwegian Government would not make any difficulties" [111] concerning the Danish territorial claims in Eastern Greenland. The court held, considering the context of the negotiations between the two states, that the oral Ihlen Declaration was binding upon the Norwegian government.[112]

There is, a fortiori, ample authority for the juridical validity of a more formal written instrument such as the Balfour Declaration. In form the Balfour Declaration is a unilateral pronouncement by the British Government. The three years of negotiations leading to its issuance, and particularly the last several months of intensive negotiations, reveal that, in substance, it is a multilateral agreement.[113]

---

[109] Harvard Research, Treaties 667.
[110] Legal Status of Eastern Greenland, P.C.I.J., ser. A/B, No. 53 (1933).
[111] Id. at 36.
[112] Id. at 73.
[113] Stein passim demonstrates the negotiating context and the agreement character of the Declaration.

Neither the Balfour Declaration nor any other basic understanding or agreement can have any single "natural and ordinary" or "clear and unambiguous" meaning apart from its relevant context of conditions.[114] At the minimum, this context must include the objectives of the participants and the principal purposes sought to be effectuated. Where the instrument interpreted embodies an agreement, an understanding of its negotiating history affords indispensable insight in its interpretation.[115] A basic agreement which, like the Balfour Declaration, has been negotiated over a period of years, is the result of the negotiating process which preceded it and which gives it meaning. The unilateral negotiating proposals which were abandoned in order to achieve multilateral agreement are particularly significant portions of the negotiating history. Without such compromises or recessions, there would be no basic agreement in many instances.

Senator Elihu Root, a distinguished former Secretary of State, gave appropriate emphasis to the crucial importance of negotiations in a statement made with reference to the Hay-Pauncefote treaty:

> If you would be sure of what a treaty means, if there be any doubt, if there are two interpretations suggested, learn out of what conflicting public policies the words of the treaty had their birth; what arguments were made for one side or the other, what concessions were yielded in the making of a treaty. Always, with rare exceptions, the birth and development of every important clause may be traced by the authentic records of the negotiators and of the countries which are reconciling their differences.[115a]

A thoughtful approach to the interpretive process is summarized in the *Harvard Research:*

> The process of interpretation, rightly conceived, cannot be regarded as a mere mechanical one of drawing inevitable meanings from the words in a text, or of searching for and discovering some preexisting specific intention of the parties with respect to every situation arising under a treaty. It is precisely because the words used in an instrument rarely have exact and single meanings, and because all possible situations which may arise under it cannot be, or at least are not, foreseen and expressly provided for by the parties at the time of its drafting, that the necessity for interpretation occurs. In most instances, therefore, interpretation involves *giving*

---

114 Harvard Research, Treaties 937-39; 946-48.
115 Id. at 937, 948-66.
115a Quoted in 5 Hackworth, Digest of International Law 259 (U.S. Dep't State, 1943).

a meaning to a text—not just any meaning which appeals to the interpreter, to be sure, but a meaning which, in the light of the text under consideration and of all the concomitant circumstances of the particular case at hand, appears in his considered judgment to be one which is logical, reasonable, and most likely to accord with and to effectuate the larger general purpose which the parties desired the treaty to serve.[116]

These traditional criteria will now be employed in providing juridical interpretation of the Balfour Declaration.

(2) The Negotiating History: Participants, Purposes and Proposals

It has been stated that the Balfour Declaration, though unilteral in form, is shown by its negotiating history to be a multilateral agreement in substance.[117]

The participants in the negotiations comprised four readily identifiable groups. The first group was the Zionists, represented by the principal Zionist leaders in Great Britain, including Dr. Weizmann, the president of the English Zionist Federation, and Mr. Nahum Sokolow, a member of the Executive of the World Zionist Organization. The second group was composed of the anti-Zionist Jews of England. Their leaders included Edwin Montagu, Secretary of State for India in the British Government at the time of the issuance of the Declaration, and Mr. Claude Montefiore, an eminent Englishman and Jew. The third participant comprised the Arabs of Palestine, who were either Moslems or Christians by religion. This group did not appear as an active negotiator, but its interests in the subject had to be taken into account by the other participants. The fourth participant was the British Government, which, in addition to attempting to advance its own national self-interest, served as conciliator and arbitrator among the other participants.[118]

Though the Zionists' purposes were those of political Zionism, Dr. Weizmann was well aware that Zionist political objectives had to accord with those of the British. He wrote of Palestine as "the Asiatic Belgium" and as "the barrier" protecting the Suez Canal.[119] Leonard Stein, the authoritative historian of the Balfour Declaration and a Zionist, has described Weizmann's understanding of the situation:

---

[116] Harvard Research, Treaties 946.
[117] Text at note 113 supra.
[118] The textual paragraph is based upon Stein passim.
[119] Quoted in Stein 127.

The Declaration [sought by the Zionists] itself presupposed that the Jewish people counted for something in the world and that the ideas bound up with the connection between the Jews and Palestine had not lost their potency. But the war years were not a time for sentimental gestures. The British Government's business was to win the War and to safeguard British interests in the post-war settlement. Fully realising that these must in the end be the decisive tests, Weizmann was never under the illusion that the Zionists could rely on an appeal *ad misericordiam*. Zionist aspirations must be shown to accord with British strategic and political interests.[120]

When the drafting began in the British Foreign Office, its conception was that the Government would declare itself in favor of establishing "a sanctuary for Jewish victims of persecution" [121] in Palestine. This conception had little relevance to Zionist political purposes. A preliminary Zionist draft prepared by Sokolow and others stressed "the principle of recognizing Palestine as the National Home of the Jewish people." [122] An official Zionist draft proposal transmitted by Lord Rothschild to Mr. Balfour on July 18, 1917, read as follows:

> 1. His Majesty's Government accepts the principle that Palestine should be reconstituted as the National Home of the Jewish people.
> 2. His Majesty's Government will use its best endeavours to secure the achievement of this object and will discuss the necessary methods and means with the Zionist Organisation.[123]

This draft contained three central Zionist objectives in the wording: "that Palestine should be reconstituted as the National Home of the Jewish people." The first objective was that the Zionist national home enterprise be "reconstituted," or established as of legal right, without regard to the existing rights of the Palestinian Arabs. The second objective was that all Jews (the comprehensive claimed entity of "the Jewish people") be recognized in law as constituting a single nationality grouping. The third objective was that a juridical connection be recognized in law between "the National Home" and "the Jewish people."

Two ensuing drafts were prepared in August 1917. One of the

---

[120] Stein 126.
[121] Id. at 468.
[122] Ibid.
[123] Id. at 470. This draft, each of the three successive drafts considered in the text, and the final Declaration are reproduced by Mr. Stein in a single Appendix. Id. at 664.

August drafts followed the official Zionist draft proposal very closely and reproduced *verbatim* the wording containing the three central Zionist objectives. Stein describes this draft, termed the Balfour draft, as a "slightly amended version of the Zionist draft." [124] The other August draft, termed the Milner draft, eliminated the crucial Zionist wording and substituted much weaker wording in its place.[125] Stein refers to Milner's draft as "a considerably watered-down version of Balfour's [August] formula." [126] The Milner draft led the way to much more drastic curtailment of Zionist nationalism in the penultimate and final drafts of the Declaration. Each of the drafts considered thus far had one feature in common. They contained no safeguard clauses. Such clauses were to achieve preeminence in the penultimate and final drafts of the Declaration.

Leopold Amery, an assistant secretary of the Cabinet, stated that shortly before the War Cabinet meeting of October 4, 1917, he was asked by Lord Milner, a Cabinet member, to draft "something which would go a reasonable distance to meeting the objections both Jewish and pro-Arab, without impairing the substance of the proposed declaration." [127] The ensuing Milner-Amery draft provided not only a "pro-Arab" safeguard but an explicit pro-Jewish and anti-Zionist one as well:

> His Majesty's Government views with favour the establishment in Palestine of a national home for the Jewish race and will use its best endeavours to facilitate the achievement of this object, it being clearly understood that nothing shall be done which may prejudice the civil and religious rights of existing non-Jewish communities in Palestine, or the rights and political status enjoyed in any other country by such Jews who are fully contented with their existing nationality and citizenship.[128]

This was the draft which Dr. Weizmann regarded as such "a painful recession." [129] Apparently the first of the "two limiting provisos" [130] was intended to satisfy Lord Curzon,[131] a Cabinet member who was not a friend of the Zionists, while the second was in-

---

[124] Id. at 520.
[125] Id. at 521.
[126] Ibid.
[127] Quoted in Stein 520.
[128] Stein 521. The last two words "and citizenship" were added subsequently. Id. at 525 n.31.
[129] Text at note 101 supra.
[130] Stein 522.
[131] Ibid.

serted to meet Montagu's anti-Zionist objectives.[132] Stein acknowledges with candor "the progressive watering down"[133] of the official Zionist draft submitted by Rothschild in July and accepted in substance by Balfour in August. Stein recognizes that this was clearly a response, not only to the pressure of the Jewish anti-Zionists, but also to the fact that in "dealing with the Palestine question there were other claims and interests to be considered besides those of the Jews."[134]

The "other claims and interests" involved were those of the Palestinian Arabs. Both the British Government and the anti-Zionists were concerned, for different reasons, with protecting the Arabs' existing rights and interests. The British Government was then engaged in military operations against Turkey[135] and hardly would be welcomed in Palestine as a liberator if Arab rights were to be violated.[136] Consistent with this, the basic humanitarianism of the anti-Zionist proposals attempted to ensure fair treatment for the Arabs. Thus only the Zionists were opposed to safeguarding the "other claims and interests."

After completion of the October 4 draft, it was sent by the Government, with an invitation for comments upon it, as a proposed declaration, "from Zionist leaders and from representative British Jews."[137] The anti-Zionist position was well summarized in the views of Claude Montefiore.[138] He objected to the phrase "a national home for the Jewish race" as implying that "Jews generally constitute a nationality."[139] In his views "such an implication is extremely prejudicial to Jewish interests."[140] He continued that "emancipation and liberty" are "a thousand times more important than a 'home.' . . . It is very significant that anti-Semites are always very sympathetic to Zionism."[141]

---

[132] Ibid.; Weizmann 206.

[133] Stein 522.

[134] Ibid.

[135] See generally 1 Esco Study 72-73.

[136] Field Marshal Allenby's proclamation upon British entry into Jerusalem contained the promise of protection for each of the three religions practiced in the city. It is quoted in 1 Esco Study 73.

[137] Stein 524; Mr. Stein describes the seeking of the views of the anti-Zionist "representative British Jews" as a "concession to Montagu" which made Weizmann indignant. Id. at 518.

[138] Mr. Stein states of Montefiore: "By reason of his lofty character, his learning and his philanthropy, and of his high standing and reputation outside as well as inside the Jewish community, he was an inportant and impressive figure in Anglo-Jewish life and was recognized by the Zionists themselves as an opponent worthy of respect." Stein 175.

[139] Quoted in Stein at 525.

[140] Ibid.

[141] Id. at 525-26.

Whatever may have been the subsequently expressed views of Dr. Weizmann, the Zionists accepted the Milner-Amery draft.[142] In spite of their resentment over the "progressive watering down," [143] the Zionists were sufficiently realistic to recognize that they were unlikely to obtain anything better.[144] In spite of Zionist opposition, the safeguard clauses had come to stay.

The text of the Milner-Amery draft was telegraphed by Mr. Balfour to Colonel House, the confidential adviser to President Wilson, on October 6, with the request that it be submitted to the President.[145] After prompting by Colonel House, President Wilson authorized a favorable, although a general and informal, response to the proposed draft.[146]

On October 9, Weizmann had telegraphed the same draft to Justice Brandeis in the United States.[147] Brandeis and his associates found the draft unsatisfactory in two particulars. They disliked that part of the draft's second safeguard clause which read, "by such Jews who are fully contented with their existing nationality and citizenship," and wished to substitute "the rights and civil political status enjoyed by Jews in any other country." [148] In addition, Brandeis apparently proposed the change of "Jewish race" to "Jewish people." [149] In both particulars the final declaration appeared to be changed because of these views.[150]

The proposed declaration was submitted to the British Government for approval in final form.[151] It was so approved on October 31, 1917, and issued two days later in the letter from Balfour to Rothschild.[152]

One of the most significant features of the final Declaration was the

---

[142] Weizmann, Sokolow, and Lord Rothschild "welcomed" the draft. Stein 527.
[143] Stein 522.
[144] Weizmann 207-08; supra note 142.
[145] Stein 528.
[146] Id. at 529-30.
[147] Id. at 530.
[148] Id. at 531.
[149] Ibid.
[150] Ibid. Mr. Stein is very equivocal concerning the reasons for the change in the second safeguard. Id. at 531-32. The important result is that the second safeguard was strengthened.
[151] On two previous occasions the British Government had refused to issue earlier versions of the Declaration. Id. at 549.
[152] General and informal assent to the Declaration by France and Italy was obtained after its issuance:

> That neither Government had been consulted in advance is plain from Balfour's replies to question in Parliament. That both disliked the Declaration is shown by the efforts needed to induce them to endorse it. In each case it fell to the Zionists or their friends to extract the endorsement, and in each case it was communicated, not to the British Government, but to the Zionists.

Id. at 587.

Zionist failure to achieve British public law assent to any of their three central juridical objectives in their official July draft.[153] In lieu of what the Zionists sought, they received a limited and equivocal political promise clause. Even more significantly, the first safeguard survived intact while the final draft of the second safeguard was strengthened by eliminating reference to Jews in countries other than Palestine who were "fully contented with their existing nationality,"[153a] and making the second safeguard applicable, without exception, to "Jews in any other country" than Palestine.

(3) The Compromise Agreement Embodied in the Declaration

(a) The Political Promise Clause

Mr. Stein introduces his consideration of the meaning of the political promise clause with the following paragraph:

> What, then, were the Zionists being promised? The language of the Declaration was studiously vague, and neither on the British nor on the Zionist side was there any disposition, at the time, to probe deeply into its meaning—still less was there any agreed interpretation.[154]

After conceding that the Declaration failed to provide assurance that the British Government would assume direct responsibility for the establishment of the Zionist national home enterprise,[155] Stein's analysis continues:

> What the British Government did undertake was to use its best endeavours to 'facilitate' (no more) 'the establishment in Palestine of a national home for the Jewish people'—not, as it had been put in the Zionist draft and as Balfour would, apparently, have been prepared to concede, the reconstitution of Palestine as the national home of the Jews.[156]

The "studiously vague" character of the political promise clause, to use Stein's description, is also revealed by the wide variety of "Zionist" support for the Declaration. Thus, Achad Ha'am, who

---

[153] See the text accompanying note 123 supra.
[153a] See the text accompanying note 128 supra.
[154] Stein 552.
[155] Ibid. Stein adds, with ambivalence, that Weizmann and his associates "had from the start regarded as fundamental" direct British assumption of responsibility for the national home enterprise, but did not expect it to be given to them. Ibid.
[156] Stein 552-53.

had participated in the negotiations leading to the Declaration, supported the final Declaration. Similarly, Justice Brandeis supported it when issued. The support of the humanitarian Zionists just named, and others as well, was welcomed by the political Zionists during the negotiations and after the issuance of the Declaration. This humanitarian support subsequently was to prove embarrassing to the political Zionists because of the wide divergence between the humanitarian and political Zionists' interpretations of the political promise clause.[157]

It has been explained that the political promise clause was exchanged for the Zionist promise to deliver political support of "the Jewish people" for British political objectives during and after the war.[158] Mention of the political support to be provided by the Zionists may possibly have been omitted from the Declaration because the negotiating history already had made it clear that it was the price to be paid by the Zionist leaders. A more pragmatic explanation may be that, if the Declaration had been explicit concerning the political bargain involved, many Jews in the states of their respective na-

---

[157] Justice Brandeis is well known as a humanitarian. He regarded the Balfour Declaration as the end of the political work of Zionism, whereas Weizmann regarded it as another beginning. Dr. Weizmann wrote:

> What struck me as curious was that the American Zionists, under Justice Brandeis, though fully aware of what was going on in England and in Palestine, nonetheless shared the illusions of our Continental friends; they too assumed that all political problems had been settled once and for all, and that the only important task before Zionists was the economic upbuilding of the Jewish National Home.

Weizmann 241. See id. at 306.

Concerning Brandeis' disillusionment with political Zionism, see Berger, Disenchantment of a Zionist, 38 Middle East Forum No. 4, p. 21 (1962). Mr. Stein writes of the "irreconcilable differences on questions of principle" between Brandeis and Weizmann which led "to an open breach." Stein 581.

The translator's introduction to Achad Ha'am, Ten Essays on Zionism and Judaism (Leon Simon transl. 1922) reproduces Achad Ha'am's interpretation of the Declaration's political promise clause. Achad Ha'am pointed out that in the negotiations and the final Declaration the political Zionists failed to achieve their objectives. Id. at xvi-xx. He concluded that:

> This position, then, makes Palestine common ground for different peoples, each of which tries to establish its national home there; and in this position it is impossible for the national home of either of them to be complete and to embrace all that is involved in the conception of a "national home." If you build your house not on untenanted ground, but in a place where there are other inhabited houses, you are sole master only as far as your front gate. Within you may arrange your effects as you please, but beyond the gate all the inhabitants are partners, and the general administration must be ordered in conformity with the good of all of them.

Id. at xviii.

The late Judah L. Magnes had a similar humanitarian value orientation. See his Toward Peace in Palestine, 21 Foreign Affairs 239 (1943). Compare Weizmann, Palestine's Role in the Solution of the Jewish Problem, 20 Foreign Affairs 324 (1942).

[158] See the text and authorities cited at note 86 supra.

tionalities would have repudiated expressly the Zionist leaders' claim to act for them and to deliver their loyalties. In any event, as actually drafted, the Declaration could more easily be represented as an unsolicited humanitarian act of the British Government in behalf of oppressed Jews. In addition, the political promise clause, in its drastically changed wording, could be interpreted accurately as a humanitarian act which should be supported by all men of good will. This interpretation of the political promise clause is even more compelling when it is read in the context of the safeguards. Thus, the British Government and the political Zionists were in the happy position of having humanitarian motives attributed to them and humanitarian interpretations applied to the Declaration because of the narrowed political promise and the inclusion of the safeguard clauses.[159]

Probably the clearest feature of the political promise clause of the Declaration, viewing "with favour the establishment in Palestine of a national home for the Jewish people," is its limited substance in comparison to the wording of the official Zionist draft of July 1917. Standing alone, the political promise is certainly as vague as Stein claims it to be. In comparison with the Zionist negotiating objectives, it must be construed as having a very restricted political meaning and perhaps even a humanitarian one. More precise interpretation of the political promise will be made after consideration of the meaning of the safeguard clauses.

(b) The Safeguard Clauses

In contrast to the relative uncertainties of the political promise clause, the safeguard clauses have a high degree of clarity. In lieu of generalizations such as "view with favour" and "best endeavours to facilitate," the safeguards are introduced by unequivocal language. It would be difficult indeed to draft clearer language than the words "it being clearly understood that nothing shall be done which may prejudice"[160] the safeguarded rights. Rather than merely stating that nothing shall be done which may injure or damage the safeguarded rights, the wording went further and prohibited "prejudice" to those rights. The words, "it being clearly understood," prove that, whatever the vagueness or ambiguity of the political promise clause,

---

159 The humanitarian views of Justice Brandeis and Achad Ha'am are referred to supra note 157.

160 The Balfour Declaration is reproduced in the text accompanying note 81 supra.

it must be interpreted as subordinate to and conditioned upon the implementation of the safeguarded rights. Both safeguard clauses were placed in the Declaration contrary to the explicit negotiating objectives of the Zionist leaders.[161]

The first safeguard clause reassured the "non-Jewish communities in Palestine" against prejudice which might result from the political bargain made between the British Government and political Zionism. The first clause refers to "the civil and religious rights" of the non-Jewish communities in Palestine. A Zionist interpretation has urged that such rights do not include either "political status" or "rights" without qualification or limitation.[162] A more likely explanation is that the specific wording referred to the rights actually enjoyed by the Arabs under Ottoman rule, which were deemed to include, among others, such basic ones as freedom of religion and the right to own land.[163] The first safeguard has been distorted by interpreting protection accorded to "the civil and religious rights" of Palestinian

---

[161] Their inconsistency with the official Zionist draft proposal of July 18, 1917, and the three central political objectives embodied in it is obvious. See the text accompanying note 123 supra.

[162] Frankenstein, The Meaning of the Term "National Home for the Jewish People," Jewish Yb.I.L. 27, 29-30. More typical Zionist "interpretation" is to ignore the safeguard clauses.

[163] Hadawi, The Loss of a Heritage (1963) reveals violation of the first safeguard clause even if it is narrowly construed. Peretz, Israel and the Palestine Arabs (1958) passim, shows systematic violation.
A sympathetic observer of Israel has written:
> She [Israel] should abolish the military government and rely on her excellent secret service to apprehend spies and saboteurs. Having at last opened the *Histadrut* to Arab membership, she should now treat the problem of Arab unemployment with exactly the same urgency as the finding of jobs for new immigrants. She should give back to its Israeli-Arab owners as much expropriated land as possible, mindful that every *dunam* of it now yields more in disaffection in Israeli-Arab hearts than in crops.

Schwarz, The Arabs in Israel 167 (1959).
American Jewish Committee & Jewish Publication Society of America, 63 American Jewish Yearbook 499 (1962) describes the Anti-Defamation League of B'nai B'rith as follows: "Seeks to eliminate defamation of Jews, counteract un-American and anti-democratic propaganda, and promote better group relations." Forster & Epstein, The Trouble-Makers: An Anti-Defamation League Report (1952) makes a valuable contribution in exposing anti-Semitism, even though it accepts uncritically some Zionist-Israel postulates. In attacking Arabs, at 169-96, the authors display intellectual confusion concerning the distinction between Zionists and Jews. The same authors then "indict" Arabs for religious prejudice:
> [W]e do indict those Arabs who use religious hatred and prejudice to achieve their ends. We do indict those Arab delegates, diplomats, and others, who peddle suspicion and distrust of Jews to the four corners of the world, and would disenfranchise them wherever they live in order to accomplish their objectives in the Middle East. We do criticize, and strongly, that Arab activity which victimizes the Jew and creates dissension in our country.

Id. at 195.

Arabs as implying juridical authority for a "Jewish" state in which the Arabs of Palestine would become a protected minority.[164]

In view of the fundamental protective purpose of the safeguard clauses, a narrow and destructive interpretation of the first safeguard clause should be rejected. It must be given a broad scope because it was inserted in opposition to the comprehensive claims of political Zionism concerning Palestine. In addition, if Palestine were to be brought under British military rule, and perhaps subsequently under an internationally supervised regime such as the League of Nations Mandate system,[165] it was essential to have the good will and cooperation of the Palestine population. The first indispensable step in obtaining such cooperation was assurance that their "civil and religious rights" would not be prejudiced.

Political Zionism also threatened the single nationality status of Jews in other countries. Anti-Zionist Jews insisted upon inclusion of the second safeguard to protect themselves from Zionist nationalism.[165a] Especially dangerous was prejudice, not to mention injury, caused by involuntary inclusion in the claimed nationality of "the Jewish people." The comprehensive terms of the clause effectuate the protection, since it includes both "rights" and "political status" of Jews in any other country than Palestine.

(c) The Consistency of the Clauses in the Compromise

An interpretation which recognizes that each of the three clauses of the Declaration is an integral part of the negotiated compromise provides clarification of the meaning of the political promise clause.[166] Since the safeguard clauses protected existing rights, they would have to be interpreted, even if there were no clarifying wording in the Declaration, as having at least equal juridical significance with the political promise clause. On the basis of such an assumption, the safeguards still would be interpreted as limiting the political promise clause. The text of the Declaration, however, by providing that "it being clearly understood that nothing shall be done which may prejudice" the safeguarded rights, accords the latter an express preeminent position in the Declaration.

---

[164] Supra note 162.

[165] The Palestine Mandate is examined in the text accompanying notes 210-22 infra.

[165a] See the text accompanying note 132 supra.

[166] It is elementary learning that all provisions of an agreement must be interpreted. Harvard Research, Treaties 947.

Further clarification is provided by the generalizations in the political promise and the specifics in each of the safeguard clauses. The political promise clause's generality, as well as the unequivocal negotiating history, prevents it from being construed as a limitation upon the safeguards. The express purpose of the specific safeguards, however, is to limit the political promise. Because each of the three clauses is an integral element in a compromise agreement, they must be construed as consistent with one another.[167] An interpretation of the political promise clause which accords with the safeguards is one which limits the political promise to the requirements of humanitarianism. In this interpretation, the political promise extends only to "a national home" for some Jews who desire it. Such a political promise is consistent with both the rights and nationalistic aspirations of the Palestinian Arabs and the single nationality status of Jews in any other country. The political promise, so interpreted, meets the objectives of the humanitarians including Achad Ha'am and Brandeis. It does not meet the objectives of the political Zionists which were specifically rejected by the British Government. In summary, one juridical interpretation of the political promise clause is that it provides sanctuary for Jews without impinging upon the rights of Palestinian Arabs or the rights of Jews in any other country.[168]

(4) Zionist Distortion of the Second Safeguard Clause

The preeminent character of the safeguard clauses has presented a problem to Zionist interpreters of the Declaration. Typically, the Zionists have ignored the safeguards. An article by Professor Feinberg of the Hebrew University entitled "The Recognition of the Jewish People in International Law" [169] is important because it gives

---

[167] An objective interpreter cannot lightly assume that a text which has been agreed upon following negotiations conducted over a period of years contains inconsistent provisions. By "objective interpreter" the writer does not refer to one who lacks moral values and corresponding juridical objectives.

[168] Another juridical interpretation of the political promise clause is provided in the text accompanying notes 198, 199 infra.

Mr. Stein, as lawyer, approaches the humanitarian juridical interpretation. See the text accompanying notes 154, 155, and 156 supra. Mr. Stein, as Zionist, then retreats from it. After having compiled the negotiating history demonstrating Zionist failure, which facilitates juridical analysis, and providing a measure of close juridical analysis, he makes this statement: "The Declaration was a political and not a legal document, and the *crucial* words did not lend themselves to close analysis." (Emphasis added.) Stein 553. Mr. Stein, in typical Zionist fashion, does not interpret the safeguards (although he spells out their crucial importance in the negotiations). If Stein did interpret the safeguards, as a lawyer, he would be compelled to interpret the political promise clause even more narrowly than he does.

[169] Jewish Yb.I.L. 1.

direct attention to the second safeguard clause. The article begins with a survey of the historic humanitarian interventions in behalf of persecuted Jews. Professor Feinberg examines the juridical grounds for the interventions under a heading entitled, significantly, "Rights of Jews, not of the Jewish People." [170] He states that the "chief characteristic" of the humanitarian interventions before the First World War was that "the Jewish question was not dealt with in its entirety, as a question concerning a nation or a people and requiring a political solution." [171] He then contrasts individual rights with collective rights:

> These interventions had in common the further characteristic that they aimed at protecting only individual and not collective rights. The struggle for rights which the Jews pursued in their respective countries was carried on under the banner of the emancipation of the individual Jew, and aimed only at obtaining religious freedom and civil and political rights.[172]

From the Zionist perspective, the humanitarian protection of Jews *as individuals* was an undesirable situation. In Professor Feinberg's view the possession of "only" individual rights by Jews is changed by the Balfour Declaration.[173] In Feinberg's words, "[T]he Jewish question was raised to the level of a question involving a nation as a whole, i.e., an entity entitled to separate national existence and to the organization of its life within the framework of the State." [174]

After emphasizing the "binding effect" [175] of the Declaration, Professor Feinberg spells out his interpretation of the political promise clause:

> The right to the National Home is granted to the Jewish people as a whole, and not to any part of it; it is granted not to Zionists or to Jews who have settled in Palestine or who will settle there, but to all Jews wherever they may be.[176]

The most startling feature of the foregoing interpretation is that it is a violation of the second safeguard clause. In elementary juridical

---

170 Id. at 5.
171 Ibid.
172 Ibid.
173 Id. passim.
174 Id. at 7.
175 Id. at 9.
176 Id. at 17.

conception, a right necessarily involves a correlative duty.[177] In Feinberg's view the "right to the national home" is granted to "all Jews wherever they may be." This national right is difficult to separate, either in theory or in practise, from the correlative duty of national allegiance. The additional national allegiance which appears to be involved in the national right is inconsistent with the existing single nationality status and allegiance of Jews in the states of their respective nationalities. The protection of this single nationality status of Jews was the principal purpose of the second safeguard.

Feinberg continues with a detailed examination of the second safeguard clause:

> It was also on the basis of the above view that, as early as 1917, when the Balfour Declaration was drafted, it was thought necessary to remove any doubt as to the status of those Jews who would not settle in Palestine. To this end the second part of the Declaration provided that "nothing should be done which might prejudice . . . the rights and political status enjoyed by Jews in any other country." [178]

The foregoing analysis would not be subject to criticism if "the status of those Jews who would not settle in Palestine" were interpreted consistently with the negotiating history of the Balfour Declaration agreement.

Professor Feinberg, however, then states:

> Neither the Czechoslovaks nor the Poles required any such provision, as no international rights were granted to members of those peoples who lived outside the limits of the future States of Czechoslovakia and Poland . . . . The Building up of the National Home could not have been effected without the collaboration and assistance of Jews throughout the world; and it was for the purpose of representing them in all that concerned the establishment of the National Home that the Jewish Agency was created. Under these circumstances it was seen fit to secure that the grant of the National Home, and the ensuing right of all Jews to take part in the upbuilding of that home, did not in any way affect their status and allegiance as citizens of the countries to which they belonged.[179]

The second safeguard clause is thus construed by Feinberg as providing international legal protection for Zionists (termed "Jews" by

---

[177] See generally Hohfeld, Some Fundamental Legal Conceptions as Applied in Judicial Reasoning, 23 Yale L. J. 16, 30-32 (1913).
[178] Feinberg, Jewish Yb.I.L. 1, 17.
[179] Id. at 17, 18.

him) exercising the system of national "rights" and correlative obligations necessary for the building of the "National Home." The legal
protection of such Zionists is apparently regarded as protection from
the states of their regular nationalities, since their participation in
Zionist political activities is interpreted as not affecting "their status
and allegiance as citizens of the countries to which they belonged." [180]
Thus, the additional Zionist nationality status attributed to "the
Jewish people" is interpreted as consistent with the recognized
nationality "status and allegiance" of Jews in their respective states
in spite of the second safeguard clause. These astonishing conclusions
are reached by mere statement of the Zionist juridical objective of
protecting Zionists outside Palestine by giving them international
legal authority to participate in the activities of Zionist nationalism
without regard for the municipal laws of the respective states of their
recognized nationalities. Professor Feinberg's methodology is simply
to assume the answer to the question in issue, that is, whether or not
such international rights were granted to Zionists. The alleged Zionist
rights are explained by stating that no other "peoples" (Czechoslovaks and Poles) required such a provision "as no international
rights were granted" to them.[181] Then the postulate of Zionist nationalism is restated, with appropriate changes in terminology, as
the conclusion of the analysis. In Feinberg's words, "the ensuing
right of all Jews" [182] (i.e., Zionists) is provided in the second safeguard clause of the Declaration. If the human values at stake were
less important, the quaint old game of legal ring-around-the-rosy
might be amusing. By the same "logic," if it is postulated that the
moon is made of green cheese, then it becomes obligatory to conclude, *inter alia*, that green cheese is that of which the moon is
made.[183] The human values are so crucial, however, that the Feinberg fallacy must be exposed.

The Feinberg interpretation is so inconsistent with the negotiating
history and the ultimate compromise embodied in the Declaration
that it does not deserve consideration on its merits. His interpretation is, nevertheless, a highly ingenious and original one. He attributes
to the French international law authority, Paul Fauchille, the con-

---

[180] Ibid.
[181] Id. at 18.
[182] Ibid.
[183] Systematic exposure of the fallacies of such legal "logic" or "reasoning" is provided by Francis, Three Cases on Possession—Some Further Observations, 14 St.
Louis L. Rev. 11 (1928), reprinted in Fryer (ed.) Readings on Personal Property 85
(1938).

clusion that the Balfour Declaration and informal assent to it[184] "undoubtedly constituted the recognition of the Jewish people as a nation." [185] M. Fauchille writes of the Balfour Declaration, as embodied in the Treaty of Peace with Turkey signed at Sevres in 1920:

> But Article 95 takes care still to add that "nothing shall be done which may prejudice the civil and religious rights of existing non-Jewish communities in Palestine, or the rights and political status enjoyed by Jews in any other country." In the clearest way, this was to recognize both the existence of a Jewish nation and the rights of Israelites to international protection in all states in which they reside or whose nationals they have become.[186]

The last sentence in the Fauchille quotation introduced by the words, "In the clearest way," leaps to the conclusion of juridical recognition of "the existence of a Jewish nation." Such a conclusion is inconsistent with the compromise agreement embodied in the Declaration and, in particular, the second safeguard. The second portion of Fauchille's last sentence referring to the "rights of Israelites to international protection in all states in which they reside or whose nationals they have become" might possibly be regarded as sufficiently ambiguous so that it could be construed as consistent either with Professor Feinberg's interpretation of the second safeguard clause or the interpretations based upon the negotiating history and the ultimate compromise agreement. If Fauchille's word, "Israelites," is employed to refer to "Zionists," then the Feinberg interpretation[187] appears to be partially supported. If "Israelites" is accorded its more accepted meaning of "Jews," then the Fauchille interpretation gives considerably less support to Feinberg. The principal ambiguity in the

---

[184] See supra note 152.
[185] Feinberg, Jewish Yb.I.L. 1, 15.
[186] 1 Fauchille, Traité de Droit International Public 316 (1923). (Translation by Mrs. Vera Taborsky and the writer.)
[187] Professor Feinberg's article ends with the following paragraph:
    There is an old dictum which may be regarded as a canon of interpretation in Jewish matters, even though it is not to be found in treatises on international law. The dictum is etched in the long and turbulent history of the Jews, and its severity has even been enhanced in our own days: *Judaeorum causae non es aequitate sed rigore juris decidendae sunt.*
Jewish Yb.I.L. 1, 26. The last sentence quoted is translated by Professor John F. Latimer of The George Washington University as follows: "Jewish juridical causes must be decided not on the basis of justice or equity but according to the strictness of the law."
    In the view of the present writer, the juridical causes of individual Jews, as of all adherents of religions of universal moral values, and even as of those individuals who do not profess a religion, must be decided according to law including the preeminent objectives of justice and equity which the law is intended to effectuate.

Fauchille statement, however, concerns the character of the "international protection" accorded to Israelites. The negotiating history, previously examined, demonstrates that it was protection from Zionist nationalism.

(5) The Limited "Jewish People" of the Balfour Declaration: The Zionists Only

It has already been stated that Dr. Weizmann's claimed constituency of "the Jewish people" in the negotiations leading to the Balfour Declaration was a fabrication subsequently conceded by him.[188] What then was the actual constituency intended to be included within the phrase "the Jewish people"?

During the negotiations, Dr. Weizmann and the other Zionist negotiators attempted to negotiate in behalf of "the Jewish people." [189] In their conception "the Jewish people" consisted of: (1) the Zionist negotiators along with other Zionist leaders and the avowed members of the Zionist movement; (2) Jews in any country other than Palestine.[190] There was no doubt that the Zionist leaders had the right to speak for the Zionists. The central controversy in the negotiations, however, concerned the right of the Zionists to speak for Jews in any country other than Palestine. Montagu and the other anti-Zionist leaders directed their principal effort to limiting the Zionists to their real constituency and denying them the right to act for Jews who were not Zionists.[191] The anti-Zionist purpose of maintaining the single nationality status of Jews in any other country than Palestine was maintained implacably throughout the negotiations.[192] The full measure of the anti-Zionist success is set forth unequivocally in the second safeguard clause. The complete failure of the Zionist leaders' claim of authority to act for Jews in any coun-

---

188 See the text accompanying note 88 supra.

189 It is clear that the meaning of "the Jewish people" was drastically limited from October 4, 1917, when the anti-Zionists succeeded in having the second safeguard clause placed in the Milner-Amery draft. See the text accompanying notes 127-132 supra.

190 The textual statement is based upon the Zionist negotiating objectives. See Weizmann 176-94, 200-08, and passim; Stein 502-32, 543-56, and passim.

191 Mr. Stein admits this, by implication only. Stein passim. "[N]or could anything be better calculated to prejudice his [Montagu's] work in India, than a British declaration which, as he saw it, would imply that he belonged, as a Jew, to a people apart, with its home—the real focus of its loyalties—in Palestine." Id. at 498-99.

192 Primary authority for the textual statement is found in the negotiating history and particularly in the Milner-Amery draft (reproduced in the text accompanying note 128 supra) where the second safeguard first appeared.

try other than Palestine is demonstrated by the strengthening of the second safeguard as it appeared in the final Declaration.[193]

What, then, did "the Jewish people" of the political promise clause include, in the light of the exclusion of Jews in any other country than Palestine from the Zionist constituency? It is a drastically restricted "Jewish people" limited to contemporary Zionists or those who would become Zionists in the future.

The question is raised: If "the Jewish people" excludes the "Jews in any other country" and thus limits Zionist nationalism to its genuine constituency of Zionists, why was not the term "Zionists" substituted for "the Jewish people" in the political promise clause? A realistic answer must recognize that, in spite of the crucial juridical significance of the Declaration, it had other purposes as well. The Zionist negotiators had offered, as *quid pro quo*, the support of their claimed international constituency of Jews to the British Government for British political objectives. Even though the second safeguard fully protected Jews "in any other country" than Palestine, the British Government welcomed political support from all sources. The phraseology of the Declaration was designed, *inter alia*, to make it appear as a humanitarian act by the British Government. There is no doubt that the Declaration had substantial propaganda value to Great Britain and the Allies.[194] A classic study of propaganda during the First World War states: "General Ludendorff regarded the Balfour Declaration as the cleverest thing done by the Allies in the nature of war propaganda, and lamented the fact that Germany had not thought of it first." [195]

None of the additional purposes of the Declaration could have been achieved if "the Jewish people" had been candidly described as "Zionists" or "Zionist nationalists" in the political promise clause. Humanitarian concern with the plight of oppressed Jews would not have been aroused by a political promise in behalf of "a national home for the Zionists." Similarly, such a clause would have eliminated the appearance of humanitarian intent on the part of the British

---

[193] Text accompanying note 153 supra.

[194] Balfour recognized the propaganda value of the Declaration. Stein 544. So did Lloyd George. Id. at 546-47. Propaganda reasons are referred to in 1 Esco Study 115. "The essential reason, accounts agree, was strategic and had to do with the need of strengthening Great Britain's lifeline to the East." Id. at 117. "Through the Balfour Declaration Great Britain ultimately strengthened and extended her position in the whole Near East." Id. at 118.

[195] Lasswell, Propaganda Technique in the World War 176 (1927). See Stein 533-42 concerning Zionist contacts with the German Government. A cautious German Government statement concerning Zionists and Palestine, issued on Jan. 8, 1918, is quoted in Stein at 602-03.

Government.[196] For British political objectives, consequently, it was indispensable to use "the Jewish people" intact in wording but limited in meaning by the second safeguard clause.

The Zionists were opposed to any limitation of the content of their "Jewish people" concept but failed to achieve this negotiating objective. The Zionists as political realists, however, were aware of the benefits which might accrue to them from even the carefully limited word symbols. Non-Zionists and other potential supporters of Zionism might be led to believe that something akin to "the Jewish people" of Zionist nationalism had been recognized in public law. In addition, the Zionists *qua* "Zionists" could not succeed in the Zionist "national home" enterprise without support from outside Palestine. Only by making the "national home" appear to be a haven for oppressed Jews were the Zionists able to recruit more Zionists while simultaneously obtaining humanitarian support for British and Zionist political objectives. Of all the possible selections of word symbols, "the Jewish people" [197] was the most likely to assist in promoting Zionist political objectives consistent with the stringent juridical limitation of the second safeguard clause. The anti-Zionists were secure in the knowledge that Jews (as opposed to Zionists) had their existing "rights and political status" fully protected by the ultimate compromise Declaration.[198]

In summary, the second safeguard clause of the Declaration limited Dr. Weizmann by law to his genuine constituency of the Zionists by subtracting his false constituency of "Jews in any other country" than Palestine. The ensuing juridical result is that though the word symbols "the Jewish people" were used in the political promise clause, they referred to a restricted "Jewish people" which was limited to the Zionists alone. This juridical interpretation recognizes that "the Jewish people" of the political promise clause is employed as a palatable euphemism for "Zionists" or "Zionist nationalists." Whatever doubt may have existed concerning the character of Dr. Weizmann's constituency during the negotiations, it was removed by the clear cut anti-Zionist victory spelled out in the second safeguard of the compromise Declaration.

---

196 The humanitarian appearance was needed to enhance the juridical, propaganda, strategic, and other objectives.

197 As to the ambiguity of the term, see the text accompanying note 28 supra.

198 In addition, domestic constitutional law provides similar protection. For example, the United States Government is prohibited by the First Amendment to the Constitution from discriminating among its citizens on a religious basis. See text accompanying notes 320-24 infra. It should be noted that the Jews of Palestine were not protected by the terms of either safeguard clause.

It has been demonstrated previously that one juridically sound interpretation of the political promise clause is that it provides humanitarian sanctuary for Jews.[199] Its alternative juridically sound interpretation is that it is limited to present and potential Zionists only. The common element in these alternative interpretations is that each is consistent with the compromise Declaration including the safeguards.[200] In contrast, the centural feature of Zionist interpretation of the political promise clause is its violation of the safeguards.[201]

(6) The Continuing Validity of the Balfour Declaration

From its issuance on November 2, 1917, until the present, the Balfour Declaration has been relied upon by the Zionist Organization,[202] and since 1948, by the State of Israel[203] also, as authority for Zionist juridical claims. In particular, it has been viewed by the Zionist-Israel sovereignty as granting international juridical authority for "the Jewish people" nationality claims.[204]

The Balfour Declaration came into existence as an explicit international agreement binding, *inter alia*, the British Government, as such, and as the Mandatory Government in Palestine.[205] It might be argued that Israel is bound by the Declaration, including both safeguards, as the successor government to the Palestine Mandatory Government.[206] It could also be argued that the United Nations General Assembly Resolution of November 29, 1947,[207] which recommended partition of Palestine, obligated Israel to the Balfour Declaration. As to both the recommended Arab and "Jewish" states, the

---

[199] Text accompanying notes 167, 168 supra.

[200] Any *juridical* interpretation of the political promise must be consistent with the safeguards.

[201] See, e.g., Weizmann 211 and passim; Feinberg, Jewish Yb.I.L. 1 passim; Frankenstein, Jewish Yb.I.L. 27 passim.

[202] In addition to the specifics considered in this study see, generally, Jewish Agency Documents passim.

[203] In addition to the specifics considered in this study see, generally, Israel Office of Information (New York), Israel's Struggle for Peace (1960).

[204] The "Jewish people" concept was used by the Zionist negotiators as one of the devices employed to obtain the Balfour Declaration political promise and now that very restricted promise is used to advance the nationality claims based upon the "Jewish people" concept.

[205] The Declaration was incorporated into the League of Nations Mandate for Palestine which is examined in the text accompanying notes 210-22 supra.

[206] See C. H. Alexander, Israel in Fieri, 4 Int'l L.Q. 423 (1951) which states: "[A]t the time of withdrawal of the Mandatory Power the new Sovereign was already at hand. Continuity of rights and duties is provided by general principles of International Law, the breach of which would make the State of Israel a tortfeasor." The same writer makes rigid distinctions between different types of international duties. Id. at 427. He is aware that Israel denies that it is a successor to the Mandatory Government. Ibid.

[207] U.N. Gen. Ass. Off. Rec. 2d Sess. 131-50 (A/519) (1947).

resolution provided: "The State shall be bound by all the international agreements and conventions, both general and special, to which Palestine has become a party." [208]

It is even more convincing to contend that the Balfour Declaration is now a part of customary international law. Even though the Balfour Declaration was originally an explicit international agreement, it has now become established as customary international law through the implicit agreement, by toleration and acquiescence, of states other than Israel in the context of the repeated Zionist-Israel claims advancing it.[209] Since the Zionists have so continued the validity of the Declaration as international law, they are confronted with the extremely difficult situation brought about by their violation of both safeguard clauses. It would not be an adequate defense to the charge of violation of customary international law at this late date for the Zionists to claim that there was no intention to incorporate the safeguard clauses of the Declaration into customary law. If such a defense were attempted, it would have to be rejected as being too late and because of the preeminent character of the safeguards.

3. The League of Nations Mandate for Palestine (1922)

The basic elements of the Mandate system were enunciated in the League of Nations Covenant. The applicable article provides:

> To those colonies and territories which as a consequence of the late war have ceased to be under the sovereignty of the States which formerly governed them and which are inhabited by peoples not yet able to stand by themselves under the strenuous conditions of the modern world, there should be applied the principle that the well-being and development of such peoples form a sacred trust of civilisation and that securities for the performance of this trust should be embodied in this Covenant.[210]

By the terms of the Covenant the "sacred trust of civilisation" was to be exercised for the benefit of the people inhabiting the respective territories. This applied, prima facie, to the existing inhabitants of Palestine, whatever the religious identification of individual Palestinians.[211] This provision of the Covenant, protecting territories

---

208 Id. at 138.
209 The implicit agreement-making processes of customary law are considered systematically in the text accompanying notes 306-17a infra.
210 League of Nations Covenant art. 22(1).
211 Palestine was not a member of the League and, consequently, Palestinians were not directly represented in it.
There was no Arab resentment or hostility to Jewish immigration, as such, in

"inhabited by peoples," is clearly inconsistent with "the Jewish people" nationality claims based upon the religious identification of individuals who are the inhabitants of many territories. Dr. J. Stoyanovsky, a Zionist legal writer, has nevertheless labored to make these nationality claims, which in his view are recognized in the Palestine Mandate, appear to be consistent with the Covenant.[212]

The Council of the League of Nations designated Great Britain as the Mandatory Power for Palestine, and the Palestine Mandate went into force on September 29, 1922.[213] The second paragraph of its preamble incorporated the Balfour Declaration. It shortened the political promise clause but set forth both safeguard clauses with only one word changed: "which might prejudice" was substituted for "which may prejudice." [214] The third paragraph of the preamble provided:

> Whereas recognition has thereby [through the Balfour Declaration] been given to the historical connection of the Jewish people and to the grounds for reconstituting their national home in that country.[215]

---

contrast to the Arab attitude concerning Zionist immigration. The Zionists referred to Zionist immigration as "Jewish." See 2 Esco Study passim and index heading "Immigration, Jewish" at 1320. "Immigration, Zionist" does not appear in the index. Compare the candid reference to "Zionist Immigration into Palestine" in Hourani, Near Eastern Nationalism Yesterday and Today, 42 Foreign Affairs 123, 130 (1963). As late as 1918, and entirely consistent with the juridical interpretations of the Balfour Declaration, "The Sherif [of Mecca], in turn, welcomed the Jews to the Arab lands on the understanding that a Jewish state in Palestine would not be in the offing." Zionist Diplomacy 32.

[212] Stoyanovsky, The Mandate for Palestine: A Contribution to the Theory and Practice of International Mandates 42-47 (1928), cited hereafter as "Stoyanovsky." Dr. Stoyanovsky appears to perceive some inconsistency between the Zionist nationality claims and the League Covenant: "The peculiarity of the national home policy seems to be the extension of this principle [protecting existing inhabitants] so as to include the Jewish people in the category of the above peoples." Id. at 43.

[213] Stoyanovsky 33.

[214] Citations to the League Palestine Mandate are taken from the Convention between the U.S. and Great Britain concerning Palestine of Dec. 3, 1924 (proclaimed by the President on Dec. 5, 1925) by which the U.S. agreed, inter alia, to the Palestine Mandate and the Balfour Declaration as described in the text: 44 Stat. pt. 3, p. 2184. The word changed in the text of the safeguards certainly did not weaken them. The omission of "and will use their best endeavours to facilitate the achievement of this object" may be construed to weaken the British political promise clause to which the United States agreed. It is not necessary, of course, to rely on such an interpretation because of the juridical interpretations of the political promise. See text accompanying notes 167-68, 198-200 supra.

[215] 44 Stat. pt. 3, p. 2184. The Zionists could argue plausibly that the Mandate wording, recognizing "the historical connection," is highly significant, except for the fact that it resulted from the rejection of their recommended wording. "Zionists wanted to have it read: 'Recognizing the historic rights of the Jews to Palestine.'" Weizmann 280. Curzon, then the British Foreign Secretary, rejected the Zionist claim of "rights" unequivocally. Ibid. It is clear that he was obligated to reject the Zionist claim by both safeguard clauses as well as by the "rights and political status" enjoyed by British Jews under municipal law.

The Zionists interpreted the Mandate in the same way that they had interpreted the Declaration. Dr. Weizmann, in a contemporary Zionist interpretation, advanced "the Jewish people" nationality claims:

> [T]he value of the Mandate, apart from being a great success of Zionism, consists in the recognition of the Jewish people. This is of immense value, which will bear fruit and will open up new perspectives as yet hidden from our weak eyes, while we are engaged in our daily task.[216]

Dr. Stoyanovsky advanced the same claims in the guise of a careful juridical interpretation:

> There can hardly be any question now whether Jews constitute a distinct national entity in the eyes of international law. This seems to have been laid down, on the one hand, by the various treaties containing what is known as minority clauses, and on the other, by the mandate for Palestine providing for the establishment in that country of a *national* home for the Jewish people. If, therefore, the question of the national character of the latter may remain open—as in fact it does—for purposes of ethnographical or sociological research, it seems to have been definitely settled from the point of view of international law. The status of Jews no longer constitutes a mere political issue within certain States, or a diplomatic issue between States, on the ground of humanitarian protection afforded to them by such Powers as Great Britain, France and the United States; Jews as such have now become subjects of rights and duties provided for by international law.[217]

The Weizmann and Stoyanovsky interpretations, of course, reflect the meaning which the Zionists sought to impose upon the Mandate and not the meaning of the Mandate. They are fallacious for the same reasons that the Zionist interpretations of the Declaration are fallacious.[218] The Weizmann interpretation impliedly violates the second safeguard clause. The Stoyanovsky interpretation, on the other hand, expressly violates it. His interpretation imposes "the national character" of "the Jewish people" upon Jews in any country other than Palestine without regard to the second safeguard clause. In his interpretation, "Jews as such" have become members of a

---

[216] Address, Carlsbad, Germany, Aug. 25, 1922. Goodman (ed.), Weizmann 175, 179.

[217] Stoyanovsky 55.

[218] Text accompanying notes 89-108 supra.

"distinct national entity" recognized by international law without regard to their individual preferences.

A comprehensive analysis of the provisions of the Palestine Mandate dealing with Zionism and its "national home" enterprise is beyond the scope of the present study.[219] It may be appropriately mentioned, however, that article two of the Mandate made the Mandatory responsible for placing Palestine "under such political, administrative and economic conditions as will secure the establishment of the Jewish national home." [220] The Zionist "national home" enterprise referred to in the Mandate preamble was specifically limited by the inclusion of both safeguards. Consequently, it is inaccurate and misleading to attribute a broader meaning to the Zionist "national home" and the related claimed nationality of "the Jewish people" in the Mandate than that in the Balfour Declaration upon which the Mandate is based. Even though article two of the Mandate refers to "*the* Jewish national home," [221] it has to be interpreted as consistent with the phrase "a national home" set forth in the preamble. Whether the phrase is "the" or "a" national home, it must be interpreted as being limited by the preeminent safeguard clauses in the preamble to the Mandate.

The League of Nations Mandate for Palestine is significant because it involved explicit agreement by the League of Nations to the provisions of the Balfour Declaration. It should be recognized that this amounts to multilateral approval of the Declaration compromise agreement. It does not change the interpretation of the Declaration including the two alternative juridical interpretations of the political promise clause which have been explained.[222]

---

[219] General description is provided in U.S. Dep't State, Mandate for Palestine (Near Eastern Series No. 1, Pub. No. 153, 1931).

Zionist interpretation is provided in Feinberg, Some Problems of the Palestine Mandate (1936) and Stoyanovsky, Law and Policy under the Palestine Mandate, Jewish Yb.I.L. 42.

An analysis of the Zionist pressure politics utilized to implement Zionist nationalism (where juridical attempts had failed) is beyond the scope of this study. See Zionist Diplomacy 32-33, 39-87; Jewish Agency Documents passim and 226-27 concerning the "Declaration Adopted by the Extraordinary Zionist Conference, Biltmore Hotel, New York City, May 11, 1942."

[220] 44 Stat. pt. 3, p. 2184 at 2185.

[221] Ibid. (Emphasis added.)

[222] See text accompanying notes 167-68, 198-200 supra.

The interpretation of the Palestine Mandate in the text postulates that the incorporation of the Declaration in the Mandate incorporates the Declaration's negotiating history which gives it meaning. If it should be postulated, unrealistically, that the Declaration was incorporated without its negotiating history, then the interpretation of the Mandate in the text is supported by the clear and preeminent character of the safeguards and the ambiguities in the political promise clause.

4. The Anglo-American Convention on Palestine (1924)

The nominal subject of the Anglo-American Convention was the rights of the United States Government and its nationals concerning Palestine. For present purposes the significance of the Convention is that it made the United States a party to the Balfour Declaration agreement. The entire League of Nations Mandate, including the substance of the Balfour Declaration, was set forth in the preamble to the Convention.

Article two of the Convention provided:

> The United States and its nationals shall have and enjoy all the rights and benefits secured under the terms of the mandate to members of the League of Nations and their nationals, notwithstanding the fact that the United States is not a member of the League of Nations.[223]

Of "all the rights and benefits," probably the most obvious was the protection accorded by the second safeguard clause to American Jews.

Article seven provided:

> Nothing contained in the present convention shall be affected by any modification which may be made in the terms of the mandate, as recited above, unless such modification shall have been assented to by the United States.[224]

This article empowered the United States to object to any changes in the Mandate which affected American citizens.[225] A change in the second safeguard clause would affect American citizens. Thus, the United States Government obtained an additional means of preventing any infringement of the nationality status of its citizens based upon their religious identification.

American Jews are entitled to rely upon United States adherence to the entire Balfour Declaration, including the safeguards, as embodied in the Anglo-American Convention.[226] Such reliance is il-

---

[223] Supra note 220, at 2191.

[224] Id. at 2192.

[225] For Zionist criticism of the United States' interpretation of the Convention as limiting its power to prevent modifications to those situations in which Americans were affected, see Feinberg, The Interpretation of the Anglo-American Convention on Palestine 1924, 3 Int'l L.Q. 475 (1950).

[226] They are still entitled so to rely because of the present status of the Balfour Declaration as customary law. See the text accompanying notes 202-09 supra. The Anglo-American Convention, as such, is no longer in force. See U.S. Dep't State, Treaties in Force 99-100, 192-204 (1964).
American Jews are entitled, fundamentally, to rely upon the First Amendment

lustrated by the actions of Louis Marshall, a distinguished lawyer. In 1929, Marshall wrote to a German Jew who, like himself, rejected Zionist nationalism but deemed it desirable to obtain from the League of Nations an interpretation of the phrase "national home for the Jewish people." [227] At the outset, Marshall stated, "I am not a nationalist, and . . . I take pride in my American citizenship and in my loyalty to Judaism." [228] After stating that there was "no occasion whatsoever for requesting" [229] such an interpretation, Marshall declared:

> There can be no clearer reservation than that contained in concise terms in the Balfour Declaration and adopted by the other documents to which I have referred [the League of Nations Mandate for Palestine and the British White Papers of June 3, 1922, and October 4, 1922]:
> *"It being clearly understood that nothing should be done which might prejudice the civil and religious rights of existing non-Jewish communities in Palestine, or the rights and political status enjoyed by Jews in any other country."*
> The American non-Zionists have found it unnecessary to make any reservation on this subject, and I am sure that they would be unwilling to unite in any application to the League of Nations looking for a definition.[230]

to the Constitution prohibiting religious discrimination. See the text accompanying notes 318-24 infra. Subordinate municipal law authority for adherence to the Balfour Declaration may be found in the Joint Resolution Favoring the establishment in Palestine of a national home for the Jewish people. 42 Stat. pt. 1, p. 1012 (Approved, Sept. 21, 1922). The Joint Resolution included the first safeguard clause of the Balfour Declaration with variations in the wording. It omitted the second safeguard but this is not significant juridically since its provisions must have been regarded as obviously applicable to Americans. In any event, it is clear that a joint resolution cannot diminish the constitutional prohibition against religious discrimination.

[227] 2 Reznikoff (ed.), Louis Marshall, Champion of Liberty: Selected Papers and Addresses 775 (1957).

[228] Ibid.

[229] Id. at 777.

[230] Ibid. Marshall, as an American lawyer, quoted the safeguards, including the word "might," as they appeared in 44 Stat. pt. 3, p. 2184.

Marshall referred to "American non-Zionists." In 1929, this term included anti-Zionists also, as clarified in the text accompanying note 19 supra.

The Anglo-American Convention is no longer in effect, as such, though the Balfour Declaration included in it is valid as customary law. See the text accompanying notes 202-09 supra. The Treaty of Friendship, Commerce and Navigation Between the U.S. and Israel, Aug. 23, 1951, [1954] 1 U.S.T. & O.I.A. 552, 5 T.I.A.S. No. 2948 (Effective April 13, 1954), contains two specific denials of the right to engage in political activities, although one such denial is considered sufficient in many similar treaties. The last sentence of art. 8, sec. 3 states: "Nothing in the present Treaty shall be deemed to grant or imply any right to engage in political activities." Art. 13, sec. 4 states: "The present Treaty does not accord any rights to engage in political activities." Systematic Zionist-Israel violation of these provisions in the United States is revealed in Senate Committee on Foreign Relations, Hearing on Activities of Nondiplomatic Representatives of Foreign Principals in the United States, 88th Cong., 1st Sess., pt. 9 (May 23, 1963); pt. 12 (Aug. 1, 1963). "The hearings of the

B. "THE JEWISH PEOPLE" NATIONALITY CLAIMS ADVANCED SINCE THE ESTABLISHMENT OF THE STATE OF ISRAEL

1. The Declaration of the Establishment of the State of Israel (1948)

An analysis of the constitutive process which created the State of Israel, including the claimed juridical authority for its creation, is beyond the scope of the present study.[231] The Declaration of the Establishment of the State of Israel, however, is significant in the present analysis because it contains "the Jewish people" nationality claims. The following excerpts from the Declaration manifest the continuing Zionist objective of advancing "the Jewish people" nationality claims in the context of public law:

(1) ERETZ-ISRAEL was the birthplace of the Jewish people. Here their spiritual, religious and political identity was shaped. . . .

(2) In the year 5657 (1897), at the summons of the spiritual father of the Jewish State, Theodore Herzl, the First Zionist Congress convened and proclaimed the right of the Jewish people to national rebirth in its own country.

(3) This right was recognised in the Balfour Declaration of the 2nd November, 1917, and reaffirmed in the Mandate of the League of Nations which, in particular, gave international sanction to the

committee have offered some guidance, but the nine chosen cases were selected not because they were typical but rather because they illustrated a range of activities which the committee believed were *inimical* to the interests of the United States and should be dealt with in new legislation." (Emphasis added.) Senate Committee on Foreign Relations, Report on Foreign Agents Registration Act Amendments, S. Rep. No. 875, 88th Cong., 2d Sess. p. 5 (Feb. 21, 1964).

[231] Zionist views are suggested in the ensuing text in the quotations in which the Zionist nationality claims are advanced.

For critical appraisal of a portion of the Israeli constitutive process see Roosevelt, The Partition of Palestine: A Lesson in Pressure Politics, 2 Middle East J. 1 (1948).

United States Foreign Policy: Compilation of Studies (Prepared under the direction of the Senate Committee on Foreign Relations, 86th Cong., 2d Sess., 2 vols., 1960) provides a systematic and thoughtful appraisal of U.S. foreign policy. Study No. 13 concerning U.S. Foreign Policy in the Middle East was prepared by the Staff of the Senate Committee on Foreign Relations; it appears in vol. 2 at pp. 1269-1387. "The Palestine Problem" is examined, id. at 1303-16. The views of retired Foreign Service Officers concerning Israel and the Middle East are printed, id. at 1459-62. The staff of the Senate Committee on Foreign Relations summarized their views as follows: "It was unanimously agreed that the manner in which Israel was created had an unfortunate effect on our relationship with the Arab nations." Id. at 1459. See also [1943] 4 Foreign Rel. U.S. 747-829 (1964) indicating United States official concern with Zionist political activities.

In 1954, Mr. Henry A. Byroade, then Assistant Secretary of State, stated:

To the Israelis I say that you should come to truly look upon yourselves as a Middle Eastern State and see your own future in that context rather than as a headquarters, or nucleus so to speak, of worldwide groupings of peoples of a particular religious faith who must have special rights within and obligations to the Israeli state.

The Middle East in New Perspective, 30 Dep't State Bull. 628, 632 (1954). See also Byroade, Facing Realities in the Arab-Israeli Dispute, 30 Dep't State Bull. 708 (1954).

historic connection between the Jewish people and Eretz-Israel and to the right of the Jewish people to rebuild its National Home. (4) The catastrophe which recently befell the Jewish people— the massacre of millions of Jews in Europe—was another clear demonstration of the urgency of solving the problem of its home-lessness by re-establishing in Eretz-Israel the Jewish State, which would open the gates of the homeland wide to every Jew and confer upon the Jewish people the status of a fully-privileged member of the comity of nations. . . .

(5) THE STATE OF ISRAEL will be open for Jewish immigra-tion and for the Ingathering of the Exiles; . . . .

(6) WE APPEAL to the United Nations to assist the Jewish people in the building-up of its State and to receive the State of Israel into the comity of nations. . . .

(7) WE EXTEND our hand to all neighbouring states and their peoples in an offer of peace and good neighbourliness, and appeal to them to establish bonds of cooperation and mutual help with the sovereign Jewish people settled in its own land. . . .

(8) WE APPEAL to the Jewish people throughout the Diaspora to rally round the Jews of Eretz-Israel in the tasks of immigration and upbuilding and to stand by them in the great struggle for the realization of the age-old dream—the redemption of Israel. . . .[232]

Excerpt (1) refers to, *inter alia*, the "political identity" of "the Jewish people." Excerpt (2) illustrates the consistent character of the claimed nationality entity of "the Jewish people" from 1897 to 1948. Except (3) sets forth the familiar Zionist nationalist claims based upon Zionist interpretation of the Balfour Declaration and the League of Nations Mandate.[233]

Excerpt (4) affords a clear illustration of the Zionist political solution to anti-Semitism and Nazi criminality. This political solu-tion had not changed from the time of Theodor Herzl. The excerpt claims that the Zionist State of Israel is "the Jewish state" and claims to confer "the status of a fully-privileged member of the comity of nations" upon "the Jewish people." The word "homeland" in the excerpt is not used to refer to the State of Israel as the home of its regular nationals without regard to their religious identification. "[T]he homeland" is deemed to be the homeland of "every Jew." Excerpt (5) emphasizes the last point by showing that Jews living

---

[232] The excerpts from the Declaration in the text are numbered by the present writer for convenience in the ensuing analysis. 1 Laws of the State of Israel (au-thorized translation from the Hebrew) 3-5 (May 14, 1948), cited hereafter as "Israel Laws." The Declaration is also in Badi (ed.), Fundamental Laws of the State of Israel 8-11 (1961), cited hereafter as "Fundamental Laws."

[233] See note 215 supra.

outside of the State of Israel are treated in Zionist public law as living in exile. Excerpt (6) further emphasizes the Zionist public law claim that the State of Israel is the state of "the Jewish people" and not of its regular nationals alone.

Excerpt (7) is ambiguous. It refers to the "sovereign Jewish people" as "settled in its own land." This could be interpreted as referring only to the "sovereign" character of that part of "the Jewish people" living in the State of Israel. Even if it is interpreted in such limited fashion, the word "sovereign," as it appears in the context of the excerpt, tends to identify Jews in states other than Israel with the State of Israel in public international law without regard to their individual preferences and regular nationality status.

Excerpt (8) provides an alternative in the form of an emotional "appeal" to the juridical claims already considered. Individual Jews who reject the Zionist claim of juridical connection between them and the State of Israel may be induced to give practical assistance to the State of Israel if the objectives of Zionist nationalism are re-formulated as an "appeal."

In summary, the Declaration of the Establishment of the State of Israel reveals no change or diminution in the character of the Zionist-Israel juridical claims to constitute "the Jewish people" nationality entity and confer membership in it. This Declaration provides a highly effective platform from which to advance the nationality claims in public law. In the same way that Brandeis and the other humanitarians regarded the Balfour Declaration as an end to the political work of Zionism,[234] some today may regard the establishment of the State of Israel as the culmination of Zionist nationalism. The excerpts from the Declaration of the Establishment of the State advancing "the Jewish people" nationality claims in international law indicate a very different situation. The Zionists conceive of the State of Israel as an additional public body, to be associated with the existing Zionist Organization in achieving Zionist political objectives.[235] The establishment of "the Jewish people" nationality claims

---

[234] See note 157 supra.

[235] See Zionist Diplomacy at 106 entitled, Epilogue: The Remaining Task for Political Zionism.
A director-general of the Israeli Foreign Ministry has written:
It is a commonplace of our Foreign Service that every Envoy Extraordinary and Minister Plenipotentiary of Israel has a dual function. He is Minister Plenipotentiary to the country to which he is accredited—and Envoy Extraordinary to its Jews. This has come to be accepted generally—by other

in law is the central juridical task of each of these two Zionist public bodies.

2. The World Zionist Organization-Jewish Agency Status Law (1952)

Prior to the establishment of the State of Israel, the Zionist Organization achieved status as a public body through the Balfour Declaration,[236] the League of Nations Mandate for Palestine,[237] and the

---

> governments in the "free" world, . . . by the Jews of the diaspora, and by every one in Israel.

Eytan, The First Ten Years: A Diplomatic History of Israel 192-93 (1958).

> [T]he Foreign Ministry of Israel probably brings more money into the public chest than any other ministry, except the tax-collecting Ministry of Finance. No computation has ever been made of the value, in terms of money, of Israel's representatives abroad. They are constantly engaged in the campaigns for voluntary funds contributed by Jews all over the world, in popularizing Israel bond issues, in securing official loans (as from the American Export-Import Bank) and grants-in-aid, in negotiating commercial agreements and stimulating trade in general, and in a variety of other revenue-producing activities. If it were not for them, there would be a heavy slump in Israel's income.

Id. at 225.

> A pro-Zionist writer has stated:
> [T]he level of aid given to her [Israel] has been quite exceptional. During the first fourteen years of Israel's existence, the United States government has in fact awarded her close to $850,000,000 of aid in various forms, mostly outright grants of one kind or another. On a per capita basis of the recipient country, this is probably the highest rate of American aid given to any country. Moreover, the American government never seriously attempted to question the classification of the billion dollars of donations made by American Jews as tax-exempt "charity," though this money went, in effect, into the general development budget of Israel.

Safran, The United States and Israel 278 (1963).

[236] It received some status before the Declaration by the conduct of negotiations with various governments. See the text accompanying notes 65-74 supra.

[237] Art. 4 of the Mandate provided:

> An appropriate Jewish agency shall be recognized as a public body. . . .
> The Zionist organization, so long as its organization and constitution are in the opinion of the Mandatory appropriate, shall be recognized as such agency . . . .

44 Stat. pt. 3, p. 2184 at 2185.

The Permanent Court of International Justice has interpreted the foregoing provisions:

> This clause shows that the Jewish agency is in reality a public body, closely connected with the Palestine Administration and that its task is to co-operate, with that Administration and under its control, in the development of the country.

The Mavrommatis Palestine Concessions, P.C.I.J., ser. A., No. 2, p. 21 (1924).

In 1946 an impartial and respected fact-finding committee concluded:

> There thus exists [through the Jewish Agency] a virtual Jewish nonterritorial State with its own executive and legislative organs, parallel in many respects to the Mandatory Administration, and serving as the concrete symbol of the Jewish National Home. This Jewish shadow Government has ceased to cooperate with the Administration in the maintenance of law and order, and in the suppression of terrorism.

Anglo-American Committee of Inquiry, Report to the United States Government and His Majesty's Government in the United Kingdom, April 20, 1946, p. 39 (U.S. Dep't State Pub. 2536, 1946).

Anglo-American Convention on Palestine.[238] Since its establishment in 1948, the State of Israel has sought to maintain the public body status of the Zionist Organization as a means of advancing Zionist nationalism. The purpose of the 1952 Status Law is to implement this goal.

The following excerpts from the Status Law reveal the integral juridical relationship between the Zionist Organization and the State of Israel:

> 1. The State of Israel regards itself as the creation of the entire Jewish people, and its gates are open, in accordance with its laws, to every Jew wishing to immigrate to it.
>
> 2. The World Zionist Organisation, from its foundation five decades ago, headed the movement and efforts of the Jewish people to realise the age-old vision of the return to its homeland and, with the assistance of other Jewish circles and bodies, carried the main responsibility for establishing the State of Israel.
>
> 3. The World Zionist Organisation, which is also the Jewish Agency, takes care as before of immigration and directs absorption and settlement projects in the State.
>
> 4. The State of Israel recognises the World Zionist Organisation as the authorised agency which will continue to operate in the State of Israel for the development and settlement of the country, the absorption of immigrants from the Diaspora and the coordination of the activities in Israel of Jewish institutions and organisations active in those fields.
>
> 5. The mission of gathering in the exiles, which is the central task of the State of Israel and the Zionist Movement in our days, requires constant efforts by the Jewish people in the Diaspora; the State of Israel, therefore, expects the cooperation of all Jews, as individuals and groups, in building up the State and assisting the immigration to it of the masses of the people, and regards the unity of all sections of Jewry as necessary for this purpose.
>
> 6. The State of Israel expects efforts on the part of the World Zionist Organisation for achieving this unity . . . .
>
> 7. Details of the status of the World Zionist Organisation—whose representation is the Zionist Executive, also known as the Executive of the Jewish Agency—and the form of its cooperation with the Government shall be determined by a Covenant to be made in Israel between the Government and the Zionist Executive. . . .[239]

The first section of the Status Law enunciates a fundamental precept of Zionist nationalism: The State of Israel is not created for its

---

[238] In this Convention, the United States agreed to the entire Palestine Mandate including art. 4 quoted supra note 237. See the text accompanying notes 222-23 supra.

[239] 7 Israel Laws 3 (1952); Fundamental Laws 285.

own regular nationals alone but, rather, for "the entire Jewish people." This may be appraised as a Zionist claim to identify further "the entire Jewish people" (not only that part possessing Israeli nationality) with the State of Israel in law.

The second section recognizes with candor that the Zionist Organization was the principal creator of the State of Israel. In other words, "the Jewish people" was not sufficiently organized to create the State of Israel. Consequently, the Zionist Organization, as the self-appointed agent for its alleged constituency of "the Jewish people," created the State. The reference to "other Jewish circles and bodies" acknowledges non-Zionist support for political Zionism.

The third section indicates that the Zionist Organization (under that name or under the name "Jewish Agency") continues to perform the same functions after the enactment of the Status Law as it did before. The fourth section refers particularly to the long continuing governmental functions of the Zionist Organization within Palestine and the State of Israel. The sections of the Status Law do not create public body status for the Zionist Organization. They recognize its pre-existing and continuing public body or governmental status.[240]

The fifth section is applicable to the individual members of the alleged "Jewish people" entity living in other states than Israel. In traditional Zionist public law conception, they are regarded as "exiles" whose "gathering in" is "the central task" of both the State of Israel and the Zionist Organization.[241] In addition, the State "expects the cooperation of all Jews, as individuals and groups," in implementing Zionist political objectives. "The unity" (meaning,

---

[240] The same conclusion is reached in Lasky, Between Truth and Repose 51 (1956).

[241] Israeli nationality law, as opposed to "the Jewish people" nationality claims, is beyond the scope of the present study. It is important to note, however, that Israeli nationality law is designed to facilitate the acquisition of Israeli nationality by that part of "the Jewish people" living outside Israel. See the Law of Return (1950), 4 Israel Laws 48, as amended 8 Israel Laws 144; Fundamental Laws 156, as amended 8 Israel Laws 332. Sec. 1 of the Law of Return provides: "Every Jew has the right to come to this country as an *oleh* (Jew immigrating to Israel)."

See also the Nationality Law of 1952, 6 Israel Laws 50, as amended 12 Israel Laws 99; Fundamental Laws 254, as amended Fundamental Laws 410.

See Ravenna v. Ministeri Interno (Italy Tribunal of Rome, February 25, 1958), 26 Int'l L. Rep. 376 (1958-II) holding that the acquisition of Israeli nationality by an Italian Jew was not "spontaneous" within the meaning of Italian law. The result was that the Italian Jew did not lose her Italian nationality. The court indicated that it would have been "very difficult for the applicant to make an express declaration that she *did not desire*" to acquire Israeli nationality as required by Israeli law of Jews. Id. at 379. See the severe Zionist criticism of the case in Bar-Yaacov, Dual Nationality 245-47 (1961).

of course, political unity rather than religious unity) "of all sections of Jewry" is regarded as necessary for Zionist purposes. The excerpt from the sixth section refers to the public or governmental function of the Zionist Organization in achieving the Zionist political unity of Jews in states other than Israel.

The seventh section refers to an agreement between Zionist State and Zionist Organization. The ensuing "Covenant" [242] between the Israeli Government and the Zionist Executive allocates specified governmental functions to the Zionist Executive. These include the "organizing of immigration abroad and the transfer of immigrants and their property to Israel" [243] and Zionist participation in economic development activities in Israel. It provides that the Zionist Executive is to coordinate activities in Israel within the scope of its functions "by means of public funds." [244] The Covenant also establishes a "Coordination Board" for "the purpose of coordinating activities between the Government and the Executive in all spheres to which this Covenant applies. . . ." [245]

In summary, the Status Law and Covenant embody the central provisions of the integral public law relationship between the State of Israel and the Zionist Organization. The Law and Covenant provide for an allocation and coordination of governmental functions to further the common Zionist objectives of State and Organization. [246]

---

[242] The Covenant is reproduced in Lasky, supra note 240, at 63-65.

[243] Covenant sec. 1.

[244] Ibid.

[245] Covenant sec. 8.

[246] The conclusion as to the public or governmental character of the Zionist Organization—Jewish Agency is supported by the authorities in supra note 237. Contrast with this conclusion the statements of Mr. Gottlieb Hammer, Executive Vice-Chairman of the Jewish Agency for Israel, Inc. (identified by Mr. Hammer as an organization under American control), in his testimony under oath. He stated that he would refer to the Jewish Agency for Israel, Jerusalem, as the "Jerusalem Agency." Senate Committee on Foreign Relations, Hearing on Activities of Non-diplomatic Representatives of Foreign Principals in the United States, 88th Cong., 1st Sess., pt. 9 at 1216 (May 23, 1963). He then continued:

> Since 1948, when the State of Israel was established, the Jerusalem Agency has performed no political functions.
> The Jerusalem Agency is a unique organization. It is a nongovernmental body . . . .

Ibid.

In response to a question by Senator Fulbright concerning the relationship of the Jewish Agency for Israel, Jerusalem, to the State of Israel, Mr. Hammer replied in part:

> I think I should make it clear they are not part of the Government, they are not a governmental agency, nor are they an agency of the Government.

Id. at 1227.

The Jewish Agency for Israel, Jerusalem, is the same Jewish Agency referred to in the Israeli Status Law. See the text accompanying notes 236-46 supra. Sec. 3 of the Status Law shows clearly that the Jewish Agency and the World Zionist Organization are the same entity.

Because of this juridical structure, the State of Israel and the Zionist Organization taken together may be realistically described as a single Zionist-Israel sovereignty.

In addition, the Status Law spells out a clear governmental interference by a foreign sovereign in the lives of "Jews in any other country" than Israel. The juridical consequence is a violation of the "rights and political status" specifically protected by the second safeguard clause in the Balfour Declaration. This also involves a violation of the equal domestic rights of American Jews protected by the First Amendment to the Constitution. The practical consequence is injury to individual American Jews which goes beyond mere "prejudice" to their "equal rights and political status."

3. *The* Eichmann Trial Judgment (*1961*)

The Nazi murder of millions of innocent men, women, and children is probably the most tragic event of the present century. All moral individuals of whatever national or religious identification share revulsion at those who perpetrated these crimes. The largest group of victims was designated by the Nazis as "Jews." Other designated groups included, *inter alia*, "Poles," "Gypsies," "Slavs," and "Ukranians." Many other civilians throughout Europe were murdered by the Nazis even though they could not be included properly in even the most extended definitions of the specified victim groups. These crimes have been established by overwhelming evidence, including documents prepared by the Nazis themselves, in the forty-two volumes of *The Trial of the Major War Criminals Before the International Military Tribunal* at Nuremberg,[247] as well as in other post-war trials.

The jurisdictional authority, insofar as crimes against civilians were concerned, involved in the principal *Nuremberg Trial*[248] and the subsequent proceedings[249] was derived from the concept of crimes against the common humanity of all. The juridical concept of crimes against humanity (as opposed to a concept of crimes against the victims and their co-religionists alone) was firmly established in international law by the principal *Nuremberg Trial* and other post-World War II trials.[250] The jurisdictional authority derived from

---

[247] Official Text in the English Language (1947), cited hereafter as "I.M.T." See the Judgment of the Tribunal, 1 I.M.T. 171.

[248] 1 I.M.T. 226-28, 232-38.

[249] See, e.g., United States v. Ohlendorf (The Einsatzgruppen Case), 4 Trials of War Criminals Before the Nuernberg Military Tribunals 1, 496-500 (1948).

[250] Supra notes 248-49.

crimes against humanity is a very extensive one which is usually termed universality of jurisdiction. "Universality," in this jurisdictional sense, authorizes any state having custody of the accused to try him without regard to the geographic location and time elements of the acts alleged to constitute the crime against humanity. In addition, the national state trying the accused may not discriminate upon the basis of the national identity of the accused or that of the alleged victim.[251]

The evidence produced before the Israeli trial court in the case against Adolph Eichmann appears to be ample to establish his guilt for crimes against humanity. If the principal charges against Eichmann had been crimes against humanity,[252] there is no doubt that Israel would have been entitled to invoke universality of jurisdiction. It would, of course, have been required, in order to meet the juridical criteria, to apply universality of jurisdiction without regard to the national identity of the accused or of the victims.

It is particularly significant that the Israeli court in the *Eichmann Trial Judgment* paid only lip service to the concept of crimes against humanity.[253] Principal emphasis was placed upon the Zionist concept of "crimes against the Jewish people." [254] This involved the

---

[251] The requirements of universality of jurisdiction stated in the text are based upon the decisions of the post-World War II trials conducted by the United States and its allies. A similar formulation appears in McDougal & Feliciano, Law and Minimum World Public Order: The Legal Regulation of International Coercion 717-18 (1961). See also 1 Oppenheim-Lauterpacht, International Law 753 (8th ed. 1955).

[252] Eichmann was also charged with crimes against humanity, but the principal charges were "crimes against the Jewish people." See the Israeli Nazis and Nazi Collaborators (Punishment) Law (1950), 4 Israel Laws 154, Fundamental Laws 162, defining "crime against the Jewish people." This Israeli statute was applied in The Attorney-General of the Government of Israel v. Adolf, the son of Karl Adolf Eichmann, Criminal Case No. 40/61, District Court of Jerusalem, Israel, Dec. 11-12, 1961, affirmed Criminal Appeal No. 336/61 Supreme Court of Israel, May 29, 1962, cited hereafter as "Eichmann Trial Judgment."

[253] The Israeli trial court did not appear to understand the distinction between defining the crime in terms of the victims' identification and defining it in terms of the common humanity of all. It stated:
> It is hardly necessary to add that the "crime against the Jewish people", which constitutes the crime of "genocide" is nothing but the gravest type of "crime against humanity" . . . .
Eichmann Trial Judgment p. 22, heading #26. In a conception of law based upon respect for the individual, "crimes against humanity" are of equal gravity without regard to the religious identification of the victim. Definition of crime by the victim's religion involves the immoral implication that crimes against Jews are not crimes against common humanity.

[254] Eichmann Trial Judgment passim. In Criminal Appeal No. 336/61, the Supreme Court of Israel in affirming the Eichmann Trial Judgment, in reference to the alleged "connecting link between the State of Israel and the Jewish people," stated: "It should be clear that we fully agree with every word said by the Court on this subject in Paragraphs 31-38 of its judgment." Id. at p. I 24, heading #12, last para.

claim of the alleged "Jewish people" nationality status of Eichmann's victims. Similarly, the Israeli court preferred to base its jurisdictional claim to try Eichmann principally upon the alleged legal link between the State of Israel and "the Jewish people" rather than upon the recognized authority of universality of jurisdiction.[255]

A sense of reality concerning the *Eichmann Trial Judgment* can be achieved by examination of the following excerpts from it:

> If there is an effective link (and not necessarily an identity) between the State of Israel and the Jewish people, then a crime intended to exterminate the Jewish people has a very striking connection with the State of Israel.
>
> The connection between the State of Israel and the Jewish people needs no explanation. The State of Israel was established and recognised as the State of the Jews. . . . It would appear that there is hardly need for any further proof of the very obvious connection between the Jewish people and the State of Israel: this is the sovereign State of the Jewish people.
>
> * * *
>
> In the light of the recognition by the United Nations of the right of the Jewish people to establish their State, and in the light of the recognition of the established Jewish State by the family of nations, the connection between the Jewish people and the State of Israel constitutes an integral part of the law of nations.
>
> * * *
>
> The Balfour Declaration and the Palestine Mandate given by the League of Nations to Great Britain constituted an international recognition of the Jewish people, (see *N. Feinberg,* "The Recognition of the Jewish People in International Law" Jewish Yearbook of International Law 1948, p. 15, and authorities there cited), the historical link of the Jewish people with Eretz Israel and their right to reestablish their National Home in that country.[256]

It is significant that the claim of juridical connection between "the Jewish people" and the State of Israel is set forth, not as a claim, but as though it were already established as "an integral part of the law of nations." The *Eichmann Trial Judgment*, with its wide humanitarian appeal, was thus exploited by Zionism as an instrument for advancing "the Jewish people" nationality claims in international law.[257] The price paid for this approach was the sacrificing of

---

[255] Ibid.

[256] Eichmann Trial Judgment, cited supra note 252, at p. 32, headings #33-34, pp. 34-35, heading #38.

[257] Penetrating criticism of the Eichmann trial is provided in T. Taylor, Large

reliance upon the established concept of crimes against humanity and ensuing universality of jurisdiction. The almost certain result was lack of jurisdictional authority. Such a result was acceptable to Zionists because of the great opportunity presented to advance "the Jewish people" claims in a supposedly judicial context. The Zionist objection to *basing* the claim to jurisdictional authority upon the established concepts of crimes against humanity and ensuing universality of jurisdiction, as opposed to merely giving lip service to them, is that the established concepts recognize the membership of Jews in the common humanity of all. Such recognition is inconsistent with the purpose of "the Jewish people" nationality claims to separate Jews from other individuals in public law.

Thus, in the Zionist public law conception of the *Eichmann Trial Judgment*, the regular nationality status of Jewish victims of the Nazis was ignored or minimized in favor of their alleged nationality status as members of "the Jewish people." The Zionist objective was to show that only the Zionist State of Israel seeks to protect the Jewish victims of the Nazis.[258] The principal *Nuremberg Trial* and the subsequent proceedings demonstrate unequivocally that the United States and other states employed the concept of crimes against humanity and ensuing universality of jurisdiction without discrimination based upon the religious or national identity of the victims or the accused.[259]

4. The Joint Israel-Zionist Communique of March 16, 1964

A joint meeting of the Israeli Cabinet and the Zionist Executive was held on March 15, 1964.[260] The Joint Communique issued on the following day illustrates further the integral relationship and

---

Questions in the Eichmann Case, N.Y. Times Magazine 11 (Jan. 22, 1961). Lasok, The Eichmann Trial, 11 Int'l & Comp. L.Q. 355, 372-74 (1962) provides some criticism. See also Silving, In Re Eichmann: A Dilemma of Law and Morality, 55 Am. J. Int'l L. 307 (1961).

[258] The same conclusion is reached in Rogat, The Eichmann Trial and the Rule of Law 15-17 and passim (1961).

[259] In addition, no discrimination was permitted where victim or accused lacked either religious or national identity or both. See, e.g., United States v. Ohlendorf, supra note 249, at 499 involving crimes against humanity where the victims were identified, factually but without juridical discrimination, as German Jews. Many Jews in Germany were deprived of their German nationality by municipal law.

[260] Reported in the semi-official Jerusalem Post, March 16, 1964, p. 1, col. 1; p. 8, cols. 3, 4.
Arts. 40-45 of the Constitution of the World Zionist Organization concern the Executive of the World Zionist Organization. These articles are reproduced in Senate Committee on Foreign Relations, Hearing on Activities of Nondiplomatic Representatives of Foreign Principals in the United States, 88th Cong., 1st Sess., pt. 9 at 1412 (May 23, 1963); part 12 at 1768 (Aug. 1, 1963).

cooperation between the Zionist State and the Zionist Organization. On its face, the Communique is designed to interfere in the lives of nationals of states other than Israel. It is reproduced in full:

> A joint meeting of the Government of Israel and the Executive of the World Zionist Organization, which took place yesterday in Jerusalem, was devoted to the examination of the problems facing the Jewish people in the Diaspora, in view, on the one hand, of the denial to Jews in certain countries of religious and cultural liberties and, on the other hand, of the dangers of assimilation affecting Jewish communities elsewhere.
>
> The members of the Executive expressed the determination of the Zionist movement, whilst continuing to discharge its functions in the spheres of immigration, absorption and settlement on the land, as provided for in the Covenant, to concentrate and invigorate its efforts in the Diaspora in the fields of the education of children and the youth, as well as by active participation in the activities of Jewish communities and Jewish international organizations.
>
> It was explained that the purpose of these endeavours will be to strengthen the attachment of Jewish communities in the Dispersion to the State of Israel as a centre of their spiritual life; to enlist their effective sharing in the responsibility for the further development of the State and the safeguarding of its future; to intensify among them the consciousness of the unity of the Jewish people, the solidarity of its various parts and its vigil for self-preservation through an organized effort; to assist in the extension and development of Jewish education with a view to imparting to the young generation the values of Judaism and its spiritual heritage, to spread the knowledge of the Hebrew language and Israel's renascent Hebrew culture, and to awaken and cultivate the mental readiness and active desire to settle in Israel.
>
> On behalf of the Government of Israel, the Prime Minister expressed his agreement with this analysis of the situation and the programme of action entailed thereby, of which the primary aim is the preservation of the identity and unity of Jewish people in all the lands of the Dispersion and the strengthening of its emotional and material ties with the State of Israel.
>
> It was agreed that the effort aiming at the enhancement of the Zionist spirit in Jewish life is a matter of joint concern for the State of Israel and the World Zionist Organization. Consequently, the Government gave expression to its vital interest in the Zionist Executive's plan of action in the Diaspora and its readiness to lend full assistance to its realization.[261]

The first paragraph acknowledges explicitly that the joint meeting concerned the affairs of Jews in states other than Israel. It also sets

---

[261] Text of Joint Communique in Jerusalem Post, March 16, 1964, p. 8, col. 4.

forth a traditional Zionist concept by expressing concern about "the dangers of assimilation affecting Jewish communities elsewhere." The phrase, "the dangers of assimilation," may be interpreted, in the light of Zionist objectives, as referring to integration into the secular aspects of life in the state of a Jew's regular nationality. Thus, secular integration and accompanying individual equality of rights for Jews and their fellow nationals who are not Jews is regarded as dangerous to Zionist nationalism.

The second paragraph emphasizes the continuing practical implementation of the govermental functions allocated to the Zionist Executive by the Covenant. The reference to "the education of children" may appear to be a non-political matter if read out of context. In relation to the objectives of political Zionism, it must be interpreted as education for Zionist nationalism. "Jewish communities," in Zionist conception, refers to a grouping of Jews for secular purposes and not to a voluntary religious fellowship.

The third paragraph states the purpose of strengthening "the attachment" of secular "Jewish" communities to the State of Israel in a "spiritual" manner. This appears to be Zionist exploitation of religious values for political purposes. It also refers to the "Dispersion" of Jews. Zionist nationalism is to be implemented by awakening and intensifying among such dispersed Jews "the consciousness of the [political] unity of the Jewish people" and "the mental readiness and active desire to settle in Israel." The phrase "self-preservation" must be taken as meaning the self-preservation of "the Jewish people" rather than the self-preservation of individual Jews and their religion of Judaism. "The Jewish people" is viewed as comprised of various parts which must maintain political "solidarity" by "an organized effort." Obviously, the "organized effort" is a politically organized one.

The penultimate paragraph in the Communique states that "the primary aim" of the Zionist-Israel sovereignty "is the preservation of the identity and unity of Jewish people" in "all the lands of the Dispersion." In addition, the importance of strengthening the "emotional and material" ties of such Jews with Israel is stressed. "Emotional" is interpreted, in the light of Zionist objectives, as exploitation of humanitarian and philanthropic motives for political purposes. The final paragraph states the Israeli Government's interest in, and full support of, Zionist political interference with Jews in any other country than Israel.[262] In summary, the Joint Communique illustrates continuing Zionist-Israel efforts in public law to implement Zionist nationalism wherever Jews live.[263]

In an address of March 23, 1964, concerning the same subjects dealt with in the Joint Communique, Israeli Prime Minister Levi Eshkol stated:

> To us falls the responsibility of securing the future of the Jewish people. Zionists must not draw a distinction between the two complementary sections: the State and the people.[264]

The foregoing dichotomy indicates the "two complementary sections" of "the Jewish people" nationality without equivocation. In Zionist conception "the Jewish people" nationality comprises: (1) the State of Israel (or at least its "Jewish" nationals together with the apparatus of the Zionist State); and (2) all Jews in states other than Israel without regard to their individual preferences and juridically recognized nationality status. In the official view of the Israeli Prime Minister, an artificial distinction must not be drawn between "the two complementary sections." If the distinction were stressed unduly, it would, in Zionist conception, minimize the common "Jewish people" nationality of both sections.

The *Israel Digest* attributed another significant point to the Israeli Prime Minister in the same address:

> [E]ver since the emergence of the State, the Zionist Movement had been re-examining itself, not because there had been any change in its mission, but because it must establish goals and objectives in accordance with the present-day circumstances in the life of the State of Israel and the Jewish people.[265]

There is ample evidence of the consistent character of the Zionist political "mission" from the First Zionist Congress to the present. One of the principal conclusions of the present study is that the character of "the Jewish people" claimed nationality has been maintained consistently since the First Zionist Congress.

---

[262] An editorial comment stated: "In re-affirming the State's link with Zionism, the Government is seeking to strengthen the link of the State and People of Israel with the Jewish people." Jerusalem Post, March 16, 1964, p. 1, col. 1.

[263] Some individuals, and perhaps organizations as well, have accepted assurances from Israeli officials which are quite inconsistent with the conclusions of the present study. Among the examples, see the one provided in Appendix A.

[264] 7 Israel Digest (American Edition published by Jewish Agency-American Section, Inc., New York) No. 8, p. 2 (April 10, 1964).

[265] Ibid.

IV. INTERNATIONAL LAW LIMITATIONS UPON THE COMPETENCE TO CONSTITUTE A NATIONALITY ENTITY AND TO CONFER MEMBERSHIP IN IT: APPLICATION TO "THE JEWISH PEOPLE" NATIONALITY CLAIMS

The competence to constitute a nationality entity and confer membership in it is limited by law. The juridical limitations are as applicable to "the Jewish people" nationality claims as to any others.

A. THE FUNCTIONAL SIGNIFICANCE OF NATIONALITY LAW

Professor Silving has aptly summarized the practical political importance of nationality law as follows:

> Nationality Law is closely connected with the political structure of a country, more so than most branches of law. It determines who shall be a "citizen," and thus what shall be the composition of the "nation." The concept of "nationality" prevailing in a country importantly reflects its political philosophy, which is also expressed in a country's attitude towards "foreign nationality." [266]

Nationality membership is "the principal link" between individuals and the protection afforded to them by international law.[267] Thus, individuals abroad are accorded the standard of treatment prescribed for aliens under international law by virtue of their nationality membership in a particular state.[268] The state whose national is abroad may intervene diplomatically to protect him according to the principles of international law.[269]

Nationality, or citizenship, membership is traditionally regarded as imposing reciprocal obligations between a state and its individual nationals. In a typical formulation of this basic concept, the United States Supreme Court has stated:

> Citizenship is membership in a political society and implies a duty of allegiance on the part of the member and a duty of protection on the part of the society. These are reciprocal obligations, one being a compensation for the other.[270]

---

266 Silving, Nationality in Comparative Law, 5 Am. J. Comp. L. 410 (1956).
267 1 Oppenheim-Lauterpacht, International Law 645 (8th ed. 1955), cited hereafter as "Oppenheim-Lauterpacht."
268 Borchard, The Diplomatic Protection of Citizens Abroad (1915).
269 Ibid.
270 Luria v. U.S., 231 U.S. 9, 22 (1913).

An elementary "duty of protection" on the part of a political society or state is the protection of its national's or citizen's status against foreign attack. In the contemporary world of conflicting nationality claims, democratic states cannot afford complacency. If a democratic state did not protect the status of its nationals, the consequence would be a subversion, in the functional sense of the term, of the individual's democratic value orientation including his "duty of allegiance." The central point has been enunciated by Professors McDougal and Leighton:

> It should need no emphasis that one condition of the survival of a free society is a vision, fortified with reasonable hopes of fulfillment, by the peoples of the world of what a free society can offer. Loyalties that are not indissolubly tied to democracy can be captured . . . .[271]

Application to "the Jewish People" Nationality Claims

"The Jewish people" nationality claims have a central role in advancing Zionist nationalism in many public law contexts considered in the present study. These claims are used to change the juridical status of Jews in states other than Israel. In states like the United States of America, where each individual possesses equal nationality status, the objective is to add to the existing nationality status of Jews a further membership in "the Jewish people" nationality entity.

Any such additional nationality status, based upon the religious identification of individuals, is functionally subversive of their equal nationality status. Whether it is regarded as adding to or subtracting from their equal status, it changes such equality to inequality. In Zionist conception, the additional "Jewish people" nationality may be deemed necessary to compensate for the postulated inadequacy of a Jew's regular nationality status. In Orwellian conception, such an additional nationality could be deemed to result in a status of "equal but . . . more equal." [272] In democratic conception, such an additional nationality status must be recognized as subversive of the equal nationality status of each citizen.

---

[271] McDougal & Leighton, The Rights of Man in the World Community: Constitutional Illusions Versus Rational Action, 14 Law & Contemp. Probs. 490, 530 (1949).

[272] Orwell, Animal Farm 148 (1946).

B. Limitations upon the Competence to Constitute Nationality

1. The Constituting Entity Must Be a National State

The universally recognized nationality entity in the contemporary world community is the national state. In the typical nationality situation, an individual has the single nationality status of a particular state. It is widely agreed that a state must have at least three juridical qualifications:[273]

First, there must be a permanent population. A population, in this sense, may be regarded as a group of individuals who live together in a common political community. All of the individuals comprising this population must share a common national identification. In religious belief, racial identification, national origin, and other similar matters they may be quite different from one another.

Second, there must be a fixed geographical territory or country which the population inhabits. A nomadic tribe or group does not comprise a state.

Third, there must be an organized government exercising control over the population within the fixed territory. A community of anarchists, even though inhabiting a fixed territory, does not comprise a state. A government is necessary for the maintenance of both a municipal public order system and an international one.

2. The Constituted Entity Must Be the Nationality of a State

In addition to national states there are other significant group participants in the contemporary world community, including international public organizations or bodies,[274] political parties, pressure groups, and private associations.[275] Without minimizing the importance of such international groups, none of them has the unique juridical competence of the national state to constitute its nationality entity. Even where a particular international organization or public body is controlled by the same political elite which controls a state,

---

[273] The ensuing textual statements are based upon 1 Oppenheim-Lauterpacht 118-19 and 1 Hyde, International Law: Chiefly as Interpreted and Applied by the United States 22, 23 (2d rev. ed. 1945), cited hereafter as "Hyde."

[274] This category includes the Zionist Organization. See the text accompanying notes 236-46 and note 17 supra.

[275] McDougal, International Law, Power and Policy: A Contemporary Conception (1953), 82 Hague Academy Recueil Des Cours 137, 227 (Ch. 4 entitled Participants in the World Power Process Other than Nation-States) (1954). See also Schwarzenberger, Power Politics, ch. 8 (1951).

it is only the latter which constitutes a nationality entity. As Lord Acton has stated:

> The nationality formed by the State, then, is the only one to which we owe political duties, and it is, therefore, the only one which has political rights. The Swiss are ethnologically either French, Italian, or German; but no nationality has the slightest claim upon them, except the purely political nationality of Switzerland.[276]

Application to "the Jewish People" Entity Claim

One of the features of "the Jewish people" nationality entity claim which requires its rejection in international law is that it does not comprise the nationality of a national state. Even though "the Jewish people" is claimed to have a juridical relationship to the State of Israel,[277] it is obvious that the nationality of "the Jewish people" is not the same as the nationality of the State of Israel.[278] It is an additional "nationality" entity in the sense that it is composed of individuals identified by religion who are the nationals of the states of their respective nationalities. It is designed to remain such an additional nationality until the time when all the "exiles" are "ingathered" to the Zionist State of Israel.[279] It may be assumed that the State of Israel is a state in the sense of having population, territory, and government. This would have some relevance to an examination of Israeli nationality law.[280] It has little or no relevance to evaluation of an alleged additional "nationality" entity which is claimed to have existed for half a century before the establishment of the State of Israel.[281] During that time "the Jewish people" was claimed to comprise an additional "nationality" entity by the Zionist Organization public body in many juridical contexts.[282] Since 1948 "the Jewish people" has been claimed, in the same way, as such a "nationality"

---

[276] Acton, Essays on Freedom and Power 190 (1949). See 2 Hyde, supra note 273, at 1064-66.

[277] See the Eichmann Trial Judgment, in the text accompanying note 256 supra.

[278] Supra note 241.

[279]   Since I called, at the beginning of my remarks, for absolute allegiance to the Jewish revolution, I shall now make a few concluding remarks about the goal, of our revolution: *It is the complete ingathering of the exiles into a socialist Jewish state.*
Ben Gurion, The Imperatives of the Jewish Revolution (1944) in Hertzberg (ed.), The Zionist Idea: A Historical Analysis and Reader at 606-19 (1959).

[280] Supra note 241.

[281] Herzl, The Jewish State: An attempt at a Modern Solution of the Jewish Question (original pub. 1896; D'Avigdor & Israel Cohen transl. 1943), and text at supra notes 32-36; The Zionist Basle Program examined in text accompanying notes 59-60 supra; Zionist Diplomacy passim.

[282] Sec. III A supra.

entity by both the Zionist Organization and the Zionist State of Israel.[283]

Another feature of the claimed "Jewish people" additional "nationality" entity is that it is divided into two parts in Zionist conception as enunciated by Prime Minister Eshkol.[284] The two parts are: (1) the State of Israel (or at least the "Jewish" nationals of that State) together with its Zionist governmental apparatus; and (2) all Jews in states other than Israel. It is apparent that each of the parts of "the Jewish people" has a different normal and juridically recognized nationality status. The part in Israel has Israeli nationality. Individual Jews "in any other country" than Israel have the nationality status of their respective countries. For these further reasons, neither the State of Israel nor the Zionist Organization has the juridical competence to constitute "the Jewish people" additional "nationality" entity.

C. Limitations upon the Competence to Confer Membership: The Recognized Procedures for Conferring Nationality

Given the existence of a state nationality entity, the problem remains as to which individuals may have its nationality membership conferred upon them. Though a state has wide discretion in conferring its nationality status, there are certain international law limitations upon the recognized procedures employed to confer nationality membership.

1. Membership by Birth or Naturalization

The first sentence of the Fourteenth Amendment of the United States Constitution summarizes the two principal methods of conferring nationality membership:

> All persons born or naturalized in the United States, and subject to the jurisdiction thereof, are citizens of the United States and of the State wherein they reside.

Nationality at birth may be acquired either through the territorial principle of *jus soli*,[285] prescribed in the Fourteenth Amendment,

---

[283] Sec. III B supra.
[284] See text accompanying note 264 supra.
[285] 2 Hyde 1068-73; 1 Oppenheim-Lauterpacht 651-52.

or by the principle known as *jus sanguinis*,[286] where the child at birth acquires the nationality of one or both of his parents.

The second method of acquiring nationality membership is through naturalization.[287] The provisions of the municipal nationality law must not conflict with the applicable limitations of international law.[288] Through its naturalization procedure, an individual who is an alien by birth may acquire nationality membership in a state through his *voluntary* choice.[289]

2. Membership in More Than One Nationality Entity: Dual Nationality

Illustration of dual nationality is provided from Hackworth, *Digest of International Law:*

> The classic example of dual nationality is that of a person born in one country of nationals of another country, who acquires the nationality of the former by reason of the place of birth, *jure soli*, and that of the latter by virtue of the nationality of the parents, *jure sanguinis*.[290]

The United States recognizes ordinary dual nationality and the juridical limitations upon it.[291] One such limitation is that one state may not intervene effectively in behalf of its national who has voluntarily identified himself with his other national state, as by establishing his residence there.[292]

The common feature of these recognized procedures is fairness or reasonableness in conferring nationality membership upon individuals. The reasonableness of conferring nationality membership based upon birth within the national territory is obvious. The child's acquisition of his parent's natonality at birth also contains an element of reasonableness. The acquisition of nationality membership through naturalization based upon consent rather than coercion is eminently reasonable. Consensual naturalization promotes the democratic objec-

---

[286] 2 Hyde 1073-78; 1 Oppenheim-Lauterpacht 651-52.

[287] 2 Hyde 1087-93; 1 Oppenheim-Lauterpacht 654-56.

[288] The Nottebohm Case in the text accompanying notes 297-301 infra; 2 Hyde 1066; Briggs, The Law of Nations: Cases, Documents, & Notes 460 (2d ed. 1952), cited hereafter as "Briggs."

[289] See the official view of the United States emphasizing voluntariness in the text accompanying note 302 infra. See also 2 Hyde 1088-90.

[290] 3 Hackworth, Digest of International Law (U.S. Dep't State) 352 (1942), cited hereafter as "Hackworth."

[291] 3 Hackworth 353.

[292] Cases and other authorities are collected in id. at 353-62.

tive of permitting maximum individual voluntariness in political membership and participation.[293]

Application to "the Jewish People" Membership Claim

Is the procedure employed in conferring "the Jewish people" nationality upon individuals deemed to be through membership at birth? If the answer is affirmative, then such a conferring of nationality status at birth by religious identification is not consistent with the principle of *jus soli*, the principle of *jus sanguinis*, or any other principle recognized in public international law.

Is the membership in "the Jewish people" nationality entity conferred upon individuals by naturalization? If the answer is affirmative, it does not conform to the recognized procedures for naturalization. Its attempted conferment is involuntary in two respects. It has no regard for the consent of the individual concerned or the consent of his national state. More specifically, it includes all Jews simply because they are Jews and without regard to the individual consent of any member of the supposed nationality entity. "The Jewish people" membership claim makes no exception for United States citizens who are Jews, even though many such United States citizens are pro-democratic and consequently anti-Zionist. In addition, attempted conferring of membership in "the Jewish people" is without the consent of states other than the State of Israel. One of the principal purposes of the reiterated Zionist "Jewish people" membership claim in international law contexts examined in section III of this study is to obtain the assent of governments other than the Government of Israel through the processes of implied agreement in customary international law.[294] The United States Government is, of course, constitutionally prohibited by the First Amendment from assenting to "the Jewish people" membership claim (and entity claim, as well) either expressly or by implication.

Is "the Jewish people" additional "nationality" entity a type of dual-nationality? In Zionist conception, the alleged membership of Jews in "the Jewish people" is not deemed to be a substitute for their juridically recognized nationality status.[295] Such nationality status

---

[293] Compare the Zionist conception of "membership and identity" quoted in the text accompanying note 327 infra.

[294] Customary law making is examined in the text accompanying notes 306-17a infra.

[295] The textual statement is implicit in the attempts to implement "the Jewish people" membership claim. It is made explicit in the lives of Zionist leaders such as Dr. Weizmann, who was a naturalized British subject while claiming to be also

of Jews "in any other country" than Israel is deemed to be actually or potentially inadequate.[296] Consequently, "the Jewish people" nationality is intended to provide additional nationality membership to supplement or correct the alleged inadequacy of such Jews' recognized nationality status. Even though "the Jewish people" is an additional "nationality," it does not meet the juridical criteria for dual or multiple nationality in international law. Such criteria require that membership in each of the two or more nationalities be conferred by recognized procedures. None of the recognized procedures permits conferment of nationality membership according to the religious identification of individuals.

D. Limitations upon the Competence to Confer Membership: The "Genuine Link" Requirement for Conferring Nationality

The significant test of the scope of discretion accorded to a state in conferring its nationality membership is the extent to which other states are bound to honor such nationality membership. The International Court of Justice has considered this issue in the *Nottebohm Case* (Liechtenstein v. Guatemala).[297]

Mr. Nottebohm was a German national who resided and conducted his business affairs in Guatemala from 1905 until 1943, when he was removed from the country as an enemy alien. On October 9, 1939, a little more than a month after the beginning of the Second World War, Nottebohm applied for naturalization in Liechtenstein. After having apparently complied with all the requirements of Liechtenstein municipal law, he was naturalized effective October 13, 1939. In early 1940, he obtained a Liechtenstein passport and returned to Guatemala and the conduct of his business activities until 1943. Liechtenstein, relying on the nationality membership thus conferred by it, subsequently intervened diplomatically with Guatemala. It claimed that Guatemala had violated international law in its treatment of Nottebohm as a German and thus an enemy alien. The counsel for Liechtenstein formulated the issue before the Court as follows: "[T]he essential question is whether Mr. Nottebohm, having acquired the

---

a member of "the Jewish people." Stein 117. For explicit statement of conflict between Zionist nationality obligations and juridically recognized nationality obligations, see the last quotation from former Israeli Prime Minister Ben Gurion in Appendix A.

[296] Such actual or potential inadequacy, in Zionist conception, follows from the basic Zionist postulate of ineradicable anti-Semitism. See, e.g., Herzl, supra note 281.

[297] [1955] I.C.J. Rep. 1.

nationality of Liechtenstein, that acquisition of nationality is one which must be recognized by other States." [298] After conceding that each state is permitted a measure of discretion to confer its own nationality membership, the Court stated:

> [A] State cannot claim that the rules it has thus laid down are entitled to recognition by another State unless it has acted in conformity with this general aim of making the legal bond of nationality accord with the individual's *genuine connection* with the State which assumes the defence of its citizens by means of protection as against other States. [299]

The Court determined that there was no genuine connection between Mr. Nottebohm and Liechtenstein. [300] Consequently, it refused to give effect to the acts of Liechtenstein purporting to confer its nationality upon Nottebohm. The Court's reasoning emphasized the relationship between fact and law in conferring nationality membership:

> According to the practice of States, to arbitral and judicial decisions and to the opinions of writers, nationality is a legal bond having as its basis a social fact of attachment, a genuine connection of existence, interest and sentiments, together with the existence of reciprocal rights and duties. It may be said to constitute the juridical expression of the fact that the individual upon whom it is conferred, either directly by the law or as the result of an act of the authorities, is in fact more closely connected with the population of the State conferring nationality than with that of any other State. Conferred by a State, it only entitles that State to exercise protection vis-à-vis another State, if it constitutes a translation into juridical terms of the individual's connection with the State which has made him its national. [301]

The last sentence from the opinion just quoted is particularly important. Absent the necessary factual connection or "genuine link" between the individual and the state which has attempted to confer nationality membership upon him, other states are not juridically required to honor the purported nationality membership.

The decision and reasoning of the International Court of Justice in the *Nottebohm Case* are highly persuasive. It is important, never-

---

[298] Id. at 17.
[299] Id. at 23. (Emphasis added.)
[300] Id. at 26 and passim.
[301] Id. at 23.

theless, to recognize that the *Nottebohm Case* merely added a judicial determination to what had long been understood to be the applicable customary law. The same principles had been recognized by the United States in 1929. In its letter of March 16, 1929, replying to questions submitted to governments by the preparatory committee of the Hague Conference for the Codification of International Law, the United States stated its official position:

> While, as indicated, the Government of the United States has always recognised the fact that the acquisition or loss of the nationality of a particular State are matters which pertain primarily to domestic policy and are therefore to be determined by the domestic law of that State, it does not admit that a State is subject to no limitations in conferring its nationality on individuals. It has proceeded upon the theory, which is believed to be sound, that there are certain grounds generally recognised by civilised States upon which a State may properly clothe individuals with its nationality at or after birth, but that no State is free to extend the application of its laws of nationality in such a way as to reach out and claim the allegiance of whomsoever it pleases. The scope of municipal laws governing nationality must be regarded as limited by consideration of the rights and obligations of individuals and of other States. The reason for this is that true nationality involves a reciprocal relationship. It not only confers upon the individual certain rights and privileges with regard to the State of which he is a national, but gives to the State the right to claim the allegiance and obedience of the individual and to give him diplomatic protection when he is in a foreign State.[302]

Application to "the Jewish People" Membership Claim

The existing limitations of public international law have been developed to protect the primary human values which are involved in nationality law. The requirement that the constituted nationality entity must be that of a state with a genuine nationality link protects individuals from a multiplicity of nationality claims based upon religion or other factors which are juridically irrelevant to the individual's nationality status. The "genuine link" requirement limits the conferment of nationality status to those situations in which the individual has "a genuine connection of existence, interest and sentiments" with the state conferring its nationality and "is in fact more

---

[302] League of Nations, Conference for the Codification of Int'l Law, Bases of Discussion: 1 Nationality 118, 145-46 (1929). Many other states indicated similar views. Id. passim. See Briggs 460-62, concerning the United States' official position against "forced naturalization."

closely connected with the population" of such state than with that of any other. The "interest and sentiments" must be secular rather than religious ones. Thus the *Nottebohm Case*, in considering various nationality links and alleged links, did not even mention Nottebohm's religious identification, if any. Mr. Nottebohm's continuing political, business, and social connections with Nazi Germany, however, were contrasted with his lack of such genuine connections with Liechtenstein.[303] It is clear that in "the Jewish people" membership claim there is no semblance of the required "genuine link" between the identification of an individual as a Jew and *any* juridically recognized nationality.

"The Jewish people" membership claim is based upon the religious identification of individuals.[304] Nothing in either the *Nottebohm Case* or in the customary law formulations of the same basic juridical principles suggests that the "genuine link" requirement may be met by conferring nationality membership according to the religious identification of individuals. "The Jewish people" membership claim is invalid, consequently, under the existing criteria of public international law. In the same way, supposed nationality concepts such as "the Christian people" would be equally invalid. It requires but little imagination to envision the legalistic chaos and ensuing human despair which would result from juridical acceptance of nationality membership based upon the religious identifications of individuals.

V. APPRAISAL OF "THE JEWISH PEOPLE" NATIONALITY CLAIMS: INVALID UNDER PUBLIC INTERNATIONAL LAW

The central conclusion of section III of this study is that the Balfour Declaration agreement and the later international agreements concerning the same subject denied the Zionists juridical authority for

---

[303] [1955] I.C.J. Rep. at 25-26.

[304] The textual statement refers to the fact that Jews are claimed as members of "the Jewish people" entity. It is recognized that Zionists are claimed as members of the same entity. Zionists are placed in the alleged entity accurately because individual Zionists claim additional membership in "the Jewish people" whatever their juridically recognized nationality membership. As to individual Jews, they are claimed as members of "the Jewish people" by the Zionists. Jews are a highly diverse group as to many factors, including nationality, language, political opinions concerning Zionism and other subjects, and race. See supra note 12. The only identification they share is adherence to Judaism. Zionist nationalism, in spite of its preeminent political character, has had to rely upon the religious identification of individual Jews to bring them within "the Jewish people" membership claim because there is no other criterion shared by Jews. See the text accompanying notes 7-12 supra. Cf. Feinberg, The Recognition of the Jewish People in International Law, Jewish Yb.I.L. 1, 18 and n. 34.

"the Jewish people" nationality claims. The safeguard clauses of these agreements are so unequivocal that they must be construed as prohibiting the claims. The central conclusion of section IV is that the claims to constitute "the Jewish people" nationality entity and to confer membership in it fail because they are inconsistent with the applicable basic principles of public international law.

In spite of the present invalidity of "the Jewish people" nationality claims, the State of Israel and the Zionist Organization continue to advance them in the context of customary international lawmaking processes.[305] It is because the Zionists lost the negotiations analyzed in section III and because the Zionist nationality claims are now legally invalid as demonstrated in section IV that the Zionist public bodies attempt to validate them through customary law. These nationality claims are indispensable to Zionist nationalism and, if the Zionists fail to establish them in public law, Zionist nationalism will also fail. May these nationality claims be validated juridically through customary lawmaking or prescribing processes?[306]

A. The Attempt to Establish "the Jewish People" Nationality Claims through Customary International Law

Customary international law is regarded traditionally as having two constituent elements.[307] First is the existence of a particular, uniform pattern of conduct in the past. Without more, this conduct may be dismissed as mere "usage" which does not attain the status of "custom." The second element required for customary international lawmaking is an *opinio juris* or element of moral "oughtness" ascribed to the past uniformities in conduct.

In order to prescribe international law by custom it is not necessary for the past uniformities in conduct to have existed for a long period of time.[308] The time element is significant as evidence, which may be provided in other ways, of contemporary expectations of decision-

---

305 Examples are set forth in the text of sec. III B supra.

306 The contemporary importance of prescribing international law by custom was stated in Committee VI (Legal) of the U.N. General Assembly by Senator Albert Gore, representative from the United States, Nov. 21, 1962: 47 Dept. State Bull. 972 (1962).

307 The textual statements are based upon the analysis of customary law in McDougal, Lasswell & Vlasic, Law and Public Order in Space 115-19 (1963).

308 In The Scotia, 81 U.S. (14 Wall.) 170 (1871), the international maritime practice which the U.S. Supreme Court applied as customary law had existed only for eight years. The decision reflected the common interest in safe navigation. Individual rights were not adversely affected.

makers as to the existence of customary international law. Professor Lauterpacht states:

> As usages have a tendency to become custom, the question presents itself: at what stage does a usage turn into a custom? This question is one of fact, not of theory. All that theory can say is this: Wherever and as soon as a line of international conduct frequently adopted by States is considered legally obligatory or legally right, the rule which may be abstracted from such conduct is a rule of customary International Law.[309]

To prescribe international law by custom, it is not necessary that the consent of all national states be obtained: The assent of states may be manifested expressly or impliedly. Consent by implication includes silence and acquiescence when juridical claims are advanced by others. Such acquiescence has been accurately described by Professor Hyde:

> The requisite acquiescence on the part of individual States has not been reflected in formal or specific approval of every restriction which the acknowledged requirements of international justice have appeared, under the circumstances of the particular case, to dictate or imply. It has been rather a yielding to principle, and by implication, to logical applications thereof which have begotten deep-rooted and approved practices. Moreover, such a yielding seems to be inferred from the absence of objections to recurrent acts assertive of freedom to commit particular forms of conduct, or to apply principles in a particular fashion.[310]

Emphasizing the juridical significance of the failure "to make appropriate objection," Professor Hyde has written:

> It should be observed, however, that acquiescence in a proposal may be inferred from the failure of interested States to make appropriate objection to practical applications of it. Thus it is that changes in the law may be wrought gradually and imperceptibly, like those which by process of accretion alter the course of a river and change an old boundary.[311]

The American Law Institute's *The Foreign Relations Law of the United States* considers the highly relevant situation of a past

---

[309] I Oppenheim-Lauterpacht 27.
[310] 1 Hyde 5.
[311] Id. at 9.

uniformity in conduct or practice "for which there is no precedent in international law":

> *Objection to practice as a means of preventing its acceptance as a rule of law.* The growth of a practice into a rule of international law depends on the degree of its acceptance by the international community. If a state initiates a practice for which there is no precedent in international law, the fact that other states do not object to it is significant evidence that they do not regard it as illegal. If this practice becomes more general without objections from other states, the practice may give rise to a rule of international law.
>
> Because the failure to object to a practice may amount to recognition of it, the objection by a state to the practice of another is an important means of preventing or controlling in some degree the development of rules of international law.[312]

In what type of situation should a state object to a practice "as a means of preventing its acceptance as a rule of law"? The same publication of the American Law Institute states:

> A state subjects a person to its laws when it provides, by statute or otherwise, that its law is applicable to him as well as when it actually applies its law to him through its courts or other law enforcement agencies.[313]

Section III B of this study provided examples, "by statute or otherwise," of "the Jewish people" nationality claims made expressly applicable to Jews in states other than Israel. The national states of such Jews should reject "the Jewish people" nationality claims to prevent their being prescribed as customary international law.

It is not necessary that a state's nationals be adversely affected before it objects to the prescription of customary law. Indeed, a state should object before this happens. This point is amplified in *The Foreign Relations Law of the United States:*

> *Objection by a state prior to being adversely affected.* In many cases, a state is not adversely affected until the rule prescribed is actually enforced. In such cases, nevertheless, registering opposition to the prescription of the rule through appropriate means such as diplomatic correspondence may serve a significant purpose. . . .

---

[312] Restatement: The Foreign Relations Law of the United States § 1, comment (d) (Proposed Official Draft, 1962), hereafter cited as "Restatement."
[313] Restatement, Introductory Note to part 1 (Jurisdiction), at 23.

[T]he growth of a practice into a rule of international law depends on the degree of its acceptance by the international community. In putting on record the view that the state prescribing the rule lacks jurisdiction to prescribe it, another state not only precludes the suggestion that it recognizes the prescribing of the rule as legal but may contribute as well to the prevention of the development of a rule of international law sanctioning the legality of the action.[314]

The quoted analysis refers to the informal processes of claim, counter-claim, and decision between foreign ministries and state departments which involve prescribing and applying customary law. The juridical status of unilateral claims, including "the Jewish people" nationality claims, is appraised and decided by national officials, excluding those of the claimant state. Toleration and acquiescence by these officials, in customary law context, may result in favorable decision.

National and international judicial tribunals also prescribe and apply customary international law. Classic formulation was provided by Justice Gray, writing for the United States Supreme Court, in the case of *The Paquete Habana:*

> International law is part of our law, and must be ascertained and administered by the courts of justice of appropriate jurisdiction, as often as questions of right depending upon it are duly presented for their determination. For this purpose, where there is no treaty, and no controlling executive or legislative act or judicial decision, resort must be had to the customs and usages of civilized nations . . . .[314a]

In the famous *Lotus Case,*[315] decided by the Permanent Court of International Justice, the French Government failed to object to Turkish legislation prior to its application to a French national in a Turkish court. The French Government claimed unsuccessfully that the application of the Turkish criminal legislation to the French national was invalid under international law. One of the bases for the decision was that:

> [T]he Court does not know of any cases in which governments have protested against the fact that the criminal law of some coun-

---

314 Restatement § 8, comment (c).

314a 175 U.S. 677, 700 (1900).

315 Case of the S.S. "Lotus," P.C.I.J., ser. A, No. 10 (1927).

try contained a rule to this effect or that the courts of a country construed their criminal law in this sense.[316]

The significance of the *Lotus Case* is that the decision against the French government was based partly upon its failure to object to a provision of Turkish law before an actual case or controversy had arisen. The Turkish legislation, however, was in existence prior to the high seas collision between the French and Turkish merchant ships which led to the litigation. Apparently, the French Government assumed that no practical problems existed for France and its nationals and, consequently, timely protest was not made.

In summary, "the Jewish people" nationality claims are not advanced only upon the basis of Zionist interpretation of the Balfour Declaration and ensuing international agreements. The Zionist-Israel sovereignty also continues to attempt to prescribe these claims through customary international law. One of the most dramatic contemporary attempts is embodied in the *Eichmann Trial Judgment*.[317] Unless national states make appropriate objection to these nationality claims, they might become prescribed as customary law. It should be recognized that it requires more to prescribe as customary law claims which derogate from the rights of individuals than claims which do not.[317a]

B. JURIDICAL REJECTION OF "THE JEWISH PEOPLE" NATIONALITY CLAIMS

Even if the Balfour Declaration did not exist, the United States Government would be required by its Constitution, which prohibits religious discrimination among its citizens,[318] to reject the Zionist-Israel "Jewish people" concept and the juridical claims based upon it. Quite recently, in fact, the United States Government did reject the central concept of "the Jewish people" nationality claims. The rejection contains nothing new in United States constitutional law principles, but it is highly significant in terms of its specific applica-

---

[316] Id. at 23.

[317] See the text accompanying note 256 supra.

[317a] Supra note 308.

[318] The First Amendment states: "Congress shall make no law respecting an establishment of religion, or prohibiting the free exercise thereof. . . ." The Fourteenth Amendment (applicable to the states) contains "due process of law" and "equal protection of the laws" clauses. The Fifth Amendment (applicable to the Federal Government) contains a "due process of law" clause but not an express equal protection clause. The Supreme Court has, however, unequivocally held the Federal Government to at least the same standard of equal protection which is applicable to the states. Bolling v. Sharpe, 347 U.S. 497 (1954).

tion to the "Jewish people" concept. The rejection is enunciated in the letter of April 20, 1964, from the Department of State to the American Council for Judaism.[319] The second paragraph of this letter reads:

> The Department of State recognizes the State of Israel as a sovereign State and citizenship of the State of Israel. It recognizes no other sovereignty or citizenship in connection therewith. It does not recognize a legal-political relationship based upon the religious identification of American citizens. It does not in any way discriminate among American citizens upon the basis of their religion.

The first sentence quoted reflects recognition of the State of Israel and *its* nationality membership. The second sentence rejects any "other sovereignty or citizenship" in connection with the State of Israel. The Zionist Organization public body may be regarded as another "sovereignty" connected with the State of Israel. The other citizenship (or nationality) connected with the State of Israel is that of the claimed "Jewish people" nationality.

The third sentence in the quoted paragraph is a rejection of the "legal-political relationship based upon the religious identification of American citizens" involved in "the Jewish people" nationality claims. The last two quoted sentences reflect juridical obligations of the United States Government which are binding upon it in United States constitutional law as well as in public international law.[320]

The penultimate paragraph of the Department's letter states:

> Accordingly, it should be clear that the Department of State does not regard the "Jewish people" concept as a concept of international law.

"Accordingly" is the key introductory word. Since it follows the statements of basic United States constitutional obligation, it must be interpreted as governmental rejection of the "Jewish people" concept according to its constitutional obligation to do so.[321] There is

---

319 Appendix B.

320 See supra note 318. In addition to the public international law obligations examined in the present study, the United States, along with other members of the United Nations including the State of Israel, has agreed to promote human rights in the world community without "distinction" as to "religion." Article 55 (c) of the United Nations Charter provides that "the United Nations shall promote: . . . universal respect for, and observance of, human rights and fundamental freedoms for all without distinction as to race, sex, language or religion."

321 The press reporting of the governmental rejection included, *inter alia*: N.Y. Herald Tribune, May 8, 1964, p. 3, cols. 1-2; N.Y. Times, May 8, 1964, p. 9, col.

no constitutional alternative to official rejection of this juridical concept, since it is fundamentally inconsistent with the constitutional prohibition against discrimination upon religious grounds.

Among the earlier precedents is one applied by the Department of State in response to religious discrimination against some Americans by Tsarist Russian officials. It was the Tsarist practice to refuse to visé United States passports of American Jews (but not of other

---

1; Washington Post, May 9, 1964, p. A4, col. 5; Christian Science Monitor, May 19, 1964, p. 3, cols. 1-3.

The Zionist reaction pointed up the significance of the rejection of the "Jewish people" concept. Max Nussbaum, president of the Zionist Organization of America, was quoted as stating:

The oneness of the Jewish people is not legal or political but emotional and spiritual and cultural. . . . That is our position and that has always been our position. It is also the position of the Israeli Government.

N.Y. Times, May 8, 1964, p. 9, col. 1.

The semi-official Jerusalem Post in editorial comment conceded that:

The State Department itself has elaborated the statement as deriving from the principle that there must be no differentiation between American citizens on account of religion or race, which is a perfectly proper view from the U. S. standpoint.

Jerusalem Post, May 10, 1964, p. 1, col. 1. But the balance of the comment was devoted to establishing "the Jewish people" as recognized in law:

It does not diminish the fact that the U.S. recognized the existence of the Jewish people at the time when the League of Nations Mandate for the creation of the Jewish National Home in this country was given to Britain, and that its present recognition of Israel as a sovereign state, and of Israel citizenship, which derives its legal basis in part from the Balfour Declaration, is ultimately also based on the recognition of the existence of the Jewish people as a national unit. . . . There is today a Jewish people exposed to a variety of economic and social disabilities in many countries—not excluding even the United States itself.

Ibid.

I. L. Kenen wrote under the heading, "Misuse of A Letter," that the letter of April 20, 1964, had been misinterpreted to mean "that the Zionists believe that Jews have a political connection with Israel. (*They don't.*)" 8 Near East Report No. 11, p. 42, col. 3 (May 19, 1964).

Dr. S. Margoshes, one of the principal Zionist ideological protagonists in the United States, wrote:

The concept of a Jewish people and of Jewish peoplehood may be new, of [sic] even obnoxious, to Mr. Talbot, as it is obviously obnoxious to Mr. Coleman [president of The American Council for Judaism]; that does not alter the fact that the concept is recognized by international law.

The Day-Jewish Journal, May 12, 1964, p. 1, col. 1.

An editorial in a periodical with the masthead statement, "Dedicated to the advancement of Judaism as a religious civilization, to the upbuilding of Eretz Yisrael as the spiritual center of the Jewish People, and to the furtherance of universal freedom, justice and peace," stated:

Naturally, having set up a straw man, it is easy to knock it down; and this is precisely what the Talbot letter has done. . . . But Mr. Talbot goes further. He collaborates with the ACJ [American Council for Judaism] in attempting to destroy the entire concept of the Jewish people. Thus he adds, in his letter: "Accordingly, it should be clear that the Department of State does not regard the 'Jewish people' concept as a concept of international law." But this is clearly contrary to the facts. As early as 1917, the Balfour Declaration referred to the "establishment in Palestine of a national *home for the Jewish people* . . . ."

30 Reconstructionist No. 8, pp. 3-5 at 3, 4 (May 29, 1964).

Americans) for travel to Russia. Although less comprehensive than the Zionist-Israel discriminations, these Tsarist Russian discriminations also had a domestic impact within the United States.[322] The juridical position of the United States was set forth unequivocally in a communication of June 25, 1895, to the Tsarist Government. After quoting the First Amendment provisions concerning religion, it continued:

> Thus, you see, my Government is prohibited in the most positive manner possible by the very law of its existence from even attempting to put any form of limitation upon any of its citizens by reason of his religious belief. How, then, can we permit this to be done by others? To say that they can thereby be discriminated against by foreign Governments, and are only safeguarded against their own, would be a remarkable position for us to occupy.[323]

Another diplomatic communication to the Tsarist Government on July 8, 1895, concerning the same subject, stated the United States Government's position emphatically:

> Our Constitution does not say that Congress shall not make a law simply "prohibiting" or "authorizing" a religious exercise or belief, as your excellency seems to understand.
> It says that "Congress shall make no law respecting an establishment of religion, nor prohibiting the free exercise thereof." Certainly if a law deprives any people or person of a certain faith, because of that faith, of all or of any part of the rights, privileges, and immunities enjoyed by any other citizen, or class of citizens, it is made "respecting" that religion, and it militates against "the free exercise thereof" as much so as if the sect had been mentioned in the title of the act and the consequences had been named as pains and penalties for the conscientious belief and observances entertained and practiced.[324]

In summary, the United States executive branch was required by the Constitution to reject Tsarist religious discriminations applied to Americans in 1895. The Constitution places the same obligation upon all branches of the Government to reject any discriminations based upon religion which are applied to Americans today. This is recognized in the letter of April 20, 1964, rejecting the central "Jewish people" concept in its application to American nationals. Unless there

---

[322] [1895] Foreign Rel. U.S. 1056-74 (1896).
[323] Id. at 1064.
[324] Id. at 1067.

should be drastic change in the political character of Zionist nationalism and its "Jewish people" concept persistently advanced in public law contexts, the United States Government will have the opportunity to reject it in numerous specific situations in the future. In doing so, the United States Government will be faithful to the Constitution and to long established executive branch precedents in applying it.

The *Harvard Research in International Law* provides authority for the concluding juridical rejection of "the Jewish people" nationality claims:

> It may be difficult to precise [*sic*] the limitations which exist in international law upon the power of a state to confer its nationality. Yet it is obvious that some limitations do exist. . . . Thus, if State A should attempt to naturalize all persons living outside its territory but within 500 miles of its frontier, it would clearly have passed those limits; or similarly if State A should attempt to naturalize all persons in the world holding a particular political or *religious* faith or belonging to a particular race.[325]

The quoted text does not consider a situation as extreme as that involved in "the Jewish people" nationality claims. It assumes the existence of a valid state nationality entity and considers the juridical validity of imposition of *its* nationality membership upon individuals holding a particular "religious faith." This situation is stated to be one which has "clearly" exceeded the permissible "limits" of public international law. The even more aberrational factual and juridical elements in "the Jewish people" nationality claims must, a fortiori, make them invalid under international law.

C. Moral Rejection of "the Jewish People" Nationality Claims

In fulfilling its constitutional and international juridical obligations by rejecting the discriminatory "Jewish people" concept, the United States is also justified by the most fundamental considerations of morality. Not the least of these fundamentals is separation of religious and political values sufficient to permit the exercise and development of religions of universal moral values free from political

---

[325] Harvard Research, Draft Convention on Nationality, 23 Am. J. Int'l L. Supp. 1, 26 (1929). (Emphasis added.)

interference and coercion.[326] The practical implementation of such value separation requires the separation of corresponding religious and political organizational structures. Similarly, this requires that clear differentiation be made between identity of and membership in religious organizations, on the one hand, and political organizations, on the other.

A significant insight into the Zionist conception of "membership and identity" is provided by a contemporary writer:

> It is perhaps the greatest irony of the [*Eichmann*] trial that its two antagonistic forces—Israel and the Nazis—have both asserted the older view of membership and identity. In saying this, it is necessary to be very careful because of the emotional consequences of any comparison of any kind with the Nazis. I am not saying Israel is like the Nazis. Referring back ultimately to an intensely humane Old Testament and Talmudic tradition differs completely from following a brutal and uniquely destructive charismatic leader. Nevertheless, they are at one in their opposition to the rootless, cosmopolitan, and atomized individual; and in each case this opposition is so intense that it may permit no accommodation with the liberal spirit.[327]

The quotation appropriately emphasizes the involuntary and coercive aspects of the "membership and identity" conception of Zionist nationalism. Such a conception is inconsistent with democracy and individual equality including religious freedom and secular integration.

As long ago as 1896, Theodor Herzl reacted to the fundamental problems posed for Zionist nationalism by democracy and individual equality:

---

[326] See Editorial: The Church-State Legacy of John F. Kennedy, 6 Journal of Church and State 5, 9-10 (1964):
> Confronted with challenges and complexities unknown to [his] . . . early predecessors, Kennedy nonetheless expressed in clear and unmistakable terms a strong commitment to the separation of church and state . . . . In church-state relations, Kennedy was no neutralist. . . . He expressed strong opposition to clericalism of any kind and that type of bloc voting which determines the support of a political candidate on the basis of religion. . . .

Contrast the mixture of religious and secular matters in Silberg, Law and Morals in Jewish Jurisprudence, 75 Harv. L. Rev. 306 (1961) which is a translation of a lecture delivered by an Israeli Supreme Court justice ten years earlier.

[327] Rogat, The Eichmann Trial and the Rule of Law 21-22 (1961). Rogat attributes the Zionist conception to "Israel."

Concerning the Nazi conception of "membership and identity" see the statutes and other documents collected in The German Reich and Americans of German Origin (sponsored by a group of fourteen individuals, 1938). Among the lawyers in the sponsoring group were Felix Frankfurter, George Wharton Pepper, and Henry L. Stimson. Id. at vii.

It might further be said that we ought not to create new distinctions between people; we ought not to raise fresh barriers, we should rather make the old disappear. But men who think in this way are amiable visionaries . . . . Universal brotherhood is not even a beautiful dream. Antagonism is essential to man's greatest efforts.[328]

There is no reason to believe that Zionist nationalism will succeed in imposing its conception of "membership and identity" where similar ones of the past have failed.[329] Democratically oriented individuals, while sympathizing with those who appear to desire an intellectual or physical ghetto,[330] will not surrender their individual freedom and equality under law for any mess of pottage.[331] Professor Hans Kohn has enunciated the democratic promise of creative freedom for all men:

Modern Jewish life with its great promise of creativeness in freedom is based on Enlightenment and Emancipation everywhere. Enlightenment and Emancipation are nowhere secure against the resurgence of atavistic forces. Enlightenment and Emancipation have to be defended and revitalized everywhere and at all times. This is the difficult task of modern life of which the Jews form part. . . . [332]

---

[328] Herzl, The Jewish State: An Attempt at a Modern Solution of the Jewish Question 107-08 (D'Avigdor & Israel Cohen transl. 1943). Zionist contempt for "brotherhood" or humanitarianism is not merely theoretical. Morris L. Ernst has described Zionist attacks upon himself because he undertook to assist President Franklin D. Roosevelt in providing humanitarian asylum for refugee Jews in places other than Palestine. Ernst, So Far So Good 176-77 (1948). See Zionist Diplomacy 92-94 concerning Zionist subordination of humanitarian values to political objectives.

[329] Many ancient ways of life have been shattered by the new forces of democracy and science, challenging as they do the evils of past and present at many points. The dignity of man and the consent of the governed hold no terrors for the scientific study of government, with its indifference to privilege, its trend away from the thralldom of force, fear, and want. The finest reasoning and the most decisive experiments point in the direction of the goals which humanity hopes to attain.

Merriam, Systematic Politics ix, x (1945).

[330] See Israel versus the Jews, The Economist (London), 399, 400, col. 2 (Feb. 1, 1964):

[W]hat the rabbis [in the State of Israel], who for the first time in history possess state coercive powers, fail to see is that in the contemporary world a religious people can coexist with a secular state. Indeed, modern man requires this freedom if he is to be religious. He will not be forced to observe, much less to believe.

[331] It was a great day for the human race—the new day of Creation—when the idea dawned that every man is a human being, an end in himself, with a claim for the development of his own personality, and that human beings had a dignity and a worth, respect for which is the firm basis of human association.

Merriam, supra note 329, at 59.

[332] Kohn, Zion and the Jewish National Idea, 46 Menorah Journal 17, 46 (1958). The same value orientation appears in Berger, A Partisan History of Judaism (1951).

Jews, with the adherents of other religions of universal moral values, as well as those who adhere to such moral values for other reasons, must continue to expand and perfect the existing heritage of enlightenment and emancipation for the individual. This high task requires the expansion and perfection of juridical systems based upon democracy, individual equality, and religious freedom in both the international and national communities.

(See note 263 of the present study.)

[American Jewish Committee & Jewish Publication Society of America, 53 American Jewish Yearbook 564-568 (1952).]

On August 23, 1950, Mr. David Ben Gurion, then Israeli Prime Minister, stated in an address at an official luncheon tendered by him in honor of Mr. Jacob Blaustein, then President of the American Jewish Committee:

> It is most unfortunate that since our State came into being some confusion and misunderstanding should have arisen as regards the relationship between Israel and the Jewish communities abroad, in particular that of the United States. These misunderstandings are likely to alienate sympathies and create disharmony where friendship and close understanding are of vital necessity. To my mind, the position is perfectly clear. The Jews of the United States, as a community and as individuals, have only one political attachment and that is to the United States of America. They owe no political allegiance to Israel. . . . We, the people of Israel, have no desire and no intention to interfere in any way with the internal affairs of Jewish communities abroad. The Government and the people of Israel fully respect the right and integrity of the Jewish communities in other countries to develop their own mode of life and their indigenous social, economic and cultural institutions in accordance with their own needs and aspirations. Any weakening of American Jewry, any disruption of its communal life, any lowering of its sense of security, any diminution of its status, is a definite loss to Jews everywhere and to Israel in particular.

53 American Jewish Yearbook at 564.

In reply to the address, which included the foregoing, Mr. Blaustein stated, *inter alia*:

> Your statement today, Mr. Prime Minister, will, I trust, be followed by unmistakable evidence that the responsible leaders of Israel, and the organizations connected with it, fully understand that future relations between the American Jewish community and the State of Israel must be based on mutual respect for one another's feelings and needs, and on the preservation of the integrity of the two communities and their institutions.

I believe that in your statement today, you have taken a fundamental and historic position which will redound to the best interest
not only of Israel, but of the Jews of America and of the world.
I am confident that this statement and the spirit in which it has
been made, by eliminating the misunderstandings and futile discussions between our two communities will strengthen them both
and will lay the foundation for even closer cooperation.

Id. at 568.

Compare the official views of Prime Minister Ben Gurion, expressed to a different audience, about a year later:

First of all there is the collective duty of the Zionist Organization and of the Zionist Movement to assist the State of Israel in all
conditions and under any circumstances towards accomplishment of
4 central matters—the Ingathering of the Exiles, the building up of
the country, security and the absorption and fusion of the Disper-
sions within the State.

This signifies assisting the State whether the government to which
the Jews in question owe allegiance desire [sic] it or not . . . . We are
speaking about countries in which the citizen is free to go against
his government's will, as the Jews of England did in the days of
the White Paper. They have given an example of civic courage.
When the official policy of their government was anti-Zionist, they
persevered in their Zionist rebellion and were not afraid of being
spoken about as disloyal to their country; these were English citizens
and not citizens of Israel, and they had duties as well as rights in
England, and nevertheless they showed no fear. They live in a
country where a citizen may oppose the policy of his government. . . .

When we say "one Jewish nation" we must ignore the fact
favourable or unfavourable as the case may be, that this Jewish
nation is scattered over all the countries of the world and that Jews
living abroad are citizens of the states in which they live—desirable
or undesirable, no matter which—and that they possess rights or
demand rights or we demand rights for them. They also have duties.
And we, for whom this duplicity has ended and who are residents
of the State of Israel living here and talking its language and fighting
for the State of Israel, must not disregard the situation of those
Jews who are not among us. . . .

Article entitled, Tasks and Character of a Modern Zionist, based on
a speech by Prime Minister Ben Gurion delivered at the World Conference of Haichud Haolami on Aug. 8, 1951, Jerusalem Post, Aug.
17, 1951, p. 5, cols. 3-8 at cols. 4-6.

DEPARTMENT OF STATE

WASHINGTON

April 20, 1964

Dear Mr. Berger:

We have carefully studied your letter of March 14, 1964, drawing the Department of State's attention to the "<u>sui generis</u> character of 'the Jewish people' concept," and urging clarification of the Department's views with respect to the "'Jewish people' claim." You state: "The central point is that the Zionist-Israel sovereignty uses 'the Jewish people' concept as the basic juridical claim directed against the Jews in states other than Israel who insist upon maintaining their single nationality status." "Its principal function," you state, "is to change the legal status of Jews from that of individual nationals of Jewish religious faith to members of a juridically recognized transnational nationality group with additional 'rights' and obligations to the Zionist-Israel sovereignty. The core of 'the Jewish people' concept is its nationality characteristics..."

The Department of State recognizes the State of Israel as a sovereign State and citizenship of the State of Israel. It recognizes no other sovereignty or citizenship in connection therewith. It does not recognize a legal-political relationship based upon the religious identification of American citizens. It does not in any way discriminate among American citizens upon the basis of their religion.

Accordingly, it should be clear that the Department of State does not regard the "Jewish people" concept as a concept of international law.

I remain doubtful that a formal meeting of the type you describe would lead to useful results. As in the past, however, appropriate officers of the Department will be willing to discuss any problem that may arise and the Department will always be happy to continue the dialogue whenever occasion warrants.

Sincerely yours,

Phillips Talbot
Assistant Secretary

Mr. Elmer Berger,
    Executive Vice President,
        American Council for Judaism,
            201 East 57th Street,
                New York, New York.

The Anti-Zionist Phobia: Legal Style*

BEN HALPERN

THE LATEST WEAPON in the anti-Zionist arsenal of the American Council for Judaism is a State Department letter to the ACJ Executive Vice-President, Rabbi Elmer Berger, over the signature of Assistant Secretary Phillips Talbot, dated April 20, 1964. While politely declining to hold a conference with ACJ representatives on the alleged menace of Zionism, Mr. Talbot affirmed that the "Department of State does not regard the 'Jewish people' concept as a concept of international law."

We do not know what preceded this letter, which manifestly replies to previous correspondence, presumably extensive and insistent. But there is now available what may be a version of the brief presented in order to persuade the State Department to issue its statement on the international legal status of the "Jewish people" concept. The June, 1964 issue of the *George Washington University Law Review* carries an extensive discussion (pp. 983-1075) of "The Zionist-Israel Juridical Claims to Constitute 'the Jewish People' Nationality Entity and to Confer Membership in It." The "appraisal in public international law" of these alleged claims is by Prof. W. T.

Mallison, Jr., of the George Washington University law faculty, who tells us he "has served, from time to time, as consultant to the American Council for Judaism." It is safe to assume, then, that his argument represents substantially the same kind of documentation as may have been presented to the State Department. Thus we may consider what the latest version of anti-Zionist argument is worth in an authoritative presentation, and see whether it has gained any substance by resort to legal counsel.

The Charge Sheet

Prof. Mallison contends that the World Zionist Organization and the State of Israel, forming a "single Zionist-Israel sovereignty," have been trying to "constitute a 'Jewish people' nationality" and "confer membership in it" upon all Jews—without regard "for the consent of the individual concerned or the consent of his national state" (pp. 992f., 998ff., 1036-1043, and 1056, among many others). He further charges that "any such additional nationality status, based upon the religious identification of individuals, is functionally subversive of their equal

* Ed. Note: See also Ben Halpern, *The Drafting of the Balfour Declaration*, 7 HERZL YEAR BOOK 255 (1971).

nationality status" (p. 1051). So far there is nothing new. This is standard ACJ agitation; and the new wording for the charge of Zionist dual loyalties is in the familiar ACJ tradition of tortuous obfuscation.

The old vinegar has, nevertheless, been poured into a new bottle; or, to put it directly, the same old goods has been put in a new package to attract a new market. The wrappings of the new package concern mainly questions of "public international law." The author piles up allegations of fact and points of law subordinate to the main charges and purportedly supporting them. The major contentions may be outlined as follows:

1. After a "record ... of failure and frustration in public international law" up to the First World War, the Zionists pretend they obtained recognition of their " 'Jewish people' nationality claims" through the Balfour Declaration (pp. 1000ff.) In fact however, according to Mallison, the Balfour Declaration does not recognize, but decisively repudiates, the claims which the Zionists allegedly made regarding Palestine, including the claim to "constitute a 'Jewish people' nationality entity":

> "One of the most significant features of the final Declaration was the Zionist failure to achieve British public law assent to any of their three central juridical objectives ..." (p. 1015f.).

He then argues that the Balfour Declaration is a "multilateral agreement" resulting from negotiations between the Zionists, the British government, British anti-Zionist Jews, and the Arabs of Palestine.* It follows, ac-

cording to Prof. Mallison, that both the Zionists and the State of Israel are bound under the "Balfour Declaration agreement" *not* to impose an "additional nationality status" on Jews in other countries, as he says they have been doing (p. 1029ff.) Furthermore, he claims that the Anglo-American Convention on Palestine (1924) "made the United States a party to the Balfour Declaration agreement." Accordingly (even though he notes that the Anglo-American Convention is no longer in force), "the United States Government obtained an additional means of preventing any infringement of the nationality status of its citizens based upon their religious identification"; and "American Jews are entitled to rely upon the United States adherence to the entire Balfour Declaration, including the safeguards ... " (p. 1034).

2. A second stage in the alleged attempt of Israel and the Zionists to "constitute a 'Jewish people' nationality entity" and "confer membership" in it begins, according to Mallison, with the rise of Israel. This "attempt" is made in a number of documents interpreted by Mallison as presenting the alleged claims. Such an attempt fails, he then argues, because it does not come within the "juridical limitations" which restrict "competence to constitute a nationality entity and confer membership in it" (pp. 1036ff., 1050ff.).

3. Having thus been twice foiled, the "Zionist-Israel sovereignty" is now embarked on a third attempt to encompass its fell design:

> " ... because the Zionists lost the [Balfour Declaration] negotiations analyzed in section III and because the Zionist nationality claims are now legally invalid as demonstrated in section IV, ... the Zionist public

---

* While the Arab party "did not appear as an active negotiator, ... its interests in the subject had to be taken into account by the other participants" (p. 1011).

bodies attempt to validate them through *customary law*" (p. 1060ff., emphasis added).

This tactic, Prof. Mallison fears, could easily succeed, for "unless national states make appropriate objection to these nationality claims, they might become prescribed as customary law." Mr. Talbot's letter to Rabbi Berger is then cited as a "highly significant" repudiation of "the 'Jewish people' concept" and of the "sovereignty or citizenship" status allegedly imposed by the World Zionist Organization upon the "claimed 'Jewish people' nationality."*

4. As a final flourish (pp. 1060ff.), and in sporadic outbursts throughout the brief, Prof. Mallison rejects the alleged " 'Jewish people' nationality claims" on "moral" grounds.

The Method of "Proof"

This is a formidable list of topics, and the arguments about them are correspondingly copious and complicated. But it is quite another question whether everything in the brief is relevant or material.

Thus there is a long initial section of definitions (pp. 983-1000) of terms like "Jew," "Zionist," "Zionist-Israel sovereignty," in the meaning Prof. Mallison arbitrarily assigns to them. This proves nothing *per se* about Zionist claims or intentions. Other sections deal with the questions, who are parties to a purported "Balfour Declaration agreement" (pp. 1030-1036), or who is competent to "constitute a nationality" (in Mallison's sense) and "confer membership" in it (pp. 1050-

1061), and so on. Whether any of this is material depends on Mallison's success in proving the prior points: that the Balfour Declaration has, indeed, the character he attributes to it, or that there is, in fact, a "Zionist-Israel sovereignty" which is actually trying to "constitute a 'Jewish people' nationality entity" such as he describes and "confer membership in it" upon all Jews without their consent.

The latter, cardinal points are *not* discussed directly by Prof. Mallison. He does argue *about* them at length in scattered passages throughout his brief. His method of argument on these crucial questions requires no technical legal competence, as it is very familiar and commonly used among laymen— for instance, by husbands and wives, or street urchins, why try to win arguments by begging the question. Prof. Mallison, too, deals with the question of the alleged "Zionist-Israel sovereignty" and " 'Jewish people' nationality claims" very simply—by begging the question.

His method is to define arbitrarily certain terms—"Jew," "Jewish people," "public," "nationality"—which everybody uses. From his own definitions of these terms he derives certain legal consequences, expressing them in neologisms like "Zionist-Israel sovereignty" or " 'Jewish people' nationality claims"—which nobody uses except anti-Zionist propagandists. He then shows that "Jewish people," "national," "public," etc. appear in Zionist statements or other pertinent documents. He thereupon attributes to the Zionists the intention to constitute the legal consequences ("Zionist-Israel sovereignty") or claim the legal status (" 'Jewish people' nationality") of the terms based on *his* definitions (e.g., pp. 994, 996-998, 1000-1001, 1004-1006, 1012, 1024, 1032-1033, 1036-1039, 1043-

---

* This document is compared by Prof. Mallison to the American notes of June 25 and July 8, 1895 to the Tsarist government concerning discrimination against American Jews who sought visas for travel in Russia (pp. 1065ff.) .

1048). In every one of these instances what the *Zionists* mean by the terms they use bears no relation whatever to the definition Mallison gives them; as will be evident when we examine some examples in detail. Accordingly, the ACJ legal consultant has proved nothing, out of his special legal competence, on these cardinal points.

But one cannot say the ACJ's purposes have not been served. Propaganda does not need solid proof to be effective as defamation. In *no* case cited, as we have noted, do the Zionists use the terms "Jewish people," "national," or "public" in the arbitrary or specific sense of Mallison's definitions; consequently, they do *not* make the claims he ascribes to them. In *some* of the cases, moreover, the Zionists explicitly *deny* the very implications stated by Mallison and by so many anti-Zionist propagandists before him. This seems to be too blatant a contradiction for Mallison to ignore. He then says, in substance, that the Zionists are liars and plotters who are simply trying, in their devious way, to conceal their true intentions: for example p. 999—"calculated ambivalence" (Prof. Mallison apparently does not know what "ambivalence" means) and "calculated ambiguity"; p. 1003—"ambivalence"; pp. 1004, 1026—"fabrication." On pp. 1017f. and 1026 the Jews and British together are accused of deceit in using the term "Jewish people" instead of "Zionists" in the Balfour Declaration; a point to which we shall return.

The impression should not be given that Prof. Mallison is reluctlantly driven to the use of such defamatory expressions in order to defend major points against contradiction. He seizes on the slightest pretext to vilify Zionists, with no apparent limits of taste or decency. There is, for example, a footnote on p. 1021 (n. 167) where

Mallison is discussing whether the Balfour Declaration is to be interpreted as a consistent document. Anyone who disagrees with him on this rather technical point is described as "one who lacks moral values and corresponding juridical objectives." Or, to get closer to home, note Mallison's interpretation on p. 1048 of an "Israel-Zionist" reference to the "emotional ties" of Jews to Israel; he labels this as "exploitation of humanitarian and philanthropic motives for political purposes." Or his outrageous insinuation on p. 1045ff. that, far from being sincerely concerned with the basic issues in the Eichmann trial, the Israelis (the Zionists, he says) exploited "its wide humanitarian appeal ... as an instrument for advancing 'the Jewish people' nationality claim in international law." In cases like these the defamation is *not* incidental to the legal argument, but the legal "argument" is a cover for · the defamation. The incredible emptiness of the argument as argument makes this conclusion inescapable for the entire brief.

"Zionist-Israel Sovereignty"

This term first occurs in Prof. Mallison's brief (p. 922) in a preliminary section which he calls "The Clarification of Word Symbols." He tells us that *"Zionist-Israel sovereignty* is used to refer to the integral relationship between the State of Israel and the Zionist Organization." The pertinent question here is, who uses the term in this way; or, indeed, who uses the term at all? As it is apparently an expression coined by Mallison or his ACJ clients, it tells us nothing in itself about the Zionists. Prof. Mallison claims, however, that "the Israeli Status Law of 1952 and the ensuing Covenant between the Government of Israel and the Zionist Executive of 1954" prove his point. We turn then to his discussion of these documents.

But we turn in vain. There are two implied "proofs," and neither directly argues the point in question, whether the State of Israel and the World Zionist Organization are a "single sovereignty."

The first "proof" is made up of references to Herzl's diplomatic contacts with governments, who thereby accorded "a measure of recognition for the Zionist Organization as an international public body" (p. 1000); and of bare references to the texts of the Balfour Declaration, the Mandate for Palestine and interpretations of it, and the Anglo-American Convention on Palestine, which recited in its preamble the full text of the Palestine Mandate. All this reduces, in substance, to Article IV of the Mandate, which recognizes "an appropriate Jewish agency" as a "public body" and recognizes "the Zionist organization . . . as such agency."

The question is whether "public body," the term used in the Mandate to describe the Jewish Agency, is understood by anyone but Mallison as equivalent to "sovereignty" or "governmental." The authoritative comment on this point is by the Permanent Court of International Justice, in the Mavrommatis Case. Mallison briefly cites this case as though it supports his view but does not discuss it (p. 1039). The issue in the case was whether the Palestine Administration was liable for compensation to a Greek citizen who had obtained certain Ottoman concessions to provide electricity in Palestine because, after the Mandate was established, it granted a concession for the purpose to Pinchas Ruttenberg. The legal issue depended on the meaning given to the term

"public control." From the text of the decision in the case it is crystal-clear that the Court did *not* regard the terms "public body" or—quite obviously— "public control" as signifying "an integral relationship" to a government, a relationship so close that a "public body" or a company or agency under "public control" constitutes a "single sovereignty" with any government that grants it such a status. The Court says (p. 19ff of the decision):

> " . . . it does not appear to be correct to maintain that the English expression 'public control' only covers cases where the Government takes over and itself directs undertakings of one kind or another. The expression is also used to indicate certain forms of action taken by the State with regard to *otherwise private undertakings.*

> " . . . Article 28 of the Ruttenberg concessions lays down that 'the undertakings of the company under this convention shall be recognised as a *public utility body* under Government control' " (emphasis added).

In this context (p. 21 of the decision) the Court then describes the Jewish Agency's status, in the passage cited by Mallison:

> "This clause [Article IV of the Palestine Mandate] shows that the Jewish agency is in reality a public body, closely connected with the Palestine Administration and that its task is to co-operate, *with* that Administration and *under its control,* in the development of the country" (emphasis added).

The meaning is clear: the Ruttenberg electric company was a "public utility body" and the Jewish Agency was a "public body" under the Administration of the Palestine Mandate. Both are *non-governmental bodies*— the one, a private business enterprise, the other, a private membership organization—with public functions: that is, they have been given a special legal status to carry out functions approved, as a matter of policy, by the government; and accordingly they operate under a certain degree of governmental control. The instrument that grants them the necessary legal status to carry out their functions is, in the case of the Ruttenberg company, a concession, and, in the case of the Jewish Agency, the Palestine Mandate itself. The Jewish Agency, then, enjoyed under the Mandate a certain status under public international law; but it was certainly not the status of a government. If there were any doubt about this matter, it was made quite explicit in the (Churchill) White Paper of 1922, which was the authoritative interpretation of the Palestine Mandate. We read there that

> "It is also necessary to point out that the Zionist Commission in Palestine, now termed the Palestine Zionist Executive, *has not desired to possess,* and does not possess, any share in the general administration of the country. Nor does the special position assigned to the Zionist Organisation in Article IV of the Draft Mandate for Palestine imply any such functions. That special position relates to the measures to be taken in Palestine affecting the Jewish population, and contemplates that the Organisation may assist in the general development of the country, *but does not entitle it to share in any degree in its Government"* (emphasis added).

There is a second set of "proofs," stated at greater length, to support Mallison's contention that the State of Israel and the World Zionist Organization constitute "a single sovereignty." Four pages are devoted to a discussion of the World Zionist Organization-Jewish Agency Status Law (1952), and the Covenant implement-

ing the law; but not a single word directly confronts the issue. Instead, Prof. Mallison simply refers (p. 1041; emphasis added) to "the long continuing *governmental* functions of the Zionist Organization" as though he had already proved they existed;* and to its "continuing *public body or governmental* status," as though not only he, and other ACJ spokesmen whom he relies on, but everyone assumed that "public body" was equivalent to "governmental" or "sovereign" with reference to the World Zionist Organization and the Jewish Agency.**

That is the whole "proof." All other references to "Zionist-Israel sovereignty," of which there are many, are not arguments but accusations, and serve only to hammer away at a propaganda theme. But one further point needs mention before leaving the topic.

Prof. Mallison holds (p. 1041) that the World Zionist Organization-Jewish Agency Status Law (1952) did not *create* a "public body status" for the Zionist Organization, but merely rec-

---

* Indeed, in note 246 he brazenly refers to a previous footnote 237 as having established this point. Note 237 is the citation of Article IV of the Mandate and the decision in the Mavrommatis case, already discussed. In addition, it quotes an irrelevant, non-legal passage from the Anglo-American Inquiry Committee's report.

** It is interesting that Prof. Mallison does *not* state in his introductory section on definitions that he intends to use "public" as equivalent to "governmental" or "sovereign." He slips this definition in by a mere prepositional phrase, in the form cited—"public body or *governmental status."* His definitions of "Jews," "Zionists," etc. may be arbitrary, but at least they are open and explicit; and there is even some slight recognition that other interpretations of these terms are possible. But this cardinal definition, equating "public" with "governmental," upon which his whole argument rests, is nowhere openly or explicitly stated. His other key definition, of the term "nationality," is also slipped in much in the same way.

ognized its "pre-existing and continuing public body or governmental status." If so, Winston Churchill's 1922 interpretation still remains authoritative. Prof. Mallison simply ignores it. The same point that Churchill made—that the Jewish Agency is a "non-governmental body," that it is "not part of the Government"— was made by an Agency spokesman, Mr. Gottlieb Hammer, at recent Senate hearings. These statements *are* quoted by Prof. Mallison (p. 1042, n. 246). He does so in a way that leaves no doubt he regards Mr. Hammer's remarks as one more instance of Zionist duplicity—or perhaps even of perjury, since he takes pains to mention that they were made "under oath." Perhaps if he had quoted Churchill's instead of Mr. Hammer's repudiation of the charges he makes, he might have found it more difficult to confine himself to insinuation instead of proper argument. But with Mallison, as we shall have occasion to note, even this is far from certain.

"The 'Jewish People' Nationality Claim"

There is obviously a close connection between the term "Zionist-Israel sovereignty" and the expression " 'Jewish people' nationality entity," both of which serve Mallison as battlecries. If there is a "Zionist-Israel sovereignty," then there must be a "nationality" in which the sovereignty is exercised—to wit, the Jewish people. On the other hand, if a "nationality entity" means what Mallison says it means—that is, a national state with full sovereign authority, including compulsory powers over its citizens— then a " 'Jewish people' nationality entity" implies a "Zionist-Israel sovereignty." If Mallison could prove that the Zionists do, in fact, intend or claim

to "constitute a 'Jewish people' nationality entity," in his meaning of this characteristic expression, then he might claim some justification for dismissing as deliberate deception all Zionist denials that the World Zionist Organization is part of the Israel government.

How does Prof. Mallison seek to prove this crucial point, on which his whole brief stands or falls? The answer is the same as before. He does not try to prove it; he assumes it by definition. One sentence, completely undocumented, constitutes his entire discussion of the question. It reads (p. 1052), "The universally recognized nationality entity in the contemporary world community is the national state."

This is palpably false. All Prof. Mallison had to do to check this unqualified assertion that the national state, and only the national state, is the universally recognized nationality entity today was to consult the card catalogue of his university library and note the titles devoted to nationality entities other than national states. Surely the George Washington University has copies of such standard writers as Carleton Hayes, Louis Snyder, or, for that matter, Hans Kohn—a writer whom Prof. Mallison does not hesitate to quote when it serves his purpose. Or, if this procedure was too arduous, it would have served just as well to look up "nation" in any standard dictionary. Or, if he wished to limit himself to legal documents, he could easily have learned of the existence of national minorities treaties, concerning "nationality entities" other than national states; and it should not have been difficult to discover that in the Soviet Union today Jewish citizens carry identity papers describing their nationality as Jewish, with no relation whatever to a Jewish national state or other sovereign Jewish national entity.

Prof. Mallison could, if he wished, reject such usages on "moral" grounds and condemn them as undemocratic or in any other way he liked, provided he proved his point by pertinent arguments. But what he has done is—without an iota of evidence and in the face of facts easily available to, literally, any schoolboy—to *ignore* any usage but the one he needs for his case; and even more, he has implicitly denied the quite unmistakable existence of such usages.

This enables him to apply the only method by which a brief such as his could be written. Wherever he finds "nation," "nationality," "people," or any similar term in Zionist statements or other pertinent documents, he automatically interprets them as "national state" or "sovereignty" or equivalent expressions. He never tries to prove that this meaning, and not another possible meaning—say "a people connected by ties of blood generally manifested in community of language, religion, customs, etc.," which is the first meaning of "nation" in Webster—is what the documents really mean. Then, when Zionists say specifically that the "Jewish people" is a term which relates to Webster's definition of "nation," not to Mallison's, he simply says they are employing "calculated ambiguity." Words mean what Mallison says they mean; there is no meaning but Mallison's meaning —and anyone who says otherwise is a liar.

This is not proper argument. It is libel. The fact that a professor of law has written it and published it in a law review only makes it vicious libel.

It may be argued that even if the documents Mallison analyzes do not, in *every* case, use "national," "people," etc., in the sense of his definitions,

there may be *some* documents in his brief that support his case. In that event, it would still be wrong of him to accuse opponents of lying merely because they use words in a valid sense other than Mallison's, but he might nevertheless have a basis for his major contentions. *May I add, accordingly, that I have checked every one of Mallison's analyses. In not one case does the document mean what Mallison says it means for his own purposes; in each and every case the Zionists have something else in mind—just as they say they do.*

To go into each analysis would be to stretch out this essay beyond endurance. I shall therefore confine myself, by way of illustration, to the analysis of the Balfour Declaration and alleged "Zionist claims" relating to it.

The Balfour Declaration

Prof. Mallison devotes his most assiduous attention to the Balfour Declaration and its "negotiating history." This is the analysis where he shows the greatest originality, arriving at conclusions no one ever dreamed of before. If there were any substance to his conclusions, he would have achieved a veritable breakthrough in the interpretation of a chapter in diplomatic history. But in actuality—possibly owing to the fact that he is out of his proper field here, dealing with a problem of history, not of law—his analysis is completely amateurish and his conclusions entirely baseless.

According to Prof. Mallison's reconstruction (p. 1012), the alleged Zionist claims were made in the first clause of a draft proposal for a declaration, submitted by Lord James Rothschild on July 18, 1917, which read as follows:

"1. His Majesty's Government accepts the principle that Palestine should be reconstituted as the National Home of the Jewish people."

As analyzed by Mallison's method, this brief statement is shown to conceal, among other "central Zionist objectives," the following claim: " ... that *all Jews (the comprehensive claimed entity of the 'Jewish people')* be recognized in law as constituting a *single nationality grouping"* (emphasis added). The interpretation rests again on the assumption that such words as "national" and "people" always and only mean what Mallison says they mean, and no other significance is allowed. But Prof. Mallison may believe that some support is given to his reading by his account of the "negotiating history" of the Balfour Declaration and by comparing the language above with the final text.

For, according to Mallison, the Zionist claim he has read out of the July 18 draft proposal was *specifically rejected* in a later draft prepared for the British Cabinet by Leopold Amery, which served as the base for the final Declaration. A "safeguard clause" was inserted in this document, providing that it should be "clearly understood that nothing shall be done which may prejudice ... the rights and political status enjoyed in any country by such Jews who are fully contented with their existing nationality." This "safeguard" against "the incursions of Zionist nationalism" was then strengthened, according to Mallison, by none other than Justice Louis D. Brandeis. He suggested that the final clause of the Balfour Declaration read, "rights and civil political status enjoyed by Jews in any other country." In this way, all Diaspora Jews—not only those "fully contented with their existing nationality and citizenship"—were

protected against the menace of Zionism.

Such an interpretation of the Balfour Declaration's "negotiating history" confronts readers with a set of riddles. On Mallison's account, most of those concerned were acting in an irrational manner, with little or no regard for their objectives as he has defined them. The "safeguards" inserted in the Balfour Declaration unequivocally repudiated the objectives of the "official Zionist draft," according to Mallison—but the Zionists accepted it. Nor is that all: some Zionists—"Brandeis and his associates"—deliberately proposed changes which strengthened one of the anti-Zionist "safeguards." As for the anti-Zionist Jews, through the Balfour Declaration they had obtained (incipient) "public law" guarantees against the "incursions of Zionist nationalism"; yet it is they who still opposed the Balfour Declaration. To credit Mallison's "historical" reconstruction of what happened, we should have to assume that almost everyone involved in the "negotiating history" was stricken with lunacy.

The whole construction rests 1) on considering the July 18, 1917 draft proposal a statement which emanated from Zionist quarters alone, without British involvement, and then 2) counterposing to it anti-Zionist proposals from which 3) Leopold Amery drew his "safeguard" clauses. In view of this history, the "safeguard" clauses should be interpreted as repudiating the original Zionist claims. On this basis one could then interpret the original "Zionist claims" as, indeed, intended to prejudice the rights and civil political status of all Jews, wherever they lived. Q. E. D.

Now, this is sheer moonshine from beginning to end, and the standard contemporary account of the subject, Leonard Stein's *The Balfour Declara-*

tion, upon which Mallison relies continually, contains all the information that makes this obvious. Not only bias but hopelessly amateur scholarship was needed to reach Mallison's fantastic conclusions from this source.

The facts are: 1) the July 18, 1917 draft was *not* a proposal independently formulated by the Zionists as their bargaining position. It was virtually a direct transcription of a Foreign Office formula, defining Zionist aims succinctly and broadly in a way Lord Balfour had already indicated he was ready to accept.

2) There were no anti-Zionist drafts proposed in opposition to this proposal after July 18 which could explain the difference in the final Declaration of November 2, 1917.

3) Leopold Amery, who devised the so-called "safeguard" clauses upon which Mallison builds his case, tells us that these additions to the July 18 draft "gave away nothing that was not self-evident."

What the "negotiating history" of the Balfour Declaration makes entirely clear is, in fact, that these "safeguard" clauses, like the rest of the Declaration, can be traced directly to Zionist ways of thinking and expression, which the British adopted, not to any anti-Zionist source. However one may interpret them, they cannot be regarded as repudiating Zionist claims on the basis of their "negotiating history."

A draft proposal for a British Palestine proposal in favor of the Jews *was* made by anti-Zionists in March, 1916. This proposal was abandoned by the British in the act of undertaking serious negotiations with the Zionists and was never considered as an alternative thereafter. It differed from the Zionist desiderata in two major respects: it wanted no reference to a *"national* home for the Jewish people" and

no special status (e.g., as a "public body") for a Jewish agency in Palestine; and, of course, the anti-Zionists did not welcome any recognition granted to the Zionist Organization in the transmittal of the Declaration to their spokesman. On these essential points the Declaration at no point in its "negotiating history," from the draft proposal of July 18 to the final Declaration of November 2, 1917, made any substantive concessions to the anti-Zionists. The drafting changes that took place responded to no proposals of the anti-Zionists and, of course, were not regarded by them as satisfying their wishes in any way.

The "safeguard" clauses, in particular, echo language and thoughts voiced by Zionists, rather than anti-Zionists, in the debates of that period. The main points at issue were the meaning and practical implications of the expression "national home for the Jewish people." The anti-Zionists, like Mallison today, held that these terms implied that all Jews throughout the world were being involved in a political entity—the Jewish people—in a way that must cast doubt on their allegiance and endanger their rights in the countries of which they were severally citizens. The Zionists heatedly *denied* that the terms in dispute had any such meaning or bore any such implication. In the words of Lord Rothschild, "We Zionists cannot see how the establishment of an autonomous Jewish State . . . can be considered in any way subversive to the position or loyalty of the very large part of the Jewish people who have identified themselves thoroughly with the citizenship of the countries in which they live."

This is the direct antecedent of the so-called "safeguard" clause which reads, according to Mallison (p. 1014): "it being clearly understood that nothing shall be done which may prejudice . . . the rights and political status enjoyed in any other country by such Jews who are fully contented with their existing nationality and citizenship." Its meaning is the same as the meaning of its direct literary progenitor: not a repudiation of the Zionist claims inherent in the phrase "national home for the Jewish people," but an interpretation of those claims in the same way the Zionists interpreted them— which is to say, a *denial* of the interpretation anti-Zionist spokesmen in those days (like Mallison today) placed upon them. What Amery meant, speaking for the British government, is the same as the London *Times* editorialist meant in his comment of May 29, 1917: "Only an imaginative nervousness suggests that the realisation of territorial Zionism, in some form, would cause Christendom to round on the Jews and say, 'Now you have a land of your own, go to it!' " It was a somewhat gratuitous assurance, to anyone who needed assuring, that, in issuing the Balfour Declaration, His Majesty's Government was not being anti-Semitic.

An interpretation such as that of Mallison in the face of this evidence, all available to him, stems from a paranoidally suspicious frame of mind. Not analysis but a phobia is at work—whether Mallison's or that of his clients. If anything further is needed to prove this diagnosis, a brief consideration of one more item should be conclusive.

Prof. Mallison interprets the Balfour Declaration as a bargain struck between two parties (among others): the British government and the Zionists, on behalf of their "claimed constituency." The Zionists claimed to speak for all Jews, but the British repudiated this claim through the "safeguard" clause protecting Diaspora Jews other than Zionists. This left the Zionist membership—and after Brandeis' emendation of the last clause of the Declaration, those in Palestine—as the beneficiaries of the British promise. Why then, asks Prof. Mallison, did not the Balfour Declaration read "a national home *for Zionists*" instead of "a national home for the Jewish people"? (p. 1027) The question is not, as you see, an imaginary one made up by a hostile critic in order to confute Mallison; it is an issue that bothers him sufficiently to raise it himself, quite seriously. For, indeed, if the Balfour Declaration had been made in favor of "Zionists" instead of "the Jewish people" —an expression Mallison can cope with only by encasing it in quotation marks —his interpretation of the document could have relied on the text as written.

But Prof. Mallison is not one to be daunted by the wording of a text. He explains the regrettable verbal deficiencies of the Declaration simply enough: *it did not pay* the British or the Zionists to make the *true nature* of their agreement clear. Consequently, they decided not to be "candid" and, deliberately and concertedly, avoided using the word "Zionists." They chose instead to replace it with the expression "Jewish people" as a "palatable euphemism."

Now, how does Prof. Mallison *know* all this? Nowhere does he refer to anyone who is actually on record at the time concerned as considering a reference to a "Zionist" national home or a "Zionist" people, neither among friends nor foes of the document; the historical fact is that no one ever did. Indeed, it is *historically inconceivable* that anyone could have proposed such phrasing at the time. The use of "Zionist" instead of "Jewish" in relation to the Jewish national home (or, later, the State of Israel) is one of those neologisms which Mallison's Jewish clients, together with Arab propagandists, invented in our own time. Its specific function is to allow the whole technique and much of the actual material of traditional anti-Semitic propaganda to be used against Israel, and the Jews who support Israel by an overwhelming consensus, while denying that one is anti-Semitic. To apply this usage to the period of the Balfour Declaration is not only a grotesque anachronism; it is rewriting history in the style of a demonological myth.

The Talbot Letter

When the Balfour Declaration came out, Zionist leaders were not pleased with its provisos assuring the Arabs and Jews in the Diaspora that no harm would come to them because of the promise to help establish a home in Palestine for the Jewish people. What was said there was exactly what Zionists themselves had been arguing; in Amery's words, it "gave away nothing that was not self-evident." But precisely because what the provisos said *was* self-evident, to state it explicitly in the Declaration, said Chaim Weizmann, might seem to "impute possible oppressive intentions to the Jews."

The language of Mr. Talbot's letter to Rabbi Elmer Berger shows plainly that, to an extent, similar motives were at play here as in the framing of the added provisos of the Balfour Declaration. For some reason, the State Department felt obliged to assure Rabbi Berger that the United States is not anti-Semitic. Its recognition of the State of Israel implies no recognition of any "other sovereignty or citizenship in connection therewith" or any "legal-political relationship based upon the religious identification of American citizens." Thus were laid to rest, presumably, the demons that haunt the dreams of American Council for Judaism leaders and their legal consultants; but which have no reality in the world of Zionist activity or "claims" or "intentions." Mr. Talbot also affirmed that the State Department "does not regard the 'Jewish people' concept as a concept of international law." This is, strictly speaking, correct: for the Palestine Mandate's recognition of the Jewish people (*not* in quotation marks; and *not* as a nation-state entity, but as an historical reality with historic connections and claims) was superseded in international law upon the creation of Israel; and the "Jewish people" (in quotation marks) concept is a figment of the imagination of the ACJ and its consultants. To make its good will quite clear, the State Department also explicitly affirmed that our government is not anti-Semitic: "it does not in any way discriminate among American citizens upon the basis of their religion."

When similar remarks were inserted in the Balfour Declaration, they too gave undue consideration to phobias. But, at least, in that case the provisos were made in a context of unquestioned beneficence toward the whole Jewish people, and were patently meant to reassure those who had unfounded fears of an act of kindness.

What good purpose did Mr. Talbot's letter serve? What benefit did it confer upon all Jews, to balance, let alone outweigh, the harm done by bolstering the self-importance of a lunatic fringe group in the Jewish community?

Sovereignty over Palestine

HENRY CATTAN

The territories which are now occupied by Israel are the following:

the territory which was envisaged for the Jewish state in accordance with General Assembly resolution 181 (II) of November 29 1947 and

the various territories which Israel has seized in excess of the General Assembly resolution. These territories comprise:

i. More than half the areas which General Assembly resolution 181 (II) of November 29 1947 had reserved for the Arabs of Palestine and which were to constitute the territory of the proposed Arab state. These additional areas were occupied by Israel in 1948 and 1949.[1]

ii. The City of Jerusalem, which under the same General Assembly resolution was to have been subject to an international regime administered by the United Nations. Israel occupied the New City of Jerusalem in 1948 and the Old City of Jerusalem in 1967.

iii. The West Bank of Jordan, the Sinai Peninsula and the Golan Heights—being territories of Jordan, Egypt and Syria respectively. Israel seized these territories in June 1967.

iv. The Gaza Strip was also seized by Israel in June 1967.

The above-mentioned territories are shown in Appendix VII.

It is proposed to examine here the question of sovereignty over such territories and the legal status of Israel in regard to such territories. This legal question may not be of much interest to the layman but it has an important bearing upon the eventual solution.

In its common usage, the term sovereignty means the supreme power of a state over a certain territory and its people regardless of the legitimacy of its origin. But sovereignty involves also a broader and more fundamental concept: the legal and inalienable title of a king or a nation to a territory. It was on the basis of this concept of legitimacy of title that the pre-Napoleonic sovereigns were restored to power and

[1] See Section 2 of Part I.

Europe was reconstructed after 1815.[2] It is on the basis of the same concept that the nationhood of Poland was preserved during the long interregnum between 1795 and 1919 until it finally triumphed with the restoration of its international personality. The same broad concept explains the survival of Austria's sovereignty during the period of its forced union with Germany in 1938 until its formal re-establishment in 1945. In all these cases, sovereignty was not extinguished by the forceful occupation of territory or by conquest. Consequently, a distinction exists between legal and political sovereignty, the latter meaning factual dominion and control and the former signifying the rightful and inalienable title of a people to a territory. Such a distinction corresponds to the difference that is made between sovereignty in law and sovereignty in fact.[3] Professor Schwarzenberger has made the distinction between legal and political sovereignty as follows: 'The last word is still not with law, but power. On such a level, the counterpart to legal sovereignty is political sovereignty.'[4] Mr. Ian Brownlie has made the same distinction by contrasting the 'assumption of the powers of government' with 'de jure sovereignty'.[5] It is in the sense of legal sovereignty that the term sovereignty is used hereinafter.

I SOVEREIGNTY OF THE ORIGINAL INHABITANTS OF PALESTINE

Notwithstanding the political vicissitudes in Palestine during the last fifty years, legal sovereignty still lies today in the original inhabitants of the country as they existed at the time of the detachment of Palestine from Turkey at the end of the First World War.

Prior to the occupation of Palestine by the British Army in 1917 during the First World War, Palestine formed an integral part of Turkey, which was a sovereign and independent state. The inhabitants of Palestine, Moslems, Christians and Jews, all Arabic-speaking peoples, were then Turkish citizens and enjoyed, as we have already seen, equal rights

---

[2] See Guglielmo Ferrero, *The Reconstruction of Europe* (translation by Jaeckel, New York, 1941), and C-M. de Talleyrand, *Mémoires*, Vol. II.

[3] As to this distinction, see Gaston Jèze, *Etude Théorique et Pratique sur l'Occupation* (Paris, 1896), p. 46.

[4] G. Schwarzenberger, *The Fundamental Principles of International Law* (Hague Recueil, 1955), p. 215.

[5] Ian Brownlie, *Principles of Public International Law* (Oxford 1966), pp. 100–102.

with the Turks in government and administration.[6] The Turkish constitution made no distinction between Turk or Arab or between Moslem
or Christian or Jew. Turks and Arabs, therefore, shared sovereignty
over all the territories of the Turkish Empire regardless as to whether
such territories were Turkish or Arab provinces. This situation continued
until the detachment of the Arab provinces, including Palestine, from
Turkey at the end of the First World War. Such detachment was at first
de facto, and resulted from the military occupation of Palestine by the
British Army in 1917 and then became *de jure* by Turkey's renunciation
of its sovereignty over the Arab territories in accordance with the
Treaty of Lausanne of July 24 1923.

The British military occupation of Palestine in 1917 did not give
sovereignty to the occupying power nor take away the sovereignty of
the inhabitants. Apart from the fact that under international law the
military occupation of enemy territory does not give the occupier a
territorial title, it was clear that the avowed objective of the Allied
Powers during the First World War was not the acquisition of territory
in the Middle East. This is evident from the various pledges and formal
assurances given to the Arabs by Great Britain and its Allies between
1915 and 1918 regarding the future of the Arab territories. These
pledges and assurances were mentioned in Section 1 (1) of Part I.[7] It
should be remarked that the reference to the British pledges and assurances given to the Arabs during the First World War does not signify
that such pledges and assurances are made a foundation for the Arab
claim to Palestine. The title of the Palestinian Arabs to Palestine does not,
and cannot, depend upon the pledges and assurances of a third Power
which, moreover, possessed neither sovereignty nor dominion nor any
right whatsoever over the country. Their title rests upon their ownership of the country from time immemorial. That the title of the Palestinians to Palestine dates from time immemorial is literally true, not a
figure of speech. Frequently, the date of the Arab occupation of Palestine is related back to the Moslem Arab conquest of the country some
thirteen centuries ago. This is not historically accurate. The Moslem
conquest of Palestine in A.D. 637 was not the starting-point of the occu-

[6] See Section 1 (1), of Part I, *ante*.

[7] For the text of these pledges and assurances see the Report of the Committee set up by
the British Government to consider the McMahon–Hussein Correspondence and
statements made on behalf of His Majesty's Government in 1918, *Cmd.* 5964, and
George Antonius, *The Arab Awakening* (Khayats, Beirut).

pation of the country by the Palestinians. The Arabs, including the Palestinians, are a pre-Islamic people. They lived in Palestine and other parts of the Middle East before the advent of Islam and the Moslem conquest. As we have seen earlier in Part I, the Palestinians were the descendants of the Philistines and Canaanites, and have lived continuously in Palestine since the dawn of history, even long before the ancient Hebrews set foot in the country.

The Covenant of the League of Nations, approved by the Paris Peace Conference on April 28 1919, and incorporated into the Treaty of Versailles on June 28 1919, also discarded any idea of annexation by the occupying powers of the territories seized from Turkey and Germany during the First World War. The Covenant dealt in Article 22 with the future of the Arab communities and territories of the Turkish Empire and also with the future of the former German Colonies. Article 22 of the Covenant established a new status under international law for the Arab communities detached from the Turkish Empire and, it is important to note, recognized their 'existence as independent nations'. Article 22 began with the statement:

> To those colonies and territories which as a consequence of the late war have ceased to be under the sovereignty of the States which formerly governed them. . . .[8]

Its fourth paragraph stated:

> Certain communities formerly belonging to the Turkish Empire have reached a stage of development where their existence as independent nations can be provisionally recognized subject to the rendering of administrative advice and assistance by a mandatory until such time as they are able to stand alone.[9]

Mr. Duncan Hall has observed: 'Underlying Article 22 was the assumption of independent national sovereignty for mandates. The

[8] See Appendix I. The term 'colonies', as distinct from 'territories', must be understood to refer to the former German colonies in Africa. The Arab provinces of the Turkish Empire were not colonies, as already noted, since they formed an integral part of Turkey.

[9] The use of the expression 'communities belonging to the Turkish Empire' is misleading. The Arab provinces 'belonged' to the Turkish Empire in the sense that they formed part of this country, but not in the sense in which a colony 'belongs' to the mother country. It has been made amply clear that Arabs and Turks enjoyed equal rights and shared sovereignty over the whole Turkish Empire.

drafters of the Covenant took as their starting-point the general notions of "no annexation" and "self-determination".'[10] In the case concerning the International Status of South-West Africa (1950) the Court held that in Article 22 of the Covenant of the League of Nations 'two principles were considered to be of paramount importance: the principle of non-annexation and the principle that the well-being and development of such peoples form a sacred trust of civilization'.[11] The inhabitants of the mandated territories were the beneficiaries of this trust.[12]

The legal effect under international law of the detachment of Palestine from the Turkish Empire and of the recognition by the League of Nations of the community inhabiting it as an independent nation was to make of this country a separate, independent and international political entity. The community which then inhabited Palestine thus became a subject of international law in which was vested the legal sovereignty over the territory in which it lived.

But although Palestine acquired its own sovereignty as a result of its detachment *de facto* from Turkey and the recognition of its people as an independent nation by the Covenant of the League of Nations, the formal renunciation by Turkey of its sovereignty over its former Arab provinces occurred only some time later. The Supreme Council of the Principal Allied Powers sought to impose upon Turkey the Treaty of Sèvres of August 10 1920. This Treaty, however, was not ratified by the Turkish Government, which objected to some of its provisions. Ultimately, the Allied Powers had to negotiate with the Turkish nationalists, who had abolished in 1922 the Sultanate and declared the Ottoman Government to be no longer in existence. The Turkish nationalists accepted the separation of the Arab provinces and concluded with the Allied Powers the Treaty of Lausanne of July 24 1923 after certain provisions of the abortive Treaty of Sèvres had been withdrawn and abandoned. Among the provisions of the abortive Treaty of Sèvres to which the Turkish authorities had taken objection and which were abandoned was the provision concerning the Jewish national home. The Treaty of Sèvres had provided in Article 95 that the parties agreed to entrust, by application of Article 22 of the Covenant of the League of Nations, the

---

[10] H. Duncan Hall, *Mandates, Dependencies and Trusteeships* (Carnegie Endowment for International Peace, Washington, 1948), p. 80.

[11] *I.C.J. Reports*, 1950, p. 131.

[12] *Ibid.*, p. 132.

administration of Palestine to a Mandatory to be selected by the Principal Allied Powers, and that the Mandatory would be responsible for putting into effect the declaration made on November 2 1917 by the British Government in favour of the establishment in Palestine of a national home for the Jewish people.[13] Turkey refused to subscribe to this provision. Instead, Article 16 of the Treaty of Lausanne provided as follows:

> Art. 16. Turkey hereby renounces all rights and title whatsoever over or respecting the territories situated outside the frontiers laid down in the present Treaty and the islands other than those over which her sovereignty is recognized by the said Treaty, the future of these territories and islands being settled or to be settled by the parties concerned.

It is significant that by excluding any reference in the Treaty of Lausanne to the declaration of November 2 1917, Turkey, as the state which had possessed sovereignty over Palestine in the past, did not, upon renunciation of such sovereignty, mortgage the future of Palestine with any obligation relating to the establishment of a Jewish national home. The Treaty left the future of Palestine, and other Arab territories, to be decided by 'the parties concerned'. This expression was not defined, but it can only mean the communities which inhabited these territories, since they were the parties primarily concerned.

It is also significant that the renunciation by Turkey of 'all rights and title' over the Arab territories detached from it was not made in favour of the signatory Powers or of any Power in particular. This is in contrast with Article 15 in the same Treaty wherein 'Turkey renounces in favour of Italy all rights and title' over certain specified islands. The difference between the two renunciation provisions can be ascribed to two reasons: first, it was not the intention that the Principal Allied Powers or any one of them should acquire sovereignty over the Arab provinces; secondly, the Arab communities in the provinces detached from Turkey were the original inhabitants and already possessed sovereignty over their own territories. Hence they were not in need of any renunciation to be made in their favour, in contrast with Italy, which needed a renunciation of sovereignty in its favour to enable it to acquire sovereignty over the islands which came under its occupation. In this regard Turkey's

---

[13] See the text of Article 95 of the Treaty of Sèvres in Hurewitz, *Diplomacy in the Near and Middle East* (D. Van Nostrand, New Jersey, 1956), Vol. II, p. 84.

renunciation by the Treaty of Lausanne of its sovereignty over the Arab territories is comparable to Spain's relinquishment of its sovereignty over Cuba by the Treaty of Paris, 1898. In both cases the renunciation of sovereignty was not made in favour of the occupying Power. In the case of Cuba Spain's renunciation was held to vest sovereignty in the inhabitants:

> In the present case, as the United States expressly disclaimed any intention to exercise sovereignty, jurisdiction, or control over the island, 'except for the pacification thereof', the ownership of the island, upon the relinquishment by Spain of her sovereignty over it, immediately passed to the inhabitants of Cuba, who, in the resolutions referred to, were declared to be free and independent, and in whom, therefore, abstractly considered, sovereignty resided.
>
> Had the language been 'Spain cedes to the United States the island of Cuba' as by Article II she did Porto Rico, that would have divested her of all title to and, by consequence, all sovereignty over Cuba, both of which would then immediately have passed to the United States, as they did in the case of Porto Rico; subject, however, to the rights of the people. True, when, pursuant to the treaty, the United States occupied the island, the inhabitants thereof during such occupancy undoubtedly owed allegiance to the United States, i.e., fidelity and obedience for the protection they received, but that did not divest them of their inherent rights. (*Galban and Company, A Corporation* v. *the United States*, 40 Ct. Cls. (1905), 495, 506–507.)[14]

Although Palestine had as a result of these developments become a separate and independent political entity, distinct from the political entity of which it previously formed part, and possessed of its own sovereignty, its people were prevented from the exercise of full and effective sovereignty as a result of two circumstances: the existence of a military occupier, and subsequently the grant in 1922 by the Council of the League of Nations of a mandate to the British Government to administer Palestine.

It is necessary, therefore, to consider whether the grant to the British Government of a mandate over Palestine affected the sovereignty of its inhabitants.

Conflicting views have been expressed in the past as to who possessed sovereignty in the case of a mandated territory. Some have argued that

[14] Hackworth, *Digest of International Law*, Vol. I, page 425.

sovereignty lay in the Principal Allied Powers [15] or in the League of Nations [16] or in the mandatory [17] or jointly in the League of Nations and the mandatory [18] or in the inhabitants of the mandated territory. [19] All the various views which have been expressed on the point—except that which considers sovereignty to reside in the inhabitants of the mandated territory—have now been abandoned or discredited. None of the views that sought to vest sovereignty elsewhere than in the inhabitants of the mandated territory appears to rest on an acceptable legal or logical basis.

It is obvious, on the one hand, that the Peace Treaties concluded with Germany and Turkey at the end of the First World War did not embody any renunciation by these states of their sovereignty over the territories detached from them in favour of the principal Allied Powers or the League of Nations or the mandatory Power. It is equally obvious, on the other hand, that it was not the intention of the Covenant of the League of Nations or the mandates that the principal Allied Powers or the League of Nations or the mandatory Power should acquire sovereignty over the mandated territories. The terms of the mandates granted by the League of Nations in respect of former Turkish and German territories did not involve any cession of territory or transfer of sovereignty to the mandatory Power. The International Court of Justice has recently confirmed this principle with regard to the mandate for South-West Africa. The Court said:

> The terms of this Mandate, as well as the provisions of Article 22 of the Covenant and the principles embodied therein, show that the creation of this new international institution (i.e., the mandate) did not involve any cession of territory or transfer of sovereignty to the Union of South Africa. The Union Government was to exercise an international function of administration on behalf of the League, with the object of promoting the well-being and development of the inhabitants. [20]

[15] Hoijer, *Le Pacte de la Société des Nations* (1926) (Spes, Paris, 1926), p. 374.

[16] Redslob, *Le Système des Mandats Internationaux*, p. 196.

[17] H. Rolin, Le Système des Mandats Internationaux, *Revue de Droit International et de Législation Comparée* (1920), p. 302.

[18] Quincy Wright, Sovereignty of the Mandates, *AJIL* (1923), p. 698.

[19] P. Pic, Le Régime du Mandat d'après le Traité de Versailles, *RGDIP*, Vol. 30, 1923, p. 334; Millot, *Les Mandats Internationaux*, p. 91; Stoyanovsky, *La Théorie Générale des Mandats Internationaux*, p. 92.

[20] Advisory Opinion of the International Court of Justice regarding the Status of South-West Africa, *I.C.J. Reports* (1950), p. 132.

The view that sovereignty over a mandated territory lies in its inhabitants received the support of several writers, and was summarized by Mr. Van Rees, Vice-President of the Permanent Mandates Commission, as follows:

> Enfin, un dernier groupe d'auteurs—divisé en deux fractions—le seul groupe qui a tenu compte du principe de non-annexion adopté par la Conférence de la Paix, soutient que les auteurs du Pacte ont voulu tenir en suspens ou bien la souveraineté elle-même sur les territoires sous mandat pour une période équivalente à la durée des mandats respectifs (Lee D. Campbell, *The Mandate for Mesopotamia and the principle of trusteeship in English law*, p. 19; A. Mendelssohn Bartholdi, *Les Mandats africains* (traduction), Archiv für politik und Geschite, Hamburg, 1925) ou bien *l'exercice* des pouvoirs souverains dont furent provisoirement chargées certaines nations en qualité de tuteurs. D'après ce dernier point de vue la souveraineté elle-même serait détenue, depuis la renonciation des anciens Empires, par les communautés et les populations autochtones des différents territoires. En d'autres termes, les anciens Empires ayant renoncé à leurs droits et titres sur les territoires en question sans qu'il y ait eu transfert de ces droits et titres à d'autres Puissances, la souveraineté, qui appartient à ces divers peuples et communautés jusqu'au moment de leur soumission à l'Allemagne et à la Turquie, renait automatiquement du fait de la renonciation susdite. (Paul Pic, *Le régime des mandats d'après le Traité de Versailles*, *RGDIP*, Paris, 1923, p. 14; Albert Millot, *Les mandats internationaux*, Paris, 1924, pp. 114–118; J. Stoyanovski, *La théorie générale des mandats internationaux*, Paris, pp. 83 and 86.)[21]

The same author pointed out that the view which held that sovereignty lies in the indigenous communities and populations of the mandated territory 'is the only one which at least takes into account the principle of non-annexation unanimously adopted by the Peace Conference'.[22]

The concept of sovereignty is not strained by recognizing the attribute of sovereignty to the inhabitants of mandated territories. Westlake has said: 'The duties and rights of States are only the duties and rights of the men who compose them.'[23] Article 22 of the Covenant of the League of Nations specifically recognized, as we have seen, the existence

---

[21] D. F. W. Van Rees, *Les Mandats Internationaux* (Rousseau, Paris, 1927), p. 20.

[22] Translation from D. F. W. Van Rees, *Certains Aspects du Régime des Mandats Internationaux* (Bibliotheca Visseriana, 1931), p. 21.

[23] Westlake, *Collected Papers*, p. 78.

of certain communities as independent nations. Independence implies sovereignty. In its resolution adopted in 1931 the Institute of International Law described the communities under mandate as subjects of international law.[24] The international personality of communities under mandate first recognized by the Covenant of the League of Nations has now come to be accepted as a principle of international law.[25] Pélichet has observed:

> La personnalité internationale ne fut longtemps reconnue qu'aux Etats. Ce n'est qu'à la fin du XIXe siècle, sous l'influence de Mancini et de l'école italienne, qu'on admit que certaines collectivités, étrangères aux Etats, pouvaient relever du droit des Gens et en devenir des sujets. Cette opinion a de plus en plus prévalu.[26]

One of the first writers who proclaimed the principle that sovereignty lies in the inhabitants of the mandated territory was Professor Pic. He said:

> Les rédacteurs du Traité de Versailles, s'inspirant avant tout d'un droit pour les peuples de disposer d'eux-mêmes, ont formellement proclamé qu'il n'y aurait *aucune annexion* des territoires sous mandat par une puissance quelconque, pas plus par la collectivité des Etats ayant nom Société des Nations et siégeant à Genève, que par tel ou tel Etat particulier. Ces territoires appartiennent virtuellement aux populations ou communautés autochtones, dont la Société des Nations s'est constituée le défenseur, et au regard desquelles elle joue un peu le rôle d'un conseil de famille. Or, en droit interne, un conseil de famille n'a, pas plus que le tuteur qu'il désigne, et dont il controle les actes, de droit privatif sur les biens du pupille.[27]

A somewhat similar view was held by Professor Quincy Wright with respect to the 'A' mandates. He observed:

> Communities under 'A' mandates doubtless approach very close to sovereignty.[28]

[24] *AJIL* (1932), p. 91.
[25] See in this regard E. Pélichet, *La Personnalité internationale distincte des collectivités sous mandat* (Rousseau, Paris, 1932), p. 183.
[26] E. Pélichet, *op. cit.*, p. 51.
[27] Professor P. Pic, *op. cit.*, p. 334.
[28] Quincy Wright, *Sovereignty of the Mandates*, AJIL, Vol. 17, 1923, p. 696. Mandates were classified into three types: 'A', 'B' and 'C'. This classification was made in a 'descending order of political individuality' according to their international status and the degree of authority given to the mandatory. The 'A' mandates applied to Iraq, Palestine, Syria and Lebanon. The 'B' mandates applied to German possessions in West

The Earl of Birkenhead thought that the 'A' mandated territories had a close similarity to protected States. He observed:

> The question as to the sovereignty of the mandated territory raises difficulties. It may lie in the League of Nations, in the mandatory State or in the mandated territory. With regard to the 'A' territories their close similarity to protected States would suggest a solution; but ... the 'B' and 'C' territories may have to await the happening of some crucial event ... before its juristic position can be unquestionably defined.[29]

Referring to Palestine and Syria in particular, the same author said:

> The position of Palestine and Syria is that they were integral portions of the Turkish Empire (which has renounced all right or title to them: Article 16 of the Treaty of Lausanne, 1923), they have become, administratively, partially dependent now upon an appointed mandatory State, but they are acknowledged—in the terms of Article 22 of the Covenant—to be entitled to provisional recognition of independence. ... The status of Palestine and Syria resembles very closely that of States under suzerainty.[30]

Millot also vested sovereignty in the inhabitants of the mandated territory. He based his view upon Article 22 of the Covenant of the League of Nations and the intention of the Peace Conference which ended the First World War. Regarding the Arab territories detached from the Turkish Empire he said that Article 22 of the Covenant has declared these territories to be provisionally independent States and remarked that 'independent' means 'sovereign'.[31]

Stoyanovsky has argued that the people of a mandated territory are not deprived of the right of sovereignty but are deprived only temporarily of its *exercise*. The right of sovereignty belongs to the inhabitants of the mandated territory 'by virtue of the principles of nationality and self-determination which are the foundations of modern international law'.[32] The distinction between sovereignty and its exercise in the case of mandated territories is comparable to the distinction made

---

Africa. The 'C' mandates related to German possessions in South-West Africa and to certain South Pacific Islands. It is to be remarked that only in the case of 'A' mandates were the communities concerned recognized by Article 22 of the Covenant as independent nations.

29 Earl of Birkenhead, *International Law*, 6th ed., p. 99.
30 Earl of Birkenhead, *op. cit.*, p. 40.
31 Millot, *Les Mandats Internationaux*, pp. 91 et 115.
32 Stoyanovsky, *La Théorie Générale des Mandats Internationaux*, p. 83.

under private law between ownership and its exercise in cases of guardianship, curatorship or other forms of tutelage.

Pélichet has advanced the view that communities under mandate enjoy real, not only virtual, sovereignty:

> La jouissance des droits de souveraineté est détenue réellement, et non point virtuellement par les collectivités.[33]

In regard to Palestine, Pélichet pointed out that the United Kingdom, as the mandatory Power, has concluded agreements with Palestine, as the mandated territory. Thus a community under a mandate can acquire rights, conclude agreements and assume international obligations. In consequence, he concluded:

> Nous estimons que la théorie de la souveraineté des peuples sous mandat est celle qui convient le mieux à l'esprit comme à la lettre de l'article 22.[34]

In his separate opinion concerning the International Status of South-West Africa, Lord McNair expressed the opinion that the mandate system does not fit into the old conceptions of sovereignty. According to Lord McNair sovereignty over a mandated territory is 'in abeyance'.[35]

The principle that sovereignty lies in the people of the mandated territory itself was recently applied to territories held under trusteeship in accordance with the Charter of the United Nations. Mandates and trusteeships possess the same legal affiliation. In the case of Società A.B.C. *v.* Fontana and Della Rocca, the Italian Court of Cassation held that 'sovereignty over the territory of Somaliland is vested in its population, although, under Article 2 of the Trusteeship Agreement, the administration of the territory, for the period specified in the Agreement, has been entrusted to Italy'.[36] The same view was expressed by Oppenheim, who observed:

> In considering the question of sovereignty over trust territories—a question which is by no means of mere academic importance—the distinction must be borne in mind between sovereignty as such (or what may be described as residuary sovereignty) and the exercise of sovereignty. The latter

---

[33] E. Pélichet, *op. cit.*, p. 100.
[34] E. Pélichet, *op. cit.*, p. 108.
[35] Advisory Opinion of the International Court of Justice regarding the Status of South-West Africa, *I.C.J. Reports* (1950), p. 150.
[36] Decision dated August 10 1954, *International Law Reports* (1955), Vol. 22, p. 77.

is clearly vested with the trustee powers subject to supervision by and accountability to the United Nations.[37]

We can, therefore, conclude this inquiry by remarking that the grant by the Council of the League of Nations of a mandate to the British Government to administer Palestine did not deprive its people of their right of sovereignty. The legal status of Palestine under international law during the British mandate and upon its termination on May 15 1948 can, therefore, be summarized as follows: during the currency of the mandate the people of Palestine enjoyed an independent international status and possessed sovereignty over their land; Palestine possessed its own identity, which was distinct from that of the mandatory power; its administration was theoretically its own though, in fact, it was in the hands of the mandatory; the Government of Palestine, as representative of the people of Palestine, concluded agreements with the mandatory power and became party, through the instrumentality of the mandatory, to a number of international treaties and conventions; however, the full exercise of sovereignty by the people of Palestine was restricted in certain respects by the powers of administration entrusted to the mandatory power by the League of Nations; upon the termination of the mandate the mandatory's powers of administration came to an end and, as a result, the restrictions upon exercise of full sovereignty by the people of Palestine ceased, so that by virtue of this right as well as by virtue of their right of self-determination they became entitled to govern themselves and to determine their future in accordance with normal democratic principles and procedures. The first and fundamental rule in any democracy is the rule of the majority. This rule, however, was not respected by the General Assembly of the United Nations, which recommended in 1947, in circumstances and under political pressures already mentioned, the partition of the country between Arab and Jewish states. The events which followed and the emergence of Israel have prevented the Palestinian people from exercising their right of sovereignty over their own land. The question which we have now to consider is whether the emergence of Israel and its occupation in 1948 and 1949 of various territories of Palestine did deprive the people of Palestine of their sovereignty. In other words, did Israel acquire legal sovereignty over such territories? For reasons of

[37] Oppenheim, *International Law* (Longmans, London, 1955), Vol. I, 8th ed., p. 236.

clarity in the discussion rather than because of any difference in conclusions, this inquiry into the legitimacy or illegitimacy of Israel's title will be made separately in respect of the territory destined for the Jewish state by the United Nations partition resolution and of the other territories which Israel seized in excess of the same resolution.

2 HAS ISRAEL ACQUIRED LEGAL SOVEREIGNTY OVER THE TERRITORY ALLOCATED TO THE JEWISH STATE BY THE PARTITION RESOLUTION?

The question as to whether Israel has acquired sovereignty over the territory which was allocated to the Jewish state by the partition resolution can be examined in the light of three political developments with a view to determining whether any one of them could have conferred title or sovereignty upon Israel. These three developments are: the Balfour Declaration of November 2 1917; the United Nations resolution on the partition of Palestine of November 29 1947, and the forcible occupation by Israel in 1948 and in 1949 of the territory earmarked for the proposed Jewish state by the said resolution.

a   *No grant of sovereignty was or could have been involved in the Balfour Declaration*

The Balfour Declaration, which the Zionists have utilized almost as a document of title for the establishment of a Jewish state in Palestine, never possessed any juridical value. At no time did the British Government as the author of such declaration possess any right of sovereignty over Palestine, whether on the date on which the Balfour Declaration was made or at any time thereafter, which could have enabled it to recognize any rights in favour of the Jewish people in or over Palestine. Hence the British Government was not in a position validly to grant any title or any rights to the Jews over Palestine because a donor cannot give away what does not belong to him. Professor W. T. Mallison, Jr., has observed:

Perhaps even more fundamental than analysis of the Balfour Declaration agreement is the issue of the juridical authority of the British Government to make a promise of political support in favor of Zionist nationalism.[38]

It has also been remarked that,

The most significant and incontrovertible fact is, however, that by itself the (Balfour) Declaration was legally impotent. For Great Britain had no sovereign rights over Palestine; it had no proprietary interest; it had no authority to dispose of the land. The Declaration was merely a statement of British intentions and no more.[39]

Moreover, neither party to the Declaration, namely, the Zionist Jews and the British Government, intended that it should convey any territorial rights to the Jews or result in their acquisition of sovereignty over Palestine. On the one hand, the Zionists, at least outwardly, emphatically denied that the Jewish national home mentioned in the Balfour Declaration did envisage the establishment of a Jewish state or the grant of sovereignty to the Jews. Writing in 1919, Sokolow, who is the Zionist historian, stated:

It has been said, and is still being obstinately repeated by anti-Zionists again and again, that Zionism aims at the creation of an independent 'Jewish State'. But this is wholly fallacious. The 'Jewish State' was never a part of the Zionist programme.[40]

Mr. Norman Bentwich, a Zionist Jew who held for several years the office of Attorney-General of Palestine during the British Mandate, has declared on a number of occasions that sovereignty was no part of the Jewish national home. He said:

State sovereignty is not essential to the Jewish national ideal. Freedom for the Jew to develop according to his own tradition, in his own environment, is the main, if not the whole demand.[41]

He also wrote:

It has often been made an objection to Zionist hopes that the Moslem Arabs now in possession of Palestine lands, already numbering more than a

[38] W. T. Mallison, Jr., The Zionist—Israel Juridical Claims to Constitute the 'Jewish People' Nationality Entity and to Confer Membership in it: Appraisal in International Law, *The George Washington Law Review*, Vol. 32, p. 1002, June 1964.

[39] Sol M. Linowitz, Analysis of a Tinderbox: The Legal Basis for the State of Israel, *American Bar Association Journal*, Vol. 43, 1957, pp. 522–523.

[40] Sokolow, *History of Zionism*, xxiv.

[41] Norman Bentwich, *Palestine of the Jews* (London, 1919), p. 195.

quarter of a million, cannot be ejected. . . . But it is neither to be expected, nor is it desired, that the Jews should occupy and appropriate the whole country.[42]

Mr. Bentwich defined the concept of the Jewish national home as not implying the grant of rights of political sovereignty but as offering the opportunity for cultural development. He said:

> The idea of a national home for a homeless people is now embodied in this single mandate (The Mandate for Palestine). . . . It signifies a territory in which a people, without receiving rights of political sovereignty, has, nevertheless, a recognized legal position and the opportunity of developing its moral, social and intellectual ideas.[43]

In 1934, Mr. Bentwich distinguished between a national home and a state in the following terms:

> A national home, as distinguished from a state, is a country where a people are acknowledged as having a recognized legal position and the opportunity of developing their cultural, social and intellectual ideals without receiving political sovereignty.[44]

Mr. Bentwich thought that the Jews should integrate within Palestine together with the Arab inhabitants:

> The Jewish people on their side do not ask for political power or national sovereignty. . . . They have no need or desire to rule over others. Ultimately, they would ask within the territory to form an integral part of the government of the land, together with the Arab inhabitants.[45]

On the other hand, the British Government as author of the Balfour Declaration did not intend to grant any political sovereignty to the Jewish people in Palestine. In its Statement of Policy of 1922, the British Government declared that the interpretation which His Majesty's Government place upon the Declaration of 1917, 'need not cause alarm to the Arab population of Palestine. . . . His Majesty's Government

---

[42] *Ibid.*, pp. 206–207. It may be remarked in passing that his reference to the Moslem Arabs numbering 'more than a quarter of a million' was a gross underestimate of the number of Moslem Arabs who inhabited Palestine at the time.

[43] Norman Bentwich, *The Mandates System* (Longmans, London, 1930), p. 24.

[44] Norman Bentwich, *Palestine* (E. Benn, London, 1934), p. 101.

[45] *Ibid.*, p. 288.

have not contemplated . . . the disappearance or the subordination of
the Arabic population. . . . They would draw attention to the fact that
the terms of the (Balfour) Declaration referred to do not contemplate
that Palestine as a whole should be converted into a Jewish National
Home, but that such a Home should be founded in Palestine.'[46] This
interpretation of the Jewish National Home was again confirmed in the
Statement of Policy issued by the British Government in October
1930.[47] In the Statement of Policy of May 1939 the British Government
dealt at length with the meaning it attributed to the Jewish national
home:

> 3. The Royal Commission and previous Commissions of Enquiry have
> drawn attention to the ambiguity of certain expressions in the Mandate,
> such as the expression 'a national home for the Jewish people', and they
> have found in this ambiguity and the resulting uncertainty as to the objec-
> tives of policy a fundamental cause of unrest and hostility between Arabs
> and Jews. . . .
> 4. It has been urged that the expression 'a national home for the Jewish
> people' offered a prospect that Palestine might in due course become a
> Jewish State or Commonwealth. His Majesty's Government do not wish to
> contest the view, which was expressed by the Royal Commission, that the
> Zionist leaders at the time of the issue of the Balfour Declaration recognized
> that an ultimate Jewish State was not precluded by the terms of the Declara-
> tion. But, with the Royal Commission, His Majesty's Government believe
> that the framers of the Mandate in which the Balfour Declaration was em-
> bodied could not have intended that Palestine should be converted into a
> Jewish State against the will of the Arab population of the country. That
> Palestine was not to be converted into a Jewish State might be held to be
> implied in the passage from the Command Paper of 1922, which reads as
> follows:

>> Unauthorized statements have been made to the effect that the purpose
>> in view is to create a wholly Jewish Palestine. Phrases have been used
>> such as that 'Palestine is to become as Jewish as England is English'. His
>> Majesty's Government regard any such expectation as impracticable and
>> have no such aim in view. Nor have they at any time contemplated . . . the
>> disappearance or the subordination of the Arabic population, language or
>> culture in Palestine. They would draw attention to the fact that the
>> terms of the (Balfour) Declaration referred to do not contemplate that

[46] Cmd. 1700, p. 18.
[47] Cmd. 3692.

Palestine as a whole should be converted into a Jewish National Home, but that such a home should be founded in Palestine.

But this statement has not removed doubts, and His Majesty's Government therefore now declare unequivocally that it is not part of their policy that Palestine should become a Jewish State. They would indeed regard it as contrary to their obligations to the Arabs under the Mandate, as well as to the assurances which have been given to the Arab people in the past, that the Arab population of Palestine should be made the subjects of a Jewish State against their will.[48]

Finally—and this is the most important consideration—whatever may have been the meaning and intention of the Balfour Declaration—the people of Palestine, who were the party most directly concerned as the owners of the country, were not consulted about the British promise to the Jews. They never gave their consent to the establishment of a Jewish national home in Palestine and never accepted the British Declaration. Neither did the other Arabs accept the Balfour Declaration. The Agreement made between Emir Faisal and Dr. Chaim Weizmann on January 3 1919 regarding the carrying into effect of the Declaration of November 2 1917 might appear to be an exception. It should be observed, however, that Emir Faisal possessed no representative capacity that entitled him to speak on behalf of the Arabs of Palestine or of the Arabs generally, or to commit the Arabs to an acceptance of the Balfour Declaration. Emir Faisal was then attending the Peace Conference at Paris in 1919 to secure political support for the claims of the Kingdom of Hejaz. In the so-called Faisal–Weizmann Agreement he is described as 'representing and acting on behalf of the Arab Kingdom of Hejaz'. He did not represent or act on behalf of the Arabs of Palestine or the Arabs generally. Mr. George E. Kirk has observed,

> At this stage the Palestine Arabs had never been consulted; they had given no mandate to Faisal to negotiate on their behalf; and his agreement with the Zionist leader could not be considered binding on anyone but himself and his father.[49]

Faisal's Agreement with Weizmann was repudiated by the Syro-Palestinian Congress of 1921. Even as regards Emir Faisal himself, the

[48] *Cmd.*, 6019, pp. 3 and 4.
[49] George E. Kirk, *A Short History of the Middle East* (Methuen and Co., London, 1948), p. 151.

Agreement lapsed in accordance with its own terms on the strength of a condition therein included by Emir Faisal that if the Arabs did not obtain their independence as demanded by him or if the slightest modification or departure were made to his demands the Agreement would be 'void and of no account or validity'. Since the conditions which he attached were not fulfilled, the Agreement never acquired validity.[50]

At the Anglo-Arab Conference of London in 1939, the Committee set up to consider the McMahon-Hussein Correspondence (1915–1918) came to the conclusion that it was evident from the statements made during and after the war that 'His Majesty's Government were not free to dispose of Palestine without regard for the wishes and interests of the inhabitants of Palestine, and that these statements must all be taken into account in any attempt to estimate the responsibilities which—upon any interpretation of the Correspondence—His Majesty's Government have incurred towards those inhabitants as a result of the Correspondence'.[51]

The Arabs have continuously protested against the Balfour Declaration from the first day it came to their knowledge. The Palestine Arabs have strenuously fought the Declaration. There cannot be the least doubt that their rights are not and cannot be impaired, diminished or in any way affected by a Declaration made by a third party against their interests. It is equally clear that the Jews did not gain any title or other right whatsoever in Palestine on the basis of the Declaration. From the juridical standpoint, therefore, any claim by the Jews to Palestine on the basis of the Balfour Declaration is entirely groundless, if not plainly nonsensical.

b　　*No title was derived by Israel under the resolution on the partition of Palestine adopted by the General Assembly of the United Nations on November 29 1947*

We now turn to consider whether Israel has or could have acquired any title or sovereignty over the territory earmarked for the Jewish state by virtue of the resolution of November 29 1947, which recommended

---

[50] George Antonius, *The Arab Awakening* (Khayats, Beirut), pp. 285 and 286. George Antonius remarks that the main interest of the Faisal–Weizmann Agreement 'is in the evidence it affords of the lengths to which Faisal was prepared to go in the sense of Arab–Jewish co-operation so long as that did not conflict with Arab independence': p. 286.

[51] Report of the Committee, March 16 1939, *Cmd.* 5974, p. 11.

the partition of Palestine between Arab and Jewish states. This inquiry does not concern the wisdom or justice of partition or the circumstances of political pressure and undue influence by which the resolution was obtained. These aspects were considered earlier in Section 1 (3) of Part I. The present inquiry will be limited to an examination of the legal effect of the resolution and, in particular, of the question whether the General Assembly of the United Nations could juridically give any title to the Jews or to a Jewish State over any part of the territory of Palestine.

The legal position in this regard is quite clear and obvious. The United Nations are an organization of States which was formed for certain purposes mentioned in the Charter. At no time did this organization possess any sovereignty or other power in or over Palestine. The United Nations could not give what they did not possess. Neither individually nor collectively could the members of the United Nations alienate, reduce or otherwise affect the sovereignty of the people of Palestine, nor dispose of their territory, whether by partition or otherwise. Nor could the United Nations in any way impair or diminish the political rights of the original inhabitants or grant to alien immigrants any territorial or political rights in Palestine. Not only did the United Nations possess no sovereignty over Palestine but they did not even possess any power to administer the country. The League of Nations had assumed the power to supervise the administration of mandates established after the First World War in accordance with Article 22 of the Covenant. With the dissolution of the League of Nations the power of supervision which it possessed over mandates came to an end. Such a result was recognized by the resolution adopted at the last meeting of the League of Nations held on April 18 1946. The resolution stated that 'on the termination of the League's existence, its functions with respect to the mandated territories will come to an end'.[52] At the same meeting the Chinese delegate pointed out that the Charter of the United Nations made no provision for the assumption by the United Nations of the functions of the League with respect to mandates.[53] The Trusteeship system envisaged by Article 77 of the Charter of the United Nations did not apply to territories held under mandate except to the extent that they might be placed

[52] Twenty-first Ordinary Session of the Assembly of the League of Nations, *Document A.33*, 1946, pp 5–6.
[53] *Ibid.*, p. 3.

thereunder by means of trusteeship agreements. Mr. Duncan Hall has summarized the position in these words:

> In the case of mandates, the League died without a testament. . . . There was no transfer of sovereignty to the United Nations. . . . Sovereignty, wherever it might lie, certainly did not lie in the United Nations.[54]

Not possessing any sovereignty or any right of administration or any other right whatsoever over Palestine, the United Nations could not legally determine, as they sought to do in 1947, the future government of Palestine by recommending the partition of the country between Arab and Jewish states. Such action completely lacked any juridical basis. The Palestine Question was brought on the agenda of the General Assembly of the United Nations as a result of a request made by the mandatory power to the Assembly for a recommendation to be made under Article 10 of the Charter concerning the future government of Palestine. Article 10 provides as follows:

> The General Assembly may discuss any questions or any matters within the scope of the present Charter . . . and, except as provided in Article 12, may make recommendations to the Members of the United Nations or to the Security Council or to both on any such questions or matters.

On the assumption that the Palestine Question was one of 'the questions or matters within the scope of the Charter' within the meaning of Article 10, and that consequently the General Assembly could discuss such a question or matter and make a recommendation to Members of the United Nations or to the Security Council, it is clear that the General Assembly had no power to make any recommendation that would be incompatible with the rights of the people of the country. In particular, the General Assembly did not possess the power to decide, impose or recommend the future form of Government of the country or to decide its partition between its original inhabitants and foreign immigrants, or otherwise to interfere with the sovereignty of its inhabitants. The question of the future government of Palestine was a matter which fell within the exclusive competence of its people and had to be decided in accordance with ordinary democratic principles and procedures. Any recommendation made by the General Assembly to the mandatory power whose functions were about to terminate could not

[54] H. Duncan Hall, *op. cit.*, p. 274.

affect the mandated territory, its integrity or the rights of its people. Any such recommendation, unless accepted by the original inhabitants of the country, had no value, either in law or in fact. Mr. P. B. Potter has observed that:

> The United Nations has no right to dictate a solution in Palestine unless a basis for such authority can be worked out such as has not been done thus far.
>
> Such a basis might be found by holding that sovereignty over Palestine, relinquished by Turkey in the Treaty of Lausanne, passed to the League of Nations, and has been inherited by the United Nations, a proposition which involves two hazardous steps. Or it might be held that the Mandate is still in force and that supervision thereof has passed to the United Nations, which is much more realistic but still somewhat hazardous juridically. The Arabs deny the binding force of the Mandate, now or ever, as they deny the validity of the Balfour Declaration on which it was based, and again they are probably quite correct juridically.[55]

Professor Quincy Wright has recently expressed the view that 'The legality of the General Assembly's recommendation for partition of Palestine was doubtful.'[56]

The same view was expressed by Professor I. Brownlie who said:

> It is doubtful if the United Nations 'has a capacity to convey title', *inter alia* because the Organization cannot assume the role of territorial sovereign ... Thus the resolution of 1947 containing a Partition plan for Palestine was probably *ultra vires* (outside the competence of the United Nations), and, if it was not, was not binding on member states in any case.[57]

The Palestinian Arabs questioned in 1947 the competence of the United Nations to recommend the partition of Palestine or otherwise prescribe the manner of its future government. In this regard, Sub-Committee 2 to the Ad Hoc Committee on the Palestine Question stated in its report dated November 11 1947 as follows:

> 15 (c) Before considering the effect of the provisions of the United Nations Charter on the Mandate, it should be pointed out that the United

---

[55] Pitman B. Potter, The Palestine Problem Before the United Nations, *AJIL* (1948), Vol. 42, p. 860.

[56] Quincy Wright, *The Middle Eastern Crisis*, an address to the Association of the Bar of the City of New York, November 1968.

[57] I. Brownlie: *Principles of Public International Law* (Clarendon Press, Oxford, 1966), pp. 161–162.

Nations Organization has not inherited the constitutional and political powers and functions of the League of Nations, that it cannot be treated in any way as the successor of the League of Nations in so far as the administration of mandates is concerned, and that such powers as the United Nations may exercise with respect to mandated territories are strictly limited and defined by the specific provisions of the Charter in this regard.

Competence of the United Nations

16. A study of Chapter XII of the United Nations Charter leaves no room for doubt that unless and until the Mandatory Power negotiates a trusteeship agreement in accordance with Article 79 and presents it to the General Assembly for approval, neither the General Assembly nor any other organ of the United Nations is competent to entertain, still less to recommend or enforce, any solution with regard to a mandated territory. Paragraph 1 of Article 80 is quite clear on this point, and runs as follows:

'Except as may be agreed upon in individual trusteeship agreements, made under Articles 77, 79, and 81, placing each territory under the trusteeship system, and until such agreements have been concluded, nothing in this Chapter shall be construed in or of itself to alter in any manner the rights whatsoever of any States or any peoples or the terms of existing international instruments to which Members of the United Nations may respectively be parties.'

18. In the case of Palestine, the Mandatory Power has not negotiated or presented a trusteeship agreement for the approval of the General Assembly. The question, therefore, of replacing the Mandate by trusteeship does not arise, quite apart from the obvious fact alluded to above that the people of Palestine are ripe for self-government and that it has been agreed on all hands that they should be made independent at the earliest possible date. It also follows from what has been said above, that the General Assembly is not competent to recommend, still less to enforce, any solution other than the recognition of the independence of Palestine, and that the settlement of the future government of Palestine is a matter solely for the people of Palestine.[58]

As previously observed in Section 1 (3) of Part I, all the requests which were made in 1947 by the Arabs at the United Nations for an advisory opinion by the International Court of Justice on the legal issues, including the question of competence of the General Assembly

[58] Document A/AC 14/32, November 11 1947, *Official Records of the Second Session of the General Assembly, AD HOC Committee on the Palestine Question*, pp. 276–277.

to recommend or implement partition, were turned down as a result of the political pressures exercised in favour of partition.

In adopting the resolution of November 29 1947 the General Assembly completely ignored the wishes of the people of Palestine and acted contrary to the will of the majority of the population. The principle of majority rule, which is one of the dogmas of modern civilization, was utterly ignored in 1947 in the case of Palestine. The partition resolution was pre-eminently a political decision which was engineered by Zionism and its friends in violation of the principles of law, justice and democracy. At no time was the partition resolution accepted by the Palestinians or by the Arab states. The partition resolution, therefore, lacked all juridical basis, was not within the powers of the General Assembly, and could not confer any valid title upon Israel over such part of Palestine as was earmarked for the Jewish state.

The conclusion herein reached that Israel cannot derive any valid title under the partition resolution is further strengthened by the consideration that, as previously mentioned, the Jewish state which emerged in 1948 and assumed the name of Israel was not established in conformity with the partition resolution. The manner of establishment of Israel and its organic structure have deviated in every material respect from the basic provisions of the United Nations resolution, whether they be territorial, demographic, political or constitutional. By forcibly displacing the Arab inhabitants of the Jewish state and by usurping a large part of the territory of the proposed Arab state, the Jews have created in Palestine something entirely and radically different from what the United Nations had contemplated in 1947. Territorially, Israel is not the Jewish state which was envisaged by the resolution of the United Nations. Demographically, Israel is not the Jewish state which was contemplated by the United Nations. Politically and constitutionally also, Israel cannot be considered to be the Jewish state envisaged by the United Nations. The Jewish state as envisaged by the General Assembly resolution was Jewish only in name, for in fact, as previously noted, it would have had an Arab majority.[59] Israel, as formed in 1948 and as it exists today, is a racist state in which its Arab population was reduced by

[59] The proposed Jewish state would have had a total population of 1,008,800 consisting of 509,780 Arabs and 499,020 Jews: U.N. Document A/AC 14/32 November 11 1947, Official Records of the 2nd session of the General Assembly, Ad Hoc Committee, 1947, p. 291. See also Section 1 (3) of Part I, *ante*.

methods already considered to about ten per cent of its original number. Thus, by its seizure of a large part of the territory of the proposed Arab state and by displacing the majority of its Arab population, Israel has completely distorted the concept of the Jewish state as originally envisaged by the United Nations. It is evident that the United Nations never intended to create a racist and theocratic state from which the original inhabitants of the country, both Moslems and Christians, would be ousted. Organically, Israel is not, and cannot be considered to constitute, the Jewish state whose creation was proposed by the United Nations in 1947, and hence cannot lay claim to the territorial and other rights, whatever their value, which were intended by the partition resolution for a materially different political and demographic entity.

c   *No title was gained by Israel as a result of conquest or occupation*

Before May 14 1948 the state of Israel did not exist. On that date, a number of Jews—largely of foreign origin and most of them not even possessing the nationality of the country—proclaimed the existence of the state of Israel and proceeded by force of arms to seize a substantial area of Palestine after driving away its Arab inhabitants. Can such seizure give a legal title to Israel? The answer is obvious. Israel cannot under international law claim title to the territories which it seized in 1948 and 1949 either by conquest or by occupation.

The right of conquest does not exist any more. It is now established by the consensus of the civilized community that military conquest is not a ground of acquisition of territory. War cannot give title. This principle, which was recognized by Article 22 of the Covenant of the League of Nations, was expressed in no uncertain terms by the United Nations during the fifth emergency special session of the General Assembly which was convened in the summer of 1967 following Israel's aggression. The same principle was also reaffirmed by the Security Council in its resolutions of November 22 1967 and May 21 1968, both of which emphasized 'the inadmissibility of the acquisition of territory by war' (Appendices VIII and IX).

Neither can Israel derive any title by occupation. Several considerations relating to the nature of the territory which was seized, the identity of the occupiers and the circumstances of the occupation negate the acquisition by Israel of any legal title to such territory.

In accordance with accepted principles of international law, occupation as a means of acquiring territory can only be conceived in the case of a *terra nullius*. 'Occupation can only come into play when there is a *res nullius* to be occupied.'[60] Palestine was at no time *terra nullius*, so that it was not open for occupation nor capable of acquisition by any state or any group of alien settlers. Palestine belonged to the Palestinians, i.e., its original inhabitants who had been established there for centuries.

Turning to the identity of the occupiers, it has already been observed that they were mainly aliens—both in origin and nationality. The bulk of the Jews who seized a large area of Palestine and proclaimed the State of Israel on May 14 1948 were foreign immigrants—some of whom had been admitted by the mandatory power as 'legal immigrants' while others had penetrated the country illegally[61]—and who in all cases had entered the country against the wishes of its original inhabitants.[62] Only a small number of the Jews who lived in Palestine in 1948 were indigenous inhabitants, and these were mostly opposed to the concept and establishment of a Jewish State. Moreover, the majority of the Jews who proclaimed the state of Israel in 1948 were not even citizens of Palestine. Although the mandatory power facilitated the acquisition of Palestinian citizenship by Jewish immigrants and did not require more than two years' residence in order to give them the country's nationality, the total number of certificates of naturalization granted by the Government of Palestine between 1925 and 1945 to all categories of immigrants—Jews and others—did not exceed 91,350.[63] The number of Jewish immigrants who had acquired Palestinian citizenship up to 1945 was 132,616 persons.[64] Thus the total number of Jews who possessed Palestinian citizenship in 1948—comprising both the original Jewish inhabitants of

---

[60] Earl of Birkenhead, *International Law*, 6th ed., p. 93; Oppenheim, *op. cit.*, p. 555.

[61] The Palestine Government estimated the number of Jewish illegal immigrants in 1945 to have been between 50,000 and 60,000: Government of Palestine, *A Survey of Palestine*, Vol. I, p. 210.

[62] Most of Israel's political leaders, past and present, have come from Russia, Poland, South Africa and other countries, and cannot even claim to belong to the country by birth on its soil. Mr. Ben Gurion, Israel's former Prime Minister, has taken pride in asserting that he came to Palestine in 1906 as a Russian tourist on a three-months' visa and simply overstayed: Ben-Gurion, *Israel, Années de Lutte* (Flammarion, Paris, 1964), p. 9.

[63] Government of Palestine, *A Survey of Palestine*, Vol. I, p. 208; Government of Palestine, *Statistical Abstract*, 1944–1945, pp. 36 and 46.

[64] Government of Palestine, *A Survey of Palestine*, Vol. I, p. 208.

Palestine and naturalized Jewish immigrants—hardly reached one-third of the Jewish population[65] or one-ninth of the total population. In these circumstances, the establishment of Israel by a minority group of foreign settlers who in the main did not even possess the citizenship of the country cannot be viewed as the act of a section of the original inhabitants seceding from the mother country. It would be a ludicrous situation under international law if a minority of alien settlers owning no more than 6 per cent of the land should, by reason of a successful military seizure of 80 per cent of the area of the country, be deemed to have acquired title and sovereignty over the territory which they have usurped.

The circumstances of the occupation also negate the acquisition of any valid title by Israel to the territory which it has seized. The territory of Palestine was wrested from its owners by violence exercised by a small but strongly organized alien minority which displaced by terrorism, expulsions and fear the majority of the original inhabitants. Thus, the very origin of Israel's occupation was wrongful and illegitimate and its seizure of Palestine territory was a usurpation of a land that does not belong to it. Oppenheim points out that where an act alleged to be creative of a new right is done in violation of an existing rule of international law, it 'is tainted with illegality and incapable of producing legal results beneficial to the wrongdoer in the form of a new title or otherwise'.[66] Oppenheim further mentions that the Permanent Court of International Justice has repeatedly held that an act which is not in accordance with law cannot confer upon a state a legal right.[67]

3 HAS ISRAEL ACQUIRED LEGAL SOVEREIGNTY OVER TERRITORIES SEIZED IN EXCESS OF THE PARTITION RESOLUTION?

The legal position with respect to the territories which Israel seized in 1948 and 1949 in excess of the territorial limits of the Jewish state as

[65] Official Records of the 3rd Session of the General Assembly, First Committee, Part I, p. 849.

[66] Oppenheim, *op. cit.*, pp. 141–142.

[67] Order of December 6 1930 in the case of the *Free Zones of Upper Savoy and the District of Gex* (2nd phase): *P.C.I.J.*, series A, No. 24; Order of August 3 1932, concerning the *South-Eastern Territory of Greenland*, *ibid.*, series A/B, No. 48, p. 285; Advisory Opinion of March 3 1928, the case of the *Jurisdiction of the Courts of Danzig*, *ibid.*, series B, No. 15, p. 26.

fixed by General Assembly resolution 181 (II) of November 29 1947 is also quite obvious.[68] On the one hand, the considerations already discussed that preclude the acquisition of legal sovereignty by Israel over the territory envisaged by the partition resolution for the Jewish state apply with equal force to the areas which Israel has seized in excess of the said resolution. Neither conquest nor occupation can give Israel any valid legal title to such territories. On the other hand, Israel's seizure of territories earmarked for the Arab state and the New City of Jerusalem can give it no title for the reason that such seizure is not only incompatible with international law but also constitutes a violation of General Assembly resolution 181 (II) of November 29 1947 which fixed and defined the geographical limits of the Jewish state, the Arab state and the City of Jerusalem. Juridically, therefore, Israel can have no possible claim to the territories which it seized in excess of the partition resolution, for it is inconceivable that it could acquire rights by violating a General Assembly resolution.

Israel has in turn invoked the partition resolution to justify its occupation of the territory envisaged for the Jewish state, and rejected and violated the same resolution by its seizure of territories earmarked for the Arab state.[69] In 1948 Count Bernadotte made it plain that Israel was not entitled to consider provisions of the partition resolution which are in its favour as effective and treat certain others of its provisions which are not in its favour as ineffective. In his reply dated July 6 1948 to the Israeli Government's letter of the preceding day wherein it objected to the Mediator's suggestions for a peaceful settlement of the Palestine Question on the ground of their 'deviations from the General Assembly resolution of November 29 1947',[70] Count Bernadotte stated as follows:

2. . . . You have not taken advantage of my invitation to offer counter-suggestions, unless I am to understand that your reference in Paragraphs 1 and 2 of your letter to the resolution of the General Assembly of November 29 1947 implies that you will be unwilling to consider any suggestions which do not correspond to the provisions of that resolution.

3. In paragraph 1 of your letter it is stated that my suggestions 'appear to ignore the resolution of the General Assembly of November 29 1947'. . . .

[68] The territories which Israel seized in excess of the partition resolution were described in Sections 2 and 3 (3) of Part I and are shown in Appendix VII.
[69] See Ben-Gurion, Israel, Années de Lutte (Flammarion, Paris, 1964), pp. 59 and 61.
[70] U.N. Document A/648, p. 9.

6. As regards paragraph 4 of your letter, I note that your Government no longer considers itself bound by the provisions for Economic Union set forth in the November 29 resolution for the reason that the Arab State envisaged by that resolution has not been established. In paragraphs 1 and 2, however, the same resolution is taken as your basic position. Whatever may be the precise legal significance and status of the November 29 resolution, it would seem quite clear to me that the situation is not of such a nature as to entitle either party to act on the assumption that such parts of the resolution as may be favourable to it may be regarded as effective, while those parts which may, by reason of changes in circumstances, be regarded as unfavourable are to be considered as ineffective.[71]

Israel may not blow hot and cold. It is elementary that Israel cannot claim title to the territory envisaged for the Jewish state under the General Assembly resolution and deny the title of the Palestinians to the territories envisaged for the Arab state under the same resolution. Such an attitude is tantamount to a denial by Israel of its birth certificate. In his Progress Report to the General Assembly of the United Nations, Count Bernadotte took the position, almost as a matter of course, that Israel is not entitled to retain the areas which it had occupied in excess of the partition resolution. He said in his Progress Report:

(C) The disposition of the territory of Palestine not included within the boundaries of the Jewish State should be left to the Governments of the Arab States in full consultation with the Arab inhabitants of Palestine, with the recommendation, however, that in view of the historical connexion and common interests of Transjordan and Palestine, there would be compelling reasons for merging the Arab territory of Palestine with the territory of Transjordan. . . .[72]

Count Bernadotte's view that Israel was not entitled to retain the areas which it seized in excess of the General Assembly's resolution was shared by the U.S. representatives at the third session of the General Assembly of the United Nations held at Paris in 1948. Dr. Philip C. Jessup, then U.S. representative, indicated the position of the United States as being that if Israel desired additions to the boundaries set forth

[71] Count Bernadotte's Progress Report to the General Assembly dated September 16 1948 (U.N. Document A/648) contains extracts only from the said letter. However, the full text of Count Bernadotte's letter to the Provisional Government of Israel dated July 6 1948 which contains the passages quoted above is set out in his diary published under the title *To Jerusalem* by Hodder and Stoughton, London, 1951, pp. 153–158.
[72] U.N. Document A/648, p. 18.

in the resolution of November 29 1947 'it would have to offer an appropriate exchange, acceptable to the Arabs, through negotiation'.[73] Similarly, Mr. Rusk for the United States declared at the same session that 'any modifications in the boundaries fixed by the resolution of 29 November 1947 could only be made if acceptable to the state of Israel. That meant that the territory allocated to the State of Israel could not be reduced without its consent. If, on the other hand, Israel wished to enlarge that territory, it would have to offer an exchange through negotiation.'[74]

The U.S. Government maintained its view that Israel cannot keep territory seized in excess of the partition resolution when it appeared during the meetings of the Conciliation Commission for Palestine held in Lausanne in 1949 that Israel's obdurate attitude regarding territory and refugees was preventing any settlement on the basis of the Lausanne Protocol. On May 29 1949 the U.S. Government addressed through its Ambassador, Mr. James G. McDonald, a note to Israel which:

> Expressed disappointment at the failure of Eytan (Israel's representative) at Lausanne to make any of the desired concessions on refugees and boundaries; interpreted Israel's attitude as dangerous to peace and as indicating disregard of the U.N. General Assembly resolutions of November 29 1947 (partition and frontiers), and December 11 1948 (refugees and internationalization of Jerusalem); reaffirmed insistence that territorial compensation should be made for territory taken in excess of November 29 resolution and that tangible refugee concessions should be made now as essential preliminary to any prospect for general settlement.[75]

During the debate in 1949 on Israel's application for admission to membership of the United Nations, Israel explained the discrepancy between the territory which it held at that time and the territory envisaged for the Jewish state by the resolution of November 29 1947 as follows:

> All the areas occupied by Israel's forces at this time are so occupied with the agreement concluded with Arab States under the resolution of November 16.[76]

---

[73] Official Records of the 3rd Session of the General Assembly, Part I, 1948, First Committee, pp. 682 and 727.

[74] Official Records of the 3rd Session of the General Assembly, 1948, *supra*, p. 836.

[75] James G. McDonald, *My Mission to Israel* (Simon and Schuster, New York, 1951), pp. 181–182.

[76] Official Records of the 3rd Session of the General Assembly, 1949, Part II, p. 347.

The 'resolution of 16 November' to which reference is made in the aforementioned statement was resolution No. 62 of the Security Council dated November 16 1948. This resolution took note that 'the General Assembly is continuing its consideration of the future Government of Palestine in response to the request of the Security Council in its resolution 44 (1948) of April 1 1948' and called upon the parties involved in the conflict to seek agreement with a view to the immediate establishment of the armistice. The 'agreement' mentioned by Israel's representative as a basis for its occupation can, therefore, only refer to the Armistice Agreements which had then been concluded with Egypt, Lebanon and Jordan under a resolution of the Security Council which envisaged that 'the future Government of Palestine' was still under consideration by the United Nations. This can only mean that the whole question of Palestine was in suspension. Furthermore, Israel's occupation of Palestinian territory under the Armistice Agreements is not and cannot be a source of title. In fact, the Armistice Agreements specifically provided that the armistice lines are not to be construed as political or territorial boundaries and are delineated 'without prejudice to the ultimate settlement of the Palestine Question'.

In order to justify the seizure of various areas falling outside the boundaries of the proposed Jewish state, Israel has suggested that it did not limit itself to the territorial boundaries of the partition resolution because the Arabs themselves had rejected the partition plan. According to Israel, the Arab refusal to accept partition and the military intervention of the Arab states have rendered the partition resolution null and void. This, in its view, opened the way for Israel to grab as much territory as it could. Israel's argument is specious and, of course, devoid of any legal basis. The Arabs had a perfect legal right to oppose the dismemberment of their country and to defend the territorial integrity of their homeland. The Arab refusal to accept partition and the ensuing strife between Arabs and Jews could in no way confer upon Israel the right to seize any part of the territory of Palestine and much less to usurp the territories reserved by the United Nations for the original people of Palestine. The fact that the latter were aggrieved by the partition resolution and considered it to be null and void and not binding upon them cannot be invoked by the Jews as an excuse for aggravating the wrong and usurping the remainder of Palestine. The Arab–Israeli conflict of 1948 did not take away, diminish or affect the rights of the Palestine Arabs nor enlarge the rights of the Jews. As regards the intervention of the Arab states, it was proclaimed in 1948 that the object of their intervention was to go to the help of the Palestinians who were the victims of Jewish terrorism and were threatened by the superior military force of the Jews. Lieutenant-General Burns has remarked that the Arabs outside Palestine had as much right to come to the assistance of Arabs in Palestine as Jews outside Palestine to come to the assistance of Jews within.[77] Israel's seizure in 1948 and 1949 of territories outside the geographical limits of the Jewish state as fixed by the partition resolution is a clear and obvious usurpation committed in violation of the General Assembly resolution. The United Nations did not consider that the Arab–Israeli conflict of 1948 affected in any way their resolutions on Palestine or that the results of the conflict enlarged the rights of the Jews in Palestine, for, as noted earlier, the General Assembly accepted Israel into the fold of the United Nations only after 'recalling its resolutions of November 29 1947 and December 11 1948 and taking note of the declarations and explanations made by the representative of the Government of Israel before the Ad Hoc Committee in respect of the implementation of the said resolutions'.[78] This took place on May 11 1949 long after the end of the 1948 conflict. Furthermore, as already mentioned in Section 2 of Part I, the Jews themselves have largely contributed to the defeat of the partition resolution by their seizure before the end of the mandate of the greater part of the territories reserved for the Palestine Arabs by such resolution. Hence, they cannot, in order to justify their seizure of territories in excess of the partition resolution, say that such resolution has lapsed as a result of the armed conflict of 1948.

In the light of the preceding considerations it is safe to say that Israel did not and could not gain title either to the territory which, as a result of an excess of competence and authority, the General Assembly designated as the area of the proposed Jewish state or to the territories which the General Assembly designated as the area of the proposed Arab state. The legal status of Israel in relation to the entirety of the territory which it occupied prior to June 5 1967 is identical with its status in relation to the territories which it seized since June 5 1967: it is the status of a belligerent occupier. And it is indifferent whether Israel is considered a

[77] E. L. M. Burns, *Between Arab and Israeli* (George G. Harrap & Co., London, 1962), p. 127.
[78] Resolution No. 273 (III) of May 11 1949. See Section 3 (2) of Part IV.

belligerent occupier or a conqueror. In neither case can it acquire sovereignty. 'Israel, alone among all the countries of the world, possesses not a single square inch of territory which she could assuredly proclaim to be her own in perpetuity.'[79] Israel does not possess any recognized frontiers but only armistice lines. Its relationship with its neighbours is still technically today a state of war suspended by the Armistice Agreements of 1949 and the cease-fire resolutions of the Security Council of June 1967. It is settled under international law that a belligerent occupier does not acquire sovereignty.[80] The legitimate sovereign, though prevented from exercising his authority, retains legal sovereignty. Professor Jèze has pointed out that the belligerent occupier acquires a 'sovereignty in fact but not in law':

> Cette prise de possession, qui repose exclusivement sur la force, n'entraine pas au profit du vainqueur l'acquisition du territoire occupé. . . . Supposons d'abord que l'Etat dont le territoire est envahi se refuse à traiter, et que le vainqueur maintienne son occupation. La domination de l'Etat victorieux sera une souveraineté de fait et non de droit. . . . Tant que des protestations se feront entendre, il y aura bien une domination de fait, mais non un état de droit.[81]

The basic attributes of sovereignty were set out in the French Constitution of September 3 1791 which declared: 'sovereignty is one, indivisible, inalienable and imprescriptible'. Title over Palestine lies in its original inhabitants, in whom sovereignty vested upon detachment of the country from Turkey. Their sovereignty over their ancestral land is 'one, indivisible, inalienable and imprescriptible' and extends to the whole territory of Palestine regardless of any partition, occupation, usurpation or lapse of time.

The people of Palestine have never given their consent to any transfer of title over their country nor have they recognized any sovereignty in the occupier. 'In present day international law', observes Professor Schwarzenberger, 'it is by itself not sufficient to transform wartime occupation into a transfer of sovereignty. Even in the relations between

[79] Hedley V. Cooke, *Israel, A Blessing and a Curse* (Stevens and Sons, London, 1960), p. 186.

[80] Oppenheim, *International Law* (Longmans, London, 1963), 7th ed., Vol. II, p. 618.

[81] Gaston Jèze, *Etude Théorique et Pratique sur l'Occupation* (Paris, 1896), pp. 44–46. See also Ian Brownlie, *Principles of Public International Law* (Oxford, 1966) who refers to the continued existence of legal personality under international law despite that the process of government in an area falls into the hands of another state, pp. 100–102.

belligerents, not to speak of third States, the title requires to be consolidated by positive acts of recognition or consent or, at least, by acquiescence of the former territorial sovereign.'[82]

It might perhaps be argued that Israel is a state which is recognized by a large number of other states. Such recognition, however, is not general. Israel is not recognized by the Arab states nor by a large number of other states. More important still, Israel is not recognized by the original people of Palestine in whom sovereignty lies. The fact of recognition by other states cannot give to Israel what it lacks: legal sovereignty. Under international law recognition does not confer sovereignty. The recognition or non-recognition of a state is not determined at present under international law by considerations relating to its legitimacy or regularity of origin. Professor Philip C. Jessup has observed that the practice of basing recognition on constitutional legitimacy instead of on actual existence and control of the country has not as yet been widely enough accepted to be acknowledged as having the force of customary law.[83] Recognition by other states does not remove the vice with which an occupation is tainted:

> La reconnaissance par les Puissances ne peut avoir au point de vue juridique aucune influence sur la validité de l'occupation. . . . La reconnaissance du fait accompli par les Puissances civilisées est impuissante à couvrir le vice qui entache la prise de possession.[84]

Nor does lapse of time make legitimate Israel's wrongful occupation of Palestine. Professor Giraud has observed that in contrast to private law, no prescription is envisaged by international law to regularize irregular situations.[85]

---

[82] G. Schwarzenberger, *International Law*, 3rd ed., p. 302.

[83] *AJIL* (1931), p. 721.

[84] Gaston Jèze, *Etude Théorique et Pratique sur l'Occupation* (Paris, 1896), p. 298.

[85] E. Giraud, *Le Droit International et la Politique*, Académie de Droit International, *Recueil des Cours*, 1963, Vol. III, p. 425.

The Question of Sovereignty over Palestine

NATHAN FEINBERG

If I were asked to sum up the contents of Henry Cattan's book "Palestine, The Arab and Israel, The Search for Justice" [1] in a few sentences, I believe that the best way of doing so would be to quote a number of the author's contentions and statements in his own words. "Israel", he writes, "is an illegitimate and unnatural creation" [2]; "the essence of the [Arab–Israel] conflict... is the basic injustice of 1948" [3]; "the first misconception concerns the possibility of acceptance by the Arabs of the factual situation created by Israel in 1948" [4]; "the liquidation of the consequences of the conflict of June 1967 alone will not solve the basic issues involved in the Palestine Question" [5]; "the establishment of a just and lasting peace requires much more than the withdrawal of Israeli forces from the territories occupied during the recent conflict [of 1967]" [6]; "the people of Palestine have never given their consent to any transfer of title over their territory nor have they recognized any sovereignty in the occupier" [7]; "the Palestine injustice cannot be buried under

---

1. Henry Cattan, *Palestine, The Arabs and Israel, The Search for Justice* (hereafter quoted as Cattan, *Palestine*) (London, 1969).
2. *Ibid.*, p. 138. 3. *Ibid.*, p. 139.
4. *Ibid.*, p. 140. 5. *Ibid.*, pp. 181—182.
6. *Ibid.*, p. 182. 7. *Ibid.*, p. 274.

a *fait accompli*" [8]; "Israel has often said that 'the clock cannot be turned back'.... But... history shows that many a time the clock was, in fact, turned back to redress a glaring injustice or to remove a colonialist implantation. If justice is to be done in Palestine and peace to be restored to the Middle East the clock must be turned back." [9]

Yet the question arises: how does one turn back the clock of history? Nor is the question pertinent only today, twenty three years after the establishment of the State of Israel. The United Nations Mediator, Count Bernadotte, asked the very same thing just seven weeks after Israel came into being. In his reply of 5 July 1948 to a letter in which the Arab League had proposed the elimination of Israel as an independent political entity and the establishment of a unitary Arab State in Palestine, with full rights and guarantees for the Jewish minority, Bernadotte put the grave counter-question: how could this be done by peaceful means? "I am fully convinced", he wrote, "that there is no possibility whatever of persuading or inducing the Jews to give up their present separate cultural and political existence and accept merging in a unitary Palestine in which they would be a permanent minority. The alternative method of achieving the Arab objective would be to wipe out the Jewish State and its Provisional Government by force. This course as Mediator, I obviously cannot recommend." [10]

8. *Ibid.*, p. 141.   9. *Ibid.*
10. U.N. Doc. A/648, *Progress Report of the United Nations Mediator on Palestine* (1948), p. 24.

Cattan's book, as its contents indicate, is aimed, first and foremost, at the law-abiding and peace-loving reader, who cannot be won over to the Arab cause by advocacy of the use of force.[11] Accordingly, the author finds it necessary to adopt other means of achieving his purpose and, to this end, formulates two legal propositions, on the basis of which he seeks to show that "turning the clock back" is both lawful and possible. The first of his propositions is that, despite the decisions on Palestine taken by international bodies and despite the establishment of the State of Israel, the Arabs of the former British Mandated territory still hold sovereign rights over Palestine today. The second is that, in view of the special circumstances in which the State of Israel came into being and the undertakings that it assumed on becoming a member of the United Nations, the latter Organization is competent to reexamine the Partition Plan of 1947 and impose on Israel any settlement which the United Nations may deem proper to redress the injustice suffered by the Arabs in consequence of the Plan.

Let us begin then by examining these two propositions, which constitute the central theme of Cattan's book. After that, a number of the other questions raised will be considered.

11. In Cattan's book one does not find the routine accusations made in the Arab literature that Israel is "a colonial fact", "a colonial phenomenon", "a beach-head of the capitalist world", "the ally of the capitalist Powers". See, for example: *Colloque de Juristes Arabes sur la Palestine — La Question Palestinienne, Alger 22-27 Juillet 1967* (hereafter quoted as *Colloque*) (Alger, 1968), pp. 44, 57, 110.

I. The Question of Sovereignty over Palestine

Cattan devotes a special appendix to the subject of sovereignty. He is right in saying that "the question of sovereignty over Palestine is of a strictly juridical nature" [12] and that it "has an important bearing upon the eventual solution [of the Arab–Israel conflict]" [13]. However, his conclusions on this matter are extremely arbitrary and without any foundation in current international law.

1. *"Legal sovereignty" and "political sovereignty"*

In his book, Cattan draws a distinction between "legal sovereignty" and "political sovereignty". According to his definition, the latter means "factual dominion and control" over a certain area of land, whereas the former is "the legal and inalienable title... of a nation to a territory" [14]. "Notwithstanding the political vicissitudes in Palestine during the last fifty years", he holds, "legal sovereignty still lies today in the original inhabitants of the country as they existed at the time of the detachment of Palestine from Turkey at the end of the First World War." [15]

The first point to make in this connection is that "legal sovereignty" and "political sovereignty" are not accepted terms in public international law. To the best of my knowledge they do not appear in any of the many textbooks on this branch of the law; nor are they mentioned in the *Dictionnaire de la terminologie du droit interna-*

12. Cattan, *Palestine*, p. 183.   13. *Ibid.*, p. 242.
14. *Ibid.*, pp. 242, 243.   15. *Ibid.*

tional — published in 1960 under the auspices of Professor Basdevant — where all the various meanings of the term "sovereignty" are clarified and defined [16]. Professor Schwarzenberger did, it is true, resort to these two terms some years ago in his lectures at the Hague Academy of International Law — and it is on these lectures that Cattan bases himself. But Schwarzenberger used the terms in a completely different sense from that which Cattan seeks to give them. For Schwarzenberger, political sovereignty is not the antithesis of legal sovereignty; his contention is that, in the atomic age, not all of the States which enjoy legal sovereignty are equally sovereign in the political sense. "At present", he writes, "[only the States] which are able to produce the superweapons of our age or are relatively immune against their application... have freedom of decision in situations in which, owing to lack of such weapons or means of effective protection against their application, other States may consider it advisable to act differently from how they would if they were sovereign in the political sense." [17] Cattan also cites the jurist

16. See : *Dictionnaire de la terminologie du droit international* (Paris, 1960), pp. 573—579.
17. G. Schwarzenberger, "The Fundamental Principles of International Law", *Recueil des Cours de l'Academie de Droit International* (hereafter quoted as *R.A.D.I.*), tome 87 (Paris, 1956), p. 215.
    The sentence cited by Cattan from Schwarzenberger's lectures ... "the last word is still not with law, but power" (Cattan, *Palestine*, p. 243) — does not appear in the lectures as a general statement in an independent sentence. It expressly relates to the differences of opinion between the two existing blocs and is preceded by the words : "It would mean to ignore

Brownlie on this point [18]; but the two terms in question do not appear either in the pages of Brownlie's book to which he refers the reader [19], or on the following page where the same subject is dealt with [20]. Nor do I find any authority there for the substantive meaning which Cattan attributes to those terms. Moreover, Cattan's attempt to weave into the present context the question of the conquest of one State by another — such as the conquest of Austria by Nazi Germany — is quite irrelevant [21]. The conquering State does not acquire sovereignty — not even "political sovereignty", to use Cattan's terminology — but "authority", as provided by Article 42 of the Annex to the Fourth Hague Convention of 1907, respecting the laws and customs of war on land.

Yet a further indication of the extent to which Cattan's use of the concept of sovereignty is arbitrary is to be found in the following passage from his own book: "Prior to the occupation of Palestine by the British Army in 1917, during the First World War, Palestine formed an integral part of Turkey... . The Turkish constitution made no distinction between Turk or Arab or between Moslem or Christian or Jew. Turks and Arabs, therefore, shared sovereignty over all of the territories of the Turkish Empire regardless as to whether such territories were Turkish or Arab provinces." [22] And a few pages

that, at least in the overall relations between West and East" (Schwarzenberger, op. cit., p. 215).
18. Ian Brownlie, Principles of Public International Law (Oxford, 1966), pp. 100—102.
19. Cattan, Palestine, p. 243.   20. Brownlie, op. cit., p. 103.
21. Cattan, Palestine, p. 243.   22. Ibid., pp. 243—244.

further on, he reiterates this point in these words: "It has been made amply clear that Arabs and Turks enjoyed equal rights and shared sovereignty over the whole Turkish Empire." [23] Is it really possible to contend, in all seriousness, that the Arabs shared with the Turks — in the time of the Sultan Abdul Hamid, or under the Young Turks — sovereignty over the whole of the Ottoman Empire?

Whatever the terminology that Cattan may choose to employ, it can be assumed that, in using the phrase "legal sovereignty", he had in mind what it is usual to call "self-determination", or in French — "droit des peuples à disposer d'eux-mêmes". I have already taken the opportunity in an earlier publication [24] of discussing in some detail the place of the question of self-determination in the Arab–Israel conflict, both from a legal point of view and from political and moral points of view. Accordingly, I can confine my remarks here to a summary of the main conclusions [25]. In that earlier work, I stressed the fact that right up to the present day there are differences of opinion as to whether self-determination of peoples is a binding rule of positive international law, or merely a political principle or moral postulate. But one point is clear beyond any doubt: it was not a binding rule of law

23. *Ibid.*, p. 245, note 9.
24. N. Feinberg, *The Arab-Israel Conflict in International Law, A Critical Analysis of the Colloquium of Arab Jurists in Algiers* (Jerusalem, 1970), pp. 44—55.
25. I shall adopt the same course in the case of other arguments in Cattan's book on which I have already expressed my views in my book on the *Colloque*.

at any of the many stages on the road towards the emergence of the State of Israel — neither on 2 November 1917, the date of the Balfour Declaration; nor on 24 July 1922, when the Palestine Mandate was finally defined by the Council of the League of Nations; nor on 29 November 1947, when the General Assembly of the United Nations passed its Resolution on the partition of Palestine; nor on 15 May 1948, the date of the establishment of the State of Israel. Support for this conclusion can even be found in the work of the Algerian jurist Mohammed Bedjaoui [26], who opened and closed the Colloquium of Arab jurists in Algiers and whose views — one may assume — will not be without weight among advocates of the Arab case. It would seem to follow, then, that the distinction and terms underlying Cattan's discussion of the question of sovereignty have no basis whatsoever in international law; and, if our assumption is correct that by "legal sovereignty" Cattan meant the right of self-determination, then neither on the day of the establishment of the State of Israel, nor in the period preceding that event, was that principle recognized as a binding rule of positive international law.

2. Turkey's views on the Jewish National Home and the Treaty of Lausanne

Cattan contends that Turkey opposed the setting up of the Jewish national home and that in Article 16 of the Treaty of Lausanne, which it signed in 1923, it renounced

26. See: Mohammed Bedjaoui, *Law and the Algerian Revolution* (Brussels, 1961), pp. 241—243.

its rights over Palestine to the Arabs [27]. These claims are without any foundation in law or in fact.

(a) *The Treaty of Sèvres.* Because the Balfour Declaration is mentioned in the Treaty of Sèvres (which remained unratified), but not in the Treaty of Lausanne, Cattan draws the conclusion that "Turkey refused to subscribe to... [the] provision [regarding the national home]" [28]. But this is completely to ignore the fact that the Treaty of Sèvres was signed two years before the confirmation of the Palestine Mandate by the Council of the League of Nations, whereas the Treaty of Lausanne was signed exactly one year after its confirmation. In the circumstances, it was quite logical and reasonable for those who drafted the Treaty of Lausanne to refer, in Article 16, to "the future of these territories [that Turkey renounced] being settled or to be settled by the parties concerned"; and, in so far as Palestine is concerned, it is the words "being settled", not "to be settled", that apply, for — as we have already seen — the decision on the settlement had already been taken on 24 July 1922, with the final drafting of the Palestine Mandate by the League of Nations [29].

27. Cattan, *Palestine,* pp. 246—247; and see *ibid.,* p. 18.
28. *Ibid.,* p. 247.
29. The fact that the Palestine Mandate only came into force fourteen months after its confirmation by the Council of the League of Nations is attributed by Cattan to Turkey's objection to the Jewish national home (*ibid.,* p. 18). But this is not the case. The real reason for the delay was the dispute between France and Italy as to certain provisions of the Mandate for Syria and the Lebanon, and France's demand that the latter Mandate come into force at the same time as the Palestine

(b) *Article 16 of the Treaty of Lausanne.* In Cattan's opinion, "the parties concerned" referred to in Article 16 are "the communities which inhabited these territories, since they were the parties primarily concerned" [30]. This interpretation is unconvincing. The words "the parties concerned" were used in Article 16 because it was impossible to resort to the usual term "the Contracting Parties", since that included not only the Principal Allied Powers, but also Greece, Romania and Yugoslavia. Nor was it possible to use the term "the Governments concerned" — as was done, for example, in Articles 49 and 92 of the Treaty — for the Covenant of the League of Nations, which was already in force at the time when the Treaty was being drafted, entrusted the Council with an important — and even decisive — role in the framing of the Mandates. Clearly, then, the words "the parties concerned" can in no way be regarded as referring to the Arabs [31].

Mandate. On 29 September 1923 the French and Italian representatives notified the League of Nations that the differences between their two countries had been reconciled, and on the very same day the Mandates came into force. See: *League of Nations, The Mandates System, Origin—Principles—Application* (Geneva, 1945), pp. 20-21; *League of Nations, Permanent Mandates Commission* (hereafter quoted as *P.M.C.*) *Minutes of the Second Session* (Geneva, 1922), p. 10.

30. Cattan, *Palestine*, p. 247.
31. Cattan also dwells on a difference in the wording of Articles 15 and 16: whereas in Article 15 Turkey renounces certain territories "in favour of Italy", there is no indication in Article 16 in whose favour it renounced. On the strength of this difference, he draws the conclusion that, in the case of Palestine, there was no need for any clarification, since "the original in-

(c) *The provisions as to Palestinian nationality.* There is yet another point which proves that Turkey had no objection to the establishment of the Jewish national home in Palestine. In the draft of the Treaty presented to the Turkish delegation on 31 January 1923, it was provided — in Article 35 — that "Jews of other than Turkish nationality who are habitually resident in Palestine on the coming into force of the present Treaty will have the right to become citizens of Palestine by making a declaration in such form and under such conditions as may be prescribed by law" [32]. And in the letter sent from Ankara on 4 February 1923 to the heads of the British, French and Italian delegations, Ismet Pasha,

habitants ... already possessed sovereignty over their own territories" (*ibid.*). If the position with regard to Palestine were really as Cattan presents it, there would have been no point at all in speaking of "the future of the territories ... being settled", for sovereignty — according to his approach — was automatically vested in the Arab inhabitants of Palestine. In fact, Cattan himself points out the true reason why Article 16 makes no mention of the entity in whose favour the territories are renounced when he writes: "it was not the intention that the Principal Allied Powers or any one of them should acquire sovereignty over the Arab provinces" (*ibid.*). Nor does Cattan's reference, in this context, to a judgment given in the United States in 1905, in connection with the treaty on Cuba between the United States and Spain, support his argument. In that case the Court was concerned with the transfer of sovereignty to the inhabitants of Cuba who "were declared to be free and independent" (*ibid.*, p. 248), whereas Palestine was placed under a Mandatory regime and the Mandatory was expressly bound to set up a Jewish national home there.

32. *Cmd. 1814, Turkey No. 1 (1923), Lausanne Conference on Near Eastern Affairs, 1922—1923* (London, 1923), pp. 697—698.

head of the Turkish delegation, declared, *inter alia,* that
Turkey unreservedly accepts the proposed arrangement
as to citizenship [33]. The said provision of Article 35 was,
it is true, eventually omitted from the final text of the
Treaty of Lausanne; this, however, was not because
Turkey changed its mind about accepting the arrangement, but because of certain misgivings from the point
of view of the French law on citizenship, raised at the
Conference by the French representative, who, by the
way, took the opportunity of pointing out that, in principle, he had no objection to the provision in question [34].

3. *The "sovereignty" of the original inhabitants of Palestine by virtue of the Mandates system*

Cattan seeks to base the "legal sovereignty" — to use his
terminology — of the original inhabitants of Palestine
over this territory on the international Mandates system,
too. To this end, he relies on one of the many doctrines
as to the question of sovereignty over Mandated territories
prevalent in the period of the League of Nations. According to this doctrine, sovereignty over such a territory
did not reside in the Principal Allied and Associated
Powers, or in the Mandatory Power or the League of Na-

---

33. *Ibid.,* pp. 837–841.
34. *Conférence de Lausanne sur les affaires du Proche Orient
(1922–1923), Recueil des Actes de la Conférence, deuxiéme
série, tome 1er, Procès-verbaux et documents relatifs à la seconde
partie de la Conférence* (Paris, 1923), p. 23; see also N. Feinberg, "The Principles of Palestinian Citizenship as laid down
by International Law", *Some Problems of the Palestine
Mandate* (Tel Aviv, 1936), pp. 47–64.

tions, but in the inhabitants themselves. Cattan's contention is that "all these various views... — except that which considers sovereignty to reside in the inhabitants of the Mandated territories — have now been abandoned or discredited. None of the [others]... appears to rest on an acceptable legal or logical basis." [35]

It is worth making quite clear at the outset that Cattan's claim, that the doctrines which he dismisses have been abandoned, is unfounded. In 1950, Kerno, addressing the International Court of Justice on behalf of the Secretariat of the United Nations Organization, stressed, in the course of his survey of the various doctrines as to sovereignty over Mandated territories, that despite the abundance of legal theories "there exists no consensus, nor even a clearly discernible preponderance of opinion" [36]. This is not the occasion to establish which of these doctrines was, and is now, the correct one. For the purposes of the present discussion I am prepared to accept the one adopted by Cattan; but, even so, this does not prove the accuracy of his thesis. By Article 22, paragraph 8, of the Covenant of the League of Nations, the terms of the Mandates were to be "explicitly defined" in each case by the Council of the League [37]. Cattan has taken the easy way out and completely ignored the provisions of the Palestine Mandate. But, of course, he cannot by doing so eradicate the following facts: the second

35. Cattan, *Palestine,* p. 249.
36. *International Court of Justice, Pleadings, Oral Arguments, Documents, International Status of South West Africa, Advisory Opinion of July 11th, 1950,* p. 192.
37. *Ibid.,* p. 191.

paragraph of the preamble to the Palestine Mandate — the international constitution, in accordance with whose provisions the Mandated territory of Palestine was to be administered — embodies the Balfour Declaration [38]; in the second Article, the Mandatory was made "responsible for placing the country under such political, administrative and economic conditions as will secure the establishment of the Jewish national home"; the sixth Article called on the Mandatory to "facilitate Jewish immigration under suitable conditions and encourage... close settlement by Jews on the land"; the seventh requires the Mandatory to "facilitate the acquisition of Palestine citizenship by Jews who take up their permanent residence in Palestine"; and in the White Paper of 1922, published by the British Government as a definition of its future policy in Palestine immediately prior to the confirmation of the Mandate, we find this statement — "it is essential that it [the Jewish people] should know that it is in Palestine as of right

38. The Spanish member of the Permanent Mandates Commission, Professor L. Palacios, defined the Balfour Declaration as "the very soul of the Mandate" (*P.M.C., Minutes of the Twenty-Seventh Session,* Geneva, 1935, p. 198). And the British Royal Commission of 1936, too, under the chairmanship of Lord Peel, held that "unquestionably, ... the primary purpose of the Mandate ... is to promote the establishment of the Jewish National Home" (*Cmd. 5479, Palestine Royal Commission Report,* London, 1937, p. 39). Again, in 1946, the Anglo-American Committee of Enquiry of that year also came to the conclusion that "though extensive safeguards were provided for the non-Jewish peoples, the Mandate was framed primarily in the Jewish interest" (*Cmd. 6808, Report of the Anglo-American Committee of Enquiry regarding the Problems of European Jewry and Palestine,* London, 1946, p. 61).

and not on sufferance" [39]. In the face of these clear and express provisions, what possible legal significance is to be attributed to Cattan's claim that the Jews who immigrated to Palestine during the Mandate were "mainly aliens — both in origin and nationality" [40], or that "Ben Gurion... came to Palestine... as a Russian tourist" [41], or there was an "implantation in Palestine of a foreign people" [42]. In support of his case, Cattan cites extensive passages from the book of van Rees, Vice-Chairman of the Permanent Mandates Commission [43]. But surely, in reading that book he cannot have failed to notice the following words on the Palestine Mandate and the return of the Jews to Palestine: "In virtue of the Balfour Declaration, brought in the opening passage of the Mandate, [the Jewish people] is — in effect — a part of the inhabitants of Palestine." [44] And some two years later, at one of the sessions of the Permanent Mandates Commission, van Rees declared: "[the Jewish] people would not enter the country as foreigners... ." [45]

39. *Cmd. 1700, Palestine, Correspondence with the Palestine Arab Delegation and the Zionist Organization* (London, 1922), p. 19.
40. Cattan, *Palestine,* p. 267.
41. *Ibid.,* p. 267, note 62.
42. *Ibid.,* p. 25. See also, in the same vein, pp. 28, 39, 266, 268.
43. *Ibid.,* p. 250.
44. D.F.W. Van Rees, *Les mandats internationaux, Les principes généraux du régime des Mandats,* tome 1 (Paris, 1928), p. 100. The passage cited here and subsequent passages cited in English from works in French or other languages are in the writer's own translation.
45. *P.M.C., Minutes of the Seventeenth (Extraordinary) Session* (Geneva, 1930), p. 39. Cattan also refers to a resolution, adopted in 1931 by the Institute of International Law, which

4. *The Balfour Declaration and the Palestine Mandate*

Turning to the question "whether Israel has acquired sovereignty over the territory which was allocated to the Jewish State by the partition resolution", Cattan remarks that it "can be examined in the light of three political developments... . These three developments are : the Balfour Declaration of November 2, 1917; the United Nations resolution on the partition of Palestine of November 29, 1947, and the forcible occupation [sic !] in 1948 and 1949 of the territory earmarked for the proposed state by the said resolution." [46]

I find it difficult to understand why Cattan includes the Balfour Declaration in that list and not the Palestine Mandate. He may have done so because it is so much easier to treat the Declaration as if it claimed a legal significance, which it does not have, and then proceed to prove that it lacks that significance, than to put for-

---

"described the Communities under the Mandate as subjects of international law" (Cattan, *Palestine*, p. 251). But that resolution is no authority for his thesis as to the "legal sovereignty" of the Arabs over Palestine, for what it said, *inter alia*, was this: "the Mandate is created in each case by act of the Council of the League of Nations" and "that act of Mandate defines the obligations of the Mandatory Power" (H. Wehberg, *Institut de Droit International, Tableau général des résolutions, 1873-1956,* Bâle, 1957, p. 18). And, as already pointed out, the Palestine Mandate imposed on the Mandatory Power the task of setting up a Jewish national home in Palestine. Moreover, throughout the years of its existence, the League of Nations fully exercised its supervisory powers to ensure that this obligation was faithfully carried out.

46. Cattan, *Palestine,* p. 255.

ward any persuasive legal arguments against the validity of the Palestine Mandate.

At all events, Cattan reiterates the old Arab contention that "at no time did the British Government as the author of such declaration possess any right of sovereignty over Palestine, whether on the date on which the Balfour Declaration was made or at any time thereafter, which could have enabled it to recognize any rights in favour of the Jewish people in or over Palestine" [47], and that "from the juridical standpoint, therefore, any claim by the Jews to Palestine on the basis of the Balfour Declaration is entirely groundless, if not plainly nonsensical" [48]. "The Balfour Declaration", he adds, "... never possessed any juridical value." [49]

This line of argument is pointless. The Balfour Declaration was never intended to determine the fate and future of Palestine. All that that document provided was that "His Majesty's Government *view with favour* [50] the es-

47. *Ibid.*   48. *Ibid.,* p. 260.

49. *Ibid.,* p. 255. It is surprising that Cattan also sees fit to rely on Professor Mallison's article (Cattan, *ibid.,* p. 256), for in it Mallison specifically expresses the view that "the Balfour Declaration is now a part of customary international law" and that while "the Anglo-American Convention on Palestine, 1924, is no longer in effect, as such, ... the Balfour Declaration included in it is valid as customary law ...". See: W. T. Mallison Jr., "The Zionist-Israel Juridical Claims to Constitute 'The Jewish People' Nationality Entity and to Confer Membership in it: Appraisal in Public International Law", *The George Washington Law Review,* vol. 32 (Washington 1964), p. 1030 and p. 1035, note 230. I confess that it is difficult to grasp the full meaning of this statement; but one thing is clear — it can hardly be said to add to the force of Cattan's case.

50. Italics added.

tablishment in Palestine of a national home for the Jewish people and *will use its best endeavours* [51] to facilitate the achievement of this object..." [52]. There was nothing at all wrong in giving such a promise. It was no more an infringement of international law than was giving promises to the Arabs and other nations during the War. The Balfour Declaration became a binding and unchallengeable international obligation from the moment when it was embodied in the Palestine Mandate, which the distinguished judge, Moore, went so far as to define — in his opinion in the Permanent Court of International Justice in the Mavrommatis Case — as "in a sense an [international] legislative act of the Council" [53]. That the Palestine Mandate was *sui generis* in so far as international Mandates are concerned in no way detracts from its legality [54]. Cattan's constant reference to the Balfour Declaration, while intentionally ignoring the fact that it

51. Italics added.
52. By the way, the Balfour Declaration was not the first to be issued in support of Zionist aspirations. It was preceded by the declaration given on 4 June 1917 by Jules Cambon, Secretary-General of the French Foreign Office, to Nahum Sokolow, one of the leaders of the World Zionist Organization, in these words: "The French Government, which entered this present war to defend a people wrongfully attacked, and which continues to struggle to assure the victory of right over might, can but feel sympathy for your cause ['the renaissance of the Jewish nationality in the land from which the people of Israel were exiled so many centuries ago'], the triumph of which is bound up with that of the Allies." See: N. Sokolow, *History of Zionism, 1600—1918*, vol. II (London, 1919), p. 53.
53. *Permanent Court of International Justice, Series A, No. 2, The Mavrommatis Palestine Concessions* (1924), p. 69.
54. See Feinberg, *The Arab-Israel Conflict*, pp. 38–44.

formed part of the Mandate, makes his case meaningless from a legal point of view.

5. *The power of the General Assembly of the United Nations in respect of the Resolution on the partition of Palestine*

Cattan stresses that his "inquiry does not concern the wisdom or justice of partition...", but whether the Partition Resolution was within the Assembly's powers at all. In his opinion, "the legal position in this regard is quite clear and obvious [55].... The partition resolution... lacked all juridical basis, was not within the powers of the General Assembly, and could not confer any valid title upon Israel over such part of Palestine as was earmarked for the Jewish state [56].... The Arabs had a perfect legal right to oppose the dismemberment of their country and to defend the territorial integrity of their homeland." [57]

55. Cattan, *Palestine,* p. 261. See also: *ibid.,* p. 262.
56. *Ibid.,* p. 265. See also: *ibid.,* pp. 268, 269.
57. On this point, Cattan rests his case on passages from the report of Sub-Committee II of the 1947 Assembly's Ad Hoc Committee on the Palestine Question (*ibid.,* pp. 263–264). He also draws on the Sub-Committee's conclusions on a number of other occasions (*ibid.,* pp. 28, 29) and even introduced, in an appendix to his book, a map prepared by it on land-ownership in Palestine in 1945 (*ibid.,* p. 210). It is pertinent to remark here that Sub-Committee II was composed solely of representatives of those States which, in principle, opposed the partition plan, as put forward by the majority of the members of U.N.S.C.O.P. (United Nations Special Committee on Palestine), and favoured the establishment of "an independent, unitary State", as put forward by a minority. On the Sub-Committee were the representatives of six Arab States and of Pakistan, Afghanistan and Colombia. There was

It is surprising that Cattan — like certain other jurists — resorts to this argument that the Assembly exceeded its powers, for, already in 1950, the International Court of Justice, in its Advisory Opinion on South West Africa, unanimously held that "the competence to determine and modify the international status... [of a Mandated territory]" rests with the Mandatory, acting with the consent of the United Nations Assembly [58]. Cattan cites the statement made by the Chinese representative, at the winding up session of the League of Nations in 1946, that the Charter of the United Nations contains no provision for the assumption by the United Nations of the League's functions with regard to Mandates [59]. But, whatever weight Cattan may attribute to the opinion of China's representative, the fact remains that the International Court has held otherwise. "The Court", writes Professor Bastid, "... has held that the Assembly of the United Nations replaces the organs of control already existing as part of the machinery of the League of Na-

---

a feeling that, to avoid the appearance of one-sidedness, its composition should be altered, and the representatives of two Arab States were prepared to vacate their places in favour of neutrals or of countries which had not definitely committed themselves to any particular solution of the Palestine Question. The Chairman of the Sub-Committee, Colombia's representative, did not see fit to accede to the proposal made in this connection and, in consequence of this refusal, he resigned. The representative of Pakistan was elected in his place. See: *Yearbook of the United Nations, 1947—1948* (New York, 1949), p. 240.

58. *International Status of South-West Africa, Advisory Opinion*: *I.C.J. Reports 1950*, p. 144.

59. Cattan, *Palestine*, p. 261.

tions" [60]; and she then goes on to say: "The Court has equally recognized [the Assembly's] power to modify the international status [of a Mandated territory]." [61] This includes the power to change the status of a Mandated territory by setting up two States. Thus, for example, the Mandate for Syria and the Lebanon of 1922 expressly provided that, on its termination, two separate States would be set up — not a single unitary State. Moreover, when — in 1937 — the British Royal Commission voiced the possibility of the partition of Palestine, and the Council of the League of Nations and the Permanent Mandates Commission were asked to consider that proposal, no questions at all were raised as to the illegality of partition. Nor did the United Nations regard itself as incompetent to approve the partition of the trust territory of Ruanda-Urundi into two States — Rwanda and Burundi — despite the fact that the trusteeship agreement of 1946 contained no express or implied authority for partition of the territory. And, in 1962, the Assembly of the United Nations felt under no obligation to reject *a limine*, on grounds of illegality, the plan for the partition of South West Africa, but went on to discuss the substantive merits of that plan [62].

---

60. S. Bastid, "La jurisprudence de la Cour Internationale de Justice", *R.A.D.I.*, tome 78 (Paris, 1952), p. 665.
61. *Ibid.*, p. 667.
62. For details on this question see: Feinberg, *The Arab-Israel Conflict*, pp. 55—71.

6. *The status of Israel's territory under the Armistice Agreements*

Since, as we have seen, Cattan denies Israel's sovereignty even over the territory allotted to it in the Partition Resolution, it goes without saying that he does not recognize its right to territories beyond the boundaries provided for in that Resolution but included within its boundaries under the Armistice Agreements [63]. In addition to his general arguments in support of his thesis, he invokes — in the present context — yet another reason: "Israel's occupation of the Palestinian Territory under the Armistice Agreements" "is not and cannot be a source of title" [64], for in each of them (with Egypt, Jordan, the Lebanon and Syria) it is "specifically provided that the armistice lines are not to be construed as political or territorial boundaries and are delineated 'without prejudice to the ultimate settlement of the Palestine Question' " [65]. The first point to make here is that in the above sentence, cited by Cattan from the text of the Armistice Agreements, the word "peaceful" is omitted between the words "ultimate" and "settlement", without this omission being indicated, as is customary, by a dotted line or dashes. Moreover, each of the four Agreements stipulates that "no provision... shall in any way prejudice the rights, claims and positions of either Party", words which constitute an unequivocal acknowledgement of the fact that Israel, too, has rights, claims, and so on. Secondly, it is

63. Cattan, *Palestine,* pp. 157, 160.
64. *Ibid.,* p. 272.   65. *Ibid.*

difficult to understand why Cattan ignores the many other provisions of the Armistice Agreements which are of so much greater significance than the one that he refers to. Thus, each of the Agreements states that its purpose is "to facilitate the transition from the present truce to permanent peace in Palestine"; that "the right of each Party to its security and freedom from fear of attack by the armed forces of the other shall be fully respected"; that "no aggressive action by the armed forces... of either Party shall be undertaken, planned or threatened against the people or the armed forces of the other"; that neither Party shall "... advance beyond or pass over for any purpose whatsoever the Armistice Demarcation Lines"; and that the Parties are not "to revise or to suspend the application" of the provisions forbidding the use of force, even by mutual consent. In the light of these perfectly clear provisions, there is only one possible answer to the question of the legal status of the territories outside the boundaries delineated by the Partition Resolution : the Arab States undertook to respect the armistice lines and refrain from revising them unless Israel give its consent to such revision in the course of the drafting of a "permanent peace settlement" [66]. I should add that, even if this prohibition were not expressly included in the Armistice Agreements, it would apply by virtue of Article 2, paragraph 4, of the Charter of the United Nations, which forbids the threat or use of force against "the territorial integrity or political independence of any State" [67].

66. See: Feinberg, *The Arab-Israel Conflict*, pp. 76–79.
67. In a textbook on international law published in the Soviet

And those who in 1970 drafted the "Declaration on Principles of International Law concerning Friendly Relations and Cooperation among States in accordance with the Charter of the United Nations", formally and unanimously adopted by the twenty-fifth General Assembly, saw fit to declare in express terms that the prohibition against the threat or use of force also applies to "international lines of demarcation such as armistice lines" [68].

7. The contention that Israel has no claim to sovereignty over a single square inch of Palestinian soil

Cattan concludes his discussion of the question of sovereignty with the following statement: "The legal status of Israel in relation to the entirety of the territory which it occupied prior to June 5, 1967 is identical with the status in relation to the territories which it seized since June 5, 1967: it is the status of a belligerent occupier. And it is indifferent whether Israel is considered a belligerent occupier or a conqueror. In neither case can

---

Union in 1969, we read: "In so far as a general armistice is a decisive step towards the restoration of peace — and that is the only normal position from the point of view of international law — every attempt to evade the armistice and renew hostilities ... must be regarded as constituting an act of aggression .... A general armistice cannot, therefore, be cancelled and is, in principle, to be considered to be of unlimited duration". See: *The Academy of Sciences of the Soviet Union, Course of International Law*, vol. 5, (Moscow, 1969), p. 405 (Russian).

68. Resolution 2625 (XXV), U.N., *General Assembly, Official Records, Twenty-Fifth Session*, Suppl. No. 28 (17/8028), 1970, p. 122.

it acquire sovereignty." [69] Here, again, Cattan seeks to strengthen his general legal thesis by adducing additional arguments. One is that "Israel does not possess any recognized frontiers" and, in this connection, he cites the following sentence from H. O. Cooke's book — "Israel a Blessing and a Curse": "Israel, alone among all the countries of the world, possesses not a single square inch of territory which she could assuredly proclaim to be her own in perpetuity." [70] But the absence of permanent frontiers does not detract from the status of a State as a sovereign State. In December 1920, Albania became a member of the League of Nations, as a sovercign and independent State, even though it had no fixed boundaries at that time [71], a fact which the Permanent Court of International Justice referred to in one of its opinions without comment or reservation [72]. And in 1921, Lithuania became a member of the League despite its boundary dispute with Poland [73]. "Both reason and history demonstrate", stressed Professor Jessup, in the course of the Security Council meeting at which Israel's application for admission to the United Nations was debated, "that

69. Cattan, *Palestine*, pp. 273–274.
70. *Ibid.*, p. 274.
71. See: F. P. Walters, *A History of the League of Nations* (Oxford, 1960), p. 123, where it is said: "As for Albania [when it became a member of the League], her frontiers were still undefined ... ."
72. *P.C.I.J.*, Series B, No. 9, *Question of the Monastery of Saint Nahum* (1924), p. 10.
73. See: N. Feinberg, "L'admission de nouveaux membres à la Société des Nations et à l'Organisation des Nations Unies", *R.A.D.I.*, tome 80 (Paris, 1953), p. 329.

the concept of territory does not necessarily include precise delimitation of the boundaries of that territory." [74]
And Professor Guggenheim justly remarks that, "bearing
in mind the principle of effectiveness, it is not necessary
that the law of nations establish rules of an imperative
nature regarding the need to demarcate the territory of
the State.... New States can, therefore, be recognized in
international law even if their frontiers have not yet been
definitively settled." [75]

The second reason adduced by Cattan is that "Israel is
not recognized by the Arab States nor by a large number
of other States. More important still, Israel is not recognized by the original people of Palestine in whom sovereignty lies." [76] Here, too, the non-recognition of Israel
by the Arab States, and by a number of other States supporting them [77], cannot derogate from Israel's status as a
sovereign State or impair its rights as a legal international
entity. The Institute of International Law — the highest

74. U.N. Doc. S/PV. 383, 2 December 1948, p. 11.
75. See: P. Guggenheim, *Traité de droit international public*,
    tome I (Genève, 1953), pp. 379—380. See also: *North Sea
    Continental Shelf, Judgment, I.C.J. Reports 1969*, p. 32.
76. Cattan, *Palestine*, p. 275.
77. Cattan's claim is that the number of States which have not
    recognized Israel is "large" (*ibid.*, p. 275). But Professor
    Quincy Wright describes the position far more accurately
    when he speaks of "its [Israel's] recognition by most States"
    and goes on to point out that even the Arab States recognized
    Israel, with qualifications, in a declaration to the United
    Nations Conciliation Commission on May 12, 1949; by this
    he means the Protocol signed on that date, to which we shall
    refer, later on, in a different context. See: Quincy Wright, "The
    Middle East Problem", *American Journal of International Law*,
    vol. 64, No. 2 (1970), p. 271.

scientific body in this branch of law — has held that "the existence of a new State, and all the juridical consequences of such existence, are not affected by the refusal of one, or more States, to recognize it" [78]. And this same principle was embodied in the Charter of the Organization of American States, confirmed in 1948 at the Bogota Conference, in these words: "The political existence of the State is independent of recognition by other States. Even before being recognized, the State has the right to defend its integrity and independence, to provide for its preservation and prosperity and consequently to organize itself as it sees fit... ." [79] In his lectures at the Hague Academy of International Law, Professor Rousseau dwells on the illogical and inconsistent nature of current international practice, whereby one State withholds its recognition from another, despite the collective recognition extended to the other State by its very admission as a member of the United Nations. In this context he refers to the non-recognition of Israel by the Arab States and criticizes the Secretariat of the United Nations for having yielded to this practice and even upheld it. Indeed, he goes on to define the resultant situation as "the contamination of legal principles by political opportunism" [80]. It

78. H. Wehberg, *op. cit.*, p. 11.
79. "Charter of the Organization of American States, Bogotá, April 30, 1948", *American Journal of International Law*, vol. 46, No. 2, Official Documents (1952), p. 46.
80. Ch. Rousseau, "Principes de droit international public", *R.A.D.I.*, tome 93 (Leyde, 1958), p. 457. Professor Rolin, too, in his lectures at the Hague Academy of International Law, has expressed the view that, once a State has been admitted to the United Nations, "old Members must no longer contest

seems clear, then, that Cattan's argument, that Israel has no permanent boundaries and is not recognized by a number of States, is of no significance in so far as its status as an independent State is concerned and does not detract, in any way, from the rights that it enjoys as such.

the international personality of the new Member .... The new State can claim the protection extended to it by the general international law, in particular — respect for its independence, inviolability of its territory, the right to a flag. All that can be denied it is the active or passive exercise of the *jus legationis*" or, in other words, the other States cannot be compelled to enter into diplomatic relations with it. See: H. Rolin, "Les principes de droit international public", *R.A.D.I.* tome 77 (Paris, 1951), pp. 332–333. And Brownlie writes: "Few would take the view that the Arab neighbours of Israel can afford to treat her as a nonentity: the responsible United Nations organs and the individual States have taken the view that Israel is protected, and bound, by the principles of the United Nations Charter governing the use of force" (Brownlie, *op. cit.*, p. 85). See also: Feinberg, *The Arab-Israel Conflict*, pp. 71—79.

The Palestine Question

SEMINAR OF ARAB JURISTS ON
PALESTINE, ALGIERS, JULY 22-27, 1967

PART ONE

HISTORICAL "RIGHTS"

The fight in which the Arabs are engaged to ensure the integrity of Palestine is the struggle of a people for its liberty and for the recovery of its fundamental right to reoccupy the land which is its own. Israel has made the most strenuous efforts to justify her existence as a state set up in the heart of the Arab nation, but neither the Arab nation nor any man who respects the law could possibly consider as legal a "solution" involving the expulsion of millions of Arabs from their fatherland and their replacement by non-Arabs. And these jurists rightly invoke the principles of international law to affirm the nullity of such acts as regards international legality.

Skilful propaganda has attempted to induce world public opinion to accept certain ideas which the most superficial examination reveals as false! Sometimes this propaganda stresses the existence of historical rights as a foundation for the rebirth of the Jewish State from the ashes under which it had been buried for two thousand years. Sometimes it strives to set the creation of Israel within the framework of the struggle of nationalist movements which have fought to secure recognition for the right of those communities, whose aspirations they have embodied, to self-determination. Sometimes again it recalls the persecutions to which the Jews have always been subjected to justify the creation of a State in Palestine under whose protection they could henceforth live in peace. And, finally, it sometimes lays stress on the 1947 resolution of the United Nations on the Partition of Palestine, and on certain so-called international acts which preceded it, in an attempt to prove that the State of Israel has an unquestionable juridical basis.

I. — THE FALSIFICATION OF HISTORY

If this formula of historical "rights" is to be invoked at all, it is the Arabs, and the Arabs alone, who have any right to do so. An objective analysis of historical facts and the lessons that can be learnt from them, establishes without any doubt that Palestine has never been anything but a specifically Arab land, inhabited by a people speaking the same language, united by the same cultural aspirations, nurtured by the same aspirations and linked by common interests.

1) PERMANENCE OF THE ARAB CHARACTER OF PALESTINE

Arab for nearly four thousand years, Palestine has preserved this Arab character, although several human groupings or States have conquered it in the course of history.

a) It is recognised that, as the Old Testament tells us, Palestine was the place where tribes of Canaanite Semites settled; the geographical origin from which these tribes sprang proves them to have been Arabs. *The Hebrew tribes did not enter Palestine* until the 13th or 14th century B.C. when, under the leadership of Joshua, they conquered certain parts of it. They found there a flourishing civilisation; the Bible provides ample evidence of its prosperity. The Canaanites had been established in Palestine since the Neolithic period and were descended from tribes of Semitic stock whose original cradle was, according to theories generally accepted today in the scientific world, in the Arabian peninsula.

Historically, therefore, the ancient Hebrews were not born in Palestine. And when they did come to Palestine for a brief period of time, they never occupied the whole of what is now Israel. The coastal plain remained in the hands of the Philistines, who gave it their name (Palestine.)

The basic fact that must be emphasised in subsequent discussion, therefore, is that the land of Canaan, which was inhabited by Canaanites, who were Semites and therefore Arabs, was later conquered by alien Hebrew tribes.

But this Jewish entity was not to last long. Divided into two hostile kingdoms, Israel and Judah, it was soon overwhelmed, from the 7th century B.C. onwards, by successive invasions of Persians, Macedonians, Assyrians and Babylonians. Then, in the year 64 B.C., Rome seized Jerusalem and extended her dominion over Palestine, which was then inhabited by Jews, Idumeans, Itureans, Ammonites and Arabs. It is from the year 120 A.D., when the emperor Hadrian crushed the revolt of the Jews and drove them out of Jerusalem, that Palestine can be considered as having become an Arab province once more. The *Provincia Arabia* of the Roman Empire was, in fact, Palestine which, after having been subjected to the influence of Christianity, became Moslem in the 7th century.

It is clear from these facts that the Jewish political presence in Palestine came to an end almost at the beginning of our era, and that the period during which it did exist was not long enough for it to prevail over Arab legitimacy.

b) By putting an end to the Latino-Roman, later Byzantine, dominion of Palestine, the Arab victories came as a liberation for the Christian and Jewish communities. The dying Empire had confined both Christian and Jew in a system of rigid discrimination, of which an abundant religious literature has given a merciless description. Five centuries after the abolition of this system, Syrian authors, particularly Michael in the 13th century, were still emphasising the liberating character of Arab power.

All these communities welcomed Arab rule, especially the Jews, who were to become some of the Arab rulers' most loyal subjects.

c) The period of the Crusades was marked by the persecution of the people of Jerusalem and the depradations inflicted on all communities, Muslim, Jewish and Christian alike. It was not until the Ottoman conquest of Palestine by Sultan Selim in 1516, that the protection of these believers was secured. It was the same for the Jews in other places. It should be recalled that, at the beginning of the XVIIth century, Cardinal Ximenes, Prime Minister of Ferdinand III of Spain, ordered that they be expelled from Andalusia,[1] along with such of the Arab minority as still remained in the country. The only places of refuge then open to the Jews were the Arab Maghreb and the Ottoman Empire.

In Istanbul, Izmir and other towns of the eastern Mediterranean

---

[1] - There had been a first exodus of Jews from Spain after the persecutions of 1492.

there are still communities of Spanish Jews who have preserved their traditions, their rites and even their ancient Castilian language.[2] This survival is due to the protection which they enjoyed under the Ottoman regime and, later, to the immunities written into the constitution of modern States.

d) The Arabs accepted Ottoman rule, to which they had been subjected since the XVIth century, because they believed that they were living under the traditional system of the Islamic Caliphate. However, they rapidly recovered their nationalist feelings, and it was not long before they revolted and shook off the Ottoman yoke.

The occasion for this was provided by the First World War, when the Sublime Porte found itself committed on the side of Germany. The Arabs then began their revolution for liberation; with the support of the Allies who, in an exchange of letters known as the "Hussein-MacMahon Correspondence," promised to recognise the independence of the Arab States detached from the Ottoman Empire. It was these promises, in fact, which induced the Arabs to revolt during the summer of 1916. They first succeeded in liberating the Hejaz; from there, their army advanced to occupy Jericho and Damascus. At the same time, Great Britain, from her base in Egypt, launched an attack on Palestine in 1917 and succeeded in occupying it, thanks to Arab support. Great Britain then set up a military administration in Palestine, which meant that she was to administer the territory in this manner until such time as its inhabitants, of whom 90% were Muslim and Christian Arabs, were in a position freely to decide their own destiny.

The lessons provided by the analysis of these historical facts may be summarised as follows:

a) The Hebrew tribes, in fact, were no more than one among many waves of immigration, and the Kingdom of the Jews was only able to maintain its sovereignty in Palestine for a very limited period, two thousand years ago.

b) Before the arrival of the Hebrews, Palestine had always

---

[2] - Some of these communities speak a derivative language, *Ladino.*

been Semitic-Canaanite, that is to say, Arab, in view of the fact that the Semite is, geographically speaking, of Arab origin. It was Christianised under the Roman and Byzantine Empires, but this event, of course, in no way changed its Arab character. Finally, after the fall of Byzantine and the Arab victories of the VIIth century, Palestine of course continued to be an Arab land where Moslems, Christians and Jews lived in freedom and in peace.

c) The Jews recognised Ottoman no less than Arab sovereignty, the former having taken upon itself all the obligations arising from Islamic Caliphate. Under both the Jews found that protection which neither the Byzantine Empire nor the other European States were willing to grant them.

It is thus clear that all legal and political links between the Jews and Palestine have been severed for the past two thousand years.

Historical rights are closely linked with the effective exercise of sovereignty. This being the case, the Jews are in no position to invoke such rights; if they do so, then the Arabs must be allowed to claim sovereignty over Spain, which they ruled for nearly eight centuries. Such claims find no support in international law.

d) On the other hand, the claims formulated by the Arabs immediately after the secession of Palestine from the Ottoman Empire, are based upon the soundest principles of international law, particularly that of self-determination. Moreover, the Arabs could avail themselves of the promises made by Great Britain in the Hussein-MacMahon Correspondence, especially in the letter sent by the latter to the Sharif Hussein on October 25th, 1915, in which England declared her readiness to recognise the independence of the Arabs within the frontiers traced by the Sharif, and to guarantee the integrity of the Holy Places.

This policy was opposed by the Zionist movement, which passed through several stages before it finally took the political form given to it by the man who may be considered as its founder, the Austrian journalist Theodor Herzl, author of the book "The Zionist State," published in 1896. At a congress, held at his suggestion in

Basle on August 29th, 1897, Herzl mooted the idea of the creation of a Jewish national home in Palestine. Despite the opposition of several Jewish communities, he was able to get the congress to adopt a Zionist programme for the creation of a Jewish homeland in Palestine which would bring together immigrants from various countries.

To justify this solution, which left world Jewry profoundly divided, the Zionist movement expounded the theme of the existence of a Jewish people, a Jewish race, a Jewish nation, and announced, quite untruly, that the Jews are the descendants of the ancient Hebrews, and that they have much more than their religion in common. It was a surprising point of view to adopt, so surprising indeed, that the Zionists felt it necessary to launch a vast propaganda campaign designed to get this new "truth" accepted both by the European States, which were reluctant to give their positive support to the establishment of a Jewish national home in Palestine, and by the Jews living in many countries, who were by no means convinced that they belonged to the same people, the same race and the same nation.

2) THE ZIONIST CONCEPT OF A JEWISH NATION

When Weizmann, the president of the Zionist movement, decided to take action to put an end to the hesitations of the Allied Powers, divided by colonial rivalries and little inclined to provoke unfavourable reactions in the Arab world, he held conversations mainly with the representatives of the British and French governments, Mr Sykes and M. Picot.

Certain Jewish circles, in Britain and elsewhere, were opposed to this concept, asserting that Zionist ideas were inconsistent with the principles of the Jewish religion and were liable to weaken the position of the Jews who were already integrated into European societies. Similarly, the American-Jewish Committee and the Franco-Jewish Alliance were opposed to the Zionist movement for exactly the same reasons.

Writing as a Jew, Sir Edwin S. Montagu, Secretary of State

for India in the Lloyd George government that, in 1917, ratified
the Balfour Declaration, in which Great Britain "promised" Palestine
to the Jews, said: "Zionism has always seemed to me to be a mis-
chievous political creed, untenable by any patriotic citizen of the United Kingdom. If a Jewish Englishman sets his eyes on the Mount of
Olives and longs for the day when he will shake British soil from
his shoes and go back to agricultural pursuits in Palestine, he has
always seemed to me to have acknowledged aims inconsistent with
British citizenship and to have admitted that he is unfit for a share
in public life in Great Britain, or to be treated as an Englishman...
It is quite true that Palestine plays a large part in Jewish history
but so it does in Christian history. The Temple may have been
in Palestine, but so was the Sermon on the Mount and the Crucifixion."[3]

Nevertheless, the Zionist movement continued its activities
with the object of securing recognition for Palestine as the "un-
forgettable historical fatherland" of the Jews, despite the denials
of history and sociology.

With unusual perseverance, it portrayed the Jews as one nation,
one people and once race.[4] And yet, as has been shown by an
expert on the subject who is himself of Jewish faith, not to mention
many others, the Jews do not "constitute a clan, a tribe, a nation
in the strict sense of the word... In the light of their past, it is
strange that the Jews should be considered as a distinct race and
that such efforts should be made to prove it... There exists no
decisive evidence to support the claim that the Jews constitute a
racial entity, at least in the sense of the traditional criteria of racial

---

[3] - Excerpt from secret documents published by the British Government.
Text number CAB.24/24. *The Antisemitism of the Present Government*, by
Sir Edwin S. Montagu, August 25th, 1917, quoted by Sami Hadawi in:
"Les revendications 'bibliques' et 'historiques' des Sionistes sur la Palestine,"
Les Temps Modernes, Le Conflit judéo-arabe, dossier, 1967, no. 253 bis,
Paris, p. 98.

[4] - See, in particular, Marcel Bernfeld: *Le Sionisme*, thesis for Doctorate
in Law, Paris, 1920, Jouve edit., 458 pp., (the author was responsible for
the Zionist movement in France. It requires a good deal of indulgence to
read his astounding conjectures on the concepts of nation, race, people. (Cf.
The first part of the book entitled *La Nation Juive*, pp. 29-121.)

classification."[5]

Examination reveals the "historical rights" of the Jews over Palestine to be non-existent. They are all the more inconsistent in view of the fact that the Jews who came from Europe to Palestine cannot be regarded as heirs to the ancient Hebrews of the Holy Land. For, in fact, many Europeans were converted to Judaism in the Middle Ages. The Turkish Kingdom of the Khazars in southeast Russia, under its King Bulan, adopted the Jewish religion in 740 A.D. In the 18th century a wide movement of conversion to Judaism, inspired and encouraged by the Byzantine Jews, reached the Caucasian Russians, whose descendants, scattered throughout central Europe, Russia, Poland and the United States, gave Israel its immigrants and even its present political leaders. There were also yellow Jews and black Jews from Malabar and Cochin, and the Felashas of Ethiopia. Any attempt therefore to consider the Jews as a race and a people when they are no more than a religious community—and a non-homogeneous one at that, for it is divided into sects[6]—constitutes an unauthorised exploitation of their religious feelings, as will be shown later.

Nevertheless, Zionism continues to base itself on the expression "Jews," or "Judaism," to emphasise that it is political, and not religious in character, implying the existence of a Jewish nationality, distinct by its race, its culture, its language, its history, and its aspirations.

The objections to these claims can be briefly summed up as

---

[5] - Harry L. Shapiro (head of the Department of Anthropology of the American Museum of National History): *Le Peuple Juif: une histoire biologique,* Geneva, UNESCO, 1960, pp. 74-75. Cf. Also the works of Juan Comas, professor of anthropology at the University of Mexico, on the notion of race.

[6] - Traditionally, a distinction is made between the *Sephardim,* Mediterranean and Oriental Jews, the *Ashkenazim,* European Jews, the *Karaites,* Iraqi and Egyptian Jews, and the *Hassidim,* Jews of the Mea Shearim quarter of Jerusalem. It is also to be noted in passing that Israel is notorious for practising discrimination even between her own Jews: it is always the "Orientals" — the Sephardim and Karaites who are the victims. Cf. "Israel et les Pays Arabes dans le Moyen-Orient depuis 1948," *Les Cahiers de l'Histoire,* Paris, October-November, 1967, No. 70, pp. 18-23.

follows:

a) The Jews do not constitute a homogeneous racial unit. A few fanatical Jews may believe that they descend from pure and choice Semitic elements, but studies refute this belief, which is, in fact, a pure myth. In reality, the Jews, like all other religious groupings, have their origins in different races.

b) The Jews do not have one common language, for the languages which they speak are those of the communities in which they live. Thus, in reviving Hebrew and encouraging the Jews to speak it, the Zionists are imposing a foreign language on the communities concerned.

c) There are as many diversities in the customs and traditions of the Jews as there are different communities in which they live.

d) The Jews do not have a common history. They have lived, during the last twenty centuries, dispersed in various states. They have adopted the ways of life of the people amongst whom they have lived.

The Jews only constituted a state, in the proper sense of the term, for short periods of history. The kingdom of David and Solomon lasted only 78 years, as against four thousand years of Arab Palestine. Likewise, the two kingdoms of Judah and Israel, which succeeded the unified kingdom, had a very limited role in Jewish history. Israel was absorbed by the Assyrian Empire as far back as 722 B.C.; Judah fell into the hands of Persia in 587 B.C. The memories of these short-lived kingdoms belong more to the realm of faith and emotion than to political and social history.

Consequently, the Jews have, in fact, no common language, no common history, no common origins. The link which unites them is an exclusively religious one, not a national one, as Zionism maintains. Non-Zionist Jews acknowledge this truth.

In 1878, the Chief Rabbi of England, Herman Auler, said: "Ever since the invasion of Palestine by the Romans, the Jews have ceased to be a political community. We Jews rally politically to the countries in which we live. We are simply, English, French, Germans. We have, of course, religious beliefs which are our own. Yet, in this case, we do not distinguish ourselves from other citizens who practise another religion. We cooperate with them for the prosperity of the country which has received us and we claim the rights and the obligations of its citizens."[7]

The American rabbi Weiss reaffirmed this concept in 1883. Jewish rabbis throughout the world have acknowledged it. In the resolution adopted by the Jewish Congress held in Pittsburg, U.S.A., in 1885, it is stated: "We Jews do not consider ourselves as a nation, but simply as a religious community. Therefore, we do not envisage the return to Palestine, nor do we wish to revive any of the laws relative to the Jewish State."

Thus, at the time when Zionism was born and being developed, ministers of the Jewish religion rejected the idea of the existence of a Jewish people united by a common nationality, and the non-Zionist Jewish Communities have continued to oppose this concept. It will be seen, therefore, that the concept of a Jewish nation, based as it is on fallacious promises, belongs historically to the same category as the myths created to serve the infamous ends of the various imperialist regimes, which have always collapsed with the regimes that created them. These myths, do, of course, succeed for a time in misleading a world opinion which has little knowledge of historical facts, which facts, moreover, have been distorted by a gigantic propaganda machine to suit its own political requirements.

Does not the same apply to Zionism's fraudulent exploitation of religious and humanitarian sentiments with the object of winning universal sympathy and deceiving world Jewry?

---

[7] - Cf. W. Mallison Jr: "The Zionist-Israel juridical claims to constitute the Jewish people nationality entity and to confer membership in it: appraisal in public international law," *George Washington Law Review*, 1964, vol. 32, number 5, June 1964, pp. 983-1075.

[8] - Sir Edwin Montagu, Secretary of State for India, himself of Jewish faith, stated (*op. cit.*): "It is no more true to say that an English Jew and a Moorish Jew belong to the same nation than it is to say this about an English Christian and a French Christian."

3) FRAUDULENT EXPLOITATION OF RELIGIOUS AND HUMANITARIAN FEELINGS

It has been rightly said that the creation of the State of Israel could not have been more artificial and unlawful. By appealing now to religious sentiments, now to humanitarian feelings aroused by the persecutions suffered by the Jews, the partisans of the State of Israel have sought to convince people that there were solid grounds for the foundation of such a state.

In fact, however, there is no relation in international law between the creation of a State and religion or persecutions.

A. – *Religious Feeling and Sovereignty Rights :*

The Jews, both those converted to Judaism and those who originally came from Palestine, have, throughout the centuries, lived as minorities in various countries of the world. They have thus acquired the same rights and nationality as the other citizens of these countries. They have been able to practise their religion in freedom. But some Jewish anagogical interpreters have gone so far as to claim that the promises contained in the Holy Books gave the Jewish "people" the right to recover their sovereignty over Palestine, their "promised land." After its first congress held in Basle in 1897, the Zionist political movement strove to strengthen this religious factor so as to establish a connection between the Jews and Palestine.

This movement did all it could to combine Jewish religious concepts with Zionist political designs on Palestine. But what of the religious sentiments that attach Moslems and Christians to Palestine?

Moreover, Zionist exegesis of the Biblical texts in question is quite wrong; of course, the idea of the establishment of a state on a basis of arguments derived from the Bible is utterly unacceptable to twentieth century thinking, but were this not so, the conclusion that it was to *the Arabs* that God promised Palestine would be unavoidable.[9]

But considerations of a religious nature have no place in contemporary international law. Sovereignty, according to this law, is based only on certain well-defined juridical and political facts such as the uninterrupted and effective exercise of sovereignty over the territory of the State.

According to the rules of international law established since the 18th century, a territory can only be subjected to the sovereignty of the occupier through actual occupation. In laying down con-

---

[9] - Old and New Testament scholars have established the following facts;

a) The 4,000-year old Biblical promise ("Unto thy seed have I given this land, from the river of Egypt unto the great river, the river Euphrates") was intended for *all the descendants* of Abraham, that it to say, the *Arabs* (who claim descent through Ishmael,) as well as the Jews, who claim descent through Israel.)

b) Even more significant is the fact that, when Abraham made a covenant with God through circumcision, (Genesis XVII, 8) and all the land of Canaan was promised to him for an everlasting possession, it was *Ishmael, ancestor of the Arab tribes, who was circumcised, for Isaac had not then been born.* If, therefore, one were to follow Zionist reasoning, Palestine was "promised" by God exclusively to the Arabs.

c) In any case, the divine promises were annulled by the apostasy of the Jews.

d) The prophecy of the "Return" was fulfilled when the Jews returned to Judaea after their captivity, re-erected the walls of Jerusalem and rebuilt the Temple; the Holy Scriptures contain no mention of a "Second Return." So that the creation of Israel which is presented as the "Return after 2,000 years," *contradicts the Biblical promise on which it is allegedly based.* There are Jews in Jerusalem itself who consider that the creation of Israel, for this reason in particular, runs counter to their faith (Cf. infra, note 19);

e) The texts refer to Israel not as a geographical, ethnic or political entity, but as the universal community of believers, the *Israel of God.*

On all these questions see in particular, the work of Dr. Elmer Berger, Chief Rabbi; of Dr. Alfred Guillaume, Professor of Old Testament Studies at London University; Dr. William H. Stinespring, professor of New Testament and Semitic Studies at Duke University in North Carolina and Pastor of the Presbyterian Church, (*Zionism and the Bible*); Dr. Ovid R. Sellers, formerly Old Testament Professor, Dean of McCormick Theological Seminary, and pastor of the United Presbyterian Church; and the Very Reverend Jonathan G. Sherman, Suffragan Bishop of the Diocese of Long Island, New York; particularly in *Israel according to the Holy Scriptures,* Cedar Rapids, Ingram Press, all cited by Sami Hadawi in: "Les Revendications 'bibliques' et 'historiques' des Sionistes sur la Palestine," *Les Temps Modernes,* Paris, 1967. no. 253 bis, pp. 91-105, (op. cit.). See also Samarrai: "Palestine, Arab or Jewish?" *Arab Journal,* vol. 1, no. 2-3, Spring-Summer, 1964.

ditions for the transfer of territories from the sovereignty of one
State to that of another, international law has never admitted
claims based on religion. There exists no obligation to create a
State for the adherents of a given faith. Civil law only requires of
the citizen allegiance and loyalty to the State in which he lives,
regardless of his religion. And if the Jews, like the followers of
other religions, consider themselves dedicated to a specific mission,
they can perfectly well fulfill that mission while retaining the
nationality of the States in which they live.

B. – Persecutions and the Creation of the State of Israel :

The incredible process which has resulted in the Arab people
of Palestine being obliged to pay for the persecutions of the
Jews amounts to a really astounding transfer of collective responsibility. No less astonishing is the assertion that the Nazi persecutions
confer on the Jewish "people" the right to live in their own State,
and, to make things worse, in a country which does not belong to
them.

According to this concept, it would be perfectly legal to
create a special State, under whose authority the Jewish "people"
could at last find the protection which had hitherto been denied
them.

But this very association of the two expressions "persecution"
and "creation of a State" is, from a juridical point of view, absolutely illogical. International law has never acknowledged the
validity of the equation: persecution = creation of a State, and it
can consider only juridical rights in judging the legitimacy or the
legality of the State of Israel.

Experts in international law and international relations have
severely criticised the view that political links among Jews do
exist, that there is a nationality common to all Jews. These experts
point out that Zionist objectives, by their very nature, go beyond
the creation—illegal at that—of a Jewish State, and tend towards the establishment of a system of guarantees for the Jews

with the object of finding a solution of the problem created by the pogroms of Europe.

But the only tie which unites Jews is religion, as it is for Christians, or other believers sharing a common faith. This tie has no connection with that of nationality, which gives the right to self-determination and also permits of the creation of a State.

For it is utterly erroneous to see any connection between the alleged rights of the Jews in Palestine and self-determination. The Zionists did not liberate themselves from foreign domination but have, on the contrary, seized for themselves a country inhabited by another people. Their entire policy has been that of the expulsion of a people so that they might settle in its place.

The right to self-determination, which is the right of every people to govern itself, and freely to choose its political, economic, social and cultural future, forms an integral part of the law of nations. It is one of the declared objects of the Charter of the United Nations (Art. 1, par. 2) and it is included among the provisions of the Convention on Economic and Social Rights, adopted by the United Nations General Assembly in 1966. Recognising the right of every people to determine its own future, the World Organisation acknowledges the necessity of resorting to a referendum, or some other form of democratic consultation, before the future of hitherto non-self-governing territories is decided, out of respect for the right of every people to determine its own future.

However, it goes without saying that such a principle can only be applied in the case of a people living on its own land which it has occupied continuously and undisputedly, and not in the case of a religious community reassembled in Palestine after two thousand years of dispersion.

The application of this principle to the Palestine problem confirms the right of the Palestinian nation to independence and excludes all possibility of creating a Jewish State. Religion has, by the will of the Zionists, been transfigured into a means for the political relocation of all Jews, through the creation of the myth of a common nationality.

4) THE ZIONIST CONCEPT OF NATIONALITY

Even before Israel set up herself as a State, the *Leit-motiv* that all Jews belonged to a single nation was one of the main weapons employed by Zionist propaganda. And it has been quite easy to prove the inconsistency of this concept of a nation common to all Jews, a concept which, artificial though it is, has succeeded in catalysing the aspirations of the Jews to return to Zion. Consequently, the Zionist concept of nationality is a very peculiar one: on the one hand it rejects and condemns the integration of Jews in the various States in which they live; on the other hand it considers it perfectly normal that Jews should enjoy the advantages of dual nationality.

The uncompromisingly *imperialist character of Zionist thinking* is revealed in a collection of letters written by Dr. Elmer Berger, Executive Vice-President of the anti-Zionist American Council for Judaism. Recalling a conversation with the Israeli Consul in New York, Dr. Berger writes: "When I told him my point of view that if the Jew, no matter where he is, succeeds in integrating himself among others, the Jewish problem as such disappears... he immediately replied that this kind of integration was contrary to Israeli aims."[10]

In adopting this attitude the Israeli consul was merely reflecting the official attitude of Israel, which condemns the integration of Jews into the various communities in which they live. At the 25th World Zionist Congress which met in Jerusalem in 1961, Ben Gurion said: "Ever since the day the Jewish State was born and the doors of Israel were opened to all Jews, every one of them, if he has any religious belief at all, has committed a daily breach of the precepts of Judaism and of the Torah by remaining in the Diaspora." He called all Jews living outside Israel "impious."

In 1950 the Zionist parliament passed the "Law of the Return," which, one of the most reactionary nationality laws in the world,

---

[10] - *Cf.* Revue *Al-fikr al-mu'asir* (Contemporary Thinking), Cairo, September, 1967. The letters collected by Dr. Berger date back to 1955.

is based on the narrowest racial and confessional principles. This law opens up the State of Israel to all the Jews of the world—this clearly indicated Israel's imperialistic and expansionist intentions[11]—and opens it up to Jews only[12]—which makes it possible to see the philosophy which lies behind this law in its true perspective.[13]

Israel claims rights over all the Jews of the world. Through the intermediary of the World Zionist Organisation, it imposes on them something remarkably like a tax, and also claims to control their lives and their destiny by methods which do not always respect the sovereignty of other States.

"This sort of superior right," we read in *Les Cahiers de l'Histoire,* "exercised by Israel over the Jews, explains certain disputes of a private nature, one of which, the affair of the Finaly children, was headline news about ten years ago. Born of Jewish parents

---

[11] - Cf. *infra, passim* and particularly pp. 41 and 75.

[12] - The definition of a Jew has given rise to a number of complex problems. Every child of a *Jewish mother* or every person officially converted to Judaism is considered a Jew. But a great number of immigrants into Israel had previously contracted mixed marriages and kept a non-Jewish identity. Thus a non-Jewish woman arriving in Israel could not, according to Jewish law, hand down the quality of Jewishness (which is regarded as the basis of Israeli nationality) to her offspring, although the father was Jewish.

As regards converts, their situation is even more astonishing: "The absurdity of the Zionist claim is best illustrated in the case of the American negro actor Sammy Davis, Jr., ...who embraced Judaism some years ago. According to Zionist logic, as formulated in the Israeli *Status Law* and the *Law of the Return,* Davis is now considered to be living in 'exile' in his homeland, America, pining for the day to return 'home' to Palestine! Ironically, while a total stranger in language, colour, culture and race, can acquire the right to live in Palestine merely by adopting Judaism, the Moslem and Christian inhabitants of the Holy Land—whose physical descent from Abraham can hardly be questioned, if the 'Biblical' promises have any legitimacy in the 20th century at all—are denied the right to live in the country of their birth!" (Sami Hadawi, *op. cit.,* pp. 101-102.)

[13] - Cf. *Infra,* p. 75, for the legal status of the Arabs of Palestine. particularly in matters of nationality and public liberties. The *Law of the Return* requires of the Palestinian Arabs to apply for naturalisation; failure to do this makes them *aliens in their own land,* which, in fact, is precisely what happens! Naturalisation is not granted to the Arab unless the Israeli Minister of the Interior "deems it useful," i.e. it is left to the discretion of the Minister. and is subject to conditions almost impossible to fulfil.

who were later deported and died in exile, and brought up by a
Catholic family to whom they had been entrusted, the Finaly children
were abducted in France and taken to Israel. In this case, personal
preferences manifested by the children and family considerations
were overruled by a law which requires that *every Jewish child be
considered a potential Israeli.*"[14]

One is tempted to speak of dual nationality—many Americans,
Germans, Poles or Russians today have links with two parties at
once—one which gives them the protection of its laws and into
which one would have thought they might have become integrated;
the other, Israel, towards which they are attracted by feelings which
receive constant encouragement. Evidence for the existence of this
double allegiance is provided not only by the *"Law of the Return"*
which is "a practical instrument for expansion,"[15] but also by the
activity of a whole range of Zionist organisations which have Israeli
legal status but operate throughout the whole world.[16]

---

[14] - *Les Cahiers de l'Histoire:* "Israel et les pays arabes dans le Moyen-
Orient depuis 1948," no. 70, Paris, October-November, 1967, p. 18.

[15] - *Les Cahiers de l'Histoire, op. cit.,* same page.

[16] - After the creation of the State of Israel, in which they played an
extremely important part, the Jewish Agency, the Zionist Congress and the
Jewish National Fund were given the status of Israeli *"national institutions."*
They became responsible for this double allegiance throughout the world by
maintaining permanent contact between the Jews of the Galuth, the Diaspora,
and the Israelis.

A law defining the status of the World Zionist Organization was passed
by the Knesset on November 24th, 1952. It calls upon the Jewish Agency,
which had built the "Jewish National Home" and, later, Israel, to continue
to maintain a closely-knit, powerful and effective network of solidarity with
Israel and political and financial support for the Zionist cause. On November
27, 1952, three days after the passing of this law, a pact was signed between
the Israeli Government and the Jewish Agency recognising the latter as the
representative organ of the Jewish world.

The Zionist Congress, which is the supreme organ, and which meets
every three years in Israel, is elected by all the Jews in the world who
pay the *Shekel* (registration-fee.) At present Israel holds 38% of the seats
in this body, the United States 29% and the other countries of the Galuth
33%.

(On the activity of the Zionists in the United States, *cf* the publication
of the U.S. Congress: "Activities of Non-Diplomatic Representatives of Foreign
Principals in the United States," *Hearing before the Committee on Foreign
Relations. U.S. Senate, 88th Congress, 1st Session,* Part 12, May August,
1963. Senator Fullbright presided over the U.S. Senate Enquiry Committee.)

However, it is true to say that Zionist excesses in this field have aroused reaction and resistance, and that many Jews refuse to consider themselves as being other than American, French, etc., citizens. Thus, on March 14, 1964 the American Council for Judaism, which is strongly anti-Zionist, addressed a letter to the State Department calling for a clarification of the official position of the American government in this respect. The government stated that no *legal-political relationship can arise from the religious affiliation of American Jews, who continue to be exclusively American citizens free from all allegiance as regards Israeli sovereignty.*[17]

Other statements could be cited in which Jewish personalities express their refusal to consider themselves as Israeli citizens or as members of the Jewish "people."[18]

---

[17] - In his reply to the American Council for Judaism, Mr. Phillips Talbot, Assistant Secretary at the Department of State, wrote as follows:

"We have carefully studied your letter of March 14, 1964, drawing the Development of State's attention to the *"sui generis* character of the "Jewish people' concept," and urging clarification of the Department's views with respect to the "Jewish people' claim." You state: *"The central point is that the Zionist-Israeli sovereignty uses the concept of 'Jewish people' as the basic juridical claim against the Jews in states other than Israel who insist on maintaining their single nationality. Its principal function, you state, "is to change the legal status of Jews"* from that of individual nationals of Jewish religious faith to members of a juridically recognised trans-national nationality group with additional 'rights' and obligations to the Zionist-Israel sovereignty..."

"The Department of State... does not recognise a legal-political relationship based upon the religious affiliation of American citizens... Accordingly, it should be clear that the Department of State does not regard the concept of 'the Jewish people' as a concept of international law." (Our italics). Facsimile of the original text of the letter, dated April 20, 1964 in W.T. Mallison. Jr.: "The Zionist-Israel Juridical Claims to Constitute 'The Jewish People' Nationality Entity and to Confer Membership in it: Appraisal in Public International Law," *The George Washington Law Review*, 1964, *op. cit.*, p. 1075.)

[18] - Following the more than pressing, not to say threatening, appeal for Jewish solidarity, made by Mr Edmond de Rothschild in June 1967, Mlle Jacqueline Hadamard. after recalling her Jewish ancestry and the sufferings endured by her family in Nazi Camps, expressed her dissent in the following words: "...*He speaks of a Jewish people which does not exist.* There are in a great many countries people of Jewish faith who have nothing else in common; or people who may have similar origins but whose ideas and philosophies are totally different, for they live integrated into the communities in which they have taken root. Such is my case... No, I do not belong to the Jewish people. *Like the majority of French Jews, I belong to the*

Recent claims by certain French Jews to double allegiance have caused great annoyance to the French Government.[19]

This wholly imperialistic Israeli concept of nationality reminds one of the famous law passed by Wilhelm II in 1914, the "Delbruck Law," which made it possible for a German to hold any other nationality he chose in addition to his German nationality.[20] It aroused so many protests that the Allied and Associated Powers inserted an article in the Treaty of Versailles obliging the Weimar Republic to rescind it.[21]

Modern public law imposes upon every citizen unconditional loyalty to the State of which he is the subject. Rightly concerned to ensure the juridical homogeneity of the State and to avoid any depersonalisation of the notion of citizenship, it admits no infringement of this rule.

Therefore, any claim to self-determination advanced by men who have no common nationality and who are united only by a common religion, must be unlawful.

The feeling, which has been so carefully nurtured despite the weakness of its scientific basis, of belonging to one people, one race, one nation, and of having the same history, the same language and the same religion, has certainly, time and space notwithstanding,

---

[18] - Cont'd

French people...". (Le Monde, 9-10 August, 1967.)

[19] - "Certain (Jews)," writes André Fontaine, "who are totally assimilated, consider that the blood which flows in their veins does not impose on them obligations towards their cousins who live outside France, any more than the fact of having an Italian or German great-grandfather would impose obligations on an American citizen towards Italy or Germany. There are even religious Jews—they are to be found even in Jerusalem, in the Mea Shearim Quarter—who consider that the existence of a Jewish State is contrary to their faith." (André Fontaine: "La double allégeance," *Le Monde,* 11 January 1968, p. 1 and 4.

[20] - Cf. The French text of the law in *Annuaire français de législation étrangère,* 1913, p. 138 et S; the English text in *The American Journal of International Law,* 1914 supplement, p. 217 ets., the German text in *Reichgesetzblatt,* 1913, no. 46, p. 583 et s. For comments on this law, see Haenning: "Une fourberie allemande, la loi Delbruck," *Revue du droit international privé,* 1913, p. 971 and D.J. Hill: "Dual Citizenship in the German Imperial and State Citizenship," *American Journal of International Law,* 1918, p. 356.

[21] - *Treaty of Versailles,* Article 278.

served as a cement in building the Zionist structure and in giving its aims a concrete form. But now that the objective has been attained and this feeling has fulfilled its socio-political purpose, Zionism practically admits that the secular *Leit-motivs* it has employed to unify the Diaspora have disregarded historical and scientific truth: *"What binds the Jews together,"* says David Ben Gurion, *"is not religion, because the Zionist Movement includes atheists as well as pious elements, nor race, which has vanished after so much dispersion, nor language, since Hebrew almost died out for several centuries and since the majority of world Jewry does not know it and cannot speak it. The real bond which unites Jews throughout the whole world is their faith in a return to Israel."*

This statement, though belated, has the merit of being frank and completely refutes Zionist "historical rights" based on myths. It also has the virtue of attracting attention once again to the essential nature and the real objectives of Zionism, which cannot hope to bring the 14 million Jews of the world to Palestine revealing its essentially expansionist and colonial character.

II. — ISRAEL, A COLONIAL PHENOMENON

Israel is the most recent creation of the European colonialism and expansionism of the 19th and 20th centuries. It is perhaps not the purest nor the most perfect of such creations, because many political experts of good faith would hesitate to label the Israeli pheno-menon as colonialist. But a study of the objective elements which have accompanied the birth of Israel, and of the condition of the Arab minority in the country, leaves no room for doubt. The creation of Israel is the outcome of a colonial process and Israel's anti-Arab racialism is an integral part of colonialist thinking.

1) THE CREATION OF ISRAEL, OUTCOME OF A CO-LONIAL PROCESS

Certain definitions of colonialism give an accurate description of the vicissitudes experienced by Palestine, its partition and the creation of the Jewish State. A colony is an "assemblage of persons leaving their country to people another," or "the colony is a foreign country, generally subjugated by right of conquest, and placed under the political and economic protection of the conqueror." But the definition provided by the sociologist,[22] more comprehensive than that of the dictionary, gives the essence of the colonial phenomenon in one sentence: "One can speak of colonisation when there is occupation with domination, and emigration with legislation." If we accept this lucid definition the Israeli phenomenon is certainly a colonial phenomenon, even though the traditional picture of life in Israel, as depicted by skilful propaganda, bears little relation to one's usual idea of colonialism.

It is certainly difficult to believe that these "dignified Arabs of Israel shown in government publications solemnly casting their votes in the democratic ballot box" are really the victims of colonialism, or that "the kibbutznik, with his pure innocent face, radiant with idealism, working with his hands on the land once trodden by the feet of Solomon, Isaiah and Jesus, the long degradation of his ancestors in the ghetto now a thing of the past,"[23] is really a colonialist.

But colonialism is not an entity with precisely defined outlines; the student of social sciences will agree with M. Rodinson when he says that: "All are agreed on the essential, the nucleus; ...but at the periphery, there is no clear definition, with the result that the terminology employed differs widely as between groups, schools of thought and even individuals." Here we intend to concentrate on three facts that clearly demonstrate that the creation of Israel must take its place in the long series of colonial phenomena.

These facts are a) that Zionism is a movement inspired by colonialism; b) that it is related to European expansionism; c) that the progressive settlement of Palestine was achieved by colonisation; and, finally, that colonial settlement in Palestine has been able to develop and grew only at the expense of the Arab population.

---

[22] - René Maunier: *Sociologie coloniale*, Paris, 1932, p. 37.
[23] - Maxime Rodinson: "Israel fait colonial?," *Les Temps Modernes, op. cit.*, p. 23.

A. – Zionism and Colonialism

Zionism is a philosophy; it is also an ensemble of means and techniques designed to enable it to attain its objectives.

The modern Zionist movement, initiated by Theodor Herzl's "*The Jewish State*," published in 1896, is resolutely colonialist. The founder of Zionism had one essential aim: to create a Jewish State. At first he suggested either Argentina or the Holy Land as alternative locations for the future State. But it was not long before he came out in favour of Palestine, and this was the choice of the first Zionist Congress, held in Basle in 1897. The objective declared by this first Congress was the creation in Palestine of a Jewish homeland guaranteed by public law, and one of the means to be employed was the "rational colonisation of Palestine by the settlement of Jewish farmers, artisans and industrialists."[24]

Further means proposed by the Congress included "organising and associating all Jews through the agency of local associations and general federations, to the extent allowed by the laws of the country in which such associations are established, strengthening the feeling of personal dignity and the national consciousness of the Jewish people," and "taking first steps towards securing the consent of governments, which is necessary for the achievement of the aim of Zionism."

The Basle programme was not implemented immediately, one reason being that Zionist opinion was divided when it became known that on August 17, 1903 the British Government had offered Herzl a territory in British East Africa.

The VIth Zionist Congress (1903) was allotted the task of deciding between Palestine and Uganda. With this end in view it appointed a committee to examine the possibility of settling Jewish settlers in the British territory.

This committee having decided against Uganda, the VIth Congress witnessed the triumph of Zione-Zion (these in favour of the choice of Palestine) and adopted the following very significant

---

[24] - *Cf.* Bernfeld: *op. cit.,* p. 341.

motion: "The Zionist Organisation stands firmly by the fundamental principle of the Basle programme, namely, 'the creation of a home-land guaranteed by public law for the Jewish people in Palestine,' and rejects both as an aim and as a means, every *colonising* action outside Palestine *and the neighbouring countries.*"

Thus the Zionist Congress frankly proclaimed the principle of colonising action in Palestine and of expansionism in the direction of the neighbouring territories, a fact which throws a glaring light on recent events.

Zionist claims were subsequently clarified and confirmed. The geographical ambitions of Zionism were defined in a memorandum submitted by the World Organisation to the Versailles Peace Con-ference in Versailles on February 3, 1919. In this memorandum the Zionists demarcated the frontiers of the State which they desired to create. "These frontiers comprised territories which today belong to Arab countries such as southern Lebanon, the east and west banks of the Jordan, a part of the northern Hejaz and all the Sinai peninsula. Ever since its creation, Israel has been striking stealthy blows at the neighbouring Arab countries in the hope of conquering not only these territories but others as well."[25]

Herzl himself specified what the geographical configuration of the future State was to be. "For our future trade we must be located on the sea, and for our large-scale modern agriculture we must have a large area of land."[26] "Our slogan should be: the Palestine of David and of Solomon."[27] "The area: 'from the river of Egypt to the Euphrate'."[28]

But it was quite obvious that a doctrine so clearly stated could not prevail without logistic assistance derived from the financial solidarity of Zionists throughout the world.

---

[25] - Burhan Dajani: "Les risques d'explosion du problème palestinien," *Les Temps Modernes, op. cit.,* p. 136.
[26] - *The Complete Diaries of Theodor Herzl,* Raphael Patay, English translation by Harry Zohen, Herzl Press and Thomas Yassilov, Part one, p. 133.
[27] - *ibid,* p. 432.
[28] - *ibid,* Part II, p. 711.

The creation of the *Jewish National Fund* by the VIth Zionist Congress in 1901 was, according to its promoters, intended to secure the purchase of lands in Palestine, which were to remain the inalienable property of the Jewish people. Moreover, in 1899, the IInd Congress had decided to establish the *Jewish Colonial Bank,* a limited company with headquarters in London, having a capital of two million pounds sterling. But, as Mr. Bernfeld has so aptly remarked,[29] the Jewish Colonial Bank, "although created as an ordinary bank to deal in credit operations, and to stimulate agriculture, commerce and industry in Palestine, and in the Orient, nevertheless *pursued an essentially political aim."*

In fact it was considered by its promoters, such as Dr. Bodenheimer, as the "most appropriate organ to enter into negotiations with the Turkish Government for the concession and purchase of lands." Herzl stated that the negotiations between the Bank and the Turkish Government were to have as their objective "the acquisition of a large concession with all the sovereign rights which are customarily granted to *Charter Companies."* In the eyes of the Zionists, the Turkish charter (or concession) was to be the prelude to a European Charter embodying guarantees by public international law.

The Jewish Colonial Bank was conceived as a political instrument to ensure the creation of a legally guaranteed homeland.

With the whole arsenal of ideological, economic and juridical weapons at the ready, all that remained to be done was to secure the active cooperation of the Great Powers. The skill of Zionism lay in the way it integrated the means at its disposal with European expansionism.

B. – Zionism and European Expansionism

At the time when Herzl and his friends made their definite choice of Palestine as the place where the future Jewish State was to be planted, the consent of the Great Powers was indispensable, if such a vast political plan was to have any chance of success. Herzl, who played a decisive role in the creation of Zionism and in its

---

[29] - Bernfeld: *op. cit.,* p. 415 (our italics.)

subsequent orientation, was well aware of the strength the Zionist cause could derive from the approval of the principal European Powers, and realised that their active interest in that cause was the *sine qua non* of its triumph.

As it turned out, each partner was only too ready to help the other—an immoral alliance if ever there was one—with Zionism placing all its hopes and all its power of influencing others in the support which it was to offer to, and to receive from, European States in the process of expansion; while the latter, realising how important the establishment of a Jewish State could be for the defence and security of their spheres of influence, decided to help and support Zionism. Should one call it a contract, this deal without a name, concluded at the cost of the freedom of the Palestinian people, to the exclusive benefit of the Zionists and their associates?

There can be no doubt that the Zionist leaders were aware that an exceptional opportunity would be offered them if they could get their movement adopted by the European imperialisms which, with their power of expansion, were in a better position to ensure its rapid and complete success. Herzl put it in simple words: "If His Majesty the Sultan gave us Palestine we could undertake to put the finances of Turkey in order. For Europe, we should form part of its bulwark against Asia; we should be the advance guard of civilisations against barbarism. As a neutral State, we should keep in constant touch with all Europe, which would have to guarantee our existence."[30]

We may note in passing the casual effrontery with which certain values, that all civilisation regard as essential, are reduced to the level of merchandise. In June 1896 Sultan Abdul-Hamid gave Herzl the answer he deserved: "The Turkish Empire does not belong to me but to the Turkish people. I cannot give away any part of it. Let the Jews spare their millions. When my Empire is divided up they can have Palestine for nothing. But it will only be our dead body which is cut up; I shall never agree to vivisection."[31]

---

[30] - Herzl: *L'Etat Juif*, Paris, 1926, p. 95.
[31] - Quoted by Rodinson, *op. cit.*, p. 38.

Zionism not only agreed, but actually requested to act as the privileged instrument of European imperialistic policy, in return for the grant of Palestine to the Jews. For such, indeed, were the conditions. A study of the history of the Zionist movement reveals that Zionism's first and only preoccupation was to build a State, a homeland guaranteed by public law. It was never content with creating a Jewish spiritual centre or scattered agricultural colonies, of which Herzl said that they were a method inspired by "the erroneous principle of progressive infiltration:" "Infiltration is bound to come to a bad end, for the moment will surely come when the government, at the request of the population which feels itself threatened, will stop further Jewish immigration. Consequently, emigration has really no *raison d'être* unless it is based on our guaranteed *sovereignty*. *The Society of Jews* will negotiate with the sovereign authorities of the territories in question, under the protection of European Powers, should this be agreeable to them."[32]

Aware of the rapid decline of "The Sick Man," these powers had begun, in the Sykes-Picot Agreement of 1916, to carve out spheres of influence for themselves in the Middle East, and made provision for an international administration in Palestine. But this agreement, concluded to control Anglo-Franco-Russian competition in this part of the world, was soon made obsolete by the triumph of the Bolshevik Revolution in 1917.

Great Britain took the lead in a spectacular manner, with the Balfour Declaration. This letter, addressed by Lord Balfour, British Secretary of State for Foreign Affairs, to Lord Rothschild, contained the following words: "His Majesty's Government view with favour the establishment in Palestine of a national home for the Jewish people, and will use its best endeavours to facilitate the achievement of this object, it being clearly understood that nothing shall be done which may prejudice the civil and religious rights of existing non-Jewish communities in Palestine, or the rights and political status of Jews in any other country."

---

[32] - Quoted by Rodinson, *op. cit.,* p. 32.
[33] - *Cf.* Dr. Jacques Khoury: *La Palestine devant le monde*, 1953, p. 9.

One is struck immediately, before one grasps the exact meaning
of this paragraph, by the surprising expression used to designate
the Arabs of Palestine ("the non-Jewish communities"). Taken
literally, it means that Palestine is regarded as a Jewish country, and
all its inhabitants other than Jews as aliens or immigrants! It suggests
that a country can, paradoxically, take the name of its alien minority
rather than that of the majority of its native inhabitants! And yet,
at the time of the Balfour Declaration, the Arabs formed 92% of
the population of Palestine.

It should be emphasised at the outset that British support in
the matter was decisive—not that the support of the other Great
Powers was by any means negligible. In general, reference is made
only to the Balfour Declaration of November 2, 1917, whereas in
reality the Zionist movement payed particular attention to securing
identical declarations from other Great Powers.[34] But the fact remains
that it was Great Britain which was to take up the Zionist Cause
most enthusiastically and this fully explains the notoriety of the
Balfour Declaration, a notoriety it retains to this day. The British War
Cabinet received a note from Weizmann which read as follows: "In
submitting our resolution we have entrusted our national and Zionist
destiny to the Foreign Office and the Imperial War Cabinet, in the
hope that the problem would be considered in the light of *imperial*
interests and the principles for which the Entente stands."[35]

By agreeing, in the middle of the war, to support Zionist
ambitions, and to subscribe to this peculiar interpretation of history,

---

[34] - *Cf.*, for example the letter addressed on June 4, 1917 (prior to the
British Declaration) to Sokolow by Jules Cambon, Secretary General of the
French Ministry of Foreign Affairs; the letter of February 14, 1918 from
Stephen Pichon, French Minister of Foreign Affairs, to Nahum Sokolow;
the letter to the same addressed on May 9, 1918 by the Italian Ambassador
in Paris in the name of Baron Sonnino, Italian Minister of Foreign Affairs;
the letter of August 31, 1918 from United States President Wilson to Rabbi
Stephen Wise, Zionist representative. In these documents France, Italy and
the United States take upon themselves the obligations of Lord Balfour.
They are published in the doctorate thesis of Bernfeld on *Le Sionisme, op. cit.,*
pp. 17-20.

[35] - Weizmann: *Trial and Error,* London, East and West Library, 1950,
p. 258.

which recognises Palestine as a Jewish land, Great Britain showed her lively interest in controlling the future of the Middle East. In this she was only following one of the established principles of her foreign policy. In a report he wrote as early as 1840, (well before the birth of Zionism) Lord Shaftesbury recommended that the Asiatic part of the Arab world be separated from the African part by the establishment of a British-protected State between them. Similarly, a memorandum addressed to Palmerston, British Minister for Foreign Affairs, on September 25, 1840, contained a plan for the colonisation of Palestine. The British consulate established in Jerusalem in 1838 (the first Western consulate to be opened in the Holy City) included the Jews among those subject to its jurisdiction, and put them under its protection.

Again, well before the Balfour Declaration, in letters dating back to August, 1840, and February, 1841, Palmerston instructed his ambassador in Turkey to promote the settlement of Jews in Palestine, with the object of thwarting any attempt by Mohammed Ali to achieve the union of Egypt with Syria.[36]

Almost a century later, it was the Zionist leaders, under Weizmann, who asked Great Britain to exercise a protectorate over the future Jewish State.[37] France, meanwhile, through George Picot, had unsuccessfully claimed a protectorate over the same area, Palestine, a claim which was rejected by the Zionist leaders.[38] Great Britain accepted this role because she saw in Zionism a means for implementing her imperial plans. There were many obvious reasons for her

---

[36] - Cf. Hamed Sultan: *Secondary Juridical Aspects of the Palestine Question*, Cairo, 1967, pp. 76-77 (in Arabic). "This *'entente cordiale'* between imperialism and Zionism," writes the author, "is not a new phenomenon. It existed before the birth of official Zionism. Imperialism has always looked upon the creation of a Jewish State in the Middle East as a means of preventing the rebirth of Arab nationalism, which it considered hostile to its interests in the region. When Mohammed Ali, Pasha of Egypt, entered into conflict with the Ottoman Sultan and considered the creation of an independent Arab State which would include all the Arabic-speaking Ottoman provinces, Great Britain, seeing the plan taking concrete shape, recommended the colonisation of Palestine by the Jews of Europe as a means of counteracting nascent pan-Arabism."

[37] - Weizmann: *op. cit.,* p. 243.

[38] - Weizmann: *op. cit.,* p. 240.

attitude. The moving of a pawn into the heart of the Ottoman Empire, made impossible the achievement of the Egyptian-Syrian unity envisaged by Mohammed Ali. Nor was Great Britain averse to acquiring a reliable base on the route to India by establishing there a State whose population would be well aware of the debt it owed to Great Britain. This point of view was described by the great historian Harold Temperley, in his *History of the Peace Conferences*.[39] "Great Britain" he says, "had special motives which prompted her to adopt the policy she followed in Palestine. These motives become obvious when one stops to consider the advantage of covering the Suez Canal from the East by a country whose population well knew how much help they had received from Great Britain and whose interest it was to retain that help, quite apart from the support it was certain to receive from Jews the world over."

One further observation must be made. The establishment of a protective glacis to the east of the Suez Canal was all the more necessary for Great Britain in view of her realisation that she would have to counter-balance the influence exercised by her importunate ally, France, to whom something would have to be given, either in Lebanon or in Syria.

Once the victory of the Allies was secured, it remained only to implement the Balfour Declaration, a deliberately ambiguous document, since it referred to a "Jewish national home," which did not fit into any precise juridical category. It was most desirable to maintain this obscurity about Anglo-Zionist intentions to avoid alarming the Hashemite dynasty, to which Great Britain had pledged its support. But it was not difficult to prophecy, as did Golda Meir on August 21, 1921 : "It is not the Arabs the English will choose to colonise Palestine, it is us."[40]

Meanwhile, the important thing was not to provoke an armed uprising by speaking of a Jewish State at a time when people were beginning to become aware of something which had hitherto been ignored by everyone, the Arab National Movement. Even the Zionists

[39] - Harold Temperley: *History of the Peace Conferences*, Vol. IV, p. 171.
[40] - Cf., Mary Syrkin: *Golda Meir,* Paris, Gallimard, 1966, p. 63.

were displeased to hear Tardieu announce, before the Council of Ten in February, 1919, that France would oppose neither the placing of Palestine under British trusteeship nor the formation of a Jewish State. Weizmann was to write later: We ourselves had refrained from using them."[41] (i.e. these words).

Both British and Zionists had to advance surreptitiously by proclaiming to the world something totally different from what they had in mind, and on which they were in entire agreement. Hence the *White Paper*, or Churchill Memorandum, of June 3, 1922 which endeavoured to minimise the significance of the Balfour Declaration in order to forestall the recurrence of violent Arab reactions: "Phrases have been used such as that Palestine is to become 'as Jewish as England in English.' His Majesty's Governments regard any such expectation as impracticable and have no such aim in view... The terms of the Declaration (Balfour) referred to do not contemplate that Palestine as a whole should be converted into a Jewish National Home, but that such a home should be founded in Palestine... Nor have they at any time contemplated... the disappearance or the subordination of the Arabic population, language, or culture in Palestine."[42]

It was with the formal consent of the Zionists to such an interpretation of the Balfour Declaration—an interpretation which excluded a Jewish State—that the draft Mandate was submitted to the League of Nations. This Mandate, which was granted to Great Britain on July 24, 1922 embodied the Balfour Declaration.

At this stage of the historical evolution of the Palestine question, one cannot but subscribe to the conclusion of M. Rodinson's well-documented and subtle analysis. "The Arabs had every right to regard the implantation of a new foreign element in the land of Palestine (an element which, at that time, was mainly European) as having been imposed on them by a European Power, thanks to the victory of a group of European Powers over another group to which

---

[41] - Weizmann, *opp. cit.,* p. 306.
[42] - Quoted by Rodinson: *op. cit.,* p. 50.

the Ottoman Empire had attached itself."[43]

The Zionist leaders had good reason to believe that the Mandate over Palestine, inasmuch as it embodied the terms of the Declaration, was the ideal platform from which they could feed and control the current of immigration with a view to forming a majority Jewish population which would, eventually, lead to the emergence of a Jewish State. Officially, at any rate, there was no further mention of such a State, but the idea of creating it remained the driving force of the Zionist Organisation.

Subsequently, the close alliance between the Zionists and the British, undermined by increasingly serious differences, turned into open hostility. This was an illustration of the classical phenomenon of tension between a mother country and its colony, such as existed between France and the European settlers in Algeria. Great Britain, which had, by force of circumstances, played the role of the mother country, in protecting the Jewish colonisation of Palestine, came increasingly into collision with the Jewish colonisers. Concern for her interests led her to be more tactful in her dealings with the Arabs and to favour the Zionist cause less and less. *Such was the case with the White Paper published in 1939.* The dispute between the Zionists and the British later degenerated into actual armed conflict.

Then, when the United Nations adopted its Partition Plan, and Great Britain decided to withdraw her troops from Palestine on May 15, 1948, the Israel-Arab confrontation became inevitable, as the Arab countries could not accept the United Nations decision.[44]

---

[43] - M. Rodinson: *op. cit.,* p. 46.

[44] - One must understand, as did M. Rodinson, what were the feelings of the Arabs at that time, when thirty years of a policy of slow erosion, authorised by the Balfour Declaration, culminated in the dismantling of their country. "Europe had collectively sent colonisers whose objective was to seize part of the national territory. At a time when the Palestinian Arabs themselves could easily have thrown out these colonisers, they were prevented from doing so by the nations of Europe, together with America, acting in concert. The Arabs had already been morally disarmed by the false assurance that all that was intended was the peaceful settlement of a few unfortunate and harmless groups of people who were to remain in the minority. Then, when the real designs of these groups came out into the open, when the

In short, the development of the political phenomena can be summed up in a series of observations that admit of no doubt whatsoever.

The ideological Zionist Movement was of European origin. The success of Zionism was due to the Balfour Declaration, a British political act given decisive importance by the victory and the subsequent approval of the Allies. The first Arab-Israeli war of 1948 brought to the fore the Jewish community, settled in Palestine and supported by all the European-American nations, and especially by Europe, which was happy to rid itself of unwanted elements.

From this general phenomenon of expansion by European countries into the under-developed world, Zionism has advanced to establish in it a sort of economic and political condominium based on the sacrifice of the legitimate rights of the native Arab population. What does it signify, as far as the Arab population is concerned, if Israel is a socialist State, when its creation was the result of fraud and force? And even if it is socialist, *it certainly remains a bridgehead for the capitalist world in the heart of the underdeveloped world. The connecting link between its Zionist origin and its present role is only too obvious. As a result of Zionism's initial choice Israel is the ally of the capitalist Powers.*

At the beginning, as well as at the present stage of the evolution of Israel, we find capitalism and imperialism, and between then and now there has been Jewish settlement, which is a colonial phenomenon, a colonial act.

(44 - Cont'd)

collective power they had slowly built up under the protection of the Mandate was disclosed, the European-American world, united despite its internal differences, from the socialist USSR to the ultra-capitalist U.S.A., wanted to force the Arabs to submit passively to the *fait accompli*. In the eyes of the Arabs, the conclusion of the Second World War brought a bitter repetition of the end of the First." After this lucid analysis of the responsibilities incurred by the Great Powers, M. Rodinson writes: "Did not the 1922 Mandate itself stipulate that 'nothing shall be done which prejudice the rights and the position of the other sections of the population?" And did not the American Presidents Roosevelt and Truman promise, in letters to Ibn Saud on April 5, 1945 and October 28, 1946, not to take any decision without 'full consultation' of Arabs and Jews, and to decide nothing which would be contrary to Arab interests?" (Maxime Rodinson. *op. cit.* pp. 60-61.)

C. – *Jewish Settlement in Palestine*

Everything has happened as though Palestine was an uninhabited land, as though the Arabs who lived in it would be indifferent to the occupation of their land. But, as Neville Mandel has remarked,[45] contrary to the view generally held, Arab resistance to Jewish colonisation began well before the 1914 War. Arab nationalism had been opposed to Zionist colonisation since 1850. The first immigrants bothered their heads but little about the Arabs of Palestine, such dealings as they had being with the Ottoman authorities who governed Palestine at that time.

It is in the light of these considerations that Jewish immigration into Palestine must be described.

a) The first wave of immigrants (the first *aliya*) covers the period that ended in 1917. By 1914 there were probably some 85,000 Jews living in Palestine. (This figure fell to 56,000 during the First World War.)

It was, therefore, essential for the Zionists, after the Allied victory, to make sure that the minority Jewish population of Palestine increased rapidly.

b) There followed a second period, which ended with the creation of the.State of Israel. In 1920, the Jewish Agency was authorised to bring into Palestine 16,500 immigrants per year, and by 1922 the proportion of Jews to the other inhabitants of Palestine was 11%. However, this percentage was to increase rapidly, totalling 17.7% in 1931 and 28% in 1936, the annual quotas having been considerably exceeded as a result of clandestine immigration. The Simpson Report of June 20, 1930, highlighted the importance of the so-called "tourist" phenomenon and recalled that in 1925, 33,800 immigrants had settled in Palestine. It held the Jewish Agency responsible for these violations of the immigration law, violations which it was impossible to check once the clandestine immigrants were settled in Palestine. The same Report also noted the consequen-

---

[45] - Neville Mandel: *Turks, Arabs, and Jewish Immigration into Palestine, 1882-1914,* London, 1965, pp. 77 to 108.

ces to employment of this uncontrolled immigration, which resulted in unemployment among Arab workers. Simpson concluded that it was essential either to stop or control this influx, so as to prevent a further deterioration in the living conditions of the native population. Similar concern had been expressed in the 1922 *White Paper,* or Churchill Memorandum, mentioned above, which stated that immigration would be limited by the "economic capacity of the country to absorb new arrivals."

The second *White Paper,* issued in 1930, after the Simpson Report, again limited immigration. But these restrictions, as MacDonald assured Weizmann in a letter dated 13 February 1931, were not to be considered as a reversal of previous policy.

Whatever the intentions expressed, the undeniable fact remained that five years after the publication of the White Paper, 143,000 immigrants had entered Palestine. The Mandatory Power was either unable or unwilling to stem this tide, which had been swollen by the first racialist measures taken by the Hitler regime.

In 1939, the attitude of Great Britain underwent a change, as a result of her increasing awareness of Arab opposition to the creation of a Jewish State. The White Paper of May 17, 1939 proposed the establishment, within a period of ten years, of an independent Palestinian State in which not more than one third of the population would be Jews. To attain this objective, the British document stipulated that Jewish immigration was to be restricted to a total of 75,000 over the five years following its publication, and that thereafter "no further immigration was to be allowed unless the Arabs of Palestine are prepared to acquiesce in it." Finally, it stipulated that the number of clandestine, or illegal, immigrants would be deducted from the fixed quota.

The above measures, as well as the following excerpt from the White Paper, reflect a change in the British attitude: "His Majesty's Government sees nothing, either in the Mandate or in subsequent statements, which corroborates the view that the establishment of a Jewish National Home in Palestine could not be achieved unless immigration were allowed to continue indefinitely."

Once again, the quotas fixed by the White Paper were exceeded, and the Jewish population of Palestine continued to increase. At the end of 1943, the Jews numbered 539,000 out of a total population of 1,676,000, or 32%.

c) With the creation of Israel, a third phase opens. From 1949 to 1954, the number of Jews rose from 758,000 to 1,500,000, and reached 1,800,000 in 1958. Thus were fulfilled the hopes of the Zionist Organisation of America which, in its meeting at the Biltmore Hotel in New York on May 11, 1942, had demanded unrestricted immigration under the sole control of the Jewish Agency.

The State of Israel had made immigration a cornerstone of its policy. As early as 1950, the famous Law of the Return, passed on July 5 of that year,[46] contained a pressing appeal to all Jews, every one of whom, no matter where he lives, has the right to come to the country as an immigrant. Israeli policy of populating Palestine with Jewish immigrants was given concrete form in this law, which has proved a useful instrument in the service of Israeli expansionism. "The Arab States neighbouring on Israel," we read in *Les Cahiers de l'Histoire,* "have constantly feared that *immigration was the basis of an endless process of correlation, with the Jews demands for lands to settle their immigrants geared to their bringing in immigrants in order to be able to claim more lands... The Arabs were therefore justified in looking on the creation of the State of Israel not as the beginning of an era of stability, but as the starting point of an expansion, the only object of which, according to the Israelis themselves, was the ingathering of the Diaspora."[47]*

The concentration of Jews on Palestinian soil which, during the past 25 years, has been going on at a rapid pace, significant enough in itself because of its colonial nature, acquires an even greater significance when one realises that it must inevitably be accompanied by the progressive dispossession of the Arabs.

---

[46] - Cf. *supra.* pp. 38 and 40 and *infra.* p. 65.
[47] - *Les Cahiers de l'Histoire: op. cit.,* p. 18.

D. – *Progressive Dispossession of the Arabs*

To understand and appreciate the methods followed by Israel in the acquisition of land, we must divide the operation into two stages: a first, which begins with the first attempts at colonisation and ends in 1948; and a second, from 1948 up to the present day, which has been characterised by the policy followed by Israel.

a) *Until* 1948, the Zionist Organisation's land-acquisition policy in Palestine was implemented in an ostensibly regular manner.

The Jewish National Fund created in 1907, which was supported by the Jewish Colonial Bank, acquired lands by purchase from their Arab owners. On this basis, an attempt has been made to establish the legitimacy of Jewish settlement in Palestine and to justify the fact that in 1930 the Jews owned 1,170,000 dunums, as against 400,000 in 1914.

But colonisation is not necessarily accompanied by the brutal procedure of confiscation. Very often the colonial phenomenon of land acquisition has evolved within the strictly regular framework of a mutual contract. But it must be remembered that the alien coloniser is, in fact, in a privileged position; there is a whole series of shifts, tricks, and administrative facilities which make it easy for him, at small cost to himself, to extend his domains at the expense of the native. The history of French colonisation in Tunisia[48] and in Algeria[49] provides excellent illustrations of such ostensibly legal practices.

Indeed, an analysis of colonial history shows that settlers have usually acquired lands by purchase, confiscation being rarely resorted to. Yet, nobody could maintain that such transactions are not in fact colonial phenomena.

These general remarks were necessary in order to place the policy of the purchase of Arab lands in Palestine in its true context, i.e., the context of colonialism. Add to this the evidence provided

---

[48] - Paul Sebag: *La Tunisie, essai de monographie,* Paris. 1951, p. 36 sqq.
[49] - *Cf.,* F. Borella: "Le droit public économique algérien," *Revue algérienne des sciences juridiques, économiques et politiques,* 1966, p. 513.

by Zionist practice, and the true dimensions of the Israeli colonial phenomenon will be clearly seen.

The inalienability of Jewish lands is asserted by the Constitution of the Jewish Agency (Article 2), which, adopted in Zurich on August 14, 1929, also includes provisions intended to consolidate and extend the Jewish nature of such appropriation. Paragraph 5 stipulates that only a Jew can work on Jewish land, those who employ non-Jewish labour being liable to a fine.

However, this embargo on the employment of Arab labour in the development of Jewish lands must not be used as an argument in support of the claim that Israeli settlement in Palestine is of a non-colonial nature. Here, again, direct exploitation of the native is not an inevitable and invariable feature of the colonial phenomenon. In America, India, New Zealand and Australia, the English did not, strictly speaking, exploit the native population by employing local manpower, yet British expansionism was certainly a colonial phenomenon.

According to the Simpson Report of June 20, 1930, Jewish colonisation of Palestine had by then resulted in 29% of Arab families being dispossessed of their lands. As a result, the Mandatory Power started concerning itself, somewhat late in the day, with the transfer of lands. After the publication of the *White Paper* of 1939, the *"Land Transfer Regulations Act"* divided the country into three zones:

— Zone A, (4 million acres, 63% of the total area) in which the transfer of Arab lands to Jews was forbidden.
— Zone B, (2 million acres, 32% of the total area) in which the purchase of lands by Jews was permissible under certain conditions.
— Free Zone (332,000 acres, 5% of the total area) where the purchase of land was unrestricted.

The area of Jewish lands has increased continuously: it totalled 928 square kilometres in Mandatory Palestine in 1941, and reached 3,240 square kilometres in 1961. The period of the British Mandate was particularly propitious to the extension of Zionist landholding:

at the beginning of the Mandate, Zionist-held lands totalled 650,000 dunums but increased to 2,075,000 dunums towards the end of the Mandate.[50] The rate of increase was extremely high after 1948.

b) In fact it was with the creation of Israel that the first of a series of measures was taken, all of which were designed to secure the rapid dispossession of Arabs. With these measures, we pass from the stage of "acquisition to that of confiscation."[51]

No sooner had the 1948 war ended, than Arab lands close to the frontier (Upper Galilee, the Arab region of the central part of Israel, and the zone adjacent to the Gaza Strip) were placed under military government. In these areas the military authorities applied the *Absentees' Property Law* in such a manner that a general redistribution of lands was effected in favour of the Jews, particularly in upper Galilee. Emergency military regulations traced boundaries so arbitrarily that owners of lands within these limits could not enter them without permission from the military authorities. Or, "having ordered the Arabs to live in their villages, which made it impossible for them to cultivate distant properties, the military authorities carried out by decree land transfers which were often to the disadvantage of the Arabs."[52]

A similar summary procedure was established at that time to enable the civil authorities arbitrarily to declare any Arab town or village an "abandoned area." As a result of a 1948 regulation, many Arabs were considered as absentees and their properties regarded as abandoned properties, although in fact they had never left Israel.

The law of March 10, 1953 which replaced this emergency regulation, stated that all land reserved, seized, distributed or put to use since May 14, 1948, in order to ensure the needs of vital

---

[50] - *La politique internationale,* Cairo, October 1967, p. 153 (Al Ahram edition).

[51] - For all these questions, see W. Schwarz: *The Arabs in Israel,* London, 1959, p. 96; Don Peretz: *Israel and the Palestine Arabs,* Washington, The Middle East Institute, 1958, p. 152. See also "Les Arabes en Israël," in *Les Temps Modernes, op. cit.,* p. 792 sqq.

[52] - *Cf. Les Cahiers de l'Histoire, op. cit.,* p. 24 sqq.

development, settlement or security, and neglected by its titular owner, was declared to be the property of the Development Authority. By virtue of this law and other laws which preceded it, 16,000 hectares of land belonging to the Arab minority were confiscated. The central committee of the courageous little group called *Ihud* protested against this Land Acquisition Law "which really means the theft of lands owned by inhabitants of the State. They are farmers like you. They are citizens of Israel like you. There is only one difference between them and you: they are Arabs and you are Jews." No land belonging to Jews has been "acquired" by virtue of the provisions of this law of 1953, which is all the more iniquitous in that the compensation it envisaged was based on land prices in 1950, and this, in effect, meant that those whose lands were expropriated were compensated at a ridiculously low rate.

The so-called *Law of Limitations,* of 1958, stipulated that landowners desiring to register their lands had to prove possession for twenty years, not only ten years as previously. Thus Arab landowners who had failed to claim their property deeds under the old legislation, were unable to apply for the registration of their lands in their name.

This racialist legislation, which resulted in the spoliation of what remained of the native population, inevitably invites comparison with legislation in the Union of South Africa. There, legislation has progressively prohibited Africans from acquiring real estate, and through the Group *Areas Act* of 1950, has dealt a final blow to all forms of landholding by Africans.

The above should have been sufficient to reveal the anti-Arab racialism of the State of Israel. Let us now examine the subject in greater detail.

2) THE ANTI-ARAB RACIALISM OF ISRAEL IN CO-LONIAL THINKING

As Rodinson has so pertinently remarked:[53] "The idea of

---

53 - Rodinson: *op. cit.,* p. 68.

creating a purely, or predominantly Jewish State in Arab Palestine in the 20th century, could only lead to a colonial-type situation, with the development of a *racialist* mentality and, finally, to a military confrontation of the two ethnic groups."

In fact, anti-Arab racialism has been institutionalised to the extent of becoming one of the distinguishing characteristics of Israeli legislation, in the same way that anti-black racialism predominates in the legislation of the South African Union.

A) In the field of political rights and liberties the discrimination, as regards citizenship and nationality, is fundamental, because it is a discrimination based on religion.

The *Law of the Return* of July 5, 1950,[54] according to which "every Jew has the right to come to this country as an immigrant," should be compared with the Nationality Law of 1952, Article 2 of which stipulates that "every immigrant, within the meaning of the Law of the Return, shall become an Israeli."

Thus, acquisition of Israeli nationality is subordinated to the quality of being a Jew, a matter which constitutes a discriminatory practice resulting in the refusal of the benefits of such nationality to Arabs, whether they be Christians or Moslems.[55] In other words, the *Law of the Return* is a naturalisation law applicable exclusively to Jews.

But private international law on naturalisation has different rules in this respect. It does acknowledge that every State has discretionary competence in this matter, but insists that certain basic rules must be applied. These cover such matters as a medical examination, good character, and a longer or shorter probationary period; the law also generally stipulates a minimum age for applicants for naturalisation. But, in the civil law of naturalisation, there is no place for the element of religion, whereas in Israel this is first condition laid down for the acquisition of Israeli *nationality*.

The Arabs have no right of political association. Their political representation in the Israeli parliament is not in proportion to their

---

[54] - *Cf. supra.* pp. 39 and 41.
[55] - *Cf.* Lehmann, in *Journal du Droit International*, 1963, p. 694.

importance in the State of Israel. With only six seats out of 120, the Arabs, who constitute 11% of the total population, are not adequately represented. Moreover, no Arab holds a responsible post in any of the organs of the State of Israel. Finally, as regards freedom of expression and freedom of the press, these rights have been denied the Arabs by the Supreme Court in Jerusalem.[56]

B) Public freedoms are also the object of restrictive measures on the part of the Israeli authorities. Freedom of movement and residence, recognised by Article 13 of the Universal Declaration of Human Rights, is "organised" in such a manner that the Arabs are in fact unable to exercise it.

The *Law and Administration Ordinance*,[57] inspired by the Defense Emergency Regulations enacted by the Mandatory Power in 1945, authorises the Israeli Minister of Defence to limit the movements of the Arab minority and the exercise by them of other individual liberties, by means of emergency regulations. These regulations have established "Defence Areas" within which there are "security Zones" where the Minister can exercise his authority, either directly, or by delegating it to other officers.

In this way three military security zones, which no person had the right to enter, were created. Those who were permanent residents of these zones could not leave them without prior permission from the authorities. Violations of these restrictions made the offender liable to either expulsion or to imprisonment and fines, or both. Sentences, against which there was no appeal, were passed by military tribunals unhampered by any form of procedural restrictions.

In these Zones,[58] the commissioners had extremely wide powers. They were authorised to remove or deport the inhabitants of the Zones, to seize and to hold "any goods, articles or objects," to enter

---

[56] - Cf. "Les Arabes en Israël," *Les Temps Modernes, op. cit.*, pp. 804 and 805. In South Africa a series of legislative texts has limited to the minimum the exercise of public freedoms and political rights. They are the *South Africa Act of 1909*, the *Publication and Entertainments Bill of 1957*, and the *Unlawful Organisation Act of 1960*,

[57] - Cf. *Laws of the State of Israel*, vol. I, p. 8.

[58] - The three Zones created were the Northern Area in Galilee, the central sector or "Little Triangle" and the sub-district of Beersheba.

and search at any moment, to limit the movement of persons, to impose restrictions in the field of employment and business, to issue deportation orders, to place any person under police supervision, or to force him to live where ordered.

The commissioners could also confiscate any land in the interests of public security; they had extensive powers to requisition and to impose military occupation and charge the cost of it to the inhabitants, to impose a curfew, and to suspend postal and all other public services.

Don Peretz[59] has accurately summed up the position of the Arabs as follows: "Arabs in these areas lived under a complex of legal restrictions. Their movement into, out of, and within security zones was regulated by the military. Legal residents could be banished and their properties confiscated. The populations of whole villages could be removed from one area to another. The only authority entitled to deal with infringements of emergency regulations was a military court, whose decisions were not subject to the jurisdiction of the Civil Courts of Appeal."

Moreover, even Jewish lawyers have condemned the application of these emergency laws.[60] Meeting in Tel-Aviv on February 7, 1947, they recalled that the laws deprived citizens of their fundamental freedom, and constituted a threat to the principles of legality and individual liberty. Such laws, they said, which were liable to lead to dictatorial government, should be rescinded.

This hope was not to be fulfilled. On the contrary, the laws in question have been the instrument of a policy aimed at the eviction of both Christian and Moslem Arabs who had remained on their lands. In its desire to create a predominantly Jewish State, Israel stepped up its drive to induce the Arabs to quit. The Arabs had no other choice but to leave Palestine, thus making room for Jewish immigrants.[61]

---

[59] - Don Peretz, *op. cit.,* chap. VII, pp. 95 and 96.

[60] - *Cf.* "Les Arabes en Israël," *Les Temps Modernes, op. cit.,* p. 808 sqq.

[61] - In South Africa, the movements and residence of negroes are subject to regulations which first appeared in the *Natives Labour Registration Act* (1911) the most recent version being the *Natives Act of 1952.* The latter

C) Everything possible has been done to restrict the exercise of what might be called concrete freedoms, such as the right to education and to work.

The organisation of Secondary education for the Arabs in Israel is most inadequate. There are only six schools, which function under most unsatisfactory conditions. Libraries, laboratories and books are almost non-existent; the buildings are inconvenient or very old. Teachers are recruited more for their submissiveness than for their competence. A total of only two thousand pupils attend these mediocre secondary schools. This situation has resulted in a very low standard of education, as is attested by the fact that only 5.4% of the pupils pass the *bagrut* (Matriculation) examination. Furthermore, examinations in Hebrew and Hebrew literature are compulsory for Arab secondary school pupils of whom, naturally only a very small number reach the university.[62]

Thus, instead of the system being organised so as to provide equal opportunities for Arabs and Jews, education for Arabs is systematically neglected to impede the formation of an Arab elite.

It is a fact too, that the Arab minority is being proletarianised as a result of the reduction in the number of Arab landowners. Arab labourers employed in mines, industry and public works, are restricted to inferior jobs, and rigorous working conditions often compel them to move from one part of the country to another; 50% of Arab

---

([61] - Cont'd)

substitutes a control booklet for the various laissez-passer documents *(Reference Book)* and coordinates the old system of *Pass Laws* controlling and restricting the movements of negroes. Moreover, a negro can only reside in a zone specified by the law with prior and express authorisation, which can be refused for a variety of reasons. No African can reside for more than 72 hours in an urban zone, or a designated zone, unless he was born therein or is a resident thereof, or has continuously worked therein for more than ten years. The law grants discretionary powers to any responsible civil servant who "has reason to believe" that an African, who finds himself in an urban zone, is "idle, has loose morals or is capable of disturbing public order," to arrest him "without a warrant" and to charge him before a Commissioner for Native Affairs or a Magistrate.

[62] - *Cf.* "Les Arabes en Israël," *Les Temps Modernes, op. cit.,* pp. 800 and 802. It is to be noted that a similar discriminatory regime in education exists in South Africa. *The Bantu Education Act* establishes separate schools and curricula for whites and blacks.

workmen, in fact, are constantly changing both the places where they work and the kind of work they do. They constitute a social group which has no means of defence against exploitation. The government admits very few Arabs to the public service (1.5%) although the Arab population, even after several exoduses, still constitutes one tenth of the population of Israel.[63]

The best analysis of the situation is provided by Rodinson in the following passage:

"Relations between Israelis and Arabs *have been relations of domination rather than of exploitation*. Whatever the particular reasons for the flight of the Arabs from Israeli territory, which has reduced their number from two thirds to one tenth of the population, the general cause is undoubtedly the determination of the new settlers, who have gradually infiltrated into Palestine over the past sixty years, to make themselves the dominant element in a Jewish national State."[64]

This State was created by world Zionism in conformity with a colonialist philosophy. The weakness and absurdity of its historical foundations have been dealt with above. Joseph Reinach, like other well-known and distinguished Jews (Judah Magnes, Martin Buber, Dr. Elmer Berger, Maxime Rodinson...) wrote in the *Journal des Débats* of March 30, 1919: "As there is neither a Jewish race nor a Jewish nation, as there is only a Jewish religion, Zionism is a folly —a triple historical, archaeological and ethnic error."

One must add to this that it was also a legal error, as Zionism was completely lacking in the legal titles necessary for the creation of Israel.

---

[63] - Similar remarks can be made about South Africa. *The Labour Regulation Act* of 1911, the *Workmen's Wages Protection Act* of 1911, the *Natives Urban Areas Act* of 1923 apply the principle of *apartheid*. The Africans are restricted to harsh, inferior jobs and are not allowed to compete with the whites for whom skilled jobs carrying authority and responsibility are reserved. The *Natives Law (Amendment) Act* of 1957 empowers the Minister of Labour to extend freely the application of the laws of 1911. The barrier erected to prevent Africans from obtaining jobs reserved for whites has been strengthened. The latter receive salaries much higher than those of the Africans, who are not allowed to look for work as and where they like: they are obliged to register their names in the general unemployment roll.

[64] - Maxime Rodinson: *op. cit.*, p. 80.

PART TWO

LEGAL TITLES

An erroneous interpretation of history has succeeded in winning some credence for the thesis that the Jews have historical rights in Palestine. And just as religious and humanitarian feelings have been exploited to create a trend in world public opinion favourable c Israel, so has legal argumentation been employed in an attempt to prove the legality of that State. But the legal aspect of the establishment of Israel as a State has flaws which cannot but lead the impartial observer to a different conclusion.

Although not yet fully codified, international law does assume the existence of a number of rules which, had they been strictly enforced, would have made impossible not only the abuse of its authority by the Mandatory Power in Palestine, but also the astonishing Partition resolution adopted by the United Nations, and the recognition of Israel by certain members of the international community.

This spate of legal irregularities committed since the Balfour Declaration would have been impossible, had it not been for the impotence of the League of Nations and the United Nations to enforce respect for their Covenant and Charter, and the complicity or indifference of several of the States concerned.

The first observation to be made in this respect is that the League of Nations Covenant was violated during the execution of the Palestine Mandate. Secondly, it will be shown that the United Nations Partition resolution for Palestine was null and void. Thirdly, it will be shown that the legal status of Israel has been invalid ever since the creation of the State.

I. — VIOLATION OF THE LEAGUE OF NATIONS COVENANT BY THE PALESTINE MANDATE

The Mandates system, however flexible it may be thanks to the existence of different classes of Mandates, includes a rule common to all, of which Article 22 of the League of Nations Covenant can be considered as the principal source. The Charter of the Mandate for Palestine is this constitutional text presented in a form applicable to a community.

The problem we are faced with is to discover whether the regulations governing the Mandate are in conformity with the general rules relating to the Mandatory system, or if it is to be seen as a mere variation on the mandatory formula no more, and no less, significant than were the Mandates over Irak, Transjordan or Syria, or as a patent violation of the League of Nations Covenant.

A comparative analysis of the Mandatory System based on Article 22 of the Covenant and the Mandate for Palestine, leads one to the observation that the texts are compatible only insofar as the provisions of the Mandate for Palestine which reproduce the Balfour Declaration are considered null and void.

In other words, one is inevitably led to the conclusion that the Mandate for Palestine, embodying as it does substantial departures from the basic principles of the Mandatory System, conforms only ostensibly to those principles. Let us now examine the following two aspects of this proposition:

1) THE PALESTINE MANDATE OSTENSIBLY COMPLIES WITH THE BASIC PRINCIPLES OF THE MANDATORY SYSTEM

Article 22 of the League of Nations Covenant, which is the Charter of the Mandates System, enumerates a number of principles applicable to territories and colonies which have ceased to be under the sovereignty of certain States, but which are still incapable of governing themselves under the exacting conditions of the modern world. "The well-being and development of such peoples form a sacred trust of civilisation, and it is fitting that guarantees for the proper execution of this trust should be embodied in this Covenant."

Although this text uses the words 'mandate' and 'trust', it is obvious that these two concepts, derived as they are from private law, could not form a legal basis for the formal investiture of a government with political rule over a community. The basic characteristic of this concept is, in the words of Article 22, that it constitutes a "sacred trust of civilisation," a clear formula reflecting a well-defined political will on the part of the authors of the Mandatory System to facilitate the progress of peoples who had not yet reached complete maturity.[1]

If we are to insist on an analogy with a concept in private law, it is the concept of *trust* that immediately comes to mind.[2] This specifically Anglo-Saxon institution imposes upon the trustee a purely moral obligation. Such is the position of the Mandatory State, which should administer the territory entrusted to it by fulfilling such obligations as it has accepted, for the exclusive benefit of the inhabitants of this territory.[3]

The territory under Mandate is, in fact, entrusted to the Mandatory State not as absolute property, but in the same manner as a trustee is put in possession of the property he is entrusted with. Briefly, this obligation means that the Mandatory should act for the sole benefit of the Mandated territory. And his powers to administer it do not in any way include the right to dispose of it.

However, this reference to an institution of private law is not strictly necessary. To clarify the concept of Mandate it is sufficient to indicate that the expression was not used, either in Article 22 or in other special regulations, in a technical sense, but merely to indicate that the Mandatory acted in the name of the League of Nations.

On July 20, 1922 the League approved the Mandate for Palestine, which was an instrument defining the degree of authority, control and administration to be exercised by the Mandatory Power, in accordance with Article 22, para. 8, of the Covenant.

In connection with the particular legal status of Palestine, the following two observations must be made. These observations are also valid as regards all other Mandates.

---

[1] - Cf. A. McNair, Opinion given in the question of South West Africa. *Recueil des Arrêts, Avis consultatifs et Ordonnances.* C.I.J., 1950, p. 22 sqq.

[2] - Cf. Brierly, in *British Yearbook of International Law*, 1929, pp. 217-219.

[3] - Cf. J. de Villiers, Supreme Court of the Union of South Africa, *Rex v. Christian* (quoted by McNair. *op. cit.*, p. 26.)

A. In the first place, there is no fusion of the juridical organisation of the Mandatory State with that of the community placed under Mandate.

The judicial system in the Mandated territory is quite distinct from that of the Mandatory State, and must fully guarantee the rights of foreigners as well as the indigenous population.

Foreign relations are reserved for the Mandatory Power (Article 12) which negotiates and signs treaties on behalf of the Mandated territory, as its own treaties are not applicable to that territory; it is required to extend diplomatic and consular protection to the citizens of Palestine. Like all other countries placed under a Mandate, Palestine has no competence in the international field.

The guarantee of the territorial integrity of Palestine is provided for in Article 5, which makes it incumbent on the Mandatory State to ensure its protection against any cession or lease of all or part of its territory, and against the establishment therein of any foreign Power.

However, there is one exception to the general scheme outlined above: Article 1 specifies that the Mandatory Power shall have full power of legislation and administration within such limits as may be laid down by the terms of the Mandate. This is tantamount to saying that the Mandatory Power can apply its own legislation. But, apart from this particular feature, the statute for Palestine, like the majority of other Mandate charters, assures the community of a certain degree of juridical autonomy.

B. The second observation that must be made is that the *Mandatory Administration is compelled to assume obligations* in which can be discerned some of the standards of positive international law.

Freedom of conscience and the free exercise of all forms of worship, compatible with public order and good morals, are stipulated in Article 15 of the Mandate for Palestine.

The Mandatory Power is authorised to recruit volunteers for such forces as may be necessary for the maintenance of peace and order and for the defence of the country (Article 17).

It is under obligation to take all necessary measures to safeguard the interests of the community by ensuring that the country is developed. And, subject to any international obligations accepted by it the Mandatory Power has full power to determine ownership or public control of all the natural resources of the country, or of public works, services and utilities established or to be established. It is also required to introduce a land system appropriate to the needs of the country (Article 11).

The institution of the Mandate had a civilising aim; the Mandatory Power was called upon to develop the culture of the inhabitants, to enrich the artistic heritage of the community put under Mandate. Thus Article 21 entrusted Great Britain with the task of drafting an antiquities law.

International control was provided for, as in the case of the other Mandates, in the form of a compulsory annual *report* to the Council of the League of Nations, required by Article 24 of the Palestine Mandate. The provisions of the Mandate could not be modified without the Council's consent (Article 27). As regards the termination of the Mandate, it follows from Article 28 that this could only come about by the establishment in Palestine of an independent government.

Thus, the rights and obligations vested in Britain by the Palestine Mandate can be classified in two categories. In the first come those which directly concern the administration of the territory and which correspond to the "sacred trust of civilisation" mentioned in Article 22 of the Covenant. The second category includes those which are related to the supervision and control machinery of the League of Nations and constitute the sum of the guarantees established for the accomplishment of this special mission entrusted to the Mandatory Power.

In the *Mavrommatis* decision of August 30, 1924, the International Court of Justice gave a precise definition of the extent and scope of the powers of the Mandatory State. According to the Court, the Mandatory had no right to exercise administrative power in a discretionary manner, and the expression "public control" referred to in Article 11 should be understood in its English meaning, i.e. in the sense of method of administration.

Limits were thus placed on the exercise by the Mandatory State of its power of administration.

The rights and obligations of the Mandatory Power which we have just examined conform entirely with Article 22 of the League of Nations Covenant, and particularly with paragraph 4 of that Article.

But this respect paid to the principles of the Mandatory System is only apparent, since three Articles of the Palestine Mandate, Articles 2, 4 and 6, violate the Covenant of the League of Nations.

2) THE MANDATE FOR PALESTINE, A VIOLATION OF THE LEAGUE OF NATIONS COVENANT

Article 2 of the Mandate repeats the promise made a few years earlier by Lord Balfour. It says: "The Mandatory shall be responsible for placing the country under such political, administrative and economic conditions as will secure the establishment of the Jewish national home, as laid down in the preamble, and the development of self-governing institutions," and "also for safeguarding the civil and religious rights of all the inhabitants of Palestine, irrespective of race and religion."

The incorporation of the Balfour promise[4] in the Mandate creates doubts both as to its legality and as to its real intention.

A. – Nullity of the Balfour Declaration

The promise of November 2, 1917, by which Great Britain pledged "the establishment in Palestine of a national home for the Jewish people" is invalid on several counts.

(a) *The Balfour Declaration concerned a territory* with which Great Britain had no legal relation and which she bestowed on a party that was not qualified to receive it.

---

[4] - It is interesting to note that, as a result of urgent and insistent Zionist intervention, this "promise" was at first inserted by the San Remo Conference in the draft peace treaty with Turkey. This was on April 24, 1920. But the Treaty of Lausanne of July 24, 1923, which replaced the unratified Treaty of Sèvres of August 10, 1920, and established definite peace with the Ottoman Empire, made no mention at all of this promise. The Mandate did not come into force until September 29, 1923.

It is sufficient to recall that it was not until June 20, 1922 that the Mandate was granted by the League of Nations, and that the effective occupation of the territory of Palestine was achieved progressively, Gaza being occupied on November 16, 1917, and Jerusalem on December 9 of the same year.

Furthermore, the Balfour Declaration is not the result of an agreement between States. It is no more than a letter addressed by Lord Balfour to a private person with no title to enter into an official contractual obligation, since its recipient, Lord Rothschild, a Zionist British subject, did not even represent the Jewish Community which, in any case, was not a subject of international law.

(b) *But even admitting that Great Britain* considered that she had the right to act by virtue of her military occupation of Palestine, the law of war would not have allowed her to dispose of the occupied territory.[5] The entry of the British Army into Palestine, therefore, did not result in the substitution of British for Ottoman sovereignty over Palestine. Furthermore, had not the British Government stated on several occasions that the purpose of the occupation of Palestine by her troops was to liberate it from Turkish sovereignty and to establish therein a national government?[6]

(c) *The Balfour Declaration is prejudicial* to the acquired rights of the Palestine population.[7] These rights were expressly recognised by the Allies, who repeatedly affirmed that the non-Turkish peoples, subject to Ottoman rule, should be liberated and given national governments deriving their authority from the free will of the people.[8]

---

[5] - *Cf.* the preamble of the Hague Convention No. IV on the Laws of War, in which it is made clear that occupied territories remain under the protection of the rules of international law.

[6] - *Cf.* Allenby's statement on December 9, 1917, the day of his entry into Jerusalem.

[7] - *Cf.* W.T. Mallison Jr.: "The Zionist Israel Juridical Claims," *George Washington Law Review,* vol. 32, 1964, p. 1002.

[8] - *Cf.* Statement of President Wilson of 1917, approved by the Allies, which mentions the liberation of non-Turkish peoples subject to the Ottoman regime.

(d) *But above all the Balfour Declaration is inconsistent* with certain provisions of the Covenant.

First of all, it is inconsistent with Article 20, which, it should be recalled, states that: "The members of the League severally agree that this covenant is accepted as abrogating all obligations or understandings *inter se* which are inconsistent with the terms thereof, and solemnly undertake that they will not hereafter enter into any engagements inconsistent with the terms thereof.

In case any Member of the League shall, before becoming a Member of the League, have undertaken any obligations inconsistent with the terms of the Covenant, it shall be the duty of such Member to take immediate steps to procure its release from such obligations."

The opinion so pertinently expressed by M. Jules Basdevant, formerly President of the International Court of Justice, enables us to pass judgment on the British attitude. "No State has the right to extend at will its own competence at the expense of other States and other peoples. International law does not recognise the British State as having competence other than over its territories and over its own subjects and nationals."[9] But the land of Palestine, inhabited by Arabs for thousands of years, has never been a British territory.

Furthermore, the Balfour Declaration contradicts one of the major principles established by the Covenant of the League of Nations in 1919, the principle that, as regards the colonies and territories which, as a result of the war, were removed from beneath the sovereignty of the defeated countries, the well-being and development of their peoples were the sacred trust of civilisation. From the application of this principle derives the prohibition to annex or colonise these territories and the obligation to guarantee the sovereignty of all peoples living in them. Article 22 of the Covenant of the League of Nations placed these territories under the international Mandatory System, which automatically implied respect for their integrity and for all rights of their respective populations. What is more, the countries placed under Mandate were to be assisted to attain their independence.

9　J. Basdevant: *Cours de Doctorat,* Paris, 1936-1937, p. 198.

However, it must be admitted that Great Britain took care to incorporate its promise in the Mandate granted it by the Council of the League on July 24, 1922. But it is permissible, even today, to question the legal validity of the Council's decision, in view of the fact that the objectives of the Covenant had been clearly defined, as had the duties of the Mandatory to lead the peoples entrusted to its care toward progress and independence.

But, peculiar as this exceeding of its competence by the League Council may seem, the fact remains that the Balfour Declaration, recapitulated in the Mandate, in no way tended towards the creation of the State of Israel. The Mandate was the means by which Great Britain was able to facilitate the realisation of Zionist aims. The ingenuity lay in awaiting a concatenation of circumstances favourable to the creation of the Jewish State in Palestine, the opportunity to act being left to the Jews themselves. The basic rule in this policy was to avoid Arab reaction as far as possible and to guarantee the Zionist movement Britain's constant support.[10] The Balfour Declaration's position in international law has been aptly described by Arthur Koestler as: "A promise made by one nation to another nation to cede to it the territory of a third nation." This statement would be accurate but for the fact that the receiving nation had never been a nation in the sociological sense. The robbed nation, consisting of the Arabs of Palestine, who alone had the right to freely determine its future, was not consulted.

B. – The Real Meaning of the Balfour Declaration

Admitting, for the sake of the argument, that the Balfour Declaration is valid in the eyes of international law, the promise to establish a Jewish national home must, if it is to be reconciled with the principles of the Mandatory System, be interpreted in the light of :

---

[10] - Cf. Report of the Commission to Study the Hussein-MacMahon Correspondence Appointed on March 6, 1939. Documents of the British Conference on Arab Palestine held in London in 1939, principal documents on the Palestine Case, p. 30 sqq.

(a) *The history of the negotiations between the Zionist leaders and the British Government;*

(b) *A comparison of the texts proposed by each side and the text finally adopted;*

(c) *The rules of interpretation accepted by international law;*

(d) *Various legislative acts of the British Government regarding Palestine: these texts should not be regarded as cancelling each other but should, in every case, be appropriately interpreted so that each law is given its due weight and thereby allowed to contribute its particular value to the whole.*

According to this way of thinking, the Balfour Declaration is in conflict with the obligations arising from the Hussein-Mac-Mahon negotiations, at the close of which Great Britain undertook officially to recognise the independence of the Arab States. Subsequently, she tried to escape from this impasse by stating that Palestine was not part of the areas to which she had promised independence. She pointed out that Palestine held a special position, in view of the fact that it was regarded as a holy land by the three great monotheistic religions; and that, being situated close to Egypt, it would be illogical to hand it over to the Arabs. She also maintained that the MacMahon correspondence did not allude to the parts of Syria situated to the west of Damascus, Homs, Hama and Aleppo, that is, according to Britain, Palestine, though in fact this description is more applicable to Lebanon.

But this interpretation is without importance, for Great Britain acted inconsistently with even those provisions of the Hussein-MacMahon agreement which expressly stipulated guarantees for the Holy Places, guarantees which were strengthened by the cooperation foreseen between Great Britain and the Arabs.

The exclusion of Palestine from the field of British promises —which, according to the British interpretation, did not cover the above mentioned areas of Syria—was in reality a consequence of the fact that these areas were the ones over which France was anxious to exert her influence. These areas are situated along the coast of northern Syria and are close to Beirut. But Palestine is not included in the said areas, for it is situated to the south, not to the north of Syria. Furthermore, Palestine was mentioned among the territories proposed by the Sharif Hussein with regard to which MacMahon had made no reservations whatsoever.[11] In fact, British promises contained in the Hussein-MacMahon correspondence make no reservation whatsoever as regards the inclusion of Palestine in the Arab Kingdom envisaged in the correspondence, nor, indeed, is there any mention of the Jewish national home or of Jewish interests.[12]

In fact, the promise to create a Jewish national home must be regarded as humanitarian rather than political in character.[13] And, from a legal point of view, the clause granting Jews a national home was intended to provide the Jews with a refuge without impinging on the rights of Palestinian Arabs or the rights of Jews in any other country.[14]

The safeguard clause contained in the promise (safeguarding the rights of the non-Jewish population) is as important as the promise itself. Interpreted broadly, as indeed it should be, this clause is inconsistent with the view of a Jewish State in which the Arabs would be reduced to the status of "protected minorities."

Was the Mandatory State to devote all its attention to the Jews of Palestine, ignoring the aims of the Mandate, or was it to guarantee the protection of the natives, to safeguard their interests and to guide them towards self-government?

Was the creation of a Jewish national home in conformity with Article 5 of the Mandate, which laid upon the Mandatory Power the obligation to see "that no Palestine territory shall be ceded or leased?"

There is really no difference between the cession of all or part of a territory to a foreign Power and the granting of facilities to a group of foreigners to settle in it with a view to securing it for

---

[11] - See the *Report of the Commission to Study the Hussein-MacMahon Correspondence of March 16, 1939, op. cit.,* p. 30 sqq.
[12] - *Cf.* Mallison, *op. cit.,* pp. 1003 and 1030.
[13] - *Cf.* Mallison, *op. cit.,* p. 1018.
[14] - *Cf.* Mallison, *op. cit.,* p. 1021.

themselves.

Are we to conclude from this that the Mandate is entirely invalid?

Reference to the concept of trust, or trusteeship, makes it possible to reply that the illegality of the act committed by the trustee, or the mandatory, does not entail the nullity of the trustee-ship or the mandate. Only the vitiated act is null and void.

Thus the Mandate for Palestine remains in conformity with the Covenant of the League of Nations, except in its provisions regarding the creation of a Jewish national home, which in turn have led to the creation of a Jewish State and to the disappearance of Palestine.

We arrive at the same conclusion when we consider that the formal creation of an international civil service—which was really what happened when Mandates were entrusted to various Powers— is valid only insofar as it is in conformity with the provisions of the Covenant which, of course, are of overriding validity. All provisions of the particular law which contravene the general provisions of the Covenant are to be considered as null and void.

We hope that we have now made it sufficiently clear that the Covenant did not open the door to a partition of Palestine, and that the normal conclusion of Mandates A was the acquisition of statehood by local governments.

All this explanation would have been completely unnecessary if the creators of the Mandatory System had considered themselves more bound by the spirit and the letter of the Covenant. This unfortunate precedent, which led the highest international bodies to break away from the rule of law, was not to remain an isolated case. The United Nations has also taken certain liberties with the Charter.

II.—THE ILLEGAL ACTION OF THE UNITED NATIONS

There is no doubt that the United Nations was competent to deal with the Palestine problem. However, this did not mean that it was at liberty to take any decision it fancied. In this respect, the

Partition resolution is absolutely null and void.

1) COMPETENCE OF THE UNITED NATIONS IN THE PALESTINE QUESTION:[15]

The Palestine problem was submitted to the United Nations as early as 1947, when the Organisation decided to adopt a "Partition Plan" for Palestine.[16] Before considering the problem of the competence of the United Nations in this matter, let us see how the question came to be submitted to it.

A. – Course of Events :

(a) *In February* 1947 the United Kingdom Government, realising its inability to solve the problem, intimated that it was "not prepared to administer Palestine indefinitely." The reason given was that Jews and Arabs "were unable to agree on the solution desired by it." Following the admission of failure, the United Kingdom Government requested the inclusion of the Palestine question in the Agenda of the second Ordinary Session of the General Assembly, specifying that the latter should, in accordance with the provisions of Article 10 of the Charter, make recommendations regarding the future status of Palestine.[17] It also proposed the holding of a special session of the General Assembly for the purpose of constituting a special committee to make a preliminary study, which the General Assembly would examine during its next ordinary session. A counter-proposal put forward by five Arab countries requested that "the termination of the British Mandate over Palestine and the declaration of its independence" should also be considered during the special session.

But these countries were unable to get this very important

---

[15] - It is a question of competence at the time when Great Britain gave up her Mandate over Palestine.

[16] - Resolution No. 181 (II) of November 29, 1947. This resolution was adopted by the U.N. General Assembly during its Second Ordinary Session by 33 votes against 13 with 10 abstentions. The plan calls for the creation in Palestine of two States, Arab and Jewish, with a special status for Jerusalem. There was also to be an economic union.

[17] - Letter of April 3, 1947 addressed by the United Kingdom delegation to the Acting Secretary-General.

item included in the agenda, and the General Assembly confirmed this failure by 24 votes against 15, with 10 abstentions.[18] After the Political Committee had heard statements by the representatives of the Jewish Agency and the Arab Higher Committee, the General Assembly finally met and adopted two resolutions on May 15, 1947.[19] The first created a Special Committee on Palestine, consisting of eleven members, with extremely wide powers, "to ascertain and record facts, and to investigate all questions and issues relevant to the problem of Palestine."[20]

This Committee, which was called U.N.S.C.O.P.,[21] was instructed to draw up, by September 1, 1947, a report for submission to the General Assembly, in which it was to make "appropriate proposals for the solution of the Palestine problem."

At the same time the Assembly, in its resolution No. 107, called "upon all governments and peoples, and particularly upon the inhabitants of Palestine, to refrain from ... the threat or use of force or any other action which might create an atmosphere prejudicial to an early settlement of the question of Palestine."

The Special Committee, unable to reach a unanimous decision on a single solution, submitted two different plans to the Assembly.

The majority plan, adopted by seven members of the Committee, recommended the partition of Palestine into two States (one Arab and the other Jewish) linked by an economic union, and the internationalisation of Jerusalem under United Nations trusteeship.

The minority plan, adopted by the other four members, recommended the creation of a federal State, with Jerusalem as its capital.

(b)*The Ordinary Session of the General Assembly*[22] finally set up an *Ad Hoc* Committee to consider the Palestine question and,

---

[18] - Sohn: *Cases and Materials on United Nations Law*, p. 456 sqq.

[19] - Resolutions No. 106 and 107.

[20] - It is, perhaps, surprising that such a mandate could have been interpreted as including authority to enquire into Nazi crimes against the Jews (*Cf.* Plessier: *Etat juif et monde arabe*, p. 254.)

[21] - United Nations Special Committee on Palestine.

[22] - 90th Plenary Session of September 23, 1947.

in particular, to examine three points; the British proposal, the Arab proposal on the termination of the Mandate and the recognition of independence and, finally, the report of the Special Committee.[23] The *Ad Hoc* Committee appointed from among its members a conciliation group and two sub-committees.

The first sub-committee recommended the adoption of a resolution on the basis of the plan for Partition accompanied by economic union: it proposed only slight modifications of the recommendations made by the majority of U.N.S.C.O.P.

The second sub-committee submitted three proposals, *one of which was most important:* it suggested that the General Assembly, before making any recommendations whatsoever, should ask the International Court of Justice for an advisory opinion on eight legal questions and in particular, on the following two:

(g) *"Whether the United Nations is competent to recommend either of the two plans and recommendations of the majority or minority of the United Nations Special Committee on Palestine, or any other solution involving partition of the territory of Palestine, or a permanent trusteeship over any city or part of Palestine, without the consent of the majority of the people of Palestine.*

(h) *Whether the United Nations or any of its Member States, is competent to enforce or recommend the enforcement of any proposal concerning the Constitution and future government of Palestine, in particular, any plan of partition which is contrary to the wishes, or adopted without the consent of, the inhabitants of Palestine."*[24]

The *Ad Hoc* Committee rejected the first seven points by 25 votes to 18 with 11 abstentions; the eighth, i.e., point *l* of the plan, was just rejected by a vote of 21 to 20 with 13 abstentions.

The *Ad Hoc* Committee did, however, adopt the Partition plan by 25 votes to 13, with 17 abstentions; two members being absent.

Such a result, secured through strong Zionist pressure, was

---

[23] - *Repertory of Practice Followed by the U.N. Organs*, vol. 1, p. 469-470.

[24] - *Repertory, op. cit.*, and Sohn, *op. cit.*, p. 457.

certainly no indication that, in the General Assembly, the Committee's report would receive the two thirds majority required for its adoption. Despite the approval by the "Two Great Powers" of the Committee's Partition proposal, the result remained uncertain because of the impressive number of abstentions. Besides Great Britain, which abstained because she was only willing to accept a solution on which both sides could agree,—such a solution was, of course, purely hypothetical—France did the same because she desired to maintain a certain measure of neutrality. Several Latin American countries, Greece and Yugoslavia refused to support the Partition plan.

It is undeniable that, at that time, very strong pressure was brought to bear upon several States by the Zionists and the United States. Many countries which had voted one way in Committee found themselves obliged to vote in a different way at the Plenary Session. Harry Truman, former President of the United States, makes no secret of this in his "Memoirs."[25] With eleven months to go before the presidential elections in America, he found that he could not relinquish the valuable support of the Zionist vote; he therefore rallied to the support of the Partition plan: "I instructed the State Department to support the Partition plan."[26]

From that time on the representatives of the United States impressed upon every delegation the necessity to adopt a "positive attitude;" the means employed was more often intimidation than persuasion. In this way Belgium, France, Haiti, Liberia, Luxemburg, the Netherlands, New Zealand, Paraguay and the Philippines found themselves obliged to reconsider their vote at the Plenary Session.

At the same time, the Zionists subjected several delegations to extreme and embarrassing pressure. This pressure took several forms, the most readily available being blackmail by charges of anti-Semitism. Every question raised about the future of the Palestinian people, every query about the right to establish the "National Home" in a land already inhabited, every qualm expressed as regards the

---

[25] - Harry Truman: *"Memoirs."* Paris. Plon edit.. 1956.
[26] - *ibid.,* vol. II, p. 188.

competence of the United Nations to create a State, to impose it on a people and, by the same token, to condemn that people to exile— were construed as so many insults to the dead of the Nazi camps. Zionist excesses were such that they almost jeopardised the Jews' own objectives. Mr. Truman's feelings were so aroused by this Zionist campaign that Dr. Weizmann deemed it necessary to minimise its importance by attributing it to "uncontrolled elements:" "It is freely rumoured in Washington that our people have exerted undue and excessive pressure on certain delegations and have thus 'over-played' their hand. I cannot speak for unauthorised persons..."[27]

Commenting on this incident in retrospect, President Truman admitted that "the facts were that not only were there pressure movements around the United Nations unlike anything that had been seen there before, but that the White House, too, was subjected to a constant barrage. I do not think I ever had as much pressure and propaganda aimed at the White House as I had in this instance. The persistence of a few of the extreme Zionist leaders —actuated by political motives and engaging in political threats— disturbed me and annoyed me. Some were even suggesting that we pressure sovereign nations into favourable votes in the General Assembly."[28]

President Truman intimates that he himself was not influenced by these pressures, but in his "Memoirs," published in 1949, Dr. Weizmann writes that the adoption of the Partition resolution was mainly due to the intervention and efforts of President Truman.

This emotional campaign had a profound influence on the decisions of several delegations, in view of the wide range of the Leit-motivs employed: antisemitic blackmail, exploitation of Nazi persecutions, the sufferings of the Jews in central Europe—not to mention the weight of twenty billion dollars of credits which the

---

[27] - Dr. Weizmann's letter to President Truman, New York Times, November 27, 1947 and H. Truman, "Memoirs," op. cit., vol. II. p. 191.

[28] - H. Truman: op. cit., vol. II. p. 192.

United States granted to certain countries at that time.[29]

In this affair the Zionists not only engaged the responsibility of the United States, but also dragged in their wake nations which, after long hesitation, finally consented to sacrifice both the people of Palestine and international ethics.

The General Assembly simply confirmed the Partition plan proposed by the Ad Hoc Committee.[30] This resolution was not approved by the immense majority of Asian and African countries, and certainly not by any country geographically close to Palestine.

Foreseeing difficulties in the implementation of its recommendations, the General Assembly requested that:

"(a) *The Security Council take the necessary measures as provided for in the plan for its implementation;*

. . . . ;

(c) *The Security Council determines as a threat to the peace, breach of the peace, or act of aggression, in accordance with Article 39 of the Charter, any attempt to alter by force the settlement envisaged by this resolution."*

But in view of the pertinent objections raised in the Council as to the competence of the General Assembly and of the Security Council in this affair, the latter did not give effect to the resolution nor did it issue any directives to the Committee which was to implement it.[31]

The United States at first employed the power of persuasion, and later all sorts of pressure, to secure the adoption of resolution 181 (II), but was forced to modify its position in view of the magnitude of the difficulties and of Zionist excesses. Thus, during the meeting of the Security Council in November 1947, the U.S. representative expressed the desire that no date should be fixed

[29] - *Le Monde,* November 2-3, 1947.

For an account of all the pressures and intimidations resorted to by the Zionists, seethe excellent study by Kermit Roosevelt: "The Partition of Palestine, a Lesson in Pressure Politics," *Middle East Journal.* January, 1948. p. 1-16. Regarding Zionist activities in the U.S.A. see also *supra* p. 41 and 42, note 16, on the work of the U.S. Senate Committee presided over by Senator Fullbright.

[30] - Resolution 181 (II) of November 29, 1947 entitled: "The future government of Palestine."

for the discussion of the Assembly resolution. Then, on March 19, 1948, the United States proposed to the Council another plan which was tantamount to the abandonment of resolution 181 (II).

The delegate of India, having questioned the validity of the Assembly's recommendations, requested the United Kingdom to pledge itself in advance to accept the recommendations of the Assembly on Palestine. The United Kingdom refused to implement any resolution which would not be "compatible with the aspirations of the peoples concerned."

Resolution 181 (II), therefore, could have no effect whatsoever. A final blow was dealt to it when the Security Council, refusing to decree coercive measures, asked for an extraordinary session of the General Assembly. The opening, on March 30, 1948, of an extraordinary session of the Assembly "to find a solution" to the Palestine problem could only mean the abandonment of the Partition plan. In fact, the resolution of May 14, 1948, appointing a mediator for Palestine, *suspended* the application of the partition resolution.

In view of all this, it will be readily believed that the resolution was only adopted after lively debates on the question of competence.

B. — The Problem of the Competence of the United Nations

The United Nations is undoubtedly a world Organisation, but does this legally authorise it to intervene in the Palestine affair?[32] To answer this question, we need to examine two hypotheses: that the United Nations is the successor of the League of Nations, and that the competence of the present Organisation, in the case under

---

[31] - The Council confined itself to calling "upon all permanent members to make recommendations to it regarding the guidance which the Council might usefully give to the Palestine Committee." In its resolution of April 2, 1948 (doc. A/532 of April 10, 1948, p. 2) the Committee confirmed that it had received no guidance or instructions from the Council regarding the implementation of the General Assembly resolution.

[32] - It is to be noted that this question of the competence of the United Nations is here examined only as an interlocutory question so that, regardless of any conclusion which may reach, there remains the problem of the legality or illegality as to the substance of the resolutions adopted.

consideration, is limited.

(a) *Is the United Nations a continuation of the League of Nations as regards the mandate over Palestine?*

In its resolution of April 18, 1946, the League of Nations Assembly expressly declared that "on the termination of the League's existence its functions with respect to the Mandated territories will come to an end," but observed that principles corresponding to those enunciated in Article 22 of the Covenant are incorporated in Chapters XI, XII and XIII of the United Nations Charter."[33]

It should be noted, in this connection, that these chapters deal with the trusteeship system and that this system only applies in the case of particular (trusteeship) agreement;[34] Palestine was not the object of such an agreement. But Article 80, paragraph 1, stipulates that, with the exception of the particular trusteeship agreements, "and until such agreements have been concluded, nothing in this Chapter shall be construed in or of itself to alter in any manner the rights whatsoever of any state or any people or the terms of existing international instruments to which Members of the United Nations may respectively be parties."

It is on this basis that a number of jurists have refused to acknowledge that there could be any question of succession between the two Organisations in matters relating to Mandates.

According to Kelsen, "the United Nations did not succeed to the rights of the League of Nations as regards the former Mandated territories." He considers that there is no legal continuity in the relations of these two systems for "one had ceased to exist long before the other came into existence."[35]

It is to be noted first of all that Kelsen does not assert that the Mandate has lapsed; he merely specifies that "the trusteeship

---

[33] - Cited by P. Guggenheim: *Traité de droit international public,* vol. I, p. 226, note 2, *Cf.,* also, International Court of Justice, *Recueil,* 1950, p. 134.

[34] - Article 77, paragraph 1, reads as follows: "The trusteeship system shall apply to such territories... as may be placed thereunder by means of trusteeship agreements."

[35] - H. Kelsen: *The Law of the United Nations,* London, 1951, pp. 596-597.

system did not automatically replace the Mandate system,"[36] and this is clearly indicated in Article 77 of the Charter; on the other hand Article 80, paragraph 1, clearly states that the Mandates, which are all international acts creative of rights and obligations for States and peoples, remain in force until such time as they are replaced by trusteeship agreements.[37] Besides, the continued existence of Mandates and the obligations proceeding therefrom seems to be quite obvious.

The International Court of Justice affirms that: "From all aspects, the *raison d'être* of obligations resulting from Mandates and their first objective remains. As the fulfillment of these obligations did not depend on the existence of the League of Nations they could not become obsolete simply because this organ of supervision had ceased to exist; nor could the right of the population to see the territory administered according to these rules be conditional on the existence of the League."[38]

The judges, even when they have not agreed with certain aspects of the solution recommended by the Court in this opinion, have made a point of emphasising the continued existence of the obligations of the Mandatory: Sir A. McNair, in particular, is of the opinion that international obligations arising out of the Mandate continue to exist.[39] He considers that: "The dissolution of the League of Nations . . . has not put an end to Mandates . . . I cannot say that I know of the existence of any event of which it could be said that it has, by implication, put an end to the Mandate.[40]

Thus, a first fact is established: the Mandate remains in force after the disappearance of the League of Nations.

---

[36] - *Op. cit.,* p. 596. The U.N. Charter, in Article 80, paragraph 2, stipulates that: "Paragraph 1 of this article shall not be interpreted as giving grounds for delay or postponement of the negotiation and conclusion of agreements for placing mandated and other territories under the trusteeship system...".

[37] - Advisory opinion rendered by the International Court of Justice on July 2, 1950 on South West Africa, *Recueil des arrêts, avis consultatifs et ordonnances,* 1950, p. 133.

[38] - *Recueil,* I.C.J., 1950, p. 133.

[39] - Individual opinion, *Recueil,* I.C.J., 1950, p. 162.

[40] - McNair, *op. cit.,* p. 157.

Moreover, although the object of the Mandate is a "sacred trust of civilisation," it also has the characteristics of an international civil service.[41] From this point of view, the Mandate system has a statutory nature, and this status is specified "in each particular case by an act-law which is the charter for the Mandate."[42] But, in chapters XI, XII and XIII, relative to the trusteeship system,[43] the United Nations Charter stipulates an equivalent status. It is therefore unquestionable that the United Nations has succeeded the League of Nations, for the U.N. is an international organ other than that provided for in the League of Nations Covenant, and is endowed with similar, though not identical, functions.[44] This succession has been very clearly affirmed by the International Court of Justice as regards one aspect of the Mandate which had been questioned by certain writers: succession in the powers to supervise the execution of a Class C Mandate. Therefore, the succession of the United Nations to the League of Nations in matters relating to Mandates becomes *a fortiori* imperative when the Mandate is a Class A one, and *also when the Mandatory Power relinquishes the administration of a territory, as Great Britain did*. To refuse to recognise this succession of the two international Organisations in this field, especially in the particular case of Palestine, would involve ignoring this "sacred trust of civilisation," which is one of the essential contributions of modern international law.[45]

It follows from this brief explanation that the United Nations not only could, but was obliged to, assume responsibility for the Palestine problem after Great Britain had made known her wish to relinquish the Mandate.

[41] - G. Scelle: *Précis du droit des gens,* Paris, 1932, vol. I, p. 170. Art. 22 of the League of Nations Covenant specifies that "the well-being and development of such peoples (those not yet able to stand by themselves) form a sacred trust of civilisation."

[42] - G. Scelle, *op. cit.,* p. 170-171; See also Alvarez, dissenting opinion, *Recueil des Arrêts,* I.C.J. 1950, p. 182.

[43] - See aforementioned resolution of the League of Nations of April, 1946.

[44] - I.C.J. *Recueil des Arrêts...* 1950, p. 136.

[45] - Disregard of this "sacred trust" would constitute a serious violation of the U.N. Charter, whose Article 73 reads as follows: "They (the Members of the Organisation) accept as *a sacred trust* the obligation to...".

(b) *Other Charter provisions confirm this competence:*

Apart from situations involving a threat to the peace, a breach of the peace or an act of aggression, it is the U.N. General Assembly which, by virtue of Article 10 of the Charter, is empowered to discuss any questions or any matters within the scope of the Charter. Furthermore, the Assembly may, on the basis of Article 14, recommend all appropriate measures to ensure "the peaceful adjustment of any situation, regardless of origin, which it deems likely to impair the general welfare or friendly relations among Nations." Thus the Assembly has a general competence which gives rise to "few remarks."[46]

More particularly, as regards the mandated territories, the General Assembly is competent, "by virtue of Article 10 of the Charter, to proceed with the consideration of the Mandate ... and to make recommendations in regard to that Mandate."[47] This view is confirmed by the decisions of the International Court of Justice.[48] In the Palestine question, the United Nations was competent in 1947, but its powers regarding the basic nature of the solution to be adopted were not unlimited.

2) LIMITATIONS OF U.N. POWERS AND NULLITY OF THE PARTITION RESOLUTION:

The United Nations General Assembly can only take action within the limits laid down in the Charter. In the Palestine case, its powers are further limited by the provisions of the Mandate.

A. – Limits set by the Provisions of the Charter :

But even if it is admitted, for the sake of the argument, that the United Nations is not bound by the obligations laid down in the Mandate and that the Organisation is only competent by virtue of its Charter, the General Assembly must, none the less, respect the principles contained in the Charter if its recommendations are to have any validity.

---

[46] - M. Sibert, *Droit International Public,* vol. II, p. 751.
[47] - McNair, *op. cit.,* p. 162. Alvarez, *op. cit.,* pp. 182, 184 and 185.
[48] - Opinion on South West Africa, *Recueil,* I.C.J. 1950, p. 137.

In addition to the provisions of Articles 10 and 14, the Partition resolution on Palestine also violates the principle embodied in Article 1, paragraph 2, of the Charter, which sanctions the right of peoples to self-determination.

"It is doubtful if the United Nations," writes Professor Brownlie, "has a 'capacity to convey title,' *inter alia* because the Organisation cannot assume the role of territorial sovereign ... Thus the resolution of 1947 containing a Partition plan for Palestine was probably *ultra vires* (outside the competence of the United Nations,) and, if it was not, was not binding on member States in any case."[49]

(a) *The General Assembly has acted contrary to the provisions of Articles 10 and 14 of the Charter,* which empower it to recommend resolutions and not to make decisions. For, in effect, there is "a distinction between making a recommendation and adopting a plan prejudicial to the territorial integrity of a people and their political and legal status, and appointing a committee of the Assembly to carry out that plan."[50] The Partition plan contained in the resolution undoubtedly implied coercion, because one of its clauses provided that any attempt to alter by force the settlement set forth in the resolution should be considered as a threat to the peace, breach of the peace, or act of aggression within the meaning of Article 39. What is involved is a solution to be imposed by force and is, therefore, not a simple recommendation. But, it is an incontrovertible fact that the Assembly can only adopt resolutions capable of being implemented by force within the framework of the "Uniting for Peace" resolution of November 3, 1950. Any measure of a different nature constitutes a violation of the Charter. "Article 14 authorises the General Assembly only to make recommendations. But this resolution goes beyond simple recommendations."[51]

---

[49] - I. Brownlie: *Principles of Public International Law,* Clarendon Press, Oxford, 1966, pp. 161-162.
[50] - *Repertory of Practice of the United Nations, op. cit.,* vol. I, p. 471.
[51] - H. Kelsen: *The Law of the United Nations,* London, 1951, p. 195, note 7; L. di. Qual, *Les effets des résolutions des Nations Unies,* Paris, L.D.G.J., 1967, p. 283. (*Bibliothèque de droit international,* vol. 37).

The General Assembly can, no doubt, by virtue of Article 14, make recommendations to States, even those which are not Members of the United Nations. However, the Partition resolution went beyond recommendations since it provided for the creation of a five-member Committee and for the administration of Palestine by this Committee during a transitional period. The Assembly was competent to make a recommendation to the United Kingdom, but it was in no way competent to transfer the administration of Palestine to a committee established by the General Assembly. The resolution was an actual decision of the General Assembly to administer a territory on behalf of the United Nations.

But to decide that the United Nations shall administer a territory for the purpose of establishing two States therein, cannot be within the competence of any Organ of the United Nations.[52]

It must also be noted that the General Assembly has no competence to implement a "decision."[53] Nor is it empowered to request the Security Council to take enforcement measures by virtue of Article 14, as it did in the case of the Partition resolution.[54] In fact, the Council is not competent to implement the recommendation[55]

---

[52] - H. Kelsen: *Op. cit.,* p. 197. Analysing the statements made on this point by Irak, Pakistan and Cuba, particularly at the Plenary Session of November 25, 1947, the author considers that their "arguments are correct from a strictly legal point of view." The representative of Syria added that the constitution of the Committee entrusted with the task of administering Palestine was illegal, its members having been appointed by the President of the Assembly and not by the Assembly itself, which was a breach of Article 84 of the Rules of Procedure (S/PV. 254, p. 21.)

[53] - Cf. The statement of the Syrian representative (doc. A/Cl/Sr. 1200) which refers to other recommendations rejected by the different states. The limitations of Article 14 of the Charter are quite clear, as are also the dispositions of Chapter VI.

[54] - Cf., The statement of the Syrian representative, doc. S/PV.260, p. 13.

[55] - Cf., Hans Kelsen: *op. cit.,* p. 287. Article 36 of the Charter only refers to methods of adjustment, whereas the creation of two States goes further; and even if the Council had power to act on the basis of this Article, it would not have been able to do so until after the enquiry prescribed by article 34 was completed. Article 39, which envisages a situation constituting a threat to the peace, was inoperative in the case in question: "The Charter does not empower the Security Council to enforce a political settlement, whether it was in pursuance of a recommendation made by the Assembly or of one made by the Council itself... The Council's action should not have as an aim the imposition of partition but the maintenance of peace." (Security Council, 253rd meeting, Feb. 24, 1947, p. 41.)

and, as we know, it refrained from taking any measures.

Some observers believe there is an inconsistency in the attitude of the Arab States, which all voted against the resolution and asked in vain that the International Court of Justice be consulted on the Partition plan; for while they criticize Resolution 181 (II), they invoke other resolutions of the Assembly, for example, those concerning the Palestine refugees. In reality, the Arab States, in asking for the return of the refugees, are invoking *a right* recognised by the General Assembly. Likewise, when they demand the application of the principle of self-determination, they are invoking *another right*, which the Assembly does not create but merely affirms.[56] In other words, while a resolution cannot destroy the force of a principle of law, neither can it create a right which does not otherwise exist.

More particularly, the Assembly has no power to oppose the right of peoples to self-determination.

(b) *The consequences of the principle of self-determination as applied to Palestine:*

The legality of the recommendations of the Assembly was subordinate to respect for the principle of self-determination.

In this connection, two hypotheses must be considered:

According to the first, the Assembly could have secured the consent of the Palestinians by means of a plebiscite before any recommendation was made. However, not only was this plebiscite not held, but in addition, a proposal that the International Court of Justice be requested to give an advisory opinion on the powers of the United Nations in this matter was rejected.[57]

In default of a plebiscite, respect for the principles of self-determination, and of the territorial integrity of Palestine, implied that the very most the General Assembly could do was to adopt a resolution recommending that the rights of the Jewish community as a *minority* be guaranteed. In creating a Jewish State by the Parti-

---

[56] - The resolution does not *create* rights but merely *enunciates* them.

[57] - Cf. *supra*, pp. 107-108. This is point *h* of the proposals made by the second *ad hoc sub-committee*. Cf. also Sohn, *op. cit.*, p. 457.

tion resolution, the United Nations went beyond the simple protection of a community, by giving it an international status. In so doing, the United Nations committed a grave violation of the Charter, a violation which, in itself, deprives resolution 181 (II) of any legal basis whatsoever.

According to United Nations practice, self-determination is the right of the majority to exercise power *within a political entity*. In other words, it is necessary that there should be stable frontiers, so that political change may be brought about, within the framework of these frontiers, through self-determination.[58] This cannot apply to the Jews, who are scattered throughout the world and are united by no juridical links.[59]

(c) *Moreover, the Partition resolution could not be justified by the Charter provisions relating to non-self-governing territories:*

This is, in fact, the only case where the United Nations can create new States by detaching territory which is "not yet autonomous" from the colonial Power. Besides, the birth of a new State is the natural consequence of the Trusteeship system set up by the United Nations Charter. But these provisions do not apply in the case of Palestine.[60]

For Palestine was not subject to the Trusteeship system, but to that of the Mandate, and, more particularly, of Mandate A. But the aim of the latter system was the independence of Palestine in

---

[58] - R. Higgins: *The Development of International Law Through the Political Organs of the United Nations*, p. 104.

[59] - *Cf., supra*, Part one: *The Historical "Rights,"* pp. 37-38 and *infra*, pp. 143-144. The principle of self-determination is a dominant general principle which the United Nations cannot violate for, according to Ian Browlie, it fors part of the *jus cogens*.
According to A. Taylor (*Prelude to Israel*, New York, 1959, Chapter IV: The creation of Israel), President Truman considered that the Balfour Declaration was in conformity with the principles of Wilson on the right of peoples to self-determination. "One cannot," says Taylor, "but note the *'enormous error'* of President Truman, for the Balfour Declaration is in basic contradiction with the principle of self-determination which, if applied to Palestine, would have prevented the establishment of a Jewish State for a population which was, in the main, non-Jewish."

[60] - *Cf.*, A. Mathiot: "Le statut des territoires dépendants d'après la Charte des Nations Unies," *Revue Générale du droit international public*, 1946, p. 159 sqq.

respect of its territory as a whole, not the independence, through splintering them, of the various human communities who happened to be living there. Moreover, the Charter provisions only apply with reference to a colonial power. It would have been ridiculous, in this case, to consider the Arab majority as a colonial Power.

In actual practice, the principle of non-interference by the United Nations in the internal affairs of any State embodied in Article 2, paragraph 7, of the Charter, does not, in general, apply to territories which are not yet independent. The United Nations reserved for itself the right to look into the colonial policy of the Powers.[61] But if this principle cannot be invoked by a colonial Power against the international Organisation, the United Nations, in turn, is strictly forbidden to interfere in relations between ethnic groups in a dependent territory, except in cases where the object of such interference is to hold a plebiscite.[62]

It follows therefore, that not only did the Charter not authorise the United Nations to adopt such a resolution, but that it actually prohibited it. The Assembly had power to act only within the framework of the Mandate for Palestine.

B. – Limitations Set by the Provisions of the Mandate:

As we have seen, the Mandate remained in force after the disappearance of the League of Nations, and the United Nations inherited the responsibilities arising from the provisions of the Mandate. Therefore, if the General Assembly was competent to deal with the Palestine question, it was obliged, in its search for a substantive solution, *to act solely within the framework of the Mandate* and to respect its provisions. Its freedom was in this case limited by the provisions of the Charter, as we have seen.

Briefly, the existence of an applicable juridical text obliges

---

[61] - Of particular significance were the resolutions adopted by the United Nations in connection with the Algerian Affair, which France tried in vain to have regarded as an "internal affair."

[62] - In this connection *cf.*, for example, General Assembly resolution 637 of December 16, 1952.

the Assembly to adopt only solutions which are in conformity with the provisions of that text.

This is what is called, in national law, the principle of the link between competence and the substance of applicable law. The General Assembly only acquires its general *political* competence when faced with a *situation* which is not subject to any legal text from which an appropriate solution can derive. But when such a legal provision exists, the competence of the Assembly ceases to be political and becomes juridical.

The Mandate laid down a limited number of solutions; nevertheless, the United Nations remained free to choose, within these limits, whatever solution it deemed appropriate, with due consideration of the facts of the situation as regards the capacity of the Palestinian people to govern itself. Had such capacity been acknowledged in 1947, the answer to Britain's request could have been none other than the declaration of Palestine's independence; the problem would have received a definite solution.

But if, as actually happened, the General Assembly was not to recognise the Palestinian people as being capable of governing themselves, it was obliged to choose one of the following two solutions:

— Either that the administration of Palestine be continued by the United Nations itself, by application of the Trusteeship system provided for in the Charter;[63]

— Or else to entrust this administration to a third party, not directly concerned, by concluding a trusteeship agreement with it. The Partition resolution is therefore basically void, because it is

---

[63] - This solution was recommended by the United States Government in 1948. At the 271st session of the Security Council on March 19, 1948, the U.S. representative stated that his "government believes that a temporary trusteeship for Palestine should be established under the Trusteeship Council of the United Nations to maintain the peace and to afford the Jews and Arabs of Palestine, who must live together, further opportunity to reach an agreement regarding the future government of that country." A Trusteeship Plan for Palestine was submitted by the U.S. delegation to the Special Session of the General Assembly (Document A/Cl/277 referred to by Kelsen, *op. cit.*).

contrary to the provisions of Article 5 of the Mandate, which affirms that no Palestine territory "shall be ceded or leased to, or in any way placed under the control of, the government of any foreign power."

It is quite obvious, therefore, that the creation of Israel has no legal basis whatever either in the Mandate or in the Partition resolution. That is why Israel tends more and more to rely on facts and events which have occurred since 1948, while by the same token, it drops the first two arguments, which are legal ones.

III. — PERMANENT ILLEGALITY OF ISRAEL SINCE 1948:

Some people have believed, and even asserted, that the creation of the State of Israel has ceased to be a phenomenon of "juridical pathology." Admitting, at least by implication, that its creation was of questionable legality, they have considered that a continued existence for nearly twenty years has purged it of the blemishes which disfigured its entry upon the international scene. But the twenty years which have elapsed since the United Nations adopted the Partition resolution have not strengthened Israel's position which, far from being consolidated by the lapse of time, remains as precarious as ever from a legal point of view.

Time has in no way strengthened the position of Israel. A mere *de facto* existence for twenty years has not brought about a miraculous change in its legal status and has not endowed it with legality in the eyes of international law. Yet this is the thesis advanced by the Zionists and a few others who, basing their attitude on the continued existence of Israel, believe that this continued existence has modified the legal situation by devolution of the contested territory to another sovereign.

Moreover, paradoxically enough, the same people who invoke the principle of prescription on Israel's behalf, recognising the right of the Jews to return to Palestine after an absence of two thousand years, deny this right to Palestinians driven out of their land hardly twenty years ago.

In short, Israel claims the right to remain where it is on the basis of *acquisitive prescription*. But even supposing that it was permissible to invoke this method of acquiring territorial sovereignty in connection with the Palestinian problem, it must be noted that Israel does not fulfil the conditions required by international law as regards prescription.

Furthermore, the refusal of the Arab countries to recognise Israel has perpetuated the illegal position of this "State," a position which, furthermore, has been made worse by Israel's constant refusal to implement the resolutions of the United Nations.

1) ISRAEL CANNOT AVAIL ITSELF OF THE CONCEPT OF ACQUISITIVE PRESCRIPTION:

Admitted, though with many limitations in both law and in practice, the concept of acquisition of title by prescription received a jurisprudential application in the judgement delivered on April 4, 1929 in the *Island of Palmas Case* and, implicitly, in the judgement by the P.C.I.J. (Permanent Court of International Justice) of April 5, 1933 regarding Eastern Greenland.

Is it reasonable to suppose that this concept which is applied by international tribunals only with great caution, recognised by only a few writers,[64] and but rarely incorporated into conventional law, should have enabled Israel to establish a valid legal title?

Even if we admit that acquisition by prescription is recognised in international law,[65] we must, in order to give a correct answer to this question, consider the conditions for the validity of acqui-

---

[64] - The Internationalists are very divided on the existence and validity of prescription. More than half of them, and they are not the least important, refuse to acknowledge it. Among those who support the concept is Louis Delbez: *Principes généraux de droit international public,* Paris, 1964, p. 269. Against it is Ian Brownlie; *Principles of Public International Law,* Clarendon Press, Oxford, 1966: "Since acquiescence is by itself a source of right, an independent notion of prescription has no place in international law" (p. 146). *Cf.* for the point in question by Roger Pinto: "La prescription en droit international," *Recueil des Cours de l'Académie de droit international de La Haye,* 1955, vol. 87, p. 390. For bibliography, see Verykios: *La prescription en droit international,* thesis, Paris, 1934.

[65] - *Cf.,* M. Sibert: *Traité de droit international public* vol. I, Paris, 1965. This work adopts the most unfavourable attitude as far as Palestine is concerned, that of admitting the validity of prescription in international law.

sitive prescription in the light of the facts of the Palestine problem. Then, and only then, shall we be in a position to conclude whether or not Israel was entitled to acquire the land of Palestine by prescription.

Prescription is a well-defined legal process in internal law, but it is not so precisely defined in public international law. The rules concerning the duration of prescription or the nature of possession, cannot be removed bodily from one juridical system to the other. Those who acknowledge the existence of prescription in international law do not regard this process as a mere question of time.

What, then, are the conditions for acquisitive prescription or, to put it differently, what should be the characteristics of the possession which serves as a basis for such prescription?

— *Possession must be "nec clam et nec precario,"* i.e., not clandestine and not carried out on behalf of others;

— Possession must be *"nec vi,"* that is, it should not be accompanied by force. Who would dare to maintain that such was not the case as regards Palestine?

— Possession must be uninterrupted and uncontested.

A study of these three conditions reveals that the duration of possession alone is not sufficient for the validation of title, as the British Government maintained.[66]

Since as early as the arbitral award given on June 5, 1911 in the *Chamizal Arbitration*[67] between the United States and Mexico, arbitral jurisdiction has been concerned to ascertain if the possession invoked by the former was "not troubled, uninterrupted and peaceful." In that case it established that not one of these conditions was fulfilled and, in particular, that possession was far from being peaceful. Possession lacked "one of the characteristics serving as a basis for prescription."

The arbitral award in question also had the merit of clearly showing that one of the conditions for prescription was that it should be uninterrupted. Arbitral jurisdiction did not, however,

---

[66] - Cf.. Anglo-Venezuelan dispute over Guiana, decision of 1899, *Revue de droit international public,* 1901, p. 78.

[67] - Cf., *American Journal of International Law,* 1911. p. 785 sqq.

merely adapt the methods of municipal law, which insists that the interruption of prescription must be established by a lawsuit; it showed itself flexible and admitted that a diplomatic protest was sufficient.

Here again, the indications which emerge from court decisions in this matter are of value in that they spell out the conditions which must be fulfilled. Both the history of Palestine and international practice provide elements which can only be viewed and interpreted as acts which interrupt prescription.

Thus, the fact that the Palestinian people, did not submit to force as soon as the attack took place, and the fact that they did not cease to demand their return to their usurped homeland, interrupt prescription.

Thus, also, the United Nations resolutions reaffirming the right of the Palestinian people to return to their homeland, are acts which interrupt prescription. International law requires that prescription be continuous, publicly known and uninterrupted, but it also requires that it be *peaceful*. In this respect, the arbitral decision in the *Island of Palmas Case*[68] had occasion to emphasise that possession must be peaceful. The arbitrator Max Huber established that there was no force.

As regards the duration of possession, no general rule can be deduced from the study of international law. Some arbitrations require immemorial possession, while others require possession for sixty years. Certain writers speak of thirty or fifty-year periods. Be that as it may, even though international law does not contain definite and precise rules, it at least requires a period of time longer than that which has elapsed since the creation of Israel.

Thus Israel cannot claim to have acquired Palestine through prescription, because possession was either impaired by violence or of too short duration. Neither Israel's occupation of Palestine, nor her successive expansions, entitle her to claim it as hers by "usucaption," if only because the State at whose expense prescription is

---

[68] - *Cf.* McNair and Lauterpacht: *Annual Digest of Public International Law Cases,* (Years 1927-1928), p. 103 sqq.

claimed has never stopped protesting. In these conditions, no transfer of sovereignty can have been validly effected.

Those who originally subscribed to the theory that prescription was valid in this case, were eventually obliged to abandon it, because they were convinced that it could not be a proper basis for Israel's right to keep territories acquired illegally, and it is further to be observed that the same negative conclusion can be reached through other channels.

Is there any need to recall that Israel could not have established herself except by force, as an alien minority usurping the rights of the majority? Or that this minority has driven the people of Palestine out of their land, so that they have been forced to live in exile for the past twenty years? A fundamental principle of international law, that of self-determination, has been violated. The people of Palestine should have been given the right to decide their own future by democratic procedure. The fact that a solution by force was substituted for this rule of international law obviously cannot confer any semblance of legality on the entity called Israel.

This is all the more so inasmuch as, according to a recently formulated doctrine,[69] the *"jus cogens,"* which is a body of rules in international law of an imperative nature, performs the same role as the concept of public order in municipal law. Thus the *jus cogens* has come to exercise a dominant function in international law, for there is an increasing tendency to consider that the rules of which it is composed (and which, according to Professor Brownlie, include the principle of self-determination) cannot be broken by the members of the international community or by international organisations. The rights and prerogatives attributed to the *jus cogens* are inalienable and imprescriptible. In the field of organisation, the international community reserves a prominent place for the *jus cogens*. Article 37 of the draft Law of Treaties, drawn up by the International Law Commission of the United Nations, regards every treaty which is contrary to the *jus cogens* as null and void.

---

[69] - *Cf.*, Ian Brownlie, *op. cit.*, p. 417-418. *Cf.* also *supra*, part one relative to "historic rights," pp. 37-38 and p. 144.

To sum up, it is clear from the above analysis that Israel has not complied with any of the basic conditions of acquisitive prescription, and can therefore not take advantage of it. It is also evident that Israel's unwarranted invocation of acquisitive prescription constitutes a breach of an essential rule of international law, and fundamentally vitiates the position of Israel.

In default of prescription, can recognition by all States constitute a basis for arguing that the creation of Israel was legal?[70]

The Arab States have never recognised the situation arising from the "creation of Israel." They have not recognised the State of Israel, and the States not directly concerned should have refrained from recognising such a creation brought about by force. The Stimson doctrine obliged them to do so. This doctrine, as Professor Delbez pointed out, "is a prolongation and complement of the theory of prescription. It establishes that possession should be peaceful and uncontested, and provides the rule with a positive sanction, non-recognition."[71]

2) THE NON-RECOGNITION OF ISRAEL:

Israel has not been recognised by the Arab States. A certain number of States, including the United States and the U.S.S.R., have recognised her. The Arab States were perfectly justified in refusing to recognise Israel, even after her admission to the United Nations. Furthermore, it seems clear that the illegality of Israel should have led the other States to withhold their recognition.

A. – Refusal of the Arab States to Recognise Israel

The Arab States consider that Israel is a colonial phenomenon which developed and expanded in the land of Palestine at the expense of the Palestinian people, in whose hands alone remains the right of sovereignty. They claim that the United Nations, in adopting the Palestine Partition resolution, has ignored the fundamental right of the Palestinian people to self-determination, and has

---

[70] - Cf., J. Charpentier: *La reconnaissance internationale et l'évolution du droit des gens.* Paris, Pedone, 1956.

[71] - L. Delbez, *op. cit.,* p. 270.

violated the provisions of the Charter. The General Assembly has, in fact, broken its own rules of competence.

They deplore the fact that the Security Council, far from punishing Israeli acts of aggression, has sided with Israel. In so doing, it has made it impossible to preserve the legitimate rights of the Palestinian people. Furthermore, it has failed in its mission to guarantee international peace and security in this region of the world.

Moreover, even the countries which recognize Israel, on the basis of the Partition resolution, cannot but admit that this resolution has been violated by Israel. For she has occupied territories failing outside the boundaries fixed by the resolution, and has also occupied other territories inside the armistice lines, which cannot be considered as international frontiers in the juridical sense of the word.

These countries reject Israel's claim to base her sovereignty on the right of conquest, a highly inadmissible claim, since Article 4, paragraph 4, of the Charter, prohibits the use of force in international relations.

For these reasons, the Arab States, notwithstanding the admission of Israel to the United Nations on May 11, 1949, have refused to recognise her, and consider themselves entirely justified in doing so.

(a) There is, indeed, a school of thought which holds that admission to an international organisation necessarily and automatically implies recognition of the new member by the old members. Georges Scelle has defended this point of view, asserting that there is a legal obligation to recognise any State admitted to the League of Nations.[72] This theory has been taken up by contemporary writers. Lauterpacht[73] and Guggenheim[74] have formulated the following juridical equation: admission = recognition.

(b) *However, this thesis* has been vigorously contested by an

---

[72] - *Cf.* Georges Scelle: *Revue Générale de droit international public,* 1921.
[73] - *Cf.* Lauterpacht: *Recognition in International Law,* 1947.
[74] - *Cf.* Guggenheim: *Traité de droit international public,* Vol. I, p. 190.

important group of writers, who have observed that it is in utter contradiction with the present practice of members of the international community.

Thus, Kunz,[75] Cohn[76] and Briggs[77] have severely criticised the thesis of Guggenheim and Lauterpacht.

Quite recently, Brownlie[78] went over to the camp of those who consider that there is no juridical obligation to recognise a new member. He develops a double line of reasoning which is of particular interest.

In the first place, he writes, to speak of a juridical obligation is, in fact, to beg the question. It cannot be said that obligation exists except vis-à-vis a subject of international law. But, as regards the State which refuses to extend recognition, the entity to be recognised is not yet a subject of international law; therefore no obligation to recognise it is owed to this entity. Recognition, as a sovereign act, is optional, and has a political and discretionary nature. There is no juridical obligation in this matter.

In the second place, as to whether the recognition of a state is affected by its admission to the United Nations, Brownlie observes that it is wrong to hold that such admission involves *ipso jure* recognition of the new member by all the old members of the Organisation, regardless of how they voted on the question of admission. He points out that there is nothing in the Charter, or in the rules of international law outside the Charter, which obliges a State withholding recognition, *to grant political recognition to the new member and to establish with it bilateral relations,* which remain entirely discretionary.[79]

There is, therefore, no legal obligation to recognise new mem-

---

[75] - Kunz, *American Journal of International Law,* Vol. 44, 1950, p. 713-719.

[76] - Cohn, *Law Quarterly Review,* 1948, p. 404-408.

[77] - Briggs, *American Journal of International Law,* Vol. 43, 1949, p. 113-121.

[78] - Ian Brownlie: *Principles of Public International Law,* Clarendon Press, Oxford, 1966, pp. 85-90.

[79] - *Cf. Memorandum of the U.N. Secretariat General,* Document S/1. 466 and Hans Kelsen: *The Law of the United Nations, op. cit.,* p. 946.

bers admitted by the World Organisation. The position of the Arab States towards Israel is thus unassailable from a legal point of view.

But if the old members are under no legal obligation to grant recognition, are they not under a legal obligation to refuse recognition?

B. — Israel's Illegality, Basis of the Refusal to Extend Recognition

The obligation to withhold recognition from new States falls upon all the members of the international community when the creation of these new States is accompanied by manifest irregularities or by acts of violence.

We need only consider the Partition resolution, and the series of successive territorial expansions brought about by force, to realise that Israel is the resultant of a series of extremely grave illegalities.

The Stimson Doctrine, which was accepted by the League of Nations, since a resolution unanimously adopted on March 11, 1932 forbade members to recognise new States created by force or conquest, has been ignored by the United Nations. Was it because the authors of the Charter, regarding this doctrine as having fallen into decline, preferred to substitute for the system of *a posteriori* condemnation established by it, a system based on the prevention of violence?

In any event, the Stimson Doctrine belongs to positive customary law, to those general principles of law mentioned in Article 38, paragraph 3, of the Statute of the International Court of Justice. It is also in keeping with Article 2, paragraph 4, of the Charter, which outlaws force; it imposes a penalty for the violation of this obligation. Finally, it is one of the factors which, should the occasion arise, prevent acquisitive prescription from coming into play.[80]

Indeed, the doctrine of non-recognition, which is a tribute paid to legality, has been "forgotten" in Israel's favour by a number of

[80] - L. Delbez: *Principes généraux du droit international public*, Paris, 1964, p. 164.

States which have recognised her. For these states, effective existence has been a preferential factor; they would certainly have adopted an attitude more respectful of the law had they complied with the old principle *"ex injuria jus non oritur,"* which is one of the general principles referred to above.

The illegality of Israel, as a State whose creation was based on force and the violation of the general principles of law, has certainly constituted an insurmountable legal obstacle to its recognition by other States.

The Arab States were, therefore, quite justified in refusing to extend their recognition to Israel, which cannot offer in her defence an alleged *"de facto"* recognition which she claims to have been accorded to her.

C. – De Facto Non-Recognition : Existence of a State of War

In default of *de jure* recognition, Israel, in an attempt to find a legal basis for her existence, might hope to avail herself of eventual *de facto* recognition by the Arab States as such a legal basis. But this has not come about, as a result of the continuation of the state of war which, in this case, is of a specific nature, inasmuch as it constitutes *a fundamental refusal on the part of the Arab States to recognise any right on the part of Israel to create a State.*

(a) *The specific nature of the state of war between the Arab States and Israel:*

Classical doctrine considers that a state of war is established by the setting in motion of a body of juridical rules regulating relations between belligerents themselves and between the latter and third parties.[81] Belligerency itself is recognised even in the case of entities which are not states;[82] it is, therefore, not necessary to be a State in an international law sense for certain rules of the law of war to be applied.

War, properly so-called, implies the combination of two ele-

---

[81] - Notably P. Reuter: *Droit international public,* Paris 1963, p. 290.
[82] - Mme. Paul Bastid: *Cours de droit international,* 1965-66, p. 1029.

ments: a state of war, and hostilities amounting to actual combat between armed forces. Insofar as it is lawful, war is regarded as a procedure for the settlement of a disagreement, transformed by its gravity into a dispute, between two States.[83] The State which begins a war is practising "diplomacy by other means,"[84] with a view to punishing the State which persists in its refusal to meet its demands. Such a procedure does not in any way put in question the legal existence of the State involved.[85]

In the case of Palestine, the state of war existing between the Arab States and Israel acquires a special significance; it does not mean a temporary disagreement between the parties capable of being settled; *it is a radical, fundamental refusal to recognise any right on the part of the Jewish community to create a Jewish State in Palestinian Arab territory. It is due to this special nature that it constitutes an insurmountable obstacle to a* de facto *recognition of Israel by the Arab States.*

(b) *The beginning of the state of war in Palestine in 1948:*

On May 14, 1948, the Jews proclaimed "the State of Israel" and expressed their determination to suppress any attempt on the part of the Arab majority to oppose the creation of this State. The acts of violence committed during the period which preceded the proclamation of the Jewish State did not, for that matter, stop; on the contrary, they took on new and bigger dimensions. The purpose of these acts was to sow terror in people's hearts and, consequently, to force the Arabs to leave Palestine and seek refuge in the neighbouring Arab States.

It was then that the Palestinians asked the Arab States to help them in maintaining order inside Palestine, with a view to safeguarding their persons and their belongings. Moreover, this request was made by representative bodies, the *"Arab Higher Committee"* and the *"All-Palestine Government."* The latter was proclaimed by

---

[83] - P. Guggenheim: *Traité de droit international public,* Vol. II, p. 98.

[84] - Mme. Paul Bastid, *op. cit.,* p. 1028.

[85] - It is certain that an ordinary war does not put an end to recognition between two States when such recognition took place before the beginning of hostilities.

the Arab majority in reply to the proclamation of Israel, and had a seat on the Council of the Arab League, which decided to give a favourable response to the Palestinian request.

Furthermore, the disturbances caused by the Jews inside Palestine wre so widespread that they constituted a real threat to the other Arab States themselves: a threat which gave them the right of legitimate self-defence in accordance with Article 51 of the Charter. Subsequent events were to prove how real this threat was.

Thus, in 1948, the Arab States did not wish to" crush a minority" but simply to restore security, in accordance with the request of the majority in Palestine, bu putting an end to illegality which also threatened public order in their own countries.

(c) *The state of war did not end with the Armistice Agreements:*

It is generally conceded that an armistice does not put an end to the state of war; it does no more than suspend war operations by an agreement between the belligerent parties; the local or general nature of the armistice, and its duration, do not modify its effects.[86] Only a peace treaty or, failing that, an express statement, puts an end to a state of war existing between the belligerents after the cessation of hostilities. It is true that contemporary armistices, on account of their substantive provisions, and especially because of the evolution of international law, no longer confer upon the parties as many rights as the old armistices. The belligerents can no longer resume hostilities after the signature of an armistice agreement, even if a dispute should arise between them. In fact, "the outlawing of war and the obligation to find a peaceful solution to all international disputes today no longer permit of freedom of action being left to the parties to an armistice agreement, and particularly the fieedom to resume hostilities."[87]

---

[86] - Art. 36 of the IVth Hague Convention of 1907; P. Guggenheim, *op. cit.,* Vol. II, p. 335, note 1; M. Lachs: *Nouvelle fonction des armistices contemporains,* in *Hommage d'une génération de juristes au Président Basdevant,* p. 315 sqq.

[87] - M. Lachs, *op. cit.,* p. 315 sqq. This shows clearly that when Israel claims that the Armistice Agreements are no longer valid, she is committing yet another violation of international law.

All the same, even though present day armistices limit the freedom of the parties concerned, they have not yet acquired the quality of putting an end to the state of war. To produce such a result, an armistice agreement should settle the very cause of the conflict, i.e. it should be equivalent in its provisions to a peace treaty. But the Armistice Agreements, far from having this meaning, were no more than an indispensable step towards the liquidation of armed conflict and the restoration of peace in Palestine.[88] Moreover, all the Armistice Agreements clearly indicate that "they do not in any way constitute peace treaties" and that they shall not "prejudice the rights, claims and positions of either party hereto in the ultimate peaceful settlement of the Palestine question.[89]

Thus a state of war continues to exist between Israel and the Arab States, because the Armistice Agreements have settled only the second element in concept of war, namely, hostilities.

The aggressive behaviour of Israel, particularly in 1956 and 1967, has proved that the Arab States were, in fact, justified in taking precautions against attacks which did not fail to materialise.

(d) *A state of war is not incompatible with the Charter of the United Nations:*

The Charter forbids the use of force or the threat of force (Article 2, paragraph 4). War is, therefore, an unlawful act in modern international law; its first element, consisting as it does of actual fighting, is undoubtedly so, but its second element, (state of war) is none the less unlawful, in that it constitutes a threat to use force.

As a counterpart to this prohibition, Article 51 of the Charter recognizes the right of the State which is attacked to defend itself. This right would be void of any real meaning if it did not also confer upon a State, which has not yet been attacked, but which has good and obvious reasons to fear an armed aggression, the right to prepare

---

[88] - Art. 1, paragraph 4 of the Armistice signed between Egypt and Israel on February 24, 1949.

[89] - Art. XI of the same agreement. All the other Armistices contain similar provisions.

for its own defence. For Article 51 of the Charter to have its full meaning, it is necessary to recognise that such a State has the right to take advantage of the juridical rules which establish a state of war not only when it has actually been attacked.

In fact, as far as the Palestine question is concerned, the very existence of Israel constitutes aggression; but even supposing that it did not, the expansionist activities of Israel since 1949 have constituted a real and indubitable threat to all the Arab States, particularly those which border on Israel.

As far as this group of countries is concerned, therefore, a state of war, according to the provisions of international law, continues to exist. Its special nature prevents Israel from availing herself of an eventual *de facto* recognition on the part of the Arab States.

The argument that used to be put forward, that membership of the United Nations was incompatible with a state of war claimed by a member State to exist with another member State, has been declared by legal doctrine to be "wholly inadmissible,"[90] and considered as scarcely compatible with the realities of international life, even under the Charter of the United Nations.[91]

3) THE NON-IMPLEMENTATION OF UNITED NATIONS RESOLUTIONS:

Despite the great number of resolutions on the Palestine problem which have been adopted by the United Nations; action by this Organisation has, paradoxically, yielded very few practical results. The non-implementation of its resolutions has been due to two factors: violation by Israel of the decisions of the General Assembly and the Security Council, and the inadequacy of the World Organisation.

A. — *Violation of U.N. Resolutions By Israel*

The failure of the United Nations has, essentially, been due to

---

[90] - Bengt Broms, *The Legal Status of the Suez Canal*, Helsinki, 1961, p. 210, note 4.

[91] - Baxter, *The Law of International Waterways*, Cambridge, Mass.; 1964, p. 222, note 163.

deliberate ill will on the part of Israel, which has persistently refused to submit to its decisions. Thus the Partition resolution, although favourable to Israel, which secured it in violation of the Charter, has not been respected by her. Israel has seized territories over and above those demarcated in the Partition plan. Thus, too, the various General Assembly resolutions on the return of the refugees, have remained a dead letter.[92] Likewise, the resolution of the General Assembly relative to the Status of Jerusalem[93] has not been implemented by Israel, and the Armistice Commission created by the Security Council has been boycotted by her.[94]

But it is mainly as regards the attacks of regular troops of the Israeli army, on the territories of neighbouring Arab States, that the violations by Israel of U.N. resolutions have been most flagrant, and the condemnations by the Security Council most severe.[95] The same has been true of the resolutions adopted by the General Assembly since the invasion of Egyptian territory in 1956, which have not been implemented by Israel.[96]

---

[92] - The relevant General Assembly resolutions are the following: Resolution No. 302 of December 8, 1949; Resolution No. 394 of December 14, 1950; Resolution No. 512 of January 26, 1952; Resolution No. 614 of November 6, 1952; Resolution No. 720 of November 17, 1953; Resolution No. 818 of December 4, 1954; Resolution No. 916 of December 3, 1955; Resolution No. 1018 of February 28, 1957; Resolution No. 1191 of December 12, 1957; Resolution No. 1315 of December 12, 1958.

On the contradiction involved in Arab acceptance of certain resolutions and rejection of others, see *Supra,* p. 127-128. Violation by Israel of resolutions declaratory of a right, or of those which are in conformity with the principles of international law and the Charter, is in fact tantamount to violation of the international law applied by these resolutions.

[93] - General Assembly resolution No. 303 of December 9, 1949.

[94] - Security Council resolution No. 48 of April 23, 1948.

[95] - Security Council resolutions of May 18, 1951, of November 24, 1953, of March 29, 1955, of January 19, 1956 and of April 9, 1962. Especially as regards the resolution of April 1962, the Israeli parliament categorically rejected it. (See "Israel Digest," Vol. V, No. 9, April 27, 1962.)

[96] - General Assembly resolutions of November 2, 1956, of November 4, 1956, of November 7, 1956, of November 24, 1956, of January 19, 1957, of February 2, 1957. The General Assembly, especially in its resolution of February 2, 1957, "deplores the non-compliance of Israel to complete its withdrawal behind the armistice demarcation line despite the repeated requests of the General Assembly," and calls upon Israel "to complete its withdrawal behind the armistice demarcation line without delay."

By its deliberate and persistent refusal to implement the binding resolutions of the Security Council and the principles of international law embodied in the resolutions of the General Assembly, Israel has placed herself in an illegal situation, over and above the illegality of her creation.[97]

Nevertheless, the non-implementation of U.N. resolutions on the Palestine question is not only due to deliberate non-compliance on the part of Israel; it is also a result of the inadequacy of the World Organisation itself.

B. — Inadequacy of the United Nations

When a Member State commits a breach of the Charter provisions, or when it deliberately refuses to comply with resolutions rightfully adopted by the Security Council or the General Assembly, it is mandatory upon the United Nations to take measures against such a state. These measures are threefold: sanctions, suspension of rights and privileges, and expulsion.

In case of a threat to peace, a breach of the peace or any act of aggression, the Security Council may, in accordance with Chapter VII of the Charter, decree a whole range of sanctions[98] against the recalcitrant State. But the Security Council which, according to the Charter, is responsible for the maintenance of peace, has been remiss in its duty by failing to impose sanctions against Israel.

Furthermore, the General Assembly can, by virtue of Article 5 of the Charter, decide that a Member State should be suspended from the exercise of its rights and privileges.[99] And if a Member

---

[97] - On the binding force of Security Council decisions see, in particular, M. Virally: *La valeur juridique des recommandations des Organisations internationales*, A.F.D.I., 1956, pp. 83-90; L. Cavare: *Le droit international public positif*, Vol. I, p. 665; Ch. Chaumont: *L'O.N.U.*, pp. 47-48; L. di Qual: Les effets des résolutions des Nations Unies, Paris, L.G.D.J., 1967, p. 283. (*Bibliothèque de droit international*, Vol. 37).

[98] - See on this point, L. Cavare: *Le droit international public positif*, vol. I, 1961, pp. 684-690.

[99] - The power of the General Assembly is exercised in conjunction with that of the Security Council. On the recommendation of the latter the General Assembly can pronounce suspension from the exercise of rights and privileges of membership. (Art. 5 of the Charter.)

State "persistently violates the principles contained in the Charter,"[100] the General Assembly may, on the recommendation of the Security Council, expel it from the Organisation. In failing to adopt these various measures with regard to Israel, the General Assembly has failed to perform its duties.

Moreover, not only should the General Assembly or the Security Council have taken the necessary steps against Israel with a view to restoring peace; it was also incumbent upon the Members of the United Nations to help each other to implement the decisions of the Security Council in accordance with Article 48 of the Charter. In particular, it is stipulated in paragraph 2 of Articles 48 that the decisions of the Security Council shall be carried out by United Nations Members directly.[101]

In accordance with the provisions of the Charter, the Member States of the United Nations are responsible for implementing the resolutions voted by the Security Council or the General Assembly. This responsibility is clearly binding on all parties individually and collectively. And, in particular, the members of the Security Council bear a special responsibility for implementing these resolutions. Furthermore, the member States which have voted for the resolutions condemning the Israeli action also share in the responsibility for the non-implementation of these resolutions.

---

[100] - Article 6 of the U.N. Charter.

[101] - According to the provisions of Articles 24, par. 1, and 25 of the Charter, the Members of the United Nations "agree that in carrying out its duties under this responsibility the Security Council acts on their behalf," and they "agree to accept and carry out the decisions of the Security Council." This principle of collective action by the Security Council and of the collective responsibility of the members of the Security Council therefore derives from the provisions of Articles 24, 25 and 48 of the Charter. On this point, see M. Virally: " La valeur juridique des recommandations des Organisations internationales," article quoted in *Annuaire français de droit international*, 1956, p. 84.

PART THREE

IMPLICATIONS OF THE CONFLICT

By creating the State of Israel in 1948 under notoriously illegal conditions, the Zionists entered into conflict with the Arabs who had already been pillaged and threatened.

The proclamation of the State, and the war which followed it, accelerated the exodus and expulsion of the Palestinians from their homeland. They became refugees, with all that this implies in the way of suffering and bitterness.

The Zionists were not content to secure for themselves the territories which the Partition resolution had given them at the cost of serious juridical irregularities and heavy political and moral responsibilities. After numerous attacks they succeeded in occupying part of Jerusalem, for which the United Nations had reserved at least an international status.

Violating the truce and Armistice Agreements, and unmoved by United Nations condemnation of their actions, Zionist troops continued their advance until they reached and, quite improperly, occupied the Jordanian village of Umm Rashrash on the Gulf of Aqaba, where they established by force the port of Elath, thus creating a new political problem in the Gulf.

They then proceeded to jeopardise the economies of the neighbouring countries—Lebanon, Syria and Jordan—by starting, in violation of the provisions of the international law of rivers, to divert the waters of the Jordan.

Finally, their expansionist policy, which since 1948 has found concrete expression in a series of aggressive acts, including the seizure of Palestine, the occupation of New Jerusalem, and the conquest of Umm Rashrash, has been revealed in an even more outrageous manner since their aggression of June 5, 1967. In utter disregard of the rules of the law of war and military occupation, they have annexed Syrian, Jordanian and Egyptian territories, and established themselves on one of the banks of the Suez Canal, an Egyptian waterway, which they intend not only to use but also to control. Alas, the dream of "Greater Israel," from the Nile to the Euphrates, which so clearly illustrates Israel's determination to expand, and which the Arabs have constantly denounced to sceptical and indifferent world opinion, assumed a new and more decisive form in June 1967.

Palestinian refugees, Jerusalem, the Gulf of Aqaba, the river Jordan, the Suez Canal, these are some of the implications of the Arab-Zionist conflict.

Chapter I

The Status of Jerusalem

Few cities in the world have such emotive force and such spiritual wealth as Jerusalem. Its exclusive privilege of being the meeting place of the three great monotheistic religions has ever made it the focus of the religious fervour of Moslems, Christians and Jews alike. It was not part of its destiny that it should become first the object, then the victim of Israeli ambitions; its threefold religious vocation predisposes it to a sort of ecumenism, which is quite incompatible with its present situation as an occupied city.

Open as it is to so many different religious influences, Jerusalem, as long as it remained under Arab control, offered a most liberal welcome to all and allowed every man absolute freedom to practise the religion of his choice. From time immemorial, the believer has been able to go there to worship his God in the Temple or Sanctuary which Arab sovereignty has preserved intact for centuries.

And yet, despite the fact that this situation gave satisfaction to everybody, the status of Jerusalem as an Arab city, i.e. as a city in which everybody enjoyed freedom, gradually deteriorated from the moment when that fatal process was put in motion which was to lead the U.N. to decide on the partition of Palestine and the internationalisation of Jerusalem.

The contemporary history of Jerusalem is that of an Arab city, wrested from its legitimate sovereign, endowed in 1947 with an international status, then divided in 1948, finally to be annexed by Israel in 1967. Under the cloak of a regime of internationalisation

—a regime which was never applied and which was enacted with little or no regard to Palestinian sovereignty—Israel has expanded her empire, at first seizing part, then all, of Jerusalem.

Today, internationalisation is advanced as the best possible solution; no one remembers the simple truth that Jerusalem is an Arab city which, in logic and in justice, should be restored to the Arab homeland.

Should this debatable decision of the makers of international law lead us to consider as right an internationalisation which, after all, is no more than the culmination of a whole series of aggressions? How can one admit that the internationalisation of a territory acquired by force is capable of satisfying both the despoiled victim and equity? Jerusalem divided, Jerusalem annexed, Jerusalem internationalised, such, then, is the turbulent history of the city, to be crowned with the "happy ending," so satisfactory to some, but not to the Arabs who will never be able to forget that Jerusalem is first and foremost an Arab city.

I. — JERUSALEM PARTITIONED :

Until Jerusalem, Arab for thousands of years, was conquered by the Zionists, the faithful of the three greatest monotheistic religions in the world could visit it for the practice of their faith. Free access to the Holy Places, freedom of conscience for all the city's inhabitants, protection of all religious sanctuaries were assured and even organised, because, in 1878, the Congress of Berlin had established a partition in time and space of religious edifices and laid down conditions for the practice of each faith.

Although an Arab city, Jerusalem never either established or permitted any kind of discrimination against Jews or Christians. Based as it was on freedom, mutual respect and equality, the status of Jerusalem and the Holy Places gave satisfaction to all. There was nothing in the situation to justify the relinquishing of such a liberal regime of full freedom, for one of internationalisation. And yet, this is what the United Nations decided in its resolution of November

29, 1947, which internationalised Jerusalem as well as partitioning Palestine.

1) FROM FREEDOM TO INTERNATIONALISATION:

It is difficult to understand how an international regime could be imposed on an Arab city with a clearly defined sovereign, whose consent, to say the least, was required to this statutory change. All known regimes of internationalisation presuppose the consent of the State territorially competent, which must indicate its willingness to surrender its sovereignty in a treaty, as happened, for example, in the case of Tangiers or Trieste. Nothing of the sort happened in the case of the internationalisation of Jerusalem, where the opinion of the territorial sovereign was not asked, and where a status was imposed in accordance with which the city was set up as a *corpus separatum* administered by the United Nations, this status applying not only to Jerusalem but also to Bethlehem.

The authority entrusted with the administration was required to protect the spiritual and religious interests of the three monotheistic religions, as though they had hitherto not been perfectly protected to everybody's benefit.

Such was the erroneous *juridical* solution of a simple problem, which could only be properly solved by respecting the rights of the territorial sovereign. It was inevitable that the latter should reject a settlement which so flagrantly ignored these rights.

2) FROM INTERNATIONALISATION TO PARTITION:

The international regime decreed by the resolution of November 29, 1947 never saw the light; war between Jordan and Israel broke out immediately after the departure of British troops. A truce agreement of November 30, 1948, followed by an armistice agreement on April 3, 1949, sanctioned a *de facto* partition of Jerusalem.

It was thus that Israel achieved territorial gains by the occupation of New Jerusalem and obtained more than the United Nations had illegally granted it two years before. Jordan asserted its sovereignty over the oldest part of the city, in which the Holy Places were situated.

This was a *de facto* partition of Jerusalem, with its boundaries traced by the ceasefire line, not a legal partition implying relinquishment of territorial sovereignty over the new part of the city.

Some have regarded the various agreements of Novembr 30, 1948 and of April 3, 1949 as constituting ratification by the United Nations of the partition of Jerusalem, since these agreements were made in the presence of the U.N. Mediator, and approved by the Security Council. But an armistice is no more than a provisional measure, which in no way prejudices the rights of the parties concerned.

If, purely for the sake of the argument, we admit that the partition of Jerusalem constituted a regime acceptable to international law, we must also admit that the attack of June 5, 1967, accompanied as it was by a total Israelisation of the city, violated that regime in a most flagrant manner.

II. — JERUSALEM ANNEXED :

Any doubts that may have been entertained about the real intentions of Israel with regard to Jerusalem, were dispelled by General Dayan after the conquest of the city. Standing before the Wailing Wall, he gave free expression to his joy, and uttered words which indicated that the Jewish State intended to annex Jerusalem. At about the same moment the Chaplain General of the Israeli army exclaimed: "A people recovers its capital; a capital recovers its people; never shall they be separated again."

Today, it is a fact that Israel considers that it has reconquered the "high place of her national past" and that she intends to organise worship in the Holy Places as she wishes.

Furthermore, the declaration proclaiming the unification of the two sectors of the city reveals Israel's intention of annexing it permanently, an attitude which was condemned by the U.N. General

Assembly during its extraordinary session of June, 1967. In its resolution of July 4, 1967, the General Assembly condemned the annexation of the Jordanian sector, and called upon Israel to rescind all measures leading to a modification of the status of the city.

Israel, however, has taken no steps to rescind any of the annexation measures. On the contrary, after the Knesset, by its decision of December 22, 1949, had proclaimed Jerusalem as the capital of the State, and after the transfer, since that date, of most of her ministries to that city, Israel maintains her policy, despite the resolutions of the United Nations and condemnation by world public opinion.[1] By abandoning the Arab population to the brutality of her troops,[2] Israel has behaved as a conqueror and, under cover of an alleged "unification," has annexed the whole of Jerusalem.

The Holy City, so rich in history, in which the spirit of tolerance and respect for all communities formerly prevailed, lies today under the domination of a partisan and persecuting State. The Arabs, Moslems as well as Christians, are threatened, and access to the Holy Places is subject to the disturbing fanaticism of Israel.

Such is the sad balance sheet of United Nations action in Palestine as it stands today. Ignoring the natural right of Palestine to preserve its integrity, that of Jerusalem included, the World Organisation has shown itself incapable of securing respect even for the international status of Jerusalem, a status which itself could not satisfy the city's legitimate sovereign, since it mutilated the city's territory and deprived that sovereign of part of it.

III. — JERUSALEM INTERNATIONALISED ?

This question mark reflects more than the anxious surprise of the Arab peoples vis-à-vis the internationalisation plan: these

---

[1] - The great majority of countries have refused to establish their embassies in Jerusalem. *Cf.* on this point the article by Farag Moussa in "International Policy" (*As-Siyasa ad-Dawliya*), *Al-Ahram*, Cairo, October, 1967.

[2] - On the horrors committed by Israeli troops in Jerusalem, see the accounts given by Father Paul Gauthier and Sister Marie Thérèse in the damning pamphlet published by *Témoignage Chrétien*, Paris, Cahier No. 47.

peoples are today resolutely hostile to the plan.

In this connection, a fundamental observation must be made, before proceeding to any discussion of the question of Jerusalem. This is that the problem of internationalisation was not raised until after Israeli expansionism had again decided to question the sovereignty of Palestine over a part of its territory—as long as this region of the world remained under Arab sovereignty the question of internationalisation was never raised.

The difficulties came from outside, with massive Jewish immigration and the Jewish community's lust for conquest. The United Nations bowed to these pressures to such an extent that, far from enforcing respect for Arab sovereignty, it approved this disastrous plan for internationalisation. But the development and progress of international law is not tied to the replacement of an indisputable sovereignty by an internationalisation which is as questionable in its legality as it is inopportune in its planning.

1) THE INTERNATIONALISATION SOLUTION OF QUESTIONABLE LEGALITY:

We have already briefly indicated why the internationalisation of Jerusalem is illegal, but this blunder on the part of the United Nations is so grave that it must be stressed again.

The World Organisation, based as it is on the principles of the equality of States and of mutual respect for territorial sovereignty, is itself bound, as is each of its members individually, to respect these basic principles. It is not, therefore, in a position to decide that part of a territory, with a well-defined sovereign, shall be subjected to an international regime without the consent of this territorial sovereign. It has no competence to make such a decision, which could only be made by the States concerned, including the legitimate territorial sovereign, within the framework of a multilateral treaty.

Moreover, there is no relation whatsoever between the necessity for establishing an international regime and the fact that a city is a holy one, even if, as in the present case, it is the cradle of the three great monotheistic religions. Jerusalem is a city which, due to its numerous Holy Places, attracts Moslems and Christians, who have always met within its walls in mutual respect.

It is only Israel's claim to total hegemony over Palestine, to the building of a Greater Israel, to make of Jerusalem the capital of the New State,[3] that led some to believe that Jerusalem must be internationalised, if peace was to return to this region of the world, and especially to this high place of spiritual meditation.

2) THE INTERNATIONALISATION OF JERUSALEM INOPPORTUNE :

The internationalisation of Jerusalem is clearly not only an illegal solution, but one that is out of date and inapplicable in the present political context in the Middle East, for three basic reasons:

(a) In the first place, the attitudes to internationalisation previously adopted have been radically modified, as far as most States are concerned, by the aggression of June 5, 1967.

Admittedly the Holy See, through Pope Pius XII, called for internationalisation in 1948 and 1949, and recently too it has been considered that this principle, as elaborated by the Trusteeship Council on April 4, 1950, "could constitute a fair settlement of the question."[4]

But all the Arab States, however, divided they may have been on the subject in the past, are now unanimous in their rejection of internationalisation as a solution, because it would sanction aggression. Israel too, if, indeed, her attitude has to be mentioned, no longer supports the internationalisation of the Holy Places, which she proposed in a memorandum of May 15, 1950, because she has annexed the entire city of Jerusalem.

The third Israeli aggression of 1967 has made the Arab peoples conscious of their profound unity and rekindled their national sentiments; they cannot again accept that an illegal conquest be per-

---

3 - Cf. *supra*, p. 177-178.
4 - Cf. *Le Monde,* June 13, 1967.

petuated by the establishment of an international regime.

(b) In the second place, the United Nations has been unable to secure respect for the various internationalisation plans drawn up by its Organs, so liable have they all been to criticism.

This is true of the resolutions of November 29, 1947 and of December 11, 1948, as well as the third attempt in the resolution of December 9, 1949, by which the General Assembly called on the Trusteeship Council to draft a Statute for Jerusalem. The Council adopted the Statute on April 4, 1950.

Other resolutions have been adopted, such as that passed by the Special Political Committee on December 11, 1952. This resolution no longer spoke of internationalisation, confining itself to vague recommendations. It was rejected by the General Assembly.

In 1952, another resolution recommended direct negotiations "bearing in mind the objectives and the resolutions of the United Nations;" it received 24 favourable votes. It was interpreted as implying a renunciation of the General Assembly and as underlining the non-compulsory nature of U.N. resolutions.

All this goes to show that, if an international regime were to be adopted, and accepted by the Arab States—which is purely hypothetical—the United Nations would be neither able nor willing to get it respected.

c) But the Arab States cannot approve internationalisation, which would validate the occupation by force of an indisputably Arab city, and remove it from its natural sovereign.

An integral internationalisation of Jerusalem, set up as a *corpus separatum,* including Bethlehem and Nazareth, with guarantees of freedom of access to all pilgrims and foreign visitors regardless of nationality or creed, would only be conceivable if there had been discrimination in the past, i.e. before 1948.

It is unnecessary to recall that the Arab regime always functioned in the best interests of the different religious communities, ensuring equality among them in law and in practice, as well as mutual respect for one another's faith.

The idea of internationalising Jerusalem is an idle fancy, which cannot possibly provide a final solution for the problem of the Holy Places. If, through weakness, this situation is allowed to come about, an entity which has been Arab for thousands of years will be fettered by a completely artificial status, and the natural rights of a community to be itself will be disregarded, a community of men who will never forget who they are, whence they came and where they wish to go.

This ignorance of a fundamental truth has led to the invention of legal structures which are undoubtedly ingenious, but so unreal that not even their foundation stone has been laid.

The entire international community owes it to itself to re-examine the problem of the Holy Places, starting with this elementary premise: Jerusalem, a Holy City, is also an Arab city.

Then, as in the past, Israel and Ishmael will be able to worship and to meet in a Jerusalem regained, and the Christians too, as the *Osservatore Romano*[5] hoped, will be able, "in the ever living reality of the Old Testament, to follow anew the earthly itinerary of the Redemption" along the paths trodden by the feet of the Son of Man.

---

[5] - Quoted by *Le Monde,* June 13, 1967.

Chapter II

The Palestine Arab Refugees

The Arab tragedy in Palestine was not confined to Israel's confiscation of a territory. Usurpation was accompanied by the forcible dispossession of the inhabitants and their expulsion from their country. At the present moment they number more than a million and a half persons, mainly women and children, both Moslems and Christians, cast on the roads by an unjustified and concerted action, aimless, without resources and deprived of their natural home. "The refugees," said the Director of U.N.R.W.A. before the United Nations in 1964, "are still living today in dire poverty, often under pathetic and, in some cases, appalling conditions. Despite the sustained efforts of U.N.R.W.A. and of the host Governments and other collaborating agencies, there are families who still live in dwellings which are unfit for human habitation... and who face starvation."[1]

Faced with these realities, the Zionists maintain that it is the Arabs who are responsible for the creation and the continuance of this problem. In their view, it is up to the Arabs to receive and to help the Palestine refugees and, eventually, to integrate them into their own peoples. Has not Israel, so runs the argument, absorbed all the Jews who came from different States, particularly those from the Arab World?

---

[1] - U.N. Document, A/6013, U.N.R.W.A., *Report* for period 1st July, 1964 to 30 June, 1965. pp. 4-5.

This view reduces the refugee problem to a simple transfer of populations. As we shall see, the only object of this reasoning is to increase the confusion, permanently kept alive by the Zionists, about the realities of the Palestine case. Furthermore, it evades the question of Zionist responsibility by passing it on the Arab countries.

In so doing, Israel gravely misrepresents both the degree and the nature of the obligations of the Arabs towards the Palestinians; on the one hand, she sets aside, and at little cost to herself, the international obligations she has accepted, and on the other, she passes in silence over the failure, for which she herself is primarily responsible, of United Nations action to achieve a satisfactory settlement of the refugee problem.

The whole Arab attitude can be summed up as a rejection of the political genocide of the Palestinians.

Israel's attempt to reduce the refugee problem to a simple transfer of populations, attractive though it may seem at first sight to reasonable men is, in fact, an example of Israeli Machiavellianism. Israel has indeed, assimilated Jews from, for example, the North African countries, but it is quite clear that this integration was not only desired and hoped for, but that it was basically positive, in that it aimed at the unification, at the ingathering of Jews dispersed throughout the world, to fuse them in a single crucible.

But can Israel be brought to admit that the integration of the refugees in Arab countries might have different consequences? The same remedy applied in two different situations will obviously not have the same results.

In the first case the object of the proposed integration is unity, but in the second it can only lead to the splitting up, to the disintegration of the Palestinian people.

Moreover, it should be recalled that a population transfer presupposes some agreement, albeit tacit, among the parties concerned. But it is well known that the refugees have but one desire, to return to their homes and not to go farther away from them for fear of losing all hope of recovering them.

The Palestinian people constitutes an entity. To split it up in order to integrate it better, is purely and simply to dissolve it and remove it altogether from the international scene.

Once the usurpation is legalised, the Palestinian people eliminated and genocide accomplished, Israel, finally cleansed of all flaws, will leave it to the bar of History to condemn the Arab countries as unwitting butchers of a brother people.

I. — ATTITUDE OF ARAB STATES

Contrary to Zionist assertions, the Arabs have never failed to meet their obligations arising out of the solidarity which unites them with their Palestinian brethren. This concrete and effective solidarity is limited by the political considerations mentioned above: no state can assume responsibility for the political genocide of the Palestinian people by entirely integrating the refugees.

1) ARAB AID IS OF MANY KINDS:

In the first place, this aid aims at meeting the basic needs of the refugees. It stems from a natural human solidarity. Furthermore, the feeling of the Arab States of belonging to one community has led them to adopt measures calculated to guarantee protection and security for the refugees by the granting of the rights and privileges attached to citizenship.

A. – Material Aid

This is not the place to draw up a balance sheet of the very considerable material aid given by the Arabs. They have, either directly or through specialised international organisations, made a contribution, entirely out of proportion to their economic potentials, to meet the vital needs of the refugees (food, clothing, medical care, etc...).

This contribution is indisputable, and no one has tried to deny it. Reference to the relevant statistics, should this be required, will suffice to reveal the facts beyond any possibility of doubt.

B. – Legal Protection

The Arab States which have given refuge to the immense majority of the Palestine refugees have, since 1948, made a number of decisions with the object of giving them protection and at the same time solving the many legal, economic and social problems involved in the situation.

In implementation of these decisions, measures have been taken to facilitate acquisition by the refugees of the nationality of their host countries, along with the rights and obligations of the citizens of these countries. In this respect the example of Jordan, which has been followed by other Arab countries, may be taken as typical.

The Jordanian Ordinance No. 56 of 1949 makes the following stipulation: "All persons permanently resident in the territory of the Hashemite Kingdom of Jordan, who formerly held Palestinian nationality, are deemed to have acquired Jordanian nationality. Consequently, they have the rights and obligations of Jordanians."

The government incorporated the provisions of this Ordinance into the nationality law of March, 1954. As a result of this text, is considered a Jordanian:– any person who has acquired Jordanian nationality by virtue of ordinance No. 56 of 1949:– and any person who was a Palestinian citizen before May 15, 1948, and who, at the time when this law was promulgated, was a permanent resident of the Hashemite Kingdom of Jordan.

The Law of 1954 goes further than the Ordinance of 1949, in reducing the formalities required for the granting of Jordanian citizenship to the minimum.

Other States have similarly made it easy to acquire their nationality, and this has enabled thousands of refugees to acquire the rights and obligations of the citizens of those countries.

But Arab solidarity is limited by the political dimensions of the problem:

2) REFUSAL TO ASSUME RESPONSIBILITY FOR THE POLITICAL GENOCIDE OF PALESTINE:

As has just been explained, the Arab States have offered the Palestinians a legal framework favourable to their integration; *but the overwhelming majority of Palestinians, whose sole desire is to return to their country, have objected to this assimilation.*

As early as 1953, the Director of U.N.R.W.A., addressing the United Nations states: "The salient fact which continues to condition the mood of the refugees and to influence the policies of Middle Eastern governments on this question, is the desire of the refugees to return to their country."[2]

The regrouping of the Palestine Arab peoples is evidence of a refusal: *"A refusal, first of all, to crumble, to disperse, to disintegrate by being integrated into other States, even if they are sister states. By clinging together, the Palestinians have been able to spare themselves the 'diaspora' which the Israelis had destined for them. Although Arab Palestine no longer exists as a State, through the refugee camps it remains an organised body.*

But these camps are not merely the organised expression of the Palestinian nation; they are also the sociological form which the protest of this people against its expatriation and its expropriation has taken.[3]

This rejection by the Palestinians of any form of settlement of their situation which does not safeguard their inalienable rights and which does not lead to their return to their country, is a fundamental element in the attitude of the Arabs. Consequently, they are not satisfied with merely meeting the requirements of human solidarity, natural as it may be, even when to this is added the feeling of belonging to the same community.

These considerations mean that the responsibility of the Arab States towards the refugees involves their political obligation, that

---

[2] - U.N. Document: GA/AH/356, November 22, 1953.

[3] - Jean-Pierre Provins: "Les Camps de Réfugiés Palestiniens," in *Un jour ou l'autre Israël disparaîtra, Le Communiste,* édit., 42 Rue René Boulanger, Paris, p. 37.

is, their concern to take into account and to ensure respect for the legitimate rights of the interested parties themselves.

Thus the human solidarity incumbent upon the Arabs vis-à-vis every Palestinian refugee, is inevitably limited by their political responsibility towards the Palestinian people as a whole and towards history.

II. — RESPONSIBILITY OF ISRAEL

The baselessness of the Israeli argument of Arab responsibility is evident. By reversing the facts of the case, Israel attributes the unhappy fate of the refugees to inaction on the part of the Arabs. In so doing, she seeks to hide her own prime responsibility as the usurper of the homeland of these refugees. This has already been said. But what concerns us here is that Israel also wants to evade the obligations imposed on her by international law to settle this painful problem.

It is surely unnecessary to recall that the Zionist State bears the prime responsibility. This responsibility is twofold:

— On the one hand, Israel has failed to satisfy the conditions laid down by the United Nations for her admission to membership in the Organisation;

— On the other hand, her policy of discrimination against those other refugees of a different kind viz., the Palestinians who have remained in their homes, constitutes a flagrant breach of morality and of the principles firmly laid down by law and jurisprudence for the protection of minorities.

1) REPATRIATION OF THE REFUGEES, ABROGATING CONDITION FOR ISRAEL'S ADMISSION TO THE U.N.:

Normally, every Member State of the United Nations is bound by the obligations arising out of the Charter. It undertakes to respect them from the very first day of its admission.

Israel, on the other hand, was the only State to be admitted on condition that she carried out certain specific resolutions of the

General Assembly, more particularly those regarding the question of the refugees. This situation must be stressed. The heavy obligations with which Israel is burdened are in proportion to the exceptional nature of such a condition, which indicates without any doubt the prime responsibility of the Zionists.

A. – Right of the Refugees to Repatriation and Compensation

Faithful to the principles affirmed in Article 13 of the Universal Declaration of Human Rights,[4] the United Nations General Assembly has always recognised the right of the refugees to return to their homes. As early as 1948 the Assembly recommended that they should be permitted to do so "at the earliest practicable date" and that compensation should be paid for "loss of or damage to property."

These provisions were originally embodied in resolution 194 (III) of December 11, 1948 which was subsequently recapitulated in numerous later resolutions. Paragraph 11 of this resolution stipulates "that the refugees wishing to return to their homes and live at peace with their neighbours should be permitted to do so at the earliest practicable date, and that compensation should be paid for the property of those not choosing to return and for loss of or damage to property which, under principles of international law or in equity, should be made good by the Governments or authorities responsible."

At its fourth ordinary session in 1949, the General Assembly expressly reaffirmed the provisions of paragraph 11. A year later, it adopted measures to ensure that, when they were repatriated, the refugees should not be discriminated against "in law or in fact." Resolution 394 (V) of December 14, 1950, called "upon the governments concerned to undertake measures to ensure that refugees, whether repatriated or resettled, will be treated without any discrimination either in law or in fact."

---

4 - "Everyone has the right to leave, and return to, any country, including his own."

B. – Non-Fulfillment of the Abrogating Condition and Nullity of Israel's Admission to the U.N.

The General Assembly has established a direct relationship between the admission of Israel to the United Nations and the implementation of resolution 194 (III) mentioned above. This link is clearly expressed in the actual text of resolution 273 (III) of May 11, 1949 concerning the admission of Israel to the United Nations.

"Noting . . . the declaration by the State of Israel that it 'unreservedly accepts the obligations of the United Nations Charter and undertakes to honour them from the day when it becomes a member of the United Nations,

"Recalling its resolutions of 29 November 1947 and 11 December 1948 and taking note of the declarations and explanations made by the representative of the Government of Israel before the *ad hoc* Political Committee in respect of the implementation of the said resolutions,

"The General Assembly,

" . . . . ,

decides to admit Israel to membership in the United Nations."

Israel has not honoured the obligations she thus subscribed to before the largest possible body of public opinion and, what is more, on the occasion of her solemn admission to the United Nations. On the contrary, she has shifted her own responsibility for the Arab refugees to the lap of Arab countries.

Already in its resolution 394 of 14 December 1950, the General Assembly of the United Nations noted that no repatriation, no resettlement and no economic and social rehabilitation of the refugees had been carried out, and that the payment of compensation had not been effected. Since that date the General Assembly has on several occasions noted that the provisions of paragraph 11 of resolution 194 (III) concerning repatriation, have not been put into effect. Such censure, indicating the condemnation of Israel, has clearly not disturbed the Zionists at all.

Thus, Israel has not only pledged her responsibility for the refugees, but has also released the United Nations from its obligations towards her, so that the Organisation would be perfectly justified in expelling her.

The close link established by the General Assembly in the same resolution, between the admission of Israel and the implementation of resolution 194 (III) of 11 December 1948, makes it possible to affirm *that it was the intention of the United Nations to confer upon the application of this resolution the character of an abrogating condition.*

By her systematic opposition to the return of the refugees, Israel has failed to fulfil the terms of this condition. By the same token she has stripped of all legality the resolution which admitted her to the International Organisation.

2) THE "INTERNAL REFUGEES"

The protection of minorities is solidly established in law. This is evidenced by a large volume of jurisprudence and the numerous recommendations of the General Assembly. Israel has subscribed to these resolutions; but has she also respected her undertakings?

Bullying, harrassing, destroyed homes, occupied lands, laissez-passers and barbed wire prove that she has not done so. Only one conclusion can be drawn from this: Israel does not respect her own pledges and, in short, treats the Palestinians who remained behind *as nothing more nor less than a new kind of refugees, second class citizens stripped of their rights, internal refugees.* Living in ghettoes, they are condemned to exile in their own country.[5]

A. – Racial Discrimination

Before the aggression of June 5, 1967, 250,000 Palestinian Arabs still lived in Israel. This minority is discriminated against.

The Arabs are deprived of the right to equal pay for equal work; Their opportunities for education and work are restricted.

---

[5] - On their situation see also the development of this question, *supra*, pp. 75-82.

For the last 20 years, the Arabs living in Israel have been restricted to "Zones" and live under martial law.

They are subjected to a system of military permits which severely restricts their freedom of movement. These permits are issued only by the military authorities or by the police.

The mere fact of their moving from one place to another inside Israel leads to the Arabs being regarded as absentees; in this manner their properties have been confiscated. Furthermore, the arrival of every wave of new immigrants results in the expulsion of the inhabitants of yet another Arab village and their replacement by these immigrants.[6]

Like the racialist legislation in South Africa, that of Israel gives the head of the Israeli army the right to arrest and imprison any Arab for a whole year without having to give any reasons for his detention. Frequent resort to this legislation explains why hundreds of Arab youths are behind bars in Israeli gaols. In matters of detention, the Arabs have no real guarantees.

It should also be observed that acts of violence are frequently committed against the Arab minority. These acts are sometimes obviously deliberate massacres with the object of arousing panic and forcing the Arabs to flee the Jewish zone, or to leave Israel for good.

B. – Israel's Policy of Discrimination Constitutes a Breach of International Law

International law prohibits all forms of discrimination against

---

[6] - cf. *supra*, pp. 69-74. "Israel," according to *Les Cahiers de l'Histoire,* (*op. cit.,* October-November, 1967, pp. 71-72,) "was in no hurry to integrate the refugees and adopted a series of measures to keep them separate, the principal measure being the *Absentee Law,* which deprived fugitives of their property. After the war, the term "Absentee" was extended to include all those who, for some reason or other, were not in their homes. Finally, in 1953, a law authorised the State to nationalise lands for public purposes; 70,000 hectares of Arab lands were thus expropriated to be distributed among *Israeli* settlers. *During this whole period Israel did not show good will by attempting to settle the problem of the refugees...* For the majority of them there was no hope for the future. The sons and grandsons of the refugees have no other assets than the rights of their fathers over Palestine."

minorities in a State. This principle has been admitted both by decisions of international courts and by conventional law.

(a) *Application of the principle of non-discrimination by the courts:*

The Permanent court of International Justice has formally recognised the principle of racial and religious non-discrimination.

In its opinion of February 4, 1932 *(treatment of Polish nationals in the territory of Dantzig)* the P.C.I.J. prohibits, in fact as in law, all discrimination based on nationality, racial origin, or language. In another opinion of February 6, 1935 on *schools in Albania,* the P.C.I.J. states that "minority nationals should be on a footing of perfect equality with the other nationals of the State." The Court adds that there is "an obligation to ensure to social groups incorporated in a State whose population is of a race, religion and language distinct from theirs, the possibility of peaceful existence and friendly collaboration with that population..."

Certain implications arise out of this principle.

All minorities are entitled to protection of life and the fundamental freedoms (recognition of equality in matters of civil and political rights.)[7]

Conventional law has also sanctioned this principle.

(b) *Confirmation of the principle of non-discrimination by conventional law and by the United Nations:*

Already acknowledged in numerous bilateral treaties, the principle was recognised by the League of Nations Covenant, which specified a procedure for the protection of minorities.

The peace treaties of 1947, also, admitted and recognised this principle.

As regards the United Nations, Article 7 of the Universal Declaration of Human Rights lays down identical principles (equal protection by law of minorities; principle of non-discrimination.)

---

[7] - *Cf.* P.C.I.J., 26 April, 1928, *Case of Minority Schools in Upper Silesia;* P.C.I.J., opinion of May 15, 1931 on *Access to these same Schools;* P.C.I.J., opinion of April 6, 1935 on *Minority Schools in Albania.*

On 20 November 1963 the General Assembly of the United Nations unanimously (therefore, including Israel) adopted a resolution on the elimination of all forms of racial discrimination. Basing itself primarily on general principles, the Assembly regards "discrimination among human beings for reasons of race, colour or ethnic origin as a repudation of the principles of the United Nations Charter." Then, proceeding to the sphere of its practical application, the resolution contemplates the adoption of specific concrete measures with a view to putting an end to all forms of racial discrimination.

Furthermore, on December 21, 1965, the General Assembly adopted an "international convention on the elimination of all forms of racial discrimination." Israel, which adhered to this convention on March 7, 1966, is bound by this instrument, Article 2 of which stipulates that "the States parties to the convention condemn racial discrimination and undertake to follow, by all appropriate means and without delay, a policy leading to the elimination of all forms of racial discrimination..."

There can be no doubt that Israel violates the provisions of the convention to which she has adhered. In particular, she does not respect Article 5, i.e., the right to equal treatment before the courts and all other organs administering justice; the right to personal safety; the right to freedom of movement, and, finally, the right to just and favourable conditions of work, to protection against unemployment, to equal pay for equal work, to just and favourable remuneration.

In conclusion, Israel's discriminatory and inhuman treatment of what has become the Arab minority in Palestine, constitutes a breach of positive international law, and especially of the convention on the elimination of all forms of discrimination, to which Israel has subscribed.

III. — JEWISH EXPANSIONISM INCREASES UNITED NATIONS RESPONSIBILITY

In pursuance of her expansionist policy, Israel encourages

Jewish immigration, and systematically refuses to repatriate the refugees.

The unhappy lot of the Arab minority is consistent with such a policy. The only object of the discrimination practised against the members of this minority is to speed up their departure, so as to make it easier to settle an ever-increasing number of Jewish immigrants.

Always consistent, Israel opposes every measure which runs counter to her expansionist policy, and in particular the U.N. recommendations for the repatriation of Palestinians and the treatment of the Arab minority in accordance with law and morality.

The United Nations has, indeed, evinced a sincere desire to aid the refugees, but this good intention has not been followed by decisive action. In its humanitarian and charitable endeavours, as well as in its political action, the United Nations, has been conspicuously inadequate.

1) HUMANITARIAN AND CHARITABLE MEASURES:

To give a practical application to its intentions, the United Nations established the United Nations Relief and Works Agency for Palestine Refugees in the Near East (U.N.R.W.A.) by resolution 302 of 8 December 1949, reaffirmed by other resolutions, which extended the Agency's mandate. A successor to the United Nations Relief Office for Palestine Refugees, U.N.R.W.A. has striven to carry out the economic reinstatement of the refugees amidst a multitude of political and material difficulties. Its task is to make international assistance available for the Arab refugees through direct relief or through a policy of works programmes, aimed at the rehabilitation of the refugees without prejudice to their rights to repatriation and compensation.

The fact remains that, in 1966, the number of refugees registered with the Agency was about 1,400,000, of whom 900,000 lived in camps located in Jordan, Syria, Lebanon and in the Gaza Strip.

Apart from the United Nations, certain charitable organisations have given aid to the refugees (food, clothing, etc...) with the help of U.N.R.W.A.

But in spite of all its efforts, U.N.R.W.A. has been able to achieve only very limited results, because of the inadequacy of its financial resources. Daily food rations distributed among the re- fugees amount to barely 1,500 calories per person in the summer and 1,600 calories in the winter. They do not include meat, fresh vegetables or fruit, and are below the required minimum for an individual.

In other fields, the results achieved by U.N.R.W.A. are no less limited. Efforts made to provide education and vocational training for young refugees are definitely below actual requirements.

Furthermore, the events of June 1967, with their disastrous consequences, have greatly increased the difficulties of U.N.R.W.A., and put it in the same critical position as that which almost destroyed it a few years ago.

Besides, hundreds of thousands of needy refugees, who for one reason or another are not entitled to relief by U.N.R.W.A., live in tragic insecurity. For them, as for the refugees who do receive assis- tance, "continued efforts aiming at enabling them to become econo- mically self-sufficient," as the Director of U.N.R.W.A. recommend- ed, have been deplorably unsuccessful.

What does the future hold in store? There is no doubt that the deadlock which has been reached in finding a solution to the refugee problem can only engender violence in this part of the world. The only solution possible, in equity and in law, would be the return of the refugees to their homes. It is monstrous that one million Palestinians should still be living in tents under conditions wholly unacceptable by the normal standards of human life, while the Zionist movement continues to issue pressing appeals for new immigrants which it hopes to uproot from the countries of their birth.

2) POLITICAL FAILURE OF THE UNITED NATIONS:

In 1947, the United Nations Organisation gave its approval

to a Partition Plan for Palestine. This being the case, it clearly has a share in the responsibility for the subsequent disturbances which compelled the Arabs to flee from their homes.

If the United Nations has obligations of a moral nature towards other categories of refugees, it owes Arab victims more than a mere protection in principle. Besides, the General Assembly has recognised the right of the refugees to repatriation and to compensation for loss of or damage to property.

The General Assembly resolution of 29 November 1947 stipulated guarantees for the protection of Arab property rights and forbade all encroachments upon these rights.

Moreover, resolution 194, of 11 December 1948, stipulated that *"the refugees wishing to return to their homes ... should be permitted to do so at the earliest practicable date."*

This same resolution instructed the Conciliation Commission to facilitate the *repatriation,* resettlement and economic and social rehabilitation of the refugees and the payment of compensation, and to maintain close relations with the Director of the United Nations Relief Agency for Palestine Refugees and, through him, with the appropriate organs and agencies of the United Nations.

The aim of this resolution was to placate both parties without finding a solution to the problem. Thus, the United Nations appointed the Conciliation Commission as a trustee over the rights and properties of the refugees, and requested it to facilitate for them, in the name of the United Nations, the exercise of all their rights.

This task is confirmed by paragraph *C* of the resolution of 14 December 1950, which stipulated that the Conciliation Commission should continue consultations with the parties concerned regarding measures for the protection of the rights and property of the refugees.

Israeli legislation designed for the impounding of the property of Arab refugees is based on the assumption that they are "absentees." But they cannot properly be regarded as absentees—theirs is an enforced absence, imposed on them by Israel, in contravention of United Nations resolutions.

Not one of these resolutions has been implemented by Israel.

The same is true of resolution No. 99, adopted by the *Security Council on 17 November 1950*, which requested the Mixed Armistice Commission to give urgent attention to the Egyptian complaint concerning the expulsion of Palestinian Arabs, and called upon both parties to give effect to the decisions of the Commission regarding the repatriation of these Arabs.

This resolution of the Security Council, like others, has remained a dead letter.

Under these circumstances, are we not justified in asserting that United Nations action in favour of the refugees, which is an obligation resulting from the Partition resolution of 1947, has met with a serious reverse?

Every year, the refugee question is listed on the agenda of the United Nations, and every year the International Organisation reaffirms the rights of the refugees.

However, such good will is not sufficient. Action must be taken to make it possible to implement the resolutions, by providing effective sanctions for them. The absence of such sanctions against Israel has been the cause of the United Nations' most injurious failures, and has played into the hands of Zionist expansionism, of which it is the refugees who have been the victims.

CONCLUSION

There is a *logic of numbers.*

Fourteen million Jews, scattered throughout the world, are willy-nilly regimented by Israel and her powerful organizations, thanks to a dual political allegiance which many of them accept willingly, and, in so doing, often reverse the order of priorities and give priority to their loyalty to Israel.

Zionist ideology is based on the conviction that all the Jews of the world must achieve a national existence in the historic land of the Twelve Tribes. Israel is determined to put an end to what it persists in regarding as their dispersion, even though the majority of them are unwilling to leave the country in which they and their remotest ancestors were born, for an unknown land.

This theory of relocation which is the very essence of Zionism, makes many demands: it lays down with the utmost vigour the course to be followed by Zionism which, consequently, is inevitably confronted by the temptations of expansionism. Israel, established in conditions of illegality and terror which are only too familiar, cannot, even if she so wishes, abandon her permanent search for "living space." For the past century, during which she has been trying to make her appearance on the world scene, to reconstitute a people through an empire, Israel's policy has been a model of consistency. From the small agricultural colonies to the Jewish National Home, which, people claimed to believe, was no more than a cultural and religious relocation of people, strictly limited in numbers; from the jigsaw puzzle-State conceived by the United Nations to the warring State of 1948; from the conquering Israel of 1956 to the "Greater Israel"of 1967—every stage has been marked by this age-old will to expand. Israel is blithely following a plan which *purely and simply imperils the very existence of several Arab countries* as independent States, after having already erased Palestine from the map of the world. In the three major armed encounters of 1948, 1956, and 1967, Israel has always been the aggressor, and every time her territory has been enlarged by the hostilities.

It seems quite futile to recall this logic of numbers. To bring all Jews together, Israel must enlarge herself; this makes it necessary to push back the Arabs, and for this to be achieved they must be attacked. This policy has a thousand pretexts for expansion ready at hand to delude public opinion. Thus, in 1965 Mr. Abba Eban asserted that the Arabs, who at first asked for the return of Palestine to the Arabs, then, more modestly, for Israel to retire to the 1948 frontiers, would one day be obliged to ask for no more than a return to the 1966 or 1967 frontiers.[1] This is an unabashed admission of the permanent character of Israel's expansionist aims, and of the premeditation of the attack of 1967; it reveals an unruffled confidence in the force of arms; and finally, alas, it is an indication of Israel's utter contempt for the Arabs.

It is sometimes alleged that the denunciation of Zionism's expansionist aims is groundless, inasmuch as the fourteen million Jews in the world have no intention of abandoning their respective countries, even if they do regard Israel as a second homeland, or even, in some cases, their first homeland. In reality, it is of little consequence to know whether the Jews *in fact* desire or refuse to emigrate to Israel. The important thing to remember is that Zionism, both in theory and in structure, has made this Return of all the Jews its basic premise, and always behaves on the assumption that, one day, these fourteen million will settle in Eretz Israel. To demand lands on which to settle immigrants, then to clamour for immigrants to occupy the lands acquired, to claim the waters of the Jordan to meet the needs of an increasing population and then to call for such immigration in her prayers, indeed in her legislation, to conquer new territories in the expectation, albeit problematic, of the influx of individuals towards Israel, then to broadcast an urgent appeal to world Jewry to populate the vast Arab territories annexed in June, 1967—this is the vicious circle in which, through a sort of infernal

---

[1] - Abba Eban in: *Foreign Affairs,* July, 1965.

logic, the expansionist dynamism of Israel is imprisoned.

Mr. Ben Gurion was thus able to affirm to the students of the Hebrew University of Jerusalem in 1950 that "the Israeli *empire* (sic) should include all the territories situated between the Nile and the Euphrates." By what means? "It will be erected by *invasion* as well as by diplomacy." "I agree to form a government," he added on the occasion of his investiture in 1952, "on condition that I am allowed to use all possible means to enable us to extend towards the South." In such a profession of faith lay the seeds of the Suez adventure of 1956. The same man, in a recent letter to the President of the French Republic, continued to claim for *Eretz Israel* "the lands lying both to the east and to the west of the river Jordan" on the ground that ... "such was the country of Joshua."[2]

The map of this "Greater Israel," engraved on the pediment of the Knesset, Tel-Aviv's parliament, is a permanent reminder to the Israeli legislator of his country's annexationist aims in the other Arab countries, after Palestine, a permanent provocation, and a blow to the independence and sovereignty of neighbouring States, which, however, does not shock those who have been conditioned to look upon Israel as a peaceful country in constant danger of extermination at the whim of the Arabs.

From the earliest days of the Zionist movement, its adherents have set themselves territorial objectives going far beyond the present frontiers of Israel. There have, admittedly, been profound differences of opinion in this field, as appears in Herzl's *Memoirs*, in the Memorandum[3] submitted to the Peace Conference at Versailles on 3 February, 1919, and in certain other documents, but Zionism's geographical ambitions, ready though they have always been to adapt themselves to circumstances, have always included among their objectives South Lebanon, Sinai, Northern Hejaz and the east and west banks of the Jordan. A Zionist writer, who certainly wished to be thought moderate, was to define the front-

---

[2] - Mr. Ben Gurion's letter to General de Gaulle, *Le Monde*, 10 January, 1968, p. 3.

[3] - *op. cit.*, (*cf. supra*, p. 50).

iers as including Judaea, Samaria, Galilee and ... "the country beyond the Jordan,"[4] adding: "A Palestine extending from the Mediterranean to within a certain distance from the Hejaz railway and from the river Litani to a point well to the south of Gaza and of the Dead Sea, including the latter, would meet *the needs of the Jewish people.*"[5]

The series of expansions carried out by Israel during the past twenty years, and the course which events have taken since 5 June 1967, are certainly alarming. What we are witnessing is the gradual *Anschluss* of a number of Arab States, all of which are members of the United Nations, all of whose sovereignty and territorial integrity are guaranteed by international law, but with no assurance that their constant aggressor will be stopped or penalised by the international community, or even that this aggressor will be designated as such. On 6 June, 1967, a Parisian journalist, either misled or biased, put out the stupid falsehood of an Arab attack on Israel. Today, it has at least been recognised that Israel not only began the hostilities but had also premeditated and carefully prepared her attack.[6]

* * *

Thus the logic of numbers calls forth the logic of expansionism, as Zionism's basic ideology, the course it has followed and its ever more strongly worded statements, which scorn evasion in their unabashed arrogance, all bear witness.

But this logic of numbers, which makes a reality of the will of all the Jews in the world to relocate themselves, also implies another logic, that of Jewish refusal to assimilate, that of *self-segregation*. Zionism is uncompromising in its rejection of the

---

[4] - Marcel Bernfeld: *Le Sionisme, op. cit.,* p. 386.

[5] - Bernfeld: *op. cit.,* p. 387. (our italics).

[6] - Eric Rouleau, Jean-Francis Held, Jean and Simone Lacouture: *Israël et les Arabes. Le Troisième Combat,* Paris, éditions du Seuil, 1967, pp. 119 and 122.

assimilation of Jews by non-Jewish societies, its object being to encourage the Jews of the Diaspora to emigrate to Israel. This policy has been pushed to extremes and has led certain Zionists to extol the "purity of the race" so that "God's chosen people" might fulfil their special destiny.

By allowing themselves to be regimented by the Zionists, even to the point of behaving as persons with dual nationality, or even, in some cases, as Israelis first and foremost, the Jews of the world have borne witness to the existence and the strength of this self-segregation.[7] Herzl wrote that the conservation of the "Jewish people and race" in their pure state is due to the Hebrew marriage laws which "forbid the mixing of races."

This logic of self-segregation and of loyalty to Israel also implies *racial exclusiveness,* i.e. it calls not only for the immigration of Jews into Israel but also for the radical eviction of non-Jews from the land "destined for the Jews." It is in this manner that Zionism has succeeded in bringing about the "final solution" of the "Arab problem" and has created a "Palestine without Arabs." We can now understand the driving out of the refugees just as we have already understood the driving force behind expansionism.

At its last ordinary session, the United Nations recalled the impressive list of its resolutions on the refugees, resolutions which have not been implemented, and noted "with deep regret" that the repatriation of these Palestinians has not taken place.[8]

The United Nations will not realise the futility of its repeated speeches until it understands what the Israeli edifice is made of:

---

[7] - Cf. the penetrating studies of Mr. Fayez A. Sayegh: *Zionist Colonialism in Palestine,* Beirut, 1966, p. 54.

[8] - Resolution 2341 (XXII) of the General Assembly recalling its resolutions 194 (III) of 11 December 1948, 302 (IV) of 8 December 1949, 512 (V) of 26 January 1952, 614 (VII) of 6 November 1952, 720 (VIII) of 27 November 1953, 818 (IX) of 4 December 1954, 916 (X) of 3 December 1955, 1018 (XI) of 28 February 1957, 1191 (XII) of 12 December 1957, 1315 (XIII) of 12 December 1958, 1456 (XIV) of 9 December 1959, 1604 (XV) of 21 April 1961, 1725 (XVI) of 20 December 1961, 1856 (XVII) of 20 December 1962, 1912 (XVIII) of 3 December 1963, 2002 (XIX) of 10 February 1965, 2052 (XX) of 15 December 1965, and 2154 (XXI) of 17 November 1966.

self-segregation throughout the world, immigration into Israel, expansionism and, finally, exclusiveness, which casts the non-Jew outside the Jewish nation. All pleas made to Israel to allow the Palestinians to return to their homeland stem from a ludicrous ignorance of the forces lying behind the Zionist system.

The effectiveness of the United Nations can be measured by its capacity to jam the infernal machine which we have just taken to pieces, which pieces run the gamut from self-segregation to dual loyalty, from immigration to aggression, from expansionism to racial exclusiveness. This presupposes that the Powers which hold some sway in this world, are prepared at long last to say what the director of the *Journal de Genève* said in August 1967: that *"Israel is going too far"* in continuing to annex Arab territories. This would also presuppose that the majority of Jews in the world have realised that the time has come for them to refuse to continue in the service of Zionism, and that States will no longer tolerate that in their territory the Zionists should seize certain attributes of their sovereignty and lord it over Jewish communities, so as to keep them in strict and chauvinistic obedience to Israel, and to ''excommunicate'' them when they dare state too frankly what they are, i.e. no more and no less than citizens of the various States in which they were born. Finally, this would presuppose that the States should urgently—in all the meanings of the word urgent—call on the Israelis to withdraw from the occupied territories.

* * *

This occupation itself also has peculiar features, which can only be explained by reference to the basic premises of Zionist ideology.

In the view of publicists, military occupation following a war is of an extremely precarious nature, and confers very limited rights upon the occupying Power. It has no effect on the sovereignty of the State over that part of its territory which is occupied by foreign troops.[9] Modern international law considers occupation as "an occurrence due to war, based upon, and maintained by, force." It is here that military occupation differs from annexation. The first cannot confer upon the occupier sovereignty over the territory seized.

But today, since the aggression of June 1967, Israel is not only committing an abuse of power in certain territories, by exceeding the competence recognised for an occupying Power, but is also fundamentally violating international law in other areas in which occupation has become annexation.

Annexation cannot legally take place unless the territorial sovereign expressly renounces his territories which have been occupied. In 1949, Mr. Abba Eban, then Israel's representative at the United Nations, maintained that his government had annexed territories beyond the limits laid down in the Partition Plan, by virtue of the consent of the neighbouring countries, a consent which, he claimed, derived from the Armistice Agreements![10] Who is going to believe this astounding plea? This is no doubt the reason why today, after the annexations of 1967, it is not even considered necessary to given explanations. Statements pour forth, full of quiet confidence. Decisions find their justification in force. On June 27, 1967, the Knesset "voted" the annexation of the Arab part of Jerusalem, thus admitting that this was the only real objective of the aggression of June 5. To the United Nations resolution of 4 July calling on Israel "to revoke all measures already adopted and to refrain from taking any action which could alter the status of Jerusalem," Israel replied that annexation is in its view "irreversible and irrevocable."

Following the example set by his Minister of Defence, Mr. Moshe Dayan, for whom "Israel cannot go back to the ridiculous frontiers of 1948," and his Foreign Minister, Mr. Abba Eban who "does not believe that the map of June 5th can be re-established,"

---

9 - Debbasch (Odile): *L'occupation militaire,* thesis, Paris, 1962. Articles 42, 43, and 48 of the *Règlement de La Haye* of 1907 stipulate that the belligerent, by occupying enemy territories, does not acquire sovereign power over it.

10 - Security Council, 433rd meeting. 4 August, 1949.

the Prime Minister of Israel, Mr. Levy Eshkol, affirmed on 6 September 1967 that there is "no more natural frontier than the Suez Canal."

Jerusalem annexed, the territories on the West bank of the Jordan "liberated," the frontiers of Israel advanced to the Suez Canal, the Golan heights in Syria absorbed, such is the "Grand Plan" of Zionism, which is in the process of being realised. It will not come as a surprise to anyone except those who, against all reason, look upon Israel as a peaceful country. But it is only the inexorable logic of numbers and expansionism that can fully explain this phenomenon, which is outside the law, against the law and against right. Israel's aggression was launched to annex territory and to expand. Having succeeded, it would be absurd if the aggression did not have this result.

There is also a sort of *logic of the absurd,* which would like the Arabs, in response to Israel's progressive aggrandisement, to reduce the problem of Israel to the dimensions of her latest conquests. As Semites, it is suggested, the Arabs should bury in the grave of family quarrels what their Israeli cousins took from them in the course of their first two aggressions, and argue only about what they have lost since 5 June 1967. As realists, they should know that no other course is open to them after their crushing defeat.

This invitation to the Arabs to submit to territorial acquisitions, old or recent, which only pave the way for others, suggests the abandonment of the view of the Palestine problem as a whole to trap the Arabs in a discussion restricted to the latest, but certainly not the last, Israeli territorial thrust. There might be some small merit in being "realistic" in this manner, if this shifting of the whole problem could at least provide the Arabs with the certainty of being definitely secure from further Israeli expansionism. But, in fact, what is being recommended to the Arabs is an "escalating realism." They are constantly being asked to accept the event which has just taken place while discussing the one which Israel is always in a position to bring about. This realism has both a name: "ostrich policy," and a consequence: progressive anaemia of the Arab nation, which neither began nor ended on 5 June 1967. *What is called in question is, first of all, what has been done since the disastrous United Nations Partition resolution which carried within itself the seeds of all subsequent aggressions; and then, and this is the most important thing, the necessity to jam the machines which are carrying Zionism towards self-segregation, expansionism and racial exclusiveness.*

It is no more a problem today of deciding what is to be done with the territories occupied by Israel after her third aggression, than it may well be tomorrow of discussing the fate of those territories which Israel may conquer as a result of a fourth aggression launched to achieve the final realisation of her old dream of "Greater Israel."

Here lies the tragedy. Israel, fired by her Zionist philosophy, contains in herself, and through herself, all the risks of explosion in the Arab Middle East.

How tragic and unique is the fate of the Palestinian people! At a time when decolonisation, already begun after World War I, had enabled many peoples to recover their lost freedom, Palestine, already far advanced along the road to independence, was deprived of it at the very moment when she was ready to accede to it. A strange distortion of the curve of history!

Given a local government in 1920, promised early independence, Arab Palestine is the exception, the freak case of a young nation still-born as a result of the blows of Zionism. That is why this tragedy, a deliberate shunting error on the open line which leads to decolonisation, is more cruel and more unbearable in a world which is freeing itself from the demons of domination.

Resolution Adopted by the Seminar on

27 July 1967

The Seminar of Arab Jurists, meeting in Algiers from 22 to 27 July 1967:

Having studied the legal aspects of the Palestine problem;

In view of the fact that the Arab people has exercised its sovereignty over Palestine where it has lived continuously and unchallenged;

In view of the fact that, after the First World War, Palestine was placed under a League of Nations Mandate with a view to preparing it for independence under the leadership of a national government;

In view of the fact that the principle of self-determination confirmed by the Charter of the United Nations and by successive resolutions of the General Assembly, should apply to the Palestinian people which claims its right to freedom and independence;

In view of the fact that the creation of Israel in 1948 is a colonial phenomenon of aggression, resulting from the alliance of the world Zionist movement with imperialism; that this creation has resulted in the expulsion of the Arabs from their homeland in which they constituted the majority and in the settlement of foreign immigrants having no historical, political or cultural links with this land;

In view of the fact that in establishing herself on a narrow ethnic basis, and a fictitious one at that, and in her determination to be the State of the Jews, Israel is essentially a racialist phenomenon, practising, as regards the native Arab inhabitants, who have been reduced to a persecuted minority, a policy of racial discrimination which is evident in her legislation regarding nationality, agricultural property, work or education;

I. — Declares :

(a) that the United Nations resolution of 1947 concerning the Partition of Palestine is null and void, the General Assembly having no competence to create States or to put an end to their existence, especially when by so doing it infringes the right of peoples to self-determination;

(b) that the birth of Israel on a basis not recognised by international law is not of a nature to give rise to a regular situation to which could be assured that protection acknowledged by international law in situations that are legal;

(c) that the rules regarding acquisitive prescription are not applicable in this case, as the Palestinians have never given up their claim to their homeland and have continuously asserted their legitimate rights in it;

II. — Affirms :

(a) that the Arab refugees have an inalienable and imprescriptible right to return to Palestine, in accordance with the successive resolutions adopted during twenty years by the United Nations, and to put an end to foreign immigration;

(b) that Jerusalem, an Arab city over which Arab States have successively exercised their sovereignty in conditions which guaranteed the protection and freedom of access to the Holy Places, has been annexed by Israel since its latest aggression of June 1967, in conditions which the U.N. General Assembly has condemned in two resolutions adopted during the XXIst extraordinary session; and that the internationalisation of the City does not constitute an alternative solution consistent with respect for Arab sovereignty or with the right of peoples to self-determination, and cannot be considered as the ideal status for the protection of the Holy Places;

(c) that the diversion of the waters of the Jordan by Israel is an unlawful act, incompatible with established rules for the utilisation of the waters of international rivers, and constitutes an infringement of the rights of Syria, Lebanon and the Kingdom of Jordan;

III. — Observes:

(a) that the Gulf of Aqaba, historically an Arab gulf, forming part of the territory of Arab States, over which they have continuously exercised their sovereignty, is, moreover, connected with the Red Sea by a navigable opening which, according to the rules of the law of the sea, forms part of Arab territorial waters like all the waters of the Gulf; and that the illegal presence of Israel on the Gulf, which began in 1949, after the conclusion of the Armistice Agreement with Egypt, following the irregular occupation of the Arab village of Umm Rashrash and its transformation into the port of Elath, only allowed Israel to pass through the Gulf of Aqaba and the Straits of Tiran as a result of her aggression against Egypt in 1956;

(b) that the Constantinople Convention of 1888 and the Declaration of 1957 by the Egyptian government do not confer upon Israel any right of passage through the Suez Canal, particularly as the Convention recognised Egypt's right to adopt measures of self-defence in the Canal.

IV. — Condemns:

the latest aggression against the Arab countries and deplores the failure of the United Nations Organs to apply the principles of the Charter for the restoration of right;

V. — Decides:

(a) to expound the results of its work in a book which will be published in several languages for the benefit of world public opinion;

(b) to organise, in a place, and on a date, to be fixed later, an enlarged juridical seminar to include, besides Arab jurists, jurists from other parts of the world.

The Arab-Israel Conflict in International Law

NATHAN FEINBERG

At the end of July 1967 a number of Arab jurists met in Algiers to discuss the legal aspects of the Arab–Israel conflict. One of the resolutions adopted at the meeting was to publish its conclusions in book-form, and in several languages, with the aim of winning the attention of public opinion all over the world. The book appeared first in French,[1] in 1968. Surprisingly, there is no mention of names of the participants in the Colloquium or their number. All that is said in the foreword is that those attending were divided into three groups: one — on "historical 'rights' ", under the chairmanship of Professor Edmond Rabbath of Beirut; the second — on "juridical title" — under the chairmanship of Professor Mustafa Kamil Yasseen,[2] Iraqui delegate to the United Nations Organization in Geneva; and the third — on "the implications of the conflict" — under the chairmanship of Mrs. Aïcha Rateb, Professor at the University of Cairo.

1. *Colloque de Juristes Arabes sur la Palestine — La Question Palestinienne, Alger, 22–27 Juillet 1967* (hereinafter quoted as *Colloque*) (Alger, 1968) p. 219. In the meantime an English translation of the book has also appeared: *Seminar of Arab Jurists on Palestine, Algiers, 22–27 July 1967 — The Palestine Question,* translated from the French by Edward Rizk, Beirut, Institute for Palestine Studies, 1968. The present study is based on the original French text. Passages cited in English are not taken from the Beirut edition, which I did not have before me at the time, but, together with the passages cited in English from other French works, are my own translation.
2. The name is erroneously given in the book as Yassen, instead of Yasseen.

The authors have not found it necessary to give a summary of the views expressed in each group, but make do with a general survey of the subjects on each agenda.[3] They reproduce the text of the resolutions formulated at the meeting and the opening and closing addresses of Mohammed Bedjaoui, Minister of Justice and Keeper of the Seal of Algeria. In his closing address, Bedjaoui complimented the participants and stressed: "As jurists, you have tackled all of the basic issues of the Palestinian conflict without by-passing a single one of them. In doing so, you have reviewed the [Israel] case in a most objective manner.... You have brought no passion into your debates. All of which has added — if there were any further need — to the depth of your reflections and to the force of your analysis."[4]

It is clear that for a jurist — Arab or Jew — to come to consider such a passionately controversial issue as the Arab–Israel conflict *from a legal standpoint,* without allowing his judgment to trail after his feelings or losing sight of the boundaries between the fields of law and politics, which it is so necessary to distinguish,[5] calls for a

3. Part one of the book, in which the work of the first group — on historical rights — is discussed, will be referred to here as "the first report"; part two — on juridical title — "the second report"; and part three — on the implications of the conflict — "the third report".
4. *Colloque,* p. 220.
5. The authors themselves distinguish between legal argument and political argument. They resort to this distinction, for example, in dismissing the contention of the United States that the Straits of Tiran are an international waterway open to free navigation. In their opinion, this claim "clearly has a purely

tremendous intellectual effort. It may be that, circumstances being as they are, it is difficult for those involved to
reach the stage of complete objectivity; but, at all events,
they must surely display that minimum degree of detachment, lacking which every supposedly legal argument becomes a purely political one, and sometimes mere propaganda. Fortunately, the jurist, it would seem, does have
one fairly useful criterion by which to decide whether
any given argument is worth a hearing or not — namely :
would any serious lawyer be prepared to put it forward
in his pleadings before the International Court of Justice
with a reasonable chance of its acceptance by the judges?
As we shall see, the book does not stand up to this test;
its authors have not hesitated to make assertions for which
there is no legal basis whatsoever. Nor is this all : with
regard to some of the things that they have to say, it is
doubtful whether any responsible person would permit
himself to say them. Indeed, a feeling of deep enmity towards Israel marks the book from start to finish — so
much so that its authors have lost their sense of proportion and do not shrink from resorting to the old Arab
propaganda libel of a "map of Greater Israel" adorning

political content [sic!] and is quite untenable by the jurist"
(*Colloque*, p. 180). Similarly, the declarations of the many States
which, at the emergency special session of the General Assembly
of the United Nations in 1956 and at the regular session that year
and at the beginning of 1957, called for a free right of passage
through the Straits of Tiran, are regarded by them as a manifestation of the desire of those States "to support Israel against
the Arab countries" and "therefore, the validity of these objections is negligible" (*Colloque,* p. 181, note 38). It is clear that
what is meant is their *legal* validity.

the façade of the Knesset building.[6] Millions of tourists —
Jews and non-Jews — have visited Israel during the
twenty-one years of its existence and can bear witness
before any tribunal in the world that this is no more than
a figment of the imagination. The following fact, too,
gives some indication how far the authors are from an
approach *sine ira et studio* to their task : throughout almost the whole of the book the word "Juif" is printed
with a small "j",[7] the word "Arabe" with a capital "A".
It may be doubted whether this typographical stratagem,
intended to hurt the honour of the Jewish people, has, in
fact, achieved its purpose; one thing is clear : it has
added nothing to the authors' own dignity or to the
persuasive force of their argument.

One may well ask whether a publication which em-
ploys devices such as these warrants serious critical analysis
at all; I have, however, come to the conclusion that it
does, if only for the benefit of those students of international law and relations who are not familiar with the
details of the subject and may feel the need for a study
which sheds light on it from the Israel and Zionist point
of view.

It is not my intention here to answer every one of the
findings, interpretations, assertions and assumptions in the
book. Only the more important of them will be dealt
with, and no attempt will be made to go into most of the
details on specific questions reviewed in the report on "the

6. *Ibid.,* p. 206.
7. See, for example, pp. 24, 25, 27, 28, 29, 31, 33, 35, 41, 52, 60,
   65 and 85.

implications of the conflict". Needless to say, failure to refer to any particular question examined in the book is in no sense to be taken as tacit acquiescence in the authors' approach. It should also be underlined that my purpose is not to examine the policy of the Arab countries towards Israel, from its establishment till the present day, in the light of the rules of international law; nor is the aim to dwell on the innumerable infringements of those rules by those States — from their war of aggression against Israel in 1948 up to the endless violations of the cease-fire order of June 1967, including their encouragement of, and close cooperation with, the terrorist organizations. These matters will only be mentioned insofar as is necessary to refute the arguments raised in the book against Zionism, the Mandate for Palestine and the establishment of the State of Israel. The enquiries as to the ways of resolving the Arab-Israel conflict are also outside the scope of our deliberations.

Let us begin, then, with a few general remarks that may throw light on the authors' method of work and the manner in which they argue their case — both leave much to be desired.

I. GENERAL REMARKS

1.   In the foreword — as we have seen — the names are given of the chairmen of the three groups; but the reader is not told whether each chairman is responsible for that part of the book which deals with the work of his particular group, or whether all three are jointly respon-

sible for the whole. At all events, the different parts are not always in complete harmony and some of the statements are clearly contradictory. Thus, for example, in the first report it is said that Zionism is "the product... of colonialism" [8] and that its emergence was "inspired by colonialism".[9] In the second, by contrast, one finds that "the promise of the establishment of a Jewish national home assumes a humanitarian, rather than a political character".[10] And the question arises — how does one reconcile colonialism and humanitarianism?

2. In the second report, also, Israel is said to have been accepted into the United Nations Organization on the resolutory condition [11] that it implement the General Assembly's Resolution of 11 December 1948, in particular with regard to the question of the refugees; and, since Israel has not fulfilled this condition, the validity of its

8. *Colloque,* p. 43.

9. *Ibid.,* p. 45.

10. *Ibid.,* p. 83. G. Antonius, Secretary-General of the Arab delegations to the London Conference of 1939, in his comments of 27 February 1939 on the statements submitted by the Lord Chancellor, Lord Maugham, to the Committee set up by the British Government to consider the 1915—1916 correspondence between McMahon and Hussein, dismisses the claim that "in drawing up the Balfour Declaration he [Balfour] was doing anything that would involve a Jewish claim to an independent State in Palestine"; and he goes on: "It is none the less a historical fact that in drawing up the Balfour Declaration Mr. Balfour did have a future Jewish State in Palestine definitely in mind". See *Cmd. 5974, Report of a Committee Set up to Consider Certain Correspondence between Sir Henry McMahon... and the Sharif of Mecca in 1915 and 1916* (London, 1939), p. 43.

11. *Colloque,* p. 142.

acceptance, it is argued, has lapsed.[12] "The United Nations", states the report, "intended to give the implementation of... [the] resolution [of December 1948] the character of a resolutory condition." [13] This is a classic example of an assertion which, from the legal point of view, is untenable. There is no provision whatsoever in the Charter of the United Nations for the acceptance of a member conditionally. Nor is there any provision as to the possibility of automatic termination of membership. Under Article 6 of the Charter, a member may be expelled from the Organization by the General Assembly upon the recommendation of the Security Council.[14]

And, incidentally, the statement of the report is quite unfounded. Suffice it to quote the words of Inis L. Claude Jr. on the point. "The Assembly voted on 11 May 1949 to accept Israel as a member of the world organization. In so doing, it recalled its resolutions of 29 November 1947 and 11 December 1948, and formally took note of the declarations and explanations concerning the implementation of those resolutions which had been made by the representative of Israel before the *Ad Hoc* Political Committee. These references, however, did *not* constitute a declaration that Israel had assumed definite obligations to permit unlimited repatriation or to guarantee

12. *Ibid.,* p. 143.
13. *Ibid.,* p. 144.
14. In the second report, it is said that "the [United Nations] Organization has every ground for expelling [Israel] from it..." (*Colloque,* p. 144). It is difficult to understand how the contention that membership is automatically terminated can be reconciled with the assertion that there must be a decision to expel.

minority rights to its present or future Arab population. The best evidence that Israel had made no such commitments was provided by the speeches of Arab delegates in the plenary meeting at which the resolution was voted; they regarded the admission of Israel as a repudiation of their demand for capitulation on the repatriation issue by the applicant state, and they asserted with bitterness that Israel 'had given no definite assurances'." [15]

Here is yet another example of a legal argument without the least foundation: the third report accuses Israel of discrimination against the Arab minority within its jurisdiction. "International law", it states, "forbids all discrimination directed against the minorities of a State."[16] In support of this contention, the authors cite two advisory opinions given by the Permanent Court of International Justice — one, on 4 February 1932, on the treatment of Polish nationals in the territory of the Free City of Danzig; the other, on 6 February 1935, on the minority schools in Albania. But they altogether ignore the fact that what is said in those opinions refers to minorities placed under the system of international protection in force between the two World Wars: in the territory of Danzig — by virtue of Article 104 (5) of the Peace Treaty with Germany of 28 June 1919 and the Paris Convention of 9 November 1920; and in Albania — by virtue of the declaration on minorities made by its representatives to the Council of the League of Nations on 2 October

15. Inis L. Claude, Jr., *National Minorities, An International Problem* (Cambridge, Mass., 1955), p. 181.
16. *Colloque,* p. 146.

1921. Surprisingly, too — as if this were not enough — the report goes on to say that "the principle [of non-discrimination] has also been recognized by the Covenant of the League of Nations, which lays down a procedure for the protection of minorities".[17] Yet it is a well-known fact that the Covenant contains no provision at all — express or implied — on minorities and their protection. As for the factual content of the allegation, Israel is said to commit "acts of violence against the Arab minority. These acts have even taken the form of planned massacres...."[18] There is no more truth in this than in the assertion that the Covenant of the League includes a provision for the protection of minorities. It may be added that, about a month after the meeting of jurists in Algiers, one Arab scholar — Albert Hourani of St. Anthony's College, Oxford — was sufficiently candid (in an article in the *Observer*) to define the position of the Arabs in Israel as "tolerable". He did, indeed, mention the restrictions placed on them by the Military Government — without hiding the fact that, in the last few months preceding the writing of his article, some of these had been removed; but he also acknowledges, with praiseworthy impartiality, that the Arabs do "enjoy [in Israel] civil and political rights".[19]

3.   The authors do not seem to regard themselves as being under any obligation to be accurate — either as to

17. *Ibid.,* p. 147.
18. *Ibid.,* p. 146.
19. Albert Hourani, "Palestine and Israel", *The Israel–Arab Reader, A Documentary History of the Middle East Conflict,* ed. by Walter Laqueur (New York, 1969), p. 276.

facts or in citing passages from documents or articles, even when these are presented within quotation marks. Thus, for instance, they cite the Balfour Declaration within quotation marks without being faithful to the text. Instead of "the establishment in Palestine of a national home for the Jewish people", they write "the establishment of a Jewish national home in Palestine".[20] Since — as we shall see — they go out of their way to prove that a Jewish people, as such, does not exist, they should have been meticulously exact on this point.

In the second report it is said that, during the First World War, the Allied Powers made "numerous declarations reaffirming that the non-Turkish peoples under Ottoman rule must be freed and granted national governments [21] deriving their authority from the free will of the populations themselves".[22] In a note on this passage, they

20. *Colloque,* pp. 50 and 78. It is pertinent to mention here that in the first report a passage is cited in quotation marks from a letter sent by Philip Talbot — in the name of the State Department of the United States — to the American Council for Judaism; two sentences are omitted from that passage without any indication of the omission (by a dotted line, for example) being given as is customary. Among the words omitted are the following: "The Department of State recognizes the State of Israel as a sovereign State and citizenship of the State of Israel. It recognizes no other sovereignty or citizenship in connection therewith." See W. T. Mallison Jr., "The Zionist-Israel Juridical Claims to Constitute 'the Jewish People' Nationality Entity and to Confer Membership in it: Appraisal in Public International Law", *George Washington Law Review,* vol. 32 (Washington, 1964), p. 1075.

21. The word wrongly appears as "government" instead of "governments".

22. *Colloque,* p. 79.

adduce as authority for it a declaration made by President Wilson in 1917 (the date is not given) and approved by the Allies. But the truth is that President Wilson never promised the non-Turkish peoples of the Ottoman Empire independent national governments : he did not do so in his speech of 22 January 1917 — and that is undoubtedly the one intended in the report; nor did he do so in his "fourteen points" of 8 January 1918, in his four "principles" of 11 February 1918, in his four "ends" of 4 July 1918, or in his five "particulars" of 27 September of that year. With regard to the speech of 22 January 1917, which — as said — is the most relevant, Professor Mandelstam stresses that "this *minimum of rights* [which Wilson proclaimed] is in no way to be equated with the recognition of *each* nation's right to independence; it cannot otherwise be understood than as autonomy".[23]

The second report is in further error in stating that four of the eleven members of the United Nations Special Committee on Palestine (hereinafter "U.N.S.C.O.P.") voted against the Partition Plan.[24] To be precise, only three of them voted against it; the fourth — the Australian

---

23. See André Mandelstam, "La protection des minorités", *Recueil des Cours de l'Académie de Droit International* (hereinafter quoted as *R.A.D.I.*), tome 1 (Paris, 1925), p. 399. In the 10th and 12th of Wilson's Fourteen Points, too, there is no mention of independence, either for the peoples of Austro-Hungary or for the non-Turkish nations of the Ottoman Empire; all that is promised is the "unmolested opportunity of autonomous development". Indeed, of the Fourteen Points, only the thirteenth — the one dealing with Poland — provides for the establishment of an independent State.

24. *Colloque,* p. 86.

representative —abstained.[25] Equally unfounded is the statement in the first report that Tardieu's declaration, that France would not object to a British Mandate in Palestine and to the establishment of a Jewish State, was made at a meeting of the Supreme Council of the Peace Conference;[26] he made the declaration in the course of an interview with a correspondent of *Le Temps*.

The following sentence, too, serves to illustrate how unreliable the authors are: "By virtue of Article 10 [of the Charter] the General Assembly may discuss all questions and matters that fall within the framework of the Charter, apart from a threat to peace, a breach of the peace or an act of aggression." [27] For does not Article 11 of the Charter expressly lay down that "the General Assembly may discuss any questions relating to the maintenance of international peace and security"? And Article 12 adds that, if the issue is not on the agenda of the Security Council, the Assembly may also make recommendations on it.

4. Many parts of the book are worded in an imprecise and ambiguous manner. For example, in criticizing the vote on partition, taken in the General Assembly on 29 November 1947, it is said: "It is quite incontestable that the Zionists and the United States brought very considerable pressure to bear on many of the States.... The

---

25. *United Nations, Official Records of the General Assembly* (hereinafter — *G.A.O.R.*), *Second Session, Suppl. No. 11, United Nations Special Committee on Palestine, Report to the General Assembly*, vol. I (Lake Success, 1947), p. 8.
26. *Colloque*, p. 54.
27. *Ibid.*, p. 96.

former President of the United States, Mr. Harry Truman, has not hidden this fact in his *'Memoirs'*. Eleven months before the American presidential elections, he could not afford to forgo the invaluable assistance of the Zionist votes and he therefore joined the ranks of the advocates of the partition plan: 'I gave instructions to the Department of State to extend America's support to the partition plan'." [28] This passage is likely to create the impression that Truman himself said in his Memoirs that he could not afford to forgo the Zionist votes. That is not so; what in fact he wrote was this: "I was of the opinion that the proposed partition of Palestine could open the way for peaceful cooperation between the Arabs and the Jews.... [T]he partition proposal impressed me as the most practicable way to make progress in that direction [the advancement and development of the Middle East so that it can support from twenty to thirty million more people]. It was always my hope that a solution could be worked out without bloodshed." [29]

The wording of the following sentence in the book is no less questionable: "In accordance with the principles of the Charter, the member States of U.N.O. are responsible for the implementation of resolutions passed by the Security Council or the General Assembly." [30] Since when, and according to what provision of the Charter, do the States have to implement the Assembly's resolutions (apart

28. *Ibid.*, p. 88.
29. *Memoirs by Harry S. Truman, vol. II, Years of Trial and Hope* (New York, 1956), pp. 156—157.
30. *Colloque*, p. 122.

from those relating to the internal life of the Organization and in a few exceptional cases)? It is not irrelevant to point out, by the way, that, since the establishment of the United Nations and up to April 1968, the Assembly has passed some 2,370 resolutions, while the number of operative paragraphs in them amounts to some ten to fifteen thousand.[31]

5. There are very many mistakes in the book as to the dates of events, names of persons, article or paragraph numbers, and so on. Some are, possibly, merely printing errors; the others are the result of carelessness. Thus, on page 74 it is said that the Palestine Mandate was confirmed on 20 July 1922; on page 76 — on 20 June 1922; and on page 78 — on 24 July 1922, which is the correct date. The name of Dr Brownlie is incorrectly given as Browlie six times.[32] The British Government referred the question of the Mandate to the United Nations in 1947, not — as is said on page 85 — in 1957, and on 2 April, not 3 April, as is said in note 17 on the same page. The provision of the United Nations Charter prohibiting war is in Article 2(4), not in Article 4(4) as said on page 111. The intention on page 75 is to Article 5 of the Palestine Mandate, not to Article 2; and on page 93, note 36 – to Article 80(2) of the Charter, not Article 77(2). And what is the point of calling Churchill's memorandum

31. F. B. Sloan, "Implementation and Enforcement of Decisions of International Organizations", *Proceedings of the American Society of International Law, April 25—27, 1968* (Washington, 1968), p. 3.
32. See *Colloque,* p. 9; p. 9, note 49; p. 101, note 59; p. 105, note 64; p. 108, note 69; and p. 109.

of 1922, in English, White Manifest [33] instead of White Paper? Furthermore, works are cited as authority without any mention of the relevant pages in them,[34] and how can one explain a reference to the last page of a work, where the reader actually finds the end of the table of contents? [35]

We may now turn to an examination of the specific legal problems dealt with in the book.

II. The Existence of the Jewish People and its Historical Connection with Palestine

The authors completely deny the very existence of the Jewish people and state categorically that the Jews are no more than "a religious community" [36] and that "religion is all that links the Jews together, just as in the case of Christians or of any other persons who subscribe to the same faith".[37] In their opinion, the Jews have no common language, history or roots.[38] I doubt whether there is any point at all in taking up this proposition : the fundamental basis of the principle of national self-determination is the recognition of the right of the group of persons concerned to define for themselves what they are and to decide upon their own fate; it is the denial of the right of others

33. *Colloque,* p. 54.
34. See, for example, p. 109, note 70; p. 111, notes 72—73; p. 164, note 12; p. 165, note 15; p. 167, note 17.
35. *Colloque,* p. 120, note 97.
36. *Ibid.,* p. 30. See, too, *ibid.,* pp. 31, 221.
37. *Ibid.,* p. 36.
38. *Ibid.,* p. 31.

to decide for them and on their behalf. "It is commonly accepted today" said Professor George Scelle, in his lectures at the Hague Academy of International Law, "that every collective, united by links of conscious solidarity — of which the members thereof, *themselves,* are the judges — should be regarded as 'a people'...." [39] And as for the Jews in particular, Scelle wrote some years earlier : "What characterizes a nation is certainly not race — for there is no longer a pure race; it is a combination of manifestations of conscious solidarity — some of an historical nature, others of an intellectual, religious, social or even emotional nature — which together result in the creation of a collective desire for common life, an organization of solidarity and a permanent relationship. If, in truth — as Renan was one of the first to say — it is this psychological element which constitutes the very essence of nationality, there can be no doubt that the whole body of Jewish communities together can be considered one nation or one people. Moreover, the prevalent opinion of jurists concerned with the right of peoples is that the voluntary element, rather than the ethnic one, is what must be borne in mind in determining whether the solidary aspirations of a particular group deserve to be satisfied. It is not even essential that the group have common ethnic or traditional roots for it to constitute a nation or a people, or for its aspirations to be legitimate." [40] He goes on —

39. G. Scelle, "Règles générales de la paix", *R.A.D.I.,* tome 46 (Paris, 1934), p. 407 (italics added).
40. G. Scelle, "Les caractéristiques juridiques internationales du foyer national juif", *Palestine, Revue internationale,* tome 2

"undoubtedly, the Jews are exceptional in this respect that, as a result of their dispersion, they lack some of the elements of solidarity encountered in the case of other peoples — in particular the solidarity that derives from the fact of living in close geographical proximity. On the other hand, it can be contended that their traditions, customs, the persecutions they have endured, their religious practices and mystic aspirations are so firmly integrated — *certainly far more so than in the case of other peoples* — for the very reason that they have not assimilated with the political groups in whose midst they have lived or settled." [41] The French jurist, Fauchille, holds the same view. In discussing the Balfour Declaration and the other declarations in favour of Zionism made by the Allied and Associated Powers, he states: "The Great War of 1914—1919 brought with it official recognition of the nationhood of yet another persecuted

(Paris, 1928), p. 100. Professor Scelle adopts here, then, the well-known doctrine of Ernst Renan, as expressed in his classic definition of the term "nation" — a definition which, in Scelle's opinion, is widely accepted by jurists: "For us a nation is a soul, a spirit, a spiritual family, deriving from past memories, sacrifices, moments of glory, very often common sorrows and regrets; and from a present desire to go on living together. That is what forms a nation; it is not speaking the same language or belonging to the same ethnic group; it is the fact of having done great things together in the past and the desire to do more of them in the future. The nation is a spiritual principle, a result of the profound complex of history." Cited from O. Nippold's lecture, "Le développement historique du droit international depuis le Congrès de Vienne", *R.A.D.I.*, tome 2 (Paris, 1925), p. 40.

41. Scelle, *Palestine*, 1928, p. 100 (italics added).

people : namely, the Jewish people." [42] And the *Dictionnaire de la terminologie du droit international,* prepared under the auspices of the well-known jurist, Basdevant, defines the term "people", *inter alia,* as a group of persons united by "community of race and traditions and the existence of a common conscience", and then continues that in this sense "one speaks of the Jewish people".[43]

One might go on adding to the list of jurists, historians and other scholars for whom there are no doubts as to the identity and existence of the Jewish people. But it is really unnecessary to rest our case on the learned opinions of scholars — for the fact is unequivocally endorsed in many instruments of positive international law. Thus, the Palestine Mandate, finally defined by the Council of the League of Nations on 24 July 1922, expressly recognizes the existence of the Jewish people, its historical connection with Palestine and its right to re-establish its national home there; the Mandate also recognizes the Zionist Organization, or other body set up by it (the enlarged Jewish Agency), as the representative of the Jewish people in all matters affecting the establishment of the national home.[44] The decision of the International

42. P. Fauchille, *Traité de droit international public,* tome 1, première partie, *Paix* (Paris, 1922), p. 314.
43. *Dictionnaire de la terminologie du droit international* (Paris, 1960), p. 450.
44. The authors of the book take the very strange course of ignoring completely the express and clear provisions of the Palestine Mandate on the question of the Jewish national home, as if they were not part of that document at all. An outstanding example of this is to be found in the following

Military Tribunal in Nuremberg, among whose judges
were nationals of the four Great Powers, expressly establishes that "atrocities against the Jewish people were
committed"; [45] and when, subsequently, on almost every
single page of that judgment, reference is made to the
murder of "the Jews" in the various countries of Europe,
the intention is to members of the Jewish people — in the
ethnic, not the religious sense; for in the holocaust both
Jews converted to other faiths and persons of Jewish
origin were also exterminated. Again, in the preamble to
the agreement drawn up in 1952 between Israel and the
Federal Republic of Germany, it is said that "unspeakable

passage from the preamble to the resolution adopted at the
Algiers meeting: "Whereas, after the First World War, Palestine was placed under a Mandate of the League of Nations,
with a view to preparing it for independence under the direction of *a* national *government...*" (*Colloque,* p. 216) (italics
added).

And the question arises how the preamble to that resolution can be reconciled with the following passage from G.
Antonius, whom no one can suspect of wrongly interpreting
the Palestine Mandate to Arab disadvantage: "They [the
decisions of the San Remo Conference] gave the Mandate
for it [Palestine] to Great Britain, on terms in which the
recognition of the independence of that territory was purposely
omitted" (G. Antonius, *The Arab Awakening, The Story of
the Arab National Movement,* London, 1938, p. 351). Antonius
also dwells on the demand made in 1923 by King Hussein
that the safeguard of "*civil and religious* rights" of the Arabs
in Palestine, as provided for in the Mandate, "be extended to
include *political and economic* rights as well", and on Britain's
refusal, as Mandatory Power, to accede to this demand (*ibid.,*
p. 333).

45. *Cmd. 6964, Judgment of the International Military Tribunal
for the Trial of German Major War Criminals, Nuremberg*
(London, 1946), p. 4.

criminal acts were perpetrated against the Jewish people during the National-Socialist regime of terror".[46] One may also mention in this context the U.N.S.C.O.P. Report; this states that "both the Balfour Declaration and the [Palestine] Mandate involve international commitments to the Jewish people as a whole" [47] — not, that is to say, the Jewish population then domiciled in Palestine, but the whole Jewish people, dispersed throughout the world. Finally, the existence of the Jewish people is recognized in Article 80 of the Charter of the United Nations, which safeguards the rights of any "States" and any "peoples" under the Mandates, until the conclusion of trusteeship agreements. As we shall see, those who drafted the Charter used the term "peoples" in the plural, and not "people" in the singular, in order to guarantee the rights of the Jewish people under the Palestine Mandate.

It is worth remarking at this point that, with the termination of the Palestine Mandate on 15 May 1948 and the establishment of the State of Israel, the status of the Jewish people in international law — as the bearer of the right to a national home in Palestine — was indeed extinguished. But this does not mean the abrogation of the very existence of the Jewish people. The recognition of that people by the Mandate, as detailed above, was partly declarative and partly constitutive: it was decla-

46. *Ministry for Foreign Affairs, Documents Relating to the Agreement between the Government of Israel and the Government of the Federal Republic of Germany (signed on 10 September 1952)* (Jerusalem, 1953), p. 125.

47. *G.A.O.R., Second Session, Suppl. No. 11,* p. 32.

rative as to the existence of the Jewish people in the Diaspora and its historical connection with Palestine; constitutive as to the rights granted to the Jewish people for the purposes of establishing a national home and setting up a Jewish Agency. Clearly, recognition, which is declarative in content, cannot be revoked; accordingly, the recognition of the Jewish people's existence remained valid even after the termination of the Mandate — though no longer, it is true, as a recognition of a political entity endowed with certain rights in international law, but rather of a sociological one, united by historical tradition and a sense of spiritual identity and a common fate.

The authors also emphatically deny the existence of an historical connection between the Jewish people and the land of Palestine.[48] Here again, in so doing, they turn a blind eye on the fact that this connection is expressly recognized in positive international law and ignore, too, the history of the Jewish people. Throughout its long exile that people remained faithful to the country of its origin and never ceased to dream of a "return to Zion" and the rebirth of its national life within the framework of a State. This "historical connection" is no mere myth, as the authors of the book suggest; it is an unchallengeable reality. All through the ages, there have been Jews living in Palestine, while the whole way of life of those in the Diaspora — both on the ordinary days of the year and on festivals — has always been inextricably bound up with events in the history of the people when it dwelt

48. *Colloque,* p. 216.

in its homeland. For two thousand years, Jews all over the world have prayed for rain at precisely that time of the year when it is needed in Palestine — not when it is needed in the lands where they lived. In every period there have been migrations of Jews to Palestine — of 300 rabbis from France and England, for example, at the beginning of the thirteenth century. From time to time Messianic movements have arisen : that of David Alroy in the twelfth century; of Shlomo Molcho in the sixteenth; of Shabtai Zvi in the second half of the seventeenth; and of Ya'akov Frank in the eighteenth. In a book on *Nationalism,* written in Great Britain on behalf of the Royal Institute of International Affairs by a team of experts headed by Professor E. H. Carr, we read that "Jewish national feeling [in the Diaspora] could never have remained so strong if Jerusalem had been blotted out and the place of it forgotten...".[49] Even Professor Toynbee, whose negative attitude to Zionism is well enough known, acknowledges that "the Jews do, in... [his] opinion, have a right to a special position in Palestine which no other present-day non-Palestinians possess".[50] There are, then, no grounds whatsoever for the theory of a Zionist movement emerging at the end of the nineteenth century as an artificial phenomenon, an in-

49. *Nationalism, A Report by a Study Group of Members of the Royal Institute of International Affairs* (Oxford, 1939), p. 253.
50. *Jewish Rights in Palestine,* by Professor Arnold J. Toynbee; *Jewish Rights in Eretz Israel (Palestine),* by Professor Solomon Zeitlin; *Correspondence,* reprinted from the *Jewish Quarterly Review,* New Series, vol. 52, Nos. 1, 4 (Philadelphia, 1961—1962), p. 4.

novation, a *deus ex machina.* It is, in fact, the embodiment of the old Jewish historical aspiration, in a modern
and secular form.[51] And even the authors themselves confess that "the opposition of the Arabs to Zionist settlement began well before the 1914 War". "Since 1850",
states the first report, "there have been manifestations
of Arab nationalism against Zionist colonialism" [52] — that
is to say, long before 1897, the year in which the Zionist
Organization was set up.

To strengthen their case as to the non-existence of the
Jewish people and the absence of any historical connection between it and Palestine, the authors of the book
turn for support to statements made on this subject by
well-known Jewish personalities from the anti-nationalist
camp — men such as Edwin S. Montagu and Joseph
Reinach.[53] It is surprising to find jurists attaching so
much weight and significance to statements of that kind,
which are in direct conflict with the express recognition
of the Jewish people's existence in so many international

---

51. The fact that Zionism is a secular movement — not a religious
    one — is emphasized in A. R. Taylor's book, *Prelude to Israel,
    An Analysis of Zionist Diplomacy, 1897—1947* (New York,
    1959), pp. V, VI, 4.
52. *Colloque,* p. 57.
53. See *Colloque,* pp. 28, 70; see, too, *ibid.,* p. 41, note 18. The
    assertion made, at p. 70 of the book, that Yehuda Leib Magnes
    and Martin Buber identified themselves with Reinach's view —
    "Zionism is pure nonsense, a triple error: historical, archaeologi-
    cal and ethnic" — is, it should be stressed, a grave insult to
    their memory. Both Magnes and Buber were, throughout their
    lives, faithful Zionists, firm in their approval of the principle
    of the Return to Zion, though they differed on the official
    policy of the Zionist Organization.

instruments. As for the actual content of the statements, the Jewish people and the Zionist movement have never attempted to constrain persons of Jewish origin into identifying themselves with their people. But, by the very nature of things, a Jew who has chosen to assimilate with another people can no longer be regarded as qualified to appear as spokesman and arbiter on Jewish affairs. There have always been — in the history of peoples which have undergone a process of national revival — individuals, and sometimes whole sectors of society (generally the upper classes), that have estranged themselves from their own people's national liberation movements and even fought against them. But they have never succeeded in curbing any such movement or frustrating the aims that it has set itself. In this context, it is pertinent to recall the following episode in the annals of the Arab national movement. On 13 February 1919, a Syrian delegation, headed by Chekri Ganem, appeared before the Supreme Council of the Peace Conference and, in the name of the Central Syrian Committee, argued passionately that there is a "distinction between Syrian nationality and that of the Arabs"; [54] that "the Syrians are no Arabs" ; [55] that there are no "affinities... between the native of Hedjaz and the Syrian, the nomad and the settler on the soil".[56] The members of that delegation went so far as to declare that they preferred to be "handed back to Turkey. She

54. See *Papers Relating to the Foreign Relations of the United States, The Paris Peace Conference, 1919,* vol. III (Washington, 1943), p. 1028.
55. *Ibid., loc. cit.*
56. *Ibid.,* p. 1029.

will massacre us a little more, but with her we shall at least preserve a hope of one day being able to escape." [57] The authors of the book will no doubt argue that this episode in no way detracts from the image of the Arab nationalist movement. They must equally confess that the opposition to Zionism of individual Jews, or of insignificant and uninfluential groups like the American Council for Judaism, makes no difference at all to the fact that the Jewish people as a whole is united today by close-knit ties of solidarity with the State of Israel,

57. *Ibid.,* p. 1038. The Syrian delegation based its opposition to Feisal, *inter alia,* on a fear of "any kind of theocratic Government, founded on the confusion of civil and religious power" (*ibid.,* p. 1030), of the place reserved for the Islamic faith in the Arab countries, and of the clerical policy that would prevail in them (*ibid.,* p. 1031). And it is interesting to note, by the way, that, some forty years after these doubts were expressed, the Arab League was criticized by a group of scholars and statesmen who, at the request of the Carnegie Endowment for International Peace, prepared a report in Athens on Greece and the United Nations. This is what they had to say: "What is particularly worrying is that the Arab League rests on a religion — Islam, and, in this way, rallies all Muslims to its cause to set up a religious bloc, with a view to uniting Arab and Muslim culture. As with all religious movements, its propaganda is activist. Undoubtedly, this would be quite legitimate if it [the propaganda] were limited to the religious sphere and did not serve an expansionist policy. But this is not the case here. The Muslim activities of the Arab League are incompatible with the spirit and the provisions of the Charter and its tactics are contrary to the procedures prescribed therein." See *Etudes nationales sur l'organisation internationale, La Grèce et les Nations Unies,* préparées par la Société d'études internationales d'Athènes et la Dotation Carnegie pour la paix internationale (New York, 1957), pp. 167—168.

proud of its existence, deeply concerned about its fate and future, and prepared to do all in its power to strengthen it and help it to develop and flourish.

III. The McMahon–Hussein Correspondence

The authors have seen fit to raise once again the question of the contents of the letters exchanged in 1915 and 1916 between Sir Henry McMahon, British High Commissioner in Egypt, and Hussein, Sharif of Mecca and subsequently King of the Hedjaz. It was with regard to this correspondence that one astute writer remarked that "gallons of ink have been spilled" on the discussions on it.[58] The Arabs claim that, in it, Palestine was promised to them as part of the territory in which Britain undertook to recognize and support an independent Arab State, or a confederation of Arab States. The British Government never accepted this interpretation of the correspondence, and on a number of occasions dismissed it as unfounded. As the Arabs reverted to the matter at the Round Table Conference of British and Arab delegations, held in London in 1939, a Joint Committee was set up to consider the contents of the letters and draft its conclusions. But, despite the appeasing attitude towards the Arabs which marked the Conference, the Committee failed to reach agreement. The British representatives informed their Arab counterparts in writing that "they maintain that on a proper construction of the correspondence Palestine was

58. See Paul L. Hanna, *British Policy in Palestine* (Washington, 1942), p. 22.

in fact excluded [from the area] in which Great Britain
was to recognize and support the independence of the
Arabs".[59] But the truth is that, even if the Arab interpretation of the letters were the correct one, McMahon's
letters clearly could not determine the future of territories
that would be occupied by the Allies in the Middle East.
The authors of the second report themselves admit, in
effect, that promises of this kind, given in the middle of
a war, cannot establish the future status of such territories.[60] The decision can only be taken at the end of
the war, when it is expressed in an international instrument drafted by the competent body — Congress, Peace
Conference, Ambassadors' Conference or the like. Certainly, if the settlement finally reached does not accord
with solemn promises made by a State, and the reason
for this is that the State has neglected to take appropriate
action to give effect to its promises, the recipient will
have grounds for complaint against it; but this does not
lessen the legal validity of the said settlement.

The fate and future of Palestine were determined
by the Council of the League of Nations, which, by virtue
of Article 22, paragraph 8, of its Covenant, had the
power to define the terms of all Mandates; and on 24
July 1922 [61] that body decided upon the terms of the

59. See *Cmd. 5974*, p. 10. Nonetheless, the British representatives
    agreed that "the language in which [Palestine's] exclusion
    was expressed was not so specific and unmistakable as it was
    thought to be at the time" (*ibid*).
60. *Colloque*, p. 78, note 5.
61. For reasons connected not with the Palestine Mandate itself,
    but with the relations between France and Italy on the ques-

Palestine Mandate, and imposed on the Mandatory Power the responsibility for implementing the Balfour Declaration. Nor, be it said, was the Balfour Declaration itself any more than a promise, until its incorporation in the Mandate — albeit a binding promise insofar as the relations between the British Government and the Jewish people were concerned.[62] The authors of the second report are wrong, then, when they say that, in issuing the Declaration, the British Government "disposed of conquered territory"[63] over which it had no sovereignty and thereby infringed the rules of international law. The text of the Declaration on this point is clear and unambiguous: "His Majesty's Government *view with favour* the establishment in Palestine of a national home for the Jewish people, and *will use their best endeavours to facilitate the achievement of this object....*"[64] Unlike the McMahon–Hussein correspondence, which was secret and *officially* published only in 1939, the Balfour Declaration was indeed a public document from the moment when it was issued, and immediately won the approval of the rest of the Great Powers and of many other States.[65] But even this fact could not endow the Declaration with greater validity than that of any other pro-

tion of the Mandate for Syria and the Lebanon, the Palestine Mandate only came into force on 29 September 1923.

62. See, on this point, N. Feinberg, "The Recognition of the Jewish People in International Law", *The Jewish Yearbook of International Law, 1948* (Jerusalem, 1949), pp. 8—12.
63. *Colloque,* p. 78.
64. Italics added.
65. See Fauchille, *op. cit.,* p. 315.

mise — though it did, it is true, considerably improve the chances of its serving as the basis for a future settlement.

Since Palestine was under Turkish rule, Turkey's consent to the arrangements to be made was necessary in accordance with international law. This was given in the Treaty of Lausanne of 23 July 1923. In contrast to the Treaty of Sèvres of April 1920 (which was not ratified by Turkey), the Treaty of Lausanne does not, in fact, expressly mention the Balfour Declaration. But that is of no legal significance, contrary to what the authors of the second report seek to imply.[66] By Article 16, Turkey renounced all rights to the territories outside its frontiers, as laid down in the Treaty, the future of those territories "being settled or to be settled by the parties concerned".[67] And, since the decision as to Palestine was taken a year before the signing of the Treaty, there was absolutely no need for Palestine and the Balfour Declaration to be expressly mentioned in it.

It is surprising that, in a number of passages in the book, the authors speak of Palestine as a territory "under Arab sovereignty"[68] and of the Arabs as "the territorial sovereign"[69] and "the legitimate sovereign";[70] they even affirm that "the Jews recognized Arab sovereignty no less

66. *Colloque*, p. 77, note 4.
67. *Cmd.*, 1929, *Treaty of Peace with Turkey and other Instruments* (London, 1923), p. 20.
68. *Colloque*, p. 131.
69. *Ibid.*, p. 128.
70. *Ibid.*, pp. 126, 131.

than Ottoman sovereignty".[71] If what is meant here is the right of self-determination of peoples — the subject is considered below; if, on the other hand, the reference really is to sovereignty in the conventional sense, as defined — with all its connotations — in the *Dictionnaire de la terminologie du droit international*,[72] then the assertions are, legally, unfounded. Palestine, as we have seen, was under Turkish rule — without interruption from 1517; and even before that year, it was never under Arab rule. As the U.N.S.C.O.P. Report says: "...not since 63 B.C., when Pompey stormed Jerusalem, has Palestine been an independent State." [73]

It is worth our pointing to yet another flaw in Arab reliance on the McMahon-Hussein correspondence: already in 1919, when the Arabs submitted their territorial claims to the Paris Peace Conference, not only did they not include Palestine in the territory for which they demanded Arab independence; they expressly excluded it, leaving it aside to be dealt with separately. On his appearance before the Supreme Council of the Conference on 6 February 1919, the Emir Feisal, Chief of the Delegation of the Hedjaz (which had already been recognized as an independent State, with Hussein as its king), asked for the independence of all Arabic-speaking peoples in Asia from the line Alexandretta-Diarbekir southward; he then dwelt specifically on the difficulties

71. *Ibid.*, p. 26.
72. *Dictionnaire de la terminologie du droit international*, pp. 573—579.
73. *G.A.O.R., Second Session, Suppl. No. 11*, p. 32.

that would confront him in reference to Syria and expressed his readiness to recognize Lebanese independence on certain conditions; while, with regard to Palestine, we read in the official protocols of the Peace Conference as follows: "Palestine, for its universal character, he left on one side for the mutual consideration of all parties interested. With this exception, he asked for the independence of the Arabic areas enumerated in his memorandum." [74] A second memorandum, also signed by the Emir Feisal, on 1 January 1919, serves to prove, in the words of U.N.S.C.O.P., that "the special status of Palestine was recognized in Arab circles".[75] In it Feisal lists the "provinces of Arab Asia", as he calls them, whose unification he demands; Palestine is not included. Insofar as Palestine is concerned, he acknowledges the need for a special regime.[76]

It is not necessary to consider here other documents from the days of the Peace Conference — by which I mean, primarily, the agreement signed in London on 4 or 5 January 1919 between "His Royal Highness the

---

74. See *Papers Relating to the Foreign Relations of the United States,* vol. III, p. 891; see, too, David Hunter Miller, *My Diary of the Peace Conference, with Documents,* vol. XIV (New York, 1928), p. 230.
75. *G.A.O.R., Second Session, Suppl. No. 11,* p. 34.
76. See the full text of the memorandum: Hunter Miller, *op. cit.,* vol. IV, pp. 297—299. Incidentally, Feisal stresses in it, in the part dealing with the aims of the Arab nationalist movements, "of which [his] father became the leader", that his "father has a privileged place among Arabs, as their successful leader and as the head of their greatest family and as Sharif of Mecca"; see *ibid.,* p. 297.

Emir Feisal, representing and acting on behalf of the Arab Kingdom of Hedjaz, and Dr. Chaim Weizmann, representing and acting on behalf of the Zionist Organization",[77] and the Emir Feisal's letter to Professor Felix Frankfurter of 5 March 1918.[78] In that letter Feisal acknowledges Zionist aspirations and shows readiness to come to an understanding and agreement with the Zionist movement. The two official documents submitted to the Peace Conference are sufficient to establish unchallengeably that, in appearing before the Conference as the authorized representative of the Arab nationalist movement and in drafting Arab territorial claims, the Emir Feisal excluded Palestine from the territories demanded by that movement.

IV. THE LEGALITY OF THE PALESTINE MANDATE

For some reason, the authors of the book have found it necessary to re-open the debate on the legality of the Palestine Mandate — a subject which was gone into thoroughly when the Mandate was in force. Their contention is that its provisions on the establishment of a Jewish national home in Palestine are contrary to Article

77. See the full text of the agreement: *ibid.*, vol. III, pp. 188—189; G. Antonius, *op. cit.*, pp. 437—439.
78. See the text of the letter: *Book of Documents Submitted to the General Assembly of the United Nations Relating to the Establishment of the National Home for the Jewish People* (New York, 1947), p. 18; see, too, *Felix Frankfurter Reminiscences Recorded in Talks with Dr. Harlan B. Phillips* (London, 1960), pp. 155—157.

22 of the Covenant of the League of Nations, to the effect that "the well-being and development of... [the] peoples" placed under a mandatory regime "form a sacred trust of civilization".[79] The sole aim of all Mandatory rule is, in their opinion, "to guarantee the protection of the natives and safeguard their interests with a view to guiding them towards self-government",[80] but not to trouble about the future of some other people from outside the territory in question.

The first answer to this is that, when the Council of the League was asked to confirm the text of the Palestine Mandate, it was fully aware of the Arabs' legal arguments on the matter. Yet those arguments failed to carry conviction with the Council; nor did they convince the Permanent Mandates Commission, which, in the period 1924—1939, as the organ responsible for supervising the implementation of Mandates, discussed the problems involved in the Palestine Mandate each year and devoted two extraordinary sessions to them in 1930 and 1937. Moreover, when the Greek Government brought before the Permanent Court of International Justice its claim against the British Government regarding concessions contested by the Greek national, Mavrommatis, the question of the legality of the Palestine Mandate did not arise at all. When U.N.S.C.O.P. heard the Arab case on this issue, it dismissed it, being of the opinion that "there would seem to be no grounds for questioning the validity of the Mandate for the reason advanced by the Arab

79. *Colloque,* p. 73.
80. *Ibid.,* p. 83.

States".[81] Most important of all is the fact that, even before the U.N.S.C.O.P. hearings, the Palestine Mandate won the approval of the San Francisco Conference, which would certainly not have given its support had it believed that the contents of the Mandate were unlawful. We have here in mind Article 80 of the Charter of the United Nations — already mentioned — laying it down that, "until such agreements [Trusteeship Agreements] have been concluded, nothing in this Chapter [dealing with the international trusteeship system] shall be construed in or of itself to alter in any manner the rights whatsoever of any State or any peoples or the terms of existing international instruments to which Members of the United Nations may respectively be parties". From the history of this article, known as the conservatory or safeguarding clause, it is clear enough that its provisions apply to the Palestine Mandate and that those who drafted it used the word "peoples" in the plural — and not "people" in the singular — so that there should be no room for doubt that the rights guaranteed to the Jewish people by the Palestine Mandate were still valid and operative.[82]

The Arab delegations at the San Francisco Conference made innumerable attempts to prevent the use of the word "peoples". Egypt proposed a text which read "the

81. *G.A.O.R., Second Session, Suppl. No. 11*, p. 35.
82. See Ruth B. Russell, *A History of the United Nations Charter, The Role of the United States, 1940—1945* (Washington, 1958), pp.827—830; *International Court of Justice, Pleadings, Oral Arguments, Documents, International Status of South-West Africa, Advisory Opinion of July 1950*, pp. 215—217.

rights of the people of any territory or the terms of any Mandate",[83] thereby seeking to make clear that "only the rights of the inhabitants of the territory were protected".[84] On the rejection of that proposal, Syria submitted a similar one,[85] which also fell away. Equally unsuccessful was the Iraqui representative's wording — "the rights of the people of that territory" [86] — which was clearly intended to imply non-recognition of the rights claimed by any people from outside the territory in question.

It is clear, then, that the representatives of the Arab States at the San Francisco Conference did not succeed in preventing the confirmation of the Palestine Mandate in its entirety — including, therefore, those of its provisions which deal with the Jewish people's rights in its national home.

As for the actual substance of the Arab contention from the point of view of the Covenant of the League of Nations, the following points may be made:

a) Article 22 of the Covenant, whereby the Mandates system was created, does, it is true, detail three categories of Mandate; but it does not stipulate as to any one of them what territories it is to include. Article 22, paragraph 4, speaks of *"certain* [87] communities formerly belonging to the Turkish Empire"; Article 22, paragraph 5 — of

83. *Documents of the United Nations Conference on International Organization,* vol. X (San Francisco, 1945), p. 477.
84. See Russell, *op. cit.,* p. 828.
85. *Documents of the United Nations Conference on International Organization,* vol. X, p. 487.
86. *Ibid.,* pp. 515—516.   87. Italics added.

"other peoples, *especially* [87] those of Central Africa"; and Article 22, paragraph 6 — of "territories *such as* [87] South West Africa and certain of the South Pacific Islands". Moreover, Article 22, paragraph 4, does not impose an obligation to place any territory at all of those formerly belonging to Turkey under such rule, for it does not use the word "shall' or even "will" — but "can". The only conclusion that can be drawn is that a Mandate need not necessarily be drafted according to the pattern of one of the three said categories. Legally, then, the fact that — in contrast to the preamble to the Mandate for Syria and the Lebanon, where Article 22, paragraph 4, is referred to — the Palestine Mandate uses the phrase: "for the purpose of giving effect to the provisions of Article 22", without mentioning any one of the paragraphs of that article, is unimpeachable.

b) In the Advisory Opinion on the Mandated territory of South West Africa, given by the International Court in 1950, it is said that the Mandates system was created to prevent the annexation of territories conquered by the victors in the First World War; to advance "the well-being and development" of the inhabitants of the territory as a "sacred trust of civilization"; [88] and to serve "the interest... of humanity in general".[89] In view of this definition, and since, first, the Principal Allied and Associated Powers and, subsequently, the League of Na-

87. Italics added.
88. *International Status of South-West Africa, Advisory Opinion, I.C.J. Reports 1950*, p. 131.
89. *Ibid.,* p. 132.

tions reached the conclusion that it was in the interest of humanity that a solution be found for the national problem of the homeless Jewish people, there was nothing to prevent the Palestine Mandate being drafted as it was.

c) The authors of the book attribute supreme importance to the sentence in Article 22, paragraph 1, of the Covenant reading: "The well-being and development of such peoples form a sacred trust of civilization." [90] They find in this principle "one of the main contributions of modern international law",[91] and in the failure to abide by it "a grave violation of the Charter of the United Nations".[92] But, as Lord McNair has emphasized in his separate opinion in 1950, "no technical significance can be attached to the words 'sacred trust of civilization' ".[93]

d) Article 22, paragraph 8, of the Covenant, already referred to above, gave the Council of the League the ultimate power of determining the texts of the Mandates. In the well-known Report on Mandates, drawn up by the Belgian representative, Paul Hymans, and confirmed by the Council on 5 August 1920, it was emphasized that the provisions to be included in Mandates "will inevitably vary *according to the nature of the territory* or the people subject to the Mandate".[94] There can be no doubt that

---

90. See *Colloque*, pp. 73, 76, 94, 95.

91. *Ibid.*, p. 95.

92. *Ibid.*, p. 95, note 45.

93. *International Status of South-West Africa, Advisory Opinion, I.C.J. Reports 1950*, p. 148.

94. *Société des Nations, Les responsabilités qui incombent à la Société des Nations en vertu de l'article 22 (Mandats), Rap-*

the "nature" of Palestine — its past and its place in the history of the Jews and in Jewish life — is what justified the drafting of the Palestine Mandate in a manner which differed from the accepted pattern. There was here no breach of the underlying principles of the Mandates system or denial of the aims which that system set itself.

V. The Right of Self-Determination

Like a thread running through the whole of the book is the authors' claim — made both independently and incidentally to their other arguments — that the Balfour Declaration of 1917 and the endorsement of it by the League of Nations in the Palestine Mandate of 1922, and, subsequently, the Partition Resolution adopted by the United Nations in 1947 and the establishment of the State of Israel in 1948 constitute a violation of the right of self-determination of peoples ("le droit des peuples à disposer d'eux-mêmes").[95] They make this point, in a determined and categorical way, as a *legal* argument; but the truth is that it is far from convincing, for they completely ignore the fact that on none of the dates on which the four events took place was the principle of self-determination recognized as a binding rule of positive international law — and, if there was no norm, there could be no infringement.

Under President Wilson's inspiration, the Paris Peace

port présenté par le Conseil à l'Assemblée, 20/48/161 (Genève, 1920), p. 13 (italics added).

95. See *Colloque,* pp. 25, 36, 81, 87, 110.

Conference of 1919—1920 turned to the "right of self-determination" (or "principle of nationalities" [96]) as its guiding rule in all that concerned the delineation of the map of Europe. But it was never elevated to the status of an absolute principle at the Conference, to be followed whatever the circumstances and regardless of all other factors and considerations. "Without any doubt", wrote Professor Dupuis, "the Paris Conference gave the principle [of nationalities] a more prominent place than any preceding Congress had; but... it refused to apply it in its entirety" [97] and treated it as "a purely political factor and not as a legal principle applicable to all peoples whose fate has to be determined." [98] Professor Mandelstam writes in the same sense : "The Wilsonian doctrine recognizes, in principle, the need to satisfy national aspirations, but it reserves the examination of substantive justice for each individual case.... Where there is a conflict between the State and the nations which form part of it, there will be no uniform solution : sometimes it will be more favour-

---

96. Generally, the two terms — "the right of self-determination of peoples" and "the principle of nationalities" — are used interchangeably, although, from a theoretical point of view, they differ in content. The principle of nationalities is a substantive principle with real content, whereas that of self-determination is a technical and formal one. If, for example, in the plebiscite held in 1935 on the future of the Saar, the decision had been in favour of union with France, the result would have been contrary to the principle of nationalities, but consistent with the principle of self-determination.

97. Charles Dupuis, "Règles générales du droit de la paix", *R.A.D.I.*, tome 32 (Paris, 1931), p. 37.

98. *Ibid.*, p. 38.

able to the State, sometimes to the nation — according to the supreme interests of human society." [99]

If we turn now to the period between the two World Wars, there is — we find — only one official legal document dealing with the subject, namely — the Aaland Islands Opinion, given in 1920 by an *ad hoc* committee of eminent jurists set up by the League of Nations — among its members being F. Larnaude and Max Huber. While examining the question of the status of those islands, the committee found it necessary to go into the issue of the right of self-determination and this is what it said : "Although the principle of self-determination of peoples plays an important part in modern political thought, especially since the Great War, it must be pointed out that there is no mention of it in the Covenant of the League of Nations. The recognition of this principle in a certain number of international treaties cannot be considered as sufficient to put it upon the same footing as a positive rule of the Law of Nations.... The fact must, however, not be lost sight of that the principle that nations must have the right of self-determination is not the only one to be taken into account. Even though it be regarded as the most important of the principles governing the formation of States, geographical, economic and other similar considerations may put obstacles in the way of its complete recognition. Under such circumstances, a solution in the nature of a compromise may ap-

---

99. See Mandelstam, *op. cit.*, p. 399. See, too, Scelle, *R.A.D.I.*, tome 46, pp. 408—411; Claude, *op. cit.*, pp. 12—13.

pear necessary according to international legal conception and may even be dictated by the interests of peace."[100]

Article 1, paragraph 2, and Article 55 of the Charter
of the United Nations, in contrast to the Covenant of
the League of Nations, do mention the principle of self-
determination. But even its inclusion in the Charter did
not convert it into a norm of international law. Suffice it
to refer, in this context, to Chapter XI of the Charter,
which acknowledges the right of the colonial States to
continue administering the non-self-governing territories
and even defines the task imposed upon them as a "sacred
trust". On this, Professor Giraud rightly comments: "A
State which fulfils a sacred trust cannot be regarded as
a violator of international law." [101] Opinions are divided,
however, on the question whether the principle of self-
determination has, in the course of time, become a binding norm of international law — in particular, since the
United Nations General Assembly in 1960 unanimously
approved the "Declaration on the Granting of Independence to Colonial Countries and Peoples". A clear
expression of the conflicting views is to be found, *inter
alia,* in the deliberations conducted since 1964 by the
Special Committee on Principles of International Law
concerning Friendly Relations and Cooperation among
States.[102] Even now, some of the members of that Com-

100. *League of Nations, Official Journal, Special Supplement No.
    3, The Aaland Islands Question, Report of the Committee of
    Jurists* (London, 1920), pp. 5—6.
101. E. Giraud, "Le droit international public et la politique",
    R.A.D.I., tome 110 (Leyde, 1966), p. 744.
102. *United Nations, General Assembly, Report of the Special*

mittee deny the binding nature of the principle; others argue that it is "no longer to be considered a mere moral or political postulate" but "rather a settled principle of modern international law".[103] The wording — "*no longer*

Committee on Principles of International Law concerning Friendly Relations and Cooperation among States, Document A/6230 (New York, 1966), pp. 91—100; Document A/6799 (New York, 1967), pp. 29—37; Document A/7326 (New York, 1968), pp. 52—66; Document A/7619 (New York, 1969), pp. 48—68.

103. See *ibid.*, Document A/6230, p. 92; Document A/6799, p. 30; Document A/7326, p. 59. The Indian jurist, R. Rao, who is one of the members of the Special Committee and was, in 1966, its chairman, is of the opinion that "the view is near unanimously held among the various States, including those of Afro-Asia, that the right of self-determination, while made applicable to the traditional colonies by the Charter and the 1960 Declaration, has no application to independent States". He goes on to point out that, in Afro-Asian regions, smaller States, adjacent to Big Powers, have not attained independence or have become satellites. Referring, in this connection, to the fate of the Mongolian, Tibetan and other peoples in countries adjoining China and Russia — viz., one of inexorable absorption in either of the two great States, or, in the alternative, a satellite status — he continues: "The conclusion may not be inapt that self-determination is more a function and consequence of geography, than a right in law." Rao also points out that the Covenant on Civil and Political Rights and that on Economic, Social and Cultural Rights, upon which the General Assembly of the United Nations agreed in 1966 and both of which give prominence of place to the provision that "all peoples have the right of self-determination", were not ratified by a single State" (R. Rao, "The Right of Self-Determination: Its Status and Role in International Law", *Internationales Recht und Diplomatie*, Köln, 1968, pp. 24—28). It should be mentioned that since Rao wrote his article the two Covenants have been ratified, or acceded to, by six States; but, by their terms, they have to be ratified, or

to be considered" [104] — implies that even those who uphold its binding nature attribute to it the status of a legal principle not insofar as the past is concerned but only with regard to the present and the future. [105] The attempts made by some members of the Committee to resolve the differences have not, up to now, borne fruit and opinions remain divided.[106]

These conclusions, which undoubtedly relate to the most important legal argument in the Arab case, are upheld by Mr Bedjaoui himself — who, as we have said, opened and closed the meeting of Arab jurists — in a work of his published in 1961. The views which he expresses there, we may surmise, will not be without weight in the eyes of our authors. In his book, Bedjaoui exhaustively surveys the development of the principle of self-determination in the course of the last fifty years. After examining its influence on the work of the Paris Peace Conference and on political life in the time of the League of Nations, he commends its incorporation in the Charter of the United Nations; but, in his opinion, too, only as

        acceded to, by thirty-five States before coming into force.
104. Italics added.
105. For a similar approach, see Giraud, *op. cit.*, pp. 744—749; and in contrast, for the standpoint of those who deny the legal validity of the principle, J. H. W. Verzijl, *International Law in Historical Perspective,* vol. I (Leyden, 1968), pp. 321—326; O. Schachter, "The Relation of Law, Politics and Action in the United Nations", *R.A.D.I.,* tome 109 (Leyde, 1964), pp. 228—232; R. Y. Jennings, *The Acquisition of Territory in International Law* (Manchester, 1961), pp. 78—79.
106. *Report of the Special Committee on Principles of International Law, Document A/6799,* p. 80; *Document A/7326,* pp. 67—68.

"a fundamental principle of international morality".[107]
And then he goes on to say: "After fifteen years of
constant discussion on international platforms, the right
of peoples to self-determination has become a driving
force, a dynamic principle, in world affairs. Little by
little the United Nations sought to go beyond the purely
moral limits of this principle and to give it a positive content. After the experience of a decade they tried to transform a vague moral principle into a precise rule of law
with clearly defined methods of enforcement." [108] So we
see that Bedjaoui's accurate and unambiguous survey,
as well, shows us clearly that, at the time when the international instruments concerning the Palestine Mandate
and the establishment of the State of Israel were drafted,
the principle of self-determination was no more than a
political and moral principle. And it is an accepted rule
of intertemporal international law that the legality of an
action is determined in the light of the law in force when
it was effected and not of the law prevailing when its
validity is challenged. "[This] rule", writes Professor
Jennings, "... is elementary and important. It is merely
an aspect of the rule against retroactive laws, and to that
extent may be regarded as a general principle of international law." [109] In a legal sense, then — and it is in
this sense, according to our authors, that the issues were
discussed in Algiers — there is no foundation for the pro-

107. Mohammed Bedjaoui, *Law and the Algerian Revolution*
     (Brussels, 1961), p. 242.
108. *Ibid., loc. cit.*
109. Jennings, *op. cit.*, p. 28.

position repeatedly put forward in their book that the realization of Zionist aims involved a breach of a binding norm of international law.

It may well have been sufficient to rebut the legal arguments on self-determination; but it will not be out of place to devote a few words to the political and moral aspects of the matter. There is no justification whatsoever for criticizing the two central organs of mankind — the League of Nations and the United Nations — for having recognized the need, and even the duty, to solve, once and for all, the problem of the national existence of the homeless Jewish people, and for having acceded to Zionist claims, in view of the historical connection of that people with Palestine. Professor Scelle has compared the Balfour Declaration with the Italian Government's "Guarantees Law" of 1871 on the status of the Holy See and of the' Pope. Just as that Law, he states — formally Italian, but international in content — established the status of the international relations of the Papacy, so, too, the Balfour Declaration, "issuing though it did from one single government, is a manifestation of international solidarity and public utility regarding the situation of the Jews, dispersed among the nations. It is a recognition of the need to give legal expression to the particular solidarity of the Jewish community within the general solidarity of the international community." [110] The Enquiry Commission set up by President Wilson to prepare a draft map of the world on the basis of the peace programme traced out by him in

110. Scelle, *Palestine,* 1928, pp. 102—103.

his famous "Fourteen Points" did not feel that there was any inconsistency between Zionist demands and Wilson's concepts and principles — including the principle of self-determination; it even recommended, in a most clear and express manner, the establishment of an independent Jewish State in Palestine. "It is right", says the Commission, in the explanatory remarks to its Report of 21 January 1919, "that Palestine should become a Jewish State, if the Jews, being given full opportunity, make it such. It was the cradle and home of their vital race, which has made large spiritual contributions to mankind, and is the only land in which they can hope to find a home of their own, they being in this last respect unique among significant peoples." [111] The Permanent Mandates Commission, too, to which all of the arguments of the Arab world were exceedingly well known, did not hesitate to define the Zionist cause — in its 1937 Report — as "a measure of higher justice which cannot be carried out without a sacrifice from their [the Arabs'] side", [112] and, in that same Report, the Commission explains its approach in these words: "the collective suffering of Arabs and Jews are not comparable, since vast spaces in the Near East, formerly the abode of a numerous population and the home of a brilliant civilisation, are open to the former, whereas the world is increasingly being closed to settlement by the latter." [113] And Mr Gromyko, the repre-

111. Hunter Miller, *op. cit.*, vol. IV, p. 264.
112. *League of Nations, Permanent Mandates Commission, Minutes of the Thirty-Second (Extraordinary) Session* (Geneva, 1937), p. 230.
113. *Ibid.*, p. 229.

sentative of the Union of Soviet Socialist Republics at the first special plenary session of the General Assembly, convened to discuss the Palestine Mandate, declared that "the aspirations of a considerable part of the Jewish people are linked with the problem of Palestine and of its future administration"; "it would be unjust not to take this into consideration and to deny the right of the Jewish people to realize this aspiration", which is "to establish their own State".[114] And a year later, at the second special session, he emphatically reiterated that "the decision on the partition of Palestine was a just decision",[115] that "the partition of Palestine into two States represented the most equitable solution, ... [since] it was compatible with the national interests of both peoples of Palestine",[116] both of which — as he had said the previous year — "have historical roots in Palestine".[117]

Underlying all of these declarations — and one could add very many more to the list — is the principle that, where two rightful claims are in conflict, the amount of suffering that will be caused by failure to satisfy each one of them must be carefully weighed and the decision must fall in favour of that which will result in the least suffering.[118] It was this principle that turned the scale in favour of the Zionist solution of the Palestine problem.

114. *G.A.O.R., First Special Session, vol. I, Plenary Meetings* (Lake Success, 1947), pp. 131, 132.
115. *G.A.O.R., Second Special Session, vol. II, Main Committees* (Lake Success, 1948), p. 20.
116. *Ibid.*, p. 18.
117. *G.A.O.R., First Special Session*, vol. I, p. 133.
118. This is also the meaning of what Dr Weizmann said on

But the decision was — it must be stressed — by no means a one-sided decision, entirely to the advantage of only one party. The 1947 Partition Plan was drafted as a compromise between the two conflicting claims; more-over, in accordance with the decision of the Council of the League of Nations of September 1922, three-fourths of the territory of Mandatory Palestine had already been excluded from the application of the provisions of the Mandate relating to the Jewish national home and transferred, in effect, to the Emir Abdullah of Trans-Jordan. But the Arabs did not merely reject the com-promise plan of 1947; they even resolved to oppose it by force and, when the State of Israel was proclaimed, the armed forces of five Arab countries invaded its ter-ritory with the declared aim of destroying it. Fifty years ago, Lord Balfour, in one of his speeches, expressed the hope that "they [the Arabs] will not grudge that small notch [the territory of Palestine] — for it is no more geographically, whatever it may be historically — that small notch in what are now Arab territories being given to the people who for all these hundreds of years have been separated from it...." [119] These words, surely, are doubly valid today when there are fourteen independent

relative justice to the Anglo-American Committee. "There is", he stressed, "no absolute justice in this world" and the Committee must "move on the line of the least injustice". See the minutes of the *Public Hearings before the Anglo-American Committee of Inquiry, Jerusalem (Palestine), 8 March, 1946,* p. 29 (stencil).

119. *Speeches on Zionism, by the Right Hon. the Earl of Balfour,* edited by Israel Cohen (London, 1928), p. 24.

Arab States — all members of the United Nations —
whose territories extend over almost twelve million square
kilometres. The area of the State of Israel within the
Armistice Agreements lines was only 20,700 square
kilometres.

VI. The "Illegality" of the Partition Plan

In the opinion of the authors of the book, the Resolution of 29 November 1947 on the partition of the Mandated territory of Palestine is of no "legal validity"; [120] it
is without "any legal basis"; [121] and is, therefore, "fundamentally void",[122] "an absolute nullity".[123] They rest
this contention on three grounds: a) the Resolution exceeds the powers granted to the Assembly by the Charter
of the United Nations; b) it infringes the right of self-
determination of peoples; c) it is contrary to the Palestine
Mandate.

We have dwelt on the right of self-determination in
the preceding section. As for the other two grounds, it
should be noted, in the first place, that in the many
deliberations of the International Court of Justice on the
Mandate for South West Africa — in the years 1950 to
1966 — the Partition Resolution was frequently referred to
in the course of the pleadings, and its legality was never
questioned.[124] Moreover, in its Advisory Opinion of 1950,

---

120. *Colloque*, p. 80.   121. *Ibid.*, p. 100.
122. *Ibid.*, p. 217.   123. *Ibid.*, p. 84.
124. See *International Court of Justice, Pleadings..., International
    Status of South-West Africa, Advisory Opinion of July 11th,*

the Court itself saw fit to refer to it as follows: "This conclusion [that the Assembly and the Mandatory Power together have the competence to modify the international status of a Mandated territory] is strengthened by the action taken by the General Assembly...",[125] the action in question being no other than the Resolution of 29 November 1947 on Palestine. Lord McNair, in his separate opinion, even makes express reference to the Resolution.[126] Clearly, if it were illegal, or in any way defective from a legal point of view — as the Arab jurists argue — then the Judges of the International Court would not have relied on it.

The authors do not challenge the fact that, by virtue of Articles 10 and 14 of the Charter of the United Nations, the Assembly was competent to consider every matter concerning Mandates and make recommendations regarding them. But — they hold — the Partition Resolution of 1947 was more than a mere recommendation. "The Partition Plan", states the second report, "... undoubtedly assumed an obligatory character, since, by one of its clauses, every attempt to alter by force the arrangements made thereunder is regarded as a threat to the peace, a breach of the peace or an act of aggression within the meaning of Article 39 of the Charter." [127] As

1950, pp. 134, 137, 213, and p. 236, note 1; *I.C.J. Pleadings, South West Africa, 1966*, vol. II, pp. 68—70; vol. VII, pp. 294—297; vol. VIII, pp. 161—166, 493—500; vol. IX, pp. 175—187, 436—443.

125. *I.C.J. Reports, 1950,* p. 142.
126. *Ibid.,* p. 157.
127. *Colloque,* p. 97.

Professor Viralli has already so rightly remarked, experience teaches that, when States refuse to accept the recommendations of the Assembly, they do not simply rest their case on their lack of binding force; in most instances, they also challenge the legality of the recommendations and contend that they are unconstitutional and *ultra vires*.[128]

We have no intention here of going into the question whether the Assembly, when asked by Great Britain as the Mandatory to determine the future of the Palestine Mandate, was competent only to make recommendations or also to pass a binding resolution. The matter is a subject of controversy in the legal literature.[129] The Security Council — and this fact is stressed in the second report[130] — did not consider itself bound to implement the Resolution and refused, therefore, to do so. Let us assume, for the purposes of our enquiry, that the theory of the authors of the book is correct — namely that the

---

128. M. Viralli, "La valeur juridique des recommandations des organisations internationales, *Annuaire français de droit international,* tome II (Paris, 1956), p. 87.

129. Among those who hold the resolution to be binding are, for example, Pierre F. Brugière, *Les pouvoirs de l'Assemblée générale des Nations Unies en matière de politique et de sécurité* (Paris, 1955), p. 231; Giraud, *op. cit.,* p. 732, note 51. Of those taking the opposite view, the following may be mentioned: C. Eagleton, "Palestine and the Constitutional Law of the United Nations", *American Journal of International Law,* vol. 42 (Washington, 1948), pp. 397—398; L. M. Goodrich and E. Hambro, *Charter of the United Nations, Commentary and Documents,* second and revised edition (London, 1949), p. 152.

130. *Colloque,* p. 99.

Assembly was not entitled to pass a binding resolution in the matter. Even so, there is no ground whatsoever for challenging its legality. There was nothing invalid — as the authors argue — about the Assembly's recommendation that the Security Council regard every attempt to alter by force the settlement envisaged by the Resolution as a breach of Article 39 of the Charter and take appropriate action. It is surprising to find that, in this context, they choose to turn to Professor Kelsen for support,[131] when Kelsen himself unequivocally repudiates the claim that "the Assembly is not competent to recommend to the Security Council enforcement measures",[132] and, in another passage of his work, again emphasizes that, in proposing that the Security Council resort to enforcement measures in time of need, the General Assembly recommended nothing "that was not in the competence of the Security Council".[133] He does, indeed, go even further, rejecting the approach of the representative of the United States, which was that, under the Charter, the Security Council is only qualified to remove a threat to peace, but is absolutely forbidden to enforce recommendations. Kelsen regards

131. *Ibid.,* p. 98.
132. H. Kelsen, *The Law of the United Nations, A Critical Analysis of its Fundamental Problems* (London, 1950), p. 210, note 7. Kelsen does, indeed, hold that the Resolution could have been implemented by virtue of Article 10 of the Charter, not by virtue of Article 14. His assumption is that the Resolution was, in fact, based on Article 14, though this is not expressly stated in it (*ibid.*).
133. *Ibid.,* p. 288, note 1.

this interpretation as contrary to the Charter.[134] In his opinion, the Security Council is bound to implement the Assembly's recommendations not only when attempts are made to prevent their implementation *by force,* but also if it "considers noncompliance with a recommendation made by the Assembly as a threat to the peace under Article 39 [of the Charter]".[135] And, in referring directly to the Partition Resolution, he says: "If the Security Council considered the partition [of Palestine] as suggested by the General Assembly as necessary for the maintenance of international peace, that is to say if the Council considered non-implementation of the partition plan as a threat to international peace, the Council was authorized by the Charter to take the measures referred to in Articles 39, 41, 42, for the purpose to maintain or restore peace by enforcing the partition plan." [136]

The authors adduce another reason for their contention that the Assembly exceeded its powers, challenging the clause in the Resolution providing for the setting up of a five-man commission to take over the administration of the affairs of Palestine, temporarily, on the withdrawal of the armed forces of the Mandatory. [137] This provision — they hold — is, by its very nature, not a recommendation, but an executive act — the transfer of the administration of the Mandate, for an interim period, to a commission set up by the Assembly itself; and, as such, it is *ultra vires.*

134. *Ibid., loc. cit.*   135. *Ibid.,* p. 459.
136. *Ibid.,* p. 288, note 1.   137. *Colloque,* p. 98.

This point was argued at considerable length, and with great persistence, by the representatives of the Arab States at the 1947 Assembly of the United Nations. It may be that even then it was out of place, for only fifteen days before the passing of the Resolution on the partition of Palestine, the same Assembly had *unanimously* voted to set up a Temporary Commission on Korea and to impose upon it executive duties in order to "facilitate and expedite the fulfilment of the... programme [recommended by the Assembly] for the attainment of national independence of Korea and withdrawal of occupying forces..."; [138] and the next Assembly went yet further, resolving to extend the duties of that Commission; but no one challenged the legality of that Resolution.[139] One thing, at all events, is clear : in view of the practices evolved by the United Nations during the twenty-four years of its existence, and in the light of the opinions of the International Court of Justice on the extent of the Assembly's competence, there are no grounds for questioning the legality of the Partition Resolution simply because it embraced the said provision. The annual Assemblies of the United Nations have not only established commissions which can, perhaps, be regarded as performing mediatory or conciliatory functions of the Assembly itself; the 1956 Assembly even decided upon the establishment of an Emergency Force, to

138. *Yearbook of the United Nations, 1947—1948* (New York, 1949), p. 88.
139. *Yearbook of the United Nations, 1948—1949* (New York, 1950), pp. 293—294.

be placed on Egypt's border with Israel, and upon the clearance of the Suez Canal — and it made the Secretary-General responsible for the arrangement necessary for implementing those measures. Underlying all these decisions was an organic and dynamic interpretation of the Charter of the United Nations, which — in the words of Judge Charles de Visscher — is "a treaty of a constitutional character",[140] and, therefore, must not be narrowly interpreted. This same approach has also been adopted by the International Court of Justice, when, on several occasions, it has been asked to give its opinion on the scope of the Assembly's powers. In its Advisory Opinion of 1949 on "Reparation for Injuries Suffered in the Service of the United Nations", the Court holds: "It must be acknowledged that its [the United Nations'] members, by entrusting certain functions to it, with the attendant duties and responsibilities, have clothed it with the competence required to enable those functions to be effectively discharged." [141] And further in that same Opinion the Court reiterates that "the [United Nations] Organization must be deemed to have those powers which, though not expressly provided in the Charter, are conferred upon it by necessary implications as being essential to the performance of its duties".[142] Clearly then, it is not

140. *I.C.J. Reports 1950*, p. 187.
141. *Reparation for Injuries Suffered in the Service of the United Nations, Advisory Opinion: I.C.J. Reports 1949*, p. 179.
142. *Ibid.*, p. 182. See, too, *Certain Expenses of the United Nations (Article 17, paragraph 2, of the Charter), Advisory Opinion of 20 July 1962, I.C.J. Reports 1962*, p. 165.

the Court's opinion that the United Nations is not entitled to do anything not expressly permitted by the Charter; it adopts the opposite view — namely, the doctrine of implied powers.[143] Mr. Vallat has quite properly pointed out that, even when the Assembly decides upon executive action, it does not have the intention of passing an enforceable decision; from a legal point of view, its resolution remains no more than a recommendation. If, for example — Vallat explains — the Assembly were to decide upon the setting up of a commission composed of nine members, from certain countries, this is obviously a recommendation to those nine countries to appoint representatives to the commission and to all other countries to cooperate with it. "Whether consciously or not", he writes, "this doctrine has often been relied upon by the Assembly and has come to be part of the constitutional law of the United Nations." [144]

Nor is any authority for the contention that the Partition Resolution is illegal to be found in the legal literature specifically devoted to an examination of the questions involved in the Assembly's recommendations — that is

---

143. See F. A. Vallat, "The Competence of the United Nations General Assembly", *R.A.D.I.,* tome 97 (Leyde, 1960), p. 268 and *passim; Lino du Qual, Les effets des résolutions des Nations Unies* (Paris, 1967), pp. 226—227; K. Skubiszewski, "The General Assembly of the United Nations and its Power to Influence National Action", *Proceedings of the American Society of International Law, April 23—25, 1964* (Washington, 1964), p. 159.

144. See Vallat, *op. cit.,* p. 256. See, too, Lino du Qual, *op. cit.,* pp. 118—119.

to say, in the works of Sloan,[145] Eagleton,[146] Johnson,[147] Brugière [148] and Lino du Qual.[149] In referring to the Resolution, Professor Viralli emphasizes that the fact that the Security Council and the Assembly eventually gave up all intention of enforcing its implementation is of little importance, for "the question here is one of political outlook and does not affect the legal validity of... [the] recommendation".[150]

The authors of the book also challenge the very content of the Resolution. They regard the proposal to partition the Mandated territory and set up two separate States there as an action which exceeds the Assembly's power.[151] But, on this point, too, their argument is legally unsound. In its Advisory Opinion on South West Africa, given in 1950, the International Court of Justice un-

145. F. B. Sloan, "The Binding Force of a Recommendation of the General Assembly", *The British Year Book of International Law*, vol. 25 (Oxford, 1948), pp. 1—33.
146. Eagleton, *op. cit.*, pp. 397—399.
147. D. H. N. Johnson, "The Effect of Resolutions of the General Assembly of the United Nations", *The British Year Book of International Law*, vol. 32 (Oxford, 1957), pp. 97—122.
148. Brugière, *op. cit.*, pp. 1—431.
149. Lino du Qual, *op. cit.*, pp. 1—274.
150. Viralli, *op. cit.*, p. 86. Professor Sibert does, it is true, raise a number of questions as to the competence of the Assembly to partition the territory of Palestine; but he, too, it would seem, does not consider the Partition Resolution illegal, for, if he had so considered, he would not have praised the Assembly for having fitted the Resolution into the network of "international relations", thereby demonstrating "a large measure of constructive audacity" (M. Sibert, *Traité de droit international public,* tome deuxième, Paris, 1951, p. 768).
151. *Colloque,* p. 97.

animously held that "the competence to determine and modify the international status... [of a Mandated territory] rests with the Mandatory, acting with the consent of the United Nations".[152] And, in fact, it was Great Britain, as the Palestine Mandatory, that raised the question of the future of that territory in the United Nations. True, in its many statements to the Assembly at the regular and special sessions of 1947 and, subsequently, at the special session of 1948, at the meetings of the Security Council and in the two Houses of Parliament, the British Government did express certain reservations when asked whether it would accept the Assembly's Resolution. But a careful study of all these statements shows conclusively that the reservations do not really refer to the actual acceptance of the Resolution, but to Britain's readiness to assume — either alone or in a major role — responsibility for its implementation. And, incidentally, from a legal standpoint, this responsibility did not even rest on the British Government — for, on the termination of the Mandate, Great Britain was under no greater duty to take steps to implement the Resolution than any other country. In a speech made in the *Ad Hoc* Committee of the Second Assembly, in 1947, the British representative, Creech-Jones, declared that "he could not easily imagine circumstances in which the United Kingdom would wish to prevent the execution of a settlement recommended by the Assembly regarding the future structure of Palestine.... It had recognized the place of

152. *I.C.J. Reports 1950,* p. 144.

international authority in settling a grave conflict of interest over Palestine;" [153] and, some months later, in his speech to the Security Council on 24 February 1948, he recalled the words of the British Foreign Minister, Mr Bevin, in Parliament, to the effect that, while Britain "cannot itself undertake, either individually or collectively in association with others, to impose [the United Nations'] decision by force", His Majesty's Government "has no intention of opposing [that] decision". Creech-Jones then reiterated that Great Britain "has loyally accepted the recommendations of the General Assembly" and went on to trace out the expenditure of life and money which Britain had sacrificed in Palestine in the course of more than twenty-five years. Referring to this as having brought his Government "infinite anxiety and trouble", he explained that this was why it was no longer prepared to assume any further responsibility for, or to participate in, the implementation of the decision by force.[154] Mr Ernest Gross, on his appearance before the International Court of Justice on behalf of Ethiopia and Liberia, in connection with the issue of South West African Mandate, analyzed and explained the British Government's position on the Palestine Partition Resolution, summing it up in these words: "The British delegate, in fact, understandably drew a distinction between

153. *G.A.O.R., Second Session, Ad Hoc Committee on the Palestinian Question* (Lake Success, 1947), p. 97.
154. *United Nations, Security Council, Official Records* (hereinafter quoted as *S.C.O.R.*), 253rd meeting, 24 February 1948, pp. 272—273.

acceptance of the General Assembly's recommendations, on the one hand, and unwillingness to bear sole responsibility for carrying them out, on the other hand." [155] It seems clear, then, that the British Government, while — for the reasons given above — showing great caution in wording its agreement to the Partition Resolution, did, at all events, agree to it. And, since the Assembly and the Mandatory have — according to the aforementioned Opinion of the Court, given in 1950 — competence to "determine and modify the international status" of a Mandated territory, there is no ground for challenging the Partition Resolution from the point of view of its content.

The authors put forward yet another reason for invalidating the Resolution and for contending that it is null and void : namely, that it is absolutely incompatible with Articles 5 [156] and 28 [157] of the Palestine Mandate. Article 5 imposed on the Mandatory the responsibility "for seeing that no Palestine territory shall be ceded or leased to, or in any way placed under the control of, the Government of any foreign Power". The sole purpose of this provision — if one does not attempt to read into it what is not there — was to prevent the Mandatory doing any thing which might affect the territorial integrity of the Mandated territory or its political independence of any foreign State. There is no hint or suggestion in it of the territorial arrangements to be made on

155. *I.C.J. Pleadings..., South West Africa, 1966,* vol. IX, p. 183.
156. *Colloque,* pp. 75, 83, 104.
157. *Ibid.,* p. 76.

the termination of the Mandate. Moreover, even when the Mandate was in force, the provision made in Article 5 applied solely to the Mandatory — not to the League of Nations itself. Indeed, there were cases in which the Council of the League did decide upon the modification of the borders of mandated territories: in 1921–1922 — with regard to that between Ruanda-Urundi and Tanganyika; and in 1930–1931 — with regard to that between Iraq and Syria.[158]

Article 28 of the Palestine Mandate stipulates: "In the event of the termination of the Mandate... the Council of the League of Nations shall make such arrangements as may be deemed necessary for safeguarding in perpetuity, under guarantee of the League, the rights secured... [in the Articles dealing with the Holy Places], and shall use its influence for securing, under the guarantee of the League, that the Government of Palestine will fully honour the financial obligations legitimately incurred by the Administration of Palestine during the period of the Mandate, including the rights of public servants to pensions or gratuities." The argument here is that, since this Article refers to "the Government" — not "Governments" — of Palestine, what was intended was the establishment of one State and, accordingly, the recommendation to set up two States constitutes an infringement of the Mandate. To interpret Article 28 as dealing with the question whether, on the termination of the Mandate, one or two States were to be set up in

158. *I.C.J. Pleadings...*, *International Status of South-West Africa*, 1950, pp. 226—227.

Palestine just does not stand to reason. The one and only purpose of the Article was to guarantee rights as to the Holy Places, and as to certain financial interests, which it was felt necessary to safeguard. The Mandate for Syria and the Lebanon, confirmed by the Council of the League of Nations only a month or so after the confirmation of the Palestine Mandate, serves to prove this point. Despite the fact that Article 1 of it expressly provides for the establishment of two independent States on the termination of that Mandate — namely, Syria and the Lebanon — Article 19, which, like Article 28 of the Palestine Mandate, deals with the guaranteeing of financial interests, uses the same expression "Government" in the singular, not the plural, in both the French and English texts — the two official languages of the League. And just as the use of the word "Government" in the Mandate for Syria and the Lebanon did not preclude the establishment of two States,[159] neither can it be held to have done so in the case of the Palestine Mandate: its use there is in no sense decisive of how the Mandate was to be terminated.

159. From time to time, the Permanent Mandates Commission of the League of Nations received petitions regarding the union of Syria and Lebanon. This is what Professor Rappard, the Commission's rapporteur, had to say on some of them in the report which he submitted in 1935: "As, moreover, the Mandate for Syria and Lebanon, while not expressly precluding the union of those two territories, does not enjoin it, it seems to me obvious that the Commission cannot endorse the view of these petitioners." See *Permanent Mandates Commission, Minutes of the Twenty-Seventh Session* (Geneva, 1935), pp. 208, 234.

The authors of the book speak of the Partition Resolution as "a surprising resolution".[160] But the truth is that it came as no surprise: ten years earlier a Royal Commission, appointed by the British Government to examine the situation in Palestine, had proposed a plan of partition. The Permanent Mandates Commission of the League of Nations devoted a special session in 1937 to clarification of all the problems arising out of the proposal and reached the conclusion that it was a positive way of solving the Palestine question.[161] In September 1937, the Council of the League authorized Great Britain to go on investigating the solution in detail. Nor was the League alone in finding no fault in the termination of a Mandate by way of partition. The United Nations' position on that issue was exactly the same. When, in 1958, the Good Offices Committee on South West Africa voiced the idea of partitioning this Mandated territory and suggested that the feasibility of partition be examined, the suggestion was not dismissed *a limine* as illegal. On the contrary, it was the subject of a long and searching debate in the Fourth Committee of the General Assembly and in the Assembly

160. *Colloque,* p. 72.
161. *Permanent Mandates Commission, Minutes of the Thirty-Second (Extraordinary) Session,* pp. 225—230. It is worth mentioning here that in 1939, after having discussed the new policy which Great Britain announced in the White Paper of that year, the Mandates Commission stated that *all* members agreed in thinking that the Partition plan should be borne in mind at the appropriate moment as one of solving the Palestine problem. See *Permanent Mandates Commission, Minutes of the Thirty-Sixth Session* (Geneva, 1939), p. 275.

itself.[162] And it should not be forgotten that, in that case, the question involved was not the establishment of two States, but a partition whereby one part of the Mandated territory was to be placed under Trusteeship, the other transferred to the Union of South Africa. Many of the participants in the debate rejected the plan, on the ground, *inter alia,* that the United Nations cannot agree to the subjection of part of the population of a Mandated territory to a regime of *apartheid,* thereby giving legal sanction — as it were — to that regime.[163] A few years later, in 1962, the General Assembly debated a proposal to establish two States — Rwanda and Burundi — in the territory of Ruanda-Urundi, on the termination of the Trusteeship under which it had been placed in December 1946; the Assembly took note of the fact that the efforts to maintain Ruanda-Urundi as a single unit had not been successful and approved the establishment of two sovereign and independent States. Among the sponsors of the draft Resolution were four Arab States, and all ten Arab States then members of the United Nations voted in favour of it. No one questioned the legality of the decision, notwithstanding the fact that there was no authority — express or implied — in the Ruanda-Urundi Trusteeship Agreement for partition of the territory.[164]

162. See *Yearbook of the United Nations, 1958* (New York, 1959), pp. 311—319.
163. See, for example, the speech of Mr Krishna Menon, India's representative in the Fourth Committee of the General Assembly in 1958. *G.A.O.R., Thirteenth Session, Fourth Committee, 13 October 1958* (New York, 1958), p. 97.
164. *Yearbook of the United Nations, 1962* (New York, 1963), pp. 455—460.

Summing up, then, it can be said that all the arguments advanced by the authors against the legality of the Partition Resolution of 29 November 1947 — both with regard to the competence of the General Assembly and from the point of view of the actual contents of the Resolution and of the Palestine Mandate itself — are completely unfounded.

VII. Non-Recognition of Israel

The book gives much space and prominence to the question of the non-recognition of Israel by the Arab States. "Israel", it says, "has not been recognized by the Arab States"; [165] Israel is "an entity which the Arab States have never recognized as a State"; [166] Israel is "simply a human entity [which], in Egypt's eyes, has never constituted a State"; [167] "in Egypt's eyes, Israel has never attained the status of [a State]" ; [168] the Arab States, refusing to recognize Israel, regard Israel as "not yet a subject of international law".[169] And it goes on to refer to "those who consider Israel a State" [170] and "the supposed 'State' of Israel".[171] The Arabs cannot even recognize Israel *de facto,* for "a state of war" exists between them "which..., on the part of the Arab States, reflects *an absolute negation of the very right of Israel to create a State".*[172] "This ['state of war'] does not signify some transient discord which can be settled by the parties.

165. *Colloque,* p. 110.
167. *Ibid.,* p. 201.
169. *Ibid.,* p. 112.
171. *Ibid.,* p. 227.

166. *Ibid.,* p. 180.
168. *Ibid.,* p. 192.
170. *Ibid.,* p. 165.
172. *Ibid.,* p. 114.

It is an absolute and fundamental negation of the very right of the Jewish community to set up a Jewish State in the Arab territory of Palestine." [173]

The question of the existence of a "state of war" will be discussed in the following section. As for non-recognition, the only conclusion to be drawn from the foregoing conglomeration of assertions is that, because the Arab States do not recognize Israel, they can treat it as if it were not a State; or, in the words of Professor Quadri, in his criticism of the constitutive doctrine of recognition : "The unrecognized State must be considered *an outlaw,* without any protection under international law, in a state of civil death, like a mere *object* of the law." [174]

It is very doubtful whether even the most extreme advocates of the constitutive theory will derive much satisfaction from the fact that such far-reaching conclusions are sought to be drawn from it — conclusions that are likely simply to derogate from any validity, which the theory may have and lay bare the absurdity of it. "The attempts to regard a State which is not recognized as legally non-existent", writes Quadri, "appear to us truly incongruous or mere political expediency.... No one, for example, could raise any doubts today as to the existence of... the State of Israel.... [A] new State, from the very fact of its existence, enjoys all the benefits deriving from general international law." [175] As Judge Sir

173. *Ibid.,* p. 115.
174. R. Quadri, "Cours général de droit international public", *R.A.D.I.,* tome 113 (Leyde, 1966), p. 447.
175. *Ibid.,* pp. 450—451. Professor Baxter, too, regards the non-

Gerald Fitzmaurice, stresses: "The extreme constitutive theory fell into disrepute, at any rate with jurists." [176] "Since... it is generally agreed by all schools of thought that the new State or member... is automatically *bound* by international law, and since the existence of an obligation necessarily entails the enjoyment of any corresponding rights, it follows that the new State or member must have the right to claim the observance of international law in respect of itself." [177] Professor Waldock points out that the "effects [of the constitutive theory] when applied to the very existence of a State are really quite inadmissible. For a State, by merely declining to recognize a new State, could logically claim that no rules of international law, not even those concerning respect for territorial sovereignty and maritime law, are in force between it and the unrecognized State." [178] And Professor Sørensen holds that "in no circumstances can the new State, which has not yet been recognized, be regarded as a non-existent entity. Its authority may be so

recognition of Israel as a "fiction"; but it is not clear why, in this context, he writes that both parties indulged in fictions, as if Israel, as well, were not ready to recognize its neighbours, or — to be precise — to enter into diplomatic relations with them, for those States were established before Israel and had no need at all of Israel's recognition. See R. Baxter, *International Waterways, With Particular Regard to Interoceanic Canals* (Cambridge, 1964), p. 209.

176. Sir Gerald Fitzmaurice, "The General Principles of International Law, Considered from the Standpoint of the Rule of Law", *R.A.D.I.*, tome 92 (Leyde, 1958), p. 25.

177. *Ibid.*, p. 17.

178. Sir Humphrey Waldock, "General Course on Public International Law", *R.A.D.I.*, tome 106 (Leyde, 1963), p. 148.

manifest that it would be absurd not to acknowledge its status as a subject of international law." [179] "The practice of States", we find in the last edition of Brierly's book, "does not support the view that they have no legal existence before recognition.... A State may exist without being recognized, and if it does exist in fact, then, whether or not it has been formally recognized by other States, it has a right to be treated by them *as a State*." [180]

In Professor Waldock's opinion, the majority of writers hold that recognition of a new State is essentially declaratory; [181] and that, it may be noted, is the accepted view not only in the Western world, but in the Eastern bloc as well.[182] The text-book on international law published by the

179. M. Sørensen, "Principes de droit international public, cours général", *R.A.D.I.,* tome 101 (Leyde, 1961), p. 132.

180. J. L. Brierly, *The Law of Nations, An Introduction to the International Law of Peace,* sixth edition, edited by Sir Humphrey Waldock (Oxford, 1963), p. 139. See also P. J. Nkambo Mugerwa: "It is generally admitted that an unrecognized State cannot be completely ignored. Its territory cannot be considered to be no-man's-land; there is no right to overfly without permission; ships flying its flag cannot be considered stateless, and so on" (in the *Manual of Public International Law,* edited in 1968 by Max Sørensen, p. 269).

181. See Waldock, *op. cit.,* p. 149. The declarative doctrine was adopted in 1936 by the Institute of International Law in a resolution on "the recognition of new States and new governments" (H. Wehberg, *Institut de droit international, tableau général des résolutions (1873—1956),* Bâle, 1957, pp. 11—13). It was also endorsed in the Convention on Rights and Duties of States, signed in Montevideo at the Seventh Conference of American States, in 1933. See M. O. Hudson, *International Legislation, A Collection of the Texts of Multipartite International Instruments of General Interest,* vol. VI (Washington, 1937), pp. 620—625.

182. *The Academy of Sciences of the U.S.S.R., Course on Inter-*

Soviet Academy of Sciences in 1967–1969 describes the declaratory theory as a "truly scientific" one,[183] whereas the constitutive theory is attributed to "reactionary circles".[184] Like many Western jurists, the authors of this text-book hold that there is a *duty* to recognize a new State. "A new sovereign and peace-loving State", they say, "no matter where it is or what the extent of its territory, the size of its population, the character of its public regime, the form of its government and of its political structure, has the right to full and unreserved recognition in accordance with the principle of equal rights." [185] To withhold recognition is, in their opinion, not only "an unfriendly act; in view of paragraphs 2 and 3 of Article 1 of the Charter of the United Nations... it is also an illegal act." [186] Professor Sørensen, who deals extensively with the duty of recognition, pays particular attention to cases such as that of the establishment of the State of Israel. "It also happens", he writes, "that a new State is set up by decision of an international organ, such as the General Assembly of the United Nations. This is especially the case wnen a trust territory attains independence. The international decision is constitutive insofar as concerns the new status of the territory, which — from the date prescribed by the international organ — is a subject of international law. If the decision is by resolution of the General Assembly, the new status binds all — both the States which

national Law, vol. III (Moscow, 1967), p. 11 (in Russian).
183. *Ibid.*, p. 9.   184. *Ibid.*, p. 10.
185. *Ibid.*, p. 26.   186. *Ibid.*, p. 12.

voted for the resolution and, equally, those which voted against it — and even, it would seem, States which are not members. Recognition is superfluous." [187]

In his book on self-defence, Bowett raises the specific question whether a State which has not been recognized enjoys the protection of Article 2, paragraph 4, of the Charter, which forbids States to use force, or the threat of force, in their international relations. Referring, *inter alia,* to the stand taken by the United Nations on the invasion of Israel's territory by the Arab States in 1948, he reaches the conclusion that the United Nations "will not interpret statehood too literally and limit the obligation of Article 2(4) to cases of attack against a recognized State; more particularly, they [the United Nations] will not allow the attacker, by withholding recognition from its victim, to evade the prohibition." [188]

These, then, are the views on recognition which prevail today in the science of international law. All that the Colloquium of Arab jurists has to say on the matter is arbitrary and with no least foundation in the rules of international law.

Discussion on the recognition of Israel necessarily gives rise to yet another question : How can the non-recognition of Israel be reconciled with the contents of the Armistice Agreements signed by the Arab States (Egypt, the Lebanon, Jordan and Syria)? It is true that each Agreement stipulates that no provision "shall in any way pre-

187. Sørensen, *op. cit.,* p. 130.
188. See D. W. Bowett, *Self-Defence in International Law* (Manchester, 1958), pp. 153—154.

judice the rights, claims and positions of either Party hereto in the ultimate peaceful settlement of the Palestine question" (Article 2, paragraph 2, of the Agreement with Jordan). But, at the same time, the express purpose of each Agreement is declared to be "to facilitate the transition from the present truce to permanent peace in Palestine" (the preamble to the Agreement with Jordan, clause 1) and "with the view to promoting the return of permanent peace in Palestine" (Article 1); both parties are stated to regard the Agreement as "an indispensable step toward the liquidation of armed conflict and restoration of peace in Palestine" (Article 1, paragraph 4); both declare that "no aggressive action by the armed forces — land, sea or air — of either Party shall be undertaken, planned, or threatened against the people of the armed forces of the other" (Article 1, paragraph 2) and that the Agreement "shall remain in force until a peaceful settlement between the Parties is achieved" (Article 12, paragraph 2). The Agreements forbid the parties to "commit any warlike or hostile act against the military or para-military forces of the other Party" or "...advance beyond or pass over for any purpose whatsoever the Armistice Demarcation Lines" (Article 3, paragraph 2). They also forbid them to revise the provisions of Article 1 or 3, even by mutual consent (Article 12, paragraph 3).

In view of these far-reaching provisions, the tendency, very rightly, has been to regard the Armistice Agreements as non-aggression treaties.[189] And the question

189. W. M. Jordan, "Recent Developments in the Handling of International Disputes", *Annual Review of United Nations*

therefore arises — as we have said — how can these commitments be reconciled with the assertion in the book that the Arab States deny the very right of the Jewish community to set up a State and will never give it their recognition? [190] Does not the undertaking to refrain from violating the armistice lines, accompanied as it was by the prohibition to alter it even by mutual consent (otherwise, of course, than in negotiations for a peace treaty), constitute recognition of the very existence of the State of Israel and of its right to continue to exist? Moreover, the Arab States themselves contend that the Agreements are still valid today. Indeed, at the Security Council meeting on 31 May 1967, the Egyptian representative dismissed Israel's claim that the Israel-Egyptian Armistice Agreement was no longer valid and proposed a formal resolution calling on the Council to confirm the existence of that Agreement and revive the Mixed Armistice Commission.[191] And, even after the Six-Day War, at the Council's session of 15 November 1967, the representative of Syria, the most radical of the Arab States in its hostile attitude towards Israel, criticized the Israel Foreign Minister's statement that the Armistice Agreements were a dead letter.[192]

Affairs, 1950 (New York, 1950), p. 69.

190. *Colloque,* p. 115.

191. *U.N. Document S/PV. 1345, 31 May 1967,* pp. 51—53.

192. *U.N. Document S/PV. 1377, 15 November 1967,* pp. 13—16. At the Security Council meeting on 30 June 1969, the Lebanese delegate, too, argued that the Armistice Agreement with his country was still in force. See *U.N. Document S/PV. 1482, 30 June 1969,* pp. 21—22.

Several writers have also pointed out how illogical and inconsistent it is to talk of non-recognition and, at the same time, assert that a "state of war" exists. Dr Brownlie mentions cases in which States were not prepared to acknowledge that they were at war with another State because they refused to recognize that other's international personality; and he adds that "Egypt and other Arab States have maintained a state of war with Israel, though they do not recognize its existence as a State".[193] Professor Verzijl even regards the Arab States' claim that they are in a "state of war" with Israel as "a clear, if tacit, admission of Israel's international personality; for, how is it possible, from a legal point of view, to be at war with a non-existent State?" [194]

VIII. The Existence of a "State of War"

As we have observed, the authors of the book assert that a "state of war" exists between the Arab States and Israel.[195] And the fundamental question arises whether the relationship of member States of the United Nations Organization leaves room for such a situation. Some years

193. I. Brownlie, *International Law and the Use of Force by States* (Oxford, 1963), p. 398 and *ibid.*, note 4.
194. Verzijl, *op. cit.*, vol. II (Leyden, 1969), p. 589.
195. See *Colloque*, p. 114. See also *ibid.*, p. 173 ("a state of war continues to govern the reciprocal relations" of Israel and the Arab States); and page 184 (the closing of the Straits of Tiran to Israel ships in May 1967 was based on "the international custom, whereby States have the right, in case of war, to exercise control over passage through straits bordering their territories").

ago, the writer published a monograph on this subject; in it, the whole range of issues involved was analyzed in detail and the conclusion reached was that the contention of the existence of a "state of war" can in no way be reconciled with the provisions of the Charter of the United Nations.[196] The provisions of Article 2, paragraph 4, prohibiting the use, or the threat, of force, are, of course, no guarantee against developments which might, in consequence of a breach of them, lead to hostilities between member States of the Organization, and even to military operations on a very wide scale. But it is impossible to maintain that, on the cessation of such hostilities (generally, by a cease-fire order of the Security Council), a State can lawfully argue that it is at war with the State with which it has been in conflict. How can the very institution which has prohibited the use of force in all forms (except for cases of self-defence and collective punitive measures) be prepared to acknowledge, explicitly or implicitly, the existence of a status basically incompatible with the prohibition that it has itself prescribed? The authors draw a distinction between a "state of war" accompanied by hostilities and one not so accompanied; the former, in their opinion, is forbidden, the latter, permissible, under the Charter.[197] There is no foundation for this distinction in current international law. A State which

196. N. Feinberg, *The Legality of a "State of War" after the Cessation of Hostilities, under the Charter of the United Nations and the Covenant of the League of Nations* (Jerusalem, 1961), pp. 1—86.
197. *Colloque,* pp. 118—119.

contends that it is at war with another State thereby gives expression to its *animus belligerendi*. "One may ask", writes Professor Wehberg, "whether a declaration of war, not immediately followed by the use of force, would be a violation of Article 2, paragraph 4. There can be no doubt that this question must be answered affirmatively, because it would be at least a *threat* to use force, which is forbidden just as the actual use of force is." [198] This approach is no less valid in respect of the declaration of the existence of a "state of war". Moreover, the distinction is not merely meaningless from a theoretical point of view; it is unfounded in practice, too. The Arabs have never qualified their assertion as to the existence of a "state of war" with a declaration that they have no intention of resorting to force; indeed, not a few express statements by official and responsible Arab factors are evidence to the contrary.[198a]

198. H. Wehberg, "L'interdiction du recours à la force, le principe et les problèmes qui se posent", *R.A.D.I.*, tome 78 (Paris, 1952), p. 73.

198a. The official Notes sent by the Governments of the United Arab Republic and Syria to the Soviet Union at the beginning of 1964, in answer to the proposal of the U.S.S.R. concerning the conclusion of a treaty on the peaceful settlement of all territorial disputes, bears this out emphatically. In the Notes, the two Arab Governments expressed their readiness to accede to the proposed treaty, but made a formal reservation, namely, that their obligations under it should not apply to their dispute with Israel. See F. Monconduit, "La Note Khrouchtchev du 13 décembre 1963 relative au règlement pacifique des litiges territoriaux", *L'Annuaire Français de Droit International,* tome X (Paris, 1964), p. 62.

It is also pertinent to recall the discussions which have been taking place since 1964 in the Special Committee on

The following sentence from the book is particularly surprising : "The doctrine now is that the argument put forward in the past, whereby membership of the United Nations is incompatible with the assertion by one member of the Organization of the existence of a 'state of war' against another member, is 'totally inadmissible' and irreconcilable with the realities of international life, even under the Charter of the United Nations."[199] The meaning

Principles of International Law concerning Friendly Relations and Cooperation among States on the prohibition of use of force, embodied in Article 2, paragraph 4, of the United Nations Charter. The four Arab States represented in the Committee (Algeria, Lebanon, Syria and the United Arab Republic) are among the States which have strongly opposed the proposal that, in the resolution to be drafted on the subject, activities forbidden in connection with State boundaries be expressly declared to extend to international lines of demarcation as well. This extension was to relate to the provisions enjoining States to refrain from the threat or use of force to violate the existing boundaries of another State; to refrain from organizing or encouraging the organization of irregular or volunteer forces or armed bands for incursions into the territory of another State; and to refrain from committing terrorist acts in another State. To meet the objection to the reference to international lines of demarcation on the theoretical ground that this would endow them with the status of permanent boundaries, those members of the Committee, who favour the extension proposed that, in the resolution to be adopted, it be clearly emphasized that such mention was without prejudice to the rights, claims or position of the parties concerned with regard to the territories in dispute. But this proposal, too, has so far proved unacceptable to the objectors. See *Special Committee on Principles of International Law...*, *Document A/6230* (1966), pp. 38—39, 46; *Document A/6799* (1967), pp. 17, 21; *Document A/7326* (1968), pp. 18, 28—30, 39—40, 43—51; *Document A/7619* (1969), pp. 13, 18, 20—23, 27—28, 37—47.

199. *Colloque*, pp. 118—119.

of the words "put forward in the past" ("l'argument jadis avancé") is not clear : are there no jurists who advocate this today? And what basis is there for the uncompromising statement that doctrine now regards the existence of a "state of war" as permissible under the Charter? In the first place, the truth of the matter is that doctrine has devoted very little attention to the subject. In a discussion of it in April 1968, at the American Society of International Law, Lauterpacht, one of the two principal lecturers, rightly stressed : "Strangely enough, the discussion of the legal consequences of Article 2 (4) has only rarely touched directly upon the question with which the present paper is primarily concerned — namely, whether... any State can still lawfully bring into being a technical condition of war." [200]

The authors cite, in support of their argument, two jurists in whose opinion the existence of a "state of war" is lawful within the framework of the United Nations.[201] But this is far from justifying the claim that doctrine *as a whole* is based on it. Thus, for example, Professor Scelle wrote, in 1957, that "once hostilities have come to an end — especially on the intervention of the international society — the state of *belligerency* must be considered as a situation no longer existent from a legal point of view, for it is contrary to a basic norm of the

200. E. Lauterpacht, "The Legal Irrelevance of the 'State of War' ", *Proceedings of the American Society of International Law, April 25—27, 1968* (Washington, 1968), p. 63.
201. The reference is to Professor R. R. Baxter and Professor Bengt Broms. See *Colloque,* pp. 180—181.

Charter".[202] And, in a more recent book by Dr Higgins — published in 1963 — we find: "The contention of any State that it acts under rights of belligerency is to be rejected as incompatible with the Charter and current international law."[203] Of the literature which has appeared since the publication of the book which we are analyzing, we may mention Lauterpacht's lecture, referred to above,[204] and, in particular, the following words of Professor Quincy Wright: "A 'state of war' is, therefore, 'outlawed'. Israel as a State and a member of the United Nations, is recognized under the Charter as the 'sovereign equal' of all other members. The Arab States as fellow members of the United Nations cannot, therefore, be in a 'state of war' with it."[205] And, returning to the question a few pages on, he holds: "The claim that a 'state of war' exists... is not valid."[206] No less unequivocal is the view expressed by Professor Verzijl. He, too, is of the opinion that the claim of the Arab States is "in no sense compatible with common membership of the United Nations."[207]

202. See *Annuaire de l'Institut de Droit International, Session d'Amsterdam,* tome 1 (Bâle, 1957), p. 581. See, too, L. Gross, "Passage through the Suez Canal of Israel-Bound Cargo and Israel Ships", *American Journal of International Law* (Washington, 1957), pp. 566—568.
203. R. Higgins, *The Development of International Law through the Political Organs of the United Nations* (Oxford, 1963), p. 216.
204. E. Lauterpacht, *op. cit.,* pp. 58—68.
205. Quincy Wright, "Legal Aspects of the Middle East Situation", *Law and Contemporary Problems,* School of Law, Duke University, vol. 33 (Durham, 1968), p. 17.
206. *Ibid.,* p. 20. See, too, *ibid.,* p. 28.
207. Verzijl, *op. cit.,* vol. II, p. 589.

XI. A Few More Unfounded Facts and Assertions and Incorrect Interpretations

As we have already emphasized, it is not the aim of this analysis to examine every statement made in the book. There are, however, a few more unfounded facts and assertions, and some incorrect interpretations, which, it is felt, cannot be passed over without at least a brief comment.

1. *The White Paper of 1939*. The authors have seen fit to stress, on two occasions, that in 1939 the British Government published a White Paper in which it imposed grave restrictions on the development of the Jewish national home.[250] But they are completely silent on the fact that the majority of the members of the Permanent Mandates Commission of the League of Nations — which was the body called upon to supervise the Mandatory Powers and see that they complied with the duties imposed upon them by the Mandates — came to the conclusion that it could not be stated that "the policy of the White Paper was in conformity with the Mandate, any contrary conclusion appearing... to be ruled out by the very terms of the Mandate and by the fundamental intentions of its authors".[251]

2. *The Partition Plan and the Special Session of the Assembly in 1948*. The convening of a special session of the General Assembly in March 1948, to discuss the possibility of placing Palestine temporarily under a trusteeship, signifies — in the opinion of the authors of the book — "the abandonment of the partition plan".[252] The Assembly was, it is true, convened for the purpose

---

250. *Colloque*, pp. 55, 59.
251. *Permanent Mandates Commission, Minutes of the Thirty-Sixth Session*, p. 275.
252. *Colloque*, pp. 91, 92. And, incidentally, the Assembly was not convened for the purpose of "finding a solution for the Palestine problem" — yet the words "finding a solution" are given in quotation marks — but "to consider further the question of the future Government of Palestine" (*G.A.O.R., vol. I, Plenary Meetings*, p. V).

mentioned; but a formal proposal to set up a Trusteeship regime in Palestine was never moved, and all that came before the Assembly's First Committee was a working paper drafted by the Government of the United States.[253] Moreover, when that Government realized that temporary trusteeship did not attract support, it dropped the idea. Even when the representative of the United States first broached it, in his speech to the First Committee, he expressly emphasized that "the temporary trusteeship should not be considered as a substitute for the plan of partition"; [254] and the representative of the Soviet Union declared, in the Assembly, that, even if a decision had been reached in favour of a temporary Trusteeship, "that would in no way affect the partition decision, which remained valid".[255] And, it should be noted, not only was the Partition Resolution not revoked by the special session of the Assembly; on the contrary, when the news of the proclamation of the State of Israel was received at its last meeting, on 14 May 1948, the President of the Assembly marked the occasion by declaring that the Assembly "must greet the advent of a new free people to the concert of nations".[256]

3. *The Arab Invasion of Israel in 1948.* The authors seek to justify the invasion of the State of Israel by the Arab armies as follows: On the creation of the State of

253. See *Yearbook of the United Nations, 1947—1948*, p. 259.
254. *G.A.O.R., Second Session, vol. II, Main Committees,* p. 9.
255. See *ibid., vol. I, Plenary Meetings,* p. 38. See, too, *ibid., vol. II, Main Committees,* p. 119.
256. *Ibid., vol. I, Plenary Meetings,* p. 47.

Israel on 15 May 1948, the Palestinian Arabs appealed
to the Arab States "to come to their help and maintain
order in Palestine", and this appeal was made on the
part of representative organs — the Supreme Arab Committee and the Government of all Palestine.[257] Even if this
description were in accordance with the facts, it could
in no sense minimize the patently aggressive character
of the invasion. The truth of the matter is that the decision to send troops into Israel was made by the Arab
States not after the establishment of the State of Israel,
but before the approval of the Partition Plan. We refer
here to the secret decision reached by the Political Committee of the Arab League on 19 September 1947, at
Sofar in the Lebanon.[258] As for the "Government of all
Palestine", it was only set up on 23 September 1948,[259]
that is to say four months *after* the establishment of the
State of Israel — so there could be no appeal on the
part of that body in May 1948. These two facts are unchallengeable : they are recorded by Boutros Ghali, Professor at Cairo University, in his monograph on the Arab
League, which — as he himself acknowledges in it — was
written on the strength of a study in the generally inac-
cessible archives of the League.[260]

257. *Colloque,* p. 116.
258. B. Y. Boutros-Chali, *The Arab League, 1945—1955,* International Conciliation, No. 498 (New York, 1954), p. 411. See
also idem, "La crise de la Ligue Arabe", *Annuaire Français
de Droit International,* tome XIV (Paris, 1968), p. 106.
259. *Ibid.,* p. 412.
260. See *ibid.,* p. 394. See, too, the foreword to that number by
the editor of the "International Conciliation" series.

The second reason given in justification of the invasion is equally characteristic. The disorder in Palestine — it is claimed — "presented a real threat to the other Arab States themselves" and, therefore, "gave them the legitimate right of self-defence under Article 51 of the Charter".[261] This is an extremely strange contention not only from a legal point of view, but no less so factually, for the Arabs were sure that they would have no difficulty at all in overcoming the poor defence forces of the State of Israel — which had only just been created and had, as yet, no organized army — and wiping it out. The measure of their confidence in a speedy victory over Israel is attested by the following words of Azzam Pasha, Secretary-General of the Arab League, uttered in Cairo on the proclamation of the State : "This will be a war of extermination and a momentous massacre which will be spoken of like the Mongolian massacres and the Crusades." [262]

261. *Colloque,* p. 116.
262. *B.B.C. News Broadcast, May 15, 1948.* On the eve of the Six-Day War also, the Arabs were sure of their imminent victory: "The Arab people", declared President Nasser, for example, on 25 May 1967, "is firmly resolved to wipe Israel off the map and to restore the honour of the Arabs of Palestine" (*U.N. Document A/PV. 1526, 19 June 1967,* p. 41); and, a few days later, on 31 May, Ahmed Shukeiry, the then head of the Palestine Liberation Organization, when asked what would happen to native-born Israelis if the Arab attack succeeded, replied — "Those who survive will remain in Palestine. I estimate that none of them will survive" (see Th. Draper, "Israel and World Politics", *Commentary,* vol. 44, No. 2, New York, 1967, pp. 35—36 — quoted from a monitored radio broadcast).

4. *Zionism — A "Colonial" Movement.* The Zionist movement is defined in the book as "a movement of colonialist inspiration" [263] and the State of Israel as "a colonial fact", [264] "a colonial phenomenon", [265] "a colonial phenomenon of aggression", [266] "the most recent product of European colonialism and expansionism in the nineteenth and twentieth centuries". [267] The authors do, indeed, acknowledge that Israel "is not perhaps the purest and most perfect product [of colonialism] in this sense, that real, true politicologues would hesitate to attach the colonialist label to the Israeli phenomenon..."; [268] but, it is, for them, without any doubt, "a beach-head of the capitalist world in the midst of the undeveloped world". Israel is even accused of being "the ally of the capitalist Powers". [269] We have already dwelt on the fact that the Zionist movement, as the liberation movement of the Jewish people, was created with a view to restoring to that people normal conditions of national life in its historic homeland. It may be that, in attaching the "colonialist" label, the authors meant that Britain's own imperial interests were among the factors which moved the British Government to make the Balfour Declaration. But since when does a humanitarian project cease to be humanitarian and become reprehensible simply because those who support it are likely to derive some political benefit as a result of their support? Was there

263. *Colloque,* p. 45.
264. *Ibid.,* p. 44.
265. *Ibid.,* p. 110.
266. *Ibid.,* p. 216.
267. *Ibid.,* p. 43.
268. *Ibid., loc. cit.*
269. *Ibid.,* p. 57.

no justification for the war against the slave trade in the middle of the nineteenth century simply because Britain was likely to strengthen its domination of the seas in consequence of its part in it? And was not the termination of the slaughter of Armenians in the Ottoman Empire, at the end of the nineteenth century, a clearly humanitarian enterprise, even though selfish imperialist considerations moved the Powers to intervene?

It is equally difficult to grasp the legal significance of the claim that Israel is a State which maintains friendly relations [270] with capitalist Governments. What norm of international law is violated by such relations? Are not States bound by Articles 1 and 2 of the Charter of the United Nations and by the principle of "co-existence" to maintain peaceful relations with all other States?

5. *Zionism as "Aggression"*. As we have already said, Zionism, in the opinion of the authors of the book, is a "colonial phenomenon of *aggression*"; [271] and in yet another passage they say: "The very existence of Israel is an aggression." [272] Here, too, one's understanding fails to appreciate the true meaning of the words. Who, in effect, is here accused of aggression? Is it the League of Nations for having entrusted the Mandatory Power with the task of setting up a national home in Palestine for the Jewish people and for having supervised the im-

270. "Friendly relations" has been preferred to the term "ally", for it is well-known that Israel is not a member of any of the existing military alliances.
271. *Colloque,* p. 216 (italics added).
272. *Ibid.,* p. 118.

plementation of this international obligation for nearly twenty years? Or, perhaps, the United Nations, which — as a compromise between two conflicting national claims — found the partition of Palestine, and the establishment of a Jewish State in one part of it, a just and reasonable solution? Or is it the United States and the Soviet Union as the principal promoters of the Partition plan — the Soviet Union having supported partition even during the deliberations on the postponement of its implementation and on the placing of Palestine under a temporary trusteeship?

6. *The Question of Dual Nationality*. The authors argue that Israel "arrogates to itself rights over Jews throughout the world"; [273] that "fourteen million Jews, dispersed all over the world, are — *whether they like it or not* — governed by Israel and its powerful organs, thanks to a dual political allegiance, which many of them willingly accept, sometimes going so far as to reverse the order of priority in favour of Israel".[274] Or, in other words, the Jews conduct themselves — they say — as "dual nationals and even as Israelis first and foremost"; [275] "the Israeli conception of nationality [is] purely imperialistic" and reminds one of the infamous German Law of Delbrück of 1913.[276] The allusion here is to an enactment allowing every German citizen to hold, in addition to his German nationality, that of another State. There is, in fact, nothing new in this assertion; it was continuously and persistently advanced by the Arabs in

273. *Ibid.*, p. 39. 274. *Ibid.*, p. 203.
275. *Ibid.*, p. 208. 276. *Ibid.*, p. 42.

connection with the setting up of the national home at the time of the Mandate. And Professor Scelle had this to say about it, more than forty years ago: "It is quite wrong to attribute to the Jewish home the risk of a return to the abuses of the Law of Delbrück." [277] It is true that the State of Israel today calls on world Jewry — in much the same way that the Zionist Organization did, in the past, with regard to the national home — to join the ranks of those building Israel, to settle in Israel and to contribute to the development and strengthening of the State.[278] But it has never regarded Jews living outside its

---

277. See Scelle, *Palestine,* 1928, p. 107.
278. The Law of the Return, of 1950, which recognizes the right of every Jew to immigrate to Israel and acquire Israel nationality, is defined in the book as "one of the most reactionary documents in the world" (*Colloque,* p. 38). It is difficult to grasp what is wrong with the Law. Already in Articles 6 and 7 of the Palestine Mandate, which was — after all — drafted by the League of Nations and not by the Government of Israel, the Mandatory was required "to facilitate Jewish immigration" into Palestine and "the acquisition of Palestinian citizenship by Jews who take up their permanent residence in Palestine". Could the State of Israel, on its establishment as the national home of the Jewish people, have reasonably been expected not to draw the conclusions naturally deriving from its very creation? It is interesting to note that yet another people — the Armenians — whose position is, in more than one respect, similar to that of the Jews, also conducts propaganda for the return of its sons to their homeland, Armenia; and, in doing so, it is encouraged and supported by the Soviet authorities. We may pertinently cite here a passage from an article published in Pravda on 12 January 1966; in it, an Armenian journalist greets the arrival of the ship 'Armenia' at a Russian port: "... Aboard this ship there were many Armenians once doomed to the cruel fate of a life far away from the homeland, who

borders as tied to it in any political or legal sense. All the statements made by the Government of Israel are clearly based on this conception.[279]

had built nests on foreign soil under foreign skies, people in whose hearts a song of yearning had always sounded, in whose eyes there always lived the reflection of a cherished dream — to see reborn Armenia.

"And now they are arriving, from great distances, in Soviet Armenia, some to live permanently, some to see relatives, some as tourists, simply to soothe the yearning for their native land and to enjoy the sweet 'smoke of the fatherland'.

"... Soviet Armenia has today become that promised land upon which are fixed the eyes of the Armenians scattered all over the world, that sacred land, that holy land to which their yesterdays are bound. Nearly 200,000 Armenians have returned to Armenia. This is a historical process of gathering and uniting a nation..." (M. Decter, "Silence and Yearning: A Report and Analysis of the Status of Soviet Jewry", *Congress bi-Weekly,* vol. 33, No. 16, New York, 1966, p. 37).

279. It should be mentioned that, on the acceptance of Israel as a member of the United Nations, M. Sharett, in his maiden speech to the General Assembly at its plenary meeting on 11 May 1949, declared that "the State of Israel claimed no allegiance from Jews in other lands. As a sovereign entity it rested on the loyalty of its own citizens and was alone responsible for its actions and policies" (*G.A.O.R. Third Session, Part II, Plenary Meetings,* New York, 1949, p. 332). We should also recall that, in explaining to the Knesset, on 5 May 1952, the Bill on the status to be granted to the World Zionist Organization in Israel, Mr Ben-Gurion, then Prime Minister, emphasized that "every Jew [living outside Israel] is subject, like the non-Jew, to the laws and the policy of his country, but his ties with the other members of his people are subject to the free will and the personal inclination of each and every Jew" (see *Divrei HaKnesset, Second Knesset, First Session, 5—7 May 1952,* No. 27, p. 1890). Nor is it out of context to refer to the agreement signed in 1950 (and reconfirmed in 1961) between Mr Ben-

7. *The Refugee Question.* While denying the binding force of the Partition Resolution on the grounds that resolutions of the Assembly are only recommendations, the authors nevertheless build their pleading on the refugee question on the binding force of the Resolution of 11 December 1948. To overcome the patent inconsistency in their approach, they contend that the latter Resolution is declarative, not constitutive. "In demanding the restoration of the refugees", it is said, "the Arab States invoke a *right* recognized by the General Assembly"; [280] "[Israel] wants to evade the duties with which is has been encharged by international law...." [281] The words "a right recognized by the General Assembly" refer to Article 13, paragraph 2, of the Universal Declaration of Human Rights of 1948, which proclaims the right of every man "to return to his country".[282] The resort to this argument is very surprising, for there is complete consensus of opinion in the legal literature that the Universal Declaration is not a legally binding document. One need only mention the names of a few of the renowned jurists who express this view : Kelsen,[283] Lauter-

Gurion and Mr Blaustein, one of the leading spokesmen of American Jewry; it was stressed that the State of Israel represents only the Jews living within its boundaries and that it is neither its wish nor intention to interfere in any way in the internal affairs of the Jewish communities abroad (*Jerusalem Post,* No. 10020, 2 May 1961).
280. *Colloque,* p. 99.
281. *Ibid.,* p. 141.
282. *Ibid.,* p. 142.
283. Kelsen, *op. cit.,* p. 40.

pacht,[284] Charles de Visscher,[285] Guggenheim [286] and Giraud.[287] Moreover, if the authors of the book really believe that refugees have a right to return by virtue of the Declaration, then the question arises : Why do they ignore the express provision of the International Covenant on Civil and Political Rights, unanimously drafted by the Assembly in 1966 and submitted to the States for their signature — so that those which sign and ratify it will be bound by it? Article 4 of that Covenant provides that a State which is a party to it is entitled, *in time of public emergency,* not to perform the obligations undertaken (apart from a few, of which the right to return is not one).[288] Surely, in view of what they have to say about the very existence of the State of Israel being an abhorrent crime and about the fate awaiting it, the authors will not challenge the fact that Israel is in a state of emergency, or of "public emergency which threatens the life of the nation", in the words of the said Article.

Another point totally ignored in the book is that

284. Hersch Lauterpacht, "The Universal Declaration of Human Rights", *The British Year Book of International Law,* vol. 25 (1948), pp. 354—381. See also idem, *International Law and Human Rights* (London, 1950), p. 419.

285. Ch. de Visscher, *Théories et réalités en droit international public,* troisième édition (Paris, 1960), p. 165.

286. P.Guggenheim, *Traité de droit international public,* tome 1 (Genève, 1953), p. 303.

287. E. Giraud, "Le droit international public et la politique", *R.A.D.I.,* tome 110 (Leyde, 1966), p. 756.

288. *Resolutions Adopted by the General Assembly during its Twenty-First Session, 1966, Official Records, Supplement No. 16 (A/6316)* (New York, 1967), p. 53.

Article 11 of the 1948 Resolution, which deals with the return of refugees who so desire, or the payment of compensation to those who do not, allows for the return only of refugees "wishing to... live in peace with their neighbours", and even this — not at once, but "at the earliest practicable date". What is more, that provision constitutes but a small part of a resolution comprising no less than fifteen clauses, which together are a single whole; and one of those clauses calls on the parties "to seek agreement by negotiations conducted either by the Conciliation Commission or directly, with the view to the final settlement of all questions outstanding between them",[289] a demand which the Arab States have refused to comply with up to the present day.

The book attributes Israel's objection to the return of the refugees to its adherence to the principle of "auto-segregation... [which] also implies *racial exclusivism*".[290] Professor Giraud's explanation of that objection is, surely, far more convincing. In his lectures at the Academy of International Law in 1963, after stressing that "numerous and categorical declarations on the part of the Arab Governments have made it clear that their objective is the very destruction of Israel", he goes on : "The resettlement of the Arab refugees in Israel, creating — as it would — insoluble difficulties and weakening considerably the political and military power of Israel — would, it

289. *G.A.O.R., Third Session, Part I, 1948, Resolutions* (Paris, 1948), pp. 21—25.
290. *Colloque,* p. 209.

seems, be only one stage towards the final objective, which is the destruction of the State of Israel." [291]

8. *Jerusalem*. In the chapter of the book devoted to Jerusalem, the fact is emphasized that Jerusalem is "an Arab City",[292] "above all an Arab City",[293] "an authentic Arab City".[294] It is also asserted that this "holy city", in which "a spirit of tolerance and respect for all communities formerly prevailed, is now subject to the op-

291. See Giraud, *R.A.D.I.*, tome 110, p. 513, note 38. Already over twenty years ago, the Egyptian Foreign Minister, Salah-el-Din, declared that, "in demanding the return of the Palestinian refugees, the Arabs mean their return as masters, not slaves; or, to put it quite clearly — the intention is the extermination of Israel" (the Egyptian daily *Al-Misri*, Cairo, 11 October 1949). And President Nasser, too, in an interview with the correspondent of *Zürcher Woche* on 1 September 1961, stated that "if the refugees return to Israel — Israel will cease to exist". Six years later, Abdullah el-Yafi, Prime Minister of the Lebanon, did not hesitate to admit in the Lebanese House of Representatives that "the day on which the Arab hope for the return of the refugees to Palestine is realized will be the day of Israel's extermination (the *El-Hayat* newspaper, Beirut, 29 April 1966). It is in place to add that Professor Henri Rolin, in his speech to the Belgian Senate on 8 June 1967, expressed his astonishment that the neighbouring Arab States, and the Muslim countries which declare their solidarity with them, despite a total population of some 200 million, had not yet been able to absorb one and a half million Arab refugees. "The Arab countries", in his opinion, "must give up fostering a kind of permanent abscess and maintaining this new ghetto of refugees, in which a germ of revenge and reconquest [of Palestine] is nourished." See *Sénat — Annales parlementaires, No. 58, Séance du jeudi 8 juin 1967* (Bruxelles, 1967), pp. 1537—1538.
292. *Colloque,* pp. 126, 134, 135.
293. *Ibid.,* p. 127.
294. *Ibid.,* pp. 128, 134.

pressive rule of a partisan State. The Arabs — Muslims and Christians alike — are in danger, and access to the Holy Places is under the frightening shadow of Israel's fanaticism".[295]

This claim as to the city's Arab character is wholly unfounded, as the figures on the composition of Jerusalem's population in the last hundred years unarguably prove.[296] And if the meaning of the authors is that Jerusalem is one of Islam's three Holy Places, they cannot deny that it does not have the standing reserved for the other two. In his lectures at the Academy of International Law in the Hague in 1966, on the principles of international law in the light of Islamic doctrine, the Lebanese jurist, Professor Mahmassani, pointed out that Muslim jurists and publicists divided the world into two large territories : dar-al-Islam and dar-al-harb. Dar-al-Islam, which is the territory of Islam, is of three categories : the "Holy Lands" — Mecca and Medina; Hedjaz; and the remaining Islam lands — that is to say, "the countries which are subject to the sovereignty of [an] Islamic State or States and are governed by Islamic law". The name of Jerusalem is not even mentioned in this context in Professor Mahmassani's lectures.[297]

295. *Ibid.,* p. 130.
296. See Julius Stone, *No Peace — No War in the Middle East, Legal Problems of the First Year* (Sydney, 1969), pp. 19—20. See also, on the deliberations in the United Nations on Jerusalem since 1947, E. Lauterpacht, *Jerusalem and the Holy Places* (London, 1968), pp. 13—36.
297. S. Mahmassani, "The Principles of International Law in the Light of Islamic Doctrine", *R.A.D.I.,* tome 117 (Leyde, 1967), pp. 250—251.

As for "the spirit of tolerance and respect for all communities" which the authors so proudly acclaim, the undeniable fact is that, throughout the period of its rule in East Jerusalem, Jordan prevented Israel from "free access to the Holy Places and cultural institutions and use of the cemetery on the Mount of Olives", in patent breach of Article 8, paragraph 2, of its Armistice Agreement with Israel. Nor was that all, for, in that same period, Jordan destroyed thousands of Jewish graves in Jerusalem and Hebron and used the tombstones for the purposes of army camps, roads, stables and even latrines;[298] while, in the Old City, it demolished no fewer than thirty-four of the thirty-five ancient synagogues there and desecrated Scrolls of the Law and other religious articles.[299]

9. *The Gulf of Aqaba and the Straits of Tiran.* The first reason put forward in the book to justify the closing of the Straits of Tiran to Israel ships is that, from a legal point of view, Israel is not a riparian State of the Gulf of Aqaba, having conquered Eilat after signing the Armistice Agreement with Egypt and in breach of that Agreement.[300] But the truth is that, in Article 7 of the Agreement, it was expressly stipulated that it did not

298. See *Survey of the Committee [appointed by the Jerusalem Municipal Corporation] to Examine the Desecration of the Mount of Olives and Hebron Cemeteries* (with photographs) (Jerusalem 1967), pp. 1—32 (in Hebrew).
299. See *Desecration,* Ministry for Foreign Affairs (Jerusalem, 1967). See also *U.N. Document A/7064/Add. 1, 6 March 1968,* and *Document S/PV. 1482, 30 June 1969,* pp. 36—37.
300. *Colloque,* pp. 170—174.

constitute a settlement of the issues pertaining to areas comprising the Eastern Front (that is to say, including Eilat); those issues, it was provided, would be dealt with in a separate agreement with a third party — namely, Jordan. And, in fact, by the terms of the Armistice Agreement with Jordan — signed on 3 April 1949, when Eilat was already in Israel's hands — and according to the maps appended to it, Eilat remained a part of Israel's territory. The question has been most carefully studied in the articles of Professor Gross [301] and Dr Lapidoth,[302] who also examine, and bring forward factual material and substantive reasons to disprove, the other Arab arguments on this matter — that the Gulf of Aqaba is "an historic bay", "a national gulf", "a *mare clausum*".

10. *Israel — "An Aggressor State"*. Israel is accused in the book of having been the aggressor "in each one of the three major armed confrontations — in 1948, 1956 and 1967", and each time "the hostilities brought with them territorial aggrandisement [for Israel]".[303]

301. Leo Gross, "The Geneva Conference on the Law of the Sea and the Rights of Innocent Passage through the Gulf of Aqaba", *American Journal of International Law,* vol. 53 (Washington, 1959), pp. 564—594; idem, "Passage through the Strait of Tiran and in the Gulf of Aqaba", *Law and Contemporary Problems,* Duke University, vol. 33, pp. 125—146.

302. R. Lapidoth, "Le passage par le Détroit de Tiran", *Revue générale de droit international public,* tome 73, No. 1 (Paris, 1969), pp. 30—51. See also Sh. Rosenne, "Directions for a Middle East Settlement — Some Underlying Legal Problems", *Law and Contemporary Problems,* Duke University, vol. 33, pp. 62—64.

303. *Colloque,* p. 204.

With regard to the War of 1948, the authors themselves confess that is was the Arab States which opened the fighting. And Trygve Lie, who was Secretary-General of the United Nations at the time, even awarded it a "place of honour", for — as he puts it — "the invasion of Palestine by the Arab States was the first armed aggression which the world had seen since the end of the [Second World] War".[304]

As for the Sinai Campaign of 1956, this was Israel's response to the operations of the armed gangs of fedayun, which, throughout the first eight years of Israel's existence, were continually sent to carry out acts of murder and sabotage within its borders; to the denial of free passage through the Suez Canal and the Straits of Tiran; to Egypt's repcated declarations that it was at war with Israel; and to its open and concealed threats to destroy the State of Israel and wipe it off the map.[305] In an article published in 1963 on the "Prohibition of the Use of Force — Theory and Practice of the United Nations", Professor Giraud enumerated fifteen cases in which States had resorted to force in violation of the Charter; Israel does not appear in that list. "Israel's position with regard to the United Arab Republic", he writes, "was different [from that of France and Britain]. It had

---

304. Trygve Lie, *In the Cause of Peace, Seven Years with the United Nations* (New York, 1954), p. 174.
305. See the speeches of Israel's Foreign Minister in the Security Council and the General Assembly: *S.C.O.R., 749th meeting, 30 October 1956,* pp. 8—18; *G.A.O.R., First Emergency Special Session, Plenary Meetings and Annexes* (New York, 1956), pp. 20—25.

grounds for complaining of the use of limited, but real force against it...." [306] Professor Quincy Wright, too, does not define the Sinai Campaign as an act of aggression. Having examined the reasons given by Israel in justification of the action as one of self-defence, he reaches the conclusion that "all these considerations involve difficult questions of law and fact which would seem to invite judicial inquiry". [307]

Finally, insofar as the Six-Day War is concerned, suffice it to refer here to what the eminent Belgian jurist, Professor Henri Rolin, had to say: "In the application of rules of law, I consider myself a scrupulous and objective jurist. And I hereby declare that, when the acts of war I have mentioned were accompanied by declarations such as those I have just read to you [passages from speeches of President Nasser and others], they constituted a grave and imminent threat to Israel, placing it in a legitimate position of self-defence.

"If one of us were to see his home the object of nightly attacks and bullets piercing his window-panes — and if, on one occasion, when the incident was accompanied by cries of 'death' and 'kill him', he were to go out armed with a gun to disperse the aggressors — I assure you that no tribunal, no court of law in Belgium, would refuse to vindicate his action on grounds of self-defence.

---

306. Giraud, "L'interdiction du recours à la force — la théorie et la pratique des Nations Unies", *Revue générale de droit international public,* 3e série, tome 34 (Paris, 1963), p. 533, note 20.
307. Quincy Wright, "Intervention, 1956", *American Journal of International Law,* vol. 51 (Washington, 1957), p. 271.

Israel — I am convinced — was in just that position...." [308]

Nor should it be forgotten that the United Nations — both in the Security Council and at the special session of the General Assembly convened immediately after the Six-Day War — rejected all the proposals demanding that the State of Israel be declared aggressor. Even the cease-fire order issued by the Security Council on 6 June 1967 did not call on Israel to return to the *status quo ante*; and no proposal in this direction was adopted in the special session of the Assembly. Clearly, if the members of the United Nations had been of the opinion that this was a case of aggression, they would have ordered the immediate restoration of the position prevailing before the War.

11. *Annexation of Territory*. Some of the statements in the book lead one to ask oneself whether they were really made in earnest. In their summing up, for example, the authors return to their contention that Israel wants to settle fourteen million Jews in Palestine. [309] "Slowly but surely", they say, "we shall witness a progres-

---

308. See Rolin, *Annales parlementaires*, pp. 1535—1536. Professor Quincy Wright, who holds both Egypt and Israel responsible for the Six-Day War, comments *inter alia*: "...It would appear that the well-authenticated acts of Egypt, especially its insistence that a 'state of war' existed and its policy to terminate the existence of Israel, accompanied by the closure of the Straits of Tiran and extensive mobilizations on the Israel frontier, could be regarded as amounting to an 'armed attack' on Israel" (Quincy Wright, *Law and Contemporary Problems*, Duke University, p. 27).

309. *Colloque*, p. 205.

sive *Anschluss* of divers Arab States, all of them members
of the United Nations, their sovereignty and territorial
integrity guaranteed by international law; yet it is uncertain whether the international community will put
a stop to the aggression or impose sanctions on the aggressor." [310] Mohammed Bedjaoui, in his speech of welcome to the participants in the Colloquium, went as far
as to list the territories that Israel would annex as follows :
"Israel — encouraged by its present successes — cherishes
the hope of annexing, little by little, Syria, Jordan, Lebanon, Iraq and part of the United Arab Republic." [311]
One thing is not clear — why he says only "part of the
United Arab Republic", not the whole of it. The authors,
at all events, do not just make do with guesses as to the
future; they categorically assert that "[the Zionists] disregarding the rules of the law of war and military occupation, *have annexed* Syrian, Jordanian and Egyptian territories...".[312] That these words are no mere slip of the
pen can be seen from the following two phrases : "the
annexations carried out in 1967";[313] "the extensive Arab
territories *annexed* in *June 1967*".[314] Here, again, we
may ask : How can responsible jurists unhesitatingly make
assertions which they know — or ought to know — are
wildly unfounded? [315] Israel did, it is true, decide upon

310. *Ibid.*, p. 207.
311. *Ibid.*, p. 18.
312. *Ibid.*, p. 124 (italics added).
313. *Ibid.*, p. 212 (italics added).
314. *Ibid.*, p. 205 (italics added).
315. See J. Dehaussy, "La crise du Moyen-Orient et l'O.N.U.",
     Journal de droit international, tome 95 (Paris, 1968), p. 878.

the administrative union of East and West Jerusalem; but
it did nothing that could be regarded as annexation
of the territories occupied in the defensive war of June
1967.[316] Israel has accepted the Security Council's Resolution of 22 November 1967 [317] and its only demands are
that the "secure and recognized boundaries" referred to
in that Resolution be determined in direct negotiations
between the parties concerned; that all the other issues
still to be settled find their solution in those negotiations;
and that the "just and lasting peace", of which the Resolution speaks, be achieved. In the last session of the
General Assembly, in 1969, the Israel Foreign Minister,
Mr Eban, renewed his appeal to the Arab States to enter
into negotiations — without any prior conditions — for
the settlement of the conflict. In unequivocal terms, he
emphasized that "the word 'non-negotiable' is not a part
of Israel's vocabulary. You ask: 'What can be discussed
and proposed in these negotiations?' I answer: 'Everything'. You ask: 'What is excluded from discussion?' I
answer: 'Nothing'." [318] True, the Government of Israel is
not prepared to withdraw from the cease-fire lines until
the Arab States display their readiness to recognize the
existence of Israel, repudiate their three 'nos', adopted at
the Khartoum Conference of 1 September 1967 — no
peace, no recognition, no negotiation — and agree to
maintain relations with Israel, in accordance with the

316. Stone, *op. cit.,* pp. 17—21.
317. See *U.N. Document A/PV. 1686, 8 October 1968,* p. 41. See
     also *U.N. Document A/PV. 1418, 1 May 1968,* pp. 68—70.
318. *U.N. Document A/PV. 1757, 19 September 1969,* p. 93.

Charter of the United Nations. But, as Dr Higgins rightly points out : "There is nothing in either the Charter or general international law which leads one to suppose that military occupation, pending a peace treaty, is illegal. The Allies, it will be recalled, did not claim title to Berlin in 1945; but neither did they withdraw immediately they had entered it. The law of military occupation, with its complicated web of rights and duties, remains entirely relevant, and until such time as the Arab nations agree to negotiate a peace treaty, Israel is in legal terms entitled to remain in the territories she now holds." [319]

Conclusion

The Colloquium of Arab jurists was, as we have already seen, held with a view "to analyzing the legal problems involved in the Palestine question". In their foreword, the authors stress that they can offer no "magical solution [to those problems]. To find the solutions is the task and the honour of the statesmen".[320] A study of the book hardly verifies this statement, for one finds in it the formulation of principles and dogmas whose practical political meaning is plain. Of primary importance in this regard is the second paragraph of the

319. R. Higgins, "The June War : The United Nations and Legal Background", *Journal of Contemporary History*, vol. 3, No. 3 (London, 1968), p. 271. See also Quincy Wright, *Law and Contemporary Problems*, Duke University, p. 24.
320. *Colloque*, p. 8.

first article of the Resolution drafted at the Algiers meeting; it reads as follows: "...the nature of the birth of Israel, on a basis not recognized by international law, is not such as to give rise to a normal state of affairs, attracting the protection guaranteed by international law to legal situations." [321] The content of this provision is absolutely unambiguous: it is an assertion — no more and no less — that the State of Israel does not enjoy the protection of the rules of international law; and the consequence is that the Arab States have the right to conduct themselves towards Israel and act against it without being bound by any of the norms of international law. Mr Bedjaoui was even prepared to declare openly that the Arabs "are stead-fastly determined to destroy Israel as a State and political entity set up on Arab soil". [322]

And the question arises: How does one destroy a State without resorting to violence and infringing the Charter of the United Nations and the most fundamental norms of international law? It simply does not stand to reason that those taking part in the Algiers Colloquium could have thought it conceivable that the State of Israel would agree to give up its independence of its own free will and — as it were — commit suicide. Professor Verzijl rightly stressed in his last article in 1969 that the existence of the State of Israel "is an irreversible fact, however unpalatable to the Arabs, and an indubitable legal phenomenon that can no longer be denied". [323]

321. *Ibid.*, p. 217.
322. *Ibid.*, p. 226.
323. Verzijl, *op. cit.*, vol. II, p. 564.

The book which we have analyzed was not written to uphold one particular interpretation of a given provision of a certain treaty. Its manifest purpose is to provide a legal basis for the denial of the very right of a State to exist — with all that this involves. It is a sad and extremely distressing fact that, in their deliberations in Algiers, the Arab jurists not only failed to contribute to the advancement of peace and understanding between the Arab States and Israel; they have not even refrained from abusing international law by turning it into a means of forwarding the anti-Israel policies of their countries. The attempt is made — openly in Bedjaoui's speech, by innuendo in the book itself — to justify, legally and in a supposedly scientific manner, the extinction of a State set up with the support and encouragement of the two central institutions of mankind (the League of Nations and the United Nations Organization), a State which has been in existence for twenty-one years, is a member of the United Nations and maintains friendly diplomatic and consular relations with some hundred countries throughout the world. The attempt was doomed to failure from the very outset.

Errata: (1) On p. 391, n. 10, l. 8, insert "did not think he" at the beginning of the line.
(2) On p. 399, l. 13, "76" should read "78" and, on l. 14, "78" should read "80".
(3) On p. 418, ll. 25-26, read "When U.N.S.C.O.P. heard the Arab arguments on the illegality of the Mandate, it dismissed them, being of the opinion that . . . ."
(4) On p. 457, n. 192, l. 5, read "*1498, 13 August 1969*, p. 11."

The Palestinian Arab Resistance Movement:
Its Significance in the Middle East Crisis

MICHAEL HUDSON

T HE MOST IMPORTANT consequence thus far of the 1967 Arab-Israeli war has been the emergence of the Palestinian resistance movement as a major factor in the Middle East. Neither Israel, the Arab states, nor the great powers can any longer ignore its existence and significance, for it has shown that it can affect the interests, if not the destinies, of them all. The Palestinian guerrillas helped trigger the June war[1] and have effectively reactivated the Palestinian Arab struggle against Israel. They have flourished, not withered, under massive Israeli retaliations and have shown that they can maintain a level of sabotage and terrorism too high for Israel to shrug off as unimportant. While several Arab governments have been plunged into disrepute as a result of the war, the Palestinian partisan organizations have themselves attained a degree of political legitimacy and popularity throughout the Arab states whether "conservative" or "radical"—a fact significant for the future internal political development in the Arab world. The Palestinian organizations, by exacerbating the risks of a Middle East confrontation, are beginning to draw the attention of the great powers to their long-standing grievances not simply as refugees, but as a political community with national aspirations. Today the Palestinians, for better or worse, have a renewed sense of political identity and are developing effective organizations for political and military action.

These are among the conclusions that emerge from extensive interviews with members of the Palestinian partisan organizations and with journalists, professors and government officials in Egypt, Jordan, Israel, Lebanon, Libya, Tunisia, Algeria and Morocco.

The movement has taken firm root throughout the Arab world; its partisans and supporters are everywhere. Walls in Beirut and Cairo are plastered with recruiting posters for Fatah* and the other guerrilla organizations and graffiti

---

1. Charles W. Yost, "The Arab-Israeli War: How It Began," *Foreign Affairs,* 46, 2 (January 1968), 304-20, 318.

* An acronym, from *f-t-ḥ*, the initial letters of the Arabic words for "Palestine Liberation Movement," reversed to mean "opening" in the sense of military victory.

△ MICHAEL HUDSON is associate professor of political science at Brooklyn College of the City University of New York. The support of the American Philosophical Society, the Brooklyn College Research Center in Comparative Politics and Administration, and the Yale World Data Analysis Program is gratefully acknowledged.

reminding passers-by of the Palestine cause.[2] The press from Lebanon to Morocco gives full play to operations of these *fidā'iyīn,* or "sacrificers." The nightly broadcasts of Fatah tell of the latest expeditions and try to educate young Palestinians about the villages and lands that once belonged to their fathers.[3] Spectacular incidents in the smoldering Arab-Israeli war, such as the Israeli raid on Beirut airport, bring on massive demonstrations in support of the Palestinian resistance. Recruiting centers are open in most Arab countries and the supply of recruits, which increases after every Israeli retaliation, far exceeds the absorptive capacity of the commando groups. In Kuwayt and elsewhere the Palestinians are developing an administrative infrastructure for procurement, finance, education and welfare not unlike the Jewish Agency of the British Mandate era;[4] the Palestinian Arabs hope that these quasi-governmental structures will someday comprise the nucleus of a Palestine Arab state. The movement is generously financed, largely from Palestinians and other Arabs in the oil producing states. Arab governments finance the Palestine Liberation Organization and provide facilities in varying degrees for all the guerrilla groups. Even more significant is the broad base of the movement: Palestinians of all classes are participating, financially and otherwise, in contrast to their fitful and ineffective political efforts since the Balfour Declaration of 1917. But the Palestine cause is not just the cause of the Palestinians anymore. Non-Palestinian Arab opinion of all political shades is with the movement. This popular solidarity has been an important factor in the increasing, though sometimes reluctant, support offered by Arab governments in behalf of the movement. If the Palestinian movement can curb the splintering tendency that has crippled other modernizing political movements in the Arab world, it will be here to stay. "I think they've got a going concern," observes a Western journalist with excellent connections in the area.[5]

Some Western observers profess skepticism about the importance of the Palestinian resistance in the Middle East crisis. Israeli officials too have attempted to discount its effectiveness, variously referring to the guerrillas as criminal, poorly trained, amateurish, and as tools of Arab governments that wish to promote skirmishes for their domestic political considerations.[6] Some

2. Elie Salem calls our attention to the symbolic significance of wall inscriptions in Beirut since the June war: "Back-Alley Politics," unpublished paper, Political Studies Department, American University of Beirut, summer 1968, 12 pp.

3. For the educated, there is also a large and growing amount of literature, often copiously documented, on the history of the Palestine question, produced by the Palestine Liberation Organization Research Center. Al-Fatah publishes a magazine, *Al-Thawra Al-Filistiniyya* (The Palestinian Revolution); the PLO military organizations publish *Sawt Filistin* (Voice of Palestine); and the communiqués and pronouncements of all the major groups are prominently displayed in the leading dailies and weeklies. A spate of books has appeared on guerrillas in general and *fidā'iyīn* in particular.

4. See, e.g., John K. Cooley, "Kuwait provides Arabs with prosperous rear base," *Christian Science Monitor,* March 26, 1968, p. 1.

5. Cf. Anouar Abdel-Malek, "La Résistance Palestinienne," *Le Monde,* February 13, 1969, p. 3.

6. A recent expression of the "puppet" theory may be found in Alfred Friendly, "Text of Interview with Israel's Foreign Minister Eban," *The Washington Post,* March 6, 1969, p. E23.

American observers doubt that the movement reflects a truly deep-rooted national feeling on the part of Palestinians and therefore will "wither away" under repeated Israeli pressure. Inadequate information makes it difficult to assess the movement's power, but there are reasons for doubting whether this degree of skepticism is justified. On the military level, Israel is superior, not only to the guerrillas but also to all the Arab armies put together, in full-scale war. Despite this disproportion the guerrillas have been able to apply selective violence and inflict significant psychological and political damage. Since the June war, sabotage and terrorist incidents have provoked new massive retaliations, notably against the Jordanian towns of Karamah, Irbid and Salt, and the Beirut airport—retaliations that were politically damaging to Israel and beneficial to the resistance. Moreover, the commandos have been able to carry out border incidents virtually on a daily basis since summer 1968 despite vigorous Israeli countermeasures. These activities have rightly been described as "pinpricks," militarily; but their persistence has given them a disproportionately irritating political and psychological effect. Even more effective in this sense than border incidents, however, have been the spectacular acts of terror carried out far from the front lines: these include bombings in Tel Aviv and Jerusalem and attacks against Israeli airliners in Europe. In addition, the Palestinian organizations have stimulated the Arab states toward increasing their military pressures against the Israeli units on the cease-fire lines, notably along the Suez Canal. The Palestinian partisans have contributed to Israel's sense of political frustration, a climate which promotes political "hawkishness" and diplomatic intransigence and which benefits the resistance movement.

Palestinian Political Consciousness

In the political domain, a sense of Palestinian political community has reemerged after two decades of quiescence. It draws much of its cohesion from the common experience of the loss of the homeland. This experience is complex and deeply rooted. For Palestinians, the 1967 war was not the only common bond of misfortune. The 1948 war is probably even more binding a memory, with its own sad folklore, passed down through narratives and literature. The general strike and uprisings of 1936-1939 and the sporadic violence of the early and late 1920s, in protest of the Jewish National Home policies of the British, comprise other layers in the accretion of national consciousness.[7]

There are positive ties as well. Foremost is a love for the land of Palestine itself. This attachment, not surprisingly, is very deep among the former peasantry, the largest component of the Palestinian community: life as landless refugees has, if anything, only sharpened this attachment, and the feeling has

---

7. Dr. Taufiq Canaan, *The Palestine Arab Cause* (Jerusalem: The Modern Press, 1936, ["seventy-fifth day of the general strike"] 22 pp.) for an early and cogent statement of the Palestinian Arab position.

been transmitted to a new generation that has never seen Palestine. This specific attachment to lands is sometimes not appreciated by Western observers, but it helps explain why plans for resettlement in other parts of the Arab world have been so cooly received. At the turn of the century Theodor Herzl and other Western European Zionists could rationally discuss alternative geographic locations for the Jewish national home—Uganda, Argentina, Palestine—but among the Palestinian Arabs there is no debate as to the location of their homeland. In addition to the land, Palestinians have an active appreciation for other features of their culture—a culture that is Arab but that also possesses distinct regional characteristics. Notable are the elaborate costumes, handwork, weaving and crafts of the different districts. In addition to these highly developed artifacts of a peasant culture, the educated Palestinian strata are developing an art and literature on national themes. Then there are the subtle, everyday nuances of speech and inflection, the "in" jokes of the community, the social patterns of the Palestinian diaspora that are difficult for the outsider to perceive but that comprise nonetheless an important aspect of Palestinian communal consciousness.

While these bonds may be stronger than many Western analysts believe, the Palestinian political culture also displays several important non-integrative characteristics. There has never been a state of Palestine under indigenous Arab control; indeed there has never been a Palestine state of any kind in modern times, until the British Mandate. The Palestinian Arabs themselves have been scattered beyond their homeland for 20 years and many of them have been assimilated in varying degrees within neighboring Arab states or beyond. As a community they have suffered the traditional impediments to political development apparent throughout the Arab world: the rather rigid class structure that impedes vertical linkages and the regional and familial cleavages detrimental to horizontal integration. Furthermore, while Palestine has been the frame of reference for its Arab inhabitants and former inhabitants ever since the Zionist threat was perceived, Palestinians have devoted the greater part of their political energies since 1948 to promoting Arab unity in general. Palestinians, for example, have played a major rôle in the Arab Nationalist Movement. From 1948 until the June war the Palestinians were almost politically inert with respect to the Palestine problem. Although the Arab Higher Committee, led by Ḥājj Amīn al-Ḥusaynī, remained in existence throughout this period it was politically insignficant, and the establishment of the Palestine Liberation Organization in 1964 under the leadership of Aḥmad Shuqayrī produced as much cynicism as commitment among middle-class Palestinians.

The factor that has crystallized the latent Palestinian national consciousness in spite of these weaknesses is modernization. Modernization is the process through which parochial, timeless and sacred world views are transformed into universalistic, change (progress)-oriented, and instrumental modes of thinking; in which simple, family-oriented social systems become differentiated and complex in structure. The instruments of modernization—companies, factories, bureaucracies, mass communications, education and, above all, science and technology—have transformed much of the world in this century.[8] Modernization has been carried by merchants, missionaries, colonizers and armies in the Arab Middle East, as elsewhere in the Third World.[9] What are the implications of modernization for politics, and especially for nationalism? According to an eminent student of this subject, modernization can greatly accelerate the nation-building process, if the basic common elements in the political culture exceed the divisive tendencies.[10] Although we still lack a thorough empirical study of the question, it would appear that modernization has promoted more solidarity than disintegration among the Palestinians. Ironically, two of the chief carriers of modernization into Palestine—the British Mandate and the Zionist movement—were also responsible for frustrating Palestinian national aspirations.

The political modernization of the Palestinians may be considered to have fallen in two stages. Under Ottoman and British rule, many Palestinian Arabs were drawn into the government service, and opportunities for higher education were opened up. This Palestinian élite was politically conscious, but it was cosmopolitan, with an attachment to the entire Arab East rather than a commitment to a Palestine state. Furthermore, it was internally divided along sectarian and family lines.[11] Under the persistent and growing Zionist challenge, however, members of this élite came to realize that the Palestine area was endangered; many also perceived that their own vaguely defined political goals and the traditional divisions within the "gentry" gravely aggravated this danger. But their response was too little and too late. Despite the resistance of this modernized stratum and indeed the neighboring Arab world as well, the Zionist movement succeeded in establishing political control in a large area of Palestine. By 1949 the great bulk of this élite had been forced out and

---

8. David E. Apter, *The Politics of Modernization* (Chicago: University of Chicago Press, 1965), esp. Ch. 2.

9. Bernard Lewis, *The Middle East and the West* (London: Weidenfeld and Nicolson, 1963), provides a succinct overview. George Antonius, *The Arab Awakening* (London: Hamish Hamilton, 1938) remains indispensable on the stimuli to political consciousness in the Arab East. On the "implantation" of modernization generally, see Apter, Chs. 4 and 5.

10. Karl W. Deutsch, *Nationalism and Social Communication* (Boston and New York: The Technology Press of M.I.T. and John Wiley and Sons, 1953), 97-104, 127-36. See also his article, "Social Mobilization and Political Development," *American Political Science Review*, LV, 3 (September 1961), 493-514, p. 501: ". . . social mobilization may be expected . . . to promote the consolidation of states whose peoples already share the same language, culture, and major social institutions; while the same process may tend to strain or destroy the unity of states whose population is already divided into several groups with different languages or cultures or basic ways of life."

11. William R. Polk, David Stamler, and Edmund Asfour, *Backdrop to Tragedy* (Boston: Beacon Press, 1957), 225-304, esp. 241-247, 265-272.

had taken up residence in neighboring countries; leadership of the Palestinians still rested, nominally at least, with it.

The second stage of modernization involved the bulk of the 700,000 Arabs who were displaced in 1948, the displaced peasantry. Deprived of land and livelihood, they existed on a Spartan international dole, mostly in refugee camps. Grim as they were, the refugee camps functioned as a kind of hothouse of political modernization. The United Nations administration was efficient with its meager resources: refugee health levels were generally similar to those elsewhere in the Arab world and nutrition was minimally adequate, at least by medical standards. The birth rate was high and infant mortality low.[12] Even more important was the fact that refugee children were educated.[13] It was inevitable that they should learn better than their parents about the loss of "their country." Many refugee children received university and technical training and found work in the oil producing states; some did very well for themselves and moved into the professions and business, demonstrating an upward mobility that might not have occurred for years had they remained on their plots of land in Palestine. Precisely because it was harsh, the disastrous confrontation with the West and with Zionism tended to break up the traditional parochial social structure that had inhibited effective political organization under the Mandate.

12. About 20 per cent of the Palestinian population was estimated to belong to the middle class or higher and did not have to depend on UNRWA assistance (Statement of Dr. John H. Davis, Director of UNWRA, to the January 1961 World Refugee Year Conference, Geneva; p. 1); the living standards of this group were clearly superior to those of the refugees and comparable to the Arab middle class in general. Among the refugees under UNWRA jurisdiction the basic winter daily caloric intake *per capita* is 1600 (See, e.g. *Report of the Commissioner-General of the United Nations Relief and Works Agency for Palestine Refugees in the Near East*, July 1966-30 June 1967, (A/6713), 33, 63). Compared to 75 nations reporting caloric data for the 1965 period, the Palestinian refugees ranked 74th on this indicator. (Data courtesy of Charles L. Taylor, from the Revised Edition of *The World Handbook of Political and Social Indicators* (Yale World Data Analysis Program, forthcoming). The Palestinian caloric intake, however, is exactly the same as the medically-determined minimal nutritional allowances for "normally healthy" evacuees "not engaged in essential emergency work" (Michael G. Wohl and Robert S. Goodhart, *Modern Nutrition in Health and Disease* (Philadelphia: Lea and Febiger, 1960, p. 1047). In terms of inhabitants per hospital bed, the Palestinian refugee figure in 1966-67 (663) was higher (i.e. worse) than Jordan, Egypt, Tunisia, Algeria, Lebanon and Kuwayt, and lower (i.e. better) than Morocco, Iraq, Syria, Sudan, Saudi Arabia, South Arabia and Yemen. (The Arab states data is, however, for circa 1960; Bruce M. Russett, *et al*, *World Handbook of Political and Social Indicators* (New Haven: Yale University Press, 1964; pp. 208-10). The overall annual rate of population increase, calculated from UNRWA figures was around 3.5 per cent, a figure which ranked 13th out of 111 countries in the period ca. 1958-61 (Russett *et al*, 46-48). In terms of survival, the Palestinian Arabs therefore seemed to be at least holding their own.

13. The 1966-67 *UNRWA Report* (p. 35) estimates that over 75 per cent of refugee children of school age were in fact attending elementary and preparatory level schools. This figure is comparable with the unadjusted school enrollment percentages reported to UNESCO. Out of 120 countries reporting data for the 1963-64 period the Palestinian refugees ranked 13th, on a level with France and Czechoslovakia. In terms of other aspects of social mobilization, such as exposure to the mass media, there can be little doubt that the Palestinians have been thoroughly mobilized. According to Deutsch, "the growth in the numbers of these socially-mobilized people produces mounting pressures for the transformation of political practices and institutions. . . ." ("Social Mobilization and Political Development," 498).

The 1967 war revived the Palestine question and brought forth a new generation of leaders. This leadership shuns the traditional rhetoric and emphasizes organization, rationality and training. It is acutely conscious of the dangers of political factionalism. It learns Hebrew and studies Israeli military techniques. It tries to know the enemy and makes realistic appraisals of the great powers' interests in the area. Because it is disciplined and purposeful it exerts influence on the Middle Eastern scene far out of proportion to its material strength.

Structure of the Movement: Fission and Fusion

Like the Algerian National Liberation Front in its early development, the Palestinian resistance movement is a loosely coordinated collection of organizations with varied constituencies in the Palestinian community and the Arab world. If one dates the beginning of active resistance from 1965, one may observe a process of fission and fusion within the movement. In 1964 the Arab states summit conference established the Palestine Liberation Organization as the official voice of the Palestinian community and gave it quasi-diplomatic status and financial support. The PLO's main governmental patron was the United Arab Republic and its constituency among the Palestinians was with the "established" bourgeois and professional notables. The PLO attempted to build up a Palestine Liberation Army in the Gaza strip. At the same time, however, the clandestine Fatah organization was emerging. Some Fatah members felt that the PLO was a sham and that its establishment was a cynical attempt by the UAR and other Arab governments to contain rising anti-Israel feeling. The Ba'thi régime in Syria at the time, itself at odds with the UAR, appears to have supported Fatah, and the neo-Ba'thi régime which assumed power in February 1966 was even more cooperative. A visitor to Damascus in summer 1966 could easily spot the guerrillas in their mottled green uniforms in the streets and public places, and Syrian officials made it very plain they hoped to provoke a war by encouraging sabotage.

While the Arab states were still reeling from the June 1967 defeat, Fatah was beginning to expand and other groups were coming into existence. Of the several dozen other groups that emerged, two were of particular importance—Ṣā'iqah, a commando movement reportedly closely directed by the Syrian army, and active on the Syrian and Jordan River fronts, and the Popular Front for the Liberation of Palestine. The Popular Front grew out of the merger of three small groups, the most important of which was the Arab Nationalist Movement. Galvanized by the 1948 defeat, a Christian Palestinian, George Habbāsh, founded the ANM to recover Palestine and realize the long-standing ideal of one Arab nation. The ANM decided that the recovery of Palestine— the heart of the Arab nation—could only be achieved through prior unification of the existing Arab régimes. Thus it supported Jamal 'Abd al-Nāṣir in the middle 1950s as the strongest available unifier, but it eventually moved ideologically to the left of Nāṣir. Through the Popular Front the ANM returned to the problem of recovering Palestine; but it returned with a radical socialist ideology it did not have in 1948 and which its comrades-in-arms in Fatah and the PLO do not share.

The PLO meanwhile had been almost completely discredited by the 1967 war, sharing in the disgrace of its governmental patrons. The Palestine Liberation Army, inadequately trained and armed, had easily been overrun by Israeli forces, and the echoes of Mr. Shuqayrī's vitriolic speeches only cast further disrepute on the Palestinian establishment that had followed him. Reconstituted under the new leadership of Yaḥyā Hammūdah, the PLO held a third Palestine National Assembly in Cairo in July 1968 (the first one had been in 1964 and the second in January 1968) to which the previously excluded guerrilla groups sent delegates. This attempt at fusion was only partly successful: the PLO and Fatah shared major control, with lesser place being given to the Popular Front. Ṣāʻiqah was excluded and the reorganized Palestine Liberation Army, nominally under control of the PLO executive, shortly asserted its autonomy when several of its senior officers mutinied in Damascus.

Another step toward fusion took place at the next Palestine National Assembly conference in February 1969, again in Cairo. Fatah, largest of the guerrilla organizations, won control of the Assembly: its representatives took four seats on the 11-man Executive Committee and its spokesman, Yāsir ʻArafāt, was elected chairman. Of the other Executive Committee seats, two went to Ṣāʻiqah, one went to a former PLO executive member, and three went to independents. Ṣāʻiqah was back in the fold, Fatah was consolidating its primary position, and the major organizations of the Palestinian resistance now had an "official" face to present to Arab governments and the world. All these developments were indicative of fusion. But the Popular Front was now excluded. Not only was the Popular Front not represented but the Front itself was splintering. The parent faction, led by George Habbāsh, and the one responsible for the spectacular terrorist operations, was opposed by a more ideologically rigorous Marxist faction led by Naʼif Hawatmah. The Hawatmah faction split away and called itself the Popular Democratic Front. A third component of the original Popular Front, but not tied to the Arab Nationalist Movement also split away; it was led by a major in the Syrian Army, Aḥmad Jabrīl, and was called the General Command of the Popular Front. Furthermore, at the time of this assembly it was not entirely clear whether Yāsir ʻArafāt could control the breakaway Palestine Liberation Army.

Despite these fissiparous tendencies, the trend has been toward consolidation of structures under the aegis of Fatah. Formation of a Palestinian Armed Struggle Command in April 1969 was intended to improve military cooperation among the guerrillas, and it included the previously dissident PLA and PDF. The principal cleavages are ideological and tactical, and on each the Fatah-PLO group diverge from the Popular Front and the PDF. Fatah and the PLO eschew all political ideology beyond the principle of liberating Palestine and making it a democratic country. They avoid taking sides in the Arab cold war—the rivalry between the conservative, pro-Western régimes and the radical, socialist republics, and instead draw support from all of them. The Popular Front and the PDF leadership is committed to inculcating a revolutionary, egalitarian spirit not only among the Palestinians (including Israelis) but among all Arabs, and it seeks to establish "liberation" beachheads in a number of conservative Arab states. On the tactical level, the Fatah-PLO position is again relatively moderate: it believes in developing solid organization and chipping away at Israel, slowly but steadily, over a long period, and concentrating its operations against the Israeli military and administrative apparatus. The Popular Front, on the other hand, has tried to develop an organization inside the occupied areas and to carry out spectacular acts of terrorism against Israeli civilians. The Popular Front is to Fatah what the Irgun was to Haganah. And just as the various rival Jewish partisan organizations could cooperate to some extent, so it would seem to be with the Palestinian groups: fusion rather than fission has been the dominant theme.

How Fatah Views the Situation

Fatah is the largest and oldest of the resistance organizations. Fatah is committed to the liberation of all of Palestine from Zionist political control. It believes that armed violence is the only way to accomplish its objective. "Liberation" means not only the "destruction of the imperialist base" but also the eradication of Zionist society by striking at its industrial, agricultural and financial institutions. The political, military, economic and intellectual roots of Zionism must be so thoroughly destroyed that they can never rise again.[14]

Fatah was founded in 1956 as a small secret society but did not begin active operations against Israel until 1965. From then up to the June war it carried out increasingly provocative acts of sabotage, usually from across the Syrian border. The June war helped Fatah succeed in the first stage of its plan for the liberation of Palestine: it created a climate in which the Palestine question became again the principal issue in the Arab world. To this end the Israelis cooperated by convincing the Arabs that they intend to stay in the occupied territories. "I knew we were going to lose the war," said a resistance leader, "but that didn't bother me as much as the possibility that the Israelis might withdraw immediately. If they had, our cause would have been set back for years: the Palestinians would have been further demoralized, Israel would have won a tremendous moral victory, and the Arab governments would have agreed

---

14. Fatah, *Tahrir al-Aqtar al-Muhtala* (Liberation of the Occupied Lands) Number 8 in the series "Revolutionary Studies and Experiences" (No place, no publisher, 1968; 24 pp.), 16-17.

to suppress the resistance as part of the price for withdrawal. Fortunately, the Israelis gave us a break." After the war Fatah successfully renewed its harassment tactics in order to prevent a new *status quo* from emerging around the battle lines. The Israeli command, fearing that Fatah might succeed in organizing active resistance among the Arabs in the occupied areas and in Israel itself, attempted to wipe out the concentration of guerrilla bases just east of the Jordan River. The Israelis evidently expected that King Husayn's army would allow them to carry out the operation since the commandos seemed to threaten his régime. But when the Israelis attacked the town of Karamah on March 31, 1968, they were surprised by unexpectedly stiff opposition from the commandos and the Jordan army together. This battle, though hardly a military victory for the Arabs, gave the Palestinian resistance a huge boost. Arab public opinion was delighted that the commandos had parried the Israeli assault. Before the June war, according to a reliable Palestinian source, Fatah numbered no more than 200-300 men; by the time of the Karamah battle it had increased to around 2,000; but in the three months following the Karamah battle it had burgeoned to 15,000.

Fatah sees the political structures of Israel as an especially malignant mutation of classical imperialism. In the classical case an alien régime is imposed on a politically underdeveloped people for the economic betterment of the mother country. The imperial administration is confined to a small élite. Such was the British Mandate in Palestine. A more destructive type of imperialism involves the implantation of a colonial population, such as occurred in French Algeria. But the intrusion of Zionism into Palestine has been even more devastating because the massive colonization was accompanied by the systematic expulsion of the bulk of the indigenous population, the Palestinian Arabs. In as much as the Maoist doctrine of liberation movements requires that the insurgents operate in a favorable environment, "like fish in the sea," Israel in its pre-June 1967 boundaries was a very difficult target, for the Palestinian Arabs had dwindled from two-thirds of the total population before 1948 to only ten per cent. Even so, Fatah's leaders believed that Israel, barred from the Arab world and a "colony" of world Jewry and the United States, was in a precarious economic and strategic position. When Fatah began active operations in 1965 it was thus obliged to resort to border raids, in hopes of provoking Israel into a larger confrontation in which its vulnerability could be exploited. After the June war "Greater Israel" was a more vulnerable target than it had been—especially if the Arabs in the occupied areas could be organized for cooperation in resistance.

Fatah representatives seem well aware of the formidable obstacles before them. What it fears most, says a spokesman, is not new aggression by Israel against Egypt, Jordan or Syria—indeed, it could benefit from such a thing—but rather the possibility that there will be a diplomatic solution. If the great powers and United Nations efforts in this direction should fail the movement is certain to gain new momentum; but should they succeed it might be set back for years, since it would once again face active opposition from the Arab governments. Fatah knows that Arab governments view it now with ambivalence. Of their general sympathy there is no doubt. Furthermore, it is clear that the commandos have relieved these governments of some of the popular displeasure with their disastrous performance in the war. At the same time, however, Fatah activities are the chief obstacle to a diplomatic arrangement that would require Israeli withdrawal from at least some of the territories it occupied in 1967; Jordan and the UAR have repeatedly shown their interest in such an arrangement.

In Jordan's case, the differences with Fatah go beyond disagreement about a diplomatic solution. If protracted warfare continues, Jordan suffers not only in human and economic terms, it also risks revolution or even extinction as a political entity. If the tide should turn against Israel, with the commandos in the vanguard, Jordan still would face at least the permanent loss of the West Bank. While it is quite possible that Jordan would lose in a diplomatic settlement as well, the losses would be relatively fewer. For their part, the commandos (especially the Popular Front) have considered the Hashimite régime almost as much an enemy as Israel itself. Both before and immediately after the June war, King Husayn tried actively to curb guerrilla activities across Jordan's frontier; and while his control has slipped markedly he still seeks to influence commando operations.

The government of Lebanon is confronted with a similar problem. Tolerance of guerrilla operations invites massive Israeli retaliation, specifically the occupation of part of southern Lebanon including the Litani River. But suppression of the guerrillas produces governmental crises and the threat of civil turmoil. The relatively pro-Western stance and "moderation" of both Jordan and Lebanon only exacerbate the conflict with the Palestinians. Adroit diplomacy and a common appreciation of the Israeli challenge have permitted an uneasy *modus vivendi,* but the fundamental conflict is recognized by all concerned: it is not just a question of Palestinian military *versus* governmental accommodation *vis à vis* Israel, but of revolutionary pan-Arabism—symbolized by the commandos—*versus* bourgeois political oligarchies.

Egypt, however, is the most important country to the commandos. Until the Karamah battle, President Nāṣir had accepted the estimate of his former intelligence chief, Ṣalāḥ Naṣr, that Fatah was controlled by the anti-Nāṣir Muslim Brotherhood, but after that battle he changed his mind and began cautiously to support the guerrilla organization. While the Egyptians have used their own guerrillas rather than Fatah to operate across the Suez Canal, they have given Fatah a radio voice, some financing behind the scenes, and qualified public support. Indeed, UAR support has become increasingly warm as the Israelis have strengthened their fortifications on the Suez Canal. Egyptian-Palestinian relations, however, are not entirely harmonious. The commandos understand Egypt's interest in a diplomatic settlement, and worry about it, because it is Egypt that will determine what, if any, diplomatic terms the Arab states will accept.

This concern was evident in the comments of a Fatah spokesman in Cairo in August 1968 on an editorial by Muḥammad Ḥasanayn Haykal in *al-Ahrām,* which extolled the courage of a martyred Fatah commando:

> Look carefully at this article. On the surface it is a sentimental eulogy to our cause, but this is simply for the masses, to show that Egypt is 100 per cent behind the Palestinian resistance. If you look farther on you see that Haykal is arguing that the Palestinian resistance is secondary in importance to the Arab governmental policy. If this policy is to wait indefinitely for the Arab states to prepare for a new confrontation, then we must wait; if they accept an expedient diplomatic solution that requires us to stop our operations "temporarily" then we must stop. We do not accept Mr. Haykal's ideas. *We* are directing the liberation struggle, not the Egyptian government; these governments will work for us because they know that their people support us.

In strictly military terms Fatah's insistence on the primacy of guerrilla operations, especially against an enemy as strong as Israel in land as open as Palestine, may seem unrealistic. But politically it serves to legitimize the guerrilla activism that could force Arab armies into a battle in which they would in fact play the primary rôle.

Fatah is also aware that it has no friends among the superpowers. It believes that American diplomats regard the resistance as an obstacle in the way of peacemaking efforts. It doubts that any US government would ever recognize any Palestinian Arab political claims in Palestine other than through the Kingdom of Jordan. Most important, it realizes that the US is committed to the sovereign existence of Israel and its territorial integrity, though just what territory is encompassed by that pledge is not clear. American opposition, however, does not deter Fatah from pursuing its activities. The Palestinians are encouraged by the difficulties of the US in Vietnam and the resulting disinclination among Americans to get involved in new protracted conflicts in the world. This disinclination, they feel, allows them to cause continual disruptions within Israel, provoking it into irrational and expensive counter-measures, without inviting an intervention by the Sixth Fleet. US intervention would also be deterred by the Soviet presence.

The position of the Russians is more subtle and more dangerous, in the view of Fatah. While the Soviet Union has been indirectly helpful in making available arms and in championing the cause of liberation wars in general, it has also upheld the right of Israel to exist and it has exerted pressures on the guerrillas to mute their activities. Russian efforts to jog the disputing states toward a settlement have been received with anger and concern in Palestinian circles. Soviet pressures to throttle the movement are far more of a problem than American pressures because the Soviet Union now has more influence than the United States with the key Arab governments in Syria, Egypt, Iraq and Algeria. If the Soviets should decide that they can have *rapprochement* with the US in the Mediterranean without sacrificing (to the Chinese, perhaps) the new influence they have over the Arabs then the Palestinians would have a problem. But they feel they can cope with it. Since Soviet success in the Arab world is a function of its solidarity with the Arabs on Palestine, they argue, and since the Palestinian resistance now speaks more authoritatively on that question than any Arab government, it behooves the Russians to think carefully before trying to suppress it.

Finally, there is Israel. How can the Palestinians expect to defeat a dedicated, thoroughly trained and brilliantly led citizen army of 300,000? Fatah representatives reply that they cannot defeat it either directly or alone, but that defeat in this sense is not the immediate objective. What the resistance does have in mind is waging a campaign of protracted violence against the vital institutions of the Israeli state, avoiding situations in which the Israelis can bring to bear their superior organization and technology. The Arab armies play an important rôle here by applying constant pressure and providing tactical support on "Greater Israel's" borders. This violence in turn has three beneficial results: domestically, it depresses Israeli morale; it discourages new investment, tourism and economic development; it exacerbates existing political divisions as the leadership fails to stop the sabotage. Second, it paves the way for organization of the Arabs in the occupied areas and in Israel itself for active resistance. Israeli attempts to punish this resistance only fuel it. Third, the violence forces the Israelis to retaliate harshly and indiscriminately against the surrounding Arab countries, but in so doing Israel only diminishes its reputation in the international community and forces the Arab governments into even greater solidarity with the Palestinians.

The Israeli authorities have consistently and categorically denied that Fatah and the other guerrilla organizations are a serious threat. A retired Israeli intelligence officer, whose views presumably coincide with current official analyses of the guerrillas, dismisses Fatah's published strategic doctrine as unsound, its military accomplishments as minimal, and its efforts to promote organized resistance among the Palestinians in the occupied areas as a complete failure. Furthermore, he speculates that the movement will eventually die out as the Arab public comes to realize these facts.[15] American sources, both diplomatic and journalistic, also minimize the disruptive effects of the commandos against Israel. Casualty rates among the commandos are fearfully high

---

15. Y. Harkabi, *Fedayeen Action and Arab Strategy*, Adelphi Papers, Numbers 53 (London: The Institute for Strategic Studies, December 1968, 43 pp.).

and Israeli efforts at sealing its borders with fences and other devices are reported to be very successful.[16] Fatah declarations of its own accomplishments are said to be deliberately and grossly exaggerated.

Fatah, for its part, consistently and categorically claims that its operations are increasingly effective, that Israel systematically exaggerates its accomplishments in killing and capturing guerrillas and that Israel conceals a great many of the raids and incidents that actually occur. Fatah representatives do not deny that their losses are high, but they point out that guerrilla warfare is bound to be bloody; dying on a guerrilla mission is far better than the living death of the refugee camps. Fatah is ready to accept unfavorable casualty ratios; if it takes the loss of six commandos to kill one of the enemy, the struggle is worth making. Despite the obstacles, Fatah members appear absolutely confident that they will prevail.

Palestine Liberated

The new Palestinian leaders are generally reluctant to speak about plans for Palestine after the liberation because they feel such talk is premature: they do not want to alienate any present sources of support or divide the movement unnecessarily. But some of them, particularly those in the Popular Front, see dangers in not planning ahead. If the question "Liberation for what?" is not openly discussed, they contend, it may be difficult to mobilize the Palestinians for what is expected to be a long struggle. A clearer program may also ease the way to accommodation with the Jewish population. At the present time there is no such clear program. Some of the differences among the guerrillas arise over the future direction of Palestine. Yet it is possible to discern a certain core of agreement among representatives of the different tendencies.

Certainly a crucial issue is what would happen to the Israelis under a government dominated by Palestinian Arabs. There is general agreement that the Jews would be given the choice of living peacefully in the state of Palestine, with full civil rights, or else of leaving. "We do not intend to drive them out as they drove us out," said a PLO spokesman, "We think that there is room in Palestine for six million Palestinians—Arabs and Jews. The only condition is that they accept to live as peaceful citizens." The more militant resistance people are less liberal and more noncommittal, though none advocates wholesale deportation of the Israelis. One Fatah spokesman, for example, declared that all Jews living in Palestine before 1948 (and their subsequent offspring) would be allowed to stay but the others would have to leave. A Popular Front representative remarked that the Palestinian resistance had no malice for the Israeli population but neither did it assume responsibility for their welfare:

---

16. See e.g., Philip Ben, "The Arabs Are Not Ready to Make Peace," *The New Republic*, March 15, 1968, p. 18.

these people, after all, had with few exceptions supported the Israel government's harsh policies toward the Palestinian Arabs.

Constitutionally, a new Palestine state would probably be republican. Even relatively conservative Palestinians are doubtful that King Husayn would be acceptable, although that possibility is not ruled out. One PLO spokesman suggests that there might emerge a federation between the new Palestine Republic, with its eastern boundary at the Jordan River, and the Kingdom of Transjordan, now reduced to its original boundaries. If the new state were a republic, however, and up to 40 per cent of its new population (greatly enlarged by the repatriation of over a million Palestinian Arabs) remained Jewish, it is obvious that it would not be exclusively an Arab state. It is no less obvious that such a state would only be viable if a political formula could be worked out in which both sides would be secure. Such a formula presumably would create a national, bi-cultural Palestine and somehow convert Israeli Jews and Palestinian Arabs, respectively, into Jewish and Arab Palestinians.

Yet once the power of the state of Israel was broken, say some resistance spokesmen, the establishment of a viable state along these lines would be difficult but not impossible; nor would it be repressive to the Jews. The "de-Zionizing" of the Jewish population would require essentially its renunciation of the goal that "Palestine be as Jewish as England is English." This would mean abolition of the Law of the Return, under which Jews throughout the world are eligible for automatic citizenship in Israel. It would also mean relinquishing those deeply-rooted symbols of a Jewish state—the flag and the name of Israel. Israeli political parties and quasi-governmental institutions would have to be radically reorganized. It would not mean, assert the Palestinians, the infringement of any religious practices which Jews of all tendencies now enjoy in Israel. Israelis would have to accept the return of all the exiled Palestinian Arabs, to undergo common hardships in the massive relocation, and to live peacefully with them.

Would the new Palestine republic become "just another Levantine state"? Whether becoming more Levantine is desirable or not is debatable, but it seems clear that the resistance does not want to impose traditionalist leadership and values in the new state. To the intellectuals even in the less ideological resistance groups liberation means much more than a change of government from Zionist to Arab control. It means a social revolution as well, a revolution that would change the Arab society and politics perhaps even more than the Jewish. "It is not enough simply to wear khaki and shoot to have a revolution," asserts a Popular Front spokesman, "and the Palestinian youth are not giving their lives just to restore the oppressive rule of landlords and big businessmen in Palestine. It is not possible to have a revolution in the world today that is not leftist." Resistance leaders are trying to win over those sectors in Israeli society that are poor and discriminated against, notably the Arabic-speaking

Eastern Jews, to persuade them that the Palestine liberation will liberate Arab and Jew alike from imperialist exploitation. In foreign policy, the Palestinians are oriented toward the Third World in their desire for national self-determination and liberation from foreign control. They are emphatic in their declarations that they want no entangling alliances with East or West and that they intend to be neutral in great power rivalries.

Some Concluding Observations

It is difficult from a distance to measure the disruptive impact of Fatah and the other groups on Israel. That their military effects have been exaggerated cannot be doubted, and many Palestinians close to the organizations criticize them for this deception. On the other hand, Israeli attempts to belittle them and to minimize their significance, while understandable, do not seem to paint an accurate picture either. Reports from journalists and travelers in Israel suggest that there may be some truth to the allegation by Fatah that more incidents occur than are reported. Organized resistance, ranging from petitions to demonstrations and sabotage, has in fact been reported from all the main towns in the occupied areas despite very severe Israeli reprisals; in view of the manifest capacity of Israel further to "de-Arabize" the occupied areas this degree of defiance is significant.[17] Terrorist and sabotage rings have in fact been established; a few have been uncovered but incidents continue to occur. The Israeli defense budget has risen to two and a half times its pre-June 1967 size.[18] If the average monthly Israeli casualty rate is around 75, then the country's security situation, in one sense at least, would seem to have deteriorated since before the June war.[19] The government of Israel, despite its low opinion of guerrilla capabilities, has come to regard their activities with some concern, if one may judge from its public security precautions and its statements in international forums.

With the second anniversary of the June war, it appeared that commandos had developed to the point where they could persistently harass Israel. In accordance with their rather vague theoretical stages of revolutionary growth, they had succeeded in mobilizing the Palestinian community and establishing a modest infrastructure. They had also been successful in winning support, in

17. See, e.g., the articles by John K. Cooley in *The Christian Science Monitor* of May 5, 21, and 24, 1969.

18. According to a Reuters News Agency report, quoting an Israel Defense Ministry spokesman. *Christian Science Monitor*, April 12, 1969.

19. *Time*, December 13, 1968, p. 35, reports over 900 Israeli casualties from commando operations in 1968. Overall Israeli losses from commando and regular Arab forces in the nearly two years following the June war were put at 350 dead and 1500 wounded, according to official Israeli sources. In addition, some 400 soldiers were officially reported to have died in "vehicular and training accidents." According to *The New York Times* correspondent in Israel, there was ". . . a gnawing suspicion among Israelis, denied vigorously and regularly by army spokesmen, that the casualty rate is even higher than officially admitted." *The New York Times*, May 18, 1969.

varying amounts, from the Arab governments and promoting a more active rôle for the Arab armies against Israel. They appeared to be growing in numbers and capability, and they were becoming sufficiently entrenched in the Arab states to make their eradication quite difficult, either by "moderate" Arab governments or by Israel, despite its military superiority. But they were a long way from posing a vital threat to Israeli security.

Perhaps even more significant, however, has been the resurrection of a Palestinian political identity on a more modern base than was the case before 1948. The Palestinians are developing a political community—a sense of national consciousness, and rudimentary political and administrative structures. Their new influence on the Middle Eastern scene has had at least one salutary effect: it has drawn attention back to the long-neglected root of the Palestine problem: the Palestinian Arabs, alone among the people of the area, do not have a national home of their own. Few would contest their rightful claims to self-determination, and nobody would deny that they were promised a state in Palestine by the international community. Power, we are taught, is a more important determinant of international behavior than moral or legal claims; what the resistance has begun to do is exert a small amount of power in behalf of their claims. They may lack the power to achieve their solution to the Middle East crisis—the eradication of Zionism in Palestine—but if there is to be any solution it would seem both necessary and desirable that they be a party to it. Indeed, it is conceivable that the Palestinian resistance movement— its militant rhetoric notwithstanding—may hold the key to a just peace in the Middle East.

The Palestinians as a Political Entity

SAMIR N. ANABTAWI

One of the most interesting developments to come out of the Middle East conflict of 1967 is the increasing awareness on the part of Westerners as well as Middle Easterners of the Palestinians as a distinct political community. For nearly twenty years the Western world has viewed the Palestinians in charitable and humane terms, a people whose lamentable lot was the regrettable product of irreconcilable regional and world forces. From time to time visual and touching accounts were given of the miserable conditions of their existence in refugee camps, thus spurring well-meaning individuals and organizations to increase or supplement the amount of aid that had been given to them. If any questions were raised, they were raised around such technical matters as to whether the Palestinians were evicted from their homeland or whether they left of their own volition, whether UNRWA figures regarding the number of refugees were indeed accurate, whether the seven cents' worth of daily rations per refugee was too much or too little, whether the United States and other Western Powers should increase or diminish their voluntary contributions, how many could be realistically repatriated to Israel in the eventuality of a political solution, and how best to resettle the remainder in the Arab countries with or without international or Big Power assistance. In short the Palestinians were regarded as a tragic people whose suffering should and could be alleviated if common human decency and genuine goodwill on the part of all were to prevail. That this blight on the conscience of mankind was allowed to exist for nearly twenty years was deemed to be the result of ambitious and immoral politicians who sought to perpetuate the refugee status of the Palestinians and to use them as a football in a political game aimed at furthering their selfish goals.

In the Middle East itself, the view of the Palestinian refugee has been quite understandably somewhat more complex. The Israelis, in the main, saw the refugees as an unfortunate and underdeveloped people whose sordid life could have been ameliorated long ago were it not for the cynical leadership in the neighboring Arab states. Those Israelis who may have felt some pangs of guilt in this human tragedy, and there are more of those than many Arabs think, often assuaged their conscience by arguing that the Arab refugees were after all the problem of their kinfolk, that the Palestinians left their native homes of their own accord and with the prodding of radio broadcasts from neighboring Arab capitals, that except for a relatively small number Israel could not in any event allow the refugees who so wished to return to their native lands without jeopardizing its security and upsetting its ethic composition, thereby calling into question its very *raison d'être*. Besides, many felt, Israel had absorbed a vast number of Jewish immigrants from Arab lands, and in effect an exchange of populations had for all intents and purposes taken place. Since Israel had settled those Jewish immigrants, it was only fair and proper that the Arab states should settle the Arab immigrants in their midst.

In the Arab world, interestingly enough, there has not been over the years one single and uniform attitude that was all pervasive toward the Palestinians. Instead, there were, and perhaps still are, despite all that has transpired since the June War, a number of attitudes depending on the ideological orientation and the socio-economic status of the observer. To the rabid nationalist the Palestinians were first and foremost an uncomfortable reminder of what he keenly felt to have been the worst calamity to befall the Arab nation in modern times. His sense of personal involvement in their lot did not stem from his humanitarian impulses, or from his sense of compassion, but from his political consciousness and his nationalistic perceptions and aspirations. I do not wish to imply that such a person is necessarily callous or insensitive to the plight of many of the refugees, but merely to state that his feeling of outrage was more directed at the origins and political consequences of the Palestine problem than the result of his revulsion at the nature of the refugees' existence. Indeed, it is doubtful that many Arab nationalists have been fully acquainted with the conditions of life in the refugee camps, and even if they have it is quite possible that their sense of empathy might have been blunted by their familiarity with not too dissimilar standards of living which they probably observed among their own compatriots. Nevertheless, it is his feeling of shame that the Arabs were unable to stem the forces of Zionism that wounds him; it is his sense of soiled honor that grieves him; it is his frustration at having been unable to erase a grave political injustice that gnaws at him. And the Palestinians are a living presence that endlessly brings to recall those distressingly uncomfortable multitudes of passions. The intensity of these emotions is often so overwhelming that it generates as a defensive mechanism a disposition to lash out at the Palestinians themselves and to accuse them of having been the cause of the current Arab predicament.

There are, however, those Arabs whose ideological commitment to the 'Arab cause' is less complete, and to whom Palestinians have not been as much a source of deep anguish as they have been a stumbling block in the pursuit of personal and/or limited national aspirations. I refer here to those individuals who, while sharing in the all-pervasive yet somewhat vague yearning for Arab unity and glory, and while capable in times of heightened Arab-Israeli tensions of emotional involvement, are nonetheless more intimately concerned with the attainment of more personal goals and the satisfaction of material desires. On a day-to-day basis it is not the refugees in the camp that concern them, but the educated, skilled, urbanized, and entrepreneurial Palestinians who have insinuated themselves into all sectors of the neighboring Arab societies, and who gradually came to be perceived as competitors in the marketplace, education, etc., even in certain corridors of power. Ordinary feelings of resentment, jealousy, envy and hostility, common to all such sociological situations wherein real or imaginary fears of displacement give rise to class or group tensions, were further aggravated by the Palestinian literati who (1) continued to maintain their separate national identity often despite the acquisition of the legal benefits of citizenship from the host countries; (2) assumed a posture of superiority through derogatory references to the governmental, administrative, and organizational machinery of the Arab states, as well as through constant reminiscences about how things were done in Palestine; and (3) chided other Arabs for their lack of preparation and weak resolve in their confrontation with Israel. Understandably enough all this and much more hardly served to endear this Palestinian diaspora who in the eyes of many have come to be looked upon as the 'new Jews' in their midst. Indeed, charges of ingratitude were often levelled against them, and many a Palestinian could recall being told in the heat of an argument to leave the country if he did not care for the way things were.

It would be presumptuous and inaccurate, of course, to suppose that the above classifications exhaust all the feelings and attitudes regarding the Palestinians that are current throughout the world and in particular the Arab portion of it. There are probably as many reactions to the Palestinians as there are individuals. However, what is above all else common to all these views is that none of them sees the Palestinians as a corporate political entity, possessed of preferences and aspirations, and having an independent will of its own that is sufficiently crystallized as to have merited consideration in the determination of affairs in the region during the past twenty years. On the contrary, the underlying supposition that is frequently betrayed in the discourse of individuals, at all levels of public accountability, be they Arab or non-Arab, is that the Palestinians are a malleable group that can be politically distended or constricted, as the case may be, to conform to the shape of any political agreement that may ultimately emerge. They are essentially regarded as a "problem," an "impediment," a "cancer," as C. P. Snow recently put it, whose solution, removal, or excision must be accomplished in order that the larger and more significant goal of peace can be reached. Just exactly how this task is to proceed, or what will become of the Palestinians is never clearly spelled out. Instead, vague generalities are given. The now celebrated November 1967 resolution of the U.N. Security Council calls for a "just settlement of the refugee problem." World leaders speak of an 'honorable' solution. Others talk of 'fair' compensation. Some discuss 'minimum' repatriation, while still others advocate 'resettlement.' Aside from the simple fact that no one seems to know exactly what is meant by 'just,' 'honorable,' or 'fair,' or how many would be repatriated, or where the remainder would be 'resettled,' there is the implicit assumption that the Palestinians will meekly accept, and comply with, whatever scheme that may be worked out by others. Indeed, one suspects that the Palestinians are regarded as morally obligated to submit to any solution that may be devised by the international community no matter how repugnant or unpalatable they may deem it. Even certain Arab leaders, in their attempts to find a solution to the current impasse, assure the world that once agreement has been reached with Israel regarding her withdrawal from occupied territory, the Palestinians would no longer pose a 'problem,' and if they did they would be muzzled.

How is it that a people have come to be seen in this light? What regional and global forces have come to play during the past two decades which would gradually cause what was once an active and corporate Palestinian Arab community to be viewed as an amorphous entity whose character can be molded to suit the predilections of others? What factors made a rapidly multiplying population so recede into the background for more than twenty years? And why is it that the present Palestinian movement, as symbolized in part by the activities of the fedayyeen, should have taken the world by surprise?

Answers to such questions are not easily obtained, and I do not pretend to have them. Neither can they be found in the simplistic and glib accounts that are ordinarily given in the press and which surprisingly enough receive credence in academic circles. Certain clues, however, may be derived from an examination of some aspects of the struggle for Palestine during the past half century.

Even though the current Arab-Israeli impasse is viewed by the world community with justified alarm, and despite the fact that it has captured the attention of the major statesmen of our time, it should be remembered that in its early history, what came to be known as the Palestine Question barely merited more than a footnote in the chronicles of the post World War I period. The Balfour Declaration which now looms so large in the minds of many hardly had the resounding international repercussions that, say, the Truman Doctrine had thirty years later. The struggle for Palestine between the Palestinian Arabs and Jews was regarded, first and foremost, as an internal one which, despite its significance to certain world-wide interests, was hardly one with which the international community was concerned. Britain was, as the mandatory power, definitely involved. But its role tended to seek a balance between what eventually proved to be irreconcilable commitments made to the principal parties. The League of Nations, though technically exercising suzerain powers over the country had, owing to its internal and constitutional make-up, no more than superficial involvement in the dispute which gradually took on the character of a communal strife, albeit with occasional international overtones.

However, when the United Kingdom, for reasons beyond the scope of this inquiry, decided to unburden itself of what it eventually came to feel as a taxing responsibility by placing the future of the Mandated territory before the U.N., the Palestine Question had already begun to assume international proportions. The plight of Jews in Europe during the War and the horrid revelations of the Nazi extermination camps captured the sympathy of human beings everywhere and brought international support, particularly from the United States, to the idea of the establishment of a Jewish state already long advocated by Zionist groups.

The 'internationalization' of the Palestine problem placed the Palestinian Arab community at a distinct political disadvantage. Lacking adequate organization, inexperienced in the by-ways of mid-twentieth-century diplomacy, wanting the necessary apparatus with which to wage a diplomatic offensive, unskilled in the techniques of propaganda, devoid of the unequivocal support of a Major Power or the staunch advocacy of a powerful constituency therein, the Palestinian Arabs were in no position to mount an effective campaign in international forums. They were further handicapped by a leadership that was heavily tinged with semi-feudal and theocratic colorations and which was not at all receptive to dissent or at least open inquiry which is a necessary requisite of rational planning. If anything, it was given to unyielding and exaggerated rhetoric that was often a source of embarrassment to friends and disenchantment to those who might otherwise have been in their camp.

It was almost natural in such circumstances for the Arab States to step forward and to fill this diplomatic void. They were, after all, independent political units, recognized by the international community, possessed of all the trappings of sovereignty, and having representation in world capitals as well as in the United Nations. Their reach and influence extended into circles to which the Palestinians had no access. Furthermore, the Arab States had only recently banded together to form an international regional organization (the Arab League), which provided the mechanisms for unified and concerted action that aimed at magnifying their diplomatic effectiveness.

Whatever else these transformations may have accomplished, they caused the entire Palestinian Question to be cast in an entirely different light. It was no longer perceived as a localized dispute between the Arabs and Zionists of Palestine, but as a much wider confrontation between Arab and Jew, encompassing far larger communities. From this vantage point the Palestinians' identity was gradually being submerged or diluted in his Arabdom, a development which was further accentuated by the outbreak of armed hostilities in which the armies of the neighboring states took part and which, significantly enough, came to be known as the first Arab-Israeli War.

The consequences of the 1948-49 conflict are now a matter of history. They have been analyzed and dissected in countless books. Strategy has been studied, heroism extolled, accountabilities unravelled, deficiencies noted, and remedies exhorted. Rarely, however, has attention been devoted to its impact on the Palestinians in political terms.

Aside from the fact that the majority of Palestinian Arabs found themselves all of a sudden as refugees, with all the human, legal, economic, social and psychological liabilities that this naked status entailed, politically speaking they were a bludgeoned group. Scattered throughout the neighboring states, denied the requisites of freedom of movement across state boundaries, their leadership discredited and defunct, whatever rudiments of organization they possessed in Palestine was now tattered and irrelevant. Furthermore, the immediate and burning issue before them was no longer the fundamental question of the future of Palestine, but of their right to return to their homes, lands and property, and to escape the privations and indignities which their newly acquired refugee status often brought. Efforts to revive the old political networks through the establishment of a government met with little enthusiasm on the part of the younger westernized Palestinian intelligentsia that was often contemptuous of the policies and personalities of the past and which could no longer be intimidated into silence. Besides, the creation of a vigorous and vociferous Palestinian movement would not have met with universal blessing from every Arab quarter. For all of its intrinsic tragedy, the Palestinian problem nevertheless did not eliminate old rivalries or dissipate deeply harbored ambitions. Indeed, in some instances it provided new opportunities for aggrandizement and the satisfaction of long-held desires.

In any event, the political initiative had long passed from the Palestinians to the Arab States who, in the aftermath of defeat, became steeped in a tumultuous soul-searching that unleashed a period of severe political instability and which gave added impetus to a long-felt desire to adjust a pattern of relationships with the Great Powers that derived from an imperial past. The general consensus was that the Palestine Question could not be tackled until internal political and economic stability was accomplished, a goal that was, in turn, deemed attainable only after the shackles of the colonial era had been entirely removed. So for the next few years the Palestinians had to take a back seat to such matters as the renegotiation of the Anglo-Egyptian Treaty of 1936, the Egyptian Revolution of 1952, agrarian reform, withdrawal of British troops from the Suez Base, the future military ties with the West, Baghdad Pact, Aswan Dam, Glubb Pasha, etc.

One should not assume that what eventually ensued in the next several years after 1948-49 was the result of a well-conceived and rational process. Some of it was, of course, the product of planning. But much of it was the by-product of accident, fortuitous circumstances and of what that great sixteenth-century Florentine secretary (Machiavelli) called the caprice of fortune.

The 1956 Suez Crisis, far from refocusing attention on the Palestinians, served only to divert attention from them. The conflict over Palestine, once a localized, and subsequently an 'internationalized' dispute, had now become global in its overtones. It now brought the ominous prospect of U.S. and U.S.S.R. involvement in addition to that of England and France. The issues posed had now transcended those of the region; the peace of the world was deemed at stake. The likelihood of nuclear warfare in an ever-shrinking universe in which local and regional conflicts could no longer be neatly separated from total world disorder had rapidly impinged on the consciousness of thinking human beings everywhere.

However, even when the spectre of nuclear disaster had faded, the Palestinians did not come into view. The international community was far too concerned with the immediacy of the issue attending Suez to pay them heed. Instead, the resources of the United Nations, and the surprisingly fertile imagination of its statesmen, were devoted to such matters as the future of the Canal, the modalities of British, French and Israeli withdrawal from Egypt, the creation, deployment and mandate of a United Nations Emergency Force, demilitarization, Sharm el-Sheikh, Straits of Tiran, Gulf of Aqaba, shipping, etc. One might say that, ironically enough, the more complex and magnified the Palestine Question became, the less visible were the Palestinians.

The events of 1967 hardly served to change the picture. Aside from the spate of humanitarian resolutions calling upon Israel to allow the new refugees to return to their homes, resolutions similar to the scores that had been passed over the last twenty years by various organs of the U.N., and which perhaps by their very repetitiveness seemed to have deprived them of their potency, the Palestinians did not seem to count a great deal in the new equations. Indeed, if anything, they were pushed even further into the background. True enough, the November 1967 Security Council resolution "affirm(ed) ... the necessity ... for achieving a just settlement of the refugee problem." But the bulk of that resolution was directed at such questions as the termination of belligerency, withdrawal of Israeli forces, acknowledgment of sovereignty, boundaries, territorial inviolability, navigation though international waters, inadmissibility of territorial annexation by conquest, demilitarization, designation of a Special Representative, and so on and so forth.

However, even though they may have been drowned out in the U.N. by what they may have considered tangential matters, in the Middle East itself the Palestinians were coming into their own. In the aftermath of the shattering defeat of the Arab armies, all the elements converged to bring them into prominence.

It was obvious to nearly everyone that the traditional and orthodox methods employed by the Arab States in dealing with Israel had proven themselves a failure. It was also clear that the highly vocal Arab leadership which had been so shrill prior to the War had now been tarnished, if not altogether disgraced. It was further evident that the remnants of the old Palestinian leadership, as symbolized by Ahmed Shukairy, which still pretended to speak in the name of the Palestinians, and which was heavily reliant on, and indeed subservient to, the will of the Arab League and some of its members, could no longer claim the Palestinians' allegiance. And in the probing self-examination and remarkably open debate that followed the Six-Day War, the voices of hitherto silent and none too prominent younger Palestinians came to be heard. These were in the main the voices of the children of the old Palestinian middle and lower-middle classes that despite their severe dislocation somehow managed to provide their sons and daughters with a university education. These offspring were individuals who were much more performance oriented than their elders, far less given to pompous pronouncements, a little better adept at organizational skills, and far more possessed of a sense of political realism.

An examination of the history of the past two decades finally convinced them of the futility of their dependence on the Arab States. They could clearly see that far from saving Palestine for the Palestinians, the Arab States only succeeded in surrendering more of the territory to Israel after each try. And far from holding what remained of it in trust for the Palestinians after 1949, they dispensed with it in a manner suited to their interests. Furthermore, some of the Arab States were now so anxious to preserve their own territorial integrity that in exchange for Israeli troop withdrawals they were ready to concede the loss of Palestine through the recognition of Israel and the ending of all claims to belligerency.

The general feeling among this younger generation of Palestinians was that the road back to Palestine could only be paved by the Palestinians themselves. They drew inspiration from the activities of the Algerians, Cubans and Vietnamese, and a few of them were well-versed in the literature of guerilla warfare and national liberation. Some went so far as to establish contacts with these groups and even received training and support from them. Gradually, the rudimentary beginnings of a few guerilla organizations came to be formed.

It was not, however, until after the 1967 June War that they finally came into prominence. The few attacks that they mounted in Israel and in the occupied areas were seized upon by the Arab masses and their governments as a sign that the struggle with Israel had not yet ended, that resistance was still in effect, and that while the Arabs may have lost a few battles the war itself was far from over. Contributions came pouring in from all corners of the Arab World. Money, supplies and weapons were sent. And in the publicity given the Israeli raid on Karameh in Jordan, recruits were easily obtained. Somehow the movement captured the imagination not only of the Palestinians in the refugee camps, but also of the ones in the universities, medicine, law, engineering and other professions. Donations of skills became readily obtained. Bases were established, clinics installed, and schools staffed. Almost overnight what was only an incipient movement turned into a well-structured and intricately woven organization, with a will of its own that is increasingly becoming an important factor in the new Middle East equation.

Expressed in plain and simple language, the object of the movement, according to some of its leaders, is the return of the Palestinians to their homes in a Palestine that would be de-Zionized. In other words, Palestine would revert to its old self when it consisted of two communities working in harmony side by side as they once did, under a political arrangement wherein Judaism would not bestow any special privileges. Just exactly what sort of government would be established, whether a 'balance' would be built into the political system, how Arab property would be restored and what would become of the Jews currently in possession of it, are not clearly spelled out. The impression is that at the moment the attention of this new Palestinian leadership is focused far more on the operational and military aspects than on the long-range political ones. Nevertheless, they seem tenacious in their determination to return to Palestine regardless of the obstacles and possible consequences. Toward that goal they are willing to sacrifice almost anything and to risk the ever-increasing likelihood of escalation and total conflict. Neither will they allow the Arab Governments to assume control over them, or to restrict them in their military conduct, as the current clashes in Lebanon have shown. Indeed, some have been known to express the belief that no Arab Government should be allowed to remain aloof from the struggle, and if its involvement ultimately resulted in military defeat and occupation by Israeli forces, then the chances for ultimate victory would be enhanced. In such circumstances the Israelis would then constitute a minority within a framework far better suited to waging guerilla warfare.

It is not my purpose to indulge in forecasting the likelihood of this possibility coming into being, but to indicate the type of thinking and activity that seems to be rampant among Palestinians. There is the tendency in certain quarters, particularly in Israeli ones, to play down the military effectiveness of the fedayyeen. The argument usually presented is that the Palestinians are obviously no match for the Israeli Army, that they are merely a small thorn in its side, and that in the final analysis they fall in the category of a nuisance that cannot, in all realism, pose a serious threat to the survival of the Jewish State.

Such a view, to my mind, is myopic. It merely concentrates on the present and places far too much emphasis on its military aspects, as the Israeli policy regarding the Palestinians clearly indicates. The sending of Israeli jets across the Jordan River or into Syria to strike at Fatah and other bases has become an almost daily affair. Inside the occupied territories unrest is met with incarcerations, expulsions, curfews, demolition of homes and other forms or threats of sanctions. Policies of this kind are probably due to the increased role of the professional military in the decision making process, the emergence of a new form of nationalism in Israel, and the readiness to submit to demands for reprisals from the rank and file. But it is also due, one suspects, to a distorted and uncomplimentary picture of the Arab in general, and the Palestinians in particular, in the Israeli mind. The image carried is that in the final analysis he is incompetent, lacking in organization, discipline or resolve, unable or unwilling to comprehend reality, having an infinite capacity for self-delusion, capable of understanding only force, and ever unlikely to sacrifice personal comfort for the demands of national goals. These and many other unflattering associations, further re-enforced by three Israeli military victories, have somehow planted in many an Israeli a *Herren* mentality where the Arab is concerned, one not unlike the intellectual framework which governed the behavior of nineteenth-century Europeans toward their colonial subjects. Indeed, so prevalent is this image that it has even been transmitted overseas to American shores.

The simple fact is that despite assertions to the contrary, many Israelis do not know the younger generation of educated and Westernized Palestinians. There are a great many Israelis, born since the creation of Israel twenty-one years ago, whose contacts and associations have been almost exclusively with the Palestinian minority in Israel which in the main is not one that has been able to achieve great economic and educational attainments. There are not many Arab students studying in Israeli universities. Nor are there many Arab scientists, doctors, or engineers working in Israeli laboratories, hospitals, or factories. The Palestinian Arabs now in Israel largely fall in the lower rungs of the socio-economic ladder. Besides, they are politically suspect, and feelings of hostility and suspicion further accentuate the gap or distance to which class discrepancies give rise.

Neither can it be said that the 'Arabicized' or 'Islamicized' Jew who came from the Arab countries is acquainted with this new breed of Palestinian. Indeed, whatever their previous conceptions may have been toward the Arabs in general they very likely had, since coming to Israel, undergone great transformations. Largely unskilled and uneducated, the Arabs in Israel were their competitors in the labor markets. Furthermore in their efforts not to be confused with the Arabs, they reacted in accordance with classic sociological patterns by seeking to dissociate themselves from them and by quickly incorporating the dominant values of the European group which again were replete with derogatory stereotypes of the Arab.

The one thing that Israelis, and incidentally many others, do not seem to realize is that the current Palestinian movement is directed by an impressive elite whose academic credentials would do credit to any country. It is not anything like that which dominated the various paramilitary groups that came into being prior to the establishment of Israel and which some older Israelis may still remember. There are estimates that there may be as many as fifty thousand Palestinians today holding university degrees. And an increasing number of these have been

moved by the activities of the fedayyeen to join in the general movement. It is interesting to note that Yasir Arafat, the present head of
the Palestine Liberation Organization, is a university trained engineer,
and that the leader of the Front for the Liberation of Palestine is a
medical doctor—a graduate of the American University of Beirut.
Admittedly the rank and file are not of such educational attainments
and many are recruited from the refugee camps. But they are receiving
superior training and direction which is already becoming a source of
greater discomfiture to Israel.

I do not mean to suggest that they are likely to attain such an overwhelming military capacity that they could defeat Israeli forces in open
combat. But by their activities they may spur a greater number of Palestinians, presently under Israeli occupation, to join the struggle. Elements are quickly converging which may propel a substantial body of
Palestinian youth to participate in the resistance movement. There are
already conditions of privation in Gaza. Unemployment is widespread,
and under-employment is high. Secondary school graduates—and bear
in mind that this June the third class will have graduated since the
occupation, with 4,500 in each class—are cut off from universities in
Arab lands and face a future of continued idleness with severe consequences to their lives and to those of their families. Despair may drive
them to acts which may in turn bring on an ever-widening cycle of sabotage and repression whose consequences can only bear ill to the future
of the region.

For Israel the resort to military measures cannot help but in the end
prove morally and institutionally corrosive. A society cannot maintain
its professed character with repression in its midst. The impact of emergency laws enacted, of violence and counter-violence, of the deep ha-
treds that are engendered, would most assuredly shake the foundations
of any society. Reliance on force would become automatic, and the
continued and increased suspension of civil liberties would be constitutionally debilitating. Indeed, the greatest threat to Israel, it seems
to me, is the one that may rise from within itself as a result of its increasing dependence on military means. No society espousing democratic principles can ultimately maintain its values and at the same time
become a praetorian state.

The Palestinians, the Israelis must realize, if any peace is to be
achieved in the region, are a living reality. It does not do Israel, the
Middle East, or the world, any service to pretend that they never
existed. Unlike what many Zionists would have had the world believe,
Palestine was not a land without a people to be earmarked for a people
without a land. Neither was it a desert which Israelis in the span of
twenty years made bloom. Palestinians lived there for centuries. They
ploughed their fields, planted their crops, ran their small industries and
tended their commerce. They were not, of course, as technologically
advanced as the European Zionists who came to settle in their midst.

But that does not mean that the Palestinians are a kind of *untermenschen* that can be continuously expelled to give way to settlement and security questions. Neither does it mean that they can be herded into a corner of the West Bank, integrated economically but deprived of citizenship rights. Such notions are outmoded and untenable. The economic cannot be separated from the political, or the other way around. Nor are the Palestinians, in any case, willing to concede that the Universal Declaration of Human Rights affirming that man is endowed with inalienable rights that include life, liberty and dignity falls short of covering them. And unless Israelis recognize this, I fear that the worst is yet to come.

Vanderbilt Univ.   SAMIR N. ANABTAWI
Nashville, Tenn.

The Position of the Palestinians in the Israeli-Arab Conflict and Their National Covenant (1968)

Y. HARKABI

Part I

THE PALESTINIANS IN THE ISRAEL-ARAB CONFLICT*

These days a sharp controversy is raging among us concerning the place of the Palestinians in the conflict, their collective identity and the question whether they are the party with whom Israel can negotiate a peace settlement.

Their self-definition as Palestinians gives them a strong sense of common identity. The overwhelming majority of them preserved their identity and attachment to Palestine despite the passage of time, their hardships and dispersion. This is also true of the period which preceded the Six Day War. Children who were born to Palestinian parents in other countries did not identify themselves to foreigners in terms of the country where they were born; they said rather, "I am from Haifa" or "I am from Jaffa," thus demonstrating their Palestinianism in a specific and concrete way.

It is true that states like the UAR and Iraq evoked the idea of "the Palestinian entity" in meetings of the Arab League from 1959 on, doing so for tactical reasons within inter-Arab rivalries, and the Palestine Liberation Organization was established by a decision of the Arab rulers at their First Summit Conference. However, the call for the Palestinians to organize themselves and assume the central role in the struggle against Israel came *also* from within the ranks of the Palestinians themselves. Such ideas recur with great forcefulness in the writings of Palestinians at the beginning of the sixties. This applies also to the fedayeen organizations. Though most of them were formed and continued to exist owing to the support of

---

3. By Y. Harkabi, Lecturer in Int'l Affairs, Hebrew Univ., formerly Brig. General and Head of the Strategic Research Dept. of the Ministry of Defense of Israel. This document was obtained through the courtesy of the Consulate Genera of Israel. (Translated by Y. Karmi.)

* Revised text of a lecture given at Tel-Aviv University on May 18, 1969 in memory of Moshe Haviv. Appeared in *Ma'ariv* November 21, 1969.

one or another Arab state, it would be a mistake to regard the Palestinian organizations as mere pawns that serve the aims of the Arab states.

A number of factors contributed to this feeling of identity and attachment to Palestine. First and foremost, the factor of a common place of origin, shared experiences, and common fate and suffering in the past and present. Another factor was the difficulty of absorption into Arab countries economically and, no less, socially. Despite the common language and cultural background, and notwithstanding Arab nationalism, the Palestinians felt like strangers in Arab countries and expressed this in their poetry. It is significant that one collection of poems was called "Hymns of the Strangers."* Their admission to feeling like strangers in Arab countries contradicts the basic conception of Arab nationalism, which has emphasized Arab unity, manifested in the feeling of being at home in every Arab country. In this matter, as in others, Arab nationalist ideology is not in tune with the feelings of the individual. The fact that a considerable segment of the Palestinians has been living *en masse* in refugee camps has also contributed to their preservation of group identity. The Zionist example may also have had some influence. A conflict is a competitive situation, and the preservation by the Jews of their attachment to Palestine served as an example to be emulated. It is as though the Palestinians said, "We are no less than the Jews, who preserved a tie to this country for a long period of time." Tibawi notes that "a new Zionism" was formed among the refugees.

Among the refugees a state of mind developed which stigmatized assimilation into Arab societies as an act of disloyalty. A committee of the Norwegian Institute for the Study of Peace, which investigated the situation in the Gaza Strip in 1964, was impressed by the unity of presentation and consensus in the argumentation of the refugees. They noted in this respect: "It is difficult to imagine a social group with a more homogeneous perception and definition of the past and the present than the refugees in the Gaza Strip. Regardless of age, income or educational level and the social status in general of the men we spoke with, the definition seemed to be the same—at least in so far as they wanted to present it to foreigners." Their report relates that among the refugees there was even a prevailing tendency to disparage efforts at improving living conditions in the camps, lest this imply the admission that these were permanent living places. The report notes that Palestinians tended to

---

* A. L. Tibawi, "Visions of the Return: The Palestine Refugees in Arabic Poetry and Art," *The Middle East Journal*, 17 (1963), pp. 507-526.

prefer short-term work contracts in Arab countries, again lest they be considered of little faith regarding the anticipated imminent "return." A need was generated to demonstrate a faith that, indeed, they soon would return to "the homeland." The refugees began calling themselves officially "returnees" (*'â'idûn*) instead of "refugees," in accordance with a decision of the First Congress of the Palestine Liberation Organization. There may have been an expectation that the psychological mechanism of "self-fulfilling prophecy" would operate, that is, the very name "returnees" assures not only that the hope would not fade but more, that it would be realised. The word *'awda*, "return," or "repatriation," was made a principal slogan. In the recesses of their heart many refugees probably doubted that hope for "the return" would materialize in the near, or even distant, future. But, according to the report of the Norwegians, the mechanism of "pluralistic ignorance" operated among them; that is, each one was apprehensive that only he was of little faith, as though the others were wholly confident in an early return, and as a result no one dared make his doubts public. Ideas that are repeated, even if not believed at first, are slowly assimilated in human consciousness, for otherwise a "cognitive dissonance" is created. It is uncomfortable to live in two different conceptual frameworks, what is said and what is believed, and ultimately belief is adjusted to what is said. Because of the stigma of absorption into Arab countries it was presumably easier for a Palestinian to become assimilated before 1948 than afterwards. Nevertheless, many were absorbed in Arab and other countries.

In their preservation of group attachment there was also an element of protest and negation of their situation as refugees, which is translated into the hope that one day redemption would come and they would return to their land. The return is seen as a collective salvation and messianic vision. Tibawi speaks of "the mystique of the return."

The form of attachment to Palestine varies with the generations. In the attachment of the *older generation* to the country there was a concrete factor: longing for property they left and their former way of life. Among the older generation a process of "idylization" of the way of life before "the disaster" operated against the background of negating life in the present. By selective memory, the shadows of Arab life in the land were forgotten, and the village house expanded with the passage of time and became a palace. In their stories to their children the parents probably described their life before the war in 1948 as a period of glory and a heroic struggle.

There may have been in this an element of apology by the father before his son, to this effect: "Don't look at me in my decline, for the life of the camp has destroyed me. Once I was a man." It is significant that 'Arif al-'Arif entitles his book, *al-Firdaws al-Mafqûd* (*Paradise Lost*).

Among the *younger generation*, which constitutes the majority of the Palestinians, the attachment is not directly experiential. The younger generation did not experience the hardships of the 1948 war and the exodus. Their quest to return does not stem from longing for some property, as in their parents' case, but from negation of their present life and from an *ideological* position: the wrong that was inflicted on the Palestinians, Israel's aggressiveness, and the requirement that justice be done and Israel liquidated. The education that the youth received brought them to the point where the village life of most of the parents ceased to enchant them. The return does not appear as a return to the village of their parents but as a political act in which the Palestinians become the sovereigns over Palestine and all their problems, as it were, are solved.

Paradoxically, the ideological attachment of the youth, though indirect, is by no means weaker than the concrete, direct attachment of the parents. The vehemence of the ideological and learned attachment can be much stronger than that of the concrete and direct attachment.

The Six Day War, and the possibility given to many Palestinians to see Israel, and even to visit their place of origin, could impair the concrete attachment, for it became clear to the visitors that the property for which they longed, and in whose imagined existence they sought consolation, was no longer. The concrete attachment to the country is more vulnerable to the concrete reality expressed in changes that took place in the scenery and the consolidation of the State of Israel, while the ideological attachment of the younger generation is more immune to these facts.

Illusion ultimately disappoints. This applies to us also. It is best for us to acknowledge facts of reality without attempting to deny them. An acknowledgment that the Palestinians have an attachment to Palestine need not produce in us a state of anxiety. The conflict is also a contest of attachments. Our awareness that the Arabs also have an attachment to the country need not impair our own. I emphasize this because I have found that there is among us a degree of fainthearted reluctance to see some of the facts of the Arab-Israeli conflict as they are. An example of this is the reaction

I have found in Israeli audiences to evidences of Arab attachment to Palestine.

In lectures before an Israeli audience I sometimes read a paragraph from Nasir ad-Din an-Nashashibi's book, *Return Ticket* (Beirut, 1962). Toward the end of the book (p. 205) the author says:

> Every year I shall say to my little son: "We shall return my son, and you will be with me; we shall return; we shall return to our land and walk there barefoot. We'll remove our shoes so that we may feel the holiness of the ground beneath us. We'll blend our souls with its air and earth. We'll walk till we come to the orange trees; we'll feel the sand and water; we'll kiss seed and fruit; we'll sleep in the shade of the first tree we meet; we'll pay homage to the first martyr's grave we come across. We'll turn here and there to trace our lives. Where are they? Here with this village square, with this mosque's minaret, with the beloved field, the desolate wall, with the remains of a tottering fence and a building whose traces have been erased. Here are our lives. Each grain of sand teaches us about our life. Do you not remember Jaffa and its delightful shore, Haifa and its lofty mountain, Beth Shean and the fields of crops and fruit, Nazareth and the Christians' bells, Acre and the memories of al-Jazzar, Ibrahim Pasha, Napoleon and the fortress, the streets of Jerusalem, my dear Jerusalem, Tiberias and its peaceful shore with the golden waves, Majdal and the remnant of my kin in its land?"

When one reads this paragraph, even if he be poisoned by the abundant words of abuse and calumny against Israel found in Nashashibi's book which preceded this paragraph, he will admit, even if reluctantly, that there is here an expression of genuine longing and love for the country.

I found that an older audience, upon hearing this, would be moved. The divulgence that an Arab too may have an emotional attachment to this country was a confusing and ominous surprise. In a younger audience the reaction was different. Among them the prevailing tendency was to accept the plain meaning of the words as something natural and understandable. In their reaction the youth said, in effect, "If the author wishes to run barefoot, let him run and get himself stuck by thorns." I think that, despite its frivolousness, such a reaction is more healthy.

Whoever is moved by these manifestations of human longing for this country, and whose heart is touched by this phenomenon, should have no illusions concerning its significance for us. The refinement expressed in feelings of yearning does not, by any means, become refinement toward the Israelis. On the contrary, on the following page Nashashibi describes the effect his words will have on his son:

> I shall see the hatred in the eyes of my son and your sons. I shall see how they take revenge. If they do not know how to take revenge, I shall teach them. And if they agree to a truce or peace, I shall fight against them as I fight against my enemy and theirs. I want them to be callous, to be ruthless, to take revenge. I want them to wash away the disaster of 1948 with the blood of those who prevent them from entering their land. Their homeland is dear to them, but revenge is dearer. We'll enter their lairs in Tel-Aviv. We'll smash Tel-Aviv with axes, guns, hands, fingernails and teeth, while singing the songs of Qibiya, Dir Yasin and Nasir ad-Din.* We shall sing the hymns of the triumphant, avenging return. . . .

Truly, it is a tragic complication in which we are enmeshed. In the presence of the intention of annihilation we cannot permit ourselves to become soft, and at times not even to assume a humanistic stance, for this may imply responsiveness to the quest of our annihilation, and this is a self-contradiction.

The leaders of the Palestinians made special efforts to preserve the Palestinian attachment of the members of their flock and to nurture it by means of education, writing of history, collection of folklore, and the like. In brief, efforts were made to mould a Palestinian people although it had no territory. In this also the Jews, as a people without territory and government, served as an example. It was easy for the Palestinian leadership and intelligentsia to find work and become absorbed in Arab countries. But for the sake of the political goal they were callous to the suffering of their people and exerted pressure upon them not to become absorbed but to remain in their camps. This duplicity was not hidden from the refugees, who regarded the Palestinian leadership with a great deal of reservation. It is difficult to place trust in a leadership which establishes itself in convenient positions and leads a normal way of life while at the same time demanding of its flock that it live wretchedly. This may have been one of reasons why the tendency among the refugees to organize themselves was late in coming.

It is understandable that among the Palestinians especially,

---

* A village east of Tiberias which is frequently mentioned in Arabic literature as an example of Jewish terrorism. 'Arif al-'Arif relates that ten Arabs were killed there (an-Nakba, Vol. I, p. 205).

along with their attachment to Palestine, pan-Arab sentiments would be more prevalent than among other Arab groups. Through their dispersion and wanderings many of the Palestinians became acquainted with Arab countries and sometimes even attached to them, whereas Egyptian, Syrian and Lebanese Arabs tend to know one country, and patriotism toward their homeland predominates pan-Arab sentiments.* In this also they can draw an analogy with Jews. Just as the Jews, owing to their dispersion, tended toward cosmopolitanism, so the Palestinians tended toward pan-Arabism. It is not accidental that the Qawmiyyûn al-'Arab movement, which so emphasized the idea of Arab unity, emerged from amid the Palestinians.

Acquaintance with the Arab states did not always endear these states to the Palestinians, for they indeed had their fill of bitters with them. Their loyalty to ideas of pan-Arabism may have arisen among them as a compensation for the grievances they had against the individual Arab countries. The Palestinians had complaints against the Arab countries for several reasons: they did not fulfill their obligations to the Palestinians, imposed discriminatory restrictions upon them, and manipulated the Palestinian problem within their own rivalries. The Palestinians were a fermenting factor in the Arab countries. Several of the Arab states were apprehensive about their influence and consequently clipped their wings. The Palestinians have also had many grievances on the social level, for many Arabs were indifferent to their suffering and did not treat them as brethren in distress.

The Palestinians gave vent to their grievances in their literature (Ghassan Kanafani's novels for example). But it would be simplistic to conclude from these literary accounts that, because of their resentment of Arab countries, they will be amenable to agreement with us. The heart of man is sufficiently wide to encompass hostility toward more than one enemy, and the enemy of his enemy does not automatically become his friend. Along with grievances toward the Arab countries the Palestinians also have feelings of gratitude, for they did derive benefits from these countries. Even if they experienced difficulties of absorption, they could find work and send their chil-

---

* Arab ideologues tend now to distinguish between the one Arab "nation" and the many Arab "peoples," such as the Egyptians, Iraqis and so on. They call attachment to the nation *qawmiyya*, "nationalism," whereas attachment to the people, and especially its land, they call *waṭaniyya*, which recently took on the sense of "patriotism." Correspondingly, there are also those who distinguish between the general homeland of all the Arabs, *al-waṭan al-'âmm*, and the homeland of a specific people, which is called *al-waṭan al-khâss*.

dren to to study in their colleges. The recognition that in the confrontation against Israel they ultimately depend on the support of the Arab countries, especially in the military struggle, is another factor which inhibits the development of enmity toward them. The result, therefore, is not dissociation from the Arab countries but a complex attitude that contains an element of ambivalence: friendship and distrust at the same time.

Arabic belles-lettres are certainly a more faithful mirror of what is happening in the public than the political literature written according to the dictate of rulers. There is more spontaneity in its expressiveness than there is in publicistic writing   [sic]. However, in evaluating political positions one should distinguish well between the position on the popular level and the one on the government level. For example, in the literary depiction of English life in the years 1938-1939 enmity toward the Germans was not at all conspicuous, but an inference from this to England's position as a state would be misleading. From literary descriptions of the life of the Japanese farmer it was probably impossible to infer that there existed a conflict between Japan and the United States critical enough to produce an explosion as great as the attack on Pearl Harbor. In general, the individual is not preoccupied in his private life with a national conflict. He worries about his personal problems, first and foremost his daily bread, especially in countries where poverty prevails. Therefore, it would also be an error to derive lessons concerning the political position of a group of Palestinians or Egyptians from literary descriptions of the life of the individual in that group. If the conflict preoccupies the Egyptian as an individual slightly, this by no means implies that it is marginal to Egypt as a state. If the average Egyptian is not filled with enmity toward Jews and Israel, this is not translatable into political terms. Egypt as a state may be bitterly hostile toward Israel. Political leadership determines political objectives, and it is not necessarily influenced daily by popular conceptions. The direction of influence is generally the opposite, for recognized and accepted leaders, even if they are not helmsmen of the state, influence their people more than their people influence them. Political opinions and views among the public are not formed spontaneously as much as they are the effect of influence by that circle called "the moulders of public opinion": local leaders, journalists, authors and, at their head, the political leadership. Popular emotions do not create an international conflict. For the most part, people do not make war because they hate; they hate because they make war. It is political conflict that incites hatred. Notions that are current among the people may have significance in so far as they bear upon their support of the government. But again, this requires qualification, especially as regards Arab countries. Regimes did not come to power in Arab countries because they had popular support necessarily, but having achieved power they could create it. The regimes in Arab countries can be unpopular, or become unpopular, and nevertheless retain their position for a long time.

A question that is being argued with great fervor is whether the Palestinians are a people or nation. But there is no accepted criterion or definition by which to decide who is a people or nation. It cannot be determined, for example, what the necessary components are which form a nation. Neither territory nor language are a necessary criterion. The Jews, for example, had no territory, and there are nations which have no language of their own, or which speak a number of languages. It was not without reason that Ernest Renan defined the nation subjectively as "a daily plebiscite." That is, the human group determines according to its feelings and mutual attachment whether it is a nation or not. The argument that the Palestinians are not a nation because such a nation has not existed in the past is not persuasive. No nation existed primordially, and all were the product of an historical process, generally by affiliation to a governmental center. The distinction between people and nation on the one hand, and non-people and non-nation on the other, is not a dichotomous division. It seems better to view nationhood as a continuum, on the one side of which there is a group of people among whom there is no cohesion, and on the other side of which there is a group whose cohesion has been realized. This continuum implies that the existence of the nation is relative. For example, the Swedes, if it is possible to say so, are "more a nation" than the Turks, the Turks more a nation than the Pakistanis, the Pakistanis more a nation than the Tanzanians, and so on. The Palestinians are found somewhere on this continuum, and their national status will be determined by what happens to them. If at some point a Palestinian state is created, this status will reach maturity and be reflected also in subjective feelings.

Until 1948 the conflict was basically between Israel and the Palestinians. The intervention of the Arab states caused the role of the Palestinians to diminish. After May, 1948 their position in the conflict became marginal. The pendulum swings back in the first half of the sixties, when the Palestinians again gain prominence. It should be noted that this emergence parallels a process of *rad-*

icalization in the concept of the form of warfare against Israel. Ideas appear to the effect that the conflict involves "a war of national liberation," in which the Palestinians will be the vanguard, and the war, at least in its early stages, will take on the form of guerrilla warfare. It should be remembered that, in the meantime, changes of the guard had started in the Palestinian leadership, and a younger generation emerged, of a predominantly Leftist state of mind, which advocated activism in the struggle with Israel and disparaged the "passivity" (salbiyya) of the previous generation. This state of mind of the younger generation was first given a literary expression. The younger generation deliberated and expressed thoughts in periodicals and books concerning the most efficient form of combatting Israel. Only afterwards were these ideas given organizational form in the shape of the fedayeen groups, the chief of them being Fatah.

A great change took place in the status of the Palestinians as a result of the Six Day War. The stature of the Palestinians, which was bowed by their defeat in 1948 and their exile, was raised, for after the downfall of the Arab armies the fedayeen actions gained renown for them in Arab countries and outside, and the Palestinians were transformed from an inferior factor into standard-bearers of Arab nationalism and a source of pride. Again, this is not always translated into the concrete, practical attitude of the population in Arab countries toward them. Their support remains on a national and political level and is not always expressed in real action to mitigate the suffering of the Palestinian refugees.

In the past the conflict was presented as though it had two levels: the first, the national-geopolitical antagonism between Israel and Arab nationalism; and the second, the problem of the Palestinians. Arab ideologues emphasized that the antagonism on the national level was the principal one, and that even if the issue of the Palestinians were solved and the refugees settled, still the principal antagonism between Israel and Arabdom would remain.

As a result of the war the situation has been reversed and, according to current fashion, the contradiction with the Palestinians is presented as the essence of the conflict, for this is allegedly a struggle for national liberation. Arabs explain, especially to foreigners, that the antagonism is not that of the large Arab states versus a small state like Israel but of an oppressed people against a strong, colonialistic, oppressive state. David has become Goliath. It is maintained that the antagonism of the rest of the Arab states is a by-product of the Palestinian cause. Thus, the geopolitical issue is demoted, if only temporarily and for purposes of presentation. The ecology of the conflict is shifted. It is not between states but between a government and a people struggling for its liberation, and by definition a just war that deserves support. The "liberation" of the Palestinians is not the elimination of their subjugation but the establishment of their sovereignty over Palestine.

The paradox in this switch is that when the conflict was marginal for public opinion in Arab countries it was represented as a conflict between the Arab states and Israel, while precisely when the importance and saliency of the conflict increased in the national life of neighboring states it is not represented as a conflict between them and Israel but between the Palestinians and Israel.

Since the importance of the Palestinians in the conflict has grown, the question arises: can a settlement emerge from them?

The Palestinians are divided into two main groups. The first consists of those who live in the West Bank (Judah and Samaria) and the Gaza Strip. Many in this group are apprehensive about a renewal of the war, for they may assume by extrapolation that in the contest between Israel and the Arabs they are liable to be the principal victims. For this reason, it is no wonder that these people would want a settlement which might prevent a renewed eruption of the war. They could also explain to the Arab countries that such a settlement with Israel will benefit the Arabs, for it would bring about withdrawal of the Israeli military presence from the territories that are occupied. This settlement, they could contend, is not the final word, and would not be a barrier when the Arab states regain their strength, making it possible for them to reopen the war. In fact, the idea of a Palestinian state arose in Arab countries. It was brought up by the Egyptian journalist, Ahmad Baha' ad-Din (in his book, *The Proposal for a State of Palestine and the Controversy Surrounding It*). However, he did not intend a state that would make peace with Israel but "a confrontation state" that would include Jordan. This state would make a military pact with the other Arab states and serve as the base for the onslaught against Israel. It should be noted that the idea is not new; it is merely the metamorphosis of an idea that arose previously concerning the establishment of "The Republic of Palestine." The issue was brought up by General Qassem in 1959 and arose again during the first stages in the establishment of the Palestine Liberation Organization at the beginning of 1964, and then afterwards when relations between the organization and the Jordanian rulers became strained.

The leaders of the Arab states, including the leaders of the Palestinian organizations, took a strong, unequivocal stand against a Palestinian state in any agreement with Israel. Most of those who debated the proposal of Baha' ad-Din, whose articles he includes in his book, rejected it. They pointed out that the present time is not appropriate for this proposal because the establishment of a Palestinian state would arouse opposition among circles close to the government of Jordan and thus produce an internal rift, weakening the front against Israel.

An agreement by the Palestinians of the West Bank to a settlement with Israel in face of opposition by the Arab rulers would brand them as traitors. One must not underestimate the deterrent force of this stigma for them. More serious from their point of view is the fear that a settlement with Israel would cut them off from the places of dispersion where their families are—from sons, daughters and relatives in Arab countries. This is how the Arab countries might penalize them. The Palestinians on the West Bank cannot, therefore, allow themselves a settlement for human and family reasons. It is no surprise that so few expressed support for the idea of a Palestinian state.

The Palestinians of the West Bank want two things; the catch is that they are incompatible. It is possible that many of them wish a settlement with Israel, but on condition that the Arab League and the Arab states endorse it. They face the dilemma: on the one hand, fear of war and the desire for a settlement that would prevent it; and on the other, apprehension of separation from their families and national ostracism. It is no wonder that, when they are forced to choose between leaving the situation as is with all its dangers and a settlement in defiance of the Arab countries, they tend to elect the first alternative.

A strong stand against the idea of a Palestinian state on the West Bank was taken by the Palestinian National Council in its Fourth Congress, which took place in Cairo beginning on July 10, 1968.* Among its political resolutions, under the heading, "The Dubious Calls for Creation of a Fraudulent Palestinian Entity," it is stated:

> The Zionist movement, imperialism and the tool of both, Israel, are making efforts to reinforce the Zionist aggression against Palestine and to strengthen the Israeli military victory of 1948 and of 1967 by establishing a Palestinian entity in the territory conquered after the aggression of June 5th, an entity

---

* The Palestinian National Council is the highest institution of the Palestine Liberation Organization, which now amalgamates virtually all the Palestinian organizations.

which will bestow legality and permanence on the State of Israel. This is an act which entirely contradicts the right of the Palestinian Arab people to the whole of its homeland of Palestine. This fraudulent entity is actually an Israeli colony which will finally liquidate to Israel's advantage the Palestinian problem. At the same time, it will be a temporary stage which will enable Zionism to evacuate the Arab inhabitants from the Palestinian territories which were conquered after the aggression of June 5th. Moreover, there will be the possibility of setting up a vassal ('amil) Palestinian Arab administration, upon which Israel will depend in its contest with the Palestinian revolution. There also enter into this framework the imperialist and Zionist programs to place the Palestinian territories conquered after June 5th under international administration and protection.* Whence the National Council declares its absolute denunciation of the idea of the fraudulent Palestinian entity in the territories of Palestine conquered after June 5th and, together with this, denunciation of every form of international protection. Likewise, it declares that every Arab individual or group, Palestinian or non-Palestinian, calling for the vassal entity and international protection, or supporting it, is the enemy of the Palestinian Arab people and the Arab nation. (The official report of the Congress, pp. 39-40.)
The declaration concerning "the enemy of the people" is, in effect, a threat against life.

Presenting the problem as though what is required for a settlement with the Palestinians is Israel's recognition of them is a distortion. This indictment on the tongue of Israelis only abets [sic] the slander against Israel, that it is the principal barrier to peace. If among some circles in the world our image has become tarnished, not only the extremists among us, but even many of those who claim to be men of peace, are responsible. Israel, in fact, has already recognized a Palestinian entity, as implied in its very acceptance of the Partition Resolution in 1947, which determined the establishment of a Palestinian Arab state in our neighborhood. The problem was, and remains, quite the opposite: not recognition on our part of their right to a section of this country but the non-recognition on the part of the Palestinians and the Arabs of our national right to a separate national existence of our own. In the Palestinian position there was a consistent totalistic demand for exclusive possession.

---

* This has to do with the idea of demilitarizing the West Bank for a number of years under UN protection. It was suggested by foreign consuls in conversations with men of the West Bank and was considered by its leaders.

This appeared in the form of opposition to the Partition Plan, and appears today in the demand for "general liberation" and sovereignty over the whole territory of Palestine. (The reader will find documentation of this in the version of the Palestinian National Covenant in Part II.) Our declaration from morning to evening that we recognize the Palestinians is entirely irrelevant to the possibility of establishing a Palestinian state through an agreement with us, even within the Armistice demarcation lines.

The second Palestinian group consists of those found outside the present boundaries. They have nothing to lose from the continuation of the conflict, as do the Arabs of the West Bank. Their leaders have capitalized on the conflict and thrive on it. Men like Yassir Arafat and George Habash acquired a high status only owing to the conflict. In their case there is rabid opposition to a compromise solution. They vehemently oppose any political settlement, regardless of boundaries or conditions, because their opposition is to the principle of a Jewish state in any size or shape. They formulated this opposition to a political settlement in their "National Covenant," in its new version adopted by their Congress in Cairo of July, 1968 and reinforced it with explicit resolutions. The National Covenant is the Palestinians' basic political document and it was approved by most of the terrorist organizations.* Concurrence with it is a condition for joining the "Command of Armed Struggle," which now makes joint announcements for most of the terrorist organizations. What is said in it has more weight and importance than the declaration of any Palestinian spokesman. For understanding the Arab position, especially that of the Palestinians, there is not a more important document. Article 21 of this charter asserts: "The Palestinian Arab people, in expressing itself through the armed Palestinian revolution,** rejects every solution that is a substitute for the complete liberation of Palestine. . . ." The right of self-determination becomes the right of "restoring" the whole territory of Palestine. The Jews now living in the country have no right of national self-determination. Many Palestinian leaders outside the country affirm that they do not fear another war, nor even another defeat of the Arab states. On the contrary, it appears that they are interested in embroiling the Arab states in the conflict as much as possible. The position of the Palestinians toward us is

---

* See below, Part II.

** "The armed Palestinian revolution" is an idiom from the lexicon of Fatah. It is expressed in the fact that the Palestinians take upon themselves the chief role in the struggle against Israel by undertaking fedayeen actions.

polarized. Their hostility toward Israel is much more central in their world-view than was the hostility of the Nazis to Jews. However, they now choose to hide their aim of destroying Israel in euphemistic expressions, such as, "the dezionization of Israel," or "the restoration of the rights of the Arabs in Palestine," which does not alter the basic meaning, namely, the annihilation of Israel.

Even though the Arabs' confidence in their ability to achieve their aim was shaken by the Six Day War, the radicalism of the Palestinian leadership outside the country increased as a result of the war. This can be deduced from comparison of the Covenant in its first version of May, 1964, from the time of Shukeiry, with the version adopted under the influence of Yahya Hamuda and Yassir Arafat concerning the fate of the Jews in the free Palestinian Arab state after it is "liberated" and Israel annihilated. The former version can be interpreted to the effect that the Jews who lived in Palestine in 1947 would be recognized as Palestinians, that is, would be able to remain; whereas in the new text, as revised in the fourth session of the National Council (July, 1968), it is explicitly stated that only Jews who lived permanently in Palestine before 1917 would be recognized as Palestinians. This implies that the rest are aliens and must leave. It is indeed difficult to agree with the claim of some people, that the Arabs have become more realistic and their position more moderate, if a hallowed and authoritative document like the National Covenant specifies the aim of banishing almost two and a half million Jews.

What can be a more flagrant contradiction of the slogan they brandish today concerning a "pluralistic society"? It should be mentioned that the representatives of all the Palestinian organizations participated in the Congress, including the principal fedayeen groups. The Popular Front for the Liberation of Palestine, which is critical of the Palestine Liberation Organization, did not criticize this article. The importance of such articles in the Covenant is not in their practical value but in the state of mind reflected in them. Shukeiry did speak of throwing the Jews into the sea and used many vilifying expressions, but his position was in principle less radical. In view of the extremism of the official Palestinian and Arab position, what value is there to the words of an Arab student outside the country who tries to lend moderation to his remarks, whether out of false piety or an effort to conform to the general atmosphere and find favor in foreigners' eyes, while in closed gatherings of Arab students he holds the official position, and upon returning to his country shows the same tendency to conform to the radical atmosphere of the Arab countries? Even if we assume that he was sincere in his remarks, their value is nil over against the collective position. Moreover, there is no sign of any dissociation from this formulation of the Covenant by any Arab group, including Arab student organizations abroad. In no Arab newspaper or other publication was there even the slightest afterthought about the wisdom of this formulation. In the meantime, another two Congresses were held and the Covenant was not amended. It seems that there is no more decisive evidence regarding the essence of the Palestinian Arab position.

One may ponder what induced the Palestinian Congress which assembled in Cairo on July 10, 1968 to introduce this change which is so radical regarding the Jews "who would be permitted" to remain in a Palestinian state. We shall probably have to wait for solid information until clarifications are published by the participants in the Congress, or until its minutes or those of the Covenant Committee appointed to formulate it become known. In the meantime, it is possible to guess what factors prompted this. It may be that the very emphasis by Palestinian spokesmen that the state will be "democratic" necessitates the reduction of the number of Jews to a small minority. It is also possible that the radicalization of their position as result of Fatah's gaining control of the Palestine Liberation Organization produces greater doctrinal consistency: since Zionism is despicable, it is necessary to purge the country of all the Jews who came after the first political recognition that was granted to Zionism in the Balfour Declaration. Fatah defines the purpose of the war thus: "The action of liberation is not only the liquidation of an imperialistic base but the obliteration of a society" (Fatah pamphlet, *Taḥrîr al-Aqṭâr al-Muḥtalla wa-Uslûb al-Kifâḥ ḍidd al-Isti'mâr al-Mubâshir* [*The Liberation of the Occupied Territories and the Means of Combatting Direct Colonialism*], new edition, September, 1967, p. 16; Fatah Yearbook, 1968, p. 39). It may also be that the qualitative superiority of the Israeli and Israeli society, which was conspicuous in the Six Day War, in contrast to Arab individual and societal weakness, engenders apprehensions about living together with a significant Jewish minority; hence the need that it be small. Reduction of the number of Jews in Palestine is inherent in the Arab position. If to the outside world they now prudently avoid specifying that it will be done by violent means, as a compensation, the dimensions of the reduction have increased.

The Palestinian Arab position, as expressed in pronouncements of Palestinian spokesmen, is not only a demand to return to Palestine as its sovereigns but that Palestine should return to the Arabs as Arab, that is, after its foreign population is purged from it. It is not accidental that in their descriptions of its "liberation" they frequently use the verb "purify." Professor Fayez Sayegh, the chief Arab propagandist in the United States, who was a member of the Executive Committee of the Palestine Liberation Organization and the founder of the Palestine Research Organization, formulates the position in the following words: "Peace in the land of Palestine and its neighbors is our fondest desire. The primary condition for this is the liberation of Palestine, that is, the condition is our return to an Arab Palestine and the restoration of Palestine to us *as Arab*" (Emphasis added. *Ḥafna min Ḍabâb* [*A Handful of Mist*], PLO Research Center, Beirut, July, 1966, p. 19), Shafiq al-Hut, the head of the Beirut branch of the Palestine Liberation Organization, writes in the same spirit: "Disregarding the Palestinian entity is only a part of the Zionist imperialist plot, the aim of which is the liquidation of the people of Palestine and prevention of its attaining its right in the struggle for liberation of its usurped country, restoration of it as free and Arab, and returning its people to it as free and sovereign, abounding with honor and glory" (Haqâ'iq *'alâ Ṭarîq at-Taḥrîr* [*Truths on the Way to Liberation*], PLO Research Center, Beirut, November, 1966, p. 6). Publications of Fatah usually end with the motto, "Long live a free Arab Palestine," emphasizing the Arab character the population must have.

Among the Arabs the Palestinians outside the country are the most radical and uncompromising group. Their leaders and intellectuals acquired positions and influence in Arab public life, and they are the chief inciters against Israel. These Palestinians are not hostile to Israel on account of the hostility of the Arab states but the opposite: the hostility of the Arab states is caused to a great degree by the hostility of the Palestinians. Nasser reiterates the statement, "We shall not concede the rights of the Palestinians," that is, he presents himself as fighting their war. Nasser repeatedly defines the Palestinian problem as one of "a people" and its "fatherland," that is, the people must become sovereign over its fatherland. Nasser indicated that he would agree to a peace settlement after a just solution from the point of view of the Palestinians was found. He could agree to the Security Council Resolution of November 22, 1967 because this condition was included in it. The problem is that according to his interpretation this justice means the sovereignty of the Palestinians over their homeland. The injustice inflicted on the Palestinians is not only in their loss of property but is implicit in the circumstance that their homeland and sovereignty were taken from them. Less than restoration of sovereignty is not "just," and a partial justice is a self-contradiction because it permits the injustice to remain. Thus, the use of the language current among the Arabs, "a just solution of the problem of the Palestinians," is actually a euphemism for the destruction of Israel. The existence of Israel and a just solution of the problem of the Palestinians, as the Palestinians and Arabs define it, are thus incompatible.

A complication is created which is the essence of the Arab-Israeli conflict at the present stage. The Palestinians on the West Bank can hardly allow themselves to reach a settlement with us on account of the Arab states. The Arab states are bound to a degree that should not be minimized [sic] by their commitment to the Palestinians, especially those outside our borders. In this triangle, therefore, the Palestinian leadership outside our borders is the principal barrier to a settlement.

At the present stage the Palestinians outside the country are more influential than those of the West Bank. The relationship is asymmetrical. The Palestinian leaders outside the country have influence over the Palestinians of the West Bank, but it is doubtful if the leaders of the West Bank could influence the Palestinians outside to change their position. This change is possible only by means of the suppression of their organizations by the Arab states. Indeed, between them and the Arab states there are seeds of antagonisms which may develop into a confrontation.

One should not overlook the status and influence this Palestinian leadership outside the country has. However, when it becomes clear to what extent it has failed, especially in relying on fedayeenism, when this does not produce the anticipated results, its status is bound to be weakened. When the Arab states discover to what extent continuation of the conflict is destructive from their aspect, draws them into political disintegration, and denies them any possibility of national progress and recovery, they may take action against the Palestinian organizations outside the country. Then there will be an opening for negotiation and a settlement between Israel and the Palestinians nearby, and between Israel and the Arab countries.

WORKS CITED

al-'Arif, 'Arif. an-Nakba: Nakbat Bayt al-Maqdis wal-Firdaws al-Mafqûd (The Disaster: The Disaster of Palestine and the Paradise Lost). 5 vols. Sidon-Beirut: al-Maktaba al-'Asriyya, 1947-1955.

Baha' ad-Din, Ahmad. Iqtirâh *Dawlat Filasṭîn wa-mâ Dâra ḥawlahâ min Mu-nâqashât (The Proposal for a State of Palestine and the Controversy Sur-rounding It)*. Beirut: Dar al-Adab, 1968.

Galtung, I. and J. *A Pilot Project from Gaza*. Peace Research Institute, Oslo, February, 1964.

al-Hut, Shafiq. *Ḥaqâ'iq 'alâ Ṭarîq at-Taḥrîr (Truths on the Way to Liberation)*. PLO Research Center. Beirut, November, 1966.

Munazzamat at-Taḥrîr al-Filasṭîniyya (PLO). al-Majlis al-Waṭanî al-Filasṭînî al-Mun'aqad fî al-Qâhira fî 10-17 Tammûz (Yûliyô), 1968 (The Palestinian National Council, which Convened in Cairo July 10-17, 1968). Official Report.

an-Nashashibi, Nasir ad-Din. *Tadhkirat 'Awda (Return Ticket)*. Beirut: al-Maktab at-Tijari, 1962.

Sayegh, Fayez. Hafna *min Ḍabâb (A Handful of Mist)*. PLO Research Center. Beirut, Julŷ, 1966.

Tibawi, A. L. "Visions of the Return: The Palestine Refugees in Arabic Poetry and Art," *The Middle East Journal*, 17 (1963), pp. 507-526.

Part II

THE PALESTINIAN NATIONAL COVENANT*

The Palestinian National Covenant is perhaps the most important document of this stage of the Israel-Arab conflict, especially with regard to the Arab side. It represents a summation of the official position of the Palestinian organizations in the conflict.

The previous version of the Covenant was adopted by the First Palestinian Congress, which convened in Jerusalem in May, 1964 at the time of the establishment of the Palestine Liberation Organization. In the official English translation of the previous version it was called "Covenant" and not "Charter," in order to emphasize its national sanctity, and the introductory words to the Covenant conclude with an oath to implement it. The Congress stipulated that a Palestinian National Council, the highest institution of the Palestinian organizations, would meet periodically, and that a two-thirds majority of the Council members would be required to amend the Covenant. As a result of the changes which came about in the Palestine Liberation Organization after the Six Day War the Palestinian National Council convened in Cairo for its fourth session on July 10-17, 1968 and amended the Covenant. It should be noted that representatives of almost all the Palestinian

---

* Appeared in *Maariv* December 12, 1969.

organizations existing in Arab countries participated in this session, including all the fedayeen organizations. Fatah and the fedayeen organizations under its influence had thirty-seven representatives in the National Council of one hundred members and the Popular Front had ten. Fatah's style is recognizable in the new Covenant. This amended version was certainly not formulated casually; it represents a position that was seriously considered and weighed. The amended version is here presented. In order to highlight the changes we shall compare this version with its predecessor.

The main principles which were set down in the Covenant are:

In the Palestinian State only Jews who lived in Palestine before 1917 will be recognized as citizens (Article 6).

Only the Palestinian Arabs possess the right of self-determination, and the entire country belongs to them (Articles 3 and 21).

Any solution that does not involve total liberation of the country is rejected. This aim cannot be achieved politically; it can only be accomplished militarily (Articles 9 and 21).

Warfare against Israel is legal, whereas Israel's self-defense is illegal (Article 18).

For the sake of completeness the Covenant is presented here in its entirety.

THE PALESTINIAN NATIONAL COVENANT*

THIS COVENANT WILL BE CALLED "THE PALESTINIAN NATIONAL COVENANT" (AL-MÎTHÂQ AL-WAṬANÎ AL-FILASṬÎNÎ).

In the previous version of the Covenant of May, 1964 the adjective "national" was rendered by *qawmî*, the usual meaning of which in modern Arabic is pan-Arab and ethnic nationalism, whereas here they use the adjective *waṭanî*, which signifies nationalism in its narrow, territorialistic sense as patriotism toward a specific country. This change intends to stress Palestinian patriotism.

---

* The body of the document is translated from the Arabic original. Articles of the 1964 Covenant repeated here are rendered on the basis of the official English translation of that Covenant but with alterations of style and terminology. The same procedure is followed in translating quotations from the earlier Covenant cited in the commentary (Y.K.)

ARTICLES OF THE COVENANT[4]

ARTICLE 1) PALESTINE IS THE HOMELAND OF THE PALESTINIAN ARAB PEOPLE AND AN INTEGRAL PART OF THE GREAT ARAB HOMELAND, AND THE PEOPLE OF PALESTINE IS A PART OF THE ARAB NATION.

In most Arab constitutions it is simply stipulated that the people of that country constitutes an integral part of the Arab nation. Here, because of the special problem of territory, it is also stressed that the land is an integral part of the general Arab homeland. The previous version in the Covenant of 1964 was more vague: "Palestine is an Arab homeland bound by strong Arab national ties to the rest of the Arab countries which together form the Great Arab Homeland." The combination "the Palestinian Arab people" recurs often in the Covenant and is also intended to stress the special status of the Palestinians, though as Arabs.

ARTICLE 2) PALESTINE WITH ITS BOUNDARIES THAT EXISTED AT THE TIME OF THE BRITISH MANDATE IS AN INTEGRAL REGIONAL UNIT.

The same formulation as in the previous version. It is implied that Palestine should not be divided into a Jewish and an Arab state. Although it is an accepted tenet of Arab nationalism that existing boundaries should be abolished, since they were artificially delineated by the imperialist powers, here they are sanctified. The expression "that existed at the time of the British Mandate" is vague. The article is subject to two interpretations: 1) The Palestinian State includes also Jordan and thus supersedes [sic] it; 2) The West Bank is detached from Jordan.

ARTICLE 3) THE PALESTINIAN ARAB PEOPLE POSSESSES THE LEGAL RIGHT TO ITS HOMELAND, AND WHEN THE LIBERATION OF ITS HOMELAND IS COMPLETED IT WILL EXERCISE SELF-DETERMINATION SOLELY ACCORDING TO ITS OWN WILL AND CHOICE.

The decision concerning the problem of the internal regime is deferred until after the liberation. The crux of this article is to postpone the decision concerning the relation to the Kingdom of

---

4. Text of the Covenant is printed in all upper case type. Commentary by Y. Harkabi appears in upper and lower case type.

Jordan and Hashemite rule. There is also the emphasis here that only the Palestinian Arabs possess a national legal right, excluding of course the Jews, to whom a special article is devoted below.

ARTICLE 4) THE PALESTINIAN PERSONALITY IS AN INNATE, PERSISTENT CHARACTERISTIC THAT DOES NOT DISAPPEAR, AND IT IS TRANSFERRED FROM FATHERS TO SONS. THE ZIONIST OCCUPATION, AND THE DISPERSAL OF THE PALESTINIAN ARAB PEOPLE AS RESULT OF THE DISASTERS WHICH CAME OVER IT, DO NOT DEPRIVE IT OF ITS PALESTINIAN PERSONALITY AND AFFILIATION AND DO NOT NULLIFY THEM.

The Palestinian, therefore, cannot cease being a Palestinian. Palestinianism is not citizenship but an eternal characteristic that comes from birth. The Jew is a Jew through the maternal line, and the Palestinian a Palestinian through the paternal line. The Palestinians, consequently, cannot be assimilated. This article implies that Palestinian citizenship follows from the Palestinian characteristic. This is the Palestinian counterpart to the Law of Return.

ARTICLE 5) THE PALESTINIANS ARE THE ARAB CITIZENS WHO WERE LIVING PERMANENTLY IN PALESTINE UNTIL 1947, WHETHER THEY WERE EXPELLED FROM THERE OR REMAINED. WHOEVER IS BORN TO A PALESTINIAN ARAB FATHER AFTER THIS DATE, WITHIN PALESTINE OR OUTSIDE IT, IS A PALESTINIAN.

A reinforcement of the previous article. This definition refers solely to the Arabs. With reference to the Jews the matter is different. This is because being Palestinian is basically equivalent to being Arab.

ARTICLE 6) JEWS WHO WERE LIVING PERMANENTLY IN PALESTINE UNTIL THE BEGINNING OF THE ZIONIST INVASION WILL BE CONSIDERED PALESTINIANS.

In the section on resolutions of the Congress, in the chapter entitled "The International Palestinian Struggle" (p. 51), it is stated: "Likewise, the National Council affirms that the aggression against the Arab nation and its land began with the Zionist invasion of Palestine in 1917. Therefore, the meaning of "removal of the traces of the aggression" must be removal of the traces of the aggres-

sion which came into effect from the beginning of the Zionist invasion and not from the war of June, 1967. . . ."

"The beginning of the Zionist invasion" is therefore at the
time of the Balfour Declaration. This conception is current in Arab
political literature. In the 1964 version the corresponding article
was: "Jews of Palestinian origin will be considered Palestinians if
they are willing to endeavor to live in loyalty and peace in Palestine." The expression "of Palestinian origin" is vague, for the article
does not specify which Jews are to be considered of Palestinian
origin. Since in the previous article (5 in the new version, 6 in the
old) the date which determines being Palestinian is set at 1947, the
implication could be that this applies also to the Jews. Since the
aim is the return of the Arab Palestinians, it is necessary to make
room for them. However, in the meantime, Jews have taken up
residence in Arab dwelling-places, especially those Jews who immigrated after 1947; hence also from a practical aspect it is necessary to remove these Jews in particular.

The Jews who will not be recognized as Palestinians are therefore aliens who have no right of residence and must leave.

The National Covenant is a public document intended for
general distribution. The Executive Committee of the Palestine
Liberation Organization specified in its introduction to the official
report of the proceedings of the Congress as follows: "In view of
the importance of the resolutions of the Palestinian National Council in its session convened in Cairo from July 10 to 17, 1968, we
published them in this booklet so that the Palestinians in every
place may read them and find in them a policy and a program. . . ."
(pp. 17-18).

One might expect that those hundred members of the National
Council would have recoiled from adopting such an extreme position which could serve as a weapon against the Palestinians. The
fact that they did not is itself of great significance and testifies to
the severity of the Palestinian Arab position.

A year and a half has elapsed since the Covenant was amended,
sufficient time to raise criticism against this manifestation of extremism. However, until now no Arab body, including the Popular
Front for the Liberation of Palestine, which is usually critical of
the Palestine Liberation Organization and Fatah, has dissociated itself from the position presented in this article. To the best of my
knowledge, no article has been published in an Arab newspaper
that raises criticism against it. This silence is also highly significant.

The amended version of this article points to a radicalization of the Palestinian Arab position. It contains decisive evidence as to the nature of the slogan Arab leaders brandish concerning a "pluralistic, democratic state." Pluralism that is expressed in the elimination of two million four hundred thousand Israeli Jews is nothing but throwing dust in the eyes.

Arab spokesmen add that the aim is for the Palestinian state to be secular, as opposed to Israel, which they condemn as an anachronistic state founded upon a religious principle. It should be noted, however, that in all the constitutions of the Arab states (except Lebanon) Islam is explicitly established as the state religion. The Syrian constitution of 1964 stipulates that the president of the state must be a Muslim. In most of the constitutions it is also emphasized that the *Shari'a* (Islamic Law) is the source of the laws of the state. Fatah appealed to a congress held in al-Azhar University in September, 1968 to consider contributions to the fedayeen *Zakât* (a religious alms tax) and warfare against Israel, *Jihâd*. Thus they wage a religious war in order to establish a secular state. The crown of democracy, with which Palestinian spokesmen adorn the Palestinian state, also arouses scepticism in view of the Arabs' failure to set up democratic regimes.

Even if the Palestinians, realizing how this article damages their cause, amend it, such an amendment would be tactical and reactive, a response to foreign criticism, while the 1968 version reflects the more spontaneous mood.

ARTICLE 7) THE PALESTINIAN AFFILIATION AND THE MATERIAL, SPIRITUAL AND HISTORICAL TIE WITH PALESTINE ARE PERMANENT REALITIES. THE UPBRINGING OF THE PALESTINIAN INDIVIDUAL IN AN ARAB AND REVOLUTIONARY FASHION, THE UNDERTAKING OF ALL MEANS OF FORGING CONSCIOUSNESS AND TRAINING THE PALESTINIAN, IN ORDER TO ACQUAINT HIM PROFOUNDLY WITH HIS HOMELAND, SPIRITUALLY AND MATERIALLY, AND PREPARING HIM FOR THE CONFLICT AND THE ARMED STRUGGLE, AS WELL AS FOR THE SACRIFICE OF HIS PROPERTY AND HIS LIFE TO RESTORE HIS HOMELAND, UNTIL THE LIBERATION—ALL THIS IS A NATIONAL DUTY.

The second part, the preparation for the struggle, is new and was formulated under the influence of the special place that is now given to fedayeenism.

ARTICLE 8) THE PHASE IN WHICH THE PEOPLE OF PAL-
ESTINE IS LIVING IS THAT OF THE NATIONAL (*WAṬANĪ*)
STRUGGLE FOR THE LIBERATION OF PALESTINE.
THEREFORE, THE CONTRADICTIONS AMONG THE PAL-
ESTINIAN NATIONAL FORCES ARE OF A SECONDARY
ORDER WHICH MUST BE SUSPENDED IN THE INTEREST
OF THE FUNDAMENTAL CONTRADICTION BETWEEN
ZIONISM AND COLONIALISM ON THE ONE SIDE AND THE
PALESTINIAN ARAB PEOPLE ON THE OTHER. ON THIS
BASIS, THE PALESTINIAN MASSES, WHETHER IN THE
HOMELAND OR IN PLACES OF EXILE (*MAHĀJIR*), ORGA-
NIZATIONS AND INDIVIDUALS, COMPRISE ONE NA-
TIONAL FRONT WHICH ACTS TO RESTORE PALESTINE
AND LIBERATE IT THROUGH ARMED STRUGGLE.

It is necessary to postpone internal disputes and concentrate on
warfare against Israel. The style of "secondary contradictions" and
"fundamental contradictions" is influenced by the language of Fatah
and the younger circles. In the previous corresponding article it is
stated: "Doctrines, whether political, social or economic, shall not
divert the people of Palestine from their primary duty of liberating
their homeland. . . ."

ARTICLE 9) ARMED STRUGGLE IS THE ONLY WAY TO
LIBERATE PALESTINE AND IS THEREFORE A STRATEGY
AND NOT TACTICS. THE PALESTINIAN ARAB PEOPLE
AFFIRMS ITS ABSOLUTE RESOLUTION AND ABIDING DE-
TERMINATION TO PURSUE THE ARMED STRUGGLE AND
TO MARCH FORWARD TOWARD THE ARMED POPULAR
REVOLUTION, TO LIBERATE ITS HOMELAND AND RE-
TURN TO IT, [TO MAINTAIN] ITS RIGHT TO A NATURAL
LIFE IN IT, AND TO EXERCISE ITS RIGHT OF SELF-
DETERMINATION IN IT AND SOVEREIGNTY OVER IT.

The expression "a strategy and not tactics" is from the lexicon
of Fatah expressions (see Y. Harkabi) *Fedayeen Action and Arab
Strategy* [Adelphi Papers, No. 53, The Institute for Strategic Studies,
London, 1968], p. 8). They use it with reference to fedayeen activities: they are not a support weapon but the essence of the war.
"The armed struggle" is a broader concept, but here too stress is
placed on action of the fedayeen variety. "The armed popular revolution" signifies the participation of the entire people in the war

against Israel. It is depicted as a stage that will be reached by means of broadening the activity of the fedayeen. They are merely the vanguard whose role is to produce a "detonation" of the revolution until it embraces all levels of the people.

The radicalism in the aim of annihilation of the State of Israel and the "liberation" of all its territory eliminates the possibility of a political solution, which is by nature a compromise settlement. Such is the reasoning in this article and in Article 21. There remains only the way of violence.

ARTICLE 10) FEDAYEEN ACTION FORMS THE NUCLEUS OF THE POPULAR PALESTINIAN WAR OF LIBERATION. THIS DEMANDS ITS PROMOTION, EXTENSION AND PROTECTION, AND THE MOBILIZATION OF ALL THE MASS AND SCIENTIFIC CAPACITIES OF THE PALESTINIANS, THEIR ORGANIZATION AND INVOLVEMENT IN THE ARMED PALESTINIAN REVOLUTION, AND COHESION IN THE NATIONAL (*WAṬANĪ*) STRUGGLE AMONG THE VARIOUS GROUPS OF THE PEOPLE OF PALESTINE, AND BETWEEN THEM AND THE ARAB MASSES, TO GUARANTEE THE CONTINUATION OF THE REVOLUTION, ITS ADVANCEMENT AND VICTORY.

This article is new. It describes the "alchemy" of fedayeenism, how its activity broadens and eventually sweeps the entire people. The masses in Arab countries are described in the language of Fatah as constituting "the supportive Arab front," the role of which is not only to offer aid but to assure that the Arab states will not deviate, on account of local interests and pressures, from their obligation to support the Palestinian revolution.

ARTICLE 11) THE PALESTINIANS WILL HAVE THREE MOTTOES: NATIONAL (*WAṬANIYYA*) UNITY, NATIONAL (*QAWMIYYA*) MOBILIZATION AND LIBERATION.

Here there is no change. These mottoes are inscribed above the publications of the Palestine Liberation Organization.

ARTICLE 12) THE PALESTINIAN ARAB PEOPLE BELIEVES IN ARAB UNITY. IN ORDER TO FULFILL ITS ROLE IN REALIZING THIS, IT MUST PRESERVE, IN THIS PHASE OF ITS NATIONAL (*WAṬANĪ*) STRUGGLE, ITS PALESTINIAN PERSONALITY AND THE CONSTITUENTS THEREOF, IN-

CREASE CONSCIOUSNESS OF ITS EXISTENCE AND RESIST ANY PLAN THAT TENDS TO DISINTEGRATE OR WEAKEN IT.

The idea of Arab unity requires giving priority to the pan-Arab character over the local character. From the aspect of a consistent doctrine of unity, stressing local character or distinctiveness is divisive because it strengthens difference, whereas unity rests on what is common and uniform. The issue of the relation between local distinctiveness and pan-Arab unity has much preoccupied the ideologues of Arab nationalism. The conservative circles tend to stress the need for preserving local character even after unity has been achieved. By this means Arab unity will be enriched through variegation. The revolutionary circles, on the other hand, stress unity and homogeneity. This is based either on a practical consideration, that internal consolidation will be reinforced in proportion to the reduction of distinctive factors, or on the view that the local character is part of the heritage they wish to change. The controversy between distinctiveness and unity is also reflected in the conception of the structure of unity. Those who seek to preserve distinctiveness deem it necessary to conserve the existing political frameworks in a loosely confederated unified structure. Those who stress unity tend to try and obliterate the existing political frameworks, along with their boundaries, which were merely the adjunct of a colonial system, with the object of achieving a more consolidated political structure. This controversy may be represented as an antinomy in which Arab nationalism is caught: Unity which tries to suppress the distinctive character of its parts will arouse local opposition; unity which conserves the local distinctive character may abet [sic] divisive tendencies.

This article intends to answer the charge that stressing Palestinian distinctiveness is an objective that conflicts with Arab unity (in the language of Arab nationalism, the sin of Shu'ûbiyya or Iqlîmiyya). This charge was heard, for example, from within circles of the Qawmiyyûn al-'Arab movement, who were dedicated to the idea of Arab unity. Previous to the Six Day War this charge also had a practical aspect, namely, the assessment that excessive stress on the Palestinianism of the struggle against Israel diminished the role of the Arab states as direct participants in this confrontation. The response to this charge is, therefore, that preservation of Palestinian distinctiveness is merely a temporary necessity, to be transcended in favor of Arab unity. There is, however, a contradiction between this contention and the previous assertion of the eternity of the Palestinian personality.

ARTICLE 13) ARAB UNITY AND THE LIBERATION OF PALESTINE ARE TWO COMPLEMENTARY AIMS. EACH ONE PAVES THE WAY FOR REALIZATION OF THE OTHER. ARAB UNITY LEADS TO THE LIBERATION OF PALESTINE, AND THE LIBERATION OF PALESTINE LEADS TO ARAB UNITY. WORKING FOR BOTH GOES HAND IN HAND.

This again is an antinomy. Victory over Israel requires concentration of all Arab forces upon the struggle, a concentration made possible only by the establishment of a supra-state authority to control all these forces, that is, a common government. Nasser repeatedly warned that unity is a precondition for initiating war against Israel. But attaining unity is a long-range affair. Consequently, war against Israel is deferred until a remote time, because undertaking a war without unity would only lead to defeat. On the other hand, unity can be attained only by the detonation of a spectacular event, like victory over Israel. The ideologues of Fatah were much preoccupied with this issue (see *Fedayeen Action and Arab Strategy*, p. 9). Their response is contained in their slogan: "The liberation of Palestine is the road to unity, and this is the right substitute for the slogan, 'unity is the road to the liberation of Palestine.' " Actually, this article offers a verbal solution, circumventing the problem of priority by characterizing both events as contemporary, just as in the previous version of the Covenant.

ARTICLE 14) THE DESTINY OF THE ARAB NATION, INDEED THE VERY ARAB EXISTENCE, DEPENDS UPON THE DESTINY OF THE PALESTINE ISSUE. THE ENDEAVOR AND EFFORT OF THE ARAB NATION TO LIBERATE PALESTINE FOLLOWS FROM THIS CONNECTION. THE PEOPLE OF PALESTINE ASSUMES ITS VANGUARD ROLE IN REALIZING THIS SACRED NATIONAL (*QAWMI*) AIM.

This is a common notion in the Arab position. It is often stated in Arab political literature that the Palestine issue is *fateful* for the very Arab existence. It is maintained that the existence of Israel prevents the Arabs from achieving their national goal. Furthermore, the existence of Israel necessarily leads to its expansion and the liquidation of the Arabness of additional Arab lands. The Palestinians have an interest in stressing the fatefulness of the struggle against Israel and its centrality for the whole Arab world. They thus spur on the others to take an active role in the struggle against Israel. It may be that there is also hidden here the intention to lend symmetry to the conflict. Thus, both sides threaten each other with extinction, and the Arabs are not alone in this. A formula for division of labor is also presented here. The Palestinians will be the vanguard marching before the Arab camp.

ARTICLE 15) THE LIBERATION OF PALESTINE, FROM AN ARAB VIEWPOINT, IS A NATIONAL (*QAWMĨ*) DUTY TO REPULSE THE ZIONIST, IMPERIALIST INVASION FROM THE GREAT ARAB HOMELAND AND TO PURGE THE ZIONIST PRESENCE FROM PALESTINE. ITS FULL RESPONSIBILITIES FALL UPON THE ARAB NATION, PEOPLES AND GOVERNMENTS, WITH THE PALESTINIAN ARAB PEOPLE AT THEIR HEAD.

The goal is, therefore, twofold: defense of the rest of the Arab countries and removal of Zionism from Palestine.

FOR THIS PURPOSE, THE ARAB NATION MUST MOBILIZE ALL ITS MILITARY, HUMAN, MATERIAL AND SPIRITUAL CAPABILITIES TO PARTICIPATE ACTIVELY WITH THE PEOPLE OF PALESTINE IN THE LIBERATION OF PALESTINE. THEY MUST, ESPECIALLY IN THE PRESENT STAGE OF ARMED PALESTINIAN REVOLUTION, GRANT AND OFFER THE PEOPLE OR PALESTINE ALL POSSIBLE HELP AND EVERY MATERIAL AND HUMAN SUPPORT, AND AFFORD IT EVERY SURE MEANS AND OPPORTUNITY ENABLING IT TO CONTINUE TO ASSUME ITS VANGUARD ROLE IN PURSUING ITS ARMED REVOLUTION UNTIL THE LIBERATION OF ITS HOMELAND.

There is the implied concern lest, without the support of the Arab states, the drive of "the Palestinian revolution" will dissipate. The distinction of this version as compared with its predecessor, is mainly in the accentuation of "the active participation" of the Arab states and the issue of "the armed Palestinian revolution," which is certainly to be attributed to Fatah's ideological influence upon the Palestine Liberation Organization.

ARTICLE 16) THE LIBERATION OF PALESTINE, FROM A SPIRITUAL VIEWPOINT, WILL PREPARE AN ATMOS-

PHERE OF TRANQUILITY AND PEACE FOR THE HOLY LAND, IN THE SHADE OF WHICH ALL THE HOLY PLACES WILL BE SAFEGUARDED, AND FREEDOM OF WORSHIP AND VISITATION TO ALL WILL BE GUARANTEED, WITHOUT DISTINCTION OR DISCRIMINATION OF RACE, COLOR, LANGUAGE OR RELIGION. FOR THIS REASON, THE PEOPLE OF PALESTINE LOOKS TO THE SUPPORT OF ALL THE SPIRITUAL FORCES IN THE WORLD.

ARTICLE 17) THE LIBERATION OF PALESTINE, FROM A HUMAN VIEWPOINT, WILL RESTORE TO THE PALESTINIAN MAN HIS DIGNITY, GLORY AND FREEDOM. FOR THIS, THE PALESTINIAN ARAB PEOPLE LOOKS TO THE SUPPORT OF THOSE IN THE WORLD WHO BELIEVE IN THE DIGNITY AND FREEDOM OF MAN.

The very existence of Israel and the lack of a Palestinian homeland create alienation in the Palestinian, for these deprive him of his dignity and bring him to a state of subservience. As long as Israel exists the Palestinian's personality is flawed. This is an addition in the spirit of Fatah which was not in the previous version, and it is probably influenced by recent revolutionary literature, such as the teaching of Franz Fanon.

ARTICLE 18) THE LIBERATION OF PALESTINE, FROM AN INTERNATIONAL VIEWPOINT, IS A DEFENSIVE ACT NECESSITATED BY THE REQUIREMENTS OF SELF-DEFENSE. FOR THIS REASON, THE PEOPLE OF PALESTINE, DESIRING TO BEFRIEND ALL PEOPLES, LOOKS TO THE SUPPORT OF THE STATES WHICH LOVE FREEDOM, JUSTICE AND PEACE IN RESTORING THE LEGAL SITUATION TO PALESTINE, ESTABLISHING SECURITY AND PEACE IN ITS TERRITORY, AND ENABLING ITS PEOPLE TO EXERCISE NATIONAL (*WATANIYYA*) SOVEREIGNTY AND NATIONAL (*QAWMIYYA*) FREEDOM.

As in the previous version, the existence of Israel is illegal; therefore war against it is legal. In Palestinian literature there is a frequent claim that the fedayeen assaults against Israel are legal, while the self-defense and reactions of Israel are illegal, for their aim is to perpetuate the state which embodies aggression in its very establishment and existence. To the foreign observer this distinction between the legality of attacking Israel and the illegality of the response may appear as sham innocence that is indeed even ludicrous.

Nevertheless, it may be assumed that there are Arabs for whom this is not only a matter of formal argument but a belief.

Ibrahim al-'Abid, in an article entitled "The Reasons for the Latest Israeli Aggression" (The Six Day War), writes: "Fedayeen action is a right of the people of Palestine because the right of national liberation is an extension of the right of peoples to self-defense, and it is the right which the United Nations Charter affirmed as an original natural right" (Anis Sayegh, ed., *Filastîniyât*, PLO Center for Research, Beirut, 1968, p. 107).

ARTICLE 19) THE PARTITIONING OF PALESTINE IN 1947 AND THE ESTABLISHMENT OF ISRAEL IS FUNDAMENTALLY NULL AND VOID, WHATEVER TIME HAS ELAPSED, BECAUSE IT WAS CONTRARY TO THE WISH OF THE PEOPLE OF PALESTINE AND ITS NATURAL RIGHT TO ITS HOMELAND, AND CONTRADICTS THE PRINCIPLES EMBODIED IN THE CHARTER OF THE UNITED NATIONS, THE FIRST OF WHICH IS THE RIGHT OF SELF-DETERMINATION.

It is often found in Arab literature that the Mandate and the Partition Resolution, though accepted by the League of Nations and the United Nations Organization, have no legal force. They represent an aberration and not a norm of international law. The reason for this is that they contradicted the fundamental principle of the right of self-determination. This article is copied from the previous version.

ARTICLE 20) THE BALFOUR DECLARATION, THE MANDATE DOCUMENT, AND WHAT HAS BEEN BASED UPON THEM ARE CONSIDERED NULL AND VOID. THE CLAIM OF A HISTORICAL OR SPIRITUAL TIE BETWEEN JEWS AND PALESTINE DOES NOT TALLY WITH HISTORICAL REALITIES NOR WITH THE CONSTITUENTS OF STATEHOOD IN THEIR TRUE SENSE. JUDAISM, IN ITS CHARACTER AS A RELIGION OF REVELATION, IS NOT A NATIONALITY WITH AN INDEPENDENT EXISTENCE. LIKEWISE, THE JEWS ARE NOT ONE PEOPLE WITH AN INDEPENDENT PERSONALITY. THEY ARE RATHER CITIZENS OF THE STATES TO WHICH THEY BELONG.

Again an identical formulation. This article incorporates the principal claims concerning historical right: The Jews lived in Palestine for only a brief time; their sovereignty over it was not exclusive; the Arabs did not conquer it from them and need not restore it to them; and the Arabs remained in the country longer than the Jews. Moreover, a state embodies a national, not a religious, principle. The Jews, as having merely religious distinctiveness, do not need a state at all, and a Jewish state that makes of Judaism a nationalism is a historcial and political aberration. Therefore, Zionism, as a manifestation of Jewish nationalism, distorts Judaism.

Since the State of Israel is not based on a true nationalism, it is very often described in Arabic as "an artificial entity." This is also brought as proof that Israel can be destroyed. This conception is also at the basis of fedayeen theory: since the Jews have no real nationalism, terror will cause their disintegration to the point that they will consent to relinquish Jewish statehood.

The conception that the Jews do not constitute a national entity is a vital principle for the Arab position. For if the Israelis are a nation, then they have the right of self-determination, and the claim that only the Palestinian Arabs have the right of self-determination, and that only they must decide the national character of the country, is not valid. Moreover, the Arab claim for exclusive national self-determination appears in all its starkness as chauvinism that demands rights for itself while denying the same rights to the other.

ARTICLE 21) THE PALESTINIAN ARAB PEOPLE, IN EXPRESSING ITSELF THROUGH THE ARMED PALESTINIAN REVOLUTION, REJECTS EVERY SOLUTION THAT IS A SUBSTITUTE FOR A COMPLETE LIBERATION OF PALESTINE, AND REJECTS ALL PLANS THAT AIM AT THE SETTLEMENT OF THE PALESTINE ISSUE OR ITS INTERNATIONALIZATION.

This rejection of any compromise settlement is an addition to the previous version. In the resolutions of the fourth session of the Palestinian National Council a long and detailed section is devoted to the rejection of the Security Council Resolution of November 22, 1967 and any peaceful solution, with insistence upon the intention to undermine any attempt in this direction.

ARTICLE 22) ZIONISM IS A POLITICAL MOVEMENT ORGANICALLY RELATED TO WORLD IMPERIALISM AND HOSTILE TO ALL MOVEMENTS OF LIBERATION AND PROGRESS IN THE WORLD. IT IS A RACIST AND FANATICAL MOVEMENT IN ITS FORMATION; AGGRESSIVE,

EXPANSIONIST AND COLONIALIST IN ITS AIMS; AND FASCIST AND NAZI IN ITS MEANS. ISRAEL IS THE TOOL OF THE ZIONIST MOVEMENT AND A HUMAN AND GEO-GRAPHICAL BASE FOR WORLD IMPERIALISM. IT IS A CONCENTRATION AND JUMPING-OFF POINT FOR IM-PERIALISM IN THE HEART OF THE ARAB HOMELAND, TO STRIKE AT THE HOPES OF THE ARAB NATION FOR LIBERATION, UNITY AND PROGRESS.

In this new version there is an accentuation of Israel's relation to world imperialism and intensification of its denunciation. This is in the spirit of the Leftist sentiments that prevail among the up-and-coming Arab generation. The claim that the hostility of Zionism is directed, not only against the Arabs, but against all that is good in the world, is also an addition. Thus, warfare against Israel is ele-vated from an Arab interest to a universal humanistic mission.

ISRAEL IS A CONSTANT THREAT TO PEACE IN THE MIDDLE EAST AND THE ENTIRE WORLD. SINCE THE LIBERATION OF PALESTINE WILL LIQUIDATE THE ZION-IST AND IMPERIALIST PRESENCE AND BRING ABOUT THE STABLILIZATION OF PEACE IN THE MIDDLE EAST, THE PEOPLE OF PALESTINE LOOKS TO THE SUPPORT OF ALL LIBERAL MEN OF THE WORD AND ALL THE FORCES OF GOOD, PROGRESS AND PEACE; AND IMPLORES ALL OF THEM, REGARDLESS OF THEIR DIFFERENT LEANINGS AND ORIENTATIONS, TO OFFER ALL HELP AND SUP-PORT TO THE PEOPLE OF PALESTINE IN ITS JUST AND LEGAL STRUGGLE TO LIBERATE ITS HOMELAND.

ARTICLE 23) THE DEMANDS OF SECURITY AND PEACE AND THE REQUIREMENTS OF TRUTH AND JUSTICE OBLIGE ALL STATES THAT PRESERVE FRIENDLY RELA-TIONS AMONG PEOPLES AND MAINTAIN THE LOYALTY OF CITIZENS TO THEIR HOMELANDS TO CONSIDER ZIONISM AN ILLEGITIMATE MOVEMENT AND TO PRO-HIBIT ITS EXISTENCE AND ACTIVITY.

The attachment of Jews to Israel expressed in Zionism creates dual-nationality and political chaos. Arabs apparently do not sense the contradiction in this claim. Despite the prevalence of supra-national tendencies among circles in the progressive world, with which the Palestinians claim to have an affinity, a narrow, formal nationalistic approach is stressed here, which maintains that a man cannot cherish a loyal attachment to any factor apart from his own state.

ARTICLE 24) THE PALESTINIAN ARAB PEOPLE BELIEVES IN THE PRINCIPLES OF JUSTICE, FREEDOM, SOVER- EIGNTY, SELF-DETERMINATION, HUMAN DIGNITY AND THE RIGHT OF PEOPLES TO EXERCISE THEM.

ARTICLE 25) TO REALIZE THE AIMS OF THIS COVENANT AND ITS PRINCIPLES THE PALESTINE LIBERATION OR- GANIZATION WILL UNDERTAKE ITS FULL ROLE IN LIB- ERATING PALESTINE.

This article (with the omission of the conclusion, "in accor- dance with the fundamental law of this organization") is identical to the previous version. In this and the next article the Palestine Liberation Organization is presented as the umbrella organization bearing the general responsibility for the struggle of all the Pales- tinians against Israel.

ARTICLE 26) THE PALESTINE LIBERATION ORGANIZA- TION, WHICH REPRESENTS THE FORCES OF THE PAL- ESTINIAN REVOLUTION, IS RESPONSIBLE FOR THE MOVEMENT OF THE PALESTINIAN ARAB PEOPLE IN ITS STRUGGLE TO RESTORE ITS HOMELAND, LIBERATE IT, RETURN TO IT AND EXERCISE THE RIGHT OF SELF- DETERMINATION IN IT. THIS RESPONSIBILITY EXTENDS TO ALL MILITARY, POLITICAL AND FINANCIAL MAT- TERS, AND ALL ELSE THAT THE PALESTINE ISSUE RE- QUIRES IN THE ARAB AND INTERNATIONAL SPHERES.

The addition here, as compared with the previous version, is that the organization assumes also the role of bringing into effect the regime it prefers after the victory.

ARTICLE 27) THE PALESTINE LIBERATION ORGANIZA- TION WILL COOPERATE WITH ALL ARAB STATES, EACH ACCORDING TO ITS CAPACITIES, AND WILL MAINTAIN NEUTRALITY IN THEIR MUTUAL RELATIONS IN THE LIGHT OF, AND ON THE BASIS OF, THE REQUIREMENTS OF THE BATTLE OF LIBERATION, AND WILL NOT IN-

TERFERE IN THE INTERNAL AFFAIRS OF ANY ARAB STATE.

The obligation of neutrality, therefore, is not absolute but is qualified by the requirements of the battle of liberation.

ARTICLE 28) THE PALESTINIAN ARAB PEOPLE INSISTS UPON THE ORIGINALITY AND INDEPENDENCE OF ITS NATIONAL (WAṬANIYYA) REVOLUTION AND REJECTS EVERY MANNER OF INTERFERENCE, GUARDIANSHIP AND SUBORDINATION.

The Palestinian movement is not the tool for any Arab state and does not accept orders from any outside authority.

ARTICLE 29) THE PALESTINIAN ARAB PEOPLE POSSESSES THE PRIOR AND ORIGINAL RIGHT IN LIBERATING AND RESTORING ITS HOMELAND AND WILL DEFINE ITS POSITION WITH REFERENCE TO ALL STATES AND POWERS ON THE BASIS OF THEIR POSITIONS WITH REFERENCE TO THE ISSUE [OF PALESTINE] AND THE EXTENT OF THEIR SUPPORT FOR [THE PALESTINIAN ARAB PEOPLE] IN ITS REVOLUTION TO REALIZE ITS AIMS.

This is a new article, which includes a threat that the friendship of any state toward Israel will entail the enmity of the organization. A similar principle was established in the First Arab Summit Conference.

ARTICLE 30) THE FIGHTERS AND BEARERS OF ARMS IN THE BATTLE OF LIBERATION ARE THE NUCLEUS OF THE POPULAR ARMY, WHICH WILL BE THE PROTECTING ARM OF THE PALESTINIAN ARAB PEOPLE.

In other words, there is a future in the fedayeen or military career.

ARTICLE 31) THIS ORGANIZATION SHALL HAVE A FLAG, OATH AND ANTHEM, ALL OF WHICH WILL BE DETERMINED IN ACCORDANCE WITH A SPECIAL SYSTEM.

ARTICLE 32) TO THIS COVENANT IS ATTACHED A LAW KNOWN AS THE FUNDAMENTAL LAW OF THE PALES-

TINE LIBERATION ORGANIZATION, IN WHICH IS DE-
TERMINED THE MANNER OF THE ORGANIZATION'S
FORMATION, ITS COMMITTEES, INSTITUTIONS, THE
SPECIAL FUNCTIONS OF EVERY ONE OF THEM AND ALL
THE REQUISITE DUTIES ASSOCIATED WITH THEM IN
ACCORDANCE WITH THIS COVENANT.

ARTICLE 33) THIS COVENANT CANNOT BE AMENDED EX-
CEPT BY A TWO-THIRDS MAJORITY OF ALL THE MEM-
BERS OF THE NATIONAL COUNCIL OF THE PALESTINE
LIBERATION ORGANIZATION IN A SPECIAL SESSION
CALLED FOR THIS PURPOSE.

Arab Palestine: Phoenix or Phantom?

DON PERETZ

BECAUSE many Palestine Arabs are stateless under international law, their importance has frequently been overlooked in the numerous parleys and in the skein of complex international negotiations over the Middle East crisis. The Palestine dispute, as it is euphemistically labeled in the United Nations, has appeared on the annual agenda of the U. N. General Assembly for over twenty years, generally under the guise of assistance to refugees. Neither the principal antagonists nor the major powers officially acknowledge existence of the Palestinians as a nation-party to the dispute.

In a recent interview Israeli Prime Minister Golda Meir emphasized that there is no such thing as either a Palestinian nation or people. Palestine Arabs are considered by the Government of Israel as little different from those of the surrounding Arab states. When queried about creation of a new Arab Palestine on the West Bank, Prime Minister Meir pointed out that it would be too small; only if it were part of Jordan or Israel could the area remain viable. Furthermore, she emphasized, there is no representative body speaking for the so-called Palestinians. Had the Arabs who fled in 1948 not urged Jordan's King Hussein into the June 1967 war the Hashemite Kingdom might well have become the successor state to Palestine. Israel's experience with the already existing fourteen Arab states discourages it from supporting the creation of still another. Furthermore, to treat the Palestinians as a political entity would be inconsistent with Israel's internal and external policies. At present the Israeli Government considers its principal antagonists to be the Arab states of Jordan, Syria, Iraq and, to a greater extent, the United Arab Republic. The major goal of Israel's Arab policy is to reach agreement with the U.A.R., whose President Nasser is considered the chief obstacle to peace. The Israelis believe that only after he has been convinced of the need to come to terms with Israel will other Arab nations follow suit.

The reluctance of Israel and the major powers to recognize the Palestinians only inflames the latters' already deep hostility toward the West. Their situation is not unlike that of other self-identified national groups in the Middle East which sought international recognition during this century—such as the Armenians, the Jews and the Kurds.

The national identity of the Palestine Arabs has gone through a cycle of: discovery in the 1920s, political failure in the 1930s, near abandonment in the 1940s, disillusionment in the 1950s and '60s, and rebirth, rediscovery and new expectations since 1967.

II

Prior to establishment of the British Mandate at the end of World War I, there was no distinctive Palestinian people, nor political entity. The land and its inhabitants were considered backwater regions of the less developed Ottoman Syrian provinces. Only after establishment of the British Mandate in 1920, and the rise of Jewish nationalism in the country, did a distinctive Palestinian Arab consciousness emerge in response to the challenge of these two forms of European intrusion. In that era Palestinian Arab nationalism, led by a coalition of Muslim landed gentry and upper-middle-class Christian Arab families, resembled nationalist movements then emerging elsewhere in the Arab East. Some 80 percent of its constituency was a politically unsophisticated rural peasantry. There was little if any ideology, and that little was devoid of social content. Major emphasis was on elimination of foreign control and influence—in the case of Palestine, British controls and European Jewish influences. The Palestinian Arab national effort culminated in the abortive rebellion between 1936 and 1939; it failed because of massive use of British armed force and lack of internal cohesion among nationalist leaders. Nevertheless, heroes of this rebellion are still eulogized by the new nationalist organizations; their military failures and inability to form a cohesive political movement are overlooked.

The major revision of Great Britain's policies in Palestine, embodied in the 1939 White Paper, was a great victory for Palestine-Arab nationalism since it made an independent Arab state seem inevitable. Nevertheless, most of the country's Arab leaders slipped into lethargy and paralysis of action which was to last nearly thirty years. By the end of World War II, Jewish nationalism in Palestine was much more dynamic, well organized and politically effective. Both within the country and abroad, Zionists and their supporters surpassed the Palestine-

Arab nationalists in militant political activity, finally voiding the White Paper and achieving their goal of statehood. The disjointed and inchoate Palestine-Arab nationalist movement reached its nadir in 1947–48 with defeat and exodus of the Arab population from Jewish-held areas.

Until termination of the Mandate in 1948, both Arab and Jewish residents of the country were identified as British subjects, although they did not hold British citizenship. When Israel was established, its Jewish and some of its Arab inhabitants became citizens of the new state. More than one million Palestine Arabs were left in an international limbo, with no recognized citizenship status. Within the next decade, Palestinians who remained in the Hashemite Kingdom and in those parts of Palestine annexed to it acquired Jordanian citizenship; a small number of Christian Palestinians qualified for Lebanese citizenship, and the others—some 700,000—have remained stateless persons until today. Syria, while refusing citizenship to Palestine refugees, granted them most, but not all, citizenship rights. Lebanon was reluctant to offer citizenship to the large number of Muslim Palestine refugees it harbored for fear they would destroy the delicate balance between the country's Christians and Muslims. Egypt, already one of the world's most overpopulated nations, kept most of the Palestinians under its jurisdiction penned up in the tiny Gaza enclave, which was governed as though it were still a separate country rather than part of the U. A. R.

During the next two decades "Palestinian Arab" became synonymous with "Palestine refugee" in international consciousness. Even in Arab countries and among the Palestinians themselves there was little distinction, and annual debates over the refugees at the United Nations and the activities of UNRWA further blurred any clear difference. The most visible evidence of Palestinian existence was the network of refugee camps where tensions between the inhabitants and natives of host countries forcefully delineated the occupants from other Arabs.

Jordan needed its Palestinians as a population base for the new Hashemite Kingdom, but all the other Arab states encouraged the displaced Arabs to retain their national identity. This was not difficult since few were socially accepted in the host countries and many non-Palestinian Arabs regarded the outsiders as a disruptive and troublesome element. Palestinians therefore main-

tained their old social structure and family ties, formed their
own political groups, intermarried with each other and continued to regard themselves as a distinctive national group.
Recognition of this identity was further encouraged by the
United Nations through the network of relief, social and particularly educational services provided to Palestine refugees
through UNRWA. In the UNRWA schools, where refugee
children were educated by Palestinian teachers, a new generation of ardent Palestine patriots was raised. The most zealous
proponent of militant activism against the "intruder state" of
Israel was this new generation of U.N.-educated youth.

Various Arab governments attempted to exploit the distinctive
character of the Palestine Arab community before 1967. Jordan,
Iraq, Syria and Egypt encouraged and gave sustenance to Palestine Arab nationalist groups of one type or another. Usually
these groups were instruments of national policy of various Arab
governments, which provided them with political and material
support, including arms for so-called commando organizations
which supposedly operated independently. Inter-Arab efforts to
give political respectability and national élan to the Palestinian
movement resulted in formal recognition of the Palestine Liberation Organization at the 1964 summit meeting of Arab leaders in Cairo. While Ahmed Shukairy, recognized by the conference as leader of the PLO, led it through a maze of verbal
pyrotechnics, up to 1967 it had failed to gain real political autonomy or to galvanize strong popular support. In effect, it remained an instrument of inter-Arab policy manoeuvres.

After the 1967 fiasco, Palestinians were disillusioned with
nearly all the established leadership, organizations and governments; Shukairy and the old-line leadership associated with him
were discredited. Wherever there were large concentrations of
Palestinians, diverse new groups emerged, led by a younger
generation unfettered by the political and social commitments
of its elders. The new leadership reflected the transformation of
the Palestine Arab community that had occurred during the
"lost" generation. Living in or near to urban areas, most Palestinians had lost their peasant skills and outlook, acquiring many
of the views and sophistications of town and city. Several hundred thousand were employed in urban trade, commerce, industry and ancillary occupations. More than one hundred thousand
had developed skills in the Arabian oil states. In two decades,

approximately 50,000 Palestinians attended universities, nearly equaling the number of young professionals trained by Israel during this period. The new generation of Palestinians had all the attributes of a displaced minority group, including great aspirations for upward mobility, political restiveness, and a core of revolutionary-minded young men who aspired to "reëstablish the homeland."

Several dozen new Palestinian organizations were created within two years of the 1967 defeat. By far their greatest emphasis was on military or paramilitary activity aimed at Israel. Disillusioned with failures of conventional tactics against Israel and with Arab government fiascos, most of the new groups drew inspiration from guerrilla techniques and activities modeled on those of Algeria, North Viet Nam and Latin American revolutionaries. The objective was no longer that of Arab governments such as the U.A.R. or Jordan—to achieve Israel's withdrawal from the occupied territories and to circumscribe and delimit its frontiers—but to obliterate completely the Jewish state.

In the ebb and flow of inter-Arab politics since 1967, the new Palestinian groups have merged, subdivided, reunited and again fragmented, finally organizing themselves into three or four principal political-military organizations: the Palestine Liberation Organization; *Fatah;* the Popular Front for the Liberation of Palestine; and *Saiqa.* While there are political differences and diversities in the type of commando or terrorist activity each advocates, personality clashes rather than ideology often account for the variety of organizations. They differ generally from the pre-1967 groups in their asserted independence from Arab governments, in the growing number of young intellectuals and professionals they have enlisted in their ranks, and in the extent of support they have received from Arabs generally and from Palestinians in particular. While most of the organizations indirectly draw subsidies from Arab governments, including Kuwait and Libya, they have also succeeded in rallying substantial private contributions from wealthy Palestinians and other zealous supporters throughout the Arab world.

The reliability of commando communiqués is highly questionable, but their political effect throughout the Arab East is becoming increasingly obvious. Within the last two years they have created a new identity for the Palestinians. "Refugee" is no longer synonymous with "Palestine Arab." Increasingly, "Palestinian" is identified with the commando warrior rather than with the downtrodden displaced person. This is evident among Arab students, intellectuals, professionals and the man in the street, from Casablanca to Kuwait. While much commando activity is exaggerated if not entirely fictitious, there is sufficient substance to their achievements to have created a commando mystique. Posters on university campuses and in government offices and shopping centers; the daily radio bulletins and pronouncements by commando leaders; and the Arabic press—all have created in Arab consciousness the image of a new Palestinian who, unlike the traditional and now aging military leadership, is young, vigorous, intelligent, self-sacrificing, intensely patriotic and single-mindedly dedicated to reëstablishment of Arab Palestine. This image pervades even the thinking of commando critics such as Lebanese and Jordanian officials, who recognize that fedayeen terrorism in Israel serves only to weaken their own stability.

Not only Israel but several Arab governments are targets of commando activities. Some leaders of the organizations aim to overthrow any politician who might interfere with their guerrilla strategy against Israel; others have set their sights on total revolution of Arab political life. Among the former are leaders of Fatah and PLO who can coöperate with conservative monarchs or with radical socialists. Within the past year these two less revolutionary-minded groups have been involved in machinations behind the scenes to topple the ruling establishments of Jordan, Lebanon, Saudi Arabia and Libya. In Jordan and Lebanon, commando leaders have sought, with some success, to gain control of strategically located territories for training recruits, or for striking across the Israeli border. The commandos are reported to have taken over fourteen of the fifteen refugee camps in Lebanon and to have free access to most camps in Jordan. This has led to a de facto partition in which King Hussein's government has been forced to acquiesce. Because of the wide support enjoyed by the commandos among Jordan's largely Palestine Arab population, the Hashemite Kingdom has found it impossible to repress them and on occasion it even coöperates in providing covering fire for their movements across the frontier. Consequently Jordan has become the recipient of nearly daily artillery and air strikes, which have leveled towns, disrupted agricultural life in the river valley and threatened both political and economic stability.

In Lebanon, where Palestinians are a small minority but have considerable support among the population, the commandos threaten to end the country's relative isolation from direct military confrontation with Israel. Since the first Arab-Israeli war of 1948 the Lebanese-Israeli border has been more or less free of the military clashes that have periodically erupted between Israel and Syria, Jordan and Egypt. While willing to permit the organizations free movement, fund raising and propaganda activity within its borders, the Lebanese Government has been reluctant to countenance establishment of guerrilla enclaves. The dilemma has torn the government apart, divided the population into pro and anti commandos, and led to threats of both Syrian and Israeli intervention on behalf of or against the Palestinians. But now the commandos are asserting themselves in all areas they deem vital—including the Lebanese frontier. They recognize no right of withdrawal from confrontation with Israel, insisting that every Arab and Arab state has an obligation to join the "War of Liberation."

Members of even the "conservative" organizations were involved in an aborted coup in Saudi Arabia this fall resulting in arrest and imprisonment of several score high-ranking Saudi army officers. In Libya, where hundreds of Palestinians have found niches as teachers, physicians and professionals, they played a role in the successful overthrow of the monarchy. The new Libyan Republic's first civilian Prime Minister is a Haifa native whose family left when clashes between Jews and Arabs made life in Palestine difficult. He has asserted his and his government's full support for liberation of his former homeland.

Public approval of the commandos has become so widespread that Egypt's President Nasser has been placed in the ambiguous position of offering them his blessings at the same time that he calls for implementation of the U.N. November 1967 resolution. More recently, the Soviet Union has also withdrawn its disapproval of the commandos as a reactionary and disruptive element. Now they have been awarded Soviet accolades as fighters for independence of the people of Palestine.

The most wide-ranging goals have been stated by the small but influential and hyper-activist Popular Front for the Liberation of Palestine. Led by a zealous Christian Palestinian, George Habash, the PFLP emerged from the militant Arab Nationalist Movement, an organization of intellectuals whose goals were considered so revolutionary that it was banned in most Arab nations after its creation several years before the 1967 débâcle. Although it now concentrates its activities on the Palestine issue, its goals encompass the Arab world. The PFLP is splintered into Marxist and more Marxist factions. The most zealous would, with the aid of the Chinese Communists or any other equally revolutionary group, strive now for total revolution throughout the Arab world using any tactic necessary to bring down the political and social structure of all "corrupt" Arab states.

Attacks by the Front on commercial aircraft and civilian centers within Israel and abroad are an embarrassment to less zealous compatriots and to Arab governments. It was a PFLP attack on an Israeli commercial airliner that precipitated the raid on the Beirut airport last year, followed by dissolution of the Lebanese Government and continued internal political crisis. Since the Israeli Government holds accountable Arab countries from which such attacks are planned or undertaken, PFLP tactics threaten continued political crisis in the Arab world. At parleys between the Lebanese Government and various commando leaders conducted last summer in Beirut, the Front openly stated its aim to bring down the country's "reactionary" communal political system.

III

It is increasingly evident that instead of being a tool of Arab governmental policies, the new Palestine organizations are striving to reverse the pattern of control and to exercise strong influence on those governments which at one time controlled Palestinian destinies. The commandos have in effect become an instrument of pressure for more militant action by governments such as Lebanon, Jordan and the U.A.R. The support that commandos have rallied among university students and other leaders of Arab opinion has undermined the few voices of moderation existing prior to 1967.

The commando mystique clearly extends to Arab citizens of Israel and those in the occupied territories. A survey conducted in 1968 by Hebrew University sociologists indicated that Arab defeat in the Six Day War increased respect for the state among Israeli Arab schoolchildren but also greatly intensified feelings of hatred toward Israel, deepened Arab consciousness and made more determined than ever before the resolve to wage still another war against the Jewish state. With each passing month of Israeli occupation, the number of young Arab Israeli supporters of the commando movement grows. During the first half of 1969, the number of youths who were apprehended for supporting commando activities was nearly one hundred. While small in relation to the Arab population of Israel, the number exceeds the total of Israeli Arabs arrested for such activities since the state was established twenty years ago.

One of the most serious aspects of this phenomenon is that it threatens to undermine relationships laboriously built up since 1949 between the Government of Israel and its Arab minority. Though not ideal, relations had slowly become tolerable. Israeli Arabs had come to be recognized as citizens and many had voluntarily, even willingly, accepted this status. During the past twenty years Israel's universities have graduated several hundred Arabs. While many have been dissatisfied with their minority position, a considerable number found a place in Israeli society. Arabs worked in lower- and middle-level government posts and a few rose to become police officers. However, with increased commando activity, there is growing apprehension among both Israeli Arabs and Jews about the future of amicable relationships between the communities. After every incident the arrest of scores of Arabs and destruction of suspected terrorist homes by Israeli security authorities embitter feelings in both communities. Those who for twenty years strove to liberalize Israel's policies toward its Arab minority find themselves increasingly isolated; this is reflected in the recent election results, which increased by a substantial percentage the number of Knesset members favoring a hard line toward the Arabs.

So far, commando military escapades along the frontiers and terrorist activities within Israel have failed to disrupt life or to have a serious impact on its ever increasing military capacity. The border fighting has claimed 80 percent of the more than 2,000 casualties sustained by Israel since the 1967 War (nearly 500 of them fatal); 10 percent were inside the occupied areas and 10 percent in pre-1967 Israel. This fall Defense Minister Moshe Dayan noted that casualty figures had increased from an average of 50 a month in the year after the war to an average of 157 in the third postwar year. While the casualty rate from Arab confrontations is still less than the number suffered in automobile accidents in Israel, it has an obvious impact on public attitudes and further explains the turn toward militancy evident in the 1969 elections.

Indirectly the economy has been affected by the labor shortages caused by the large number of men under arms and by the need for reservists to serve up to age 55. Nevertheless, the economy is booming again, though foreign currency reserves are falling to a dangerously low level and the military budget eats up to 21 percent of Israel's GNP—three times more than in most modern nations.

There is also fear among civil libertarians that security restrictions in the Arab community could lead to increasingly restrictive measures against all dissidents, including Jews. While the vast majority of Israelis support their government's internal and external Arab policies, the small critical minority feels that it may be threatened if commando activities lead to expanded interference by security authorities in Israel's internal life.

IV

In recent months some commando intellectuals have become aware of the importance of winning over potential Jewish dissidents within Israel as well as gaining support in the West. Policy-planning groups in the high command of PLO, now recognized as the representative body of most commando organizations with the exception of the PFLP, have opened discussions about long-range plans in the occupied territories. However, they have failed to come forward with a program that would elicit support or even interest among any substantial number of Israelis or their supporters. At best their political goals are vague and ill-defined.

The commandos state categorically that they seek to destroy the government and state of Israel, its Zionist institutions and its exclusive Jewish character; they brook no compromise based on the pre-1967 borders or even the 1947 U. N. partition resolution. Some leaders have indicated that Palestine would become an Arab state; others have been more ambiguous. None has publicly recognized the possibility of coexistence between Arab and Hebrew nationalism, both of which have the identical attributes of a linguistic base, a rich cultural and historical heritage and deeply instilled popular consciousness, and both of which derive from a major religio-national ethos.

Hebrew broadcasts of the commando organizations directed

to Israel are listened to with derision rather than fear or hope of discovering any serious political intent. The recently announced objective of converting Palestine into a democratic secular state in which all Jews, Muslims and Christians will live in equity is not believed because of the long years in which the people as well as the state of Israel were threatened. The organizations have yet to define clearly the kind of government they propose, the status of minority groups, whether or not the country is to be an Arab state, or what is to become of its Hebrew-speaking residents who retain an attachment to their language and cultural, social and political institutions. The tragedy in this situation—and the root of conflict—is that each group denies the other the right of such identity and strives to assert exclusive control over the area that each believes to be the essential heartland of its national life.

The Palestine Arab nationalist movement represented in the varied groups that have been created since 1967 is still run through with many of the difficulties and shortcomings that have characterized modern Arab politics. The mystique and slogans full of emotional overtones tend to vitiate clear-cut, well-defined policy goals. The tendency to rely on exaggerated battle communiqués, while fortifying their image and mystique, undermines political credibility among those whom the commandos seek most to influence—the Jews of Israel, as well as influential outsiders. Above all there is lack of cohesive leadership. While the Fatah commando and PLO leader, Yasir Arafat, is the most visible and most colorful personality, he still lacks the charisma that Egypt's President Nasser so successfully capitalized on to become the pre-1967 leader of Arab nationalism. During the past two years there have been several instances in which members of one commando group have sought to undermine competing organizations. Yet despite these shortcomings the Palestine movement and the new organizations have become a factor of significance which cannot be ignored in any settlement of the Middle East crisis.

As the more militant groups strike out with increasing frequency at targets such as American oil companies, they threaten to sever the supply of oil to the West. The Front and other commando organizations have threatened to extend their attacks against other Western "imperialist" targets in the Middle East, but if they do so they will merely weaken further the already tenuous relations between the United States and the few remaining friendly Arab governments in the region.

Some Palestinians have demanded that they be represented in the deliberations convened to deal with the crisis. This presents an international dilemma. Although some Third World nations are moving toward recognition of a Palestine entity, so far even the U.A.R. has dragged its feet on clarification of long-range policy toward Palestine. Jordan hesitates, since recognition of the Palestine entity would give approval to partition of the Hashemite Kingdom. Neither the United States nor Great Britain can sanction territorial fragmentation of one of their chief Arab allies in the area.

Yet it would be in the interest of all parties concerned if the Palestinians had a recognized voice in negotiations. There are a number of issues in the dispute that are of only indirect concern to the non-Palestinian Arab states, but must sooner or later result in direct contacts between Israelis and Palestine Arabs. These include the return or compensation for Palestine Arab property now held by Israel; the future of Jerusalem, which is not only a Jewish but a Palestinian Arab city; and the status of several hundred thousand stateless persons who left Israeli-held territory in 1948 and 1967. While Israel wants to negotiate with states as far removed from these issues as the U.A.R. or Syria, negotiations would be much more likely to succeed if they were carried on between those whose vital interests are most involved. As for the United States, it will find American interests and American friendships in the area becoming increasingly endangered if steps are not taken soon to reach an accord with what is now the most disruptive element in Middle East politics—the Arabs of Palestine.

The Liberation of Palestine Is Supported
by International Law and Justice

ISSA NAKHLEH

In 1919 Palestine, Iraq, Lebanon and Transjordan were recognized as independent states by all the nations assembled in Paris for the Versailles Peace Conference, and at the same time they were temporarily placed under Mandates of the League of Nations.

The Mandate for Palestine was entrusted to Great Britain. The population of Palestine in 1919 was 95% Moslem and Christian Arabs and 5% Jews.

The Mandate system was created by Article XXII of the Covenant of the League of Nations for the administration of the non-Turkish provinces of the Ottoman Empire and former German colonies. The States placed under Mandates fell into three classes: Class "A" included Palestine, Iraq, Syria, Lebanon and Transjordan; Class "B" comprised Togoland, the Cameroons, Tanganyika and Ruanda; Class "C" included Southwest Africa, German Samoa, New Guinea and others.

According to Article XXII of the Covenant of the League of Nations the countries of the Class "A" Mandate, which included Palestine, "were recognized as provisionally independent nations, subject to the rendering of administrative advice and assistance by a Mandatory until such time as they are able to stand alone."

Under international law Palestine was recognized as a State, with territory, with fixed boundaries and with a population "whose wellbeing and development formed a sacred trust of civilization." The British Mandatory organized a civil administration which it called the Government of Palestine. That Government consisted of an Executive, a Judiciary and ten Departments, which administered the affairs of the country. The Government of Palestine was headed by a High Commissioner and a Chief Secretary, aided by various Assistant Secretaries. Palestine citizenship was created by the Palestine Citizenship Order-in-Council which defined who were to be considered citizens of Palestine. Palestine passports were issued to citizens. The Government of Palestine took part ir many important international conferences and became a member of several international agencies.

These facts are proof that Palestine had all the qualifications of a State under international law. However the indigenous population of Palestine were unable to exercise their sovereignty due to the presence there of the British High Commissioner and other British officials.

Britain Denies Palestine Self-Determination

All countries placed under Mandates have become independent and are now members of the United Nations with the exception of Palestine and a few others.

In the 29 years following 1919 the British Mandatory failed to carry out its mandate to give the population of Palestine independence and self-determination. Throughout that period Great Britain continued dumping alien Jews into an Arab country and using the Balfour Declaration as justification.

The Balfour Declaration confirmed the infamous and perfidious conspiracy by which in 1916 Great Britain betrayed her Arab allies in World War I by promising world-wide alien Jews "a Jewish national home in Palestine" as the price the Zionist Jews demanded for using their influence to railroad the United States into World War I as Great Britain's ally. Samuel Landman, a London solicitor and legal adviser to the World Zionist Organization, described, in his *Great Britain, the Jews and Palestine* (London, 1936), the Balfour Declaration as follows: " . . . the best and perhaps the only way (which proved so to be) to induce the American President to come into the War was to secure the co-operation of Zionist Jews by promising them Palestine, and thus enlist and mobilise the hitherto unsuspectedly powerful forces of Zionist Jews in America and elsewhere in favour of the Allies on a *quid pro quo* contract basis."

As soon as this conspiracy became known to the Arabs they protested vigorously, demonstrated and demanded their liberty and independence. From 1919 to 1939 many Arab uprisings took place. British military forces, reaching 200,000 British troops in 1936–1939, crushed Arab resistance using the most unjustified and ruthless methods. More than 50,000 Palestinian Arabs were killed during the 29 years of British rule in Palestine. More than 100,000 Palestinian Arab nationalists were imprisoned or thrown into concentration camps. Many British Commissions were sent from London to investigate the situation in Palestine. Each and every one of them came to the identical conclusion — that the Mandate was "unworkable because there existed two incompatible obligations, one to the indigenous Arab population and the other to Jews."

Jews Resort to Terrorism

Ultimately the British Government issued the 1939 White Paper, promising Palestine self-determination and limiting the further immigration of Jews to Palestine. This White Paper enraged the international Jewish Agency and Zionists throughout the world. While Great Britain was engaged in a life and death struggle in World War II, terrorist gangs of Jews in Palestine — the Hagana, the Irgun and the Stern gangs — waged an armed insurrection, committing the most barbaric atrocities and acts of terrorism against the British forces, the Government of Palestine and the civilian Arab population. Many thousand victims were killed, maimed or wounded. According to official British documentary evidence David Ben-Gurion and his Jewish Agency colleagues plotted, planned and ordered the execution of these crimes and atrocities.

Palestine Question Submitted to United Nations

In 1947 the Government of the United Kingdom decided it could no longer handle the situation in Palestine and referred the problem to the United Nations. When the General Assembly of the United Nations met in a special session in April 1947, there were in Palestine 1,350,000 Moslem and Christian Arabs who were Palestine citizens by birth, about 200,000 Jews naturalized Palesstine citizens and about 450,000 alien Jews, mostly illegal immigrants.

A United Nations Special Committee on Palestine was appointed to investigate the problem and make recommendations for political settlement. The influence of the Western Powers and Zionist machinations produced a "majority plan" for partitioning Palestine. The "minority plan" proposed a Federal State.

By pressure, undue influence and power politics a resolution proposing reference of the Palestine issue to the International Court of Justice to determine whether the United Nations had authority to partition Palestine or any other country was rejected in the General Assembly.

As the result of pressure and improper manipulation by the Western Powers the General Assembly of the United Nations adopted the resolution of November 29, 1947, recommending the "partition" of Palestine into an Arab State, a "Jewish State" and an International Zone for the Jerusalem-Bethlehem area.

Civil War broke out in Palestine immediately after the adoption of the United Nations "partition resolution." The Security Council discussed the situation in Palestine and considered it a threat to international peace, adopting resolutions for a cease fire and truce. It recommended a special session of the General Assembly to "consider further the future Government of Palestine." The Second Special Session of the General Assembly convened on April 16, 1948. The United States submitted proposals for placing Palestine under Trusteeship, whereby the Trusteeship Council would exercise supervisory powers over Palestine, appointing a Governor-General.

While the United Nations was in session searching for a peaceful solution to this problem, the minority of Jews in Palestine by force and violence, aided and abetted by British troops, expelled more than one million Moslem and Christian citizens from Palestine from their ancestral homeland, occupying their homes and properties, robbing them of all their personal possessions. Jews owned less than 1% of Palestine, yet they plundered and occupied all private and public property in 80% of Palestine. The minority of Jews in Palestine was about 30% of the total population, less than one-half were naturalized Palestine citizens and the balance illegal alien immigrants.

British-Zionist Conspiracy

It is an historic fact that prior to the month of April, 1948, Palestine Arabs were winning the fight against the Jews throughout the country. Arabs dominated more than 82% of the area of Palestine. Jews were unable to travel on highways between important cities. All Jewish quarters in Jerusalem were about to surrender. Jews lost every battle they fought against Palestine Arabs. In the 1951 *Year Book* of occupied Palestine, pages 44–45, David Ben-Gurion confirms the victories of Palestine Arabs, stating "by March [1948] anyone without faith could find ample justification for believing the end was near . . . This last week in March was the black week."

The massacre of Arabs in Deir Yasin occurred on April 10, 1948. Terrorist Jews massacred more than 350 aged Arab men, women and children with barbarism exceeding that of the Nazis. Terrorist Jews stripped ten Arab women naked, forced them into a truck, displaying them in a victory parade throughout the Jewish quarters, later turning them loose in the outskirts of the Arab quarters.

The British then carried out their part of the bargain by supplying Jews with all types of the most modern weapons, including Centurian tanks. British forces disarmed Arabs in every city, town and village throughout Palestine. The British military forces took part in battles between Jews and Arabs, insuring victory for the Jews. This British-Zionist conspiracy resulted in the expulsion of Arabs from Tiberias, Haifa, Jaffa, Acre, Safad, Beisan, modern Jerusalem and all villages surrounding these towns. When the disarmed Arab civilian population were threatened with massacre by the terrorist Jews, the British military forces, representing the British Mandatory Power and as such responsible for law and order, were considerate enough to urge the Arabs to surrender and generous enough to offer army trucks and lorries to evacuate Arab civilians to enable them to take refuge in neighboring Arab countries!

Could there have been a more honorable way by which Great Britain, the Mandatory Power, fulfilled her obligation to lead Palestinians to independence and self-determination? Zionist claims of victory were made to deceive world public opinion. Zionists know they did not win a war honorably on the field of battle. It was a "British-made" victory. British armed forces aided and abetted Jews, enabling them to win the second round against the Palestine Arabs after April 1948. Great Britain used her then powerful influence in the Arab world to prevent Palestine Arabs from taking part in the war after May 15, 1948.

Zionists Defy United Nations

In spite of the fact that the United Nations General Assembly was still meeting in the Special Session called to search for a peaceful solution of the Palestine problem, the international Jewish Agency on May 14, 1948, proclaimed their so-called "Declaration of Independence."

The Jews in occupation of Palestine called themselves the so-called "State of Israel" and organized a so-called "Provisional Government." The international Zionist gangsters believed they could thus wipe the State of Palestine off the face of the map by a stroke of their pen and by "proclaiming" their "Declaration of Independence." The Jews, a minority in Palestine, by force and violence violated the territorial integrity of Palestine and the political independence of the Moslem and Christian Arab majority of Palestine. The Jews expelled more than one million Arab citizens from their ancestral homeland in defiance of Article 2, Paragraph 4, of the United Nations Charter which "forbids the threat or use of force against the *territorial integrity or political independence of any State,* or in any other manner inconsistent with the purpose of the United Nations."

Points of International Law

These are the facts of the Palestine tragedy. But what is the position according to international law, the United Nations Charter and the Charter of Human Rights? Can a naturalized Palestine citizen who is a Jew expel a native Palestine citizen who is a Moslem or a Christian? If not, can a Jew, who is an alien illegal immigrant in Palestine, do so? If a minority of Jews by force and violence occupied 80% of Palestine, what right do these Jews have in Palestine as occupants under international law? Can these Jews legally claim they are a "Jewish State"? Can these Jews claim sovereignty in Palestine under international law?

Citizens Cannot Expel Citizens

A citizen of a State cannot expel another citizen. A State cannot expel or exile a native citizen. Since the First World War the international community has endeavored to lay rules for the protection of minorities and safeguarding their rights to life, liberty and religious freedom. The maxim adopted was that all citizens were to be equal before the law, enjoy the same civil and political rights without any distinction due to race, language or religion. It also provided that minorities or any State could petition the League of Nations if these rights were violated.

The preamble of the United Nations Charter reaffirms faith in fundamental human rights, in the dignity and worth of the human person, in the equal rights of men and women, of nations large and small. The Declaration of Human Rights guarantees against violation of the rights of the individual. These principles of international law support our contention that the minority of the naturalized Palestine Jews could not expel the majority of the citizens of Palestine from their ancestral homeland and deprive them of their citizenship, their political, religious and civil rights, and their right to political independence and self-determination.

If international law affords protection to minorities and guarantees their rights and freedom, is it not legal and logical to assume that the same protection of the law is afforded to the majority against the minority? What would be the position under international law if the 3,500,000 Jews in New York State expelled the 13,500,000 Christians and proclaimed themselves "Israel-on-the-Hudson"? What would be the position under international law if the 7,000,000 French Canadians expelled the 12,000,000 British Canadians and proclaimed themselves the "State of Joan of Arc"? What would be the position under international law if the colored minority of Georgia expelled the white majority and proclaimed themselves the "Republic of Ham"?

Aliens Cannot Expel Citizens

If naturalized Jews in Palestine cannot deprive Palestine Arabs of their rights, under what principle of international law and justice can alien Jews, legal or illegal residents in Palestine, deprive the indigenous Arab Palestine population of sovereignty and birthright in their homeland?

According to the principles of international law, "the natural home and field of activity of every human being is his home State. He cannot claim any right to be admitted to, or settle in, foreign States. If admitted, he is merely a guest who must put up with the conditions offered him. He must obey the general laws of the land. Being a foreigner he must put up with the lack of many advantages conferred on the natives. If he is not satisfied, he can leave the country."(Ross: *A Textbook of International Law*). In the present case alien Jews illegally in occupation of Palestine claim every right and deny the lawful indigenous population all their rights.

Jews Used Force in Defiance of the United Nations

Commenting on the use of force and any change that might take place in Palestine, Senator Warren Austin, United States Ambassador to the United Nations, in a statement to the Security Council on April 1, 1948, described the legal position in Palestine as follows: "So long as there is a Mandate no other country or people has a right to use military force in Palestine. Until an agreement is entered into which transmits this responsibility from the United Kingdom to its successor, or until an agreement is made with the United Nations, the Security Council has the responsibility of trying to maintain order and peace in Palestine." (Security Council official records).

Yet, by an armed insurrection and in defiance of the General Assembly of the United Nations and the Security Council, Jews occupied 80% of Palestine and "proclaimed" themselves the counterfeit so-called "State of Israel."

Occupants Acquire No Rights or Sovereignty

The rules of war in international law deal with the occupation by one State of the territory of another State. At the same time it considers the occupation by armed insurrection as a military occupation to which the principles of international law apply. The concensus of opinion of international lawyers confirms the following principles:

1. "Insofar as the Covenant of the League of Nations, the Charter of the United Nations and the General Treaty for the Renunciation of War prohibit war, they probably render invalid conquest on the part of the State which has resorted to war." (Lauterpacht: *Oppenheim's International Law*).

2. "The occupant does not in any way acquire sovereign rights in the occupied territory but exercises a temporary right of administration on a trustee basis. . . . The legitimate government of the territory retains its sovereignty but . . . the

latter is suspended during the period of belligerent occupation." (von Glahn: *Occupation of Enemy Territory*).

3. "Military occupation does not confer title or extinguish a nation. As long as the people of the occupied country do not accept military conquest, so long as they can manifest, in one way or another, their inalterable will to regain freedom, their sovereignty even though flouted, restricted and sent into exile still persists." (Philip Marshall Brown, in: *American Journal of International Law,* Volume 35).

4. "Mere seizure of territory does not extinguish the legal existence of a government." (Charles Cheney Hyde: *International Law as Applied by the United States*).

5. "The occupant is not entitled to alter the existing form of government, to upset the constitution and domestic laws of the territory occupied or set aside the rights of the inhabitants." (War Office [London], *Manual of Military Law*).

6. "The most important principle of law is that occupation does not displace or transfer sovereignty." (McNair: *Legal Effects of War*).

7. "The rights of the inhabitants of an occupied territory are also safeguarded against abuse and violation. They owe no allegiance of any sort to the occupying power. Their family honor and rights, and private property, must be protected. Individual or mass forcible transfers, as well as deportation of the inhabitants from occupied territory to the territory of the occupying power or that of any other country, are prohibited regardless of their motive." (von Glahn: *Occupation of Enemy Territory*).

The *Manual of Military Law,* published by the British War Office, and Professor von Glahn in his book *Occupation of Enemy Territory,* sum up what an occupant may or may not do in the occupied territory as follows: "It would be unlawful to change the constitution or form of government of the occupied territory, or replace the existing language of the occupied area with the language of the occupant. The nationality of the inhabitants of the occupied area does not change. *The occupant is forbidden to change the internal administration of the area or establish a new State or assist in the maturing of plans to do so."*

Occupation of Palestine by Jews Illegal

These principles of international law establish beyond any shadow of doubt that the occupation of 80% of Palestine by a minority of Jews was illegal. Under international law Jews could not establish a State in Palestine. They could not change the internal administration in the country. They could not substitute a new governmental structure. They could not change the nationality of the inhabitants. They could not replace the Arabic language. They could not expel, exile or forcibly transfer the population of Government of Palestine or occupy, appropriate, dispose of, or use the private property of the inhabitants of the country. They could not commit outrageous acts, atrocities and massacres against the inhabitants.

The international Zionist leaders led by David Ben Gurion and his associates committed in Palestine "war crimes and crimes against humanity" as defined by Article 6 of the Nuremberg Charter, of which Nazi leaders were convicted by the International Military Tribunal and hanged.

Admission to United Nations Cannot Legalize Occupation

When confronted with these cogent arguments some people ask, "What about the admission of the so-called 'State of Israel' to the United Nations?"

We maintain that such admission cannot give the minority of Jews in Palestine, the occupants by force of 80% of Palestine, any right or sovereignty because the United Nations has no authority to do so. One of the purposes of the United Nations in Article 1 of the Charter is *"to bring about by peaceful means and in confor-*

mity with the principles of justice and international law, adjustment or settlement of international disputes or situations which might lead to a breach of the peace."

The words "by peaceful means" and "in conformity with justice and international law" are imperative. The United Nations cannot contravene, violate or ignore the principles of international law and justice. The occupation of Palestine by force and violence by alien Jews and the expulsion of more than one million inhabitants can hardly be said to have been accomplished by "peaceful means," or are consistent with the principles of justice and international law.

The United Nations, as well as all its members, are bound by the doctrine of non-recognition and therefore cannot recognize in any way the illegal occupation of Palestine by Jews. Lauterpacht in his book *Recognition in International Law* and McMahon in his book *Conquest and Modern International Law* state: "The doctrine of non-recognition is based on the view that acts contrary to international law are invalid and cannot become a source of legal rights to the wrongdoer. That view applies to international law, one of the general principles of law recognized by civilized nations. The principle *ex injuria jus non oritur* is one of the fundamental maxims of jurisprudence. An illegality cannot, as a rule, become a source of legal right to the wrongdoer."

"After the end of hostilities there is full room for the application of the principle that no rights and benefits can accrue to the aggressor from his unlawful act." (Lauterpacht: *Oppenheim's International Law*).

Dr. T. C. Chen in his book *International Law of Recognition* states the position clearly as follows: "It is generally believed that the duty of non-recognition is implied in the Covenant of the League of Nations, Article 10 of which reads 'The members of the League undertake to respect and preserve as against external aggression the territorial integrity and existing political independence of all members of the League.' The refusal to treat a violation as legal seems to be the minimum exertion that ought to be required from other members consistent with their obligations under the Article. The Charter of the United Nations does not contain a guarantee clause similar to Article 10 of the Covenant, yet members of the United Nations have pledged themselves to the purposes and obligations enumerated in Articles 1 and 2 of the Charter. It is hardly possible that recognition of illegal acquisitions could be compatible with these obligations."

Therefore the resolution of the General Assembly of the United Nations had no effect under international law and did not legalize the unlawful occupation of Palestine by Jews.

Admission of So-Called "Israel" to United Nations Illegal

The admission of so-called "Israel" to the United Nations was contrary to international law and to the letter and spirit of the United Nations Charter. A so-called "State of Israel" never existed in fact or in law. It was nothing but an illegal "proclamation" and illegal occupation by a minority of Jews. Furthermore, such admission was obtained by undue pressure and deceit and therefore it is void. This so-called "Provisional Government of Israel," which consisted of international Zionist gangsters, aliens from many foreign lands, representing Zionists throughout the world, submitted an application for membership in the United Nations! On December 17, 1948, the Security Council rejected that application.

The Western Powers submitted the application to the General Assembly in April 1949 and was referred to the Political Committee for further discussion. Many delegates questioned Zionist representatives whether they intended to abide by resolutions of the General Assembly regarding Palestine. The Committee was given affirmative assurance by Abba Eban, a citizen of the Union of South Africa who had no relation to Palestine. His answers were misleading. He gave the impression that Jews intended to abide by United Nations resolutions on Palestine. The Western Powers exerted strong pressure upon delegates in the Political Committee for the admission of the so-called "State of Israel."

Strong pressure by the Western Powers was again exerted in the General Assembly for adopting the resolution of May 11, 1949, for admitting the so-called "State of Israel" to the United Nations.

The General Assembly recalled "its resolution of 29 November 1947 and 11 December 1948 and took note of the declarations and explanations made by the Representative of the Government of Israel [a citizen of the Union of South Africa] before the *Ad Hoc* Political Committee in respect of the implementation of the said resolutions."

Therefore the admission of the so-called "State of Israel" for membership in the United Nations was a qualified admission. Furthermore, Article 4 of the United Nations Charter provides that the United Nations can only admit as a member "a peace-loving State which accepts the obligations of the Charter and able and willing to carry out these obligations."

The so-called "State of Israel" never was a State. It consisted of a minority of Jews, alien illegal immigrants, transplanted into Palestine, who, by an armed insurrection, in violation of international law, expelled more than one million citizens from Palestine and stole all their assets. How could they be a "peace-loving" nation? How could they carry out obligations under the United Nations Charter when their very existence, their occupation of 80% of Palestine and the crimes committed by them against its inhabitants are the greatest mockery of the United Nations Charter?

For these cogent reasons, it is submitted that the admission of these international Zionist gangsters to the United Nations was void *ab initio* and had no validity under international law. It could not possibly convert robbery and looting into an act of benevolence nor transmit crimes into acts of decency nor transform aggression into "peace-loving."

Jews Have No Rights or Sovereignty in Palestine

Applying the principles of international law to the present

position of the Jews in Palestine, their presence there is nothing but illegal occupation. Unlawful occupation cannot give Jews rights or sovereignty in Palestine. "Sovereignty-in-Exile" is still vested in the 2,000,000 Moslem and Christian indigenous citizens of Palestine.

The Palestine Arabs never have accepted and never will recognize the "British-made" conquest of Palestine by Jews. In the words of a great American scholar and lawyer, Philip Marshall Brown, expressed in Volume 35 of the *American Journal of International Law:* "As long as they [the Arabs of Palestine] do not accept military conquest, as long as they can manifest, in one way or another, their inalterable will to regain freedom, their sovereignty, even though flouted, restricted and sent into exile, still persists. A nation is much more than outward form of territory and government. It consists of the men and women in whom sovereignty resides. So long as they cherish sovereignty in their hearts their nation is not dead. It is not to be denied the symbols and forms of sovereignty on foreign soil or diplomatic relations with other nations."

Italy occupied Ethiopia in 1936. The King of Italy was proclaimed the Emperor of Ethiopia. Eight nations in Europe were occupied by the Nazis in World War II. Their inhabitants were subjected to Nazi rule. Their Governments fled. These eight nations established Governments-in-Exile in London. After many years they regained their sovereignty and independence when the illegal occupation of their respective countries terminated. The fate of aggressors is well known – no matter how long their aggression endures. It will not be long before the Arabs of Palestine liberate their motherland.

The illegal occupation of Palestine by Jews will soon come to an end. The right and the obligation of Moslem and Christian Arabs of Palestine to liberate their ancestral homeland are supported both by international law and well-established precedents.

Peace and the Palestinians

JULIUS STONE

I. INTRODUCTION

The idea of a "Palestinian Entity," articulated concurrently among the Arab States and the Palestinian refugees, is a creature of the past decade. The establishment of a Palestine Arab State had been proposed long ago, of course, in the Partition Resolution of 1947[1] and accepted on behalf of the future state of Israel.[2] The subsequent invasion of the newly formed Israeli state by six Arab countries thwarted its establishment. Although condemned even by the Soviets,[3] the invasion left Jordan and Egypt in military occupation of substantial parts of the abortive Palestine Arab State: the West Bank of the Jordan River, the Gaza Strip and East Jerusalem. Had the concept of a Palestine Arab State not thus come to grief, the specific "nationhood" of its population, scarcely manifest at the time, would perhaps have grown with the responsibility and experience of statehood. That possibility did not materialize. It was not until the decade of the 1960's, and probably not until after the 1967 war, that "Palestinianism" in the specific sense made its entrance on the international stage. The fact that this entry was made in an explosive context of political passion and armed violence should not cloud the long term issue which it raises.

The notion of a "Palestinian Entity" was invoked by Arab States at Arab League meetings in 1959[4] against a background of

* S.J.D., Harvard University; D.C.L., Oxford University. Challis Professor of International Law and Jurisprudence, University of Sydney. This article was prepared during a visit by the author to the Hebrew University of Jerusalem in the late Spring of 1970. Later developments, such as the stand of Egypt and Jordan against the "liberation terrorist groups in relation to the U.S." peace initiative, the successive crises between Jordan and these groups and the Jordanian defeat of the Syrian intervention, illustrate the main theme.

1. G.A. Res. 181(II), U.N. Doc. A/519, at 131 (1947).
2. 3 U.N. GAOR, Ad Hoc Comm. on the Partition of Palestine (1947). The Israeli representative at the meetings was the Jewish Agency for Palestine.
3. 4 U.N. SCOR, 306th meeting 7 (1948). Remarks of the Ukrainian delegate.
4. N.Y. Times, Sept. 3, 1959, at 3, col. 1; id., Sept. 4, 1959, at 3, col. 2; id.,

mutual quarrels as well as the struggle against Israel, the ultimate goal being Israel's dismemberment.[5] Since the 1967 war, the claims of this "entity" have evolved into a central factor offered as material to the current Middle East conflict.[6] Clearly, very substantial preliminary questions arise as to the relevance of such an "entity" to the merits of the conflict. At the outset, one may challenge the genuineness of the supposed association of Palestinian "people" or "nation" with this "entity" in the sense that those are symbols which today imply entitlement to political independence.[7] The second major question concerns what bearing the "entity" could have at this stage of history on the military and political facts or moral issues which characterize the present Arab-Israeli conflict. This article will discuss both questions with primary focus on the latter.

II. PALESTINIAN "ENTITY" AND "NATIONHOOD"

Even scholars rather sympathetic to Arab claims have pointed out that when the British White Paper of 1939[8] had apparently made an independent Arab State inevitable, "most of the country's Arab leaders slipped into lethargy and paralysis of action which was [sic] to last nearly thirty years."[9] Therefore, whatever interpretation might be given to the sporadic and mostly localized attacks by Arabs on Jews in 1920, 1929 and 1936 to 1939,[10] it still remains a puzzle how and why Palestinian Arab nationalism, had it already existed, could have remained inert and passive during the critical years which followed 1939. As late as 1948, the main role of the Palestinians during the Arab States' attack against the new State of Israel was either to accept life under the new State or to leave

---

Sept. 6, 1959, at 24, col. 3; id., Sept. 7, 1959, at 3, col. 1; id., Sept. 9, 1959, at 8, col. 3. A complete account of the issues at the Conference is noted in the referenced N.Y. Times articles.

5. Id.

6. See S. Shamir, The Attitude of Arab Intellectuals, in The Anatomy of Peace in the Middle East 5, 21 (1969). On the role of the new elites among the Palestinians, see Harkabi, The Position of the Palestinians in the Israel-Arab Conflict and Their National Covenant, 3 N.Y.U.J. Int'l L. & Pol. 209 (1970).

7. The attempt at association lies behind the deliberate use of the Arabic term for "nation" to symbolize Pan-Arab nationalism (qawniyya) and the term for "peoplehood" to represent the several independent Arab countries (wataniyya). See The Palestinian National Covenant, 3 N.Y.U.J. Int'l L. & Pol. 228 (1970) and commentary thereon by Harkabi, note 6 supra.

8. Parliamentary Papers 1939, Cmd. No. 6019.

9. Peretz, Arab Palestine, Phoenix or Phantom?, 48 Foreign Affairs 322, 323-24 (1970).

10. See generally C. Sykes, Crossroads to Israel (1965).

their homes to seek shelter with the Arab States and their armies. Pending more persuasive historical studies, these facts seem to point to a movement merely stirred and manipulated, and then only sporadically, by forces outside Palestine.

III. THE "ENTITY" AS A FACTOR IN THE PRESENT CONFLICT

Assuming, however, that either in 1960, 1967 or 1970 the demand for a Palestinian "entity" has acquired a genuine relation to the notion of a Palestinian Arab "peoplehood," a second question arises. What bearing would this assumed fact have on the present military and political situation or the moral position of each side? The answer is neither simple nor easily determined.

Obviously, a specific Palestinian consciousness associated with the idea of establishing a Palestinian "entity" which emerged in the 1960's must, in some sense, be a factor in the present stage of the Middle East conflict. Yet chronology does not allow this factor to be decisive in judging events which took place a half century or even a generation before, in 1917, or 1922, or 1948. An emergent nationalism cannot be treated as if it had developed decades before for purposes of facilely ignoring entitlements previously fixed and acted upon. Thus to ignore chronology would result in an arbitrary reconstruction of both events and rights of peoples, as they presented themselves after World War I, to claim a share in the distribution of the territories of the defeated Turkish Empire.

A. *After World War I*

As a matter of historical fact, the principal claimants in the distribution of the vast, formerly Turkish territories embracing the whole of the Near and Middle East were the Arab and Jewish peoples.[11] The Arabs, of course, were dispersed over the entire area with a number of cultural and political centers, but no particular center in Palestine. One scholar[12] has observed that during this period "there was no distinctive Palestine people, nor political entity." He adds that "the land and its inhabitants were considered backwater regions of the less developed Ottoman Syrian provinces."[13] Another scholar[14] has recalled that even at the height of

---

11. See S. Hadawi, Bitter Harvest—Palestine Between 1914-1967 (1967).
12. Peretz, supra note 9, at 323.
13. Id.
14. J. Parkes, History of Palestine from 135 A.D. to Modern Times (1949).

Arab, and later Turkish, hegemony over the area, Palestine was never exclusively Arab or Moslem anymore than it was exclusively Jewish or Christian, either in population or in cultural and religious concerns. The departure or re-entry of Jews and Christians reflected the degrees of persecution or tolerance of successive local rulers. A part of the Jewish people, driven from Palestine by invading conquerors, remained as dispersed communities throughout the Middle East. Another part ventured into Europe and North Africa. Still another remained in Palestine. But for Jews everywhere Palestine continued into the modern era to be the focus of religious and national life, just as it had also been the center of Jewish political life during the earlier millenium of the kingdoms of David and Solomon and, later, of the Hasmoneans.[15]

This perspective clearly indicates that Jewish and Arab nationalisms, each embracing its own cluster of scattered populations, each sharing specific cultural, religious and historical experiences deeply rooted in the Middle East region, simultaneously claimed the territories liberated during World War I from Turkish sway. Modern concepts of national self-determination necessitate careful identification of claimants to post-war distributions of territory.[16] This point is particularly valid when applied to the assumed recent emergence of a Palestinian "peoplehood." For the assertion that Israel came into existence on the basis of injustice to the Palestinian people distorts historical fact. The Arab claimant after World War I included Arabs throughout the entire area. The Palestinian Arabs were merely a peripheral rather than a distinctive segment whose interests as such were taken into account. Consequently, to present a Palestinian "entity" and people, presumably emergent in the 1960's, as a claimant against Israel now, is an unwarranted and dubious game with history.

The following conclusions about the distribution of territory after World War I and the implementation of the distribution during succeeding decades are in order. First, Jewish and Arab claims in this vast area came to the forum of justice together, not by way of Jewish encroachment upon an already vested and exclusive Arab domain. Second, the allocation made to the Arabs, as implemented by the creation of the existing Arab sovereignties, was markedly greater in area and vastly richer in resources than the "Palestine" designated as the "Jewish National Home." Third,

---

15. M. Louvish, Challenge of Israel 16 (1968).

16. Examples of previous instances are discussed in J. Kunz, The Changing Law of Nations 180, 217 (1968).

by successive steps thereafter, the initially penurious satisfaction of Jewish claims was further reduced. A portion of the original allocation was cut away in 1922 (some 70,000 of 96,000 square kilometers, including the more sparsely populated regions) to establish the State of Transjordan,[17] now renamed Jordan. The partition proposal of 1947[18] included further excisions to establish the Palestine Arab State.[19] Most of the areas designated for that Arab State were in fact seized, and thereafter held until 1967, by Egypt and Jordan in the course of the first armed attack against Israel in 1948.

Contemporary ideologues have attempted to tear the Palestine refugee question from this checkered context of history. Yet it twists and parodies both history and justice to present the Palestine issue as a struggle between the Jews of the world on one hand and the Arabs *of Palestine* on the other in which the Jews seized the major share. The struggle was rather between the Arabs of the Middle East region, including some hundreds of thousands living in Palestine, and the Jews of the world in which the Arabs took a lion's share and from which more than a dozen Arab States emerged. Neither at the time of distribution nor during later decades, moreover, was there any identifiable *Palestinian* Arab people, much less any center of Arab cultural or political life in Palestine.[20] There were Arabs who had lived in Palestine for centuries just as there were Jews who had lived in Iraq, Yemen and other parts of the region for centuries. All were to pay a price for the inheritances their respective nations received.

B. *Aftermath to the Distribution: Refugees*

In the aftermath of these allocations, some 500,000 Arabs were said to have been forced to leave their homes in Palestine.[21] An equal number of Jews were also coerced into leaving their homes and property throughout the various Arab dominions.[22] Marginal interests among major claimants often suffer some degree of wrong even in the course of a just distribution. However, the duty of redress for such wronged marginal interests generally attaches to those who benefit from the overall distribution. The measure of that duty should be gauged according to a rational and proportional division

---

17. A. Reversky, Jews in Palestine 340 (1935).
18. G.A. Res. 181(II), U.N. Doc. A/519, at 131 (1947).
19. Id.
20. Peretz, supra note 9, at 323.
21. Israel Ministry of Foreign Affairs, The Arabs in Israel 89 (1958).
22. Israel Office of Information (New York), Israel's Struggle for Peace 106 (1960).

of responsibilities. The wrong in the Middle East resulted from the initial territorial settlement and continued in a process as drawn out as that from which *all the Arab States, as well as* Israel, emerged. Correctly seen, any injustice which the Arabs of Palestine suffered was as much a function of the creation of the present Arab States as it was a direct result of the establishment of Israel.

Israel, in any case, accepted the responsibility to resettle and rehabilitate fully one half of the one million displaced persons involved, namely the Jews from Arab lands.[23] In addition, she offered to accept a similar responsibility for a significant number of displaced Arabs and offered, as part of a settlement, to receive back some 100,000 Palestinian refugees.[24] The Arab States, with vastly greater areas and resources, have not accepted responsibility to assist in the resettlement of Jewish refugees displaced in the course of the Arab-Israeli conflict. Only a few, moreover, undertook any substantial resettling of displaced Arabs.[25] Instead, the Arabs have sought to keep the "refugee" question alive as a political weapon against Israel, sometimes, as with the U.A.R. in Gaza, by confining the refugees in virtual concentration areas on the borders of Israel.[26] The notion of a Palestinian "entity" derives much of its artificiality from cold calculation in the use of this weapon.

The context in which the burden of making amends to Arabs and Jews displaced as a consequence of the post World War I distribution must be approached is that very distribution itself. As demonstrated above, the distribution overwhelmingly favored the Arabs. The moral principle involved is clear: marginal wrongs occurring in the course of a distribution should be righted by those who benefited from the distribution in proportion to that

---

23. A. Eban, My People, The Story of the Jews 488-93 (1968).

24. Despite the fact that Israel's offer was never acted upon, Israel reports to have allowed back 48,500 Arabs from divided families as of 1960. Israel Office of Information (New York), supra note 22, at 107.

25. H. Cook, Israel: A Blessing and a Curse 200 (1960). A certain number of the Arab refugees have also been absorbed into some Arab states, notably Lebanon and Jordan. This merely highlights the default of the other Arab states. Egypt, for example, literally confined its displaced kindred in Gaza, left the responsibility of their subsistence with U.N. agencies and concerned itself mainly, for twenty years, with channeling refugee resentment against Israel. Even in Jordan, where some assistance has been provided, there has been a willingness to place the heavy burden for refugee operations on the United Nations. See 55 Palestinian Refugees Today 4 (1968). The anti-Government activity by Palestine liberation groups in Lebanon and particularly Jordan is, in part, the fruit of neglect.

26. At least the Israelis view its use as political. See Discussion, Arab-Israel Parley: Step Toward a Political Settlement, in A Middle East Reader 430 (I. Gendzier ed. 1969).

benefit. It applies equally to Jews and Arabs regardless of whether the controlling assumption is that Arab refugees fled from Palestine as a result of intimidation by Israelis during the 1948 Arab invasion[27] or, as the Israelis assert, because they chose to join the invaders in hope of securing personal safety, possessions and perhaps even some spoils in the event of an Arab dismemberment of Israel.[28] Any final share of responsibility imputed to Israel to aid the half million Arab refugees must necessarily make allowance for the heavy burdens she assumed toward a half million Jewish refugees from Arab countries, particularly in view of the small share of resources allotted to her in the post-war distribution.

The enunciation of this principle does not mean that the international community has no role to play in refugee resettlement and rehabilitation in the area. Obviously, the international community has its own interest in fostering reconciliation and in easing tensions. However, prior standards set within the international community merely highlight the default in the duty to insure that justice is done with respect to the refugee problem in the Middle East. The record since World War II shows a remarkable recognition of the duty to resettle and rehabilitate refugees,[29] stimulated no doubt by international concern for the stabilization of frontiers and the reduction of tensions. These standards are even more plainly drawn when circumstances permit exchanges of populations.[30] The Arab-Israeli impasse would seem to be exactly such a case. But significantly, the Arab position has been characterized by motives which run counter to those of the international community: to increase tension with Israel and undermine the stability of frontiers.

C. *Title by Conquest*

Those who support the Arab cause assert that the claims of Palestinian Arabs do not rest merely on their displacement. A

27. The Institute for Palestine Studies (Beirut), The Palestine Question 53 (1968).

28. Israel Ministry of Foreign Affairs, supra note 21, at 7.

29. Since World War II, there have been numerous instances of massive resettlements of refugee populations. See L. Holborn, World Refugees (1960) in regard to West Germany; E. Rees, Century of the Homeless Man (1957) in regard to Austria; Balogh, World Peace and the Refugee Problem, 75 Recueil des Cours Academie de Droit International 363, 396-405 (1949).

30. The standards of civilized duty are even plainer when circumstances permit exchanges of population which will ease majority-minority relations and, therefore, tensions across new frontiers. See e.g., the Greco-Turkish exchange of population after World War I or the less orderly Hindu-Moslem exchanges in the Indo-Pakistani partition of 1948.

second ground offered for the validity of the claims is the seventh century Arab conquest of Palestine.[31] That conquest is juxtaposed against the fact that Jews displaced from Iraq and Yemen had never conquered Iraq or Yemen. The argument raises the important question of whether a military victory in the course of an ancestral incursion thirteen centuries ago is entitled to some moral priority over Israeli victories in two wars of self-defense in this century and, if so, on what grounds.

First, the seventh century Arab conquest is antedated by the older Israelite conquest of the same area from the Hittites and Philistines in the thirteenth century B.C. and the undoubted governance of the land by a succession of Jewish judges and kings for many centuries thereafter.[32] Therefore, those beguiled by claims of title based on ancient Arab conquest cannot consistently dismiss the even more ancient Jewish conquest. And those who place emphasis on more recent Arab conquests must recognize the present State of Israel by its even more recent military ability repeatedly to defeat the neighboring Arab States of the region.

It is, of course, absurd to attribute moral value to either the modernity or antiquity of conquest, as such. Title based on ancient conquest no longer supported by possession is doubly absurd. Such a concept would call for the dismemberment of many existing states in the event descendants of their earliest known conquerors could be found. An intriguing choice of claimants might be presented for the right to displace the English in the United Kingdom or to take title in the various states of North and South America. Israel's possession, based on rightful entry under international law[33] and twice successfully sustained, does not rest on such questionable grounds.

Indeed, according to the more advanced anticolonialist ideas of our age, it is Arab claims in Palestine which require justification. For instance, application of Alexandrowicz's thesis concerning "reversion to sovereignty" of peoples overrun by foreign dominators[34] to the Palestine question would render the Arab position rather threadbare. Alexandrowicz took the view that the descendants of an ancient civilization, which formerly controlled its own affairs but was subsequently submerged under foreign domination, must be regarded as having maintained their sovereignty throughout.

31. Hadawi, supra note 11, at 37-39.
32. See generally A. Sachar, History of the Jews (5th ed. 1968).
33. G.A. Res. 181(II), U.N. Doc. A/519, at 131 (1947).
34. Alexandrowicz, New and Original States: The Issue of Reversion to Sovereignty, 45 Int'l Affairs 465 (1969).

Therefore, when restored to their original land, they join the international community as an old state, reverting as of right to its former sovereignty, rather than as a new state seeking recognition.[35]

This theory is quite obviously responsive to the spirit of decolonization. It expresses a principle of morality and justice more surely, perhaps, than it expresses an established technical doctrine of international law. In any case, its application to the Arab-Israeli conflict is most interesting. For it is clear that no identifiable people now survives which can demonstrate any special relation to Palestine prior to the centuries of Jewish statehood there. The Palestinian Arabs, from the standpoint of history, were but colonists under the wing of imperial conquerors. As indicated before, they never established any specific local civilization or independent political life. Even in terms of advanced anticolonialist concepts therefore, the Palestinian claims remain unconvincing.

D. *The Issue of "Majorities."*

The Palestinian Arabs have commonly argued that the fact that more Arabs than Jews lived in the area that was designated as the "Jewish National Home" in 1917[36] is decisive. A majority which controls a state often does assert a right to forbid access by others which might disturb its predominance. Conceivably, one could extend some analogous right to a majority which, though not in control, has built a distinctive national life. However, as already discussed, the Arabs of Palestine did not show any specific national distinctiveness at any relevant time. Until recently, they identified themselves as residents of particular cities or districts rather than as Palestinians.

Moreover, the Arab claim to exclude Jews after World War I on the basis of their own numerical majority and currently, in the Palestinian National Covenant,[37] retrospectively to expel all those who entered thereafter is both unrealistic and inconsistent. If applied to present times, when Jews predominate numerically in Palestine, the claim would result in vesting exclusive control in the Jewish majority. Nor does it make any sense to proceed in terms of power to exclude new entries but not to include re-entries. For a significant number of those currently enrolled as "Palestine

---

35. Id. at 478-80.

36. Hussein, My War with Israel 131 (1969); A. Nutting, The Tragedy of Palestine from the Balfour Declaration to Today, in The Arab-Israeli Impasse 54 (M. Khadduri ed. 1968).

37. The Palestinian National Covenant, art. 6, supra note 7, at 230.

refugees" with UNRWA have never lived in that part of Palestine which is now Israel.[38]

In the past, the Arabs did succeed by putting pressure on the former British Mandatory in limiting re-entry of Jews to the mandate-declared "Jewish National Home."[39] Tests of "economic absorptive capacity"[40] were then imposed against the Jews and restrictive estimates, which history has since shown to have been quite arbitrary, were made. The tests were based on the assumption that Jewish entry would result in Arab displacement. But it is clear that Jewish re-entry and settlement did not create an Arab refugee problem.[41] For during the critical years of World War II, the Mandatory Power continued to hold a considerable reserve of public lands, accesss to which was barred to Jewish settlement.[42] This policy, in turn, created a seller's market in land which enabled Palestinian Arabs to reap high profits. Indeed, it was common knowledge, noted by Royal Commissions prior to the institution of restrictions on Jewish landholding, that the reactivation of the land by Jewish resettlement was accompanied by substantial immigration from surrounding Arab countries and increased rather than diminished the local Arab population.[43]

The problem of displaced Arabs, now part of the hard core of the Arab-Israeli problem, was therefore not a product of Jewish re-entry but a by-product of Arab resort to military force in 1948.[44] The validity of this conclusion is not affected by the outcome of the debate as to whether the displacement of Arabs was voluntary or as a result of Israeli pressure.[45] An assessment of the evidence

38. The numbers have grown so quickly that the UNRWA has reported difficulty in distributing food due to the large number of third generation refugees. 43 Palestinian Refugees Today 5-6 (1965).

39. Parliamentary Papers 1939, Cmd. No. 6019.

40. Royal Institute of Int'l Affairs, Great Britain and Palestine 1915-1945 60 (1946).

41. It is significant in this regard that art. 5 of the Covenant admits as Arab citizens of the proposed Palestine Arab State only those Arabs living permanently there until 1947 even though art. 6 dates "the Zionist invasion" from 1917. Even in the Arab version of history, then, it is assumed that no substantial number of Arabs were displaced before 1947.

42. D. Peretz, The Middle East Today 270 (1963).

43. Peel Royal Comm'n, Cmd. No. 5479, at 241-42 (1937).

44. The official Israeli view is somewhat harsher. See speech of A. Eban, 8 U.N. GAOR 215 (1953): "Can Governments really create a vast human problem by their aggression, possess the full capacity to solve it, receive international aid toward its solution and then, with all that accumulation of responsibility upon their hands, refuse to join in the acceptance of any permanent responsibility for the faith and future of their own kith and kin?"

45. Notes 27 and 28 supra.

relating to the major movements, for example of the Arab community from Haifa, indicates that they were inspired by feelings of solidarity with the advancing Arab forces. Those feelings were accompanied, no doubt, by a general fear of impending hostilities in some cases and, in others, by hopes of gain after an Arab victory.[46] Such movements should be regarded as voluntary even though those who left naturally hoped to return either as adherents and followers or as beneficiaries of the invading armies. The choice made by these Arab refugees is easy to understand. Correspondingly, it is difficult to see how Israel, or any other state in a similar situation, having repelled the Arab attack, could be expected to invite their wholesale return. Adherence to the enemy in time of war is not easily countenanced anywhere. Israel's offer to readmit and resettle 100,000 refugees (about 20% of the total) and acceptance of 28,000 returnees whose status was legalized may be regarded as a fair response.[47] But whether an Arab from Haifa, who in 1948 deliberately chose to leave his home and his Jewish fellow citizens in obedience to the call of Arab armies, now manifests painful personal nostalgia or real feelings of "national" resurgence, is a difficult judgment to make. Fanatical campaigns to inculcate hatred against Israel among the refugees do not render the task easier.

E. *In Summary*

In light of the history sketched above, Arab claims of a "Palestinian entity" are unconvincing. If some notion of a Palestinian peoplehood is accepted as a present fact, it would certainly become relevant to the present prospects of an eventual peace among the Arabs themselves and between the Arabs and Israel. However, that notion did not justify the destruction of the 1947 partition

---

46. Statement of Valid al-Qamhawi, in Disaster in the Arab Fatherland, quoted in T. Harkabi, Time Bomb in the Middle East 20 (1970): "These factors, the collective fear, moral disintegration and chaos in every domain were what displaced the Arabs from Tiberias, Haifa, Jaffa and tens of cities and villages." Harkabi claims that the supposed massacre of Arabs at the village of Dir Yassin in Apr., 1948, later alleged to have triggered the flight, was scarcely mentioned in the contemporary reporting and only began to be offered as an explanation many months later.

47. See U.N. Conciliation Comm'n General Progress Rep., 5 U.N. GAOR, Supp. 18, U.N. Doc. A/1367/Rev. 1 (1950). Between 1952 and 1954, all outstanding balances and safe custody articles of refugees in Israeli banks were agreed to be released. Israel also helped to identify and assess refugee land holdings. The Arabs have, of course, insisted from the beginning that no consideration of Israel's security could be taken into account as regards repatriation of all refugees. Id.

plan by military aggression. Nor does it justify the larger design of destroying Israel's existence. Lastly, the inculcation of hatred and lust for revenge in younger generations who probably do not share feelings of nostalgia for a lost homeland, must negate, if unchecked, whatever possibilities remain for a lasting peace in the future.

II. JORDAN AS THE PALESTINIAN ARAB STATE

A. *Masking the Real Issues*

An important part of the present conflict arises precisely from a desperate search to find scapegoats for mistakes and failures. One might expect that the refugees as well as the Arab States should seek to project onto Israel the blame for their own failures and for the frustrations occasioned by mutual rivalries. However, the Arabs have also found a number of other objects of wrath in addition to Israel: imperialism, an Arab-Soviet invention entitled "Nazi-Zionism" and, at critical moments, the United States and United Kingdom.[48] But the difficulties of the Palestinians in fixing their group identity and in defining their homeland are at least in part due to their reluctance to face the fact that it is the existence of Jordan rather than of Israel which results in a deprivation of their claimed rights.

The Palestine promised to the Jewish people in 1917 embraced both Cisiordan and Transjordan.[49] This area lay on both sides of the Jordan River and was within the mandate requested by Britain and granted by the League of Nations in 1922.[50] At that time, however, at Britain's insistence and over the protest of Jewish organizations, Transjordan was taken out of the mandate provision for the establishment of a "Jewish National Home" and allocated to the creation within Palestine of the Emirate of Transjordan.[51] Therefore, when Transjordan became independent in 1946, this state, under the name of Jordan, was then and is now the Arab State within Palestine. The area currently called the West Bank and Gaza and Jerusalem remained within the confines provided for the "Jewish National Home" until 1948 when the State of Israel was established. The subsequent Arab attack resulted in the Jordanian seizure of the West Bank and East Jerusalem,

---

48. The Palestinian National Covenant, art. 22, supra note 7, at 241.
49. C. Weizman, Trial and Error 208 (1949).
50. 3 League of Nations Off. J. 1007 (1922).
51. Id.

while Egypt helped itself to Gaza. This territorial expansion by
Jordan, whatever its international standing,[52] only reconfirmed
Jordan's character as an Arab State within Palestine. The fact that
it was not called the Palestine Arab State was either a semantic
evasion or an idiosyncracy of the Hashemite monarch, for neither
of which Israel could be held responsible.

It is noteworthy in this regard that as early as 1937 the Peel
Commission considered the potential capacity of Transjordan to
receive immigrants. The Commission Report noted that the area
allotted to Transjordan was nearly two and a half times as large
as the residual area of Palestine and contained only about a
quarter of its population. It expressed the hope that, if fully developed, Transjordan could hold a much larger population. However, proposals for immigration into Transjordan were dismissed
on the ground that Arab antagonism to Jewish immigration was
as bitter there as in residual Palestine.[53] Accordingly, in 1937 also, it
was apparent that in reality Jordan was the Palestinian Arab
State.

Transjordan, then, on its creation in 1922 either had the function of a Palestinian Arab State or of simply another throne for
a Hashemite to sit upon. The latter function ceased to suffice after
1948 when Palestinians constituted sixty percent of Jordan's population.[54] It is even less compelling when Palestinian "peoplehood"
is assumed to be a present reality in search of a homeland. The
available rational solution is for Jordan, with or without the West
Bank and Gaza, to *be* the Palestinian Arab State. King Hussein's
regime has rejected this solution even during its military occupation and attempted annexation of the West Bank prior to 1967.[55]
For the Arabs, turning the demand for self-determination into a
demand for the dismantling of Israel, in which Jordan and other
Arab States could join, has had the attraction of avoiding, or at
least postponing, the day when the Palestinians and the Jordanian
Government must settle the real issue between themselves. It also
has had the advantage of deflecting attention from the divisive
ambitions of Syria, Iraq and Egypt in the ultimate fate of both

---

52. G.A. Res. 181(II), U.N. Doc. A/519, at 131 (1947).

53. Peel Royal Comm'n, supra note 43, at ch. 11.

54. Peretz, supra note 42, at 262, 293.

55. According to the Al Fatah spokesman in Cairo, on Sept. 24, 1970, "the
only solution to the Jordan crisis is for the King to abdicate and leave the country." The Australian, Sept. 25, 1970. Conversely, for an account of the Bedouin
royalist position, see the report filed by the correspondent of The Guardian,
London, The Australian, Sept. 25, 1970.

the West and East Banks of the Jordan River which a Jordanian-Palestinian Arab settlement would bring to a head.[56] In this situation all parties concerned, but especially the Palestinian groups in their relative weakness, find it easier to join a common campaign of hate against Israel than face their internecine disagreements, the solution of which must precede an Arab-Israeli settlement.

Presently, the Arab accusations focus on the charge that Israel's refusal to recognize the claims of Palestinian Arabs blocks the emergence of "Palestinian consciousness" into Palestinian statehood.[57] A segment of Israeli public opinion also advocates that Israel should immediately declare its recognition of a Palestinian Arab right of self-determination.[58] The argument proceeds not upon the assumption that such recognition requires the dismantling of Israel but in the hope of hastening the development of favorable conditions for Palestinian political emancipation in Jordan and the territory of the West Bank. An Israeli reaffirmation of this sort would serve to re-emphasize Israel's continued support for the principle of self-determination in these waning days of the age of decolonization. It might also turn the attention of the Arab States and Palestinians to the real issues which they must first adjust among themselves.

An Israeli reaffirmation of a Palestinian right of self-determination should not, however, lead anyone to the delusion that it could be at all decisive for peace. For Israel's *further* recognition of a Palestinian right of self-determination is, in the existing situation, probably redundant. As already observed, the real question of self-determination centers on the *raison d'être* of the Kingdom of Jordan if not as the Palestine Arab State. People living in Jordan should be permitted to decide that question for themselves.

B. *The Palestinian National Covenant*

It appears clear, especially after the 1968 revision[59] of the Palestinian National Covenant, that the course chosen by the Palestinian groups and the Arab States to avoid facing the issues dividing them is to target demands against Israel which, on their face, are a plain call for Israel's destruction. The 1964 version of what

---

56. M. Kerr, The Arab Cold War 151 (2d ed. 1967).
57. Peretz, supra note 9, at 323-24.
58. See V. Avineri, Israel Without Zionists (1968).
59. The Palestinian National Covenant, note 7 supra.

is presently Article 6 of the Covenant[60] stated that "Jews of Palestinian origin will be considered Palestinians if they are willing to endeavor to live in loyalty and peace in Palestine." This was a theoretically conceivable basis for negotiating a "truly binational" state. In the 1968 amended version, however, only "Jews living permanently in Palestine until the beginning of the Zionist invasion will be considered Palestinians."[61] The Conference[62] made clear that for this and other purposes "the Zionist invasion" was deemed to have begun in 1917.[63] The path chosen by the Palestinian groups renders *any* peaceful settlement with Israel impossible. For it demands, as a precondition, the liquidation of Israel in the form of the expulsion of more than two million of its present citizens. The Covenant makes no reference, moreover, to the need for an asylum for these prospective refugees.

The added difficulties in achieving peace created by this intransigent call for Israel's dismemberment are not eased by skepticism that it represents the views of Palestinians generally. Important differences exist in the claims and postures of Palestinians living in the administered territories and those outside. Perhaps those now living side by side with the Israelis would conform with varying degrees of sincerity, if publicly questioned, to the views expressed in the Covenant. Most Arabs in the Israeli administered territories, however, are concerned with living their daily lives free from terrorist violence and from the Israeli authorities' countermeasures or from guerrilla reprisals for collaboration with Israel. The degree of cooperation with terrorist groups is not significant.[64] The violence which the terrorists find necessary to exert even against the strongly anti-Israel Gaza Arabs suggests, conversely, that there may be some willingness to cooperate with the Israelis.[65]

---

60. The Palestinian National Covenant, 1964 Version, art. 6, 3 N.Y.U.J. Int'l L. & Pol. 199, 200 (1970).

61. The Palestinian National Covenant, art. 6, supra note 7, at 230.

62. Harkabi, supra note 7, at 230.

63. Id.

64. Peretz, supra note 9, at 330. There are serious attempts now being made by both the Israelis and the Palestinians to induce the Arabs living in Israel to support each side. Id.

65. According to a report in the Jerusalem Post, Apr. 6, 1970, at 3, ". . . the main purpose of these terror acts is to prevent the local population from cooperating with the occupying power . . . . At present the terror acts are directed mostly against Gaza Strip citizens who are employed in Israel." In Mar., 1970 alone, 103 Gaza inhabitants were wounded and seven killed by Arab terrorist attacks, five killings being deliberate murders. According to reports of Aug., 1970, there had been 15 political murders by terrorists between mid-July

On the other hand, uncertainty as to a future territorial settlement also deters such cooperation with the Israelis as might result in exposure to the malice of a future Arab regime.

By way of contrast, Palestinians living outside the administered territories lack, as the account of Article 6 of the Covenant indicates, any motives of restraint. Their leaders have a stake in encouraging irresponsibility and in sharpening and widening the conflict. They are rabidly opposed to what Article 21 of the Covenant expresses as "all plans that aim at the settlement of the Palestine issue."[66] Article 21 rejects every solution that is a substitute for "a complete liberation" of Palestine.[67]

IV. Conclusion

The Arab States will block the road to a peaceful settlement as long as they continue to endorse the claimed "vanguard" role of the Palestine "liberation" groups.[68] While this position has had the effect of diverting attention from military setbacks, it is an expediency which results in the avoidance of the real issue that must be resolved between Jordan and the Palestine Arabs. The fact remains that it is Jordan which historically and demographically holds the key to the solution of the Palestinian question. By evading this issue, the Arab States are committed to military efforts going well beyond their vital concerns.

This situation represents a fatal circle not only of Arab defeat and frustration in war, but also of the defeat and frustration of long term Arab interests, not to mention those of the Palestinians or of the rest of the world. Until some degree of "self-liberation" is achieved by the Arab States from the more impossible demands of the leadership of the Palestine "liberation" groups, no Israeli initiative can release West Bank and Gaza Arabs from the pressures of terrorism and manipulation so that fruitful negotiations might begin. Peace ultimately will come, if at all, from the self-interested recognition by Jordan or Egypt, or both, that the aims of the present Palestinian leadership cannot succeed in the forseeable future. In the meantime, the price will be paid primarily by the Arab States in terms of the welfare of their people and the stability of their governments.

---

and mid-August, "apparently trying to liquidate Arabs suspected of collaborating with the Israel authorities." The Australian, Aug. 13, 1970.

66. The Palestinian National Covenant, art. 21, supra note 7, at 240.

67. Id.

68. Peretz, supra note 9, at 325.

The Arab-Israeli Conflict—Real and Apparent Issues: An Insight into Its Future from the Lessons of the Past

M. CHERIF BASSIOUNI AND EUGENE M. FISHER

OBSERVATIONS ON THE NATURE OF CONFLICT RESOLUTION AND THE INTERNATIONAL PROCESS

The Arab-Israeli confrontation provides the world community with one of history's greatest opportunities for implementation of the "Rule of Law" as a substitute for the "Rule of Force" in international relations and institutionalized conflicts. Thus far, unfortunately, the opportunity has proved elusive and the challenge has gone unanswered. The world community continues to clamor for peace, order, and justice, but yet is unable or unwilling to attain any of those avowed goals.

The resolution of conflicts in a consensual system of law, such as international law, is rendered difficult by the· lack of fact-finding processes, inadequate analytical methodology, non-compulsory adjudication, and unenforceable dispositions and determinations. However, unlike most international conflicts, the Arab-Israeli dispute is not clouded by seriously controverted facts. Virtually all of its elements are grounded in issues which are susceptible to legal formulation and, hence, of juridical adjudication and determination.

In juridical controversies, the manner in which the relevant issues are formulated is frequently outcome-determinative. Notwithstanding, modern world conflicts have been shaped by what is referred to as "world public opinion." (The most significant aspect of this state of affairs is that world public opinion can, and frequently does formulate issues which, through repetition, become so solidified that they sometimes cannot be altered by the very parties to the conflict.) When one considers the informational sources of world public opinion, it is clear that all too often they are either the product of a guided or controlled governmental policy or subject to the more subtle, but almost

* Professor of Law, DePaul University; Fulbright-Mays Professor of International Criminal Law and Visiting Professor of Law, University of Freiburg, 1970. LL.B., University of Cairo, 1961; J.D., Indiana University, 1964; LL.M., John Marshall Lawyer's Institute, 1966.
** Member of the Indiana Bar.

equally, effective pressure of nongovernmental, politically-oriented interests. Additionally, one cannot overlook the impact of propaganda upon such already doubtful credentials. This word, often misused, is a euphemism for the propagation of information, which can range from biased to falsified, by means of "facts" scientifically dispensed by interested governments or political pressure groups acting directly or through covert channels. Ever since Paul Joseph Goebbels mastered it in the 1930's, propaganda has become a weapon of such magnitude that its effectiveness can be raised to the level of indirect or subjective aggression. Its subliminal impact affects world public opinion by implanting a version of the facts which is conducive to the formulation of issues in a controlled (outcome-determinative) manner. And when considering the American system of criminal justice, in which trial by public opinion has been recognized as devastatingly prejudical from a psychological and legal point of view, one can only imagine the effects of propaganda on a discipline such as international law, in which, in addition to such psychological considerations, world public opinion becomes forum and fact-finder, free to formulate and sustain the issues by a selective and often discriminating choice of supporting facts.

The observer will not fail to recognize that in the Arab-Israeli conflict, world public opinion has been shaped and conditioned by exposure to a biased version of the facts as a paper curtain has apparently fallen on any aspect of the conflict which supports the Arab position. In spite of these obstacles, however, intellectual honesty, as well as the tradition of the legal profession, requires that this position be examined.

The "international process"[1] of conflict resolution usually becomes operative when the parties to the controversy submit to one of its classical devices, i.e., conciliation, negotiation, mediation, arbitration or adjudication. However, quite often one of the parties will undertake a "holding pattern," awaiting further development, or perhaps, termination of the crisis.

In either case, the basic consideration will not only be predicated upon proposed resolutory grounds; rather, such delaying tactics will generally be pursued in conjunction with a guided campaign to condition world public opinion to a particular version of the conflict.

---

1 The term "international process" includes all aspects of international interrelationships, encompassing political and diplomatic action by one nation-state vis-à-vis another as well as the workings of international organizations through which conflicts may be channelled.

Accordingly, this period will be characterized by an escalation of propaganda efforts which are often destined to conceal the real issues behind apparent ones. Whether the issues advanced by the parties or by world public opinion are indeed real will become evident only when the international process attempts to fashion a solution to the conflict. When reasonable solutions are thwarted or rejected, it will then be clear that the apparent issues were camouflage for the real ones which were concealed, in whole or in part, for reasons better known to the concealing party or parties. While these observations may appear elementary, they do provide a foundation for the proposition that, even though virtually all of the issues arising from the Arab-Israeli confrontation can be juridically formulated, no juridical solution to the conflict has been achieved because the issues, as presented, are not in fact real.

THE LEGAL ISSUES[2]

The following schematic statement of the apparent issues arising from the Arab-Israeli conflict (formulated in a manner heretofore unseen in American professional publications and virtually never disclosed in rather obviously prejudiced popular literature) is presented to demonstrate that a juridical solution is certainly within the realm of the possible. Theoretically, the conflict could immediately be removed from the opposing parties and placed in the context of international adjudication, with justiciability of the issues almost assured. As stated previously, the fact that it is not substantiates the proposition that the issues that lie at the heart of the conflict are not those apparent issues, but rather psychological and political issues which will be explored below. Additionally, this discussion will illustrate that even if these apparent issues are in fact real, the Arab position is the meritorious one.

1. In 1947 the United Nations, as successor to the League of Nations, decided to partition the "provisionally independent State of Palestine" into a "Jewish" and "Arab" State.[3] By virtue of what authority did the United Nations assume such a right?[4]

2. Assuming that the United Nations, under its trusteeship

---

2 See Bassiouni, *Some Legal Aspects of the Arab-Israeli Conflict* 14 THE ARAB WORLD 41 (special ed. 1968), to be reprinted in *The Arab-Israeli Confrontation of 1967* (I. Abu-Lughod ed. 1970); Wright, *Legal Aspects of the Middle East Situation*, 33 LAW & CONTEMP. PROB. 5 (1968).

3 G.A. Res. 181, U.N. Doc. A519 at 131 (1947).

4 See generally El-Farra, *The Role of the U.N. Vis-à-Vis the Palestine Question*, 33 LAW & CONTEMP. PROB. 68 (1968).

articles, possessed sufficient authority to make such a decision, should it not have complied with the Palestinian peoples' right to self-determination as a condition precedent to the partition; and if the people elected separate States, should not the allocation of territory to each State have been on the basis of citizenship and property ownership?[5] Would the failure to do so render the partition decision void or voidable?

3. Assuming the legitimacy and validity of the United Nations action in Palestine, would not Israel's borders be confined to its allotted partition share? If this position is correct, would not all territory subsequently acquired by force of arms constitute illegal occupation and, therefore, violate international law (*jus ex injuria non oritur*)?[6]

4. Does the United Nations have a supervisory duty over the obligations it imposed upon the creation of Israel, such as the obligation to repatriate and compensate the Palestinian Arabs, who have been denied such rights in violation of both international law and various United Nations resolutions?[7]

---

[5] *See* notes 120-30 and accompanying text *infra*. It should also be noted that in 1920 the Arab population of Palestine was 90 percent Christian and Moslem and 10 percent Jewish. By 1930, as a result of increasing British immigration quotas to European Jews, that segment of the population rose to 19 percent and by 1940, it became 30 percent of a total population of 1,530,000. By then Great Britian pledged to keep a lid on immigration so as to maintain a one-third to two-thirds ratio. Between 1940 and 1947, no less than an estimated 250,000 Jews entered Palestine illegally, *i.e.*, without an immigration visa. In 1947 the Arab non-Jewish citizens owned all but 12 percent of the registered real property. These figures appear in DOCUMENTS ON BRITISH FOREIGN POLICY 1919-1939 (E. Woodward & R. Butler eds. 1951) and are referred to in W. YALE, THE NEAR EAST ch. 28 (1958). It is believed, however, that these figures are approximated and not exact.

[6] Notwithstanding the figures cited in note 5 *supra*, the Partition Plan allocated 58 percent of Palestine to Israel. *See* notes 3-5 *supra*; Bassiouni, *supra* note 2, at 42-43.
After the 1948-1949 war, Israel's territorial occupation of Palestine increased by 23 percent, and by 1967 it included all of Palestine and parts of Egypt, Syria and Jordan. The principle of invalidity of acquisition of territory by force of arms finds its legal foundation in the Kellogg-Briand Pact of 1929. *See* R. FERRELL, PEACE IN THEIR TIME 266 (1968); *The Fourteen Points of President Woodrow Wilson*, in DOCUMENTS OF AMERICAN HISTORY 137 (7th ed. 1969); THE INTER-AMERICAN CONVENTION ON RIGHTS AND DUTIES OF STATES art. 2; THE DRAFT DECLARATION OF RIGHTS AND DUTIES OF STATES arts. 9, 10, 11; U.N. CHARTER art. 2, para. 4 and specifically S.C. Res. 242, 22 U.N. SCOR, 1382d meeting 8 (1967). *See generally* Q. WRIGHT, THE OUTLAWRY OF WAR AND THE LAW OF WAR (1953); Wright, *The Meaning of the Pact of Paris*, 27 AM. J. INT'L L. 39 (1932).

[7] The U.N. Charter trusteeship provisions specify in article 79:
Nothing in this chapter shall be construed in or of itself to alter in any manner the rights whatsoever of any states or any peoples or the terms of existing international instruments to which members of the United Nations may respectively be parties.
In this context it should be noted that article 5 of the Palestine Mandate provided for "safeguarding of the civil and religious rights of all the inhabitants of Palestine, irrespective of race and religion." The Mandate will be discussed subsequently. For a discussion of British Policy implementing the Mandate, see PARLIAMENTARY PAPERS CMD No. 1700, at 18 *et seq.* (1922); CMD No. 1785 (1922); CMD No. 6019, at 2-3 *et seq.*

5. If Israel is a legally constituted State by virtue of the United Nations partition decision, did the Arab States commit aggression when they attacked Israel in 1948? In the event, however, that the decision of the United Nations was either without authority or in violation of international law, was the Arab States' action that of a third party intervening on behalf of the Palestinian Arabs in the course of a civil war?[8]

6. Assuming the validity of the United Nations partition resolution, did it create the State of Israel proper or was that State created by its own subsequent declaration of independence? Under the former interpretation, Israel's borders are limited to the territory allocated by the United Nations; but under the latter, did Israel become the state successor of the "provisionally independent State of Palestine," thereby freeing itself from any such limitation?[9]

7. Having subsequently conquered all of the territory of Palestine, would Israel not then, in fact, have become the successor State of Palestine?[10] In this case, would the Palestinian Arabs be entitled to

---

(1938-1939). *See* Count Bernadotte's report incorporated into Secretary General Trygve Lie's report to the Security Council in 2 U.N. SCOR, Supp. 1948, at 103-104. Specifically, the right of the Palestinians to return and to be compensated was first established in G.A. Res. 194, U.N. Doc. A/810 at 21 (1948), and has been often reiterated. Israel pledged implementation of this right to the U.N. Conciliation Commission, and this pledge was incorporated in the Commission's Lausanne Protocol, 2 U.N. GAOR, U.N. Doc. A/927 at 6 (1949).

From 1949 to date, 22 U.N. Resolutions reaffirmed Resolution 194, not including Res. 242, Nov. 22, 1967, which also mentioned the settlement of the refugee problem. Israel's admission to the U.N. in 1949 was conditioned upon its compliance with the U.N. Charter membership requirements which include compliance with international obligations.

The Resolutions accepting Israeli membership of May 11, 1949 state in paragraph 4 that Israel "unreservedly accepts the obligations of the U.N. Charter and undertakes to honour them from the day when it becomes a member of the U.N." G.A. Res. 273, U.N. Doc. A/900 at 18 (1949). The Lausanne Protocol was signed the following day to emphasize Israel's obligations not only as a creation of the U.N., but also as a member of the U.N.

8 For a discussion of third party interventions in civil wars and/or international wars, see, *e.g.*, R. HULL & I. NOVOGRAD, LAW AND VIET NAM (1968); Moore, *International Law and the United States' Role in Viet Nam: A Reply*, 76 YALE L.J. 1051, 1091-93 (1967). *Cf.* Falk, *International Law and the United States' Role in the Viet Nam War*, 75 YALE L.J. 1122, 1154 (1966); Partan, *Legal Aspects of the Vietnam Conflict*, 46 B.U.L. REV. 281 (1966); Wright, *Legal Aspects of the Viet Nam Situation*, 60 AM. J. INT'L L. 750 (1966); Comment, *The United States in Vietnam: A Case Study in the Law of Intervention*, 50 CALIF. L. REV. 515 (1962). *See also* Bassiouni, *The War Power and the Law of War: Theory and Realism*, 18 DEPAUL L. REV. 188 (1968); Wright, *The Concept of Aggression in International Law*, 29 AM. J. INT'L L. 373 (1935); *Symposium — Legality of United States Participation in the Viet Nam Conflict*, 75 YALE L. J. 1085 (1966).

9. Palestine was the only nation in Class *A* of the League of Nations' Mandate which did not receive its independence even though it was referred to in the Mandate as a "provisionally independent state." *See* LEAGUE OF NATIONS COVENANT art. 22 and the "Mandate" discussed at notes 121-31 and accompanying text *infra*. For a discussion of state succession, see generally D. O'CONNELL, THE LAW OF STATE SUCCESSION (1956); L. OPPENHEIM, INTERNATIONAL LAW (8th ed. 1955).

10 After the 1967 war, all of Palestine fell under Israeli occupation and the question of state succession may arise more significantly again. *See* G. HACKWORTH, DIGEST OF INTERNATIONAL LAW 360-77 (1943); I. HYDE, INTERNATIONAL LAW 358-438 (2d ed. 1945). For

equal citizenship rights in the successor State? Would the denial of these rights on such a basis constitute a violation of international law?

8. Is Israel entitled to claim a right of free and innocent passage in the Straits of Tiran and the Gulf of Aqaba?[11] Would that right accrue to Israel as a State whose borders are limited to the territory allotted under the partition plan or because it is the successor State of Palestine? Can that right, depending upon the basis of its existence, be abridged by a "state of belligerency," or by Israel's violations of international law, such as the military conquest of additional territory or its refusal to repatriate and compensate the Palestinian Arabs? Alternatively, is the Gulf of Aqaba an internal waterway possessing historical characteristics which would not be available to a new state?[12] Is the 1958 Geneva Convention[13] applicable in determining the right of access to the Gulf and the Straits, regardless of whether Israel is a lawful riparian nation? Would it apply to a state which acquired riparian territory by force of arms, or only if Israel is to be considered the state successor of Palestine? Does the closing of the Straits to Israeli navigation constitute an act of aggression, a violation of international law, or a *casus belli* as Israel claimed in 1967?[14]

9. The right to free and innocent passage through the Suez Canal raises questions which again pertain, in part, to the origin of Israel. As the successor State of Palestine, which was part of the Turkish Ottoman Empire at the time of the 1888 Constantinople Convention, Israel is entitled to free and innocent passage, and so are goods directed to its territory on board other flag-carrying vessels.[15] However, could

---

the most recent American position see 2 M. WHITEMAN, DIGEST OF INTERNATIONAL LAW 754-936 (1963). *See also* A. KEITH, THEORY OF STATE SUCCESSION 5 (1905); D. O'CONNELL, *supra* note 9, at 156-69, 571-73; L. OPPENHEIM, *supra* note 9, at 944-45.

11 *See* Bassiouni, *supra* note 2, at 49-51; *cf.* L. BLOOMFIELD, EGYPT, ISRAEL AND THE GULF OF AQABA IN INTERNATIONAL LAW 50 (1957); Selak, *A Consideration of the Legal Status of the Gulf of Aqaba,* 52 AM. J. INT'L L. 660 (1958).

12 For an analogous situation see the case of the Guatemala-Honduras boundary arbitration of 1933 which involved the Bay of Fonseca. Bay of Fonseca Case (Guatemala-Honduras), 2 U.N.R.I.A.A. 1307 (1933-1934). A contrary view can be seen in the Corfu Channel Case, [1949] I.C.J. 28. The Arab position that it is a *mare clausum* appears in 12 U.N. GAOR 223 (1957). Since 1841, the ports on the Gulf of Aqaba had been recognized as Egypt's by the Turkish Ottoman Empire and acknowledged by Israel in a Ministry of Foreign Affairs' publication, BACKGROUND PAPER ON THE GULF OF AQABA 5 (May 1956). The American position can be found in 36 DEP'T STATE BULL. 482-89 (1957).

13 THE GENEVA CONVENTION OF HIGH SEAS, TERRITORIAL SEA AND CONTIGUOUS ZONES art. 16, para. 4, recognizes a right to innocent passage. *See also* art. 14, para. 4, which states: "Passage is innocent so long as it is not prejudicial to the peace, good order or security of the coastal state." *See* note 15 *infra*.

14 The closing of the Gulf of Aqaba in May 1967 was deemed a *casus belli* by Israel. *See* Sharabi, *Prelude to War: The Crisis of May-June 1967,* 14 THE ARAB-WORLD 23-29 (special ed. 1968).

15 M. HEFNAWY, LES PROBLEMES CONTEMPORAINS DU CANAL DE SUEZ (1953); Bassiouni, *The Nationalization of the Suez Canal and the Illicit Act of International Law,* 14 DEPAUL L. REV. 258 (1965); *cf.* Dinitz, *The Legal Aspects of the Egyptian Blockade of the Suez*

that right be limited to non-strategic goods or abridged by reason of the existence of a state of belligerency between Egypt and Israel or by reason of Israel's forceful occupation of Arab territory in violation of international law and its denial of the Palestinians' rights, which were enunciated by the United Nations and were in accordance with Human Rights Conventions and international law in general? If Israel is the product of its own declaration of independence, rather than the resolution of the United Nations, and is not deemed the successor State of Palestine, can it then claim a right to passage under the 1888 Convention? If so, on what legal basis? If the claim is based upon status as a third-party beneficiary, for whose benefit was the right to passage stipulated (even though Israel did not exist at the time)?[16]

10. The United Nations condemned Israel for its attack against Egypt in 1956. Was Egypt subsequently authorized to prohibit passage of Israeli or Israeli-bound vessels through the Tiran Straits and the Canal? Was Israel guilty of aggression in 1967,[17] and what legal consequences derive from its policy of preemptive attack?

11. Is Israel's continued occupation of territory beyond the 1947 partition lines a continuous violation of international law and a condition of permanent aggression?[18] Does Israel's continued violation of the rights of the Palestinian Arabs have the same effect?[19] And finally do such actions activate the Palestinians' rights to self-defense and

---

Canal, 45 GEO. L.J. 175 (1956). The American position is indicated in U.S. DEP'T OF STATE, THE SUEZ CANAL PROBLEM 16-19 (1956). *See also* the Egyptian Embargo Act of Feb. 6, 1950, which did set forth the basis for searching and seizing material destined to aid Israel's strategic war potential and which relied upon article 10 of the 1888 Constantinople Convention. This allowed Egypt to take measures to insure its own safety, and is discussed in Bassiouni, *supra* at 266-88. *See also* Bassiouni, *supra* note 2, at 47-49.

16 *See* Bassiouni, *supra* note 15, at 288-329 and *supra* note 2, at 5-6; *cf.* Wright, *supra* note 2 at, 20-22. *See also* Report of the Committee on Use of International Rivers and Canals, I.L.A. Hamburg, at 58 (1960); L. OPPENHEIM, *supra* note 9, at 926-927.

17 The contention was made at the Security Council, *See* 22 U.N. SCOR, 1347th meeting 17-21 (1967); *see also* Res. 242 (1967) which ordered Israel's withdrawal from occupied territory; notes 18, 24 *infra*.

18 The question remains unresolved by Res. 242 (1967); but, it states:
> *Emphasizing*
> The inadmissibility of the acquisition of territory by war . . . , (1) withdrawal of Israeli armed forces territories occupied in the recent conflict.

However, Moshe Dayan has stated:
> Our fathers had reached the frontiers which were recognized in the Partition Plan. Our generation reached the frontiers of 1949. Now the Six-Day Generation has managed to reached Suez, Jordan and the Golan Heights. This is not the end. After the present cease-fire lines, there will be new ones. They will extent beyond Jordan — perhaps to Lebanon and perhaps to central Syria as well.

The Times (London), June 25, 1969, at 1, col. 1. For a discussion of the Resolution see Bassiouni, *The Middle East in Transition: From War to War*, 4 INT'L LAW 379 (1970). *See also* Levie, *The Nature and Scope of the Armistice Agreement*, 50 AM. J. INT'L L. 880 (1956).

19 *See* note 7 *supra*.

the rights of neighboring States to collective self-defense under the United Nations Charter and general principles of international law.[20]

12. The partition plan contemplated an internationalized Jerusalem with free access for all faiths.[21] Did the Jordanian occupation of Old Jerusalem from 1948 until 1967 constitute a violation of international law? Did Israel's 1967 annexation of the same territory and its refusal to heed subsequent United Nations resolutions condemning this action also constitute a violation of international law?[22] Would a doctrine of better title be applied? In that case, would the result not depend on the "clean hands" of the party seeking equity under the International Court of Justice's *exacquo et bono*?

13. Does Resolution 242 of November 22, 1967, commanding (the word *commanding* can be at issue since there is disagreement on whether or not this resolution is recommendatory or resolutory) Israel's withdrawal from territory occupied in that conflict include *all* territory? Must the withdrawal be accomplished prior to any guarantees of secured and recognized borders for Israel, or is the resolution unconditional and peremptory? In the latter case, Israel would be in violation of this United Nations resolution in particular and of international law in general, since territory acquired by force is invalid and illegitimate.[23] If Israel is to comply with the resolution, would its return to pre-1967 lines sanction these lines as the permanent borders of its legitimate territory, or would that still be in issue?[24]

14. Could Israel's claim to be the political institution representing the "Jewish people," in violation of accepted principles of nationality status under international law, be considered an act of subversion against those countries having "nationals" of the Jewish faith?[25] Could Israeli-sponsored attempts to induce such nationals to abandon their citizenship in favor of Israel, coupled with its claim of representation, constitute a subversive condition amounting to indirect aggression against such nations and, in view of this in-gathering policy, a permanent threat to Israel's neighboring States?

15. Does the effective deprivation of the Palestinian peoples' rights, including their right to return, to be compensated, to live and

---

20 *See* note 8 *supra.* U.N. CHARTER arts. 50-51; S. BOWETT, SELF-DEFENSE IN INTERNATIONAL LAW (1958).

21 G.A. Res. 304, U.N. Doc. A/1251 at 12 (1949); G.A. Res. 194, U.N. Doc. A/810 at 21-23 (1948).

22 G. A. Res. 2253, 22 U.N. GAOR Supp. 1 at 4, U.N. Doc. A/6798 (1967) (Emer. Sess. V) (by a vote of 116-0-2).

23 For a discussion of Resolution 242, see Bassiouni, *supra* note 18.

24 *See* Levie, *supra* note 18.

25 *See* notes 36-67 and accompanying text *infra.*

organize on territory allotted them by the United Nations in 1947, in addition to violating United Nations resolutions,[26] Human Rights Conventions,[27] and international law in general, constitute a violation of the 1948 Genocide Convention?

16. Does the avowed propaganda of some Arab news media, promising the annihilation or destruction of Israel by its neighboring Arab States, coupled with their military alliances, offensive armaments, and military preparedness constitute direct aggression, or to a lesser degree, indirect aggression,[28] or conspiracy to commit genocide in violation of Genocide Conventions?[29] Does it justify Israel's preemptive and reprisal policies?

PSYCHO-POLITICAL UNDERPINNINGS OF THE CONFLICT

As previously noted, the most startling observation which arises from even a cursory examination of the conflict is that the facts giving rise to these issues are, for the most part, uncontroverted.[30] This is rather unique in the history of modern conflicts, although certainly many secondary facts are disputed. Arguments are made with respect to the actual number of pre-1967 Palestinian Arabs and Jews, the number of legal and illegal Jewish immigrants between 1936 and 1947, and the number of Palestinian Arab refugees after the 1948 and 1967 wars. Claims of initial aggression and reprisals are also a matter of factual contention. However, these arguments are not material to the formulation of the issues proper. Thus, while the lack of a fact-finding process has been one of international law's most glaring weaknesses, it has not been one of the factors in this conflict. The parties admit the material facts and are, therefore, in agreement with them — even though only by implication. Furthermore, the United Nations has maintained a close fact-finding operation from the inception of the problem in 1947.[31]

---

26 See notes 5 & 6 supra.

27 See THE UNIVERSAL DECLARATION ON HUMAN RIGHTS AND THE CIVIL AND POLITICAL RIGHTS COVENANT, G.A. Res. 217, U.N. Doc. A/555, at 71 (1948).

28 J. STONE, AGGRESSION AND WORLD PUBLIC ORDER (1958). For a discussion of propaganda and its effects, see J. WHITTON & A. LARSON, PROPAGANDA: TOWARDS DISARMAMENT IN THE WAR OF WORDS (1964); Symposium — International Control of Propaganda, 31 LAW & CONTEMP. PROB. 437 (1966).

29 E.g., the Genocide Convention of 1948.

30 See note 28 and accompanying text supra.

31 An Ad Hoc Commission formed in 1947 filed several reports with the U.N. Secretary General and the General Assembly, among them 2 U.N. GAOR, at 209, U.N. Doc. A/AC/13/32. Count Bernadotte was dispatched by the U.N. in 1948 and reported to the Secretary General on September 19, 1948. Many reports followed, including some by his successor Ralph Bunche. See reports by the U.N. Conciliation Commission work in Switzerland in 1948, the Jordan Waters Commission, the Mixed Armistice Commission following the 1949 Rhodes Armistice under U.N. auspices, the United Nations Emergency

Jurists will readily recognize that, notwithstanding its limitations, international law has formulated a sufficient legal framework for a juridically based resolution of the issues raised by this conflict. Consequently, one must question why such a juridically based solution has not been found.[32] The authors submit that the reason why no viable alternative to the use of force has been offered, or, if proposed, has not been adopted, is because the underpinnings of the conflict are psycho-political rather than legal. This article proposes to explore these psycho-political underpinnings, in order to gain a better understanding of their effect on the prospects of peaceful resolution.

The crux of these psycho-political differences lies in the view that Israel is the fulfillment of the first stage of the Zionist dream of *Eretz Israel*. The in-gathering of all the Jews to reestablish the "Jewish people" on the "land of Israel," in fulfillment of the prophecy and in keeping with the divine covenant, is to be implemented by a strong State capable of insuring the safety of its people and attaining their political, religious, spiritual, and cultural goals. Unfortunately, the Zionist leaders chose to build this State on what they understandably claimed as ancestral territory — in total disregard of what had come to be, in over 13 centuries, the land of the Arabs.

Palestine, as part of the Arab land, plays a much greater role than that of being mere real estate. It is the geopolitical link of the "Arab nation" — an equally political concept, also resting on historical arguments, but much more realistic and natural to the area and its indigenous population. Arab nationalist secularism is not as well formulated, dogmatically or ideologically, as Zionism, but that is because it requires less artificial dogmatic formulation. It is predicated on the historical unity of the Islamic nation, which was founded by the Arab people in the seventh century (Palestine became part of it in 640 A.D.) and united by the universalism of Islam.[33] The aspirations of the Arab people are currently linked by common modern experiences, language, religion, culture and, to a large extent, future political expectations. The geographic continuity of the Arab States is a political and eco-

---

Forces after 1956 and the cease-fire line observers after 1967. U.N. Secretary General U Thant made several trips to the area and reported twice to the Security Council on May 19 and 26. For a discussion of these reports see C. VON HORN, SOLDIERING FOR PEACE 127-40 (1967). *See also* Anabtawi, *The United Nations and the Middle East Conflict of 1967*, 14 THE ARAB WORLD 53-60 (special ed. 1968).

32 This author, as Chairman Pro-Tem of an Ad-Hoc Commission composed of eighteen professors of international law, made such a proposal which was presented to the members of the U.N. Security Council.

33 Bassiouni, *Islam: Concept, Law and World Habeas Corpus*, 2 RUTGERS-CAMDEN L. REV. 160 (1969).

nomic factor which also militates in favor of these regional aspirations. Thus far, however, the political basis of these future aspirations is undefined and thereby constitutes what is probably the most significant impediment to Arab expectations. To that extent, the present conflict over Israel is its most binding element; yet, it is clear that Israel is not the *raison d'être* of Arab nationalism but merely its contemporary catalyst.

The central issue underlying the entire conflict, then, is Zionism versus Arab nationalism. The two doctrines are, in their original form, irreconcilable. It is this conflict of concepts which explains why no juridically-based solution has been adopted. Neither side has been willing to alter its ideological course. Arabs and Zionists are suspicious and fearful of each other, and coexistence cannot be envisioned by either as long as such positions are maintained. Thus, in addition to the very nature of the ideological conflict, derivative psychological factors must also be considered. These factors are varied, and can be said to have their roots in mutual fear and distrust. Lately, however, there has evolved the conviction that the destruction of the opposite ideology is essential. Both sides now regard this as an objective because their popularized social psychology is impregnated with the conviction that if one ideology is bent on the destruction of the other, the survival of either can be insured only by the preemptive destruction of the other. In other words, as Mr. Eban aptly referred to it (but only one-sidedly), each side is bent on "politicide" (to say the least). The initial respective claims of righteousness and legality are now replaced by rationalizations of survival and self-preservation, at which point logic, reason and law fade away behind allegedly justifiable extremism. To understand the present stage of the situation and to explore its future, we must first examine these underlying factors which support and fuel the conflict at present, and thereby affect its future development.

Recent events in the Middle East underscore the failure of the governments and peoples of most Western countries to understand or even recognize the true nature of the conflict between Israel and her adversaries. This struggle began more than 50 years ago between the Arabs of Palestine and Zionist Jews. Powerfully aided by the Western powers, the Zionists were determined to restore Palestine to the status it had once enjoyed for a brief time: an independent Jewish State. The recent emergence of a rapidly coalescing Palestine liberation movement, planned, led, and carried forward by Palestinians, demonstrates that the Arab-Israeli conflict continues to bear the imprint of its original form — a bitter war between a people who had inhabited Palestine continuously for more than 1300 years and those who would deny the Palestinians their claim to nationhood or their national right to self-determination.[34] When this basic conflict between contending claims of nationhood and nationality — that of the Palestinians seeking the reestablishment of their State and that of a "Jewish people" claiming sovereignty, to the exclusion of the Arab Palestinians in particular and non-Jews in general, in a "national home" — is at last resolved, other issues between Israel and the Arab States (most of which derive from this central issue) can be expected to wither into relative insignificance and virtually certain peaceful resolution.

To understand the Palestinian claim to nationhood, we must first study the validity of the Jewish claim to nationhood and sovereignty within the same disputed territory.

The basis for such a scheme of study rests upon the fact that Palestine existed before Israel (1948). Correlatively, it is the Palestinian people who are presently dispossessed of a homeland they are now seeking to recover, by force of arms if necessary, against those who claim a superior right. The surrounding Arab States are only secondary parties to that issue and are, therefore, only derivatively involved as third-party intervenors.

One must be mindful of the very significant fact that Zionism is an international doctrine of which Israelism and Judaism are but constitutive factors. Conversely, Arab nationalist secularism is indigenous and regional. While the former political doctrine draws support from its international base, the latter remains local. Opportunities for foreign intervention in the conflict have, since its inception, resulted from the international character of Zionism, which has been able to attract foreign support. In contrast, the search by the Arabs for foreign support was a reaction to that of the Zionists and, as such, was belated. Simi-

---

[34] The Israeli position on this subject is manifested by its leaders' positions.
Asked whether the Palestinians were not also entitled to their homeland, Premier Levi Eshkol answered: "What are the Palestinians?"
NEWSWEEK, Feb. 17, 1969, at 18.
Asked about the role of the Palestinians in any future peace settlement, Foreign Minister Abba Eban said: "They have no role to play."
Le Monde, Jan. 20, 1969, at 2, col. 3.
The Palestinians "are not a party to the conflict between Israel and the Arab states." Ruling by the Israeli Military Court at Ramallah.
Jewish Observer, April 18, 1969, at 1, col. 2.
There was no such thing as Palestinians. . . It was not as though there was a Palestinian people in Palestine considering itself as a Palestinian people and we came and threw them out and took their country away from them. They did not exist.
Statement by Golda Meir, The Times (London), June 15, 1969, at 1, col. 3.

larly, the Arabs were forced to turn to those who, for other reasons, opposed the solicited supporters of Israel. Thus the entry of this conflict into the "cold war" was caused by Israel's successful polarization policy, which allied the Western powers to it and effectively compelled Arab alignment with anti-Western nations.

THE JEWISH PEOPLE QUESTION: SOCIAL, POLITICAL, HISTORICAL, AND LEGAL DEVELOPMENT OF ITS NATIONALITY CLAIM AND PALESTINE

The claim for the existence of a "Jewish people" as a legally and juridically recognizable entity rests primarily on the historical, religious, and sociological background of the Jews in Palestine and on the premise (widely accepted in Western lands) that these factors entitle Jews of diverse national origins to establish and maintain a sovereign State in Palestine. The claim presupposes the continuous existence of a Jewish nationality group deriving from Jewish history in Palestine, notwithstanding the individual assumption of various nationalities by its claimed membership over the centuries. To understand this claim, a knowledge of that history is required.

Recorded Palestinian history is rooted in the Old Testament of the Bible, although modern research has produced supplementary knowledge. Arabs migrating from Yemen had settled in Palestine as early as 3500 B.C.,[35] while the Hebrews, led by Moses, came there 2,000 years later. The first Hebrew kingdom was established by King David circa 1010-970 B.C., and the chief symbol of Hebrew culture and thought has always been the temple built by David's son, Solomon, in Jerusalem circa 970-930 B.C.[36] Although at one point Hebrew rule extended as far as the borders of Egypt and Assyria, before David and after Solomon no central government exercised undisputed dominion over Palestine (the kingdom of David and Solomon lasted only about 70 years).

In 65 B.C., Roman legions seized Jerusalem, and thereafter, until 1948 A.D., there was no independent Jewish rule in Palestine. For seven centuries Palestine remained a Roman, then Byzantine province. From 640 A.D. until 1948, the country was wholly Arab in character, history and tradition. Palestine existed as part of the nation of Islam, and although it remained subject to the political control of the Ottoman Empire for over 600 years, it preserved and maintained its local character as an Arab country.

---

35 A. NUTTING, THE ARABS ch. 7 (1965).
36 Tibawi, *Jerusalem: Its Place in Islam and Arab History*, 14 THE ARAB WORLD 9-22 (special ed. 1968).

After the Romans destroyed Jerusalem in 135 A.D., successive waves of Jewish emigration swelled the Jewish communities in Egypt and Mesopotamia, flowed into Syria, and moved across the Mediterranean to Greece. Another wave followed the Arab conquest in 640 A.D., as the Jews resettled in North Africa and Iberia. It is especially significant that Jews in all Arab-ruled countries accepted assimilation into the Arab nation (as Prime Minister David Ben-Gurion conceded in interviews with American newsmen in 1964),[37] and yet preserved their religious affiliation. The Muslim Arabs practiced a degree of religious tolerance which was unmatched in the Western world until the advent of the French Revolution; Jews and Christians were permitted to practice their religious creeds while enjoying the civic, political, and economic benefits of citizenship. In sharp contrast, an era of Christian persecution of the Jews followed the downfall of Moslem rule in Spain. Those Jews who survived the Grand Inquisition without converting to Christianity, either retreated to Arab North Africa or sought refuge in Central Europe. However, those adopting the latter course quickly discovered that the religious freedom available to their co-religionists in the Arab world was unavailable in Europe. They were driven into walled ghettos by Pope Paul IV, a practice which was to be frequently adopted by other European rulers. Indeed, the vicious brutality of the treatment imposed upon European Jews during the Middle Ages shocks the modern mind, and one marvels that any survived. No figures can be cited with certainty, but scholarly estimates indicate that there were approximately four million Jews in the world in the early years of the Diaspora and only about one and a half million by 1700.[38]

After the French and American Revolutions introduced new concepts of individual rights to the world community, Judaism began to flourish again. Yet, in many areas, particularly Eastern Europe, persecution continued. Even in the Western countries, Jews remained the victims of social and economic discrimination, the spread of anti-Jewishness[39] culminating in the *Dreyfus* case.[40] Similarly, the frequent pogroms and massacres in Russia continued to demonstrate that the status of Jews was still insecure, their safety and well-being remaining

---

[37] Moskin, *Prejudice in Israel*, LOOK, Oct. 5, 1965, at 127.

[38] ROYAL PALESTINE COMMISSION REPORT ch. 1, ¶ 26 (1937) [hereinafter ROYAL COMM.].

[39] Use of the word "anti-semitism" is purposely avoided; Semites include Arabs, and just as Arabs cannot be anti-semites, it is believed that, since Europe had no Arab minorities living therein, her experience was with Jews and the discrimination anti-Jewish oriented.

[40] *See* note 13 *supra*.

in jeopardy; and in Eastern Europe, conditions continued to resemble markedly those which existed in medieval times. In those lands of continuing oppression, large scale emigration seemed to offer Jews their brightest hope. Accordingly, huge majorities of migrating Jews turned to the West, particularly Great Britain and the United States. However, some did "return" to Palestine; while there were some 12,000 Jews in that land in 1845, this number increased to 80,000 in 1914, the difference due, in large part, to European immigrants.[41]

Zionists vigorously contend that throughout 18 centuries of dispersion, Jews everywhere nourished a memory of, and prayed for return to, a Palestine homeland. Nevertheless, history raises serious doubts as to this claim, and indicates that their attachment to Palestine was religious, spiritual, and perhaps even cultural (even though strong Arab influence makes it unseemly), rather than political or temporal. A continuing spiritual attachment to the birthplace of their religious faith cannot be denied, but desire for a physical return there is historically doubtful. In the Arab countries, as we have noted, Jews were thoroughly Arabized. To cite one example, Maimonides (Moshe ben Maimon) served as court physician to the famed Salah-El-Din (Saladin) and wrote his still revered *Commentary on the Mishma* and *Book of Commandments* in Arabic at Fostat, a suburb of Cairo. Similarly, many Jews served as the ambassadors of Muslim rulers and occupied other high government posts throughout the history of the Islamic nations. Jews taught at Arab universities, pursued advanced study in medicine, science, history, and philosophy, and wrote freely concerning both sacred and secular subjects. Indeed, a century before Prophet Muhammad's time, a Himyarite Arab ruler at Sa'nāa, Dhu Nuwas, adopted Judaism and took his people into that faith with him.[42]

Russian Jews appear to have kept the story of a Jewish homeland in Palestine glowing as a beacon of hope, but it seems unlikely that they had any direct historical or ancestral link with the birthplace of Judaism. History has recorded no mass migration of Jews to Russia. Rather, Russian Jews seem to have descended from the Khazars, a Turkish-speaking people who once ruled southern Russia. About 800 A.D., a Khazar king, along with his subjects, converted to the Jewish faith,[43] and although the Khazars subsequently relinquished their political power to the Muscovites, they continued to cling to their reli-

---

[41] ROYAL COMM. at 9, ¶ 19.
[42] A. NUTTING, *supra* note 35, at 24.
[43] D. DUNLOP, HISTORY OF THE JEWISH KHAZARS (1954).

gious faith, keeping it alive until modern times. Significantly, however, the Khazar Jews had no access to learning after their fall from power. Even the history and the laws of Judaism were preserved almost entirely in oral tradition, and it is extremely likely that Russian Jews of the 19th century knew little or nothing of their actual ethnic origin. In such circumstances, the natural tendency was to identify themselves with all other followers of Judaism, their brethren in faith, and to believe in an ancestral link with Palestine which did not in fact exist.

The yearning of Eastern European Jewry for a better, brighter future promoted a sense of Jewish nationalism in which Palestine — Zion — was the goal. Branches of a new nationalist movement, *Hoveve Zion* (Love of Zion), began to appear in Eastern Europe during the late 1800's. This was the origin of the Zionist movement, which achieved wide notice and international attention when Theodor Herzl, angry and bitter over the flagrant injustice of the *Dreyfus* case in 1894, wrote his pamphlet, *Der Juden Staat (The Jewish State)*,[44] contending that only a sovereign Jewish nation capable of dealing with other nations on a basis of equality could protect Jewish rights throughout the world.

From the anger and indignation aroused by both the Dreyfus affair[45] and Herzl's works, there came into existence a new World Zionist Organization established at Basel, Switzerland, in 1897. With Herzl as its first international president, the group set, as its prime objective, the creation for the "Jewish people" of a Palestinian home *secured by public law*.[46] Herzl saw in the World Zionist Organization a symbolic embodiment of the sovereign will of the "Jewish people," a kind of government in exile of the Jewish State which he hoped to help establish. Despite his belief that such a body could win international recognition as the accepted representative of the "Jewish people," this task was virtually insurmountable at that time. The primary obstacle was the Organization's contention that it represented a constituency scattered throughout the world, whose members had long since acquired full citizenship in the States they inhabited, and who had no interest whatsoever in a program designed to establish for them a

---

44 Der Juden Staat, published originally in Vienna in 1894, has been republished in many languages and is still in print. T. Herzl, The Jewish State: An Attempt at a Modern Solution of the Jewish Question (S. D'Avigor & A. Cohen transl. 1943).

45 In 1894, a French military court sentenced Captain Alfred Dreyfus, a Jew, to life imprisonment for treason. His conviction was based on the testimony of gentile fellow officers who committed perjury to protect a gentile aristocrat. Theodor Herzl reported the trial for *Neue Freie Presse of Vienna*.

46 *See* note 11 *supra*.

new national status or identity based solely upon the fact of their Jewishness.

In terms of contemporary nationality law, the Zionist claim to represent a Jewish nation, in which every Jew is and remains a de facto natural citizen, until he claims it de jure is unprecedented, without legal foundation in international law, and difficult to sustain. Although citizenship is a question of municipal law, the competence to constitute a nationality entity and to confer membership in it, while emanating from municipal law, is nonetheless limited by international law.[47] The constituting authority must be a State, and the constituted entity must be the nationality of that State, as conferred by the former to a juridical subject whose links with the conferring state warrant the grant of nationality.[48] Even a sovereign State lacks unrestricted power to confer nationality.[49] There must be a factual connection or "genuine link" between the individual and the State which attempts to confer nationality, with its legally binding and enforceable duties and obligations upon him. This mutuality of citizen-state obligations was well expressed in the case of *Lurie v. United States*:[50] "Citizenship is membership in a political society and implies a duty of allegiance on the part of the member and a duty of protection on the part of the society. These are reciprocal obligations, one being a compensation for the other."[51] Accordingly, statehood differs from nationhood, in that the former is predicated on a political concept subject to the regulation of international law, while the latter is a label for an association predicated on factors other than juridicial. Only a State, then, can confer nationality, subject to the limitations of international law.

---

47 "Nationality Law is closely connected with the political structure of a country. . . . It determines who shall be a 'citizen' and thus what shall be the composition of the 'nation.'" Silving, *Nationality in Comparative Law*, 5 AM. J. COMP. L. 410 (1956). "The competence to constitute a nationality entity and confer membership in it is limited by law. The juridical limitations are as applicable to the Jewish people nationality claims as to any others." Mallison, *The Zionist-Israel Juridical Claims to Constitute "the Jewish People" Nationality Entity and to Confer Membership in It. Appraisals in Public International Law*, 32 GEO. WASH. L. REV. 983, 1050 (1964). *See also* L. OPPENHEIM, *supra* note 9, at 645. *See also* The Times-Morocco Nationality Decrees [1923] P.C.I.J., ser. B, No. 4; The Hague Convention on Conflict of Nationality Laws, April 12, 1930, 179 L.N.T.S. 89; Koessler, *Subject, Citizen, National and Permanent Allegiance*, 56 YALE L.J. 58, 65-75 (1946); McGovney, *Our Non-Citizen Nationals, Who Are They?*, 22 CALIF. L. REV. 593 (1934); Note, *Developments in the Law — Immigration and Nationality*, 66 HARV. L. REV. 643, 703-04 (1953).

48 *See also* M. PANHUYS, THE ROLE OF NATIONALITY IN INTERNATIONAL LAW (1959); Mallison & Koessler, *Rights and Duties of Declarant Aliens*, 91 U. PA. L. REV. 321 (1942); Harvard Research in International Law, *Nationality*, 23 AM. J. INT'L L. 11 (special supp. 1929).

49 *See* notes 47 and 48 *supra* and note 52 *infra*.

50 231 U.S. 9 (1913); *see also* note 57 *infra*.

51 231 U.S. at 22.

Organized Zionism prior to the creation of the State of Israel was not in any sense the type of "State" contemplated by public law, and until the establishment of Israel, there was no "political society" constituted as a State which was capable of granting "Jewish" nationality. In regard to the second requirement, various factors are to be considered in determining the existence of a "genuine link" between an existing State and those upon whom it seeks to confer nationality, and the nature of those factors will determine their significance. Habitual residence is one such factor; others include the center of individual interests, family ties, participation in public life, service in the military forces of the conferring country, attachment to the interests of a given State as manifested by cultural conduct, and declaration of the individual's intentions.[52] Furthermore, the sentiments forming the link must be secular; religious attachment alone is not enough, for if that factor, without more, was regarded as sufficient, the procedure would be discriminatory, and as such, of internationally enunciated human rights.

Application of these criteria to the "Jewish people" issue is difficult, but we believe that on the facts, they support the following findings:

1. The only States capable of conferring Jewish nationality were the ancient Hebrew States in Palestine and their successor States, whenever bound by the obligations thus created.
2. *Only* those Jews who have maintained the effective link between themselves and the ancient Hebrew states by successfully resisting assimilation into another nationality have not

---

[52] Lichtenstein v. Guatemala, (Nottebohm Case) [1955] I.C.J. 4. Genuine link includes the following requirements: (a) some social basis both in an objective sense in terms of tangible interest and a subjective sense in terms of sentiments to ideals, cultural and perhaps religious attachment; and (b) reciprocal rights and duties between the individual and the state. Hence, the basis utilized in countries such as Israel, Red China and Russia, where citizenship can be granted only on ideological grounds, would not be sufficient to be recognized under international law. The main arguments advanced by the court in favor of the "genuine link" requirement are: (1) its use in cases of dual nationality; (2) the definition of nationality by third states as a legal bond having as its basis a social fact of attachment, a genuine connection of existence, interests and sentiments, together with the existence of reciprocal rights and duties; (3) the writing of publicist; (4) the tendency of nationality laws which make naturalization dependent on conditions indicating the existence of a link; (5) the practice of certain states to refrain from exercising protection in favor of a naturalized person when the latter has, in fact, severed his links with his new country (Bancroft treaties); and (6) the existence of article 5 of the Hague Convention (1930) which called for a genuine link. Hence, the court derived from custom and general principles the added requirement, beyond naturalization by a state, of a "genuine link" between that state and the individual to whom it wishes to afford diplomatic protection. The case was discussed in Kunz, *The Nottebohm Judgment*, 54 Am. J. Int'l L. 536 (1960).

abandoned their citizenship in those ancient states, and thus, in the successor States. Every Jew who participated in the public life of any other State, swore allegiance to such a state, or by some other positive act, exercised the rights of citizenship in such a State *at any time since the original conferring or adoption of nationality in one of the ancient Hebrew states,* must be held to have abandoned his Jewish nationality for himself and his children. This would seem to exclude practically all modern Jews from any contemporary Jewish nationality status.

3. Those Jews whose direct ancestors were never members of the nationality group represented by the ancient Hebrew States have never enjoyed Jewish nationality, and therefore, could not be members of a continuing "Jewish people" in any political sense. This conclusion would apply specifically to the Jewish Khazars of Russia and to the Jews of Yemen.[53]

This restrictive view of the "Jewish people" question is vigorously contested by the Zionists, who maintain an open-ended concept of Zionism and thus, of Jewish nationality status. This concept, which finds its clearest expression in the Israeli Law of Return,[54] enjoyed its most telling victory when Israel secured reparations from West Germany for German acts against all European Jews, regardless of their nationality, even though the State of Israel did not exist at the time of those acts (1939-1945).

Zionists contend that no Jew has ever broken the effective link because the people of the Diaspora were exiled from Palestine by force, and were prevented from returning. Hence, the Zionists claim that any prescriptive loss of nationality would be unconscionable. However, this view ignores the fact that after the Arab conquest in 640 A.D., the Arab rulers of Palestine rescinded the Roman decree of exclusion against Jews, and that some Jews of the Diaspora did indeed take up residence in the country.[55] For these very few, the Zionist claim of a continuing Jewish nationality would certainly have to be acknowledged. But for the enormous majority of Jews who accepted the

---

53 *See* notes 42 and 43 *supra.*

54 In 1950, the Israeli Knesset (parliament) enacted a "Law of Return," which recognizes every Jewish immigrant as a full citizen as of the moment of his arrival and confers upon him the right to exercise all the functions of citizenship forthwith. This will be discussed further in note 62 *infra.* For a critical discussion of the practical application of this law, see Galanter, *A Dissent on Brother Daniel,* COMMENTARY, July 1963, at 10-17.

55 *See* Tibawi, *supra* note 36.

rights and obligations of nationality in other States *after Palestine was reopened to them*, the Zionist claim would appear to possess no validity.

As intimated previously, the Zionist claim of a continuing Jewish nationality poses significant problems of dual nationality, especially for Jews in the United States. That issue is beyond the scope of this article, but it may be proper to mention here the principal question thus raised: Can a Jewish American claim the Jewish nationality that Zionism contends he possesses (even though he does not, in fact, assert it), and at the same time, remain compatible with those citizenship obligations imposed by the Constitution and laws of the United States?[56] For those who do not claim or accept Israeli offers of citizenship, there is no conflict. As to those who do not refuse or repudiate the offer, but subjectively further its purposes by monetary contributions, political allegiance, and other forms of support, the question is at least open to exploration.[57]

---

[56] The issue of dual nationality, especially as it affects U.S. citizens, continues to present problems. David Ben-Gurion, former prime minister of Israel, defined Zionist loyalty to Israel in these terms: "The basis of Zionism is neither friendshhip nor loyalty but the love of Israel, of the State of Israel . . . . It must be an unconditional love. There must be a complete solidarity with the state and the people of Israel." Address by David Ben-Gurion before the Action Committee, World Zionist Organization, in Jerusalem, April 25, 1950, in A. LILIENTHAL, THE OTHER SIDE OF THE COIN 76 (1965). Nahum Goldmann, President of the World Zionist Organization, has said "American Jews must have the courage to openly declare that they entertain a double loyalty, one to the land in which they live and one to Israel. Jews should not succumb to patriotic talk that they owe allegiance only to the land in which they live." Jewish Daily Forward, Jan. 9, 1959.

[57] See Afroyim v. Rusk, 387 U.S. 253 (1967), which overruled Perez v. Brownell, 356 U S. 44 (1957), and held that expatriation must be based upon the voluntary relinquishment of nationality as manifested by the intent of the party. Justice Harlan's dissenting opinion supports the *Perez* holding on the ground that Congress has the power to decide what conduct is deemed in "derogation of undivided allegiance to this country." 356 U.S. at 68. The majority, by implication, would hold that finding a breach of allegiance is an offense under American law but not sufficient to warrant expatriation in the absence of a showing of intent. The Justice Department maintains the attitude that for administrative purposes, and until the courts have clarified the scope of *Afroyim*, the Nationality Act of 1940 continues to be held applicable and that voluntary relinquishment of citizenship is not confined to a written renunciation, as under section 349 (a) (6), (7) of the Act. 8 U.S.C. § 1481 (a)(6),(7) (1964). But it can also be manifested by other actions declared expatriative under the Act, if such actions are in derogation of allegiance to this country, even if in those instances *Afroyim* leaves it open to the individual to raise the issue of intent. The burden of proof of such intent is on the party asserting it. *Afroyim* suggests that this burden is not easily satisfied by the Government. In Nishikawa v. Dulles, 356 U.S. 129 (1958), Mr. Justice Black had stated that the voluntary performance of some acts can "be highly persuasive evidence in the particular case of a purpose to abandon citizenship." *Id.* at 139 (concurring opinion). Yet some kinds of conduct, though within the proscription of the statute simply will not be sufficiently probative to support a finding of voluntary expatriation. In each case the administrative authorities must make a judgment, based on all the evidence, whether the individual comes within the terms of an expatriation provision and has in fact voluntarily relinquished his citizenship. The principles of *Afroyim* reach and, therefore, include all of sections 349(a) and 350 of the Act, insofar as it relates to dual nationals born or naturalized in the United States, and section 405(c) insofar as it purports to continue the effectiveness of individual losses of nationality under

Zionists argue that their concept of a continuing "Jewish people" throughout the history of mankind, as predicated on the notion of the "chosen people," was implicitly recognized in the Balfour Declaration. This view completely ignores one very important provision of the Declaration: "It being clearly understood that nothing shall be done which may prejudice the . . . rights and political status of Jews in any other country."[58] This provision was specifically designed to avoid the juridical and political consequences of open-ended Zionism, which the mandatory powers contemplated with apprehension.[59]

The concept of a subjective Jewish nation, existing through more than 19 centuries without territory, government, or political continuity, and imposing obligations and limitations upon all adherents of the Jewish religious faith, regardless of ethnic origin, choice of nationality or time of conversion to Judaism (or for that matter continued adherence to Judaism), has no foundation or precedent in any recognized legal doctrine. The United States has specifically and expressly rejected it, as is evidenced by a letter dated April 20, 1964 and addressed to Rabbi Elmer Berger (then executive vice president of the American Council for Judaism), wherein Assistant Secretary of State Phillips Talbot officially asserted:

> The Department of State recognizes the State of Israel as a sovereign State and citizenship of the State of Israel. It recognizes no other sovereignty or citizenship in connection therewith. It does not recognize a legal-political relationship based upon the religious identification of American citizens. . . . Accordingly, it should be

the similar provisions of sections 401 and 404 of the Nationality Act of 1940. *See also* Schneider v. Rusk, 377 U.S. 163 (1964); Perri v. Dulles, 230 F.2d 259 (3d Cir. 1956); *In re* Becher, I. & N. Dec., interim decision No. 1771 (Att'y Gen. 1967); Speer, *The Place of Foreign Law in Expatriation Cases*, 4 INT'L LAW 139 (1969).

[58] *See* L. STEIN, THE BALFOUR DECLARATION app. IV (1961).

[59] A decision of mandatory powers including the United States was made on April 25, 1920

> to accept the terms of the mandates' article as given below with reference to Palestine on the understanding that there was inserted in the *proces-verbal* an undertaking by the mandatory powers that this would not involve the surrender of the rights hitherto enjoyed by the non-Jewish communities in Palestine.

For a discussion of the viewpoint that the nationality of native inhabitants of the mandated territories is definitely different from that of the nationals of the Mandatory Power, see G. HALL, MANDATES, DEPENDENCIES AND TRUSTEESHIPS 77-80 (1948); L. OPPENHEIM, *supra* note 9, at 220-22; Goldie, *Wong Man On v. Commonwealth of Australia*, 1 INT'L & COMP. L.Q. 557 (1952); Wright, *Status of the Inhabitants of Mandated Territory*, 18 AM. J. INT'L L. 306 (1924). While most of the trusteeship agreements concluded by the United Nations are silent as to the nationality of the inhabitants of the trust territories, the trusteeship agreement for the former Japanese mandated islands provides in article 11 that the United States, as administering authority, "shall take the necessary steps to provide the status of citizenship of the Trust Territory for the inhabitants of the Trust Territory." Trusteeship Agreement for Japanese Mandated Islands, July 18, 1947 T.I.A.S. No. 1665, 8 U.N.T.S. 181.

clear that the Department of State does not regard the "Jewish people" concept as a concept of international law.[60]

Professor W. T. Mallison, Jr., one of the foremost authorities on this subject, proposes recognition of what he has termed "limited, political membership" in the "Jewish people." It is Mallison's contention that the "Jewish people" referred to in the political promise clause of the Balfour Declaration, included only those who, at that time were, or thereafter might become, Zionists. In his view, a *limited* "Jewish people" concept was recognized in international law and put into effect through such international agreements as the Balfour Declaration and the League of Nations Mandate over Palestine, which incorporated that Declaration.[61]

It would appear that Professor Mallison's definition must be further clarified. Recognition of a "Jewish people" nationality group, entitled to be regarded, collectively and individually, as members of a *political society* in international law, must be based upon a declaration of their intention to abandon all preexisting allegiance to any other political society. A rejection of this contention would render their position analogous to that of a citizen of country *A* who has not publicly declared his intent to transfer his allegiance to country *B* but, in fact, admits his allegiance to the latter without the knowledge or consent of the former. On the other hand, adoption of that contention would mean that only those contemporary or future Zionists who intended (by virtue of a public act) to join the "Jewish people" nationality as an alternative to their previously existing political affiliations could be recognized as members of the "Jewish people." An exception would occur whenever the States involved permitted dual citizenship under their municipal laws. In this regard it is interesting to note that neither the Zionist Organization nor the State of Israel has ever accepted any limitation on membership in the "Jewish people." In *Attorney General of Israel v. Eichmann*,[62] the Jerusalem

---

60 This letter is quoted in Mallison, *Legal Problems Concerning the Juridical Status and Political Activities of the Zionist Organization; Jewish Agency: A Study of International and United States Law*, 9 WM. & MARY L. REV. 556, 561 (1968).

61 *Id.*

62 Crim. Case No. 40/61 (Dist. Ct. Jerusalem, Israel, Dec. 11-12, 1961), *aff'd*, Crim. App. No. 336/61 (Sup. Ct., Israel, May 29, 1962).

> The connection between the Jewish people and the State of Israel constitutes an integral part of the Law of Nations. . . . The Balfour Declaration and the Palestine Mandate given by the League of Nations to Great Britain constituted an international recognition of the Jewish people. . . .

Id.

Israeli nationality law should be distinguished from the "Jewish people" nationality claims, an endeavor which is beyond the scope of the present study. It is important to note, however, that Israeli nationality law is designed to facilitate the acquisition of

District Court, in a judgment affirmed by the Supreme Court of Israel, stated on May 29, 1962 that

> [t]he connection between the Jewish People and the State of Israel constitutes an integral part of the law of nations. . . . The Balfour Declaration and the Palestine Mandate given by the League of Nations to Great Britain constituted an international recognition of the Jewish People.[63]

In that case, Israel purported to be acting in behalf of every European Jew that was subject to the terrors of Hitler's regime, without regard to their place of residence or nationality. Similarly, almost immediately thereafter, the State of Israel claimed and collected reparations from the Government of West Germany for the losses sustained and the suffering endured by *all* Jews during the Nazi terror.

It is clear that the open-ended "Jewish people" nationality concept violates the generally accepted view of nationality status in international law. The dicta of both the League of Nations and the United Nations, as well as unilateral pronouncements by various governments are simply not a source of international law.[64] Moreover, there has been no broad international agreement on the significance or validity of the "Jewish people" concept, even in the narrow sense proposed by Professor Mallison. It follows, we submit, that the "Jewish people" concept is not a valid concept of international law, and cannot be recognized as such solely because of Israel's unilateral declaration of adherence to it (particularly in view of the fact that it contravenes and violates the rights of others, *i.e.*, the Palestinian people).[65]

The confusion arising out of the "Jewish people" question is

Israeli nationality by that part of the "Jewish people" living outside Israel. *See* Law of July 5, 1950, Law of Return, [1950] 4 LAWS OF THE STATE OF ISRAEL 114, *as amended*, 8 ISRAEL LAWS 144; [1950] FUNDAMENTAL LAWS 156, *as amended*, 8 ISRAEL LAWS 332. Section 1 of the Law of Return provides that "[e]very Jew has the right to come to this country as an 'oleh' [Jew immigrating to Israel]." *See also* Law of April 1, 1952, Nationality Law, [1952] 5 LAWS OF THE STATE OF ISRAEL 50, *as amended* 12 ISRAEL LAWS 99; Fundamental Laws 254, *as amended*, [1952] FUNDAMENTAL LAWS 410.

63 Crim. Case No. 40/61 (Dist. Ct. Jerusalem, Israel, Dec. 11-12, 1961).

64 The sources of international law are embodied in article 38 of the statute of the International Court of Justice which states:

> 1.) The court whose function is to decide in accordance with international law such disputes as are submitted to it, shall apply: (a) international conventions, whether general or particular, establishing rules expressly recognized by the contesting States; (b) international custom, as evidence of a general practice accepted as law; (c) the general principles of law recognized by civilized nations; and (d) subject to the provisions of Article 59, judicial decisions and the teachings of the most highly qualified publicists of the various nations, as subsidiary means for the determination of rules of law. 2.) This provision shall not prejudice the power of the Court to decide a case *ex aequo et bono*, if the parties agree thereto.

I.C.J. Stat. art. 38.

65 *See* notes 52 & 59 *supra*.

understandable. Prior to the creation of the State of Israel, a political concept which would replace nationality or citizenship and compel some form of political allegiance, was tactically indispensable to the Zionist scheme. Once the State was established and the legal power to confer Israeli citizenship was gained, the "Jewish people" concept had to be legitimized. The solution to what would otherwise have proven a legally cumbersome question was found in the distinction between Israeli citizenship conferred by the State's civilian authority and "Jewish nationality," which was borrowed by Israeli law from the *Halakah*. The reader must be cautioned in his interpretation of this intricate legal concept in Hebrew law. *Halakah*, or the religious law of the Hebrews, applies to the *Le'om*, or "peoplehood." From this religious premise, it is easy to attach the political overtones which Zionism had created with respect to the definition and significance of the "Jewish people" political concept. Zionists played on the religious feelings of Jews, utilizing the rabbis' desire to maintain their exclusive jurisdiction over religious matters by conveniently preserving a misleading category of Jewish nationality in addition to Israeli citizenship. Israeli identity cards and birth certificates not only have those two categories listed separately, but to further accentuate the point, a third category for religion is added. Thus, an Israeli Jew is a citizen of Israel, a Jewish national and a Jew by faith. Orthodox Jews, as well as non-Zionist groups such as the American Council for Judaism, reject this proposition. There are probably two main considerations for the Zionist approach: (1) to preserve the fiction of the political dogma embodied in the Zionist "Jewish people" concept, as it was developed prior to the establishment of the State; and (2) to perpetuate this doctrine. The purposes of its perpetuation are: (a) to attract, recruit and induce more Jewish immigration into the State by perpetuating a political link between the original Zionist idea and its political embodiment, *i.e.*, the State of Israel; and (b) to claim, in this concealed manner, Israel's "protective jurisdiction" over all Jews of the World.

These considerations are laden with the implication, which many Jews specifically reject, that no Jew can escape his Jewish nationality. Consequently, adoption of this doctrine would give Israel a color of jurisdiction over Jews who, according to this dogmatic proposition, would only be "citizens by convenience" of another State. The danger of such a doctrine is that it saps the very foundation of allegiance to the State to which a citizen belongs. To that extent, it subverts the citizen's allegiance by claiming some right to it and by conferring upon him privileges which are usually attributable only to one's own citizens. Certainly, the collection of reparations for Nazi wrongs against the "Jewish people," the Law of Return and the continued solicitation of non-Israeli Jews for financial support and immigration clearly indicate a claim by Israel on all Jews of the world. It is the authors' opinion that there is no surer way to invite anti-semitism.

The prospects for change were rekindled by the *Shalit* case,[66] in which the Israel Supreme Court, in a rare en banc decision, held by a vote of 5 to 4 on January 26, 1970, that all Israeli citizens are Israeli nationals, and that official registries should record the nationality of a Jewish citizen as Jewish, even though he would not be a Jew under *Halakahic Law*. While the decision removes religious considerations from the determination of nationality, it reinforces the Zionist concept of "Jewish people" by leaving the category in existence (although devoid of religious significance). Politically, the decision secularizes nationality, so that it now has only the meaning which former Premier David Ben-Gurion once attributed to it, *i.e.*, that anyone who wishes to be considered a Jew is part of the "Jewish people." This is not, however, an altruistic open credo, for what would otherwise prevent the Palestinian Arabs from declaring themselves "Jews" and claiming a right to return under the Law of Return. Ben-Gurion's view was a political necessity which still exists. Israel continues to seek the "return" of Russian Jews. That country will not recognize Israel's claim to its citizens even if they are of the Jewish faith, and like the United States, rejects the Zionist doctrine of "Jewish people." As indicated earlier, Russian Jews are descendants of the Khazars and indeed, many are the offspring of mixed marriages in which the mother was not Jewish. Under *Halakahic Law*, if the mother is not Jewish, the offspring would not be Jewish either. This was the problem which confronted Shalit. His wife was a Gentile and his children were not considered of Jewish nationality. Thus, prior to *Shalit*, most Russian Jews could not qualify as members of the "Jewish people" in a religious sense, and the Law of Return, under which they hypothetically would have emigrated to Israel, hinged on membership in the "Jewish people."

Notwithstanding the furor of the rabbinical centers of Israel, the *Shalit* decision furthered the Zionist doctrine, and was capitalized upon by the Israeli Cabinet, which proposed two laws to the Knesset. One stipulates that converts to Judaism, as well as the children of a Jewish mother are Jewish nationals. As for citizenship (and return) all

---

[66] Sup. Ct. of Israel, Jan. 26, 1970.

members of an immigrant family in which one spouse is Jewish would
be regarded as Jewish nationals.[67]

THE EMERGENCE OF THE ZIONISTS AS AN "INTERNATIONAL PUBLIC BODY"

In any consideration of the juridical status of Zionism and the
State of Israel, it is essential to distinguish sharply between Israelis
(nationals of the State), Zionists (adherents to a political doctrine) and
Jews (members of a religious community).[68] It is true that most Jews
in the Western countries, particularly the United States (and some
non-Jews as well), provide emotional and financial support to Zionism
and Israel, and exercise political influence on behalf of either one or
both. However, it is also true that many Jews actively dissociate themselves from Zionism.[69] One may certainly be a Jew without being a
Zionist, and one may be a Zionist though not a Jew; an Israeli is a
citizen of that State and theoretically can be neither a Jew nor a
Zionist. These facts in themselves dispute the "Jewish people" concept,
as it is defined and used by the World Zionist Organization, *i.e.*, as
the foundation of the State of Israel.

The Zionists contend that acceptance of the Zionist (*not* Jewish)
claim to Palestine has been legalized through the exercise of diplomacy
and world power politics, and that the participation of Zionists in
international agreements has rendered it imperative that the Zionist
Organization be established as an international public body recognized
as a limited subject of international law. Obviously, the validity of
these contentions must be explored in detail.

Legal personality is a legal fiction through which a legal system
attributes rights and obligations to an entity. This proposition is
applicable to both the domestic and the international legal orders.
The existing subjects of international law are free to extend the application of international law to any entity which they see fit to admit
into the realm of the international legal system.[70] Indeed, public

---

67 For a commentary on the *Shalit* case and the proposed legislation described, see
TIME, Feb. 9, 1970, at 44; TIME, Feb. 2, 1970, at 50; The Los Angeles Herald Examiner,
Jan. 23, 1970; The Detroit News, Dec. 7, 1969, at 17B. For an interesting political com-
mentary, see The Chicago Daily News, Jan. 26, 1970, at 2.

68 U. Avnery, a member of the Israeli Knesset, has proposed an Israel without Zionism.
U. AVNERY, ISRAEL WITHOUT ZIONISTS (1960).

69 The American Council for Judaism, already referred to in connection with Zionist
nationality claims, is an anti-Zionist organization dedicated to maintaining and preserving
a sharp distinction between Judaism as a religious faith and the political concept of a
"Jewish people." It is the largest and best known such group and has actively opposed
the Zionist-Israeli position on Jewish nationality.

70 G. WEISSBERG, INTERNATIONAL STATUS OF THE U.N. 21-22 (1961).

bodies are usually constituted as subjects of international law by means of multilateral agreements among States. However, no one State possesses the authority to establish any public body as a subject of international law by unilateral act or fiat. Nevertheless, such bodies may be said to *achieve* status under international law. This generally requires an appraisal of their substantive powers and the application of empirical tests. Professor Lauterpacht proposed these criteria:

> In each particular case the question whether a person or a body is a subject of international law must be answered in a pragmatic manner by reference to experience and to the reason of the law as distinguished from a preconceived notion as to who can be subjects of international law.[71]

The average international organization may be said to have an international personality in view of its functions:

> An organization [such as the Zionist Organization] could not carry out the intentions of its founders if it was devoid of [an] international personality. It must be assumed that its members, by entrusting their functions to it . . . have clothed it with the competence to enable those functions to be effectively performed.[72]

The Zionist Organization sought to gain recognition as an international public body (1) by explicit recognition from various States, and (2) through multilateral agreements among States in which its existence was explicitly mentioned. The most intensive of these efforts involved the negotiations preceding the Balfour Declaration. That Declaration is said to constitute recognition by the British Government of the Zionist Organization as a public body. It manifested the British view that the Organization had status to receive the political promise clause and *to be subjected to the limitations imposed in the safeguard clause* (both of which will be discussed below). This did not amount to recognition as an international public body by the community of nations, but it was the first step in that direction.

When, as a consequence of its political alliance with the British Government, the Zionist Organization was permitted to participate in the drafting of the League of Nations Mandate for Palestine, the Zionists were able to gain more, but not all, of their political objectives. Article 4 of the Mandate Agreement provided that "an appropriate Jewish agency shall be recognized" *as a representative of the Jewish inhabitants of that country.*[73] Without considering here the question of the Mandate itself, we must conclude that by this act, the

---

71 H. LAUTERPACHT, INTERNATIONAL LAW AND HUMAN RIGHTS 12 (1950).

72 U.N. Reparations Case, [1949] I.C.J. Rep. 4.

73 For the complete text of the Mandate Agreement, see 44 Stat. 2184 (1924).

international community of nations recognized the Zionist Organization as a public body, speaking on behalf of the Jews of Palestine. As can be seen from the full text of article 4, certain legal limitations were imposed upon the operations of the Jewish Agency, the new name of the Zionist Organization (these limitations will be discussed in a subsequent section). Finally, any reasonable doubt that might exist concerning the public body status of the agency was resolved by the decision in the first of the *Mavromattis Concession Cases*.[74] There the International Court of Justice held, with respect to article 4 of the Mandate, that: "This clause shows that the Jewish Agency is in reality a public body, closely connected with the Palestine Administration and *under its control in the development of the country*."[75]

The principal juridical consequence of the attainment of public body status is *subjection to the law*. There can be no grant of power and status as a public body without accompanying legal obligations. These include, at a minimum, both the specific legal limitations imposed in the Mandate Agreement and the general legal limitations and commitments which apply to all subjects of international law.[76] Thus, recognition as a public body not only presupposes ability to undertake and carry out assumed obligations, but imposes the duty, under sanction of law, to discharge in fact all such assumed obligations. One may indeed question the recognition granted the Zionist Organization as a public body on these grounds.

The Arab Experience with International Agreements, International Organizations, and the Western Powers

The Arab world labors under two basic notions, the first is that Israel's creation was the product of perfidious plotting and treacherous tactics, including both power politics and military force. The second is that Zionists are abetted by the Western powers, who see in Israel an extension of European colonization of the Arab world. To understand these beliefs, one must examine the progression of Zionism in Palestine, Israel's relationship, if any, with Great Britain and the Western world, and the conspiracy against the Arab world which apparently exists between them. An analysis of various international agreements, and their significance in international law, will illustrate how Great Britain, the Western world, and Israel have in fact, manipulated and distorted international law to the point where the Arab

---

74 Mavromattis Concession Cases, [1925] P.C.I.J., ser. A, No. 2, No. 5; [1927] P.C.I.J., ser. A, No. 11.

75 *Id.*

76 *Id.* This is also discussed in Mallison, *supra* note 60, at 566.

world, in particular, and most of the Third World in general, share the belief that international law is the product and tool of Western imperialism.

The declaration establishing the State of Israel cited the Balfour Declaration of 1917 as one of the legal guarantees for its creation. However, opponents of this view contend that the Balfour Declaration had no legal effect because Great Britain did not possess jurisdiction, sovereignty, or physical possession of Palestine either at the time of the declaration or when the State of Israel was proclaimed in 1948. Furthermore, they argue that no right exists under the terms of the Mandate Agreement of 1922 to transfer a trust confided by the League of Nations to Britain alone. They also assert that prior and subsequent to the date of the Balfour Declaration, Great Britain had already given conflicting pledges to Arab leaders.[77] Thus, the Arabs understandably denounce the Balfour Declaration, and point instead to their reliance upon their treaty relations with Great Britain.

An understanding of some basic concepts of international law is necessary in order to analyze these conflicting contentions. Although some international instruments are called *treaties eo nomine*, there exists a wide vocabulary from which names for such instruments may be chosen, *e.g.*, pact, convention, protocol, agreement, arrangement, declaration, act, statute, covenant. All these terms have been used to designate international contractual instruments in recent times, and in most cases, if not all, the choice of one term over another has little or no substantive significance.[78] Thus, only the substance of the instrument is relevant — not its label.

International agreements, to be binding, must be made between subjects of international law. The case for the status of the Zionist Organization in international law has been discussed previously,[79] and, as was illustrated, is one of marginal validity. That Great Britain and the Arab States were subjects of international law is beyond all question.

An international instrument need not be bilateral or multilateral, and need not follow a specific legal form to be a binding document.[80] In regard to the interpretation of an international instrument, its negotiating history is of prime importance insofar as that history reveals or indicates the intent of the contracting parties.[81] In Great

---

77 F. KHOURI, THE ARAB-ISRAELI DILEMMA 7-10, 14 (1968).

78 Mallison, *supra* note 47, at 1009.

79 *See* notes 36-67 and accompanying text *supra*.

80 HARVARD RESEARCH IN INTERNATIONAL LAW, TREATIES 937-39 (1932).

81 M. McDOUGAL, H. LASSWELL & J. MILLER, THE INTERPRETATION OF AGREEMENTS AND

Britain, the legislative history of the issues involved is included in the interpretation of treaties to aid in ascertaining the intentions and objectives of the British government. It is clear, then, that various proposals, which are offered unilaterally by the parties to an international instrument, and abandoned or compromised in the course of the negotiations, are particularly important and significant to the interpretation of the parties' intent.[82] Furthermore, an understanding of the negotiating history affords indispensable insight into its interpretation. Therefore, the key to interpretation of any of the terms involved is the political and historical context in which the agreements were made.[83] In this respect, the aim of the Zionists was perhaps paramount, and was best expressed in the following terms:

> The advantages Zionism appeared to bring to any diplomatic arrangement arose from Herzl's claim, through his position as president of the World Zionist Organization, to represent [with the potential to activate and direct] "the Jewish people" dispersed throughout the world. It was ironic that Herzl [and Weizmann too — some years later] should have projected this claim in negotiations with various governments, since *the reality was that Herzl, to a great extent, sought major-power support to enhance Zionist influence among those [Jews included] who opposed Zionism's objectives.* Herzl, for example, aimed to have the British government induce its own citizens of Jewish faith to "collaborate" with him.[84]

Herzl had begun negotiations with the British government as early as 1902, and his successors continued talks with the British at intervals thereafter.[85] During the period of 1916 through 1918 when the agreements considered here were negotiated, Great Britain maintains two primary objectives: to enlist the support of the Arab world against the Ottoman Empire, and to enlist Jewish support against both

---

WORLD PUBLIC ORDER (1967). The process of interpretation, rightly conceived, cannot be regarded as a mere mechanical drawing of inevitable meanings from the words in a text, or of searching for and discovering some preexisting specific intention of the parties with respect to every situation arising under a treaty. It is precisely because the words used in an instrument rarely have exact and single meanings, and because all possible situations which may arise under it cannot be, or at least are not, foreseen and expressly provided for by the parties at the time of its drafting, that the necessity for interpretation occurs. In most instances, therefore, interpretation involves "giving" a meaning to a text — not just any meaning which appeals to the interpreter, to be sure; but a meaning which, in light of the text under consideration and of all the concomitant circumstances of the particular case at hand, appears in his considered judgment to be one which is logical, reasonable and most likely to accord with and to effectuate the larger general purpose which the parties desired the treaty to serve.

82 *Id.*

83 *See* notes 80-81 *supra.*

84 COMPLETE DIARIES OF THEODOR HERZL 1304 (R. Patai ed. 1960) (emphasis added).

85 American Council for Judaism, *The Making of Zionist Diplomacy*, 32 ISSUES 43 (1947).

the Ottoman Turks and the Central Powers (Germany and Austro-Hungary).[86]

While the British were striving to gain the support of both the Arab world and the Jews, the immediate goal of the Zionists in Great Britain and the United States was to obtain a guarantee from the Allies that, in the event of a Turkish defeat, Palestine would be recognized as a Jewish Commonwealth open to unrestricted immigration. To this end, Chaim Weizmann, a prominent Jewish chemist in Great Britain (then leader of the World Zionist Organization and first President of Israel), building upon a reservoir of good will developed since Herzl's time, gained the sympathy and active collaboration of a number of important public figures in Great Britain.[87] Contrasted with the announced goal of the Zionists was the early manifestations of Arab nationalism; seeking to establish independent Arab States, various Arab leaders were responding to Britain's request for aid to drive the Turks out of the Arab lands. To secure the assistance of both the Arabs and Zionists, while serving their own best interests, Britain obligated itself to both sides through various commitments.

A. *The Hussein-McMahon Correspondence*

The Arab insistence that a British agreement with Arab leaders on the disposition of Palestine antedated the Balfour Declaration relies primarily on an exchange of letters in December of 1915 between Sheriff Hussein of Hejaz and Sir Henry McMahon, British High Commissioner at Cairo.[88] As previously noted, Britain stood in urgent need of help in her plan to expel the Turks from Palestine, Syria, Lebanon, Iraq, and the Arabian Peninsula.[89] In this correspondence, Hussein promised to declare war against Turkey and to raise an Arab army to assist the British in their military campaign. For their part, Commissioner McMahon, under instructions from London, pledged that Britain would "support the independence of the Arabs" in the large area bounded on the north by the 37th parallel (approximately the northern boundary of Syria), on the east by the Iranian border down to the Persian Gulf (enclosing Iraq), and in the south by the Arab Gulf States. When Hussein demanded that the Western boundary be established at the Red Sea and the Mediterranean, McMahon accepted the Red Sea border but excluded from his pledge the coastal belt of

---

86 G. LENCZOWSKI, THE MIDDLE EAST IN WORLD AFFAIRS 70 (1962).

87 *Id.* at 78.

88 *Id.* at 76; *see also* British Command Papers, CMD No. 5957 (1939). *See also* G. ANTONIUS, THE ARAB AWAKENING chs. 7-9 (1946).

89 W. YALE, THE NEAR EAST 243-44, 256-58 (1954).

Syria lying to the west of the districts of Damascus, Homs, Hama, and Aleppo. This meant that the Arabs would be denied Lebanon and the Alawi country to the north. Although Palestine was not explicitly mentioned in these letters, the Arabs have always contended that the region promised to them included Palestine.[90] On the other hand, Winston Churchill declared when Arab delegates presented their claim:

> This reservation [in the letters] has always been regarded by His Majesty's Government as covering the wilayet of Beirut and the independent Sanjuk of Jerusalem. The whole of Palestine west of the Jordan was thus excluded.[91]

B.   *The Sykes-Picot Accord*

McMahon's pledge to Hussein preceded by several months the Anglo-French accord, the Sykes-Picot agreement, on the Middle East.[92] This pact, concluded on May 16, 1916, provided that upon cessation of hostilities, France was to get the area known as Cilicia (Syria and Lebanon), Britain, southern Mesopotamia (Iraq) with Bagdad, and the ports of Haifa and Acre in Palestine while Palestine was, in general, to be internationalized. Since secrecy was considered essential, the terms of this agreement were never communicated to Hussein.

Clearly, the Sykes-Picot agreement was incompatible with Great Britain's earlier pledge to Hussein which, disregarding the dispute over Palestine, specifically assigned Mesopotamia to the Arabs. These two agreements were followed 18 months later by the Balfour Declaration.

C.   *The Balfour Declaration*

In form, the Balfour Declaration is a unilateral statement of British policy, but the years of negotiation that preceded its issuance, particularly the last three months of intensive discussion, reveal it as a tripartite agreement[93] among the British, the Zionists, and representing a substantial majority of British Jewry, the British Anti-Zionists.[94]

---

90 G. LENCZOWSKI, *supra* note 86.

91 *Id. See also* ROYAL COMM. at 20, ¶ 8.

92 G. LENCZOWSKI, *supra* note 86, at 72. The provisions of the Sykes-Picot accord were incorporated into a corollary agreement with Russia which purported to recognize Russia's postwar claim to Constantinople. These documents were discovered in tsarist files after the October Revolution of 1917 and were published as evidence of western imperialist chancery. In this manner, the world first learned the details of the Sykes-Picot scheme. 42 Stat. 1012 (1922).

93 Zionist leaders maintain that, although unilateral in form, the Declaration was clearly a bilateral international instrument and that all its terms were binding upon both Great Britain and the Zionists. That the Declaration was at least bilateral is obvious; that it constituted an international instrument is at best highly debatable, both because the Zionist Organization had not yet attained the apparent status of an international public body and because of the intent of the parties at the time of the making of the Declaration.

94 Their purpose was to guard the interests of Jews already assimilated into the nationalities of other countries. L. EPSTEIN, BRITISH POLICIES IN THE SUEZ CRISIS 180-87 (1964).

David Lloyd George, then Prime Minister of Great Britain, and Foreign Secretary Sir A. J. Balfour, believed that the strong Jewish influence in the Russian revolutionary movement made a favorable response to Zionist aspirations essential. It was also deemed important to woo Jewish support in the United States where, before America's entrance into the war, the sympathies of the principal Jewish leaders, all of German or Austrian background, lay with the Central Powers. Zionists also argued, and many Britons believed, that an Allied pronouncement in favor of Zionism might influence Austro-German Jewry and help to induce disaffection and disloyalty within the enemy States. Therefore, Sir Mark Sykes (of the Sykes-Picot agreement of 1916) was instructed to initiate formal negotiations, on behalf of the Allies, with Nahum Sokolow, the representative of the Zionist Organization. During these talks the Zionists insisted upon a British protectorate over Palestine, and although this would have constituted yet another contradictory pledge, the British government was not adverse to it.

In any attempted analysis of the Balfour Declaration, two factors must be carefully weighted and contrasted:

1. *The Political Promise Clause:*

> His Majesty's Government views with favour the establishment in Palestine of a national home for the Jewish people, and will use their best endeavors to facilitate the achievement of this object.[95]

2. *The Safeguard Clause:*

> [I]t being clearly understood that nothing shall be done which may prejudice the civil and religious rights of non-Jewish communities in Palestine, or the rights and political status enjoyed by Jews in any other country.[96]

The political promise clause can be considered to have been a political defeat for the Zionist objectives. It is clear that the British considered impracticable, at best, any thought of making Palestine *as a whole* available as a Jewish national home or State, and at no time during their negotiations did they entertain any such purpose.[97] What the British did, in fact, was to promise to "facilitate" — nothing more — the establishment of a "national home" for the "Jewish people." In 1937, however, they modified their interpretation of this clause somewhat, and although still unwilling to commit themselves to the establishment of a Jewish national State, they indicated that the question

---

95 *See* L. STEIN, *supra* note 58, app. II.
96 *Id.*
97 CORRESPONDENCE WITH THE PALESTINE ARAB DELEGATION AND THE ZIONIST ORGANIZATION, FIFTH REPORT, CMD No. 1700, at 19 (1922).

of eventual statehood would depend mainly upon the goal and enterprise of the Jews.[98] Since the British contemplated the home as
encompassing those Jews already in Palestine, they never feared an
onslaught of immigration or any change in the demographic balance
of Palestine (an Arab majority was to be maintained).

The Zionists, however, never bound themselves to such a rigid
construction of the political promise clause, but viewed it as the initial
step in the implementation of their plans. They proposed to assure
that Jews would, in the first instance, settle in Palestine, in sufficient
numbers to guarantee their safety, and then, through an ever-increasing tide of immigration, establish their numerical and political predominance. If, when that point was reached, Palestine should be accorded self-government, the country could then become a Jewish commonwealth with full equality of rights, extended to the new Arab
minority.[99] From this point, it would be but one short step to transform Palestine into a refuge for World Jewry in the hope that Palestinians would be driven to resettle in neighboring Arab States.

It is difficult to determine from these conflicting interpretations,
whether British and Zionist leaders contemplated that a *portion* of
Palestine was to become a Jewish commonwealth, with a small Arab
minority, or whether all of Palestine was to become a Jewish commonwealth with a large Arab minority. In view of the avowed Zionist
objectives (rather than their long-range expectations) and Britain's
contradictory promises to Arab leaders, the clause when drafted, must
be construed to have had a very restricted political meaning. In this
context, it becomes important to note that the State of Transjordon
was partially carved out of Palestine in 1920, three years *after* the
Balfour Declaration and two years *before* the creation of the Palestine
Mandate, and Great Britain specifically exempted that Arab region
from the terms of the Declaration.[100]

In contrast, the safeguard clause seems clear and unequivocal. The
words "*it being clearly understood*" prove that however vague or ambiguous the political promise clause might be, it was subordinated to
and conditioned upon the implementation of the safeguard clause
which reassured the non-Jewish population of Palestine that there

---

98 ROYAL COMM. at 24, ¶ 20.

99 L. STEIN, *supra* note 58, at 553.

100 The prime British purposes in the creation of Transjordan would appear to have
been political and military: to establish and preserve unhampered control of the territory
bordering Syria and to permit easy defense against any French designs on the Mosul-
Kirkuk oil field, which had been promised to France under the Sykes-Picot agreement,
then occupied and held by British troops in defiance of this accord.

would be no resulting injury to their rights from the political bargain struck between Britain and the Zionists. The specific words employed referred to actual rights enjoyed by Arabs under Ottoman rule, which were deemed to include, *inter alia*, such basic rights as freedom of religion, the right to own land, and mobility within the territory. Since the Arab population of Palestine included both Muslims and Christians, it was indispensable that their religious rights not be prejudiced.[101] Therefore, it was implicit in the guarantees embodied within the safeguard clause that the rights of Christians and Muslims to the maintenance and protection of their shrines and religious exercises would be assured. As to their civil rights, the ultimate independence of Palestine was intended to be achieved through the implementation of gradual self-determination.

Since the clauses of any document must be interpreted in a chronological order to achieve an internal consistency, it is clear from the history of negotiations behind the Declaration that the British government agreed to support — if not, indeed, specifically to protect and secure — the recognition and observance of the rights of the non-Jewish population.

One vital item evidencing this intent was the creation of Transjordan, already referred to.[102] A second was the White Paper on Palestine issued by the British government in June of 1922, which said in part:

> Unauthorized statements have been made to the effect that the purpose in view is to create a wholly Jewish Palestine . . . that Palestine is to become "as Jewish as England is English." His Majesty's Government . . . have no such aim in view. . . . [T]he terms of the Declaration referred to do not contemplate that Palestine as a whole should be converted into a Jewish National Home, but that such a Home should be founded *in Palestine*.[103]

During the period between the two world wars, the Arabs and their partisans argued that the political and safeguard clauses of the Declaration, far from being supplementary, were in fact and in law,

---

101 B. Weinberg, *The Zionist Commission for Palestine*, 1960, at 40 (unpublished thesis, Dep't of History, Roosevelt Univ.).

102 *See* note 100 and accompanying text *supra*.

103 CMD No. 1700, *supra* note 97, at 18. In May 1939, the British government again reiterated this same view:

> His Majesty's Government therefore now declare unequivocally that it is not part of their policy that Palestine should become a Jewish State — they would indeed regard it as contrary to their obligations to the Arabs under the Mandate, as well as to the assurances which have been given to the Arab people in the past, that the Arab population of Palestine should be made the subjects of a Jewish State against their will.

PALESTINE — STATEMENT OF POLICY, FIRST REPORT, CMD No. 6019, at 4 (1939).

contradictory. After World War II, the British government itself veered toward this view. On February 25, 1947, Foreign Secretary Ernest Bevin told the House of Commons:

> There is no denying the fact that the Mandate [which incorporated the Balfour Declaration] contained contradictory promises. In the first place it promised the Jews a National Home and in the second place, it declared the rights and position of the Arabs must be protected. Therefore, it provided what was virtually an invasion of the country by thousands of immigrants and at the same time said that was not to disturb the people in possession.[104]

D. *The Hogarth Message*

When Sheriff Hussein learned of the contents of the Balfour Declaration, he demanded an explanation from the British government and protested that the Declaration violated the pledge made to him two years earlier. Britain responded by sending Commander D. C. Hogarth with a message which he delivered to Hussein on January 4, 1918, assuring the Arab emir that Britain's decision to assist the return of the Jews to Palestine meant only "so far as is compatible with the existing population" and did not contemplate establishment of a Jewish State.[105] Hussein accepted this explanation, and his son, Emir Faisal, later discussed with Chaim Weizmann the terms and conditions under which immigrant Jews might enter Palestine.[106]

With Britain committed to recognition of their organization and to at least a partial acceptance of their program, the Zionists turned to the other Allied Powers in an effort to win approval for the Balfour Declaration. France approved it on February 11, 1918, and Italy approved it 12 days later. President Woodrow Wilson signified his endorsement in a letter to Rabbi Stephen S. Wise on October 29, 1918.[107]

In this manner, the Zionists were able to attain the status of unofficial allies of the Western powers. For example, the London Foreign Office went so far as to extend them the privilege of the British diplomatic pouch.[108] In return, the Zionists were expected to render valuable assistance in the prosecution of the war. What contribution they may have made to that objective is uncertain, but David Lloyd George told the Palestine Royal Commission in 1936:

---

[104] I. TANNOUS, THE ENRAGING STORY OF PALESTINE AND ITS PEOPLE 11 (1965) (pamphlet published by Palestine Liberation Organization).

[105] F. KHOURI, *supra* note 77, at 8-9.

[106] The Faisal-Weizmann Agreement is discussed at notes 110-14 and accompanying text *infra*.

[107] F. KHOURI, *supra* note 77, at 8-9.

[108] *Id.*

Zionist leaders gave us definite promises that if the Allies committed themselves to giving facilities for the establishment of a national home in Palestine they would do their best to rally Jewish sentiment and support throughout the world for the Allied cause. They kept their word.[109]

E.   *The Faisal-Weizmann Accord*

As indicated earlier, the Arabs considered the Allied proposal to separate Palestine from Syria a breach of the McMahon pledge.[110] Historically, they had always considered Palestine more closely linked to Syria than to any other part of the Arab nation. Hussein, however, appeared to have attained most of his objectives by October of 1918. His emirate of Hejaz was recognized as a sovereign State and he was accorded recognition as its king. In addition, his son, Emir Faisal, was to take part in the Paris peace conference as a representative of that kingdom. At this conference Faisal was persuaded not only to accept but also to welcome the policy set out in the Balfour Declaration, and his statement to the members of the conference was conciliatory in tone:

> In Palestine the enormous majority of the people are Arabs. The Jews are very close to the Arabs in blood. . . . Nevertheless, the Arabs cannot risk assuming the responsibility of holding level the scales in the clash. . . . that [has] in this province so often involved the world in difficulties. They would wish for the effective supervision of a great trustee, so long as a representative local administrative organization commended itself by actively promoting the material prosperity of the country.[111]

Even more conciliatory was the agreement reached between Faisal and Chaim Weizmann, President of the World Zionists, on January 3, 1919. The text of this agreement was in English, except for an important reservation inserted by Faisal at the end of the document. The agreement recited that the

> surest means for the consummation of their [Arabs' and Zionists'] national aspiration is through . . . closest cooperation of the Arab State and Palestine . . . Arab and Jewish duly accredited agents shall be established and maintained in their respective territories. . . . The definite boundaries between the Arab State and Palestine shall be determined by a commission to be agreed upon. . . . The constitution and administration of Palestine shall afford the fullest guarantee for carrying into effect the [Balfour Declaration]. . . . All necessary measures shall be taken to . . . stimulate immigration

---

109 ROYAL COMM. at 31, ¶ 35.
110 *See* note 105 and accompanying text *supra.*
111 F. KHOURI, *supra* note 77, at 12.

of Jews into Palestine on a large scale. . . . In taking such measures
the Arab peasants and farmers shall be guaranteed in their rights.[112]

However, since Faisal's authority to act derived from his father Hussein, who considered Palestine to be part of the realm promised
him, Faisal added a final proviso, handwritten and in Arabic, to the
Declaration.

> Provided the Arabs obtain their independence as in my Memorandum dated the 4th of January, 1919. . . . [If] the slightest modification were made I shall not be bound . . . by a single word of this
> Agreement, which shall be deemed void and of no account or validity.[113]

As no available source material includes the text of Faisal's memorandum of January 4, it would appear that this document was, at the
time of signing the agreement, still to be written or that the date "4th
of January" was in error. In any event, unbiased historians agree that
the Faisal-Weizmann accord was never made effective.[114]

F. *The Effects of These Agreements and the Background of the Mandate*

An international agreement is binding upon the parties, and any
subsequent agreement between either of the parties to the original agreement and a third party cannot derogate from the terms of the original
accord without being considered a breach thereof. Similarly, rights
acquired by a party to an international agreement cannot be undone
by a subsequent conflicting promise to another party. However, if
such a conflicting promise is actually made, the third party will acquire
no rights superior to those of the parties to the original compact —
there can be no derogation of the existing or acquired rights of others.
The acceptance of this doctrine is mandated by the world community's
need for international order and stability; for without such a doctrine,
no agreements could be relied upon as a source of rights, duties, and
obligations.

The Arabs, therefore, claim that as first in time they are first in
right; and hence, any benefits accruing from their agreements with the
British are superior to the subsequent and contradictory promises made
to the Zionists.

Faced with the need of securing multilateral international confirmation of the Balfour Declaration and of ensuring its inclusion in

---

112 *Id.*
113 *See* text accompanying note 112 *supra.*
114 B. Weinberg, *supra* note 101, at 40.

the peace treaties after the defeat of Turkey, the Zionists encountered substantial opposition, even within Great Britain. For example, while the Declaration was still being debated within the British government, Edwin Montagu, the only Jew with direct access to such matters, was an implacable foe of political Zionism.[115] In addition, the Board of Deputies of British Jews, the largest Jewish organization in Britain, campaigned against the Zionist program.[116] Even in the United States, the Zionist movement encountered substantial opposition. In fact, the Zionists were unable to attract effective political support because the prevailing sentiment among Jewish Americans reflected the view posited 36 years earlier at a conference of Jewish reform rabbis.[117]

> We consider ourselves no longer a nation but a religious community. And therefore expect neither a return to Palestine, nor a sacrificial worship under the administration of the sons of Aaron, nor the restoration of any of the laws concerning the Jewish state.[118]

Nevertheless, because Great Britain had included the Zionist program, or part of it, as official British policy, the United States Government acceded in the end.

By the time the peace treaties marking the end of World War I were drafted, world opinion had seemingly forced the framers of those treaties to conform to President Wilson's 14 points, the new principles of non-imperialism and national self-determination; even though that program conflicted sharply with British, French, and Italian plans. Pushed to its logical conclusion, the 14 points would have nullified nearly all of the agreements involving the postwar disposition of the conquered Turkish province. A device designed to compromise, and in some measure circumvent, President Wilson's principles for the benefit of the victorious allies' imperial interests was found in the mandate system embodied in the Covenant of the League of Nations.

G. *The League of Nations Mandate*

The mandate system was without precedent in the history of international law. Theoretically, mandated territories were potentially sovereign states, temporarily under the tutelage of one or another major power until such time as, in the League's judgment, full independence was merited. The Mandated Territory was to be under the control of the Mandatory Power which, in turn, was responsible to

---

115 L. STEIN, *supra* note 58, at 484.
116 L. EPSTEIN, *supra* note 94, at 182.
117 W. YALE, *supra* note 89, at 147.
118 *Id.*

the Permanent Mandates Commission of the League of Nations. Since the League itself and all its agencies were in fact managed and dominated by the major powers, the arrangement was a cozy one for ambitious European empires. For example, while the degree of control and authority to be exercised by the Mandatory Power was to be explicitly defined by the Council of the League of Nations,[119] mandated territories were classified according to their degree of political ripeness, again, as determined by the League. In Class *A* were those considered provisionally independent, *i.e.*, most ready for complete independence. Palestine was a Class *A* mandate, a "provisionally independent" state. Essentially, the theory behind the mandate system envisaged the independence of the mandated territory as the only natural conclusion of the mandate; the Palestine mandate, like the others, encompassed no other provisions for its termination.

On April 20, 1920, the Supreme Allied Council allocated the Palestinian Mandate to Great Britain. In March of 1921, the British detached all territory east of the Jordan River from Palestine — this territory had historically been a part of Palestine since before the arrival of the Hebrews led by Moses — and established the emirate of Transjordan. On June 30, 1922, the United States Congress adopted a resolution essentially identical to the Balfour Declaration, with the added provisio that religious buildings and holy places in Palestine were to be adequately protected.[120] On July 22, 1922, the League formally confirmed Great Britain as the Mandatory Power for Palestine, while France was granted the Mandate over Syria. The Syrian Mandate which then included Lebanon, was part of a plan to placate France for the violation of the Sykes-Picot accord, and was approved despite the bitter opposition of both the Syrian leaders and their people.[121]

---

[119] To those colonies and territories which as a consequence of the late war have ceased to be under the sovereignty of the States which formerly governed them and which are inhabited by peoples not yet able to stand by themselves under the strenuous conditions of the modern world, there should be applied the principle that the well-being and development of such peoples form a sacred trust of civilization and that securities for the performance of this trust should be embodied in this Covenant.

LEAGUE OF NATIONS COVENANT art. 22, para. 1.

Mallison, *supra* note 47, at 1030, states:

By the terms of the Covenant the "sacred trust of civilization" was to be exercised for the benefit of the people inhabiting the respective territories. This applied, prima facie, to the existing inhabitants of Palestine, whatever the religious identification of individual Palestinians. This provision of the Covenant, protecting territories "inhabited by peoples," is clearly inconsistent with "the Jewish people" nationality claims based upon the religious identification of individuals who are the inhabitants of many territories.

[120] 42 Stat. 1012 (1922).

[121] President Woodrow Wilson, with Allied approval, sent an American commission

On the other hand, while the Palestinian Arabs were demanding immediate independence, their leaders were willing to accede to an American or British mandate. However, because the United States was not a member of the League it could not become a Mandatory Power. Thus, the Arabs had no choice but to accept Britain in that role.[122]

On December 3, 1924, the United States and Great Britain entered into a convention setting forth the respective rights of the two countries and their nationals in Palestine. This pact recited the entire text of the Mandate Agreement, including its preamble, thus confirming complete American acceptance of all its provisions.[123] The preamble of the Agreement reiterated the terms of the Balfour Declaration, which were specifically incorporated into article 2 of the Agreement. By the terms of article 4, the Zionist Organization was appointed to advise and cooperate with the mandatory administration on matters relating to the Jewish National Home; and the administration was to enact a nationality law whose provisions would facilitate the acquisition of Palestinian citizenship by Jews who might take up permanent residence in Palestine. Finally, under the terms of article 28, the League was to make such arrangements as might be deemed necessary for safeguarding, in perpetuity, free access to holy places, religious buildings, and sites should the Palestine Mandate be terminated.[124]

Concerning the question of sovereignty during the period of the Mandate, there has been no general agreement among scholars. Some authorities contended that sovereignty, though temporarily in suspension, resided in the inhabitants of the mandated territory, while others found sovereignty in the League of Nations, or even in the Mandatory Power, either alone or acting in concert with the League. Still other views were offered, but perhaps the most logical suggestion placed sovereignty in the League, which had asserted its supreme authority

---

(the King-Crane Commission) to the Middle East to determine the wishes of the peoples there. This group recommended establishment of a wholly independent Syria (including Lebanon) and strongly opposed establishment of a Zionist-Jewish entity in Palestine. See F. KHOURI, supra note 77, at 13.

122 The allegation that the wishes of the Palestine community had been ignored in the selection of a Mandatory Power has to be considered in light of the July 2, 1919 resolutions of the General Syrian Congress. There, in considering the possibility of the establishment of a mandate of Arab countries under certain conditions, the Congress named the United States as its first choice to serve as a Mandatory Power and Great Britain as its second.

123 44 Stat. 2184 (1924).

124 Mallison, supra note 47, at 1034. Cf. Feinberg, The Interpretation of the Anglo-American Convention on Palestine 1924, 3 INT'L L. Q. 475 (1950).

over Palestine and had delegated the exercise of that authority to the
Mandatory Power.[125] Whatever view we care to take as to the question
of sovereignty, the Arabs asserted that the Mandate violated article
22 of the League Covenant for two reasons: first, because the community of Palestine was not recognized as an independent nation,
and second, because the Mandatory Power was granted full legislative
and administrative control over the Mandate by the League's Council.
In opposition to this claim it has been argued:

(a) that the provisional recognition of "certain communities
     formerly belonging to the Turkish Empire" as independent
     States is permissive, i.e., the words are can be provisionally
     recognized, not will or shall;

(b) that the penultimate paragraph of article 22 prescribed that
     the degree of authority to be exercised by the Mandatory
     Power shall be determined by the Council of the League as
     the need arises;

(c) that acceptance by the Allied Powers of the policy incorpor-
     ated within the Balfour Declaration made it clear from the
     beginning that Palestine would be treated differently from
     Syria and Iraq; and that this difference was confirmed by the
     Supreme Council in the Treaty of Sévres and by the Council
     of the League in granting the Mandate.[126]

Again, however, one must also consider the fact that the decision to
establish a mandate system and to bring Arab communities within its
purview was the product of an assembly of States in which no Arab
country had any voice whatsoever. Therefore it was apparent that the
territories inhabited by the Arabs were being bartered and parceled out
like common objects for everyone's benefit but their own.

     To this date, there has been much controversy over the relative
weight to be accorded the provisions in the Mandate Agreement regarding the National Home and those that concerned self-government;
in other words, whether they were consistent with each other. Some
have suggested that between these obligations the Mandate recognizes
no primacy, no order of importance, and that they were in no way
irreconcilable. Others, however, contend that the primary purpose
of the Mandate, as expressed in its preamble and its provisions, was

---

125 See generally L. STEIN, supra note 58. Reference is not made to the United Nations
trusteeship provisions because the conditions and intent of the mandate system differs
from the trusteeship system and because the context of the Palestine question has no
parallel under the trusteeship system.
126 See, e.g., L. STEIN, supra note 58.

to promote the establishment of a Jewish National Home, therefore subordinating the obligations to develop self-governing institutions. However, both positions are merely conjectural because they represent a narrow view of the overall question. This controversy was, however, of practical significance. If, for example, the country was to be administered so as to promote self-governing institutions, those conditions would in fact destroy the concept of a Jewish National Home; indeed, the Arab majority would never permit its establishment. Hence, it would appear that although difficulties were expected, the Mandate failed to recognize that these dual obligations would, in fact, prove incompatible.

The Mandate for Palestine is significant in international law because it contained an explicit agreement by the League to the provisions of the Balfour Declaration clearly amounting to international approval of the Declaration's compromise agreement. It thus becomes plausible to argue that the claims of the Zionist Organization, as embodied in the practices of Israel, are now a part of customary international law to the extent that they comply with its requirements.

Customary international law is traditionally regarded as the sum of two constituent elements; the first being the existence of a particular uniform pattern of conduct in the past which, without more, may be dismissed as mere recurring conduct which does not attain the status of custom. The second element requires an *opino juris* or an element of moral "rightness" ascribed to the past uniformities in conduct. To prescribe international law by custom does not require that the past uniformities in conduct must have existed over a long period of time. Time is only significant as evidence of continuity and the contemporary expectations of decision-makers as to the existence of the custom, so that it can acquire the characteristics of customary international law.[127]

It is, of course, clear that the growth of a practice into a rule of international law depends upon the degree of its acceptance by the international community. If a State initiates a practice hitherto without precedent in international law, the fact that other States do not object is significant evidence that they do not consider it contrary to international law. If this practice becomes more general, as evidenced by common usage without objections from other States, the practice may give rise to a rule of customary international law.[128] This explains

---

[127] *See* 3 M. WHITEMAN, DIGEST OF INTERNATIONAL LAW 75-90 (1964) and citations therein.

[128] Mallison, *supra* note 47, at 1061-63.

Israel's consistency in continuing Zionist policy and the Arab States' persistence in denying its validity.

THE UNITED NATIONS PARTITION OF PALESTINE AND THE CREATION OF THE STATE OF ISRAEL

As Jewish immigration to Palestine increased, Arab opposition grew more and more intense. The Arabs demanded self-determination, and from the early 1920's insisted upon the establishment of a democratic, parliamentary form of government. In pursuit of this policy, they rejected an early British suggestion for an Arab Agency which would be equivalent to the Jewish Agency. Ultimately, however, various Arab groups did form a coalition called the Arab Higher Committee.

Added impetus to Jewish immigration was generated by the rise of Hitler's despotic regime in Germany; the consequent Jewish exodus alone accounted for more than 60,000 new arrivals in 1935.[129] This, however, resulted in renewed Arab unrest. In 1937 the Arabs rebelled, and their struggle continued until finally suppressed by British troops in 1939. Although the revolt was unsuccessful it had two far-reaching effects. First, the Jews in Palestine formed several guerilla units, the predecessors of the Israeli army; and second, it brought about the inevitable British reaction to every manifestation of Arab unrest — after each new crisis a commission visited Palestine to investigate, and each time it went back to London with a voluminous report. This time, however, the report of the Palestine Royal Commission of 1936-1938 took on added significance. With all hope for an Arab-Jewish reconciliation abandoned, the Commission proposed partition: the division of Palestine into an Arab State, a Jewish State, and a neutral enclave around Jerusalem and Bethlehem under continued British administration. While the Arab Higher Committee virtually rejected the scheme, the Jewish Agency was willing to accept it, with some reservations.

With war coming in Europe, and the continued unrest in the Arab countries, intensified by universal Arab resentment to British support of Zionism in Palestine, a dangerous threat was posed to the security and stability of the entire British-Arab empire. As a result, on May 17, 1939, Great Britain issued a White Paper[130] establishing new principles for the administration of the Palestine Mandate and reversing its earlier policy. Britain now proposed the creation, within

---

[129] ROYAL COMM. at 1938.
[130] British White Paper, CMD No. 6019 (1939).

10 years, of an independent Palestinian State linked with Great Britain by special treaty. On the two most important issues, land and immigration, the new policy marked a virtual acceptance of the Arab position. Jewish immigration was to be limited to a total of 75,000 persons during the ensuing five years, and thereafter no immigrant was to be admitted without specific Arab approval. In addition, the British High Commissioner in Palestine was authorized to regulate, limit, or prohibit the further transfer of Arab-owned land to Jewish ownership, and Palestine was to be partitioned into Arab, Jewish, and neutral zones under the same administration.

The 1939 White Paper shocked the Zionists and precipitated a violent reaction, the Permanent Mandates Commission of the League of Nations declared the Paper wholly incompatible with the terms of the Mandate,[131] but Britain held steadfast to her newly announced policy; the hope of preserving her Arab empire for strategic reasons was more important than Zionists protests.[132]

The first years of World War II witnessed a lull in the Palestinian dispute. Finally, in May 1942, the American Zionist Organization issued a manifesto called the Biltmore Program[133] which declared that the Balfour Declaration was no longer valid and called for the establishment of an independent Jewish State. To this end, the manifesto further urged the creation of a strong Jewish army for the defense of, and the construction of a governmental structure for the administration of, the new State. In Jerusalem the Jewish Agency defied the mandatory authorities and adopted the Biltmore Program as official Zionist policy. As the war ended, tens of thousands of illegal immigrants entered Palestine, and Arab-Zionist tensions reached a new peak.

In February 1947, the British government announced that it was not prepared to continue indefinitely to govern Palestine itself merely because Arabs and Jews could not agree upon the means of sharing its government between them. Accordingly, on April 2, 1947, Britain asked the General Assembly of the United Nations to make recommendations, under article 10 of the Charter, concerning the future government of Palestine, and suggested convocation of a special Assembly session for the purpose of constituting and instructing a special committee to prepare a preliminary study for consideration by the Assembly at its next regular session. Thereafter, five Arab States

---

131 L. SOHN, THE UNITED NATIONS IN ACTION 4 (1968).

132 The Suez Canal ran through Arab territory, and while the Red Sea was an Arab lake, it was through these waters that Britain ran her imperial lifeline to the Arab lands, India, and the islands of the Indian Ocean and the Pacific.

133 F. KHOURI, *supra* note 77, at 29-30.

asked that the special session consider the termination of the Mandate over Palestine and the declaration of its independence. The General Assembly refused to include the Arab request in its agenda and instead, named a special committee with the widest powers to ascertain and record fact and investigate all questions and issues relevant to the problem of Palestine. On the same day, the Assembly called upon all nations to refrain from invoking the use of force. Although the Arab Higher Committee refused to cooperate with the United Nations Special Committee on Palestine (UNSCOP), Arab representatives testified before the committee.

As a consequence of these hearings, UNSCOP reported two sets of recommendations: a majority plan calling for the partition of Palestine into Jewish and Arab States with economic union and an international trusteeship for Jerusalem, and a minority plan for a federal union with autonomous Arab and Jewish regions.[134] This majority report, with some modifications, was adopted by the Ad Hoc Committee on the Palestine Question which had been created by the second session of the General Assembly to study the UNSCOP report. Initially this plan met with substantial opposition, but in the plenary session, some States changed their votes, and on November 29, 1947, a two-thirds majority of those voting approved the plan for partition.[135]

Great Britain had approached the General Assembly in the expectation that that body could offer recommendations under article 10 of the Charter, according to which the Assembly could *discuss* any question within the scope of the Charter and *make recommendations* to members of the United Nations or to the Security Council. Essentially the question involved the form of government to be established for a territory whose population was not yet self-governing. Such a question was clearly within the competence of the United Nations under the declaration regarding non-self-governing territories in Chapter XI of the Charter and the provisions of Chapter III concerning the international trusteeship system. Article 14 (*recommendations* for the peaceful adjustment of any situation likely to impair the general welfare or friendly relations among nations) could also be con-

---

134 L. SOHN, *supra* note 131, at 45-47.

135 This majority was achieved only through strong pressures applied by the United States. The methods used were bitterly criticized by Secretary of Defense James Forrestal (see THE FORRESTAL DIARIES 180, 363 (W. Millis ed. 1951) and Sumner Welles, Undersecretary of State (see S. WELLES, WE NEED NOT FAIL (1948)). Other U.S. officials and historians have also asserted that the Partition Resolution, G.A. Res. 181, U.N. Doc. A/519 at 131 (1947), was "steamrollered" through the General Assembly by the United States.

sidered relevant to the Palestine situation.[136] It is clear, however, that any action by the General Assembly pursuant to articles 10 and 14 amounts to a mere recommendation and cannot be *enforced* by the Assembly acting alone. The central question, then, becomes: What is the *binding* effect of a General Assembly *recommendation* with respect to non-self-governing territories?

It may be said that the United Nations has clear jurisdiction with respect to countries formerly mandated under the League of Nations. This jurisdiction is set out in detail with regard to procedures and powers insofar as they concern conversion of a mandate to a trusteeship agreement. The way is left open for utilizing other solutions to the problems of an existing mandate. In a resolution adopted by the United Nations on April 18, 1946, the judgment was expressed that the functions previously performed by the League should be assumed by the United Nations. The League took further note of the intentions of the Mandatory Powers to continue to administer the mandated territories in accordance with the terms of the mandates until other arrangements could be agreed upon. Subsequently, in an advisory opinion on July 11, 1950, the International Court of Justice clarified the power of the General Assembly with respect to former mandates.[137] The Court held that there were decisive reasons for an affirmative answer to the question of the *obligation* of the Mandatory Power to submit to the supervision and control of the United Nations.[138] The *obligation* of the Mandatory Power to accept international supervision and submit reports of its stewardship is thus an integral part of the mandate system. In fact, the authors of the system considered that effective performance of this "sacred trust of civilization" required that administration of mandated territories be subject to international control and supervision; even to the extent that the necessity for supervision be continued despite the disappearance of the supervisory organ itself.

Having determined that the General Assembly was the legally qualified successor to the League of Nations, and, as such, could exercise the supervisory functions previously carried out by the League over the mandated territories, the Court further concluded that *the Mandatory acting alone has not the competence to modify the international status of the mandated territory*,[139] that competence to deter-

---

136 Mr. El-Khouri expressed the Syrian view in the Ad Hoc Committee that neither article 10 nor article 14 applied. L. SOHN, *supra* note 134, at 45.

137 Advisory Opinion on the International Status of South West Africa, [1950] I.C.J. 128.

138 *Id.* at 130.

139 *Id.*

mine and modify the international status of the mandated territory rests with the Mandatory acting with the consent of the General Assembly. The Court next declared that under articles 79 and 85 of the Charter the General Assembly was granted the authority to approve alterations or amendments to trusteeship agreements. By analogy it can then be inferred that the same procedure is applicable to any modification of the international status of a mandated territory which would not result in the acquisition of trusteeship for the mandated territory.

Article 79, referred to by the Court, provides that the terms of trusteeship shall be approved as provided in articles 83 and 85. Under article 83, the Security Council was granted jurisdiction over all functions of trusteeships in "strategic areas," whereas article 85 gives jurisdiction to the General Assembly in "non-strategic areas." Carried to its logical conclusion, the opinion of the Court would lead to the view that the Mandatory Power cannot unilaterally terminate the mandate and that any solution must be approved by the Security Council or the Assembly. The solution decided upon by the appropriate body would then be binding upon all member States. However, no method is prescribed to determine what may or may not be a "strategic area." Of paramount significance in this context is article 80, which prohibits the alteration in any manner of the existing rights of the population of trust territories. After the passage of the plan for partition, the United Nations Palestine Commission set up by the resolution was confronted by the refusal of the British to let the Commission enter Palestine, despite clear evidence of the impending collapse of the mandate administration.

As a result, on February 16, 1948, the Commission asked the Security Council to provide it with an adequate, non-Palestinian military force. The Council denied this request and another, proffered by the United States, which would have allowed the Council itself to enforce the terms of the partition resolution. Meanwhile, in Palestine disorders increased and on April 1, 1948, the Security Council asked the Secretary General to consider further the question of the future government of Palestine. On April 17, the Council called upon all parties to cease military operations and asked the British government to use its best endeavors to achieve a peaceful settlement. Subsequently, the Assembly met in special session on April 19, 1948, and considered several trusteeship proposals with respect to both Palestine as a whole and the City of Jerusalem. On May 14, 1948, the Assembly adopted a resolution abolishing the Palestine Commission and authorizing the appointment of a United Nations mediator to bring about a peaceful settlement in Palestine.[140] On that same day, May 14, Britain withdrew from Palestine; the mandate thus expired and the Jewish community declared the birth of the State of Israel, a unilateral declaration which resulted in the immediate recognition of Israel, as an independent sovereign state, by the United States and several other members of the world community.[141] Simultaneously, the Arab States declared that the collapse of peace and order in Palestine constituted a direct threat to peace and security in the Arab States themselves. On these grounds, the Arab States intervened on behalf of the Palestinian Arabs and opened a period of conflict that still continues. Shortly after Israel's declaration of independence, the General Assembly passed the famous and often reconfirmed resolution 194 of December 11, 1948, which in paragraph 11 recognized that under international law the Palestinian people were entitled to return to their homeland and to receive economic compensation.[142] Today, the Palestinians still claim their right to return and to be restored to their civil and political rights as nationals of Palestine or its successor State. It was not until December 10, 1969, that the United Nations "[r]eaffirm[ed] the inalienable rights of the people of Palestine." The words *people of Palestine* constitute the first official recognition that it is no longer a "refugee" question, but one of nationhood. This resolution recalls prior United Nations' resolutions from 1948 to December 1968. Twenty years of resolutions noting, affirming, directing, calling upon, and emphasizing Palestinians' rights to no avail. The historical significance of this resolution warrants its partial inclusion in this text:

Part B. *The General Assembly,*
Recognizing that the problem of the Palestine Arab refugees has arisen from the denial of their inalienable rights under the Charter of the United Nations and the Universal Declaration of Human Rights,
Gravely concerned that the denial of their rights has been aggravated by the reported acts of collective punishment, arbitrary detention, curfews, destruction of homes and property, deportation and other repressive acts against the refugees and other inhabitants of the occupied territories,

---

140 G.A. Res. 186, U.N. Doc. A/555, at 5 (1948).
141 As former Secretary of State, Dean Acheson puts it:
[Israel was] recognized the same day by President Truman on a *de facto* basis while his representative at the United Nations, Dr. Philip C. Jessup, was under instructions, speaking in the General Assembly in favor of a temporary trusteeship.
D. ACHESON, PRESENT AT THE CREATION 258 (1969). Such duplicity is still vivid in Arab memory.
142 G.A. Res. 194, U.N. Doc. A/810, at 21 (1948).

Recalling Security Council resolution 237 (1967) of 14 June 1967,

Recalling also its resolutions 2252 (ES-V) of 4 July 1967, and 2452 A (XXIII) of 19 December 1968 calling upon "the Government of Israel to take effective and immediate steps for the return without delay of those inhabitants who have fled the areas since the outbreak of hostilities,"

Desirous of giving effect to its resolutions for relieving the plight of the displaced persons and the refugees,

1. *Reaffirms* the inalienable rights of the people of Palestine;

2. *Draws the attention* of the Security Council to the grave situation resulting from Israeli policies and practices in the occupied territories and Israel's refusal to implement the above resolutions;

3. *Requests* the Security Council to take effective measures in accordance with the relevant provisions of the Charter of the United Nations to ensure the implementation of these resolutions.

1827th plenary meeting,
10 December 1969.[143]

THE RIGHT TO SELF-DETERMINATION IN PALESTINE UNDER THE LEAGUE OF NATIONS AND THE UNITED NATIONS

The Arab nations claim that the guarantees accorded the Zionists and the actions of the United Nations subsequent to Israel's self-declaration as a State violated the Palestinian Arabs' right of self-determination.[144]

Self-determination originated as a *political* doctrine that first manifested itself in the French and American Revolutions. It refers, in its political context, to the free and genuine expression of the will of the people, and accordingly includes the right of the people to determine their own political, economic, and cultural status, together with what form of government shall attain permanent sovereignty over their territory, natural wealth and resources.

It has been said that every ethno-cultural group which constitutes the majority in a cultural area has the right to create a national State of its own. On the other hand, the theory has been advanced that the right of self-determination transcends such majority-minority divisions, and is applicable only to nations. This latter term connotes large groups of people inhabiting and identified with a particular territory, sharing common historical traditions, normally speaking a common

---

[143] A/Res./2535 (xxiv).

[144] M. WHITEMAN, *supra* note 127, at 66-73; Bos, *Self-Determination by the Grace of History*, 15 NETHERLANDS INT'L L. REV. 362 (1968).

tongue, who *feel* that they form a single and exclusive community, sharing compatible views as to their future political and civil association.

The right of self-determination may also be said to apply to any reasonably designated group, and this is the crux of the problem. It is not that individuals ask to form an independent state; it is that there are several groups of people in the world, who may or may not be "nations," which demand self-determination and its corollary, political independence. There is no agreement as to where to draw the line, and thus the political doctrine has failed to find a juridical foundation that would lend itself to legal implementation without resort to insurrection or a "war of liberation."

Essentially the doctrine of self-determination gained recognition as a principle of international law after World War I; indeed, procedures for the realization of this right were incorporated into the mandate system itself. It is clear, however, that under article 22 of the League of Nations Covenant,[145] the right of self-determination was reserved to non-self-governing territories. The mandate system was thus justified as a means of aiding the establishment of self-governing institutions in the mandate countries. Therefore, to the extent that the mandate country was subject to the "tutelage" of the Mandatory Power, the right of self-determination was reserved for the people of the mandated territory.

In an effort to facilitate the eventual creation of a Jewish National Home, the greatest restrictions upon the right of self-determination under any mandate were imposed on the Palestinian people. To the extent that this attempted reconciliation of such antagonistic goals, placed *greater* restrictions upon the right of self-government, it can definitely be said that the establishment of the Jewish National Home conflicted with the right of self-determination.

Although article 2, which enumerates the principles of the United Nations, does not specifically refer to the right of self-determination, the doctrine was in fact incorporated into the United Nations Charter. Article 1 declares that the purpose of the United Nations is to develop friendly relations among nations "based on respect for the principle of equal rights and self-determination of peoples."[146] It is clear that the use of the singular noun "principle" indicates that "equal rights and self-determination of peoples" are considered elements of a single principle. The same phrase occurs in article 55 which deals not with political but with social and economic matters. Many scholars feel,

---

[145] LEAGUE OF NATIONS COVENANT art. 22.
[146] U.N. CHARTER art. 1.

however, that the enunciation of the principal of self-determination in the Charter is not the embodiment *in toto* of the positive aspects of that concept.[147] For example, Hans Kelsen in *The Law of the United Nations* has stated:

> If the "peoples" in Article 1, paragraph 2 means the same as "nations" in the Preamble, then "equal rights and self-determination of peoples" in Article 1, paragraph 2 can only refer to the sovereignty of states.[148]

It can be said, therefore, that while the Charter did not establish self-determination of peoples in the ethno-political sense as a principle of the organizational structure of the United Nations, by incorporating it in the material sense it did provide a general and recognized principle of international law.[149] References to self-determination, however, appear in Chapter XII (International Trusteeship System). These sections refer to self-government and independence even though not specifically to self-determination, and are the counterparts of article 22 of the Covenant of the League of Nations. Other provisions of the Charter also evidence this principle. Article 73 (referring to trusteeship obliga-

---

[147] L. BLOOMFIELD, EVOLUTION OR REVOLUTION? THE UNITED NATIONS AND THE PROBLEM OF PEACEFUL CHANGE (1957); H. LAUTERPACHT, INTERNATIONAL LAW AND HUMAN RIGHTS (1950); A. RÖLING, INTERNATIONAL LAW IN AN EXPANDED WORLD (1960); F. SAYEGH, THE ARAB-ISRAELI CONFLICT 9 (N.Y. Arab Information Center, 1964); Scelle, QUELQUES REFLEXIONS SUR LE DROIT DES PEUPLES À DISPOSER D'EUX MÊMES (1957); Bowett & Emerson, *Self-Determination, 1966 Proceedings* AM. SOC'Y INT'L L. 130, 138; de Nova, *The International Protection of National Minorities and Human Rights*, 11 How. L.J. 275, 276 (1965); Lauterpacht, *Règles Générales du Droit de la Paix*, Hague Rec. 1937 — IV; *From Protection of Minorities to Promotion of Human Rights*, 1948 JEWISH Y.B. INT'L L. 119.

[148] H. KELSEN, THE LAW OF THE UNITED NATIONS (1950).

[149] *See* M. SHUKRI, THE CONCEPT OF SELF-DETERMINATION IN THE UNITED NATIONS (1965); Bowett, *Self-Determination and Political Rights in Developing Countries*, 1966 *Proceedings* AM. SOC'Y INT'L L. 129. The subsequent history of the United Nations corroborates the proposition that it is more than a recognized concept and has become a general principle of international law. *See, e.g.,* the General Assembly's request of the Commission on Human Rights to study ways and means "which would ensure the right of peoples and nations to self-determination." G.A. Res. 421, 5 U.N. GAOR Supp. 20, at 43, U.N. Doc. A/1775 (1950). At its Seventh Session the General Assembly stated that "all peoples shall have the right of self determination." G.A. Res. 545, 6 U.N. GAOR Supp. 20, at 36-37, U.N. Doc. A/2119 (1952). The Commission on Human Rights prepared several resolutions on the matter which were adopted by the General Assembly. G.A. Res. 837, 9 U.N. GAOR Supp. 21, at 21, U.N. Doc. A/2890 (1954); G.A. Res. 9 U.N. GAOR Supp. 21, at 20, U.N. Doc. A/2890 (1954); G.A. Res. 738, 8 U.N. GAOR Supp. 17, at 18, U.N. Doc. A/2630 (1953); G.A. Res. 612, 7 U.N. GAOR Supp. 20, at 5, U.N. Doc. A/2361 (1952); G.A. Res. 611, 7 U.N. GAOR Supp. 20, at 5, U.N. Doc. A/2361 (1952); G.A. Res. 648, 7 U.N. GAOR Supp. 20, at 33, U.N. Doc. A/2361 (1952); G.A. Res. 637, 7 U.N. GAOR Supp. 20, at 26, U.N. Doc. A/2361 (1952). *See also* Colonial Resolution, G.A. Res. 1514, 15 U.N. GAOR Supp. 16, at 66, U.N. Doc. A/L. 323 (1960). At its Tenth Session the General Assembly examined the draft articles of the Covenant on Civil and Political Rights and the Covenant on Economic, Social and Cultural Rights which were adopted Dec. 16, 1966, G.A. Res. 2200, 21 U.N. GAOR Supp. 16, at 49, U.N. Doc. A/6546 (1966). *See also* Eagleton, *Self-Determination in the United Nations*, 47 AM. J. INT'L L. 88 (1953).

tions) clearly imposes a duty, deemed "a sacred TRUST," to ensure, with due respect for the particular culture, the political, economic, social and educational advancement, the just treatment and the protection against abuses of the peoples concerned, thus, *"to develop self-government, to take due account of the political aspirations of the peoples. . . ."*[150] In addition, article 76 which sets forth the basic objectives of the trusteeship system states:

> To promote the political, economic, social and educational advancement of the inhabitants of the trust territories and their progressive development towards self-government or independence as may be appropriate to the particular circumstances of each territory and its peoples and *the* freely expressed wishes of the peoples concerned and as may be provided by the terms of each trusteeship agreement.[151]

Finally, article 21 of the Universal Declaration of Human Rights adopted by the General Assembly provides that "[t]he will of the people shall be the basis of the authority of government. . . ."[152]

The United Nations has indeed a prolific history of resolutions seeking to uphold and implement the principle of self-determination. Notwithstanding these pronouncements, Professor Sohn states:

> With regard to the principle of self-determination, although international recognition was extended to this principle at the end of the First World War and it was adhered to with regard to the other Arab territories, at the time of the creation of the "A" Mandates, it was not applied to Palestine, obviously because of the intention to make possible the creation of the Jewish National Home there. Actually, it may well be said that the Jewish National Home and the *sui generis* Mandate for Palestine run counter to that principle.[153]

The American position is, in that respect, theoretically in full support of the concept. Professor Moore quotes Thomas Jefferson who, as Secretary of State in 1792, with reference to the recognition of France's revolutionary government stated:[154] "It accords with our principles to acknowledge any government to be rightful which is formed by *the will of the nation, substantially declared.*"[155] Less remote is the particular significance which the doctrine has assumed with the

---

150 U.N. CHARTER art. 73.
151 U.N. CHARTER art. 76.
152 G.A. Res. 217, U.N. Doc. A/555, at 71 (1948).
153 L. SOHN, CASES AND MATERIALS ON UNITED NATIONS LAW 429 (1967).
154 1 J. MOORE, DIGEST OF INTERNATIONAL LAW 120 (1906).
155 *Id.*

international dislocation of the present century. In a speech, President Wilson proposed

> [t]hat no nation should seek to extend its polity over any other nation or people, but that every people should be left free to determine its own polity, its own way of development, unhindered, unthreatened, unafraid, the little along with the great and powerful.[156]

Reminiscent of the Wilsonian philosophy is the Atlantic Charter which in expressing the ideals of the United States and Great Britain established:

> They respect the right of all peoples to choose the form of government under which they live; and they wish to see sovereign rights and self-government restored to those who have been forcibly deprived of them.[157]

The same was embodied in the Declaration of Yalta on February 11, 1945, with respect to Europe; and what had been the position of the United States and France became that of the Allies and a cornerstone of the United Nations principles. Yet the principle was violated more often than it was implemented. It was given effect in Algeria, but violated or ignored in such cases as Formosa, Hyderabad, Kashmir, Palestine, the Congo, Cuba, Hungary, Viet Nam, Nigeria (Biafra), Goa, Angola, Czechoslovakia and in the matter of "Germany's unification" — to speak only of the most notorious instances.

Consequences of Arab Experience with International Law and Its Structures, the Western Powers and Israel

The Arab people, throughout their experience with Western powers, have, by and large, been the object of colonial domination, military occupation, and economic exploitation. Finally, with the creation of the State of Israel they have witnessed the implantation of a new State, composed of alien people, to occupy a portion of their territory. Israel thus became in the eyes of the Arabs not only the creation of the same Western powers who colonized them, but an extension thereof. Not only was the land Israel occupied usurped but the question of its future intentions became paramount. The first

---

[156] *A League for Peace*, S. Doc. No. 685, 64th Cong., 2d Sess. 7-8 (1917). *See also* his address before a joint session of Congress, Jan. 8, 1918 (For. Rel. Supp. 1, Vol. I) for his fourteen points.

[157] Declaration by President Roosevelt, Prime Minister Churchill (Aug. 14, 1941), in A Decade of American Foreign Policy: Basic Documents (1941-1949). *See also* Kunz, *The Present Status of International Law for the Protection of Minorities*, 48 Am. J. Int'l L. 282 (1954).

indication of its future course was its refusal to repatriate the Palestinians, while pursuing an active policy of recruiting immigrants from abroad. The pattern was obvious; Palestinian rights and aspirations were to be subordinated to Israel's in-gathering policy. The gradual swelling of Jewish immigration coupled with the avowed pledge of Israel to "return" all Jews, paralleled events that led to the gradual expansion of the territory under Israel's occupation. The conclusion was that Israel's main purpose lies in gradual expansionism to accommodate a progressive flow of Jewish immigration at the expense of the Arab peoples. Thus, it appears that such an objective is incompatible with the goals of Arab national regionalism and is itself a new form of imperialism.[158] When one considers Western support

---

158 The efforts of Zionism first produced the Balfour Declaration (discussed at notes 93-104 and accompanying text *supra*.) The next step was a massive world-wide propaganda campaign designed to convey the impression in world public opinion that only the "promise clause" was relevant in the entire instrument. The Declaration then found its way to the Preamble of the mandate provisions of the League of Nations Covenant; Zionists thus shared in the administration of Palestine and immigrants started to enter. Eventually, established quotas were ignored and illegal immigration flooded Palestine. In an effort to cloak this illegality in an air of respectability, the propaganda machine, playing on post-World War II sympathies, developed such incidents as depicted in the book and film *Exodus* into both legend and epic. Several hundred thousand Jews from over forty nations came to Palestine between 1939-1946 (no precise figures can be cited). Notwithstanding the fact that the Arab population numbered 900,000 and Jewish citizens and residents (official immigrants not yet citizens) numbered 450,000, in addition to which there were an estimated 250,000 illegal Jewish immigrants, the partition plan gave the proposed Jewish state 58 percent of Palestine. After 1948 Israel took 23 percent more of that portion of Palestine allotted by the Partition Plan to the "Arab State."

As to its neighboring states, Israel committed aggression in 1956 and started the military operations of the 1967 war. The occupied territories from then on have been settled by Israelis and there are indications of Israel's intention to annex some or all of that territory, as they have made it clear with respect to Jerusalem notwithstanding the United Nations condemnation of its annexation. *See* notes 17-23 *supra*. Within Israeli-held territory the Palestinian's experience is more startling.

It started with forcible expulsions, examples of which are indicated below:

1. On February 28, 1949, 700 refugees were expelled from the village of Kfar Yasif.

2. On June 5, 1949, the inhabitants of Hisam, Qatia and Jauneh in Galilee were expelled from their villages.

3. On January 24, 1950, the inhabitants of Ghasbyia were expelled.

4. In March 1950, the inhabitants of Batal were expelled.

5. On August 17, 1950, the inhabitants of Mijdal were expelled.

6. In February 1951, the inhabitants of 13 villages in Wadi Ara were expelled over the Israeli frontier.

7. On November 17, 1951, a military detachment surrounded the village of Buwaishat, expelled the inhabitants and dynamited their homes.

8. In September 1953, the inhabitants of Umm-el-Faraj were expelled from their village, which was immediately blown up.

Along with expulsion, several laws in Israel "legalized" expropriations:

1. The *Law on the Acquisition of Absentee Property of 1950*, which stipulates that the land and the property of a person declared an "absentee" is transferred to the Custodian of Absentee Property. Law of March 14, 1950, Absentees' Property Law, [1950] 4 LAWS OF THE STATE OF ISRAEL 68. "Absentee" is defined as

[a]ny person who is a citizen of Israel, but who left his place of residence between

for Israel in light of the Arab experience with the same powers and their international structures, it is understandable that a sense of hope-

November 29, 1947 and the day on which the State of Emergency was abrogated, . . . if he went: (a) to a place which before 1 September 1948 was outside the land of Israel; (b) to a place inside the land of Israel but occupied at that time by hostile forces. Paragraph 28 empowers the Custodian to decide "in writing that a person or a group of persons are absentees," at which time "this person or group of persons shall be regarded as absentee."

Such language speaks for itself. Let it suffice to say that it has resulted in the confiscation of hundreds of thousands of *dunums* (measure of land) without due process of law.

Indeed, land which was part of the Islamic *Wagf* or religious trusts was transferred to the custodian of absentee property. This included one-sixth of the total area of Palestine's usable land in 1950.

2. *Article 25 of the Defence Laws* (State of Emergency, 1945) empowers the Military Governors to declare specific closed areas which no one can enter or leave without a written permit from the Military Governor.

3. *The Emergency Laws* promulgated by the Minister of Defence in 1949 "empower the Minister of Defence to declare any area inside the Land of Israel a Security Area." Law of July 27, 1949, Emergency Regulations (Security Zones) (Extension of Validity) (No. 2) Law, [1949] 3 LAWS OF THE STATE OF ISRAEL 56.

4. The *Emergency Articles for the Exploitation of Uncultivated Lands* is the link in the chain of laws for the expropriation of Arab lands. This law empowers the Minister of Agriculture to "take possession of uncultivated land, to ensure it is cultivated in cases where 'the Minister is not satisfied that the owner of the land has begun, or is about to begin, to cultivate it, or is going to continue to cultivate it.'" Official Gazette, October 15, 1948, at 3.

Sabri Jiryis explains the use of these laws as follows. The Minister of Defense, by virtue of the Emergency Laws of 1949, declares a certain area a closed area, or a security area, entry to which without a written permit from the Military Governor is a grave security offence. At the same time, of course, the Military Governor is unwilling, "for reasons of state security," to grant such permits to the owners of the land, which soon becomes "uncultivated land." When this happens, the Minister of Agriculture immediately issues an order to the effect that the land is "uncultivated." This in turn gives him the right, "in order to ensure that it is cultivated," to have such land cultivated either "by laborers engaged by him" or by "handing it over to another party to cultivate it." The other party is always the neighboring Jewish colonist. According to the original version of the Emergency Articles, the Minister of Agriculture could not keep such uncultivated land for more than two years and eleven months from the date he takes possession of it. But this period was later extended to five years by an "extension order." And eventually the ownership of such land reverted to the State.

There are five more of these laws. Each of them effectively enabled the state to grab more and more land. Jiryis feels that the estimate of one million *dunums* of land expropriated from Arabs living in Israel can be regraded as reasonable and accurate. Accounts of several incidents follow:

Radio Israel confirmed the fact that nearly 300 hectares of land in East (Arab) Jerusalem had been requisitioned by the Israeli Government; about 7,000 Jewish families will be able to live there.

L'Orient, January 11, 1968.

Israel announced the expropriation of 838 acres of the former Jordanian sector of Jerusalem.

Herald Tribune, January 16, 1968.

Hundreds of Israeli citizens gathered today in front of the Land Registration Department to buy 265 lots of land offered for sale in Arab Jerusalem by the Israeli Government.

Al-Anwar, March 1968.

A decree signed by the Israeli Minister of Finance, Mr. Pinhas Sapir, makes legal the expropriation of 190 acres on the road to Ramallah. This expropriation

lessness and frustration resulted. The consequence was a realization that international law and international organizations are tools used to attain desired goals by certain nations and that impartiality or equal treatment for non-Western or nonaligned nations is a futile expectation.

In short, if the Mandate was valid and properly carried out, why were the rights of the Palestinians disregarded? The United Nations, as the successor to the League of Nations, partitioned the State, which Israel thereafter expanded territorially. In the interim, the United Nations spoke of self-determination, protection of civil, religious, and political rights, and repatriation of Palestinians. It also condemned the annexation of Jerusalem, affirmed its commitment to the principle that force is not a valid means of acquiring territory, and ordered Israel's withdrawal from occupied territory after 1967. Despite these laudable positions, the practical results for the Arabs were to the contrary. Not one of these principles or decisions was implemented; thus, the route of peaceful resolution failed. Arabs took to arms — in fact and in words — when all else, in their eyes, had failed. Perhaps Israel's worst accomplishment thus far has been its military victories, which have left its opponents more aggrieved and wronged than before, and thus, only too eager to recover the accrued losses. Somehow it seems that what has transpired can only lead to further escalation. Israel cannot seem to "shoot its way to peace," and the Arabs cannot seem to "swallow Israel with gun powder."

Everyone who has followed the development of this conflict has at one time or another asked a rather simple question: Why has there been no dialogue between the parties? Indeed, we have all witnessed a dual monologue, each side advocating its own position while, at the

---

is intended for the establishment of a Jewish settlement.

Le Monde, April 20, 1968.

The Israeli authorities announced that they will expropriate 300 *dunums* in the neighborhood of Jerusalem on the pretext of wanting to plant a forest and name it the forest of peace, on the occasion of the unification of Jerusalem.

L'Orient, May 22, 1968.

The Mufti of Jerusalem protested against the expropriation of 29 acres that belongs to Muslim Waqf property. The Mufti went on to say that there were 5 mosques, 4 schools, and between 1,000 and 15,000 houses on the land.

L'Orient, June 5, 1968.

Mr. Ruhi el-Khatib, the Arab Mayor of Jerusalem, declared that 116 *dunums* had recently been expropriated in the Arab sector of Jerusalem. The Israeli authorities had thus seized 1,048 apartments and houses inhabited by 6,000 Arabs in addition to 437 shops employing 700 people, 4 mosques, 4 old palaces and 2 schools.

Le Monde, June 20, 1968.

And so the program of expropriation of Palestinians continues while territorial expansion at the expense of neighboring states corroborates Arab distrust of Israel's alleged peaceful intentions.

same time, it remains oblivious to the other. The only lesson to be derived from this state of affairs is that both sides long for a "judge." The tradition of the Semitic people — whether Muslims, Christians or Jews — has been one of acceptance of law and obedience to its judgments. To that extent, the statesmen and diplomats of the world community have ignored this significant factor which would have required a process, a legal process, to direct this dual monologue. But lest the reader misunderstand us, the Rule of Law is not a matter of mere technicalities, and moral authority is not political power, just as peaceful solutions cannot only be predicated upon material consideration. To understand the Arabs, and we venture to say the Israelis as well, we cannot accept the proposition that their peaceful coexistence be viewed only in terms of material well-being. Ignoring the sense of historic dignity of the Arab peoples has resulted, and will continue to result, in misdirected efforts, just as Arab misunderstanding of Jewish history has proven an overwhelming stumbling block. So as not to avoid answering the question presented above, Arabs *will* engage in dialogue and *are* ready to accept peace with the people of Israel; the question is not will they, but *how* will they and why?

Negotiations are a means and not an end to effect a compromised result, which the parties cannot assess or anticipate without direct contact, thereby leading to a gradual rapprochement, brought about by their shared goals or mutually agreed upon interests. Before even reaching the question of substance, that of form is very significant. The argument may be reminiscent of the Paris peace talks which at one time hinged on the shape of the conference table. It is, nonetheless, a fundamental fact that the road to peace with the Arabs is not the gun or the pocketbook, but the language of the heart in the proper accompanying form. Regardless of how this argument may sound to the Western mind, it is a true historic reflection of Arab culture. To a proud nation humbled by defeat, the memory of past greatness and glory is indispensable and explains the necessity for the preservation of its moral integrity.

As to the question of substance, strong advocates of "negotiations" refute any a priori consideration of the relative positions of the parties with respect to their goals and interests; thus precluding any examination of the degree of flexibility of these positions. To ignore irrevocable or uncompromising announced positions accompanied by overt conduct to that effect implies that negotiations as to these given questions are doomed to failure. Consider the issue of territory occupied by force by Israel, and more significantly Jerusalem. The United Nations has declared that these territories are to be returned. The Israeli response, evidenced by its annexation policies, was an avowed refusal to comply, to what extent can subsequent "negotiations" be distinguished from "capitulation"? The historical parallel recalls Pope Pius VII who, in response to Napoleon's occupation of the Papal States and requested negotiation for their return, is reported to have answered from his prison in Savona: "No special treaty was required to return stolen property."[159]

As negotiations are intended to produce what Israel avows its goals to be, i.e., security, Israel's objective has been to trade its military supremacy for legitimacy. Somehow it is felt by many that military supremacy is no substitute for legitimacy or voluntariness, just as submission is not the same as consent. Condonation does not erase the original transgression, but at least it has an element, even though ex post facto, of voluntariness. Its validity is dependent upon the degree of prior or subsequent coercion, be it military, political, economical or psychological.

The reader must be alerted to the significance of the values embodied in such word symbols as "peace" and "security," since these conditions are the goals of the desired negotiations. Their significance will be determined by the social values ascribed to them by those who will be expected to adhere to them. On that assumption, the values embodied in the concepts of peace and security must be contemplated within the historical, cultural, social, and psychological framework of the Arab world; spawning from its roots in Islam to contemporary social psychology (including the Arab experience with Israel and its supporters). The term *Arab*, while in itself a subject of fascinating conjecture, must be accepted, notwithstanding its historical transformations, as indicating at least a people linked by the religious, spiritual, and cultural heritage of Islam as well as by the Arabic language. While one may question the absolute relevance of this observation, it is made with direct reference to the question of peace and security.

For some 12 centuries, the Arabs, as the major ethnic component of the Muslim State, viewed the world as divided into *Dar El-Islam* and *Dar El-Harb. Dar El-Islam* was also *Dar Es-Selm*, the land of peace, contrasted by the land of war. *Dar Es-Selm* represented the ideological value which Islam ascribed to the freedom of propagation of Islam in that given part of the world. But due to the fundamental universalism of Islam, that part of the world to which Islam could not be propa-

---

159 J. HEROLD, THE AGE OF NAPOLEON 363 (1963).

gated in peace was a denial of that fundamental concept of freedom so dear to Islam's first adherents, the Arabs. The alternative was to break open these barriers to freedom, whereupon it would be proclaimed as *Dar El-Harb*. Another observation, significant at this point, is the etymological origin of the word "peace," which in Arabic is the same as that of *istislam*, or "surrender." Indeed, so slight is the semantic variation between the two words that it compels the conclusion that the use of the word "peace," if not in the proper formal context, could mean *istislam* and not *salam*, or "surrender" and not "peace."[160]

Historically, *selm* or "peace" is value-related to the concept of "freedom." Freedom of thought, speech, choice, religion, movement and all forms of human and ideological activities deemed fundamental among the natural rights of man, as embodied in Islamic precepts. Translated to the contemporary problem, the alien ideology of Zionism is, therefore, a basic impediment to "peace," as it stands in contradiction and opposition to the free propagation of "Arabism," the successor, popular ideological concept to Islam — successor, not in the religious sense, but in terms of its acceptance as the common denominator of the people. As such, Arabism, replacing what Islam had once been, is the new ideological and psychological bond of the Arabs. Hence, the effective prohibition of the propagation or dissemination of Arabism by Israel in what is deemed Arab land, is tantamount to a direct challenge to Arabism's very existence. This explains the readiness of Arabs to accept such formulas as Israel's "de-Zionization" or "Arabization." There is probably no literal significance attached to these proposed notions, for one can hardly envision a Pole, Russian, Hungarian, German or other, being literally "Arabized" for what that may mean. The significance of the point lies in the ideological, value-oriented goal of the State, be it called Israel, Palestine, or as could be suggested, "the United Arab Republic of Israel and Palestine," if a new name is all it would take.

In essence, it is not whether that State will adhere to Arab nationalism, for that would be asking of it more than other Arab States, but whether it is open to the possibility. Thus, presently Israel not only disrupts the geographic contiguity of the Arab states, but also disrupts its ideological continuity. Whether we are dealing with an open-ended Zionist ideology or a limited one (narrowed by emerging nationalistic tendencies, brought about in Israel by its "Sabras"), such an Arabiza-

---

160 Bassiouni, *supra* note 33, at 160.

tion concept if presented as a superior or supplanting ideology will be hopelessly unacceptable to Israel. However, if it were offered as a broadening concept, relating "the Love of Zion" to "the Love of the Arab World," of which it is geographically a part, the concept would have some chance of being favorably received; and, therefore, the ideological confrontation may not be unavoidable. Obviously, this would require a reconsideration of the "Jewish people" concept, to which Israel's ruling class still adheres, as it was formulated in the wake of European anti-Semitism. With over 60 percent of Israel's population consisting of native born, and over half a million Sephardic Jews (Arab Jews), and now a larger segment of Muslim and Christian Arabs, Israel is not and will not be the same exclusivist State it had once hoped to be. Already signs of its transformation are appearing, even though it is premature to foretell their future course.

THE ARAB-ISRAELI CONFLICT AND THE "ARAB REVOLUTION"

Most writers believe that the central issue in Middle East affairs is the conflict over Palestine. Reporters, editors, commentators, and politicians interpret virtually every event in this context. In the end, their judgments are often dangerously misguided because they start from this premise to the exclusion of other considerations.

Certainly, the military and political conflict between Israel and some of her Arab neighbors has been the most spectacular feature of Middle East affairs for more than 20 years. It demands our notice, enlists our sympathies and grips our interest; but it is not and cannot be the most significant Middle East problem. If Israel should vanish from world maps tomorrow, the Arab regions would continue to live in torment and turmoil. Even if Israel is the apparent catalyst today, its role is aggravated by its ability to exploit an existing situation to its best interest.

A hundred million Arabs are casting aside the ways and ideas of an older time and looking forward to building a new Arab world. What has been, passes away; what shall be, is yet dimly seen as the Arab people strive to realize their rising expectations. This, too, is conflict. On one side stand those who cling to a dead past; on the other are those who plan and struggle to build toward something better. This is revolution. When the fact of Arab revolution is recognized and accepted, the events of the last two decades reveal a clear, unmistakable historical pattern. Men and movements, wars and political maneuvers fall into historical perspective as readily as the pieces of a jigsaw puzzle mate to reveal their ordained pattern.

Exclusive concern for Israel confuses the judgment of those who look upon the struggle merely as between Israel and the neighboring Arab States, thus misunderstanding the true nature of Middle East problems and failing even to recognize the basic character of the Palestine issue itself. Indeed, the observer can clearly see, if he will, the fact that every guerrilla infiltration, every commando raid, every act of sabotage has been the work, not of Israel's neighboring States, but of Palestinians determined to regain their homeland. States like Egypt, Lebanon, Jordan and Syria, which have given refuge to displaced Palestinians, as indeed they have, and made little effort to interfere with the activities of Al Fateh and other Palestinian groups, recall that, for a decade, the United States has given protection to refugees from Cuba, who have fought with arms obtained inside the United States; and large numbers of Americans have not only cheered but also aided them in the 1961 abortive Cuban invasion. The Palestinian freedom fighters are one segment of the Arab popular revolutionary trend. To oppose them is to accelerate local revolutionary movements which already threaten to burst throughout the entire Arab world.

An understanding of the roots of this trend is necessary. After the rise of nationalism and access to independence by the Arab States, economic necessity brought about Arab socialism. Arab socialism was not and is not the communism of the Soviet Union or China, nor is it the "Middle Way" of the Scandinavian countries; it is as an Arab program derived from Arab experiences to serve Arab needs. It did not spring from any body of socio-economic theory and has no organized ideology. It is still an inchoate movement, feeling its way forward, testing ideas, keeping those that work and discarding those that fail, governed by experience and undaunted by the problems that lie ahead. While it is groping for answers, one certain fact emerges — its immediate objective is socio-political and economic justice. Exactly where the priority lies and where the emphasis is to be laid is what truly differentiates among the Arab regimes in power today and distinguishes the various local revolutionary movements.

The very first manifestation of the Arab revolution is that where it advances, kings vanish, such as in Egypt, Iraq, Yemen and Lybia. Monarchies have been replaced by military dictatorships, but the following phase is one of popular movements to replace the sectarianism which has characterized the first phase. As French and British power evaporated in the Middle East and American power undertook to replace it with uncertainty and lack of purpose, it inherited an enmity which it had not sown, while fostering the belief that its goals are neo-imperialistic as its policy often may have suggested. Like the French and British before them, American policymakers concerned themselves with the effort to maintain the political and economic status quo. Only then, so it was believed, could the enormous American interests in Arab oil be protected and the militarily strategic location that so recently had been a Franco-British enclave be preserved. America thereby earned the title of "colonial heir," and when it finds itself assuming the wardship of Israel, the effect of these roles on Arab-American relations is devastating.

The third phase of the Arab-Israeli war in 1967 brought the Soviet Union into the Middle East as a military power to reckon with, just as the Suez Canal crisis of 1956 has provided the political opening that Russia had sought in vain through long generations. Today, the Mediterranean, long a British lake, then an American *mare nostrum*, is no longer a closed sea. Soviet power already deprives the United States of the ability to determine the course of events in the Mediterranean basin, and the Soviet presence suggests that Western attempts to dictate the Arab future have now been foreclosed.

The role of the Soviet Union in Arab affairs is derivative of American-Israeli polarization of the conflict. The most telling fact is that no communist party exists in the Arab States, and the people have no sympathy for the Soviets. But the political alliance at the international level is a necessity dictated by America's one-sided position. Thus, the Soviet Union's influence in the outcome of the conflict is a factor which is a consequence of the American position and can, therefore, be controlled by the United States. Socialist doctrine is strong in the Arab world, but Marxism is relatively weak among left-wing thinkers, who, whatever doctrines they relate to, almost invariably adapt it to the context of Arab nationalism. Russian communism is not an element of the Arab revolution, and no strings pulled in Moscow will affect its course or future.

The Arab revolution transcends any local dispute and internal question. The struggle of the Arab peoples against what they believe is neo-imperialism and social inequities continues unabated in search of a more positive identity. One thing remains certain — the Arab peoples look forward to an Arab nation, and in the process of such a quest lies the difficulty of finding a common political ideology for all Arab peoples. The larger question of the Arab revolution does not absorb (though it encompasses), the many different and varied internal problems of each Arab State. Amidst these, Israel is only one problem — even though it appears to loom so largely over the others.

CONCLUSION

Those who founded and still govern Israel, although some of Palestinian birth, were and are Europeans. They were bred in a European culture, though it may have been affected by common religious tradition. As the British historian Hugh Trevor-Roper has observed, the history of European and other Western Jewry is an integral part of European history.[161]

The customs, traditions and systems of law developed among the Arabs and other non-European peoples have had no discoverable impact on international law as it now exists. Arabs are products of an Islamic culture that has its roots in the Judaeo-Christian heritage but differs sharply from that which the same has become in the Western world. Yet, existing international law demands that Arabs abide by such customs, practices and precedents, in the shaping of which they have had no part whatever. It may justly be said that they are compelled to play for very high stakes under rules compiled by their antagonists and adversaries.

It is significant that the acceptance of the Zionist Organization as an international public body, the Palestine Mandate, and the incorporation of the Balfour Declaration in the Mandate Agreement were all decreed by Europeans, in direct defiance of declared and demonstrated Arab interests — that an ancient country dominated by Islamic tradition and culture has, in crude fact, been seized and appropriated for a new extension of the areas dominated by European culture.

The concept of law and the Rule of Law is not alien to either the Arabs or Islam itself. The Islamic heritage is one of law in its purest form.[162] In fact, the history of the present conflict demonstrates that from its inception the Arabs have sought to rely upon the precepts of international law and its organized structures to resolve the problem. It was not until their realization of its failure that the present escalating trend of self-help has materialized.[163]

A sound historical hypothesis is that events of a crude and violent nature — war, revolution, the rise of tyranny — are usually not triggered by ideas, ideals and beliefs which are the result of thought in evolution. Ideology is seldom the catalyst that induces violence, although it is often the target at which the opponents of revolutionary, and even evolutionary, change aim.

---

161 Trevor-Roper, *Jewish and Other Nationalisms*, COMMENTARY, Jan. 1963, at 15-29.
162 Bassiouni, *supra* note 33, at 120.
163 Bassiouni, *supra* note 18. *See* note 158 and accompanying text *supra*.

In the Middle East today there exists two basic ideological conflicts — Arabism versus Zionism and Arab revolutionism versus reactionalism. It is the situational factors derived from these ideological conflicts which constantly threaten the peace and security of the Middle East; and as to the first, it is a political challenge to the Rule of Law in its quest for the peaceful resolution of world conflicts. In this regard, two basic points must be considered.

1. If the Arab-Israeli conflict is to be considered a permanent feature of the Middle East, deriving solely from irreconcilable ideologies, the conclusion is inevitable that peace and security will be possible only when one or the other can be annihilated or thoroughly subjugated by military force.

2. If, however, conflict is not deemed a permanent condition in the relations of Middle East peoples but a consequence of competing aspirations and struggling ambitions amenable to solutions other than inevitable collision, then the conclusion must be that the risk of violence between the parties can be obviated by a resolution of those situational factors that produce the violence.

Significantly, every violent episode throughout the history of the conflict has resulted from a situational factor only indirectly related to the central ideological conflict. The direct causes of these episodes have rarely, if ever, been within the individual or exclusive control of any contestants, yet despite the professed desire of the parties to prevent it, conflict has resulted. If this assumption is accurate, then elimination of those situational factors would remove the risk of military confrontation which threatens world peace. The legal and political aspects of the Arab-Israeli conflict have been widely discussed, and in another forum one of the authors of this article stated: "In the history of modern world conflict, there is no other instance where the very nature of the conflict can be examined in its entirety in a legal context."[164] This does not imply that a legal determination is possible in the present practice of world affairs. Almost all the "political" issues of the Palestine question and the conflict between Israel and some of the Arab states are superimposed upon legal claims and moral rationalizations, or vice-versa. Thus, it is theoretically possible, and quite realistic in an anachronistic sense, to resolve the entirety of the Arab-Israeli conflict on a legal basis. Therefore, the Arab States and the United Arab Republic, in particular, seek to submit some or all of these legal issues to the International Court of Justice; Israel consistently refuses.

---

[164] Bassiouni, *supra* note 2, at 51.

> The lack of compulsory international adjudication of world conflicts provides the perfect escape for any nation which lives in the world community by means of self-serving might to the detriment of the peace-serving maintenance of world public order. The resolution of world conflicts by the Rule of Force and not by the Rule of Law is the most constant threat to world public order.[165]

Although sporadic military encounters will occur, the bitter Arab-Israeli quarrel may well end, not in ultimate military confrontation but in the rapidly proceeding Arabization of the Zionist state. This process will be the result of the large influx of Jewish immigrants from Arab lands — men and women bred not in a Western but in an Islamic and Arabic culture — and the many Arabs living under Israeli rule. The Europeans who established Israel and still dominate both its politics and economy have been reduced to less than one-third of Israel's population. Experience and simple logic suggest that no minority can long control any country. Already Israel has ceased to be the European state in an Arab sea that its founder envisioned, and the Arabization of Israel is starting.[166]

The very real likelihood is that before many years pass, Israel will be ruled by its majority, by people who are either themselves Arabs or have a history of 13 centuries of friendly coexistence with the Arabs. At their vanguard will be the "Sabras" — born and raised in Israel. They will view their future as part of the Arabs region and not as a beholden outpost of European Zionism.

This, of course, will depend upon Israel's realization that the arrogance of her present power must abate, if and when Arab power is not one day to repay it in kind.

In this event, the Arab-Israeli conflict that so dominates world public interest in Middle East affairs will simply wither away. Arabs will see no need to arm themselves for either defense or aggression against their Arab neighbors. Meanwhile, however, the "Arab revolution" will go on for several generations. Precisely what path it will take or how fast it will advance no one can say, but that revolution in the Arab lands will continue seems as certain as anything natural can be.

The "Arab Revolution" will dominate the search for identity and realization of the emerging Arab masses who long for no more than to enjoy life, liberty and the pursuit of happiness in human dignity.

---

165 Bassiouni, *supra* note 2, at 51-52.
166 *See* G. FRIEDMAN, THE END OF THE JEWISH PEOPLE (1967). *See also* U. AVNERY, *supra* note 59.

Yet, the most fundamental moralizing effect of religion remains smothered. Islam has not played its full and mature role in the development of this course of events. The contribution of Islam can have untold effects upon the development of the Arab world and its future institutions. Islam remains, however, the main barrier against communism in the Arab world and must be regarded as the main tenet of moral strength in the Arab world of today and tomorrow.

There are too many imponderables to predict the immediate future, but certainly the long-range course of the Arab world is unmistakably clear; and Israel or Palestine, whatever the label, will be part of that Arab world of tomorrow.

The Palestine Arab Refugee Problem

LOUISE W. HOLBORN*

IN THE tangled Middle East situation, one of the most sensitive issues has been the situation of the Palestine Arab refugees.[1] A broad humanitarian but also highly political problem with deep emotional underpinnings, the more than a million Arab refugees remain a major factor in the tension between the Arab states and Israel. This has been the case since, with the creation of the State of Israel in 1948 and the subsequent war between Israel and her Arab neighbours, thousands of Arabs fled their former homeland. The problem was intensified by the conflict of 1956. It reached still more threatening dimensions with Israel's lightning victory in June 1967, which brought under her control large new areas including the Gaza Strip, Jerusalem, the Jordanian West Bank, and the Ali Qunaytirah section in Syria, and thus caused a further flight of refugees from these territories.

At the root of the Arab refugee problem is the continuing state of war, actual or tacit, between Israel and the United Arab Republic, Syria, Jordan and Lebanon, which have never accepted Israel's existence. The refugees have thus been kept in a continual state of expectation that at some future date there will be a return to the territory that was once called Palestine. From the point of view of the Arab

* Professor of Government, Radcliffe Institute, Cambridge, Mass.

[1] Of the extensive writings on the problem, the following general sources may be cited: John Campbell, *Defense in the Middle East* (rev. ed., New York, 1960). Roney Gabbey, *A Political Study of the Arab-Jewish Conflict: The Arab Refugee Problem* (Geneva, 1959). Frank Gervasi, *The Case for Israel* (New York, 1967). Sami Hadawi, *Palestine in the United Nations* (The Arab Information Center, 1964). Manfred Halpern, *The Politics of Social Change in the Middle East and North Africa* (Princeton, N.J., 1963). Robert W. Macdonald, *The League of Arab States* (Princeton, N.J., 1965). Don Peretz, *Israel and the Palestine Arabs* (Washington, D.C., 1958). Benjamin Rivlin and Joseph S. Szyliowicz, *The Contemporary Middle East* (New York, 1965). Nadav Safran, *The United States and Israel* (Cambridge, Mass., 1963). Fayez A. Sayegh, *The Arab-Israeli Conflict* (The Arab Information Center, 1964). Georgianna G. Stevens (ed.), *The United States and the Middle East* (Englewood Cliffs, N.J., 1964). Basic U.N. Documents are listed in U.N. General Assembly, Official Records, Twenty-second Session, Supplement No. 13, Doc. A/6713. *Report of the Commissioner-General of the United Nations Relief and Works Agency for Palestine Refugees in the Middle East*, 1 July, 1966-30 June, 1967 (cited as UNRWA *Annual Report, 1967*), pp. 1-2. For recent developments and resolutions of the General Assembly and Security Council, see *UN Monthly Chronicle*, Vol. 4, Nos. 6-9, June-October 1967.

states, to accept the refugees as integrated members of their communities, even when the refugees have secured jobs and have produced second and even third generations within Arab territories, would be a denial of this objective. For Israel, which already has a settled Arab population of more than a quarter of a million, and which has welcomed Jewish refugees from many of the Arab countries into its own community, the continued insistence that the refugees should be allowed back into the Jewish state is felt to be both irrational and a threat to its survival.[2]

Confronted with this intractable situation, Western nations, and particularly the United States, Great Britain, Canada and France have sought through U.N. agencies, in particular the U. N. Relief and Works Agency for Palestine Refugees in the Near East (UNRWA), and periodic special conferences and/or mediations, to lessen the tension not only by extending emergency relief to the Arab refugees in their camps and makeshift villages but also by providing the kind of economic and educational aid that could enable these people, and particularly the young, to develop skills useful to themselves and to others. Today the problem has become still more acute because of its newly extended dimensions and the heightened political antagonisms resulting from the June war.

Although the flight of the Arab refugees during the June war and its aftermath was not different in kind from earlier outward movements, it formed a high watermark both in numbers and in the extent of territory into which the refugees flooded. Prior to the June war two-thirds of all the refugees under the care of the UNRWA lived in the Gaza Strip and on the West Bank of the Jordan River where fighting occurred. Many more refugees were created as thousands crossed the Jordan to the East Bank with the advance of the Israeli army. Although the Israeli government maintained that its forces would refrain from acts of coercion, and would permit the refugees to remain where

---

[2] By the end of the British mandate in 1948 an estimated 900,000 Palestine Arabs lived in the territory which became the state of Israel. About 170,000 Arabs stayed after the first Arab-Israeli war. See Peretz, *Israel and the Palestine Arabs*, p. 95. By the end of 1966 the Arab population of Israel had increased to 313,000 through the return of some refugees and natural increase. See Walter Pinner, *The Legend of Arab Refugees* (Tel Aviv, 1967), p. 66; and for Jewish refugees from Arab states see F.T.H. Witkamp, "The Refugee Problem in the Middle East," in Research Group for European Migration Problems, *Bulletin* (The Hague), Vol. 5, No. 1, January/March 1965, p. 26; and Harry B. Ellis, "The Arab-Israel Conflict Today," in Stevens, *The United States and the Middle East*, p. 142.

they were, there were many reasons for this mass flight which has been estimated to include 350,000 new refugees.[3] Probably the most powerful incentive was fear of being caught in Israeli-controlled territory. This fear affected not only the refugees or pre-1967 vintage, but also many Jordanian officials and soldiers who were caught behind the advancing Israeli forces. In addition many fled for economic reasons, either out of fear of losing their UNRWA rations, or of being separated from the monthly remittances sent from relatives working and living in Kuwait or other countries.

Flight also occurred from other areas in which major hostilities took place. UNRWA's Commissioner-General reported that within Syria 115,000 people took flight, 35,000 fled from the Sinai Peninsula to Egypt, and 3-4,000 soldiers of the Palestine Liberation Army also fled to Egypt.[4]

At the specific request of the government, UNRWA began for the first time to operate in the U.A.R., where the problem assumed new dimensions. Many Egyptians had moved from the east bank of the Suez Canal, which was occupied by Israeli forces, and on government initiative large groups also moved from the west bank of the Canal into the interior. In addition, some 1,000 Palestinians from Gaza and Jordan, who were in the U.A.R. for educational and other reasons and were stranded, have been aided by international voluntary agencies.

Although the fighting temporarily dislocated UNRWA's work and facilities, it was possible to reestablish them quickly in large measure because of the relations long existing with the relevant governments and non-governmental organizations. By mid-July new camps had been established, new supply routes were open, and many schools

[3] U.N. General Assembly, Official Records, Fifth Emergency Special Session, Doc. A/6787, *Report by the Secretary-General under General Assembly Resolution 2252 (ES-V) and Security Council Resolution 237 (1967)*, August 18, 1967; *U.N. Monthly Chronicle*, Vol. 4, No. 8, August-September, 1967, p. 31; and United Nations General Assembly, Official Documents, Twenty-second session, Special Political Committee, *Report of the Commissioner-General of the United Nations Relief and Works Agency for Palestine Refugees in the Near East*, Doc. A/SPC/121, 13 December 1967, p. 1.

[4] U.N. General Assembly, Official Records, Fifth Emergency Special Session, Doc. A/6723, *Note by the Secretary-General submitting a report of the Commissioner General of the United Nations Relief and Works Agency for Palestine Refugees in the Near East*, June 19, 1967; *ibid.*, Doc. A6723/Add. 1, July 4, 1967; and the reports by the Secretary-General's special representative, Mr. Nils Göran Gussing in U.N. General Assembly, Official Records, Fifth Emergency Special Session, Doc. A/6797, *Report by the Secretary-General under General Assembly Resolution 2252 (ES-V) and Security Council Resolution 237 (1967)*, September 15, 1967.

were in operation once more. While widespread dislocation continued, the worst emergency needs were met. Unfortunately, the agreement painstakingly achieved by the International Red Cross with both sides for the return of large numbers of refugees to the West Bank of the Jordan, where UNRWA had the necessary camps, installations and other facilities, had relatively little effect.[4a] That only fourteen thousand of the 100,000 specified in the agreement took advantage of it was perhaps partly due to the fact that the Israeli government had reserved the right to pass on all applications as security risks, but probably more to the general fear or unwillingness to live under Israeli control. Both sentiments were openly encouraged by the Jordanian government.

In the June crisis the United Nations was constantly concerned with the humanitarian aspects of the situation. On June 14 the Security Council called upon the government of Israel "to ensure the safety, welfare and security of the inhabitants of the area where military operations had taken place and to facilitate the return of those inhabitants who had fled since the outbreak of hostilities." The Council also recommended to the governments concerned "the scrupulous respect of the humanitarian principles governing the treatment of prisoners of war and the protection of civilians and persons in time of war contained in the Geneva Convention of August 12, 1949."[5] On June 26 the President of the General Assembly appealed to all members, both as signatories of the Charter and morally obliged "human beings," to make contributions to ease the suffering and misery of the refugees. On July 4 the Assembly, welcoming the Security Council resolution, unanimously endorsed the efforts of UNRWA, "to provide humanitarian assistance . . ." on an emergency basis and as a temporary measure, "to other persons in the area who are at present displaced and are in serious need of assistance as a result of the recent hostilities."[6] Governments and organizations have contributed money as well as food, medical supplies, tents, blankets. Some assistance was on a bilateral

[4a] For the text of the Agreement (dated June 14, 1967), see UNRWA *Annual Report, 1967*, Annex III, p. 99.

[5] The text of Resolution S/RES/237 (1967) is reproduced in *UN Monthly Chronicle*, Vol. 4, No. 7, July 1967, p. 32.

[6] U.N. General Assembly, Official Records, Fifth Emergency Special Session, Supplement No. 1, Doc. A/6798, *Resolutions adopted by the General Assembly during its Fifth Emergency Special Session 17 June-18 September 1967, Resolution 2252 (ES-V). Humanitarian Assistance*, p. 3.

basis, some was channelled through UNRWA, the Red Cross and Red Crescent organizations, some through other voluntary agencies. Major aid in feeding persons not registered with UNRWA was provided by F.A.O., the World Food Program, and UNICEF. Voluntary agencies have and are playing an important part, not only in supplies and contributions, but also in helping the staff to run some of the facilities.[7]

Thus the emergency measures have been a combined operation of governments directly concerned, other governments, national and international voluntary agencies, and many individuals in many parts of the world. UNRWA, long established in the area and closely connected with the refugees, coordinated these relief works and was also able to provide information of general concern. However, its greatest burden was to continue the activities of the Agency in the difficult situation with respect to all persons within its mandate.

* * * *

In the light of this highly complicated and tense situation what hope for a long-term solution can be found in looking back at earlier efforts and proposals? From the earliest days of the Arab-Israeli conflict the United Nations, which had been so closely connected with the creation of Israel, has been concerned with the refugee situation. Count Folke Bernadotte, the U.N. Mediator appointed in 1948, first brought the refugee problem officially to world attention. Everything that has been done subsequently through the United Nations and its established agencies has its foundations in the key Resolution 194 of December 11, 1948, in which the General Assembly established a Conciliation Commission (C.C.P.) and instructed it to take "steps to assist the governments and authorities concerned to achieve a final settlement of all questions outstanding between them." Although a "final settlement" has not yet been reached, much has been attempted to ameliorate not only the situation of the refugees but also that of the area as a whole.

The guidelines laid down in the 1948 resolution focused on the economic development of the area as well as on the particular needs of the refugees. It instructed the Conciliation Commission "to seek arrangements which will facilitate the economic development of the area, including arrangements for access to ports and airfields and the use of

---

[7] UNRWA *Annual Report, 1967*, p. 16: and International Council of Voluntary Agencies, *Surveys* (Geneva, 1967).

transportation and communication facilities." It was also declared that "Refugees wishing to return to their homes and live in peace with their neighbours should be permitted to do so at the earliest practicable date, and that compensation should be paid for the property of those choosing not to return and for loss of or damage to property which, under the principles of international law, or in equity, should be made good by the governments or authorities responsible." The Conciliation Commission was "to facilitate the repatriation, resettlement and economic and social rehabilitation of the refugees and the payment of compensation, and to maintain close relations with the Director of Relief for Palestine Refugees and through him, with the appropriate organs and agencies of the United Nations." These last two paragraphs form the basis for the Arab claim that Israel has never lived up to the basic U.N. pronouncement of this issue.[8]

To aid in implementing these resolutions UNRWA was established in December 1949, directed "to carry out in collaboration with local governments the direct relief and works programs as recommended by the economic survey commission," and "to consult with the interested Near Eastern governments concerning measures to be taken by them preparatory to the time when international assistance for relief and works project is no longer available." The latter provision proved a dead letter, but in response to the former UNRWA assumed the responsibility for providing the Arab refugees with relief, health and medical services, housing, clothing, child care and educational and vocational training. Despite the great physical and political difficulties, it has conducted its huge operation with an impressive combination of humanity and efficiency. Indeed, many of the young people under its care have received better schooling, medical attention and social welfare than ordinary residents of the states in which UNRWA has operated.

That there have been major problems both of administration and of financial obligations is unquestionable. The staff of UNRWA, whose lower ranks are drawn to a large extent from the Arab refugee community, has always had to work within the limits set by the Arab states—the "host countries": Egypt, Syria, Lebanon and Jordan—within which their operations took place. No less serious is the steady increase in the numbers of those listed as refugees for whom UNRWA is

---

[8] For the Arab point of view, see Gabbey, *A Political Study of the Arab-Jewish Problem*; Pevity, *Israel and the Palestine Arabs*; and Macdonald, *The League of Arab States*, p. 90.

responsible. The original number of refugees who fled from the State of Israel was estimated at 726,000, but by May 31, 1967, 1,344,576 persons were registered with UNRWA.[9] By the eve of the June war about 70 per cent of the total population of the Gaza Strip (then administered by Egypt), more than 36 per cent of Jordan's population, nearly 8 per cent of the Lebanese and 2 per cent of the Syrian population. About 80 per cent of the refugees were farmers, unskilled workers, the aged, the sick, and their families. The other 20 per cent were business and professional men, property owners, skilled labourers and their families. About nine-tenths of the refugees were Moslem, the rest Christian.[10]

The rather startling increase in the number of refugees is owed to a number of causes. The initial working definition of a refugee eligible for relief was: "A person normally resident in Palestine who has lost his home and his livelihood as a result of the hostilities and who is in need." UNRWA changed this definition to: "A person whose normal

[9] The 1949 estimate is found in U.N. Conciliation Commission for Palestine, *Final Report of the United Nations Economic Survey Mission for the Middle East*, United Nations Publications, 28 December 1949, Part I, p. 18; see also UNRWA *Annual Report, 1967*, Tables 1 and 2, pp. 59-60. The following table illustrates the refugees in all four host countries who were registered with UNRWA (Source: UNRWA *Annual Report, 1967*, p. 59, Table 1):

June 30, 1950	June 30, 1958	May 31, 1967
960,021	1,053,628	1,344,576

The May 31, 1967, figures involve 254,247 families, of whom 95,031 families (39.6 per cent) lived in 54 camps. *Ibid.*, Tables 4 and 8, pp. 62 and 66.

The following table illustrates the number of Palestine Arab Refugees resettled by 1965, as reported in the Jordan Arabic daily, *Falastin*, September 28, 1965:

Kuwait	50,000
South Arabian Peninsula	26,000
Iraq	9,000
Egypt	8,000
Total	93,000

[10] The following table shows the age distribution of UNRWA registered refugees at May 31, 1967 (Source: UNRWA *Annual Report, 1967*, Table 2, p. 60):

Country	Below 1 year	1-15 years	15 years and over	Total
Jordan	11,993	255,985	454,709	722,687
Gaza	8,984	120,941	186,851	316,776
Lebanon	3,481	64,432	92,810	160,723
Syria	3,794	59,620	80,976	144,390
Total	28,252	500,978	815,346	1,344,576

residence was Palestine for a minimum of two years immediately preceding the outbreak of the conflict in 1948, and who, as a result of this conflict, has lost both his home and means of livelihood."[11] This definition has since been extended to cover the children of such persons. To be eligible for assistance a refugee must reside in one of the four host countries in which UNRWA operates and must be in need.

It has been very difficult, however, to adhere rigidly to these definitions. People who, living right on the border, might still have their home but were cut off from their land, had to be included. There were numerous Bedouins whose place of residence could not be clearly established, but who were in need. There were also refugees who had some money at the outset but who later became destitute and had to be rehabilitated.

Moreover, as was also experienced with displaced persons living for long in camps in Europe, the phenomenon of "being a refugee" has become institutionalized. Even if refugees found adequate economic opportunities they became reluctant to turn in their UNRWA cards which for many years had been the only source for a sense of security. With this card, "real hunger" was practically excluded. One could send one's children to school with it; one obtained free medical aid with it, and exemption from taxes as well. UNRWA itself reported that "The ration card has become, in fact, so much a part of the lives and economy of the refugees that it is not at all unusual for it to be used as a tangible asset upon the strength of which substantial sums can be borrowed."[12]

There were also false registrations and concealment of family deaths. When refugees became self-supporting, there was a reluctance to make this fact known. Testifying before the Senate Sub-Committee on Refugees and Escapees on July 14, 1966, Secretary of State Dean Rusk declared, "There are almost half a million refugees who have registered refugee status but who, in fact, have jobs, and some of them at some distance from the camps, living reasonably normal lives. They want to retain their registered status, yet we would like to see con-

[11] U.N. General Assembly, Official Records, Ninth Session, Supplement No. 17A, Doc. A/2717/Add. 1, *Special Report of the Director and the Advisory Commission of the United Nations Relief and Works Agency for Palestine Refugees in the Near East*, p. 2, para. 19.

[12] U.N. General Assembly, Official Records, Ninth Session, Supplement No. 17, Doc. A/2717, *Annual Report of the Director of the United Nations Relief and Works Agency for Palestine Refugees in the Near East, 1 July 1953-30 June 1954*, p. 3, para. 16; and Witkamp, "The Refugee Problem in the Middle East," p. 12.

tinuation of the rectification of the roles, so that the funds that are available will be used as wisely as possible."

The Arab position on repatriation has been from the first to demand that all refugees, who once lived in Palestine, should be accepted, and that establishment of the right of repatriation must precede discussion of all other facets of their dispute with Israel. At the Lausanne Conference held in the spring of 1949, in response to Resolution 194, the Israelis made a slight move away from their otherwise intransigent position that the refugees must be "resettled in Arab lands," by offering to accept 100,000 of the refugees (including in that number 10,000 women and minors to be reunited with their families domiciled in Israel) but only if they had the right to determine the location of their settlement, and whether they were security risks. This proposal was not accepted and the conference broke up.[13] The Arabs had refused to talk directly to the Israelis on the ground that face-to-face negotiations were tantamount to diplomatic recognition, and the positions of the two sides became increasingly rigid.

On acceptable compensation, the two parties have also been unable to agree. Under great international pressure, the Israelis agreed theoretically to consider the question of compensation outside the framework of a general peace settlement, although in general they have insisted that the refugee problem must be dealt with as part of an overall peace settlement. The Israelis also released most Arab refugee funds that had been frozen in Israeli banks. Neither move was accepted on the part of the other side as an acceptable means of opening negotiations.

The third, and ultimately most hopeful approach to a solution of the Arab refugee problem, has been large-scale economic development of Arab lands. In mid 1949 the Technical Committee on Refugees of the Conciliation Commission, after examining the economic situation in those countries of the Middle East affected by the Palestine war of 1948-49, advanced a comprehensive plan to enable the relevant governments to undertake development programmes to overcome the dislocation created by the war, to integrate the refugees into the economic life of the area on a self-sustaining basis within a short period of time, and to promote economic conditions that would be conducive to the maintenance of peace and stability in the area. It recommended

---

[13] For further agreements on the reunion of broken families, see Peretz, *Israel and the Palestine Arabs*, pp. 50f.

the reduction of the Arab refugee relief rolls from 940,000 to 625,000 by January 1950, and proposed gradually replacing relief by a series of works projects through which refugees could be gainfully employed. It estimated that a total of $54.9 million would be needed for relief and works projects for the eighteen-month period within which the Commission believed it would be possible to solve the refugee problem.

These recommendations were accepted by the Fourth General Assembly. The initial relief agency, U.N. Relief for Palestine Refugees, was succeeded by UNRWA, which was established in the hope of bringing both the political and the practical aspects of the refugee problem into a single focus through economic means.[14] Works programmes were developed but had almost no long range effect. Basically, the Arab governments believed that their support of this programme would undermine the right of the refugees to return to their former homes in Israel. The latter contributed almost nothing to the cost of UNRWA projects from which they greatly benefited. At the end of 1952 UNRWA reported to the General Assembly that "the Agency found itself financing and operating labor camps to build public works which the governments themselves would have built the following year." Moreover, when the projects were finished, the refugees returned to their tents and ration lines. None of them was economically integrated. When its public works fund began to run out, UNRWA decided to bring that part of its programme to a close. These works had created neither permanent benefit for the refugees nor financial relief for the United Nations. Instead they had cost five times the amount necessary for simple relief.

The Arab states then requested financial support for a new three-year programme designed to reintegrate the refugees into the economic life of the Middle East, either by repatriation or resettlement. This plan also failed. In February 1957 the Director of UNRWA, reporting to the U.N. General Assembly that little change had occurred in the refugee situation, stated that:

The reason lies in the realm of politics, and in deep-seated human emotions. It does not lie simply in the field of economics. UNRWA can

14 See the U.N. Conciliation Commission for Palestine, *Final Report of the United Nations Economic Survey Mission for the Middle East*, Parts I and II; and for the text of Resolution 302 (IV), December 8, 1949, U.N. General Assembly, Official Records, Fourth Session, 1949, *Resolutions*, pp. 23-25.

enable some hundreds of refugees to become self-supporting each year through small agricultural development projects, grants to establish small businesses and the like, but it cannot overcome the fact that refugees as a whole insist upon the choice provided for them in the General Assembly Resolution 194 that is, repatriation or compensation.

In an effort to resolve the conflicting claims, President Eisenhower in 1953 sent Eric E. Johnston as his personal representative to the Middle East.[15] Johnston's compromise plan, which won the approval of both Arab and Israeli engineers, was to allocate 60 per cent of Jordan River waters to Lebanon, Syria, and Jordan and 40 per cent to Israel. The Arab technicians' acceptance of the sharing of riparian rights represented a first tacit recognition of Israel's existence, yet at the political level neither side agreed to the implementation of the plan.

At the United Nations the United States, Britain and France submitted a resolution favouring the diversion project, if the rights of all parties could be safeguarded. It was vetoed by the Soviet Union on January 22, 1954. Since that time the diversion issue has been unresolved in both the United Nations and the Middle East.

In 1959 Secretary-General Dag Hammarskjöld was asked by the General Assembly to make recommendations for the "reintegration of the refugees into the economic life of the Near East, either by repatriation or resettlement." He reported that reintegration of Palestine refugees would be possible only "within the context of general economic development."[16] He suggested that outside capital assistance to the Arab countries would be needed in the amount of $1.5 billion between 1960 and 1965. The cost of providing jobs for an additional refugee labour force of some 380,000 persons (as of 1959) would require a further $1.5 billion of external capital investment. The magnitude of this cost of integration effectively cooled international enthusiasm, but his estimate remains a realistic evaluation of the cost of future efforts toward either repatriation or resettlement.

In 1961, at the request of the Conciliation Commission, Dr. Joseph E. Johnson, President of the Carnegie Endowment for International

---

[15] See Georgianna G. Stevens, *Jordan River Partition* (Stanford 1965).

[16] U.N. General Assembly, Official Records, Fourteenth Session, Doc. A/4121, *Proposals for the continuation of United Nations assistance to Palestine, 15 June 1959.*

Peace, made a new study of the refugee problem.[17] He proposed that "refugee heads of families, insulated by the United Nations from pressure from any source, should be allowed to choose voluntarily between a return to Palestine and compensation." The United States and other members of the United Nations, including Israel, were to contribute to this compensation. Israel was to have the right to run a security check on each refugee opting for return. "Those refugees who had lacked property in Palestine," he suggested, "would receive a reintegration allowance, wherever they might choose to go. Such allowances would be administered through the United Nations, which also would act as a cushion between the two sides during the long process of settlement."[18]

Mr. Johnson's proposals were rejected by the Israel government in January 1962 with a reiteration of a Knesset resolution of November 1961, which asserted that Arab refugees could not return to Israel and that the only solution to the problem was thus in settlement in the Arab states.[19] From their side the Arab governments did not openly reject the proposals but reasserted their persistent stand that Israel must first accept in principle the provisions of Resolution 194.

*　*　*　*

As the handling of the Arab refugee problem has thus been left chiefly to UNRWA, it is particularly important to examine in more detail both UNRWA's organization and its work.

UNRWA was set up as a temporary non-political organ of the U.N. General Assembly, and its existence has been extended several times by it, the last extension being to June 30, 1969. As of December 31, 1966, it had a staff of 11,516 persons, of whom 112 were international staff and 11,404 locally recruited, virtually all Arab refugees. By the end of 1967 it had received total contributions amounting to $590,975,149, from more than 40 nations. About 98 per cent were pledges by the United States, Great Britain, Canada, and France. The

[17] He served as Special Representative of the Commission from August 1961 to January 1963. See Joseph E. Johnson, "Arab versus Israel, A pertinent challenge to Americans," an address delivered to the 24th American Assembly, New York, October 23, 1963.

[18] Harry B. Ellis, "The Arab Israeli Conflict Today," in Stevens, *The United States and the Middle East*, pp. 142-43.

[19] Mrs. Golda Meir, Israeli Minister for Foreign Affairs, before the Special Political Committee, December 14, 1962. U.N. General Assembly, Official Records, Seventeenth Session, Special Political Committee, pp. 240-42.

host countries contributed $10,821,324. The Soviet Union, which had voted for the establishment of UNRWA, has never contributed to its expenditures.[20]

In providing food, shelter, preventive and curative health services, social measures, and educational and vocation training for the refugees, UNRWA has received valuable cooperation and aid from U.N. Specialized Agencies, especially I.R.O., W.H.O., F.A.O. and the World Food Program, UNICEF and UNESCO. In his 1962 Annual Report, Dr. John Davis, then Commissioner General, pointed out the critical needs of refugee youth and UNRWA's important role in satisfying those needs. From that time on UNRWA put its emphasis on further expansion of its educational and vocational programmes in close cooperation and guidance by UNESCO. The achievements in this regard are suggested by the numbers involved. From 1951-1967 the number of elementary and secondary school pupils attending UNRWA-UNESCO schools rose from 43,112 to 186,967. By May 31, 1967, 246,451 refugee pupils were enrolled in 440 UNRWA-UNESCO schools. In addition, a further 47,993 refugee boys and girls attended government and private schools to which UNRWA paid subsidies. 1,855 men and 237 women were enrolled in UNRWA-UNESCO vocational and technical education centres during the 1966-67 school year. Since the training programme

---

[20] The following table shows the main government contributions, May 1, 1950-December 31, 1967 (Source: UNRWA *Annual Report, 1967*, Table 20, pp. 77-82):

I. Western Countries

United States	$411,218,069
United Kingdom	100,524,004
Canada	21,039,426
France	13,714,303
Sweden	6,619,064
Germany	4,388,021
Australia	3,583,103
New Zealand	2,380,000
Switzerland	1,448,814
Netherlands	1,198,509
Italy	1,141,326
Norway	1,089,066
Israel	406,547

II. Arab Host Countries

United Arab Republic	5,471,162
Gaza Authorities	1,199,919
Jordan	1,891,833
Lebanon	728,967
Syrian Arab Republic	1,529,443

began in 1953 there have been nearly 7,500 graduates, most of whom are now at work throughout the Middle East in the host as well as in other countries. Thus UNRWA's training programme to provide skilled workers and technicians has become a significant channel of technical assistance to the area.

The agency has a staff of 4,640 teachers, 207 handicraft instructors and, in Syria, 56 home economic instructresses. Increasing emphasis has been placed on teacher training to raise the standard of instruction in UNRWA schools. Three UNRWA/UNESCO teacher training institutions are in operation, and in 1964 the UNRWA-UNESCO Institute of Education established its programme of in-service training of teachers with the aim of improving the qualifications of teachers in UNRWA schools without interrupting the teaching. UNRWA also awards university scholarships to specially qualified students. During the 1965-66 academic year 621 scholarships were granted to refugees to attend universities. Thus a pool of training and experience is being established which can have long term consequences for the Middle East.

The Arab-Israeli conflict in June 1967 vastly complicated all these efforts in the short run, but awakened hopes that the very decisiveness of the military victory might create a new climate of opinion within which genuine solutions could be sought. The objective must be to help the Arab refugees to become productive and fully accepted citizens. Their greatest need is for political identity, economic security, and social acceptance.

The West, under the leadership of the United States, has been searching for a comprehensive settlement. In President Johnson's five principles for peace of June 19, 1967, the second is "justice for refugees."[21] The Soviet Union and the Arab countries have been adamant in their demand for the withdrawal of the Israeli armies from the occupied territories before any decisions in regard to refugees would be made.

However, on November 22 the Security Council unanimously adopted a British resolution which parallels to a certain degree President Johnson's five principles and which "affirms the necessity for achieving a just settlement of the refugee problem,"[22] and approved the appoint-

---

[21] "Principles for Peace in the Middle East," *Department of State Bulletin*, Vol. VII, No. 1463, July 10, 1967, pp. 33-34. See also Ambassador Goldberg's reiteration of the same points, *ibid.*, p. 49.

[22] For full text, see *New York Times*, November 23, 1967.

ment of a mediator, the Swedish diplomat, Mr. Gunnar Jarring. If a political settlement is reached through his efforts, the refugee problem will be tackled along with it.[23] This will require both the collective responsibility and cooperation of the Israeli and Arab governments. It would mean giving equal political and civil rights to the refugees wherever they reside, a cessation of anti-Israeli propaganda and a freeing of UNRWA to operate according to its own principles and without the political influence of local governments which have hamstrung it in the past.[24]

The way will then be open for massive economic and educational aid to the whole Middle East. A special co-ordinating role in the solution of this problem will inevitably be played by UNRWA with its knowledge and far-reaching experience. Its general educational and vocational programme should be expanded with the aim of integrating the younger generation into the overall programmes of economic development.

These developments can be stimulated both bilaterally and internally. The United Nations and its various agencies can contribute not only to the integration of the refugees in their territories but also to the accelerated modernization of the Arab countries. Such agencies can assist in the solution of the manifold problems of the area within the framework of regional and international planning. Donor countries, both Western and Communist, could then concentrate upon construction rather than relief and makeshift plans.

[23] U.N. General Assembly, Official Records, Twenty-second Session, Supplement No. 1A, A/6701/Add 1, *Introduction to the Annual Report of the Secretary-General on the Work of the Organization 16 June 1966-15 June 1967*, pp. 6-8. See also Don Peretz, "The Arab Refugees: A Changing Problem," *Foreign Affairs*, Vol. 41, No. 3, April 1963, pp. 558-70; and Cecil Hourani, "The Moment of Truth," *Encounter*, Vol. XXIX, No. 5, November 1967, pp. 3-14.

[24] One of the restraining factors on the planning of the UNRWA has been the fact that prior to submission to the General Assembly the Commissioner-General's Annual Reports have had to be discussed by the Advisory Commission, established by the Assembly (Resolution 302 (IV) paragraph 8) that consists of the principal contributing governments (the United States, Great Britain, France, Belgium and Turkey) and of the four host countries.

Legal Status of Arab Refugees

GEORGE J. TOMEH

INTRODUCTION

It is a source of special gratification to participate in a symposium on the Middle East Crisis, in which not only is attention focused on the basic legal issues but in which these issues are considered as a test of international law. If in the course of the last fifty or even the last twenty years the underlying legal principles had been observed—respect for the rights of peoples, the duties and responsibilities of states, and the sanctity of international pledges and undertakings—the recent history of the Middle East would not have been the tragic sequence we have witnessed. Now, in this moment of anxiety and concern experienced by the Arab states, it is understandable that the Arabs should plead unremittingly for their usurped rights. They expect to make this plea in an environment of understanding for the great issues of mankind, the issues of war and peace, of equity, of sovereign and human rights—the environment of our world's faltering steps toward international law and under such law.

I

SCOPE OF THE PROBLEM

The problem of the legal status of the Arab refugees involves the issue of their rights, the basis of these rights, how these rights have been affirmed or denied, what recourse is open to the refugees and what recourse is open to those concerned on their behalf, against the denial of their rights.

A. Definition and Number of Refugees

The Palestinian Arab refugees are primarily those victims of the 1947-48 tragedy, resulting in a mass exodus of the Arabs of Palestine, who have been living in exile since then. These are the *old refugees*. They number 1,344,576 registered with the United Nations Relief and Works Agency for Palestine Refugees (UNRWA) according to the last census, with 722,687 in Jordan, 316,776 in Gaza, 160,723 in Lebanon, and 144,390 in Syria.[1] There is a second generation of refugees, children of parents themselves born after May 1948. These and the inhabitants of border villages who lost their property or their livelihood, or both, but did not lose the bare walls of their homes, have been ineligible for UNRWA assistance, despite ex-

---

* M.A. 1944, American University, Beirut; Ph.D. 1951, Georgetown University. Ambassador Extraordinary and Plenipotentiary, Permanent Representative of the Syrian Arab Republic to the United Nations.
[1] Report of the Commissioner-General of the United Nations Relief and Works Agency, 22 U.N. GAOR, Supp. 13, tables 1 and 2, at 59, 60, U.N. Doc. A/6713 (1967).

treme need.[2] UNRWA relief has always been withheld from 282,000 in villages on the Jordan frontier and in the Gaza Strip. Unquestionably, any Palestinian shut out from his homeland and stripped of money and property falls within the category of refugee. Half a million Palestinian Arabs, however, in addition to the numbers above given, have migrated and are self-supporting in the Arab states, the United States, Canada, South America, and other countries.

A second category of *intermediate refugees* includes over 11,000 Arab inhabitants of the Demilitarized Zones between Israel and the neighboring Arab countries and other areas who were made refugees without provision for help from UNRWA because they were expelled by Israel after July 1, 1952, the deadline for eligibility.[3]

The *new Arab refugees* are the victims of the June 5 war. According to the Report of the Commissioner-General of UNRWA submitted to the Twenty-second Session of the U.N. General Assembly, 234,000 Arabs were refugees from Jordan, Syria, and the Sinai Peninsula following the crisis of June 5, 1967, in addition to 100,000 "old" refugees who fled their refugee camps (where they were registered with UNRWA) when these were overrun by the Israeli army.[4] These numbers are on the increase day by day while the Israelis, systematically as in the past, apply terrorist methods to empty the Arab lands of their Arab inhabitants.

II

RIGHTS OF THE REFUGEES

A. Basic Human Rights

Since the events of the June 5 war, which are still fresh in our minds, the rights of the new refugees have been definitely defined. The Security Council on June 14, 1967 adopted Resolution 237,[5] and the General Assembly reaffirmed it by an overwhelming majority on July 4.[6] The Security Council Resolution specifically calls upon the Government of Israel "to ensure the safety, welfare and security of the inhabitants of the areas where military operations have taken place and to facilitate the return of those inhabitants who have fled the areas since the outbreak of hostilities." Both resolutions requested the Secretary-General to follow their effective implementation and to report thereon. The Secretary-General did report on these matters on September 15, 1967, after having sent a Special Representative, Nils Gussing, to the Middle East.[7] As therein reported and subsequently up until the present time, Israel has persistently refused to implement the two resolutions and

---

[2] Report of the Commissioner-General of the United Nations Relief and Works Agency, 20 U.N. GAOR, Supp. 13, at 4-5, U.N. Doc. A/6013 (1965).

[3] *Id*. at 4.

[4] Report of the Commissioner-General, *supra* note 1, at 11.

[5] 22 U.N. SCOR, 1361st meeting 1 (1967).

[6] G.A. Res. 2252, U.N. GAOR, 5th Emer. Spec. Sess., Supp. 1, at 3, U.N. Doc. A/6798 (1967).

[7] U.N. Doc. A/6797, Sept. 15, 1967.

has adopted further illegitimate measures against the civilian population left in the occupied territories.

We submit it is clear that the Palestinian Arab refugees have certain inalienable rights:

1. the right of sovereignty over Palestine
2. the right to nationality—the Palestinian nationality
3. the right to individual property, together with the right to compensation for property arbitrarily expropriated or taken by force
4. the right of return
5. civil and religious rights
6. the right of visitation to the Holy Places
7. the rights of Palestinians inside Palestine

These rights are not mere claims. There are international documents to validate them—treaties, statements, declarations, pledges, and scores of U.N. resolutions. The denial of these rights constitutes, in essence, what is referred to as the Problem of the Palestine Arab Refugees, which has been and will continue to be the powderkeg of the Middle East. The first such transgression of these rights was the Balfour Declaration,[8] which Henry Cattan has denounced in the following words:

> The Balfour Declaration of 1917 which the Zionists have utilized almost as a document of title for the establishment of a national home in Palestine has never possessed any juridical value. Emanating from the British Government which at no moment possessed any right of sovereignty over Palestine the Balfour Declaration could not validly recognize a right of sovereignty in favour of the Jews because a donor can not dispose of what does not belong to him.[9]

Historically, Syria, an integral part of the Arab world, stretched from the Taurus mountains on the north to Egypt on the south, with no intervening linguistic, natural, or racial boundaries of importance, and unbroken, in the nineteenth century, by any national frontier. The sea on the west, the mountains on the north, the desert south and east gave it unity. But by 1922 this area had been carved up in the interests of power politics. Palestine was one of the fragments, created to implement the Balfour Declaration and satisfy World Zionism. The official report of the Shaw Commission, which the British sent to Palestine in 1929, contained the comment: "Viewed in the light of the history of at least the last six centuries, Palestine is an artificial conception."[10]

In spite of these transgressions, pledges came from the Great Powers to safeguard Arab rights. One could cite the safeguard clause of the Balfour Declaration itself: ". . . it being clearly understood that nothing shall be done which may prejudice the

---

[8] The text is officially quoted in CMD. No. 5479, at 22 (1937).
[9] H. CATTAN, TO WHOM DOES PALESTINE BELONG? 5 (1967).
[10] CMD. No. 3530 (1930), reprinted in J.M.N. JEFFRIES, PALESTINE, THE REALITY 2 (1939).

civil and religious rights of existing non-Jewish communities in Palestine." The Anglo-French Declaration to the Arabs of (undivided) Syria and Mesopotamia on November 7, 1918 is explicit: "The object aimed at by France and Great Britain . . . is . . . the establishment of National Governments and administrations deriving their authority from the initiative and free choice of the indigenous populations."[11]

The King-Crane Commission, which was dispatched to the area by President Wilson so that he could ascertain the wishes of the population, recommended, in its report issued June 29, 1919, "that the unity of Syria be preserved, in accordance with the earnest petition of the great majority of the people of Syria." In the words of the report:

> The Commissioners began their study of Zionism with minds predisposed in its favour, but the actual facts in Palestine coupled with the force of the general principles proclaimed by the Allies and accepted by the Syrians have driven them to the recommendation here made.
>
> . . . .
>
> . . . For "a national home for the Jewish people" is not equivalent to making Palestine into a Jewish State; nor can the erection of such a Jewish State be accomplished without the gravest trespass upon the "civil and religious rights of existing non-Jewish communities in Palestine . . . ."[12]

Article 22 of the Covenant of the League of Nations signed on June 22, 1919 is of particular importance, because it was the basis of what later came to be known as the "A" Mandates over Palestine, Transjordan, Iraq, Lebanon, and Syria: "there should be applied the principle that the well-being and development of such peoples form a sacred trust of civilization and that securities for the performance of this trust should be embodied in this Covenant."[13]

Remembering the rights of the Palestine Arab refugees claimed above, let us very briefly look into the Palestine Mandate itself. Article 5 stipulated that "The Mandatory shall be responsible for seeing that no Palestine territory shall be ceded or leased to, or in any way placed under control of, the Government of any foreign Power"; article 7 stated that "The Administration of Palestine shall be responsible for enacting a nationality law. There shall be included in this law provisions framed so as to facilitate the acquisition of Palestine citizenship by Jews who take up their permanent residence in Palestine."[14]

Specific attention should be paid to article 7, because of the right of the refugees to Palestinian nationality, which has been referred to above. The article is unequivocal that the nationality is the Palestinian nationality, that the Jews who take up their permanent residence in Palestine may take up this nationality. Now this

---

[11] Joint Anglo-French Declaration, Nov. 7, 1918, reprinted in CMD. No. 5479, at 25 (1937).

[12] [1919] 12 FOREIGN REL. U.S. 745, 792 (1949), reprinted in 2 J. HUREWITZ, DIPLOMACY IN THE MIDDLE EAST—A DOCUMENTARY RECORD 1914-1956, at 66, 69, 70 (1956).

[13] 3 TREATIES, CONVENTIONS, INTERNATIONAL ACTS, PROTOCOLS AND AGREEMENTS BETWEEN THE UNITED STATES AND OTHER POWERS 1910-1923, at 3336, 3342 (Redmond ed. 1923).

[14] CMD. No. 1785 (1922), reprinted in 2 J. HUREWITZ, *supra* note 12, at 106, 108.

same nationality is denied to the people who comprised, when that article was formulated, ninety-eight per cent of the total population of Palestine, namely, the Arabs.

The history of Palestine from the institution of the Mandate until 1939 was the history of an Arab people in almost continuous armed rebellion as they saw themselves gradually subjugated by piecemeal conquest which became full conquest in 1947. They saw their right to self-determination being denied and minority status imposed upon them.

Meanwhile, the British government realized the conflict of interests between Arabs and Jews in Palestine. It would be cumbersome to discuss all the British statements of policy issued during this period affirming, time after time, Arab rights under the Mandate. Only two will be mentioned here. First, the Churchill Memorandum or "White Paper" of 1922, which states:

> Unauthorized statements have been made to the effect that the purpose in view is to create a wholly Jewish Palestine. Phrases have been used such as that Palestine is to become "as Jewish as England is English." His Majesty's Government regard any such expectation as impracticable and have no such aim in view. Nor have they at any time contemplated, as appears to be feared by the Arab Delegation, the disappearance or the subordination of the Arabic population, language or culture in Palestine. They would draw attention to the fact that the terms of the Declaration referred to do not contemplate that Palestine as a whole should be converted into a Jewish National Home, but that such a Home should be founded *in Palestine*.[15]

Second, the British statement of May 1939, known as the MacDonald "White Paper," reaffirmed the obligation under the Mandate "to safeguard the civil and religious rights of all the inhabitants of Palestine," and asserted that "His Majesty's Government believe that the framers of the Mandate in which the Balfour Declaration was embodied could not have intended that Palestine should be converted into a Jewish State against the will of the Arab population of the country."[16]

These documents and pledges are not obsolete—not matters of academic interest only. They are ineradicable facts, to be reckoned with in assessing later events, and the denial to the Arab people of Palestine, by the act of the Great Powers in backing Zionist nationality claims and institutions, of their right to self-determination. That was the "original sin." One has to remember that Syria, Lebanon, Transjordan, and Iraq all became independent states. Palestine alone, of the "A" Mandate countries, did not, and this was not a mere accident of history.

Even fifty years ago, according to the pronouncements of the Great Powers, the indissoluble, immutable character of fundamental human rights and the concept

---

[15] BRITISH POLICY IN PALESTINE, CMD. No. 1700, at 18 (1922), reprinted in 2 J. HUREWITZ, *supra* note 12, at 103, 104.

[16] PALESTINE: STATEMENT OF POLICY, CMD. No. 6019, at 2, 3 (1939), reprinted in 2 J. HUREWITZ, *supra* note 12, at 218, 219, 220.

of right could not be altered by any act of man. If legality and ethics have not been dissipated in the interval, we must observe that the Zionist state of Israel, the aggressor in the June 5 war, had dubious rights to be in Palestine in the first place. Small wonder, then, that in the League of Nations and now in the United Nations the Palestine problem with its derivative disputes has been interminably on their agenda.

B. Rights as Recognized by United Nations

We turn now to the present, to see in what manner Israel has acted while the United Nations attempts, in debate and through processes of law, to adjudicate the derivative disputes.

The birth certificate of the State of Israel was General Assembly Resolution 181 of November 29, 1947,[17] recommending the annexed Plan of Partition with Economic Union.[18] Political forces were then at play to secure a favorable vote on Partition, at any cost and by any means. The Arab delegations requested that legal aspects of the Palestine question be referred to the International Court of Justice,[19] as the recourse provided by article 36 of the U.N. Charter, and by article 26 of the Mandate, which provided:

> The Mandatory agrees that if any dispute whatever should arise between the Mandatory and another Member of the League of Nations relating to the interpretation or the application of the provisions of the mandate, such dispute, if it cannot be settled by negotiation, shall be submitted to the Permanent Court of International Justice . . . .

It should be noted that Egypt and Iraq, which were among the sponsors of this request, had been members of the League of Nations, which made the provision just quoted unequivocal in its application. When the most important of these requests for adjudication was voted on, however, the count was 20 for, 21 against.[20] One vote decided the fate of Palestine.

This same birth certificate outlined the provisions of the declaration of independence of Israel. Article 10 of Part I of the Plan of Partition stipulated that "The Constituent Assembly of each State [*i.e.*, the proposed Jewish and Arab states] shall draft a democratic constitution for its State and choose a provisional government to succeed the Provisional Council of Government appointed by the [U.N. Palestine] Commission." The constitution, according to paragraph (d) of this article, was to guarantee "equal and non-discriminatory rights in civil, political, economic and religious matters and the enjoyment of human rights and fundamental freedoms."

---

[17] 2 U.N. GAOR, Resolutions, at 131 (1947).

[18] *Id.* at 132.

[19] 2 U.N. GAOR, Ad Hoc Comm. on the Palestinian Question 299-300 (1947).

[20] *Id.* at 203.

On May 14, 1948 Count Folke Bernadotte was appointed Mediator[21] pursuant to a resolution of the General Assembly.[22] In his report to the Third Session of the General Assembly, he stated:

> 6. [N]o settlement can be just and complete if recognition is not accorded to the right of the Arab refugee to return to the home from which he has been dislodged by the hazards and strategy of the armed conflict between Arabs and Jews in Palestine. The majority of these refugees have come from territory which, under the Assembly resolution of 29 November, was to be included in the Jewish State. . . . It would be an offence against the principles of elemental justice if these innocent victims of the conflict were denied the right to return to their homes while Jewish immigrants flow into Palestine, and, indeed, at least offer the threat of permanent replacement of the Arab refugees who have been rooted in the land for centuries.[23]

Obviously the Zionists, who wanted a state as Jewish as England is English, could not have kept the Arabs in their state, since they would have constituted a majority in that state. Count Bernadotte goes on to affirm the large-scale looting, pillaging, plundering, and the destruction of villages without apparent military necessity. He states further: "The liability of the Provisional Government of Israel to restore private property to its Arab owners and to indemnify those owners for property wantonly destroyed is clear, irrespective of any indemnities which the Provisional Government may claim from the Arab States."[24]

But Count Bernadotte was assassinated, with one of his aides, in September 1948, in the holy city of Jerusalem, and the Security Council could only express shock at the "cowardly act" of a "criminal group of terrorists."[25] A month later the Security Council noted with concern "that the Provisional Government of Israel has to date submitted no report to the Security Council or to the Acting Mediator regarding the progress of the investigation into the assassinations," and reminded ". . . the Governments and authorities concerned that all the obligations and responsibilities set forth are to be discharged fully and in good faith."[26]

On December 11, 1948 the United Nations General Assembly adopted Resolution 194, paragraph 11 of which

> . . . resolves that the refugees wishing to return to their homes and live at peace with their neighbors should be permitted to do so at the earliest practicable date, and that compensation should be paid for the property of those choosing not to return and for loss of or damage to property which, under principles of international law or in equity, should be made good by the governments or authorities responsible.[27]

---

[21] 3 U.N. SCOR, 299th meeting 4 (1948).

[22] G.A. Res. 186, U.N. GAOR, 2d Spec. Sess., Supp. 2, at 5 (1948).

[23] Progress Report of the United Nations Mediator on Palestine, 3 U.N. GAOR, Supp. 11, at 14, U.N. Doc. A/648 (1948).

[24] Id.

[25] S.C. Res. 57 (1948).

[26] S.C. Res. 59 (1948).

[27] 3 U.N. GAOR, Resolutions, at 21, 24 (1948).

The same resolution established a Conciliation Commission with the purpose of implementing the above-quoted paragraph.

On May 11, 1949, the General Assembly voted to accept Israel as a member of the United Nations. Paragraph 4 of the preamble to this resolution took note of "the declaration by the State of Israel that it 'unreservedly accepts the obligations of the United Nations Charter and undertakes to honour them from the day when it becomes a Member of the United Nations.' "[28]

On May 12, 1949, under the auspices of the U.N. Conciliation Commission, the Lausanne Protocol was signed.[29] In the text it is stated that

> The United Nations Conciliation Commission for Palestine, anxious to achieve as quickly as possible the objectives of the General Assembly resolution of December 11, 1948, regarding refugees, the respect for their rights and the preservation of their property, as well as territorial and other questions, has proposed to the delegation of Israel and to the delegations of the Arab States that the "working documents" attached hereto be taken as basis for discussion with the Commission.[30]

To this document was annexed a map on which were indicated the boundaries defined in the General Assembly Resolution 181 (II) of November 29, 1947, which was taken as the basis of discussion with the Commission.[31]

What took place later is described by the Conciliation Commission in paragraph 23 of the Third Progress Report: "The signing of the Protocol of 12 May 1949 provided both a starting-point and framework for the discussion of territorial questions."[32] The delegation of Israel submitted proposals regarding the territorial questions, demanding that the international frontiers of Mandatory Palestine be considered the frontiers of Israel. When the Arab delegations protested that these proposals constituted a repudiation by Israel of the terms of the Protocol signed on May 12, the Israeli delegation replied that "it could not accept a certain proportionate distribution of territory agreed upon in 1947 as a criterion for a territorial settlement in present circumstances."[33]

When the Israeli army stands where it stands today, in occupied territories of three Arab states, members of the United Nations, and makes the withdrawal of its troops conditional on having "secure and agreed upon borders," one can, ironically, see how history repeats itself.

---

[28] G.A. Res. 273, 3 U.N. GAOR, pt. 2, Resolutions, at 18 (1949). The quoted words are those of the Foreign Minister on behalf of the Israeli State Council. 3 U.N. SCOR, Supp. Dec. 1948, at 118, U.N. Doc. S/1093 (1948).

[29] Third Progress Report of the Palestine Conciliation Commission, 4 U.N. GAOR, Ad Hoc Pol. Comm., Annex, vol. II, at 6, U.N. Doc. A/927 (1949).

[30] Id. at 9.

[31] G.A. Res. 181, *supra* note 17, at 150.

[32] Third Progress Report of the Palestine Conciliation Commission, *supra* note 29, at 7.

[33] Id. at 8.

C. Legal Implications of Paragraph 11 of Resolution 194 of
December 11, 1948

The provisions of pargraph 11, sub-paragraph 1, of the General Assembly Reso-lution 194 of December 11, 1948 affirm the right of the refugees to return to their homes and their right to compensation, classified as compensation to refugees *not* choosing to return, and compensation to refugees for loss of or damage to property.[34] These rights, according to paragraph 11, are to be implemented "under principles of international law or in equity." What is involved here?

In a working paper prepared by the Legal Department of the U.N. Secretariat in March 1950 for the guidance of the Conciliation Commission on the implementation of paragraph 11 of Resolution 194,[35] the principles of repatriation and compensation were dealt with at length and many precedents cited, from the periods before and after the Second World War. It points out that in the former Axis and Axis-occupied countries—France, Rumania, Italy, Bulgaria, Czechoslovakia, Holland, and Yugoslavia—various laws were passed between November 1944 and May 1945 for restitution or compensation to the victims of Nazi action. In the United States occupied zone of Germany a General Claims law was passed in 1949 for restitution to those Nazi victims who had "suffered damage to life and limb, health, liberty, possessions, property or economic advancement."

It further points out that during the Second World War the Institute of Jewish Affairs of the World Jewish Congress took up the question of compensation for Jewish refugees and in 1944 published a book, *Indemnities and Reparations*, by Nehemiah Robinson.[36] The thesis was that great injustice would result from follow-ing the general rule that states may seek indemnification from foreign nations only on behalf of their own citizens who were also their citizens at the time the injury occurred. Victims of Axis countries who later acquired the citizenship of these states or merely became residents there would be excluded. As to victims who remained in or would be willing to return to their homeland, the author makes a strong case that the United Nations must intervene on their behalf.

The working paper also refers to a refugee problem of comparatively recent date which presents some similarity with the problem of the Palestine refugees:

> The Pakistan and India Governments agreed on the principle that the owner-ship of refugees' property, movable as well as immovable, should remain vested in the refugees. Custodians were appointed to look after and manage such property on behalf of the owners. Similarly, registrars of claims were appointed and in-structed to make records of the property left behind by the evacuees.[37]

---

[34] 3 U.N. GAOR, Resolutions, at 21, 24 (1948).

[35] Historical Survey of Efforts of the United Nations Conciliation Commission for Palestine to Secure Implementation of Paragraph 11 of G.A. Res. 194(III), U.N. Doc. A/AC.25/W81/Rev. 2 (1961).

[36] N. ROBINSON, INDEMNITIES AND REPARATIONS (1944).

[37] Historical Survey of Efforts, *supra* note 35.

In contrast to all this, and the fact that Israeli, Zionist and Jewish organizations and Jewish individuals have had over a billion dollars in reparations from Germany,[38] we find Israeli legislation providing for confiscation of lands of "absentee" Arab owners. In three laws passed in 1948-49 (the Abandoned Areas Ordinance, the Absentee Property Regulations, and the Emergency Cultivation of Waste Lands Regulations) an "absentee" is defined as any person who was, on or after November 29, 1947 (the date of the General Assembly Resolution concerning partition of Palestine)—

(a) a citizen or subject of any of the Arab states
(b) in any of these states, for any length of time
(c) in any part of Palestine outside the Israeli-occupied area
(d) in any place other than his habitual residence, even if such place as well as his habitual abode were within Israeli-occupied territory.[39]

A conquered, surrendered, or deserted area was declared to be abandoned and sold by the Israeli Custodian to a Development Authority.[40]

Enquiry into this matter from the standpoint of the ownership of land in Palestine shows the unbelievable dimensions and grave iniquity of the liquidation of Arab rights and interests. It is established by official statistics of the Mandatory Government of Palestine,[41] submitted to the United Nations in 1947, that Jewish property in Palestine did not exceed a proportion of 5.66 per cent of the total area of the country. The document contains a breakdown of the areas owned in each district. In 1948, in violation of the territorial limits proposed by the U.N. Partition Resolution, and in 1949, in violation of the armistice agreements concluded with the neighboring countries, Israel seized another 1,400 square miles of the territory of Palestine, gaining control over seventy-one per cent of the total area of the country. Under the Israeli legislation referred to, the Israeli authorities have legalized the seizure of Arab refugee property and assets and provided for the subsequent wholesale confiscation of further property belonging to Arabs, whether refugees or not.

For twenty years now the Conciliation Commission has failed to secure legitimate Arab rights. Nineteen resolutions passed from 1949 up till now, affirming and reaffirming those rights, regretting or deploring the non-implementation by Israel of previous resolutions, have been completely disregarded.

As to the rights of the "intermediate" refugees, article V of the General Armistice Agreement with Syria provided for the "return of civilians to villages and settlements in the Demilitarized Zone"[42] and Security Council resolutions have urged

---

[38] Selzer, *The Diplomacy of Atonement: Germany, Israel and the Jews*, ISSUES, Summer 1967, at 23.

[39] Absentees' Property Law, [1950] Laws of the State of Israel, vol. 4, p. 68; reprinted in FUNDAMENTAL LAWS OF THE STATE OF ISRAEL 129 (J. Badi ed. 1961).

[40] See S. HADAWI, PALESTINE, LOSS OF A HERITAGE 52 (1963).

[41] 2 U.N. GAOR, Ad Hoc Comm. on the Palestinian Question, Annex 25, at 270, 292-93; Appendix VI, at 307, U.N. Doc. A/AC.14/32 (1947).

[42] 4 U.N. SCOR, Spec. Supp. 2, at 4 (1949).

on Israel their return forthwith. We get a picture of the situation from the Secretary-General's Report on the Present Status of the Demilitarized Zone Set Up by the General Armistice Agreement Between Israel and Syria:

> 16. The part of the central sector of the D/Zone which is on the eastern bank of the Jordan River is a narrow strip of land, generally controlled by Syria, while the western bank, generally controlled by Israel, is a large area. On the western bank Arab villages have been demolished, their inhabitants evacuated. The inhabitants of the villages of Baqqara and Ghanname returned following the Security Council resolution of 18 May 1951 (S/2517). They were later (on 30 October 1956) forced to cross into Syria where they are still living. Their lands on the western bank of the river, and Khoury Farm in the same area, are cultivated by Israel nationals.[43]

The question duly arises here: Does the rule of force or a political decision terminate a legal right? Does conquest give the conqueror legal title to an occupied territory? Philip Marshal Brown has given one answer: "Military occupation by itself does not confer title or extinguish a nation. . . . [S]o long as a people do not accept military conquest; so long as they can manifest, in one way or another, their inalterable will to regain freedom, their sovereignty even though flouted, restricted, and sent in exile still persists."[44]

III

RESPONSIBILITY FOR INITIATION OF HOSTILITIES

Now, it is widely assumed that the Arabs themselves were responsible for the misfortunes that befell them, because they were the ones who defied the U.N. Partition Resolution, and that all went peacefully in Palestine from November 29, 1947 until May 14, 1948, when the establishment of Israel was declared, with the Arabs attacking the new state. It has been concluded that the Arabs brought about the loss of their own rights through their aggression. Such is not the case. Emphasis on the real facts of the history of this period is not only relevant but necessary in the assessment of Arab claims.

To put the matter in perspective, I cite two official communications, one a letter sent by Brigadier General Patrick J. Hurley, Personal Representative of President Roosevelt, to the President from Cairo on May 5, 1943:[45]

> For its part, the Zionist organization in Palestine has indicated its commitment to an enlarged program for (1) a sovereign Jewish State which would embrace Palestine and probably Transjordania, (2) an eventual transfer of the Arab population from Palestine to Iraq, and (3) Jewish leadership for the whole Middle East in the fields of economic development and control.

---

[43] U.N. Doc. S/7573, at 4-5, Nov. 2, 1966.

[44] Brown, *Sovereignty in Exile*, 35 AM. J. INT'L L. 666, 667 (1941).

[45] Letter from Brig. Gen. Patrick Hurley to President Roosevelt, [1943] 4 FOREIGN REL. U.S. 776, 777 (1964).

The other was a telegram sent from Cairo by U.S. Minister Kirk in Egypt to the Secretary of State on January 23, 1943:

> On the Jewish side I have found Zionist officials of the Jewish Agency uncompromisingly outspoken in their determination that Palestine at end of this war shall become not merely a national home for the Jews, but a Jewish state despite any opposition from the 1,000,000 Arabs living there. In various ways main result of many of their efforts seems to be to goad Palestinian Arabs into breaking informal truce that has existed since war began. . . .
>
> It is no secret that the Hagana, their secret Jewish military organization, has plans fully made and is well equipped not only with small arms, but also with tommy-guns and machine guns many of them purchased from Vichy French forces in Syria and smuggled into Palestine during past 2 years.[46]

As to what really happened, rather than the propagandized version, we have the aid of I. F. Stone, American author of *Underground to Palestine* and *This is Israel*, who tells us that he

> first arrived in Palestine on Balfour Day, Nov. 2, 1945, the day the Haganah blew up bridges and watch towers to begin its struggle against the British and immigration restrictions. The following spring I was the first newspaperman to travel with illegal Jewish immigrants from the Polish-Czech border through the British blockade. In 1947 I celebrated Passover in the British detention camps in Cyprus and in 1948 I covered the Arab-Jewish war.[47]

In an article published August 3, 1967 he goes on to say:

> Jewish terrorism, not only by the Irgun, in such savage massacres as Deir Yassin, but in milder form by the Haganah, itself "encouraged" Arabs to leave areas the Jews wished to take over for strategic or demographic reasons. They tried to make as much of Israel as free of Arabs as possible.[48]

He also points out that:

> The myth that the Arab refugees fled because the Arab radios urged them to do so was analyzed by Erskine B. Childers in the London *Spectator* May 12, 1961. An examination of British and U.S. radio monitoring records turned up no such appeals and "even orders to the civilians of Palestine, to stay put."[49]

Irrefutable proof that the Zionists were the first aggressors in the war of 1947-48 is given by Menachem Begin, the   perpetrator of the Deir Yassin massacre, in his book *The Revolt*.[50] He tells us how the Haganah, the recognized "defense" force of the Zionist establishment in Palestine, having gone over to the principle of "offensive defense," joined forces with the Irgun, the terrorist group, and of the

---

[46] Letter from Minister Kirk to Secretary of State, [1943] 4 FOREIGN REL. U.S. 747-48 (1964).

[47] I.F. Stone, in review of special issue of *Les Temps Moderne* entitled *Le Conflict Israélo-Arabe*, The New York Review of Books, Aug. 3, 1967, at 12, col. 4.

[48] *Id*. at 10, col. 3.

[49] *Id*. at 10, col. 2.

[50] M. BEGIN, THE REVOLT, STORY OF THE IRGUN (1951).

signing of a secret agreement between the Jewish Agency, as the supreme authority over the Haganah, and the Irgun Zvai Leumi for attack on the Arabs. This was in January 1948, while the duly constituted Commission of the United Nations was still seeking a peaceful implementation of the General Assembly's recommendation. In a chapter entitled "The Conquest of Jaffa" he states:

> In the months preceding the Arab invasion . . . we continued to make sallies into the Arab area. In the early days of 1948, we were explaining to our officers and men, however, that this was not enough. Attacks of this nature carried out by any Jewish forces were indeed of great psychological importance; and their military effect, to the extent that they widened the Arab front and forced the enemies on to the defensive, was not without value. But it was clear to us that even most daring sallies carried out by partisan troops would never be able to decide the issue. Our hope lay in gaining control of territory.
>
> At the end of January, 1948, at a meeting of the Command of the Irgun in which the Planning Section participated, we outlined four strategic objectives: (1) Jerusalem; (2) Jaffa; (3) the Lydda-Ramleh plain; and (4) the Triangle.[51]

(According to the Partition plan, Jerusalem was to be a *corpus separatum*, and Jaffa was definitely to be part of the Arab state.) On April 25, 1948 (three weeks before the alleged Arab initiation of hostilities), Begin addressed his troops, en route to Jaffa: "Men of the Irgun! We are going out to conquer Jaffa. We are going into one of the decisive battles for the independence of Israel."[52] After an account of the battle, he assures us that "The conquest of Jaffa was one of the fateful events in the Hebrew war of independence."[53]

Thus the Palestine refugee problem originated, for Jaffa was practically all Arab in population. Before any Arab soldier set foot on the soil of Palestine, 400,000 Arabs had fled their Palestinian homeland in terror.

Of course, the Zionists had their own view of activities such as this, expressed by a member of the Haganah, Munya M. Mardor (now Director-General of the Israel Weapons Research and Development Authority) in a book entitled *Haganah*.[54] He tells of secret arms purchases in foreign countries: "We were conspirators, outside the law, and yet obeying what to us was a higher law."[55]

In the name of compromise, realism, and *fait accompli*, the Arabs are asked to recognize these achievements "outside the law" and admit the "conspirators" as lawful and legal successors to their land and rights.

Conclusion

It must have become clear that the legal imperatives affirming Arab rights in Palestine are firm and unequivocal, but that Israel and World Zionism have been

---

[51] *Id.* at 348.
[52] *Id.* at 354.
[53] *Id.* at 371.
[54] M. Mardor, Haganah (1957).
[55] *Id.* at 230.

able to flout them and disregard not only all international safeguards and guarantees prior to 1947, but also the scores of U.N. resolutions concerning Arab rights.

The argument has time and again been made that the Arabs should accept the *fait accompli* established by Israel, but between 1947 and today there has been not one but several *fait accompli* to subvert Arab rights.

The Arabs prefer to see not only what is, but what ought to be and what might be, and agree with U.S. Secretary of Labor W. Willard Wirtz when he told the Labor Ministers' Conference in Venezuela: "Change is our ally, and we face squarely those who fight change because the status quo has been good to them. The divine right of the successful is as false a notion as the divine right of kings."[56]

Does a *fait accompli* constitute a norm for international law and behavior—since we are dealing with basic legal considerations? We hold, with the two American legal authorities quoted below, that no *fait accompli* can establish a precedent to be accepted in international law so long as the victims of the *fait accompli* object to it.

In 1954 the Legal Adviser of the State Department, Mr. Herman Phleger, made this statement:

> International law has been defined as those rules for international conduct which have met general acceptance among the community of nations . . . .
>
> . . . .
>
> But there is such a thing as international law. It has had a long and honorable, though chequered, career. I predict that it will play an even more important part in world affairs in the future than it has in the past. Indeed, in this rapidly shrinking world, it becomes increasingly evident that our survival may depend upon our success in substituting the rule of law for the rule of force.[57]

From the American Law Institute comes a *Restatement of the Foreign Relations Law of the United States,* which contains the following:

> *e. Objection to practice as means of preventing its acceptance as rule of law.* The growth of practice into a rule of international law depends on the degree of its acceptance by the international community. If a state initiates a practice for which there is no precedent in international law, the fact that other states do not object to it is significant evidence that they do not regard it as illegal. If this practice becomes more general without objections from other states, the practice may give rise to a rule of international law. Because failure to object to practice may amount to recognition of it, the objection by a state to a practice of another is an important means of preventing or controlling in some degree the development of rules of international law.[58]

The *fait accompli* of Israel, doing away with Arab rights, has been objected to, not only by the Arab states, but by the majority of Members of the United Nations, who throughout twenty years past have affirmed and reaffirmed the rights of Arab

---

[56] N.Y. Times, May 11, 1966, at 18, col. 2.

[57] 1 M. WHITEMAN, DIGEST OF INTERNATIONAL LAW 2 (1963).

[58] RESTATEMENT (SECOND) OF FOREIGN RELATIONS LAW OF THE UNITED STATES § 1, comment *e* (1965).

refugees for return or compensation. The United States Government has voted consistently in favor of those resolutions, while regrettably opposing draft resolutions designed to safeguard Arab property rights.

The most succinct and telling objection to Israel's *fait accompli* that I call to mind is implicit in the words of Secretary-General U Thant, in his Annual Report to the 22nd Session of the General Assembly: "People everywhere, and this certainly applies to the Palestinian refugees, have a natural right to be in their homeland and to have a future."[59]

---

[59] 22 U.N. GAOR, Supp. 1A, at 7, U.N. Doc. A/6701/Add. 1 (1967).

II. UNDERLYING ISSUES

B. *Freedom of Navigation Through the Strait of Tiran, the Gulf of Aqaba, and the Suez Canal*

A Consideration of the Legal Status
of the Gulf of Aqaba

CHARLES B. SELAK, JR.

Of the District of Columbia Bar *

The status under international law of the Gulf of Aqaba has come to be a matter of concern not only to the several littoral states, but also to the international community. The basic issue, that of freedom of navigation in this arm of the Red Sea, has been brought into focus as a result of restrictive efforts of several of the coastal states with respect to Israeli shipping, for Arab-Israeli hostility has given political, strategic, commercial and even religious significance to a water area which, until recently, had attracted little attention. Without taking a position on the Palestine question, which remains essentially political, it is intended herein to describe the background of the Gulf of Aqaba problem, to explain the several points of view held with respect to the Gulf's status, and to consider what principles of international law may be applicable to this water area and the entrances thereto.

The Gulf of Aqaba is the eastern of two arms into which the Sinai Peninsula separates the Red Sea at its northern extremity; the western arm is the Gulf of Suez, which leads into the Suez Canal. The Gulf of Aqaba is somewhat over one hundred miles in length, and varies in width between three miles on the narrow bay at its northern end and seventeen miles at its widest point. The mouth—from Sinai Peninsula headland to Arabian Peninsula headland—is approximately nine miles in width. A valve-shaped island at the entrance, however, Tiran Island, further narrows the possibility of access to the Gulf, and, in fact, creates two entrances thereto. The western and principal entrance passes between Tiran Island and the Sinai Peninsula shore. It is approximately four miles in breadth, and has two channels, Enterprise Passage and Grafton Passage. The former, which lies close to the Sinai Peninsula coast, is the principal shipping channel into the Gulf, and the only channel which can be navigated safely by vessels of substantial size. Grafton Passage, separated from Enterprise Passage by a series of reefs, lies close to Tiran Island. Another island, Sanafir, is situated two miles east of Tiran. The eastern entrance to the Gulf passes between the two islands and the Arabian mainland, and appears seldom to be used, since reefs therein render navigation difficult except for small boats. The narrow belt of water between the two islands appears also to be non-navigable because of reefs. References in public statements have

* The views expressed herein are the personal views of the author. He wishes to express his thanks to Judge Jasper Y. Brinton, formerly President of the Court of Appeals of the Mixed Courts of Egypt, for material furnished and valuable suggestions made in connection with the article's preparation.

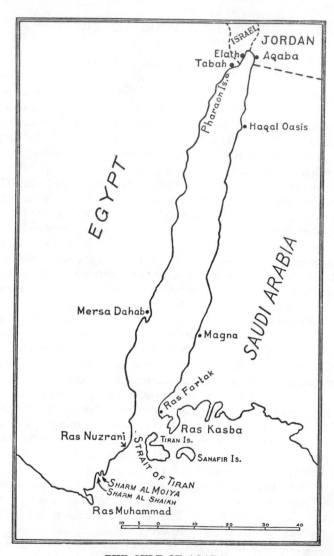

THE GULF OF AQABA

been made both to the Strait of Tiran and to the Straits of Tiran. It is unclear which designation is correct. However, the first obviously refers to the western and principal entrance, and the second to both entrances.

For over a thousand years the Gulf has been surrounded by Arab territories. By approximately 700 A.D. the Arab conquest of a large part of the area known today as the Middle East had been completed, and from that time until approximately 1517, when the Arab territories surrounding the Gulf were brought under the political control of the Ottoman Empire, the Gulf apparently was an exclusively Arab water area. From 1517 until the end of World War I the Gulf was controlled by the Empire.[1] During that long period the question of the Gulf's status does not appear to have arisen. When, however, during the Middle Ages a Crusader fleet made an incursion into the Gulf and the Red Sea from its base at the northern end of the Gulf, the whole Muslim world was shocked at the invasion of water areas which constituted a gateway of the pilgrims to the Islamic Holy Cities of Mecca and Medina.[2]

Today, four coastal states enclose the Gulf—the United Arab Republic,[3] Saudi Arabia, Jordan [for a short time a member of the Arab Union of Iraq and Jordan],[4] and Israel. Egypt, one of the partners constituting the United Arab Republic, is sovereign of the western or Sinai Peninsula coast, and Saudi Arabia of the eastern coast. Jordan and Israel each possess a small coastal strip at the very head of the Gulf. The islands of Tiran and Sanafir were under Egyptian occupation at the beginning of the Israeli drive against Egypt which commenced on October 29, 1956. Neither Egypt (UAR), Saudi Arabia, nor Jordan maintains diplomatic relations with Israel, nor, in fact, have any of them recognized its existence since its establishment in the spring of 1948.

The ancient port of Aqaba fell into decay during the Middle Ages, but

---

[1] See H. L. Hoskins, The Middle East 99 (N. Y., 1954); George Stitt, A Prince of Arabia 16 (London, 1948); George Antonius, The Arab Awakening 19 (Philadelphia, 1938); and H. J. Liebesny, "International Relations of Arabia," 1 Middle East Journal 149 (1947).

[2] See 2 Steven Runciman, A History of the Crusades 436–437 (Cambridge University Press, 1952).

[3] The union of Egypt and Syria to form the United Arab Republic was proclaimed officially on Feb. 21, 1958. N. Y. Herald Tribune (European ed.), Feb. 26, 1958, p. 2. Text of Proclamation in Egyptian Economic and Political Review, March, 1958, p. 26; for Provisional Constitution, see ibid., April, 1958, p. 23, and 13 Comunità Internazionale 409 (1958). Egypt only has a coastline on the Gulf.

[4] On March 19, 1958, Iraq and Jordan announced the terms of their new federal constitution, which recognizes King Faisal of Iraq as the senior monarch of the Arab Union. New York Herald Tribune (European ed.), March 20, 1958, p. 2. Text of Constitution in 13 Comunità Internazionale 413 (1958).

On May 27, 1958, King Faisal of Iraq was sworn in as President of the Arab Union when the Federal Parliament held its first session in Amman, Jordan. Washington Post and Times Herald, May 28, 1958, p. A5. On Aug. 2, 1958, King Husayn of Jordan announced the formal dissolution of the Arab Union of Iraq and Jordan. The Union had been de facto terminated by the Iraqi revolt of July 14, 1958. See New York Times, Aug. 3, 1958, pp. 1 and 10.

sustained a revival during the early part of the nineteenth century, and, in 1841, was recognized by the Ottoman Government as belonging, with the Sinai Peninsula, to Egypt because of its regular use by Egyptian pilgrims proceeding overland to Mecca and Medina. In 1892, after Egyptian pilgrims began to use the sea route to the Muslim Holy Places, the Ottoman Empire resumed possession of Aqaba. In 1902 the Turks occupied the neighboring post of Tabah, supposed to be Solomon's ancient port of Ezion-Geber.[5] Great Britain on behalf of Egypt objected to the occupation, and the Turks withdrew.[6] The frontier between Egypt, nominally an Ottoman province, but in effect a British protectorate since 1882,[7] and the area which later became the Palestine Mandate, was delimited by the agreement signed and exchanged at Rafah on October 1, 1906, between the Commissioners of the Turkish Sultanate and the Commissioners of the Egyptian Khedivate, concerning the fixing of a Separating Administrative Line between the Vilayet of Hejaz and Governorate of Jerusalem and the Sinai Peninsula. The frontier was fixed beginning at Umm Rash Rash or Ras Tabah on the western shore of the Gulf of Aqaba (approximately one mile northeast of the town of Tabah) and extending in a general north northwesterly direction to the Mediterranean Sea, passing 390 meters (approximately 426 yards) southwest of Bir Rafah (in the present Gaza Strip area) near that sea. Boundary pillars were erected at intervals along the frontier.[8] This boundary has remained unchanged since 1906, although it has long ceased to be a mere administrative boundary between two units of the Ottoman Empire. It is the same as that referred to as the Egyptian frontier in the Rhodes General Armistice Agreement of February 24, 1949, between Egypt and Israel.[9] The Sinai Peninsula thus was included within the territory of Egypt. Since Egypt achieved its formal independence in 1922,[10] it clearly has been sovereign

[5] Background paper on the Gulf of Aqaba, by the Ministry of Foreign Affairs of Israel (Jerusalem, May, 1956), p. 5.

[6] Article on the Gulf of Aqaba in Encyclopedia Britannica, Vol. 2 (14th ed.).

[7] Hoskins, op. cit., at p. 61, states that Egypt's status as a British protectorate "existed in most essentials since 1877 and in all since 1914." The Anglo-Egyptian agreement of Sept. 7, 1877, "to all intents envisaged Great Britain as the protector of Egyptian territorial interests." Ibid., p. 60. It was in 1882, however, that British troops actually occupied Egypt. See C. B. Selak, Jr., "The Suez Canal Base Agreement of 1954," 49 A.J.I.L. 487–505 at 490 (1955). On Dec. 18, 1914, Great Britain declared the abolition of Ottoman suzerainty over Egypt (108 Brit. and For. State Papers 185 (1914-Part II)), an act accepted retroactively to Nov. 5, 1914, by the Turkish Republic, successor state to the Ottoman Empire, through the Treaty of Lausanne of July 23, 1923 (117 ibid. 543–591 at 549 (1923)).

[8] For text of agreement, see 99 ibid. 482–484 (1905–1906).

[9] U.N. Security Council, 4th Year, Official Records, Spec. Supp. No. 3; 6 Revue Egyptienne de Droit International 299–308 (1950); J. C. Hurewitz, Diplomacy in the Near and Middle East, Vol. II, pp. 299–304 (Princeton, 1956); Israeli Foreign Ministry Background Paper on Gulf of Aqaba, op. cit., pp. 3–6.

[10] Great Britain and Egypt, 1914–1951, Royal Inst. of Int. Affairs, Info. Papers No. 19, pp. 8–9 (London, 1952).

of the western shore (Sinai Peninsula coast) of the Gulf of Aqaba from Ras Tabah southwards.[11]

The Hejaz's independence of the Ottoman Empire was recognized formally on December 10, 1916, by the United Kingdom, France and Russia, following the "Arab Revolt" against the Turks. In the summer of 1917 Colonel T.E. Lawrence and the Hejaz Army captured Aqaba. The Treaty of San Remo of April 25, 1920, gave the United Kingdom an "A" Mandate for Palestine, which included Trans-Jordan.[12] In 1922 the Palestine Mandate was divided into two parts, Palestine proper and the Amirate of Trans-Jordan, and Abdullah, son of King Husayn of the Hejaz, became Amir of Trans-Jordan. No effort was made at that time to define the border between Trans-Jordan and the Hejaz, since the Hashemite family ruled both areas. When King Husayn was forced to abdicate in 1924 as a result of the invasion of the Hejaz by the Saudi dynasty of Nejd, he took refuge in the Aqaba region. In July, 1925, a Saudi attack on the area being anticipated, Great Britain, as the Mandatory Power, ejected King Husayn, who retired to Cyprus. Britain then began to administer the Aqaba-Ma'an area as a part of Trans-Jordan.[13]

As of January 8, 1926, the Sa'ud dynasty incorporated the Hejaz into its dominions, and by the Treaty of Jidda of May 20, 1927,[14] the British Government recognized the complete and absolute independence of His Majesty the King of the Hejaz and Nejd and its Dependencies. As of September 2, 1932, King 'Abd al-Aziz ibn Sa'ud changed the name of his consolidated domain to the Kingdom of Saudi Arabia, the Arabia of the Sa'uds.

A dispute regarding the border between Trans-Jordan and the Hejaz made it expedient to append an exchange of notes to the Treaty of Jidda to provide that the frontier should run as follows:

[11] A contrary view is expressed by L. M. Bloomfield, Egypt, Israel and the Gulf of Aqaba in International Law (Toronto, Canada, 1957). Bloomfield asserts that Turkey never recognized that an area south of a line drawn from Tabah to Suez, the South Sinai Peninsula, formed a part of Egypt, and states that Egypt was merely given administrative rights over this area by the 1906 agreement (p. 139). He concludes (p. 164) that therefore Egypt "does not enjoy territorial water rights in the Gulf of Aqaba." Although he admits that neither Turkey nor the United Kingdom have made claims with respect to this area in recent times, he asserts that "this does not necessarily imply a renunciation in International Law of such claim, if it exists." (p. 142.) He suggests a U.N. trusteeship over this area to assure the maintenance of the international character of the Strait of Tiran and the Gulf of Aqaba (p. 165).

Inasmuch as the agreement of 1906 concerned only the fixing of an administrative line between Egypt, then a part of Turkey, and Palestine, also a part of Turkey, it is difficult to see why a distinction should be made between the northern and southern parts of the Sinai Peninsula. In any event, Egypt since 1922 appears to have exercised undisputed sovereignty over the whole peninsula.

[12] Stewart Perowne, The One Remains 10 (London, 1954).

[13] Article on Gulf of Aqaba in Encyclopedia Britannica, Vol. 2 (14th ed.).

[14] 11 C. V. Aitchison, A Collection of Treaties, Engagements and Sanads 189 and 227 (5th ed., Delhi, 1933). On the birth of Saudi Arabia, see Benoist-Mechin, Ibn Saud, ou La Naissance d'un Royaume (Paris, 1955), trans. into English by Denis Weaver, under the title, Arabian Destiny (London, 1957).

From the intersection of meridian 38°E and parallel 29°35'N to a point on the Hejaz Railway two miles south of Mudawwara. From this point it proceeds in a straight line to a point on the Gulf of Aqaba two miles south of the town of Aqaba.[15]

This line purported to be only a *de facto* administrative frontier, and not a definitive boundary, since the exchange of notes referred to "favorable circumstances [which] will permit a final settlement of this question."[16] King 'Abd al-Aziz, who regarded the incorporation of the Aqaba-Ma'an area into Trans-Jordan as a usurpation of territory which rightfully belonged to the Hejaz, insisted upon this qualification.

The Treaty of 1927 was extended by exchanges of notes in 1936 and again in 1943, without reference to a final boundary settlement between Trans-Jordan and Saudi Arabia. There has been no boundary settlement since Trans-Jordan on March 22, 1946, ceased to have mandate status. At the present time Saudi Arabia clearly is sovereign of the eastern littoral of the Gulf of Aqaba from a point two miles south of the town of Aqaba to the Gulf's entrance.

Jordan and Israel each possess a small coastal strip on the truncated bay at the very head of the Gulf. That of Jordan is approximately four miles in breadth, and that of Israel, five miles in breadth. When in 1922 Palestine proper and Trans-Jordan were separated, the boundary was traced from a point two miles west of the town of Aqaba northward along the Wadi al-Arabah.[17] This boundary was fixed upon in 1949 by the Jordanian-Israeli Mixed Armistice Commission as the Armistice line between Israel's territory of the Negev and the Hashemite Kingdom of Jordan (as Trans-Jordan came to be called as of April 26, 1949).[18] Israel secured control of that part of Palestine known as the Negev, including the five-mile strip on the Gulf of Aqaba, during the hostilities which followed the termination on May 15, 1948, of the British Mandate for Palestine, and the proclamation of the state of Israel at approximately the same time.[19] Israel's port of Elath (Eilat) is situated on this five-mile strip.

---

[15] Aitchison, *op. cit.*, p. 229.

[16] *Ibid.*, p. 230. And see exchange of notes between the United Kingdom and Saudi Arabian governments of Oct. 3, 1943, Treaty Series No. 13 (1947), Cmd. 7064 (British), and 145 Brit. and For. State Papers 157–158 (1943–1945).

[17] A "Memorandum on the Application of the Mandate for Palestine in Trans-Jordan" was approved at Geneva, September 16, 1922, and provided that: "Trans-Jordan . . . comprises all territory lying to the east of a line drawn from a point two miles west of the town of Aqaba on the Gulf of that name up the center of the Wadi al-Arabah, Dead Sea and River Jordan to its junction with the River Yarmuk; thence up the center of that river to the Syrian frontier." League of Nations Official Journal, November, 1922, p. 1390; 17 A.J.I.L. Supp. 172 (1923); 1 Hudson, International Legislation 120–121 (Wash., D. C., 1934).

[18] See Jordanian-Israeli General Armistice Agreement of April 3, 1949, U.N. Doc. S/1302, as corrected April 21, 1949, U.N. Security Council, 4th Year, Official Records, Spec. Supp. No. 1, Art. V, and Map I of Annex I; also U. S. Dept. of State, Documents and State Papers, Vol. I, No. 14 (May, 1949), pp. 806–809, at 807. See also Raphael Patai, The Kingdom of Jordan 48 (Princeton, 1958).

[19] See article by Harry Gilroy, " 'Pearl of Negev' may Earn its Name," in N. Y. Times, April 11, 1954, which refers to Israel's "five mile strip on the Gulf of Aqaba."

With respect to the islands of Tiran and Sanafir, Egyptian Delegate Azmi informed the Security Council on February 15, 1954, that the islands had constituted Egyptian territory since 1906, at the time of the delimitation of the frontier between Egypt and Palestine.[20] Under date of March 31, 1957, however, the Saudi Arabian Government addressed a circular note to the missions of "friendly Governments" in Jidda, which asserted that the islands "are Saudi Arabian property."[21] A memorandum attached to a letter dated April 12, 1957, from the Permanent Representative of Saudi Arabia to the United Nations, addressed to the Secretary General, stated that "these two islands are Saudi Arabian."[22] Egypt does not appear to have questioned this Saudi claim of sovereignty.

The claims of the coastal states of the Gulf with respect to breadth of territorial sea and contiguous zones may be summarized as follows:

(a) *Saudi Arabia:* Territorial Waters Decree of May 28, 1949.

Article 5. The coastal sea of Saudi Arabia lies outside the inland waters of the Kingdom and extends seaward for a distance of *six nautical miles.*

Article 9. With a view to assuring compliance with the laws of the Kingdom relating to security, navigation, and fiscal matters, maritime surveillance may be exercised in a *contiguous zone* outside the coastal sea, extending for a *further distance of six nautical miles* and measured from the base-lines of the coastal sea, provided however, that nothing in this article shall be deemed to apply to the rights of the Kingdom with respect to fishing.[23]

(b) *Egypt:* Territorial Waters Decree of January 15, 1951.

Article 5. Identical with Article 5 of the Saudi decree of May 28, 1949.

Article 9. Identical with Article 9 of the Saudi decree of May 28, 1949, except that after the phrase "extending for a further distance of six nautical miles," it continues, "beyond the six nautical miles measured from the baselines of the coastal sea; but no provision of this article shall affect the rights of the Kingdom of Egypt with respect to fishing."[24]

(c) *Jordan:* Jordan has no outlet to the high seas except the four-mile strip of coast at the port of Aqaba. Fisheries Act No. 25 of December 2, 1943, states, Article 2, that: " 'Transjordan includes that part of the sea which is contiguous to the coast of Transjordan and lies within a distance of three nautical miles from the low-water line."[25]

[20] See Verbatim Record of the 659th Meeting of the Security Council, Doc. S/P.V. 659 (Feb. 15, 1954), p. 53.

[21] Note of 29 Sha'ban 1376, corresponding to March 31, 1957.

[22] See U.N. Doc. A/3575, April 15, 1957, p. 3.

[23] Decree No. 6/4/5/3711, May 28, 1949, Umm al-Qura (Mecca), May 29, 1949; 43 A.J.I.L. Supp. 155 (1949); Laws and Regulations on the Regime of the High Seas, United Nations Legislative Series, Vol. I, p. 89 (N. Y., 1951). Italics added.

[24] Decree of Jan. 15, 1951, Al-Waqayih al-Misriyah (Official Journal), Vol. 78, No. 6, Jan. 18, 1951; Laws and Regulations on the Regime of the High Seas, *op. cit.,* Vol. I, p. 307.

[25] Laws and Regulations on the Regime of the Territorial Sea, United Nations Legislative Series, p. 522 (N. Y., 1957).

(d) *Israel:* Territorial Waters Decree of September 11, 1955, as follows:

The maritime frontier of the State of Israel is placed at a distance of *six nautical miles* from the coast measured from the low-water line, and the areas of the sea between the low-water line as aforesaid and the maritime frontier, together with the airspace above them, constitute the maritime areas of Israel.[26]

Since the Gulf of Aqaba is only seventeen miles in breadth at its widest point, and only three miles in breadth on the bay at its head, it is obvious that the several national claims to jurisdiction overlap at some points, and especially on the bay. Further, Enterprise Passage being the only practicable channel for access to the Gulf, ships proceeding to or coming from Aqaba or Elath must of necessity transit the territorial sea of Egypt. The question of freedom of navigation in the Gulf of Aqaba was raised initially by certain actions of the Egyptian Government against Israeli and Israeli-connected shipping. Egypt does not appear, however, to have brought into issue the status of the Gulf *per se.*

In 1946, two years before Israel became a state, the Arab League had instituted a boycott of the Zionists of Palestine.[27] After Israel's establishment in May, 1948, hostilities broke out between Israel and several of the surrounding Arab states, including Egypt. The Egyptian Government prescribed visit and search measures at the Suez Canal with respect to ships proceeding to Israeli ports,[28] and later extended these measures to the Gulf of Aqaba.[29]

The Egyptian Government justified such measures by asserting that the Palestine hostilities of 1948 constituted a state of war between Egypt and Israel, a condition which, it has maintained, was not terminated by the signing of the Rhodes General Armistice Agreement on February 24, 1949. Its reasoning has been that the agreement merely ended active hostilities and was not equivalent to a treaty of peace.[30] It has concluded that in

[26] Territorial Waters Decree of 24 Elul 5715 (Sept. 11, 1955), Yalkut Hapirsumim (Official Gazette), No. 442, Sept. 22, 1955; U.N. General Assembly, Doc. A/CN.4/99/ Add. 1, p. 16; 50 A.J.I.L. 1001 (1956); Yearbook of the International Law Commission, 1956, Vol. II, p. 54 (A/CN.4/ Ser.A/1956/Add. 1).

[27] See B. Y. Boutros-Ghali, ''The Arab League, 1945–1955,'' International Conciliation, No. 498, pp. 406–421 (May, 1954, but written and published in the spring of 1955).

[28] J. C. Hurewitz, ''Unity and Disunity in the Middle East,'' *ibid.*, No. 481, p. 240 (May, 1952); U.N. Press Release SC/1567, Jan. 28, 1954.

[29] According to Hoskins, *op. cit.* 70, Egyptian measures against Israeli shipping in the Gulf were undertaken in the summer of 1950, when ''the Egyptian Government proceeded to install shore batteries near the tip of the Sinai Peninsula to command the entrance to the Gulf of Aqaba. From this point of vantage control could be exercised over all shipping in the Gulf of Aqaba and vessels could be prevented from passing to the emergent Israeli port of Elath.'' The same writer states that the Egyptian Under Secretary for Foreign Affairs justified Egypt's action by asserting that ''Egypt's sovereignty over navigation in her territorial waters is affirmed by international law.''

[30] Egyptian Delegate Azmi summarized the Egyptian position in the Security Council on March 12, 1954. He stated that since ''an armed struggle has taken place between Egypt and other Arab States on the one side and Israel on the other . . . the description to be given this state of affairs is not affected by the absence of a declaration of war

consequence of this condition the international law of war rather than the international law of peace is applicable to Israeli shipping in the Strait of Tiran, and that, accordingly, passage of Israeli shipping into and through the Gulf cannot be regarded as "innocent." [31]

A recent article in the military section of an Egyptian review has raised the additional question of "Israel's right to occupy Elath itself," reasoning that since the occupation by Israeli forces of the southern Negev and Elath took place after the signing of the Rhodes General Armistice Agreement on February 24, 1949, such occupation was a violation of the agreement.[32]

---

of the traditional kind or by the lack of recognition of Israel by the Arab States, and there can be no doubt that a war has taken place between Egypt and Israel." He stated further that "an armistice, an agreement between belligerents, has never been considered to put an end to a state of war or to create a state of peace, even that type of armistice agreements which have come to be known as 'capitulation armistices,' where obviously no likelihood of further recourse to arms exists, for example the 1871 and 1918 armistices with Germany." Citing English and American authorities, including a U. S. Court of Claims decision (Walter *v.* The Government of the United States of America, June 28, 1948), he asserted "it is clear from the foregoing that an armistice does not end a war, since it is recognized that a state of war does not end until a peace treaty has been ratified."

On Egypt's visit and search measures, Mr. Azmi asserted that Egypt was exercising a legitimate right of self-defense which the duty of self-preservation gives to belligerent nations. U.N. Security Council, Verbatim Record, 641st Meeting, March 12, 1954, S/P.V. 661, pp. 10–15.

[31] An editorial in the Egyptian Gazette of March 7, 1957, at p. 2, entitled "Tiran and the Law," asserted that "since the Armistice Agreement was signed in 1949 ships of all nationalities have used the Tiran Strait with no obstruction on the part of Egypt. . . . Egypt has only insisted on stopping ships flying the Israeli flag because they do not belong to a 'neutral' state, and, as such, cannot be considered as exercising the right of innocent passage . . . international law is divided into two sections— the Law of War and the Law of Peace. What should be applied (with respect to Israeli shipping) in the case of Tiran Strait and the Suez Canal is the Law of War and not the Law of Peace . . . Egypt has officially announced that she is in a state of war with Israel, and by the mere fact of signing the Armistice Agreement, which ended the fighting, both sides admitted that the state of war exists . . . the agreement itself says that it is only a prelude to the conclusion of peace."

The editorial added that "the Tiran Strait falls in the same category as the Dardanelles (which) lead to the Black Sea. Both the Gulf of Aqaba and the Black Sea border on more than one state. But there is one difference between the Gulf of Aqaba and the Black Sea. In the case of the Black Sea the States bordering on it have been there from time immemorial but the state of Israeli is still a newcomer in the Gulf of Aqaba and has not so far received recognition of the states which control the Gulf . . . the right of innocent passage through the Dardanelles in time of peace was only introduced by a series of international treaties after years of war. The last of these treaties was the Montreux Convention of July 20, 1936, which, while accepting the principle of free navigation, gave Turkey the right to prohibit passage of ships of any state at war with her."

[32] The article, entitled "The Trouble About Aqaba," appeared in the Egyptian Economic and Political Review, February, 1957, Military Section, pp. XI–XII. It asserted that until the question of Israel's right to occupy Elath is settled, "the fundamental issue as to whether the waters of Aqaba are or are not an international waterway cannot be discussed. . . . Egypt is a belligerent, and the recent Israeli aggression . . . underlines the state of war that exists between her and the Israelis. In such circumstances the Gulf of Aqaba must inevitably play a major military part

The Israeli Government has asserted vigorously that the Gulf of Aqaba and the Strait of Tiran should be free and open to all shipping, including its own.   Through its representative on the Security Council, the Israeli Government has affirmed that "there is no value whatever in the Egyptian contention that 'an armistice does not put an end to a state of war.' " [33] The Permanent Representative of Israel at the United Nations addressed a letter dated January 29, 1954, to the President of the Security Council, to which was attached a memorandum dated January 28, 1954, which complained that

---

in her security and the security of her long Red Sea and Sinai coastline. . . . Egypt (has) legitimate rights of self-defense . . . the Israeli argument that Egypt is blocking an international waterway is defeated by the Israelis themselves, who have so far failed to give the world any precise indications as to the exact location of their allegedly legal boundaries. . . . Whether Elath is or is not Israeli territory remains a subject of debate.

". . . The fact that Israel today occupies Elath can be partly traced to the circumstances and motives affecting Britain when the Mandate boundaries were established in 1919. Aware of the military and political importance of the Gulf of Aqaba . . . Britain arranged that the Palestine Mandate territory include Elath and a few hundred yards of frontage on the Gulf to separate Egypt and the new Amirate of Trans-Jordan. With the British withdrawal from Palestine in 1948, Israeli forces occupied Elath, where they have remained ever since, a serious threat to Arab security and an unlawful obstacle violating the freedom of passage between Egypt and Jordan.

"Israeli action in the South came after the Armistice Agreement of February 24th and in clear violation of its terms . . . the Israelis were determined to secure a foot-hold on the Gulf of Aqaba . . . for only an outlet on the Gulf could enable them to gain access to the Red Sea and beyond to the Indian Ocean without being compelled to go through the Suez Canal. . . . In addition, the subsoil of the Negev contained a variety of important mineral deposits . . .

". . . the Southern Negev was since June 1948 under Jordanian control . . . the British forces in Aqaba (were) the main Jordanian defense . . . although the British Government had repeatedly expressed the view that Israel had no claim or right to occupy the area of the Southern Negev, orders came from London on March 10 (1949) . . . that British forces were not to interfere . . . unless attacked . . . Jordanian forces were faced with an intolerable situation on the night of March 10, and withdrew. The next morning unopposed Israeli forces occupied (Elath)."

[33] Israeli Delegate Abba Eban summarized the Israeli position in the Security Council on July 26, 1951, when he refered to what he called "The illegitimacy of the Egyptian blockade" and "the contradiction between this practice and the Armistice Agreement." He asserted that "this Armistice Agreement is not a mere suspension of hostilities, leaving belligerent rights intact. This Agreement, as its own text constantly reiterates, is a permanent and irrevocable renunciation of all hostile acts. . . . It is vain for Egypt to hark back to a previous era in which The Hague regulations of 1907 defined an armistice as a mere suspension of hostilities. . . . What is the relevance of this traditional concept of armistice to a specific Armistice Agreement whose text recognizes neither war nor belligerency and declares instead that: 'This Agreement . . . shall remain in force until a peaceful settlement between the parties is achieved. . . .'?" Mr. Eban further asserted that Egypt "manufactured" the "theory of a state of war" for the "sole purpose of creating a 'legal' pretext for the Suez blockade," and concluded with the statement that "my Government instructs me to declare that Israel is in no state of war with Egypt and denies that Egypt has the least right to be at war with Israel." U.N. Security Council, Official Records, 549th Meeting, July 26, 1951, S/P.V.549, pp. 3–12.

on January 25, 1954, regulations were instituted by Egypt to prevent passage of ships to the Israeli port of Eilat. Whether such interference is carried out at the Suez Canal or from Egyptian positions overlooking the Gulf of Aqaba they are equally piratical and illegal. The denial by the Security Council of Egypt's alleged rights of war renders the blockade practices in the Suez Canal and in the Gulf of Eilat (Aqaba) comprehensively illegal.[34]

The Permanent Representative, Mr. Abba Eban, was referring to the Security Council's resolution of September 1, 1951,[35] and cited it as having decided that Egyptian interference with Israeli shipping was "an abuse of the exercise of the right of visit, search and seizure," and as based on the principle that since the General Armistice Agreement of 1949 marked the permanent end of the military phase of the conflict and specifically forbade all hostile acts, "neither party could reasonably assert that it was actively a belligerent or required to exercise the right of visit, search and seizure for any legitimate purpose of self-defense." [36]

There has been some interference with non-Israeli-connected shipping proceeding to Aqaba. On July 1, 1951, the British ship *Empire Roach,* cleared by Egyptian customs authorities at Suez for the port of Aqaba, was stopped by an Egyptian patrol vessel in the Strait of Tiran.[37] In the late summer of 1955 the British ship *Anshun,* carrying Jordanian pilgrims from Aqaba to Jidda, was fired on by Egyptian shore batteries as a result of a misunderstanding.

In September, 1955, the Egyptian Government put into effect a regulation requiring vessels intending to enter the Gulf of Aqaba to secure a permit to do so from the Egyptian Blockade of Israel Office 72 hours before making the trip.[38] Israeli Prime Minister Ben Gurion told the Israeli Parliament on October 18, 1955, that this regulation was aimed at shipping destined for Elath, and characterized it as not only contrary to Security Council resolutions but also to principles of international law relating to freedom of shipping in open waters and in straits connecting seas. On September 12, 1955, the British Foreign Office issued a statement to the effect that the Gulf must be regarded as an international waterway, with free access to the ships of all nations, and on November 7 British Foreign Secretary Macmillan told the House of Commons that the United Kingdom Government had made it clear that it did not "recognize the legality of the blockade of Israel nor the right of the Egyptian Government to grant or withhold permission to ships to use the international channel at the mouth of the Gulf of Aqaba." [39] When the Jordanian Government ex-

---

[34] U.N. Doc. S/3168/Add. 1 (Jan. 29, 1954), p. 3.

[35] U.N. Doc. S/2322.

[36] U.N. Doc. S/3168/Add. 1 (Jan. 29, 1954), p. 2.

[37] Hoskins, *op. cit.* 70.

[38] Al-Akhbar (Cairo daily), Sept. 11, 1955.

[39] N. Y. Herald Tribune (European ed.), Sept. 13, 1955, p. 3; Great Britain, Parl. Deb. (Hansard), House of Commons, Official Report, Vol. 545, No. 48, Nov. 7, 1955, Col. 1454; and see comment by Moshe Perlmann, "The Middle East in the Summer of 1955," 6 Middle Eastern Affairs 258–270, at 258–259 (1955).

pressed objections to the regulation, the Egyptian Government made special arrangements for Jordanian shipping.

On October 29, 1956, Israeli forces launched an offensive against Egyptian forces in the Sinai Peninsula. Shortly thereafter Israeli troops seized Egyptian positions at Sharm al-Shaikh and Ras Nuzrani, commanding the entrance to the Gulf of Aqaba, and forced the withdrawal of such Egyptian forces as were in occupation of Tiran and Sanafir Islands.[40]

The Israeli Government was reluctant, in spite of two United Nations resolutions of February 2, 1957, "calling on Israel to complete its withdrawal behind the Armistice demarcation line without further delay,"[41] to remove its forces from positions commanding the entrance to the Gulf, lest Egyptian measures against Israeli shipping be reinstituted. It sought a guarantee that, in return for withdrawal, the Gulf would remain open to its shipping, and would be unequivocally recognized as an international waterway.[42]

Although Prime Minister Ben Gurion initially rejected, by letter of February 7, 1957, a plea from President Eisenhower for Israeli withdrawal,[43] the Israeli Government later announced, on March 1, 1957, that it had decided on "full and prompt withdrawal from the Sharm al-Shaikh area and the Gaza Strip, in compliance with General Assembly resolution 1124 (XI) of February 2, 1957." Foreign Minister Golda Meir, in making this announcement to the U.N. General Assembly, noted that:

> Our sole purpose has been to ensure that, on the withdrawal of Israeli forces, continued freedom of navigation will exist for Israel and international shipping in the Gulf of Aqaba and the Straits of Tiran.

She referred to a United States memorandum to Israel of February 11, 1957, which discussed international rights in the Gulf of Aqaba, and commented that:

> My Government has subsequently learned with gratification that other leading maritime Powers are prepared to subscribe to the doctrine set out in the U. S. memorandum of 11 February and have a similar intention to exercise their rights of free and innocent passage in the Gulf and the Straits.

Mrs. Meir added that: "In the light of these doctrines, policies and arrangements by the United Nations and the maritime Powers, my Government is confident that free and innocent passage for international and Israeli ship-

[40] Annual Report of the Secretary-General on the Work of the Organization, 16 June 1956–15 June 1957, General Assembly, 112th Sess., Official Records, Supp. No. 1 (A/3594), pp. 8–10.

[41] 36 Dept. of State Bulletin 327–328 (1957); The Times (London), Feb. 4, 1957, p. 8. The two U.N. resolutions called attention to earlier resolutions on the same subject of Nov. 2, 4, 7 and 24, 1956, and Jan. 19, 1957. See Annual Report of Sec. Gen., op. cit. 8–22.

[42] N. Y. Herald Tribune (European ed.), Jan. 5–6, 1957, p. 1, and Feb. 21, 1957, p. 1. See also Annual Report of Sec. Gen., op. cit. 22.

[43] N. Y. Herald Tribune (European ed.), Feb. 9–10, 1957, p. 1.

ping will continue to be fully maintained after Israel's withdrawal."[44] She was referring to plans for a United Nations force to assume responsibility in the Sharm al-Shaikh area.

President Eisenhower had stated on February 20 that:

> With reference to the passage into and through the Gulf of Aqaba, we expressed the conviction that the gulf constitutes international waters and that no nation has the right to prevent free and innocent passage in the gulf. We announced that the United States was prepared to exercise this right itself and to join with others to secure general recognition of this right.[45]

On March 1 U. S. Ambassador Henry Cabot Lodge on behalf of his government welcomed Israel's announcement of intention to withdraw. He told the General Assembly that:

> Once Israel has completed its withdrawal in accordance with the resolutions of the General Assembly, and in view of the measures taken by the United Nations to deal with the situation, there is no basis for either party to the Armistice Agreement to assert or exercise any belligerent rights.[46]

On the same day Ambassador Lodge referred to a United States *aide-mémoire* to Israel dated February 11, 1957, made public February 17. The *aide-mémoire* reads as follows:

> The United States believes that the Gulf comprehends international waters and that no nation has the right to prevent free and innocent passage in the Gulf and through the Straits giving access thereto. We have in mind not only commercial usage, but the passage of pilgrims on religious missions, which should be fully respected.
>
> The United States recalls that on January 28, 1950, the Egyptian Ministry of Foreign Affairs informed the United States that the Egyptian occupation of the two islands of Tiran and Sanafir at the entrance of the Gulf of Aqaba was only to protect the islands themselves against possible damage or violation and that "this occupation being in no way conceived in a spirit of obstructing in any way innocent passage through the stretch of water separating these two Is-

[44] General Assembly, 11th Sess., Off. Records, 666th Plenary Meeting, March 1, 1957 (A/P.V. 666), p. 1275. Mrs. Meir summed up Israel's policy *re* the Gulf and the Straits as follows:

"The Government of Israel believes that the Gulf of Aqaba comprehends international waters and that no nation has the right to prevent free and innocent passage in the Gulf and through the Straits giving access thereto, in accordance with the generally accepted definition of those terms in the law of the sea . . . Israel will do nothing to impede free and innocent passage by ships of Arab countries bound to Arab ports, or any other destination. . . . Israel will protect ships of its own flag exercising the signs of free and innocent passage on the high seas and in international waters. Interference, by armed force, with ships of Israel flag exercising free and innocent passage in the Gulf of Aqaba and through the Straits of Tiran will be regarded by Israel as an attack entitling it to exercise its inherent right of self-defense under Article 51 of the United Nations Charter. . . ." *Ibid.* 1276.

[45] 36 Dept. of State Bulletin 389 (1957).

[46] *Ibid.* 433 (1957); General Assembly, 11th Sess., Official Records, 666th Plenary Meeting, March 1, 1957 (A/P.V. 666), p. 1278.

lands from the Egyptian coast of Sinai, it follows that this passage, the only practicable one, will remain free as in the past, in conformity with international practices and recognized principles of the law of nations."

In the absence of some overriding decision to the contrary, as by the International Court of Justice, the United States, on behalf of vessels of United States registry, is prepared to exercise the right of free and innocent passage and to join with others to secure general recognition of this right.

Mr. Lodge added that the views expressed in the *aide-mémoire* are to be understood in the sense of the relevant portions of the Report of the United Nations International Law Commission on the Law of the Sea covering the Commission's work at its Eighth Session, from April 23 to July 4, 1956.[47]

At a press conference on March 5, 1957, Secretary of State Dulles referred to the Gulf of Aqaba problem as "a highly complicated question of international law." He observed that

> in one sense of the word the Straits of Tiran are territorial, because they are less than six miles wide and the generally accepted zone of territorial control is three miles. . . . But it is also a principle of international law that even though waters are territorial, if they give access to a body of water which comprehends international waterways, there is a right of free and innocent passage . . . the United States view is that the passage should be open unless there is a contrary decision by the International Court of Justice.

Mr. Dulles added, in response to a query regarding occupation of Tiran and Sanafir Islands after Israeli evacuation, that occupancy by Egypt had been arranged between Saudi Arabia and Egypt in 1950, when Saudi Arabia had consented to such occupation, and suggested that "we have no reason to believe that that arrangement will be altered."[48]

During consideration by the General Assembly in February-March, 1957, of the question of Israel's withdrawal from the entrance to the Gulf, the Arab delegates expressed the belief that the problem of Israel's right to free passage through the Gulf went to the very roots of the Palestine question, and ought to be dealt with in the context of a final solution of that question.[49]

Mr. Krishna Menon of India called attention to a statement of Secretary General Hammarskjold to the effect that "a legal controversy exists as to the extent of the right of innocent passage through these waters,"[50] and suggested that, such being the case, "the General Assembly cannot decide a legal controversy." He added, however, that

[47] 36 Dept. of State Bulletin 432 (1957); General Assembly, 11th Sess., Official Records, 666th Plenary Meeting, March 1, 1957 (A/P.V. 666), pp. 1277–1278.

[48] 36 Dept. of State Bulletin 482–489 (1957).

[49] See, for example, the comments of Lebanese Foreign Minister Charles Malik, General Assembly, 11th Sess., Official Records, 659th Plenary Meeting (A/P.V. 659), Feb. 22, 1957, pp. 1193–1197; and of Iraqi Foreign Minister Fadil Jamali, *ibid.*, 661st Plenary Meeting (A/P.V. 661), Feb. 26, 1957, pp. 1215–1221.

[50] Citing U.N. Doc. A/3512 (Jan. 24, 1957), par. 24.

all the existing evidence . . . is on the side that these waters are territorial waters, and the two countries concerned are Saudi Arabia and Egypt . . . I would say that this is an inland sea.

Mr. Menon based this belief upon the fact that various states have held that gulfs and bays indenting their territories with mouths wider than that of the Gulf of Aqaba are territorial.[51] All the water areas which he cited are indentations in the territory of one state only.

Statements of representatives by various maritime Powers, however, supported the position taken by Israel. On March 1, 1957, French delegate Georges-Picot observed that:

> The French Government considers that the Gulf of Aqaba, by reasons partly of its breadth and partly of the fact that its shores belong to four different States, constitutes international waters. Consequently it believes, that, in conformity with international law, freedom of navigation should be ensured in the Gulf and the straits which give access to it. In these circumstances no nation has the right to prevent the free and innocent passage of ships, whatever their nationality or type.
> . . . It considers that any obstruction of its freedom of passage would be contrary to international law and would, accordingly, entail a possible resort to the measures authorized by Article 51 of the U.N. Charter.
> . . . in its view none of the States bordering on the Gulf of Aqaba is in a state of war with any other. . . .[52]

Mr. Noble, delegate of the United Kingdom, observed on March 4 that he had listened with interest to Mr. Menon's comments, but that:

> . . . he overlooked one fact essential to consideration of this problem: the fact that, unlike the fjords of Norway or Hudson Bay in Canada, or the Hudson River here in New York, or any of the other instances which Mr. Menon quoted, the Gulf of Aqaba is not only bounded at its narrow point of entry by two different countries, Egypt and Saudi Arabia, but contains at its head the ports of two further countries: Jordan and Israel. This simple, undeniable fact is in itself enough to put it in a different category from any of the inland waters mentioned by Mr. Krishna Menon.
> It is the view of Her Majesty's Government in the United Kingdom that the Straits of Tiran must be regarded as an international waterway, through which the vessels of all nations have a right of passage. Her Majesty's Government will assert this right on behalf of all British shipping and is prepared to join with others to secure general recognition of this right.[53]

On the same day Mr. Vitetti of Italy noted that:

> . . . we consider that the Gulf of Aqaba is an international waterway and that no nation has the right to prevent free and innocent passage in the Gulf of Aqaba and through the Straits giving access thereto.

[51] General Assembly, 11th Sess., Official Records, 665th Plenary Meeting (A/P.V.665), March 1, 1957, pp. 1267–1274.

[52] *Ibid.*, 666th Plenary Meeting (A/P.V.666), March 1, 1957, p. 1280.

[53] General Assembly, 11th Sess., Official Records, 667th Plenary Meeting (A/P.V.667), March 4, 1957, p. 1284.

He challenged a statement on innocent passage which had been made by Mr. Menon in the address previously referred to, that "first of all, one must prove innocence,"[54] by observing that:

> This interpretation would nullify the rule of innocent passage, since it is obvious that, if it were valid, the littoral States would no longer have the duty of justifying their refusal of passage to a vessel on specific occasions and for specific reasons; rather, it would rest with the vessel to prove that its passage was innocent.[55]

At the same meeting the delegate of The Netherlands stated that:

> The Netherlands Government is in full agreement with the statements made by Israel, the United States, France and a number of other countries to the effect that passage through the Straits of Tiran should be free, open and unhindered for the ships of all nations. My Government bases its opinion on the following reasons:
>
> First, inasmuch as the Gulf of Aqaba is bordered by four different States and has a width in excess of the three miles of territorial waters of the four littoral States on either side, it is, under the rules of international law, to be regarded as part of the open sea.
>
> Secondly the Straits of Tiran consequently are, in the legal sense, straits connecting two open seas, normally used for international navigation.
>
> Thirdly, in regard to such straits, there is a right of free passage even if the straits are so narrow that they fall entirely within the territorial waters of one or more States. This rule was acknowledged by the International Court of Justice in the Case of the Corfu Channel (Corfu Channel case, Judgment of Dec. 15, 1949: ICJ Reports, 1949, p. 244) and also by the International Law Commission in its report for 1956 (A/3159).
>
> Fourthly, if a strait falls entirely within the territorial waters of one or more of the littoral States, there is still the right of innocent passage, but then the littoral States have the right, if necessary, to verify the innocent character of the passage.
>
> Fifthly, this right of verification, however, does not exist in those cases where the strait connects two parts of the open sea.[56]

The delegates of Belgium,[57] Sweden[58] and Denmark[59] stated support for the position that the Gulf has an international character and that its entrance constitutes an international waterway free to innocent passage of all shipping.

Mr. Pearson of Canada had suggested at the 660th Meeting of the General Assembly that "it should be agreed and affirmed by us that there should be no interference with innocent passage or any assertion of belligerent rights in the Straits of Tiran." He added at the 667th Meeting that "the Assembly should recommend and the parties should agree—as a political and not a legal act—that there should be no interference with the innocent passage of ships through the waters concerned."[60]   In

[54] *Ibid.*, 665th Plenary Meeting (A/P.V.665), March 1, 1957, p. 1271.

[55] *Ibid.*, 667th Plenary Meeting (A/P.V.667), March 4, 1957, pp. 1287–1288.

[56] *Ibid.* 1288.   [57] *Ibid.* 1296.

[58] *Ibid.* 1303.   [59] *Ibid.*

[60] *Ibid.* 1296.   For earlier statement, see *ibid.*, 660th Plenary Meeting (A/P.V.660), Feb. 26, 1957, p. 1203.

earlier meetings it had been suggested by the delegates of Ceylon [61] and Belgium [62] that the question might properly be referred for a legal solution to the International Court of Justice. When Mr. Lall of India said at this meeting that "it has not been contended seriously that the General Assembly can settle a legal issue of this nature. . . . My delegation takes the view that it cannot possibly be settled here what the legal rights are in the Gulf of Aqaba and the Straits of Tiran," [63] he was re-emphasizing a point made at an earlier meeting by his colleague, Mr. Krishna Menon.

On March 8, 1957, Secretary General Hammarskjold announced that Israeli forces had that day evacuated Sharm al-Shaikh and Tiran Island.[64] The positions which they surrendered were occupied by a 250-man detachment of the United Nations Emergency Force (UNEF), consisting mostly of Finns, which assumed control of the Gulf's entrance under an agreement between the United Nations and the Government of Egypt, an agreement which would be terminated by arrangement between the Secretary General and the Government of Egypt.[65]

A new element was added to the controversy by the entry of Saudi Arabia into the dispute. By letter of January 14, 1957, the Permanent Representative of Saudi Arabia, Shaikh Abdullah al-Khayyal, informed the Secretary General that since October 29, 1956, there had been a series of incidents whereby Israeli warships and military planes had assaulted Saudi Arabian positions near the mouth of the Gulf of Aqaba. He referred to specific instances as having taken place on January 5, 11 and 12, and stated that "the Saudi Arabian defense forces in the Aqaba Gulf have been under repeated instructions to refrain from being provoked to military action except in self-defense," and, suggesting that "the foregoing situation is likely to aggravate the maintenance of peace and security in the area," expressed the hope

> that the United Nations, in order to enforce its resolutions and to fulfill its declared intention in preserving peace and security in the region, will be able to find the means to intervene in this matter.[66]

On March 17, 1957, Mecca daily *Al-Bilad al-Saudiyah* printed an official Saudi Arabian Government statement which asserted that the Gulf of Aqaba was not an international waterway, but rather a "closed Arab gulf," and that its waters constituted "Arab territorial waters." The statement further asserted that "the Saudi Arabian Government will never allow the establishment of any right of Israel in the Gulf of Aqaba." Reference was made in the statement to the Gulf as "a natural passage for

61 *Ibid.*, 644th Plenary Meeting (A/P.V.644), Jan. 28, 1957, p. 974.

62 *Ibid.*, 649th Plenary Meeting (A/P.V.649), Feb. 1, 1957, p. 1041.

63 *Ibid.*, 667th Plenary Meeting (A/P.V.667), March 4, 1957, pp. 1301–1302.

64 *Ibid.*, 668th Plenary Meeting (A/P.V.668), March 8, 1957, p. 1314.

65 Barrett McGurn, "Guarding the Gulf of Aqaba," N. Y. Herald Tribune (European ed.), April 23, 1957, p. 4. See report of Secretary General on basic points for presence and functioning in Egypt of U.N.E.F. (U.N. Doc. A/3375), and Report of Secretary General on arrangements concerning status of U.N.E.F. in Egypt (U.N. Doc. A/3526).

66 U.N. Doc. A/3499, Jan. 15, 1957.

the caravans of Muslim pilgrims going to the Holy Places'' (Mecca and Medina). A few days earlier Mecca weekly *Hira* had contained two editorials which strongly denounced any attempt to give the Gulf an international status.

The March 17 statement was followed by a more elaborate statement in the circular note of March 31, referred to above.[67] This statement asserted that

> the straits separating these two islands (Tiran and Sanafir) are under the control and jurisdiction of the Kingdom of Saudi Arabia. Likewise, the sea-water around those islands and straits are Saudi Arabian territorial waters. The above-mentioned straits were and still are locked . . . the straits of the Gulf of Aqaba may be by no means considered open straits. Any attempt to consider these straits as international straits will be regarded as an encroachment on the Saudi Arabian Kingdom and a threat to its integrity.

The note referred to Article 10, paragraph 3, of the Constantinople Convention of 1888, and suggested that

> it appears, from the record of the negotiations which resulted in the conclusion of the Convention, that the inclusion of that provision, aimed at leaving the Gulf of Aqaba and its straits outside the scope of the order of the free passage defined for the Suez Canal . . . is an asserted recognition that the Gulf of Aqaba is a locked Arab Gulf without any international character, and that its waters together with the waters of the inlets and straits are territorial waters locked in the face of international navigation.[68]

On March 29 Israeli Prime Minister Ben Gurion told a French newspaper correspondent that "any attempt by Egypt or Saudi Arabia to impose a blockade against Israeli shipping in the Gulf of Aqaba will oblige my country to exercise its right of self-defense." [69] Although, according to a BBC broadcast of March 6, the Israeli Prime Minister had stated that his government no longer regarded the Armistice Agreement with Egypt as being in force, other official Israeli pronouncements would seem to contradict this statement. While it is unclear whether or not Saudi Arabia has ever regarded itself as being at war with Israel, there is no doubt but that no armistice agreement ever was signed with Saudi Arabia, although such agreements were signed with Egypt, Jordan, Lebanon and Syria.

[67] Note 21 above.

[68] For text of Constantinople Convention, see 3 Moore's Digest 264–266; 3 A.J.I.L. Supp. 123 (1909).

By letter dated April 12, 1957, to the Secretary General, the Saudi delegate to the United Nations presented this point of view to that body. It was contained in an attached memorandum, which asserted that ''the Gulf of Aqaba cannot be considered an open waterway and any attempt at giving it an international character will constitute an encroachment on the sovereignty of Saudi Arabia and a threat to its territorial security.'' The memorandum added that ''Israeli planes and ships some four months ago attacked positions inside Saudi Arabia, at the time when Israel forces were occupying the Egyptian territory at Sharm al-Shaikh. This proves Israel intends to force a right of passage through the Gulf, threatening the security of the area.'' U.N. Doc.A/3575 (April 15, 1957), p. 3.

[69] N. Y. Herald Tribune (European ed.), March 30–31, 1957, p. 3.

Early in May, 1957, the Saudi Arabian Government addressed a circular note to the various Muslim missions in Jidda, and sent a letter to the Secretary General of the United Nations, wherein the complaint was made that on April 30 and May 1 an Israeli naval demonstration comprising Israeli warships had taken place in Saudi and Egyptian territorial waters in the Gulf of Aqaba. Several subsequent complaints also were made. The Israeli Government denied these allegations, and also denied that it had, as alleged, committed any act of interference with the Muslim pilgrimage, or had any intention of doing so.[70]

During the June 8–13 visit of King Saud to King Husayn of Jordan, a joint *communiqué* was issued which stated that, since pilgrim travel from the port of Aqaba was unsafe because of the "aggression of Israel in this Arab Gulf," the two governments had decided to announce that travel by sea of pilgrims from the port of Aqaba was not desirable. At the end of the visit a concluding joint *communiqué* announced that the Gulf of Aqaba constitutes a "regional Arab water." The *communiqué* expressed the hope that all Muslim states would support this position. An article in *Al-Bilad al-Saudiyah* of June 27, 1957, under the headline: "The Saudi Arabian Kingdom Emphasizes its Rights in the Waters of the Gulf of Aqaba," stated that a note had been sent to the United States Government in which "the right of the Saudi Arabian Kingdom to the Arab waters in the closed Gulf of Aqaba was emphasized," and in which the statement appeared that "Saudi Arabia does not recognize any right for non-Arab ships to pass through this Gulf and the straits leading thereto."[71]

In a July 4 address to visiting Muslim leaders in Mecca, on the occasion of the 1957 pilgrimage, King Saud emphasized the Saudi Arabian position

[70] Letter dated May 7, 1957, from the Permanent Representative of Saudi Arabia to the Secretary General, U.N. Security Council (S/3825, May 9, 1957). This was followed by several letters to the President of the Security Council, alleging Israeli naval and/or air demonstrations in Saudi territorial waters in the Gulf, as follows: May 27, 1957 (S/3833, May 28, 1957); June 5, 1957 (S/3835, June 6, 1957); June 19, 1957 (S/3841, June 20, 1957); June 24, 1957 (S/3843, June 25, 1957); July 2, 1957 (S/3846, July 2, 1957); and July 10, 1957 (S/3849, July 11, 1957).

By letter dated June 10, 1957, to the President of the Security Council, the Permanent Representative of Israel to the United Nations stated that:

"The Government of Israel has noted a series of complaints by Saudi Arabia alleging that Israel naval vessels have violated Saudi Arabian territorial waters and have attacked Saudi coastal positions along the shore of the Gulf of Aqaba, and that Israel military aircraft have circled over Saudi Arabian positions.

"The Government of Israel denies these allegations categorically. The incidents alleged have never taken place. Israel naval forces are under strict instructions not to violate the territorial waters of Saudi Arabia and not under any circumstances to attack other vessels or coastal positions. . . . Israel aircraft are under strict orders to respect the airspace of all other countries. . . . The Government of Israel, so far from interfering in any way with the traditional pilgrimage, has declared its desire to place all possible facilities at its disposal. . . . Never on a single occasion has Israel prejudiced the Mecca pilgrimage in any way, nor has she any intention of doing so." U.N. Doc. A/3838 (June 10, 1957), p. 1.

[71] *Al-Bilad al-Saudiyah*, June 13, 14, and 27. *Al-Bilad* of June 29 published the text of the note from Saudi Arabia to the United States Government.

on the Gulf of Aqaba, and asked the support of the Islamic world for that position. Saudi Arabia's position on the Gulf of Aqaba was again raised during the Twelfth Session of the General Assembly, on October 2, 1957, when the Saudi representative, Ahmad Shukairy, stated that:

> The Gulf of Aqaba, basically, is not an international question. . . . The Gulf of Aqaba is a national inland waterway, subject to absolute Arab sovereignty. The geographical location of the Gulf is conclusive proof of its national character. It is separated from the Red Sea by a chain of islands, the largest being Sanafir and Tiran. The only navigable entrance—which, itself, is within Arab territory—does not exceed 500 metres. Thus, by its configuration, the Gulf is in the nature of a *mare clausum,* which does not belong to the class of international waterways. . . . The Gulf is so narrow that the territorial areas of the littoral States are bound to overlap among themselves, under any kind of measurement, even if we assume that the Gulf comprehends part of the high seas.
>
> In the second place, the Gulf of Aqaba is of the category of historical gulfs that fall outside the sphere of international law. The Gulf is the historical route to the holy places in Mecca. Pilgrims from different Muslim countries have been streaming through the Gulf, year after year, for fourteen centuries. Ever since, the Gulf has been an exclusive Arab route under Arab sovereignty. It is due to this undisputed fact that not a single international authority makes any mention whatsoever of the Gulf as an international waterway open for international navigation.
>
> It was last year, in the aftermath of aggression waged against Egypt, that the Gulf was claimed as comprehending an international waterway . . . Israel has not withdrawn from the Gulf . . . Israel warships, still in the Gulf, are one aspect of aggression. The resolution of November 2, 1956 calling for withdrawal of Israel behind the Armistice lines remains unimplemented as far as the Gulf is concerned.
>
> Israel . . . has no right to any part of the Gulf. Israel's claim . . . could only be argued on the United Nations Plan of Partition or the Armistice lines. On either ground, the claim of Israel falls to the ground. On the plan of partition, Israel cannot claim Eilat before Israel is confined to the lines of the plan. . . . With regard to the armistice lines . . . under the express provisions of the armistice agreements, the armistice lines are purely "dictated" by "military considerations"and have no political significance.
>
> Thus the area under Israel is nothing but a military control without sovereignty whatsoever. Israel has no sovereign status in the Gulf of Aqaba. Israel's position is one of aggression. . . .

Mr. Shukairy commented as follows with respect to suggestions that the legal status of the Gulf be submitted to the International Court of Justice for an opinion:

> . . . our respect for the Court is unreserved and unlimited. But the matter is not to be decided exclusively on judicial grounds. The question involves matters of the highest order pertaining to pilgrimage and other national and political considerations. As a keeper of the Holy Places, His Majesty King Saud is not prepared to expose to question any matter touching upon the Holy shrines and the free passage of pilgrims to Mecca.

On innocent passage he remarked:

> In spite of divergencies of opinion on every question falling within the province of international law, not a single legal precedent has declared a right of passage, innocent or otherwise, in a closed or inland water.[72]

On March 3, 1958, during the first meeting of the First (Territorial Sea) Committee of the International Conference on the Law of the Sea at Geneva, Mr. Shukairy recorded a Saudi Arabian reservation that his country's participation in the conference "should never be construed as recognition of Israel in any nature whatsoever." He asked that a general article be inserted in the draft convention to the effect that the text applied only to the law in time of peace and not in time of war, and stated the position that peacetime rules such as innocent passage were inapplicable not only in case of open conflict, "but even when normal relations between two states do not exist. . . . When recognition is withheld or denied, it is inconceivable how the rights and duties as set out in the draft could be applied." Mr. Shukairy warned that the Arab states will insist on denying innocent passage to Israeli shipping in all Arab waters until the "genuine state of war" in the Middle East is ended.[73]

Thus, while Israel and certain of the principal maritime Powers have expressed the position that the Gulf of Aqaba contains international waters, and that the Strait of Tiran is an international waterway through which the right of innocent passage exists for Israeli and all international shipping, Egypt and Saudi Arabia, in particular, have taken issue with this position. Saudi Arabia's position that the Gulf is an Arab *mare clausum* is, of course, most at variance with the views of those who regard it as having an international character.

Both Egypt and Saudi Arabia appear to regard Israel's possession of a five-mile strip on the Gulf as military possession without real sovereignty. On this question, it is clear that under the Palestine Partition Plan of November 29, 1947, Israel was awarded the southern Negev, including this coastline. Israel's advance into the area was made in early March, 1949, *i.e.*, after the signing of the Egyptian-Israeli Armistice Agreement on February 24, 1949. It appears, however, that at this time there were no Egyptian, but only Jordanian, troops in the southern Negev area.[74] Consequently it may be argued that the Armistice Agreement with Egypt is irrelevant with respect to the southern Negev, since Egyptian troops were not committed there. The Jordan-Israel Armistice Agreement was signed on April 3, 1949,[75] after the advance to Elath had been completed. It provided, *inter alia*, that

> in the sector from a point on the Dead Sea to the southernmost point of Palestine, the Armistice Demarcation line shall be determined by existing military positions as surveyed in March, 1949, by United Na-

---

[72] General Assembly, 12th Sess., Official Records, 697th Plenary Meeting (A/P.V.697), Oct. 2, 1957, p. 233.

[73] N. Y. Herald Tribune (European ed.), March 4, 1958, p. 1.

[74] See note 32 above.   [75] See note 18 above.

tions observers, and shall run from north to south as delineated on Map 1 in Annex I of this Agreement.

The Armistice Demarcation line, as indicated on the map, follows the Wadi al-Arabah and hence the historic boundary between Palestine and Jordan. Consequently, in terms of the Armistice Agreements, a strong argument can be made for Israel's right to possession of its coastline on the Gulf of Aqaba. Just what is the legal nature of this possession, however, is somewhat unclear. As Mr. Pearson of Canada and Mr. Shukairy of Saudi Arabia have pointed out,[76] the Armistice Agreements are not to be construed as establishing political or territorial boundaries, or to prejudge or confirm any political or territorial right or claim or boundary, and were delineated without prejudice to rights, claims and positions of the parties as regards an ultimate settlement of the Palestine question.[77] Mr. Shukairy has suggested that Israel should not be permitted to claim the Negev area until it has complied with the original Palestine Partition Plan, which would involve giving up certain other areas which were to have been Arab under that plan.[78] This point may have an important bearing upon any legal decision made with respect to the Gulf's status by an appropriate authority.

Egypt and Israel appear to differ on the nature of the Egyptian-Israeli Armistice Agreement. On the general question of an armistice agreement, the British jurist, Sir Hersch Lauterpacht, has stated:

> Armistices or truces, in the wider sense of the term, are all agreements between belligerent forces for a temporary cessation of hostilities. They are in no wise to be compared to peace . . . because the condition of war remains between the belligerents themselves, and between belligerents and neutrals, on all points beyond the mere cessation of hostilities . . . the right of visit and search over neutral merchantmen therefore remains intact as does likewise the right to capture neutral vessels attempting to break a blockade and the right to seize contraband of war . . .
>
> A general armistice is a cessation of hostilities which, in contradistinction to suspension of arms with their momentary and local military purposes, is agreed upon between belligerents for the whole of their forces, and the whole region of war . . .
>
> Everybody agrees that belligerents during an armistice may, *outside the line where the forces face each other,* do everything and anything they like regarding defense and preparation of offense.[79]

The American publicist, Charles Cheney Hyde, quotes the United States War Department Rules of Land Warfare of 1940 as defining an armistice to mean "the cessation of active hostilities for a period agreed upon be-

---

[76] See remarks of Mr. Pearson, General Assembly, 11th Sess., Official Records, 660th Meeting (A/P.V.660), Feb. 26, 1957, p. 1203, and remarks of Mr. Shukairy, *ibid.,* 12th Sess., 697th Plenary Meeting (A/P.V.697), Oct. 2, 1957, p. 233.

[77] See Art. IV, par. 3, and Art. V, par. 2, of the Egyptian-Israeli Armistice Agreement, and Art. II, par. 2, of the Jordan-Israeli Armistice Agreement. The former Agreement is cited in note 9 above; the latter in note 18 above.

[78] A/P.V.697, *op. cit.* 233.

[79] 2 Oppenheim, International Law: Disputes, War and Neutrality 546–551 (7th ed., 1952, Sir H. Lauterpacht).

tween belligerents.'' He refers to the Hague Regulations as defining armistices as ''a class of agreements purporting to suspend military operations,'' and observes that Article 37 of such regulations states that ''general armistices . . . usually precede the negotiations for peace, but may be concluded for other purposes.''[80] Hyde's general position appears to be that an armistice agreement is entered into in contemplation of, or as a first step towards, the conclusion of a treaty of peace, but is not a substitute therefor.

In a recent article entitled ''The Nature and Scope of the Armistice Agreement,''[81] Colonel Howard S. Levie observes that ''it may be stated as a positive rule that an armistice agreement does *not* terminate the state of war existing between the belligerents, either *de jure* or *de facto,* and that the state of war continues to exist and to control the actions of neutrals as well as belligerents.''[82] On the specific question of the Arab-Israeli armistice agreements, Colonel Levie states that:

> Israel complained to the Security Council asserting that the four armistice agreements (with Egypt, Jordan, Syria and Lebanon) had, in effect, terminated the state of war between all the belligerent parties. Egypt, on the other hand, contended that the state of war continued despite the armistice agreements and that the blockade (of the Suez Canal and later of the Gulf of Aqaba) was legal. The Security Council on September 1, 1951, passed a resolution calling upon Egypt to lift its blockade. (Security Council, Sixth Year, *Official Records,* 558th Meeting). This action of the Security Council has been construed as indicating that a general armistice is a kind of *de facto* termination of war. It is considered more likely that the Security Council's action was based upon a desire to bring to an end a situation fraught with potential danger to peace than that it was attempting to change a long established rule of international law. By now it has surely become fairly obvious that the Israeli-Arab General Armistice Agreement did not create even a *de facto* termination of the war between those states.[83]

Colonel Levie adds that ''it is apparent that the failure, in an appropriate case, to include within an armistice a clear provision with regard to naval blockade, and naval warfare generally, can be the cause of serious difficulties and, perhaps, even of the resumption of hostilities.'' After citing examples, including the Israeli-Egyptian Armistice Agreement, Colonel Levie observes that ''the foregoing discussion has, it is believed, indicated the necessity of including in an armistice agreement specific and precise provisions with regard to naval warfare, blockades, etc.''[84] He observes a trend, however, whereby the armistice agreement is becoming more final in character.[85]

---

[80] 3 Hyde, International Law, Chiefly as Interpreted and Applied by the United States 1783 (1945 ed.). The Hague Regulations were annexed to the Hague Convention of 1907 respecting the Law and Customs of War on Land, 2 Malloy's Treaties 2287.

[81] 50 A.J.I.L. 880–906 (1956).   [82] *Ibid.* 884.

[83] *Ibid.* 886.   [84] *Ibid.* 904, 906.

[85] *Ibid.* 906. In this connection see the address made by Department of State Legal Adviser, Herman Phleger, at the 49th Annual Meeting of the American Society of International Law, April 29, 1955, wherein he observed, referring to the Korean

A "Special Correspondent" of *The Times* of London, in a recent article, has taken a contrary position with respect to the Egyptian-Israel Armistice Agreement.[86] He has observed that:

> . . . the armistice operated to deprive Egypt of any continued right to blockade Israel or to interfere with foreign vessels bound for Israel. Normally . . . an armistice agreement does not operate to terminate the legal state of war. It is also arguable that an armistice does not even put an end to the rights of the belligerents to visit and search neutral vessels or to seize contraband and to enforce a blockade. The armistice merely ends hostilities between the armed forces of the belligerents. In all the circumstances of the dispute between Egypt and Israel, however, it seems probable that the armistice agreement did more than this.

The correspondent has relied primarily upon the Security Council resolution of September 1, 1951, to uphold his thesis that the Armistice Agreement operated to deny the exercise of belligerent rights at sea.[87] He has concluded that:

> This resolution of the Security Council creates for Egypt a legal obligation which she is not free to disregard. It will be noted that the resolution does not purport to be based so much on the special status of the Suez Canal as on the provisions of the armistice agreement. This being so, the situation resulting from the armistice would equally negative the claim of Egypt to exercise belligerent rights in the Straits of Tiran.

The Canadian lawyer, Bloomfield, in his recent book on the Gulf of Aqaba, concludes that:

Armistice Agreement, that it was "more like a treaty of peace than an armistice agreement. But that seems to be the style now. The armistice terminating hostilities between Israel and the surrounding countries, and that concluding the Indo-China hostilities, are of the same nature." 1955 Proceedings, American Society of International Law 98.

[86] March 8, 1957, p. 11.

[87] The writer cited the resolution, the particularly relevant sections of which are as follows:

"The Security Council. . . . Considering that since the Armistice regime . . . is of a permanent character, neither party can reasonably assert that it is actively a belligerent or requires to exercise the right of visit, search and seizure for any legitimate purpose of self-defense;

"Finds that the maintenance of the practice mentioned . . . is inconsistent with the establishment of permanent peace in Palestine;

"Finds further that such practice is an abuse of the exercise of the right of visit, search and seizure;

"Further finds that the practice cannot in the prevailing circumstances be justified on the grounds that it is necessary for self-defense;

"And further noting that . . . sanctions applied by Egypt to certain ships which have visited Israel ports represent unjustified interference with the rights of nations to navigate the seas . . . ;

"Calls upon Egypt to terminate the restrictions on the passage of international commercial shipping and goods through the Suez Canal wherever bound. . . ." U.N. Doc. S/2322.

No state of war existed or exists between Egypt and Israel by virtue of the fact that both are members of the United Nations Organization, and such a state of war is . . . incompatible with the obligations and duties of member states. Egypt is not entitled to exercise belligerent rights in the Gulf of Aqaba or elsewhere.[88]

Thus conflicting persuasive arguments have been advanced with respect to the nature of the Egyptian-Israeli Armistice Agreement insofar as it has a bearing upon freedom of passage for Israeli shipping in the Gulf of Aqaba. It is submitted that a definitive determination of this question may be important to any final determination of Israel's status with respect to use of the Gulf. There would seem to be no question but that the right of passage through an international waterway which lies within the territorial sea is affected by a state of war. Consequently, if Egypt and Israel are at war, and if the Rhodes General Armistice Agreement of February 24, 1949, does not have a special character which makes it more final than the traditional armistice agreement, a statement contained in a recent study on passage of ships through international waterways in wartime would be particularly relevant. Professor Baxter states the following:

The practices followed by states would seem to indicate that the recognition of any right of passage through international waterways for enemy warships when the littoral state is a belligerent would be altogether unthinkable. No more can it be expected that littoral states should deny themselves the opportunity of visiting, searching and seizing merchant ships passing through the waterway. The corresponding right of neutral warships and innocent merchant vessels to make use of the waterway must, under modern conditions, take second place to the legitimate need of the littoral state to defend itself and to derive strategic advantage from its control of the waterway. However, international law must require that the authority of the littoral state be exercised reasonably and with due regard to the seriousness of the danger anticipated.[89]

Having discussed questions raised with respect to Israeli shipping in the Gulf by the possible existence of a state of war, we may turn to a consideration of the legal status of the Gulf under the ordinary rules of international law, i.e., the law in effect in time of peace, and the bearing of these rules upon the Saudi Arabian position that the Gulf has the status of a closed water area, an Arab *mare clausum*.

Two of the conventions prepared by the United Nations Conference on the Law of the Sea which met at Geneva, February 24–April 27, 1958,[90] the Convention on the Territorial Sea and the Contiguous Zone, and the Convention on the High Seas, would seem to provide a useful point of

[88] Bloomfield, *op. cit.* 164.

[89] R. R. Baxter, "Passage of Ships Through International Waterways in Time of War," 31 Brit. Year Book of Int. Law 187–216, at 208 (1954).

[90] See article on the Conference by Arthur H. Dean, above, p. 607. The Conference was unable to reach agreement on the breadth of the territorial sea. One of the resolutions, adopted by the Conference on April 27, 1958, requests the U.N. General Assembly to study, at its 13th session (1958), the advisability of convening a second international conference of plenipotentiaries to consider further this question and other questions left unsettled by the Conference (A/CONF.13/L.56, April 30, 1958, p. 9).

departure for such consideration, inasmuch as they appear to represent the best consensus of present international opinion regarding the law of the sea. Since the problem of multinational bays was not dealt with by the Conference, resort will necessarily be made to other authorities on that question.

The threefold classification of water areas is clearly stated in Article 1 of the Convention on the High Seas, which reads: "The term high seas means all parts of the sea that are not included in the territorial sea or the internal waters of a state."[91] This threefold classification, according to H. A. Smith, "begins from the land outwards and obviously requires the delimitation of two lines—the line which divides internal from territorial waters, and the line between the territorial belt and the high seas."[92]

The Conference was unable to reach agreement on the breadth of the territorial sea. However, it has provided a method for drawing the baseline from which the breadth of the territorial sea can be measured. This baseline, according to Article 3 of the Convention on the Territorial Sea, is normally "the low-water line along the coast as marked on large-scale charts officially recognized by the coastal State." Article 4, however, provides also the possibility of employing straight baselines "where the coastline is deeply indented and cut into, or if there is a fringe of islands along the coast in its immediate vicinity," provided that "the drawing of such baselines must not depart to any appreciable extent from the general direction of the coast, and the sea areas lying within the lines must be sufficiently closely linked to the land domain to be subject to the regime of internal waters," and that "the system of straight baselines may not be applied by a State in such a manner as to cut off from the high seas the territorial sea of another State."[93]

Article 6 of the Territorial Sea Convention provides that:

> The outer limit of the territorial sea is the line every point of which is at a distance from the nearest point of the baseline equal to the breadth of the territorial sea.[94]

Article 5 provides that:

> 1. Waters on the landward side of the baseline of the territorial sea form part of the internal waters of the State.
> 2. When the establishment of a straight baseline in accordance with Article 4 has the effect of enclosing as internal waters areas which previously had been considered as part of the territorial sea or of the high seas, a right of innocent passage, as provided in Articles 14 to 23, shall exist in those waters.[95]

Article 12 provides that:

> 1. Where the coasts of two States are opposite or adjacent to each other, neither of the two States is entitled, failing agreement between

91 A/CONF. 13/L.53 (April 29, 1958), p. 2.
92 H. A. Smith, The Law and Custom of the Sea 6 (2nd ed., N. Y., 1950).
93 A/CONF. 13/L.52, p. 2.
94 Ibid., p. 3.
95 Ibid., pp. 2–3.

them to the contrary, to extend its territorial sea beyond the median line every point of which is equidistant from the nearest points on the baselines from which the breadth of the territorial seas of each of the States is measured. The provisions of this paragraph shall not apply, however, where it is necessary by reason of historic title or other special circumstances to delimit the territorial seas of the two States in a way which is at variance with this provision.

2. The line of delimitation between the territorial seas of two States lying opposite to each other or adjacent to each other shall be marked on large-scale charts officially recognized by the coastal States.[96]

The legal status of the territorial sea, and, by inference, that of internal waters, is set forth in Article 1 of the Convention, which reads as follows:

1. The sovereignty of a State extends, beyond its land territory and its internal waters, to a belt of sea adjacent to its coast, described as the territorial sea.

2. This sovereignty is exercised subject to the provisions of these articles and to other rules of international law.[97]

One of the principal limitations imposed by international law upon the coastal state's sovereignty over the territorial sea is the right of innocent passage. This right is accorded in the interest of freedom of navigation and may be described as broadly analogous to the common law easement with respect to land.[98] Articles 14 through 23 of the Convention on the Territorial Sea deal with various aspects of this right. Articles 14 through 17 are applicable to *all* ships. The provisions of these articles which seem most relevant to the present discussion are the following:

Article 14

1. Subject to the provisions of these articles, ships of all States, whether coastal or not, shall enjoy the right of innocent passage through the territorial sea.

. . . . .

4. Passage is innocent so long as it is not prejudicial to the peace, good order or security of the coastal State. Such passage shall take place in conformity with these articles and with other rules of international law.

Article 15

1. The coastal State must not hamper innocent passage through the territorial sea.

Article 16

1. The coastal State may take the necessary steps in its territorial sea to prevent passage which is not innocent.

. . . . .

3. Subject to the provisions of paragraph 4, the coastal State may, without discrimination amongst foreign ships, suspend temporarily in

---

96 *Ibid.*, p. 5.

97 *Ibid.*, p. 1. Article 2 adds that: ''The sovereignty of a coastal State extends to the air space over the territorial sea as well as to its bed and subsoil.'' *Ibid.*

98 See Smith, *op. cit.* 33–37; and C. B. Selak, Jr., ''Fishing Vessels and the Principle of Innocent Passage,'' 48 A.J.I.L. 627 (1954).

specified areas of its territorial sea the innocent passage of foreign ships if such suspension is essential for the protection of its security. Such suspension shall take effect only after having been duly published.

4. There shall be no suspension of the innocent passage of foreign ships through straits which are used for international navigation between one part of the high seas and another part of the high seas or the territorial sea of a foreign State.

Article 17

Foreign ships exercising the right of innocent passage shall comply with the laws and regulations enacted by the coastal State in conformity with these articles and other rules of international law and, in particular, with such laws relating to transport and navigation.

Article 23, applicable to warships, states that:

If any warship does not comply with the regulations of the coastal State concerning passage through the territorial sea and disregards any request for compliance which is made to it, the coastal State may require the warship to leave the territorial sea.[99]

The legal status of the high seas is set forth in Article 2 of the Convention on the High Seas, as follows:

The high seas being open to all nations, no State may validly purport to subject any part of them to its sovereignty. Freedom of the high seas is exercised under the conditions laid down by these articles and by the other rules of international law. It comprises, *inter alia*, both for coastal and non-coastal States:

(1) Freedom of navigation;
(2) Freedom of fishing;
(3) Freedom to lay submarine cables and pipelines;
(4) Freedom to fly over the high seas.

These freedoms, and others which are recognized by the general principles of international law, shall be exercised by all States with reasonable regard to the interests of other States in their exercise of the freedom of the high seas.[100]

Thus the regime of the high seas, as Smith has observed, is subject to international law alone, and national authority exercised thereon must conform to international custom or convention.[101] "As the high seas are a territory of the international community, the right of regulation must be exercised by the international community."[102]

Article 24 of the Convention on the Territorial Sea and the Contiguous Zone deals with the latter, and makes it clear that this zone is a part of the high seas. It states:

1. In a zone of the high seas contiguous to its territorial sea, the coastal State may exercise the control necessary to:

99 A/CONF. 13/L. 52, pp. 5-9.   100 A/CONF. 13/L. 53, p. 2.
101 *Op. cit.* 45-46 *et seq.*
102 Josef L. Kunz, "Continental Shelf and International Law: Confusion and Abuse," 50 A.J.I.L. 828, 829 (1956), citing C. John Colombos, The International Law of the Sea 56 (3rd ed., London, 1954).

(a) Prevent infringement of its customs, fiscal, immigration or sanitary regulations within its territory or territorial sea;
(b) Punish infringement of the above regulations committed within its territory or territorial sea.

2. The contiguous zone may not extend beyond twelve miles from the baseline from which the breadth of the territorial sea is measured.
3. Where the coasts of two States are opposite or adjacent to each other, neither of the two States is entitled, failing agreement between them to the contrary, to extend its contiguous zone beyond the median line every point of which is equidistant from the nearest points on the baselines from which the breadth of the territorial seas of the two States is measured.[103]

The Conference on the Law of the Sea did not attempt to codify the law with respect to multinational bays. Article 7 of the Convention on the Territorial Sea and the Contiguous Zone provides that: "This article relates only to bays the coasts of which belong to a single state." After defining a bay as "a well-marked indentation whose penetration is in such proportion to the width of its mouth as to contain land-locked waters and constitute more than a mere curvature of the coast," it states that:

Where the distance between the low-water marks of the natural entrance points of a bay does not exceed twenty-four miles, a closing line may be drawn between these two low-water marks, and the waters enclosed thereby shall be considered as internal waters.

The article adds that: "The foregoing provisions shall not apply to so-called 'historic bays.'"[104] One of the resolutions of the conference, however, adopted on April 27, 1958, deals with the "Regime of Historic Waters." It reads as follows:

The United Nations Conference on the Law of the Sea,
Considering that the International Law Commission has not provided for the regime of historic waters, including historic bays,
Recognizing the importance of the juridical status of such areas,
Requests the General Assembly of the United Nations to arrange for the study of the juridical regime of historic waters, including historic bays, and for the communication of the results of such study to all States Members of the United Nations.[105]

The Report of the International Law Commission covering the work of its Eighth Session, April 23–July 4, 1956, which was one of the bases for the discussion of the conventions prepared by the Conference on the Law of the Sea, stated, in the commentary to Article 7, that "the Commission felt bound to propose only rules applicable to bays the coasts of which belong to a single state. As regards other bays, the Commission had not sufficient data at its disposal concerning the number of cases involved or the regulations at present applicable to them."[106] The Report also observed, in the commentary to Article 26, that:

Some large stretches of water, entirely surrounded by dry land, are known as "lakes," others as "seas." The latter constitute in-

[103] A/CONF. 13/L. 52, p. 9.   [104] *Ibid.*, pp. 3–4.
[105] A/CONF. 13/L. 56, p. 8.   [106] See 51 A.J.I.L. 186–188 (1957).

ternal seas, to which the regime of the high seas is not applicable. Where such stretches of water communicate with the high seas by a strait or arm of the sea, they are considered as "internal seas" if the coasts, including those of the waterway giving access to the high seas, belong to a single state. If that is not the case, they are considered as high seas. These rules may, however, be modified for historical reasons or by international arrangement.[107]

The generally accepted principle with respect to gulfs and bays surrounded by the territories of more than one state has been set forth by Judge Lauterpacht as follows:

> . . . as a rule, all gulfs and bays enclosed by the land of more than one littoral state, however narrow their entrance may be, are non-territorial. They are parts of the open sea, the marginal belt (territorial sea) inside the gulfs and bays excepted. They can never be appropriated; they are in time of peace and war open to vessels of all nations, including men-of-war, and foreign fishing vessels cannot, therefore, be compelled to comply with municipal regulations of the littoral state concerning the mode of fishing.[108]

Sir Cecil Hurst has pointed out that "so-called gulfs and bays are often parts of the high seas," the descriptive title having no necessary bearing upon water areas under international law.[109] It is suggested, therefore, that in the light of Judge Lauterpacht's comments cited above, the International Law Commission's commentary regarding modification of rules regarding "lakes" and "seas" for "historical reasons or by international arrangement" [110] would be applicable equally to "gulfs" and "bays."

All gulfs and bays may be classified as either "territorial" or "non-territorial," the former consisting of internal waters of the coastal state, for normally only one state is involved, and the latter comprising a part of the high seas.[111] By these criteria the Gulf of Aqaba would appear to be non-territorial in character, with respect to which each coastal state possesses a belt of territorial sea, but which, as an entity, with the exception of such belts, would be a part of the high seas. Do historical or other considerations modify such status for the Gulf? The Saudi Arabian Government's position appears essentially to imply that the waters of the Gulf are internal waters of several Arab coastal states, either on the basis

---

107 *Ibid.* 205.

108 1 Oppenheim, International Law: Peace 460–461 (7th ed., H. Lauterpacht, 1948).

109 "The Territoriality of Bays," 3 Brit. Year Book of Int. Law 42–54, at 49 (1922–23).

110 Note 107 above.

111 See Report of the International Law Commission, *loc. cit.*, Art. 7, 51 A.J.I.L. 186–188 (1957).

Judge Lauterpacht has pointed out that: "The expression 'territorial bay' must not be allowed to obscure the facts (1) that the waters contained in territorial bays, and in the territorial portions of bays not entirely territorial, are not territorial waters and part of the maritime belt (territorial sea), but national (internal) waters, and (2) that the limit of the national waters is the datum line for the measurement of the maritime belt." Oppenheim-Lauterpacht, *op. cit.* 458, footnote.

Perhaps a more useful term for bays referred to as "territorial bays" would be "internal bays," and for bays referred to as "non-territorial bays," "open bays."

of joint control or agreed distribution of such waters. Leaving aside for the moment the problem with respect to Israel's connection with the Gulf, can justification be found for the Saudi Arabian position? The American authority, Charles Cheney Hyde, has made the following comment relevant to this matter:

Bays Bordered by Land Belonging to Two or More States.

When the geographical relationship of a bay to the adjacent or enveloping land is such that the sovereign of the latter, if a single state, might not unlawfully claim the waters as a part of its territory, •it is not apparent why a like privilege should be denied to two or •more states to which such land belongs, at least if they are so agreed, and accept as between themselves a division of the waters concerned. No requirement of international law as such deprives them of that privilege, notwithstanding the disposition of some who would leave little room for its application.[112]

The Harvard Draft Convention on Territorial Waters of 1929, George Grafton Wilson, Reporter, made the following comment in Article 6:

Where the waters within the seaward limit are bordered by two or more states, it would seem that the bordering states should be permitted by international law to divide such waters between them as inland waters. If the same waters are bordered by one state only, that state would clearly be entitled, under Article 5, to treat all of the waters as inland waters. The power of two or more states should not be smaller than the powers of one state in this respect if the states can reach an agreement.[113]

Dr. Hyde has drawn attention to the Gulf of Fonseca decision, which appears to be the only instance in which a court has held that a bay or gulf surrounded by the territory of more than one coastal state is "territorial" in nature and an "historic bay" or "closed sea." The Gulf, situated on the west coast of Central America, is enclosed by three states, Nicaragua, Honduras and El Salvador. In *El Salvador* v. *Nicaragua*, suit was brought in the Central American Court of Justice [114] to nullify a Nicaraguan grant to the United States, under the Bryan-Chamorro Treaty of August 4, 1914, of "the right to establish, operate and maintain a naval base at such place on the territory of Nicaragua bordering upon the Gulf of Fonseca as the Government of the United States may select." El Salvador argued that the Gulf was the subject of joint or community ownership, while Nicaragua asserted that its waters were apportioned among the three coastal states on the basis of an extension of the lines marking the national land boundaries. Both states agreed that it was a "closed sea."

[112] 1 Hyde, International Law, Chiefly as Interpreted and Applied by the United States 475 (2nd rev. ed., Boston, 1945).

[113] 23 A.J.I.L. Spec. Supp. 274 (1929).

[114] Established by the Central American States by the Convention of Dec. 20, 1907. 1 Hackworth's Digest 702; 2 A.J.I.L. Supp. 231 (1908).

In its judgment of March 9, 1917, the Court held the Gulf of Fonseca to be "an historic bay possessed of the characteristics of a closed sea." The rationale of the decision was: (1) The coastal states "had exercised immemorial possession accompanied by dominion both peaceful and continuous and by acquiescence on the part of other nations, from 1522 to 1821, when all were ruled by Spain, from 1821 to 1839, when all formed part of the Federal Republic of the Center of America, and from 1839 to the time of the decision, when they formed separate political entities . . . that . . . exclusive ownership has been exercised over the waters of the Gulf during the course of nearly 400 years is incontrovertible"; (2) the size and special geographic configuration of the Gulf "which safeguards so many interests of vital importance to the economic, commercial, agricultural and industrial life of the riparian states"; and (3) the necessity that the coastal states possess the Gulf in accordance with these interests and that of national defense. The Court decided that with the exception of a three-mile belt of territorial sea along the coast of each state, the three coastal states possessed the waters of the Gulf as joint owners. Honduras and Nicaragua objected to the concept of community of ownership, claiming that the Gulf was a "closed sea" on the basis of divided ownership of all the waters therein.[115] No instances of protest with respect to the closed-sea claims of the three littoral states are known.

During the General Assembly's consideration of Israeli withdrawal from the entrance to the Gulf of Aqaba in early 1957, Mr. Urquia of El Salvador alluded to the Gulf of Fonseca. He cited a comment he had made at Mexico City in 1956 to the Inter-American Council of Jurists on this question, in which, *inter alia,* he had stated the following:

> . . . The Gulf or Bay of Fonseca belongs to the category of bays known in international law as historical bays, and is therefore subject to the exclusive sovereignty of the coastal State or States, regardless of the distance or length to which it penetrates inland or its width at the mouth, provided that, as is the case for the Gulf of Fonseca, the coastal States have asserted and assert their sovereignty for reasons based on their geographical situation, their use of the Gulf for centuries, and above all, their self-defense.

Mr. Urquia added that the position of the Salvadorean Government had become known as the "Meléndez doctrine," from the name of the then President of El Salvador, and stated that

> the doctrine provides that when an arm of the sea occupies the space between two or more countries, the area of the waters *inter fauces terrae* is necessarily within the joint jurisdiction of the coastal States.

[115] Anales de la Corte de Justicia Centroamericana (1916–1917), Vols. V, VI and VII; 11 A.J.I.L. 674–730 (1917); P. C. Jessup, The Law of Territorial Waters and Maritime Jurisdiction 398–410 (N. Y., 1927).

Judge Lauterpacht has cautioned that the decision has force only with respect to the three states concerned, and has observed that while the United States appears to have acknowledged the territorial character of the Gulf, the attitude of other states is not known. *Op. cit.* 460–461, footnote 6.

He concluded by remarking that he had made this statement "as a kind of reservation with respect to what has been said here regarding the case of the Gulf of Aqaba and the Straits of Tiran." [116]

Can the Gulf of Fonseca case be regarded as a precedent to be applied to the Gulf of Aqaba? Geographically, the two water areas are approximately of similar size and restricted configuration.[117] Historically, the Gulf of Aqaba was Arab in character from approximately 700 A.D. until 1517; under Ottoman control during the period of Ottoman suzerainty over the surrounding Arab lands from 1517 until the end of World War I; and under the control of the present littoral Arab states from approximately the end of the war to the present, with mandated Palestine until 1948 occupying the coastline now controlled by Israel. The Gulf undoubtedly has strategic and defensive importance to the coastal Arab states. In addition, it has been for many centuries and remains an avenue for pilgrim traffic proceeding to the yearly Muslim pilgrimage at Mecca and Medina, although not so important as it was before the days of air travel. Some Arab authorities appear to regard the inclusion of Article 10, paragraph 3, in the Constantinople Convention of 1888 as designed to retain for the Ottoman Government a free hand in protecting the pilgrim route. These authorities seem to interpret this provision as lending support to the Saudi Arabian claim that the Gulf is a "locked Arab Gulf, without any international character." [118]

Although the Gulf of Aqaba was under Arab or Ottoman (and Islamic) control for approximately 1200 years, no formal closed-sea claim appears ever to have been made until that asserted by the Saudi Arabian Government early in 1957. However, obviously international law in its present sophisticated form did not exist throughout most of that period. In addition, it is likely that there was no need of that assertion of such a claim; foreign Powers probably were not interested in navigation in the Gulf, since it apparently had no commercial importance to them. The question of the Gulf's status might not have arisen at this time except for the fact of Arab hostility toward Israel, and the additional fact that the presence of the UNEF contingent at the entrance to the Gulf now renders Egyptian measures against Israeli shipping futile.

No precision appears to have been given to Saudi Arabia's closed-sea claim, for no agreement appears to have been reached among the three Arab littoral states to provide either for joint control of the Gulf's waters or for an apportionment thereof.

Further, both Egypt and Saudi Arabia, by their territorial sea legislation,[119] claim respectively six miles of territorial sea along their coastlines

[116] General Assembly, 11th Sess., Official Records, 666th Plenary Meeting (A/P.V. 666), March 1, 1957, p. 1281.

[117] The Gulf of Fonseca is approximately 50 miles in length and 30 in breadth. The distance between headlands is approximately 19 1/3 miles, although islands at the entrance reduce the distance to 8 miles, or 4 miles, if the Farallon Islands are considered to be the Nicaraguan boundary of the Gulf.

[118] Note 68 above.   [119] Notes 23 and 24 above.

in the Gulf, and an additional six-mile zone of contiguous waters. Although the Court in the Gulf of Fonseca case envisaged a situation in which a closed sea could have a belt of territorial sea along the coasts of the several states, the remainder of the waters being held jointly as internal waters, such a situation does not normally prevail. Ordinarily, the presence of a zone of territorial sea implies that a water area is essentially a part of the high seas. A zone of territorial sea interposes itself between the coast or the zone of internal waters, and the high seas; when a coastal indentation consists of internal waters in its entirety, the territorial sea begins seaward of a line drawn from headland to headland. A contiguous zone, according to the Convention on the Territorial Sea and the Contiguous Zone, cited above, is a part of the high seas.[120] Consequently, in spite of the existence of factors pointing to a close parallel between the Gulfs of Fonseca and Aqaba, the closed-sea claim of Saudi Arabia does contain basic weaknesses.[121]

Perhaps it is not the thought of the Saudi Arabian Government that the Gulf of Aqaba be considered in its entirety internal waters of the surrounding Arab states. The fact that large areas of waters in the Gulf, as well as the waters of the entrances to the Gulf, are territorial sea of Egypt or Saudi Arabia, may have inspired the concept that the Gulf is a closed sea. If this is the rationale of the Saudi Arabian position, however, it must be borne in mind that under the international law of peace the right of innocent passage exists with respect to the territorial sea.[122] This right, accordingly, could legally be claimed by all states not at war with the coastal states.

The Gulf of Fonseca situation appears to be unique. Water areas surrounded by the territory of a single coastal state, and thus having the status of "closed seas," which subsequently, because of political changes resulting in the establishment of more than one state on their shores, become multinational in character, generally have come to be regarded as essentially parts of the high seas, regardless of the narrowness of their entrances. Special treaty arrangements, however, usually have been necessary to establish this character.

The Black Sea is a case in point. It was a Turkish lake from 1484, when the Ottoman Empire completed the conquest of its entire littoral, until 1774, when, in accordance with provisions of the Treaty of Kutchuk-Kainardji, Russia secured a foothold on its northern coast.[123] By that treaty not only was Russia recognized as a Black Sea littoral state, but also obtained freedom of navigation—although to some extent limited—in the

---

[120] Note 103 above; p. 840 below.

[121] The London Times Special Correspondent, cited above, note 86, has observed with respect to the closed-sea argument: "At a time when the whole area was subject to Turkish sovereignty, this argument might have been tenable. This is no longer the case. The Gulf is enclosed by the shores of four independent states—Egypt, Israel, Jordan, and Saudi Arabia."

[122] See notes 98 and 99 above.

[123] Erik Brüel, International Straits, Vol. II, pp. 265–266 (Copenhagen and London, 1947).

Black Sea, and a corresponding right of passage through the Turkish Straits.[124] According to Hurewitz, the treaty "converted the Black Sea from an exclusively Ottoman lake into a Russo-Ottoman lake. It assured Russian commercial vessels unrestricted navigation in that sea and free passage through the Straits."[125] Between 1774 and 1806 the Ottoman Empire entered into a series of treaties with European Powers which provided for free navigation through the Straits by commercial vessels. A treaty of May 7, 1830, between the Ottoman Empire and the United States declared that "merchant vessels of the United States, in like manner as vessels of the most favored nation," should have liberty to enter the Black Sea through the Straits. Nothing was said regarding warships.[126] By the Treaty of Adrianople of September 21, 1829, Russia succeeded in having removed the last restrictions on the passage of its merchant vessels through the Straits. By this treaty, according to Brüel, the Ottoman Empire "undertook *expressis verbis* an obligation which was already in existence," and by 1914 the right of passage for merchant vessels through the Straits was an established rule of international law.[127]

At the present time the Montreux Convention of July 20, 1936,[128] governs the regime of the Turkish Straits. It provides "freedom of transit and navigation by sea in the Straits . . . without limit of time" for all merchant vessels in time of peace, and in time of war when Turkey is not a belligerent. When Turkey is at war, merchant vessels of states not at war with Turkey enjoy the right on condition that they do not assist the enemy, and pass by day through channels indicated by the Turkish authorities. The passage of warships both in times of war and peace is much more restricted, and when Turkey is at war or in imminent danger of war, is entirely at the discretion of the Turkish Government.[129]

Eric Brüel, in his study of international straits, has expressed the opinion that

> the fact that a legal status *sui juris* has been created for international straits in general and that regimes more or less logical have been established for particularly important straits has shown that strong normative forces are at work in this sphere . . . the direction of that development, although neither clear nor even, is at any rate not doubtful when viewed over long periods. This applies not merely to the general rules of international law relating to international straits but also in principle to the special regimes which have now been created, from the Sound Treaty with its purely negative abolition of

[124] *Ibid.* 271.

[125] J. C. Hurewitz, Diplomacy in the Near and Middle East, Vol. I, p. 54 (Princeton, 1956). For text of treaty, see *ibid.* 54–61.

[126] 1 Moore's Digest 665.

[127] Brüel, *op. cit.* 291–295. On the regime of the Turkish Straits, see also Higgins and Colombos, The International Law of the Sea 142–146 (2nd rev. ed., 1951, by C. John Colombos).

[128] 7 International Legislation 386–399 (1941); Hurewitz, *op. cit.*, Vol. II, pp. 197–203; 173 League of Nations Treaty Series 213–241 (1936–37); 31 A.J.I.L. Supp. 1 (1937).

[129] *Ibid.*, and Brüel, *op. cit.* 388–424.

a power exercised by the coastal state against the interests of the international community, to the Montreux Convention with its emphasis on the fact that special rights were granted to the coastal state not in its own interest alone but also in that of the international community . . . the principle of freedom of navigation was proclaimed in the Montreux Convention as a principle of international law independent of the will of the parties. If this principle is correctly utilized it can be of the greatest importance for the future development in this sphere.[130]

Brüel's reference to the Sound Treaty was with respect to the regime of the Danish Belts and the Sound, the only water connection between the North and Baltic Seas before the construction of the Kiel (Nord Ostsee) Canal. For centuries the Danish Kings had collected dues on traffic proceeding through these restricted water areas (the Sound's minimum width is two miles, and the minimum width of the Great and Little Belts is less), and in the "secret" articles embodied in the Armed Neutrality of 1800, Denmark, Norway and Russia claimed to maintain the Baltic Sea "perpetually as a closed sea." These states recognized, however, that in time of peace all nations could navigate through it and "enjoy the advantages of perfect tranquillity," but asserted that they had the right to take all necessary measures to guarantee it and its coasts against all hostilities. Britain, France and Holland refused to accept this position, and the right to close the Baltic Sea was definitely rejected by a general treaty on this subject, the Convention of Copenhagen of March 14, 1857. By the terms of this Convention, Denmark bound itself "not to subject any ships, on any pretext, to any detention or hindrance in the passage of the Sound or the Belts." Article 195 of the Treaty of Versailles also provided for "free passage into the Baltic to all nations," and also prohibited the erection by Germany of any fortifications or installation of any artillery commanding the maritime routes between the North and Baltic Seas.[131]

The United States entered into a separate treaty with Denmark with respect to the Danish Straits in 1857, and paid the Danish Government a lump sum of $400,000 in consideration of perpetual waiver of the Sound dues. Prior to that time the United States Government had expressed criticism of the regime of the Straits, and on October 14, 1848, Secretary of State Buchanan informed the U. S. Minister to Denmark that:

> Under the public law of nations, it cannot be pretended that Denmark has any right to levy duties on vessels passing through the Sound from the North Sea to the Baltic. Under that law, the navigation of the two seas connected by this strait is free to all nations and therefore the navigation of the channel by which they are connected ought to be free. In the language employed by Mr. Wheaton, "even if such strait be bounded on both sides by the territory of the same sovereign, and is at the same time so narrow as to be commanded by cannon shot from both shores, the exclusive territorial jurisdiction of that sovereign over such strait is controlled by the right of other nations to communicate with the seas thus connected."[132]

---

130 Brüel, op. cit. 424–425.

131 Higgins and Colombos, op. cit. 127–128.

132 1 Moore's Digest 660; citation to Wheaton's International Law (Dana's ed.).

To conclude, the fact cannot be overlooked that the Gulf of Aqaba has a multinational character, and would have such character even if Israel had no coastline on the Gulf. In spite of a current trend towards Arab unity, the three Arab coastal states are at present independent, sovereign entities. They do not appear to have entered into any sort of formal agreement to designate the Gulf a closed Arab water area, and, in fact, each coastal state has its own coastal sea legislation.[133] By the weight of international precedent the Gulf would seem clearly to be non-territorial and basically a part of the high seas, even though a considerable portion of the waters therein constitute the territorial seas of the coastal states. Not only is more than one coastal state involved, but also there is a belt of water along the center of the Gulf which is not included in the territorial sea of any of the coastal states (and, as we have noted, contiguous zones constitute a part of the high seas). Consequently, the straits at the entrance would appear clearly to constitute an international waterway, even though these waters comprise in their entirety the territorial seas either of Egypt or Saudi Arabia, and Article 16(4) of the Convention on the Territorial Sea and the Contiguous Zone would seem to be applicable:

> There shall be no suspension of the innocent passage of foreign ships through straits which are used for international navigation between one part of the high seas and another part of the high seas or the territorial sea of a foreign State.[134]

While the weight of the evidence points to this as being the general legal status of the Gulf, it does not necessarily follow that the right of innocent passage would be available to Israel in the absence of special arrangements through the United Nations. A number of the principal maritime states appear to be of the opinion that all states, including Israel, clearly may exercise this right, since no belligerent rights persist between Egypt and Israel. The Arab states, particularly the coastal states, and India, disagree. A definitive solution of this question would seem to depend in large part upon what interpretation is placed upon the Armistice Agreements *re* the problem of belligerent rights, and, as we have seen, authorities differ on this issue. While the Secretary General of the United Nations has stated on several occasions that "The international significance of the Gulf of Aqaba may be considered to justify the right of innocent passage through the Straits of Tiran and the Gulf in accordance with recognized rules of international law,"[135] he has expressed the opinion that: "A legal controversy exists as to the extent of the right of innocent passage through these waters."[136]

It is submitted that it would be well for this controversy to be settled by an appropriate juridical authority, perhaps by a decision or advisory opinion of the International Court of Justice. While the United Nations Emergency Force is at present controlling the entrance to the Gulf, and the

---

[133] Notes 23, 24 and 25, above.
[134] A/CONF. 13/L. 52 (April 28, 1958), p. 6; below, p. 838.
[135] U.N. Docs. A/3500 (Jan. 15, 1957), par. 14, and A/3512 (Jan. 24, 1957), par. 24.
[136] U.N. Doc. A/3512 (Jan. 24, 1957), par. 24.

coastal states have exercised commendable self-restraint with respect to this issue, a legal solution would seem desirable, and perhaps would help to contribute to the stability of a troubled area.

For a final and complete determination of the status of the Gulf it may be necessary to await a final settlement of the Palestine question, for it is unclear at present what is the status of Israel's coastline on the Gulf. Israel's frontiers have been established by the several armistice agreements with neighboring Arab states. These agreements by their terms provide that the frontiers are not territorial boundaries, but merely temporary lines of military control, and are not intended to prejudice rights, claims and positions of the parties as regards an ultimate settlement of the Palestine question.[137] Is Israel's coastline on the Gulf, depending as it does upon the land frontiers established by the Armistice Agreements with Egypt and Jordan, of a different legal nature than that of the land frontiers? While this would seem to be unlikely, it is a question which ought to be considered by the appropriate juridical authority.

With respect to the closed-sea claim of Saudi Arabia, should a final settlement of the Palestine question deny Israel its present coastline on the Gulf, there would seem to be no objection to the littoral Arab states, by common agreement, designating the Gulf as a closed sea, at least according to the views of several eminent authorities.[138] Also, should Israel retain its coastline, there is the possibility that the four littoral states could, by unanimous agreement, achieve the same result, since Israel would be deemed another successor state of the Ottoman Empire through the Palestine Mandate, and thus the historical, as well as the geographical and other factors, found persuasive with respect to the Gulf of Fonseca, would be applied to the Gulf of Aqaba. The preparation of the study of the "Regime of Historic Waters," which the United Nations Conference on the Law of the Sea has asked the General Assembly to arrange for, may provide an opportunity for the consideration of this question.[139]

Should it be possible for the coastal states to agree that the Gulf of Aqaba is a closed sea, there is the possibility that Articles 4 and 5 of the Convention on the Territorial Sea and Contiguous Zone [140] would be interpreted to permit innocent passage through these waters, as provided in Articles

[137] Secretary General Hammarskjold has noted this fact in his report to the General Assembly, U.N. Doc. A/3512, Jan. 24, 1957, as have Mr. Pearson of Canada and Mr. Shukairy of Saudi Arabia at the 11th Session of the General Assembly, note 76 above.

[138] Notes 112 and 113 above. This view would seem also to be implicit in the remarks of the Special Correspondent of the London Times, March 8, 1957, note 121 above.

[139] Note 105 above; p. 867 below.

[140] Art. 4(1) provides that: "In localities where the coast line is deeply indented and cut into, or if there is a fringe of islands along the coast in its immediate vicinity, the method of straight baselines joining appropriate points may be employed in drawing the baseline from which the breadth of the territorial sea is measured."

Art. 5(2) provides that: "Where the establishment of a straight baseline in accordance with Article 4 has the effect of enclosing as internal waters areas which previously had been considered as part of the territorial sea or the high seas, a right of innocent passage, as provided in Articles 14 to 23, shall exist in those waters."

14 to 23 of the same convention.[141] This would be particularly necessary because of the positions of Jordan and Israel at the head of the Gulf. However, if a special regime for the Gulf should come into existence, the governing agreement probably would make adequate provision for passage of international shipping.[142]

Pending the possible future establishment of a special regime for the Gulf of Aqaba, it would be well if agreement could be reached by the coastal states regarding their respective zones of territorial sea and contiguous zones, where there is the possibility of overlapping jurisdictions, in accordance with Articles 12 and 24 of the Convention on the Territorial Sea and the Contiguous Zone.[143]

It is to be hoped that the United Nations will continue to take all steps possible towards the achievement of a political climate in the area which will make feasible a definitive determination of the legal status of the Gulf of Aqaba, so that the shipping of the international community may be free to use this increasingly important water area, whatever its status may be found to be, without controversy.

[141] Note 99 above; see pp. 837–840 below.
[142] In this connection, see Smith, *op. cit.* 23–24.
[143] A/CONF. 13/L. 52 (April 28, 1958), pp. 5 and 9.

The Right of Passage in the Gulf of Aqaba

M. BURHAN W. HAMMAD

PART I

Geography and History Make Aqaba an Arab Gulf

A. GEOGRAPHICAL SURVEY

THE GULF OF AQABA, the Sinus Aelanites of antiquity, is a narrow bay, which stretches from the northern tip of the Red Sea, and slants toward the northeast as the right of the two arms of that sea. It is 100 miles long, between 7-17 miles wide,[1] and has a coast line of approximately 230 miles which extends 125 miles in Egypt, 94 miles in Saudi Arabia, 4 miles in Jordan and 7 miles[2] in Israel. Two ports lie at its head. Aqaba of Jordan, and Elath of Israel, originally called Um Rashrash. At its mouth where it connects with the Red Sea, and between the coasts of Saudia Arabia and Egypt are the Straits and the Tiran and Sinafir Islands. The distance between the Egyptian coast to Tiran is approximately three nautical miles; and that between Tiran and the Saudi Arabian coast is four nautical miles.[3] The straits are extremely dangerous to navigation due to several coral islets and rocks.[4] Despite continued references to the *Straits* of Tiran by United Nations personnel and men of public office, there is actually only *one* navigable

---

[1] See L. M. Bloomfield, Egypt, Israel and The Gulf of Aqaba, Toronto, 1957, p. 1, who measures the width between 12-17 miles; and see H. Hafez and M.A.R. Khalin in The Gulf of Aqaba, Cairo, p. 3, who measures it between 7-14 miles.

[2] *Ibid.* He gives this data in kilometers as follows: Total coastline 367 km, coast of Egypt 200 km, Saudi Arabia 150 km, Jordan 6 km, and Israel 11 km. See also P. A. Porter in The Gulf of Aqaba in International Waterways, Washington, 1957, Footnote p. 1; he measures Israel's coast as only 6 miles.

[3] See: Security Council Official Record, 9th year, 659th meeting, where an Egyptian Aide Mémoire to the U.S. Embassy in Cairo was read in the Security Council meeting of 15 February 1954, by which the distance is at least 3 marine miles off the Egyptian side of Sinai and 4 miles off the opposite side of Saudi Arabia.

[4] Strabo and Diodorus Siculus described "its projecting reefs, its sunken rocks, its hollowed and havenless promontories, its shoals, its whirlpools, its cross-tides, a stern succession of features, peculiar to this fearful coast, and the cause, to Aelius Callus, of the loss of so many of his ships." Quoted by Charles Forster, *The Historical Geography of Arabia* (London 1844) vol. II, p. 288, and described by Crichton as "filled with sunken rocks, sand-banks, and small islands, which throw impediments in the way of free and safe navigation." The History of Arabia, vol. I (1834) p. 65.

strait. The strait's navigable channel is 500 meters wide, and closely hugs the Egyptian Sinai Peninsula at a point known as Ras Nassrami, to the south of which lies Sharm El Sheikh.[5]

B. BACKGROUND TO THE CONFLICT.

On January 28, 1950, following an agreement between Saudi Arabia and Egypt which transferred and regulated authority over the two islands of Tiran and Sinafir to Egypt, an Aide Mémoire was sent by the Egyptian Government to the American Embassy in Cairo which reads:

"1.—Taking into consideration certain velleities which have manifested themselves recently on the part of Israel authorities on behalf of the Islands of Tiran and Sinafir in the Red Sea at the entrance of the Gulf of Aqaba, the Government of Egypt acting in full accord with the Government of Saudi Arabia has given orders to occupy effectively these two islands. This occupation is now an accomplished fact.

"2.—In doing this Egypt wanted simply to confirm its right (as well as every possible right of the Kingdom of Saudi Arabia) in regard to the mentioned islands which by their geographical position are at least 3 marine miles off the Egyptian side of Sinai and 4 miles approximately off the opposite side of Saudi Arabia, all this in order to forestall any attempt on or possible violation of its rights.

"3.—This occupation is not conceived in a spirit to hinder in whatever way it may be the innocent passage across the maritime space separating these two islands from the Egyptian coast of Sinai. It goes without saying that this passage, the only practicable, will remain free as in the past being in conformity with the international practice and the recognized principles of international law."[6]

Until 1950, passage through the straits and the Gulf was limited to the shipping of the surrounding Arab States, namely, Egypt, Saudi Arabia and Jordan. Since then, passage has been mostly confined to

---

[5] According to a map drawn by the U.S. Navy Department Hydrographic Office, only one strait is referred to which is the Strait of Tiran. Map No. 2812, Edition 3, Oct. 1919; Authorities British Admiralty Chart No. 8a, U.S. Hydrographic Office Publication.

[6] Security Council, *op.cit.*, supra note 3.

ships heading to the Jordanian port of Aqaba.[7] Prior to June 25th, 1952, when Elath was established as a harbor, Israeli ships neither sailed the gulf, nor passed through the Strait. In spite of the proclamation of Elath as a harbor, actually its role as a local or an international port was insignificant. The New York Times under date of December 9, 1955 observes:

"Only four or five ships sailing to or from the Israeli port of Elath have passed through the gulf in those seven years since the establishment of Israel."[8]

In 1954, Egypt promulgated certain regulations regarding maritime traffic through its territorial waters, in the Strait of Tiran. A naval signal station was established and vessels approaching the area were ordered to keep "a sharp lookout for signals made by this station." In August 1955, the Director General of the Egyptian Ports and Lights Administration issued a general regulation to the effect that 72 hours prior to a planned passage through the straits, the following information must be given the Egyptian authorities "name of vessel, type, nationality, exact hour of passage through the straits, general cargo, and destination."[9] These regulations were stated to be essential to the security and protection of its coast and territorial waters and in combating illicit traffic in narcotics. Between 1951-1955, very few ships were detained or fired upon by the shore batteries. Such incidents were the result of non-compliance with the directives of the Egyptian authorities. Of these only two cases pertain to ships en route to Elath.[10]

It is beyond doubt that sovereignty over the Gulf and the Strait was solely asserted by the Arab States and Egypt respectively and, despite the illegal seizure and holding of a small frontage by Israel, remains with the Arab States. This sovereignty, or authority and control over the Gulf and the Strait, together with the fact that all the territories surrounding them belonged since immemorial times to the Arabs, identifies the status juris or legal character of the straits. The 1956 invasion of Egypt by Israel resulted in Egypt's loss of comprehensive control over the Gulf and the Strait. Israel has since been able to navi-

[7] *Id.* See statistics given by the Representative of Egypt. And see also Official Statistical data of the Hashemite Kingdom of Jordan.

[8] New York Times, December 9, 1955.

[9] Journal de Commerce et de la Marine, Alexandria (August 29, 1955), Al-Ahram, Cairo, Sept. 13, 1955.

[10] Bloomfield, *op.cit.*, cites 7 incidents in this period, pp. 11-12.

gate, something which had previously been denied it. Needless to say, coercive change is unpermissible and illegal under the rules of international law. This fact has been endorsed by the United Nations Secretary General's report to the General Assembly where he referred to the change effected by the invasion of Egypt:

> "The U.N. cannot condone a change of the status juris resulting from military action contrary to the provisions of the Charter. The organization must, therefore, maintain that the status juris existing prior to such military action be re-established by a withdrawal of troops, and by the relinquishment or nullification of rights asserted in territories covered by the military action."[11]

But even if we assume that Egypt's status juris over the Gulf and the strait is questionable, it will have to be conceded that the passage of Israeli shipping is a "legal controversy."[12] That the invasion of Egypt should not affect the solution of this "legal controversy" is also pointed out by the Secretary General of the United Nations:

> "It follows from principles guiding the United Nations that the Israeli military action and its consequences should not be elements influencing the solution."[13]

Neither was the establishment of the United Nations Emergency Force envisaged as implementing any policy affecting this contested issue.

> "In accordance with the general legal principles recognized as decisive for the deployment of the U.N.E.F., the force should not be used so as to prejudge the solution of the controversial question involved. The U.N.E.F. thus, is not to be deployed in such a way as to protect any special position on these questions."[14]

Even the Permanent Representative of Israel confirmed the fact that no guarantee was given by the Secretary General for his country's

[11] Report by the Secretary General of the United Nations on the Middle East situation published in New York Times on the 25th of January 1957, Part 2, par. 1, sect. a, p. 6.

[12] See New York Times where it published a declaration given by Mr. Hammarskjold, January 25, 1957, p. 6.

[13] *Op. cit.*, supra note 11, par. 23.

[14] *Id*. par. 29, and see sect. B where the Secretary General reiterates that the force "must be impartial in the sense that it does not serve as a means to force settlement, in the interest of one party, of political conflicts or legal issues recognized as controversial."

right of passage through the Strait.[15] Despite the repudiation of their change of the status quo by the United Nations, Israel has had the support of the United States for the navigation of the Gulf in various declarations made by Secretary of State Dulles and President Eisenhower.[16] Subsequent to these declarations, the American tanker Kern Hills sailed through the Straits towards Elath.[17] Upon these declarations and the tanker passage, Israel based its contention of the establishment of the principle of innocent passage. In Israeli circles, the passage of the tanker was hailed as a milestone in "the history of the Gulf of Aqaba as an international waterway."[18]

That the United States has no legal authority to guarantee or establish such a principle is beyond question. The exercise of passage through the Gulf by Israel was an act of force as was its seizure of the land, and violation of the rules of international law, which had been endorsed by the Secretary General. Such illegality, despite any duration of time, cannot nullify or curtail Egypt's claims to authority over the Gulf. Neither can the allegation that the Strait is an international waterway be upheld.

Furthermore, it is incongruous that coercion should supplant international law as a means of settlement of disputes in disregard of commitments to the United Nations embodying basic community values.

C. AQABA IN COMPREHENSIVE PERSPECTIVE

It has to be always kept in mind that the Aqaba dispute forms part and parcel of the whole Palestine question, and that any comprehensive discussion of Aqaba must take into account a complicated set of relationships, raising questions of territorial integrity, national security, self-defense, and lawful reprisals. The Arab states vigorously oppose Israel's occupation of the coastal strip and the latter's claim of sovereign rights to passage in what Israel conceives to be an international waterway. Relying on the contrary view that the Gulf of Aqaba is a historical bay, the Arab states point to their immemorial posses-

---

[15] See: A letter dated February 10, 1957, from the Permanent Representative of Israel to the U.N. Secretary General. New York Times, February 11, 1957.

[16] See New York Times, where it indicates those declarations. April 7, 1957, p. 1. And see New York Times of February 13, 1957, where it published certain proposals by Mr. John Foster Dulles to the Israeli Government.

[17] *Ibid.*

[18] *Ibid.* The paper stated that "By this action the United States would consider the strait to be an international waterway."

sion as evidence of their right to claim the gulf as a part of their sovereign territories. And, conceiving of sovereign rights as the basis of their claim, the Arab states deny that Israel's military occupation of a part of the Gulf coastline—an occupation which is the fruit of Israeli violation of the United Nations Charter and several Security Council resolutions, as well as the terms of its armistice agreements with Egypt and Jordan—gives Israel any lawful claim to sovereignty in the disputed area. Each party's claims has, at various times, been endorsed wholly or in part by the General Assembly[19] or the Security Council. But as is shown below, the Aqaba dispute is only one of the many points of controversy that form the Palestine question. Recognizing that any attempt by one party to get satisfaction of its claims by the use of force would encourage retaliation by force and thus endanger international peace and stability, it is here urged that an ultimate peaceful solution will require that Israel be pressured into comprehensive settlement, including a reversion to the status quo ante.

PART II

The Criteria of Historic Bays Establish Aqaba as Arab

A. HISTORICAL BAY

In terms of width of mouth and proportion of such width to depth of indentation into land, Aqaba certainly conforms to the strictest physical requirements that could be laid down for a bay. Beyond these requirements, is not believed to be possible to lay down a general rule by which one may determine in all cases whether a particular gulf or bay or other body of water which forms an indentation of the coast is to be considered in whole or in part a portion of the territory of the State. Nevertheless, it must be admitted that there are certain bodies of water to which individual states by general acquiescence or long usage have acquired the absolute right or title.[20] The individual State has in practice enjoyed much latitude in determining what bays or arms of the sea penetrating its territory may be regarded

---

[19] For instance, the resolution of the General Assembly respecting the repatriation of the Arab refugees to Palestine. See: Fayey A. Sayegh, The Record of Israel At the United Nations, pp. 13-16, where he cites eight resolutions rendered by the General Assembly.

[20] See Philip C. Jessup, The Law of Territorial Waters and Maritime Jurisdiction, 1927, pp. 361-363.

as a part of the national domain and dealt with accordingly.[21] Such bays, referred to as "historic bays," are those over which, regardless of magnitude, and irrespective of the extent of the distance between their seaward headlands, coastal States have asserted a dominion respected by other States.[22]

In order to fix the international legal status of the Gulf of Aqaba, whether it is a "historic bay" according to the criteria given, it is necessary to specify the characteristics proper thereto from the threefold point of view of history, geography and the vital interests of the surrounding States. These were the characteristics investigated by the Central American Court of Justice in their judgment in the leading case of the Gulf of Fonseca.[23] This case has a direct bearing on the question of the Gulf of Aqaba due to the close analogy between the two situations.

It has been shown how the Gulf of Aqaba is surrounded by Arab coasts from all directions. This fact was acknowledged even before the Arab conquerors drove northward to the Syrian and Egyptian territories in the 8th century. The writings of many geographers on the boundaries of Arabia prove that the coasts of the Gulf of Aqaba were within these boundaries. It is important to quote here at length the various views of geographers on the boundaries of Arabia included in Crichton's work on Arabia:

"The northern frontier is not well defined, and has been subject to considerable variations. The ancients restricted it to an imaginary line, stretching between the extreme points of the Arabian and Persian Gulfs. The rest they attached partly to Egypt and partly to Syria. But the conquests and settlements of the Arabs have long extended their territory beyond this ideal boundary. On the authority of Burckhardt, the northern frontier may be taken as a line running from Suez across the isthmus of that name to the Mediterranean, near El Arish, passing along the borders of Palestine and the Dead Sea, and thence winding through the Syrian desert by Palmyra until it reaches the Euphrates above Anah, the course of which river it follows till joined by the Tigris; at which point their united streams take the name of Shut el Arab, or boundary of Arabia. Part of the

---

[21] Hyde, International Law, 2nd ed. Vol. I (1945), p. 468.
[22] Briggs, The Law of Nations, 2nd ed. (1952), p. 288.
[23] Judicial Decisions Involving Questions Of International Law, The Republic of El Salvador v. The Republic of Nicaragua, A.J.I.L., 11 (1917), p. 700.

northern frontier lies now within Damascus, which extends as far
south as Tor Hsma, a high mountain, one day's journey from
Akaba."[24]

The Greek and Roman geographers prescribed another limit to the
boundaries which also includes the areas surrounding the Gulf. Xeno-
phon carries it beyond the Euphrates, including the greater part of
Mesopotamia, or the Arabian Iraq; Ptolemy bounds it by the Chaldean
mountains on this side of the river, and northward by the city of Thap-
sacus, near Racca. The same is adopted with little variation by Diadorus and Strabo. Abdulfeda, an Arabian geographer who wrote at
about the beginning of the fourteenth century, extended the northern
boundary somewhat higher than Burckhardt, and placed it at Beles
nearly in the latitude of Aleppo, northern Syria.[25] According to Forster, among the lines of demarcation furnished by the ancients, by far
the most common are those of Ptolemy who includes in Arabia parts
of the Sinai Peninsula across the Gulf of Aqaba and parts of eastern
Syria.[26] Crichton stated that "the peninsula of Sinai may be considered
a province of Arabia."[27] Philip Hitti in his treatise, History of the
Arabs, describes the boundaries of Arabia as follows:

"The northern boundary is ill-defined, but may be considered an
imaginary line drawn due east from the head of the Gulf of al-Aqa-
bah in the Red Sea to the Euphrates. Geographically, indeed, the
whole Syro-Mesopotamian desert is a part of Arabia."[27a]

In a map annexed to Crichton's book, the Gulf of Aqaba is entitled
Gulf of Arabia, a title reiterated in several contexts as the Arabian
Gulf.[28] Forster also entitled a whole section of his book as the "Coast
of The Arabian Gulf" where it is obvious from the context that he
meant the Gulf of Aqaba.[29]

The definition of Arab boundaries is figured out in the correspondence between Sheriff Hussein of Mecca and Sir Henry McMahon,
then British High Commissioner for Egypt and the Sudan during

---

[24] Andrew Crichton, The History of Arabia, vol. I (1834), p. 37.

[25] Id., pp. 37-38.

[26] Reverent C. Forster, The Historical Geography of Arabia, vol. II (1834), pp. 116.

[27] Crichton, op.cit., supra note 24, at 52.

[27a] P. Hitti, The History of the Arabs (1951), 5th ed.

[28] Id. See the map annexed, printed by Harper & Brothers, N.Y. 1834. See also reference
to the Arabian Gulf, pp. 53, 75.

[29] Forster, op.cit., supra note 26, sect. II, pp. 116-155.

World War II. These boundaries include the territories north of Aqaba. The British Government accepted these boundaries with certain modifications which did not exclude Aqaba territories, and declared that it was prepared to "recognize and uphold the independence of the Arabs in all the regions lying within the frontiers proposed by the Sherif al Mecca."[30] Aqaba and the area around the northern and eastern coast of the Gulf were liberated by the Arab armies in their revolt against the Ottoman Empire.[31]

Arabs have been living in this area, even before Islam. Forster gives the following historical background of the people who lived in this area as follows:

"The scriptural 'Land of Median' stretched round the eastern head of the Red Sea, or the Gulf of Akaba. On the eastern shore of this gulf, accordingly, the ancient city of Median preserves to this day the record of its origin in its name. Now, along this coast, between the head of the Elanitic Gulf (the modern Akaba), and the territory of the tribal Thoumud, we meet an Arab people styled Benizomanies, in other words, Beni Zoman. But the Beni Zoman of Diadorus are, beyond doubt or question the Beni Omran of Burckhardt: a formidable race of Beduins. The tract of mountain between Hakl and Akaba is inhabited by the Arabs 'Amran.' "[32]

In a research on the Sea land of Ancient Arabia, a group of scholars at Yale University wrote:

"Aqaba alludes to an ancient city of Aqaba in the western part of Arabia, possibly in the region of the arm of the Red Sea which has long borne the name 'Gulf of Aqaba.'

The modern castle of Aqaba is located near the ruins of biblical Elath . . . It is possible, however, that a city named Aqaba existed in

[30] See The Middle East, A political and economic survey, Royal Institute of International Affairs (1951) 2nd ed. pp. 22-23.

[31] *Ibid.*, p. 22.

[32] *Ibid.*, vol. I, pp. 322-323. Quoting Burckhardt, "The Omran, inhabit the mountain between Aqaba and Moyleh (the ruins of Median are situated midway on this line) on the eastern coast of the Red Sea. The Omran are a strong tribe, of very independent spirit. Their frequent depredations render them objects of terror to the pilgrims proceeding to Mekka, who are under the necessity of passing through their territory. At the time when Mohammed Ali, Pasha of Egypt, had reduced all other Bedouins on the Egyptian Hadj road to complete subjection, the Omran still proved obstinate. In the year 1814, they attacked and plundered a detachment of Turkish cavalry near Aqaba."

antiquity in the northwestern part of Arabia in the vicinity of the northeastern projection of the Red Sea. The word Aqaba is a general Arabic term denoting mountain pass ascent or activity."[33]

It is therefore evident that the historical argument in support of the Israeli claim is exceedingly feeble. In a study undertaken by an Egyptian group on the historical origin of Elath, it is stated:

"Although there is some confusion as to the origin of Elath, it is generally accepted that the city was either the original Edomite port seized by David from the Edomites or one of its suburbs. From the date of its seizure until its capture by the Syrian King 'Regin,' Jewish occupancy did not exceed one hundred and fifty years."[34]

Since the sweep of Moslem Arab armies northward to Syria[35] and northwest to Egypt to spread their faith, the Gulf area with its adjacent territories were under the sovereignty of the Moslem Arabs or other Moslems. The Encyclopedia of Islam referred to this historical fact as follows:

"Aila [the former name of Aqaba] the only inhabited city on the Gulf of Aqaba situated on the northern edge of the Gulf since 630 A.D. and onward was directly under the Arab Moslems Authority. In Tabuk (630) Yuhanna Ruba, Lord of Aila, offered to pay a yearly tribute of 300 dinar to Mohammed, in exchange for that no harm was done to the town by the Moslem armies."[36]

It is beyond doubt that he who holds Aila, the key and the most important centre of the whole area, asserted his control and authority over the adjacent territories surrounding the Gulf. This city was of a great importance to the Moslem Arabs throughout their history, notwithstanding the changing events that had appeared during certain periods of time. The Encyclopedia of Islam gives an elaborate survey of its historical background under the Moslem era:

[33] Yale Oriental Series, Researches, Vol. I, XIX, Raymond Philip Daugherty, The Sea-Land of Ancient Arabia (New Haven, Conn., 1932).

[34] "The Trouble About Aqaba," The Egyptian Economic and Political Review, February, 1957, Cairo, Egypt, p. xi.

[35] Syria refers to the regions of Syria, Lebanon, Transjordan and Palestine. Not until the establishment of the British and French Mandates in these territories that Syria was disintegrated to the four regions referred to.

[36] Encyclopedia of Islam, vol. I, (1913), p. 210.

"A new town of Waila replaced the old which flourished as a small centre of intellectual and material culture through the period of the Caliphate Ahmed Ibin Tulun (868-883) caused a new road to be laid instead of the old caravan route which was called Akhat Aila after the neighbouring town. This was the route which passes along the Sinai Peninsula shore then to the Saudi Arabian shore. Until the twentieth century it had been under the Moslem authority when the crusaders captured it in 1116, and then obliged to surrender it to the Moslems again in 1171, when it was captured again by the Reginald Prince of Karak (crusader), Aila remained under the Moslem authority. . . ."[37]

The site of Aqaba on the head of the Gulf, which controls the adjacent areas and links Egypt, Syria and the Hedjas with each other, was of significant importance as a strategic location for commercial and pilgrimage purposes. Its commercial importance is indicated by the Egyptian research group which stated:

"In the 14th century, in nearby Aqaba, the Mamluke Sultan, El Ghairy, constructed the fortress of Aqaba, to protect the caravan routes through Elath, underlining the city's importance as one of the principal communication links between Egypt and Syria."[38]

Crichton refers to the route of the Egyptian pilgrims, "The Egyptian caravan which starts from Cairo, is under the same regulations as the Syrian. Its route is more dangerous and fatiguing, lying by Suez and Aqaba, along the shore of the Red Sea, through the territories of wild and warlike tribes who frequently attack it by open force."[39]

Kermack, writing for the Scottish Geographical Magazine, gives the following account of the importance of Aqaba to the Arabs:

"With dominance in Egypt of Mohammedism, it is worth noticing, there came into importance a Pilgrim Way from Cairo by Suez and Aqaba to the holy cities of Mecca and Medina, the 'old Suez road' which we find being repaired by medieval sultans, and which carried to the Eastern trade of raw silks, nutmegs, pepper, indigo, mace and cloves from Suez to be sold on the Nile to Venetian mer-

[37] *Id.*
[38] *Op.cit.*, supra note 34.
[39] Crichton, *op.cit.*, supra note 24, at 206.

chants at the wharves of Bulak, the fourteenth-century port of Cairo."[40]

In conclusion, the territories adjacent to the Gulf, especially those which are to the north of its head, i.e., areas included presently within Jordan and Israel, have always been an integral part of Arabia.[41] Since time immemorial and until our present day, one ethnical and homogeneous peoples, namely, the Arabs have been living in these territories. From the seventh century, these territories were under an Arab authority and control, which began with the Caliphs in Mecca, the Ummayads in Damascus, the Abbasids in Baghdad, and the Fatimids in Cairo,[42] and extended up to the beginning of the sixteenth century, when all the Middle Eastern countries became part of the Ottoman Empire. For four hundred years, Egypt, Saudi Arabia and Jordan were under the Ottoman authority and control. Consequent to the disintegration of the Turkish Empire, as a result of World War I, these three entities were proclaimed as independent and separate States.[43]

Thus, the Gulf was for nine centuries and thereafter for another four centuries, under the exclusive sovereignty of the Moslem Arab Caliphates and the Ottomans respectively. The inference to be deduced indicates the exclusiveness of the Moslem Arab Caliphate ownership over the Gulf waters, and the transfer of those rights to the Ottoman Empire. The fact that the three States adjacent to the Gulf, namely, Egypt, Saudi Arabia and Jordan, formerly belonged to a single international political entity of the Ottoman Empire, gives them the same exclusive ownership of the Gulf waters. In other words, subsequent to

[40] W. R. Kermack, "Some Geographical Notes on Ancient Egypt," Geographical Society, vol. xxxiii: 1917. Edinburgh, 1917, p. 27. See also P. Hitti, The History of the Arabs (1951) 5th ed., p. 58, where he cites Strabo who describes the importance of Aqaba "Aelena" as a major location for commercial transportation between Hedjas (Arabia) and Egypt.

[41] See M. V. Seton-Williams, "Britain and the Arab States: A Survey of Anglo Arab Relations, 1920-1949" (London, 1945), pp. 189-192. Where he refers to the fact that, under the Ottoman Empire the Hejas meant from the head of the Gulf of Aqaba to about half-way down the Red Sea. This was the basis of Saudi Arabia claims to those territories, which had been given to Transjordan. Negotiations of the boundaries were conducted between a British mission sent in 1925 to Jedah and headed by Sir Gilbert Clayton. Although the negotiations ended by signing two agreements, Saudi Arabia still maintained its claim.

[42] See: Philip Hitti, History of the Arabs (1951) 5th ed., pp. 139-484 and pp. 617-694.

[43] Id. at 750. The declaration of the British Protectorate over Egypt abolished the Ottoman suzerainty over Egypt; and see also, The Middle East, A Political and Economic Survey (1951) 2nd ed., pp. 22-30, where a description of Transjordan and Arabia independence is shown.

the dissolution of the Ottoman Empire, those three States in their character as antonomous states and legitimate successors of Turkey, incorporated into their respective territories as a result of geographical fact, and for purposes of pilgrimage and common defense, the Gulf which nature had made the main route for the holy shrines of Mecca.

B. THE FONSECA CASE

An important precedent for the Arab claims is to be found in the claims asserted, the principles embodied, and the judgment rendered in the case of the Gulf of Fonseca.

In this case, a claim inter alia for an exclusive ownership and sovereignty over the waters of the Gulf by El Salvador, Honduras and Nicaragua was made by El Salvador. This demand of comprehensive authority was mainly based on historic grounds. From the sixteenth century—asserted the claimant—when this gulf was discovered by the Spaniards, it belonged throughout the entire period of her dominion to Spain whose rights of exclusive ownership were never placed in doubt; and, upon the independence of Central America, that ownership passed into the patrimony of the Federal Republic that was formed by the five States. Those rights of exclusive ownership have been transferred to the three States referred to, by virtue of the dissolution of the Federal Republic. For a long period of time, those waters belonged to a single political entity, and upon the dissolution of that entity without having effected a delimitation among the three riparian States of their sovereignty therein, the ownership of those waters continued in common in those three States.[44] Two subsidiary facts support this claim, viz. the geographical situation of the countries surrounding the Gulf, and the objectives sought for usages of the waters which have never been exercised or even claimed by any other nation.[45]

The parallel between the claims of exclusive authority over the Gulf of Aqaba, and that over the Gulf of Fonseca is obvious. In fact, the grounds supporting to the former claim are even clearer and stronger. While the period of possession and ownership of the Gulf of Fonseca is only four centuries, on the other hand a period of thirteen centuries exists in the case of the Gulf of Aqaba. Moreover, the Ottoman pos-

[44] Judicial Decisions Involving Questions of International Law; The Republic of El Salvador v. The Republic of Nicaragua, Central American Court of Justice, A.J.I.L. 11 (1917), p. 677. See also Jessup, The Law of Territorial Waters, pp. 398 et seq.
[45] Ibid.

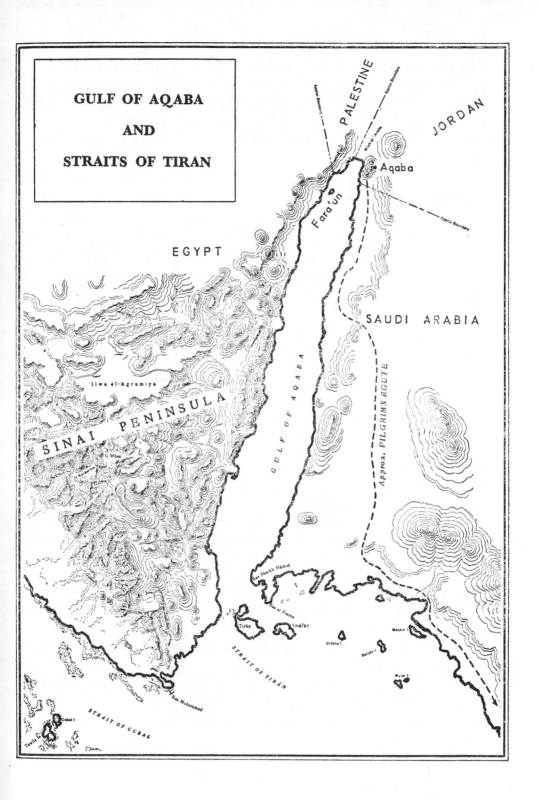

GULF OF AQABA
AND
STRAITS OF TIRAN

PALESTINE

JORDAN

Aqaba

Fara'un

EGYPT

SAUDI ARABIA

'Ilwa el-'Agramiya

SINAI   PENINSULA

GULF OF AQABA

Approx. PILGRIMS ROUTE

Ras Sheikh Hāmud

Tirān

Shūsha I.

Mecsur I.

Ras el Fisma

Sināfar

Barakn I.

Wyler I.

STRAIT OF TIRAN

Ras Muhammad

Gubal I.

STRAIT OF GUBAL

Tawila I.

session of the Gulf of Aqaba was recognized internationally within the context of the Constantinople Convention of 1888. Paragraph 3 of Article 10 of the said convention specified that the stipulations of Articles IV, V, VII, and VIII which laid down some privileges in the Suez Canal for the signatories do not apply to the Gulf of Aqaba. The paragraph reads:

"It is also understood that the provisions of the four Articles in question shall in no case stand in the way of measures which the Imperial Ottoman Government considers it necessary to assure by its forces the defence of its other possessions situated on the eastern coast of the Red Sea."[46]

Another predominant factor is the fact that the Gulf of Aqaba has been used for thirteen centuries as a main route for the purpose of pilgrimage. This objective is of great importance to the Moslems, by virtue of the fact that pilgrimage is one of the five duties of Moslems. Therefore, this route is of special interest to the Moslems throughout the world.[47]

In the judgment given by the Central American Court of Justice it was noted that "the historic origin of the right of exclusive ownership that has been exercised over the waters of the Gulf during the course of nearly four hundred years is introvertible [*sic*?]. . . During these three periods of the political history of Central America the representative authorities have notoriously affirmed their peaceful ownership and possession in the Gulf, that is, without protest or contradiction by any nation whatsoever. It is clearly deducible from the facts set forth that the Gulf of Fonseca belongs to the special category of historic bays and is the exclusive property of El Salvador, Honduras and Nicaragua; this on the theory that it combines all the characteristics or conditions that the text writers on international law, the international law institutes and the precedents have prescribed as essential to territorial waters, to wit, secular or immemorial possession accompanied by animo domini both peaceful and continuous and by acquiescence on the part of the other Nations, the special geographical configuration. . .

46 The Constantinople Convention, Art. 10, par. 3.

47 See New York Herald Tribune, April 13, 1957, p. 10. "Saudi Arabia alleges that the main use of the Gulf for the last 1,200 years has been as part of the pilgrim route to Mecca. It argues that as guardian of the Moslem holy places and of the pilgrimage routes lying within its sovereignty, the Saudi government, will not permit Israel the right to sail through the Gulf."

and the absolute, indispensable necessity that those States should possess the Gulf as fully as required by those primordial interests and the interest of national defense."[48]

In the light of the foregoing the question reduces itself to one of deciding whether the situation in the Gulf of Aqaba can be legally assimilated to that of the Fonseca Gulf. Ostensibly, the claims in both cases are identical, and their basic contentions are parallel with, of course, certain peculiar characteristics of the Gulf of Aqaba. The court's judgment is based exclusively on these geographical historical and objectives of usage bases, and actually reiterates them in several contexts. In other words the court accepted the contention that was presented by El Salvador's claim for exclusive authority over the Gulf of Fonseca. Subsequently, the court ruled unanimously that Fonseca is an historic bay possessed of the characteristics of a closed sea; and by a majority that its legal status is that of property belonging to the three countries that surround it, while Judge Gutiérrez Navas answered that the ownership of the Gulf belongs, respectively, to the three riparian countries in proportion.[49]

It is of much significance to note that the Government of the United States had recognized the claim of sovereignty set up by the three littoral states. In a note addressed by the State Department on February 18, 1914, to the Minister of El Salvador at Washington, the United States Government said categorically:

"In your protest the position is taken that the Gulf of Fonseca is a territorial bay, whose waters are within the jurisdiction of the bordering States. This position the Department is not disposed to controvert."[50]

From the parallelism between the two gulfs it may be easily deduced that the court's decision with respect to the Gulf of Fonseca should be applied to the case of the other Gulf. In other words, the Gulf of Aqaba is an historic bay possessed of the characteristics of a closed sea, and must be regarded as a property belonging to the three littoral States, namely, Egypt, Saudi Arabia and Jordan.[51]

[48] Op.cit., supra note 44 at pp. 700, 701, 705.

[49] Id. at 693. See especially the answers on the ninth to the eleventh questions.

[50] Jessup, op.cit., supra note 20 at 406.

[51] It is of interest to note the following letter published in the London Times, March 6, 1957. "It has occasionally been argued, however, that the Gulf of Aqaba is not part of the open sea, but that by reason of its virtually land-locked position it must be treated as some-

C. APPRAISAL OF AQABA AS A HISTORIC BAY

The Fonseca case has set forth the principle that certain gulfs and bays enclosed by the land of more than one littoral state are categorized as "historical bays." By the same criteria that had been applied in the former case, we concluded that the Gulf of Aqaba belongs to the same category. Not only did the judiciary adopt this principle, but other writers of international law have recognized the territoriality[52] of the bay as a general rule without any characteristics to be stipulated. Twiss squarely pointed out that this rule is embodied in the Law of Nations.[53]

> "But in case the opposite sides of a bay are inhabited by different Nations, then under the general Law of Nations, each Nation has a right to go to the central line, drawn at low water mark, as marking the extent of its Jurisdictional waters."[54]

Oppenheim, who advocates the limitation of "historic bays" to those bays which are surrounded by one state only, recognizes that the Gulf of Fonseca is an exception.[55] He also confesses that his judgment is contested by other writers who "assert that narrow gulfs and bays surrounded by the land of two different States are territorial, the central line dividing the territorial portion" of each.[56] Moreover, he recognizes that the practice of States and the opinions of writers who agree with his judgment exclude those bays which possess the characteristics of a closed sea.[57] It is important to note the generality of exception

---

thing in the nature of a private preserve of the littoral States. At a time when the whole area was subject to Turkish sovereignty, this argument might have been tenable. This is no longer the case. The Gulf is now enclosed by the shores of four independent States— Egypt, Israel, Jordan, and Saudi Arabia." Excluding Israel which is a specific case that will be discussed hereafter, this article recognized the Gulf status as a closed sea during the era of the Turks. Clearly there are no grounds for changing the status at the present time, when taking into consideration the principles Gulf of Fonseca case.

52 The expression "territorial bay" is used by Lauterpacht to imply that the waters contained in territorial bays, and in the territorial portions of bays not wholly territorial, are not territorial waters and part of the maritime belt, but national waters. Oppenheim, International Law, vol. I, 8th ed. (1955) footnote 1, p. 505.

53 Law of Nature and of Nations, L. IV. c. 5, § 8.

54 T. Twiss, The Law of Nations, Rights and Duties in Time of Peace, vol. I, 2d ed. (1884), p. 294.

55 Lauterpacht, op.cit., supra note 30, footnote 3, p. 508.

56 Id. footnote 4, p. 508.

57 Ibid.

with respect to bays mentioned. This squarely implies that the Fonseca case should not be regarded by any means as unique or unexampled. It follows that in considering the legal status of the Gulf of Aqaba the analogy of the case of the Gulf of Fonseca is reasonable and logical.

In considering the status of the Gulf of Bothnia, Heffter maintained the same thesis as applied in the Fonseca case. This Gulf has a mouth over fifty miles wide, a length of about five hundred miles and a width of from fifty to one hundred miles. It formerly lay entirely within Swedish territory and was confidently asserted to belong to Sweden. By the Treaty of Fruderickslam of 1809, Finland was ceded to Russia. Consequently Heffter declared that the Gulf belonged jointly to Sweden and Russia.[58]

The inference to be deduced from the foregoing citations indicates the possibility of considering the bays that are surrounded by more than one littoral state in the same terms as those which are surrounded by just one. On the one hand this postulate is squarely set forth both by the school of thought which does not discriminate between the two kinds of bays, and on the other hand, by the school which, although discriminating, considers certain bays as exceptions to the category of bays which are non-territorial, by virtue of being enclosed by the land of more than one littoral State. Subsequently those exceptional bays have to be categorized in terms of the other kind of bays. It is not to be understood, that this postulate denies or ignores that certain effects ensure from the tripartite authority over the historical bays. Apparently these effects are of a certain type that cannot exist in the arena of one state authority.[59] But these differences are insignificant as far as the purposes of this paper are concerned.

It is clearly deducible from the conclusion set forth in the preceding paragraph that the literature concerning historical bays can be construed to include those that are surrounded by more than one state, and that, the legal status of the Gulf of Aqaba would be envisaged within that context.

The Arab States claim for possession of the Gulf is justified by the fact that even ancient writers had accepted the principle of sovereign possession. Vattel, the Swiss jurist, wrote in 1775,

[58] Droit International de l'Europe (trans. by Bergson, ed. of 1866) sec. Quoted by Philip C. Jessup, The Law of Territorial Waters and Maritime Jurisdiction (1927).

[59] A.J.I.L., op.cit., supra note 44, pp. 710-717, where it is stated that the waters of Fonseca bay are "possession in common," and therefore a coparcener cannot dispose of the rights upon these waters without the consent of the other coparceners.

"A bay whose entrance may be defended may be possessed and rendered subject to the laws of the sovereign, and it is of importance that it should be so."[60]

It is obvious, that the Gulf of Aqaba can be easily defended, by virtue of its narrow strait. This fact was the major reason by which Ortelan, the French publicist, justified the ownership of gulfs and bays. In 1856 he wrote:

"One must place upon the same place as roadsteads and harbours, gulfs and bays, and all indentations formed by the land of one State . . . or when the entrance of such indentations can be controlled by artillery, or is defended naturally by islands, sandlands, or rocks. In all these instances, as a matter of fact, it is accurate to say that these gulfs or bays are within the dominion of the State master of the territory which encompasses them."[61]

In 1879, one of the most celebrated of British international publicists, Sir Robert Phillimore, who for many years was a legal admirer of the British Crown stated that

"Maritime territorial rights extend as a general rule over arms of the sea, bays, gulfs, estuaries which are enclosed, but not entirely surrounded by land belonging to one and the same state."[62]

As the route of pilgrimage to Mecca deems the Gulf of Aqaba enjoys a specific character that justifies the claim to be regarded as historical bay. Similar conditions were the premises of the arbitral award rendered by the Permanent Court of The Hague in 1910, in the case Great Britain v. United States.

"The character of a bay is subject to conditions that concern the interests of the territorial sovereign to a more intimate and important extent than those connected with the open coast."[63]

Dr. Drago, commenting on the award in his dissent, recognized that there are well founded national claims to particular bodies of water on the basis of usage or prescription. He maintained that

[60] Vattel, Le Droit des Gens ou Principes de la loi Naturelle (1775), vol. I, p. 142.
[61] Ortelan, Diplomatie de la Mer (1856), vol. I, p. 157.
[62] Phillimore, International Law (1879), vol. I, p. 284.
[63] Op.cit., supra 44, p. 708.

". . . it may safely be asserted that a certain class of bays which might properly be called the historical bays such as the Chesapeake Bay and Delaware Bay in North America, and the Great Estuary of the river Plate, in South America, form a class distinct and apart, and undoubtedly belong to the littoral country, whatever be their depth or penetration and the width of their mouths, when such country has asserted its sovereignty over them, and particular circumstances, such as geographical configuration, immemorial usage, and above all, the requirements of self-defense, justify such a pretension."[64]

The four conditions stipulated in the previous citation are all fulfilled with respect to the Gulf of Aqaba.[65] The third condition was regarded by Captain Stormy the premise for the inclusion of bays as internal waters. In a proposal to the Buenos Aires Conference of the International Law Association in 1922, he suggested that

"A state may include within the limits of its territorial sea the estuaries, gulfs, bays or parts of the adjacent sea in which it has established its jurisdiction by continuous and immemorial usage."[66]

The first condition was the basis of the proposal rendered by the United States Delegation to the Conference for the Codification of International Law. This proposal read as follows:

"Waters, whether called bays, sands, straits, or by some other name, which have been under the jurisdiction of the coastal State as part of its interior waters, are deemed to continue a part thereof."[67]

Sir Maurice Guyer, representative of the United Kingdom, considered a historic bay

---

[64] Jessup, *op.cit.*, supra note 58 at 379.

[65] As to the assertion of sovereignty, see King Abdul Aziz Ibn Saud Decree on May 29, 1949, which was published in the New York Times, and the letter dated April 12, 1957, from the Permanent Representative of Saudi Arabia to the U.N. addressed to the Secretary General. U.N.G.A.: A/3575. See also Saudi Arabia statement published in New York Times March 1957. "The Gulf of Aqaba is subject to the sovereignty of the surrounding Arab States. Saudi Arabia will not allow the establishment of any right for Israel in the Gulf of Aqaba." And see also the Joint Iraqi Saudi communiqué of May 17, 1957, which stated that "Aqaba is to be a closed Arab Gulf." N.Y.T. Deadline Data, p. 8. As to geography and as to immemorial usage, see pp. 9-18. And as to self defence, see passim supra.

[66] League of Nations, vol. III, Territorial Waters, Minutes of the 2nd Committee, Eleventh Meeting, p. 106. This citation was quoted by Mr. Magalhus, representative of Portugal.

[67] *Id.*, pp. 107, 197.

". . . is a piece of water more or less enclosed by land, which for one reason or another, the coastal State regards as part of its interior territory. . . . The claim that a piece of water is an historic bay does not depend on the width of the entrance to the bay, but on altogether different circumstances."[68]

An amendment submitted by the British Delegation re-iterated the third condition.

"The coastal state is able to establish a claim by usage, prescription or otherwise, that the waters of the bay are part of its national waters."[69]

The basis of discussion in that conference for a definition of an historic bay was that ". . . if by usage the bay is subject to the exclusive authority of the coastal State."[70]

Jessup in his elaborate chapter about bays, concludes his research by stating that no established rule of international law exist as to bays except to the effect that bays over which a nation has established a prescriptive claim are deemed territorial waters. "Such a prescriptive claim may be established over bays of great extent, the legality of the claim is to be measured, not by the size of the area affected, but by the definiteness and duration of the assertion. . . . The evidence of international practice and usage does not indicate that a claim to a large bay is illegal."[71]

The New York Court of Appeals in 1866, ruled in the case of Mahler v. Transportation Co. that

"The rule is one of universal recognition, that a bay, strait, sound or arm of the sea, lying wholly within the dominion of a sovereign, and admitting no ingress from the ocean, except by a channel between contiguous headlands which he can command with his cannon on either side, is the subject of territorial dominion."[72]

The Institute of International Law has admitted the territorial character of such gulfs and bays with a wider entrance as have been considered territorial for more than one hundred years.[73]

---

[68] *Id.*, p. 104.   [69] *Ibid.*
[70] *Id.*, Annex 1, Basis of Discussion No. 8, p. 179.
[71] Jessup, *op.cit.*, supra note 20, at p. 382.   [72] (1866) 35 N.Y. 352.
[73] Annuaire de l'Institut de Droit International, 13, p. 329.

Most authoritative among the references which justify the three littoral Arab States' claim that the waters of the Gulf of Aqaba are internal is the comment made by George Graflon Wilson, reporter of the Harvard Draft Convention on Territorial Waters of 1929, with reference to Article 6:

"Where the waters within the seaward limit are bordered by two or more states, it would seem that the bordering states should be permitted by international law to divide such waters between them as inland waters. If the same waters are bordered by one state only, that state would clearly be entitled, under Article 5, to treat all of the waters as inland waters. The powers of two or more states should not be smaller than the powers of one state in this respect if the states can reach an agreement."[74]

This view is compatible with Charles Cheney Hyde's comment on the same matter which reads as follows:

"When the geographical relationship of a bay to the adjacent or enveloping land is such that the sovereign of the latter, if a single state, might not unlawfully claim the waters as a part of its territory, it is not apparent why a like privilege should be denied to two or more states to which such land belongs, at least if they are so agreed, and accept as between themselves a division of the waters concerned. No requirement of international law as such deprives them of that privilege, notwithstanding the position of some who would leave little room for its application."[75]

It is relevant to note that although the Report of the International Law Commission concerning the work of the Eighth Session, April 23-July 4, 1956, did not lay down definite rules regarding the status of bays surrounded by more than one state,[76] it did not dismiss the assertions made by several states, jurists, and writers, that these bays are to be considered historical bays and their waters as internal waters.

Although the Gulf of Fonseca decision appears to be the only in-

[74] 23 A.J.I.L. Spec. Rep. 274 (1929).

[75] 1 Hyde, International Law, Chiefly as Interpreted and Applied by the United States 475 (2d rev. ed. 1945).

[76] See 51 A.J.I.L. p. 188 (1957) where the Report reads as follows: "The Commission felt bound to propose only rules applicable to bays the coasts of which belong to a single state. As regards other bays, the Commission has not sufficient data at its disposal concerning the number of cases involved or the regulations at present applicable to them."

stance in which a court has held that a bay or gulf surrounded by the territory of more than one coastal state is a "closed sea" of "historic bay," it is noteworthy that the foregoing statements are in accord with the Fonseca principle and thus provide a basis for further claims by other states to the application of the Fonseca principle. This so-called principle has also been called the "Melindey doctrine," the designation being derived from the name of the then President of El Salvador. The doctrine "provides that when an arm of the sea occupies the space between two or more countries, the area of the waters *inter fauces terrae* is necessarily within the joint jurisdiction of the coastal states."[77]

In the perspectives of the foregoing literature, an analysis of the legal status of the Gulf of Aqaba, leads to the conclusion that it is a historic bay. The criteria used, the conditions stipulated, and the premises laid down by the writers, jurists, judges, commentators and commissions, for the definition of "historic bay" are applicable to the claim of the Arab States with respect to the Gulf of Aqaba. This claim was emphasized by Mr. Ahmed Shukairy, the Saudi Arabian representative, during the twelfth session of the General Assembly, as follows:

"The Gulf of Aqaba, basically, is not an international question. The Gulf of Aqaba is a national inland waterway, subject to absolute Arab Sovereignty. The geographical location of the Gulf is conclusive proof of its national character. It is separated from the Red Sea by a chain of islands, the largest being Sanafir and Tiran. The only navigable entrance—which, itself, is within Arab Territory—does not exceed 500 meters. Thus, by its configuration, the Gulf is in the nature of a *mare clausum* which does not belong to the class of international waterways. The Gulf is so narrow that the territorial areas of the littoral States are bound to overlap among themselves, under

[77] See General Assembly, 11th Sess., Official Records, 666th Plenary Meeting (a/P.V. 666), March 1, 1957, p. 1281 where Mr. Urquia of El Salvador alluded to the Gulf of Fonseca in the context of the discussion over the Gulf of Aqaba. He cited a comment he had made at Mexico City in 1956 to the Inter-American Council of Jurists on this question, in which, *inter alia*, he had stated the following: . . . "The Gulf of Bay of Fonseca belongs to the category of bays known in international law as historical bays, and is therefore subject to the exclusive sovereignty of the coastal State or States, regardless of the distance or length to which it penetrates inland, or its width at the mouth, provided, that as is the case for the Gulf of Fonseca, the coastal States have asserted and assert their sovereignty for reasons based on their geographical situation, their use of the Gulf for centuries, and above all, their self-defense."

any kind of measurement, even if we assume that the Gulf comprehends part of the high seas.

"In the second place, the Gulf of Aqaba is of the category of historical gulfs that fall outside the sphere of international law. The
Gulf is the historical route to the holy places in Mecca. Pilgrims from
different Muslim countries have been streaming through the Gulf,
year after year, for fourteen centuries. Ever since, the Gulf has been
an exclusive Arab route under Arab sovereignty. It is due to this undisputed fact that not a single international authority makes any
mention whatsoever of the Gulf as an international waterway open
for international navigation.

"It was last year, in the aftermath of aggression waged against
Egypt, that the Gulf was claimed as comprehending an international
waterway. . . ."[78]

It might be argued that no claim for closed sea had been asserted by
the Arab States prior to the Israeli-Arab dispute over navigation
through the Gulf. Obviously, however, international law in its present
highly developed form did not exist throughout most of the 1,300 years
in which Arab and Moslem authority were exercised respectively. In
addition, it is likely that there was no need of that assertion of such a
claim; foreign powers probably were not interested in navigation in
the Gulf, since it apparently had no commercial importance to them.
The question of the status of the Gulf might not have arisen at this time
except for the fact of Arab hostility toward Israel, and the latter's occupation of the port of Elath and a narrow strip along the northern coast
of the Gulf.

The claim for a closed sea by the littoral Arab States depends, however, on the clarification of the status of Israel's coastline on the Gulf.
Before proceeding to this point it is pertinent to refer to the claims of
other states over bays and gulfs. This reference will orient us as to the
practices of these states which will offer valuable assistance in determining the status of the Aqaba Gulf.

[78] General Assembly, 12th Sess., Official Records, 697th Plenary Meeting (a/P.V. 697),
October 2, 1957, p. 233. See also, the joint communiqué which was issued by King Saud and
King Hussein during the former's visit to Jordan in June 1957. The communique after
stating that pilgrim travel from the port of Aqaba was unsafe because of the "aggression
of Israel in this Arab Gulf," the two governments had decided to announce that travel by
sea of pilgrims from the port of Aqaba was not desirable. At the end of the visit a concluding joint communiqué announced that the Gulf of Aqaba constitutes a "regional Arab
water."

D. PRACTICES OF NATION STATES

Assertions by States of exclusive authority over bays and gulfs that indent their territories have been frequent and have been respected and recognized by other states.[79] A great number of bays and gulfs have been claimed by littoral states as historic bays.

A comparative study of those gulfs with the Gulf of Aqaba would indicate that the Arab States' claim to the latter is justified. It is not within the scope of this chapter to survey all bays in the world, but certain examples are here chosen for the purpose of elucidation.[80]

Delaware Bay and Chesapeake Bay are claimed as historic bays by the United States. The former bay is ten marine miles wide at its entrance and forty miles in length from that entrance to the Delaware River.[81] The Permanent Court of Arbitration in the North Atlantic Coast Fisheries Arbitration supported that assertion by virtue of the "narrow mouth of that body of water and the landlocked nature of its whole area, make the claim a reasonable one and the United States has persisted in the assertion of this position."[82] The latter bay has an entrance twelve miles wide, is nowhere more than twenty miles wide, but is about 200 miles in length. The United States has maintained that all the waters of the bay are her territorial waters, and subject to the exclusive control and jurisdiction thereof.[83] The Court of Commissions of Alabama Claims in Stetson v. United States ruled in 1885 that Chesapeake Bay "from the earliest history of the country has been claimed territorial water, and that claim has never been questioned, that it cannot become the pathway from one nation to another . . . we are forced to the conclusion that Chesapeake Bay must be held to be wholly within the territorial jurisdiction."[84]

The Conception Bay in Newfoundland, which is forty to fifty miles deep and an average width of fifteen miles was claimed by Great Britain as belonging in its entirety to that country.[85] The British title to this body of water was considered and upheld by the Privy Council in 1877 in the case of The Direct United States Cable v. The Anglo-American Telegraph Company.[86] The title is presently exercised by Canada.

---

[79] Briggs, op.cit., supra n. 22, at 288.

[80] For a detailed study of thirty historic bays see Jessup, op.cit., supra, n. 20, pp. 382-439.

[81] Id., p. 395.   [82] Id., p. 397.   [83] Id., p. 388.

[84] Moore, International Arbitration, vol. IV, p. 4332-4341; and vol. V, p. 4675.

[85] Jessup, op.cit., n. 20 at 392.

[86] For illustration of this case, see L.R. (1876-77), 2 App. Cas. 394.

The Bay of Charleurs, with a maximum depth of one hundred miles, and a maximum width of twenty miles, opens into the Gulf of St. Lawrence through a passage sixteen miles wide, has long been claimed by the British and Canadian governments, respectively.[87] The Supreme Court of Canada in 1880 held that the bay is all within British territory.[88]

Even the huge Hudson Bay is claimed by Canada to be a historic bay. This bay, which is largely surrounded by Canadian territory, is about six hundred miles wide and one thousand miles long.[89] An Amendment Act to the Fisheries Act of July 13, 1906, section 14, reads ". . . inasmuch as Hudson Bay is wholly territorial water of Canada."[90]

France holds the Bay of Cancale to be territorial. This bay is about seventeen miles wide at its mouth and about half as deep.[91] France's claim is approved by virtue of the practical appropriation of the bay through the exploitation of its oyster fisheries over a long period of time.[92]

Russia claims exclusive authority over the Bay of Azov. This bay is two hundred thirty by one hundred ten miles, following its longest axis. Its mouth, from the Black Sea, through the Strait of Kirch, is ten miles.[93]

Holland claims comprehensive authority over the Zuyder Zee. It is divided into two portions which may be designated the inner and the outer. The latter would probably not be considered a closed sea were it not for a fringe of islands which almost completely enclose it save for narrow passage, the body of water thus enclosed is about forty miles long by twelve wide. From this area a narrow passage about nine miles wide leads into the inner portion, which is forty miles long by thirty-five wide.[94]

Sweden asserts exclusive authority over the Laholm Bay, which has a mouth of 10-12 miles. This claim was squarely approved by an opinion given by Mr. Eliel Lofgren, the Swedish Legal Adviser, to his foreign ministry in February 11, 1925. He stated that ". . . the Swedish

---

[87] Jessup, *op.cit. supra* n. 20, at 386. [88] Mourat v. McFree, 5 S. Ct. 66 (1880).

[89] Jessup, *op.cit. supra* n. 20, at 411.

[90] 5 Edw. VII cap. 13, 1906 State of Canada, p. 85.

[91] Jessup, *op.cit. supra* n. 20, at 365-366.

[92] See Hall, International Law, Sec. 41 (7th ed. 1917).

[93] Jessup, *op.cit. supra* n. 20, at 383.

[94] *Id.* at 438 and see Hall, International Law 150, 155, 158 (5th ed.), and Laurence, Principles of International Law, Sec. 74.

Government is fully entitled to claim that the entire Laholm Bay and waters out to sea be regarded as territorial waters."[95]

Norway claims the Varranger Fiord as territorial, although its entrance is thirty-two miles wide.[96]

This survey of various bays underlines certain significant points as compared with the Gulf of Aqaba. Their entrances are wider and the claims by the relative nation states are for lesser periods than in the case of the Gulf of Aqaba. No reasoning stands for regarding them as historical bays without applying the same criteria to the Gulf of Aqaba.

In conclusion, by virtue of all the characteristics analyzed, the precedents invoked, the literature written, the nation states practices, and any other criteria applied, the legal status of the Gulf of Aqaba is of the category of a historic bay.

PART III

Israel's Illegal Seizure of Coastline Creates No Rights in Gulf

The claim asserted by the littoral Arab States that the Gulf of Aqaba is a historical bay belonging to them assumes that Israel's occupation of the five mile coastline, in violation of the principles of the United Nations Charter prohibiting territorial changes by force, does not attribute to her sovereignty over that territory. Implicit in this assumption are questions relating to the status of the coastal territory itself, *i.e.*, whether it belongs to Egypt, Saudi Arabia, Jordan, or Israel; the legality of the latter's occupation of the disputed coastline following the violation of the Egyptian-Israeli Armistice Agreement and the Truce with Jordan and Egypt; and whether the Jordan-Israel General Armistice Agreement confers sovereignty to Israel over that territory. In order to ascertain the status of this coastal strip, it is necessary to survey its historical background during the last two centuries.

Subsequent to Mohammed Ali's expansion into the Ottoman Empire Provinces, the European Powers, except France and Turkey, offered him in the Convention of London in 1840 the hereditary Governorship of Egypt, and, for life, the Governorship of "Southern Syria" (or Pash-

---

[95] *Id.* at pp. 413-424. It is noteworthy that Mr. Lofgren was appointed thereafter as Minister for Foreign Affairs.

[96] Lauterpacht, *op.cit. supra* n. 52, at 506.

alik of Acre). Although the provisions of the Convention were not applied, a subsequent Separate Act was annexed to it for the pacification of the Levant. This act was signed between Great Britain, Austria, Prussia and Russia, on the one hand, and the Ottoman Empire on the other, and specified that Southern Syria (which included the Aqaba area) was to be retained by Mohammed Ali.[97] In 1841, the Sultan of Turkey issued a Firman by which Aqaba and the Sinai Peninsula were granted to Egypt because of its regular use of Egyptian pilgrims proceeding overland to Mecca and Medina.[98] In all subsequent Firmans of investiture granted to Mohammed Ali and his successors Aqaba was referred to as belonging to Egypt. In 1892, a dispute arose between Turkey and Egypt with respect to the latter's eastern frontiers. A compromise solved the dispute by nominally annexing Aqaba as well as other territories to the Vilayet of Hedjas, and by allowing Egypt to station its troops in those areas in order to protect the pilgrims' route to Mecca and Medina.[99]

[97] The Separate Act reads, in part, as follows:

"His Highness promises to grant to Mehemet Ali, for himself and for his descendants in the direct line, the administration for the Pashallic of Egypt; and his Highness promises, moreover, to grant to Mehemet Ali, for his life, with the title of Pasha of Acre, and with the command of the fortress of St. John of Acre, the administration of the southern part of Syria, the limits of which shall be determined by the following line of demarcation:

"This line beginning at Cape Ras el-Nakkora, on the Mediterranean, shall extend direct from thence as far as the mouth of the river Seisaban, at the northern extremity of the Lake of Tiberias; it shall pass along the western shore of that Lake, it shall follow the right bank of the river Jordan, and the western shore of the Dead Sea; from thence it shall extend straight to the Red Sea, which it shall strike at the northern point of the Gulf of Akaba, and from thence it shall follow the western shore of the Gulf of Akaba, and the eastern shore of the Gulf of Suez, as far as Suez." See 29 Great Britain, Parliamentary papers, 1841.

[98] Imperial Decree, Hurewitz, Documents on Near East Diplomatic History (1939), p. 51 ff.

[99] The dispute was solved by means of a telegram sent by the Grand Vizier to the Khedive on April 8, 1892, which reads, in part:

"Your Highness is aware that His Majesty the Sultan had authorized the presence at El-Wedjh, Muellah, Daba and Aqaba, on the Hedjaz littoral, as well as at certain positions in the Peninsula of Tor-Sinai, of a sufficient number of Zaptiehs (police posts) placed by the Egyptian Government, on account of the passage of the Egyptian Mahmal by land . . . El-Wedjh has, in consequence, been recently handed back to the Vilayet of Hedjas, by Irade of His Imperial Majesty, as well as the positions of Daba and Muellah; Akkaba also is now annexed to the said Vilayet."

On April 13, 1892, Sir E. Baring, Lord Cromer and the British Consul General sent a note to Tigranne Pasha, the Egyptian Foreign Minister, which reads, in part, as follows:

"The telegram from the Grand Vizier, which your excellency has done me the honour to communicate to me, makes it clear, however, that the Sinai Peninsula, that is to say,

In 1902 the Turks sent a force to occupy Taba, a city west of Aqaba and inside Egyptian territory, in an attempt to drive the Egyptians out of Aqaba. Great Britain on behalf of Egypt objected to the occupation and the Turks withdrew.[100] In 1906 another dispute over the boundaries arose between Turkey and Egypt. Great Britain, in its capacity as protector of Egypt, sent an ultimatum to Turkey demanding the demarcation of a line on Egypt's eastern provinces from Rafeh to Aqaba. Turkey demanded the recognition by Great Britain of its suzerainty over Egypt and insisted that a formal demarcation of the borders was unnecessary and inexpedient between what were practically two parts of the same Empire. Britain replied that London had neither contested nor failed to recognize the Sultan's suzerainty over Egypt, but reiterated its position with respect to the delineation of the boundaries.[101] However, an agreement was concluded at Rafeh on October 1, 1906, between the Commissioners of the Turkish Sultanate and the Commissioners of the Egyptian Khediviate, concerning the fixing of a *Separating Administrative Line*[102] between the Vilayet of Hedjas and the Governorate of Jerusalem and the Sinai Peninsula.[103] Under this Agreement the Aqaba Area retained its status as part of the Hedjas Vilayet. However, it is noted that while the exchange of letters between the participants referred to a "line of demarcation," the Agreement concerned "the Fixing of a Separating Administrative Line" between the Vilayet of Hedjas and the Governorate of Jerusalem and the Sinai Peninsula. The fact that Great Britain recognized Turkey as sovereign over Egypt and the prescription of the Administrative Line—an administrative boundary between two units of the Ottoman

---

the territory bounded to the east by a line running in a south-easterly direction from a point a short distance to the East of El-Arish to the head of the Gulf of Akaba is to continue to be administered by Egypt. The Fort of Akaba which lies to the east of the line in question, will thus form part of the Vilayet of the Hedjaz.

"Her Majesty's Government signified to the sublime Porte some weeks ago, through her Majesty's Charge d'Affairs at Constantinople, their willingness to assent to this arrangement. . . ."

Both the telegram and the note are quoted by Bloomfield, Egypt, Israel and the Gulf of Aqaba, 114, 115 (1957).

[100] Article on the Gulf of Aqaba in Encyclopedia Britannica, Vol. 2 (14th ed.).

[101] For a summary of the dispute and the subsequent negotiations, see British Documents on the Origins of the War by Gooch and Temperley, Vol. 5, The Near East, 79, 189-195 (Cmd. 3006).

[102] Emphasis supplied.

[103] For text of agreements see 99 Brit. & For. State Papers 482-484 (1905-1906).

Empire—would sustain any Egyptian claim for the Aqaba area. It is not of great importance for the purpose of this study, however, to determine the respective claims of Egypt and Saudi Arabia, the successor to the Vilayet of Hedjas in the Aqaba area, since both are Arab States and both claim that the Gulf of Aqaba is an Arab historical bay.

Hedjas remained under the Turkish sovereignty until 1916 when its independence was proclaimed and recognized formally by the United Kingdom, France and Russia following the "Arab Revolt" against the Turks. This revolt was preceded by an agreement which took the form of a series of letters exchanged between Sheriff Hussein of Mecca and Sir Henry McMahon, then British High Commissioner for Egypt and Sudan. Sir McMahon, acting on the instructions of the British government, pledged England to support "the independence of the Arabs" in the large area bounded in the north by the thirty-seventh parallel, in the east by the Iranian border down to the Persian Gulf, and in the south by the Arab Gulf States. As to the western boundary, Hussein demanded the Red Sea and the Mediterranean coast. McMahon, while readily admitting the Red Sea boundary, excluded from his pledge the whole coastal belt of Syria "lying to the west of the districts of Damascus, Homs, Hama, and Aleppo."[104] Thus the agreement prescribed the inclusion of the Aqaba area in the Arab State.[105] Following this agreement the Arab forces, the Hedjas army, captured Aqaba from the Turks in the summer of 1917. Meanwhile, Great Britain in a series of agreements plotted with France and Russia to divide the Ottoman Empire among themselves.[106] Abrogating its pledges to Sheriff Hussein, Great Britain occupied the Fertilea Crescent including the coastal strip on the Gulf of Aqaba. In 1920, Great Britain, under the Treaty of San Remo, was given a Mandate for Palestine which included Trans-Jordan.[107] Two years later the Palestine Mandate was divided into two parts: Palestine proper and the Amirate of Trans-Jordan. Under that

[104] For texts of the letters see the translations of the Arabic texts quoted in Antonius, The Arab Awakening, pp. 414, 419, 420.

[105] Although McMahon's exclusion of certain territories does not by any means refer to Palestine but only to areas far from Palestine, the British Government later contended that the Agreement excluded Palestine from the promised Arab State. For details, see Cmd. 5957 (1939); The Middle East, The Royal Institute of International Affairs, pp. 22-24 (1955); Lenczowski, The Middle East in World Affairs 76 (1952); and Seton Williams, Britain and the Arab States 122 (1948).

[106] For details about those agreements see Lenczowski, op.cit., n. 105 supra, pp. 67-83.

[107] Stewart Perowne, The One Remains 10 (1954).

division the Aqaba Maan area[108] was broken up into two separate territories belonging to the two newly-created bodies politic. Thus the five mile coastal strip was incorporated into Palestine while the residual territories, including Aqaba port, were left to Trans-Jordan. That disintegration reveals a facet of British policy in the Arab countries as indicated by an article published in the Egyptian Gazette of March 7, 1957, which reads, in part, as follows:

> "The fact that Israel today occupies Elath can be partly traced to the circumstances and motives affecting Britain when the Mandate boundaries were established in 1919. Aware of the Military and political importance of the Gulf of Aqaba, Britain arranged that the Palestine Mandate territory include Elath and a few hundred yards of frontage on the Gulf to separate Egypt, and the new Amirate of Trans-Jordan."[109]

Since Abdullah, Amir of Trans-Jordan, was the son of Hussein, King of Hedjas, no boundaries were established between the two states. But when in 1925 Hedjas was invaded and ultimately incorporated into the Saudi Arabian State, claims have been asserted by that state for the restoration of the Aqaba Maan area. Although a treaty was concluded between the British Government and Saudi Arabia on May 20, 1927, by which the former recognized the complete and absolute independence of His Majesty the King of Hedjas and Nejd and its Dependencies, a subsequent dispute over boundaries with Trans-Jordan made it expedient to append an exchange of notes to the Treaty which provided for the delineation of boundaries between Saudi Arabia and Trans-Jordan.[110] This line purported to be only a *de facto* administrative frontier, and not a definite boundary, since the exchange of notes referred to "favorable circumstances [which] will permit a final settlement of this question."[111] Saudi Arabia, which considered the incorporation of the Aqaba Maan area into Trans-Jordan as a usurpation of territory which rightfully belonged to the Hedjas, insisted upon this

[108] Maan is a city north of Aqaba. It had been linked with Aqaba, and thus had been incorporated into the Vilayet of Hedjas until the enforcement of the Mandate in 1920. The reference to Aqaba Maan area includes the provinces around both cities.

[109] An editorial in the Egyptian Gazette of March 7, 1957, p. 2, entitled "Tiran and the Law."

[110] H.C.V. Atchison, A Collection of Treaties, Engagements and Sanads 189, 227, 229 (5th ed. Delhi, 1933).

[111] *Ibid.*, p. 230.

qualification. The extension of the Treaty, in 1936 and again in 1943, by exchange of notes, did not settle the pending boundary dispute.

This historical background demonstrates that both Egypt and Saudi Arabia have valid rights to claim the disputed strip on the Gulf of Aqaba. Even though neither has recently made claims with respect to this area, their failure to do so does not necessarily imply a renunciation in international law of such claims. Consequently, it is submitted that the incorporation of the coastal strip and the Aqaba Maan area in Palestine and Trans-Jordan respectively could not be considered as final. Such incorporation, specifically with respect to the coastal strip, whether exercised by Great Britain (during the Mandate) or by Israel cannot be regarded as having been authoritatively settled and therefore is not of a "legal" nature.

Although the coastal strip was allotted to Israel under the November 29, 1947 Partition Resolution of the General Assembly, serious questions have been raised concerning the validity of the Resolution itself; the proclamation of the statehood of Israel, and the inclusion of this coastal strip in the Israeli State. The first question pertains to the competence of the General Assembly to recommend the partition of Palestine against the wishes and aspirations of the majority of its people as recognized in the principle of self-determination. The second refers to whether the recommendation of the General Assembly in its 1947 resolution (for a plan of partition with economic union) which recommendation was rejected by the Arabs of Palestine, created a right for the Jewish minority to proclaim their separate state at the termination of the Mandate. A third question is whether the final settlement of the Palestine problem should conform precisely with the resolution of the General Assembly which was in the nature of a mere recommendation.[112] This third question should not be considered alone, however, but must be examined in the light of the rejection by the First Committee of the General Assembly of several proposals by which the 1947 resolution was to have constituted "a basic starting point of the settlement by the Assembly of the Palestinian question."[113] Clearly Israel cannot claim sovereignty over the coastal strip until the

[112] It is significant that the Canadian delegation in the Security Council's discussion of the Palestine question indicated that Canada does not consider that the settlement should conform and coincide with the General Assembly's Resolution. See U.N., S.C., O.R., 3rd year, 385th Meeting, p. 24.

[113] Ibid., 384th Meeting, pp. 7-8, where Mr. El-Khouri, the representative of Syria, quoted the Australian proposal (A/C. 1/4081/Rev./1).

legal issues raised by these questions are answered by a competent judicial authority such as, for example, the International Court of Justice.

Aside from these general questions, the issue boils down to whether Israel has the right to occupy the coastal strip. Notwithstanding the fact that this strip (as a part of the general Negev area) was allocated to Israel under the partition recommendation, Israel did not physically occupy the area at the termination of the Mandate. Its occupation came later and then in violation of several resolutions adopted by the Security Council for the establishment of a truce, cease fire, and armistice in Palestine. Moreover, that occupation violated the Egyptian Armistice Agreement to which Israel is a party.

The sequence of these events is quite revealing as to the United Nations' perspective. The Security Council in establishing the truce by its July 15, 1948 resolution, ordered the participants in that arena "pursuant to Article 40 of the Charter of the United Nations, to desist from further military action."[114]

A second resolution was adopted on August 19, 1948, in which it was clearly stated that:

"d.—No party is permitted to violate the Truce on the ground that it is undertaking reprisals or retaliation against the other party;

"e.—No party is entitled to gain military or political advantage through violation of the Truce."[115]

In another resolution, adopted on November 4, 1948, the Security Council demanded that the status quo prevailing before Israel's occupation of parts of the Negev on October 14, 1948, be restored. Moreover, the Council emphasized its intention as to the application of its prior prescriptions in the resolutions of July 15 and August 19. In black letters it demanded the withdrawal of those "forces which have advanced beyond the positions held on 14th October," and again authorized the Acting Mediator "to establish lines beyond which no movement of troops shall take place."[116]

The resolution of November 4 was reaffirmed by the Council on December 29, 1948, following Israel's resumption of military coercion in the Negev area. In the latter resolution, the Council ordered the disputants "to implement without further delay the resolution of the 4

[114] Doc. S/902. For drafts see Docs. S/890, S/894, S/895, S/896, D/897, S/901.
[115] Doc. S/983. For draft see S/981.   [116] Doc. S/1070.

November and the instructions issued by the Acting Mediator in accordance with Paragraph 5 (1) of that resolution."[117] Those instructions pertain to the withdrawal of Israeli forces from positions held after October 14.

The foregoing resolutions were adopted as a result of Israel's incursions in territories which were under the control of Egypt and Jordan respectively. In adopting them, the Council ignored the fact that those territories had been allotted to Israel by the Partition recommendation and thus refused, despite the Partition allocation, to sanction the Israeli occupation. The demand put forth by the Council for the withdrawal of Israel's troops is proof of the Council's intentions. The withdrawal demand, expressed in the aforesaid resolutions, indicates that the Council prescribed a new status for these territories. This prescription was to revive and maintain the status which existed prior to October 14, 1948—the *status quo ante*. The maintenance of such status could be interpreted either as an annulment of or as a suspension of the allocations under the General Assembly's partition recommendation until the final settlement of the whole Palestinian question.

It should be remembered that the coastal strip was not occupied by Israel prior to October 14, 1948. Israel's advance to the coast strip in early March 1949[118] was not only in violation of the Security Council's prescriptions set forth in the truce and its three subsequent resolutions, but also in violation of the Egyptian-Israeli General Armistice Agreement[119] which had been concluded on February 24, 1949, in compliance with the Security Council's resolution of November 16, 1948.[120] The Armistice Agreement prescribed in Art. I, para. 2, that "no aggressive action by the armed forces—land, sea, or air—of either party shall be undertaken"; and in Art. IV, para. 1, that "no military or political advantage could be gained under the truce ordered by the Security Council. . . ." In view of these prohibitions, it is clear that Israel's possession of the coastal strip, gained by the employment of the military

117 Doc. S/1168. For Egypt's complaint see S/1151; for the Acting Mediator's reports, see S/1152, S/1153; for drafts of the resolution see S/1163, S/1167, S/1168.

118 See Cablegram dated March 20, 1949, from the Acting Mediator to the Secretary-General transmitting a Supplement Report on the situation in the Southern Negev, Doc. S/1295.

119 For the text of the Armistice Agreement, see Doc. S/1264/Rev. 1; S.C., O.R., 4th Year, Special Suppl. No. 3.

120 Doc. S/1080.

instrument, is in the nature of a military occupation only, without lawful claim to sovereignty. This is in conformity with the doctrine, well established in international law, that belligerent occupation cannot lawfully be converted into sovereignty over the occupied territory as long as the war is still in progress.[121] In other words the belligerent occupant has no sovereignty over the occupied territory and is not allowed to proceed to its annexation as long as the state of war exists. That a state of war has been existing between Israel and Egypt in spite of the conclusion of the Armistice Agreement, is emphasized by the fact that the participants have been engaging in measures of coercion through the continuous and incessant employment of the diplomatic, ideological, and economic instruments with accelerating degrees of intensity. Although the military instrument has not been continuously used, both participants have occasionally engaged in military coercion, with varying degrees of intensity, in which certain operations had more destructive and deprivational effects than the 1948 war.[122, 123]

Consequently, Israel cannot claim authority over the coastal strip because a military "occupant in no wise acquires sovereignty over such territory through the mere fact of having occupied it."[124] An occupant could claim the annexation of the occupied territory only if the state of war has ended either by the conclusion of a peace treaty or by subjugation of the vanquished.[125] The latter mode is defined by Oppenheim as "extermination in war of one belligerent by another through annexation of the former's territory after conquest, the enemy forces having been annihilated."[126] To date, neither of these events has resulted from the war between Israel and any of the Arab States. Thus, the latter are justified in refusing to recognize or accept the Israeli occupation of the coastal strip created by the use of force since such

[121] See Annex to the Hague Convention on the Laws and Customs of War on Land (Fourth Convention of the Second Hague Conference 1907); Langer, Seizure of Territory, pp. 17, 106, 117 (1947). This principle was summarized in a note of the Minister of Yugoslavia to the U.S. Dept. of State, dated May 12, 1941 (4 Dept. of State Bull. 682) as follows: "It is a cardinal principle of International Law that military occupation of a territory in the course of hostilities does not change the juridical status of the territory thus occupied and that occupation by enemy armies provides no legal basis for the establishment of a new juridical status within such territory. . . ."

[122] The frame of reference here is mainly to the 1956 invasion of Egypt by Israel.

[123] Ed. Note: There is no footnote 123 in the original.

[124] Oppenheim, International Law, Vol. II, Disputes, War, and Neutrality, 7th ed., p. 433.

[125] Langer, op.cit., n. 121 supra, at p. 117.

[126] Oppenheim, op.cit., n. 124 supra, at p. 606.

occupancy does not change sovereignty or other legal status over the occupied territory.[127]

The Arab refusal to recognize Israel's claim to authority over the coastal strip is in conformity with the Stimson Non-Recognition Doctrine. This doctrine, enunciated in 1932 by the United States Secretary of State, Henry L. Stimson, in connection with the Japanese Conquest of Manchuria, declared that the United States "cannot admit the legality of any situation de facto, nor does it intend to recognize any situation, treaty or agreement which may impair our treaty rights. . . ."[128] The non-recognition doctrine was referred to by Mr. William R. Castle, then Under Secretary of State, as a "new dictum of international law"[129] and is the "strongest moral sanction the world has ever known."[130]

Non-recognition does not stand solely as a unilateral declaration of policy on the part of one of the world's major powers, however. Repeatedly, it has been written into multilateral treaties as a basic prescription. The Declaration of Principles, addressed to the governments of Bolivia and Paraguay by the nineteen other American Republics on August 3, 1932, read in part:

> "The American Nations further declare that they will not recognize any territorial arrangement of this controversy which has not been obtained by peaceful means nor the validity of territorial acquisitions which may be obtained through occupation or conquest by force of arms."[131]

In Article 2 of the Argentine Anti-War Treaty of Non-Aggression and Conciliation, signed at Rio de Janeiro, October 10, 1933, the parties declared:

> "that as between the high contracting parties territorial questions must not be settled by violence, and that they will not recognize any territorial arrangement which is not obtained by pacific means, nor the validity of the occupation or acquisition of territories that may be brought about by force of arms."[132]

---

[127] See Harvard Draft Convention on the Rights and Duties of States in Case of Aggression. Article 4, Para. 2 provided that "Situations created by an aggressor's use of armed force do not change sovereignty or other legal rights over territory." Text 33 A.J.I.L., Supp. 823.

[128] Dept. of State Press Releases, No. 119 (Jan. 9, 1932), pp. 41-42.

[129] *Ibid.*, No. 136 (May 7, 1932), p. 418.   [130] *Ibid.*, p. 446.

[131] *Ibid.*, No. 149 (Aug. 6, 1932), pp. 100, 101.

[132] U.S. Treaty Series, No. 906.

Article II of the Convention on Rights and Duties of States, signed at the Seventh Pan American Conference in December 1933, provided that

"The contracting States definitely establish as the rule of their conduct the precise obligation not to recognize territorial acquisitions or special advantages which have been obtained by force whether this consists in the employment of arms, in threatening diplomatic representations, or in any other effective coercive measure. . . ."[133]

The foregoing conventions sustain the application of the non-recognition doctrine with respect to Israel's claim to authority over the coastal strip. This claim cannot be separated from its relevant factors which include the non-peaceful, forcible, and coercive possession of the area and the violation of proper obligations prescribed by the Security Council and undertaken by Israel in the form of the Truce and the Armistice.[134]

Indeed, the practice of non-recognition by the Arab States in this arena is, ethically, an application of the most pertinent manifestation of the postulate that a unilateral *tour de force* should not be allowed to bring about a change in the existing territorial order. Israel contends, however, that its sovereignty over the area has been established, *inter alia*, by the Hashemite Jordan Kingdom-Israel General Armistice Agreement.[135] Before examining this contention, it is relevant to mention that Israel's occupation of the area on March 10, 1949 came as a result of its military movements against the Jordanian troops stationed in the Southern Negev (including Umm Reshresh, El-Ghamir, and Ghrandal),[136] which at that time was also governed by the Truce of July 15, 1948, and Israel's occupation is obviously a violation of the latter instrument.

In connection with the Jordanian-Israeli Armistice Agreement, it is pertinent to define the term "armistice." Oppenheim regards it as an

---

133 *Ibid.*, No. 881.

134 See Briggs, Non-Recognition of Title by Conquest and Limitation of the Doctrine, 1940 Proceedings A.S.I.L., p. 75; Sir John Fischer Williams in 44 Hague Recueil 278-287 (1933); and Lauterpacht, 62 Hague Recueil 293 (1937). It should be noted that both Briggs and Lauterpacht in their consideration of the legality of Japan's occupation of Manchuria had applied the test of the violation of previous treaty obligations.

135 U.N. Treaty Series, No. 656, pp. 304-325. Reference to it will be made hereafter to the Jordan-Israeli Armistice Agreement.

136 *Op.cit.*, n. 118, *supra*.

"agreement between belligerent forces for a temporary cessation of hostilities"; it is "in no wise to be compared with peace, and ought not to be called temporary peace, because the condition of war remains between the belligerents themselves, and between the belligerents and neutrals, on all points beyond the mere cessation of hostilities."[137] The inference to be drawn from this definition indicates that the occupation of a territory by a belligerent under an armistice agreement does not confer sovereignty to the occupant.[138]

This principle has been frequently acknowledged and endorsed by the courts. In Kemeny v. Yugoslav State, the Hungarian-Yugoslav Mixed Arbitral Tribunal was confronted with the problem of deciding whether the occupation by Yugoslavia of certain territories by virtue of the Armistice Agreement concluded on November 3, 1918, sanctioned the Yugoslav State's claim to authority over those territories. The Court held that:

> "The Armistice Agreement did not have the effect of transferring sovereignty to the Yugoslav Government over the occupied territories."[139]

In Del Vecchio v. Connio, the Court of Appeal of Milan was concerned with the clarification of the status of Trieste which was occupied by Italian troops after the Armistice of 1918. In the judgment rendered the Court stated that:

> "It is universally held nowadays that warlike occupation cannot attribute to the occupying State the sovereignty over the occupied territory. . . . The conditions created by the armistice must be deemed as constituting war time occupation in regard to the territory in question."[140]

The French Court of Cassation decided that the German Colony of Togoland under French military occupation "cannot be held to be part of the national territory."[141]

In the light of these judicial pronouncements it seems clear that the

---

[137] Oppenheim, *op.cit.*, n. 124 *supra*, at pp. 546-547.

[138] *Ibid.*, p. 433, note 5.

[139] Lauterpacht, Annual Digest of Public International Law Cases, Case No. 374 (1927-1928).

[140] *Ibid.*, Case No. 320 (1919-1922).

[141] *Ibid.*, Naoum and Others v. The Government of French West Africa, Case No. 312 (1919-1922).

Jordanian-Israeli Armistice Agreement—an example of the classical type of armistice—has not conferred or established Israel's sovereignty in the coastal strip. This conclusion is strengthened by the provisions of the Armistice Agreement itself. Article 11 reads as follows:

> "With specific view to the implementation of the resolution of the Security Council of 16 November 1948, the following principles and purposes are affirmed:
>
> "1. The principle that no military or political advantage should be gained under the truce ordered by the Security Council is recognized;
>
> "2. It is also recognized that no provision of this agreement shall in any way prejudice the rights, claims and positions of either Party hereto in the ultimate peaceful settlement of the Palestine question, the provisions of this Agreement being dictated exclusively by military considerations."[142]

The Armistice Agreement established a demarcation line only to separate the two participants' forces and not as a basis for territorial claims. This was expressly provided in Article IV, para. 2: "The basic purpose of the Armistice Demarcation Lines is to delineate the lines beyond which the armed forces of the respective parties shall not move."[143] Article VI, para. 9, stipulates further that the Armistice Demarcation lines "are agreed upon by the Parties without prejudice to future territorial settlements or boundary lines or to claims of either Party relating thereto."[144]

In 1957, Mr. Shukairy, the Saudi Arabian representative to the United Nations, summarized the Arab position with respect to the coastal strip as follows:

> "Israel . . . has no right to any part of the Gulf. Israel's claim . . . could only be argued on the United Nations Plan of Partition or the Armistice lines. On either ground, the claim of Israel falls to the ground. On the plan of partition, Israel cannot claim Elath before Israel is confined to the lines of the plan. . . . With regard to the armistice lines . . . under the express provisions of the armistice agree-

---

[142] Comparable to this Article is Article III, para. 3, Egyptian-Israeli Armistice Agreement.

[143] Comparable to this Article is Article V, para. 3 of the Egyptian-Israeli Armistice Agreement.

[144] Comparable to this Article is Article V, para. 2, Egyptian-Israeli Armistice Agreement.

ments, the armistice lines are purely 'dictated by military considerations' and have no political significance.

"Thus the area under Israel is nothing but a military control without sovereignty whatsoever. Israel has no sovereign status in the Gulf of Aqaba."[145]

Mr. Pearson, the representative of Canada to the United Nations, pointed out that the Armistice Agreements are not to be construed as establishing political or territorial boundaries, or to prejudice or confirm any political or territorial right or claim to boundary, and were delineated without prejudice to rights, claims and positions of the parties as regards an ultimate settlement of the Palestine question.[146]

Mr. Selak in his article concerning the legal status of the Gulf of Aqaba agreed with the Arab claim that Israel should not be permitted to claim the Negev area until it complies with the original Palestine Partition plan and asserted that this is a point which will have an important bearing upon any legal decision made with respect to the Gulf's status by an appropriate authority.[147] Mr. Selak concluded his article by characterizing Israel's shaky claim to the coastal strip as follows:

"For a final and complete determination of the status of the Gulf it may be necessary to await a final settlement of the Palestine question, for it is unclear at present what is the status of Israel's coastline on the Gulf. . . . Is Israel's coastline on the Gulf, depending as it does upon the land frontiers established by the Armistice Agreements with Egypt and Jordan, of a different legal nature than that of the land frontiers? . . . It is a question which ought to be considered by the appropriate juridical authority."[148]

[145] General Assembly, 12th Sess., Official Records, 697th Plenary Meeting (A/f P.V. 697), Oct. 2, 1957, p. 233.

[146] General Assembly, 11th Sess., Official Records, 660th Meeting (A/P.V. 660), Feb. 26, 1957, p. 1203.

[147] Charles B. Selak, Jr., A Consideration of the Legal Status of the Gulf of Aqaba, 52 A.J.I.L. 681 (1958).

[148] *Ibid.*, p. 697.

Perhaps it should be added that Article 16 (4) of the 1958 Geneva Convention upon the Territorial Sea and Contiguous Zone will not, if generally ratified, resolve the question here in issue. This clause is relevant only if it be assumed that Israel is lawfully on the Gulf.

Even if it be assumed that Israel is lawfully upon the Gulf, the question remains further whether the Arab States may not have lawfully intended particular passage for reasons of security, self defense, and reprisal.

The Geneva Conference on the Law of the Sea and the Right of Innocent Passage Through the Gulf of Aqaba

LEO GROSS

Since the United Nations Emergency Force moved in and occupied the heights overlooking the Straits of Tiran, the Gulf of Aqaba has been quiet. Ships, including Israel flag ships, move freely in and out. The right of passage claimed by Israel and other states was discussed in the Security Council in 1954, in the International Law Commission in 1956, in the General Assembly in 1956–57, and again at the Geneva Conference on the Law of the Sea February 24–April 27, 1958, and will be analyzed here. It should be stated at the outset that Israel's boundaries, including the strip at the northern end of the Gulf of Aqaba, are not an issue here. Nor is the Arab claim that a state of war continues to exist pertinent in determining the legal status of the Gulf and the Straits, although it obviously has some bearing on the availability to Israel of the right of "innocent" passage.

1. *The Gulf of Aqaba before the Security Council, 1954*

On January 28, 1954, Israel submitted to the Security Council two complaints: one referred to the continued interference by Egypt with ships trading with Israel while passing through the Suez Canal, in contravention of the Security Council resolution of September 1, 1951;[1] and the other concerned interference by Egypt with shipping proceeding to the Israel port of Elath on the Gulf of Aqaba.[2] A draft resolution submitted by New Zealand proposed that "without prejudice to the provisions of the resolution of 1 September 1951, the complaint . . . should in the first instance be dealt with by the Armistice Commission established under the General Armistice Agreement between Egypt and Israel."[3] In the vote on March 29, 1954, this draft resolution was not adopted, there being eight votes in favor (Brazil, Colombia, Denmark, France, New Zealand, Turkey, United Kingdom, United States), two against (Lebanon, U.S.S.R.), and one abstention (China).[4] The debate was largely concerned with the question whether

[1] See Gross, "Passage through the Suez Canal of Israel-Bound Cargo and Israel Ships," 51 A.J.I.L. 530–568, particularly 564–568 (1957).

[2] U.N. Doc. S/3168. Security Council, 9th Year, Official Records, Supp., January–March, 1954, p. 1.

[3] U.N. Docs. S/3188 and Corr. 1, March 19, 1954. *Loc. cit.*, p. 44.

[4] Official Journal, 664th Meeting, March 29, 1954, p. 12. This was the second Soviet veto in the Palestinian question; the first was cast on Jan. 22, 1954, and indicated a shift in the position of the Soviet Union from abstention to active support of the Arab states against Israel.

the 1951 resolution applied to Egyptian interference in the Suez Canal only or was of a general character. Typical of the view held by members of the Council which supported the New Zealand proposal was the observation of the representative of the United States. He quoted paragraph 5 of the 1951 resolution:

> Considering that since the armistice regime, which has been in existence for nearly two and half years, is of a permanent character, neither party can reasonably assert that it is actively a belligerent or requires to exercise the right of visit, search, and seizure for any legitimate purpose of self-defense . . .[5]

and said:

> In our opinion, this principle is equally applicable to the Suez Canal and to any waters outside the Canal. . . . We believe that the Mixed Armistice Commission, in considering this specific complaint with respect to actions in the Gulf of Aqaba, must be bound not only by the provisions of the General Armistice Agreement but should also act in the light of paragraph 5 of the resolution of 1 September 1951.[6]

Egypt, in the same order of ideas, based its objections to the draft resolution, not on the legal status of the waters involved, but on the alleged rights of belligerency. While admitting the right of innocent passage through territorial waters, the representative of Egypt said:

> The passage of contraband of war through the national and territorial waters of Egypt to Israel is certainly not a case of innocent passage. It violates the most explicit provisions of Egyptian law and strengthens Israel's war effort.[7]

It is suggested that no other legal basis was open to the Egyptian representative, as, in reply to an inquiry by the United States Government, he stated that his government had explicitly and formally recognized the right of innocent passage through the Straits of Tiran in the following statement of January 28, 1950:

> This occupation (of the Islands of Tiran and Sanafir) being in no sense intended to interfere in any way whatever with innocent traffic through the stretch of sea separating these two islands from the Sinai Coast of Egypt, it goes without saying that this passage, the only practicable one, will remain free, as in the past; which is in conformity with international practice and with recognized principles of international law.[8]

There is no reference here to "national" waters. The above-quoted statement was explicitly included in the United States Memorandum to

[5] U.N. Doc. S/2298/Rev. 1. Official Records, 558th Meeting, Sept. 1, 1951, p. 2.

[6] Official Records, 663rd Meeting, March 25, 1954, p. 2. For statements to the same effect by representatives of Great Britain and France, see *ibid.*, pp. 6, 9.

[7] *Ibid.*, 661st Meeting, March 12, 1954, p. 19. The law referred to is presumably the decision of the Egyptian Council of Ministers of Nov. 28, 1953, enlarging the list of contraband goods to include food. *Cf.* U.N. Doc. S/3168, note 2 above, at p. 2.

[8] Quoted by the Israel representative in the Security Council, Official Records, 659th Meeting, Feb. 15, 1954, p. 19.

Israel of February 11, 1957,[9] which forms an integral part of the official exchanges between the two governments on the basis of which Israel finally agreed to withdraw from Sharm el Sheikh. The representative of Israel argued in the Security Council on February 15, 1954, with reference to the Strait of Tiran, that

> Where a narrow waterway is the only junction between two parts of the high seas, or the only outlet to a part of the high seas, then its international character has to be preserved, and no sovereign rights based upon the doctrine of territorial waters is inherent in any country from the viewpoint of holding up free maritime traffic.[10]

Referring to the Gulf of Aqaba, Israel's position was stated to be as follows:

> Any claim by Egypt that in the Gulf of Elath (Aqaba) it is merely exercising the rights of sovereignty in territorial waters would of course be totally frivolous since it is a physical geographical fact that there is no way for a ship to approach any place on the northern shore of that narrow gulf without passing through the territorial waters of any or all of four countries—Egypt, Israel, Jordan and Saudi Arabia.
> We should thus arrive at the absurdity that any of those four countries could at any time use its armed force in the straits of Aqaba to prevent a ship from reaching any other of the three littoral States. It is not difficult to conceive what a maritime jungle would be created by such a ludicrous theory. International law and practice on such questions is quite clear and explicit.[11]

Israel's position appeared to rest on the view that the Straits of Tiran constitute an international waterway which is open to navigation in spite of the fact that it passes through the territorial sea of Egypt; and that freedom of navigation through the Gulf is based on the theory of access to the port or ports of the coastal states. The position of the Arab states denying freedom of navigation seemed to have been based either on the existence of a state of war and consequential belligerent rights or on the "national" character of the water involved, without specifying sharply whether this character was attributed to the Straits or the Gulf. Juridically the latter position does not seem very persuasive, particularly in view of the Egyptian assurances of 1950 to the United States. It was, however, developed more concretely by Saudi Arabia which claimed the Gulf as a "closed sea."

2. *The Gulf of Aqaba as* Mare Clausum

In a "Memorandum registering the Saudi Arabian Government's legal and historical rights in the Straits of Tiran and the Gulf of Aqaba,"[12] it was claimed that both the Straits and the Gulf constitute an Arab *mare clausum,* and not an international waterway. This is based in the first

[9] "Aide-Memoire Handed to Israeli Ambassador Eban by Secretary of State Dulles, February 11, 1957," U. S. Policy in the Middle East September 1956–June 1957, Documents, p. 290 (Dept. of State Pub. 6505).

[10] Official Records, 659th Meeting, Feb. 15, 1954, p. 18.

[11] Official Records, 658th Meeting, Feb. 5, 1954, p. 16, and *ibid.,* 659th Meeting, Feb. 15, 1954, p. 18.   [12] U.N. Doc. A/3575, April 15, 1957.

place on the configuration of the area: The Gulf is 100 miles long with widths varying between 7 and 14 miles; the entrance does not exceed 9 miles and is "intercepted by the two Islands of Tiran and Sanafir" under Saudi Arabian sovereignty; the only navigable channel lies between the Island of Tiran and the Egyptian shore and does not exceed half a mile or 500 meters.[13]   In the second place, Saudi Arabia claimed that the Gulf "is of the category of historical Gulfs that fall outside the sphere of international law." The basis for this is seen in the character of the Gulf as

> the historical route to the holy places in Mecca.   Pilgrims from different Muslim countries have been streaming through the Gulf, year after year, for fourteen centuries.   Ever since, the Gulf has been an exclusively Arab route under Arab sovereignty.   It is due to this undisputed fact that not a single international authority makes any mention whatsoever of the Gulf as an international waterway open for international navigation.[14]

The Saudi Arabian Government might have added, for completeness' sake, which "international authority makes any mention whatsoever" of the Gulf as a historic gulf or bay.[15]

Juridically as well as historically this statement is of dubious value, as it would be difficult to reconcile the sovereignty of the Ottoman Empire over the whole area with "Arab sovereignty" during fourteen centuries.   However, it is unnecessary to evaluate its significance, as juridically Saudi Arabia appears to derive the historical character of the Gulf from the Suez Canal Convention of 1888:

> . . . The territorial character of the Gulf, its waters, entrance and straits, was affirmed by the Treaty of Constantinople of 1888 concerning the Suez Canal.   Article 10 (par. 3) of the said Treaty specified that the stipulations contained in that Treaty do not apply to the Arabic States lying on the Red Sea and the Gulf of Aqaba.   The records of the negotiations leading to the said Treaty clearly reveal that the Gulf of Aqaba and its straits were intended to be excluded from the proposed freedom of international navigation in the Suez Canal, thus acknowledging that the waters of the Gulf, its entrance and straits, are territorial and implying no freedom of international navigation through them.[16]

Finally, the possession of a strip of the Gulf by Israel is "nothing but a military control without sovereignty whatsoever.   Israel has no sovereign status in the Gulf of Aqaba."[17]

[13] *Ibid.*, pp. 3–4; see also statement by the representative of Saudi Arabia in General Assembly, 12th Sess., Official Records, 697th Plenary Meeting, Oct. 2, 1957, p. 233, par. 92; and at Geneva Conference on the Law of the Sea, Official Records, Vol. III, First Committee, 3rd Meeting, March 3, 1959, p. 3, par. 30: "The Gulf of Aqaba came under exclusive Arab jurisdiction."

[14] Statement in the General Assembly; *cf.* note 13 above, p. 233, par. 93.

[15] The "Memorandum concerning Historic Bays," prepared by the U.N. Secretariat for the Geneva Conference on the Law of Sea, does not mention the Gulf of Aqaba among the bays regarded as historic bays or claimed as such by the states concerned. U.N. Doc. A/Conf. 13/1 (Sept. 20, 1957), pp. 9–28.

[16] Memorandum, note 12 above, p. 4.

[17] Statement in the General Assembly; *cf.* note 13 above, p. 233, par. 96.

The first and last arguments are interdependent and will be discussed presently. The Suez Canal Convention provides no juridical basis for the asserted "territorial" character of the Gulf. Article 10, paragraph 3, does not have the significance attributed to it by Saudi Arabia. It declares:

> It is also understood that the provisions of the four Articles in question [4, 5, 7 and 8] shall in no case stand in the way of measures which the Imperial Ottoman Government considers it necessary to take to assure by its own forces the defense of its other possessions situated on the eastern coast of the Red Sea.[18]

The articles in question—4, 5, 7 and 8—are concerned with the rights and duties of belligerents in the Suez Canal and its approaches and measures of supervision. They are not concerned with freedom of navigation. Assuming, as the Saudi Arabian Government does, that the Convention relates to the Gulf, then the opposite conclusion from that drawn by Saudi Arabia appears more plausible. The principle of freedom of navigation in time of war and peace is established by Article 1 of the Convention. As this article is not excluded by Article 10, paragraph 3, it would follow, on the basis of the Saudi Arabian assumption, that it applies equally in the Suez Canal and the Gulf of Aqaba. Thus, far from supporting the claim to the "territorial character" of the Gulf, the Convention, if it applies at all, would negate it and substantiate the Israel claim to freedom of navigation, which is asserted by the United States and other maritime Powers as well.

Turning now to the first and last Saudi Arabian arguments, it can be admitted that historical titles are not unknown in international law. The International Court of Justice, in the Anglo-Norwegian Fisheries dispute, held:

> By "historic waters" are usually meant waters which are treated as internal waters but which would not have that character were it not for the existence of an historic title. The United Kingdom Government refers to the notion of historic titles both in respect of territorial waters and internal waters, considering such titles, in both cases, as derogations from general international law. In its opinion Norway can justify the claim that these waters are territorial or internal on the ground that she has exercised the necessary jurisdiction over them for a long period without opposition from other States, a kind of *possessio longi temporis,* with the result that her jurisdiction over these waters must now be recognized although it constitutes a derogation from the rules in force. Norwegian sovereignty over these waters would constitute an exception, historic titles justifying situations which would otherwise be in conflict with international law.[19]

The historic title to a gulf or bay was affirmed by the Central American Court of Justice in its Judgment of March 9, 1917.[20] The Court held:

---

[18] The Suez Canal Problem July 26–September 22, 1956, p. 19 (Dept. of State Pub. 6392).

[19] Fisheries Case (United Kingdom *v.* Norway), Judgment of Dec. 18, 1951. [1951] I.C.J. Rep. 116, at 130. See also 46 A.J.I.L. 348, at 358, 366, 369 (1952).

[20] The Republic of El Salvador *v.* The Republic of Nicaragua, 11 A.J.I.L. 674–730 (1917).

The legal status of the Gulf of Fonseca having been recognized by this Court to be that of a historic bay possessed of the characteristics of a closed sea, the three riparian States of El Salvador, Honduras and Nicaragua are, therefore, recognized as coöwners of its waters, except as to the littoral marine league which is the exclusive property of each . . .[21]

The Court arrived at the conclusion that the Gulf of Fonseca "belongs to the special category of historic bays and is the exclusive property of El Salvador, Honduras and Nicaragua" on the theory

that it combines all the characteristics or conditions that the text writers on international law, the international law institutes and the precedents have prescribed as essential to territorial waters, to wit, secular or immemorial possession accompanied by *animo domini* both peaceful and continuous and by acquiescence on the part of other nations, the special geographical configuration that safeguards so many interests of vital importance to the economic, commercial, agricultural and industrial life of the riparian States and the absolute, indispensable necessity that those States should possess the Gulf as fully as required by those primordial interests and the interest of national defense.[22]

Three pillars, then, support the historic character of the Gulf of Fonseca: first, immemorial possession established by the Spanish Crown in 1522 and continued by the three successor states;[23] secondly, the *animus domini* "both peaceful and continuous"; and, finally, acquiescence by other nations. It will be noted, however, that the Court did not attribute to the waters in the Gulf the character of internal waters and therefore did not exclude the right of innocent passage. The doctrine, even in the case of historic bays the coasts of which belong to a single state, does not seem to be unanimous whether the waters are to be regarded as "internal waters," thus excluding the right of innocent passage, or partly as "internal waters" and partly as territorial sea.[24] In the latter case there would presumably be a right of innocent passage in the territorial sea.[25]

It is doubtful whether the claim to the Gulf of Aqaba as a closed sea meets these three tests. Immemorial possession could not easily be established, although, in a sense, all the four states abutting on the Gulf may be

---

[21] *Ibid.* at 716; see also 707. [22] *Ibid.* at 705.

[23] On this point the Court said: "The historic origin of the right of exclusive ownership that has been exercised over the waters of the Gulf during the course of nearly four hundred years is incontrovertible, first, under the Spanish dominion—from 1522, when it was discovered and incorporated into the royal patrimony of the Crown of Castile, down to the year 1821—then under the Federal Republic of the Center of America, which in that year attained its independence and sovereignty down to 1839; and, subsequently, on the dissolution of the Federation in that year, the States of El Salvador, Honduras and Nicaragua, in their character of autonomous nations and legitimate successors of Spain, incorporated into their respective territories, as a necessary dependency thereof for geographical reasons and purposes of common defense, both the Gulf and its archipelago, which nature had indented in that important part of the continent, in the form of a gullet." *Ibid.* at 700.

[24] Memorandum concerning Historic Bays, note 15 above, at 63–79.

[25] See 3 Gidel, Le Droit International Public de la Mer 606 (1934). Gidel interprets the Judgment of the Central American Court in the Fonseca case in this sense.

considered as successors to the Ottoman Empire. Did the Ottoman Empire, however, manifest *"animus domini"* and was the claim to regard the Gulf as Turkish acquiesced in by other nations? Unless the advocates of the Gulf as a closed sea prove both *animus* and recognition at the time the area was under Ottoman sovereignty, the states which emerged from the progressive dismemberment of the Ottoman Empire did not succeed to a historical title to the gulf or bay. In this respect the Gulf of Aqaba situation presents no analogy at all to the Gulf of Fonseca. Failing this, it would be necessary to show that a "historic" claim arose and was recognized some time after the emergence of Egypt and Saudi Arabia as independent states and the creation of the British Mandate in Palestine out of which developed both Jordan and Israel. This would be a hopeless task and in fact has not been attempted. Egypt's official declaration of 1950 stands in the way of any such attempt. Certainly since the establishment of Israel in 1948 there has been neither a "peaceful and continuous" *animus* nor acquiescence by other nations. Unlike in the case of the Gulf of Fonseca, where all littoral states assert a historic title against outsiders, in the Gulf of Aqaba Saudi Arabia is asserting a claim against one of the littoral states, with general support from Jordan, and Egypt being precluded from supporting it.[26] In this respect, too, there is no analogy whatsoever between the juridical situation of the Gulf of Fonseca and the Gulf of Aqaba.

Certainly, the Gulf of Aqaba could be transformed into a closed sea by agreement among all the littoral states and recognition by other nations. As the then Secretary of State, Mr. John Foster Dulles, said: "If the four littoral States which have boundaries upon the Gulf should all agree that it should be closed, then it could be closed."[27] Whether in such a case the littoral states would also agree to consider the entire body of water in the Gulf or only that part outside their respective territorial seas as included in co-ownership is probably not decisive. In the case of the Gulf of Fonseca the Court assumed that Nicaragua and El Salvador exercised sovereignty individually in the maritime belts.[28] In principle, it would appear that the existence of belts of territorial seas, insofar as the littoral states in their relations *inter se* are concerned, is not incompatible with the character of a gulf or bay as a closed sea *erga omnes*.[29] The enactment of

[26] At the Geneva Conference on the Law of the Sea, the representative of Jordan expressed "his complete agreement with the observations made by the representative of Saudi Arabia" and his hope that Israel's possession of a share of the coast "would prove transient." Official Records, Vol. III, First Committee, 8th Meeting, March 7, 1958, p. 18, pars. 6 and 7. The representative of Egypt stated that, contrary to the assertion of the representative of Israel, "no single aspect of the Palestine question had yet been the object of any settlement whatever." *Ibid.*, p. 67, par. 9.

[27] News Conference Statements by Secretary of State Dulles, Feb. 19, 1957. United States Policy in the Middle East September 1956–June 1957, p. 299 (Dept. of State Pub. 6505). But see 3 Gidel, Le Droit International Public de la Mer 604, where the author considers acquiescence by other states as essential even in such a case.

[28] See note 20 above, at 711, and also the fifteenth question and the answer, at 694.

[29] For the opposite view see Charles B. Selak, Jr., "A Consideration of the Legal Status of the Gulf of Aqaba," 52 A.J.I.L. 660–698, at 693 (1958).

regulations concerning the extent of the territorial sea does not necessarily militate against a historic claim to the Gulf of Aqaba, as all states but Jordan have a coast outside the Gulf. However, the Fisheries Act No. 25 of December 2, 1943, which in Article 2 defines the territory of "Transjordan" as including that part of the sea lying within three miles from the low-water line and is maintained in force by Jordan, which has no other coastline,[30] would be a strong indication that, in the juridical view of Jordan or of the British Mandatory Administration at any rate, the historic character of the Gulf was an afterthought.

Recognition or acquiescence by third states was considered as an element in the historic title to the Gulf of Fonseca in addition to *animus* and "immemorial possession." Recognition or acquiescence or absence of protest appears to be a necessary ingredient, since a claim to a historic sea or bay appears as an encroachment upon the principle of the freedom of the high seas, or, as the International Court of Justice put it in the above-quoted passage, as "a derogation from the rules in force." Certainly the burden of proof with respect to all the elements of a historic title rests with the government or governments which claim it.[31] Certainly in the case of the Gulf of Aqaba this proof would be difficult to furnish in view of the successive changes in the number of the coastal states.[31a] The discussion at the Eleventh Session of the General Assembly on the Gulf of Aqaba failed to disclose any evidence of recognition. In any event the weight of such evidence, if it could be adduced, would have to be measured against the opposite view of Israel, which has emerged as one of the coastal states.

The Central American Court of Justice based its finding, among other factors, on the "many interests of vital importance" of the Gulf of Fonseca to the coastal states. The concept of "vital bays," that is of bays which are claimed as national or internal waters on the ground of the vital interests of the coastal state or states, does not seem to have any basis in the practice of states or in the doctrine.[32] Even if the concept were acceptable, it would be extremely difficult, in practice, to establish as national or internal the waters of a "vital bay" in the absence of agreement among the coastal states. There is obviously no such agreement with respect to the

---

[30] U.N. Legislative Series, Laws and Regulations on the Regime of the Territorial Sea, p. 522 (Sales No.: 1957.V.2).

[31] Memorandum concerning Historic Bays, note 15 above, at 91. See also *ibid.* 83–85, for doctrinal views regarding the requirement of recognition or acquiescence, and 98–102 for an analysis of the judgment of the International Court of Justice with respect to this requirement. See also the Japanese proposal of April 1, 1958, relating to Art. 7, par. 4, which, in defining historic bays, combines the elements of usage and recognition: "The term 'historic bays' means those bays over which coastal State or States have effectively exercised sovereign rights continuously for a period of long standing, with explicit or implicit recognition of such practice by foreign States." U.N. Doc. A/Conf. 13/C.1/L. 104, Conference on the Law of the Sea, Official Records, Vol. III, First Committee, p. 241.

[31a] According to Alexander Melamid, "Legal Status of the Gulf of Aqaba," 53 A.J.I.L. 412–413 (1959), there would seem to be no basis whatever for any historic or exclusive title to the Gulf in any of the riparian states.

[32] Memorandum concerning Historic Bays, note 15 above, at 85–88.

Gulf of Aqaba, although this gulf may well be vital to all or some of the coastal states. However, the interest which is considered as "vital" by them is not identic.

In conclusion, it is one thing to claim a bay as historic but another to establish a valid claim. The International Law Commission, in view of the inherent difficulties, did not attempt to include a definition of historic bays in its draft.[33] The Geneva Conference itself did not fill the gap. Instead it adopted a resolution recognizing the juridical importance of historic waters, including historic bays, and requested the General Assembly of the United Nations "to arrange for the study of the juridical régime of historic waters, including historic bays, and for the communication of the result of such study to all States Members of the United Nations." [34] However, the Conference may be deemed to have implicitly rejected the claim to the Gulf of Aqaba as a historic gulf or bay when it adopted paragraph 4 of Article 16 of the Convention on the Territorial Sea, which has been generally regarded as fitting that particular gulf.[35]

3. *The Juridical Status of the Gulf of Aqaba before the International Law Commission*

The question was raised by the Government of Israel in connection with the provisional articles concerning the regime of the territorial sea adopted by the International Law Commission at its Seventh Session in 1955. Article 18 provided that the coastal state may take measures in the territorial sea "to protect itself against any act prejudicial to its security" and for the same reason may even "suspend temporarily and in definite areas of its territorial sea the exercise of the right of passage if it should deem such suspension essential." Article 18, paragraph 4, on the other hand, read:

> There must be no suspension of the innocent passage of foreign vessels through straits normally used for international navigation between two parts of the high seas.[36]

The Government of Israel, in commenting on this, pointed out that, while agreeing with the substance, it objected to the arrangement which made it appear as if the freedom of navigation through straits were a derogation from the sovereignty of the littoral state or states, whereas it considered the latter subordinate to the former. Accordingly,

> What this means is that where access to a given port—whether an existing one or one which at some future date a State may wish to establish—is only possible by traversing a strait (in the geographical sense), then it is quite immaterial whether that strait is or is not within the

[33] See Statement by Professor François, Expert to the Secretariat of the Conference, U.N. Doc. A/Conf. 13/C.1/L.10. U.N. Conference on the Law of the Sea, Official Records, Vol. III, First Committee, p. 69, pars. 13, 14.

[34] U.N. Doc. A/Conf. 13/L.56, p. 8 (April 30, 1958). *Loc. cit.*, Vol. II, Plenary Meetings, p. 145.   [35] *Cf.* pp. 586–587 below.

[36] General Assembly, 10th Sess., Official Records, Supp. No. 9 (A/2934); and 50 A.J.I.L. 232 (1956).

waters classed as territorial sea of one or more of the littoral States, or what is the legal nature (gulf, bay, high seas) of the waters on which the harbour is situated. In such circumstances the right of passage for the ships of all nations, and quite regardless of their cargo, is and must remain absolutely unqualified, and the littoral State or States have no right whatsoever, so long as the matter is not regulated by Convention, to hinder, hamper, impede or suspend the free passage of those ships. The same rule is also true as regards warships.[37]

It is reasonably clear that the Government of Israel commented not so much on the legal status of straits in general and passage through them from one part of the high sea to another as on the legal status of a specific kind of strait, namely, that which affords the only navigable access to a port in a gulf or bay. In short, it set forth its view concerning the Straits of Tiran and the Gulf of Aqaba with emphasis on the right of access.

The International Law Commission weighted the provisions in Article 18 heavily, probably too exclusively in favor of the littoral state's right of protecting its security.[38] This imbalance was corrected to some extent at the Geneva Conference. In the Commission the comments submitted by Israel were recognized as referring to the Gulf of Aqaba, the position of which, in the view of the *Rapporteur,* Professor François, was "exceptional—possibly unique."[39] He also pointed out that

> paragraph 4 of Article 18 related to straits between two parts of the high seas, and so did not apply to the Gulf of Aqaba which, though open to the high seas at one end, merely gave access to a port at the other.[40]

Faris Bey el-Khouri agreed that the case was "exceptional" but, disagreeing with Israel, said:

> A port was not a natural feature existing from time immemorial, and if a State saw fit to establish a port at a point to which the only access was through the territorial waters of other States, it must accept the consequences. It was always open to the State in question to establish a port elsewhere or to conclude agreements with the other coastal States on the question of access to the port.[41]

Sir Gerald Fitzmaurice disagreed. In his view

> vessels would in any case enjoy the right of innocent passage through a gulf consisting entirely of the territorial waters of coastal States to a port belonging to a third State. He wondered whether the situation envisaged by the Israel Government was not already covered by article 18.[42]

---

[37] U.N. Doc. A/CN.4/99/Add. 1; 2 I.L.C. Yearbook 1956, pp. 52, 56; 50 A.J.I.L. 998 at 1005 (1956). The comment concluded as follows: "The interests of the international community must here have absolute predominance over those of the littoral States whose territorial waters have to be traversed in making for a given harbour. In this respect the passage through straits of this character is assimilated to the high seas themselves."

[38] See Myres S. McDougal, "The Crisis of the Law of the Sea," 67 Yale Law Journal 546 (1958), on the conflict between "internationalist" and "provincial" myopia.

[39] 336th Meeting, June 13, 1956, 1 I.L.C. Yearbook 1956, Summary Records of its 8th Sess., April 23–July 4, 1956, p. 202, par. 89.   [40] *Ibid.*, par. 96.

[41] *Ibid.*, par. 93.   [42] *Ibid.*, par. 94.

After a brief and desultory discussion the Commission decided that "the question raised by the Israel Government related to an exceptional case which did not lend itself to the formulation of a general rule."[43]   However, in its Report on the Eighth Session the Commission included the following comment to Article 17 (formerly Article 18):

> The question was asked what would be the legal position of straits forming part of the territorial sea of one or more States and constituting the sole means of access to a port of another State.   The Commission considers that this case could be assimilated to that of a bay whose inner part and entrance from the high seas belong to different States.   As the Commission felt bound to confine itself to proposing rules applicable to bays, wholly belonging to a single coastal State, it also reserved consideration of the above-mentioned case.[44]

This comment, along with the Commission's draft of Article 17, was before the Geneva Conference, which did not adopt it.   It was also, prior to the Conference, available to the Members of the United Nations during the Eleventh Session in 1956–1957 of the General Assembly, when Israel's demand for free and unimpeded passage through the Straits of Tiran and the Gulf of Aqaba was discussed in connection with its withdrawal from the Sinai Peninsula.

What the Commission appeared to be saying can be summarized under five heads:

1. The Straits of Tiran were not straits within the meaning of Article 17, paragraph 4, because they did not connect two parts of the high seas but a part of the high sea with a gulf or bay; therefore Article 17, paragraph 4, prohibiting the suspension of innocent passage did not apply.
2. The Straits of Tiran could be assimilated to a bay bordered by several states; therefore Article 17, paragraph 4, did not apply.
3. States had a right of innocent passage through the territorial seas of other states under Article 16, but a coastal state was authorized by the Commission to suspend temporarily such passage "in definite areas of its territorial sea" under Article 17, paragraph 3.
4. Inasmuch as the only navigable channel in the Straits of Tiran and the Gulf of Aqaba to the Israel port of Elath passed through territorial seas, therefore access to that port could be suspended by the coastal states concerned under Article 17, paragraph 3.
5. Be that as it may, it was not the task of the Commission to lay down rules for particular or even unique cases.

4. *The Juridical Status of the Gulf of Aqaba before the Eleventh Session of the General Assembly 1956–1957*

Attempts to clarify the juridical status of the Straits of Tiran and the Gulf of Aqaba were made by Israel and a number of other Members in connection with the withdrawal of Israel from the Sharm el Sheikh area.   It is not necessary to trace the deliberations of the General Assembly through its various phases, though it may be useful to indicate the principal juridical

---

[43] *Ibid.*, par. 102.

[44] General Assembly, 11th Sess., Official Records, Supp. No. 9 (A/3159), p. 20.

arguments for and against the right of free and unimpeded passage claimed by Israel.

A key to the understanding of the debates appears to be the views expressed by the Secretary General. In a note dated January 15, 1957, he stated:

> The international significance of the Gulf of Aqaba may be considered to justify the right of innocent passage through the Straits of Tiran and the Gulf in accordance with recognized rules of international law.[45]

This statement, which appeared fully to endorse the position of Israel, was somewhat modified in the Secretary General's Report dated January 24, 1957, in which, after repeating it, the following was added:

> However, in its Commentary to Article 17 of the articles of the law of the sea (A/3159, p. 20), the International Law Commission reserved consideration of the question "what would be the legal position of straits forming part of the territorial sea of one or more States and constituting the sole means of access to the port of another State." This description applies to the Gulf of Aqaba and the Straits of Tiran. A legal controversy exists as to the extent of the right of innocent passage through these waters.[46]

On the other hand, after reviewing the Security Council resolution of September 1, 1951, in which the Council called upon Egypt to terminate the restrictions which it imposed on shipping through the Suez Canal destined for Israel,[47] the Secretary General declared that

> . . . it may be held that, in a situation where the armistice régime is partly operative by observance of the provisions of the Armistice Agreement concerning the armistice lines, possible claims to rights of belligerency would be at least so much in doubt that, having regard for the general international interest at stake, no such claim should be exercised in the Gulf of Aqaba and the Straits of Tiran.[48]

The Secretary General thus formulated three propositions: First, there was a right of innocent passage through the Straits and the Gulf; secondly, there was a controversy as to the extent of this right; and thirdly, no belligerent rights should be exercised in the Gulf and the Straits. These views were to weigh heavily in the subsequent debate, although different delegations attached different weight to each of them. The second proposition, a palpable truism, was invested with an importance which appears to be quite out of proportion to its real significance. For "legal controversy" exists not merely regarding the right of innocent passage but also regarding a good deal of the law of the sea and international law in general. It is also remarkable that the positive statement made by the Commission, to wit,

[45] U.N. Doc. A/3500, p. 5, par. 14. General Assembly, 11th Sess., Official Records, Annexes, Agenda Item 66, p. 44. The Secretary General added that he "has not considered that a discussion of the various aspects of this matter, and its possible relation to the action requested in the General Assembly resolutions on the Middle East crisis, falls within the mandate established for him in the resolution of 4 November (1956)."

[46] U.N. Doc. A/3512, p. 8, par. 24. Annexes, Agenda Item 66, p. 49.

[47] On this subject see Leo Gross, "Passage through the Suez Canal of Israel-Bound Cargo and Israel Ships," 51 A.J.I.L. 530–568 (1957).

[48] U.N. Doc. A/3512, p. 9, par. 28. Annexes, Agenda Item 66, p. 50.

that "this case could be assimilated to that of a bay whose inner port and entrance from the high seas belong to different states," was virtually passed over with silence. Had this statement been given its due weight, the Members might have found it easier to disentangle the situation, for if there is a rule of international law regarding which there is practically no controversy, it is the rule that bays and gulfs with several littoral states, "however narrow their entrance may be, are non-territorial. They are parts of the open sea, the marginal belt inside the gulfs and bays excepted." Such gulfs and bays "are in time of peace and war open to vessels of all nations, including men-of-war."[49] Had this principle been taken as the starting point, the issues which remained for consideration would have been confined to the question of innocent passage and possibly the question of belligerent rights in a state of armistice.

Regarding freedom of passage, in and out of the Assembly debates, two schools of thought emerged. One, led by the United States, supported the Israeli position of freedom of passage, and the other, led by India, opposed it. The United States Government in an *Aide-Mémoire* handed to Israeli Ambassador Eban by Secretary of State Dulles on February 11, 1957, stated:

> With respect to the Gulf of Aqaba and access thereto—the United States believes that the Gulf comprehends international waters and that no nation has the right to prevent free and innocent passage in the Gulf and through the Straits giving access thereto.

After recalling the Egyptian declaration of January 28, 1950, with respect to freedom of passage through the Straits,[50] the *Aide-Mémoire* continued:

> In the absence of some overriding decision to the contrary, as by the International Court of Justice, the United States, on behalf of vessels of United States registry, is prepared to exercise the right of free and innocent passage and to join with others to secure general recognition of this right.[51]

This declaration, which President Eisenhower stated "related to our intentions, both as a Member of the United Nations and as a maritime power having rights of our own,"[52] was decisive. The first part of it was

[49] 1 Oppenheim, International Law 508 (8th ed., H. Lauterpacht, 1955). See also Gidel, *op. cit.* 593–608.   [50] See p. 565 above.

[51] United States Policy in the Middle East Sept. 1956–June 1957, Documents, p. 290 (Dept. of State Pub. 6505).

[52] White House News Statement issued at Thomasville, Georgia, Feb. 17, 1957. *Ibid.*, p. 293. The position of the U. S. Government was restated in the Statement by the Department of State of June 27, 1957, which was delivered to the Washington missions of the eleven Arab nations in reply to their collective démarche submitted to the Secretary of State on May 24, 1957, on the problems of Algeria, Palestine, the Gulf of Aqaba and the Suez Canal. The writer is indebted for copies of these statements to the Chief, Historical Division, Department of State, and the Arab States Delegations Office, respectively. Parts of the American statement were printed in the New York Times, June 29, 1957. With respect to the U. S. position concerning the Gulf of Aqaba, see also the Circular sent by the Department of State on June 5, 1957, to Clarence G. Morse, Maritime Administrator, Department of Commerce, and Ralph E. Casey, American Merchant Marine Institute, New York, N. Y., in which the Department declared: "A denial of free and innocent passage through those waters [*i.e.*, the Straits of Tiran and the Gulf

repeated textually by the Foreign Minister of Israel in announcing on March 1, 1957, Israel's plans for full withdrawal from the Sharm el Sheikh area,[53] and the representative of the United States repeated textually all relevant parts of the statement at the same meeting of the Assembly, with this addition:

> These views are to be understood in the sense of the relevant portions on the law of the sea of the report of the International Law Commission covering the work of its eighth session from 23 April to 4 July 1956 (A/3159).[54]

The American view was endorsed in substance though in varying formulas by the representatives of France,[55] Costa Rica,[56] the United Kingdom,[57] Italy,[58] The Netherlands,[59] New Zealand,[60] Australia,[61] Belgium,[62] Canada,[63]

---

of Aqaba] to vessels of United States registry should be reported to the nearest available United States diplomatic or consular officer.'' 37 Dept. of State Bulletin 112 (1957). This Circular referred to the Notice to Mariners No. 44 of Oct. 29, 1955, by the U. S. Hydrographic Office, which repeats the substance of the ''Ports and Lighthouses Administration Circular to Shipping No. 4 of 1955,'' issued by the Director General, Rear Admiral Youssef Hammad. According to this Egyptian Circular, by ''Orders dated 7th of July 1955, issued by the Minister of War and the Commander-in-Chief of the Armed Forces, the Regional Boycotting Office for Israel is appointed to be the sole authority for issuing permission to vessels to pass through the Egyptian Territorial Waters in the Gulf of Aqaba.'' The Circular requires notification of at least 72 hours prior to the entry of the vessel into the Gulf of Aqaba. *Ibid.* 113. The State Department's Circular would seem to indicate that U. S. vessels need not comply with the Egyptian requirement.

[53] 666th Plenary Meeting. General Assembly, 11th Sess., Official Records, p. 1276, par. 11. The Minister added the words: ''. . . in accordance with the generally accepted definition of those terms in the law of the sea.'' See also the statement by the Israeli representative at the 668th Meeting, March 8, 1957. *Ibid.*, p. 1325, par. 252.

[54] *Ibid.*, p. 1277, par. 33.   [55] *Ibid.*, p. 1280, pars. 58, 59.

[56] *Ibid.*, p. 1281, par. 72.   [57] *Ibid.*, 667th Meeting, p. 1284, par. 13.

[58] *Ibid.*, p. 1287, par. 51.

[59] *Ibid.*, p. 1288, pars. 56–61. The detailed reasoned statement by the representative of The Netherlands bears quoting in full: ''First, inasmuch as the Gulf of Aqaba is bordered by four different States and has a width in excess of the three miles of territorial waters of the four littoral States on either side, it is, under the rules of international law, to be regarded as part of the open sea. Secondly, the Straits of Tiran consequently are, in the legal sense, straits connecting two open seas, normally used for international navigation. Thirdly, in regard to such straits, there is a right of free passage even if the straits are so narrow that they fall entirely within the territorial waters of one or more States. This rule was acknowledged by the International Court of Justice in the case of the Corfu Channel (Judgment of December 15, 1949; I.C.J. Reports 1949, p. 244) and also by the International Law Commission in its report for 1956 (A/3159). Fourthly, if a strait falls entirely within the territorial waters of one or more of the littoral States, there is still a right of innocent passage, but then the littoral States have the right, if necessary, to verify the innocent character of the passage. Fifthly, this right of verification, however, does not exist in those cases where the strait connects two parts of the open sea. It must, therefore, be concluded that all States have the right of free and unhampered passage for their vessels through the Straits of Tiran.''

[60] *Ibid.*, p. 1292, par. 103.   [61] *Ibid.*, p. 1594, par. 124.

[62] *Ibid.*, p. 1296, par. 139.

[63] *Ibid.*, p. 1296, par. 148. It should be noted, however, that Canada's position was based on political rather than legal considerations, as in its view the Assembly should not attempt to determine legal rights in the Gulf and the Straits.

Norway,[64] Sweden,[65] Denmark,[66] and Iceland.[67] An opposite view was taken by several Members, though for reasons which are far from clear. The representative of the Soviet Union spoke of "a gross violation of the indisputable rights of Egypt and other Arab States in relation to the territorial waters of the Gulf of Aqaba and the Straits of Tiran."[68] In the opinion of the delegate of Iraq "we cannot consider passage through the Gulf as different from the passage of the refugees to their own homes." [69] The representative of Colombia, in a reasoned statement weighing the "commercial right" of passage against "the right of security," argued that the latter, "that is to say, the State's right to control navigation in its territorial waters must prevail."[70] On the other hand, he also argued "that no country has the right to prevent passage if it is innocent. A country may control it, regulate it, in order to ensure that the passage is innocent; but if it is established that the passage is innocent we would consider it an abuse of right to prevent passage." [71] This raises the issue of what constitutes innocent passage, to which the representative of India devoted some remarks. He contended, first, that the Gulf of Aqaba was an "inland sea"; [72] secondly, that it would "be possible for Egypt, in agreement with Saudi Arabia, to fill up the Gulf of Aqaba"; [73] and thirdly, that Article 17, paragraph 4, of the International Law Commission's draft articles concerning the law of the sea, did not apply to the Gulf because it does not connect two high seas; [74] and, finally, without disputing the right of innocent passage, that

> this right of innocent passage, so-called, actually means that, first of all, one must prove innocence. Innocence depends upon the character of the party claiming the passage; it depends upon the purpose of the passage, and also upon the freight that is carried.[75]

The opinions put forward by India's representatives were not unchallenged. The United Kingdom representative pointed out that the Straits of Tiran were bordered by two countries—Egypt and Saudi Arabia—and not by Egypt alone and that the Gulf of Aqaba was surrounded by four littoral states.[76] The delegate of Italy challenged India's opinion concerning innocent passage and stated correctly, it is believed, that

---

[64] *Ibid.*, p. 1300, par. 196. Norway's position was somewhat akin to that of Canada's in holding that the legal status of these waters "should be dealt with only by a legal body."   [65] *Ibid.*, p. 1303, par. 224.

[66] *Ibid.*, par. 234.   [67] *Ibid.*, 668th Meeting, p. 1319, par. 187.

[68] *Ibid.*, 667th Meeting, p. 1297, par. 159.   [69] *Ibid.*, p. 1294, par. 116.

[70] *Ibid.*, p. 1290, par. 78.

[71] *Ibid.*, p. 1291, par. 88. It may be noted here that the representative of Iraq fully subscribed to the statements made by the representatives of Colombia and India. *Ibid.*, p. 1293, par. 116.   [72] *Ibid.*, 665th Meeting, p. 1269, par. 49.

[73] *Ibid.*, p. 1270, par. 56. In his enthusiasm, the delegate of India overlooked the remaining littoral states, Jordan and Israel.   [74] *Ibid.*, p. 1271, par. 62.

[75] *Ibid.* At the 667th Meeting the representative of India specifically declared that access to the Gulf through the Straits of Tiran "cannot be arranged except with Egypt's consent," inasmuch as the waters in the Straits are Egypt's territorial waters. *Ibid.*, p. 1301, par. 210. In his view, it was not within the province of the General Assembly to decide legal controversies. *Ibid.*, p. 1269, par. 48, and p. 1301, par. 209.

[76] *Ibid.*, p. 1284, par. 12.

This interpretation would nullify the rule of innocent passage, since it is obvious that, if it were valid, the littoral States would no longer have the duty of justifying their refusal of passage to a vessel on specific occasions and for specific reasons; rather, it would rest with the vessel to prove that its passage was innocent.[77]

The question of what constitutes innocent passage was debated at some length at the Geneva Conference on the Law of the Sea and clarified along the lines indicated by the delegate of Italy.

With regard to the question of belligerent rights in a state of armistice, there also emerged two positions, although the affirmative view was not pressed for obvious reasons. Though this particular issue is not directly relevant to the question of the legal status of the Gulf and the Straits, it may be useful to refer to it briefly. As on the issue of the right of passage, the United States position on belligerency was accepted by a substantial number of Members.

The position of the United States was made clear in the *Aide-Mémoire* of February 11, 1957, in which it declared that, after Israel's withdrawal, the United States "has no reason to assume that any littoral State would under these circumstances obstruct the right of free and innocent passage."[78] In stronger terms President Eisenhower stated on February 20, 1957, as follows:

> We should not assume that if Israel withdraws, Egypt will prevent Israeli shipping from using the Suez Canal or the Gulf of Aqaba. If unhappily, Egypt does hereafter violate the Armistice Agreement or other international agreements, then this should be dealt with firmly by the society of nations.[79]

The representative of the United States declared in the General Assembly:

> Once Israel has completed its withdrawal in accordance with the resolutions of the General Assembly, and in view of the measures taken by the United Nations to deal with the situation, there is no basis for either party to the Armistice Agreement to assert or exercise any belligerent rights.[80]

Several Members, including France,[81] the United Kingdom,[82] Italy,[83] New Zealand,[84] Belgium,[85] Canada,[86] and Sweden,[87] spoke in the same vein. In

[77] *Ibid.*, p. 1287, par. 51.

[78] United States Policy in the Middle East Sept. 1956–June 1957, Documents, p. 291 (Dept. of State Pub. 6505).

[79] Radio and television address by President Eisenhower, Feb. 20, 1957. *Loc. cit.*, p. 307.

[80] 666th Meeting, March 1, 1957. General Assembly, 11th Sess., Official Records, Plenary, p. 1278, par. 36. *Cf.* also p. 1277, par. 32.

[81] *Ibid.*, p. 1280, par. 60.   [82] *Ibid.*, 667th Meeting, p. 1284, par. 14.

[83] *Ibid.*, p. 1287, par. 50.   [84] *Ibid.*, p. 1292, pars. 99–101.

[85] *Ibid.*, p. 1296, par. 140. The Belgian representative based his view also on the Charter itself: ''I pointed out on 1 February that each party to the Armistice Agreement must, in accordance with one of its fundamental provisions, refrain completely from any aggressive action against the people or the armed forces of the other. This is, moreover, an overriding principle of the Charter, except, of course, in the case of self-defence against armed aggression.''

[86] 660th Meeting, Feb. 26, 1957. *Ibid.*, p. 1203, par. 48.

[87] 667th Meeting, March 4, 1957. *Ibid.*, p. 1303, par. 225.

this context reference should be made also to the statement by the Secretary General in his Report of January 24, 1957,[88] and the resolution of the Security Council of September 1, 1951, which includes the following:

> Considering that since the armistice regime, which has been in existence for nearly two and a half years, is of a permanent character, neither party can reasonably assert that it is actively a belligerent or requires to exercise the right of visit, search and seizure for any legitimate purpose of self-defence.[89]

The contrary view was expounded by India. Its representative contended that the Armistice Agreement between Egypt and Israel of 1949 did not exclude belligerent or hostile action, and that the Secretary General's statement referred to above

> is based on the false conception that the exercise of sovereign rights in a sovereign territory, in territorial waters, is an act of belligerency. Such an exercise of sovereign rights would be no more an act of belligerency than if it were an act on the highways of Cairo. It would be an act of belligerency if it were committed anywhere else. Therefore, in the submission of my Government, the statement is based on that false conception.[90]

With respect to India's Government, it may be said that rarely has a new state committed itself to so ancient a view of sovereignty. An act of belligerency may be committed on the "highways of Cairo" as well as on the highways leading through the territorial waters of a strait. If it is a belligerent act, it does not lose this character by reason of the place where it is committed.

The views expressed by Members on the international character of the waters in the Gulf, the right of innocent passage through the Straits of Tiran unimpeded by any claim to exercise belligerent rights, were not embodied in a draft resolution.[91] They remained, therefore, the views of these Members and did not become the position of the United Nations. They are nonetheless significant. The failure of the General Assembly to take a position on this vital aspect of the Middle East crisis is all the more remarkable if one considers that one of the purposes of the United Nations is "to bring about by peaceful means, and in conformity with the principles of justice and international law, adjustment or settlement of international disputes or situations which might lead to a breach of the peace." [92]

5. The Juridical Status of the Gulf of Aqaba and the Straits of Tiran before the United Nations Conference on the Law of the Sea

The Geneva Conference succeeded in unraveling the tangled question of innocent passage through waters corresponding closely to the Straits of

[88] *Cf.* p. 575 above.

[89] U.N. Doc. S/2298/Rev. 1, Official Records, 558th Meeting, Sept. 1, 1951, p. 2.

[90] 665th Meeting, March 1, 1957. General Assembly, 11th Sess., Official Records, Plenary, p. 1270, par. 55. See also p. 1269, pars. 46, 47.

[91] The representative of Canada appeared to advocate the opposite course at the 660th Meeting on Feb. 26, 1957. *Ibid.*, p. 1203, pars. 41 ff.

[92] Art. 1, par. 1, of the Charter.

Tiran and the Gulf of Aqaba. In addition, it made more precise the meaning of innocent passage, of the duties and rights of the coastal state or states and the duties of foreign ships during their innocent passage. As all these rules bear upon the particular case here under consideration, they will be briefly considered.

a. *Innocent passage*

Article 15, paragraph 3, of the International Law Commission's draft related the innocence of the passage to conduct of the ship.[93] Several amendments were proposed to clarify its meaning. A United States proposal[94] aimed at indicating "that the sole test of the innocence of a passage was whether or not it was prejudicial to the security of the coastal State."[95] It was recognized in the debate that a close link existed between the definition of innocent passage, the rights of the coastal state, and the duties of the foreign ship regulated in Articles 17 and 18 of the Commission's draft. The American proposal was opposed as "inconsistent with existing international law" on the ground that it "would enable a State to claim that the actual passage of a ship was prejudicial to its security," whereas the real test of innocence was "the manner in which passage was carried out."[96] The First Committee appeared to be anxious to eliminate as far as possible any subjective tests which might restrict the traditional scope of innocent passage. It was probably for this reason that an eight-Power amendment submitted by Mexico to insert the words "or the interests" after the word "security" in the American proposal was defeated.[97] On the other hand, amendments submitted by India[98] and Turkey[99] were adopted. The American proposal as amended by India and Turkey became Article 14, paragraph 4, of the Convention on the Territorial Sea after adoption at the Twentieth Plenary Meeting,[100] and reads as follows:

[93] "Passage is innocent so long as a ship does not use the territorial sea for committing any acts prejudicial to the security of the coastal State or contrary to the present rules, or to other rules of international law." Report of the International Law Commission Covering the Work of Its Eighth Session, April 23–July 4, 1956. General Assembly, 11th Sess., Official Records, Supp. No. 9 (A/3159), p. 19 (hereinafter referred to as I.L.C. Report 1956).

[94] "Passage is innocent so long as it is not prejudicial to the security of the coastal State. Such passage shall take place in conformity with the present rules." Doc. A/Conf. 13/C.1/L. 28/Rev. 1. U.N. Conference on the Law of the Sea, Official Records, Vol. III, First Committee, p. 216.   [95] *Op. cit.*, p. 82, par. 22.

[96] Representative of Denmark, *ibid.*, p. 83, par. 27.

[97] Text of the eight-Power proposal in U.N. Conf., Official Records, Vol. III, p. 85, par. 4. For result of the vote see *ibid.*, p. 98, par. 37. The co-sponsors were: Chile, Ecuador, Haiti, Panama, Peru, Uruguay, Venezuela and Mexico. Speaking on this point, the representative of the United Kingdom "considered that any reference to the interests of the coastal State was also unacceptable, since it widened the whole concept to a degree which would make a farce of the right of innocent passage." *Ibid.*, p. 85, par. 7.

[98] The Indian representative proposed to insert after the word "prejudicial to" the words "the peace, good order or." *Ibid.*, p. 85, par. 3. For result of the vote see *ibid.*, p. 98, par. 39.

[99] The Turkish amendment proposed to add in the second sentence of the American proposal the words "and to the other rules of international law." *Ibid.*, p. 98, par. 40.

[100] *Ibid.*, par. 41, and Official Records, Vol. II, Plenary Meetings, p. 65, par. 3.

> Passage is innocent so long as it is not prejudicial to the peace, good order or security of the coastal State. Such passage shall take place in conformity with these articles and with other rules of international law.[101]

After the vote in committee the representative of Israel formulated a reservation on the definition of innocent passage.[102] A drafting change, proposed originally by Burma and later supported by Saudi Arabia, was accepted in the First Committee by the representative of the United States but does not appear in the final text. Burma proposed "a positive fact" for the "negative proof" called for by the American text by substituting the words "passage is innocent unless it is prejudicial . . ." for the words "passage is innocent so long as it is not prejudicial. . . ."[103] This wording would have given somewhat more emphasis to the original intent to make the passage itself rather than the ship the test of innocence. However, even without it, the text as adopted clearly puts the burden on the coastal state to show that the passage itself rather than the passage of a particular ship, its purpose or cargo, was prejudicial to the stated values of the coastal state. Thus the text rules out the concept of innocent passage propounded by India in connection with the question of passage through the Straits of Tiran and the Gulf of Aqaba.[104] It represents a stage in the struggle for a greater measure of objectivity and a corresponding reduction in the degree of subjectivity which generally characterizes the rules regarding innocent passage formulated by the International Law Commission.[105]

[101] U.N. Doc. A/Conf. 13/L.52, p. 6 (April 28, 1958). Official Records, Vol. II, Plenary Meetings, p. 133; also 52 A.J.I.L. 837 (1958).

[102] Official Records, Vol. III, p. 99, par. 43. He considered that in spite of certain improvements introduced by the American amendment, the text of the Commission's draft was more precise than the first sentence of the American amendment. The reservation was not repeated in the Plenary Meeting when the final text of Art. 14 was adopted. The final articles of the Convention do not provide for reservations.

[103] *Ibid.*, p. 83, par. 32, p. 85, par. 15; and Doc. A/Conf. 13/C.1/L.75, *ibid.*, p. 231. The acceptance of the Burmese drafting change by the representative of the United States is contained *ibid.*, p. 84, par. 46. There was no formal vote on the proposal.

[104] *Cf.* p. 578 above. But see Max Sørensen, "Law of the Sea," International Conciliation, No. 520, p. 234 (Nov. 1958). *Cf.* note 179, p. 593, below.

[105] That the Committee was concerned with this problem and was anxious to eliminate subjective judgment, although it was divided on the text best calculated to realize this objective, can be seen from the observation of the representative of the Soviet Union, who "shared the misgivings expressed by several representatives regarding the revised United States proposal, which, by referring to the passage itself as not being prejudicial to the security of the coastal State, makes a subjective interpretation of the rule possible. The text drafted by the International Law Commission was much more objective because it referred to a ship using the territorial sea for committing acts prejudicial to the security of the coastal State." Official Records, Vol. III, p. 84, par. 38. He finally voted in favor of the revised American proposal. *Ibid.*, p. 99, par. 42. In this context reference should also be made to the French amendment which introduced the concept of intent. Doc. A/Conf. 13/C.1/L.6, *ibid.*, p. 212. It was not voted upon. For observation on it by the Danish representative see *ibid.*, p. 86, par. 24; see also 3 Gidel, Le Droit International Public de la Mer 206 f.

b. *Duties of Coastal State*

Draft Article 16, paragraph 1, of the International Law Commission included a negative and a positive duty.[106] The United States proposed to strike out the latter, stated in the second sentence, on the grounds that it went beyond existing principles of international law, that it might be construed as constituting absolute liability on the part of the coastal state, and that, contrary to the view of the Commission,[107] it was not supported by the Judgment of the International Court of Justice in the *Corfu Channel* Case.[108] This proposal was adopted in Committee I,[109] and also by the Conference.[110] The first sentence of Article 16, paragraph 1, in the Commission's draft became Article 15, paragraph 1, in the Convention on the Territorial Sea.

For the purpose of this paper it is unnecessary to determine whether the adoption of the United States amendment adds to or detracts from the traditional principles. Paragraph 1 of Article 15 categorically imposes upon the coastal state the duty not to hamper innocent passage as defined in Article 14, paragraph 4. Beyond this duty the First Committee did not desire to go.[111]

c. *Rights of Protection of the Coastal State*

Article 17, particularly its paragraphs 1, 3 and 4 in the Commission's draft, was of greatest significance for the principle of innocent passage in general and the rights claimed by Israel in the Straits of Tiran and the Gulf of Aqaba in particular. Here, as in connection with the definition of innocent passage, several representatives were concerned to establish an objective standard and to eliminate subjective criteria as far as this is possible in a juridical text and in the present stage of the organization of the society of nations. As far as the first paragraph of Article 17 was concerned, the Committee's task was seen as establishing harmony and consistency with Article 14, paragraph 4, defining innocent passage. To this

---

[106] "The coastal State must not hamper innocent passage through the territorial sea. It is required to use the means at its disposal to ensure respect for innocent passage through the territorial sea, and must not allow the said sea to be used for acts contrary to the rights of other States." 1956 I.L.C. Report 19.

[107] Expressed in its commentary to Art. 16, par. 1. *Ibid.*

[108] U.N. Doc. A/Conf. 13/C.1/L.38, Official Records, Vol. III, p. 220. The United States referred particularly to the Court's *dicta* on p. 22 of the Judgment, [1949] I.C.J. Rep. 4.

[109] Official Records, Vol. III, p. 115, par. 10. The First Committee did not adopt the joint proposal of Bulgaria and the U.S.S.R., which elaborated the second sentence and excluded warships from its scope. Doc. A/Conf. 13/C.1/L.46, *ibid.*, p. 223, and p. 115, par. 9. The United Kingdom proposed to delete the second part of the second sentence beginning with "and." Doc. A/Conf. 13/C.1/L.37, *ibid.*, p. 218. In view of the adoption of the U. S. proposal, the British proposal was not put to the vote. *Ibid.*, p. 115, par. 11.

[110] Official Records, Vol. II, Plenary Meetings, p. 65, par. 3.

[111] And consequently it rejected the Yugoslav proposal, which required the coastal state "to take the steps which are necessary for the safety of navigation." U.N. Doc. A/Conf. 13/C.1/L.16, *ibid.*, p. 213, p. 114, par. 7, and p. 115, par. 12.

end the six-Power proposal to Article 17, paragraph 1,[112] was submitted, reading as follows:

> The coastal State may take the necessary steps in its territorial sea to prevent passage which is not innocent.[113]

This text met with some opposition[114] but was adopted in committee,[115] and in the Plenary Meeting,[116] and incorporated in Article 16, paragraph 1, of the Convention.

Article 17, paragraph 2, of the Commission's Draft presented no difficulty and, as adopted, became Article 16, paragraph 2, of the Convention.[117]

Paragraph 3 of Article 17 as submitted by the Commission[118] met with substantial criticism. Here clearly the Commission proposed a subjective test, namely, the untrammeled opinion of the coastal state as sole condition for suspending the right of innocent passage. Amendments were introduced by several delegations "to make the condition in the first sentence more objective"[119] and to foreclose discrimination between different flags.[120] The Netherlands delegate, in introducing the four-Power amendment to Article 17, paragraph 3, emphasized also that the proposed text was intended to incorporate the tenor of the Commission's commentary to that paragraph[121] and thus to render it more objective.[122] In the opposing view,

[112] "The coastal State may take the necessary steps in its territorial sea to protect itself against any act prejudicial to its security or to such other of its interests as it is authorized to protect under the present rules and other rules of international law." 1956 I.L.C. Report 19.

[113] U.N. Doc. A/Conf. 13/C.1/L.72; Official Records, Vol. III, p. 231. The sponsors were: Greece, Netherlands, Portugal, United Kingdom, United States, and Yugoslavia.

[114] Thus the Soviet and Mexican representatives favored the text formulated by the Commission. Official Records, Vol. III, p. 96, par. 8, and p. 99, pars. 6–9.

[115] *Ibid.*, p. 100, par. 16.

[116] *Ibid.*, Vol. II, Plenary Meetings, p. 65, par. 7.

[117] The text of Art. 16, par. 2, is as follows: "In the case of ships proceeding to internal waters, the coastal State shall also have the right to take the necessary steps to prevent any breach of the conditions to which the admission of those ships to those waters is subject." For the votes see Official Records, Vol. III, p. 100, par. 17, and *ibid.*, Plenary Meetings, p. 65, par. 7.

[118] "The coastal State may suspend temporarily in definite areas of its territorial sea the exercise of the right of passage if it should deem such suspension essential for the protection of the rights referred to in paragraph 1. Should it take such action, it is bound to give due publicity to the suspension."

[119] Official Records, Vol. III, p. 79, par. 7, observations by the British delegate.

[120] *Ibid.*, par. 6, observation by the Greek delegate.

[121] The delegate probably had this comment in mind: "In exceptional cases a temporary suspension of the right of passage is permissible if compelling reasons connected with general security require it." I.L.C. Report, 1956, p. 20. The words "if compelling reasons . . . require it," imply a measure of accountability which is totally absent in the Commission's draft. See also the Netherlands delegate's observations in Official Records, Vol. III, p. 94, par. 17.

[122] *Ibid.*, p. 88, par. 15. The text of the proposal sponsored by the four Powers (Netherlands, Portugal, U.K., U.S.A.) is as follows: "Subject to the provisions of paragraph 4, the coastal State may suspend temporarily in specified areas of its territorial sea the innocent passage of foreign ships if such suspension is essential for the

the Commission's text merely indicated who was to take the decision, and that

> Given the absence of an independent organ which could arbitrate in the matter of the application of an objective rule, the only practical possibility was to maintain a subjective criterion as contained in the International Law Commission's draft. The coastal State should certainly substantiate any action it might take, but it undoubtedly had the right to initiate action at its own discretion.[123]

This view was shared by the delegates of the Soviet Union [124] and India. The latter delegate, arguing the unavoidability of subjective discretion, stated:

> That did not, however, mean that the coastal State could act with impunity, for suspension of the right of passage would be *bona fide* only if ordered for the reasons given in paragraph 3, and the burden of proof would rest on the State alleging that such action was not *bona fide*.[125]

The Indian delegate clearly indicated the strength of the coastal state and the weakness of the state claiming innocent passage which was implied in the Commission's draft. The four-Power proposal was intended to restore a balance between the two interests involved. As the delegate of the United States pointed out, this proposal had been made "to ensure that a coastal State had the right to enforce its own regulations, but the doctrine of innocent passage must never be allowed to depend on the caprice of such a State." [126] The delegate of the United Kingdom "considered that it would be wrong to leave a coastal State to judge when and in what circumstances it should deem the suspension of innocent passage essential." [127] The four-Power proposal, as amended by Greece,[128] was adopted in the First Committee by a narrow margin,[129] and in the Plenary Meeting the whole Article 17 was adopted by a very large majority,[130] and became paragraph 3 of Article 16 of the Convention.

Paragraph 4 of the Commission's Article 17 was subjected to careful scrutiny and substantial changes.[131] It will be recalled that this provision was the subject of some debate in the Commission in connection with Israel's comment thereon and in the General Assembly in connection with Israel's

---

protection of its security. Such suspension shall take effect only after having been duly published." U.N. Doc. A/Conf. 13/C.1/L.70; Official Records, Vol. III, p. 230.

[123] Observation by the Indonesian delegate, *ibid.*, p. 94, pars. 18 and 19.

[124] *Ibid.*, p. 94, par. 29.   [125] *Ibid.*, p. 96, par. 3.

[126] *Ibid.*, p. 95, par. 33.   [127] *Ibid.*, p. 95, par. 38.

[128] The Greek proposal was to insert after the word "may" and before the word "suspend" the words "without discrimination among foreign ships." U.N. Doc. A/Conf. 13/C.1/L.31; Official Records, Vol. III, p. 93, par. 4, and p. 100, par. 18.

[129] The vote was 31 for, 27 against, with 5 abstentions. *Ibid.*, p. 100, par. 20.

[130] *Ibid.*, Vol. II, Plenary Meetings, p. 65, par. 7. The vote was 62 for, 1 against, with 9 abstentions.

[131] Its text is as follows: "There must be no suspension of the innocent passage of foreign ships through straits normally used for international navigation between two parts of the high seas."

claim that the passage through the Straits of Tiran and the Gulf of Aqaba was not subject to suspension by the coastal state or states concerned.[132] The decision of the Conference to adopt the four-Power amendment to paragraph 3 beginning with the words "subject to the provisions of paragraph 4 . . ." had already settled a point, namely, that the right of suspension was further limited by the rule to be laid down in paragraph 4. This would have been so in any event, but the inclusion of these words made the point even clearer. With reference to paragraph 4 the debate centered on two main aspects of the Commission's draft: its inclusion of the word "normally" and its omission of a rule governing access to a port through straits forming part of the territorial sea of one or more states.

The United States proposed to eliminate the word "normally" on the ground that the Judgment of the International Court of Justice in the *Corfu Channel* Case, the acknowledged basis of paragraph 4 of Article 17, did not use this qualifying term.[133] The retention of "normally" was urged by the delegate of Saudi Arabia on the ground that "the right of innocent passage could be exercised only in recognized international seaways."[134] The delegate of Portugal, while supporting its omission, would bow to the majority.[135] The delegate of the Soviet Union deemed the word "very important" and favored its retention.[136] Defending the American proposal, Mr. Dean recalled that "the Commission had not taken a vote on the insertion of the word 'normally,' which had been proposed by the USSR member at the Commission's seventh session and accepted without discussion. He therefore considered that the Committee was free to delete or retain the word in question."[137] The British delegate, supporting the deletion, pointed out that "it was vague, and might well become a future source of argument, friction and dispute between nations as to what was or was not the 'normal' use of a particular strait."[138] The decision of the Committee and the Conference was to drop the qualifying word "normally," as it was omitted from the three-Power proposal to paragraph 4 which was adopted by the Committee and the Conference. The suppression of "normally" was certainly justified in terms of the *Corfu Channel* Judgment. Whether it is likely to make much difference in practice only the future will show. For it can be contended with a degree of persuasiveness that some such qualifying concept is inherent in the phrase used by

---

[132] See p. 572 above.

[133] U.N. Doc. A/Conf. 13/C.1/L.39; Official Records, Vol. III, p. 220. It was also dropped in the Netherlands proposal, Doc. A/Conf. 13/C.1/L.51, *ibid.*, p. 224. See comment by the Netherlands representative, *ibid.*, p. 79, par. 15, and the three-Power (Netherlands, Portugal, United Kingdom) proposal, Doc. A/Conf. 13/C.1/L.71, *ibid.*, p. 231.

[134] *Ibid.*, p. 94, par. 23; see also his remarks, p. 93, par. 9.

[135] *Ibid.*, p. 94, par. 27.   [136] *Ibid.*, p. 94, par. 30.

[137] *Ibid.*, p. 95, par. 31.

[138] *Ibid.*, p. 95, par. 36. This argument was rejected by the delegate of Saudi Arabia, who recalled that the term "normally" had been used in several international instruments, and had been specifically included in the Convention and Statute on the International Régime of Maritime Ports, adopted at Geneva in 1923, to remove any doubts and ambiguity. *Ibid.*, p. 96, par. 5.

the Court, the Commission and the Conference: "straits which are *used* for international navigation. . . ." In other words, the prohibition of suspension applies only to straits which are "used . . ." When or which straits are used? Does the answer depend upon the density of the traffic,[139] the habitual choice of a strait by a particular flag, the location of a recognized route or some such criterion or a combination of several criteria? It may also be noted that the word "international" qualifies navigation and is itself not free of ambiguity.[140]

The question of securing access to a port appears to have been raised first by the Netherlands delegate saying:

> His delegation was convinced that the only just solution of the regime of gulfs, bays and estuaries bordered by two or more States was to proclaim the principle of the free access of foreign ships to every port situated on their coasts, whether the water area in question included a central part which must be regarded as the high seas, or as being placed under the undivided co-sovereignty of the coastal States, or whether it was divided up into distinct territorial maritime zones.[141]

Amendments introduced by the British and Netherlands delegations to Article 17, paragraph 4, were intended to make this objective clear.[142] The British delegate, commenting upon the amendments, declared:

> Their object was to ensure that passage was not impeded in waters which were essential to maritime communications. The main purpose of any maritime voyage was, after all, to arrive at the port of destination.[143]

The Netherlands amendment had a similar purpose, namely,

> to stress that ships should always be authorized to traverse the territorial sea for the purpose of entering a port.[144]

[139] See Arthur H. Dean, "The Geneva Conference on the Law of the Sea: What Was Accomplished," 52 A.J.I.L. 607–629, at 623 (1958).

[140] The Saudi Arabian delegate's point is borne out by the fact that the Geneva Conference used the word "normally" in spite of its vagueness. Thus in the Convention on the Territorial Sea, Art. 3 speaks of "normal" baselines and Art. 9 of roadsteads which are "normally" used. The Convention on the Continental Shelf states in Art. 5, par. 8, that the coastal state shall not "normally" withhold its consent.

[141] 6th Meeting, March 6, 1958, Official Records, Vol. III, p. 11, par. 13. At the preceding meeting, March 5, 1958, the British delegate observed in connection with the right of innocent passage through international straits: "In his delegation's view, no established and customary right of passage or access could be done away with by the unilateral action of any of the neighboring coastal States." *Ibid.*, p. 9, par. 33.

[142] The British proposed to add the words "or waters constituting the sole means of access to a port." U.N. Doc. A/Conf. 13/C.1/L.37, March 25, 1958; Official Records, Vol. III, p. 218. The Netherlands proposed a new text for Art. 17, par. 3 of which read: "There shall be no suspension of the innocent passage of foreign ships through sealanes which are used for international navigation between a part of the high seas and another part of the high seas or the territorial waters of a foreign State." U.N. Doc. A/Conf. 13/C.1/L.51, March 25, 1958; Official Records, Vol. III, p. 224. It may be noted that Portugal suggested that Art. 17, par. 4, be modified to read: "through straits and sea lanes. . . ." U.N. Doc. A/Conf. 13/C.1/L.47, March 25, 1958; Official Records, Vol. III, p. 223.

[143] Official Records, Vol. III, p. 79, par. 12.

[144] *Ibid.*, p. 79, par. 15.

At the suggestion of the Chairman of the First Committee, proposals by different delegations relating to "the same questions of principle" [145] were consolidated into a single text. The resulting three-Power proposal included the words "straits or other sealanes" from the Portuguese, and the words "or the territorial waters of a foreign State" from the Netherlands, amendments.[146] The United States decided to support this text.[147] In presenting it to the Committee the Netherlands delegate declared that

> it was insufficient to declare the high seas open to traffic without also guaranteeing the right of entry into seaports. If the right of access to ports was to be assured to landlocked States, *a fortiori*, should it be guaranteed to the maritime countries.[148]

The use of the term "sealanes" was supported by some delegations [149] and opposed by others.[150] Its use was defended by the Netherlands delegate on the ground that, although it had no special juridical significance,

> it was a term that would be easily understood by all concerned with international navigation. The term "straits" was much too narrow, because there were sea-lanes used for international navigation elsewhere than in straits.[151]

However, the reference to sea lanes was deleted and, following a proposal by the Indonesian delegate, the words "territorial waters" were replaced by "territorial sea." [152]

The fundamental part of the three-Power proposal, with which the United States had associated itself, was strongly criticized by the delegate of Saudi Arabia. He opposed it on two grounds: first, on the ground that whereas international law provided for the right of innocent passage through straits linking two parts of the high seas, "it did not provide for such a right in the case of straits linking the open sea with an internal sea or with the territorial sea of a particular State." [153] He appeared to base this position on the Judgment of the International Court of Justice in the *Corfu Channel* Case,[154] which he accepted. According to that decision he urged

> the right of innocent passage could be exercised in straits linking two areas of the high seas, but not in those linking a part of the high seas with the territorial waters of a State.[155]

---

[145] *Ibid.*, p. 80, par. 21.

[146] U.N. Doc. A/Conf. 13/C.1/L.71, March 28, 1958; Official Records, Vol. III, p. 231. This text was sponsored by The Netherlands, the United Kingdom and Portugal. The words in the British proposal were dropped. *Ibid.*, p. 93, par. 11.

[147] *Ibid.*, par. 5.   [148] *Ibid.*, p. 88, par. 16.

[149] See the Danish delegate's observation that he would support the text "on the understanding that it referred to straits only in so far as they constituted sealanes." *Ibid.*, p. 93, par. 7.

[150] Thus the delegate of Saudi Arabia declared that "so far as he knew, the word did not constitute a legal term, and was not defined by any writer on international law." *Ibid.*, p. 93, par. 9, and p. 94, par. 22. See also the remark by the Soviet delegate, *ibid.*, p. 94, par. 30.   [151] *Ibid.*, p. 94, par. 16.

[152] *Ibid.*, p. 93, par. 14, and p. 96, par. 7. It may be noted that the term "sea lanes" appears in Art. 5, par. 6, of the Convention on the Continental Shelf adopted by the Conference. U.N. Doc. A/Conf. 13/L.55.   [153] *Ibid.*, p. 93, par. 9.

[154] [1949] I.C.J. Rep. 4.   [155] Official Records, Vol. III, p. 96, par. 4.

It may be noted that this represents an attempt to use a judgment of the Court as authority for both what it decides, which is the usual case, and for what it does not decide, which is a most unusual case. Clearly the Court, in the Corfu Channel dispute, was not concerned with the situation envisioned in the three-Power proposal.

The second ground for the Saudi Arabian objection was that

> in his opinion the amended text no longer dealt with general principles of international law, but had been carefully tailored to promote the claims of one State. His delegation would be unable to support a text that covered only one specific case.[156]

This contention does not appear to be borne out by the published record of the discussion in the Committee. On the contrary, in the view of the three Powers proposing the amendment, as stated by the Netherlands representative,

> the addition of the words "or the territorial waters of a foreign State" reflected existing usage safeguarding the right to use straits linking the high seas with the territorial sea of a State.[157]

On the other hand, clearly the affirmation of this principle by the Conference gave strong support to one particular controversial case, namely, the right of passage through the Straits of Tiran and the Gulf of Aqaba to the Israeli port of Elath. The Committee adopted the three-Power proposal, with the amendments already indicated, by a roll-call vote of 31 votes to 30, with 10 abstentions.[158] In the Plenary Meeting, the delegate of the United Arab Republic asked for a separate vote on paragraph 4 of Article 17. This was opposed by the delegate of Denmark on the ground that

> the principle of freedom of navigation was indivisible, and when vessels crossed a portion of the high seas on their way to a port, it was irrelevant whether or not they had to pass through the territorial sea of another State. The effect of a separate vote would be to discriminate between ships passing through the territorial sea of a State other than their flag State on their way from one part of the high seas to another, and ships passing through the same territorial seas on their way from a portion of the high seas to the territorial sea of a third State. The coastal State would be under an equal obligation to respect the right of innocent passage in both cases.[159]

[156] *Ibid.*, p. 96, par. 6. He also declared that "his government's participation in the final act of the Conference would be conditional, among other things, on the rejection of the amendments to Article 17 at present before the Committee." *Ibid.*, p. 94, p. 25.

[157] *Ibid.*, p. 94, par. 16.   [158] *Ibid.*, p. 100, par. 21.

[159] Official Records, Vol. II, Plenary Meetings, p. 65, par. 5. He went on to justify this position by reference to Denmark's practice: "Part of the Danish coast bordered an international strait joining two parts of the high seas, and for more than one hundred years his country had maintained freedom of navigation through that strait in the interests of international trade. Such an obligation as that which his country had assumed should be counterbalanced by corresponding rights in other parts of the world, and Denmark accordingly expected that there would be free passage for its ships through straits in the territorial seas of other States." *Ibid.*, par. 6.

The motion for a separate vote on the paragraph was defeated by 34 votes to 32, with 6 abstentions, and the whole Article 17 was then adopted by 62 votes to 1, with 9 abstentions. [160]

As adopted by the Conference, Article 17, paragraph 4, became Article 16, paragraph 4, and reads:

> There shall be no suspension of the innocent passage of foreign ships through straits which are used for international navigation between one part of the high seas and another part of the high seas or the territorial sea of a foreign State.[161]

Whatever may have been the motives which prompted the three-Power proposal,[162] it is clear that, rather than deal with the broad problem of bays or gulfs the coasts of which were under the sovereignty of several states, the Conference concentrated on the specific problem of the nature and extent of the right of innocent passage. In doing so it filled a gap left by the International Law Commission, and the solution which it adopted did not follow the direction indicated by the Commission in its comment to Article 17, paragraph 4, relating to the particular question raised by Israel.   The Conference showed concern for ensuring the right of innocent passage in all conceivable situations and, while mindful of the interest of the coastal states, for protecting its character as an independent right not subordinate to any claim of sovereignty on the part of coastal states.[163]   In proceeding along this line and also in insisting on objective criteria for both the right of innocent passage and the right of protection of the coastal states, the Conference corrected in some measure the overly exclusive concern of the Commission with the latter.

d. *Duties of Ships during Innocent Passage*

Article 18, the last clause in the International Law Commission's draft devoted to an aspect of innocent passage, reads as follows:

> Foreign ships exercising the right of passage shall comply with the laws and regulations enacted by the coastal State in conformity with the present rules and other rules of international law and, in particular, with the laws and regulations relating to transport and navigation.[164]

Here, as in the case of other provisions bearing on the right of innocent passage, the aim was to ensure the application of objective standards.   The Commission's draft contained that standard in providing, in substance, that

[160] *Ibid.*, p. 65, par. 7. In explaining his abstention, the delegate of Saudi Arabia reiterated his argument that par. 4 "had been drafted with one particular case in view," and concluded: "Saudi Arabia would take the necessary steps to protect its national interests against the interpretation and application of paragraph 4." *Ibid.*, par. 8.

[161] U.N. Doc. A/Conf. 13/L.52; Official Records, Vol. II, Plenary Meetings, p. 134.

[162] It may be noted that the question of the Gulf of Aqaba was injected into the deliberations of the First Committee at their very outset by the delegate of Saudi Arabia, who claimed that this gulf "came under exclusive Arab jurisdiction." *Ibid.*, Vol. III, 3rd Meeting, March 4, 1958, p. 3, par. 30.

[163] *Cf.* the observations of the delegates of The Netherlands, the United States and the United Kingdom, *ibid.*, p. 9, par. 33; p. 94, par. 15; p. 95, pars. 33 and 37.

[164] 1956 I.L.C. Report 20.

the national laws and regulations shall be "in conformity with the present rules and other rules of international law." In the battle of amendments in the First Committee the lines were drawn between those who supported the international standard and the supporters of the national standard, that is, between those who favored the supremacy of international law and those advocating the primacy of municipal law. In short, the old contest respecting the treatment of foreigners was re-enacted with reference to innocent passage. The protagonist of national treatment was Mexico. It submitted a proposal in which the international standard was transposed from the laws enacted by the coastal state to the duty of foreign ships to observe them.[165] Explaining this proposal, the delegate of Mexico pointed out that

> there was no doubt in his delegation's view that the words "in conformity with the present rules and other rules of international law" should apply to the exercise of the right of passage by foreign ships, and not to the enactment of laws and regulations by the coastal State.[166]

He also argued that

> the obligation on coastal States to comply with rules of international law in enacting domestic laws and regulations was clearly expressed in Article 1, paragraph 2, and in Article 17, paragraph 1, of the Commission's draft.[167]

The principal argument against the Mexican proposal was the six-Power proposal, which consolidated various individual amendments and which differed only slightly from the Commission's text.[168] Commenting upon these two texts, the British delegate said that their essence

> was that foreign ships must comply with laws and regulations enacted by the coastal State, subject to the one proviso that such legislation was in conformity with the present and other rules of international law. If that proviso were omitted, there would be no limitation whatsoever on the laws which the coastal State could enact. The Mexican amendment, far from making the enactment of laws and regulations by the coastal State subject to their conformity with the rules of international law, contained a quite different proposal: that the qualification should apply exclusively to ships exercising their right of passage.[169]

---

[165] The Mexican proposal for a new text of Art. 18 was worded as follows: "Foreign ships exercising the right of passage shall comply, in conformity with the present rules and other rules of international law, with the laws and regulations enacted by the coastal State, and, in particular, with those relating to transport and navigation." U.N. Doc. A/Conf. 13/C.1/L.45; Official Records, Vol. III, p. 222.

[166] *Ibid.*, p. 96, par. 15.   [167] *Ibid.*, p. 97, par. 16.

[168] U.N. Doc. A/Conf. 13/C.1/L.72; Official Records, Vol. III, p. 231. It ran as follows: "1. Foreign ships exercising the right of passage shall comply with the laws and regulations made and published by the coastal State in conformity with the present rules and other rules of international law. 2. The coastal State has the right to take in its territorial sea the necessary steps in order to prevent infringements of the laws and regulations mentioned in paragraph 1, and to ensure the enforcement of such laws and regulations." See also *ibid.*, p. 96, par. 13. The sponsoring Powers were: Greece, Netherlands, Portugal, United Kingdom, United States, and Yugoslavia.

[169] *Ibid.*, p. 97, par. 18.

In proceeding to vote on the different proposals the Committee maneuvered itself into a procedural *cul-de-sac*, the result of which was that there remained no text for Article 18 before the Committee.   The Committee first adopted the Mexican amendment by 33 votes to 30, with 10 abstentions.[170] Thereupon five delegations withdrew their support from the six-Power proposal,[171] which the Chairman declared to have been rejected, in any event, as the result of the adoption of the Mexican amendment.[172]   The Committee then adopted one part of a joint amendment submitted by Greece and The Netherlands and rejected another.[173]   After a procedural discussion in which the incompatibility of the two adopted proposals was stressed, the Committee rejected both by 34 votes to 28, with 10 abstentions.[174]   A graceful retreat by the Chairman enabled the Committee to adopt, by 59 votes to none, with 3 abstentions, the original text of the International Law Commission.[175]   This text, with a consequential change ("in conformity with these articles" in place of "the present rules") and the insertion of the word "innocent" in the phrase "right of passage" suggested by the Drafting Committee,[176] was adopted by the Conference by 72 votes to none, with 2 abstentions, and became Article 17 of the Convention.[177]   This completed the Conference's work on innocent passage.   There can be little doubt that, in preferring the Commission's text rather than the Mexican proposal, the Conference scored a point in favor of the international standard as against the national-treatment principle.   Whether the text of Article 17 will obviate disputes relating to the applicable national enactments and their conformity with the Convention and customary international law remains to be seen.   In particular it remains to be seen whether the right to enforce these enactments, implicitly recognized in Article 17, includes the right to prevent a ship from passing through the territorial sea.[178]   It would seem that the Conference's solution leaves room for supplementary regulation by bilateral or multilateral instruments.

6. *Conclusions*

There is obviously room for differing evaluations of the work of the Conference discussed above and in particular of its contribution to the solution

---

[170] *Ibid.*, p. 101, par. 27.

[171] *Ibid.*, p. 101, par. 28.   Yugoslavia apparently remained the sole supporter.

[172] *Ibid.*, p. 101, par. 31.

[173] U.N. Doc. A/Conf. 13/C.1/L.32; Official Records, Vol. III, p. 217.   The Committee adopted the words: "The coastal State may not, however, apply these rules or regulations in such a manner as to discriminate between foreign vessels of different nationalities," and rejected the words "nor, save in matters relating to fishing and shooting, between national vessels and foreign vessels."   *Ibid.*, p. 101, pars. 34, 35.

[174] *Ibid.*, p. 102, par. 16.   [175] *Ibid.*, p. 109, par. 57.

[176] *Ibid.*, p. 256.

[177] Official Records, Vol. II, Plenary Meetings, pp. 65 and 134.

[178] *Cf.* Max Sørensen, "Law of the Sea," International Conciliation, No. 520, p. 234 (Nov. 1958).   He apparently assumes that "the coastal State is authorized to *enforce* its laws and regulations on foreign ships passing through its territorial sea, but is not allowed to prevent a ship from passing through merely on the ground of a violation of such laws or regulations."

of the question of passage through the Straits of Tiran and the Gulf of Aqaba. The intent of the Conference to reduce the element of subjectivism and to provide a better balance between the interests involved—security on the one side and freedom of navigation on the other—will probably meet with general approval. The large majorities in favor of the several articles are indicative of it. Whether the Conference actually succeeded in translating this intent into the articles dealing with vital aspects of innocent passage is debatable.[179]

Concerning the specific problem of passage through the Straits of Tiran and the Gulf of Aqaba, the contribution of the Conference is significant. The Conference, in Article 16, paragraph 4, decidedly gave its support to the point of view of all those governments which have taken their stand on the right of transit through the Straits and the Gulf. The reproach of the Arab states that the Conference was concerned with this specific problem, though approaching it through a general formula, seems to be well founded.[180] However, it is still a question whether the Conference adopted a rule the validity of which depends upon ratification of the Convention, or whether it merely confirmed an existing principle the validity of which is independent of acceptance of the Convention. The Conference received from the United Nations General Assembly the broad mandate to examine the law of the sea, "taking account not only of the legal, but also of the technical, biological, economic and political aspects of the problem." [181] The Conference does not seem to have come to any conclusion as to whether its work was primarily codificatory or in the nature of progressive development, although it debated this matter in connection with the number of ratifications to govern the entry into force of the conventions, and the inclusion of denunciatory clauses or reservations.[182] The Convention on the Territorial Sea does not state, as does the Convention on the High Seas, that it codifies the pertinent rules of international law and that its provisions are "generally declaratory of established principles of international law." [183] On the other hand, it contains no provision regarding reservations, as do the Conventions on Fishing and the Continental Shelf.[184]

With respect to the last part of Article 16, paragraph 4, however, it has been said that the Conference "adopted a new rule which clearly applied to the Israeli-Arab controversy," and that "the result reached was in accord with the general position of the United States" as laid down in the Aide-Mémoire of February 11, 1957.[185] This might be taken to mean that,

[179] Thus Sørensen argues that Art. 14, par. 4, far from restricting, "now extends the rights of the coastal State and allows it to interfere with passage on such grounds as the nature of the cargo and its ultimate destination—provided, of course, that such factors are genuinely of a character to prejudice the security of the coastal State in the specific case." Ibid. This view, if correct, would go a long way towards nullifying the right of innocent passage. [180] See Sørensen, loc. cit., p. 236.

[181] Res. 1105 (XI), Feb. 21, 1957; Official Records, Vol. II, Plenary Meetings, p. xi.

[182] Ibid., Plenary Meetings, pp. 26, 27, 52, 56, 57, 58, 59, 60.

[183] Ibid., p. 135.

[184] Cf. Art. 19 of the former and Art. 12 of the latter. Ibid., pp. 141, 143.

[185] Arthur H. Dean, "The Geneva Conference on the Law of the Sea: What Was Accomplished," 52 A.J.I.L. 607–629, at 623 (1958). For the Aide-Mémoire, see p. 576 above.

unless ratified, that rule would not be binding. On the other hand, the debates at the Conference would seem to give substance to the view that the rule was part of international law. Their evidentiary value is significant.[186] The latter view would certainly correspond quite closely to the position taken by the Members of the United Nations in the General Assembly in favor of the right of passage through the Straits and the Gulf as a right based upon existing international law.

There is a difference between their position, however, and the rule of Article 16, paragraph 4. Whereas the Members urged freedom of passage on the basis that the Gulf "comprehends international waters and that no nation has the right to prevent free and innocent passage in the Gulf and through the Straits giving access thereto,"[187] thus resting their claim essentially on the *Corfu Channel* Judgment, the Geneva Conference, while retaining this, added the further principle that there shall be "no suspension of the innocent passage of foreign ships through straits which are used for international navigation between one part of the high seas and . . . the territorial sea of a foreign State." This is a simpler way to the same port. It has the advantage which, particularly in the case of the Gulf of Aqaba, should not be overlooked, of rendering unnecessary proof of the affirmation or fact that the Gulf "comprehends international waters," about which there was some uncertainty in the International Law Commission.[188]

Should exception be taken to the validity of the principle formulated by the Geneva Conference, then the right of passage would rest, as it did before, solidly on the fact that the Straits of Tiran connect with a gulf or bay the coasts of which are under the sovereignty of several states. Such gulfs or bays have traditionally had the character of open seas, and under international law, if not under the holding in the *Corfu Channel* Case, there is a right of innocent passage through such straits to such bays or gulfs.[189]

---

[186] Philip C. Jessup, "The Geneva Conference on the Law of the Sea: A Study in International Law-Making," 52 A.J.I.L. 730–733, at 732 (1958): "The debates in the Conference would naturally contribute further evidence of what states consider to be 'a general practice accepted as law'."

[187] *Cf.* U. S. Aide-Mémoire, p. 576 above.   [188] *Cf.* p. 572 above.

[189] Gidel, note 49 above, at p. 601, affirms the right of innocent passage to the different littoral states situated on a bay. Concerning passage through straits connecting with such a bay, he says: "À partir du moment où plusieurs riverains se partagent les côtes de cette mer, celui qui détient l'entrée a, en vertu du droit international, et à moins de limitation de régimes conventionnels spéciaux, l'obligation de laisser les Etats tiers passer par cette entrée. Il paraît devoir en être de même dans le cas d'une baie. . . . On ne doit pas facilement présumer pour des espaces maritimes la condition d'eaux 'intérieures,' puisque le passage inoffensif peut n'y être pas accordé par l'Etat riverain." *Ibid.* at 603. See also the statement by the delegate of The Netherlands, p. 587 above.

Gulf of Aqaba and Strait of Tiran: Troubled Waters

CARL F. SALANS

On 23 May 1967, President Gamel Abdel Nasser of the United Arab Republic announced to the world that the Strait of Tiran and the Gulf of Aqaba would be closed to Israeli flag vessels and to vessels of other countries carrying strategic cargoes, including oil, to Israel. It was largely out of that decision that the Arab-Israeli war of June 1967 developed.

The Gulf of Aqaba is 98 miles long and varies in width from 7 to 15 miles. The United Arab Republic, Israel, Jordan, and Saudi Arabia all border on the Gulf.

The Strait of Tiran connects the Gulf of Aqaba with the Red Sea. At its narrowest point, the Strait of Tiran is about four miles wide. It has only two navigable channels, Enterprise Passage and Grafton Passage, both of which are within three miles of the U.A.R. coast and therefore within Egyptian waters. The two islands of Tiran and Sanafir, which lie athwart the Strait, have been claimed by both Egypt and Saudi Arabia, and have been occupied from time to time by Egyptian forces.

The Strait of Tiran forms the necessary passageway for access to the Israeli port of Elath at the head of the Gulf. It also provides access to Jordan's only outlet to the sea, the port of Aqaba some five miles from Elath.

The United States has for many years taken the position that the Gulf of Aqaba "comprehends"—i.e., includes or embraces—international waters and that there is a right of free and innocent passage through the Strait of Tiran and in the Gulf of Aqaba. In an aide memoire to the Israeli Embassy dated 11 February 1957, the Department of State set forth this position:

> With respect to (a) the Gulf of Aqaba and access thereto—the United States believes that the Gulf comprehends international waters and that no nation has the right to prevent free and innocent passage in the Gulf and through the Straits giving access thereto. . . .

President Dwight D. Eisenhower repeated this view in an address to the nation on 27 February 1957:

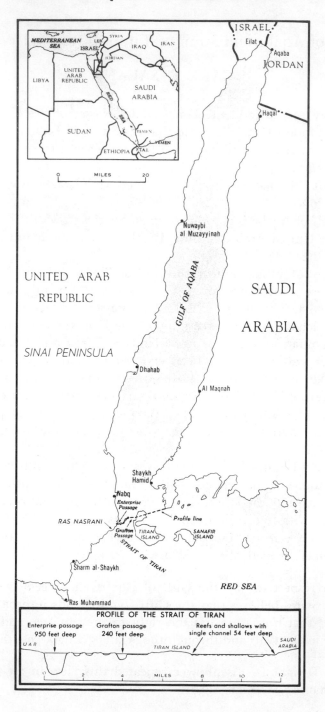

With reference to the passage into and through the Gulf of Aqaba, we expressed the conviction that the gulf constitutes international waters and that no nation has the right to prevent free and innocent passage in the gulf. . . .

We should not assume that . . . Egypt will prevent Israeli shipping from using the . . . Gulf of Aqaba. If, unhappily, Egypt does hereafter violate the Armistice Agreement or other international obligations, then this should be dealt with firmly by the society of nations.

In part, the United States bases its contention that the Gulf of Aqaba comprehends international waters on the fact that the United States recognizes only a three-mile territorial sea. Thus, because the Gulf varies in width from 7 to 15 miles, a stretch of water in the Gulf has the character of high seas.

But, more basically, the international character of the Gulf derives from the fact that four countries share its coastline. No one of these nations, or even a majority of them, can decide that the Gulf belongs to it, or to them, alone.

The Arab States, nevertheless, have argued that the Gulf consists of "Arab territorial waters" and that passage through it and through the Strait of Tiran cannot be undertaken without the consent of the Arab States. This position was asserted, for example, in a written representation made by the Arab Missions in Washington to Secretary of State John Foster Dulles on 24 May 1957:

It is evident that due to the fact that the Gulf of Aqaba is a narrow, closed Gulf covered by Arab territorial waters, and that entrance to it is also territorial water, the Gulf is by no means, physically or legally, an open sea, whereby ships of any flag can sail as on open seas, nor is the entrance to it a matter of passage, to be undertaken without the consent of the Arab States concerned.

As for the Strait of Tiran, U.A.R. President Nasser stated his government's position at a press conference held in Cairo on 28 May 1967:

The Tiran Straits are Egyptian territorial waters over which Egypt has exercised her sovereignty rights. No power whatever its might can infringe upon Egyptian sovereignty rights and any such attempt shall be regarded as aggression against the Egyptian people and the Arab nation at large. . . .

The claim of the Arab States that the Gulf of Aqaba is "Arab territorial waters" cannot be substantiated. It has not been so treated historically, nor can it logically be so viewed today. During the Ottoman
Empire and up to 1914, the Gulf was surrounded by Ottoman—not
Arab—territory. Egypt, at that time, was under Ottoman suzerainty.
Following the dissolution of the Ottoman Empire after 1914, the area
now comprising Israel and Jordan became part of the British mandate
under the League of Nations. While there was probably little international shipping in the Gulf of Aqaba during these periods, there is no
indication that the waters were regarded as closed seas. At the same
time, it is true that the Gulf of Aqaba has historically been a route of
pilgrimage to Moslem Holy Places. Apparently some pilgrims used to
travel by land to the head of the Gulf and then by ship through the
Gulf and the Red Sea to Jidda. Thus, the "Arab Sea" argument has
emotional appeal, even though the Gulf has lost much of its significance as a pilgrimage route. As pointed out earlier, the very fact that
today four countries border on the Gulf, one of which, Israel, would
not admit of its closed character, belies the Arab contention that its
waters are closed.

In fact, Eygpt herself has explicitly recognized the right of free navigation through the Strait of Tiran and the Gulf. In an aide memoire of
28 January 1950, the Egyptian Ministry of Foreign Affairs explained
to the U. S. Embassy at Cairo that Egypt's occupation of the two islands of Tiran and Sanafir at the entrance of the Gulf of Aqaba was
only to protect the islands against damage and that

> . . . this occupation being in no way conceived in a spirit of obstruct-
> ing in any way innocent passage through the stretch of water sep-
> arating these two islands from the Egyptian coast of Sinai, it follows
> that this passage, the only practicable one, will remain free as in the
> past, in conformity with the international practice and recognized
> principles of the law of nations.

U.A.R. representative to the United Nations, Ambassador El Kony,
in a speech before the U. N. Security Council on 29 May 1967, argued
that the 1950 Egyptian aide memoire was not intended to guarantee
free and innocent passage "to an enemy during a state of war." In fact,
early in 1951, Egypt promulgated regulations requiring vessels transit-
ing the Strait of Tiran to notify Egyptian authorities and to submit to
inspection. Egypt stated it did not intend to prohibit innocent passage

of warships or commercial vessels of friendly countries through the Strait of Tiran. But this was without prejudice to Egypt's "legitimate right of control as a riparian power nor to the exercise of its exceptional rights of visit and seizure of contraband. . . ." Egypt declared that "enemy" warships were forbidden access to and passage through Egyptian territorial waters, including the Strait, while "enemy" commercial vessels could have access only at the risk of seizure and detention.

While the U. S. government did not recognize the validity of the Egyptian position or the Egyptian instructions for notification of passage through the Strait of Tiran, these instructions were printed in the *Sailing Directions for the Red Sea and the Gulf of Aden* issued by the U. S. Hydrographic Office as instructions to U. S. masters and shipping companies. And presumably ships complied with these instructions on many occasions.

From the facts available, it appears that Egyptian enforcement of their policies on transit through the Strait during the early 1950s was rather spotty. There were several incidents involving detention of vessels during this period, although they were few in number, principally because of the limited traffic to the Israeli port of Elath. It was not until June 1952 that construction of the port at Elath was completed, and it was only in March 1956 that oceangoing vessels were first able to use it. Nor were there shipments of oil to Elath during this period, the oil pipeline from Elath to refineries in Haifa having been constructed in 1957-58.

In January 1957, U. N. Secretary-General Dag Hammarskjöld, in his report to the General Assembly, took the position that, while there was a right of innocent passage through the Strait, the extent of this right was subject to legal controversy:

As stated in the previous report (A/3500), the international significance of the Gulf of Aqaba may be considered to justify the right of innocent passage through the Straits of Tiran and the Gulf in accordance with recognized rules of international law. However, . . . the International Law Commission reserved consideration of the question "What would be the legal position of straits forming part of the territorial sea of one or more States and constituting the sole means of access to the port of another state." This description applies to the Gulf of Aqaba and the Straits of Tiran. A legal controversy exists as to the extent of the right of innocent passage through these waters.

The following year, the Geneva Conference on the Law of the Sea took up the very issue described by Secretary-General Hammarskjöld in his report to the General Assembly. The Conference adopted a Convention on the Territorial Sea and the Contiguous Zone, Article 16, paragraph 4, of which provides as follows:

> There shall be no suspension of the innocent passage of foreign ships through straits which are used for international navigation between one part of the high seas and another part of the high seas or the territorial sea of a foreign State.

This article ensures a right of innocent passage through an international strait even when the strait lies wholly within the coastal state's territorial waters. This provision clearly applies to the Gulf of Aqaba and the Strait of Tiran, either on the view that the Gulf comprehends international waters and therefore the Strait of Tiran connects two parts of the high seas or on the view that the Strait connects one part of the high seas (i.e., the Red Sea) with the territorial sea of the four riparian Gulf states, including Israel.

The United States, the United Kingdom, the Soviet Union, and 30 other countries are parties to this 1958 Convention. None of the Arab States have become parties, probably because of the Convention's implications for the Gulf of Aqaba and the Strait of Tiran. There is some question whether the last part of Article 16, paragraph 4, of the Convention, establishing the rule of innocent passage between one part of the high seas and the *territorial sea* of a foreign state, is a codification of existing customary international law already binding on states or is creative of a new rule of law not necessarily binding on non-signatories. This is a significant issue bearing on the rights of navigation through these waterways, but in the absence of a ruling by the International Court of Justice, it will probably remain a lawyer's debating point for years to come.

The International Court of Justice did decide a case in 1949 called the *Corfu Channel* case which supports the right of passage through international straits. In that case, brought by the United Kingdom against Albania, two British warships attempting to pass through the strait known as the Corfu Channel, between Albania and Greece, were damaged by mines laid in the channel. The Court said:

It is, in the opinion of the Court, generally recognized and in accordance with international custom that States in time of peace have a right to send their warships through straits used for international navigation between two parts of the high seas without the previous authorization of a coastal State, provided that the passage is innocent. Unless otherwise prescribed in an international convention, there is no right for a coastal State to prohibit such passage through straits in time of peace.

Both the 1958 Geneva Convention and the International Court opinion in the *Corfu Channel* case speak in terms of a right of "innocent passage" through international straits. What passage is "innocent"? Who is to determine whether passage is innocent?

Article 14(4) of the 1958 Geneva Convention on the Territorial Sea and the Contiguous Zone states a definition of innocent passage:

Passage is innocent so long as it is not prejudicial to the peace, good order, or security of the coastal state. . . .

Some light is thrown on the meaning of this definition by the World Court's decision in the *Corfu Channel* case. In that case, the Court decided that the passage of a warship was innocent if her actions did not threaten the security of the coastal state. The warships in question were British naval vessels. Great Britain was at the time an ally of Greece, which had declared itself to be in a technical state of war with Albania, the coastal state. The Court looked at the character of the *passage*, and not the character of the *vessel* as a warship, as the determinative factor in deciding whether the passage was innocent; and it found that the manner of the passage of the British warships through the Corfu Channel was such as to make that passage innocent.

Moreover, the Court made it clear in the *Corfu Channel* case that determination of innocence was not a subjective decision to be made unilaterally by the coastal state. Albania had contended that the passage of the British warships was carried out in a threatening manner and that the ship's orders were to return any fire from the Albanian coast. The Court did not accept this characterization by the Albanian government, but itself considered the behavior of the British warships in the strait and found it not to have threatened the security of Albania.

The negotiating history of the 1958 Geneva Conventions on the Law of the Sea does not indicate an intention to modify the rules regarding innocent passage established by the International Court of Justice in the *Corfu* case. It therefore seems that—to use the terms of Article 14, paragraph 4, of the 1958 Convention—the question of whether passage is prejudicial to the peace, good order, or security of the coastal state is to be determined objectively from the conduct of a particular vessel in transit and not on the basis of a subjective judgment by the coastal state concerning the character of the vessel or her cargo. Applying this test to the specific question that was raised by the Egyptian closure of the Strait of Tiran to strategic cargoes, including oil, bound for Israel, it follows that the passage through the Strait of Tiran of a merchant vessel carrying oil to Israel would be "innocent" and entitled to free passage.

The United Arab Republic, however, advanced a further argument in support of its right to close the Strait of Tiran to Israeli shipping. It asserted that it was in a state of war with Israel and that innocent passage through the Strait legitimately could be suspended by a belligerent in time of war. In its announcement at Cairo on 23 May 1967, Egypt said:

> There is a state of war between us and Israel. International law gives us the right to ban the passage of Israeli ships through our territorial waters. U. S. and British talk about innocent passage is unacceptable in a state of war.

It is fair to say that the right of innocent passage through international straits guaranteed under the 1958 Convention is a peacetime right. While the Geneva Convention does not say this in so many words, passage of an enemy vessel in time of war could hardly be considered innocent except in the most unusual circumstances.

In dealing with the assertion of belligerent rights, one has to consider, at the outset, the effect of the U. N. Charter on traditional international law concepts of belligerency. Since the coming into force of the Charter, belligerent rights are available only to a state engaged in a use of armed force that is lawful under the Charter. It is lawful, for example, for one state to use force against another state pursuant to a U. N. Security Council decision or a General Assembly decision under the Uniting for Peace Resolution, or in the exercise of the right of self-defense against armed attack, or pursuant to a decision of a regional organization for the maintenance of peace and security in the region.

None of these bases were relied upon by the United Arab Republic in closing the Strait of Tiran to Israeli shipping.

Quite apart from this, however, the United States and many other nations have considered that neither the Arab States nor Israel have been entitled to exercise belligerent rights since 1949 when they entered into General Armistice Agreements. Those four agreements, between Israel and Egypt, Israel and Jordan, Israel and Lebanon, and Israel and Syria ended the state of belligerency between the respective parties. While they were not peace treaties, the armistice agreements were intended to prohibit the parties from resorting to belligerent acts against one another during the period until permanent political settlements could be reached between Israel and the Arab States.

This view is supported by Resolution 95 of the U. N. Security Council adopted 1 September 1951, calling upon Egypt to terminate restrictions on passage of Israeli shipping through the Suez Canal. That resolution contained the following passage:

> Considering that since the Armistice regime, which has been in existence for nearly two and a half years, is of a permanent character, neither party can reasonably assert that it is actively a belligerent or requires to exercise the right of visit, search and seizure for any legitimate purpose of defense.

In his report to the U. N. General Assembly of 24 January 1957, Secretary-General Hammarskjöld confirmed this view:

> It follows from the finding of the Security Council in 1951 that . . . the parties to the Armistice Agreements may be considered as not entitled to claim any belligerent rights . . . it may be held that, in a situation where the Armistice regime is partly operative by observance of the provisions of the Armistice Agreements concerning the armistice lines, possible claims to rights of belligerency would be at least so much in doubt that, having regard for the general international interest at stake, no such claim should be exercised in the Gulf of Aqaba and the Straits of Tiran. . . .

The settlement of the Tiran-Aqaba issue made in 1957 by the United Nations in the wake of the Suez conflict supports the conclusion that the United Arab Republic could not assert a state of belligerency as a basis for closing these waterways to Israeli shipping. That settlement placed a United Nations Emergency Force (UNEF) at Sharm-el-

Sheikh, at the tip of the Sinai Peninsula overlooking the Strait of Tiran, which left the Strait and Gulf open to navigation; and rights of passage through those waters were thereafter exercised until President Nasser's announcement on 23 May 1967.

Thus, as a legal matter, the United States concluded in May-June 1967 that the United Arab Republic could not rely on belligerent rights as a basis for interfering with the Israeli right of innocent passage through the Strait of Tiran and the Gulf of Aqaba. The United States has also felt that as a practical matter it did not make much sense for the Arabs to assert this right, for they could hardly maintain the right to exercise belligerent rights vis-à-vis Israel and at the same time deny Israel's right to resort to belligerent action against the Arab States.

The various legal considerations regarding freedom of passage through the Strait of Tiran and the Gulf of Aqaba that were important in determining the United States attitude toward Egyptian closure of these waterways to Israeli shipping in May 1967 are also relevant to the efforts that are now underway to reach understandings among the parties that will ensure a lasting peace in the Middle East.

Resolution of the Middle Eastern situation will require solutions to a broad range of questions that affect Israel and the Arab States. On 22 November 1967, the United Nations Security Council adopted a resolution containing an agreed set of principles for settlement, including: withdrawal of Israeli armed forces from territories occupied in the conflict; termination of all claims or states of belligerency; respect for and acknowledgement of the sovereignty, territorial integrity and political independence of every state in the area and their right to live in peace within secure and recognized boundaries free from threats or acts of force; the achievement of a just settlement of the refugee problem; and some guaranty of the territorial inviolability and political independence of every state in the area, through measures including the establishment of demilitarized zones. The U. N. Secretary-General, pursuant to that Security Council resolution, has designated a Special Representative, Ambassador Gunnar Jarring of Sweden, "to proceed to the Middle East, to establish and maintain contacts with the States concerned in order to promote agreement and assist efforts to achieve a peaceful and accepted settlement in accordance with the provisions and principles in this resolution." In addition to the principles listed above, the Security Council Resolution singles out "the necessity for guaranteeing freedom of navigation through international waterways in the area." The history of the Arab-Israeli crisis of May-June 1967 and the negotiation of the Security Council resolution can leave no doubt that the resolution refers not only to the Strait of Tiran and the Gulf of Aqaba but to the Suez Canal as well. The resolution, adopted unanimously by the Security Council, indicates a recognition of the necessity to preserve freedom of navigation through these waterways if a recurrence of the June 1967 hostilities is to be avoided and if there is to be peace in the Middle East. It also recognizes, concomitantly, that there must be a renunciation of all claims to exercise belligerent rights if the principles of free navigation are to be protected.

The United States, of course, has been a staunch supporter of the principle of freedom of navigation through the Strait of Tiran and the Gulf of Aqaba as an essential element in a solution to the Middle East situation. On 23 May 1967, following President Nasser's closure of the Strait and Gulf to Israeli shipping, President Lyndon B. Johnson stated:

> . . . the purported closing of the Gulf of Aqaba to Israeli shipping has brought a new and very grave dimension to the crisis. The United States considers the Gulf to be an international waterway and feels that a blockade of Israeli shipping is illegal and potentially disastrous to the cause of peace. The right of free, innocent passage of the international waterways is a vital interest of the entire international community.

After the hostilities, in an address to a Department of State foreign policy conference on 19 June 1967, President Johnson outlined five basic principles for peace in the Middle East. One of these he described in the following words:

> A third lesson from this last month is that maritime rights must be respected. Our nation has long been committed to free maritime passage through international waterways; and we, along with other nations, were taking the necessary steps to implement this principle when hostilities exploded. If a single act of folly was more responsible for this explosion than any other, I think it was the arbitrary and dangerous announced decision that the Strait of Tiran would be closed. The right of innocent maritime passage must be preserved for all nations.

Although the U. S. government's immediate concern with these issues of maritime rights has been centered on the Middle East and on efforts to seek a permanent resolution of tensions in the area, the legal and political importance of the questions involved in the Middle East transcend regional boundaries. The U. S. government must also bear in mind the implications of any attempt by the United Arab Republic to close international waterways to Israeli shipping and the implications of any settlement involving this issue for broader U. S. strategic and commercial interests. The international law principles of the right of innocent passage through international straits, even when those straits consist wholly of territorial waters, is of the utmost importance to the security of the United States and to the role which the U. S. Navy plays in guaranteeing that security. U. S. defensive capabilities would be profoundly jeopardized by any erosion of the principle of freedom of innocent passage through these straits.

While the United States recognizes only a three-mile territorial sea limit, a growing number of states around the world are claiming greater areas of territorial sea. Claims have been made to four miles, twelve miles, and as much as 200 miles. Indonesia and the Philippines claim that all the waters of their respective archipelagoes are territorial in nature. If these extensive claims to territorial sea were to become established, a large number of international straits throughout the world would become subject to national sovereignty—the greater the distance claimed for territorial seas, the more straits that would be affected. The importance, therefore, of preserving the rule of international law that innocent passage through international straits may not be denied is obvious.

As Ambassador Arthur Dean, who served as Chairman of the American Delegation to the 1958 Geneva Conference on the Law of the Sea, testified before the Senate Foreign Relations Committee on 20 January 1960, "The primary danger to continuance of the ability of our warships and supporting aircraft to move, unhampered, to wherever they may be needed to support American foreign policy presents itself in the great international straits of the world—the narrows which lie athwart the sea routes which connect us with our widely scattered friends and allies and admit us to the strategic materials we do not ourselves possess."

At the same time, the United States is a major trading nation whose commercial interests are vitally linked to continued freedom of the seas. U. S. exports in 1967, for example, totaled nearly 31 billion dollars, while U. S. imports amounted to almost 27 billion. World trade was valued at approximately 200 billion dollars, in that year. This trade, which is increasing rapidly each year, and which is not only of importance to the welfare of the United States and its citizens, but also is essential to the economic development and well-being of nations and peoples around the world, depends largely on the ability of vessels of all flags to pass freely through international waterways.

Thus, the Arab-Israeli conflict, and the involvement in that conflict of the principle of freedom of passage through international straits, is of far-reaching consequence for the United States. Protection of the right of free transit through international waterways is important to the preservation of peace in the Middle East—as the events of May-June 1967 attest. But also at stake are the worldwide operations of the military forces of the United States, as well as the continued flow of international trade and commerce upon which the economic prosperity of this country and virtually every other nation of the world depends. As the United States works toward a Middle East settlement, it will have both of these interests very much in mind.

Some Legal Problems of International Waterways, with Particular Reference to the Straits of Tiran and the Suez Canal

D. H. N. JOHNSON

THE fact that the recent " six-day war " in the Middle East began with an attempt to close the Straits of Tiran and ended with those Straits re-opened to shipping, but the Suez Canal closed for the second time in eleven years, has drawn attention once again to the law affecting international waterways. Because the problem is less well known, this article will concentrate for the most part on the Straits of Tiran. A few remarks will, however, be made about the Suez Canal towards the end of the article.

INTERNATIONAL WATERWAYS—GENERAL REMARKS

What is an international waterway? The question is not easy to answer. According to the leading authority,

> " For purposes of analysis, international waterways must be considered to be those rivers, canals, and straits which are used to a substantial extent by the commercial shipping or warships belonging to States other than the riparian nation or nations. . . . The international character of a waterway, thus conceived, rests upon factual considerations, for it is only by examination of the actualities of international usage that any conclusions about the requisites of international character become possible." [1]

Nevertheless, the term " international waterway " appears to be one to which the British Government attaches significance. Speaking in the General Assembly of the United Nations on March 4, 1957, the British delegate stated:

> " It is the view of Her Majesty's Government in the United Kingdom that the Straits of Tiran must be regarded as an international waterway through which the vessels of all nations have a right of passage." [2]

This view was endorsed by the Prime Minister, during the recent Arab-Israeli crisis, when he told the House of Commons on May 31 that " the Gulf of Aqaba is an international waterway and that the Straits of Tiran do provide an international waterway into which and through which the vessels of all nations have a right of passage." [3]

---

[1] R. R. Baxter, *The Law of International Waterways* (1964), p. 3.
[2] 667th Plenary Meetings, p. 1284.
[3] H.C.Deb., Vol. 747, No. 200, cols. 205–206.

The starting point for any consideration of this branch of the international law of the sea must be the conventions adopted at the Geneva Conference on the Law of the Sea 1958—particularly the Convention on the Territorial Sea and the Contiguous Zone and the Convention on the High Seas.[4] Behind these conventions lay not less than seven years' preparatory work by the International Law Commission, during which the views of governments were repeatedly taken into account and culminating in seventy-three draft articles prepared by the Commission in the summer of 1956[5]; a protracted debate in the Sixth Committee of the General Assembly of the United Nations in the autumn of 1956; and certain further preparatory work conducted by or on behalf of the Secretariat of the United Nations during the period 1956–58.[6]

As part of the preparatory work just referred to, the Secretariat of the United Nations requested Commander R. H. Kennedy, O.B.E., R.N. (Retd.) to undertake two studies. The first, Preparatory Document No. 6, was " A Brief Geographical and Hydrographical Study of Straits which constitute Routes for International Traffic." [7] The second, Preparatory Document No. 12, was " A Brief Geographical and Hydrographical Study of Bays and Estuaries, the Coasts of which belong to Different States." [8] The Secretariat itself also prepared, as Preparatory Document No. 11, a " Guide to Instruments affecting the Legal Status of Straits." [9] These studies are invaluable to an elucidation of the problems now to be considered.

Generally speaking, the Geneva codification of 1958 eschewed unnecessary definitions. The following key provisions must, however, be noted.

FROM THE CONVENTION ON THE TERRITORIAL SEA AND THE CONTIGUOUS ZONE

Article 1

1. The sovereignty of a State extends, beyond its land territory and its internal waters, to a belt of sea adjacent to its coast, described as the territorial sea.

---

[4] Cmnd. 584. The other two conventions, dealing respectively with Fishing and Conservation of the Living Resources of the High Seas, and the Continental Shelf, are not immediately relevant. All four conventions are now in force.

[5] " Report of the International Law Commission covering the Work of its Eighth Session." *General Assembly Official Records: Eleventh Session.* Supplement No. 9 (A/3159).

[6] See the article by the present writer, " The Preparation of the 1958 Geneva Conference on the Law of the Sea " (1959) 8 I.C.L.Q. 122.

[7] A/Conf. 13/6.

[8] A/Conf. 13/15.

[9] A/Conf. 13/14. Attention should also be drawn to two other studies, namely, Preparatory Document No. 1, " Memorandum concerning Historic Bays," prepared by the Secretariat itself (A/Conf. 13/1), and Preparatory Document No. 15, a paper on " Certain Legal Aspects concerning the Delimitation of the Territorial Waters of Archipelagos," prepared at the request of the Secretariat by Mr. Jens Evensen, Advocate at the Supreme Court of Norway.

Article 2

The sovereignty of a coastal State extends to the air space over the territorial sea as well as to its bed and subsoil.

Article 5

1. Waters on the landward side of the baseline of the territorial sea form part of the internal waters of the State.

Articles 3 and 4 laid down technical rules concerning the drawing of base lines. It is these base lines which separate " internal waters " from " territorial sea." The legal difference is that, whereas a coastal state is entitled to exclude foreign shipping from its internal waters,[10] it must afford to such shipping a right of innocent passage through its territorial sea.

Article 7 was a lengthy article concerning bays. It defined a bay as " a well-marked indentation whose penetration is in such proportion to the width of its mouth as to contain landlocked waters and constitute more than a mere curvature of the coast." It also provided that " if the distance between the low-water marks of the natural entrance points of a bay does not exceed twenty-four miles, a closing line may be drawn between these two low-water marks, and the waters enclosed thereby shall be considered as internal waters "; and further that " where the distance between the low-water marks of the natural entrance points of a bay exceeds twenty-four miles, a straight base line of twenty-four miles shall be drawn within the bay in such a manner as to enclose the maximum area of water that is possible with a line of that length." However, Article 7 related " only to bays the coasts of which belong to a single State "; whilst its provisions were not to apply to " historic bays "[11] or to bays where, for the reasons given in Article 4, a " straight baseline system " along an entire coast, as opposed to closing lines across the mouths of individual bays, was envisaged. The implication of this was presumably that (i) where there is a bay the coasts of which belong to more than one state, a closing

---

[10] Save for one exception provided for in Art. 5 (2).

[11] No agreed list of " historic bays " has ever been drawn up, although a fairly clear example is Conception Bay in Newfoundland. See *Direct U.S. Cable Co.* v. *Anglo-American Telegraph Co.* (1877) 2 App. Cas. 394. An example—and possibly the only example—of a " historic bay " the coasts of which belong to more than one state is the Gulf of Fonseca. In a judgment given on March 9, 1917, in a case brought by El Salvador against Nicaragua, the Central American Court of Justice held that the Gulf of Fonseca was " an historic bay possessed of the characteristics of a closed sea " and that El Salvador, Honduras and Nicaragua were co-owners of its waters, except as to the littoral marine league which was the exclusive property of each (*American Journal of International Law*, 11 (1917), p. 693). With regard to " historic bays " it may be pointed out that, at a time when three miles was generally considered the maximum breadth of the territorial sea and six miles (or at the most 10) as the permissible length of closing lines across bays, the notion of a " historic bay " as a special category exempted from any restriction as to the length of the closing line was considerably more important that it now is if the 24 mile closing lines allowed by Art. 7 of the Geneva Convention are to become the general rule. The International Law Commission had recommended a maximum closing line of 15 miles.

line may not be drawn at all, except in the case of a " historic bay "; and (ii) in the case of " historic bays," whether the coasts of such bays belong to one or more states, the closing line is not restricted to twenty-four miles.

Articles 14 to 23 wrestled with the difficult problem of innocent passage. Although these articles bravely attempted to define both " innocent " and " passage," it cannot be said that any unambiguous conclusion emerges as to what constitutes an " innocent passage." If the coastal state and the state of the vessel concerned differ as to whether a particular passage is innocent or not, belated reference to international adjudication is always possible, if both sides agree. But clearly this is one of the most difficult issues in international law today, quite apart from the problem which arises if one or more of the states involved is, or claims to be, at war. If the coastal state is at war, it enjoys " belligerent rights " under which it may take certain steps against its enemy's ships, as well as neutral ships carrying cargoes to or from enemy ports.[12] These rights may be exercised even on the high seas; a fortiori they may also be exercised in the coastal state's own territorial sea. If, on the other hand, the coastal state is neutral, it may close its territorial sea to belligerent warships and their prizes, but it is not bound to do so.

The following further points need to be made on the Convention on the Territorial Sea and the Contiguous Zone.

(i) The convention is completely silent on the breadth of the territorial sea. An attempt was made to remedy this defect at a second conference held in Geneva in 1960, but this too failed.[13] On this critical point all that the International Law Commission had been able to say was that " international law does not permit an extension of the territorial sea beyond twelve miles " and that " the Commission, without taking any decision as to the breadth of the territorial sea up to that limit, notes, on the one hand, that many states have fixed a breadth greater than three miles and, on the other hand, that many states do not recognise such a breadth when that of their own territorial sea is less." It remains broadly true that a claim to more than twelve miles has no hope of meeting with general acceptance. A considerable number of claims up to twelve miles are put forward, but except where a claim can be justified on historic grounds (e.g., Norway's claim to four miles) the states favouring three miles decline to accept such claims.

(ii) The convention has no general article on the question of straits. This is remarkable considering the attention devoted to

12 This statement is made on the assumption that, despite the Charter of the United Nations, it is still possible for states to be engaged in " war " and to enjoy " belligerent rights." This assumption is doubtful, but that question is too large to be discussed here.

13 D. W. Bowett, " The Second United Nations Conference on the Law of the Sea " (1960) 9 I.C.L.Q. 415.

straits in the literature of international law. Article 16 (4) does, however, provide the following:

> " There shall be no suspension of the innocent passage of foreign ships through straits which are used for international navigation between one part of the high seas and another part of the high seas or the territorial sea of a foreign State." [14]

There can be no doubt that the Conference had the Straits of Tiran very much in mind when it adopted this provision and that its adoption was sufficient to explain the refusal of the Arab states to sign the convention.

According to the leading authority mentioned above, " in geographic terms, a strait is normally a narrow passage connecting two sections of the high seas." [15] Legally, the régime of a strait is affected by its breadth, in particular by the fact whether or not passage through it is possible without passing through the territorial waters of one or other of the littoral states. Thus, on the assumption that the maximum breadth of territorial waters is three miles, no special régime will in principle be required if a strait is more than six miles wide.[16] Indeed, it may be asked why, even in the case of a narrow strait, a special régime is necessary seeing that the waters in such a strait are territorial waters and that there is an undoubted right of innocent passage through such waters. The idea of a special régime for straits seems first to have arisen through the claim of littoral states to regard some straits that were more than six miles wide as territorial." Now, however, the question is seen more from the opposite point of view, namely, the right of warships of non-littoral states to pass through narrow straits. Thus, in the *Corfu Channel* case, the International Court of Justice affirmed that " States in time of peace have a right to send their warships through straits used for international navigation between two parts of the high seas without the previous authorisation of a coastal State, provided that the passage is *innocent*." [17] The Court evaded in that case the question whether there is a similar right for foreign warships to pass through the territorial sea as such, even where there is no strait. Hence the importance in certain circumstances of determining whether there is a strait or not.

There was bitter controversy at the Geneva Conference of 1958 on the question whether warships have a right to pass through the territorial sea. On that question Professor Sorensen comments:

> " The actual text of the Convention would . . . warrant the conclusion that warships have the same right in this respect

---

[14] Art. 16 (4) follows immediately after Art. 16 (3) which permits a coastal state in certain circumstances to suspend " temporarily in specified areas of its territorial sea the innocent passage of foreign ships." Such suspension, however, must be " without discrimination amongst foreign ships."

[15] Baxter, *op. cit.*, p. 3.

[16] Of course it is not as simple as that. Navigational considerations may make it necessary to keep close to one or other shore.

[17] *I.C.J. Reports 1949*, p. 4 at p. 28. Italics in original.

as other ships, but the proceedings of the Conference leave no room for doubt that this was not the intention of the majority of delegations." [18]

Because of this uncertainty it may, as already stated, be important to decide whether a particular stretch of water is a strait or not. In talking of a special régime for straits, however, it is necessary to guard against a further confusion. Some straits have been subjected to a " special régime " in the sense of a régime actually laid down by treaty. But there are very few of these. Indeed the Secretariat's Guide, referred to above (Preparatory Document No. 11), mentions only five. These are (a) the Straits of the Dardanelles, the Sea of Marmora and the Bosphorus; (b) the Straits of Gibraltar; (c) Fuca's Straits; (d) the Straits of Magellan; and (e) the Danish Straits. The special régime—such as it is— envisaged by the International Court of Justice in the *Corfu Channel* case depends solely upon factual considerations, namely, that the straits in question are " used for international navigation between two parts of the high seas."

FROM THE CONVENTION ON THE HIGH SEAS

Article 1 defines the high seas as " all parts of the sea that are not included in the territorial sea or in the internal waters of a State." Article 2 mentions " freedom of navigation " as one of the freedoms of the high seas.

During the course of the discussions at the Geneva Conference the Israeli delegate in the Second Committee (which was dealing with the régime of the high seas) advanced certain general criticisms of the manner in which the International Law Commission had approached its task. The Commission, he felt, had maintained an unduly rigid distinction between the régime of the territorial sea and that of the high seas. Its draft articles " should be redrafted or regrouped so as to include both innocent passage and passage on the high seas within the framework of freedom of navigation." To over-emphasise the distinction between the territorial sea and the high seas was to assume that

" when a ship sailed from one port to another it crossed an invisible frontier, some miles from the shore, beyond which freedom of navigation existed. In actual fact, however, a ship

---

[18] *Law of the Sea* (International Conciliation, No. 520, November 1958), p. 235.. This curious result arose in this way. The International Law Commission had proposed that coastal states might require notification of the passage of warships or even make it subject to previous authorisation. In the First Committee of the Geneva Conference the I.L.C. draft was adopted, but in plenary the Western Powers succeeded in securing the deletion of the requirement of prior *authorisation*. A number of delegations were not content with prior *notification* only, and the entire article was lost. As Arts. 14 to 17 (the general articles concerned with the right of innocent passage) appear under a subsection entitled " Rules applicable to All Ships," it is argued that warships enjoy exactly the same rights as merchant ships.

passing through the territorial sea enjoyed the right of innocent passage, which was independent of the sovereignty of the coastal state and which formed an integral part of freedom of navigation. The fact that passage through the territorial sea might be subject to qualifications did not alter the basic fact that innocent passage was exercised as a right, and not on sufferance; suspension of such passage within the territorial sea could not be arbitrary, even as a state could not arbitrarily interfere with freedom of navigation on the high seas. Moreover, qualifications of the right of innocent passage did not always exist, as in the case of international straits and bays and free access to ports."

Rather, in the Israeli delegate's view, one should lay stress on " the concept of the unity of the voyage." [19]

THE STRAITS OF TIRAN AND THE GULF OF AQABA

The description that follows is taken from the Secretariat Study of " Bays and Estuaries, the Coasts of Which belong to Different States " referred to above.[20]

" The Gulf of Aqaba is a long narrow gulf on the eastern side of the Sinai Peninsula. The western shore is Egyptian,[21] the eastern shore is Saudi Arabian and the head of the Gulf is Israeli and Jordanian territory. The islands of Tiran and Sinafar front the entrance. The length of the gulf is about ninety-six miles."

The Study goes on to explain that the breadth of the Gulf at the entrance is five and three-quarter miles; that at its widest part the Gulf is fourteen and a half miles wide but that further up the average breadth is between eight and a half and eleven miles; and that the Gulf narrows to between three and four miles wide towards the head. There are two feasible passages. One of these is the Enterprise Passage, 1,800 yards wide, between the Sinai coast and a

---

[19] Official Records of the Second Committee (A/Conf. 13/40), Twelfth Meeting, paragraphs 5–8. Similar views were expressed by the Netherlands delegate when he said: " The right to use the high seas for purposes of navigation had legal consequences that went beyond the concept of the high seas in the geographical sense of the term. No purpose would be served by proclaiming freedom of navigation on the high seas if that freedom could be enjoyed only in the geographical area of the high seas to the exclusion of territorial and internal waters. The ' freedom of navigation ' concept should imply the right of ships of all flags to engage in international trade, because in principle it covered the right to carry goods and passengers between various ports throughout the world." (Fourth Meeting, para. 10.)

[20] p. 154, *supra*. The description of the Straits of Tiran and the Gulf of Aqaba is a combined description appearing in this Study (*i.e.*, Preparatory Document No. 12). The Study covers no fewer than 48 such bays and estuaries, including Lough Carlingford and Lough Foyle. In the other Study (Preparatory Document No. 6), devoted to " Straits which constitute Routes for International Traffic," 33 straits are described.

[21] At the time of writing Israel is in possession of the Sinai Peninsula. At this time, however, her rights and duties are those of a military occupant, not a sovereign.

line of drying coral reefs. The other is the Grafton Passage, 950 yards wide, between these reefs and Tiran island.

The legal position of Tiran and Sinafar is obscure. It appears that Egypt occupied these islands in 1950 with Saudi Arabian consent. The Egyptian delegate informed the Security Council on February 15, 1954, that the two islands had constituted Egyptian territory since 1906. But in a memorandum attached to a letter dated April 12, 1957, from the Permanent Representative of Saudi Arabia to the United Nations to the Secretary-General, it was stated that " these two islands are Saudi Arabian "; and Egypt apparently raised no objection.[22]

Having regard to the width of the Gulf, and having regard also to the dispute over the breadth of territorial waters, it is not clear whether there are any high seas inside the Straits of Tiran. Obviously, if international law imposes a maximum breadth of three miles for the territorial sea, quite a considerable part of the Gulf of Aqaba constitutes high seas. If, on the other hand, international law accepts as valid claims to a territorial sea of twelve miles, as formulated by the Arab states and many others, then no part of the Gulf of Aqaba constitutes " high seas," and the status of the Straits of Tiran is affected too, since it can no longer be said of those Straits that they " connect two sections of the high seas." In that eventuality, on whatever theory any right to enter the Gulf of Aqaba—and in particular to reach the Israeli port of Eilath—may rest, it can no longer rest on the proposition that the " Straits of Tiran " are a strait in the sense of " a narrow passage connecting two sections of the high seas."

It may be necessary to draw a distinction between merely entering the Gulf of Aqaba on the one hand and navigating as far as Eilath—or for that matter the Jordanian port of Aqaba—on the other hand. If, for example, the Gulf of Aqaba constitutes " high seas," then there would be no reason why a foreign warship, enjoying its right of innocent passage through the Straits of Tiran under the *Corfu Channel* decision, should not enter the Gulf and stay for some time therein on a surveillance mission, without ever intending to reach Eilath or Aqaba. If, on the other hand, there are no high seas within the Gulf, then a mission of that kind would seem to be excluded, but it would not necessarily follow that a foreign merchant ship would not be entitled to pass through the Straits of Tiran, sail up the Gulf, and dock at Eilath or Aqaba despite any objection by the main littoral states, Egypt and Saudi Arabia.

Leaving aside the problem of defining " innocence," Article 14 of the Geneva Convention on the Territorial Sea and the Contiguous Zone states that " Passage means navigation through the territorial

---

22 See C. B. Selak, " A Consideration of the Legal Status of the Gulf of Aqaba," *American Journal of International Law*, 52 (1958), p. 660; and also L. Gross, " The Geneva Conference on the Law of the Sea and the Right of Innocent Passage through the Gulf of Aqaba," *ibid.* 53 (1959), p. 564.

sea for the purpose either of traversing that sea without entering internal waters, or of proceeding to internal waters, or of making for the high seas from internal waters." Vessels bound to or from Eilath could therefore be said to be exercising the right of passage not merely through the Straits of Tiran but also through the Egyptian and/or Saudi Arabian portions of the Gulf of Aqaba. Under the general rules of international law these states would be entitled to regulate such shipping, and possibly on occasions to suspend it temporarily, although the fact has to be faced that Israel will always tend to regard any such suspension as a threat to her security warranting an armed response in self-defence. But it is difficult to see how under general international law Egypt and Saudi Arabia could claim any permanent right to exclude such shipping altogether.

That the Arab claim to exclude ships bound to and from Eilath is weak under general international law is no more convincingly evidenced than by the heavy reliance placed on such other Arab claims as that Israel has no right to exist as a state or that the Arab states are at war with Israel.[23] Moreover, if the Arab claim were good under general international law, there might be serious repercussion upon the right of navigation in other areas where international boundaries converge, such as the Shatt Al Arab, the Gulf of Trieste and the Rio de la Plata, to mention only a few.

It may be as well also to comment upon the Israeli contention that the principle of the freedom of the seas implies in itself the right to navigate to and from the Israeli port of Eilath. This contention sounds plausible because it is certainly true that, for Israel, the freedom of the seas would be a much diminished prize if navigation were excluded from the Gulf of Aqaba. Nevertheless, it is doubtful if one principle of international law, the freedom of the seas, is of itself sufficient to generate rights that are entitled to take precedence over rights enjoyed under another principle of international law, in this case the principle of the territorial sovereignty of the intervening coastal states. This question of freedom of the seas versus territorial sovereignty was much discussed at Geneva in 1958 in relation to the problem of landlocked states. On that question Article 3 of the Convention on the High Seas asserted that " States having no sea coast should have free access to the sea." But, even in the case of landlocked states, such access was made dependent upon agreements with the intervening coastal states. Whatever geographical disadvantages she may suffer from in the Gulf of Aqaba, Israel has a Mediterranean coast as well. She cannot therefore claim any special privilege as a landlocked

---

[23] There is a certain inconsistency between the refusal of the Arab states to recognise Israel and their claim to be at war with Israel nonetheless. The inconsistency is, however, not absolute because international law admits of the possibility of belligerent communities not recognised as states (*e.g.*, the Confederacy in the American Civil War).

state. In practice, Israel must like all other states take her geographical position as she finds it. She is entitled to the benefits of the general rules of international law, no more and no less. So far as Israel's rights in the Gulf of Aqaba are concerned, these rules are the rules relating to bays, straits and passage through the territorial sea which it has been attempted to elucidate above.

There is one other question relating to the Gulf of Aqaba which needs to be considered. This is whether the littoral states, acting in agreement, are entitled to close the Gulf to foreign shipping. The question is of course academic since the littoral states are not likely to agree on such a course, Israel in particular being determined to keep the Gulf open. Nevertheless it is necessary to consider this matter as part of the general Arab contention that the Gulf of Aqaba is an " Arab Sea " on which Israel, even if it is entitled to exist at all, has no right to maintain a presence.[24]

As already indicated, Article 7 of the Geneva Convention on the Territorial Sea and the Contiguous Zone suggests that a closing line— which has the effect of turning the waters inside it into internal waters from which foreign shipping may be totally excluded—may not be drawn at all across the mouth of a bay the coasts of which belong to more than one state, unless the bay is an " historic bay." It is doubtful, however, if this restriction would apply in the case of a bay with as narrow an entrance as the Gulf of Aqaba. On any conceivable view of the breadth of territorial waters, the Gulf of Aqaba, if it belonged to a single state, could be closed. In principle, then, it would seem that the littoral states of the Gulf of Aqaba, provided they are all acting in agreement, can do what any one of them could do if it controlled the whole area—that is, close the Gulf to foreign shipping.

This being so, it is scarcely necessary to consider the Arab claim that the Gulf of Aqaba is an " historic bay." The claim rests on the long period of Arab domination of the area between 700 and 1517 and on its control by the Ottoman Empire between 1517 and 1917. But the essence of any claim on historical grounds is lack of interruption, and the sequence of events since 1917 has been too chequered to permit of the continued recognition of any historic right. (To mention only a few of these events, the Treaty of San Remo of April 25, 1920, awarded to Great Britain a Mandate for Palestine, which then included Transjordan. In 1922 a separate Mandate was created for Transjordan, which was placed under the Amir Abdullah. In 1924 Abdullah's father, King Husayn of the Hejaz, was forced to abdicate by the King of Nejd, Ibn Saud, who

---

[24] This particular Arab contention appears to be that, although Eilath was in the mandated territory of Palestine and although Eilath was also in the area awarded to the Jewish State under the United Nations Partition Plan of 1947, the Israeli occupation of Eilath was illegal because it took place on March 11, 1949, after the Israeli-Egyptian Armistice Agreement (February 24, 1949) though before the signature of the Israeli-Jordan Armistice Agreement (April 3, 1949).

in 1926 incorporated the Hejaz into his dominions, forming the present Kingdom of Saudi Arabia in 1932. As for Egypt, having been a vassal state of Turkey, she became a protectorate of Great Britain in 1914. Her independence was recognised in 1922 by Great Britain, whilst in 1923 Turkey by the Treaty of Lausanne renounced all her rights and titles over Egypt as from November 5, 1914.)

THE SUEZ CANAL [25]

Apart from the familiar contention that Israel has no right to exist, Egypt's claim to close the Suez Canal at all times to Israeli ships and cargoes destined to Israel, and from time to time to ships of all nations, rests essentially on the thesis that Egypt is at war with Israel and is entitled to take these measures in self-defence. Article I of the Constantinople Convention of October 29, 1888, respecting the Free Navigation of the Suez Maritime Canal states that " The Suez Maritime Canal shall always be free and open, in time of war as in time of peace, to every vessel of commerce or of war, without distinction of flag." Obviously this principle could not always be carried out in so bold a form, and in fact Articles IV, V, VII and VIII impose certain restrictions upon maritime belligerent Powers. Article X, however, states that " the provisions of Articles IV, V, VII and VIII shall not interfere with the measures which His Majesty the Sultan and His Highness the Khedive,[26] in the name of His Imperial Majesty, and within the limits of the Firmans granted, might find it necessary to take for securing by their own forces the defence of Egypt and the maintenance of public order." Article X also provided that " It is likewise understood that the provisions of the four Articles aforesaid shall in no case occasion any obstacle to the measures which the Imperial Ottoman Government may think it necessary to take in order to insure by its own forces *the defence of its other possessions situated on the eastern coast of the Red Sea.*" From the passage in italics it seems possible to deduce that the Constantinople Convention, although primarily concerned with the Suez Canal, might have some bearing upon the Gulf of Aqaba problem as well.

On April 24, 1957, Egypt made a Declaration, deposited with

---

[25] The reader is referred to the following: L. Gross, " Passage through the Suez Canal of Israel-Bound Cargo and Israel Ships," *American Journal of International Law,* 51 (1957), p. 530; " The Suez Canal," A Selection of Documents relating to the International Status of the Suez Canal and the Position of the Suez Canal Company, November 30, 1854–July 26, 1956, published under the auspices of the Society of Comparative Legislation and International Law (London, Stevens, 1956) and to " The Suez Canal Settlement," A Selection of Documents relating to the Settlement of the Suez Canal Dispute, the Clearance of the Suez Canal and the Settlement of Disputes between the United Kingdom, France and the United Arab Republic, October 1956–March 1959, published under the auspices of the British Institute of International and Comparative Law (London, Stevens, 1960).

[26] In 1888 Egypt was a vassal state of the Ottoman Empire, although under military occupation by Great Britain.

the United Nations, in which she undertook " to respect the terms and the spirit of the Constantinople Convention of 1888 and the rights and obligations arising therefrom." She further undertook that " differences arising between the parties to the said convention in respect of the interpretation or the applicability of its provisions, if not otherwise resolved, will be referred to the International Court of Justice." A Declaration in furtherance of this obligation was made on July 18, 1957. The possibility therefore exists of bringing before the International Court of Justice at least some of the legal issues arising from the present closing of the Suez Canal. The right to seize the Court is, however, carefully limited in the Egyptian Declarations to the parties to the Constantinople Convention and further to states who have made declarations under Article 36 (2) of the Statute of the International Court of Justice (*i.e.*, the Optional Clause). The parties to the Constantinople Convention were Great Britain, Germany, Austria, Hungary, Spain, France, Italy, Netherlands, Russia and the Ottoman Empire. Of these, the following only have made declarations under Article 36 (2): Great Britain, France, Netherlands, Turkey.

D. H. N. Johnson.*

---

* M.A.; LL.B.; Professor of International and Air Law, University of London.

Some International and Legal Aspects
of the Suez Canal Question

THOMAS T. F. HUANG

I. Introduction

The impact of the nationalization by the Egyptian Government on July 26, 1956, of the Suez Canal Company (*Compagnie Universelle du Canal Maritime de Suez*) upon international affairs is still reverberating.[1] The questions of international law and other problems to which it gives rise are manifold, but this article will be restricted to an examination of four of them: first, the international and legal status of the Suez Canal *Company;* second, the nature and legal status of concession agreements which are referred to in the text of the Convention of October 29, 1888;[2] third, the international status and control of the Suez *Canal,* particularly under the 1888 Convention; and fourth, the matter of compensation.

The fundamental legal issues have been early defined and consistently maintained by the parties concerned.[3] The Egyptian Government asserts that the nationalization of the Suez Canal Company for a public purpose, accompanied by an offer to pay compensation, was a legitimate exercise of the powers of sovereignty, and was a matter which fell within its domestic jurisdiction.[4] The governments of the United States, the United Kingdom and France have conceded the general right of a state to nationalize con-

---

* Parts of the materials used in this article are taken from a dissertation which the author is preparing for the degree of Doctor of Juridical Science at the Harvard Law School.

[1] See, *e.g.,* The Suez Canal, A Selection of Documents relating to the International Status of the Suez Canal and the position of the Suez Canal Company November 30, 1854–July 26, 1956 (London, Society of Comparative Legislation and International Law, 1956); The Suez Canal Problem, July 26–September 22, 1956 (Dept. of State Pub. 6392, 1956); U.N. Docs. S/P.V. 734–743 (Sept. 26–Oct. 13, 1956); U.N. General Assembly, Official Records, First Emergency Special Session, A/P.V. 561–572 (Nov. 1–10, 1956); United Nations Review, Vol. 3, No. 5, pp. 19 ff., No. 6, pp. 10 ff., No. 7, pp. 28 ff., 90 ff. (1956).

[2] Hereinafter referred to as "1888 Convention" unless otherwise indicated.

[3] See, *e.g.,* Egyptian Presidential Decree on the Nationalization of the Suez Canal Company, July 26, 1956, English translation in The Suez Canal Problem, *op. cit.* 30 ff., and in The Suez Canal, *op. cit.* 41–43; Tripartite Statement of Aug. 2, 1956, The Suez Canal Problem 34–35; The Suez Canal Company and Decisions Taken by the Egyptian Government on 26th July 1956 (published by the Suez Canal Company, 1956); Livre Blanc sur la Nationalisation de la Compagnie Maritime du Canal de Suez, S.A.E. (published by the Egyptian Government, Cairo, 1956); Exchange of Correspondence between the Suez Committee and the President of the Republic of Egypt regarding the future operation of the Suez Canal, Cairo, Sept. 3–9, 1956, Egypt No. 2 (1956), Cmd. 9856; and materials cited in note 1 *supra*.   [4] U.N. Doc. S/P.V. 736, p. 2.

cerns which have the national character of the nationalizing state, provided adequate, prompt and effective compensation is paid, but they challenge the arbitrary and unilateral manner in which the Egyptian Government has exercised that right *vis-à-vis* the Suez Canal Company.[5] In substance, they claim that the Suez Canal Company has acquired an international status (a) by virtue of the 1888 Convention, and (b) by virtue of the surrounding international factors, such as the international composition of the shareholders of the Company, personnel, and the manner of the operation of the Suez Canal, which rendered an international public service to the world community.[6] On the other hand, the Egyptian Government maintains that the "former" Suez Canal Company was an Egyptian company.[7] First there is raised the question: Does the Suez Canal Company in fact have an international status expressly by virtue of the 1888 Convention, or due to other circumstances? The term "international" has been employed in at least two senses: (1) in the general descriptive sense signifying a transaction cutting across the boundaries of at least two states which is devoid of legal consequences; and (2) in the technical sense from which certain legal consequences flow, such as an international obligation arising from a treaty. Second, what is the law applicable to the Suez Canal Company? Is it solely Egyptian or also French, or also international law? If the Suez Canal Company has an international status in the technical sense arising out of the 1888 Convention, then its nationalization was *ipso facto* a violation of the international obligations of Egypt under that treaty.[8]

II. The International and Legal Status of the Suez Canal Company

In the light of the positions maintained by the states concerned, as outlined above, the legality of the nationalization of the Suez Canal Company hangs upon the international and legal status of the company. The Egyptian Government claims that the "former" Suez Canal Company

[5] See Tripartite Statement of Aug. 2, 1956, The Suez Canal Problem, *op. cit.* 35; statement of U. K. representative, U.N. Doc. S/P.V. 735, pp. 3–17; statement of French representative, *ibid.* 17–24; and statement of U. S. representative, U.N. Doc. S/P.V. 738, pp. 6–13.

[6] See statements of U.K. representative in Security Council, U.N. Doc. S/P.V. 735, pp. 3–17; French representative, *ibid.* 17–24.

[7] See statement of Egyptian representative in Security Council, U.N. Doc. S/P.V. 736, pp. 1–14 at p. 2.

[8] On the Suez Canal and Suez Canal Company generally, see 1 Fauchille, Traité de Droit International Public 294–339 (Part II, 1925); Recueil chronologique des actes constitutifs de la Compagnie Universelle du Canal Maritime de Suez (3rd ed., 1950); La Documentation Française, Notes et Etudes Documentaires, No. 2, 205, Aug. 16, 1956; Whittuck, International Canals (1920); Buell, The Suez Canal and League Sanctions (1935); Hallberg, The Suez Canal: Its History and Diplomatic Importance (1931); Schonfield, The Suez Canal in World Affairs (1953); Hoskins, "The Suez Canal as an International Waterway," 37 A.J.I.L. 373 (1943); Siegfried, A., Les Canaux Internationaux et les Grandes Routes Maritimes Mondiales," 74 Recueil des Cours de l'Académie de Droit International 18–42 (1949); Wilson, "Some International and Legal Aspects of the Suez Canal," 21 Grotius Society Transactions 127 (1936).

was an Egyptian company and was subject to Egyptian law.[9] On the other hand, the governments of the United States, the United Kingdom and France [10] unanimously assert that the Suez Canal Company has an international status, and that it is subject to international law: (a) by virtue of the 1888 Convention completing the system embodied in the concessions; (b) by virtue of the Declaration of 1873; and (c) by virtue of other surrounding international factors. In addition, the Government of France [11] contends that the Suez Canal Company possesses a status *sui generis*, so that, in addition to its submission to Egyptian law, it was also amenable to French law and to public international law.

The main significance of these arguments may be summarized as follows: (1) if the Suez Canal Company has an international status in the technical sense of the term by virtue of the 1888 Convention, then its nationalization was *ipso facto* a violation of the Egyptian Government's international obligations according to public international law, even though it may be legal in accordance with the municipal law of Egypt; (2) similarly, if the Suez Canal Company has an international status by virtue of the Declaration of 1873, the same result would follow; (3) if the Suez Canal Company is subject to Egyptian law, and has Egyptian national character, its nationalization would be proper in accordance with Egyptian law, and any complaint against its nationalization would involve exhaustion of local remedies followed by diplomatic espousal of the interests of the shareholders by their respective governments; [12] (4) even if the Suez Canal Company were subject also to French law and other applicable law, excluding public international law, in its transactions and operation of the Suez Canal, this factor would not preclude its nationalization under Egyptian law; (5) under public international law, *lege lata,* an international status acquired by the Suez Canal Company by virtue of the international character of its composition, organization, personnel, and utility service rendered to the world community, would not accord it the technical international status necessary for the application of public international law, unless the question appeared before an international tribunal imbued with the power to decide the case *ex aequo et bono.*[13]

[9] U.N. Doc. S/P.V. 736, pp. 1–14 at p. 2; Egypt in 1956 was not on the list of states that have accepted the compulsory jurisdiction of the International Court of Justice in accordance with Art. 36(2) of the Statute of the Court. See I.C.J. Yearbook 1955–1956, pp. 34, 183 ff.

[10] See, *e.g.*, U.K. representative statement, U.N. Doc. S/P.V. 735, pp. 3–17; statement of French representative, *ibid.* 17–24; statement of U. S. representative, U.N. Doc. S/P.V. 738, pp. 6–13, and Tripartite Statement of Aug. 2, 1956, by the governments of the United States, the United Kingdom and France, The Suez Canal Problem, July 26–September 22, 1956, pp. 34–35 (Dept. of State Pub. 6392, 1956).

[11] U.N. Doc. S/P.V. 735, pp. 17, 18.

[12] On diplomatic protection generally, see *e.g.*, Borchard, The Protection of Citizens Abroad (N.Y., 1915); also J. Mervyn Jones, ''Claims on Behalf of Nationals Who Are Shareholders in Foreign Companies,'' 26 Brit. Year Bk. of Int. Law 225 (1949).

[13] See I.C.J. Statute, Art. 38 (2); Judge Manley O. Hudson, The Permanent Court of International Justice, 1920–1942, pp. 615–618 (N.Y., 1943); Habicht, Power of the International Judge to Give a Decision *Ex Aequo et Bono* (1935).

The foregoing problems will be examined hereinafter from the following aspects: (a) the international status of the Suez Canal Company as affected by the 1888 Convention; (b) the international status of the Suez Canal Company as affected by the Declaration of 1873; (c) international factors bearing on the international status of the Suez Canal Company; and (d) the law applicable to the Suez Canal Company: its submission to Egyptian, French and other laws.

The International Status of the Suez Canal Company as Affected by the 1888 Convention

In the course of debate in the Security Council,[14] the representative of the United Kingdom declared, *inter alia,* that the Suez Canal Company, "although technically registered in Egypt, was in substance as in name an international company enjoying concessions built into an international treaty," and the real issue, in his opinion, was the "sanctity of treaties and respect for international obligations."[15] He was apparently invoking the principle *pacta sunt servanda.* The representative of France also shared the view that the Suez Canal Company formed an essential part of the international system recognized by the 1888 Convention.[16] The representative of the United States asserted that the international law applicable to the question was the 1888 Convention.[17]

The burden of sustaining the contention that the Suez Canal Company has an international status consecrated by a particular treaty fell upon the shoulders of the representative of the United Kingdom. His thesis [18] runs as follows: The preamble of the 1888 Convention declares that it was the desire of the Powers to establish a definite system designed to

> guarantee at all times, and for all the powers, the free use of the Suez Maritime Canal, and thus to complete the system under which the navigation of this canal has been placed by the Firman of His Imperial Majesty the Sultan, dated the 22nd February, 1866. . . .[19]

This Firman (decree),[20] entered into between the Suez Canal Company and the Viceroy of Egypt, confirmed the two previous concession agreements which had been granted in 1854 and 1856.[21] Consequently, as a matter of accepted legal principle, if an instrument is concluded with the express purpose of "completing" a pre-existing system established by a prior instrument, that system becomes the necessary basis for the subsequent instrument, and the pre-existing system is impliedly continued at least

[14] See U.N. Docs. S/P.V. 734–743. [15] U.N. Doc. S/P.V. 735, pp. 3, 7, 8.
[16] *Ibid.* 17, 19. [17] U.N. Doc. S/P.V. 738, pp. 6, 8.
[18] See U.N. Doc. S/P.V. 735, pp. 3–17.
[19] 79 Brit. and For. State Papers (1887–1888) 18 ff.; English translation in The Suez Canal Problem, *op. cit.* 16 ff.; also in 3 A.J.I.L. Supp. 123 (1909).
[20] Convention entre le Vice-Roi d'Egypte et la Compagnie Universelle du Canal Maritime de Suez, le 22 Février, 1866, 56 Brit. and For. State Papers (1865–1866) 277–283; English translation in The Suez Canal Problem, *op. cit.* 9–16; Recueil chronologique des actes constitutifs de la Compagnie Universelle du Canal Maritime de Suez 39–44 (Cairo, 1930).
[21] See English translation of texts in The Suez Canal Problem, *op. cit.* 1–3, 4–9; and The Suez Canal, *op. cit.* 1, 4.

for the period for which it was first established. The 1888 Convention assumed that the operation of the Suez Canal Company would continue at least for the full period provided for by the company's concessions, especially in view of the fact that Article 14 of the 1888 Convention expressly provides that the force of the treaty shall not be limited "by the duration of the Acts of Concession of the Universal Suez Canal Company." [22]

On the other hand, the representative of Egypt contended that the mere fact that the 1888 Convention made mention of the concession agreements did not deprive them of their essentially private law character, and did not confer upon them the status of a treaty. Furthermore, he said, any alienation or limitation of Egypt's sovereign rights respecting the Suez Canal would require an express stipulation in the 1888 Convention.[23]

The representative of the United Kingdom was invoking the private law doctrine of incorporation by reference in instruments. Its application would have been stronger if the 1888 Convention had contained a statement that the concession agreement (Firman of February 22, 1866) formed an integral part of the treaty. The general principle of international law invoked by the Egyptian representative, namely, that acts in derogation of sovereignty must be expressly stipulated and may not be inferred, was applied in the case of *Radio Corporation of America* v. *China*,[24] an arbitration involving the Chinese Government and an American corporation.

Semantically, the word "complete" as used in the preamble, is susceptible of at least the following interpretations: (1) that the pre-existing concessions system confirmed by the Firman has been completely absorbed in the international system established by the 1888 Convention so as to become an integral part of the latter treaty; (2) that the 1888 Convention is merely additive, in that the pre-existing concessions system and the international system together form a whole, with the two parts separable; and (3) even though the pre-existing concessions system is mentioned in the preamble, which concededly forms an integral part of the convention, nevertheless, not being in the *dispositif*, no legal significance can flow therefrom.

The Legislative History of the Preamble of the 1888 Convention

In view of the opposing interpretations advanced by the representatives of the United Kingdom and Egypt, it is permissible to resort to *travaux préparatoires* to discover the intent of the framers of the instrument.[25] When this is done the result is rather illuminating.

---

[22] U.N. Doc. S/P.V. 735, p. 3 at p. 6. Art. 14 of the 1888 Convention provides that "the engagements resulting from the present treaty shall not be limited by the duration of the Acts of Concession of the Universal Suez Canal Company." The *travaux préparatoires* do not appear to support the view contended for. See *infra*, p. 282.

[23] See U.N. Doc. S/P.V. 736, p. 1 at p. 7.

[24] 3 Reports of International Arbitral Awards (hereafter cited as Int. Arb. Awards) 1621 ff.

[25] See Kelsen, The Law of the United Nations xiii–xvii (Preface on Interpretation) (London, 1951).

The preamble of the 1888 Convention [26] emanated from the draft convention formulated in 1885 by the International Commission [27] which had been convened to draw up an international convention to guarantee free navigation of the Canal, based upon eight points contained in the Circular which the British Government in 1883 had sent to the principal European Powers.[28] This Circular made no mention of the concession agreements or the Firman.

The French draft preamble which formed the basis of discussion at the meetings of the Subcommission which considered the question read as follows:

> [The President of the French Republic and the Contracting Parties] being desirous of confirming by a conventional act the system under which the navigation of the Suez Canal has been placed since its origin by concessions of His Highness the Khedive and the Firmans of His Imperial Majesty the Sultan. . . .[29]

The Turkish delegate expressed the view that the words "the concessions accorded by the Firman of His Imperial Majesty granted at the request of His Highness the Khedive," were more in accordance with fact.[30] The British delegate maintained that no mention of the concessions of the Khedive and the Firmans of the Sultan should be made in the preamble because they affected only merchant vessels, whereas the task of the conference was to draw up regulations for the passage of vessels of war. In his further opinion, which was expressly concurred in by the delegate of Austria-Hungary, the delegates assembled were not authorized to give sanction to the concessions and Firmans in question, and any mention of them in the preamble might indicate an indirect recognition of the respective acts.[31] The French delegate declared that, out of respect for the regard of the Ottoman Porte for historical truth, mention should be made in the preamble of "the concessions of His Highness the Khedive" and "the firmans granted by His Imperial Majesty the Sultan," but conceded the forcefulness of the British delegate's views.[32] The delegate of Austria-

---

[26] The Suez Canal Problem, *op. cit.* 16. The relevant part reads: "[The High Contracting Parties], wishing to establish, by a Conventional Act, a definite system destined to guarantee at all times, and for all the powers, the free use of the Suez Maritime Canal, and thus to complete the system under which the navigation of this canal has been placed by the Firman of His Imperial Majesty the Sultan, dated the 22nd February, 1866 (2 Zilkadé, 1282), and sanctioning the Concessions of His Highness the Khedive . . ."

[27] See Correspondence respecting the Suez Canal International Commission with the Protocols and Procès-Verbaux of the Meetings, Egypt No. 19 (1885), State. C. 4599 (1885).

[28] Extract from a Despatch from Earl Granville to Her Majesty's Representatives at Paris, Berlin, Vienna, Rome, and St. Petersburg, Jan. 3 1883, Respecting the Suez Canal, etc. Egypt No. 10 (1885), State. C. 4335 (1885).

[29] Correspondence respecting the Suez Canal International Commission with the Protocols and Procès-Verbaux of the Meetings, Egypt No. 19 (1885), State. C. 4599 (1885), p. 89.

[30] *Ibid.*   [31] *Ibid.* 89–90.

[32] *Ibid.* 237.

Hungary was at first of the opinion that the Subcommission was not only charged with the task of "confirming" the existing system, but was also to "extend" or "complete" it, but, after hearing the views expressed by the British and French delegates, veered towards the British delegate's point of view.[33]

When the full Commission considered the draft text, no material changes were made in it and no statements or declarations were further made which would in any manner alter the sense or *voeu* of the Subcommission.[34] Also, in the ensuing negotiations and diplomatic exchanges which finally led to the signing of the Convention on October 29, 1888, at Constantinople, no further discussion of the preamble appears to have taken place.[35] With minor alterations in wording, there is no material difference in the texts of the 1885 draft and the 1888 Convention.[36]

The International Status of the Suez Canal Company as Affected by the Declaration of 1873

Another international instrument cited as conferring an international status upon the Suez Canal Company is the Declaration made in 1873 by the Turkish Government.[37] In that year an International Commission met at Constantinople pursuant to an invitation by the Turkish Government to the maritime Powers to consider the question of the measurement of the tonnage of ships and the question of tolls. The Final Report of the Commission, which was formally drawn up and signed at Constantinople on December 18, 1873, had attached to it two declarations made by the Turkish delegate, which stated, *inter alia:*

> [T]he first delegate of Turkey . . . having been thereto authorized by his Government [declared]. . . .
> 2. That no modification, for the future, of the conditions for the passage through the Canal shall be permitted, whether in regard to the navigation toll or the dues for towage, anchorage, pilotage, etc., except with the consent of the Sublime Porte, which will not take any decision on this subject without previously coming to an understanding with the Principal Powers interested therein.[38]

All the delegates subsequently declared that they had been authorized by their governments to accept the provisions of the arrangements concluded, except for certain reservations made by the delegate of Holland. It has

[33] *Ibid.* 89.   [34] See *ibid.* 237–243.

[35] See 79 Brit. and For. State Papers (1887–1888) 498–534; also Correspondence respecting the proposed International Convention for Securing Free Navigation of the Suez Canal, Egypt No. 2 (1889), State. C. 5673 (1889).

[36] See text of 1885 draft, *supra*, p. 282, and text of 1888 Convention, note 26 *supra*.

[37] Despatch from the British Delegates on Tonnage at Constantinople, together with the Report and Recommendations of the Commission as to International Tonnage and the Suez Canal Dues. Commercial. No. 7 (1874), C. 943 (1874); The Suez Canal, *op. cit.* 45.

[38] Despatch, cited above, p. 11. The Members of the Commission, in their order of signature were: Germany, Austria-Hungary, Belgium, Spain, France, Great Britain, Greece, Italy, Holland, Russia, Sweden and Norway, and Turkey.

been asserted that the above Declaration was a "clear recognition and confirmation" of the interest of the user countries in the conditions of operation of the Canal.[39] The fatal defect in the rationale of "clear recognition and confirmation" lies in that fact that, if in fact the Suez Canal Company until then did not have an international status in the technical sense, then a condition precedent for the application of public international law would not have been fulfilled.

However, the Turkish Declaration is also susceptible of another interpretation. Under the so-called "Ihlen doctrine" enunciated by the Permanent Court of International Justice in the case of *The Legal Status of Eastern Greenland,*[40] the Declaration constituted legally binding international obligations upon the Ottoman Porte, and hence upon Egypt. In the *Eastern Greenland* case, the Norwegian Minister of Foreign Affairs (Mr. Ihlen) had made a statement to the Danish Minister to the effect "that the Norwegian Government would not make any difficulties in the settlement of this question [concerning the status of Greenland]."[41] The Permanent Court of International Justice held that the Norwegian Government was bound by the Ihlen Declaration. It might be contended that the Declaration of the Turkish Government in 1873 established *per se* an objective international status for the Suez Canal Company and that public international law would be applicable. In other words, notwithstanding the fact that the Suez Canal Company is an Egyptian company, the Declaration took the company out of the exclusive domestic jurisdiction of Egypt and made it a "subject" of international law. As the Permanent Court of International Justice has also declared in the case of *The Tunis and Morocco Nationality Decrees,*[42] the dividing line between domestic jurisdiction of the state and its international obligation is an essentially relative question. Therefore, the nationalization of the Suez Canal Company was a violation of the international obligations of Egypt in that it altered in a material manner the conditions of operation of the Canal.

International Factors Bearing on the International Status of the Suez Canal Company

In addition to the express references made to international agreements discussed elsewhere in this article, various other international factors have also been adduced to establish the unique status of the Suez Canal Company. One consequence of such a status has already been discussed; namely, the applicability of public international law to it. Another consequence contended for appears to be that such an international company with its unique status would not be subject to nationalization. Whether this would flow from a rule of public international law or as an exception to the municipal law respecting nationalizations is not made expressly clear.

Thus, the French representative pointed out that during the period 1856–1956, the Egyptian Government had concluded more than a hundred agreements with the company "as it would have done with a foreign

39 U.N. Doc. S/P.V. 735, p. 3 at p. 5.   40 P.C.I.J., Ser. A/B, No. 53.
41 *Ibid.* 71.   42 P.C.I.J., Ser. B, No. 4.

power"; also that the Egyptian Government had not applied the following laws to the Suez Canal Company: the Egyptian customs law; the 1947 law on the repatriation of assets of companies, and the law regarding composition of Egyptian companies.[43] It is further asserted that the company is international by virtue of its capital, which is made up of securities issued in eight European capitals and printed in five languages; by virtue of its board of directors, which includes representatives of several nationalities; and above all by virtue of its purpose, which is the operation of a public service of value to the entire world.[44]

The Court of Alexandria is reported to have stated in 1940 that

> other undertakings have a purely national purpose, while that of the Canal Company is primarily universal in character, affecting the interests of all nations.[45]

It is also claimed that Egypt does not now have the right of a grantor over an international public service which had been conceded in the latter half of the nineteenth century by the principal European Powers.[46]

Under international law, *lege lata*, it does not appear that these internationalizing factors, however important and valid they may be, can invoke the application of public international law to the present controversy. In its judgment in the *Serbian Loans Cases* in 1929, the Permanent Court of International Justice said:

> Any contract which is not a contract between States in their capacity as subjects of international law is based on the municipal law of some country.[47]

Also, in a report of the League of Nations Committee for the Study of International Loan Contracts made in 1939, the Committee was of the view that:

> Every contract which is not an international agreement—i.e., a treaty between States—is subject (as matters now stand) to municipal law. . . .[48]

However, it is believed that these internationalizing factors, inherent in concessions of international importance, constitute cogent and persuasive arguments for the application of public international law. They constitute "points of contact" or "connecting factors" which a municipal or an international tribunal, applying established rules of conflict of laws, would take into consideration in trying to find and apply the proper law of the contract or transaction.[49] It is arguable that, in the light of these inter-

---

[43] U.N. Doc. S/P.V. 735, pp. 17, 18. For some of the instruments mentioned, see Recueil chronologique des actes constitutifs de la Compagnie Universelle du Canal Maritime de Suez (1950).   [44] U.N. Doc S/P.V. 735, pp. 17, 18.

[45] *Ibid.*   [46] *Ibid.* at 19.

[47] P.C.I.J., Ser. A, Nos. 20/21 at p. 41; see also Brazilian Loans Case, P.C.I.J., Ser. A, No. 20.

[48] League of Nations Doc. C.145. M.93. 1939. 2.A., p. 21 ([May 12] 1939).

[49] See generally, *e.g.*, 2 Beale, Conflict of Laws 1042 ff.; Dicey's Conflict of Laws 579 ff. (6th ed., 1949); G. C. Cheshire, International Contracts (Glasgow, 1949);

nationalizing factors, "the general principles of law recognized by civilized nations" ought not to allow the application of Egyptian law only, but that the rights of the parties should be governed by public international law. Where a concession agreement calls for continuing performance over a long period, it transcends the bounds of mere legal rights and legal obligations, especially when that performance has been faithfully discharged by the concessionaire.[50]

The Law Applicable to the Suez Canal Company: Its Submission to Egyptian, French and Other Applicable Laws

The Government of France has also contended that, because of its unique status, the Suez Canal Company is amenable not solely to Egyptian law, but also to French and international law.[51] The main significance of the applicability of these various laws has already been noted above. It is proposed here to examine generally what laws, other than public international law, might be applicable, and in what jurisdictions proceedings might be instituted.[52]

It was generally recognized at the time that the Khedive of Egypt, under the suzerainty of the Ottoman Porte, had legal capacity to grant the concessions for the construction of the Canal, subject to ratification by the Porte.[53] Both the original concessions agreement and the second "definitive" one modifying it were in the form of a unilateral grant signed only by the Khedive of Egypt, which expressly stipulated that the concessions were subject to ratification by the Ottoman Porte, in compliance with formalities of Turkish law.[54] Negotiations for the ratification lasted ten years. Finally, the French Ambassador at Constantinople, upon instructions of the French Ministry of Foreign Affairs, in concert with a Minister of the Ottoman Porte, was instrumental in preparing a third concession agreement signed on February 22, 1866, which confirmed the two earlier ones. The last one was in the form of a bilateral agreement between the Khedive of Egypt and the Suez Canal Company represented

---

F. A. Mann, "The Law Governing State Contracts," 21 Brit. Year Bk. of Int. Law 11 ff. (1944); P. C. Jessup, A Modern Law of Nations 139 (1944); F. A. Mann, "The Proper Law of the Contract," 3 International Law Quarterly 60–73 (1950); J. H. C. Morris, "The Proper Law of a Contract: A Reply," ibid. 197–207; F. A. Mann, "The Proper Law of the Contract: A Rejoinder," ibid. 597–604.

[50] See infra, pp. 289 ff.

[51] U.N. Doc. S/P.V. 735, pp. 17, 18; also see decisions of the Egyptian Mixed Courts recognizing the special status of the Suez Canal Company, e.g., Compagnie Universelle du Canal Maritime de Suez v. Campos, Egypt, Cour d'Appel Mixte, 1947, 59 Bulletin de Législation et Jurisprudence Egyptiennes (Pt. 2) 219; Credit Alexandrin v. Compagnie Universelle du Canal Maritime de Suez, Egypt, Cour d'Appel Mixte, 1940, 52 ibid. (Pt. 2) 185.

[52] On the legal status of the Suez Canal Company generally, see 1 Fauchille, Traité de Droit International Public (Pt. II) 294–339 (1925); 2 La Pradelle et Politis, Recueil des Arbitrages Internationaux 355 (1932).

[53] See Schonfield, The Suez Canal in World Affairs 20 (1953).

[54] See The Suez Canal Problem, op. cit. 3, 9.

by Mr. de Lesseps.[55] It was not in the form of a treaty, and was confirmed by a Firman of the Ottoman Porte of March 19, 1866.[56] Juridically, the two earlier agreements were invalid without the ratification of the Porte. However, Mr. Ferdinand de Lesseps, after the establishment of the Suez Canal Company, commenced construction of the Canal before their ratification. The Ottoman Porte was of the view that his action was illegal and in 1863 demanded that Mr. de Lesseps cease construction under threat of use of force, although the Khedive of Egypt had at least acquiesced in his action. It was only with the intervention of Napoleon III, the Emperor of France, that the dispute was settled in 1864.[57]

In these various agreements the terms *"le contrat," "convention," "Actes de concession,"* were used interchangeably. Mr. de Lesseps referred to the concession agreements as a simple "contract," a "public contract" and a "contract ratified by the *Firman* of the Suzerain Power," and as a "bilateral contract." The term *"firman* of concession" has also been used.

Under the Charter (*Statuts*) [58] of the company which was annexed to the Firman of the Viceroy of Egypt in 1856, the company was constituted, with the approval of Egypt, as a joint-stock company (*Société anonyme*) "analogous to joint-stock Companies authorized by the French Government, and governed by the principles of the latter companies." [59] The Charter further provided that the company, although it would have its seat (*siège social*) at Alexandria, was to have its administrative headquarters (*domicile administratif*) in Paris and was to submit to suit (*attributif de juridiction*) in that city.[60] The 1866 Concession Agreement further provided that the company, "being Egyptian, is governed by the laws and customs of the country." [61] Questions involving the status and internal affairs of the company were to be governed by French law applicable to joint-stock companies, and were in the first instance to be submitted to arbitrators in France, "subject to appeal, as over-arbitrator, to the Imperial Court in Paris." Disputes in Egypt between the company and third parties were to be governed by local law and by treaties, applied by local tribunals. Disputes arising between the company

[55] See Correspondence relative to the Question of the Suez Canal, with the Procès-Verbaux of the Meetings held by the International Commission at Constantinople. Commercial. No. 19 (1874), C.1075 (1874), pp. 7–8.

[56] See Recueil chronologique des actes constitutifs de la Compagnie Universelle du Canal Maritime de Suez 45 (Cairo, 1930).

[57] See Schonfield, *op. cit.* 40; 1 Fauchille, Traité de Droit International Public (Pt. II) 294–304 (1925); Sentence Arbitrale de S. M. Napoleon III, Empereur des Français (6 Juillet 1864), Recueil . . . de la Compagnie Universelle du Canal Maritime de Suez, *op. cit.* 35; Sentence Arbitrale de l'Empereur des Français, sur le Compromis relatif au Canal de Suez, le 6 Juillet 1864, 55 Brit. and For. State Papers (1864–65) 1005–1021 (1870).

[58] See Statuts de la Compagnie Universelle du Canal Maritime de Suez, le 5 Janvier, 1856 (hereinafter referred to as "Statuts"), 55 Brit. and For. State Papers (1864–65) 981, 985 (1870); Recueil . . . de la Compagnie Universelle du Canal Maritime de Suez, *op. cit.* 12–27; The Suez Canal, *op. cit.* (note 1 above) 11.

[59] Statuts, Arts. 1, 73.   [60] Statuts, Art. 73.

[61] Concession Agreement of Feb. 22, 1866, Art. 16. The Suez Canal Problem, *op. cit.* 15.

and the Egyptian Government were to be submitted to local courts applying local law. Where all the parties were foreigners, litigation between them would be conducted "according to established rules." [62]

Analytically, the applicable law would be Egyptian, French, and extra-territorial law under the capitulatory system,[63] as well as other applicable law in accordance with established rules of conflict of laws. Even if the dispute were tried before an international tribunal applying public international law, as Judge Manley O. Hudson has observed,

> the general principles of law recognized by civilized nations [may] include some principles of private international law.[64]

It was early established that interpretation of the terms of the concession agreements would be solely within the jurisdiction of the Egyptian courts. Thus on October 28, 1872, the Tribunal of Commerce of the Seine handed down a decree in favor of the French company *Messageries Maritimes,* which had instituted an action in that tribunal to contest the right of the Suez Canal Company under the 1856 Concession Agreement to change the manner of levying tonnage dues. Mr. de Lesseps contested the jurisdiction of any foreign tribunal to interpret the provisions of the Concession Agreement.[65] The Ottoman Porte concurred by stating that

> the Suez Canal Company, whose principal seat is established at Alexandria, is Egyptian, and as such is amenable to the laws and customs of the Empire.[66]

Upon appeal, the case was dismissed on technical grounds.[67]

In 1874, for the first time, the construction of the term "local tribunals" was raised on the issue whether disputes involving the Suez Canal Company were to be heard before the French Consular Court or before the local Egyptian courts. An Egyptian company had instituted suit against the Canal Company in the Mixed Tribunal of Commerce at Alexandria. Since the opening of the Canal for traffic, all actions against the Suez Canal Company as defendant had been tried in the French Consular Court, although when the company was the plaintiff, actions were brought in the local courts when the defendants were foreigners or Egyptians.[68] During this early formative period both the French and British governments were of the view that the Suez Canal Company was Egyptian, and was subject to the jurisdiction of local Egyptian courts.[69] The Suez Canal Company eventually submitted to the jurisdiction of local Egyptian courts.

According to the Egyptian Government,[70] in more recent times, specifi-

---

[62] *Ibid.*

[63] On the Mixed Courts of Egypt generally, see Brinton, The Mixed Courts of Egypt (New Haven, 1930).

[64] Manley O. Hudson, The Permanent Court of International Justice, 1920–1942, p. 621 (1943).

[65] See Correspondence relative to the Question of the Suez Canal, with the Procès-Verbaux of the Meetings . . . Commercial No. 19 (1874), C.1075, pp. 20, 30, 83–84.

[66] *Ibid.* 21.   [67] *Ibid.* 165.

[68] *Ibid.* 8.   [69] *Ibid.* 15–16, 80–81.

[70] U.N. Doc. S/P.V. 736, pp. 1, 6; see also Comp. des Messageries maritimes *v.* Comp. Universelle du Canal Maritime de Suez, Sirey, Rec. Per., 1874, I, 145; Cie. Havraise

cally in 1925, 1931, 1939,[71] and in 1942, the United Kingdom Government had recognized the Egyptian national character of the Suez Canal Company and its submission to Egyptian law. The Suez Canal Company maintains an office both at London and at New York City. New York law requires that a foreign corporation doing business in New York must first obtain a certificate of authority from the Secretary of State before it can legally transact business.[72] There is also procedure available in New York for the appointment of a receiver of domestic assets of a foreign corporation that has been "liquidated or nationalized."[73] No reported case has been found as yet adjudicating the extraterritorial effect of the Egyptian nationalization decree.[74]

III. The Nature and Legal Status of Concession Agreements

Agreements between the government of a state and an individual or business association not possessing the nationality or the national character of that state, as in the case of the concession agreements of the Suez Canal Company, are of recent development in international law. It is only in still more recent times that international arbitrations and decisions involving expropriations or nationalizations of such concessions, owned wholly or predominantly by foreign nationals, can be found. Oil in the Middle East, Latin America and Africa, and basic minerals and other extractive products in all parts of the world are exploited under the concessions system. The vital effect which concessions have upon world economy, and in other spheres, warrants at least a brief consideration of the nature and legal status of concession agreements.

Péninsulaire v. Cie. du Canal Maritime de Suez, Feb. 15, 1924, Court of Appeal of Paris, Dalloz, Rec. Heb., 1924, p. 189; Case of Debbah et Consorts, June 4, 1925, Mixed Court of Appeals of Alexandria, 37 Bulletin de Législation et Jurisprudence Egyptiennes (Pt. II) 466; J. Shallam & Sons v. Compagnie Universelle du Canal Maritime de Suez, June 18, 1931, Mixed Court of Appeal of Alexandria, 23 Gazette des Tribunaux Mixtes d'Egypte (1932–1933) 304, Annual Digest and Reports of Public International Law Cases, 1931–1932, Case No. 137; Crédit Alexandria v. Hoirs Setton et Consorts, Sept. 26, 1940, 52 Bulletin de Législation et Jurisprudence Egyptiennes (Pt. II) 185; Case of Guiseppe Campos et Consorts, May 17, 1947, 59 ibid. (Pt. II) 219.

[71] See text of excerpt alleged by the Egyptian Government to be from Memorandum of the Agent of the British Government to the Mixed Court of Appeals of Alexandria in 1939, in U.N. Doc. S/P.V. 736, pp. 1, 5–6. The outcome of the case is not stated. The statement, on its face, appears rather damaging to the British case, especially the following language: "It [the Suez Canal Company] is Egyptian because it is granted a concession which has for its object Egyptian public assets and because its legal principal centre is in Egypt. It would be a legal anomaly to consider the Company at one and the same time Egyptian and non-Egyptian, i.e., universal. Such definition contradicts the general principles of law."   [72] N.Y. General Corporation Law §210.

[73] N.Y. Civ. Prac. Act. § 977 (b), (b) (1), (b) (19).

[74] On extraterritorial effect of nationalizations and expropriations generally, see Edward D. Re, Foreign Confiscations (1951); Ignaz Seidl-Hohenveldern, Internationales Konfiskations- und Enteignungsrecht (1952); "Probleme des Internationalen Konfiskations- und Enteignungsrechtes," 83 Journal du Droit International 380 ff. (1956); Kunz, "The Mexican Expropriations," Contemporary Law Pamphlets, New York University, Series 5, No. 1 (1940); Rado, "Czechoslovak Nationalization Decrees—Some International Law Aspects," 41 A.J.I.L. 795 ff. (1947).

The more recent nationalizations of major economic concessions, for example, the Anglo-Iranian Oil Company, the Patino tin mines in Bolivia, and now the Suez Canal Company, have a deterrent effect on international investments by nationals of capital-exporting countries in economically undeveloped areas which are necessary for world economic progress. It is believed that there should be adopted a rule *sui generis* applicable to concessions based upon "general principles of law recognized by civilized nations" which would not subject them to any particular system of private law, but to public international law, the law of nations.

In the award given in 1930 in the *Lena Goldfields Ltd., Case,* involving a concession to which the Soviet Union was at least a nominal party, it was stated:

> But it was submitted by him [counsel for Lena] that for other purposes the general principles of law such as those recognized by Article 38 of the Statute of the Permanent Court of International Justice at the Hague should be regarded as "the proper law of the contract" and in support of this submission counsel for Lena pointed out that both the Concession Agreement itself and also the agreement of June, 1927, whereby the coal mines were handed over, were signed not only on behalf of the Executive Government of Russia generally but by the Acting Commissary for Foreign Affairs, and that many of the terms of the contract contemplated the application of international rather than merely national principles of law. In so far as any difference of interpretation might result the Court holds that this contention is correct.[75]

The nationalization of the Suez Canal Company is, therefore, an *a fortiori* case. Also, in the award given in 1951 by Lord Asquith in the arbitration between Petroleum Development (Trucial Coast), Limited, and the Ruler of Abu Dhabi, respecting a declaration in the concession agreement that "[the parties] base their work in this Agreement on goodwill and sincerity of belief and on the interpretation of this Agreement in a fashion consistent with reason," the arbitrator concluded that the terms of the concession prescribed "the application of principles rooted in the good sense and common practice of civilized nations—a sort of 'modern law of nature.'"[76] The proposal of an International Loans Tribunal, annexed to the report of the League of Nations Committee on International Loan Contracts of May 12, 1939, included a provision that the tribunal should adjudicate

> on the basis of the contracts concluded and of the laws which are applicable . . . as well as on the basis of the general principles of law.[77]

The gap on this subject in the present legal order of the world community has been recognized in the *Survey of International Law* prepared by the Secretariat of the United Nations in 1949 for the use of the International Law Commission, which states that "while the principle of respect for

---

[75] 36 Cornell L. Q. 42, 50 (1950).   [76] 68 Law Quarterly Review 28–30 (1952).
[77] Report of the League of Nations Committee on International Loan Contracts, League of Nations Doc. C.145.M.93. 1939. II.A, at p. 41.

private rights forms part of international law, there is no adequate measure of certainty with regard to its application to various categories of private rights'' such as those founded ''in concessionary contracts.'' [78]

The term ''concession'' is not a term of art, and in the general sense embraces franchise, approbation, license, patent, charter, monopoly, grant, admission and concession.[79] There is a variety of opinion regarding its nature. Gidel, citing the definition of Aucoc,[80] defines a concession as

> a contract by which one or several persons are engaged to execute certain work in consideration of being remunerated for their effort and expenses, not by a sum of money paid directly to them by the administration after the completion of the work, but by the receipt of a return levied for a more or less lengthy period of time on the individuals who profit from the work.[81]

Mosler defines a concession as ''the grant to an individual of rights under municipal law which touch public interest,'' and states that beyond this the term ''concession'' has no fixed legal meaning.[82] Keith observes that treaty practice has been to treat a concession as merely a form of private contract.[83] In 1927, the German representative on the Permanent Mandates Commission declared that a concession was a one-sided right which depended on the sovereignty of the state, that the conditions of the concession were similar to those of a private contract, and assimilated it to European administrative contracts to which a government was a party. In his opinion, a concession might not be altered except to the advantage of the state.[84] The Report of the Transvaal Concessions Commission of 1901 did not define the term ''concession'' but proceeded to treat concessions as forms of administrative contracts.[85]

Concessions granted by the Soviet Union to foreigners during the period 1922–1927 were treated as exemptions from the prevailing legal order. It was stated:

> . . . [A] concession is a contract of the sovereign government with its class enemy—a foreign capitalist. . . . From the legal point of view, a concession implies an element of exemption from the general regime established by law. A concessionaire is granted rights with regard to the exploitation of the object of concession (in industries, concessions with regard to the industrial enterprise) which under general laws are not granted to a private business.[86]

Juridically, the term ''concession'' might signify (1) in international law, a grant by one state to another of political rights within its territory,

---

[78] U.N. Doc. A/CN.4/1/Rev. 1, p. 28 (1949).

[79] See, generally, Feilchenfeld, 4 Encyclopedia of the Social Sciences 154.

[80] Aucoc, Conférence sur les Droits administratifs, Vol. II, p. 269.

[81] Gidel, Des Effets de l'Annexion sur les Concessions 123 (1904).

[82] Hermann Mosler, Wirtschaftskonzessionen bei Änderung der Staatshoheit 79 (1948).

[83] Arthur B. Keith, The Theory of State Succession with Special Reference to English and Colonial Law 66.

[84] Official Records of the Permanent Mandates Commission, Session XII (1927), pp. 156–157.   [85] Brit. Parl. Papers, Cd. 623, 624 and 625.

[86] Vladimir Gsovski, Soviet Civil Law, Vol. II, p. 68, citing Karass, Concession, Magerovsky, Fundamentals of Soviet Law 356, 358 (in Russian, 2d ed., 1929).

as in the case of international concessions in China;[87] or (2) in municipal law, a grant of exclusive or non-exclusive rights, privileges or franchise, affecting public interest, to an individual, a public or private corporation, a state or other governmental body, or a mixed "public-private" corporation with the state and the private party as joint concessionaires.[88] The second group embraces grants or concessions made under the terms of international treaties,[89] and grants by the state, in the free exercise of its sovereignty or public powers, for the purpose of making attractive conditions for the investment of foreign capital by giving special privileges to the concessionaires in the form of tariff and tax exemptions, right of eminent domain, the guarantee of a minimum return on the capital invested, *et cetera.*

Buell attributes the existence of concessions partly to the insistence of foreign investors upon controlling the expenditure of money lent for industrial purposes. This control usually takes the form of a concession, which is

> a privilege granted by a government to an individual or group, of developing certain resources or of constructing certain public works.[90]

Concessions of this type were granted by governments in the Balkan countries, in the Near East, in China, in Mexico and throughout Latin America.

Generally, the concession or grant is of economic rights of a public or semi-public character, with or without consideration, over a defined area, for a definite or indefinite period of time, ranging from as short as 4 or 5 years to 30, 50, 70, 99 years or in perpetuity, by a governmental body which may be a unitary state, a component state, a federation, a province, a district or a municipality or a native chief of a colony.

An outstanding characteristic of the concession is that the grant is not made under legal compulsion, but at the absolute discretion of the conceding state. If this element of discretion is lacking, then in the strict sense, the grant is not a concession. That political pressure and indirect means might have been exerted to secure the grant does not necessarily invalidate the concession if the laws of the conceding state have been complied with.

The subject-matter of concessions falls into two main categories: (1) public utilities and (2) the exploitation of natural resources. Almost any kind of economic activity may be the subject of a concession. The exploitation of natural resources covers petroleum and other hydrocarbons, minerals, coal, timber, rubber, agricultural products and others too numerous to mention. In the public utilities field they embrace cables, tele-

---

[87] See W. W. Willoughby, Foreign Rights and Interests in China (Baltimore, 1930).

[88] See generally, A. Blondeau, La Concession de Service Public (Paris, 1933); R. Bullrich, La Naturaleza Jurídica de la Concesión de Servicios Publicos; Philippe Develle, La Concession en Droit International.

[89] See, *e.g.,* Act of Algeciras, signed April 7, 1906, 24 Hertslet, Commercial Treaties 742; English translation in 2 Malloy, Treaties of the United States 2157, 2178; 1 A.J.I.L. Supp. 47 (1907).

[90] Raymond L. Buell, International Relations 397–398 (1925).

graphs, shipping, roads, air transportation and the transportation of pilgrims, to mention but some of them. The concession may also be a monopoly on canal building, import and export trade or may be general commerce. The Suez Canal was a monopoly.[91] In the more important concessions the principal grant may be supplemented by auxiliary rights, such as rights over land, right of eminent domain, exemption from taxation and customs dues for a stipulated period or for the duration of the concession, right to exploit mines together with the operation of railways, stations and other appurtenances.

No legal significance can be attached to the term applied to the instrument embodying the concession. Thus, in 1670 King Charles II issued a "Royal Charter" for incorporating the Hudson's Bay Company, granting "unto them [the grantees] and their successors the sole trade and commerce of all those seas, straits, bays etc." [92] In 1825, there was an "Act of the British Parliament Relative to the Levant Company" which repealed certain acts relating to the Governor and Company of Merchants of England trading to the Levant Seas.[93] In 1838 there was a "Crown Grant" to the Hudson's Bay Company of the exclusive trade with the Indians in certain parts of North America.[94] In 1827 there was signed a "contract" by the "Supreme Government of the federal republic of Central America, of the one part, & Charles de Beneski agent of the New York Company of the other part" for the construction of a canal.[95] For the operation of its cables, the Submarine Telegraph Company received a "Charter" from the British Government in 1853;[96] a telegraph "Convention" with France;[97] and a "Concession" from the King of Denmark in 1857.[98] The British Administration in Palestine during the period of the Mandate entered into "An Agreement" for the Tiberias Baths concession;[99] a "Deed" of concession for the extraction of salts and minerals in the Dead Sea;[100] and a "Convention" regulating the transit of mineral oils of the Iran Petroleum Company through Palestine.[101] In 1933 the Persian Government and the Anglo-Persian Oil Company concluded an "Agreement" embodying the oil concession.[102] The French text of the agreement employed "Convention" interchangeably with "concession" and the British Memorial in the *Anglo-Iranian Oil Company* case submitted to the International Court of Justice [103] referred to the 1933 Agreement as the

[91] See Opinion of the Egyptian Conseil d'Etat, May, 1883, in 10 Journal de Droit International Privé (Clunet) 321 (1883).

[92] 33 Brit. and For. State Papers (1844–45) 1364–1376.

[93] 12 ibid. (1824–25) 531–535.   [94] 33 ibid. (1844–45) 1377–1382.

[95] 3 Manning, Diplomatic Correspondence of the United States, Inter-American Affairs, 1831–1860, p. 94.

[96] 56 Brit. and For. State Papers (1865–66) 1865.

[97] Ibid. 348.   [98] Ibid. 368.

[99] Report [to the Permanent Mandates Commission] on the Administration of Palestine and Transjordan for the year 1929, p. 194.

[100] Ibid. 182.   [101] Idem. for the year 1930, p. 230.

[102] League of Nations Official Journal, 1932, pp. 289 ff.

[103] Anglo-Iranian Oil Company Case—Pleadings, Oral Arguments, and Documents 74 ff. (I.C.J., 1952).

"Concession Convention" which had a double character: on the one hand, as a "contract" operating between the Iranian Government and the Anglo-Iranian Oil Company, and on the other hand, as an "implied agreement" between the Iranian and British governments, fully operative as creating an obligation in international law. The International Court of Justice, however, rejected this contention.[104] The general practice in Latin American countries requires that a concession agreement be ratified by the lgislature, and it is termed a "contract *ad referendum*." [105]

A number of international arbitral and World Court decisions involving concession agreements have almost invariably upheld the binding legal obligations which arise under such agreements.

An outstanding arbitration was the *Delagoa Bay Railway* case, in which the parties were the United States and Great Britain against Portugal, growing out of the latter's cancellation in 1889 of the railway concession in Africa. The award of compensation was made by three Swiss jurists in 1900.[106] This case is of special interest because, though the railway company was Portuguese, the beneficial ownership was in the hands of British and American nationals.[107]

The *Delagoa Bay Railway* case was relied on in the *El Triunfo* case before a United States-El Salvador arbitral tribunal in 1902.[108] In this case, compensation was awarded to American nationals, who were beneficial owners of a concession operated by a Salvadoran company with respect to steam navigation in the port of El Triunfo, after the cancellation of the concession by El Salvador. The Tribunal stated, *inter alia:*

> It is abhorrent to the sense of justice to say that one party to a contract, whether such party be a private individual, a monarch, or a government of any kind, may arbitrarily, without hearing and without impartial procedure of any sort, arrogate the right to condemn the other party to the contract, to pass judgment upon him and his acts, and to impose upon him the extreme penalty of forfeiture of all his rights under it, including his property and his investment of capital made on the faith of that contract.[109]

The abortive Treaty of Peace with Turkey, signed at Sèvres, August 10, 1920,[110] contained in Articles 310–315 elaborate provisions concerning concessions granted by the Turkish Government before October 29, 1914. These provisions served as the basis of the Protocol Relating to Certain Concessions Granted in the Ottoman Empire, concluded at Lausanne on

[104] Anglo-Iranian Oil Co. Case (Jurisdiction), Judgment of July 22, 1952, [1952] I.C.J. Rep. 93 at 112; 46 A.J.I.L. 737 at 748 (1952).

[105] See, *e.g.*, Sales of British-owned railways in Argentina and Uruguay, Brit. Parl. Papers, Cmd. 7405, 7629; Concession for the Construction of the Railroad Across the Isthmus of Panama (1847), 42 Brit. and For. State Papers (1852–1853) 1333–1352.

[106] U. S. Foreign Relations, 1900, p. 903. The contentions of the parties are set out in 2 Moore, International Arbitrations 1865–1899.

[107] See J. M. Jones, in 26 Brit. Year Bk. of Int. Law 229–231 (1949).

[108] U. S. Foreign Relations, 1902, pp. 838, 857, 859, 862.

[109] *Ibid.* 871–872.

[110] 29 Hertslet, Commercial Treaties 1126; 15 A.J.I.L. Supp. 179 (1921).

July 24, 1923, and brought into force in 1924.[111] In Article I of the Protocol, the British Empire, France, Italy, Greece, Rumania, the Serb-Croat-Slovene State, and Turkey, agreed that:

> Concessionary contracts ... duly entered into before the 29th October, 1914, between the Ottoman Government or any local authority ... and nationals (including companies) of the contracting Powers, other than Turkey ... are maintained.

Article 9 of the Protocol provides that the state acquiring territory detached from Turkey

> ... is fully subrogated as regards the rights and obligations of Turkey towards the nationals of the other contracting Powers, and companies in which the capital of nationals of the said Powers is preponderant, who are beneficiaries under concessionary contracts entered into before the 29th October, 1914, with the Ottoman Government or any local Ottoman authority.

Four cases involving the application of Article 9 were decided by the Permanent Court of International Justice—the *Mavrommatis Case* (two) in 1925,[112] the *Mavrommatis Jerusalem Concessions Case* in 1927,[113] the *Lighthouses Case* in 1934,[114] and the *Lighthouses in Crete and Samos Case* in 1937 [115]—in each of which the maintenance of, and the subrogation to, the concessions were upheld.

In the *Mavrommatis Palestine Concessions Case* before the Permanent Court of International Justice in 1925,[116] concessions granted by the Ottoman Government in 1914 were held to be valid,[117] and Articles 4 and 9 of the Lausanne Concessions Protocol were held to be applicable to them. In a later case with regard to the re-adaptation of the concessions, the Court upheld a preliminary objection to its jurisdiction.[118]

In the *Lighthouses Case* before the Permanent Court of International Justice in 1934,[119] lighthouse concessions granted by the Ottoman Government in 1913 were held to have been duly entered into and to be operative under the Lausanne Concessions Protocol of 1923 against the Greek Government. In a second case concerning *Lighthouses in Crete and Samos*, in 1937,[120] the concessions granted in 1913 were held to have been duly entered into and to be operative against Greece as a successor state under the Lausanne Concessions Protocol of 1923.

In 1924, in the case of *Germany* v. *the Reparations Commission,* an international award was handed down in which the term "concession" was defined. On the question whether the word "concession" as used in Article 260 of the Treaty of Versailles also included the right granted by a state to a private person or company to exercise a monopoly of production or sale of some product, as in the case of the Turkish Tobacco Monopoly, Mr. Beichmann (Norway), Arbitrator, said:

---

111 28 League of Nations Treaty Series 203; 18 A.J.I.L. Supp. 98 (1924).
112 P.C.I.J., Ser. A, Nos. 2 and 5 (1925). 113 *Ibid.* No. 11 (1927).
114 P.C.I.J., Ser. A/B, No. 62 (1934). 115 *Ibid.* No. 71 (1937).
116 P.C.I.J., Ser. A, Nos. 2 and 5 (1925). 117 *Ibid.* No. 5 (1925), p. 30.
118 *Ibid.* No. 11 (1927). 119 P.C.I.J., Ser. A/B, No. 62 (1934).
120 *Ibid.* No. 71.

In the word "concession" as it is employed in Article 260, are included grants of the right of exploitation of mines or deposits of petroleum, on condition that, according to the law of the country where they are situated, the grant has been made by the State or by an authority who relies for it on a special act and in virtue of a power in principle discretionary.[121]

The legal nature of a concession as a "vested" or "acquired" right was upheld in an international award in 1929 in the *Sopron Köszeg Local Railway Company* case [122] involving state succession, where the tribunal said, *inter alia,* that under most authorities and the international judgments which conform most nearly to modern views of international law,

> the rights which a private company derives from a deed of concession cannot be nullified or affected by the mere fact of a change in the nationality of the territory on which the public service conceded is operated.

From the foregoing survey, which has necessarily been of a summary nature, it is clear that there is no agreed definition of the term "concession" in international law. Still less is there any clearly established rule in international law, either conventional or customary, that all concessions are subject to the general right of expropriation or nationalization like any ordinary private contract. The few rules that are discernible have invariably been the result of precipitous or contentious actions taken and from which a rule or principle has been adduced to explain or defend the action, rather than the result of action based upon an antecedent inquiry into the rule and the extent of its application. There is a genuine need for reasonable profits, good will, and protection against outright economic spoliation for states rich in natural resources but lacking in capital to exploit them. On the other hand, an investor who invests capital in foreign states in major concessions should also be protected against measures amounting to intransigent nationalism or rampant xenophobia. Due to the disparity of the legal and "real" status of the parties to a concession agreement, the continuing relationship over a long period of time, and the mutual interest in the prosperity of the parties in the "joint venture," there are imponderables which no legal virtuosity can guard against. A concession agreement transcends the bounds of mere legal rights and legal obligations. The balance between theoretical *de jure* power and *de facto* financial power requires clearly-established equitable principles for the guidance of the parties before they plunge into the venture.

It is believed that "progressive development and codification of international law" should take care of this gap in the present legal order of the world community, so that there can be established a stable legal regime for the economic development of economically underdeveloped countries based upon "the general principles of law recognized by civilized nations."

[121] 1 Int. Arb. Awards 479.
[122] Annual Digest and Reports of Public International Law Cases, 1929–30, Case No. 34; 24 A.J.I.L. 164 (1930).

IV. The International Status and Control of the Suez Canal

In the present controversy, the fundamental principle embodied in the Convention of October 29, 1888, guaranteeing that the Canal "shall always be free and open, in time of war as in time of peace, to every vessel of commerce or of war, without distinction of flag," [123] has not been challenged. The Egyptian Government has declared its willingness to carry out the international obligations of the 1888 Convention.[124] It is objected that Egypt cannot be relied upon to have sole control and cannot be trusted in view of its past actions in blockading Israeli ships from passage in the Canal.[125] The users of the Canal have proposed the establishment of an international authority or body to take over and to operate the Canal in order to guarantee the right of freedom of passage in the Canal in accordance with the 1888 Convention,[126] which is being strenuously opposed by the Egyptian Government.[127] It is proposed to examine the problems raised from the following aspects: (a) right of freedom of passage in the Canal; (b) enforcement of the right; (c) supervision of enforcement of the 1888 Convention; and (d) legal status of the Canal.

Right of Freedom of Passage in the Canal

In the 1856 Concession Agreement, the Khedive of Egypt made a unilateral declaration that the Suez Canal "shall be open forever, as a neutral passage," to all merchant vessels on a basis of absolute equality, upon payment of the necessary fees and compliance with any regulations promulgated by the Suez Canal Company.[128] Although in municipal law such declaration might constitute an estoppel, nevertheless, it does not have the effect of neutralizing the Canal in international law. The Suez Canal Company is enjoined not to discriminate in fixing transit dues, and upon payment of such dues a merchant vessel has the right of passage.[129]

In 1873, at the Tonnage Conference, a Declaration was adopted which recognized the right of warships and auxiliary naval vessels to use the Canal as well as merchant ships.[130] This in principle, at least, admitted

[123] Convention of Oct. 29, 1888, Art. 1. English translation in The Suez Canal, *op. cit.* 49; The Suez Canal Problem, *op. cit.* 17; 3 A.J.I.L. Supp. 123 (1909).

[124] See statement of the Egyptian representative in the Security Council, U.N. Doc. S/P.V. 736, pp. 1–14; The Suez Canal Problem, *op. cit.* 317.

[125] See, *e.g.*, statement of U.K. representative in the Security Council, U.N. Doc. S/P.V. 735, pp. 3–17; statement of French representative, *ibid.* pp. 17–24.

[126] See Exchange of Correspondence between the Suez Committee and the President of the Republic of Egypt regarding the future operation of the Suez Canal, Cairo, Sept. 3–9, 1956, Egypt No. 2 (1956), Cmd. 9856; The Cairo Meeting of the Suez Committee with President Nasser, The Suez Canal Problem, *op. cit.* 303–351; text of Five-Power proposal of Aug. 21, 1956, *ibid.* 291–292; compromise Spanish proposal, *ibid.* 292–293.

[127] The Suez Canal Problem, *op. cit.* 317–322.

[128] Concession Agreement of Jan. 5, 1856, Art. 14. English translation in The Suez Canal Problem, *op. cit.* 7.

[129] See Art. 6 of the Concession Agreement of Nov. 30, 1854; Art. 15 of the Concession Agreement of Jan. 5, 1856.

[130] Despatch from the British Delegate on Tonnage at Constantinople, together with the Report and Recommendations of the Commission as to International Tonnage and the Suez Canal Dues, Commercial. No. 7 (1874), C.943, p. 11.

that conditions for passage in the Canal were under the protection of all Europe.[131] But it was not until this right was embodied in Article 1 of the 1888 Convention that it became an international right arising under an express treaty, without cavil. It is not proposed here to consider the important but separable issue of right of blockade.[132]

Enforcement of the Right of Passage in the Canal

Under the provisions of Article 9 of the 1888 Convention, Egypt is entrusted with the enforcement of execution of the treaty.[133] It is contended that the Egyptian Government cannot be entrusted solely with this task.[134] Historically, with regard to merchant ships, the 1856 Concession Agreement provided for a special Ottoman Commissioner to superintend the company in carrying out the execution of the concession.[135] In 1874, when Mr. de Lesseps threatened to close the Canal because he felt that the recommendations made by the International Commission regarding tonnage dues were illegal, the Ottoman Porte ordered the Khedive of Egypt to use force, if necessary, to enforce those recommendations.[136]

At the 1885 Conference [137] convened to establish the international system to guarantee freedom of passage for war vessels as well as merchant ships, British policy would not permit any encroachment upon the powers of the territorial sovereign, and enforcement of transit of belligerent ships in time of war was also entrusted to the Khedive. The system devised at this Conference was embodied in the 1888 Convention. Under treaty law, any change in the terms of the 1888 Convention would require the consent of the signatories. On the other hand, there is also the *clausula rebus sic stantibus* which in substance provides that, due to vital changes of circumstances, a party to a treaty might be justified in requesting a revision of the treaty on that ground.[138] It is by no means clear whether a con-

---

[131] See consideration of this Declaration, *supra*, p. 283.

[132] Respecting the Israeli position in the present controversy concerning blockade, see letter dated Oct. 13, 1956, from the representative of Israel to the President of the Security Council, U.N. Doc. S/3673. See also, generally, The United Nations and the Egyptian Blockade of the Suez Canal, A Study Sponsored by the Lawyers Committee on Blockades (New York, 1953); ''The Security Council and the Suez Canal,'' 1 Int. and Comp. Law Quarterly 85 (1952); Resolution of the U.N. Security Counsel of Sept. 1, 1951, U.N. Doc. S/2298/Rev. 1; U.N. Docs. S/P.V. 549–553, 555–556, 558; 658–664; 682–688; S/3296–3298, S/3300, S/3302; and ''Conclusions du Gouvernement Egyptien au sujet des plaintes des Gouvernement étrangers quant à la visite des navires neutres et la saisie des objets de contrebande dans les ports égyptiens,'' 7 Revue égyptienne de droit international 235 (1951).

[133] Art. 9 of the Convention of Oct. 29, 1888. The Suez Canal Problem, *op. cit.* 19.

[134] See, *e.g.*, statements of U.K. representative in the Security Council, U.N. Doc. S/P.V. 735, pp. 3–17, 9, 10; and French representative, *ibid.* 17–24, 22.

[135] See Art. 9 of the Concession Agreement of Jan. 5, 1856. The Suez Canal Problem, *op. cit.* 5–6.

[136] See Correspondence relative to the Question of the Suez Canal, with the Procès-Verbaux of the Meetings held by the International Commission at Constantinople, Commercial No. 19(1874), C.1075, pp. 138–141, 153–154.

[137] See ''Supervision of Enforcement of the 1888 Convention,'' *infra*, p. 299.

[138] See, *e.g.*, Harvard Research in International Law, Draft Convention on the Law of Treaties, 29 A.J.I.L. Supp. 662–663, 1096–1126 (1935); 1 Oppenheim's International

tracting party might unilaterally denounce the treaty. In 1941, the late President Roosevelt, in declaring the International Load Line Convention of 1930 [139] suspended and inoperative in United States ports and territorial waters, said that he was "exercising in behalf of the United States of America an unquestioned right and privilege under approved principles of international law." [140]

Supervision of Enforcement of the 1888 Convention

The 1888 Convention does not provide for procedures to be taken in case the right of freedom of passage guaranteed in the treaty was not enforced by Egypt, the party entrusted to do so in the first place. In this event, the general principles of international law would apply, namely, self-help, whether through diplomatic intervention or the ultimate employment of force. This lack of remedy, however, was not due to lack of foresight on the part of the framers of the treaty. Recourse to *travaux préparatoires* [141] makes this abundantly clear.

At the 1885 International Conference which drew up the draft convention from which the 1888 Convention is derived, there was a fundamental split over the question of supervision of enforcement of any treaty drawn up guaranteeing the right of free passage in the Canal. This basically is the problem confronting the states concerned today, namely, the establishment of an international "Users Association" to operate the Canal to ensure that the substantive right guaranteed by the 1888 Convention is enforced and made effective.[142] In 1885 a British proposal left to the territorial Power, the Khedive of Egypt, the enforcement of the treaty but no supervision over the manner in which Egypt would carry out this function.[143] The French Government, on the other hand, proposed the establishment of a permanent international commission, composed of the representatives of the Powers signatories of the 1883 Declaration of London, under the presidency of the Turkish delegate, with a delegate of the Egyptian Government sitting with a consultative voice.[144] The Italian representative also proposed that the representatives at Cairo of the Powers signatories of the Declaration of London should constitute a commission under the presidency of a special representative of Turkey.[145] The British delegate objected on the ground that it was incompatible with

---

Law 843–850 (7th ed.); 5 Hackworth, Digest of International Law 349–359; on a recent application of this clausula concerning the Suez Canal, see H. W. Briggs, "Rebus sic Stantibus Before the Security Council: The Anglo-Egyptian Question," 43 A.J.I.L. 762–769 (1949).   [139] 4 U. S. Treaty Series 5287 ff. (1938).

[140] See 5 Department of State Bulletin 114–115 (1941); 5 Hackworth, *op. cit.* 355–356 (1943).

[141] See Correspondence respecting the Suez Canal Commission, with the Protocols and Procès-Verbaux of the Meetings, Egypt No. 19 (1885), C.4599 (1885).

[142] See, *e.g.*, Exchange of Correspondence between the Suez Committee and the President of the Republic of Egypt regarding the future operation of the Suez Canal, Egypt No. 2 (1956).

[143] See Correspondence respecting the Suez Canal Commission . . . Egypt No. 19 (1885), C.4599 (1885), pp. 27, 48, 245.   [144] See *ibid.* 27, 47, 245.

[145] *Ibid.* 47, 245.

the bases contained in the 1883 Declaration which did not go beyond creating a system of guarantee only.[146]

The German, Austrian, French, and Russian delegates, supported by the Turkish, and eventually by the Netherlands delegates, asserted that freedom of passage in the Canal would be an empty phrase if the territorial Power were not included in the mutual servitude which was proposed. They cited the usefulness of the International Commission for the Lower Danube.

A compromise British proposal would have made the representatives in Egypt of the Powers signatories of the 1883 Declaration watch over the execution of the treaty. The other representatives prophetically declared that in order for the proposed international system to be effective there must be supervision of a collective and permanent character.[147]

It is readily discernible from the *procès-verbaux* of the Conference that the framers of the 1885 draft convention had not at that time foreseen that Egypt would occupy the position, nor take the step it did take in 1956. The Report of the Subcommission stated, *inter alia:*

> [The supporters of the French proposal observed] that Egypt, being a vassal of the Sublime Porte, would have neither the independence nor the authority necessary for enforcing the provisions of the treaty if she were not supported in the fulfilment of her task by an instrument of supervision emanating from a European concert; that lastly, any treaty concerning the freedom of the Suez Canal must, to be effective, provide explicitly and in a tangible form for the exercise and working of a constant supervision of its provisions.[148]

Legal Status of the Suez Canal

Under Article 10 of the 1888 Convention the Egyptian Government can take measures necessary for the defense of Egypt, including defense of the Suez Canal. Egyptian sovereignty over the Suez Canal itself has not been challenged in the present controversy.[149] It would appear that "imperium" and perhaps also "dominion" rest with the Egyptian Government. The Suez Canal Company was granted a concession "to operate" the Canal, but not ownership of the land over which the Canal flows.[150] At the end of the concession the Egyptian Government was to resume possession of the Canal without paying compensation for the Canal itself, although compensation would be paid for materials and supplies of the company.[151] The Concession Agreement of 1866 specifically provides that "The Maritime Canal and all its appurtenances" shall remain under

---

[146] See *ibid.* 26–27, 43, 88.   [147] See *ibid.* 245.

[148] *Ibid.*

[149] See statements of U.K. representative, U.N. Doc S/P.V. 735, p. 3; and French representative, *ibid.*, p. 17 at p. 21.

[150] See, *e.g.*, Concession Agreement of Nov. 30, 1854, Art. 1; Concession Agreement of Jan. 5, 1856, Art 1. On the general legal status of the Suez Canal, see 1 Fauchille, Traité de Droit International Public (Pt. II) 294–339 (1925).

[151] See, *e.g.*, Concession Agreement of Nov. 30, 1854, Art. 1; Concession Agreement of Jan. 5, 1856, Art. 16; Concession Agreement of Feb. 22, 1866, Art. 15.

the jurisdiction of the Egyptian territory.[152] Its nature has been described as being the same as that of a railroad monopoly then being granted in France.[153] It rather resembles a long-term lease of real property in private law where the lessor retains title.[154]

The 1888 Convention has preserved intact Egyptian sovereignty over the Suez Canal.[155] At the 1885 Conference [156] which drew up the draft convention from which the 1888 Convention is derived, the British policy, which prevailed, would not permit any encroachment on the rights of the territorial sovereign.[157] The international system guaranteeing this freedom of passage has been regarded as an international servitude which did not involve any restriction of the sovereign rights of Egypt.[158] Previously the Ottoman Porte had expressed the view in 1872 that Mr. de Lesseps, having only the "concessions of the undertaking," did not have the right to propose the sale of the Canal to certain European Powers then interested, or to propose the establishment of an international commission to which the Porte was opposed.[159]

Article 12 of the 1888 Convention applies the principle of equality to the use of the Suez Canal, which prohibits any of the contracting parties from seeking any territorial or commercial privileges or advantages. It further reserved "the rights of Turkey as the territorial Power." [160]

In 1882, British military forces, with the consent of the Khedive of Egypt,[161] had occupied Egypt for the purpose, among other things, of protecting the Canal from its threatened destruction by the rebel forces of Colonel Arabi.[162] The occupation continued after the rebellion was over, with the British Government maintaining that since the occupation had taken place with the consent of the territorial Power, it was not incompatible with the concept of territorial integrity of the territorial Power which was being upheld in the 1888 Convention.[163] In ratifying the 1888 Convention, the British Government had made reservation to the effect that insofar as the treaty was incompatible with the transitional and exceptional situation and would impede the liberty of action of the British Government

---

[152] Concession Agreement of Feb. 22, 1866, Art. 9.

[153] See Arnold Wilson, "Some International and Legal Aspects of the Suez Canal," 21 Grotius Society Transactions 127 (1935).

[154] See discussion *supra*, pp. 289 ff.   [155] See discussion *supra*, pp. 297 ff.

[156] See note 141 *supra*.   [157] See note 143 *supra*.

[158] See Correspondence respecting the Suez Canal International Commission . . . Egypt No. 19 (1885), C.4599 (1885), p. 110.

[159] Correspondence Respecting the Suez Canal, Egypt No. 2 (1876), C.1392 (1876), pp. 161–168.

[160] For text of Art. 12, see 79 Brit. and For. State Papers (1887–1888) 22; The Suez Canal Problem, *op. cit.* 19; 3 A.J.I.L. Supp. 126 (1909).

[161] See Proclamation of the Khedive respecting British Operations in the Isthmus of Suez and the Suez Canal, 74 Brit. and For. State Papers (1882–1883) 572 (1890).

[162] *Ibid.* 553–604.

[163] See Correspondence respecting the Suez Canal International Commission, with the Protocols and Procès-Verbaux of the Meetings, State, Egypt No. 19 (1885), C.4599, p. 1 (1884–1885).

during the occupation of Egypt, it would consider itself free to disregard any of the terms of the convention.[164] In 1904, the British and French governments concluded an agreement [165] which put the convention into effect on the condition that the international supervisory commission for the execution of the convention [166] would remain in abeyance.

Upon the outbreak of the first World War, the British Government on December 18, 1914, unilaterally terminated the suzerainty of the Ottoman Porte over Egypt, and proclaimed Egypt a British Protectorate.[167] After its defeat in the war, under the provisions of the Treaty of Lausanne, the Turkish Government renounced "all rights and titles over Egypt" as from November 5, 1914.[168] Under the provisions of the Treaty of Versailles, Germany consented to the transfer to the British Government of all powers conferred upon the Ottoman Porte by the 1888 Convention, and also recognized the British protectorate over Egypt as of August 4, 1914.[169] Similar provisions were embodied in the Treaties of St. Germain [170] and Trianon [171] concluded with Austria and Hungary respectively.

In 1922, the British Government unilaterally terminated the status of Egypt as a British Protectorate, and Egypt was declared to be an independent sovereign state,

[164] This reservation had been made earlier with respect to the draft 1885 convention. See Correspondence respecting the Suez Canal International Commission . . . State, Egypt No. 19 (1885), C.4599 (1884–1885); 79 Brit. and For. State Papers (1887–1888) 498–534; Correspondence respecting the proposed International Convention for Securing Free Navigation of the Suez Canal, Egypt No. 2 (1889), State. C.5673 (1889).

[165] See Declaration between Great Britain and France respecting Egypt and Morocco, April 8, 1904, 97 Brit. and For. State Papers (1903–1904) 39–41; Declaration between Great Britain and France respecting Egypt and Morocco, together with the Secret Articles, April 8, 1904. Art. 6 of the Declaration provides: "In order to ensure free passage of the Suez Canal, His Britannic Majesty's Government declare that they adhere to the stipulations of the treaty of the 29th October, 1888, and that they agree to their being put into force. The free passage of the Canal being thus guaranteed, the execution of the last sentence of paragraph 1 as well as of paragraph 2 of Art. 8 of that Treaty will remain in abeyance." 101 Brit. and For. State Papers (1907–1908) 1053–1059, 1056.

[166] For text of Art. 8 of the 1888 Convention, see 79 Brit. and For. State Papers (1887–1888) 20–21; The Suez Canal Problem, op. cit. 18; 3 A.J.I.L. Supp. 125 (1909).

[167] See Proclamation by the General Officer Commanding-in-Chief the British Forces in Egypt announcing the Establishment of a British Protectorate over Egypt, Cairo, Dec. 18, 1914, 109 Brit. and For. State Papers (1915) 436.

[168] See Art. 17 of the Treaty of Peace signed at Lausanne, July 24, 1923, British Treaty Series, No. 16 (1923), 117 Brit. and For. State Papers (1923) 543–591, 549; 28 League of Nations Treaty Series 12–113, 22–23; 18 A.J.I.L. Supp. 1 at 10 (1924).

[169] See Art. 147, Pt. IV, Sec. VI, of the Treaty of Versailles, June 28, 1919, 112 Brit. and For. State Papers (1919) 1–316, 79; 13 A.J.I.L. Supp. 151 at 222 (1919).

[170] See Arts. 102 and 107 of the Treaty of Peace signed at St. Germain-en-Laye, Sept. 10, 1919, 112 Brit. and For. State Papers (1919) 317–526, 363, 364; 14 A.J.I.L. Supp. 1 at 34, 35 (1920).

[171] See Arts. 86 and 91 of the Treaty of Peace signed at Trianon, June 4, 1920, 113 Brit. and For. State Papers (1920) 486–645, 520, 521; 15 A.J.I.L. Supp. 1 at 32, 33 (1921).

while preserving for future agreements between Egypt and themselves [the British Government] certain matters in which the interests and obligations of the British Empire are specially involved.[172]

The British and Egyptian governments concluded in 1936 a Treaty of Alliance [173] by which military occupation of Egypt by British forces was terminated.   However, Article 8 of this treaty permitted the stationing of British military forces in the Suez Canal Zone for a period of twenty years for the purpose of defending the Canal until such time as Egyptian forces were strong enough to do it alone.   It was specifically recognized that "the Suez Canal, whilst being an integral part of Egypt, is a universal means of communication as also an essential means of communication between the different parts of the British Empire"; and that

> The presence of these [British] forces shall not constitute in any manner an occupation and will in no way prejudice the sovereign rights of Egypt.[174]

A radical change in the British position in Egypt took place with the signing on July 27, 1954, of an agreement in which the British Government undertook to move out of the Suez Canal Zone within twenty months.   The United Kingdom Government retained the right to use the bases in case of an "armed attack" upon Egypt or upon any of the Members of the Arab League.   The agreement, which was to remain in force for seven years, recognized "the Suez Maritime Canal, which is an integral part of Egypt," as a "waterway economically, commercially and strategically of international importance."   Both parties expressed "determination to uphold the 1888 Convention guaranteeing the freedom of navigation of the Canal." [175]

V. The Matter of Compensation

The Egyptian decree [176] nationalizing the Suez Canal Company provided for the payment of the price of stock on the Paris Exchange on the day before nationalization, followed later by alternative offers to pay the average exchange price over the preceding five years, or to submit the matter

[172] See Circular Despatch to His Majesty's Representatives [Abroad] . . . London, March 15, 1922, 116 Brit. and For. State Papers (1922) 84–85.

[173] See Treaty of Alliance between the United Kingdom and Egypt, signed at London, Aug. 26, 1936, British Treaty Series No. 6 (1937), Cmd. 5360, 140 Brit. and For. State Papers (1936) 179–197; 31 A.J.I.L. Supp. 77 (1937).   On consideration of this treaty in the U.N. Security Council, see H. W. Briggs, "Rebus sic stantibus before the Security Council: The Anglo-Egyptian Question," 43 A.J.I.L. 762–769 (1949).

[174] Art. 8 of the Treaty of Alliance, 140 Brit. and For. State Papers 179 at 181 ff.; 31 A.J.I.L. Supp. 79–80 (1937).

[175] See Heads of Agreement, Anglo-Egyptian Defense Negotiations regarding the Suez Canal Base, July 27, 1954, Egypt No. 1 (1954), Cmd. 9230; Exchange of Notes, Oct. 19, 1954, British Treaty Series No. 14 (1955), Cmd. 9390; Exchange of Notes, Egypt No. 1 (1955), Cmd. 9466.

[176] Presidential Decree on the Nationalization of the Suez Canal Company of July 26, 1956.   English translation in The Suez Canal Problem, *op. cit.* 30–32; The Suez Canal, *op. cit.* 41–43.

to arbitration.[177] In any event, payment was conditional upon the Egyptian Government's taking delivery of all the assets of the company, including those located abroad.[178] The states concerned have proceeded upon the assumption that the nationalization was a *fait accompli*,[179] and that compensation would be paid in due course,[180] although some doubt has been expressed as to the economic capability of Egypt to pay.[181]

The Suez Canal Company has denounced the Egyptian offer to pay compensation as a "despoilment of the shareholders," and as "illusory" on the grounds that the Egyptian Government purported to nationalize the company's assets abroad, and did not define the following matters: currency in which it was payable; place or time limit of payment; procedure for making payment, or guarantee. Use of the stock exchange quotations was objected to as "inequitable" because they did not reflect the true value of the company's undertakings. The company has claimed indemnity for the value of the expropriated buildings and equipment; for expenses incurred after its nationalization, including wages paid, interest due, and amount spent in redeeming the company's capital and debentures, and also for loss suffered from the premature redemption of the concession, commensurate with the "true profit," and not merely twelve times the present profits.[182]

Following upon the nationalization of the company, Egyptian assets in the United Kingdom, France and in the United States were frozen,[183] both as a precautionary and as a retaliatory measure. The French Government has refused to recognize the nationalization as legal, and has declared that it would have no effect on the property of the company in France or elsewhere outside of Egypt.[184] Before the Canal was closed due to military operations, shipowners had been variously instructed by their governments to pay transit dues to the Suez Canal Company, or to the new body established by the Egyptian Government, and some were uninstructed, resulting in about 50 to 60 percent of the dues being still paid to the Suez Canal Company.[185] Reliable financial figures are hard to come by. The stock of the

[177] See statement of Egyptian representative in Security Council on Oct. 8, 1956, U.N. Doc. S/P.V. 736, p. 1 at p. 3; United Nations Review, Vol. 3, No. 5, p. 46 (1956).

[178] Art. 1 of Presidential Decree, *loc. cit.*

[179] See, *e.g.*, letter of Sept. 7 from Chairman of Suez Committee to President Nasser, in Exchange of Correspondence between the Suez Committee and the President of the Republic of Egypt . . . Egypt No. 2 (1956), p. 7.

[180] See, *e.g.*, Resolution of Security Council adopted on Oct. 13, 1956, U.N. Doc. S/P.V. 743; Requirements for a Settlement of the Suez Canal Situation, United Nations Review, Vol. 3, No. 5, pp. 19 ff. (1956).

[181] The Times (London), Aug. 2, 1956, p. 9, col. 7.

[182] See The Suez Canal Company and the Decision Taken by the Egyptian Government on 26th July, 1956 (26th July–15th September 1956), pp. 5, 19, 22–23.

[183] See *ibid.* 23; New York Times, July 29, 1956, p. 1, col. 8, p. 3, col. 1; Aug. 1, 1956, p. 1, col. 1.

[184] The Suez Canal Company and the Decision Taken by the Egyptian Government, *op. cit.* 5. See New York Times, Feb. 13, 1957, reporting the introduction of a bill in the French National Assembly declaring the company to be a French company not subject to the laws of any foreign state.

[185] The Suez Canal Company, *op. cit.* (note 182) 26–27.

Suez Canal Company has been estimated by the British Government to amount to about seventy-eight million English pounds, while the company's announced estimates place them at about U. S. $233,000,000.[186]

As calculation of compensation is essentially a technical matter of expert accounting, it is not proposed to examine the matter in this article.[187] However, a reference to certain judicial decisions and the practice of states, which constitute the principal sources of international law, may be in order.

In the case of the *Chorzòw Factory (Claim for Indemnity, Merits)*,[188] the Permanent Court of International Justice drew a clear distinction between the consequences of an expropriation which is lawful and the consequences of one which is unlawful. A lawful expropriation requires the payment only of "fair compensation" equal "to the value of the undertaking at the moment of dispossession, plus interest to the day of payment." [189] In case of an expropriation in violation of international law, such as breach of a concession agreement, the expropriating state, in addition to paying fair compensation, must also pay damages for loss sustained by the injured party.

As a result of extended diplomatic exchanges between the governments of the United States and Mexico in 1937 over the expropriation of oil and agrarian properties in the form of concessions granted to United States nationals, there emerged a rule of international law on compensation which generally has been accepted as accurate. In 1938 Secretary of State Hull wrote to the Mexican Ambassador in Washington:

> We cannot question the right of a foreign government to treat its own nationals in this fashion if it so desires. This is a matter of domestic concern. But we cannot admit a foreign government may take property of American nationals in disregard of the rule of compensation under international law.[190]

In a later note written in 1940 he said:

> The right to expropriate property is coupled with and conditioned on the obligation to make adequate, effective and prompt compensation. The legality of an expropriation is in fact dependent upon the observance of this requirement.[191]

Previously, the Netherlands Government had also declared:

> that even in cases when circumstances oblige a government to expropriate private property, it is a condition *sine qua non* that the properties expropriated must be exactly defined, and that if the authority

---

[186] New York Times, Aug. 12, 1956, p. 3.

[187] See, *e.g.*, G. Walker and R. H. B. Condie, ''Compensation in Nationalized Industries,'' in Problems of Nationalized Industry (Robson ed.) 54–72 (1952); Note, ''British Nationalization of Industry—Compensation to Owners of Expropriated Property,'' 97 U. Pa. L. Rev. 520 (1949); M. B. Cairns, ''Some Legal Aspects of Compensation of Nationalized Assets,'' 16 Law and Contemporary Problems 594–619 (1951).

[188] P.C.I.J., Ser. A, No. 17 (1927).　　　[189] *Ibid.* 46–48.

[190] 3 Hackworth, Digest of International Law 656 (1942).

[191] *Ibid.* 662.

takes immediate possession of such goods a just and prompt indemnity shall be immediately and effectively guaranteed.[192]

The general view that there is an international duty to provide compensation which exists apart from the provisions of municipal law is subscribed to by a number of writers on international law, such as Whiteman,[193] Freeman,[194] Kaufmann,[195] Gidel,[196] Fauchille and Sibert.[197]

After the second World War, especially during the period 1945–1950, large-scale nationalizations took place in such countries as France, Italy,[198] Czechoslovakia,[199] Yugoslavia, Poland, England,[200] Hungary and Rumania.[201] Respecting aliens affected by such measures, the general practice in recent years has been for the nationalizing state and the state whose nationals are affected, to conclude agreements providing for the payment by the former government to the latter of a lump sum in final discharge of all the pecuniary obligations of the nationalizing state. The government of the state receiving the compensation undertakes to distribute the sum so received among its nationals affected. The principal examples of such agreements are provided by those made by the United Kingdom with Poland in 1947,[202] with Yugoslavia in 1948,[203] and with Czechoslovakia in 1949.[204] Similar treaties have been concluded by the United Kingdom with France,[205] and between France and Czechoslovakia and Poland and between Switzerland and Czechoslovakia and Yugoslavia.[206] However, it is nowhere suggested that compensation should either be determined unilaterally or that it should take the form of vague and noncommittal promises to pay unspecified sums at uncertain dates.

On the question of payment of "prompt, adequate and effective" compensation in the nationalization of foreign property, there was a body of opinion at the 1952 Siena Session of the Institute of International Law to

[192] Documents on International Affairs (Royal Institute of International Affairs), 1938, Vol. I, p. 472.

[193] Damages in International Law 1386 (1937).

[194] The International Responsibility of States for Denial of Justice 518 (1938).

[195] 54 Recueil des Cours de l'Académie de Droit International 429 (1935).

[196] Revue de Droit International Public, 1925, p. 22.

[197] 32 Revue Générale de Droit International Public 22 (1925).

[198] See, e.g., Mario Einaudi, Maurice Byé, Ernesto Rossi, Nationalization in France and Italy (Ithaca, 1955).

[199] See, e.g., A. R. Rado, "Czechoslovak Nationalization Decrees: Some International Aspects," 41 A.J.I.L. 795–806 (1947).

[200] See, e.g., W. A. Robson, Problems of Nationalized Industry (London, 1952).

[201] See, e.g., Joyce Gutteridge, "Expropriation and Nationalization in Hungary, Bulgaria and Roumania," 1 Int. and Comp. L. Q. 14–28 (1952).

[202] British Treaty Series No. 10 (1949), Cmd. 7627.

[203] Ibid., No. 2 (1949), Cmd. 7600; see also U. S. agreement of 1948 with Yugoslavia, 62 Stat. 2658; Z. R. Rode, "The International Claims Commission of the United States," 47 A.J.I.L. 615 (1953); and Alfred Drucker, "Compensation for Nationalized Property: The British Practice," 49 A.J.I.L. 477 (1955).

[204] British Treaty Series, No. 61 (1949), Cmd. 7798.

[205] Ibid., No. 34 (1951), Cmd. 8224.

[206] See N. R. Doman, "Compensation for Nationalised Property in Post-War Europe," 3 Int. Law Q. 323–342 (1950).

the effect that a nationalizing state fulfills its obligations as to the payment of compensation by the payment of such compensation as is reasonable in the circumstances, taking into consideration the whole of its national economy.[207]

VI. SUMMARY OF CONCLUSIONS

1. It would seem that the contention that the concession agreements of the Suez Canal Company form an integral part of the Convention of October 29, 1888, because they were referred to both in the preamble and in the text of the treaty is not borne out by the *travaux préparatoires* respecting that treaty. This historic fact appears to have been overlooked so far by the states concerned in the present controversy.

2. It is at least arguable, based upon a reasonable interpretation of certain decisions of the Permanent Court of International Justice, that the Declaration made by the Ottoman Porte on December 1, 1873, established *per se* the objective international status of the Suez Canal Company, which would be a sufficient basis for the application of public international law. Consequently the company was no longer within the exclusive domestic jurisdiction of Egypt, and its nationalization was a violation of public international law. As far as is discernible, this thesis has not been widely raised.

3. There is no agreed definition in international law of the term "concession," or its character and legal status. Still less is there a clearly established right in international law on the part of a conceding state to nationalize or expropriate a concession as if it were merely a private contract. It is believed that a rule *sui generis,* based upon "the general principles of law recognized by civilized nations," and applying public international law, is the proper law to govern the legal obligations and continuing relationship of the parties, which transcend merely legal rights and legal obligations as they presently exist.

4. The proposal to establish an international body to control, operate and maintain the Suez Canal as an international waterway raises a political question, and, this article being primarily a legal analysis of limited aspects of the controversy, comment will be withheld.

[207] See 44 Annuaire de l'Institut de Droit International (Session de Sienne, 1952, II) 251–323.

Passage Through the Suez Canal
of Israel-Bound Cargo and Israel Ships

LEO GROSS

I. Introduction

The purported nationalization of the Universal Company of the Suez Maritime Canal by the Egyptian Decree of July 26, 1956, refreshed the interest of the international community in the long-lingering dispute over restrictions imposed by Egypt on the passage of cargoes bound for Israeli ports and the prohibition of the passage of Israeli ships through the Suez Canal. At the 22-Power London Conference, August 16–23, 1956, representatives of several governments referred to these restrictions [1] and

> it was pointed out that Egypt is in defiance, really, of a decision by the Security Council of the United Nations, taken in 1951 . . . which was reaffirmed again . . . in 1953, that under the terms of the Treaty of 1888 the Israeli shipping was entitled to go through and that Egypt was not entitled to bar it as it was doing.[2]

It is probably not altogether speculative to assume that it was with this situation in mind that the eighteen governments participating in the London Conference included in their Statement the following principle: "Insulation of the operation of the Canal from the influence of the politics of any nation." [3] This principle, one of the six which were to form the basis of any settlement of the Suez question, was voted upon in the Security Council on October 13, 1956, and received unanimous approval.[4]

In the recent Middle East situation, which assumed the character of an acute crisis with the military action of Israel launched on October 29, 1956, to remove the bases of the guerrilla raiders in the Gaza strip, and which was followed by the combined Anglo-French action to secure the

---

[1] See remarks made by the representatives of France, New Zealand, Iran, Netherlands and India. The Suez Canal Problem, July 26–September 22, 1956, pp. 91, 112, 128, 145, 164 (State Dept. Pub. 6392).

[2] Secretary of State John Foster Dulles at the news conference Aug. 28, 1956. *Ibid.* 298. The statement by Mr. Dulles, which is inaccurate in part, was in response to the following question: "Mr. Secretary, was Israel's right of passage through the Suez (Canal) in any way discussed at the London Conference?"

[3] *Ibid.* 308.

[4] As adopted by the Security Council, principle (3) is phrased as follows: "The operation of the Canal should be insulated from the politics of any country." In this connection principle (1) is also directly relevant: "There should be free and open transit through the Canal without discrimination, overt or covert—this covers both political and technical aspects." Security Council, Official Records, 743rd Meeting, Oct. 13, 1956, p. 18, par. 105, and Doc. S/3671.

Canal, the restrictions imposed by Egypt in the Canal also played a significant rôle. The first resolution adopted on November 2, 1956, by the General Assembly during its First Emergency Special Session, urged that

> upon the cease-fire being effective, steps be taken to reopen the Suez Canal and restore secure freedom of navigation.[5]

The Egyptian view that the state of war, initiated by Egypt on March 15, 1948, continued in spite of the General Armistice Agreement with Israel of February 24, 1949, and that Egypt derived from this certain rights of belligerency, namely, the right of visit, search and seizure, was an important element in the debates of the General Assembly and the negotiations leading to the withdrawal of Israeli troops from Egypt and the Gaza strip. It is unnecessary to review in detail the various relevant statements. Suffice it to recall that President Dwight D. Eisenhower in his address to the nation of February 20, 1957, recalled that "Egypt ignored the United Nations in exercising belligerent rights in relation to Israeli shipping in the Suez Canal and in the Gulf of Aqaba." After noting that Egypt, "by accepting the Six Principles adopted by the Security Council last October in relation to the Suez Canal bound itself to free and open transit through the Suez Canal without discrimination, and to the principle that the operation of the Canal should be insulated from the politics of any country," he declared:

> We should not assume that if Israel withdraws, Egypt will prevent Israeli shipping from using the Suez Canal or the Gulf of Aqaba. If, unhappily, Egypt does hereafter violate the Armistice Agreement or other international obligation, then this should be dealt with firmly by the society of nations.[5a]

When announcing in the General Assembly, on March 1, 1957, the plans of her government for withdrawal from Egypt, the representative of Israel, Mrs. Golda Meir, declared with reference to the above statement: "This declaration has weighed heavily with my Government in determining its action today."[6] However, neither the various resolutions adopted by the General Assembly in relation to the recent crisis nor the withdrawal of Israeli troops appear to have quieted public apprehension as to the continuation of Egypt's claim to belligerent rights. Repeated requests of the Government of Israel to secure assurances from Egypt, through the office of the Secretary General of the United Nations, "to the mutual and full abstention from belligerent acts, by land, air and sea,"[7] have been of no avail. The Secretary General reported to the General Assembly that

> the Government of Egypt reaffirms its intent to observe fully the provisions of the Armistice Agreement to which it is a party, as indicated earlier in its acceptance (A/3266) of the 2 November resolution of the

---

[5] Resolution 997 (ES–I). General Assembly, Official Records, First Emergency Spec. Sess., Supp. No. 1, p. 2 (Doc. A/3354).   [5a] 36 Dept. of State Bulletin 390 (1957).

[6] New York Times, March 2, 1957, p. 10.

[7] U.N. Doc. A/3527, Annex I: Aide-mémoire dated Feb. 4, 1957, transmitted to the Secretary General by the Permanent Representative of Israel to the United Nations.

General Assembly, on the assumption, of course, that observance will be reciprocal.[8]

A reaffirmation of this kind is of no practical value, since the Government of Egypt has at all times insisted that its restrictive practices and belligerent rights were compatible with the Armistice Agreement. It continued to do so even after the Security Council on September 1, 1951, called upon it to terminate such practices and declared that "neither party can reasonably assert that it is actively a belligerent or requires to exercise the right of visit, search, and seizure for any legitimate purpose of self-defence."[9] The position of the United States and other Members of the United Nations has also remained unchanged, and they continue to hold the view that Egypt, under the Armistice Agreement, does not possess belligerent rights.[10] It may be noted, however, that the Security Council resolution of September 1, 1951, does not express this simple view directly. The Council may have deemed it unnecessary to labor the obvious after having rejected explicitly every one of the specific arguments marshaled by Egypt in support of its practices. It is nonetheless remarkable that neither the Council nor the Assembly has yet seen its way to declare clearly and unequivocally that, between Members of the United Nations, a state of war, after termination of hostilities, is incompatible with the Charter. This, it is submitted, appears from the legal point of view to be the most promising point of departure for resolving the controversy over the Egyptian restrictions in the Suez Canal.[11] The controversy since 1949 has been the focus of legal argument principally between Israel and Egypt, and since 1951 between Egypt and the Security Council, as the latter has made its own the principal theses advanced by Israel. These arguments and counter-arguments will now be examined.

II. EGYPTIAN RESTRICTIONS AND THEIR JUDICIAL JUSTIFICATION

On May 15, 1948, Egypt announced its "armed intervention in Palestine with a view to restoring law and order, and with the object of putting an end to acts of violence committed by the Zionist bands."[12] At the same

---

[8] U.N. Doc. A/3527, Feb. 11, 1957, p. 6. Resolution 997 (ES–I), referred to above, urged "the parties to the armistice agreements promptly to withdraw all forces behind the armistice lines, to desist from raids across the armistice lines into neighbouring territory, and to observe scrupulously the provisions of the armistice agreements." Official Records, First Emergency Spec. Sess., Supp. No. 1, p. 2 (Doc. A/3354).

[9] Official Records, 6th Year, 558th Meeting, Sept. 1, 1951, p. 2.

[10] See, e.g., the statement by Secretary of State Dulles at his news conference March 26, 1957. 36 Dept. of State Bulletin 596 (1957).

[11] This paper is not concerned with the question of passage through the Straits of Tiran and the Gulf of Aqaba. Insofar as the restrictions practiced by Egypt in that area hinge juridically on the "state of war" doctrine, the arguments advanced with reference to the Suez Canal are equally applicable to it.

[12] *The Flying Trader*, Egypt, Prize Court of Alexandria, Dec. 2, 1950, Lauterpacht (ed.), International Law Reports 1950 (hereafter cited as 1950 Int. Law Rep.), p. 444. See also cablegram from the Minister of Foreign Affairs of Egypt to the President of the Security Council dated May 15, 1948, U.N. Doc. S/743; Security Council, Official Records, 3rd Year, No. 66, 292nd Meeting, May 15, 1948, p. 2.

time a state of siege was proclaimed, a shipping inspection service in the Ports of Alexandria, Port Said and Suez was established, and by Proclamation No. 38 of July, 1948, a Prize Court was set up. The Court was to "apply the rules of public international law, in their absence . . . it should decide in accordance with the principles of equity." [13]

Nearly one year after the conclusion of the General Armistice Agreement with Israel, these regulations were consolidated in the decree issued by King Farouk I on February 6, 1950 "on the procedure of ship and airplane searches and of seizure of contraband goods in connection with the Palestine War." [14] Article 2 provides for inspection by customs officers of the ship's manifest and cargo "so as to ensure that it contains no arms, munitions, war material or other articles considered war contraband and shipped directly to institutions or persons on Palestinian territory under Zionist control." Article 10 lists the categories of articles to be deemed war contraband, including fuel of every kind and "seized as prize." According to Article 3 of the decree,

> *force* may at all times be used against any ship attempting to avoid search, where necessary by *firing* so as to *force* it to stop and submit to search. Where the search subsequently reveals that the ship is not carrying any contraband it shall be permitted to continue its voyage.

Article 4 provides that

> if the crew of the ship resists the search by force, the ship shall be deemed to have lost its neutrality by reason of the hostile act. In that event the ship may be arrested, even if the search reveals that it was not carrying contraband and the cargo may be impounded for that reason, unless the owner proves his innocence.

The decree contains other rules customarily found in prize regulations, which are of no direct interest for the dispute. It is important, however, to stress the two facts: One is that the search is to be carried out by customs officials, and the other that force may be used, including firing, in order to force the ship to submit to search.

The representative of Israel also communicated to the Security Council an amendment to this decree, promulgated by the Council of Ministers on November 28, 1953, that is, more than four and one-half years after the conclusion of the Armistice Agreement. This amendment added to the list of contraband "foodstuffs and all other commodities which are likely to strengthen the war potential of the Zionists in Palestine in any way whatever." It also appeared to broaden the territorial applicability of the amended decree by providing as follows:

---

[13] *The Fjeld*, Egypt, Prize Court of Alexandria, Nov. 4, 1950, 1950 Int. Law Rep. 345 at 346.

[14] Text published in the Journal Officiel, No. 36, April 8, 1950. The English translation was submitted to the Security Council by the representative of Israel on Feb. 15, 1954, U.N. Doc. S/3179; Security Council, Official Records, 9th Year, Supp. Jan.–March, 1954, p. 6. The representative of Egypt referred to this decree as dated Feb. 9, 1950, Security Council, Official Records, 549th Meeting, July 26, 1951, p. 18, par. 69. He also listed there the regulations promulgated earlier by Military Proclamations No. 5 of May 15, 1948, No. 13 of June 6, 1948, No. 38 of July 8, 1948, and one of Nov. 4, 1949.

All the commodities heretofore enumerated shall be regarded as war contraband even when passing Egypt's territory or territorial waters in transit.[15]

These aggravations, in scope and geographical extent, of the restrictive measures were commented upon by the members of the Security Council and the Government of Israel, and they were not denied by the Government of Egypt.[16]

The legal basis of the Egyptian restrictions was discussed "from a purely academic point of view" by the Prize Court of Alexandria in the case of *The Fjeld*. Claimant argued that the seizure was null and void, as the procedure for inspection was carried out "at a time when no state of war existed"; that prior to May 15, 1948, no state of war could have existed between "the Zionist armed bands and the Arabs" and none could exist after that date because Egypt had not recognized the "Zionist State." [17] The Prize Court held that "the Palestinian conflict had begun some time before 15 May 1948 and that the Palestinian Arabs and States of the Arab League actively participated therein," and that "Egypt, in her capacity of member of the Arab League and ally of members of the League, found herself in a state of war with the Zionists, before 15 May 1948." [18] Regarding the claimant's second argument the Prize Court held that it was contradicted by the facts:

> Not only has the State of Israel been admitted to the United Nations but also on 15 May, the United States of America and Russia recognized the new State. Such recognition was unqualified and conferred upon Israel the capacity to proceed according to the laws of war, to seizures and to taking in prize so far as her enemies were concerned. The exercise of such rights by Israel against Egypt and the group of Arab States gives, no doubt, a corresponding right to Egypt to exercise the same rights against Israel. The non-recognition by Egypt of Israel as a State cannot prevent Israel from being regarded as a belligerent. Nothing in international law requires that the status of belligerency should be expressly proclaimed; such a status can result from circumstances. The Egyptian Government, by creating a Prize Court governed by the principles of international law, and by applying the rules of war in so far as concerns the treatment of prisoners and wounded and so far as concerns the conduct of hostilities, has clearly shown its desire to follow the rules laid down by international law in the Palestinian conflict.
>
> It now remains to decide the consequences of the conflict in so far as neutrals are concerned. It is established that the Palestinian conflict constitutes, from the legal point of view, a true war with international aspects. This imposes upon neutrals the duties resulting from neutrality and requires them to submit to the rights of the belligerents, whether or not such neutrals have officially proclaimed their neutrality,

---

[15] Security Council, Official Records, 9th Year, Supp. Jan.–March, 1954, p. 9.

[16] See remarks by the representatives of New Zealand, Official Records, 662nd Meeting, March 23, 1954, p. 3, par. 10; Brazil, *ibid.*, 664th Meeting, March 29, 1954, p. 5, par. 17; Israel, *ibid.*, 659th Meeting, Feb. 15, 1954, p. 17, par. 94; and Egypt, *ibid.*, 661st Meeting, March 12, 1954, p. 6, par. 28.

[17] 1950 Int. Law Rep. 345 at 347.   [18] *Ibid.* 348.

for neutrality is only one of the consequences of a state of war, and subjects neutrals, by reason only of their knowledge of such a state, to the action of the belligerents.[19]

It is important to note that the Prize Court took no notice of the General Armistice Agreement between Egypt and Israel. The Court presumably assumed, as the Egyptian Government did, that the Armistice had no effect on continued validity of the legislation concerning visit, search and seizure. If the Prize Court had taken the opposite view, that the conclusion of the Armistice Agreement put an end to the legislation of 1948, the re-enactment of virtually the identical measures by the Decree of February 6, 1950, after the conclusion of the Armistice Agreement, left the Court no choice. On this point the Court held:

> The existence of a state of war or of neutrality in so far as non-belligerents are concerned cannot be discussed by the Prize Court, for it is the duty of the Court to apply the law without examining its legality.[20]

It may well be that the Court, under the Egyptian system of law, was precluded from discussing the "existence of a state of war," both before and after the Armistice Agreement entered into force. The existence or non-existence of a state of war after the entry into force of the Agreement has been and continues to be the first point in the debates before the international forum.

It will be noted that the Egyptian decrees referred to do not deal especially with "enemy" ships. This is perhaps unnecessary as customary international law and the applicable Hague Conventions provide the necessary legal basis in time of war. The question whether and to what extent the Constantinople Convention of October 29, 1888, respecting the Free Navigation of the Suez Maritime Canal derogates from the usual rules regarding visit, search and seizure, has been considered by the Prize Court of Alexandria and debated even more extensively before the U.N. Security Council. The views expressed in the latter forum will be discussed below. In *The Flying Trader,* the Prize Court of Alexandria, after reviewing Articles 1, 4, 5, 7, 8, 9, 10, and 11 of the Convention, concluded:

> It falls to this Court to interpret the expression "the defence of Egypt and the maintenance of public order,"[21] a situation which involves the non-application of Article 4 of the Convention.
> The Court has already ruled that Egypt was truly a belligerent State possessing the right of capture *jure belli.* It follows that Egypt has in this connexion the right to take any measures necessary for its defence. The exercise of this right in no way runs counter to the provisions of Articles 4, 5, and 7, for the prohibitions contained in those articles cannot interfere with the natural right of a State to preserve its own existence, a right which cannot be the subject even of express renunciation. Egypt is the sole judge of the existence of a state of danger menacing her existence and rendering necessary cer-

---

[19] *The Fjeld,* Prize Court of Alexandria, Nov. 4, 1950. *Ibid.* 345 at 348 ff.
[20] *The Fjeld, loc. cit.* 347. [21] In Art. 10 of the Convention.

tain acts referred to in Article 4.[22]   All that the Convention requires, in the event of the carrying out of particular measures, is notification to the Powers signatory to the Declaration of London of 17 March 1885. Every armed conflict to which Egypt is a party, and especially a conflict with its neighbors, raises inevitably the question of the defence of its own territory, whatever the origin of the hostilities may be. The entire territory, land or sea, becomes, in the eyes of international law, a theatre of war authorizing the enemy to commit such acts of war therein as it may judge expedient.[23]   There flows from this the necessity of repelling aggression, whether by repulsing enemy attacks, or in preventing such attacks from taking place, which includes interrupting the means of reinforcing such attacks.

The provisions of Article 11 of the Convention, which states that measures taken by Egypt and Turkey in the exceptional cases contemplated by Articles 9 and 10 must not interfere with the free use of the Canal, cannot be construed as a restriction upon the rights of Egypt. The signatories of the Convention intended by this Article to confirm what is said in Article 1 [24] about free passage through the Canal in time of war and peace; but reasonable and necessary measures taken by Egypt do not interfere with such passage.[25]

Here again is a failure to take into account the existence of a complete armistice between Egypt and Israel, by land, sea and air.[26]   Whatever may have been the rights of the parties during the stage of active hostilities, the commission of hostile or warlike acts has been rendered illegal by the Armistice.[27]   If the commission of such acts is prohibited as between the parties to the Armistice, it follows *a fortiori* that they are prohibited

[22] In order to avoid a possible misunderstanding of the Court's argument, reference must be had to Art. 4 of the Constantinople Convention:

"The Maritime Canal remaining open in time of war as a free passage, even to ships of war of the belligerents, under the terms of Article I of the present Treaty, the High Contracting Parties agree that no right of war, act of hostility or act having for its purpose to interfere with the free navigation of the Canal, shall be committed in the Canal and its ports of access, or within a radius of 3 nautical miles from those ports, even though the Ottoman Empire should be one of the belligerent Powers." The Suez Canal Problem, *op. cit.* 17; 3 A.J.I.L. Supp. 124 (1909). It will be seen that contrary to a possible implication in the Court's language, Art. 4, far from authorizing Egypt to take any action in the Canal, expressly prohibits the exercise of any right of war.

[23] The Court referred here to 2 Oppenheim, International Law 187 (1944 ed.).

[24] Art. 1 of the Convention:

"The Suez Maritime Canal shall always be free and open, in time of war as in time of peace, to every vessel of commerce or of war, without distinction of flag."

"The Canal shall never be subject to the exercise of the right of blockade." *Op. cit.* 17; 3 A.J.I.L. Supp. 123 (1909).   [25] 1950 Int. Law Rep. at 446 ff.

[26] Art. II, par. 1, of the Egyptian–Israeli General Armistice Agreement, Rhodes, Feb. 24, 1949. U.N. Doc. S/1264/Rev. 1; Security Council, Official Records, 4th Year, Spec. Supp. No. 3, p. 2.

[27] The following articles of the General Armistice Agreement are relevant in this context: Art. I, par. 2: "No aggressive action by the armed forces—land, sea, or air— of either Party shall be undertaken, planned, or threatened against the people or the armed forces of the other"; Art. II, par. 2: "No element of the land, sea or air military or para-military forces of either Party, including non-regular forces, shall commit any warlike or hostile act against the military or para-military forces of the other Party, or against civilians in territory under the control of that Party." *Ibid.*

also in relation to third states, strangers to the conflict. The legality of Egypt's restrictions against third states has been open to question even during the hostilities, as evidenced by the protests addressed to Egypt.[28] They have become even more problematical after the end of hostilities.[29] On the strength of the Court's reasoning, Israel would have the legal right to commit acts of war—by land, sea and air—against Egypt as if the Armistice Agreement did not exist. If such acts are deemed prohibited—as they rightly are—to one party, by parity of reasoning they are also prohibited to the other.

The Court's contention that Egypt "is the sole judge" is untenable. Only the Convention of Constantinople could have conferred such an exclusive right (auto-decision), that is, the right to interpret the Convention with binding force for the other parties to it and the world at large. In the absence of such an exclusive competence, Egypt has merely the right of auto-interpretation.[30] That this was the intent of the authors of the Convention clearly appears from its Article 8, paragraph 1:

> The Agents in Egypt of the Signatory Powers of the present Treaty shall be charged to see that it is carried out. . . . In any case, they shall meet once a year to take note of the due execution of the Treaty.

The acts of the Egyptian Government have thus been placed under the supervision of the Contracting Parties.

It follows that the exception in favor of Egypt provided in Article 10 of the Convention does not escape the general supervision by the other Contracting Powers. Moreover, as the Court recognizes, the measures which Egypt "might find it necessary to take to assure by their own force the defense of Egypt and the maintenance of public order" under Article 10 of the Convention, are restricted by the requirement of Article 11, namely, such measures "shall not interfere with the free use of the Canal." The Court's statement that "reasonable and necessary measures taken by Egypt do not interfere with such passage" is for this reason not altogether in harmony with the Convention. Whether measures taken by Egypt do or do not interfere with "the free use of the Canal" is a question of fact. Certainly Egypt is authorized to take "reasonable and necessary" measures but these measures must not interfere with the "free use" of the Canal. It cannot be assumed, as the Prize Court apparently does, that any measures which Egypt regards as "reasonable and necessary" will not interfere with "free use." They

[28] Mr. Fawzi (Egypt) stated in the Security Council: "Most of the protests were lodged with the Egyptian Government even while the hostilities in Palestine were still taking place." Official Records, 553rd Meeting, Aug. 16, 1951, p. 24, par. 101.

[29] Referring to the Egyptian contention that a dispute existed between the protesting Powers and Egypt, Sir Gladwyn Jebb (United Kingdom) said: "If there were any dispute within the meaning of the Charter between one of the five delegations mentioned and Egypt, the Armistice Agreement and the whole question of Palestine would be quite irrelevant." Official Records, 555th Meeting, Aug. 27, 1951, p. 3, par. 10.

[30] Cf. Leo Gross, "States as Organs of International Law and the Problem of Auto-Interpretation," in George A. Lipsky (ed.), Law and Politics in the World Community, pp. 59–89 (1953).

very well may so interfere and in the case under consideration they have been found to do so by a large number of states.

III. Effectiveness of Egypt's Restrictions and Protests Against Them

Members of the Security Council have on four different occasions discussed the Egyptian restrictions from the legal, political and practical points of view.[31]   Members of the United Nations from the very beginning of the restrictions have also protested directly to the Government of Egypt against them.   Speaking in the Security Council the representative of Egypt stated:

> Up to today, the Netherlands has protested to the Egyptian Government no less than three times; Turkey, at least once; the United Kingdom, at least ten times; the United States, twelve times; and France, twenty-two times.   Most of the protests were lodged with the Egyptian Government even while the hostilities in Palestine were still in progress.[32]

Israel's complaints, chiefly juridical in nature, obviously also stressed the adverse effect on its economy.   In 1951 the representative of Israel stated that "vessels found to have called at any port in Israel are placed on a black list" and that the "threat of forcible interference acts as a deterrent to the normal trade which would otherwise have passed through the Suez Canal to or from Israel."[33]   The blacklist, according to the Government of Israel, contains 104 ships of "British, United States, Swedish, Greek, Norwegian, Dutch, Danish, Panamanian, Liberian, Swiss, Costa Rican and Italian nationality."[34]   The effect of blacklisting is that

[31] The first debate took place in October–November, 1950, in connection with the Israeli complaint: "Violations by Egypt of the Egyptian–Israeli General Armistice Agreement through the maintenance for seventeen months of blockade practices inconsistent with the letter and spirit of the armistice agreement," U.N. Doc. S/1794, Sept. 16, 1950.   The second debate took place at several meetings held between July 26, 1951, and Sept. 1, 1951, following the Israeli complaint: "Restrictions imposed by Egypt on the Passage of Ships through the Suez Canal," U.N. Doc. S/2241, July 11, 1951, Official Records, 6th Year, Supp. July–Sept., 1951, p. 9.   The third debate occurred at several meetings between Feb. 5 and March 29, 1954, regarding the Israeli complaint: "Enforcement by Egypt of Restrictions on the Passage of Ships trading with Israel through the Suez Canal," U.N. Doc. S/3168, Jan. 28, 1954, Official Records, 9th Year, Supp. Jan.–March, 1954, p. 1.   The final debate was concerned with the complaint by Israel arising from "the illegal arrest and detention of the Israel vessel, the *Bat Galim*, on 28 September 1954" and was spread over meetings held Nov. 3, 1954–Jan. 13, 1955, U.N. Doc. S/3300, Official Records, 9th Year, Supp. Oct.–Dec., 1954, pp. 1 ff.

[32] Official Records, 553rd Meeting, Aug. 16, 1951, p. 23, par. 98.   Similarly, the representative of the United Kingdom said: "During the past two years a number of maritime countries have made almost continuous representations to the Egyptian Government through the diplomatic channels, but all these have been of no avail."   Official Records, 552nd Meeting, Aug. 16, 1951, p. 4, par. 12.

[33] Official Records, 549th Meeting, July 26, 1951, p. 3.

[34] Letter dated Oct. 13, 1956, from the representative of Israel to the President of the Security Council, U.N. Doc. S/3673, p. 6.

cargo carried on these ships shall "be deemed intended for the enemy" and subject to confiscation and seizure, while the ships themselves would be denied the essential facilities necessary for passage through the Suez Canal. The existence of the Blacklist is, therefore, the most stringent of the deterrents whereby Egypt has prevented trading with Israel through an international waterway.[85]

In the view of Israel, "some 90 per cent of the trade which would have normally flowed through the Canal to and from Israel in the past eight years has been effectively obstructed."[36] Several ships were visited and searched, and "Egypt has confiscated and held goods of the value of $5,600,000 seized from ships exercising innocent passage in the Suez Canal."[37]

The representative of Egypt, while admitting that "some maritime Powers are, to our regret affected, although slightly, by the exercise by Egypt of its right of visit and inspection," and that "it is natural for them to want to complain," argued that "it is natural for us to want to survive."[38] Generally, the position taken by Egypt was to stress the small number of ships affected, the lenient manner in which she exercised what she claimed as her rights, and to hold out the prospect of relaxation of the measures in force. Thus the representative of Egypt spoke of "the relatively microscopic action of Egypt,"[39] and offered to show that "Egypt does little more than delay only a few ships for only a few minutes."[40] During the period

15 May 1948 to 24 February 1949, out of 8,009 merchantmen which arrived at Port Said, 548 ships were visited and only 71 ships were unloaded of contraband of war. During the same period, 282 ships reached Suez, and only two ships were visited and none was even partly unloaded. In the following three months, 2,139 ships arrived at Port Said, 195 of them were visited and only 25 were partly unloaded. During the same period 1043 ships reached Suez, nine of them were visited and none at all unloaded.[41]

In the course of the 1954 debate, the representative of Egypt declared that "since the Security Council adopted its resolution of 1 September 1951, no ship or cargo has been confiscated by Egypt" and that since then "only 55 suspected ships have been subjected to the inspection procedure

[85] *Ibid.* The blacklist includes 75 tankers. *Ibid.* 10. Blacklisting of ships is provided for in Art. 11 of the Royal Decree of 1950: Cargo shall be "deemed intended for the enemy whenever . . . (2) It is being shipped indirectly to such persons or institutions (on Palestinian territory occupied by the enemy). This shall be presumed in any of the following circumstances: . . . (g) If the consignor or consignee is listed on the *black list* kept for that purpose as a carrier of contraband for the Zionists."

[36] *Ibid.* 7.

[37] *Ibid.* 9. For a list of some of these ships, *cf. ibid.* 7–9. The representative of Israel said in the Security Council that "about 95 per cent of Israel's normal trade in products other than oil has been throttled through these restrictions, and, in the case of oil, 100 per cent of that aspect of Israel's import trade has been completely set at naught." Official Records, 661st Meeting, March 12, 1954, p. 31, par. 152.

[38] Official Records, 549th Meeting, July 26, 1951, p. 21, par. 79.

[39] *Ibid.*, 553rd Meeting, Aug. 16, 1951, p. 15, par. 62.

[40] *Ibid.*, 550th Meeting, Aug. 1, 1951, p. 3, par. 11.

[41] *Ibid.*, 549th Meeting, July 26, 1951, p. 20, par. 75.

out of 32,047 ships passing through the Suez Canal.''[42] After quoting figures showing an increase in the tonnage of goods passing through the Canal he said: "It is clear, therefore, that the measures of visit and search taken by Egypt have not in the least restricted the free use of the Canal.''[43]

Relaxation of the restrictions was referred to several times by the representative of Egypt.[44] After the Security Council failed to adopt the New Zealand draft resolution owing to the Soviet Union's negative vote, he declared that "now Egypt . . . will of its own free will move towards tolerance.''[45] The representative of Lebanon stressed that "this positive note which the representative of Egypt has afforded us . . . is something which we can all welcome and stress and end upon as a happy note.''[46] As the seizure of the Israeli ship *Bat Galim* by Egypt on September 28, 1954, was to show, Egypt's spontaneous offer of "tolerance" was either shortlived or fell far short of the Security Council resolution of September 1, 1951.

The statistics adduced by Egypt, far from proving the absence of any serious interference with non-Israeli shipping through the Suez Canal, were regarded by the representative of Israel and eight members of the Security Council as proof of the opposite, namely, the substantial effectiveness of the restrictions in deterring trade with Israel.

IV. Nature of the Restrictions

The legal nature of the Egyptian restrictions was discussed in several instances in the Security Council. Israel characterized these measures as blockade or "blockade practices" on several occasions.[47] This point is of some relevance in view of Article 1, paragraph 2, of the Constantinople Convention of 1888 which provides categorically: "The Canal shall never be subject to the exercise of the right of blockade." The Egyptian Government was accordingly at pains to show that the practices in question were technically and juridically not a blockade. Thus its representative declared in the Security Council:

> Egypt has never decreed or applied a blockade of the Suez Canal. Its action is confined to the boarding and inspection by customs employees of a very small number of suspected merchant vessels.[48]

[42] Official Records, 661st Meeting, March 12, 1954, p. 17, pars. 88–89.

[43] *Ibid.*, p. 18, par. 91.

[44] *Ibid.*, 659th Meeting, Feb. 15, 1954, p. 24, par. 130; 661st Meeting, March 12, 1954, p. 20, par. 105; 662nd Meeting, March 23, 1954, p. 12, par. 43.

[45] *Ibid.*, 664th Meeting, March 29, 1954, p. 23, par. 157.

[46] *Ibid.*, p. 24, par. 164.

[47] The Israeli complaint of Sept. 16, 1950 (U.N. Doc. S/1794), referred to "blockade practices." See also statements by the representative of Israel at 433rd Meeting, Aug. 4, 1949, p. 16; 517th Meeting, Oct. 30, 1950, p. 10 f.; 522nd Meeting, Nov. 13, 1950, p. 23; 549th Meeting, July 26, 1951, p. 13; 658th Meeting, Feb. 5, 1954, p. 12, par. 49; 659th Meeting, Feb. 15, 1954, p. 14, pars. 80, 88, 89. See also statement by the representative of the United Kingdom in which he referred to the "blockade practices in the Suez Canal," *ibid.*, 522nd Meeting, Nov. 13, 1950, p. 17.

[48] *Ibid.*, 658th Meeting, Feb. 5, 1954, p. 31, par. 163. See also 659th Meeting, Feb. 15, 1954, p. 24, pars. 127, 128; 661st Meeting, March 12, 1954, p. 6, par. 27 f., p. 15, par. 77.

This statement fails to mention the right of seizure or confiscation, which is also claimed by Egypt as a consequence of belligerency, and that the action of customs officers may be supported by force.[49]

It can readily be conceded that the right of visit, search and seizure which Egypt admittedly enforces in the Suez Canal is not identical with the right of blockade as the term is normally understood in the law of naval war. However, this is true only insofar as ships of nations other than Israel are concerned; for Israeli ships have been barred absolutely from even entering the Canal, and to that extent and in that sense it is not improper to say that Egypt has subjected the Canal to a blockade against Israeli ships within the meaning of the second paragraph of Article 1 of the Constantinople Convention. The normal meaning of blockade would, in any event, not make much sense in connection with that clause.[50]

Israel attempted only once to send a merchant vessel, the *Bat Galim*, flying her flag, through the Canal. The ship, described by the Egyptian Government as an "armed Israel vessel," during the night of September 27/28, 1954, "entered the Gulf of Suez through Egyptian territorial waters and advanced through the Gulf on its way to Suez." [51] It was further alleged that "the crew attacked two Egyptian fishing boats by automatic fire . . . sinking one of them, thus causing the death of two Egyptian fishermen," and that "this hostile act committed by armed Israelis inside Egyptian territorial waters constitutes a flagrant violation of the General Armistice Agreement." [52] The Commission investigated the allegations and by a majority vote—the Israeli delegate and the Chairman voting in favor—adopted the Israeli draft resolution and found "the Egyptian complaint regarding the *Bat Galim* case to be unfounded and that no provision of the General Armistice Agreement has been violated by Israel." [53] After the vote the Chairman stated:

[49] Arts. 1 and 3 of the Royal Decree of Feb. 6, 1950, see *supra*, p. 533. Another representative of Egypt stressed strongly the right of confiscation, saying: "To judge whether Egypt is entitled to practise the right of visit, search and confiscation of war contraband, reference must be made to the rules of international law. A state of war gives the belligerents certain rights. Foremost amongst these is the incontestable right of visit and search of ships in territorial waters, in ports, in mid-ocean, and in enemy waters, with a view to the confiscation of what is legally considered war contraband." Official Records, 659th Meeting, Feb. 15, 1954, p. 3, par. 9.

[50] The Egyptian representative quoted C. John Colombos, The International Law of the Sea, p. 539: "Blockade is the interception by sea of the approaches to the coasts or ports of an enemy with the purpose of cutting off all his overseas communications. Its object is not only to stop the importation of supplies but to prevent export as well." Official Records, 661st Meeting, March 12, 1954, p. 6, par. 29.

[51] Report dated Nov. 25, 1954, by the Chief of Staff of the United Nations Truce Supervision Organization in Palestine to the Secretary General concerning the *Bat Galim* incident, U. N. Doc. S/3323; Official Records, 9th Year, Supp. Oct.–Dec., 1954, p. 30 at p. 32, par. 8.   [52] *Ibid.* at 30, par. 2.

[53] *Ibid.* at 40, 41, pars. 34, 40. The Egyptian delegate appealed against this decision to the Special Committee provided for in the Armistice Agreement. This committee decided on Nov. 25, 1954, as follows: "The Special Committee finds that the words in the resolution, 'the Egyptian complaint regarding the *Bat Galim* case to be unfounded and' should be omitted, for the following reasons: The Mixed Armistice Commission should not adopt resolutions defining a complaint as 'unfounded,' as this may appear as

I have voted for the Israel draft resolution because conclusive evidence has not been produced that the *Bat Galim* attacked the Egyptian fishermen in the Gulf of Suez. I shall call on both parties to come quickly to an agreement for the release of the *Bat Galim* and its crew.[54]

After its judicial authorities "set aside, owing to insufficient evidence," the various charges against the crew of murder and unlawful carrying of weapons, the Egyptian Government declared on December 4, 1954, that it was prepared to release crew and cargo, and on December 23, 1954, it also declared that it was prepared to release the ship.[55] It appears that the crew was released but, according to the Israeli Government, Egypt violated her undertakings regarding the cargo and the ship.[56]

This incident appears to show that the Egyptian Government's practices regarding Israeli ships are more akin to the concept and purpose— interception of enemy ships—of a blockade than to visit and search and seizure of war contraband. If Egypt were concerned merely with visit and search, there was no reason for not allowing the *Bat Galim* to proceed on its voyage through the Canal after Egypt had satisfied itself that the ship was unarmed and that its cargo was not subject to seizure.[57] In view of these facts, admitted by Egypt, there remains the Israeli flag as the sole reason for not permitting the ship to proceed through the Canal. This has indeed been freely conceded by Egypt and defended in terms of the state of war or belligerency which she claims to exist.[58] In addition to the state of war as a ground for barring and intercepting Israeli ships, Egypt also claimed that the security of the Canal required the exclusion of such ships, as they might commit acts of sabotage within the approaches *to* the Canal or *within* the Canal itself.[59] It follows then that as long

restricting the right of either side to submit any complaint it may deem necessary; furthermore, it is unnecessary to describe a complaint in such terms after the non-adoption of the complaining party's resolution. This decision is not intended as a judgment on the facts of this particular case, as to which the Special Committee has no competence, nor is it intended as a reversal of the findings of the Mixed Armistice Commission in the resolutions as to the facts." *Ibid.* at 42 f., par. 48.

[54] *Ibid.* at 41, par. 41.

[55] See U.N. Docs. S/3326 and S/3335, *ibid.* at 44, 45.

[56] See U.N. Doc. S/3673, p. 8: "The Egyptian Government appropriated the cargo to itself, and has now commissioned the confiscated ship to the Egyptian Navy."

[57] Statement by Egyptian representative at 686th Meeting, Dec. 7, 1954, p. 16, par. 79.

[58] Said the representative of Egypt: ". . . in the state of belligerency which in our opinion still exists between Egypt and Israel, how can we allow Israel vessels to pass through the Suez Canal without interference, as the Israel representative demands?" *Ibid.* 24, par. 132.

[59] Said the representative of Egypt: "What guarantee have we that an Israel merchant vessel passing through the Canal will not be tempted to scuttle itself and thus obstruct the Canal for a considerable period, causing material losses and gravely damaging the interests of maritime Powers in general? Who can say that Israel vessels passing through the Canal will not be tempted even to lay mines in Egyptian territorial waters, either before reaching the Suez Canal or in the Canal itself? Lastly, who can say that Israel nationals on such a vessel will not try to find a way of landing in Egypt in order to damage the Canal or commit acts of sabotage in Egyptian territory?" *Ibid.*, par. 133.

as Egypt maintains the state of war with Israel, rights of belligerency are claimed which are in the range of economic warfare. As far as the ships of what Egypt calls "neutral" states are concerned, they are subjected to visit, search and seizure, whereas the ships of Israel are subjected to complete exclusion and interception in fact. Therefore, as far as Israeli ships are concerned, the effect of these measures appears indistinguishable from that of a blockade prohibited generally by the Constantinople Convention. The fundamental thesis of Egypt is the continuation of the state of war and exercise of belligerent rights in the Suez Canal as incidental to the former. It is therefore necessary to examine the validity of this thesis.

V. Continuation of State of War between Egypt and Israel as Legal Justification for Restrictive Practices

There has never been a deviation from the Egyptian thesis that a state of war continues to prevail between Egypt and Israel, and this thesis has been the chief target of the Government of Israel and of the Security Council, particularly in its resolution of September 1, 1951.

The General Armistice Agreement of February 24, 1949, with Israel "which put an end to hostilities and which was accepted as an indispensable step towards the liquidation of the armed conflict," in the opinion of the Egyptian Government, "did not put an end to the conflict and contains no provision concerning the right of visit and inspection." [60] Moreover, "the principles of international law uphold this view," [61] and the practice, "which is designed to ensure the defence of Egypt and the maintenance of public order there, cannot be construed as an infringement of the provisions of the Convention signed in 1888 concerning the Suez Canal." [62]

As regards Israeli ships in particular, Egypt contended that the Security Council resolution of September 1, 1951, which in any event it did not carry out, was inapplicable, as it was concerned with "the passage of neutral merchant vessels through the Canal for the purpose of trading with Israel, and not the passage of Israel vessels." [63]

1. *Compatibility of the Restrictive Practices with General International Law*

It may be conceded that according to general international law an armistice does not put an end to a state of war. It may also be conceded, although this was contested by Israel,[64] that the *de facto* hostilities which developed as a result of the military intervention of Egypt and other Arab States [65] resulted in a *de facto* state of war. However, what may be the ef-

---

[60] *Ibid.* 20, par. 100, and 21, par. 113.   [61] *Ibid.*, pars. 101, 103, 113.

[62] *Ibid.* 20, par. 104, and 21, pars. 105–111.

[63] *Ibid.* 23, par. 123. See also pars. 124–131.

[64] Security Council, Official Records, 549th Meeting, July 26, 1951, p. 10, pars. 10–36.

[65] This intervention has been regarded as aggression. Said the representative of the United States in the Security Council: "Probably the most important and best evidence we have on that subject is contained in the admissions of the countries whose five

fect of the Charter on the traditional doctrine of war and belligerent rights, particularly when some or all of the belligerents are Members of the United Nations, is a moot question. State practice has not always been uniform, and in some cases the cessation of hostilities has ended the state of war itself.[66] The general armistice is

> a living, dynamic war convention. . . . The elaborate armistice agreements of recent years have, in effect, rendered the preliminaries of peace obsolete. It is not inconceivable that the formal treaty of peace will suffer the same fate and that wars will one day end at the armistice table.[67]

It is, therefore, far more important to concern ourselves with the intended effect and scope of particular armistice agreements ending particular hostilities, than with the general question of the effect of an armistice on the existence of a state of war. It has been suggested that the question whether a particular armistice agreement has the effect of terminating the war is one of "construction of the particular armistice agreement concerned."[68] It may well be that an armistice agreement, even without terminating the state of war in the legal sense, puts an end to certain hostile acts such as blockade or visit, search and seizure.

2. *Compatibility of the Restrictive Practices with the General Armistice Agreement between Egypt and Israel.*

The Egyptian-Israeli General Armistice Agreement was signed at Rhodes on February 24, 1949, and entered into force on that date.[69] The Agreement was concluded pursuant to the Security Council resolution of November 16, 1948, calling upon the parties "as a further provisional measure under Article 40 of the Charter of the United Nations, and in order to facilitate the transition from the present truce to permanent peace in Palestine, to negotiate an Armistice."[70] The Agreement, pertinent provisions of which have already been quoted,[71] recognizes "the right of each party to its security and freedom from fear of attack by the armed forces of the other."[72] The Agreement prohibits all "warlike or hostile" acts against military, para-military forces and civilians, but does not specifically refer to blockades, or visit, search and seizure of vessels. Whether in the absence of a specific prohibition such acts are permitted, as Egypt argues,

---

armies have invaded Palestine that they are carrying on a war. Their statements are the best evidence we have of the international character of this aggression; it is a word which is not included in the text but which has been mentioned in the statements of these aggressors." Official Records, 3rd Year, No. 72, p. 41. The former Secretary General of the United Nations said: "The invasion of Palestine by the Arab States was the first armed aggression which the world had seen since the end of the war." Trygve Lie, In the Cause of Peace 174 (1954); *cf.* also 178 ff.

[66] Julius Stone, Legal Controls of International Conflict 639 (1954).

[67] Colonel Howard S. Levie, "The Nature and Scope of the Armistice Agreement," 50 A.J.I.L. 880–906 at 906 (1956). This day, however, in the view of the author, has not yet come. *Ibid.* 884.   [68] Stone, *op. cit.* 641.

[69] Art. 12, par. 1, U.N. Doc. S/1264/Rev. 1; Official Records, 4th Year, Spec. Supp. No. 3, p. 8.   [70] Preamble, *ibid.*, p. 1.

[71] See *supra*, p. 536.   [72] Art. 1, par. 3.

or are to be deemed prohibited by inclusion in the acts specifically banned, will be discussed presently. It is useful to recall, however, that the Armistice with Germany of November 11, 1918, specifically continued "the existing blockade conditions." [73] The Armistice Agreement in Korea of July 27, 1953, concluded "with the objective of establishing an armistice which will insure a complete cessation of hostilities and of all acts of armed force in Korea," provides in Article 2 A, paragraph 15, that the naval forces of the opposing parties "shall not engage in blockade of any kind of Korea." [74] The United Nations Command accordingly gave orders to its naval forces "to cease hostilities and blockade operations." [75] As the Egyptian-Israeli Agreement was concluded under orders from the Security Council, some light might be shed on its intended meaning by referring to the Council's debates and resolutions.

(a) *The Armistice Agreement before the Security Council: Interpretation and Construction*

The United Nations Acting Mediator on Palestine, Dr. Ralph J. Bunche, who actively participated in the armistice negotiations, stated in the Security Council on August 4, 1949:

> The Armistice Agreements are not the final peace settlement, but the only possible interpretation of their very specific provisions is that they signal the end of the military phase of the Palestine situation. . . . The entire heritage of restrictions which developed out of the undeclared war should be done away with. There should be normal access . . . there should be free movement for legitimate shipping, and no vestiges of the wartime blockade should be allowed to remain as they are inconsistent with both the letter and the spirit of the Armistice Agreements.[76]

The representatives of Israel, the United Kingdom and the United States concurred in this interpretation. The latter also stated that "the Armistice Agreements contain provisions which make them in fact non-aggression pacts." And the representative of China said: "We rejoice in the restoration of normal relations" between the parties to the Agreements.[77] It may be added here that in the course of the recent crisis in the Middle East, the Secretary General of the United Nations expressed the view, echoing the above statement by the United States representative, that Article 1 "assimilates the Armistice Agreement to a non-aggression pact, providing for mutual and full abstention from belligerent acts." [78]

The Security Council, by nine votes in favor, with two abstentions (Ukrainian S.S.R., U.S.S.R.), adopted a resolution on August 11, 1949, in

---

[73] Sir Frederick Maurice, The Armistices of 1918, p. 98 (1943).

[74] U.N. Doc. S/3079, Aug. 7, 1953; reprinted in 47 A.J.I.L. Supp. 186 (1953). It has been said that this "is probably one of the most complete naval provisions ever included in an armistice agreement." Levie, *loc. cit.* 906.

[75] U.N. Doc. S/3185; Official Records, 9th Year, Supp. Jan.–March, 1954, p. 40 at 42.

[76] Official Records, 4th Year, No. 36, p. 6. See also Shabtai Rosenne, Israel's Armistice Agreement with the Arab States 45 (1951).

[77] Official Records, 4th Year, No. 36, pp. 16, 19, 25, 27, 33.

[78] U.N. Doc. A/3512, Jan. 24, 1957, p. 5, par. 15.

which, making its own the interpretation submitted by the Acting Mediator, it

> Reaffirms, pending the final peace settlement, the order contained in its resolution of 15 July 1948 to the Governments and authorities concerned, pursuant to Article 40 of the Charter of the United Nations, to observe an unconditional cease-fire and, bearing in mind that the several armistice agreements include firm pledges against any further acts of hostility between the parties and also provide for their supervision by the parties themselves, relies upon the parties to ensure the continued application and observance of these agreements.[79]

It follows then that, although the Agreement itself is silent on the point, it has been interpreted authoritatively as prohibiting belligerent acts of visit, search and seizure. This construction is all the more indicated as the statement by the Acting Mediator was made and the resolution of the Security Council was adopted after the matter of restrictions had first been raised by Israel before the Mixed Armistice Commission. No dissent was voiced from this interpretation in the Security Council. No claim was made regarding the existence or continued existence of a state of war.

(b) *The Armistice Agreement before the Mixed Armistice Commission*
The question of the compatibility of the Egyptian restrictive practices with the General Armistice Agreement was first considered by the Mixed Armistice Commission in June, 1949, at the request of Israel in connection with a particular incident. At that time the Commission decided that "the blockade of the Suez Canal was not a subject that could be discussed in the Mixed Armistice Commission." [80]   In August, 1949, Israel submitted a second complaint of a specific character and the Commission decided:

> The Mixed Armistice Commission did have the right to demand that the Egyptian Government should not interfere with the passage of goods to Israel through the Suez Canal.[18]

Egypt appealed to the Special Committee. The Security Council, in consequence of the Israeli complaint before it, on November 17, 1950, adopted a resolution reiterating the substance of its resolution of August 11, 1949, and, "bearing in mind that the several armistice agreements include firm pledges against any further act of hostility between the parties," reminded Egypt and Israel of their obligations under the Charter and requested the Chief of Staff to report "on the compliance given to this resolution" and decisions of the Special Committee.[82]

The Chief of Staff, General Riley, reported to the Security Council on June 12, 1951, the decision of the Special Committee "on the question as to whether or not the Mixed Armistice Commission has the right to demand from the Egyptian Government not to interfere with the passing

---

[79] U.N. Doc. S/1367; Official Records, 4th Year, No. 37, p. 2 f., No. 38, p. 13.

[80] General W. E. Riley, Chief of Staff, Truce Supervision Organization, in Security Council, Official Records, 516th Meeting, Oct. 30, 1950, p. 22.

[81] *Ibid.*, and Official Records, 518th Meeting, Nov. 6, 1950, p. 20.

[82] U.N. Doc. S/1907; Official Records, 524th Meeting, Nov. 17, 1950, p. 15.

of goods to Israel through the Suez Canal.'' In view of the significance of this Report on the compatibility of Egyptian restrictions with the Armistice Agreement and the conflicting interpretations placed upon it by the Security Council, Egypt and Israel, its operative part is reproduced *in extenso:*

> In explanation of his vote, which was contrary to the stand taken by Israel, the Chief of Staff made the following statement:
>
> It is quite clear to me that action taken by Egyptian authorities in interfering with passage of goods destined for Israel through the Suez Canal must be considered an aggressive action. However, due to the limitation imposed by the text itself on the words ''aggressive action,'' this action is not necessarily against article 1, paragraph 2 of the General Armistice Agreement which states in part ''No aggressive action by armed forces—land, sea, or air—of either party shall be undertaken, planned, or threatened against the people or the armed forces of the other.''
> Similarly, I must of necessity consider that interference with the passage of goods destined for Israel through the Suez Canal is a hostile act, but not necessarily against the General Armistice Agreement, because of the limitations imposed on the term ''hostile act'' in the text of article 2, paragraph 2 of the General Armistice Agreement, which says ''No element of the land, sea or air military or para-military forces of either party including non-regular forces, shall commit any warlike or hostile act against the military or para-military forces of the other party. . . .''
> It follows, therefore, that I have no other choice but to cast my vote with Egypt that the Mixed Armistice Commission does not have the right to demand from the Egyptian Government that it should not interfere with the passage of goods to Israel through the Suez Canal.
>
> . . . . .
>
> As Chief of Staff of the United Nations Truce Supervision Organization, I am forced to base my position in this matter on the specific provisions of the General Armistice Agreement signed by Egypt and Israel. I deliberately avoid, therefore, any consideration of the status of the Suez Canal or the rights of any party with regard to it.
> While I feel bound to take this technical position on the basis of the relevant provisions of the General Armistice Agreement I must also say that the action of the Egyptian authorities in this instance, is, in my view, entirely contrary to the spirit of the General Armistice Agreement and does, in fact, jeopardize its effective functioning. It was certainly never contemplated at Rhodes that what is, in effect, an act of blockade or at least an act undertaken in the spirit of a blockade and having the partial effect of one, would be continued by one of the parties to the General Armistice Agreement more than two years after it had been signed.
> Although, in my view, there is no adequate basis for agreeing that the Mixed Armistice Commission has competence to deal with the question, it must be clear, and it certainly is to me, that the question cannot rest here. Either the Egyptian Government must, in the spirit of the General Armistice Agreement relax the practice of interference with the passage of goods destined for Israel through

the Suez Canal, or the question must be referred to some higher competent authority such as the Security Council or the International Court of Justice.

. . . . .

Because of the effect which such continued action will have on the implementation of the Armistice Agreement and the future operations of the Mixed Armistice Commission, I am compelled to direct a strong request to the Egyptian delegate to intercede with his Government to desist from the present practice of interfering with goods destined for Israel through the Suez Canal, since such acts can only be construed as inconsistent with the spirit of the Armistice Agreement.[83]

The representatives of Egypt, while belittling the significance of the Chief of Staff's finding that the interference is ''an aggressive and hostile act'' and ''contrary to the spirit of that (General Armistice) Agreement,'' [84] argued that the Report constituted a vindication of the Egyptian contention that the restrictive practices were not contrary to the Armistice Agreement.[85] Contrary to the views of Israel and other members, who argued that the Armistice Agreement was *sui generis*, the Egyptian representative claimed:

The fact that the Armistice Agreement is silent on this point (i.e. the right of visit and search), although it is fairly common practice to include a provision on this subject in armistice agreements, shows, as indeed the Mixed Armistice Commission has confirmed, that the armistice agreement of classical type concluded between Egypt and Israel expressed the joint will of the signatories and left them free to exercise their legitimate right of visit and search.[86]

Although this view was explicitly rejected by Israel (a fact which makes the assertion of ''the joint will'' rather problematical) [87] and also by the Security Council in its resolution of September 1, 1951,[88] Egypt persisted in invoking the Report in justification of its restrictive practices. It may therefore be useful to examine the Report in some detail.

[83] U.N. Doc. S/2194: Cablegram dated June 12, 1951, to the Secretary General from the Chief of Staff of the Truce Supervision Organization, transmitting a report to the Security Council; Official Records, 6th Year, Supp. April–June, 1951, pp. 162–164.

[84] The representative of Egypt claimed that these findings relate ''exclusively to his activities as a self-appointed jurist and as a gentleman-at-large.'' Official Records, 549th Meeting, July 26, 1951, p. 17. The United Kingdom representative, on the contrary, believed that ''any opinion which he expresses should command great respect in this Council.'' *Ibid.*, 550th Meeting, Aug. 1, 1951, p. 20 f, par. 95 f.

[85] *Ibid.*, 553rd Meeting, Aug. 16, 1951, p. 13, par. 52, and p. 25, par. 108.

[86] *Ibid.*, 661st Meeting, March 12, 1954, p. 9, par. 43 f. and p. 13, par. 64.

[87] *Ibid.*, 549th Meeting, July 26, 1951, pp. 9–11, and 661st Meeting, March 12, 1954, p. 29, par. 144. Israel's representative, after referring to Dr. Bunche's view, quoted *supra*, p. 545, and the Report of the Chief of Staff, declared: ''. . . all these are unanimous in asserting that whatever may be the character of other armistice agreements, this Armistice Agreement is not compatible with active belligerency or with the exercise by either party of visit, search or seizure.'' See also statement by Peruvian delegate, Official Records, 688th Meeting, Jan. 13, 1955, p. 7, par. 27.

[88] As well as by a majority of members of the Security Council in voting in 1954 for the reaffirmation of the 1951 resolution.

The Report clearly does not state that the Egyptian practices, which are called "an act of blockade . . ." are consistent with the Armistice Agreement as claimed by Egypt. It explicitly states that they are "contrary to" and "inconsistent with" the spirit of the Agreement. The Report does state, however, after what must have been careful consideration,[89] that "there is no adequate basis for agreeing that the Mixed Armistice Commission has competence to deal with the question." Members of the Security Council generally construed the Report in this sense, although some expressed a reservation on this point.[90]

The decisive consideration in determining the compatibility of the Egyptian actions with the Armistice Agreement should be, it is submitted, their aggressive and hostile character, as well as the fact that, being performed by the official forces of Egypt, they are attributable to the Government of Egypt. On the basis of these two tests and in view of the circumstance that the Government of Egypt openly insists on performing the belligerent right of visit, search and seizure, there should be no difficulty in concluding that Egyptian restrictive practices are incompatible with the Armistice Agreement.

3. Compatibility of the Restrictive Practices with the Convention of Constantinople of 1888

During the debates in the Security Council the question was frequently raised whether the Egyptian restrictions were compatible with the provisions of the Constantinople Convention. The resolution of September 1, 1951, itself makes no explicit reference to this Convention.

One of the outstanding characteristics of the Convention is the "neutralization" of the Canal, that is, the establishment in Article 1 of the principle of freedom of navigation in both peace and war for ships of all nations. Thus, even assuming the correctness of the Egyptian contention, namely, that a state of war continues to exist, Israeli ships have a right of passage through the Canal. Articles 9 and 10 authorize the Egyptian Government, as an exception to Articles 4, 5, 6, 7, and 8, to take "the necessary measures for enforcing the execution of the said Treaty" and to take such measures which it might find necessary to assure by its "own forces the defense of Egypt and the maintenance of public order." It will be noticed that the exceptions listed in Articles 9 and 10 do not include Article 1, which is therefore one which Egypt is bound to respect in all circumstances. This would be so even without the specific statement in Article 11:

[89] The Egyptian representative stated in the Security Council that "this decision of 12 June 1951 was taken after consultation with the United Nations Secretariat, particularly with the Legal Department." Official Records, 662nd Meeting, March 23, 1954, p. 9, par. 34. This consultation does not appear in public documents of the United Nations.

[90] See, e.g., the remarks by the American representative: "My Government believes that this may be technically correct, but it is difficult to consider the Egyptian actions as thereby justified merely because the officials who enforce the restrictions cannot be classified as military or para-military forces of Egypt." Official Records, 552nd Meeting, Aug. 16, 1951, p. 10, par. 45. See also remarks by the New Zealand delegate, ibid., 662nd Meeting, March 23, 1954, p. 5, par. 19.

The measures taken in the cases provided for by Articles 9 and 10
of the present Treaty shall not interfere with the free use of the
Canal.

It follows then, as the Prize Court of Alexandria held, that Egypt may
exceptionally take "reasonable and necessary measures," [91] but such measures must "not interfere with the free use of the Canal." The Convention thus lays down the limit beyond which Egypt is not authorized to go.
Egypt argued, of course, that visit and search, as well as seizure, "cannot
be regarded as prejudicing free passage through the Canal, and therefore
as contrary to the Convention of Constantinople of 1888." [92] As pointed
out already, Egypt is not the final arbiter in determining whether these
measures conform to the requirements of the Convention.[93] Members of
the Security Council did contend that they are "undoubtedly incompatible" with the Convention.[94]

The restrictive practices of Egypt having been considered at variance
with the Constantinople Convention, an even stronger case can be made
against the complete prohibition of passage of Israeli ships through the
Canal. The power to take reasonable and necessary measures is power to
regulate, not to prohibit, passage through the Canal. In this context
reference may be made to the judgment of the International Court of
Justice in the *Corfu Channel* case which clearly established this essential
distinction. After holding that the North Corfu Channel "should be
considered as belonging to the class of international highways through
which passage cannot be prohibited by a coastal State in time of peace,"
the Court went on to declare as follows:

> On the other hand, it is a fact that the two coastal States did not
> maintain normal relations, that Greece had made territorial claims
> precisely with regard to a part of Albanian territory bordering on the
> Channel, that Greece had declared that she considered herself tech-
> nically in a state of war with Albania, and that Albania, invoking the
> danger of Greek incursions, had considered it necessary to take certain
> measures of vigilance in this region. The Court is of opinion that
> Albania, in view of these exceptional circumstances, would have been
> justified in issuing regulations in respect of the passage of warships
> through the Straits, but not in prohibiting such passage or in subject-
> ing it to the requirement of special authorization.[95]

As the parallelism between this case and the Suez Canal situation,
grounded on the pretended existence of a technical state of war, is obvious,
several conclusions suggest themselves: First, if the principle laid down by
customary international law and applied by the Court governs passage
through the Corfu Straits, it follows *a fortiori* that it governs passage

[91] *Cf. supra*, pp. 535–536.

[92] Official Records, 661st Meeting, March 12, 1954, p. 15, par. 74, and p. 17, par. 87.

[93] See *supra*, p. 537.

[94] *Cf., e.g.*, the remarks of the Netherlands representative, Official Records, 553rd
Meeting, Aug. 16, 1951, p. 5, pars. 16–17; of the representative of Ecuador, *ibid.*, p. 27,
par. 123.

[95] [1949] I.C.J. Rep. 4 at 29; 43 A.J.I.L. 558 at 577 (1949).

through the Suez Canal. In the latter case the principle of customary international law is reinforced by the conventional principle of Article 1 of the Constantinople Convention. Secondly, if the principle governs the passage of warships, it follows *a fortiori* that it must govern the lesser case, namely, the passage of merchantmen. Thirdly, if in consequence of the existence of a technical state of war Albania was justified in regulating the passage of warships but not in prohibiting or subjecting it to the requirement of special authorization, the authorization granted to Egypt by the Constantinople Convention appears to be similarly limited. If Egypt claims to be entitled to impose stricter regulations, the burden of proof rests on the claimant state. Fourthly, if the measures indicated by the Court are excluded even in the case of warships, it follows *a fortiori* that they are excluded in the case of merchant vessels.

Since the view of many members of the Security Council was based on a reasoning along the lines suggested above, it may arouse some astonishment that the resolution of September 1, 1951, does not explicitly pronounce on the question of compatibility of the Egyptian practices with the Constantinople Convention. The reason may well be that the members were unsure whether the Council had competence to make such a direct pronouncement. Article 8 of the Convention provides:

> The Agents in Egypt of the Signatory Powers of the present Treaty shall be charged to see that it is carried out. In any circumstance threatening the security and free passage of the Canal, they shall meet at the summons of three of them and under the presidency of their Doyen, to make the necessary verifications. They shall inform the Khedivial Government of the danger perceived, in order that it may take proper steps to assure the protection and the free use of the Canal.

It would require going beyond the compass of this paper to examine the applicability of this procedure to the problem posed by the Egyptian restrictions.[96]

Suffice it to point out that Egypt, strongly supported by the Soviet Union, challenged the competence of the Security Council to deal with Israel's complaints on the ground that they related to the Constantinople Convention and that the procedure provided for in the Convention should be utilized.[97] Israel, the complaining state, is not a party to the Conven-

---

[96] Also, and for the same reason, an analysis is omitted of the regime established for the Canal by the United Kingdom in two World Wars, a matter which was raised at some length, though inconclusively, by the representatives of Egypt. See Official Records, 555th Meeting, Aug. 27, 1951, p. 8 f. On this aspect see R. R. Baxter, "Passage of Ships through International Waterways in Time of War," 31 Brit. Yr. Bk. of Int. Law 187–216 at 196, 206–208 (1954).

[97] The representative of Egypt said: "It is Article 8 which you should bring into operation, not the Security Council. Apply to the signatories' representatives in Cairo. You are perfectly entitled to complain of obstacles to the free passage of shipping through the Canal. I believe you know that the signatories are France, Germany, Austria–Hungary, Spain, Great Britain, Italy, The Netherlands, Russia and the Ottoman Empire. These countries exist. They even have successors. . . . You can find three to call together the signatories' representatives in Cairo. Take your com-

tion and could therefore not invoke the procedure of the Convention.[98] The Security Council did not, however, accept the Egyptian viewpoint regarding its competence in the matter. As was pointed out by several members, the Council is competent to deal with threats to the peace, including threats arising out of the non-observance of the Constantinople Convention. As the French representative stated:

> The Council is not competent to impose observance of the Constantinople Convention as such. It is, primarily and solely, the organ mainly responsible for the maintenance of international peace and security. More particularly, the Council has the paramount right of supervising the execution of the armistice agreements negotiated under its auspices between Israel and the neighboring Arab States.
>
> . . . . .
>
> . . . *The Council is competent to supervise its application in this case* in view of the special situation created between Egypt and Israel under the General Armistice Agreement of 1949.[99]

In view of this strong statement, which was shared by other members of the Council both as to the competence of the Security Council and the incompatibility of Egypt's pretended rights with its obligations under the Constantinople Convention,[100] it is probably regrettable that the Council chose not to include an explicit finding to this effect in its resolution of September 1, 1951, or in the draft resolution of 1954, and, in connection with the *Bat Galim* incident, deemed it inexpedient to declare so unequivocally.[101] Nevertheless, in the public mind the impression persists that the Security Council based its action against Egypt squarely on that ground.

4. *Egypt's Right of Self-Defense or Self-Preservation as Basis for Restrictive Practices*

In the course of the several debates centered on Israel's complaints, it became standard practice for Egyptian representatives to invoke the right

---

plaint to them. But to raise the question of free passage through the Suez Canal in the Security Council is wrong. It is completely at variance with Article 24 of the United Nations Charter.'' Official Records, 662nd Meeting, March 23, 1954, p. 14, par. 47. For the remarks of the Soviet representative see *ibid.*, 664th Meeting, March 29, 1954, p. 10, pars. 52–56.

[98] The Egyptian representative said: ''For so far as the Egyptian Government is concerned, the State of Israel has nothing to do with the 1888 Convention. It was not a signatory to the Convention; at the time the Convention was signed it was not yet in existence.'' *Ibid.*, 659th Meeting, Feb. 15, 1954, p. 23, par. 123.

[99] Official Records, 687th Meeting, Jan. 4, 1955, p. 10, pars. 56–57. See also the French statement *ibid.*, 663rd Meeting, March 25, 1954, p. 8, pars. 34–35. Italics supplied.

[100] On the first point, the representative of Belgium stated: ''As has been pointed out, the Security Council is clearly not competent to enforce the observance of the Constantinople Convention as such. It does, however, possess such competence through the Charter, insofar as it has to carry out the provisions of the Charter in order to ensure the maintenance of peace and international security. The 1951 resolution was therefore the outcome of a proper use of the Council's powers, and was not *ultra vires.*'' *Ibid.*, 688th Meeting, Jan. 13, 1955, p. 3, par. 9.

[101] This may well have been due to the belief that a resolution would be opposed by the Soviet Union.

of self-preservation or self-defense as a juridical justification for Egypt's restrictive practices. This right, said the representative of Egypt, "is universally recognized and known to transcend all other rights";[102] it is

> at the root of all existence, of all survival, individual or national . . . it is part and parcel of the Charter and the very concept of the United Nations, and . . . it is the main patrimony and the highest privilege of every individual, every community, every nation and every group of nations, except the damned and the fools.[103]

Members of the Security Council generally rejected this claim on the ground that no actual hostilities were in progress.[104] The representative of The Netherlands stated that two years after signing the Armistice Agreement Egypt

> does not require to exercise the belligerent right of visit, search and seizure for any legitimate purpose of self-defence. Besides, as far as self-defence is concerned, something has changed in our world since the closing years of the nineteenth century. Today we, the Members of the United Nations, live—or at least should live—by the Charter of our Organization.[105]

The position of the Council found expression in the resolution of September 1, 1951. It has, moreover, been restated recently by the Secretary General of the United Nations. Interpreting the assurances given him by Israel and Egypt to respect unconditionally the cease-fire injunction, subject to the right of self-defense under Article 51, the Secretary General declared that this reserve applies

> in cases of non-compliance by the other party with its obligations under the Charter, or under the Armistice Agreement, only if and when such non-compliance is found to be a reason for the exertion [Sic!] of the right of self-defence as recognized in Article 51 of the Charter. The Security Council alone can decide whether this is the case or not. The reserve for self-defence in the several cease-fire assurances and the significance it may give to compliance with the Charter, other clauses in the Armistice Agreement or relevant Security Council decisions, is thus under the sole jurisdiction of the Security Council, in accordance with the rules established.

In particular, the reservation of self-defense "could not derogate from the obligations assumed under Article 2, paragraph 2, of the Armistice Agreement between Egypt and Israel." Neither, according to his interpretation, said the Secretary General, does it "permit acts of retaliation, which repeatedly have been condemned by the Security Council."[106]

---

[102] Official Records, 549th Meeting, July 26, 1951, p. 21, par. 78.

[103] Ibid., 550th Meeting, Aug. 1, 1951, p. 8, par. 42. See pp. 6–8 for authority cited by the representative. See also the representative's observation ibid., 661st Meeting, March 12, 1954, p. 14, pars. 67–73; 659th Meeting, Feb. 15, 1954, p. 9, par. 50.

[104] See remarks by the British representative ibid., 550th Meeting, Aug. 1, 1951, p. 20, par. 93.

[105] Ibid., 553rd Meeting, Aug. 16, 1951, p. 4, par. 15.

[106] U. N. Doc. S/3596, May 9, 1956: Report of the Secretary General to the Security Council pursuant to the Council's resolution of April 4, 1956, on the Palestine Question, pp. 13, 14.

The Secretary General's interpretation is particularly illuminating and to the point as Egypt appeared to justify its practices of restriction and interception by invoking the right of self-defense or self-preservation with respect to alleged infringements of various clauses of the Armistice Agreement by Israel.[107] These acts then assume the character of retaliation, which, in the case of Israel, have been condemned by the Security Council. By parity of reasoning, such retaliatory actions by Egypt, whether or not based on or derived from the right of self-defense, are equally inadmissible.[108]

VI. SECURITY COUNCIL ACTION WITH RESPECT TO EGYPT'S RESTRICTIVE PRACTICES

1. *Resolution of September 1, 1951*

When Israel lodged its first complaint with the Security Council, a resolution was adopted on November 17, 1950, reminding the parties of their pledges of "no hostilities" and postponing further consideration until the submission of a report by the Mixed Armistice Commission.[109] In July, 1951, the Council began the consideration of the second Israeli complaint in the light of the Report of the Special Committee of June 12, 1951,[110] the relevance of which has already been discussed.[111] The Council debated the issues from political as well as juridical points of view. The majority of the members of the Security Council firmly rejected every one of the Egyptian contentions as unfounded.

The Council voted on the tripartite draft resolution, as amended,[112] on September 1, 1951. The vote was eight in favor (Brazil, Ecuador, France, Netherlands, Turkey, United Kingdom, United States of America, Yugoslavia), none against, and three abstentions (China, India, U.S.S.R.). China and India abstained because on the one hand they did not feel that the legal issues had been adequately dealt with, and on the other hand they were not convinced in view of the opposition of Egypt that the resolution

---

[107] See remarks by the Egyptian delegate in Official Records, 686th Meeting, Dec. 7, 1954, p. 25, par. 136 *et seq.*

[108] Said the Brazilian representative: "Should we accept the Egyptian thesis, we would be bound to recognize any measures of reprisal adopted by the Israel Government." Official Records, 552nd Meeting, Aug. 16, 1951, p. 12, par. 56.

[109] U. N. Doc. S/1899; Official Records, 522nd Meeting, Nov. 13, 1950, p. 15, and 524th Meeting, Nov. 17, 1950, p. 15.

[110] U.N. Doc. S/2194; Official Records, 6th Year, Supp. April–June, 1951, pp. 162–164.   [111] *Cf. supra*, pp. 546 ff.

[112] The amendment, which was adopted, related to par. 3 of the draft resolution, the original text of which was: "Noting that the Chief of Staff of the Truce Supervision Organization in his report to the Security Council of 12 June 1951 considered interference with the passage through the Suez Canal of goods destined for Israel to be a hostile and aggressive act, and contrary to the spirit of the Armistice Agreement, the effective functioning of which is thereby jeopardized." The Yugoslav delegate found this passage to be of exceptional gravity, and the American representative introduced the revision which was adopted. Official Records, 553rd Meeting, Aug. 16, 1951, p. 30, par. 142; p. 31, par. 145, and note 3.

would contribute towards peace and stability in the area. Soviet Russia never participated in the discussion.[113]

The resolution as adopted [114] reads as follows:

The Security Council,

1. Recalling that in its resolution of 11 August 1949 (S/1376) relating to the conclusion of Armistice Agreements between Israel and the neighbouring Arab States it drew attention to the pledges in these Agreements "against any further acts of hostility" between the Parties,

2. Recalling further that in its resolution of 17 November 1950 (S/1907 and Corr. 1), it reminded the States concerned that the Armistice Agreements to which they are parties contemplate "the return of permanent peace in Palestine," and therefore urged them and other States in the area to take all such steps as will lead to the settlement of the issues between them,

3. Noting the report of the Chief of Staff of the Truce Supervision Organization to the Security Council of 12 June 1951 (S/2194),

4. Further noting that the Chief of Staff of the Truce Supervision Organization recalled the statement of the senior Egyptian delegate in Rhodes on 13 January 1949, to the effect that his delegation was "inspired with every spirit of co-operation, conciliation and a sincere desire to restore peace in Palestine," and that the Egyptian Government has not complied with the earnest plea of the Chief of Staff made to the Egyptian delegate on 12 June 1951, that it desist from the present practice of interfering with the passage through the Suez Canal of goods destined for Israel,

5. Considering that since the armistice regime, which has been in existence for nearly two and a half years, is of a permanent character, neither party can reasonably assert that it is actively a belligerent or requires to exercise the right of visit, search, and seizure for any legitimate purpose of self-defence,

6. Finds that the maintenance of the practice mentioned in paragraph 4 above is inconsistent with the objectives of a peaceful settlement between the parties and the establishment of a permanent peace in Palestine set forth in the Armistice Agreement;

7. Finds further that such practice is an abuse of the exercise of the right of visit, search and seizure;

8. Further finds that that practice cannot in the prevailing circumstances be justified on the ground that it is necessary for self-defence;

9. And further noting that the restrictions on the passage of goods through the Suez Canal to Israel ports are denying to nations at no time connected with the conflict in Palestine valuable supplies required for their economic reconstruction, and that these restrictions together with the sanctions applied by Egypt to certain ships which

[113] On one occasion, for unexplained reasons, the Soviet Union insisted on a postponement of the debate for 48 hours. Official Records, 556th Meeting, Aug. 29, 1951, p. 6.

[114] U.N. Doc. S/2298/Rev. 1; Official Records, 558th Meeting, Sept. 1, 1951, p. 2. The resolution was subsequently issued as a separate document under the symbol S/2322.

have visited Israel ports represent unjustified interference with the rights of nations to navigate the seas and to trade freely with one another, including the Arab States and Israel,

10. Calls upon Egypt to terminate the restrictions on the passage of international commercial shipping and goods through the Suez Canal wherever bound and to cease all interference with such shipping beyond that essential to the safety of shipping in the Canal itself and to the observance of the international conventions in force.

The resolution notes the Report of the Chief of Staff which declared the exercise of restrictions by Egypt to be "in effect, an act of blockade," a "hostile and aggressive action" contrary to the spirit of the General Armistice Agreement.[115] It also noted the appeal addressed by the Chief of Staff to the Egyptian delegate to desist from the "present practice." The resolution rejects the Egyptian claim that it or Israel is still "actively a belligerent," and that "the exercise of the right of visit, search and seizure" is required "for any legitimate purpose of self-defense." But it will be noted that the resolution does not directly repudiate the Egyptian contention that, in spite of the Armistice, a "state of war" continues to exist, although it rejects all the consequential rights which Egypt claimed as flowing from it.[116] It must, of course, be conceded that the Security Council is free to choose the juridical or political ground on which it desires to take a stand on an issue of which it is seized. In this case the Council chose not to pronounce on what it considered a technical and probably secondary aspect of the issue, although it was pressed earnestly by Israel. It believed itself to be—and no doubt it is—legally on solid ground when it ruled in paragraphs 5, 6, 7 and 8 that the belligerent rights

[115] See *supra*, p. 547. Commenting on this on behalf of the three sponsoring Powers, the British delegate said: "The Armistice Agreement was meant to terminate all hostile acts, and it was so understood both by the parties and by the Security Council itself. . . . The restrictions which applied to Egypt were terminated by the Security Council resolution (S/1376) of August, 1949, and there can be no justification for the attempt by Egypt to maintain against Israel restrictions similar to those from which Egypt itself was released two years ago." Official Records, 552nd Meeting, Aug. 16, 1951, p. 4, par. 12.

[116] In commenting upon it the British delegate expressed himself as follows: "Egypt claims that there is a state of war and that it is therefore entitled to exercise belligerent rights. It is not necessary, in our view, for the Council to pronounce on this. Even if it were self-evident that a state of war existed—which is by no means the case, of course—this would in itself afford no justification for the maintenance of the restrictions at the present time and in the light of the present situation. What matters is not whether there is some technical basis for the restrictions, but whether it is reasonable, just and equitable that they should be maintained. This is the principle on which the draft resolution before the Council has been formulated, and it is on this issue that we consider the Council should pronounce." *Ibid.*, p. 3, par. 7. Adverting to the same theme later in his speech, he said: "For the reasons which I have already stated, the draft resolution does not attempt to say whether or not Egypt can technically claim to be entitled to belligerent rights. What the draft resolution does say is that, in the light of the Armistice Agreement and of what has taken place since it was signed, the maintenance of the present restrictions is unjustified and unreasonable and must be held to constitute an abuse of any rights which Egypt may claim to possess." *Ibid.*, par. 10.

of visit, search, and seizure claimed by Egypt were inconsistent with the armistice regime and could not be justified on grounds of self-defense. It thus construed the Armistice Agreement as one *sui generis* and in so doing rejected the Egyptian contention that it was of the classical variety and that, since it did not expressly prohibit the right of visit, search and seizure, the exercise of this right was permissible. Having done so, one may wonder why the Council found it necessary to characterize the exercise of this right of visit, search and seizure as an "abuse." While the doctrine of abuse of right is gaining ground in international law, its rôle in the system of the resolution is not clear. If the right in question is declared to be inconsistent with the armistice regime and cannot be justified as legal, was it necessary to affirm that it constituted an abuse of right?

The meaning of this affirmation becomes clear when related to the final paragraph of the resolution and to the debate in the Council regarding the compatibility of Egyptian restrictions with its obligations and rights under the Constantinople Convention of 1888. In this debate it was conceded that Egypt has certain rights under the Convention, but it was argued that these rights are limited by Article 11, which reserves the right of "free use." Both Egypt's rights and obligations are reaffirmed in paragraph 10 of the resolution, which calls on Egypt to terminate all interference with shipping through the Suez Canal "beyond that essential to the safety of shipping in the Canal itself and to the observance of international conventions in force." One of the "conventions in force" is, of course, the Constantinople Convention. It is precisely because Egypt's interference exceeded the measures permissible under the Constantinople Convention that the Council qualified the interference as "abuse of the exercise of the right of visit, search and seizure." It is for the same reason that the United Kingdom representative declared, on behalf of the three sponsoring governments, that, in calling upon Egypt to terminate the restrictions in the Suez Canal,

> we are not asking the Egyptian Government to give up any of the rights which it can legitimately claim to exercise in regard to the passage of ships through the Canal. The normal administration of the Canal must obviously continue, and the proper precautions must be taken to safeguard the Canal itself and the ships which pass through it. All this is specifically provided for in the draft resolution. The relevant international conventions must also be observed, including the Suez Canal Convention itself and any others, such as sanitary conventions, which may apply. What we want to see is the restoration of normal peacetime conditions in the Canal, providing for the unhindered passage of the ships of all nations.[117]

The Security Council thus drew a line between "reasonable and necessary" measures for safeguarding freedom of passage for ships of all nations, including Israel, and the imposition of measures of visit, search and seizure, and qualified the latter as an "abuse of right." Thus eleven months after Israel first appealed to the Security Council against Egypt's restric-

[117] *Ibid.*, p. 3, par. 11.

tions, the Council finally found the complaint well founded.   There can be no doubt that the Council proceeded slowly but it also moved deliberately.[118] Egypt's reaction consisted in restating its position that "the assumptions on which the claim of Israel was based—or on which it tried to base itself— have yet to be proved," and in fully reserving "its rights in connexion with the present debate." [119]   More specifically, the Egyptian representative argued that the resolution "is in flagrant violation of the purposes of the United Nations, as formulated in Article 1 of the Charter, which govern the functions and powers of the Security Council"; that these powers and functions mentioned in Article 24, paragraph 2, "are limited and should be strictly regulated and governed by the fundamental principles and purposes laid down in" Article 1, paragraph 1; and that the resolution "in fact proposes that the Council violate the principles and practices of international law and the stipulations of Articles 1 and 24 of the Charter of the United Nations." [120]

That the Security Council has, as the United Kingdom representative maintained, the "paramount right of supervising the execution of the Armistice Agreements" [121] cannot and has not been doubted.   In adopting the resolution the Council exercised this right.   And the obligatory character of the findings laid down by the Council stems from the binding character of the Armistice Agreement and the Suez Canal Convention as well as from the fact that the former was concluded by Egypt and Israel pursuant to a resolution adopted by the Council under Chapter 7 of the Charter.[122]

[118] After the adoption of the resolution, the French representative recalled that several postponements were granted "to give the Egyptian Government time to find a way of adapting its behavior to the obligations incumbent upon it, on the one hand under the Armistice Agreement which it had concluded with Israel, and on the other hand under the international statute of the Suez Canal," and expressed disappointment that Egypt had failed to do so.   *Ibid.*, 558th Meeting, Sept. 1, 1951, p. 5, pars. 18–19.

[119] *Ibid.*, p. 7, pars. 28–29.

[120] *Ibid.*, 553rd Meeting, Aug. 16, 1951, p. 22, pars. 94–95.   The Egyptian representative referred to Art. 1, par. 1, which states as one of the purposes "to bring about by peaceful means, and in conformity with the principles of justice and international law, adjustment or settlement of international disputes or situations which might lead to a breach of the peace."   The sentence referred to in par. 2 of Art. 24 reads: "In discharging these duties the Security Council shall act in acccordance with the purposes and principles of the United Nations."

[121] Official Records, 687th Meeting, Jan. 4, 1955, p. 10, par. 56.   The French representative referred to the Council as the "guardian" of the Armistice Agreement. *Ibid.*, 663rd Meeting, March 25, 1954, p. 8, par. 35.

[122] With respect to the Constantinople Convention, it is relevant to recall the following statement by the Belgian delegate: "The 1951 resolution was therefore the outcome of a proper use of the Council's powers, and was not *ultra vires*.   It could not, indeed, be represented in that light, since it contained nothing new and merely restated the provisions of the Convention of 1888.   Actually, it restated them only in part, for it referred only to commercial shipping, whereas the Convention was also applicable to warships.   Even if the resolution itself were not binding, its provisions would be, since they correspond to provisions which have been binding since 1888." *Ibid.*, 688th Meeting, Jan. 13, 1955, p. 3, par. 9.

2. *Egypt's Failure to Carry out the Security Council Resolution of September 1, 1951*

On January 28, 1954, Israel again complained to the Security Council that, in violation of the resolution of September 1, 1951, Egypt "has persisted in its illegitimate interference with shipping passing through the Suez Canal and has since extended the blockade to shipping passing to and from the Israeli port of Eilat on the Gulf of Aqaba"; and that moreover, these "illegal practices have been . . . recently aggravated." [123] Egypt freely admitted that it continued to act in defiance of the Security Council resolution of September 1, 1951, and its representative, in an effort to clear up the "misunderstanding" that the Egyptian measures are "entirely contrary to the Security Council's decision of 1 September 1951," declared:

> Egypt is taking action which is perhaps not in conformity with the Security Council's decision of 1 September 1951; I am prepared to recognize that. But at the same time, I would like to point out—and this is the misunderstanding I want to clear up—that when the Security Council's decision was taken, Egypt received it in a certain spirit. That spirit is illustrated in the statement made by the Egyptian representative who attended the meeting of the Security Council of 1 September 1951, at which this decision was taken. [124]

What the Egyptian representative said, in substance, was that Egypt never intended to carry out the decision of the Security Council of September 1, 1951, that it had so declared immediately after that decision was adopted, and that it would continue to do so. In a debate which was remarkable for the absence of any "tenable reason" for Egypt's refusal to comply with that resolution and equally for the absence of any "new

---

[123] U.N. Docs. S/3168 and S/3168/Add. 1; Official Records, 9th Year, Supp. Jan.–March, 1954, p. 2, par. 2 and p. 3, par. 4. The aggravation, that is, the extension of confiscatory measures to the Gulf of Aqaba and the inclusion of food among the items to be regarded as "war contraband" was instituted, said the Israeli representative, on Jan. 25, 1954. *Ibid.*, p. 3, par. 3. The decision referred to declares that "Egypt has to take sterner measures to attain the desired end" (*ibid.*, pp. 4, 5), and contrasts sharply with the alleged voluntary relaxation of the restrictive measures by Egypt. See also statement by Israel's representative, Official Records, 658th Meeting, Feb. 5, 1954, pp. 1 ff.

[124] He went on to say: "Thus Egypt accepted the Security Council's decision of 1 September 1951, within the limits of that statement, which made it clear that Egypt was not convinced that the discussion was ended, that in its view the question was not closed and that the decision did not rest on fixed and final foundations. That was our conviction in September 1951. That is still our conviction and we accordingly maintain the same viewpoint and the same position. It is therefore beside the point to state now that Egypt is acting in a manner incompatible with the decision taken by the Security Council on 1 September 1951. Egypt will continue to maintain the same position because it is convinced, as its representative said at the very moment the decision was taken, that the decision was not based on exhaustive studies or on clear opinions." Official Records, 659th Meeting, Feb. 15, 1954, p. 25, par. 135, and p. 26, par. 136. For the Egyptian representative's statement at the Sept. 1, 1951, meeting see *supra*, p. 558.

legal argument,"[125] members rejected the Egyptain "reservations" and indeed repudiated its right to make any such "reservations." Thus the New Zealand representative declared:

> We cannot accept the argument that Egypt is entitled to disregard the terms of the resolution of September 1951 by reason of a reservation entered at the time of its adoption.[126]

The Danish representative referred to Article 25 of the Charter and pointed out:

> There is no reservation to this. The obligation to accept and carry out is not limited to such decisions as you agree with and consider legal.[127]

The New Zealand representative accordingly introduced a draft resolution on March 23, 1954, which addressed itself primarily to the "incontestable and indeed uncontested fact that the clear and precise provisions of the 1951 resolution have not been complied with."[128] The draft resolution, after recalling the whole of the resolution of September 1, 1951,[129] "notes with grave concern that Egypt has not complied with that resolution," and "calls upon Egypt in accordance with its obligations under the Charter to comply therewith."[130] This paragraph, noted the French representative, "is manifestly based on Article 25 of the Charter."[131]

The United Kingdom representative, while refraining from submitting a

[125] See remarks by British and French representatives, Official Records, 663rd Meeting, March 25, 1954, p. 5, par. 23, and p. 7, par. 31. For Egyptian restatements see *ibid.*, 658th Meeting, Feb. 5, 1954, p. 26; 659th Meeting, Feb. 15, 1954, pp. 1 ff., 23 ff.; 661st Meeting, March 12, 1954, pp. 2 ff.

[126] *Ibid.*, 662nd Meeting, March 23, 1954, p. 4, par. 17.

[127] *Ibid.*, 663rd Meeting, March 25, 1954, p. 3, par. 12. He continued as follows: "All Member States in ratifying the Charter agreed to a limitation of their sovereignty. If the Council accepted that a Member State that disagreed with one of its decisions, by calling such decisions illegal was not bound by the decision, the work of the Council would become chaotic. For any State ready to shoulder the responsibility for aggression surely would be only too willing to accuse the Council of acting illegally. We might then foresee an entire technique of evasion develop. The smaller nations cannot possibly want such developments to take place." (p. 4, par. 13.)

[128] *Ibid.*, 662nd Meeting, March 23, 1954, p. 3, par. 9. See also remarks by the U. S. representative, *ibid.*, 663rd Meeting, March 25, 1954, p. 1, par. 1, p. 2, par. 5; the French representative, *ibid.*, p. 7, par. 31, p. 9, par. 41; the Brazilian delegate, *ibid.*, 664th Meeting, March 29, 1954, p. 5, par. 16; and the Colombian delegate, *ibid.*, p. 5, par. 22.

[129] Statement by the New Zealand representative, *ibid.*, 662nd Meeting, March 23, 1954, p. 5, par. 21.

[130] U.N. Doc. S/3188 and Corr. 1; Official Records, 9th Year, Supp. Jan.–March, 1954, p. 44. The final paragraph of the draft resolution refers, "without prejudice to the provisions of the resolution of 1 September 1951," Israel's complaint regarding passage through the Gulf of Aqaba to the Mixed Armistice Commission. According to statements by the American, French, and British representatives, the passage of ships through the Gulf was covered by the same principles already enunciated with respect to the Suez Canal. As the question had not yet been considered by the Commission and in order to maintain the normal procedure, it was proposed to refer the question first of all to the Commission. Official Records, 663rd Meeting, March 23, 1954, p. 2, par. 6; p. 6, pars. 27, 28; p. 9, pars. 38, 39.

[131] *Ibid.*, p. 9, par. 41.

formal amendment to the New Zealand draft resolution, put on record his government's view "that if, as I sincerely hope will not be the case, Egypt has not within ninety days complied with the resolution, the Council should stand ready to take the matter up again." [132]

The Egyptian representative declared the adamant opposition of his government, saying: "This draft resolution is not accepted by Egypt. Egypt rejects it with utmost vigour, just as it rejected the 1951 resolution." [133] The Soviet representative, intervening for the first time in the substantive discussion of the issue, challenged the jurisdiction of the Council, [134] and proposed that instead of attempting to impose a decision upon one of the parties which "has been stated by that party to be absolutely unacceptable from the outset," the Council should "appeal to both parties to take steps to settle their difference on this question by means of direct negotiations." [135]

The draft resolution was put to the vote on March 29, 1954, and not adopted, the vote being eight in favor (Brazil, Colombia, Denmark, France, New Zealand, Turkey, United Kingdom, United States), two against (Lebanon, U.S.S.R.), and one abstention (China). [136] This was the second time that the Soviet Union interposed its veto in a vote on a question relating to Palestine. [137] It marked the change from the position of abstention which the Soviet Union had followed since 1948 to one of active support of the Arab States against Israel. It must be admitted, however, that the Soviet proposal to call for direct negotiations between Israel and Egypt had some merit, particularly if these negotiations were to be conducted on the basis of the resolution of September 1, 1951. In view of the persistent refusal of the Arab States to enter into such direct negotiations with Israel, it may be doubtful that a call from the Council would have been heeded by Egypt.

It remains to note that after the vote the French representative observed that the Soviet veto "could not have caused repeal of a legally adopted resolution." [138] The representative of Israel similarly expressed his government's understanding that

> the law of the United Nations in the Suez Canal and in the Gulf of Aqaba is . . . the valid and unrepealed resolution of the Security Council adopted on 1 September 1951. [139]

[132] *Ibid.*, 664th Meeting, March 29, 1954, p. 11, par. 61; see also 663rd Meeting, March 25, 1954, p. 6, par. 26, for a similar statement.

[133] And for the same reason: "It is convinced that the two texts do not deal with the question as it should be dealt with. The legal element, which is fundamental to this dispute, is completely ignored in both." *Ibid.*, 662nd Meeting, March 23, 1954, p. 15, par. 49.

[134] This challenge, based on Art. 8 of the Constantinople Convention, has already been dealt with. See *supra*, p. 551.

[135] Official Records, 664th Meeting, March 29, 1954, p. 9, pars. 45–50; p. 10, pars. 52–56.   [136] *Ibid.*, p. 12, par. 69.

[137] The first Soviet veto occurred in connection with the question of water from the River Jordan, at the 656th Meeting, Jan. 22, 1954, p. 27, par. 135.

[138] *Ibid.*, 664th Meeting, March 29, 1954, p. 18, par. 113.

[139] *Ibid.*, p. 21, par. 141.

3. *The Security Council and the Interception of the Israeli Ship,* Bat Galim, *by Egypt*

At the end of the Security Council debate on March 29, 1954, the representative of Egypt declared that, freed from the pressure of the New Zealand draft resolution, Egypt "will of its own free will move towards tolerance." As a token of this spontaneous tolerance Egypt, six months later, on September 28, 1954, intercepted the first Israeli ship, the *Bat Galim,* which, on the strength of the September 1, 1951, Security Council resolution, attempted to pass through the Suez Canal with a cargo of meat.[140] The Egyptian charges against the *Bat Galim,* namely, that its crew attacked two fishing boats with automatic fire and killed two fishermen, are immaterial, as they were dismissed by the Mixed Armistice Commission as "unfounded."[141] The incident was discussed at several meetings of the Security Council. The discussion revealed a good deal of satisfaction at the high standard of Egyptian administration of justice in dismissing the charges against the Israeli seamen and their release, as well as at the unfulfilled promise to release the cargo and the ship. There was remarkably little disposition to examine the heart of the matter, to wit, that, contrary to the resolution of September 1, 1951, the Armistice Agreement as construed by the Mixed Armistice Commission and the Security Council, and the Constantinople Convention, Egypt had intercepted an Israeli merchantman and by separating the crew from the ship had prevented its passage through the Suez Canal. The representative of the United Kingdom, to be sure, did express his hope that the grave charges against the crew having been "withdrawn when they could not be substantiated . . . the Egyptian Government could thereafter have seen its way to letting the ship proceed on its course through the Canal, under such security restrictions as seemed appropriate in the circumstances."[142] The French delegate correctly interpreted the Egyptian statements regarding the release of the cargo and the ship "to mean that the Egyptian Government maintains its claim that it is entitled to forbid passage through the Suez Canal to any vessel flying the Israel flag and manned by an Israel crew," and asked "that Egypt should abide by the Council's decision" of September 1, 1951, to terminate the restrictions on the passage of "international commercial shipping."[143] The United States representative declared:

> Further action to give full effect to the decision of 1 September 1951, to allow the passage of the *Bat Galim,* an Israel ship, to Israel, and to cease interference with Israel shipping as well as with neutral shipping carrying goods to and from Israel, will confirm our respect for Egypt as the legitimate custodian of the Suez Canal, only recently

---

[140] The facts of this incident are discussed above, pp. 541 ff.

[141] U. N. Doc. S/3323; Official Records, 9th Year, Supp. Oct.-Dec. 1954, p. 30 at 41.

[142] Official Records, 687th Meeting, Jan. 4, 1955, p. 8, par. 46. He went on to say: "Though it would, of course, have left all the questions of principle untouched, this would at least have settled the adventures of this particular ship in a more or less satisfactory manner."

[143] *Ibid.*, p. 9, par. 52, and p. 10, pars. 58–59. The Egyptian statement will be found *ibid.*, pp. 5 ff., pars. 33–34.

reasserted by Egypt's historic agreement with the United Kingdom. Anything less than this will not be consistent with the spirit and intent of the resolution of 1 September 1951, nor, in our opinion, with its express terms.

. . . Israel has shown forbearance and restraint in the conduct of its case here. Israel might well have shown impatience and resentment that it was not granted immediate satisfaction in such a case as this, where the majority of the members of the Council have shown that they believe the right to be on Israel's side.[144]

Similar views were voiced by the representatives of Belgium,[145] New Zealand,[146] and Brazil.[147] The Egyptian contention that the 1951 resolution did not apply to Israeli ships [148] was explicitly or implicitly rejected by the representatives of all these governments. The representative of Israel expressed the hope

that the Security Council will decide to reaffirm its 1951 resolution and will continue to oppose any interference with or discrimination against the ships or cargoes of any nation or flag, including Israel.[149]

This the Council failed to do. In spite of all the brave words, no member of the Council introduced an appropriate draft resolution expressing the views of the majority and none was therefore voted upon. Instead the President of the Council summed up the sense of the discussion: On the one hand, "it is evident that most representatives here regard the resolution of 1 September 1951 as having continuing validity and effect, and it is in this context and that of the Constantinople Convention that they have considered the *Bat Galim* case"; on the other hand, "hope has been expressed that a continued attitude of conciliation on both sides will speedily bring about an agreement on the arrangements for the release of the ship and the cargo." [150]

Thus, when faced with a clear test of its authority, the Security Council bowed to the *fait accompli* completely and without any reservation. It may well be that this was done in the certain knowledge of an impending Soviet veto. But this had never in the past nor has it ever in the succeed-

---

[144] *Ibid.*, p. 12, pars. 69–70.

[145] "The Belgian delegation cannot but assume that this suggestion is inspired by a desire to bring about a settlement in conformity with the Constantinople Convention." *Ibid.*, 688th Meeting, Jan. 13, 1955, p. 4, par. 11.

[146] "May I say, quite frankly, that for Israel to set out deliberately to damage the Canal would be an act so patently against its own interests as to put the possibility beyond serious consideration. . . . There is no justification, therefore, for an Egyptian policy of exclusion against Israel ships desiring to pass through the Canal—a policy which we regard as entirely inconsistent with the intent of the 1951 resolution." *Ibid.*, p. 10, par. 46. For statements made by Peru, which endorsed the 1951 resolution, and Iran, which avoided the issue, see *ibid.*, p. 7, par. 27, and p. 8, pars. 35–37.

[147] The Brazilian delegate said: "In any case we cannot accept a breach of the Constantinople Convention, any more than we can pass over in silence the fact that a Security Council resolution is being ignored." *Ibid.*, 687th Meeting, Jan. 4, 1955, p. 14, par. 81.

[148] *Ibid.*, 686th Meeting, Dec. 7, 1954, pp. 22 ff., pars. 120–133.

[149] Official Records, 688th Meeting, Jan. 13, 1955, p. 16, par. 77.

[150] *Ibid.*, p. 20, pars. 99–100.

ing years discouraged the Council from letting the Soviet Union shoulder the responsibility before the bar of public opinion, even when lesser issues were involved. Here there was open defiance of treaties and of a standing policy and decision of the Council formulated as early as August, 1949, when it placed the seal of its approval and construction upon the Egyptian-Israeli General Armistice Agreement. Here there was an issue which has been a primary cause of the chronic and endemic tension in the Middle East, and, as subsequent events were to show, a grave threat to international peace and security. Why, then, this unmitigated fiasco, why this shirking of the Council's "primary responsibility for the maintenance of international peace and security" and the taking of "prompt and effective action by the United Nations"? A possible explanation, it is ventured to suggest, may be found in the competitive wooing of the Arab States which set in with the first and second veto cast by the Soviet Union in order to shield its prospective clients in the Middle East. An exploration of the validity of this hypothesis lies, however, outside the compass of this paper.

VII. CONCLUSIONS

Several conclusions emerge from the preceding analysis. The Security Council is undoubtedly competent to deal with the issues arising from the Egyptian restrictions. Egypt has seen fit to challenge such competence when its point of view appeared certain not to be sustained by the Council. However, at the first stage of the dispute, Egypt freely admitted that

> the General Armistice Agreement between Egypt and Israel took place under the auspices of the Security Council. The Council is therefore obviously the umpire in all matters relating to the armistice agreement. It is indeed obviously competent to deal with all matters relating to world peace and security.[151]

It is even arguable that the General Assembly would have competence under the Uniting for Peace Resolution of November 3, 1950,[152] if the Council failed to exercise its primary responsibility for the maintenance of international peace and security, owing to lack of unanimity of the permanent members. The dangers to Middle East peace were often emphasized in the Council in connection with Egypt's restrictions.[153] Indeed, the General Assembly might well be better qualified to pronounce upon the larger issue arising from the continuation of Egypt's hostile and aggressive action.

Before taking up this larger aspect of the matter, it may be well to point out that it might be profitable for the Mixed Armistice Commission to take a fresh look at the Israeli complaints and to adjust its decidedly myopic construction of June 12, 1951, of the Armistice Agreement in the

---

[151] Official Records, 514th Meeting, Oct. 20, 1950, p. 17.

[152] General Assembly Resolution 377 A (V), Official Records, 5th Year, Supp. 20, pp. 10–12 (Doc. A/1775).

[153] See Official Records, 552nd Meeting, Aug. 16, 1951, p. 12, par. 56 (Brazil); *ibid.*, p. 10, par. 45 (U.S.A.); 553rd Meeting, Aug. 16, 1951, p. 3, par. 9 (Netherlands); 663rd Meeting, March 25, 1954, p. 8, par. 34 (France).

light of the specific findings and general tenor of the Security Council resolution of September 1, 1951. Several members made this point specifically with reference to the Gulf of Aqaba, but there is no reason why this should not be done also in relation to the Suez Canal. Thus the United States representative said:

> We believe that the Mixed Armistice Commission, in considering the specific complaint with respect to actions in the Gulf of Aqaba, must be bound not only by the provisions of the General Armistice Agreement but should act also in the light of paragraph 5 of the resolution of 1 September 1951.[154]

If the Commission has to consider the Israeli complaint regarding the Gulf of Aqaba in the light of the Security Council resolution, there is every reason for it to reconsider its earlier position regarding the Suez Canal in the same light. In so doing it might conceivably remove what has turned out to be a cause of persistent, albeit fruitless, misunderstandings on the part of Egypt and also lift the cloak which it unwittingly put on the true nature of Egyptian actions.

The Security Council, in considering the legal aspects of the Egyptian restrictions in general and of the seizure of the *Bat Galim* in particular, has chosen to rest its reasoning and conclusions on its own resolutions concerning the truce in Palestine and the subsequent Armistice Agreement, on the Armistice Agreement itself and other "international conventions in force," including the Convention of Constantinople of 1888. It thus placed itself on solid ground. Even statements made more recently in connection with the Middle East crisis, in which the Israeli complaint against Egyptian restrictions and exclusions in the Suez Canal played an important part, proceeded from the same ground. Thus, in the view of the Secretary General of the United Nations:

> It follows from the finding of the Security Council in 1951 that under such circumstances the parties to the Armistice Agreement may be considered as not entitled to claim any belligerent rights. Were the substantive clauses of the Armistice Agreement, especially articles VII and VIII, again to be implemented, the case against all acts of belligerency, which is based on the existence of the Armistice régime, would gain full cogency. With such a broader implementation of the Armistice Agreement, the parties should be asked to give assurances that, on the basis established, they will not assert any belligerent rights (including, of course, such rights in the Gulf of Aqaba and the Straits of Tiran).
>
> As a conclusion from paragraphs 24–27, it may be held that, in a situation where the Armistice régime is partly operative by observance of the provisions of the Armistice Agreement concerning the armistice lines, possible claims to rights of belligerency would be at least so much in doubt that, having regard for the general international interest at stake, no such claim should be exercised in the Gulf of Aqaba and the Straits of Tiran. . . .[155]

---

[154] *Ibid.*, 663rd Meeting, March 25, 1954, p. 2, par. 6. See also the British statement, *ibid.*, p. 6, par. 27, and the French statement, *ibid.*, p. 9, par. 39.

[155] Report by the Secretary General in pursuance of the resolution of the General Assembly of Jan. 15, 1957. U. N. Doc. A/3512, Jan. 24, 1957, p. 9, pars. 27–28; 36 Dept. of State Bulletin 278 (1957).

The solution of the apparent conflict between two principal organs of the United Nations, to wit, the Secretary General's view that the prohibition of belligerent rights is not unconditional and that in some way "the parties" may assert such rights,[156] and the view of the Security Council that Egypt is unconditionally prohibited from exercising belligerent rights by the Armistice Agreement as construed by the Acting Mediator, the Security Council itself, and the Mixed Armistice Commission, is of no immediate concern here. What is of direct interest is that this conflict indicates the insufficiency of the ground on which the issue of belligerency has so far been debated and on which the Security Council based its resolution of 1951.

Between Members of the United Nations, the first standard for determining the propriety of their conduct is not an armistice agreement, not even a peace treaty, but the Charter of the United Nations. In the conflict in Palestine, the hostilities, to be sure, were brought to a close by the truce ordered by the Council and by the Armistice Agreements concluded pursuant to a Council resolution. The decisive factor, however, was the admission of Israel to membership of the United Nations on May 11, 1949.[157] Without wishing to belittle the political and legal significance of the Armistice Agreements, particularly the Egyptian-Israeli Agreement of February 24, 1949, it is submitted that the admission of Israel to membership is of decisive significance for determining the issue of belligerent rights, whether in the Suez Canal, the Gulf of Aqaba or anywhere else in the air, on sea or land. Egypt asserts categorically: "A state of belligerence exists between Egypt and Israel."[158] It asserts equally that this state of belligerency has not been terminated by the Armistice Agreement, and consequently it is authorized to exercise the belligerent right of visit, search and seizure, although Israel is not authorized to exercise belligerent rights on land or in the air The Security Council completely and in every respect rejected these pretensions, but it did so on the basis of the Armistice Agreement. The untenable character of the Egyptian assertion of a state of belligerency becomes even more obvious if it is examined in the light of the law of the Charter which is equally binding upon Egypt and Israel as Members of the Organization governed by that law. The question then can properly be formulated as follows: In the absence of authorization by the Security Council, are a state of belligerency between Members claimed unilaterally by one of them and the exercise of belligerent rights by one Member against another, compatible with the law of the Charter?[158a]

[156] See *e.g.* his statement: "Under these circumstances, it is indicated that whatever rights there may be in relation to the Gulf and Straits, such rights be exercised with restraint on all sides. Any possible claims of belligerent rights should take into account the international interests involved and, therefore, if asserted, should be limited to clearly non-controversial situations." *Ibid.*, p. 8, par. 25. Under the Armistice Agreement, what would be "clearly non-controversial situations" in which belligerent rights could be asserted?

[157] General Assembly Resolution 273 (III), Official Records, 3rd Sess., Pt. II, p. 18 (Doc. A/900).

[158] Official Records, 686th Meeting, Dec. 7, 1954, p. 21, par. 113.

[158a] "The primary issue is not what rights Egypt could exercise as a belligerent under international law, but whether it could assume the status of a belligerent at all without thereby violating fundamental obligations of the United Nations Charter." Lawyers'

If the first submission is accepted, namely, that the relations between Egypt and Israel are governed by the law of the Charter,[159] then the conclusion seems inescapable that no rights can be asserted under an agreement which is in conflict with the law of the Charter. Article 103 of the Charter clearly establishes the supremacy of the law of the Charter over obligations under any other agreement.[160] It follows *a fortiori* that in case of a conflict between an asserted right under an agreement and obligations under the Charter, the latter must prevail. A treaty or agreement inconsistent with the Charter is null and void,

> for such a treaty is an attempt to amend or abolish the Charter or parts of it in the relations of the Members, parties to this treaty. Such an effect, however, can be reached only by an amendment to the Charter the procedure of which is determined in Articles 108 and 109. In no other way can the obligations and rights of the Members stipulated by the Charter be changed or abolished.[161]

It follows, then, that rights and obligations claimed under the Armistice Agreement between Israel and Egypt which are in conflict with the Charter have been abrogated by it.[162]

It hardly needs any argument to point out the incompatibility of the Egyptian claim to a unilateral state of belligerency with the purposes and principles of the Charter. In particular, it requires no prolonged discussion to find the execution by Egypt of belligerent rights, such as visit, search and seizure, and of acts such as interception of merchantmen, incompatible with Article 2, paragraph 4, of the Charter. The acts themselves have already been authoritatively determined as aggressive and hostile acts. Moreover, Article 2, paragraph 2, applies, for the Armistice Agreement concluded pursuant to a Security Council resolution constitutes obligations assumed by Egypt and Israel "in accordance with the present Charter," which must be fulfilled in good faith. Failure to do so constitutes not merely a violation of the Agreement but of a basic principle of the Charter and of international law. Under general international law repeated and serious breaches of an armistice agreement give the injured party the right of reopening hostilities.[163] If the Armistice Agreement of

Committee on Blockades: The United Nations and the Egyptian Blockade of the Suez Canal, p. 18 (New York, 1953). See also Rosenne, *op. cit.* 82 ff.

[159] The question of recognition of Israel by Egypt and the other Arab States is irrelevant with regard to rights and duties of membership. By Egypt's own admission, legal relations—namely a state of war—exist between Egypt and Israel which are governed by international law.

[160] Art. 103: "In the event of a conflict between the obligations of the Members of the United Nations under the present Charter and their obligations under any other international agreement, their obligations under the present Charter shall prevail."

[161] Hans Kelsen, The Law of the United Nations 113 (1951).

[162] See also statements by the Israeli representative, Official Records, 516th Meeting, Oct. 30, 1950, p. 11, and 549th Meeting, July 26, 1951, p. 11; and statement by Peruvian delegate, 688th Meeting, Jan. 13, 1955, p. 7, par. 27.

[163] Stone, Legal Controls of International Conflict 644 (1954): "Certain rules seem to be established with regard to violations of armistice agreements. First, a serious breach, engaging the responsibility of the State which has committed it, gives the other belligerent state a right of withdrawal, if it so elects, and in urgent cases a right of re-opening hostilities."

1949 is of the "classic" type, as Egypt argued so persistently, and if general international law, but not the Charter, governs the relations between Egypt and Israel, then the Israel intervention of October, 1956, could be regarded as a lawful exercise of rights derived from the state of belligerency, which Egypt never fails to invoke in support of its restrictions. But that has not been the position either of Egypt or of the United Nations in the face of the Israeli intervention.[164]

In conclusion it is submitted that the time has come for the United Nations to face squarely the Egyptian claim that a state of belligerency exists with a fellow Member, and that in consequence it is entitled to exercise the belligerent right of visit, search and seizure of ships of fellow Members, and of intercepting ships of Israel, a fellow Member. In determining this basic claim, it is suggested, recourse should be had to the Charter of the United Nations rather than to the Armistice Agreement or to general international law. For what is illegal under the Charter cannot be made legal by the Armistice Agreement or general international law. In case of conflict, the higher law of the Charter must prevail juridically and consequently must be made to prevail politically and effectively. The organs of the United Nations, primarily the Security Council and the General Assembly, have an ample reservoir of power in the Charter for remedial action to remove a standing challenge to law and order, peace and justice in the Middle East.

[164] See Quincy Wright, "Intervention, 1956," 51 A.J.I.L. 257–277 (1957).

Closure of the Suez Canal to Israeli Shipping

MAJID KHADDURI

Introduction

The Arab-Israeli war of June 1967 has again raised the question as to whether Egypt can lawfully close the Suez Canal to Israeli shipping. Israel, since its establishment, has repeatedly demanded the same right of free passage accorded to other nations, but Egypt has insisted on denying her such a right despite resolutions of the United Nations Security Council calling on Egypt to terminate the restrictions imposed on the passage of Israeli shipping and goods through the Suez Canal.[1] The six-day war gave Israel the opportunity to demand again the opening of the Canal to her shipping;[2] but President Nasir, in his speech on November 24, 1967, two days after the Security Council's resolution 242 had been adopted, calling for withdrawal from occupied territory and termination of belligerency, declared in no uncertain terms that "we shall never allow Israeli ships, whatever the cost, to pass through the Suez Canal."[3] Israel's demand and Nasir's rejection call for a reconsideration of the question in the light of the new circumstances brought about by the June war and the Security Council's resolution of November 22, 1967. It is not my purpose to review the arguments of the two parties relative to the conditions preceding the June war, except in so far as they relate to the conditions after the war, since they have been thoroughly scrutinized by a number of scholars from the two opposing viewpoints.[4] In order to examine the legal aspect of the closure of the Canal specifically to Israeli shipping, I propose to deal with the question under three headings: (1) the fundamental principles governing the present legal status of the Suez Canal; (2) Israel's claim to the right of free passage; (3) Egypt's right to control of the Canal.

* B.A. 1932, American University, Beirut; Ph.D. 1938, University of Chicago. Director of the Center for Middle East Studies, and Professor, The School of Advanced International Studies, The Johns Hopkins University. Author, Independent Iraq (1951); War and Peace in the Law of Islam (1955); Islamic Jurisprudence (1961); Modern Libya (1963).

[1] The most important resolution was, of course, S.C. Res. 95 (1951). It cited S.C. Res. 73 (1949) and other resolutions and acts calling for the cessation of hostile acts and the resolution of outstanding issues between the parties.

[2] See Abba Eban's speech at the Emergency Session of the General Assembly of the United Nations on June 19, 1967, U.N. Doc. A/PV.1526 (1967) and subsequent declarations.

[3] For full text of the speech, see al-Ahram, Cairo, Nov. 25, 1967. See also N.Y. Times, Nov. 24, 1967, at 13, col. 1.

[4] Two books might be cited which deal with the divergent views in detail: B. Avram, The Evolution of the Suez Canal Status from 1869 up to 1956 (1958), and J. Obieta, The International Status of the Suez Canal (1960).

I

FUNDAMENTAL PRINCIPLES GOVERNING THE LEGAL STATUS OF THE SUEZ CANAL

When the Suez Canal was opened in 1869, Egypt had not yet attained independence. Its territory was part of the Ottoman Empire. The Khedive of Egypt, one of the Sultan's principal governors, had no power to act in entering into agreements relating to foreign affairs without the approval of the Sultan. Thus, the acts of concession issued by the Khedive in 1854, 1856, and 1866, granting the right to connect the Mediterranean and the Red Seas by a canal and to operate it, had to be ratified by the Sultan's firman (decree), issued on March 19, 1866, in order to be valid under the Ottoman law in force in Egypt.[5] However, no rights were derived from the concession by any third party nor was any surrender of the Sultan's sovereignty over the Canal ever intended. On the contrary, the acts of concession stressed Egypt's right to supervise the Canal, to enforce law and public order, and to occupy any point on the borders of the Canal whenever this was deemed necessary for the defense of the country, as a manifestation of sovereignty over the territory of the Canal. But the intent of throwing open the Canal to the free navigation of all nations without distinction of flag was made abundantly clear.

Nor was the Sultan's sovereignty over the Canal's territory restricted by the provisions of the Convention regulating the use of the Canal signed in Constantinople on October 29, 1888. The Convention of 1888 aimed at confirming the practices that had developed concerning free navigation for all nations, but no surrender of any sovereign rights was ever contemplated. For if the Sultan had given away any of his sovereign rights, he would have committed an act of servitude in derogation of his sovereignty over Egypt. The first principle governing the present status of the Suez Canal is, therefore, the principle of territorial sovereignty which was recognized by the signatories of the Convention of 1888. But to the manner in which the rights of sovereignty were to be exercised, we shall return later.

Next to the principle of territorial sovereignty is the principle that the Suez Canal is an "international waterway." This "internationality" was the product of a voluntary act on the part of the Ottoman Sultan in an effort to extend the benefits of free passage through the Canal to all nations without qualifying his sovereign rights. Even before the construction of the Canal was completed, the intent was, both in

---

[5] The concession, concluded with a private company, did not imply an international obligation on Egypt's behalf and could have been signed by the Khedive without the approval of the Sultan in accordance with the firman of appointment of the Khedive of 1841. But since the concession contained an obligation assumed by the two parties toward each other affecting third parties in their undertaking that they would not discriminate against other parties, and Article 14 of the 1866 concession provided that the canal and its ports would always be open as a neutral passage, the Sultan's approval became necessary. In the concession of 1866, it was stipulated that the Sultan's ratification was necessary. For texts of the acts of concession and the firmans of ratification, see U.S. DEP'T OF STATE, PUB. No. 6392, THE SUEZ CANAL PROBLEM: A DOCUMENTARY PUBLICATION 1-16 (1956); B. BOUTROS-GHALI, LE CANAL DE SUEZ, 1854-1957: CHRONOLOGIE DOCUMENT 10 (1958); 1 J. HUREWITZ, DIPLOMACY IN THE NEAR AND MIDDLE EAST 146-49 (1956).

the acts of concession as well as in unilateral declarations, to grant the right of free navigation to all nations. Article 14 of the Concession of 1856 reads:

> We solemnly declare, for ourselves and our successors, subject to ratification by His Imperial Majesty the Sultan, that the great maritime canal from Suez to Pelusium and the ports belonging to it shall be open forever, as neutral passages, to every merchant vessel crossing from one sea to the other, without any distinction, exclusion, or preference with respect to persons or nationalities, in consideration of the payment of the fees, and compliance with the regulations established by the universal company, the concession-holder, for the use of the said canal and its appurtenances.[6]

In this, as well as in other relevant declarations of unilateral nature, the purpose was to assure the company and all nations that the canal would always be open to free navigation. Notwithstanding these declarations, as one Israeli writer stated, "[t]he passage of ships was not a right but a privilege granted by the Ottoman Empire to other nations."[7] It is also questionable that a right was established by the Sultan's declaration made at a conference held in Constantinople, in 1873, to deal with technical matters, in which he said:

> It is understood that no modification, for the future, of the conditions for the passage through the Canal shall be permitted, whether in regard to the navigation toll or the dues for towage, anchorage, pilotage, etc., except with the consent of the Sublime Porte, which will not take any decision on the subject without previously coming to an understanding with the principal Powers interested therein.[8]

Some writers have argued, on the analogy of the *Eastern Greenland Case,* that the unilateral declaration of a Foreign Minister on behalf of his country, would be "binding upon the country to which the Minister belongs."[9] Such a declaration was, in that case, held by the Permanent Court of International Justice to be binding on the country making it. The so-called "Ihlen doctrine" may or may not be accepted, but it is of no great significance to our discussion, since an internationally binding act had been accepted by the Ottoman Porte in 1888 which established beyond any doubt the international character of the Suez Canal.

In the preamble of the Constantinople Convention[10] (October 29, 1888), the nine signatory Powers[11] stated that their intention was to establish "a definitive system intended to guarantee, at all times and to all the Powers, the free use of the Suez Maritime Canal, and thus to complete the system under which the navigation of

---

[6] THE SUEZ CANAL PROBLEM, *supra* note 5, at 7; B. BOUTROS-GHALI, *supra* note 5, at 6; and 1 J. HUREWITZ, *supra* note 5, at 148.

[7] B. AVRAM, *supra* note 4, at 31.

[8] Great Britain, *Parliamentary Papers*, Commercial 19, C. 1075, at 319.

[9] [1933] P.C.I.J., ser. A/B, No. 53, at 21, 71.

[10] For English text of the Convention, *see* Great Britain, *Parliamentary Papers*, Commercial, No. 2, Suez Canal, C. 5623 (1889); THE SUEZ CANAL PROBLEM, *supra* note 5, at 16-20; B. BOUTROS-GHALI, *supra* note 5, at 16; 1 J. HUREWITZ, *supra* note 5, at 202-05.

[11] They were Great Britain, Austria-Hungary, France, Germany, Italy, The Netherlands, Russia, Spain, and Turkey.

this Canal had been placed by the Firman of His Imperial Majesty the Sultan, dated February 22, 1866 . . . ."

Moreover, the preamble indicates the principle of "internationality" as having evolved from the inception of the Canal and that the Convention was to "complete" the legal status envisioned in early declarations. As a legal obligation, however, it is Article 1, specifying free navigation to all nations, which established the principle of internationality to include freedom of passage in time of war and peace. Article 1 reads: "The Suez Maritime Canal shall always be free and open, in time of war as in time of peace, to every vessel of commerce or of war, without distinction of flag. Consequently, the High Contracting Parties agree not in any way to interfere with the free use of the canal, in time of war as in time of peace."

In order to insure "free navigation," it was realized that a "guarantee," as stated in the preamble, was necessary. To achieve such a guarantee, the signatories provided, under Article 2, that: "They undertake not to interfere in any way with security of that Canal and its branches, the working of which shall not be the object of any attempt at obstruction."

This "security" of the Canal was to be guaranteed by the acceptance of another principle, already stated in earlier declarations, that the Canal would be neutral, although the term *neutrality* is not used in the text of the Convention. Article 4 reads:

> The Maritime Canal remaining open in time of war as a free passage . . . , no right of war, act of hostility or act having for its purpose to interfere with the free navigation of the Canal, shall be committed in the Canal and its ports . . . even though the Ottoman Empire should be one of the belligerent Powers.

All other acts on the part of belligerent Powers were forbidden in the Canal and its ports. Moreover, the Canal, as Article 1 further states, "shall never be submitted to the exercise of the right of blockade." The legal consequence of these stipulations is that the Canal, in time of war, shall be excluded from the area of warfare.[12] Thus, the neutrality of the Suez Canal, even if the Ottoman Empire were one of the belligerent Powers, is the third principle governing the present legal status of the Canal. Various terms have been used to characterize this neutral regime, from "inviolability" to "neutralization," but this should be distinguished from the neutralization of states.[13]

The three principles of territorial sovereignty, internationality, and neutrality

---

[12] This means that the neutral zone should be excluded from the region where war can lawfully be prepared or waged.

[13] See J. OBIETA, *supra* note 4, at 68-69. Colombos, however, held a different point of view on the Canal's neutrality. He said: ". . . the Suez Canal is not neutralized in the proper sense of the term, since neutrality does not admit the passage of belligerent forces across a territory . . . . It is only subject to a particular regime for the purpose of withdrawing it from all acts of hostility within its waters and protecting it from any damage or any attempt to close it to the detriment of the World's navigation." C. COLOMBOS, THE INTERNATIONAL LAW OF THE SEA 175 (4th ed. 1961).

have been assessed differently by various writers. Some, stressing internationality and neutrality, have maintained that sovereignty was restricted by the Convention of 1888 which imposed a "perpetual servitude" over Egypt in the area of the Suez Canal.[14] Others, rejecting the imposition of an international servitude, stressed the overriding principle of territorial sovereignty and recognize neither an international character for the Canal nor an implied neutrality in its zone.[15] The latter position has been maintained by writers who either tried to defend Egypt's position on the closure of the Canal against Israel or pushed to the extreme the doctrine of territorial sovereignty in the relationship among states. On the other hand, the writers who argued the case of Israel's claim to free passage have stressed Egypt's international obligations under the Convention of 1888 without qualifications. A third position, however, may be maintained in which Egypt's contractual obligations may be respected without compromising the doctrine of sovereignty. This is the position taken in this paper.

II

Israel's Claim to the Right of Free Passage Through the Suez Canal

Since its establishment more than two decades ago, Israel has repeatedly demanded the same right of free passage through the Suez Canal enjoyed by other nations, and has claimed that Egypt's closure of the Canal to its shipping had been done in violation of the general principles of international law, of the Convention of 1888, and of the Armistice Agreement of 1949. Let us examine Israel's complaints from these three legal angles.

Under the general principles of international law, according to Israel, all nations possess the right to navigate freely on the high seas, through international waterways that connect high seas, and through international rivers. This right, according to Israel, is "a cornerstone" of international law, and, therefore, cannot be denied to her as one of the members of the international community.

In the specific case of the Suez Canal, the right of free passage, clearly stated in the Constantinople Convention of 1888, was, in this area, to be enjoyed by all nations without distinction of flag. Israel, as one of the nations presumably included under the general term "without distinction of flag," was therefore entitled to enjoy the same right as other nations, but Egypt is alleged to have denied Israel such right in violation of the general principle of international law and of her obligations under the Convention of 1888.

Moreover, Egypt's restrictive measures, according to Israel, constitute an act of war in the Canal waters contrary to Articles 1 and 4 of the Convention of 1888, on

---

[14] See B. Avram, *supra* note 4, at 48-50.

[15] See Huang, *Some International and Legal Aspects of the Suez Canal Question*, 51 Am. J. Int'l L. 300-03 (1957).

the ground that Egypt possessed no right to take defensive measures in the Canal Zone.[16] Egypt proceeded to act on the assumption that she was at war with Israel, but this assumption was not justified, according to Israel, because no state—other than the Arab states—recognized such a state of war to have existed. On the contrary, the United Nations had on more than one occasion called on Egypt to open the Suez Canal presumably on the assumption that Egypt and Israel, as peace-loving members of that Organization, can no longer remain at war with one another. If they had ever been at war, as the Arab states held, such a state of war must be superseded by membership in the United Nations.[17]

Finally, the Armistice Agreement between Egypt and Israel (February 24, 1949)[18] has prohibited hostile acts. According to Israel, not only war in the military sense, but also the state of war between her and Egypt had been terminated. As stated by an Israeli jurist, the Agreement was intended to achieve four aims:

1. To facilitate the transition from the present truce to permanent peace and bring all hostilities to an end.

2. To fulfill the obligation of the Security Council to act with respect to threats to the peace, breaches of the peace and acts of aggression.

3. To delineate permanent demarcation lines beyond which the armed forces of the respective parties should not move.

4. To provide for the withdrawal and reduction of armed forces in order to insure the maintenance of the armistice during the transition to permanent peace.[19]

These aims, intended to establish eventual peace between Egypt and Israel, have been endorsed by the United Nations resolutions of 1949 and of 1951, which explicitly called upon Egypt to open the Suez Canal. Egypt's refusal to open the Canal, according to Israel, was a violation of both the Armistice Agreement and the United Nations Security Council resolutions of 1949 and 1951.[20]

Egypt, however, has refused to accept the charge that she has denied Israel's right of free passage in violation of international law. Israel has put forth a claim to free passage under international law on the ground that the Suez Canal—like any other strait—is an international waterway and, therefore, according to her, should be open to free navigation. But should the Suez Canal, even if regarded as an international waterway, be treated as other waterways, like straits, and, therefore, as subject to the same rules of international law? Straits, as "natural" waterways provided

---

[16] 9 U.N. SCOR, 658th meeting 1-25 (1954). *See also* B. AVRAM, *supra* note 4, at 119-21.

[17] This viewpoint is based on the assumption that members of the United Nations are peace-loving members and therefore no one can be at war with another member without violating the Charter of this organization. *See* H. KELSEN, THE LAW AND THE UNITED NATIONS 69 (1950); AND L.M. BLOOMFIELD, EGYPT, ISRAEL AND THE GULF OF AQABA IN INTERNATIONAL LAW 164 (1957).

[18] 42 U.N.T.S. 251, no. 654. *See also* 2 J. HUREWITZ, *supra* note 5, at 299-304.

[19] S. ROSENNE, ISRAEL'S ARMISTICE AGREEMENTS WITH THE ARAB STATES 33 (1951).

[20] *See* note 1 *supra*. For an interpretation of these views, *see* Gross, *Passage Through the Suez Canal of Israel-Bound Cargo and Israel Ships*, 51 AM. J. INT'L L. 530-68 (1957).

by nature, have existed from time immemorial and, therefore, the free passage enjoyed by all nations must be distinguished from free passage through canals which have been artificially constructed. Before a canal is opened, its territory must be under the control of some state sovereignty. Canals must, therefore, fall in a different category from straits, because they are artificial waterways opened by the express or tacit approval of the sovereign power and, *ipso jure*, the consent of the sovereign power must be first obtained. If the sovereign grants free passage by an express declaration or by an obligation under a treaty or an international agreement, it is the legal obligation undertaken by the sovereign which entitles other nations to enjoy free passage, rather than the geographical analogy with natural waterways.[21]

In the case of the Suez Canal, it was the Convention of 1888 rather than the general principles of international law that granted the right of free passage to other nations. If Israel possesses any right to enjoy free passage through the canal, such right must be derived from the aggregate right granted to other nations and not by an analogy with natural waterways which nations ordinarily enjoy under international law.

The Convention of 1888 merely confirmed the right of free passage already recognized by the Ottoman Porte before 1888 and the powers that signed this convention acquired such rights both in time of peace and war. At the time of signature, other nations were invited to adhere to the Convention, but failed to do so. With regard to non-signatory states, the question whether the Convention is obligatory on them is an open one. Israel may be said to fall in a different category of non-signatory states. As a successor state, would she not, like Egypt, be entitled to special rights?

There is no question that Egypt, already mentioned in the Convention, was granted special rights as the country immediately connected with the canal, and certain obligations were imposed on her.[22] Egypt, according to the general principles of international law, must also accept the obligations already undertaken on her behalf by the former sovereign power. Moreover, Egypt has formally declared its acceptance of the obligations under the Convention of 1888 after independence on more than one occasion.[23]

---

[21] "Unlike international rivers and straits, which are natural waterways, international canals are artificially constructed. This essentially differentiating factor has been overlooked by a number of writers who, misled by the similarity of regimes to which both international canals as well as rivers and straits are subject, have tried to find, by an analogy to the latter, a geographical or physical criterion which would serve to define an international canal."
J. OBIETA, *supra* note 4, at 24.

[22] *See* Articles 8, 9, 10, and 14 of the Convention of 1888. *Cf. supra* note 11.

[23] From 1938 in formal statements concerning the Canal following the declaration of independence to 1954, the year of signature of the treaty with Britain for evacuation of the Canal Zone. *See, e.g.,* letter from Mustafa al Sadik Bey to Lord Perth, April 16, 1938, 195 L.N.T.S. 108 (1939); Agreement between . . . Egypt and the . . . United Kingdom, October 19, 1954, 210 U.N.T.S. 1 (1955); Letter from the Minister for Foreign Affairs to Egypt to the Secretary-General . . . 24 April 1957, 12 U.N. SCOR, Supp. April-June 1957, at 8, 9, U.N. Doc. S/3818/Add. 1 (1957); statement by Egyptian Representative in Security Council, 2 U.N. SCOR 1756 (1947).

Unlike Egypt, however, Israel falls in a special category. First, she has not adhered to the Convention of 1888, which has an accession clause, and therefore may enjoy the right of free passage in time of peace like other non-signatory states to whom the right of free passage was granted before 1888, but not the right of free passage in time of war which was granted under the Convention of that year. Second, if Israel may be considered to have adhered tacitly, she must have acquired not only the right to enjoy the right of free passage, but also the obligations of the Convention. Such obligations, for instance, require that the Canal must remain neutral and not involved in the area in which war is lawfully waged, and that the Canal should not be subject to blockade. Obviously Israel has neither declared her acceptance of such obligations nor, since she carried her military operations to its very eastern bank, has she respected the neutralization of the Suez Canal.[24] Third, Egypt's territory has become the subject of an Israeli attack in 1967, which raises the question of Egypt's right to take defensive measures irrespective of whether Israel possesses the right of free passage or not. This latter point, so significantly affecting the status of the Canal, deserves to be treated separately in the following section, concerned with Egypt's right to control the Canal.

It follows from our foregoing argument that if Israel were not involved in a war with Egypt—a war in which Egypt closed the Canal as a defensive measure—Israel would be entitled to the right of free passage. There can be no doubt that Israel's attack on Egyptian territory on June 5, 1967, presumably to settle a dispute by force rather than by peaceful methods as provided by the Charter of the United Nations, was an act of war which justified Egypt's position concerning the security of the Suez Canal, since, as noted above, Israel was not entitled to enjoy the same rights and obligations as a signatory of the Convention of 1888. As a third party beneficiary, a right concerning which jurists are not all in agreement,[25] Israel might claim to enjoy certain rights to use the Canal. But in a war which Israel initiated, and in which it attacked the territorial Zone of the Canal, Egypt would be empowered to close the Canal in self-defense, no less by general law than by the very provisions of the Convention of 1888 which obligate Egypt to take measures to prohibit any state from conducting war in the Canal Zone.[26]

A controversy has raged among several writers as to whether a state of war existed between Egypt and Israel before June 5, 1967. Those who defend Israel's right to free passage through the Canal hold that belligerency between the two states created by the Palestine war of 1948-49 was terminated by the Armistice

---

[24] Although Israel did not reach the Canal Zone in the invasion of Sinai in 1956, in the June war she reached and asserted control over the eastern bank of the Canal in violation of Articles 1 and 4 of the Convention. See notes 11 and 12 *supra*.

[25] *See* LORD McNAIR, LAW OF TREATIES 309-21 (1961); HARVARD RESEARCH IN INTERNATIONAL LAW: LAW OF TREATIES 924 (J. Garner ed. 1935).

[26] In practice this seems to have been the position maintained by the Ottoman Porte and later Egypt since 1888. See J. OBIETA, *supra* note 4, at 79-87.

Agreement of February 28, 1949.[27] Moreover, the Security Council resolution of September 1, 1951, calling upon Egypt to open the Canal to Israeli shipping on the ground that hostilities had been terminated by the armistice of 1949, was asserted by some to be binding on Egypt. Egypt, according to those who supported this viewpoint, has violated the Convention of 1888 and ignored the resolution of the Security Council.[28] Those who hold an opposing viewpoint argue that the Armistice Agreement of 1949 did not terminate the state of war, since an armistice puts an end to fighting but does not establish peace. Only a peace treaty can terminate the state of war and establish peace.[29] Moreover, the Security Council resolution, based on the assumption that the intent of the Armistice Agreement was to establish peace, cannot be regarded as binding on Egypt without her consent, because the resolution was recommendatory and not mandatory in nature.[30]

The controversy between these opposing viewpoints is deemed outside the scope of this paper, which deals with the problem of the closure of the Suez Canal in the circumstances created by the war of 1967. Even if a state of war had not existed before June 5, 1967, Egypt's decision to keep the Canal closed to Israeli shipping after the June war would be justified by the measures necessary for self-defense against sudden attack on the ground that the closure of the Canal against a non-signatory to the Convention falls within Egypt's sovereign rights.

Finally, it may be asked to what extent Egypt's obligations under the Convention of 1888 have restricted her sovereign rights over the Canal? This raises the question of Egypt's right to control the Canal, which falls under the third heading of our discussion.

III

EGYPT'S RIGHT TO CONTROL OF THE CANAL

The control of the Suez Canal raises the question of the relevance of territorial sovereignty to the status of the Canal and to what extent it was restricted by an international agreement. As already stated, the internationality of the Canal may be regarded as a balancing principle between the doctrine of sovereignty and the binding obligations of an international agreement. It is in the light of this balance that Egypt's right of the control of the Canal should be assessed.

---

[27] See S. ROSENNE, supra note 19, at 82.

[28] See B. AVRAM, supra note 4, at 119.

[29] For a summary of the Egyptian point of view, see id. at 122-27.

[30] For a discussion on the nature of the U.N. resolution, see Halderman, *Some International Constitutional Aspects of the Palestine Case,* in this symposium, p. 78. Colonel Howard S. Levie makes the following remarks on the Security Council resolution of 1951:

"It is considered more likely that the Security Council's action was based upon a desire to bring to an end a situation fraught with potential danger to peace than that it was attempting to change a long established rule of international law. By now it has surely become fairly obvious that the Israeli-Arab General Armistice Agreements did not create even a *de facto* termination of the war between those states."

Levie, *The Nature and Scope of the Armistice Agreement,* 50 AM. J. INT'L L. 880, 886 (1956). *See* 2 L. OPPENHEIM, INTERNATIONAL LAW 546-51 (7th ed. H. Lauterpacht 1952).

Admitting her obligations under the Convention of 1888, Egypt has held that she has not violated Article 1 concerning "free passage" through the Canal, because the measures taken in time of war were "reasonable and necessary measures" for defense purposes, as the Egyptian Prize Court of Alexandria states.[31] It might be argued that even "reasonable" and "necessary" measures might be restricted by the Convention of 1888, since Articles 10 and 11 prohibited Egypt from actions, even for the defense of her territory, because they might interfere with the free use of the Canal. It is also argued that, as held by the World Court in the *Wimbledon* case,[32] the Canal should remain permanently free as an international waterway.

Egypt's insistence on her right to close the Canal against Israeli shipping in time of war has naturally raised the question as to whether she can close the Canal during war against any other nations including signatory powers. This seems to be different from closing the Canal against a country that had attacked Egyptian territory, including the Canal Zone. It was in the exercise of her inherent right of self-defense that Egypt denied free passage to Israel.[33] Such a situation seems either to have been taken for granted by the Convention of 1888, because it falls within the rights of sovereignty, or left undecided. Egypt's actions might, however, be justified even if the Convention is held binding upon it to grant free passage to all nations, including Israel, on the ground of the internationality of the Canal. Any such obligation would necessarily entail the reciprocal obligation on the part of Israel to respect the neutrality of the Canal and the territorial sovereignty of Egypt. It cannot be claimed that Egypt is bound by the Convention *in toto* regardless of whether Israel accepts the obligations imposed on the nine signatory powers. Such a rule would clearly be imposing an international servitude over Egypt in order to grant to Israel the right of free passage in time of peace and war and denying Egypt the right of self-defense in case of an attack on her territory. If we take this position, the purposes of the Convention would be inconsistent with the general principles of international law which recognize Egypt's right to repudiate restrictive measures on her sovereignty imposed without her consent. Nor would the Ottoman Porte have agreed to sign the Convention and acquiesce in such a servitude, because it had consistently declared before 1888 that its control over the Canal was not to be restricted by throwing the Canal's doors open to other nations.[34]

A balancing view of the principle of internationality seems to restrict Egypt's right to close the Canal in time of peace against any nation including Israel if Egypt's security were not involved. So long as Israel insists on a right of free passage under the Convention of 1888 by threatening Egypt's security, Israel seems to pursue a

[31] The Flying Trader, [1950] Ann. Dig. 440, 446-47 (No. 149) (Prize Court of Alexandria), 7 REV. EGYPTIENNE DE DROIT INTERNATIONAL 127 (1951).

[32] [1923] P.C.I.J., ser. A, No. 1.

[33] See Baxter, *Passage of Ships Through International Waterways in Time of War*, 31 BRIT. YB. INT'L L. 208 (1954).

[34] See J. OBIETA, *supra* note 4, at 78-87.

contradictory legal position by invoking one article of the Convention (Article 1) while denying Egypt's right to invoke another (Article 10).[35]

In 1956, when Egypt nationalized the Suez Canal, the Security Council passed a six-point resolution on October 13, 1956, in which it was affirmed that any settlement of the Suez Canal question should, *inter alia*, meet the following requirements: (1) free and open transit through the Canal, and (2) respect for Egypt's sovereignty.[36]

This resolution seems to embody the balancing principle of internationality by proposing to grant freedom of navigation without compromising Egypt's sovereignty. Thus, the balancing principle of internationality must be considered with due respect to Egypt's sovereignty. The principle of internationality would cease to be a balancing principle if Egypt were to be denied the right to close the Canal, as a measure of self-defense, in case of an attack. Israel can claim the right to be a beneficiary of the principle of internationality if she ceases to present a threat to Egypt's security, one of her sovereign rights.

CONCLUSION

From the time of the nationalization of the Canal, Egypt has not only reiterated her affirmation of the binding obligations of the Convention of 1888 and her respect of the principle of free navigation, but also declared that any dispute or disagreements which may arise in respect of that Convention would be settled in accordance with the Charter of the United Nations, and that any differences that may arise concerning the interpretation of that Convention would be referred to the International Court of Justice. In a letter dated July 18, 1957, addressed to the Secretary-General of the United Nations, Egypt accepted the compulsory jurisdiction of the International Court in all legal disputes that may arise from the application of the Convention of 1888.[37] Since Egypt has accepted the compulsory jurisdiction of the International Court on all legal disputes relating to the Suez Canal, Israel's claim to the right of free passage through the Canal might well be an appropriate case to be brought to the International Court for adjudication and might be regarded as an example for solving other Arab-Israeli issues on the basis of law and justice rather than force or diplomatic pressures.[38]

---

[35] Article 10, paragraph 1, of the Convention of 1888 provides:

"Similarly, the provisions of Articles IV, V, VII, and VIII shall not stand in the way of any measures which His Majesty the Sultan and His Highness the Khedive in the name of His Imperial Majesty, and within the limits of the Firmans granted, might find it necessary to take to assure by their own forces the defence of Egypt and the maintenance of public order." *Supra* note 11.

[36] S.C. Res. 118.

[37] [1956-1957] I.C.J.Y.B. 213-14, 241. *Cf.* U.N. Doc. S/3818/Add. 1, *supra* note 23.

[38] One of the states which supported Security Council resolution 95 (1951), calling on Egypt to open the Suez to Israeli shipping, might either voluntarily or upon Israel's request refer the Suez Canal dispute to the International Court of Justice in accordance with article 36, para. 1, of the statute of that Court. Article 36, paragraph 1, provides: "The jurisdiction of the Court comprises all cases which the parties refer to it and all matters specially provided for in the Charter of the United Nations or in treaties and conventions in force."

II. UNDERLYING ISSUES

C. *The Status of Jerusalem and the Holy Places*

The Status of Jerusalem:
Some National and International Aspects

S. SHEPARD JONES

I
SCOPE AND PURPOSE

If a genuine Arab-Israeli peace settlement is to be achieved as an aftermath to the 1967 war and the subsequent diplomatic efforts of the United Nations in 1967 and 1968, some understanding must be reached on the future status of Jerusalem. Of course, this is only one of many troublesome questions that evoke political malaise. The purpose of this short essay is to put the problem of Jerusalem in perspective by drawing attention to some of the background considerations that shed light on the present situation. These considerations are as much political as legal; they are both national and international, religious and secular. While the purpose is primarily to provide perspective, not to argue for a particular resolution of the future status of Jerusalem, this article does conclude with an indication of the direction and spirit within which a settlement might be sought, if the interests of all the parties are to be protected. These interests are complex and varied, and it is assumed that the cause of international peace and justice demands respect for the interests of all concerned and therefore not the complete triumph of the purposes of any one nation or religious community. The multiple interests in Jerusalem suggest the wisdom of redefining national purposes to the higher good.

II
THE NATURE OF "THE QUESTION OF JERUSALEM, 1967-68"

The more restricted "problem of Jerusalem" in its present context arises out of the suddenly upset military balance and the emotional shock produced by the lightning-like war of June 1967. A part of that reality—but not its beginning[1]—was the attack by Jordanian forces on Israel on June 5, following the outbreak of war on the Egyptian-Israeli front earlier the same day. After hard fighting there followed, on June 7, the capture of Arab Jerusalem, governed by Jordan since 1948, and Israel's announcement of June 28[2] that "the law, jurisdiction and administration of the

---

* A.B. 1930, Georgetown College; A.M. 1931, University of Kentucky; Ph.D. (Rhodes Scholar) 1936, Oxford University. Burton Craige Professor of Political Science, University of North Carolina. Author, THE SCANDINAVIAN STATES AND THE LEAGUE OF NATIONS (1939); co-editor [with D. P. Myers], DOCUMENTS ON AMERICAN FOREIGN RELATIONS (vols. I-III (1939, 1940, 1941); AMERICA'S ROLE IN THE MIDDLE EAST (1958).

[1] M. HOWARD & R. HUNTER, ISRAEL AND THE ARAB WORLD: THE CRISIS OF 1967 (Adelphi Papers, no. 41, October 1967); Yost, *The Arab-Israeli War: How It Began*, 46 FOREIGN AFF. 304-06 (1968).

[2] Under ordinance of the preceding day. Summaries at p. 8 of the Report of the Secretary-General under General Assembly resolution 2254(ES-I), U.N. Doc. A/6793, Sept. 12, 1967. Also issued as U.N. Doc. S/8146.

State of Israel" were being applied to the Old City and to an enlarged East Jerusalem, as Arab Jerusalem is now designated.

Bitter protest came from Jordan[3] and other Arab states and from non-Arab states including the United States,[4] and allegations that international law had been violated by Israel. Israel asserted that Jordan was responsible for initiating the attack on Jerusalem and must accept the consequences.[5]

The United Nations General Assembly adopted two resolutions without opposition on July 4 and 14, 1967 (the latter by a vote of one hundred to zero, with eighteen abstentions, including that of the United States[6]), declaring Israel's action "invalid," and calling upon Israel "to rescind all measures already taken and desist forthwith from taking any action which would alter the status of Jerusalem."[7] Israel refused to comply, contending that "no international or other interest would be served by the institution of divisions and barriers which would only sharpen tension and generate discrimination." The claim was made that Israel was responding to "the intrinsic necessity of ensuring equal rights and opportunities to all the city's residents."[8] This answer did not meet the major issue at stake, as the General Assembly debate made clear.[9]

Looking ahead, the Israeli Government stated that its policy of integrating all of Jerusalem "does not foreclose the final settlement of certain important aspects of the Jerusalem situation which lie at the origin of the international interest in the city." Reference was made to "the need to secure appropriate expression of the special interest of the three great religions in Jerusalem." But this statement seemed to acknowledge the concerns and interests of others as something to be considered in the future, since the Foreign Minister added: "I am confident that in an atmosphere of international tranquility substantial progress could be made toward this aim, which has hitherto had no concrete fulfillment."[10] Reference was here made,

---

[3] See, e.g., remarks of King Hussein, U.N. Doc. A/PV. 1536, June 26, 1967, at 11.

[4] See, e.g., remarks of U.S. Delegation, U.N. Doc. A/PV. 1546, July 3, 1967, at 8-10.

[5] The Israeli Foreign Minister stated to the General Assembly on June 19, 1967:

"While fighting raged on the Egyptian-Israel frontier and on the Syrian front, we still hoped to contain the conflict. Jordan was given every chance to remain outside the struggle. Even after Jordan had bombarded and bombed Israel territory at several points, we still proposed to the Jordanian monarch that he abstain from any continuing hostilities . . . .

". . . Jordan's responsibility for the second phase of the concerted aggression is established beyond doubt. Surely this responsibility cannot fail to have its consequences in the peace settlement. As death and injury rained on the city, Jordan had become the source and origin of Jerusalem's fierce ordeal. The inhabitants of that city can never forget this fact, or fail to draw its conclusions." U.N. Doc. A/PV. 1526, June 19, at 50-51.

[6] U.N. Doc. A/PV. 1554, at 41.

[7] G.A. Resolutions 2253 and 2254, U.N. GAOR, 5th Emer. Spec. Sess., Supp. 1, at 4, U.N. Doc. A/6798 (1967).

[8] Exchange of letters between the Secretary-General of the U.N. and the Israeli Foreign Minister, July 15, 1967, and Sept. 11, 1967, published in U.N. Doc. A/6793, supra note 2, at 29, 30.

[9] See, e.g., Docs. A/6743, July 3, 1967, and A/6774, July 25, 1967. See also remarks of Iraqi Delegation, U.N. Doc. A/PV. 1559, Sept. 18, 1967, at 6-16.

[10] U.N. Doc. A/6793, supra note 2, at 30.

apparently, to deprivation of access to Holy Places in the Old City of almost all citizens of Israel from 1949 to 1967, for instance to the Wailing Wall, and to acts of desecration of Jewish cemeteries.[11]

This reply should be viewed in the light of the conclusion of the United Nations Secretary-General, based on information supplied by his Personal Representative in Jerusalem,[12] that it has been "made clear beyond any doubt that Israel was taking every step to place under its sovereignty those parts of the city" not previously controlled by Israel.[13] Ambassador Thalmann reported that "The Israel authorities stated unequivocally that the process of integration was irreversible and not negotiable."[14]

The Personal Representative reported that he was told that "the Arabs recognize a military occupation régime as such and were ready to co-operate with such a régime in dealing with current questions of administration and public welfare. However, they were opposed to civil incorporation into the Israel State System," which action they regarded "as a violation of the acknowledged rule of international law which prohibited an occupying Power from changing the legal and administrative structure in the occupied territory." The population of East Jerusalem "was given no opportunity to state for itself whether it was willing to live in the Israel State community." It was claimed that the right of self-determination, in accordance with the United Nations Charter and the Universal Declaration of Human Rights, had therefore been violated.[15]

The report of the Secretary-General dated September 12, 1967 indicates that "most of the Arabs interviewed" by the Personal Representative—Arab notables in Jerusalem, both governmental and religious—stated that the Muslim population "was shocked by Israel acts which violated the sanctity of Muslim Shrines."[16]

Muslim leaders informed the Personal Representative that statements by Israeli officials and Jewish personalities "concerning Jewish claims and plans in the Temple area had had an alarming effect" on Muslim opinion.[17] The dynamiting and bulldozing of 135 houses in the Maghrabi quarter (in front of the Wailing Wall) had also aroused strong feelings. This action involved "the expulsion of 650 poor and pious Muslims from their homes in the immediate vicinity of the Mosque of Omar and the Aksa Mosque."[18]

In a letter of July 24, 1967 the Israeli Military Governor for the West Bank was

---

[11] See U.N. Docs. A/7064 and A/7064/Add. 1, March 6, 1968, a distribution of a pictorial document entitled "Desecration," issued by the Israeli Ministry of Foreign Affairs, Information Division, Jerusalem, November 1967 and transmitted to the Secretary-General of the U.N., March 5, 1968.

[12] Ambassador Thalmann, a Swiss national. He arrived in Jerusalem on August 21, 1967, and departed on September 3, 1967.

[13] U.N. Doc. A/6793, *supra* note 2, at 7.

[14] *Id.*

[15] *Id.* at 24.

[16] *Id.* at 21.

[17] *Id.*

[18] *Id.*

informed that the twenty-four signatories of the letter "had constituted themselves as the Muslim body in charge of Muslim affairs on the West Bank, including Jerusalem."[19] "This 'Higher Muslim Council,' as it is also called, designated four Arab personalities to carry out the responsibilities of public administration . . . on the West Bank, including East Jerusalem, in accordance with the applicable Jordanian law." But the decisions of the "Higher Muslim Council" were not recognized by the Israeli authorities, although publicized to the Arab population through Amman radio.[20]

The Secretary-General's Personal Representative in Jerusalem also reported the text of the statement issued June 27, 1967 by the Prime Minister of Israel concerning access to the Holy Places of Jerusalem and their administration.[21] Also reported was the "Protection of the Holy Places Law," passed by the Knesset the same day,[22] as well as the Prime Minister's statement of June 7, 1967 to spiritual leaders of all communities.[23] The statement of June 27 indicated that the Holy Places in Jerusalem "are now open to all who wish to worship at them—members of all faiths, without discrimination. The Government of Israel has made it a cardinal principle of its policy to preserve the Holy Places, to ensure their religious and universal character, and to guarantee free access." It was indicated that the policy would be carried out in consultation with representatives of the religious communities. The statutory measures provided for protection of the Holy Places from desecration and other violations.

The Personal Representative reported that these measures "were very favorably received," although some took a "wait and see" attitude.[24] The Muslim reaction has been indicated above. The Catholic Church was reported as having essentially a divergent attitude to various other Christian denominations. The Holy See remained convinced that "the only solution which offers a sufficient guarantee for the protection of Jerusalem and of its Holy Places is to place that city and its vicinity under an international régime in the form of a *corpus separatum*."[25]

III

THE UNITED STATES AND THE QUESTION OF JERUSALEM, 1967-68

On June 19, 1967 the President of the United States said there must be "adequate recognition of the special interest of three great religions in the holy places of Jerusalem."[26] On June 27, 1967 the Israeli Parliament approved legislation authorizing the Government to extend Israel's laws, jurisdiction and administration over addi-

---

[19] *Id.* at 44, 46.
[20] *Id.* at 22-23.
[21] *Id.* at 26.
[22] No. 5727-1967. Text printed in English, *id.*
[23] *Id.* at 25-26.
[24] *Id.* at 27.
[25] *Id.*
[26] 57 DEP'T STATE BULL. 33 (1967).

tional territory of *Eretz* Israel ("the Land of Israel"). On June 28 the Government of Israel defined the Old City of Jerusalem and certain other territory of the former mandate of Palestine which had been under the control of Jordan since 1948 as territory to be incorporated into an enlarged city of Jerusalem.[27] On June 28 the White House indicated that the President "assumes" that "before any unilateral action is taken on the status of Jerusalem there will be appropriate consultation with religious leaders and others who are deeply concerned" and that "the world must find an answer that is fair and recognized to be fair."[28] On June 28, the Government of Israel took administrative action under the new legislation to extend its municipal services and controls over the entire city of Jerusalem.[29] Later on that day a State Department press release[30] read:

> The hasty administrative action taken [by Israel] today cannot be regarded as determining the future of the holy places or the status of Jerusalem in relation to them.
> The United States has never recognized such unilateral actions by any of the states in the area as governing the international status of Jerusalem . . . .

On July 3, the United States Representative to the General Assembly said that "the safeguarding of the Holy Places, and freedom of access to them for all, should be internationally guaranteed."[31]

On July 7, 1967 the Executive Committee of the National Council of Churches of Christ in the United States of America adopted a resolution[32] which, in part, read:

> With due consideration for the right of nations to defend themselves, the National Council of Churches cannot condone by silence territorial expansion by armed force. Israel's unilateral retention of the lands she has occupied since June 5 will only deepen the divisions and antagonisms which separate her from those neighbors in the midst of whom she must dwell.
> The territorial frontiers of the states of the Middle East should now be definitely established by negotiation in treaties of peace and the integrity of such frontiers should be assured by international protection.

More specifically, on the issue of Jerusalem, the resolution of the National Council of Churches states:

> We support the *establishment of an international presence* in the hitherto divided city of Jerusalem which will preserve the peace and integrity of the city, foster the welfare of its inhabitants, and protect its holy shrines with full rights of

---

[27] Measures summarized in U.N. Doc. A/6793, *supra* note 2, at 8.

[28] 57 DEP'T STATE BULL. 60 (1967).

[29] *See* note 27 *supra*.

[30] 57 DEP'T STATE BULL. 60 (1967).

[31] U.N. Doc. A/PV. 1546, July 3, 1967, at 3-5.

[32] Memorandum entitled "Resolution on the Crisis in the Middle East." *See* N.Y. Times, July 15, 1967, at 28, col. 1.

access to all. We encourage the earliest possible advancement of U.N. proposals to make such arrangements practicable.

We cannot approve Israel's unilateral annexation of the Jordanian portions of Jerusalem. This historic city is sacred not only to Judaism but also to Christianity and Islam.

On July 14, Ambassador Goldberg, speaking for the United States Delegation to the Fifth Emergency Special Session of the U.N. General Assembly, reiterated that "the United States does not accept or recognize . . . as altering the status of Jerusalem" the measures taken by the Israeli government on June 28. He said further that the United States did not recognize that these measures

> can be regarded as the last word on the matter, and we regret that they were taken. We insist that the measures taken cannot be considered as other than interim and provisional, and not as prejudging the final and permanent status of Jerusalem.
>
> Unfortunately, and regrettably, the statements of the Government of Israel on this matter have thus far, in our view, not adequately dealt with this situation.[33]

Nevertheless, the United States abstained from voting on General Assembly resolution A/2254,[34] the resolution not fully corresponding to United States government views, particularly since, even as revised

> it appears to accept, by its call for rescission of measures, that the administrative measures which were taken constitute annexation of Jerusalem by Israel, and because we do not believe that the problem of Jerusalem can realistically be solved apart from the other related aspects of the Middle Eastern situation.

There are, it was said, important practical issues in addition to "transcendent spiritual interests" that must be resolved. The United States representative implied that the Assembly should have gone no further than to declare itself against any unilateral change in the status of Jerusalem.[35]

Following reports in January 1968 of Israeli plans for development of certain areas of the occupied sector of Jerusalem—being between Mt. Scopus and the former armistice line—a State Department spokesman reiterated that the United States does not recognize "any unilateral actions affecting the status of Jerusalem."[36] The United States position is that Arab territories now administered by Israel as a result of the six-day war should be administered under the law of occupation as recognized by international law, not under a right of conquest. The Department of State apparently regards the Hague Convention of 1907 as applicable to the existing situation.[37]

---

[33] U.N. Doc. A/PV. 1554, July 14, 1967, at 48.

[34] Note 6 *supra* and accompanying text.

[35] U.N. Doc. A/PV. 1554, *supra* note 33, at 48, 51.

[36] N.Y. Times, Jan. 16, 1968, at 16, col. 6.

[37] For some recent statements as to rules considered applicable, see 1 M. WHITEMAN, DIGEST OF INTERNATIONAL LAW 946-52 (1963).

IV

SOME LEGAL AND POLITICAL QUESTIONS

A question has been raised as to whether acquisition of territory by conquest is valid in the light of the United Nations Charter obligations accepted by both sides. Press reports frequently refer to "territory conquered," but the Israeli government has apparently avoided making a claim on that basis. Does the integration of Arab Jerusalem by Israel hurt the prospects for an agreed settlement of larger aspects of the Arab-Israeli confrontation? What is the legal meaning and the political effect of Israel's contention that the future of Arab Jerusalem is not negotiable? Have Israel's leaders concluded that the prospects for a settlement with the Arab states are so unlikely, because of Arab intransigence; that the integration or annexation of Jerusalem does not actually endanger prospects for a peace settlement, because the prospects for the foreseeable future, despite efforts of the Secretary-General's Special Representative, Dr. Gunnar Jarring, are hopelessly dim?

It may be useful to divide the Jerusalem question into three major aspects: (1) *who* will govern Jerusalem—*i.e.,* whose "law, jurisdiction and administration" will prevail in the future? Will the city remain unified as it was prior to 1948 and in 1967-68 or again be divided? Or will it be managed in a third way? And will the determination be made by unilateral action or by agreement? (2) What arrangements can be made to assure "adequate recognition of the special interest of three great religions in the holy places of Jerusalem," *i.e.,* to guarantee the protection of the Holy Places within and outside Jerusalem and for assurance of access thereto? (3) Should an *international presence* be maintained in Jerusalem with functions broader than that of protecting the holy places? What practical proposals can be agreed to and maintained in the face of diverging interests? These are difficult political questions which confront or may confront the interested governments. The answers can best be found through the process of negotiation. Recognizing that such negotiations must inevitably be affected by other questions lying beyond the scope of this paper, let us consider certain background facts that help put the present situation in perspective.

A. Political

How does the experience of history relate to these questions? A quick look may give a distorted image, but hopefully may suggest essential reality if only approximate. Who has governed Jerusalem and how was title gained? In the past 3500 years the city has changed hands more than twenty-five times.[38] We can begin with David who about 1000 B.C. captured the old Jebusite Town and claimed it as the City of David. Later it was conquered by one empire after another—Babylonian,

---

[38] S. PEROWNE, THE ONE REMAINS 11 (1954). *See also* REPORT OF THE COMMISSION APPOINTED BY HIS MAJESTY'S GOVERNMENT . . . TO DETERMINE THE RIGHTS AND CLAIMS . . . IN CONNECTION WITH THE WESTERN OR WAILING WALL AT JERUSALEM: DECEMBER 1930, at 9-15 (1931). Distributed as U.N. Docs. A/7057/Add. 1 and S/8427/Add. 1, Feb. 23, 1968.

Persian, Macedonian, Ptolemy, Selucid, and Roman. In 638 A.D. the Caliph Omar captured Jerusalem for Islam. Later it was held by Seljuk Turks, by Christian Crusaders, and by Egyptian Mameluks. From 1517 to 1917 Jerusalem was ruled by the Ottoman Turks, who then gave way to General Allenby of Great Britain. Following World War I, the Principal Allied Powers decided that Palestine should be a League of Nations mandate assigned to Great Britain. On July 24, 1922 the Council of the League of Nations confirmed and defined the terms of the Mandate for Palestine, with Great Britain as the Mandatory Power. The Palestine Mandate went into effect September 29, 1923.[39] When it terminated on May 15, 1948 Arabs and Jews of Palestine, and Arab armies from without, fought for possession of Jerusalem and of Palestine. The outcome confirmed the reality of what actually had already become a divided city, now occupied by Israeli and Jordan authorities,[40] with a set of conflicting claims, which, in turn, conflicted with plans and proposals of the United Nations to establish Jerusalem as a *corpus separatum* under an international régime. This proposal was part of the Plan of Partition with Economic Union, which was recommended by the General Assembly on November 29, 1947[41] in an effort to provide for the future government of Palestine, upon the termination of the British Mandate. This Plan was never fully implemented.[42]

At no time did the international community acting through the United Nations recommend that the City of Jerusalem or a portion of it be assigned to either Israel or Jordan. The claims of those two countries that they were rightful sovereigns of their parts of Jerusalem, while recognized by some states, have not been recognized by others, including the United States, the United Kingdom, France, and the Soviet Union, all of which continued to maintain embassies in Tel-Aviv and Amman.[43]

During 3000 years of history, control over Jerusalem has been almost invariably acquired by conquest.

B. Protection of and Access to the Holy Places

The historical record shows that Jerusalem has long been regarded as a place of religious significance to the adherents of three world religions all of which seek protection of their interests. Jerusalem has been revered by Jews for 3000 years, by Christians for nearly 2000, and by Moslems for more than 1300 years. Many of the shrines represent a common inheritance of three religions. Even the name of the city in Arabic (*Al-Quds*) means "The Sanctuary."[44] Although it has been said

---

[39] For text see CMD. No. 1785 (1923).

[40] P. DE AZCARATE, MISSION IN PALESTINE 1948-1952, at 182 (1966).

[41] G.A. Res. 181, 2 U.N. GAOR, Resolutions 131, 132 (1947).

[42] *See* 1 M. WHITEMAN, *supra* note 37, at 699, 701, 703.

[43] *Id.* at 594, 595, 699.

[44] P. MOHN, JERUSALEM AND THE UNITED NATIONS 427 (International Conciliation pamphlet no. 464, October 1950).

that "the business of Jerusalem is eternity,"[45] regrettably, through much of history, its spiritual significance as a city of God, of peace and of brotherly love, has been sadly tarnished by bloodshed, political intrigue and bitter rivalry for the privilege of protecting or adminstering the holy places and shrines. Religious emotion or even fanaticism has at times been exploited by temporal rulers who sought exclusive advantages not primarily those of spiritual uplift or human betterment. The diversity of religious interests—Moslem, Catholic, Jewish, Orthodox, Armenian, Coptic, Abyssinian, Syrian, Anglican and other Protestant, and with institutions established by religious bodies in Europe, Asia, Africa, and the Americas—called for some system of order and protection. In 1757 the so-called *Status Quo* was established to this end. Thereafter, Moslem *temporal* power, on the whole, did not interfere with the management of the Holy Places, but there were claims and counter-claims.[46] The system did not change greatly under the British Mandate, which in Article 13 specified that the Mandatory should preserve existing rights in connection with the Holy Places. But at times, such as 1929, there was serious rioting.[47]

C. Proposals for International Régime

When on November 29, 1947 the United Nations General Assembly recommended partition of Palestine into a Jewish state and an Arab state with Economic Union, it was recommended that the city of Jerusalem (including the existing municipality plus the surrounding villages and towns such as Bethlehem) be established as a *corpus separatum*, under a special international régime, to be administered by the Trusteeship Council on behalf of the United Nations. This régime was to include the appointment of a Governor, responsible to the Trusteeship Council, the establishment of a special police force whose members were to be recruited from *outside* of Palestine, the election of a legislative Council, and the demilitarization of the city.[48] "Jerusalem was envisaged as a *model city*, a *spiritual center*, a *seat of learning*, the influence of which could help to overcome the national and religious animosities and prejudices which for so many years have poisoned the atmosphere of the Holy Land."[49] The proposal for a *corpus separatum* seemed sensible since the General Assembly's Plan of 1947 separated Jerusalem from the proposed Jewish state by a strip of intervening Arab territory assigned to the proposed Arab state. Jerusalem under the 1947 Plan would have been a city of approximately equal Arab and Jewish population, with the Moslem Arabs somewhat more numerous than the Christian Arabs.

---

[45] PEROWNE, *supra* note 38, at 13.

[46] REPORT OF THE COMMISSION . . . , *supra* note 38, at 15-22; W. EYTAN, THE FIRST TEN YEARS 66 (1958); MOHN, *supra* note 44, at 433-38.

[47] C. SYKES, CROSSROADS TO ISRAEL 108-11 (1965).

[48] *See* Part III of the Plan, *supra* note 41; EYTAN, *supra* note 46, at 68-69. For map showing the proposed boundaries of Jerusalem, see annex B attached to the Plan.

[49] MOHN, *supra* note 44, at 451. (Emphasis added.)

A statute for Jerusalem had been drafted by the Trusteeship Council in the spring of 1948,[50] but formal adoption was postponed owing to the state of confusion into which the larger question of Palestine had been thrown by the fighting already in progress and uncertainty as to whether the November 29, 1947 Plan could be implemented.[51] The Arab Higher Committee had rejected the Partition Plan in its entirety; the Jewish Agency accepted it under protest. No international authority had been created to take the place of the British Mandatory authority in Jerusalem which had been supported by British troops for twenty-five years. These were about to depart on May 14, 1948 as the British Government had repeatedly affirmed. Yet it had been clear for months that the Partition Plan with Economic Union could not be implemented by agreement, and it could not be implemented by force alone, since it called for economic cooperation. The Plan was clearly unworkable in the light of political realities.

The divergent policies of the Powers blocked agreement in the United Nations, not of a "definition of the International interest" in Jerusalem, but of a concerted will to implement internationally-defined policy against firm resistance. International policy, defined and redefined by the General Assembly resolutions in 1947,[52] 1948[53] and 1949[54] but not consistently supported by necessary action, was brushed aside by the national policy of a few states with clear goals. Christopher Sykes aptly refers to the "melee of conflicting British and American attempts at policy."[55] The draft statutes of an international régime in Jerusalem, although at least in one case directed to be put into effect despite opposition of Israel and Jordan, were not put into effect, and "came to nothing" in the world of action. Jordanian and Israeli armed forces took and retained control of their respective parts of Jerusalem filling a vacuum with national power. A new kind of *status quo* was maintained in Jerusalem, following the Israeli-Jordan Armistice Agreement of 1949,[56] until it was again upset by force in June 1967.

When the United Nations Conciliation Commission for Palestine[57] realized the impossibility of setting up a genuine international régime (based on the idea of a *corpus separatum*) and drafted a modified statute in 1949[58] compatible with the *fait accompli* of the partition of Jerusalem between Israel and Jordan, it remained

---

[50] 3 U.N. TCOR, 2d Sess., pt. 3, Annex, at 4, U.N. Doc. T/118/Rev. 2 (1948).

[51] Proceedings summarized in Annual Report of the Secretary-General on the Work of the Organization, 1 July 1947-30 June 1948, 3 U.N. GAOR, Supp. 1, at 4-5, U.N. Doc. A/565 (1948). *See also* MOHN, *supra* note 44, at 455-56; EYTAN, *supra* note 46, at 70; AZCARATE, *supra* note 40, at 184-85.

[52] G.A. Res. 181, *supra* note 41.

[53] G.A. Res. 194, para. 8, 3 U.N. GAOR, pt. 1, Resolutions 21, 23, U.N. Doc. A/810 (1948).

[54] G.A. Res. 303, 4 *id.*, Resolutions 25, U.N. Doc. A/1251 (1949).

[55] SYKES, *supra* note 47, at 357. *See also* Report of the Trusteeship Council entitled "Question of an International Regime for the Jerusalem Area and the Protection of the Holy Places," 5 U.N. GAOR, Supp. 9, U.N. Doc. A/1286 (1950).

[56] 42 U.N.T.S. 303, no. 656; 4 U.N. SCOR, Spec. Supp. 1, U.N. Doc. S/1302/Rev. 1 (1949).

[57] Established by G.A. Res. 194, *supra* note 53.

[58] 4 U.N. GAOR, Ad Hoc Pol. Comm., Annex., vol. 1, at 10, U.N. Doc. A/973 (1949).

only a "blue-print," although one worthy of study both then and now. The draft sent to the General Assembly September 1, 1949 was "pigeon-holed without even being accorded the honor of a debate," as a result of the pressure of various delegations. Some, sympathetic with the Vatican's point of view, "were not prepared to accept anything less than integral and complete internationalization."[59] All of the Arab states except Jordan also sought a more thorough-going internationalization.

Israel, on the other hand, was antagonistic because the Conciliation Commission's plan involved too much international control. The Israeli government argued that the plan ignored the "physical facts" and "deeper truths of sentiment and allegiance," adding that "For the first time in modern history, political authority in the greater part of Jerusalem rests not on military conquest but on the will and consent of the population of the city."[60] The crux of the matter was that the Conciliation Commission was responding to the General Assembly's Resolution 194(III) of December 11, 1948 wherein the General Assembly had decided that the Jerusalem area should be accorded "special and separate treatment from the rest of Palestine" and that it should be placed "under effective United Nations control." Israel's policy did not support that objective: it favored national control of Jerusalem, its new capital, in a nation re-created after decades of struggle under Zionist leadership, catapulted to birth by the agony produced by the Nazi slaughter of millions of European Jews.

V

REFLECTIONS ON THE PRESENT
INTERNATIONAL SYSTEM AND JERUSALEM'S FUTURE

The future status of Jerusalem is obviously related to the larger question of the fundamental characteristics of the future international system of the Middle East. As for the international system of the past two decades, of which international law is only a part, if we judge it primarily by the *practice* of states rather than by the *proclaimed principles* which states affirm as principles that ought to be applied, we can only conclude that the use of force in pursuit of national policy is not altogether ruled out. Almost invariably when force is used, the claim of the exercise of the right of self-defense is asserted, and sometimes justified. The Arabs of Palestine asserted the right of self-defense in 1948 against the Partition Plan, adopted as a recommendation of the General Assembly. They regarded the Plan as immoral and illegal.[61] The Israeli Government asserted the right of self-defense to maintain

---

[59] AZCARATE, *supra* note 40, at 184. *See also* remarks of the Lebanese Delegation (Malik) to a committee of the General Assembly on May 5, 1949, 3 U.N. GAOR, pt. 2, Ad Hoc Pol. Comm. 219-26.

[60] Memorandum on the Future of Jerusalem, prepared by the Israeli Delegation, Nov. 15, 1949, at 2, U.N. Doc. A/AC.31/L. 34. *See also* remarks by the Israeli Delegation (Eban), 3 U.N. GAOR, pt. 2, Ad Hoc Pol. Comm. 230-37 (1949).

[61] The Arab Higher Committee contended, at the 2d Special Session of the General Assembly, in April 1949, that the Mandate for Palestine disregarded the right to self-determination, and that the Arabs had no alternative but "to resort to the sacred right of self-defense." The Arabs had done "'what any

national identity threatened by Arab governments in 1948, in 1956, and again in 1967.[62] The United Nations did not clarify the legal situation that existed.

In this existing international system—this system more political than juridical, this system that does not assure the rule of law or international security by collective measures to frustrate a breach of the peace—perhaps the best hope for progress towards peace and security must rest with the policies of states which surely must increasingly understand the unwisdom of continued belligerency and war. While some wars can be deterred by threat of force or reprisal, the basic Middle East problem calls for other approaches. The great imperative is for a changed approach, a new attitude on both sides, which will permit the leaders of both sides to show greater understanding of the fears, the needs, and the legitimate interests of other states. This line of thinking brings us back to the idea that governments as well as leaders of public opinion should respond to the over-riding need for national self-restraint, fairness to others, and for easing tensions between nations, thereby assisting the growth of a new spirit of confidence that men can act more wisely in the future for peace and justice. It is a new vision of the practical advantages that will accrue to those who accept a community of mutual rights and responsibilities that is needed, not a continued devotion to political myths that insist on national or group exclusiveness and enmity. On what other basis can we hope for a solid political foundation on which to develop a more adequate international law?

Surely the present need is for a more realistic understanding by peoples generally of their national and regional interests. Hostility, belligerence, non-recognition of the right of neighboring states to exist, and disregard of the rights of others to territorial integrity are basic causes of insecurity for all. Perhaps it would help in resolving the problem of Jerusalem if the parties most concerned would not overemphasize the importance of political images of Jerusalem formed centuries ago in a very different age. Historic national dreams, perhaps vital in ages past, may need updating if the fundamental interests of the peoples of our time are to be advanced. Imagine the benefits that would flow if nations would discard from national myths that which is provocative and unjust to others, thereby facilitating the growth of the more constructive aspects of nationalism and encouraging healthy international cooperation. The Jerusalem question, if viewed with this spirit, with everyone avoiding malice and vituperation, might gradually be transformed to more optimistic proportions, with reduced likelihood that Jerusalem will be in the future, as it has been all too often in the past, a center for pathetic rivalry and a continuing object of re-conquest, perhaps headed once again for destruction.

---

other Member State would have done" fought in self-defense. The Partition resolution was "ill-advised," "illegal," and "could not be carried out." U.N. GAOR, 2d Spec. Sess., vol. II, Main Committees 93 (1948).

[62] See remarks by the Israeli Minister for Foreign Affairs (Eban) to the Security Council, U.N. Doc. S/PV. 1375, Nov. 13, 1967, at 6-36; ISRAEL'S STRUGGLE FOR PEACE, chs. VIII, IX and X (Israel Office of Information, New York, 1960).

This is the time for states generally to support the efforts of the United Nations Special Representative, Dr. Jarring, as he explores with the parties most directly concerned the broader dimensions of peace-making in the Middle East.[63] Will the Arab states and Israel work to establish the foundations for peace in the spirit of that resolution? Or will shortsighted, particularistic interests of states sidetrack progress toward an agreed settlement by inducing them to nullify one or the other of the basic principles adopted unanimously in the Security Council resolution of November 22, 1967?[64] It is acceptance of the entire package which is a valid test of one's interest in peace with justice. At least this seems to have been the view of the Security Council.

One would hope that the world will not experience disappointment similar to that of 1947-1952, when an opportunity for a peaceful resolution of the Arab-Israel problem foundered. Every nation's stake in moving toward peace based on agreement is enormous. This is the prerequisite for strengthening international law in the Middle East, in view of such conflicting definitions of justice as have been spread on the United Nations record for the past twenty years.

If a new appreciation of national self-interest can be developed in the months ahead, based on a wider recognition of the futility of Middle Eastern politics of recent years, presumably some agreements would become possible. It should then become possible to agree on an acceptable formula of "the national and international interest" in Jerusalem, which could then be guaranteed by the principal Powers. The balancing of interests and claims in the Middle East becomes an imperative, in view of the uncertainties of law and the facts of power, if some tolerable stability is to be achieved. The definition of justice in such a politically divided area could hardly be expected to conform to the fullest expression of national aspirations and national morality—either Arab or Israeli. A rational solution calls for a negotiated settlement (sooner rather than later) under the auspices of a third party utilizing any arrangement agreeable to the parties most concerned, and, failing that, under an arrangement determined by the Security Council.

In the interest of long-run cooperation among the peoples and nations of the Middle East, it is believed that the advantages of a *corpus separatum* for the walled City of Jerusalem could be a desirable goal for the overwhelming majority of the members of the United Nations, and would probably serve the higher, long-range interests of Israel and Jordan. To achieve this objective, it might become desirable for the states of the world to recognize West Jerusalem as the capital of the state of Israel. So much of Israeli nationalism is centered on Jerusalem as a focal point in national political life that it would seem practical to accept this reality. However,

---

[63] A recent statement of relevant U.S. policy was made on Dec. 8, 1967, by the Under Secretary of State for Political Affairs, Eugene V. Rostow, 58 DEP'T STATE BULL. 41 (1968).

[64] For text of Resolution 242, see Rosenne, in this symposium, pp. 44, 56.

this line of thinking would reserve the walled city as an International Zone—a *corpus separatum*, but would not necessarily be restricted to it.[65]

These concluding ideas do not constitute a proposal for the future status of Jerusalem. They are suggested only as possible ideas for consideration by those concerned. Both a *national* and an *international* presence would be embraced in a greater Jerusalem. An international statute would once again be drafted, and would constitute a part of the peace settlement hopefully to grow out of Ambassador Jarring's step by step efforts to build a peace on the principles of the Security Council's Resolution 242 of November 22, 1967.

But are these ideas practical? They could become practical, when carefully re-vamped by legal and political experts—if, but only if, the parties most concerned will re-evaluate their national interests in harmony with the greater need for genuine peace. The future of Jerusalem is inevitably entwined with the larger aspects of Arab-Israeli relations. In March 1968 serious violations of the cease-fire which brought renewed consideration by the Security Council confirmed earlier impressions that the prospect for genuine peace and for a rule of law in the Middle East seemed as elusive as ever. In the interest of international peace and security, perhaps the time is near when the Security Council will act to assert its authority under the Charter.[66] If not, the outlook seems one of continued belligerency, bitterness, and danger. The Middle East is faced with important choices in 1968. We can do no other than to hope for a new vision grounded in justice and focusing on a better day.

---

[65] *See* proceedings regarding Jerusalem in the Trusteeship Council 1949-1950, summarized in the special report cited *supra* note 55. *See especially* Private Memorandum from the Archbishop of Canterbury, Oct. 31, 1949, *id*. at 9-11. The Statute for the City of Jerusalem approved by the Council, April 4, 1950, is set forth *id*. at 19. *See also* Darin-Drabkin, *Jerusalem—City of Dissension or Peace?*, NEW OUT-LOOK: MIDDLE EAST MONTHLY, Jan. 1968, at 12, for an Israeli interpretation.

[66] On May 21, 1968 the U.N. Security Council adopted Resolution 252 on Jerusalem; for text, see El-Farra, in this symposium, pp. 68, 73.

Jerusalem and the Holy Places

ELIHU LAUTERPACHT

CHAPTER I

It is generally assumed that in any peace settlement in the Middle East the solution of the question of Jerusalem and the Holy Places will play a significant part. To a large extent this is no doubt true—if only because Jerusalem is at the physical centre of the conflict and because the tension surrounding it is symbolic of the division between Israel and her neighbours. At the same time it is important that the problems of Jerusalem and the Holy Places should not be allowed to assume dimensions which will render their solution—whether on a multilateral, bilateral or unilateral basis—any more difficult than their intrinsic characteristics require.

Perhaps the very title of this paper by linking Jerusalem and the Holy Places tends to promote the confusion which affects the topic. For in truth there exist two quite distinct problems—the question of the Holy Places and the question of Jerusalem. They are brought together in people's minds because the majority of the Holy Places in the territory of what used to be Palestine happen to be situate in Jerusalem [1].

It would be an oversimplification to say that, for the Jews at any rate, concern for Jerusalem is *exclusively* a consequence of the accumulation there of Holy Places. For them, the City as such has assumed over the ages a dominant significance in their thought which, though fundamentally associated with the

---

[1] The following is a list of Holy Places compiled by the United Nations in 1949. It covers only the Holy Places in and around Jerusalem, but not elsewhere. It does not include, for example, the Holy Places associated with the residence of Jesus at Nazareth.
Christian—1. Basilica of the Holy Sepulchre (inclusive I to IX Stations of the Cross) 2. Bethany 3. Cenacle 4. Church of St. Anne 5. Church of St. James the Great 6. Church of St. Mark 7. Deir al Sultan 8. Tomb of the Virgin and Gardens of Gethsemane 9. House of Caiphas and Prison of Christ 10. Sanctuary of the Ascension and Mount of Olives 11. Pool of Bethesda 12 Ain Karim 13. Basilica of the Nativity, Bethlehem 14. Milk Grotto, Bethlehem 15. Shepherds Field, Bethlehem; *Moslem*—16. Tomb of Lazarus 17. El Burak esh-Sharif 18. Haram esh-sharif (Mosque of Omar and Mosque of Aksa) 19. Mosque of the Ascension 20. Tomb of David (Nebi Daoud); *Jewish*—21. Tomb of Absalom 22. Ancient and Modern Synagogues 23. Bath of Rabbi Ishmael 24. Brook Siloam 25. Cemetery on Mount of Olives 26. Tomb of David 27. Tomb of Simon the Just 28. Tomb of Zachariah and other tombs in Kidron Valley 29. Wailing Wall 30. Rachel's Tomb.

relics there of the Temple, exists now virtually independently of its origins [1].

Not only are the two problems separate; they are also quite distinct in nature from one another. So far as the Holy Places are concerned, the question is for the most part one of assuring respect for the existing interests of the three religions and of providing the necessary guarantees of freedom of access, worship, and religious administration. Questions of this nature are only marginally in issue between Israel and her neighbours and their solution should not complicate the peace negotiations.

As far as the City of Jerusalem itself is concerned, the question is one of establishing an effective administration of the City which can protect the rights of the various elements of its permanent population—Christian, Arab and Jewish—and ensure the governmental stability and physical security which are essential requirements for the city of the Holy Places.

There is no inherent need to confuse the two matters. Throughout the period immediately prior to the ending of the mandate in Palestine in 1948 they were approached separately. Such association as there may have been between them was the understandable consequence of the fact that in the Middle Ages wars were fought largely for religious reasons. The object of the Crusader seizure of Jerusalem was the protection of the Christian Holy Places. Comparable motives underlay the Arab re-conquest. Thus, Jerusalem and the Holy Places were thought of together.

During the four centuries from 1517 to 1917, however, Jerusalem was under the exclusive control of the Ottoman Empire. Though not an entirely satisfactory solution for either Christians or Jews, the fact remains that for four hundred years a united City was governed by a single sovereign in a manner which by and large permitted adequate pursuit of the three dominant religious faiths. Again, during the period from 1917 to 1947 when Jerusalem was under British control, first as occupants of the City during and immediately after the First World War and then as administering authorities under the League of Nations mandate granted in 1922, a single sovereign was responsible for the government of the City.

---

[1]See *Israel and the U.N.*, p. 130.

Nothing was said in the Mandate about the internationalization of Jerusalem. Indeed Jerusalem as such is not mentioned—though the Holy Places are. And this in itself is a fact of relevance now. For it shows that in 1922 there was no inclination to identify the question of the Holy Places with that of the internationalization of Jerusalem.

So in Article 13 of the Mandate we find that all responsibility "in connection with the Holy Places and religious buildings or sites in Palestine, including that of preserving existing rights and of preserving access to the Holy Places, religious buildings and sites and the free exercise of worship" is placed upon the Mandatory which in its turn "shall be responsible solely to the League of Nations in all matters connected herewith."

Upon the powers of the Mandatory in this regard one important limitation was placed:

"nothing in this Mandate shall be construed as conferring upon the Mandatory authority to interfere with the fabric or the management of purely Moslem sacred shrines, the immunities of which are guaranteed."

Article 14 required the Mandatory to appoint a special Commission to study, define and determine the rights and claims in connection with the Holy Places and the rights and claims relating to the different religious communities in Palestine. The composition and functions of the Commission were to be approved by the Council of the League.

By Article 15, the Mandatory was required to "see that complete freedom of conscience and the free exercise of all forms of worship, subject only to the maintenance of public order and morals, are ensured to all."

The Mandatory was, further, made

"responsible for exercising such supervision over religious or eleemosynary bodies of all faiths in Palestine as may be required for the maintenance of public order and good government. Subject to such supervision, no measures shall be taken in Palestine to obstruct or interfere with the enterprise of such bodies or to discriminate against any representative or member of them on the ground of his religion or nationality." (Art. 16).

The scheme thus established worked reasonably well in practice, even though no agreement on the appointment of the Commission called for by Article 14 of the Mandate could be reached until 1930.

Two features of the position during the period of the Mandate[1] may be noted: first, there was no suggestion that questions connected with the Holy Places could any the better be resolved in an internationalized city of Jerusalem; and, second, no distinction was drawn between the Holy Places in Jerusalem and those elsewhere in Palestine.

There was, therefore, a distinct element of novelty in the formal identification in 1947 of the questions of Jerusalem and the Holy Places in the shape of the proposal for the internationalization of Jerusalem[2]. This was introduced as one of the four components of the solution of the Palestine problem adopted by the General Assembly in 1947. The other three were the creation of an Arab State, the creation of a Jewish State and the establishment of an economic union between the two.

Though it cannot be said that in 1947 the idea of internationalizing Jerusalem was wholly unreasonable, at best it was highly speculative. There were international precedents. There had been an international regime in Tangier since 1906. Danzig had been under the control of the League of Nations from 1920 to 1939. The Saar had been ruled by an international commission from 1920 to 1934. The Allied powers were even then thinking about the internationalization of Trieste. But there had been no experience—other than that of the Saar—of a prolonged and successful international administration. Moreover, in the particular case of Jerusalem both the Jews and the Arabs were opposed to it—a lack of popular support which had neither characterised nor been politically relevant to the previous cases. The Jewish authorities were prepared in 1947 to waive their opposition to the internationalization of Jerusalem as part of an overall settlement of the Palestine problem. The Arabs—being opposed to any solution in Palestine other than by way of an acknowledgment of an independent state of Palestine to be ruled by Arabs—as much denied the U.N. the right to internationalize Jerusalem as they denied it the right to partition the country.

---

[1]For a summary of some aspects of this, see below, p.p. 64-67
[2]The prospect of the partition of Palestine, involving the exclusion of Jerusalem from the Jewish state, had however, been a feature of discussions on the future of Palestine since the Royal Commission's Report of 1937. See *Israel and the U.N.*, p. 130.

Some reflection of U.N. realization of the uncertainty of the future—and with it some appreciation of the ultimate severability of the political control of Jerusalem from the protection of the Holy Places—is to be found in those provisions of the Partition Resolution which referred to the duration of the special regime for the City. The regime was to remain in force in the first instance for a period of ten years from 1st October, 1948. In 1958 the Trusteeship Council was to re-examine the whole scheme in the light of the experience acquired with its functioning. At that time the residents of the City were to be free to express by means of a referendum their wishes as to possible modifications.

Now, not ten, but twenty years have passed since the General Assembly sought to fuse the questions of Jerusalem and of the Holy Places by internationalizing Jerusalem. The reasons then given by U.N.S.C.O.P. for internationalization now carry little conviction[1]. Conditions have arisen which were not foreseen in 1948. Indeed, some could hardly have been imagined at that time.

---

[1]The majority group sought to justify its proposals for Jerusalem by reference to five considerations:

(i) that as a Holy City for three faiths, the sacred character of the Holy Places should be preserved and access to them guaranteed to pilgrims from abroad;

(ii) that history had shown that religious peace had been maintained in the City because the Government was anxious to prevent controversies involving religious interests from developing into bitter strife and disorder and had the power to do so;

(iii) that religious peace in Jerusalem is necessary for the maintenance of peace in the Arab and Jewish States;

(iv) that the application of the provisions relating to the Holy Places, religious buildings and sites in the whole of Palestine would also be greatly facilitated by the setting up of an international authority in Jerusalem, with a Governor empowered to supervise the provisions and arbitrate conflicts in respect of the Holy Places; and

(v) that the International Trusteeship System is proposed as the most suitable instrument because the Trusteeship Council, as a principal organ of the U.N., "affords a convenient and effective means of ensuring both the desired international supervision and the political, economic and social well-being of the population of Jerusalem."

One may venture the comment upon these factors that, in relation particularly to the third, peace in Jerusalem has not been the pre-condition of peace between the Jews and Arabs—but rather that peace between Jews and Arabs is the pre-condition of peace in Jerusalem. Secondly, with reference to the final consideration, while in 1947 it was quite reasonable to place some reliance upon the possibilities inherent in the idea of trusteeship under direct international supervision, it is a concept for which no other application has been found in the ensuing twenty years. Indeed, the international trusteeship system, having served a useful and important purpose during the first two decades of the United Nations, is now virtually obsolete.

It is worth recalling a number of these new conditions:

—The Arab States rejected the Partition Plan and the proposal for the internationalization of Jerusalem.

—The Arab States physically opposed the implementation of the General Assembly Resolution. They sought by force of arms to expel the Jewish inhabitants of Jerusalem and to achieve sole occupation of the City.

—In the event, Jordan obtained control only of the Eastern part of the City, including the Walled City.

—While Jordan permitted reasonably free access to Christian Holy Places, it denied the Jews any access to the Jewish Holy Places. This was a fundamental departure from the tradition of freedom of religious worship in the Holy Land which had evolved over centuries. It was also a clear violation of the undertaking given by Jordan in the Armistice Agreement concluded with Israel on 3rd April, 1949. Article VIII of this Agreement called for the establishment of a Special Committee of Israeli and Jordanian representatives to formulate agreed plans on certain matters "which, in any case, shall include the following, on which agreement in principle already exists ... free access to the Holy Places and cultural institutions and use of the Cemetery on the Mount of Olives." [1]

—The U.N. displayed no concern over the discrimination thus practised against persons of the Jewish faith.

—The U.N. accepted as tolerable the unsupervised control of the Old City of Jerusalem by Jordanian forces—notwithstanding the fact that the presence of Jordanian forces west of the Jordan River was entirely lacking in any legal justification.

—During the period 1948-1952 the General Assembly gradually came to accept that the plan for the territorial internationalization of Jerusalem had been quite overtaken by events. From 1952 to the present time virtually nothing more has been heard of the idea in the General Assembly.

On 5th June, 1967, Jordan deliberately overthrew the Armistice Agreement by attacking the Israeli-held part of Jerusalem. There was no question of this Jordanian action being a reaction to any Israeli attack. It took place notwithstanding explicit Israeli assurances, conveyed to King Hussein through the U.N. Commander, that if Jordan did not attack

---

[1] *U.N.T.S.*, vol. 42, p. 314.

Israel, Israel would not attack Jordan. Although the charge of aggression is freely made against Israel in relation to the Six Days War the fact remains that the two attempts made in the General Assembly in June—July 1967 to secure the condemnation of Israel as an aggressor failed. A clear and striking majority of the members of the U.N. voted against the proposition that Israel was an aggressor [1].

In consequence, Israel is in occupation of the whole of Jerusalem and has re-unified the administration of the City. This situation has now persisted for over a year. During that time there has been unrestricted freedom of access for persons of all faiths to all the Holy Places in Jerusalem. In particular, it may be noted, Moslems have enjoyed, under Israeli control, the very freedom which Jews were denied during Jordanian occupation.

In these circumstances, it becomes relevant to ask what is to be done in the future about Jerusalem and the Holy Places? In particular, we may ask what role, if any, has the U.N. to play in this connection?

The answers to these questions involve an appreciation of the following considerations:

(i) The role of the U.N. in relation to the future of Jerusalem and the Holy Places is limited. In particular, the General Assembly has no power of disposition over Jerusalem and no right to lay down regulations for the Holy Places. The Security Council, of course, retains its powers under Chapter VII of the Charter in relation to threats to the peace, breaches of the peace and acts of aggression, but these powers do not extend to the adoption of any general position regarding the future of Jerusalem and the Holy Places.

(ii) Israel's governmental measures in relation to Jerusalem —both New and Old—are lawful and valid.

(iii) The future regulation of the Holy Places is a matter to be determined quite separately from the political administration of Jerusalem. Territorial internationalization of Jerusalem

---

[1] The relevant paragraph of the Soviet draft resolution of 18th June, 1967, (A/L.519) was defeated on 4th July, 1967, by 36 votes in favour, 57 against and 23 abstentions. On the same day an Albanian draft resolution (A/L.521) to similar effect was even more disastrously lost—22 votes in favour, 71 against and 27 abstentions.

is dead—but the possibility of functional internationalization is not. The latter means, in effect, the recognition of the universal interest in the Holy Places situate in Jerusalem and the adoption of links between Israel and the world community to give formal expression to that interest.

The remainder of this pamphlet will be taken up with a more detailed examination of these three considerations.

CHAPTER II

THE ROLE OF THE UNITED NATIONS

(a) LEGAL HISTORY OF PALESTINE TO 1947

In order to estimate the role of the U.N. in relation to Jerusalem and the Holy Places, it is necessary to look at the legal history of the territory in which Jerusalem is situated.

We need go no further back than the period immediately prior to the First World War. From 1517 to 1917 Jerusalem, as part of Palestine, was under Turkish rule. By Article 16 of the Treaty of Lausanne of 1923 Turkey renounced all rights and title over, amongst other areas, that of Palestine, "the future of these territories . . . being settled or to be settled by the parties concerned."

In the case of Palestine "the parties concerned" had already settled its future. On 24th July, 1922, the League of Nations with the assent of the Principal Allied and Associated Powers, had granted a mandate in respect of Palestine to the British Government.

We thus have the situation in which Turkey's title to Palestine devolved upon the Principal Allied and Associated Powers who, in their turn, had in effect already conveyed their rights to the League of Nations. The precise location of sovereignty over Palestine during the period of the Mandate has been a matter of academic dispute, but is now largely without practical significance. After the grant of the Mandate it is clear that sovereignty no longer rested with the Principal Allied and Associated Powers. Equally it is clear that the mere fact that the mandate to administer Palestine had been given to Britain did not convey sovereignty to her. Indeed, it was one of the fundamental elements in, and prime objects of, the Mandate system that the administering authority should not be sovereign, but should possess only those powers granted by the Mandate and in the exercise of them should be subject to the supervision of the League.

If the test of sovereignty rests in determining who had the power to dispose of any part of a territory under Mandate, the answer is that sovereignty lay in the League and the administering authority acting jointly. For example, when in 1923 Great Britain and Belgium agreed to modify the common frontier of their East African mandated areas, they requested the consent of the League to amend the Mandates accordingly.

The League of Nations was dissolved in 1946. The U.N. had been established during the previous year. There was, however, no formal conveyance by the League to the U.N. of the rights and powers of the former in relation to the mandated territories. At its final session in 1946 the League Assembly adopted a resolution which recognised that "on the termination of the League's existence, its functions with respect to the mandated territories will come to an end," but noted that Chapters XI, XII and XIII of the Charter embodied principles corresponding to those declared in Article 22 of the Covenant. The resolution also took note of the expressed intention of the Members of the League then administering territories under Mandate to continue to administer them for the well-being and development of the people concerned "until other arrangements have been agreed between the United Nations and the respective mandatory Powers."[1] The United Kingdom informed the U.N. in 1946 of its willingness to conclude Trusteeship Agreements for those territories which it administered under Mandate, save in the case of Palestine whose future, Britain was even by then obliged to say, was in a state of doubt.

(b) THE ROLE OF THE U.N. IN 1947

On 2nd April, 1947, after two years of increasing tension in Palestine, the British Government gave notice to the U.N. of its intention to place the Palestine question on the agenda of the next regular session of the General Assembly, due to start in September 1947, and stated that it would "ask the Assembly to make recommendations under Article 10[2] of the Charter, concerning the future government of Palestine." The British Government proposed that a special session of the Assembly

---

[1]See *Y.B.U.N.*, 1946-47, p. 575.

[2]Article 10 of the Charter provides as follows: "The General Assembly may discuss any questions or any matters within the scope of the present Charter or relating to the powers and functions of any organs provided for in the present Charter, and, except as provided in Article 12, may make recommendations to the Members of the United Nations or to the Security Council or to both on any such questions or matters."

should immediately be summoned with a view to constituting and instructing a special committee to prepare for the consideration of the question.

Although there was nothing in the Charter which expressly conferred upon the Assembly the power to consider the future of a mandated territory, the Assembly nonetheless accepted the competence thus attributed to it by appointing the U.N. Special Committee on Palestine (U.N.S.C.O.P.). In retrospect one is able to say that this acceptance of competence was a proper thing to do. The reason for saying "in retrospect" is that in 1947 there was no clear authority on the matter.[1] In 1950, however, the International Court of Justice in an Advisory Opinion on the *International Status of South-West Africa* expressed the view that the status of a mandated territory could be altered only with the consent of the United Nations.[2]

On this basis, the action of the United Kingdom in referring the Palestine problem to the U.N. was clearly correct. The United Kingdom was not entitled unilaterally either to terminate the Mandate or to decide upon the political future of the territory. Only the General Assembly could authorise the ending of the Mandate; and only the Assembly could, initially at any rate, make proposals for the future government of the country.

The Committee (U.N.S.C.O.P.) appointed by the Assembly forthwith entered upon its duties and eventually reported to the General Assembly in the autumn of 1947. On 29th November, 1947, as already stated, the Assembly adopted Resolution 189 (II)—the so-called Partition Resolution. This called for the division of Palestine into two States—one Jewish and one Arab, to be established within the boundaries laid down in the Resolution. There was to be an economic union between the two States. Jerusalem was to be internationalized.

(c) THE EFFECT OF THE PARTITION RESOLUTION

The Jewish authorities forthwith accepted the Resolution. It did not give them all they wanted—and in particular they did not favour the idea of an internationalized Jerusalem. But they considered that it was better to have a Jewish State in part of

---

[1] Although on 14th December, 1946, the General Assembly of the U.N. had affirmed its competence in relation to any change in the status of another mandated territory namely, South-West Africa. See Resolution 65 (I).

[2] *I.C.J. Reports 1950*, p. 128, at pp. 141-143.

Palestine, even without Jerusalem, than to have no State at all. This view, it must be recalled, however, was based upon the assumption that the resolution would be accepted and implemented by the Arabs, that it would form the basis for peace and order in Palestine, and that though Jerusalem might be internationalized it would be an open city. This assumption proved false. The Arabs rejected the resolution, which they considered to be beyond the powers of the General Assembly and to constitute an infringement of the right of the Arab people of Palestine to determine their own political future.

While, of course, it is unfortunate that the Arabs rejected the resolution, they were to some extent correct in their incidental assertion that the General Assembly was not able by resolution to dispose in a binding manner of the whole or any part of the territory of Palestine. Palestine was not the property of the U.N. to give or withhold as it pleased. The role of the U.N. was a restricted one. Its acquiescence in the termination by Britain of its obligations as Mandatory was—for the reason given above—a legal necessity. Moreover, the Assembly could, by putting forward a plan which the interested parties might accept, provide the legal basis for the settlement of the future government of the country. But resolutions of the General Assembly do not normally create legal obligations for the members of the U.N. (even if Israel and the proposed Arab State had been members at that time, which they were not); and the Partition Resolution did not have a legislative character. The Assembly could not by its resolution give the Jews and the Arabs in Palestine any rights which either did not otherwise possess: nor, correspondingly, could it take away such rights as they did possess.

The precise rights of the Jewish and Arab inhabitants of Palestine at that time cannot easily be specified—and it is questionable whether the legal position in 1947 is of more than marginal relevance to the determination of the legal position today. But some reference to the legal factors then prevailing may be helpful.

It is convenient to distinguish between the position under "general" international law, that is, under the law affecting all nations at that time; and the position in "particular" international law, that is, by reference to those special rules which might have some particular or exclusive bearing on the situation.

On the whole, general international law in 1947 was little concerned with the rights of communities which had not acquired statehood. But even then it contained the principle of self-determination—which in the following two decades has assumed great significance in international affairs.

The principle of self-determination is, however, one of indefinite and variable content. Although acknowledged in Article I of the Charter of the U.N. as one of the bases of the development of friendly relations among nations and although applied in many cases as a solvent of existing political structures and a justification for the establishment of new state units, no legal instrument exists which lays down, for example, the size of the community which is to determine its own future or the manner in which the act of self-determination is to take place. Everybody believes in the concept; few are prepared to give it a specific content unrelated to their subjective views of any particular situation. "Self-determination" may readily be invoked for the purpose of embarrassing another State; the concept is less welcome when applied by others to one's own ethnically recognizable minorities.

The vagueness of the idea was even greater in 1947 than it is now. Yet it was relied upon by the Arab States as a justification for denying the validity of the U.N. action in Palestine. Their contention was that the Arab inhabitants of Palestine should have been allowed to determine their own future. Now this argument, though superficially not unattractive, rests fundamentally upon the assumption that the concept could be applied to Palestine only as an undivided territorial unit, and without reference to the manifest fact that even by 1947 the country was clearly separable into Jewish and Arab areas. However, that assumption is of doubtful validity. As subsequent experience has shown, for example, in the cases of Togoland and the Cameroons, the process of self-determination is applicable to other than the full territorial unit that happens to bear the name of a single country. French Togoland it will be recalled was divided on the basis of the principle of self-determination between Ghana and Togo; the former German Cameroons were divided first into French and British Mandated territories of that name, and subsequently became respectively the independent republic of the Cameroons and part of Northern Nigeria.

When this is borne in mind, it can be seen that the decision of the U.N. to recommend the partition of Palestine, far from being a denial of the right of self-determination, was in fact a direct application of the principle. The Jews were not to determine the future of the Arabs, nor were the Arabs to determine the future of the Jews. Each group was to determine its own future. This the Jews subsequently did. The Arabs of Palestine did not—whether of their own volition must remain a matter of doubt. If the Arab States neighbouring Palestine had not insisted that the problem was an Arab problem rather than a Palestinian problem, the history of Arab life in Palestine over the last score of years would have been a much happier one. [1]

So much then for the application of the notion of self-determination, as the only relevant principle of "general" international law. It is now necessary to turn to the "particular" international law applicable to the Palestine situation. In this case the governing instrument is the Mandate for Palestine granted to the United Kingdom in 1922. This is the instrument by which the Principal Allied and Associated Powers—to whom Turkey's rights over Palestine had passed [2]—indicated the manner in which and the objects for which the country was to be governed. Two paragraphs of the Preamble to the Mandate are particularly important as indicating the respective rights of the interested parties:

> "Whereas the Principal Allied Powers have also agreed that the Mandatory should be responsible for putting into effect the declaration originally made on November 2nd, 1917 by the Government of His Britannic Majesty, and adopted by the said Powers in favour of the establishment in Palestine of a national home for the Jewish people, it being clearly understood that nothing should be done which might prejudice the civil and religious rights of existing non-Jewish communities in Palestine, or the rights and political status enjoyed by Jews in any other country; and
>
> "Whereas recognition has thereby been given to the historical connection of the Jewish people with Palestine and to the grounds for reconstituting their national home in that country..."

---

[1] Certainly nothing in the concept of self-determination could in 1948 have justified the Jordanian occupation of the cis-Jordanian parts of Palestine or the Egyptian occupation of the Gaza Strip.
[2] See above, p. 13.

Here, then, we have in an effective legal instrument, binding alike upon the Principal Allied and Associated Powers and upon the Members of the League, an express acknowledgment that the policy of "reconstituting" a Jewish national home was to be implemented. [1] True, the commitment was subject to the important condition that "nothing should be done which might prejudice the civil and religious rights of existing non-Jewish communities in Palestine." But the basic commitment was clear.

And in legal terms the General Assembly of the U.N. could not add to or subtract from this commitment by the direct operation of any Assembly resolution. This is not to say that the Partition Resolution was entirely without legal significance. Apart (as already indicated) from authorising the United Kingdom to end the Mandate, it also represented an indication by the General Assembly of the general direction in which it thought it proper that the political future of the country should move. While the resolution was not a title-deed to the territory of a new Jewish State (or for that matter to a new Arab State, if the one contemplated in the Resolution had been created) it represented a mark of international approbation of the creation of the new State which, while not legally essential, is not legally irrelevant. [2] It also represents another—not strictly legal— reason for questioning the propriety of the invasion of Palestine by Egyptian, Iraqi, Jordanian, Lebanese and Syrian forces in 1948. The legal reasons will be considered in the next chapter. But it was manifestly no part of the General Assembly's intentions for Palestine that it should in greater or lesser degree be carved up by its Arab neighbours.

However, the coming into existence of Israel does not depend legally upon the Resolution. The right of a State to exist flows from its factual existence—especially when that existence is prolonged, shows every sign of continuance and is recognised by the generality of nations.

---

[1] It may be recalled that on 16th September, 1922, the British Government made a declaration, subsequently confirmed by the League Council, modifying the Palestine Mandate so as to exclude Trans-Jordan from the operation of the obligation to establish a Jewish National Home.

[2] It is interesting to note that the Declaration of the Establishment of the State of Israel described the basis for the establishment of the State of Israel in the following terms: " ... By virtue of our natural and historic right and on the strength of the Resolution of the United Nations General Assembly ... " Thus the Resolution was relied upon not as the legal basis for the creation of the State, but was mentioned primarily as a relevant historical element.

Two consequences follow from this assessment of the significance of the Partition Resolution of 1947.

First, the proposal for the internationalization of Jerusalem never assumed the dimensions of a legally binding obligation. The proposal represented the U.N's assessment of one element in the creation of a viable future for a divided Palestine. The parties were free to accept or reject it. The Jews accepted it. The Arabs rejected it. The U.N.—as will be seen—eventually also acquiesced in the idea that its proposal was not to be implemented.

The Partition Resolution still stands, of course, as an indication of what the U.N. wanted in 1947.[1] Some Members of the U.N. have invoked the resolution as a justification for refusing to accept the legitimacy of Israeli sovereignty (in the period prior to June 1967) over the New City of Jerusalem.[2] But reliance upon the Resolution as a justification for such non-recognition is pseudo-legal. The Resolution cannot be regarded as justifying non-recognition of Israeli sovereignty over the New City; nor, as will be presently suggested, for denying the validity of the Israeli re-unification of the administration of the whole City. Moreover there are quite a number of Members of the U.N. who have been content to accept Jerusalem as the capital of Israel and to deal with the Israeli Government on that basis and without reservation.[3]

The second consequence of the limited legal significance of the Partition Resolution is that the boundaries therein laid down for the territories of the proposed Jewish and Arab States and for the internationalized City of Jerusalem have no permanent legal force. The position would, of course, have been otherwise

---

[1]It may even still represent the "internal" law of the U.N., in the sense that the Secretariat as an organ of the U.N. may be bound to make its conduct conform to the theory therein reflected that the area of the internationalized Jerusalem was not to form part of the Jewish or Arab State. Yet to endow the Resolution with even this degree of force at the present time is to attribute to Secretariat opinion an inflexibility which is not wholly appropriate to its functions, nor entirely consistent with the constructive vitality which generally infuses its attitudes.

[2]The following States have qualified their recognition of Israel by a reference to the U.N. resolutions on Jerusalem: Australia, France, New Zealand, Turkey, South Africa and the United Kingdom.

[3]The following States either have embassies or are diplomatically represented in Jerusalem: Bolivia, Central African Republic, Chile, Colombia, Congo (Brazzaville), Congo (Democratic Republic), Costa Rica, Dahomey, Dominican Republic, Ecuador, Gabon, Greece, Guatemala, Ivory Coast, Madagascar, Netherlands, Niger, Panama, Upper Volta, Uruguay and Venezuela.

had the Resolution been fully adopted by the interested parties as the *de facto* basis for their co-existence. But at the moment when the Resolution failed to be implemented, its description of specific boundaries ceased to be fully relevant, though it would not be appropriate to say that the proposed boundaries then became completely irrelevant. As a description of a particular boundary they became worthless; but as the reflection of the idea that there should be a boundary between a Jewish and an Arab State somewhere in Palestine the proposal still retained some value—albeit a historical rather than a legal one.

(d) DEVELOPMENTS SUBSEQUENT TO THE PARTITION RESOLUTION

This assessment of the essentially "historical" and non-legal character of the Partition Resolution is supported by consideration of two additional factors.

(i) The Rejection by the Arabs of the Political Framework for Internationalization

In the first place, the Arab States not only rejected the Resolution; they actively sought to overthrow it. Contemporaneously with the British withdrawal from Palestine the country was invaded by Egyptian, Iraqi, Jordanian, Lebanese and Syrian forces. Contemporary evidence of the fact of invasion is overwhelming, though the Arab States sought to warrant their action by invoking the need to protect the Arabs of Palestine. On 15th May, 1948, the Government of Egypt sent to the President of the Security Council a cablegram declaring "now that the British Mandate in Palestine has ended ... Egyptian armed forces have started to enter Palestine ..." The justification advanced for this action was that it was "to establish security and order in place of chaos and disorder." [1] On 16th May, the King of Jordan cabled the Secretary-General of the U.N.: "We were compelled to enter Palestine to protect unarmed Arabs against massacres ..." [2] On 21st May the Saudi Arabian Government, in a reply to a Security Council questionnaire, stated that "Saudi Arabian forces are now operating in the south of Palestine under Arab Command ... Saudi Arabia has

---

[1] *S.C.O.R.*, 3rd Yr., 292nd Mtg., p. 3.
[2] S/748, *S.C.O.R.*, 3rd Yr., Supp. for April, 1948, p. 90.

no other object in view except to put an end to this state of anarchy and to restore peace, order and security in Palestine." [1]

The view of the Soviet bloc upon these actions is worth noting (as impartially summarized in the *Year Book of the United Nations*):

> "On the question of the withdrawal of foreign troops, they asserted that the presence of foreign troops and military personnel which had invaded the country was responsible for the present disorders and the sufferings of the population. Moreover, the presence of foreign troops constituted an obstacle to the re-establishment of peace, the objective of the General Assembly. Foreign intervention was clearly manifest on the Arab side, for there was a British General Glubb Pasha and British officers commanding Trans-Jordan troops. These troops, as well as those of Egypt, Syria and Lebanon had invaded the territory earmarked for the Arab State of Palestine. This State had not been established, as provided for in the 1947 resolution. On the other hand, the State of Israel had been set up within the territorial limits established by the General Assembly Resolution. The withdrawal of troops was a necessary condition for the establishment of peace and for any settlement of the Palestine question in accordance with the 1947 resolution." [2]

The consequence of the Arab rejection of the Partition proposal and of the forcible entry of the Arab States into Palestine was that the implementation of the Partition Resolution was thereby effectively frustrated in three out of its four major elements. No Arab State was established within Palestine; there could thus be no economic union of the Arab and Jewish States. Further, the physical attack by the Arab forces upon the Jews in Jerusalem, and indeed upon the Jewish State as such, left the Israeli forces with no option but to respond in kind and maintain such hold as they could upon the areas then in Jewish possession, to the point—by way of defensive rationalisation of their positions —of moving in places beyond the lines laid down in the Partition Resolution.

---

[1] S/772, *ibid.*, p. 96.
[2] *Y.B.U.N.*, 1948-9, p. 171. Again, in the General Assembly on 9th December, 1949, the U.S.S.R. delegate said: "Even before the end of the Mandate, when Palestine was still under the official control of the United Kingdom, detachments of the Arab Legion of Transjordan commanded by British nationals had invaded Palestine. Those detachments had occupied strategic points and military bases evacuated by British troops . . ." (*G.A.O.R.*, 275th Plenary Mtg., para. 15).

(ii) THE GRADUAL EXHAUSTION OF U.N. INTEREST IN INTERNATIONALIZATION

This *de facto* abandonment of the Partition Resolution by the Parties directly concerned came in time to be matched by a similar, though not fully articulated, attitude on the part of the U.N. Although the General Assembly, quite understandably, began by treating the Resolution as a valid and effective instrument which it should seek to implement as fully as possible, in due course it gradually abandoned this position. Thus for some five years after the Resolution, the Assembly pursued further the question of the internationalization of Jerusalem.[1] After 1952, however, no more was heard in the General Assembly and the Security Council about internationalization, although the Secretariat and various individual Members of the U.N. continued on occasion to pay lip service to the idea.

Moreover, when in 1967, in the aftermath of the Six Day War, the General Assembly came to concern itself with the Jerusalem problem, it is significant that it made no mention of the idea of internationalization in the relevant resolutions. Indeed, the resolutions appear to proceed on the basis that the General Assembly accepted the immediately pre-existing division of the City into its Israeli and Jordanian-held parts.

At this remove of time it may be helpful to recall in some detail the gradual decline in the momentum with which the U.N. pushed the idea of internationalization—until eventually it was replaced by a realistic assessment of the impracticality of the concept. And in so doing, we may note the emergence of the idea of "functional"—as opposed to "territorial"—internationalisation: an idea which involves instead of the direct international government of Jerusalem simply a demonstration of international concern for freedom of access to and worship at the Holy Places. We may also observe the divisions and shifts in Arab policy: the division between Jordan and her neighbours; and the shift on the part of the Arab States other than Jordan from opposition to territorial internationalization to acceptance of it, as they gradually realised that on no other basis could they serve their political objective of ousting Israel

---

[1] For a helpful indication of the official Israeli attitude to these developments see *Israel and the U.N.*, pp. 128-140.

from Jerusalem—a motive which was only coincidentally associated with concern for the Holy Places.

Here then is the narrative of the manner in which the U.N. approached the internationalization of Jerusalem between 1948 and 1952.

1948: THE TRUSTEESHIP COUNCIL

Within five days of the adoption of the Partition Resolution, the Trusteeship Council appointed a Working Party on Jerusalem, [1] whose Report [2] was considered by the Council during the second part of its second session in February-March 1948. In these debates, the Iraqi delegate took the position, on behalf of all the Arab States, that the proposal for an international trusteeship for Jerusalem was a breach of the Charter and violated the inalienable rights of the people concerned. They were not prepared to enter into details or to participate in the discussion of the plan. "The Council would, moreover, be held responsible for an action charged with dangerous responsibilities (sic) to which the Iraqi Government declared itself in no way bound, and in regard to which it reserved complete freedom of action." [3]

In fact, the Trusteeship Council did not proceed formally to adopt the draft Statute which it had been elaborating, primarily because by the time it was ready to do so (on 20th April, 1948), the General Assembly was already undertaking, at its second special session, a further consideration of the future government of Palestine. The Council instead decided to refer the question of the Statute to the Assembly. [4] In September 1948 the U.N. Mediator on Palestine made certain proposals for the future of the territory which included a suggestion that the City of Jerusalem and the Holy Places be placed under effective U.N. control. [5]

1948: THE GENERAL ASSEMBLY

The General Assembly did not at its 1948 session consider the draft Statute for Jerusalem which had been referred to it

---

[1] *T.C.O.R.*, 2nd Sess. 1st Part., p. 140, 2nd Dec. 1947.
[2] T/122.
[3] *T.C.O.R.*, 2nd Sess., 2nd Part, 19th mtg., p. 5, 18th Feb. 1948.
[4] Trusteeship Council Resolution 34 (II).
[5] See Progress Report of 16th September, 1948, A/648, as reported in *Y.B.U.N.*, 1948-9, p. 167.

by the Trusteeship Council. Instead, on 11th December, 1948, the Assembly adopted a resolution in which, after establishing a Conciliation Commission, it resolved that the Holy Places should be protected and free access to them assured; and that "the Jerusalem area .. should be accorded special and separate treatment from the rest of Palestine and should be placed under effective U.N. control."[1] The resolution also requested the Security Council to take further steps to ensure the demilitarization of Jerusalem at the earliest possible date[2] and instructed the Conciliation Commission to present to the next session of the Assembly "proposals for a permanent international regime for the Jerusalem area which will provide for the maximum local autonomy for distinctive groups consistent with the special international status of the Jerusalem area."[3]

1949: THE ISRAEL-JORDAN ARMISTICE AGREEMENT

Yet even before the matter was further considered by U.N. organs, Israel and Jordan had signed, on 3rd April, 1949, an Armistice Agreement in which the *de facto* division of Jerusalem —and its consequent non-internationalization—was crystallized.[4]

The Agreement provided in particular that a Special Committee of two representatives of each party should be established immediately to formulate arrangements on various matters including, specifically, "free access to the Holy Places and cultural institutions and the use of the cemetery on the Mount of Olives."[5]

---

[1]Resolution 199 (III). Text in *Y.B.U.N.*, 1948-49, p. 174.

[2]When, in October 1949, Egypt raised in the Security Council the question of the demilitarization of Jerusalem pursuant to the request made in the Assembly's resolution of 11th December, 1948, the President of the Council suggested postponement of the item pending its consideration in the Assembly. (*Y.B.U.N.*, 1948-49, pp. 189-190).

[3]*Ibid.*

[4]*U.N.T.S.*, vol. 42, p. 304.

[5]See Article VIII (2). In November 1950 Israel complained to the Security Council that Jordan had violated the Israel-Jordan Armistice Agreement through ,*inter alia*, non-implementation of Article VIII relating to Jerusalem, thereby preventing access to Holy Places, impairing the water supply of the city of Jerusalem, preventing the normal functioning of the Hebrew University and the Hadassah Medical Centre and preventing normal traffic on vital roads. On 17th November, 1950, the Security Council adopted a resolution which read in part: "*The Security Council* notes that with regard to Article 8 of the Israeli-Jordan Armistice Agreement the Special Committee has been formed and has convened and hopes that it will proceed expeditiously to carry out the functions contemplated in paragraphs 2 and 3 of that Article." (S/1907. See *Y.B.U.N.*, 1950, p. 320).

1949: THE PALESTINE CONCILIATION COMMISSION

Nevertheless, the Conciliation Commission, pursuant to the instruction given to it by the Assembly, began in March 1949 to prepare proposals for a permanent international regime for the Jerusalem area. It established a Special Committee on Jerusalem and the Holy Places which in April entered into discussions with the Israeli and the Arab Governments. During these conversations, the Arab delegation indicated general acceptance of the principle of an international regime for the Jerusalem area on condition that the U.N. should be in a position to offer the necessary guarantees regarding the permanence and stability of such a regime. The Israeli Government on the other hand declared its intention to request the General Assembly to revise part of its resolution of 11th December, 1948. While the Israeli Government accepted without reservation an international regime for, or international control of, the Holy Places in the City of Jerusalem, it could not accept the establishment of an international regime for the City.[1]

By September 1949 the Commission had prepared a draft text of an instrument establishing a permanent international regime for the Jerusalem area.[2] In it the Commission proposed:

1. That the Jerusalem area should be permanently demilitarized and neutralized;

2. That the area should be divided into two zones, one Arab and one Israeli, to be administered by the respective authorities; and

3. That four principal organs, namely a U.N. Commissioner, a General Council, an International Tribunal and a Mixed Tribunal, should be set up to exercise certain specific powers concerning mainly the protection of and free access to the Holy Places in the Jerusalem area, the protection of human rights, the co-ordination of the public services of common interest and the solution of the various legal conflicts resulting from the existence of two separate zones.

---

[1]Second Progress Report of the Palestine Conciliation Commission A/838, as summarised in *Y.B.U.N.*, 1948-49, p. 198. See also *Israel and the U.N.*, p. 132.
[2]Further Progress Report (A/992) and Draft Text (A/973 and Add. 1), together with a draft declaration (A/1113); summarised in *Y.B.U.N.*, 1948-49, pp. 198-199.

1949: AD HOC POLITICAL COMMITTEE OF THE GENERAL ASSEMBLY

This proposal, and the documents associated with it, were then considered by the Ad Hoc Committee of the General Assembly in late November and early December 1949.[1] During these debates the Government of Israel proposed that the U.N. should sign an agreement with Israel relating to the supervision and protection of the Holy Places.[2] A sub-committee was established to study and report on the various proposals regarding Jerusalem. This sub-committee proposed, and the Ad Hoc Political Committee eventually adopted, a resolution which called upon the General Assembly, *inter alia*, to restate its intention that Jerusalem should be placed under a permanent international regime, which should envisage appropriate guarantees for the protection of the Holy Places.[3] During the discussion prior to the adoption of this resolution, the Jordanian delegate stated that internationalization would serve no useful purpose since the Holy Places under the control of his Government were safe and there was no need for a special regime.[4]

1949: PLENARY SESSION OF THE GENERAL ASSEMBLY

The proposal made by the Ad Hoc Political Committee was discussed in the plenary meeting of the General Assembly on 9th December, 1949. Among those who supported the proposals of the Ad Hoc Political Committee were the representatives of Argentina, Australia, Brazil, Cuba, Egypt, El Salvador, Greece, Haiti, Iraq, Lebanon, Pakistan, Peru, Syria and the U.S.S.R., mainly on the grounds that implementation of the resolution would ensure peace and security in Jerusalem and would meet the interests of both the population of the city of Jerusalem and all religious groups. The resolution was opposed by the representatives of Canada, Denmark, Guatemala, Israel, the Netherlands, Norway, Sweden, the Union of South Africa, the United Kingdom, the United States and Venezuela, primarily on the ground that its adoption might jeopardise the truce in Jerusalem, complicate the finances of the U.N., and be impossible

---

[1] *Y.B.U.N.*, 1948-49, p. 190 *et seq.*
[2] Draft attached to draft resolution A/AC.31/L.42. For text, see below, Appendix I, p. 76
[3] *Y.B.U.N.*, 1948-49, p. 191.
[4] *Ibid.*, p. 192.

to implement.[1] Instead a joint Netherlands-Swedish draft[2], supported by Canada, Chile, Iceland and Norway, proposed the internationalization of the Holy Places without disturbing the existing political situation in Jerusalem.

The Assembly then adopted, on 9th December, 1949, Resolution 303/IV[3] in which it restated its intention that Jerusalem should be placed under a permanent international regime, which should envisage appropriate guarantees for the protection of the Holy Places, both within and outside Jerusalem. The Trusteeship Council was requested to complete the preparation of the Statute of Jerusalem at its next session.

1949-50: THE TRUSTEESHIP COUNCIL

For the purpose of carrying out the task thus re-assigned to it, the Trusteeship Council held a special session from 8th to 20th December, 1949. The President of the Council was asked to prepare a working paper on the Statute in time for the next session of the Council on 19th January, 1950. The Council also adopted a resolution[4] in which it expressed the opinion that the Government of Israel, in removing to Jerusalem certain of its ministries and central departments, was likely to render more difficult the implementation of the Statute.

When the Council met again in January 1950 it had before it the President's proposals for the establishment of Jerusalem as a *corpus separatum* to be placed under a permanent international regime. The territory was to be an economic free zone, but was to be divided into three parts—an Israeli zone, a Jordanian zone and an international city, which would include all the Holy Places covered by the Status Quo of 1757.[5]

During the debate, the representatives of Egypt, Iraq and Syria objected to the division of the City into three parts. Jordan stated that it was not prepared to discuss any plan for internationalization. Israel declared that, while opposed to the internationalization of the Jerusalem area, as proposed in the Statute, it was willing to accept the principle of direct U.N. responsibility for the Holy Places.

---

[1]*Ibid.*, p. 193.
[2]A/1227.
[3]The voting was 38 to 14, with 7 abstentions. For text, see *Y.B.U.N.*, 1948-49, p. 196.
[4]T/427.
[5]*Y.B.U.N.*, 1950, p. 335. See also p. 65 below.

The Council also heard the views of various religious groups. The representative of the Patriarch of Jerusalem stated that the following, among other conditions, should be guaranteed: (i) The Status Quo of 1757 should be kept inviolate; (ii) the character of the monastic foundations belonging to each Church should be preserved; and (iii) the Holy Places and Shrines, as well as the property attached to them, should be exempt from all taxation.

The representative of the American Christian Palestine Committee expressed the view that the internationalization of Jerusalem was impossible to implement, in view of the opposition of the inhabitants of that area to any such plan. A U.N. Commission should be established which would have no territorial sovereignty but only the duty of protecting the Holy Places vis-à-vis the Governments concerned.

The representative of the Armenian Church welcomed the internationalization of Jerusalem but made certain proposals for the establishment of a legislature and the creation of a judicial organ charged with the special task of regulating differences between the religious groups and the civil authorities.

Finally, the representative of the Commission of Churches on International Affairs suggested three conditions for an international regime for Jerusalem: (i) the preservation of human rights and fundamental freedoms, particularly of religious liberty; (ii) recognition that the protection of and access to Holy Places was an international responsibility; and (iii) the return to owners of all church-owned and mission-owned property in Palestine which was occupied by either Arabs or Jews.

Eventually on 4th April, 1950, the Trusteeship Council approved a draft Statute for Jerusalem under which the City was to be constituted a *corpus separatum*, but not divided into three parts. On 14th June, 1950, the Council decided to submit to the General Assembly its special report[1] containing the Statute.

1950: AD HOC POLITICAL COMMITTEE OF THE GENERAL ASSEMBLY

This report was considered by the *Ad Hoc* Political Committee of the General Assembly between 7th and 14th December, 1950.

---

[1]A/1286.

During the debates in the Ad Hoc Political Committee both Sweden and Belgium presented draft resolutions which, in effect, dropped the idea of internationalization of the City. Sweden proposed simply that Israel and Jordan should give certain pledges to respect human rights and give free access to the Holy Places, while allowing the U.N. to supervise through a Commissioner the protection of and access to the Holy Places. But jurisdiction and control over each part of the Jerusalem area was to be exercised by the States concerned. [1] The Belgian proposal was that there should be further study of the conditions of a settlement capable of ensuring the effective protection, under U.N. supervision, of the Holy Places [2].

During the debate, the Jordanian representative while repeating his objection to the territorial internationalization of the City, did not close the door to the functional internationalization proposed by Sweden. However, he said, the Swedish draft resolution tended in certain respects to infringe the sovereignty of Jordan and he was therefore unable to accept it as it stood.

Other Arab and Moslem States opposed the Swedish proposal on the grounds that it would fail to resolve the basic issue which was how international control could harmonise the two opposing nationalisms which dominated the city, and that it was inconsistent with the resolution adopted by the General Assembly. They felt that full territorial internationalization of the City was the best solution.

The representative of Israel supported the Swedish proposal and stated that Israel would be prepared to co-operate with a U.N. Commissioner.

The Swedish proposal received support from, amongst others, Australia, Denmark, Guatemala, the Netherlands, New Zealand, Turkey, South Africa, the United Kingdom, the U.S.A., the Uruguay and Yugoslavia. [3] The Belgian draft was supported by Brazil, Chile, China, El Salvador, France, Greece and the Philippines, among others.

The Soviet delegate stated that although the resolutions of 1947 and 1949 had provided for the creation of a permanent

---

[1] A/AC.38/L.63. For text, see Appendix II below, p. 80.
[2] A/AC.38/L.71.
[3] For the text of an amendment proposed by the United Kingdom, see Appendix III below, p. 84.

international regime, it now appeared that the solution was acceptable to neither the Arab nor the Jewish inhabitants of Jerusalem. Accordingly, his Government could not continue to support those resolutions. As both drafts now before the Committee were unsatisfactory, the U.S.S.R. would abstain from voting on either of them.[1]

The Committee then voted first on the Belgian draft. As this was adopted by 30 votes to 18 with 11 abstentions, the Committee decided not to vote on the Swedish draft.

1950: PLENARY SESSION OF THE GENERAL ASSEMBLY

But when the report of the Ad Hoc Committee containing the resolution recommended by it was voted upon by the General Assembly on 15th December, 1950, without a debate, the voting in favour of the draft was 30 in favour, 18 against and 9 abstentions. As a two-thirds majority is required for the adoption in the General Assembly of a resolution on important matters, the draft resolution was not adopted. The consequence was that no further action on the Jerusalem question was taken in the U.N. between December 1950 and December 1952.

1952 (January): THE GENERAL ASSEMBLY

Although the question of Palestine was discussed in the Ad Hoc Political Committee and in the Plenary Meetings of the General Assembly in January 1952 the question of Jerusalem was not specifically raised. Nevertheless on 26th January, 1952, the Assembly adopted Resolution 512 (VI)[2] in which, after recalling its earlier resolutions on the Palestine problem and stating that it had examined the progress of the Palestine Conciliation Commission, it noted that the Commission had been unable to fulfil its mandate and stated that it considered "that the governments concerned have the primary responsibility for reaching a settlement of their outstanding differences" in conformity with the Assembly's resolutions. While this resolution does not involve any explicit abandonment of the Assembly's views on internationalization the fact that it is not expressly mentioned is a mark of the diminishing importance which the Assembly was coming to attach to that solution.

---

[1]On 17th April, 1950, the Soviet Union had informed the Secretary-General of the U.N. that it was withdrawing its support of G.A. Resolution 303 (IV) (See *G.A.O.R.*, 5th Sess., Supp. No. 1, p. 5).

[2]See *Y.B.U.N.*, 1951, p. 308.

1952 (December): The General Assembly

In 1952 the General Assembly decided quite explicitly not to re-assert the principle of internationalization. The Arab States had inscribed on the General Assembly agenda an item entitled "The Conciliation Commission for Palestine and its work in the light of the resolutions of U.N."[1] In their statements the Arab States drew attention to the fact that the Commission had been unable to implement the Assembly's decisions regarding the internationalization of Jerusalem and its Holy Places. On 11th December, 1952, the Ad Hoc Political Committee adopted a resolution in which it urged "the Governments concerned to enter at an early date . . . into direct negotiations for the establishment of . . . a settlement, bearing in mind the resolutions as well as the principal objectives of the U.N. on the Palestine question, including the religious interests of third parties."[2]

When this resolution was considered in the plenary session of the Assembly, the Philippines representative proposed two amendments to the clause just quoted, of which one was the addition at the end, after the words "interests of third parties," the words "and, in particular, the principle of the internationalization of Jerusalem." This amendment was not adopted because it failed, by a quite significant figure, to achieve the required two-thirds majority. The voting was 28 in favour, 20 against and 12 abstentions.[3] The Ad Hoc Political Committee's

---

[1]See Y.B.U.N., 1952, p. 299 et seq.
[2]Ibid., p. 252.
[3]The voting was as follows: In favour: Afghanistan, Argentina, Belgium, Bolivia, Brazil, Chile, Colombia, Costa Rica, Cuba, Dominican Republic, Egypt, El Salvador, Ethiopia, Haiti, India, Indonesia, Iran, Iraq, Lebanon, Pakistan, Paraguay, Peru, Philippines, Saudi Arabia, Syria, Thailand, Venezuela, Yemen. Against: Byelorussian S.S.R., Czechoslovakia, Denmark, Ecuador, Iceland, Israel, Netherlands, New Zealand, Norway, Panama, Poland, Sweden, Turkey, Ukrainian S.S.R., Union of South Africa, U.S.S.R., United Kingdom, United States, Uruguay, Yugoslavia. Abstaining: Australia, Burma, Canada, China, France, Greece, Guatemala, Honduras, Liberia, Luxembourg, Mexico, Nicaragua.
The following table of voting on "territorial internationalization" is taken from Israel and the U.N., p. 138:

Year	In Favour	Against	Abstentions	Result
1947	33	13	10	Resolution 181 (ii)
1948	35	15	8	„ 194 (III)
1949	38	14	7	„ 303 (IV)
1950	30		9	No resolution for
1951		no discussion		lack of two-thirds
1952	28	20	12	majority
1953		no discussion		„ „

draft resolution was itself then not adopted by a vote of 24 in favour to 21 against with 15 abstentions.

This meant that the Assembly adopted no resolution on Palestine at its seventh session, and Resolution 512 (IV) remained in force.

1952-1967: U.N. INACTION

From 1952 to 1967 the question of Jerusalem was conspicuous only by its absence from discussion in the U.N. During those fifteen years, the matter was never referred to in the General Assembly.[1] Moreover, on only three occasions has the subject been mentioned in the Security Council: in 1957, when there was some discussion of the status of certain areas lying in the areas between the Israeli and Jordanian held parts of Jerusalem; in 1958, when there was a brief reference to the question of Mount Scopus; and in 1965, when Jordan filed a complaint about a proposed Israeli Independence Day Parade to be held in Jerusalem, but did not request a meeting of the Security Council.

For all practical purposes, the idea of internationalizing Jerusalem was forgotten. Moreover, the members of the U.N. showed no concern whatsoever about the protection of the Holy Places. They were content to accept—and for fifteen years accepted—the *de facto* unilateral control of Israel and Jordan over the Holy Places within their respective jurisdictions.[2]

1967: THE GENERAL ASSEMBLY RESOLUTIONS

Then, early in June 1967, renewed fighting broke out between Israel and her neighbours. Faced by the closure of the Straits of Tiran, the prospect of a renewed blockade of Eilath and the manifest threat of the massive use of force by Egypt, Israel was compelled to adopt vigorous defensive measures. Egyptian forces were driven out of the Gaza Strip and, indeed, out of the whole of the Sinai Peninsula. Jordan failed to restrain itself and after joining on 5th June in the general attack upon Israel was driven

---

[1] The Report of the Conciliation Commission for the period covering 1953 referred to the fact that protests by the Arab States had been transmitted to it regarding the transfer of Israeli Ministries to Jerusalem. The Commission stated that it adhered to the position on this topic which it had taken in 1949. (*Y.B.U.N.*, 1953, p. 214).

[2] It may be noted that of the 30 Holy Places listed by the U.N. in 1949 only two fell within the part of Jerusalem held by Israel prior to the events of June 1967. The rest were under Jordanian control.

not only out of Jerusalem but also out of all possessions on the west bank of the Jordan River.

Israel's opponents in the U.N. reacted to those events in two ways. First, they sought to secure the condemnation of Israel as an aggressor. In this they failed miserably.[1] Secondly, they sought to attack the validity of Israeli measures affecting the government of the City of Jerusalem. In this they achieved a measure of success—albeit merely verbal.

On 4th July, 1967, the General Assembly adopted a resolution proposed by Pakistan of which the most important provisions read as follows:

"The General Assembly,

Deeply concerned at the situation prevailing in Jerusalem as a result of the measures taken by Israel to change the status of the City,

1. *Considers* that these measures are invalid;

2. *Calls upon* Israel to rescind all measures already taken and to desist forthwith from taking any action which would alter the status of Jerusalem . . ."[2]

And on 14th July, 1967, the General Assembly adopted a further resolution on the same subject in which it deplored Israel's failure to implement the resolution of 4th July, and reiterated its call to Israel to rescind all measures already taken and to desist forthwith from taking any action which would alter the status of Jerusalem.

The question which we must ask is whether these resolutions reflected any intention on the part of the General Assembly to resurrect the idea of the territorial internationalization of Jerusalem and, in particular, whether "the status of the City" about which the first resolution stated concern was the status of Jerusalem as a city chosen by the General Assembly in 1947 for internationalization. To both these questions a negative answer may properly be given.

It may be noted that the first resolution was adopted with virtually no discussion of its content. In the general debate which preceded its introduction only four States—Spain, Brazil, the Ivory Coast and Peru—had referred to the internationalization of Jerusalem; the rest had discussed the Middle East crisis

---

[1]See above, p. 11, n. 1.
[2]Resolution 2253 (ES-V). The voting was 99 in favour, none against and 20 abstentions.

in more general terms or had been concerned to assert in a variety of ways the concept that a State should not be permitted to acquire territory by force.[1] The voting on the resolution was immediately preceded by the rejection of the Soviet and Albanian draft resolutions seeking condemnation of Israel as an aggressor; and the resolution clearly represented the maximum which the General Assembly was prepared to accept at the time. Nor was the content of the second resolution any more fully scrutinised; and no attempt was made to read into it a reassertion of the idea of internationalization.

Furthermore, the language used in the resolutions is quite incompatible with any demonstration of concern for the idea of internationalization. It should be recalled in this connection that the measures to which the resolution was directed were measures of administrative re-unification of the City. To declare them invalid and to call upon Israel to rescind the measures already taken was, in effect, to demand the restoration of a status which involved a claim by Jordan to control over the Old City of Jerusalem which was completely irreconcilable with the idea of internationalization.

Thus, it may be said that the resolution goes even further than a non-assertion of the idea of internationalization. For, in laying emphasis without qualification upon the restoration of the status of the City to the position prior to the fighting, the Resolution appears to concede the acceptability of the previous occupation of each of the two parts of the City by Israel and Jordan respectively.

1968: THE SECURITY COUNCIL RESOLUTION

Finally, reference should be made to the adoption by the Security Council on 27th April, 1968, of a resolution calling upon Israel not to hold a military parade in the part of Jerusalem formerly held by Jordan and on 2nd May, 1968, of a resolution deeply deploring the holding of the parade in disregard of the earlier resolution. Neither of those resolutions—either in their terms or by reason of the debates preceding their adoption—can be regarded as indicating any revival of a U.N. interest in the territorial internationalization of Jerusalem. The basis of the Security Council's attitude as reflected in both resolutions was

---

[1]The validity of the application of this concept to the Israeli actions will be considered in the next chapter. See below, p. 51.

its concern with the maintenance of peace and security and its consequential fear that the parade would aggravate tensions in the area and have an adverse effect on a peaceful settlement of problems in the area.[1]

(e) CONCLUSIONS

At the risk of labouring the obvious, the principal conclusions to be drawn from this close survey of what has actually happened in the U.N. in relation to the internationalization of Jerusalem are the following:

(i)   During the critical period of the changeover of power in Palestine from British to Israeli and Arab hands, the U.N. did nothing effectively to implement the idea of the internationalization of Jerusalem.

(ii)   In the five years 1948 to 1952 inclusive, the U.N. sought to develop the concept as a theoretical exercise in the face of a gradual realization that it was acceptable neither to Israel nor to Jordan and could never be enforced. Eventually the idea was allowed quietly to drop.

(iii)   In the meantime, both Israel and Jordan demonstrated that each was capable of ensuring the security of the Holy Places and of maintaining access to and free worship at them—with the exception, on the part of Jordan, that Jews were not allowed access to Jewish Holy Places in the area of Jordanian control.

(iv)   The U.N. by its unconcern with the idea of territorial internationalization, as demonstrated from 1952 to the present date, effectively acquiesced in the demise of the concept. The events of 1967 and 1968 have not led to its revival.

(v)   Nonetheless, there began to emerge, as long ago as 1950, the idea of "functional" internationalization of the Holy Places in contradistinction to the "territorial" internationalization of Jerusalem. This means that there should be no element of international government of the City, but only a measure of international interest in and concern with the Holy Places. This idea has been propounded by Israel and has been said to be acceptable to her. Jordan has not subscribed to it. The various ways in which it may be implemented are explored in Chapter IV below.

---

[1] A later Security Council resolution of 21st May, 1968 (S/RES/252 (1968)), was received too late for detailed consideration in this pamphlet-but it does not appear to alter the position described above.

CHAPTER III

THE LAW AND JERUSALEM

We shall in this Chapter distinguish between, and deal separately with, those parts of Jerusalem which were under Israeli control between 1948 and 1967, i.e. in general terms, the New or western City, and those parts which fell under Israeli control as a result of the fighting in June 1967, i.e. the Old and eastern parts of the City.

(a) THE NEW CITY

It will be clear from the previous chapter that it was no part of the General Assembly's original intention as expressed in the 1948 Partition Resolution that any part of Jerusalem should be subject to the sovereignty of Israel or of any other State. Yet, as events have turned out, Israel has been in control of the New City of Jerusalem since 1948 and has claimed sovereignty over it since 1949. The question which we must examine is whether there is any element of illegality in this now long-established Israeli presence in, and claim to sovereignty over, the New City.

Israeli sovereignty over the New City of Jerusalem has rarely been challenged and is now established to a degree which renders unrealistic any contemplation of reversal of the position. Nevertheless, an understanding of the basis of Israel's rights in the New City before 1967 is fundamental to an appreciation of her rights in the Old City after 1967.

When considering rights to territory, lawyers usually prefer to speak in terms of "title to," or "sovereignty over," territory. Certainly in the case of the New City, these are what Israel claims. The New City is in the Israeli view no less a part of the territory of Israel than is, say, any part of Israel,[1] such as Tel Aviv, falling within the territory originally allotted to the Jewish State under the Partition Resolution and therefore indisputably Israeli. As will be seen, the Israeli claim to the Old City is differently couched and may therefore be different in nature.[2]

---

[1] Though see above, p. 20, for an indication of the manner in which a number of States have refrained from establishing embassies in Jerusalem for reasons said to flow from the operation of the Partition Resolution.

[2] See below, p. 50.

Concerned then, as we are, with a question of title, the normal procedure is to trace the chain of title back from the present claimant to a holder whose rights were unquestioned. If there is no defect in the chain, the present claim is deemed valid.

In scrutinizing the basis of Israeli title to the New City it is unnecessary to go farther back than the period of Ottoman rule which ended *de facto* in 1917. The transfer of Ottoman sovereignty over Palestine to the Principal Allied and Associated Powers was confirmed in the Treaty of Lausanne, 1923.[1] In the meantime, the Powers had in effect vested their rights in the League of Nations, to be exercised in fulfilment of the objects of the Mandates System.[2] As indicated earlier, the precise location of sovereignty over Palestine during the period of the Mandate is difficult to specify, but at any rate all the attributes relevant for present purposes, including the right to dispose of territory, could be exercised only with the consent of the Council of the League.

What happened when the League of Nations ceased to exist? We have the authority of the International Court of Justice for the proposition that after 1946 the status of a mandated territory could only be altered with the consent of the General Assembly of the U.N. This suggests that at least part of the League's interest in the sovereignty previously vested in it and the Mandatory had, as a result of the events of 1945-1946, devolved upon the U.N. If this is correct, what happened to sovereignty in Palestine as a result of the adoption of the Partition Resolution?

One thing is clear—namely that the United Kingdom thereupon completely dropped out of the picture. This loss of any vestige of participation in the title to Palestine was inherent in giving effect to the British wish to be relieved of the obligations of the Mandate.

There remains the question of what happened to the residual rights (such as they may have been) of the U.N. At this point further examination of the chain of title becomes so complex and speculative—and the consistent pursuit of each theory diverges so much from the material facts and the terms of the

[1]See above, p. 13.
[2]Ibid.

relevant instruments—that it is questionable whether the investi·
gation is worth maintaining.

There are, of course, a number of theories which one could
examine. One possibility is that the U.N. conveyed its residual
rights to the proposed Arab and Jewish States respectively,but
retained its interest in the area of the proposed international
City of Jerusalem. There are, however, a number of difficulties
about this approach. An important one is that the language
of the Partition Resolution clearly does not cover this theory.
There is no recital of the U.N's interest; there are no words
which effectively establish the two States; there is no reservation
of rights over the area of the international City. Instead, the
relevant operative parts of the Resolution consist of the following
paragraphs:

> "*The General Assembly*
>
> *Takes note* of the declaration by the Mandatory Power that
> it plans to complete its evacuation of Palestine by 1st August,
> 1948;
>
> *Recommends* to the United Kingdom, as the mandatory
> Power for Palestine, and to all other Members of the United
> Nations the adoption and implementation, with regard to the
> future Government of Palestine, of the Plan of Partition with
> Economic Union set out below:
>
> *Requests* that
>
> . .   . .
>
> (c) The Security Council determine as a threat to the peace,
>   breach of the peace or act of aggression, in accordance
>   with Article 39 of the Charter, any attempt to alter by
>   force the settlement envisaged by this resolution;
>
> . .   . .
>
> *Calls upon* the inhabitants of Palestine to take such steps
> as may be necessary on their part to put this plan into effect;
>
> *Appeals to* all Governments and all peoples to refrain from
> taking any action which might hamper or delay the carrying out
> of these recommendations . . ."

None of this reflects an intention to convey rights, conditionally
or otherwise.

A second reason why it would be difficult to treat the
Partition Resolution as the conveyance of the U.N's rights is
that we then run into insuperable difficulties when seeking to

reconcile the continuance of the Resolution as an effective legal instrument with the facts as they eventually unfolded.[1] We are left with so many important unanswerable questions. For example, if the Partition Resolution conveyed sovereignty to the Arab and Jewish States, what was the effect upon that transfer of the rejection of the Resolution by the Arab States? Was the proposal for an Arab State severable from the proposal for a Jewish State? Was the proposal for an international Jerusalem severable from the creation of the two new States? Or did the grant of sovereignty to the Arabs lapse while that of Israel remained effective? In any case, how can the U.N's silence regarding the retention of such (if any) of its rights as did not pass be reconciled with its complete silence on this aspect of the matter for 20 years?

One can contemplate various other theories about the orderly devolution of sovereignty in Palestine. One can even examine the implications of theories about the location of sovereignty in mandated territories other than the one adopted above as the starting point for this discussion, namely, that sovereignty was divided between the League and the Mandatory.[2] But none of these approaches provides a fully satisfactory answer to the question of sovereignty in Palestine after 1948.

It thus becomes appropriate to take note of the possibility that a territory may not have a sovereign. In such circumstances, sovereignty is said to be in "suspense." Or, to put it another

---

1. Even within the Security Council there was a divergence of views upon the effect of this Resolution. In December 1948 the Soviet view was stated in the Security Council in the following terms:

"The U.S.S.R. . . . . maintains . . . that the basis for the creation and the existence of the State of Israel and of an Arab State in Palestine is the General Assembly resolution of 29th November, 1947. That resolution is an international legal document entitling the State of Israel and the Arab State of Palestine to their creation and existence, and nobody—except, of course, the General Assembly—has a right to revoke it . . .

Modification is, of course, possible, but that is the affair of the State of Israel and not of those who are trying by force to deprive it of territory which is legally its own . . ." (S.C.O.R., 3rd Year, No. 129, 385th mtg., 17th Dec. 1948, pp. 28-29).

On the other hand, in the same debate, the Canadian representative said:

"We regard the resolution of the General Assembly as having the force of a recommendation, and we do not consider the settlement, which we hope will emerge soon in Palestine, need conform precisely to any resolution of the General Assembly." (Ibid., p. 24).

²For the summary statement of the different views, see Oppenheim's International Law, vol. I (8th ed., 1955), p. 222, n. 5.

way, there arises a lapse in or vacancy of sovereignty. Naturally, cases of this kind are rare—but the United Kingdom has gone on record in acknowledging its possibility. In 1955, in reply to a Parliamentary question about the legal aspects of the situation in the South-East China Coast, the reply was given that "Formosa and the Pescadores are therefore, in the view of Her Majesty's Government, territory the *de jure* sovereignty over which is uncertain or undetermined."[1] Subsequently, the British Government applied the same concept quite specifically to Palestine—in considering the position of the Gaza strip which had been occupied by Egypt in 1948. On 14th March, 1957, the Foreign Secretary said: "The facts about the Gaza strip seem to me to be these. No country has legal sovereignty . . ."[2]

Once the possibility of a vacancy or vacuum in sovereignty is recognized, then the situation in Palestine in 1948 is one which can readily be seen in such terms. Whatever may have been the notional intention of the General Assembly at the moment of the adoption of the Partition Resolution on 29th November, 1947, the early British withdrawal,[3] the Arab rejection of the Resolution, the creation of the State of Israel and the entry into Palestine of the neighbouring Arab States with a view to crushing Israel, all led to a situation of such juridical confusion as to exclude any tracing of an orderly devolution of sovereignty.[4]

But if there was, upon the termination of the mandate, a sovereignty vacuum in Palestine, the large question arises of how it could validly be filled. The suggestion that there was a vacuum of sovereignty does not imply that Palestine became at the end of the mandate a *terra nullius*, a land owned by no-one

---

[1]*House of Commons Debates*, vol. 536, Written Answers, col. 159, 4th Feb. 1955. See also E. Lauterpacht, "Contemporary Practice of the United Kingdom," *International and Comparative Law Quarterly*, vol. 5 (1956), p. 414. The answer was repeated in *House of Lords Debates*, vol. 212, col. 498, 13th Nov., 1958.

[2]*House of Commons Debates*, vol. 566, col. 1320. For comment, see E. Lauterpacht, *op. cit.*, vol. 6 (1957), p. 513.

[3]This had originally been planned for the end of July, 1948, but in fact took place on 14th May, 1948.

[4]It is possible, of course, that the sovereignty vacuum in Palestine at the end of the Mandate was nothing more than a reflection of a much longer standing lapse of sovereignty going back to the date when the territory was placed under Mandate. This thought is suggested by the following observation of Sir Arnold (now Lord) McNair in his Separate Opinion on the *International Status of South-West Africa:* "Sovereignty over a Mandated Territory is in abeyance; if and when the inhabitants of the territory obtain recognition as an independent State, as has already happened in the case of some Mandates, sovereignty will revive and vest in the new State." (*I.C.J. Reports* 1950, p. 150).

in which anyone was free to stake a claim by simply combining physical presence with an assertion of title.[1] Slight though the legal force of the Partition Resolution might be, it is difficult to conceive of it as having opened up Palestine to the law of the jungle, to be carved up on the basis of first come first served.

In other words, it seems reasonable to suggest that sovereignty could only be acquired by lawful action. Indeed, the scope for the right-creating effect of illegal acts in international law is exceedingly restricted; and there seems to be general consensus to-day as to the validity of the maxim *ex injuria ius non oritur* —no right can be born of an unlawful act.

It becomes necessary, therefore, to consider the legality of the various demonstrations of physical power in Palestine in the period immediately following the end of the Mandate. We must accordingly attempt an assessment of the conduct of the neighbouring Arab States and of Israel at that time.

Of the Arab States, Jordan was not a member of the U.N. and did not become one until 1955. Israel did not become a member of the U.N. until 1949. But few will be likely to dissent from the proposition that the legality of the conduct of all concerned—even in the period before Jordan and Israel became members of the U.N.—fell to be tested by reference to the Charter of the U.N. Technically, this instrument does not bind States not parties to it, but its basic principles have generally been regarded as reflecting fundamental legal obligations of all States, whether or not formally members of the U.N. Indeed, Article 2 (6) of the Charter both acknowledges and asserts this superior juridical authority for the principles of the Charter by providing that

> "the Organisation shall ensure that States which are not Members of the United Nations act in accordance with these Principles so far as may be necessary for the maintenance of international peace and security."

The principle of the Charter which is most relevant in this connection is Article 2 (4):

> "All Members shall refrain in their international relations from the threat or use of force against the territorial integrity

---

[1]See, for a similar view, Blum, "The Missing Reversioner: Reflections on the Status of Judea and Samaria," *Israel Law Review*, vol. 3 (1968), at p. 283.

or political independence of any State, or in any other manner inconsistent with the Purposes of the United Nations."

It will be recalled that immediately after the termination of the Mandate, the forces of Egypt, Iraq, Jordan, Lebanon and Syria crossed the borders of Palestine with the declared object of preventing by force the implementation of the Partition Resolution. Some of the evidence of the nature and object of this attack has already been mentioned.[1] To this may be added a reference to an explanatory footnote appended to the text of the Partition Resolution as it is printed in an official British publication—the *British and Foreign State Papers*. The note in question, after speaking of the establishment of Israel on 14th May, 1948, continues as follows: "On the following day Israel was simultaneously invaded by the armed forces of Egypt, Transjordan, Iraq, Syria and the Lebanon. Hostilities continued until January 1949."[2]

This invasion was entirely unlawful. True, Article 2 (4) of the Charter prohibits primarily "the threat or use of force against the territorial integrity or political independence of any State." And it might, therefore, be argued that in so far as the Arab States were moving into the part of Palestine allotted to the proposed, but as yet uncreated, Arab State, they were not infringing the territorial integrity of any *State*. Moreover, it could be said, from the Arab point of view, that as they did not recognize Israel as a State, the violation of the boundaries of the territory allocated to her was no breach of their obligations under Article 2 (4).

Arguments of this kind, however, carry no great weight when it is appreciated that, as was the fact, the invading Arab States did not intend to, and did not, limit their incursion to the territory of the proposed Arab State and, moreover, that the prohibition of attack upon "States" is not limited to States which have been recognized by the attacker but extends to any State which enjoys a *de facto* existence—as Israel undoubtedly did and was recognized by others as doing.

---

[1] See above, p.p. 21-22.
[2] See *British and Foreign State Papers*, vol. 154 (1949—II), p. 384, n. 1.

Another Arab justification of their attack upon Israel in 1948, and indeed of the continuance of their attitude of belligerency to Israel ever since, is this: that the true aggressor is Israel, which, by the very fact of its establishment and existence, attacks the political independence and territorial integrity of the embryonic State comprising the Arab people of Palestine;[1] and that the presence of the forces of neighbouring Arab States is warranted as a measure of collective self-defence pursuant to Article 51 of the Charter.   The difficulty with this argument is that it invites the assumption that Israel did not, does not and cannot exist as a State with its own right to survival—an assumption which is universally rejected by all save the Arab States.

If, then, there was no legal warrant for the Arab invasion of Palestine in 1948 aimed at the destruction of Israel, two consequences follow.   First, by reason of the illegality of the conduct, no Arab State could rely upon its physical occupation of any part of Palestine as a valid foundation for filling the sovereignty vacuum.   Thus Jordan was not entitled to claim any of the areas west of the river Jordan (a matter of special relevance in connection with Jordan's position in the Old City of Jerusalem —of which more will be said later) and Egypt was not entitled to assert sovereignty over the Gaza Strip.[2]

The second consequence is that, of course, Israel when attacked became entitled to defend herself.   This is a fundamental right of States in international law, and the restatement of the right in Article 51 of the Charter of the U.N. in terms which acknowledge the right of self-defence if an armed attack occurs against a Member of the U.N., does not really limit its generality.

In estimating the proper geographical limits of the development of Israeli self-defensive measures, it is necessary to recall the nature of the attack launched against the Jewish people of Palestine.   The attack was not simply an attack upon the Jewish people in the area of Palestine allocated to the Jewish State;

---

[1]For a statement of this view, see Colloque de Juristes Arabs sur la Palestine, 1967, *La Question Palestinienne* (1968), p. 115.

[2]See p. 41 above for the British attitude to sovereignty over the Gaza Strip—an attitude which, though barely elaborated, may well have been founded upon considerations similar to those examined here.   On the other hand, on 27th April, 1950, the British Government announced its recognition (subject to the exclusion of Jerusalem) of the Union with the rest of Jordan of the West Bank areas occupied in 1948.   See *House of Commons Debates*, vol. 474, cols. 1137-1139.

it was an attack upon all Jewish settlement in Palestine, where-ever situate, and including especially the Jews in the area set aside for the international City of Jerusalem. At that time, acceptance of a territorially internationalized Jerusalem was no part of Arab thinking. Their aim was to drive the Jews from Jerusalem no less than from the other parts of Palestine.

This being so, it is clear that the defensive measures adopted by the Israeli forces could not be limited to the area allocated to Israel in the Partition Plan. The Arabs by attacking the Jews outside the area of the Jewish State and by forcibly rejecting the internationalization of Jerusalem were themselves responsible for the first Israeli expansion beyond the Partition boundaries. By provoking this Israeli movement outside the boundaries of the Jewish State, the Arabs themselves legitimized the process by which Israel filled the vacancy in sovereignty in the areas which, in order to save their kin, the Israeli forces were obliged to defend and therefore to occupy.

It is on this basis—the legitimate filling of the sovereignty vacuum—that the legality of Israeli presence in the New City of Jerusalem in the period prior to the fighting of June 1967 may be seen as resting.

When the situation is analyzed in this way, the Armistice Agreements of 1949 fall into their proper place. Quite under-standably, each of these Agreements concluded between Israel and her neighbours contains a provision that the armistice lines therein laid down shall not prejudice the future political settle-ment. [1] It would not, therefore, be accurate to contend that questions of title, as opposed to temporary rights of occupation, depend upon the Armistice Agreements. Questions of sovereign-ty are quite independent of the Armistice Agreements. Thus, if Israel had, prior to the Armistice Agreement with Jordan, filled the sovereignty vacuum in any particular place, such as the New City of Jerusalem or Tel Aviv, without committing any unlaw-ful act, then her title to that place is perfected and exists apart from the Armistice Agreements.

The important function of the Armistice Agreement was to add to the general prohibition upon the use of force prescribed by Article 2 (4) of the Charter of the U.N., the specific further

---

[1]See Article II (2) of the Israel-Jordan Armistice Agreement, 1949 (*U.N.T.S.*, vol. 42, p. 304).

prohibition contained in the armistice.[1] This restricted even further the limits within which the Parties might lawfully use force and thus validly claim to step into the shoes of the defunct sovereign.

It follows, then, from all that has been said in this section, that by filling the sovereignty vacuum Israel acquired a valid title to the following parts of Palestine:

(i) those parts allotted to the Jewish State under the Partition Plan, because Israel could not, and did not, commit any infringement of anyone else's rights in perfecting its title to those parts; and

(ii) those parts of Palestine *outside* the area allotted to the Jewish State, which Israeli forces were compelled to occupy by way of self-defensive measures during the fighting of 1948-49. These parts include the New City of Jerusalem.

It may be said in passing that the U.N. appears to have acquiesced in this conclusion, primarily because over the last twenty years it has not chosen to challenge it. This is so even in relation to the New City of Jerusalem.[2]

(b) THE OLD CITY

(i) Jordan's Position in the Old City prior to June 1967

Jordan's legal position in the Old City from 1948 to 1967 can be dealt with quite briefly, since all the relevant legal considerations have been set out in the previous section. Quite

---

[1]Article I of the Israel-Jordan Armistice Agreement of 3rd April, 1949, (*U.N.T.S.*, vol. 42, p. 304) provided as follows:

"With a view to promoting the return of permanent peace in Palestine and in recognition of the importance in this regard of mutual assurances concerning the future military operations of the Parties, the following principles, which shall be fully observed by both Parties during the armistice, are hereby affirmed:
1. The injunction of the Security Council against resort to military force in the settlement of the Palestine question shall henceforth be scrupulously respected by both Parties.
2. No aggressive action by the armed forces—land, sea, or air—of either Party shall be undertaken, planned, or threatened against the people or the armed forces of the other..."
    Article III, 2, provided:
"No element of the land, sea or air military or para-military forces of either Party, including non-regular forces, shall commit any warlike or hostile act against the military or para-military forces of the other Party... or shall advance beyond or pass over for any purpose whatsoever the Armistice Demarcation Line set forth in articles V and VI of this Agreement..."

[2]See above, p.p. 23-36.

simply, Jordan's situation in the Old City is the converse of Israel's position in the New. There was never any legal justification for Jordan's entry into the Old City. In contrast with what Jordan did, Israel had not, by rejecting the plan for the internationalization of Jerusalem and moving up forces to expel the citizens of the opposing side, created a condition warranting Jordanian self-defensive measures. Thus Jordan's occupation of the Old City—and indeed of the whole of the area west of the Jordan river—entirely lacked legal justification; and being defective in this way could not form any basis for Jordan validly to fill the sovereignty vacuum in the Old City. Jordan's prolonged *de facto* occupation of the Old City was protected exclusively by the Armistice Agreement which prohibited Israel from initiating action to displace Jordan; and Jordan's occupation could last no longer than the protection thus afforded. This bulwark was abandoned when Jordan destroyed the Armistice Agreement by its attack on Israeli Jerusalem on 5th June, 1967.

Moreover, this same Armistice Agreement affirms in Article II its recognition (1) that "no military or political advantage should be gained under the truce ordered by the Security Council" and (2) that no provision of the Agreement "shall in any way prejudice the rights, claims and positions of either Party hereto in the ultimate peaceful settlement of the Palestine question." The Agreement thus effectively precludes Jordan from asserting any sovereign right to the Old City on the basis of twenty years of effective occupation.[1] Its provisions negative the right-creating effect which the facts might otherwise have had.

(ii) ISRAEL'S POSITION IN THE OLD CITY SINCE JUNE 1967

This brings us to the question of Israel's legal rights in the

---

[1] In this connection it is worth noting the reaction of the Arab League to the Jordanian attempt to annex the West Bank areas of Palestine, including Jerusalem, in April 1950. On 16th May, 1950, the Political Committee of the Arab League decided unanimously that the annexation of Arab Palestine by the Jordan Government violated the League's resolution of 12th April, 1950, which prohibited the annexation of any part of Palestine. Egypt, Saudi Arabia, Syria and Lebanon voted on 16th May, 1950, for the expulsion of Jordan from the Arab League. However, after Iraqi mediation, a compromise was reached under which Jordan declared that the annexation was without prejudice to the final settlement of the Palestine issue. This union was recognised by the British Government subject to the reservation that "pending a final determination of the status of [the Jerusalem area] they are unable to recognise Jordan sovereignty over any part of it." (See Whiteman's *Digest of International Law*, vol. 2, pp. 1163-1168).

Old City in the period subsequent to its occupation by Israeli forces in June 1967. It follows from what has been said above that the sovereignty vacuum arising in the Old City at the end of the Mandate was not filled by Jordan, whose status there was one of *de facto* occupation protected by the Armistice Agreement. Once Jordan was physically removed from the Old City by legitimate measures—as the Israeli reactions to the Jordanian attack on 5th June, 1967, undoubtedly were—then the way was open for a lawful occupant to fill the still subsisting vacancy.

That Israel would be entitled to do this, there seems—on the reasoning here set out—to be little doubt. What is less certain is whether in strictly legal terms she has in fact done so. Although, in political terms, Israeli control over the Old City has been repeatedly and emphatically asserted, and although she has declared that her position there is "not negotiable," she has not expressly and in so many words claimed "sovereignty" over the Old City. Instead she has spoken of re-unification and of reuniting the administration of the two parts of the City.

Still, if, as is suggested, the larger measures would be justifiable, then the lesser measures certainly are. And one has then only to ask on what basis the General Assembly could have asserted its view on 4th July, 1967[1] that the Israeli measures are invalid; and what effect, if any, has to be ascribed to this assertion.

To dispose of the question of effect first, the answer is simply that the Resolution of 4th July, 1967, is legally quite ineffective. Leaving aside for the moment the fact that the Resolution appears to have been formulated on the basis of a misconception of the legal position, the fact remains that General Assembly resolutions do not, in the absence of special circumstances which do not characterize the present situation,[2] create legal obligations for their addressees. Consequently, unless the Israeli measures are invalid for other reasons, the Resolution cannot make them so or require Israel to rescind them.

But are there in truth any reasons—the mere contents of the Resolution apart—for denying validity to the Israeli measures? They are not the acts of an aggressor as the Assembly by its own

[1] Resolution 2253 (ES-V). See above, p. 34.
[2] On the limits of the binding force of resolutions of the General Assembly, see Johnson in *British Year Book of International Law*, vol. 32, p. 97.

rejection on 4th June of the Soviet and Albanian draft resolutions has so clearly indicated[1] and cannot therefore be condemned on that ground. Perusal of the General Assembly debates suggests that the thought of Members at the time may have been woven of two separate strands. (i) certain ideas about the relevance of the law of belligerent occupation and (ii) some maxims about the relationship of force and territorial change.

CONSIDERATIONS OF THE LAW OF BELLIGERENT OCCUPATION

The traditional law of war, developed when there was no legal fetter upon the freedom of States to resort to war,[2] contains a chapter on "belligerent occupation." On the assumption that two States are at war with each other in a technical sense,[3] there exist rules which govern the rights and duties of each belligerent in relation to the occupation by it of its enemy's territory. One of these rules involves the distinction between "occupation" and "annexation" of enemy territory. "Occupation" is mere control of enemy territory by force of arms for so long as the belligerent is able to maintain his position or until he voluntarily gives it up. It involves no denial of the *de jure* rights of the regular sovereign, only a temporary, though possibly prolonged, *de facto* suspension of the exercise of those rights. "Annexation," on the other hand, involves an attempt by the occupant to convert his physical right of occupation into a legal title to the territory. In other words, he seeks to change "sovereignty" over the territory from his enemy to himself.

Having drawn this distinction between "occupation" and "annexation" the traditional law permitted the former but prohibited the latter. The rule was that *pendente bello*, that is, for so long as the technical condition of war lasted, a belligerent

---

[1]See above, p. 11, n. 1.

[2]That is, prior to the Kellog-Briand Pact, 1928, in which the Parties undertook not to have recourse to war for the settlement of their disputes. This and the Charter of the U.N. are the two major instruments which have effectively outlawed resort to war and the use of force.

[3]It should always be recalled that so long as "war" was lawful, i.e. before 1928, a distinction could be drawn between, on the one hand, "war" as a technical legal status which States were free to create and which might or might not be associated with hostilities and, on the other, "hostilities" or "fighting" which could, of course, occur even in the absence of a formal state of war. To-day, it is doubtful whether a formal state of war can ever validly arise; and the operation of the important humanitarian rules of warfare, such as the 1949 Geneva Conventions, has been made independent of the existence of any technical state of war.

was not entitled to annex enemy territory which he might have occupied. A transfer of title to territory in consequence of war could take place only as a result of the cession of the territory in the treaty of peace.[1]

Now it would seem that, at any rate for some States, considerations of this nature entered into the formation of their attitude to the General Assembly Resolution of 4th July, 1967, declaring the Israeli measures in the Old City of Jerusalem invalid. Thus in the debate on the resolution Lord Caradon said, on behalf of the United Kingdom, that the Israeli measures were invalid because they went beyond the competence of an occupying power as defined by international law.[2]

The correctness of the British approach as thus expressed rests upon one major assumption which appears to have been wrongly made. The assumption was that Israel had in law formally annexed the Old City of Jerusalem. For this view there is no evidence. Whatever may be the generally held opinion as to the political future of the City, the step of formal incorporation has yet to be taken. The point was made clearly by the Israeli Foreign Minister in a letter received by the Secretary-General of the U.N. on 10th July, 1967:

> "The resolution presented on 4th July by Pakistan and adopted on the same day evidently refers to measures taken by the Government of Israel on 27th June, 1967. The term "annexation" used by supporters of the resolution is out of place. The measures adopted relate to the integration of Jerusalem in the administrative and municipal spheres, and furnish a legal basis for the protection of the Holy Places of Jerusalem."[3]

The measures in question were three in number: the Law and Administration Ordinance (Amendment No. 11) Law, 1967,

---

[1]Though this was the rule, there were occasions on which it was not always honoured. For example, in 1878 the United Kingdom was allowed by Turkey to occupy and administer Cyprus. Sovereignty over the island remained in Turkey. When the First World War broke out, with Turkey and Britain on opposite sides of the line of war, Britain remained in control of the island, but the existence of the state of war put Britain in the position of a belligerent occupant. Nevertheless, in 1914 the United Kingdom unilaterally purported to annex the island. This was an unlawful act. Ultimately the illegality was cured when Turkey recognised the annexation in the Treaty of Peace.

[2]See A/PV. 1553, p. 7.

[3]See A/6753, p. 3. Reprinted in *International Legal Materials*, vol. 6 (1967), p. 846.

and accompanying Order, which extended the operation of Israeli law, jurisdiction and administration to the eastern part of Jerusalem; the Municipal Corporations Ordinance (Amendment) Law 1967, which empowered the Minister of the Interior to enlarge the area of any municipality by the inclusion of an area designated under the first measure; and the Protection of Holy Places Law, 1967. None of these instruments constituted a formal annexation of the Old City.

Once it is seen that there has been no formal annexation of the Old City, and that the measures adopted by Israel are largely consistent with the technical maintenance of a condition of belligerent occupation, the objection expressed by the United Kingdom falls to the ground.

Yet to have met the British point on its merits, as has been done here, should not be read as an acknowledgment of the correctness of the supposition that the traditional law of belligerent occupation is as such applicable to the Israeli position in Jerusalem. It must suffice for present purposes to indicate that any such supposition makes certain assumptions about the nature of the conflict between Israel and her neighbours, about the character of the Jordanian presence in Jerusalem and about the duration of the applicability of the rules of occupation which are very far from being beyond controversy in this context.

Force And Territorial Change

The reference to the law of belligerent occupation has necessitated the introduction into the present study of considerations which look technical even in the context of a legal debate. This does not make them bad, but it does warrant returning to the discussion on the basis of the general assumption that Israel has in effect annexed the Old City of Jerusalem.

When approached thus, the ground on which the legality of the Israeli actions has been denied is the proposition that territorial change as a result of the use of force is impermissible.

This proposition, stated in this unqualified form—and it is only in an unqualified form that those who use it can make it apply to the Jerusalem situation—is an erroneous distortion of a well-known and well-established principle. The correct principle has already been mentioned in this paper—*ex injuria jus non oritur*, out of a wrong no right can arise. Or, relating the proposition more closely to the situation, territorial change cannot properly take place as a result of the *unlawful* use of force. But to omit the word 'unlawful' is to change the substantive content of the rule and to turn an important safeguard of legal principle into an aggressor's charter. For if force can never be used to effect lawful territorial change, then, if territory has once changed hands as a result of an unlawful use of force, the illegitimacy of the position thus established is sterilized by the prohibition upon the use of force to restore the lawful sovereign. This cannot be regarded as reasonable or correct.

Moreover, it does not accord with the law as reflected, for example, in the discussions of the U.N. Special Committee on Principles of International Law concerning Friendly Relations and Co-operation among States. Among the principles considered by this Committee is the principle that States shall refrain in their international relations from the threat or use of force against the territorial integrity or political independence of any State or in any other manner inconsistent with the purposes of the U.N. Now it is significant to observe that in none of the various proposals for the elaboration of this principle advanced in this Committee at its second session held in July-August 1967, in the immediate aftermath of the June war, was the proposition about the consequences of the use of force ever put forward in the stark and unqualified terms upon which the critics of the Israeli position have been relying.

Perhaps it is unnecessary to do more than examine the joint proposal made by a number of States which included some of Israel's most vocal and active opponents, such as Algeria, Syria and the United Arab Republic. This draft,[1] after re-stating the basic prohibition on the use of force, then proposes that

> "5. No threat or use of force shall be permitted to violate the existing boundaries of a State *and any situation brought about by such threat or use of force shall not be recognized by other States.*"[2]

This looks, of course, like the statement of the proposition in an unqualified form. But it is followed in the very next para-

[1]A/AC.125/L.48. See the Report of the Committee to the 22nd Session of the General Assembly, A/6799, 26th Sept. 1967, para. 26.
[2]Italics supplied.

graph by the quite crucial qualification that *"the prohibition of the use of force shall not affect . . . the right of States to take, in case of armed attack, measures of individual or collective self-defence* in accordance with Article 51 of the Charter . . ."[1] Yet, once this qualification is accepted (and the facts of the fighting in June 1967 certainly bring Israel within its ambit), it quite undermines the validity of the loose assertion of the formula so readily enunciated in the General Assembly.

It may be of course that a number of Members of the U.N., while not seeking to advance the proposition except in its full and qualified form have been taking the view that Israel's action does not fall within the conception of permissible self-defence. Yet if her action was not self-defensive, it could only have been aggressive; and the General Assembly, by a most impressive majority, was unwilling to reach this conclusion.[2]

---

[1] Italics supplied
[2] See above, p. 11, n. 1.

CHAPTER IV

THE FUTURE OF THE HOLY PLACES

It is now necessary to look forward. We have already seen in this paper that the proposals for the territorial internationalization of Jerusalem have effectively lapsed; that the objectives which internationalization was intended to secure were, even when the Old City was in Jordanian hands, with one major exception, achieved; and that they have all been maintained under Israeli occupation. We have seen too that there is nothing illegal about Israeli presence in either the New or the Old parts of the City of Jerusalem.

But the fact remains that, regardless of who is sovereign or exercises jurisdictional control in Jerusalem and regardless, too, of the adequacy of the manner in which the City is administered and access to the Holy Places actually secured, there still exists among the nations and faiths of the world an interest in Jerusalem which thirsts for expression in some formal manner. The need for an international instrument may well be more psychological than organic, but there can be little doubt that the need is felt.

In reflecting upon the scope and content of this expression of interest, two things may be recalled: the nature of the interest and the theoretical range of modes in which it may be met.

We start with the commonplace that the Holy Places are of interest to three great religions—Christian, Moslem and Jewish. On the whole, those personally demonstrating this interest can be divided into two groups: those whose presence in the Holy Land is transient and those whose presence is permanent. In relation to the transients, what is required is acknowledgment of their right to come and go freely and to worship. For those who remain for the longer term, what is required is the freedom so to remain, to maintain themselves as part of a religious community in the manner hitherto prevailing, and to lead their lives free of unnecessary intrusion by the secular authority. In addition, the religious communities desire that their vested rights in the Holy Places should be respected; and all are concerned—though their concern is not always translated into effective common action—that the physical fabric of the various Holy Places should be preserved in good repair. They need too the presence of a lay authority capable of maintaining the rights of each as against the others and possibly of settling any disputes which may arise between them.

The selection of one or more devices from the wide variety of legal forms available for the reflection of international interest is a matter of political rather than legal decision. In this connection it is always important to bear in mind the distinction between national and international law. It is perfectly possible for the necessary guarantees of religious interests to be secured exclusively in terms of national law—the law of the local authorities. In fact, subject only to the declarations made by Jordan and Israel to the U.N. Conciliation Commission in November 1949, that is the basis on which the Holy Places have been regulated since 1948. Indeed, it is the basis on which the Holy Places were treated throughout the period of Ottoman rule; and, within the limits prescribed by the Mandate, this was also the position from 1917 to 1948.

Since the re-unification of Jerusalem in 1967, the Protection of Holy Places Law, 1967,[1] has provided that the Holy Places should be protected from desecration and any other violations and from anything likely to violate the freedom of access of the members of the different religions to the places sacred to them or their feelings with regard to those places. Whoever desecrates or otherwise violates a Holy Place shall be liable to imprisonment for a term of seven years.

(a) INTERNATIONAL ASSURANCES

But it is also possible to provide some assurances about the Holy Places in terms of international law. These guarantees can vary greatly both in form and in content.

(i) FORM

As regards form, the assurances could be established either in a treaty or in a unilateral declaration.

The selection of the treaty form would immediately give rise to a question about the parties; and this in its turn would to some extent depend upon the substantive content of the treaty.

---

[1] English text in U.N. doc. A/6793*, 12th Sept., 1967, p. 26, para. 140.

If it were simply a general restatement of the obligations of the local secular authority in relation to the Holy Places, the treaty could be either bilateral, between Israel and the U.N., or multilateral, between Israel and such other States as desired to manifest their interest in the Holy Places.

Clearly, there would be greater difficulty about the conclusion of a multilateral than a bilateral treaty, unless the treaty were drawn up by the U.N., and Israel and the other interested States were invited to accede. While this might be one way in which the U.N. could reassert its authority in the situation, it is questionable whether an approach along these lines would in fact achieve its stated object. Assuming that the text of the relevant instrument were to be drawn up in the General Assembly, a two-thirds majority of the Members of that body would suffice for the adoption of the text. Adoption of a text is, of course, not the same thing as making it binding upon the prospective parties. But once the text of a multilateral treaty is adopted, States, if they are to become parties, have to take it largely as it stands. Although the technique of permitting reservations may enable some States to ratify the treaty as a whole without accepting some of its more objectionable clauses, the flexibility thus introduced is limited. In these circumstances, and having regard to the strength and influence of the Arab bloc in the Assembly, especially when combined in a matter of this kind with the non-Arab Moslem States, there is the distinct possibility that the General Assembly might by a majority adopt a convention which would be unacceptable to Israel. And whether or not Israel's possibly negative attitude to such a convention might appear to all persons to be reasonable and proper would, in all the circumstances, be irrelevant. The declared object of the exercise—the adoption of a binding instrument regarding the Holy Places—would have been defeated. This outcome is not inevitable—but negotiation within the U.N. seems to be the most speculative of the approaches which may be considered.

Another alternative is that of the bilateral treaty. Here again there are various possibilities. One is that of a single bilateral treaty concluded between Israel and the U.N. This in fact was suggested by Israel in 1949. At that time, she proposed a text—the content of which still has considerable contemporary relevance and is printed for convenience of reference as Appendix I hereto. However, this approach, like that of the multilateral treaty, is also exposed (though perhaps less so) to the risk of uncontrollable marshalling of forces in the Assembly more interested in making political capital out of a frustrated negotiation than in securing the conclusion of a workable agreement. [1]

More feasible would be the conclusion of a series of bilateral agreements between Israel and each of the Parties especially interested in the Holy Places. These might include the Holy See (as representing one, but not, of course, all the Christian denominations) and Jordan. This approach would have a number of advantages. There would be scope for true negotiation based upon a genuine desire to reach accommodation. The special requirements of the different Parties could more easily be met. For example, to the extent that any formal recognition of Jordan's sovereign interest in the Moslem Holy Places of Jerusalem were possible, it could more readily be incorporated into a bilateral agreement between Israel and Jordan than into a multilateral agreement. Again, the negotiation of an accord upon the status and privileges of the Christian religious communities in Jerusalem could perhaps more easily be concluded with the representatives of one denomination than with those of all denominations. Moreover, the conclusion of a series of bilateral agreements could be spaced out over a period of time, thus eliminating the need to achieve simultaneous consensus amongst a large number of States.

The merit of the treaty approach—whether multilateral or bilateral—is that the content of the settlement is assured upon a contractual basis. There is then no scope for unilateral withdrawal or amendment, unless specially agreed upon or otherwise permitted by the text.

Nonetheless, there remains another alternative which is not necessarily exclusive of the treaty approach, but can be used as a substitute for it over either the long or the short term. This

---

[1] A variant of this device would be the adoption by the General Assembly of a suitably worded resolution, followed by formal acceptance thereof by Israel. As General Assembly resolutions are not normally binding, such acceptance by Israel would be necessary if it were to have any legal force. The Israeli proposal for the Holy Places submitted to the Trusteeship Council in May 1950 in fact suggested that a "statute" might be adopted in this way (see *G.A.O.R.*, 5th Sess., Suppl. No. 9, p. 29, para 21 (a)). Pursuit of this method to-day might well be open to the difficulties discussed above.

is the device of the unilateral declaration intended to create international obligations for the State making the declaration. True, such declarations are relatively rare; and their effect in international law is not free of doubt. All one can confidently say is that their legal force becomes more certain if one can show that any invitation implicit in them has been accepted by other States. Such acceptance would in effect convert the declaration from one of general force into one having contractual effect as between the declarant State and the State accepting the declaration.

There is one recent precedent for the making of such a declaration in relation to a matter of general interest in the Middle East. On 24th April, 1957, the Egyptian Government made a Declaration on the Suez Canal and the Arrangements for its Operation.[1] This began with the following statement:

> "In elaboration of the principles set forth in their Memorandum dated 18th March, 1957, the Government of the Republic of Egypt, in accordance with the Constantinople Convention of 1888 and the Charter of the United Nations, make hereby the following Declaration on the Suez Canal and the arrangements for its operation."

In paragraph 9, the Government of Egypt indicated that it would accept the jurisdiction of the International Court of Justice in disputes arising between parties to the 1888 Convention. The Declaration concluded thus:

> "This Declaration, with the obligations therein, constitutes an international instrument and will be deposited and registered with the Secretariat of the United Nations."

As already suggested, the precise legal quality of declarations of this kind is open to debate. The text contains, especially in the last paragraph, several indications of the intention of the Government of Egypt to constitute it an "international instrument." Yet, when the instrument is perused as a whole, it contains little in the way of statement of obligation and much instead in the way of statement of intentions. It does not contain any suggestion that it is an invitation which other States may, by an act of acceptance, crystallize into a binding commitment.

---

[1] For text, see E. Lauterpacht (ed.), *The Suez Canal Settlement* (1960), p. 35.

Equivocal though this particular text may be, it does exemplify one technique which could be used in the present situation. Certainly, it is not beyond the bounds of juridical imagination to develop a form of words which could serve unilaterally to create international obligations. From the point of view of the Government of Israel, there might be convenience in such an approach, which would permit it to demonstrate the sympathy which it undoubtedly feels for "the universal interest" in Jerusalem, while at the same time doing so in its own terms and in a manner which could not prejudice the subsequent conclusions of bilateral treaties or other arrangements.

(ii) CONTENT

We may now turn to the content of an international arrangement, whatever may be its form. Here three elements require consideration: substance, supervision and settlement. Their relevance is suggested by examination of earlier proposals regarding the position of the Holy Places.

(a) SUBSTANCE

It is convenient to approach the question of substantive content without regard to the proposals for the territorial internationalization of Jerusalem. We must assume that any further suggestion for actually placing Jerusalem under a form of international government, involving the administrative divorce of the City from the rest of Israel and the direct control of the City by an international authority, is completely excluded. If a system of national jurisdiction, albeit divided between Jordan and Israel, was acceptable for nineteen years, then it is difficult to see why the continuation of a system of national jurisdiction, albeit undivided, should now cease to be internationally tolerable.

However, the rejection of any suggestion of territorial internationalization does not mean that it is necessary for Israel to adopt any rigid stand on such matters as "sovereignty" over the Old City. While she has in the past claimed sovereignty over the New City, she has not as yet done so over the Old; and although there would appear, by reference to the considerations examined in Chapter III above, no legal reason why formal Israeli sovereignty should not be extended over the Old City, there is equally no compelling political reason why it should be. The subject is one on which it is not necessary that anything should be said—and silence on this topic could well be regarded as an important part of the "content" of the instrument (whatever its form).

At one time, particularly in 1949, during the debates in the Ad Hoc Political Committee of the General Assembly on the question of Israel's admission to the U.N., the Government of Israel stated that it was not opposed to the possibility of a limited territorial internationalization of that part of the City in which there was the heaviest concentration of Holy Places. This would, of course, have excluded the New City. Whether nearly twenty years later the Israeli Government, or people, would still be of this view, is clearly a matter for considerable doubt. Nevertheless, the maintenance by Israel of a negotiating position of some flexibility prompts one to enquire whether one possible solution, at any rate in part of the Old City, would be not a territorial internationalization, but an acknowledgment of some form of Jordanian national interest in the Moslem Holy Places.

To speculate upon the form, or even the possibility, of this essentially symbolic gesture might be to raise ideas which have no hope of implementation. It may be best therefore to make no further attempts here to give precise content to this thought. Nevertheless, it might be as well to add that the considerations which prompt this suggestion in relation to the recognition of Jordanian interests in the Old City do not necessarily move in the same way as regards other interests in the Old City. For one thing, if the gesture is thought of in terms of the flying of a Jordanian flag in the environs of the principal Moslem Holy Places, it may be recalled that the representative, for example, of the Holy See is already entitled to fly the Papal flag upon his official residence. For another, any move of this kind in relation to Jordan would partly be warranted by the fact that there is in the Old City of Jerusalem a substantial Arab population with, it may be assumed, basically Jordanian sympathies. The same consideration does not prevail in relation to any of the other parties interested in the Old City.

Once general and largely symbolic matters such as sovereignty are set aside, the substantive content of any assurance or guarantees regarding the Holy Places can readily be deduced from a number of texts which reflect the nature of the international concern for the Holy Places. The texts in question are: the Mandate for Palestine, 1922; the U.N.S.C.O.P. proposals as subsequently incorporated in the Partition Resolution of November, 1947; the Draft Declaration concerning the Holy Places etc. outside Jerusalem, proposed by the U.N. Conciliation Commission on 2nd September, 1949;[1] the Israeli and Arab Declarations made respectively on 8th and 25th November, 1949;[2] the Draft Agreement between the U.N. and Israel annexed to Israel's draft resolution of 25th November, 1949;[3] the Netherlands-Swedish draft resolution of 5th December, 1949;[4] the Cuban draft resolution of 6th December, 1949;[5] certain provisions (particularly Article 33) of the draft Statute for the City of Jerusalem approved by the Trusteeship Council on 4th April, 1950;[6] the Israeli proposal submitted to the Trusteeship Council on 26th May, 1950;[7] and the Swedish draft resolution of 5th December, 1950.[8]

These texts are clearly of much more value in dealing with the specific detail of the Holy Places in the Holy Land than are such important, but nonetheless general, unrelated and therefore less pertinent precedents, like the Conciliation Treaty and the Concordat concluded on 11th February, 1929, between the Holy See and Italy.[9]

With some variation in wording, these texts, in one way or another, provide for respect for the Holy Places; the maintenance of the vested rights of the various denominations; freedom of access to and worship at the Holy Places; and exemption of the Holy Places from taxation. The expansion of these basic concepts into acceptable form in any text on which general political

---

[1]*G.A.O.R.*, 4th Session, Annexes, Agenda Item 18, p. 30.
[2]*Ibid.*, p. 31.
[3]*Ibid.*, p. 46 (A/AC.31/L.42).
[4]*Ibid.*, p. 60 (A/AC.31/L.53).
[5]*Ibid.*, p. 62 (A/AC.31/L.57).
[6]Trusteeship Council Resolution 232 (VI).
[7]*G.A.O.R.*, 5th Sess., Suppl. No. 9, p. 29, at p. 32.
[8]*G.A.O.R.*, 5th Sess., Annexes, Agenda Item 20, p. 1 (A/AC.38/L.63).
[9]For English translation, see Royal Institute of International Affairs, *Documents on International Affairs*, 1929, pp. 216 and 227.

agreement could be reached would not appear to be a matter of any special difficulty.[1]

(b) SUPERVISION

The provisions dealing with supervision and with settlement of differences, although they have a slightly more complex history, should not give rise to greater difficulties.

When in November 1949 the U.N. Conciliation Commission requested the Arab Governments and the Government of Israel to give formal guarantees concerning the Holy Places, the Governments were invited to subscribe to a draft declaration on the subject which the Commission had prepared.[2]   The draft after referring to the main substantive headings (mentioned in the preceding section) proposed that (a) the implementation of its provisions should be under the supervision of a U.N. Commissioner and (b) disputes regarding the interpretation of the Declaration should be settled by the Tribunal which was contemplated in the Instrument then under consideration for the establishment of a permanent international regime for the Jerusalem area and, pending the setting up of this tribunal, should be reported to the Secretary-General of the U.N. for reference to the appropriate organ of the U.N.

Both Israel and the Arab States gave undertakings regarding the substantive matters in the Declaration. In their reply the Arab Governments adopted the wording of the substantive articles, but completely omitted, without any explanation or comment, the articles dealing with supervision and settlement of differences. The Israeli reply, while similarly limiting itself to acceptance of the substantive provisions, explained that, in view of the pending discussion of the subject in the General Assembly, it would be better to take up the actual formulation of the Declaration "in the light of the situation soon to be clarified."

However, when the Government of Israel commented in detail upon the Conciliation Commission's own draft instrument

---

[1]It may be noted in passing that none of the texts has shown any particular concern with the position of the religious communities as a matter distinct from the status of and access to the Holy Places. Thus, not every religious interest is likely to be reflected in the instrument of assurance.

[2]*G.A.O.R.*, 4th Session, Annexes, Agenda Item 18, p. 30 (A/1113).

establishing a permanent regime for the Jerusalem area,[1] i.e. for the implementation of the idea of territorial internationalization, it made the following remarks:

> "Articles 15 to 20 describe the responsibility of the United Nations Commissioner for the protection of Holy Places, religious buildings and sites. It is noticeable that those articles are completely self-sufficient and are not related to any of the other provisions of the instrument. Their implementation in no sense requires the exercise by a United Nations commissioner of full and permanent authority, or the operation of his organs and courts in any secular field. This fact is in itself clear and convincing proof that the exercise of United Nations responsibility for the safeguarding of Holy Places can be implemented without any of the administrative or judicial intrusions envisaged by the Commission in the secular life of Jerusalem. Neither the permanent Commissioner nor the General Council, nor the International and Mixed Tribunals, nor demilitarization, are in the slightest degree essential to the protection under international auspices of Holy Places and sites."[2]

Admittedly, these comments were made in the context of a much further reaching set of proposals than it may be hoped will again be considered in this context by the General Assembly. The comments indicate quite clearly that whatever external organ may be responsible for supervision, it should be concerned with that task only, and not with the performance of any role in the ordinary administrative life of the City. As the Israeli comments suggest a few lines later, "the supervision of the agreement on behalf of the United Nations should be the concern of a representative, and not of a commissioner endowed with executive powers."[3]

In all subsequent proposals for "functional" as opposed to "territorial" internationalization, provision is made for a U.N. representative or commissioner, whose functions were, in the Israeli proposals of 25th November, 1949, to be limited to the "exercise (of) the rights and duties conferred upon the United Nations."[4] The Netherlands-Swedish draft of December 1949

---

[1] *Ibid.*, p. 10 (A/973).
[2] *Ibid.*, p. 42 (A/AC.31/L.34, para. 65).
[3] *Ibid.*, para. 66.
[4] *Ibid.*, p. 46 (A/AC.31/L.42, Annex).

proposed a Commissioner with supervisory functions and very limited executive powers. [1] A similar suggestion was made in the Cuban draft Statute of 6th December, 1949. [2] In the proposals made in May 1950 [3] the Israeli Government proposed the appointment of a U.N. representative who

> "should constitute an independent authority deriving its powers solely and exclusively from the General Assembly itself and exercising these functions in the international right without dependence on any individual government or accreditation thereto."

However, there may have been some subsequent stiffening of the Israeli position in this connection, and it should not therefore be assumed that there would be no difficulty from the Israeli point of view in accepting the appointment of a U.N. Commissioner or representative with the function of supervising the rights of access to and worship at the Holy Places, and with power to request the Israeli Government to suspend any laws or acts which impair the exercise of those rights and to call upon the religious denominations to keep the Holy Places in repair.

(c) DISPUTES

The disputes for the settlement of which it is desirable that provision should be made in any future arrangements fall into two categories:

First, there are those disputes which can arise between the various religious denominations themselves about the enjoyment of their respective rights in the various Holy Places. As the following summary taken from Chapter 3 of the U.N.S.C.O.P. Report shows, these disputes can be complex and have in the past given rise to major international controversy. It also shows that, with one exception, the decisions in this class of case have been taken by the local secular authority.

> "6. In the absence of the special commission for which article 14 of the Mandate provided, the responsibility of settling difficulties and disputes connected with existing rights devolved entirely upon the Government. The Palestine (Holy Places) Order in Council of 1924 withdrew from the law courts of

---

[1] *Ibid.*, p. 60 (A/AC.31/L.53).
[2] A/AC.31/L.57, Arts 7 and 8.
[3] *G.A.O.R.*, 5th Sess., Suppl. No. 9, p. 29, at p. 33.

Palestine any 'cause or matter in connection with the Holy Places or religious buildings or sites in Palestine or the rights or claims relating to the different religious communities of Palestine.' Jurisdiction was vested in the High Commissioner, whose decisions were 'final and binding on all parties.'

"7. The claims in connection with the Holy Places, religious buildings or sites, or religious communities have been determined by the mandatory Government on the basis of rights and practice existing during the Ottoman regime. When the Government's decision has not been accepted, a formal protest has been made by the interested community and it has been recorded that no change in the *status quo* was held to have occurred.

"8. As regards the Christian Holy Places, century-long controversies between Powers sponsoring the respective Roman Catholic and Greek Orthodox interests were settled on the basis of the *status quo* at the end of the Crimean War; but they were not settled between the religious communities themselves. The report of the international commission appointed by the British Government, with the approval of the Council of the League of Nations, to determine the rights and claims of Moslems and Jews in connection with the Wailing Wall[1] summarises as follows the history of the establishment of the *status quo* and its present application as regards the Christian Holy Places:

"At the conclusion of peace (in 1855, after the Crimean War) the matters in dispute being still left undecided were sub-mitted to the signatory Powers, who undertook to guarantee in every respect the *status quo ante bellum*. The question of the protection of the Holy Places was again discussed during the peace negotiations at the conclusion of the Russo-Turkish War (1878). At that time it was laid down in the Peace Treaty itself that no alterations were to be made in the *status quo* without the consent of the signatory Powers. In 1878 as well as in 1855 indications as to the administration of the *status quo* were based upon the same rules as those that had been proclaimed in the decree (*firman*) issued by the Sultan of Turkey in 1852, which were in conformity in the main with a preceding *firman* of 1757 . .

---

[1]"Report of the Commission appointed by His Majesty's Government in the United Kingdom of Great Britain and Northern Ireland, with the approval of the Council of the League of Nations, to determine the rights and claims of Moslems and Jews in connection with the Western or Wailing Wall at Jerusalem: December, 1930." (London, 1931), p. 34. (The Commission was constituted as follows: M. E. Lofgren (Sweden), M. Charles Barde (Switzerland), M. C. J. van Kempen (Netherlands).) Reproduced as U.N. doc. S/8427/Add.1*, 28th Feb., 1968.

"As apportioned between the three principal Christian rites, viz., the Orthodox Greek Rite, the Latin (or Roman Catholic) Rite and the Armenian Orthodox Rite, the Holy Places and their component parts may be classified into the following categories:

(a) Certain parts which are recognised as property common to the three rites in equal shares.

(b) Other parts as to which one rite claims exclusive *jurisdiction*, while other rites claim joint *proprietorship*.

(c) Parts as to which the ownership is in dispute between two of the rites.

(d) Finally, parts the use or ownership of which belongs exclusively to one rite, but within which other rites are entitled to sense or carry out ritual services up to a limited extent in other ways.

"Certain strict principles are adhered to in the administration of the *status quo*. Thus, . . . a right granted to hang up a lamp or a picture or to change the position of any such object when hung is regarded as a recognition of exclusive possession of the pillar or the wall in question . . .

"It is easy to understand that the application of 'rights' of this nature must lead to great difficulties and often to litigation, especially as each alteration *de facto* in the prevailing practice might serve as a proof that the legal position has been altered. Therefore, the Administration has had a difficult task both in ascertaining and in maintaining the *status quo*. In controverted cases the objects in dispute have been sometimes allowed to fall into decay rather than risk the possibility that any alteration of the balance of power between the contestant rites should be permitted to ensue. Hence, if the carrying out of repairs becomes urgent, it devolves upon the Administration to have them attended to, supposing it proves not to be possible in the individual case for the parties concerned to come to an amicable agreement.'

"9. The *status quo*—as far as it has been possible to ascertain what that consists in—has also been applied by the Palestine Administration as regards Moslem or Jewish sacred places and sites, which have been objects of dispute between Arabs and Jews, particularly the Wailing Wall at Jerusalem and Rachel's Tomb near Bethlehem.

"10. It must be noted that in disputes between the Christian communities, as well as between the Moslem and Jewish communities the Mandatory Administration like its predecessor, the

Ottoman Government, possessed the police forces necessary to impose its decisions and generally to prevent religious disputes from resulting in religious strife."[1]

The generality of the Israeli rejection of the Conciliation Commission's proposals that a U.N. Commissioner be competent in such cases[2] could be read as amounting to an assertion that Israeli courts should have jurisdiction to settle such disputes. There is, however, some evidence of a modification of this view in the terms of the Israeli proposal of 25th November, 1949[3] which, while providing that such disputes should in the first place be referred to the Government of Israel, contemplates that if the issue is not thereby settled it can be referred to the General Assembly.

Israel appears to have had further thoughts on this question, prompted perhaps by the suggestion in the Netherlands-Swedish draft[4] that this class of dispute should be settled by a U.N. Commissioner. The Israeli memorandum to the Trusteeship Council of 26th May, 1950,[5] commenting on the draft Statute for Jerusalem prepared by the Trusteeship Council, puts forward an alternative proposal which suggests that a U.N. representative should, inter alia, adjudicate upon disputes between communities as to their rights in the Holy Places.

While it is possible that Israel might no longer feel that it would be right to vest this class of jurisdiction in the U.N., one can still see reasons why Israel should not herself become involved in disputes arising between the various religious denominations. In so far as they arise between non-Jewish groups, it may be better that they should not be decided by Jewish authorities; and in so far as they affect relations between Jewish and non-Jewish interests, there may again be advantage in having them decided by a non-Israeli body.

The second category of foreseeable disputes comprises those which may arise out of the interpretation and application of the instrument containing the regime for the Holy Places. Such disputes would arise primarily between the State of Israel, on the one hand, and the U.N. or some particular State on the

---

[1]*G.A.O.R.*, 2nd Sess., Supp. No. 11, pp. 36-37.
[2]See p. 63 above.
[3]Section 19. See Appendix 1 at p. 79 below
[4]*Loc. cit.* p. 61 n. 4 above.
[5]*G.A.O.R.*, 5th Sess., Suppl. No. 9, p. 29.

other; and would involve the application not of local, but of international, law. In general terms, in common with all other international disputes, it is desirable that such cases should be settled by international judicial means. This may involve either reference to the International Court of Justice or the establishment of a special arbitral body. But in the absence of any evidence of willingness by any Arab State to accept compulsory international settlement of disputes, it is not easy to make out a convincing case to persuade Israel to agree to expose herself in this way to international judicial or arbitral proceedings. If the obligatory jurisdiction of an international tribunal were in fact accepted by Israel, it would in all likelihood have to be made conditional upon strict reciprocity.

(b) A POSSIBLE DECLARATION AND STATUTE CONCERNING THE HOLY PLACES

Since it is commonly found that general ideas can more readily be assessed when presented in a specific form, I have ventured to prepare a somewhat tentative draft of the sort of Declaration and Statute which might give effect to some of the ideas canvassed in this Chapter.

INTRODUCTION TO THE DRAFT DECLARATION AND STATUTE CONCERNING THE HOLY PLACES

There are two ideas underlying this draft Declaration and Statute.

First, there should exist some instrument setting out in detail the status of the Holy Places in Jerusalem[1] and the special rights and privileges of the religious communities actively associated with them. This is the function of the draft Statute.

Second, this instrument should be given some international status, both so that its provisions may stand as international commitments of Israel and so that Israel may reciprocally expect that other States will not act in a manner prejudicial to the terms of the Declaration or seek to overthrow the situation underlying it. This is the function of the draft Declaration.

---

[1]The ideas elaborated here are restricted to the Holy Places *in Jerusalem.* Shrines elsewhere in Israel have a different background. Moreover, any geographical extension of these proposals would necessarily raise difficult questions regarding Jewish shrines in Arab territory outside Jerusalem.

It is contemplated that the Statute would need to be incorporated into the law of Israel by legislation.

The reasons which support this form of approach have already been indicated. The principal alternative would have been some sort of international treaty formally embodying the results of an international negotiation. Clearly, there would be considerable difficulties about determining which States and other interested bodies should participate in this negotiation. Further, formal discussions on the international level would certainly be much prolonged. Accordingly, since the Government of Israel has already been able to discuss matters in some detail with some of the principal interested parties, it appears simpler that the settlement should be incorporated in a unilateral offer by Israel to regulate her conduct and the treatment of the Holy Places on a basis which she already understands to be largely acceptable to those most immediately connected with the problem.

At the same time, in recognition of international interest in the problem, Israel would in effect offer the States of the world the opportunity to become parties to the settlement and to take advantage, on a basis of reciprocity, of the procedure for the judicial enquiry set out in the Declaration.

However, it should be appreciated that, although for international purposes the Statute is appended to the Declaration, the Statute is nonetheless independent of the Declaration. The Statute would govern Israel's treatment of the Holy Places regardless of whether the States of the world were prepared to signify their approval of the principles therein stated and irrespective of whether such States might desire to take advantage of the opportunity of invoking the jurisdiction of the International Court of Justice.

Draft Declaration Accompanying The Statute

1. The Government of Israel has promulgated a Statute for the Holy Places in Jerusalem the text of which is appended to and forms part of the present Declaration. [1]

---

[1] The text of the Declaration and the Statute would be communicated to the Secretary-General of the United Nations. See para. 4 of the text of the Declaration.

2. The present Declaration constitutes an international undertaking by the Government of Israel to act in conformity with the Statute. This undertaking will be effective as between Israel and those States which indicate their acceptance of the Statute and themselves undertake neither to act, nor to permit on their territories any action, [1] contrary to the letter and intent of the Statute.

3. The Government of Israel accepts the jurisdiction of the International Court of Justice in relation to any dispute which may arise between any State accepting the Statute and Israel, subject only to such State having declared that it reciprocally accepts the jurisdiction of the International Court of Justice in relation to its obligations under paragraph 2 above. [2]

4. The present Declaration will be registered with the Secretariat of the United Nations pursuant to Article 102 of the Charter of the United Nations.

DRAFT STATUTE CONCERNING THE HOLY PLACES

1. The present Statute relates to the Holy Places in Jerusalem.

2. For the purpose of this Statute

"Commissioner" shall mean the Commissioner of Holy Places appointed pursuant to Article 7 hereof.

"Community" shall include any religious body, brotherhood, order or organization with an established interest in the Holy Places.

"Council" shall mean the Council of the Holy Places established pursuant to Article 8 hereof.

"The Holy Places" are those buildings, sites, structures and localities listed in Column 1 of the Schedule to this Statute

---

[1] It seems reasonable that, at any rate in relation to the Arab States which have been making war upon Israel, Israel should ask for a reciprocal undertaking that such States will not allow their territories to be used as a basis for the preparation of acts designed to overthrow the system underlying the Statute. At the same time, it is possible that other States, having no real connection with the Arab attacks upon Israel, might find it difficult to incorporate this undertaking in their municipal law. It may, therefore, be necessary to reconsider the formulation of this provision.

[2] For the reasons set out above, this is a provision which Israel might not find it easy to include.

traditionally subject to the jurisdiction of the religion, order, or body listed in Column 2 of the said Schedule.[1]

The Minister of Religious Affairs of the State of Israel shall have the power to amend the Schedule by adding to or removing from it the name of any Holy Place or by modifying the description of the body to whose jurisdiction the place is deemed to be subject, but the Minister shall not remove the name of any Holy Place save after a determination in that sense by the Commissioner of Holy Places, and the Minister shall not modify the description of the body to whose jurisdiction a Holy Place is deemed to be subject without either the consent of the body to whose jurisdiction the Holy Place was theretofore deemed to be subject or an appropriate determination by the Commissioner of Holy Places.

FREEDOM OF ACCESS TO THE HOLY PLACES IN JERUSALEM

4. (1) There shall be freedom of access to the Holy Places in Jerusalem for all persons without discrimination as to faith, nationality, race or colour.

(2) The Government of Israel will ensure that there shall be free and ready movement by available and convenient routes of transport to and from Jerusalem from and to stated points of arrival in and departure from Israel.

(3) Persons entering Israel for the sole purpose of visiting the Holy Places may do so without visa for periods not exceeding twenty-one days. Persons intending to visit other places or to remain in Israel for longer than twenty-one days shall satisfy the entrance requirements normally applicable to visitors to Israel.

(4) All visitors to Israel, whether to the Holy Places exclusively or to other places in Israel, are at all times subject to the operation of the laws of Israel, as modified by the terms of this Statute.

(5) The Government of Israel reserves the right to exclude entirely or limit the period of visit of any person claiming to visit the Holy Places if the Government of Israel believes that

---

[1]This Schedule, which is not appended to the present Draft, should be sufficiently detailed so as to avoid, or at any rate limit, dispute as to the places which benefit from the Statute.

the visit of any such person is or may be prejudicial to the security of the State of Israel, or if the entry of such person into Israel would be contrary to existing Israeli health regulations. Any person thus excluded may require the Government of Israel to state its reasons to the Commissioner for the Holy Places.

(6) It shall be no excuse or justification in law for a person found in Israel without having satisfied the formal entry requirements to claim that he was visiting or intending to visit the Holy Places.

THE HOLY PLACES

5. (1) There shall be complete freedom of attendance at and worship in the Holy Places.

(2) No form of racial or religious discrimination shall be permitted with respect to the rights of visit and access to any of the Holy Places, except in so far as the performance of certain religious rites and ceremonies may require the exclusion from them of the adherents of other faiths during the performance of such religious rites and ceremonies.

(3) The Holy Places in Israel shall remain in the custody and subject to the jurisdiction of the communities who by law and custom have exercised rights in and over them. The rights and interests of all communities in the Holy Places in Israel shall be as they were on the 14th May, 1948, subject only to such agreed or otherwise lawful changes as may since have taken place.

(4) Any dispute between the communities as to rights in or over the Holy Places shall be determined by the Commissioner for the Holy Places [or some other special jurisdiction][1] upon hearing all interested parties and after receiving the advice of the Council for the Holy Places. Any decision of the Commissioner in this regard shall be recognised as valid and binding under the law of Israel and shall be enforceable by process in the civil courts of Israel.

(5) The organization of and the conduct of services in the Holy Places shall be regulated exclusively by the personnel of the community or communities exercising rights in and over the Holy Place.

---

[1]See above, p. 67.

(6) Any fees charged or payments required for access to the Holy Places shall not exceed those which have in the past been customary; and questions arising in this connection shall be determined by the Commissioner upon the advice of the Council.

(7) Any act or omission occurring in a Holy Place which would if it had occurred outside a Holy Place constitute a civil or criminal wrong under the law of Israel shall fall within the jurisdiction of the Israeli courts applying the law of Israel.

(8) The Israeli public authorities, whether police or other, will not enter the Holy Places save with the consent or at the invitation of the head or acting head of the community in charge of such Holy Place. Such consent shall not be necessary in circumstances of emergency, that is to say, the occurrence of violent crime, riot, civil commotion, fire or other comparable event, or the reasonable anticipation thereof.

(9) The income and receipts of the communities controlling the Holy Places shall not be subject to income tax in Israel.

(10) The Holy Places and premises occupied in connection with the Holy Places shall not be assessed to rates save in respect of the provision of police protection and fire or sanitary services.

(11) The communities responsible for the Holy Places shall pay reasonable and non-discriminatory rates for all other municipal services.

THE PERSONNEL OF THE HOLY PLACES

6. (1) The organization of the communities having rights in the Holy Places shall be governed exclusively by the rules of each such community.

(2) Whoever by the rules of each such community is its head in the Holy Places in the territory of Israel or the occupied areas shall serve as the representative of that community in the Council of the Holy Places.

(3) The communities shall have exclusive jurisdiction over their personnel in all matters which are traditionally the subject of regulation by the rules of the communities. In all other respects the law of Israel shall be applied. Any question

arising as to which body of law is applicable shall be determined by the Commissioner, whose certificate in the matter shall be accepted as final and conclusive.

(4) The freedom of dress and habit of the personnel of the communities is guaranteed as heretofore, as is their movement throughout Israel and in particular from one Holy Place under their charge to another.

(5) There shall be freedom of communication between the communities and their parent organizations outside Israel.

THE COMMISSIONER OF THE HOLY PLACES

7. (1) There shall be a Commissioner of Holy Places (hereinafter called the Commissioner) with the following functions

    (i) To exercise a general supervision over the application of the present Statute;

    (ii) To preside over the Council;

    (iii) To represent the Council;

    (iv) To report annually to the Secretary-General of the United Nations;

    (v) To make such representations or proposals as he may at any time think necessary or desirable to the Government of Israel, or to the Council, with a view to ensuring the fullest achievement of the objects of this Statute.

    (vi) Generally, to perform any other functions conferred upon him by the present Statute.

(2) The Commissioner shall be appointed by the Secretary-General of the United Nations and shall be paid by the United Nations. The assumption of his duties by the Commissioner shall be subject to the agreement of the Government of Israel. If this is withheld, the Secretary-General shall make another appointment.

(3) The Commissioner shall hold office for a period of three years from the date of his appointment. Subject to the continuing agreement of the Government of Israel, the Commissioner may be re-appointed for a further period or periods.

(4) The Commissioner shall enjoy while in Israel or in territories under Israeli control or occupation the same privileges and immunities as are accorded to the head of a foreign diplomatic mission accredited to the President of Israel.

(5)   The Government of Israel will accord to the Commissioner all facilities that he may require for the due discharge of his functions.

THE COUNCIL OF THE HOLY PLACES

8.   (1)   There shall be a Council of the Holy Places consisting of the heads of the communities interested in the Holy Places.

(2)   The Council shall perform the functions placed upon it by the present Statute, and shall serve as the organ for the representation to the Commissioner of the collective views of the religious communities interested in the Holy Places.   Each community shall however remain entitled to present its views on any matter affecting it directly to the Commissioner or to the Israeli authorities.

(3)   Communications on municipal matters shall take place between the religious communities and the local municipal authorities.   On all other matters the communities shall communicate with the Israeli Ministry of Religious Affairs.

CONSIDERATIONS OF SECURITY

9.   The provisions of this Statute are subject to the interests of the security of Israel and, in particular, so long as the United Arab Republic, Syria, Lebanon, Jordan, Iraq or any other State maintains with Israel a state of war or belligerency, whether or not accompanied by hostilities; and the State of Israel shall be entitled for such security purposes within limits dictated by the exigencies of the circumstances to restrict the liberties herein guaranteed.   The Commissioner shall hear any complaints which any community may make in this connection and may, if he thinks fit, refer the same to the Government of Israel.

APPENDICES

The texts which appear below show that for nearly twenty years there have existed firm proposals, involving a measure of U.N. supervision, on the basis of which Israel could assume clear international commitments in connection with the Holy Places. The Israeli draft agreement of 1949 (Appendix I) may not in all its details represent what Israel would to-day put forward, but it and the Swedish proposal represent two ways in which the universal interest in Jerusalem could be recognized. The Swedish proposal (Appendix II), though never put to the vote (see p. 31 above), was nonetheless in its essential elements basically acceptable to the United Kingdom, the U.S.A. and Uruguay, as is shown by the terms of their proposed amendment (Appendix III).

The texts are reprinted here because readers without access to libraries with U.N. materials may not otherwise readily be able to find them.

APPENDIX I
ISRAEL: DRAFT RESOLUTION
U.N. doc. A/AC.31/L.42

(Original text: English)
(25 November 1949)

The General Assembly

1. *Recalling* its successive resolutions which expressed the concern of the United Nations in Jerusalem by reason of the presence therein of Holy Places, religious buildings and sites;

2. *Noting* that the Declaration of Independence of Israel of 14 May 1948, provides for the protection of the Holy Places of all religions;

3. *Desiring* to maintain the existing rights in the Holy Places, and in particular those rights and practices in force 14 May 1948, and thus to give effective and practical expression to that concern,

4. *Resolves therefore:*

(*a*) To authorize the Secretary-General to sign on behalf of the United Nations an agreement (as attached) with the State of Israel relating to the supervision and protection of the Holy Places in Jerusalem;

(*b*) To request the Secretary-General to report to the fifth regular session on progress made with respect to the signature and implementation of this agreement.

ANNEX

TEXT OF DRAFT AGREEMENT BETWEEN THE UNITED NATIONS AND ISRAEL
Article 1
Definitions
Section 1

In this Agreement:

(*a*) The expression "The Holy Places" means those places, buildings and sites in Jerusalem which were recognized on 14 May 1948 as Holy Places and any other places, buildings or sites which may subsequently be considered as such by agreement between the parties;

(b) The expression "United Nations" means the internationa organization established by the Charter of the United Nations;

(c) The expression "Secretary-General" means the Secretary-General of the United Nations;

(d) The expression "Jerusalem" means the part of Jerusalem now under Israel control.

Section 2

The parties shall establish by mutual agreement a detailed list indicating what were the Holy Places in Jerusalem on 14 May 1948 for the purposes of this Agreement, and in the same way may amend such list by additions or by deletions.

ARTICLE 2
Maintenance of existing rights

Section 3

The free exercise in Jerusalem of all forms of worship in accordance with the rights in force on 14 May 1948, subject to the maintenance of public order and decorum, shall be guaranteed by law and effectively secured by administrative practice in conformity with the Declaration of Independence of Israel.

ARTICLE 3
Preservation of the Holy Places

Section 4

The Holy Places in Jerusalem shall be preserved, and no act shall be permitted which may in any way impair their sacred character. If at any time it appears to the Government of Israel that any Holy Place, religious building or site is in need of urgent repairs, it may call upon the religious community or communities concerned to carry out such repairs. The Government may carry out such repairs itself at the expense of the religious community or communities concerned, if no action is taken within a reasonable time.

Section 5

The Government of Israel shall take all reasonable steps to ensure that the amenities of the Holy Places in Jerusalem and their immediate precincts are not prejudiced.

ARTICLE 4
Access to the Holy Places

Section 6

No form of racial or religious discrimination shall be permitted with respect to the rights of visit and access to any of the Holy Places, except in so far as the performance of certain religious rites and ceremonies may require the exclusion from them of the adherents of other faiths during the performance of such religious rites and ceremonies.

Section 7

Subject only to requirements of national security, public order and decorum, health, liberty of access, visit and transit to the Holy Places in Jerusalem shall be accorded to all persons without distinction in respect of nationality in conformity with the rights in force on 14 May 1948.

Section 8

The Secretary-General and the Government of Israel shall, at the request of either of them, consult as to methods of facilitating entrance into Israel, and the use of available means of transportation, by persons coming from abroad who wish to visit the Holy Places. This shall not prevent the Government of Israel from making suitable arrangements directly or with other States for any of these purposes.

Section 9

Nothing in this Agreement shall affect in any way the application of laws and regulations from time to time in force in Israel regarding the entry of aliens, or to confer any right of entry into Israel otherwise than in accordance with such laws and regulations, or any modifications thereof, and with the terms of any international obligations assumed by Israel in this regard.

ARTICLE 5
Protection of Holy Places
Section 10
(*a*) The Government of Israel shall exercise due diligence to ensure that the sacred character of the Holy Places in Jerusalem is not disturbed by the unauthorized entry of groups of persons from outside or by disturbances, and shall cause to be provided such police protection as is required for these purposes.

(*b*) If the Secretary-General is of opinion that additional police protection is required for any of the Holy Places in Jerusalem, or for any area of Jerusalem in which a number of Holy Places are situated within a reasonable degree of propinquity, he may request the Government of Israel to increase the number of policemen regularly stationed for the protection of such Holy Places or area.

ARTICLE 6
Law and authority in relation to the Holy Places
Section 11
(*a*) The law of Israel including regulations and by-laws made by the local authorities shall apply to and within the Holy Places in Jerusalem.

(*b*) The Israel Courts shall have jurisdiction over acts done and transactions taking place within the precincts of the Holy Places.

ARTICLE 7
Public services
Section 12
The Government of Israel will exercise the powers which it possesses to ensure, at the request of the Secretary-General, that the Holy Places shall be supplied on equitable terms with the necessary public services, electricity, water, gas, post, telephone, telegraph, transportation, drainage, collection of refuse, fire protection, etc. In case of any interruption or threatened interruption of any such services, the Government of Israel will consider the needs of the Holy Places to the extent practicable, and subject to the requirements of security and the maintenance of essential services and supplies.

Section 13
Nothing in this Agreement shall be interpreted as restricting the rights of the Government of Israel or any local authority, or any of their agencies or subdivisions, officials or employees, with regard to entry into any Holy Place in Jerusalem for the purpose of enabling them to inspect repair, maintain, reconstruct and relocate utilities, conduits, mains and sewers, which may run over, through, or under such Holy Places, religious building or site.

ARTICLE 8
Exemptions
Section 14
No form of taxation shall be levied in respect of any Holy Place in Jerusalem which was exempt from such taxation on 14 May 1948. No change in the incidence of any form of taxation shall be made which would discriminate between the owners and occupiers of Holy Places, religious buildings or sites in Jerusalem, or would place such owners and occupiers in a position less favourable in relation to the general incidence of that form of taxation than existed on 14 May 1948.

ARTICLE 19
United Nations representative
Section 15
The Secretary-General and the Government of Israel shall settle by agreement the channels through which they will communicate regarding the application of the provisions of this Agreement and other questions affecting the Holy Places in Jerusalem, and may enter into such supplemental agreements as may be necessary to fulfil the purpose of this Agreement.

Section 16

Israel hereby agrees that if the Secretary-General so requests he may appoint and send a representative to Israel to exercise the rights and duties conferred upon the United Nations by this Agreement. In making such appointment the Secretary-General shall have due regard for the accepted international custom relating to the appointment of diplomatic representatives. Such representative may establish his headquarters in Jerusalem or in some other place agreed between him and by the Government of Israel, and shall be accredited to the President of Israel. For the duration of his mission the Convention on the Privileges and Immunities of the United Nations approved by the General Assembly of the United Nations on 13th February 1946, as acceded to by Israel, shall be applicable to him as well as to his staff and to the buildings he occupies, all as is more particularly laid down in the said Convention on the Privileges and Immunities of the United Nations, it being understood that nothing in this agreement shall imply the extension of the provisions of the said Convention to any Holy Place.

Section 17

The functions of the representative of the Secretary-General shall be limited to matters pertaining to the application and implementation of this Agreement; in particular it is understood that nothing shall authorize the United Nations or the Secretary-General or his representative, to intervene in matters which are essentially within the domestic jurisdiction of the State of Israel, or shall require the Government of Israel to submit any such matters to settlement under the Charter of the United Nations or under this Agreement.

ARTICLE 10
Settlement of disputes

Section 18

Any dispute between the United Nations and Israel concerning the interpretation or application of this Agreement, or of any supplemental agreement, including any dispute as to whether any place in Jerusalem was recognized on 14 May 1948 as a Holy Place which is not settled by negotiation, or other agreed mode of settlement, shall be referred for final decision to a tribunal of three arbitrators, one to be named by the Secretary-General, one to be named by the Minister for Foreign Affairs of Israel, and the third to be chosen by the two, or if they should fail to agree upon a third, then by the President of the International Court of Justice.

Section 19

Subject to the provisions of section 10, where any dispute concerning a Holy Place, religious building or site in Jerusalem arises between two or more religious communities, or sections of communities, such dispute shall, in the first instance be referred to the Government of Israel which may, in reaching its decision, seek the guidance of the United Nations. If the decision of the Government of Israel does not settle the dispute, than either Israel or the Secretary-General may refer the matter to the General Assembly.

ARTICLE 11
Final provisions

Section 20

This Agreement shall be construed in the light of its primary purpose to ensure protection of the Holy Places in Jerusalem, which is desirable, in view of the special character of Jerusalem, whose soil is consecrated by the prayers and pilgrimages of the adherents of three great religions.

Section 21

This Agreement shall be brought into effect by an exchange of notes between the Secretary-General, duly authorized pursuant to a resolution of the General Assembly of the United Nations, and the appropriate executive officer of Israel, duly authorized pursuant to appropriate action of the Knesseth.

IN WITNESS WHEREOF the respective representatives have signed this Agreement and have affixed their seals hereunto.

DONE in duplicate, in the English, French, Hebrew and Spanish languages, all authentic, at Lake Success, this . . . day of . . . in the year one thousand nine hundred and . . . .

APPENDIX II

SWEDEN: DRAFT RESOLUTION
U.N. doc. A/AC.38/L.63

(*Original text: English*)
(5 *December* 1950)

The General Assembly

Recognizing the unique spiritual and religious interests of the world community in the Holy Land,

Desiring to preserve the peace of Jerusalem,

Considering its resolutions 181 (II) of 24 November 1947, 194 (III) of 11 December 1948 and 303 (IV) of 9 December 1949,

Having regard to the special report of the Trusteeship Council regarding the question of an international regime for the Jerusalem area and protection of the Holy Places (document A/1286),

Considering that it has so far not been possible to carry into effect the resolutions of the General Assembly with regard to Jerusalem and the Holy Places,

Considering that any further delay in ensuring international protection of the spiritual and religious interests of the world community in the Holy Land is undesirable and that therefore, awaiting the taking of final measures, it is appropriate to take such measures as will henceforward ensure the respect of those interests;

Determining that for the purpose of this resolution:

"Holy Land" means the former mandated Territory of Palestine;

"Holy Places" means those Holy Places and religious buildings or sites which were regarded in Palestine on 14 May 1948 as Holy Places;

"Free Access" means those rights of access and visit to which individuals and religious denominations were entitled on 14 May 1948, together with facilities of transit to and from Holy Places, whether these Holy Places are situated within or outside the territory of the State granting facilities, subject always to the requirements of public health, public security and decorum;

"Existing rights, immunities and privileges" means such rights, immunities and privileges as existed on 14 May 1948;

"Jerusalem area" means the city of Jerusalem as defined in section B of part III of the plan set out in resolution 181 (II) of the General Assembly adopted 29 November 1947;

"Commissioner" means the United Nations Commissioner appointed under article VI of Section B of the present resolution;

Resolves

A. To *invite* the governments of the States in the Holy Land to pledge themselves before the United Nations to:

(*a*) Observe human rights and fundamental freedoms and in particular freedom of thought, conscience and religion as set forth in article 18 of the Universal Declaration of Human Rights;

(*b*) Refrain from any act that would endanger the Holy Places in their territories;

(*c*) Guarantee to nationals of their States, as well as aliens, without distinction as to nationality, free access to Holy Places in their territories;

(*d*) Observe and maintain all the existing rights, immunities and privileges as provided in article II of section B of this resolution;

(*e*) Levy no tax in respect of any Holy Places which are exempt from such taxation on 14 May 1948, and make no change in the incidence of any form of taxation which would either discriminate between the owners and occupiers of different Holy Places or would place such owners and occupiers in a position less favourable in relation to the general incidence of that form of taxation than existed on 14 May 1948;

(*f*) Maintain and respect the property rights of religious bodies;

(*g*) Reduce their armed forces in the Jerusalem area in progressive stages with a view to their limitation to normal peacetime requirements as provided in article VIII of section B of this resolution;

(*h*) Carry out in good faith the obligations and provisions laid down in section B of this resolution, and co-operate fully with the Commissioner in the task imposed on him by this resolution.

B.   Lay down, in order to ensure the protection of and free access to the Holy Places and the maintenance of existing rights, immunities and privileges of religious demonstrations, the following articles:

ARTICLE I

The Holy Places throughout the Holy Land shall be preserved and no act shall be permitted which may in anyway impair their sacred character.

ARTICLE II

Rights, immunities and privileges of religious denominations with respect to Holy Places, as well as the rights, immunities and privileges of religious bodies with respect to monasteries and missionary, educational and welfare establishments now maintained by them, shall be preserved as they existed on 14 May 1948.

ARTICLE III

1.   The supervision of the protection of and free access to the Holy Places and the maintenance of the rights, immunities and privileges referred to in article II, shall be the responsibility of the United Nations.

2.   The Commissioner appointed pursuant to article VI shall exercise this supervision on behalf of the United Nations and shall make arrangements with the governments concerned regarding the implementation of the provisions of this resolution.

3.   For the Jerusalem area such arrangements shall be subject in particular to the provisions of articles VIII, IX, X, XI and XII.   The Commissioner shall negotiate and conclude agreements with the governments concerned in order to ensure that the appropriate provisions of this resolution are carried into effect also in the Holy Land outside the Jerusalem area.   He shall report the results of his negotiations to the Secretary-General of the United Nations.

ARTICLE IV

1.   The Commissioner shall draw up an authoritative list of Holy Places which were regarded as such on 14 May 1948.   If any question arises as to whether any place, building or site was regarded as a Holy Place on 14 May 1948, the Commissioner shall decide;

2.   If any question arises between any religious denominations in connexion with any Holy Place, the Commissioner shall decide on the basis of existing rights;

3.   Before taking any decision under paragraph 1 and 2 of this article the Commissioner shall consult with members of the panel of advisers as provided in article XIV.   His decision shall be final.

4. If a place, building or site not regarded as a Holy Place on 14 May 1948 is claimed by a religious denomination to be a Holy Place of such character that it is entitled to enjoy the protection of this statute, the Commissioner may propose to the Government concerned that such a place, building or site be brought under the provisions of this resolution. In the event of the Commissioner and the government concerned failing to reach agreement, the matter shall be referred to the arbitral tribunal as provided in article XV.

ARTICLE V

Should a visitor or pilgrim or a group of visitors and pilgrims be denied free access to any Holy Place, the government denying access shall inform the Commissioner of the reasons therefor.

ARTICLE VI

1. There shall be a United Nations Commissioner to be appointed for a period of three years on the nomination of the Secretary-General by a Committee of the General Assembly consisting of the eleven members of the Security Council. This Committee shall decide by a majority of the members present and voting. The Commissioner shall be responsible to the General Assembly and may be dismissed by it. He shall report annually to the General Assembly and may also make special reports to the appropriate United Nations organs whenever he deems necessary. His headquarters shall be the former Government House in Jerusalem.

2. There shall be appointed in the same manner a Deputy Commissioner who shall be subject to the same terms of office, and shall be responsible to the Commissioner. The Deputy Commissioner shall assist the Commissioner and shall replace him in the event of his absence or disability.

3. The Commissioner and the Deputy Commissioner shall not be selected from among nationals of the State of Israel or of an Arab State or from among residents of the Jerusalem area.

4. The Commissioner shall be authorized to appoint and employ under temporary contracts the auxiliary administrative personnel necessary for the carrying out of his functions.

ARTICLE VII

The functions of the Commissioner shall be to exercise the powers conferred upon him by this resolution and to ensure its implementation.

ARTICLE VIII

1. The governments of the States administering the Jerusalem area shall gradually reduce their armed forces in that area in conformity with article VII of the General Armistice Agreement between the Hashimite Kingdom of the Jordan and Israel of 3 April 1949 and shall limit them, not later than three months after the coming into effect of a peace settlement between the States administering the Jerusalem area, to normal peacetime requirements;

2. Should the Commissioner be of the opinion that the forces maintained by either party under paragraph 1 are above normal peacetime requirements, he shall make representations accordingly to the government concerned;

3. In the event of the Commissioner and the governments concerned failing to reach agreement in the matter, it shall be referred to the Security Council.

ARTICLE IX

The jurisdiction and control of each part of the Jerusalem area shall be exercised by the States concerned, subject to the powers of the Commissioner with respect to this area and without prejudice to the rights and claims of either party in the ultimate peaceful settlement for the area.

ARTICLE X

1. The Commissioner shall be empowered:

(a) To request the governments in the Jerusalem area to modify, defer or suspend such laws, ordinances, regulations and administrative acts pertaining to the area, which in his opinion impair the protection of and free access to Holy Places or the rights, immunities and privileges referred to in article II;

(b) To request the governments to take such action or to make such orders or regulations for the maintenance of public security and safety as he deems necessary to ensure the protection of and free access to Holy Places or the safeguarding of the rights, immunities and privileges concerned.

2. The governments shall carry into effect without delay any such action which the Commissioner, in accordance with the provisions of paragraph 1 of this article, deems necessary, for the protection of and free access to Holy Places and the safeguarding of the rights, immunities and privileges concerned.

3. If a government objects to a request made by the Commissioner under this article, the matter shall be referred for a final decision to the arbitral tribunal provided in article XV. The tribunal shall decide not later than one month from the submission of a dispute. Without prejudice to the final decision of the tribunal, provisional effect shall be given by the government concerned to the action requested by the Commissioner.

4. The Commissioner shall immediately inform the Secretary-General of the United Nations of any objection of a government to a request made by him under this article.

ARTICLE XI

The Commissioner shall be empowered to employ under temporary contracts a limited number of guards for the performance of his functions in the Jerusalem area as well as to assure his own security and that of his staff. These guards shall not be selected from among nationals of the State of Israel or of an Arab State. The salaries, allowances and administrative expenses of the Commissioner, Deputy Commissioner, and the staff of the Commissioner, including guards and administrative personnel, shall be included in the annual budget of the United Nations. These salaries and allowances shall be exempt from local taxation.

ARTICLE XII

The governments in the Jerusalem area shall upon the Commissioner's request direct their respective police forces to assist the Commissioner in the performance of his duty.

ARTICLE XIII

If at any time it appears to the Commissioner that any Holy Place is in need of urgent repair, he may call upon the religious denominations or bodies concerned to carry out such repair. If in the opinion of the Commissioner the repair is not carried out or is not completed within a reasonable time, he may arrange for repairs to be carried out or completed. The expenses incurred shall be borne by the religious denominations or bodies concerned. The Commissioner shall decide, after due investigation on the basis of existing rights, which denominations or bodies are responsible for the repair.

ARTICLE XIV

The Commissioner shall appoint a panel of advisers consisting of representatives of the religious denominations and of the governments in the Holy Land. These advisers shall be nominated by the religious denominations and governments concerned. If a disagreement arises in connexion with the provisions of this resolution, the Commissioner shall consult advisers from the panel representing such religious denominations or religious bodies and governments as are concerned with the dispute. No representative of any religious denomination shall be consulted on questions relating to a Holy Place belonging wholly to another religious faith.

ARTICLE XV

1. Any dispute between the Commissioner and one of the governments of the States in the Holy Land concerning the interpretation or implementation of this resolution or of any supplementary agreements or arrangements, which is not settled by negotiation, shall be referred for final decision to an *ad hoc* tribunal of arbitrators, one to be nominated, as the case may be, either by the Hashimite Kingdom of the Jordan or by the State of Israel, and one to be nominated by the Secretary-General of the United Nations. In the event of two arbitrators being unable within seven days to agree on the choice of an umpire, the latter shall be nominated by the President of the International Court of Justice.

2. In case of a dispute between the Commissioner and both governments concerned, two arbitrators will be nominated by the respective governments concerned and two by the Secretary-General. In the event of their inability within seven days to agree on the choice of the fifth arbitrator, the latter shall be nominated by the President of the International Court of Justice.

3. The decisions of the arbitral tribunal shall be binding on the governments concerned.

ARTICLE XVI

Nothing in this resolution shall apply to purely Moslem Holy Places, religious buildings or sites and Moslem religious interests within territory controlled by the Hashimite Kingdom of the Jordan, or to purely Jewish Holy Places, religious buildings or sites and Jewish religious interests within territory controlled by the State of Israel.

ARTICLE XVII

The terms of this resolution can be reviewed only by the General Assembly.

APPENDIX III

UNITED KINGDOM, UNITED STATES OF AMERICA, URUGUAY:
AMENDMENT TO THE DRAFT RESOLUTION OF SWEDEN (A/AC.38/L.63)
U.N. doc. A/AC.38/L.73/Rev. 2

(*Original text: English*)
(13 *December* 1950)

Preamble
Replace the sixth paragraph of the preamble by the following:

"*Pending* further decisions by the United Nations with respect to the interests of the international community in the Jerusalem area;"

Operative part
Replace the operative part of the draft resolution by the following text:

"1. *Resolves* to invite the Governments of Israel and the Hashimite Kingdom of the Jordan to pledge themselves before the United Nations to:

"(*a*) Observe human rights and fundamental freedoms in the Jerusalem area, and in particular freedom of thought, conscience and religion as set forth in article 18 of the Universal Declaration of Human Rights;

"(*b*) Refrain from any act that would endanger the Holy Places in their territories;

"(*c*) Guarantee to nationals of their States, as well as aliens, without distinction as to nationality, free access to Holy Places in their territories, without prejudice to the General Armistice Agreement between the Hashimite Kingdom of the Jordan and Israel of 3 April 1949;

"(*d*) Observe and maintain as they existed on 14 May 1948 the rights, immunities and privileges of religious denominations with respect to Holy Places, as well as the rights, immunities and privileges of religious bodies with respect to monasteries and missionary, educational and welfare establishments now maintained by them;

"(*e*) Levy no tax in respect of any Holy Places which were exempt from such taxation on 14 May 1948 and make no charge in the incidence of any form of taxation which would either discriminate between the owners and occupiers of different Holy Places or would place such owners and occupiers in a position less favourable in relation to the general incidence of that form of taxation than existed on 14 May 1948;

"(*f*) Maintain and respect the property rights of religious bodies;

"(*g*) Reduce their armed forces in the Jerusalem area in progressive stages with a view to their limitation to normal peacetime requirements upon the conclusion of a peace settlement;

"2. *Resolves* to send to Jerusalem a United Nations representative to represent the interests of the United Nations in the Holy City in implementation of paragraph 1 of this resolution; and to report to the General Assembly with such recommendations as he may consider appropriate with regard to the Jerusalem question; the United Nations representative in Jerusalem shall be appointed on the nomination of the Secretary-General by a Committee of the General Assembly consisting of the eleven members of the Security Council; this Committee shall decide by a majority of the members present and voting;

"3. *Calls upon* the governments of the States in the Holy Land to co-operate fully with the United Nations representative;

"4. *Requests* the Secretary-General to furnish to the United Nations representative such staff and other facilities, as are required in the performance of his task."

Jerusalem: Keystone of an Arab-Israeli Settlement

RICHARD H. PFAFF

For the past two years, Israel has ruled over the Jordanian sector of Jerusalem. In the face of concern by the world community that Israel is altering the status of the Jordanian sector of the holy city, or "East Jerusalem" as it is now termed, the Jewish state has continued to implement its political, legal, economic, and demographic plans to integrate this part of occupied Jordan with the State of Israel.

Of all the outstanding issues of the Arab-Israeli conflict, that of East Jerusalem may well prove to be the most difficult of all to resolve. The Arab states are adamant that East Jerusalem be returned to the Arabs;[1] the Muslim community, representing one-fifth of all mankind, has vigorously expressed its opposition to Israeli "unification" of East and West Jerusalem;[2] the Roman Catholic church stands opposed to the unilateral action of Israel with regard to East Jerusalem;[3] the National Council of Churches has expressed its opposition to this action by Israel;[4] and the United Nations has repeatedly called upon Israel to rescind its action relative to East Jerusalem.[5] Furthermore, not one country has recognized this unilateral action taken by Israel. Nevertheless, Israel has not found it compatible with her interests to heed these calls from abroad. In fact, Israeli political leaders simply refuse to discuss the matter, declaring that the question of Jerusalem is not negotiable.

Since the framework of proposed settlement of the Arab-Israeli dispute is the Security Council's unanimous resolution of November 22, 1967, the Israeli position makes the prospects for peace in the Middle East difficult to envisage, for the first point of the U.N. resolution calls for "withdrawal of Israeli armed forces from territories occupied in the recent conflict." [6]

1. In March, 1968, for example, King Faisal of Saudi Arabia called for a "jihad" or holy war, in the defense of East Jerusalem; King Hussein of Jordan has repeatedly stressed that no peace settlement is conceivable without the return of East Jerusalem to the Arabs. See *New York Times*, March 7, 1968, for King Faisal's statement and the *New York Times*, February 17, 1968, December 21, 1968, and April 11, 1969, for references to King Hussein's position.

2. See part IV of this study.

3. *Ibid.*

4. *Ibid.*

5. *Ibid.*

6. For complete text of this resolution, see *ibid.*

The several other issues that make up the Arab-Israeli conflict are also important: Recognition of Israel's right of sovereign existence; withdrawal of Israeli armed forces from the Golan Heights, the West Bank, the Gaza Strip, and the Sinai Peninsula; the cessation of belligerency; secure boundaries for all parties; freedom of navigation; a just settlement of the Arab refugee problem; and the establishment of demilitarized zones are all matters that will require extensive negotiations. The issue of East Jerusalem, however, may prove decisive for success or failure in the quest for a peaceful and enduring solution of the Arab-Israeli problem; Jerusalem is of deep symbolic significance to the entire world, a holy city which is the source of emotional involvement for hundreds of millions of mankind.

It is the purpose of this study to examine Jerusalem, not only as the keystone of an Arab-Israeli settlement, but as a spiritual center of the three great monotheistic faiths: Christianity, Islam, and Judaism. While the analysis is primarily concerned with the political events that have marked the recent history of this holy city, its spiritual importance must also be briefly discussed. Because the "business of Jerusalem is eternity," the holy character of the city constitutes the basis for much of the political controversy over that city. The study begins, therefore, with an examination of Jerusalem's religious meaning.

I. THE CITY OF PEACE

Unique among the cities of this world, Jerusalem links the past with the present, man with his creator. For over 1.5 billion people, this holy city is a major, if not the major, geographical locus of their religious faith. The sacred books of Christianity, Judaism, and Islam speak of Jerusalem as a city apart from others, as a city of God.

One of the oldest cities in the world, Jerusalem has been a spiritual, as well as urban center for millenia. Egyptian sources dating from 1400 B.C. speak of this city as "Uru-Salim," or City of Peace. Even during the Bronze Age, this city flourished through its command over the commerce flowing between Pharaonic Egypt and Asia Minor. As civilized man expanded his domain from the eastern Mediterranean to encompass the globe, Jerusalem's importance as a metropolis waned, but as a religious center, its influence became universal.

Stripped of this spiritual dimension, Jerusalem is an uninviting place. Standing upon the summit of the Judean ridge, the sterile plateau of limestone upon which it rests presents an appearance that is both dreary and desolate. The Jerusalem area is cleft by deep ravines such as the Valley of Kidron and the Valley of Hinnom which descend rapidly to lower elevations. Some of Jerusalem's plateaus have rounded summits which have been dubbed, rather generously, as mounts: the Mount of Olives, Mount Zion, and Mount Scopus.

From this lofty, but sterile location, the descent to the Mediterranean is almost precipitous. The road to Tel Aviv, 33 miles away, has a drop of 2,485 feet which occurs almost entirely in the first few miles. Equally sharp is the drop from Jerusalem to Jericho toward the east. From the holy city southeast to the Dead Sea—a distance of only 15 miles—there is a descent of 3,870 feet.

The geographical location of Jerusalem, a boon when cities prospered behind the security of stone walls and narrow defiles, severely limits its economic utility today. Tourism, the sale of religious souvenirs, governmental administration, a small shoe factory in West Jerusalem, and a small but growing textile industry in East Jerusalem are features of the economic life of the city. Although both Israel and Jordan were giving special attention to the economic growth of those parts of Jerusalem under each country's control prior to June, 1967, it is still the Holy Places that sustain the Jerusalem economy.

Jerusalem, as with other Middle Eastern cities, is a composite of diverse ethnic and religious communities, for the most part clustered in discrete residential quarters. Because of Jerusalem's unique religious significance, the composition of the city reflects more sharply than other places the various religious communities that make it up.

The citizens of Jerusalem also may be separated in terms of certain spatial characteristics. The holy city has three parts. First, there is the walled city, the religious focus. Within the walled city are the three edifices that most link each of the three great monotheistic religions to the holy city: the Church of the Holy Sepulchre, the Haram esh-Sharif, and the Wailing Wall.

The walled city is an extremely small area. The walls, erected by the Ottoman Sultan Suleiman in 1542, are 38½ feet high and have a circumference of only 2.5 miles. The area they encompass is less than one-half a square mile. Within this area live—or did so prior to June, 1967—some 20,000 Arabs. This walled city of stone buildings, holy sites, and extremely narrow streets is one of the most densely populated areas in the Holy Land.

The walls form an irregular rectangle and are broken by six ancient gates. Running clockwise from the northeast corner these gates are: (1) St. Stephen's Gate (also called the Lion's Gate or Bab al-Asbat); (2) Dung Gate (Bab al-Magharabeh); (3) Zion Gate (Bab an-Nabi al-Daoud); (4) Jaffa Gate (The Hebron Gate or Bab al-Khalil); (5) Damascus Gate (Gate of the Columns, Bab al-Amud); and (6) Herod's Gate (Bab al-Zahar).

The streets of the walled city, running from the gates to the interior, divide it into four uneven quarters. The largest is the Muslim quarter, embracing over ha!f of the city (including the Haram esh-Sharif) of the northeast and eastern parts. In the northwestern area, between Damascus Gate and Jaffa Gate, is the Christian quarter. In the southwestern corner is the Armenian quarter. And along the southern edge of the walled city, between the Armenian quarter and the Haram esh-Sharif is the Jewish quarter.

The population within the walled city, excluding ecclesiastics servicing the Holy Places, has been almost entirely Arab for over a thousand years. The British Mandatory Government's census for 1931 counted 25,183 people living within the walled city at that time.[1] Of this total some 20,000 were Arabs (both Christian and Muslim), about 5,000 were Jews, and a handful Armenians. Subsequent to that date, there was a steady decline in the Jewish population within the walled city, accounting for only 4,000 in 1946, and only about 2,000 in April, 1948. Among the Arab community, Muslims outnumbered Christians (1946: 10,000 Muslims to 7,000 Christians), but if one adds ecclesiastics and Armenians, the ratio of Christians to Muslims has tended to be even over past years.

Outside the walled city, generally running north of the walls is an area populated almost entirely by Arabs. To the west of the walled city is the New City, by far the more populous section, and predominantly Jewish. Beginning in the mid-nineteenth century, a number of rich American Jews sent sizable contributions to foster a Jewish community in the Jerusalem area. In the early 1850s the North

---

1. *U.N. General Assembly, Official Records (V), Suppl. 9, Question of an International Regime for the Jerusalem Area and Protection of the Holy Places.* Doc. A/1286, p. 17.

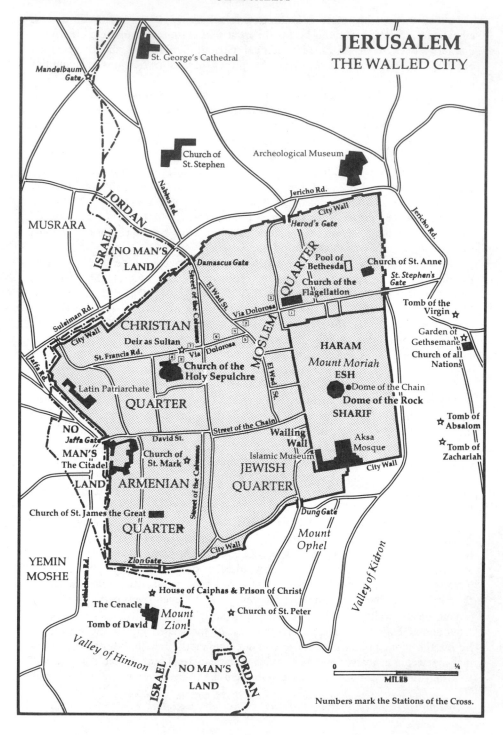

JERUSALEM
THE WALLED CITY

St. George's Cathedral

Mandelbaum Gate

Church of St. Stephen

Archeological Museum

Jericho Rd.

City Wall

Jericho Rd.

Herod's Gate

JORDAN

MUSRARA

ISRAEL

NO MAN'S LAND

QUARTER

Damascus Gate

Pool of Bethesda

Church of St. Anne

St. Stephen's Gate

Church of the Flagellation

Nablus Rd.

El Wad St.

Via Dolorosa

Tomb of the Virgin

Suleiman Rd.

City Wall

Street of the Columns

CHRISTIAN

Garden of Gethsemane

Church of all Nations

Deir as Sultan

Via Dolorosa

St. Francis Rd.

MOSLEM

HARAM

Mount Moriah

ESH

Church of the Holy Sepulchre

El Wad St.

Dome of the Chain

Dome of the Rock

Jaffa Rd.

Latin Patriarchate

QUARTER

SHARIF

Tomb of Absalom

NO

Jaffa Gate

David St.

Street of the Chain

Wailing Wall

Aksa Mosque

Tomb of Zachariah

MAN'S

The Citadel

Church of St. Mark

Islamic Museum

City Wall

LAND

ARMENIAN

JEWISH

Street of the Columns

QUARTER

Church of St. James the Great

Dung Gate

QUARTER

Mount Ophel

YEMIN MOSHE

City Wall

Valley of Kidron

Zion Gate

Bethlehem Rd.

House of Caiphas & Prison of Christ

The Cenacle

Mount Zion

Church of St. Peter

Tomb of David

Valley of Hinnon

ISRAEL

NO MAN'S LAND

JORDAN

0 ¼

MILES

Numbers mark the Stations of the Cross.

American Relief Society for the Indigent Jews of Jerusalem was founded. A major contributor to this society was a New Orleans Jew, Judah Touro.[2] In 1854 he donated funds for the establishment of a housing project near the walled city for Jews. This project was established near Zion Gate and named Yemin Moshe, or the "right hand of Moses." From this nucleus the New City grew slowly north and west of the walled city. The great bulk of the Jewish population of Jerusalem is, however, of recent vintage. Only after the establishment of the British Mandate over Palestine in the 1920s did the Jewish community in Jerusalem grow to significant size. By 1931 some 46,000 Jews were living in the New City, and by 1946 the number had grown to 95,000, the increase primarily the result of Jewish immigration to Palestine following the rise of Hitler.[3] By 1948 the Jewish population in the New City exceeded 100,000.

The rapid growth of the Jewish community upset the ecological balance in Jerusalem. There was little economic opportunity for this expanded community and the New City, or West Jerusalem, became less a part of the corporate structure of Jerusalem than an extension of the Jewish community of Palestine into the holy city. As one official Israeli statement concludes,

> The City [i.e., Israeli Jerusalem] is not even remotely self-supporting, either agriculturally or industrially, and would never have been able to maintain its population, except as part of a wider and more productive unit in the resources of which it could proportionately share.[4]

East Jerusalem, embracing the walled city and the Arab quarters north of it, grew more slowly over the decades. In 1967 the population of East Jerusalem was only 90,000 (including Arab refugees from 1948-49), while that of West Jerusalem numbered over 180,000.

In brief, Jerusalem is two cities: an Arab East Jerusalem and a Jewish West Jerusalem. It is within East Jerusalem that one finds virtually all of the Holy Places; this is, in fact, the "Jerusalem" of religious significance.[5] In contrast, West Jerusalem is modern, more expressive of Western culture, and linked politically, economically, and ideologically with the Israeli community along the Mediterranean littoral rather than with the immediate hinterland of the holy city.

Jerusalem: Holy City of Christendom

There are close to one billion Christians in the world today. They constitute the dominant religious groups in Europe, both North and South America, and in the English-speaking commonwealths. Altogether, Christians account for about one-third of mankind. While divided into many denominations, all Christians look to Jerusalem as the site where Christ's mission was concluded.

2. J. C. Hurewitz, *Middle East Dilemmas* (N.Y.: Harper & Bros., 1953), p. 107.

3. Doc. A/1286, *loc. cit.*

4. Delegation of Israel to the United Nations, *Memorandum on the Question of Jerusalem Submitted to the Trusteeship Council of the United Nations,* Seventh Session. Lake Success, May, 1950, p. 7.

5. According to United Nations Map 229, dated November, 1949, only three Holy Places are in West Jerusalem: the Tomb of David, Ein Karim (the birthplace of John the Baptist) and the Cenacle. Part of the Cenacle is in No Man's Land between the Israeli and Jordanian sectors of the holy city.

The United Nations lists the following Christian Holy Places in the Jerusalem area:

1) Basilica of the Holy Sepulchre
2) Bethany
3) Cenacle
4) Church of St. Anne
5) Church of St. James the Great
6) Church of St. Mark
7) Deir as-Sultan
8) Tomb of the Virgin
9) House of Caiphas and Prison of Christ
10) Sanctuary of the Ascension
11) Pool of Bethesda
12) Birthplace of John the Baptist
13) Basilica of the Nativity
14) Milk Grotto
15) Shepherds Field
16) The Nine Stations of the Cross, collectively also known as the Via Dolorosa.[6]

A few miles south of the walled city is the village of Bethlehem, where three of the Holy Places cited above are found. Here, where Christ was born, is the Basilica of the Nativity, the Milk Grotto, and Shepherds Field. Every Christmas, the Christian world celebrates the event that took place in this tiny village 1969 years ago.

To the east of the walled city, on the opposite side of the Valley of Kidron, is the Garden of Gethsemane, a favorite spot, the Gospel according to St. Luke tells us, to which Christ frequently retired. Here on the slopes of the Mount of Olives, He prayed the night before His crucifixion, sweated His tears of blood, was given the kiss of betrayal by Judas, and was arrested (Luke 22:39 ff). In these same gardens is located the tomb of the Virgin Mary, and a few hundred feet away the Sanctuary of the Ascension, marking the spot from which "he was parted from them, and carried up into heaven." (Luke 23:51.)

Just outside Zion Gate is the Cenacle, the forerunner of all Christian churches. This is the site of the Last Supper and the institution of the Blessed Sacrament. Here, too, Jesus appeared to the Apostles after His Resurrection, standing in their midst and saying, "Peace be unto you." (John 20:19.)

Within the walled city, the holy sites of the Christian faith are ubiquitous. Along the Via Dolorosa, a narrow zigzag alley running from the site of Pilate's house to the Holy Sepulchre, are marked the Stations of the Cross,[7] with the final Station the Holy Sepulchre itself. This is Calvary, the site of Christ's crucifixion. Here, too, within the walls of biblical Jerusalem, is the Church of St. Anne, the Church of St. James the Great, the Church of St. Mark, the Deir as-Sultan, and

---

6. *Loc. cit.*

7. The several stations indicate the spot where Jesus is condemned, His first fall, His meeting of Mary, Simon carries His cross, His second fall, etc. The present path is much higher, of course, than the original. At the convent of the Sisters of Zion, one may descend to the ancient level where the Sisters will point out to the visitor the scratches on the pavement marking the game the Roman soldiers played for Christ's robe.

the Pool of Bethesda. In addition to these recognized Holy Places within the walled city, there are also many religious sites (shrines, churches, convents, and sanctuaries) which various Christian denominations consider especially sacred. Thus, there are more than 30 Christian Communities and the Church bodies in the walled city, representing Catholic, Orthodox, Monophysite, and Protestant sects. The Catholic Church has more than 35 orders and congregations within the walled city and in other sections of East Jerusalem.

The large number of Christian groups represented in the holy city, together with the intense devotion Jerusalem evokes from all Christendom, has frequently led to ugly sectarian disputes which challenge the sacred character of this city.[8] These very disputes, however, serve to underscore the significance of Jerusalem to Christianity. The history of Christianity and the holy city of Jerusalem also reflects this admixture of the baseness of man with his search for spiritual communion. The Crusades, noble in thought, but often marked by bloodshed, were demonstrative of this contradiction in feeling and action.

For all Christianity, the Holy Places of Jerusalem assume particular importance because of this very reason; they symbolize the teachings of Christ—teachings which sought to free man from his base emotions. To Christianity, then, Jerusalem is the city where all the moral aspirations of man are brought into sharp focus.

Al-Quds: Sanctuary of Islam

For the 500,000,000 Muslims of the world, Jerusalem is also a particularly holy site, subordinate only to the cities of Mecca and Medina. It is a consecrated place and is known in Arabic (the language of Islam as well as the language of Arabs) as al-Quds, or "The Sanctuary." To the Muslim, the religion of Islam *is* the religion of Abraham, Isaac, Moses, and Jesus, all recognized as prophets of the one God (Allah). Muhammad is merely the last of God's messengers. All the apostles of God are accepted; to reject the prophets of Judaism and Christianity dooms the Muslim to everlasting hell.[9] While,

> To those who believe
> In God and His apostles
> And make no distinction
> Between any of the apostles,
> We shall soon give
> Their (due) rewards:
> For God is Oft-forgiving,
> Most Merciful.[10]

To the Muslim, both Christians and Jews are *Ahl al-Kitab,* or "People of the Book." As such they are "believers" and hold juridical right under Islamic law to live as "protected peoples" within the Islamic world. The whole corpus of Islamic dogma links the three great monotheistic faiths together. Because of the

---

8. The latest took place only two years ago. See Evan M. Wilson, "The Internationalization of Jerusalem," *Middle East Journal,* XXIII (Winter, 1969), pp. 1-13. The author of this study was witness to one such melee in 1955 when a young priest of one sect held mass during a period assigned to a different sect.

9. The Quran, Surah IV: 150-151.

10. Surah IV: 152.

incorporation of Judaic and Christian religious traditions into Islam, the city of Jerusalem has been a Muslim holy city from the very beginning of Muhammad's prophetic call.

In fact, the *giblah,* or direction of prayer, was initially toward Jerusalem, not Mecca. The Muslim *giblah* was not switched from Jerusalem until 624 A.D., more than a decade after Muhammad began preaching.[11]

Jerusalem, records the Kuran, is also the site of Muhammad's "ascent" (Miradj) at the time of his "nocturnal journey" (Isra). This was a particularly important episode in Muhammad's life, one of the rare times that his life transcended the mundane. The Kuran describes this journey as follows:

Glory to God
Who did take His Servant
For a journey by night
From the Sacred Mosque
To the Farthest Mosque
Whose precincts we did
Bless in order that We
Might show him some
Of our signs: for He
Is the One who heareth
And seeth (all things).[12]

The Sacred Mosque refers to the Kaba at Mecca (Masjid al-Haram) while the Farthest Mosque (Masjil al-Aqsa) refers to the Temple of Solomon in Jerusalem.

Islamic tradition, or *hadith,* has greatly embellished this journey of Muhammad, detailing the miraculous character of the event, his ascension from Jerusalem to heaven, even his conversation with God. A summary of the Islamic traditions dealing with this journey runs as follows:

The angel Gabriel escorted Muhammad one night from Mecca to Jerusalem. Muhammad made this journey mounted on a winged horse called al-Buraq. En route to Jerusalem, Muhammad stopped to pray at Bethlehem, "where was born Jesus the Messiah, son of Mary." [13] From there Muhammad went on to Jerusalem, tethering al-Buraq against the Temple Wall. Thus, the opposite side of the Wailing Wall, *the* holy site in Jerusalem for Jews, is also a holy site to Muslims. In fact, the very same wall is known to Muslims as the "Wall of al-Buraq."

After praying at the "Farthest Mosque," Muhammad stood upon a rock (*sakhra*) from which he then ascended to heaven. Muslims consider this rock second only to the Kaba itself, in order of sanctity. It is over this rock that the Islamic Caliph, Abd-al-Malik, built a shrine in 688-691 A.D. This shrine is the Dome of the Rock, popularly known as the Mosque of Omar. The Dome of the Rock, the al-Aqsa Mosque, and the "Wall of al-Buraq" are enclosed in an area known as the Haram esh-Sharif (Noble Enclosure).

---

11. For an analysis of this switch in the Islam *giblah* from Jerusalem to Mecca, see W. Montgomery Watt, *Muhammad at Medina* (Oxford: Clarendon Press, 1956), pp. 198-202.

12. Surah XVII: 1.

13. Imam al-Beihaqi, *Dalail an-Nubuwah,* on the authority of Shaddad ibn Aux, as cited in Charles D. Matthews, *Palestine-Mohammedan Holy Land* (New Haven: Yale University Press, 1949), p. 8.

After speaking with God, Muhammad returned to Mecca. According to Islamic tradition, it was during this visit to heaven that the obligation of prayer five times each day was established for Muslims.[14]

A number of other Islamic traditions deal with Jerusalem, too. Thus al-Bukhari states in his canonical collection of traditions that the Mosque al-Aqsa (i.e., the Farthest Mosque—Solomon's Temple) was the second mosque ever created. He further relates such traditions as "whosoever makes a pilgrimage to Jerusalem . . . God will give him a reward of a thousand martyrs," "whoever gives alms in Jerusalem to the value of a dirbum, it is his ransom from the Fire," or "God said to Jerusalem, Thou art My paradise and My sanctuary, and My choice of the lands! Who dwelleth in thee, it is a blessing (to him) from Me; and who is outside thee without just reason, it is from Mine anger at him." [15]

It is no wonder that the founder of the second caliphate, Muawiyah the Umayyad, proclaimed himself caliph in Jerusalem (661 A.D.) rather than Damascus, his capital.[16]

For more than a thousand years Muslim rule prevailed over Jerusalem. Only during three periods since 638 A.D. has sovereignty over the holy city been lost. The first time was during the Crusades, when Jerusalem fell under Christian rule following its capture on July 15, 1099. The Muslims recaptured the holy city in 1187, but lost it again to the Christians in 1229. Muslim rule was finally reestablished, however, some 15 years later.

The second period Jerusalem was lost to the Muslims followed General Allenby's expulsion of the Turks from that city in 1918. Muslim rule was restored to East Jerusalem between 1948 and 1967, but now, again, no Muslim flag flies over Jerusalem. For the tradition-minded Muslim, to whom the spiritual and the temporal aspects of life are closely interwoven, the loss of al-Quds—the Sanctuary—is more than a military or political event. It is a phenomenon of deep spiritual significance.

Judaism and the City of David

On June 7, 1967, Major General Moshe Dayan and other leaders of the Israeli army entered the walled city through St. Stephen's Gate. Without delay they proceeded directly to the Wailing Wall, where, after praying before this last remnant of the Temple, Dayan left a note that read "let peace prevail in Israel." Within a few days thousands of Jews streamed into the walled city to pray before the wall. For 14,000,000 Jews scattered throughout the world, this act marked the climax of a mission over 1800 years old, for the Jews prayed before the wall, not as tolerated subjects of another people, but as masters of all Jerusalem. Not since Rome put an end to the Second Jewish Commonwealth (70 A.D.) have Jews ruled over the walled city.[17]

The Wailing Wall, which more secularly-minded Palestinian Jews 30 years

14. Cf. *Shorter Encyclopaedia of Islam* (Ithaca: Cornell University Press, 1961), article on "Miradj."
15. These selections are from Matthews, *op. cit.*
16. Philip K. Hitti, *History of the Arabs* (New York: Macmillan, 1951), p. 189.
17. Excepting the ephemeral rule of Bar Kochba 117-135 A.D. during the Jewish revolt against Hadrian.

years earlier once dismissed as a "worthless pile of stones in a dirty Arab alley," [18] now symbolized the final return of the Jew to the Jerusalem of his forefathers.

In a sense, the entire history of Judaism these past 18 centuries has focused on the holy city. Few Jews cannot recite the psalm:

> If I forget thee, O Jerusalem
> Let my right hand forget its cunning;
> Let my tongue cleave to the roof of my mouth
> If I remember thee not,
> If I recall not Jerusalem
> On the day of my chiefest joy.
>   (CXXXVII)

The words of the great Jewish poet, Judah Halevi, reaffirm this devotion of the Jew to the holy city,

> Could I but kiss thy dust,
> So would I fain expire;
> As sweet as honey then
> My longing, my desire.[19]

Since the year 135 A.D. the basic condition of Jewry was set by its exile from Jerusalem. This exile was manifested in the scattering (diaspora) of Jews throughout the world. But despite the centrifugal forces acting upon the Diaspora Jews, a unity of the Jewish spirit has been retained. In no small way, this unity has been maintained because of the deep prophetic, literary, and liturgical relationship of Judaism to Jerusalem—City of David and site of the Temple.

To Judaism, Jerusalem is more than a holy city. It is the epicenter of the Promised Land. The writings of Judaism are replete with references to the promise God made to Abraham that the land of Canaan would ultimately belong to His chosen People.[20] So to the Jews the Land of Zion has always been home, either as apocalyptic vision, or reality. Thus immigration to Israel is termed "in-gathering"; thus General Dayan could announce that June day, 1967, that Israel had "liberated" Jerusalem.

But if Zion is "home" to the Jew, then Jerusalem is even more so:

> Jerusalem is at the center of the Land of Israel, the Temple is at the center of Jerusalem, the Holy of Holies is at the center of the Temple, the Ark is at the center of the Holy of Holies and the Foundation Stone is in front of the Ark, which point is the foundation of the world.[21]

To the Jew, all Palestine is holy, with Jerusalem the very center of this Promised Land. There is hardly a square foot of Jerusalem that does not hold historical or religious significance for Judaism. The cemeteries, particularly that on the Mount of Olives, the synagogues, particularly those that were located within the walled city, the Tomb of Absalom, the Tomb of David, the Tomb of

---

18. John Gunther, "The Realities of Zionism," *Harper's Magazine*, CLXI (July, 1930), p. 207.
19. As cited in Abram L. Sachar, *A History of the Jews* (N.Y.: Alfred A. Knopf, 1965), p. 175.
20. Genesis 17:1-8.
21. Tanhuma (Kedoshin), as cited in Arthur Hertzberg, *Judaism* (N.Y.: George Braziller, 1963), p. 150.

Simon the Just, the Tomb of Zachariah, and the several other Tombs in the Valley of Kidron—all these are but a sampling of the revered sites in the Jerusalem area for Jews.

Three great religions—all focused on a specific geographical site: For hundreds of millions this is testimony that Jerusalem must be considered apart from all other cities. Each faith makes its claim to Jerusalem; each claim is valid. To a Christian, Muslim, or Jew, Jerusalem is a point of contact between the individual and his creator. But the City of Peace is a city of people—people who serve the god of nationalism as faithfully, if not more so, than the God of Abraham. In the service of nationalism, the City of Peace becomes the city of conflict. It is to this aspect of the Jerusalem problem that we must now turn.

II. JERUSALEM UNDER THE MANDATE

At the outbreak of World War I the Ottoman Empire was but a shadow of its former greatness. Most of its Balkan and African territories had been lost and the secular power of the Sultan had been made nominal, at best, by the Young Turk revolution in 1908. Although the Empire still ruled over most of the Arab World in Asia, including the Holy Land, the stirrings of Arab nationalism in this area before 1914 suggested that they, too, would soon seek a separate political destiny. Therefore, when the Ottoman Empire joined with the Central Powers in October, 1914, Arab nationalists turned to the British for support of Arab political aspirations.

Events in Constantinople at the beginning of the war made the British more receptive to the Arabs than might otherwise have been the case. The Ottoman Sultan was also Caliph, or spiritual leader, of the Sunni (orthodox) Muslims, the dominant sect of Islam. On November 14, 1914, the Sultan-Caliph declared a *jihad* or "holy war," against the Allies. To the British who ruled over millions of Sunni Muslims in Egypt, British India, and elsewhere, the Sultan-Caliph's call was a source of potential danger, for, if heeded, widespread colonial disturbances might ensue.

To counteract the effects of this move by the Sultan-Caliph, the British needed the support of an Islamic leader whose influence would undermine the religious importance of the Caliph. They found this individual in Sherif Hussein, lineal descendant of the Prophet Muhammad and traditional custodian of the Islamic holy places in Mecca. Early in 1914 Hussein's second son, Abdullah, had already hinted to the British that Sherif Hussein might rebel against the Turks if British support were assured. So with the advent of the war and the Sultan-Caliph's call for a "holy war," the British High Commissioner for Egypt and the Sudan, Sir Henry McMahon, began negotiations by means of a series of letters with Sherif Hussein preparatory to the latter's launching an Arab revolt against the Ottoman Turks.

For the British, three major benefits could be seen in their support of Sherif Hussein. First, the call for a "holy war" by the Sultan-Caliph would lose much of its meaning; second, Arab nationalists would rally to the support of the Allies in expectation of a separate state for Arabs following the war; and third, the

Arabs would be valuable in providing military support along the desert flank in the anticipated march of General Allenby from Egypt into the Holy Land.

Before launching the 1916 Arab Revolt in support of Great Britain, Sherif Hussein of Mecca sought an understanding with the British relative to the geographical scope of the Arab State to be brought into being under British auspices subsequent to the dismemberment of the Ottoman Empire. It was Hussein's initial understanding that *all* of the area now made up of Syria, Lebanon, Jordan, Israel, Iraq, Saudi Arabia, and the sheikhdoms of the Arabian Peninsula (but excluding the Aden protectorate) would be included in this independent Arab State.[1]

The British responded by suggesting that to discuss this matter "would appear to be premature . . . in the heat of war."[2] Sherif Hussein was dissatisfied with this diplomatic hedging and continued to press Great Britain for some agreement on the area of the postwar Arab state, and,[3] under this pressure, Great Britain agreed to recognize the Arab claims, but with two important reservations. First, the Ottoman administrative districts *(vilayets)* of Baghdad and Basra would require "special administrative arrangements" (they would later become part of Iraq); and, second, that "portions of Syria lying to the west of the districts of Damascus, Homs, Hama, and Aleppo . . . should be excluded from the limits demanded."[4]

The Ottoman Empire in Asia was divided, for administrative purposes, into various *vilayets*. Each *vilayet*, in turn, was further subdivided into *sanjaks*. The *vilayet* of Syria was composed of four *sanjaks:* Hama, Damascus, Hauran, and Maan. The most southern *sanjak* in the *vilayet* of Aleppo was the *sanjak* of of Aleppo itself. The British-Arab discussions up to this point agreed that the *sanjaks* of Aleppo, Hama (which included Homs), and Damascus would go to the Arabs. It was further agreed that the *sanjaks* of Hauran and Maan would go to the Arabs. What was in dispute were the three administrative units along the Mediterranean littoral: the *vilayet* of Beirut (including the *sanjaks* of Latakia, Tripoli, Beirut, Acre, and Balqa), the quasi-independent Province of Lebanon, and the independent s*anjak* of Jerusalem. The latter, established as an independent *sanjak* in the 1880s, was not included in a larger *vilayet*, but was directly under the supervision of the Porte.

What is important to note is that neither Great Britain nor Sherif Hussein made specific reference to the proposed disposition of the *sanjak* of Jerusalem. A literal reading of the relevant correspondence would assign that *sanjak* to the Arabs. But Great Britain also suggested guaranteeing "the Holy Places against all external aggression" and that they would "recognize their inviolability." This would imply that the Jerusalem s*anjak* might have some special status even if it were to be placed within the proposed Arab state.

Sherif Hussein agreed to a temporary British administration of the *vilayets* of

1. Cmd 5957, *Correspondence between Sir Henry McMahon and The Sherif Hussein of Mecca, July 1915-March 1916* (London: H.M.S.O., 1939), letter from Sherif Hussein to Sir Henry McMahon, July 14, 1915.

2. *Ibid.,* letter from McMahon to Hussein, dated August 30, 1915.

3. *Ibid.,* Hussein-McMahon letter of September 9, 1915.

4. *Ibid.,* McMahon-Hussein letter of October 24, 1915.

Baghdad and Basra, but insisted that the Mediterranean littoral be included in the proposed Arab State.[5] To this persistence, the British could only respond that the matter would "require careful consideration" and that "the interests of our ally, France, are involved." [6]

Once again Hussein capitulated and agreed that "the northern parts and their coasts . . . we now leave to France." [7] But by this diplomatic concession, Hussein did not give up his claim to the "southern" parts, i.e., the independent *sanjak* of Jerusalem. It was on this unsettled issue that the British-Arab negotiations ended.[8]

While Sir Henry McMahon and Sherif Hussein were exchanging these letters, Sir Mark Sykes of Great Britain had visited Cairo and was privy to this correspondence. Only later Sir Henry McMahon would be aware of what Sykes was doing. In any case, Sykes and the French diplomat Georges Picot concluded the so-called Sykes-Picot agreement of May, 1916, with full knowledge of the contents of the McMahon-Hussein correspondence.[9]

The Sykes-Picot Agreement

The 1916 Sykes-Picot Agreement consists of a series of letters between Great Britain, France, and Russia concerning the period April 26 through October 23, 1916.[10] Under the terms of this agreement it was established, *inter alia,* that:

> With a view to securing the religious interests of the Entente Powers, Palestine, with the Holy Places, is to be separated from Turkish territory and subjected to a special regime to be determined by agreement between Russia, France and Great Britain.[11]

On November 2, 1917, Lord Balfour, then Britain's Secretary of State for Foreign Affairs, published a statement of policy in the form of a letter to Baron Rothschild which stated that:

> His Majesty's Government view with favour the establishment in Palestine of a National Home for the Jewish people, and will use their best endeavours to facilitate the achievement of this object, it being clearly understood that nothing shall be done which may prejudice the civil and religious rights of existing non-Jewish communities in Palestine, or the rights and political status enjoyed by Jews in any other country.[12]

Thus, when Jerusalem fell to General Allenby in December, 1917, the Arabs were under the impression it would become part of an independent Arab state,

---

5. *Ibid,* Hussein-McMahon letter, November 9, 1915.

6. *Ibid.,* McMahon-Hussein letter, December 14, 1915.

7. *Ibid.,* Hussein-McMahon letter, January 1, 1916.

8. There was some additional correspondence, but these letters deal only with military preparations then underway.

9. Elizabeth Monroe, *Britain's Moment in the Middle East, 1914-1956* (Baltimore: Johns-Hopkins Press, 1963), p. 32.

10. The text of this agreement may be found in J. C. Hurewitz, *Diplomacy in the Near and Middle East, 1914-1965,* volume II (N.Y.: W. Van Nostrand, 1956), pp. 18-22. However the preliminary accord was concluded in May, 1916.

11. As cited in Cmd. 5479, *Palestine Royal Commission Report,* July, 1937 (London: H.M.S.O., 1937), p. 21.

12. For the text of this "Balfour Declaration" see Hurewitz, *op. cit.,* p. 26.

the Jews assumed it would be part of a British-administered Palestine until unrestricted Jewish immigration into the Holy Land allowed greater Jewish political autonomy,[13] and everyone else assumed Jerusalem would be part of an internationalized zone—everyone except President Wilson of the United States who thought that the people of Palestine should have the right to determine their own political future.[14]

The post-World War I formula for Palestine was a blow to the incipient Arab nationalist movement. After fighting alongside the British for two years, they felt a British administration of Palestine as a cover for the establishment of a Jewish National Home in that area was a dubious reward for Arab efforts.

For the Zionists, the postwar settlement, while not entirely meeting their wishes, was a wedge into Palestine. Symbolic of their intention to establish a truly National Home in Palestine was their founding of the Hebrew University. On July 14, 1918, before General Allenby had fully established his administration in Jerusalem, Dr. Chaim Weizmann (then a leader of British Zionists and later to be the first president of Israel) laid the foundation stone of the new university on Mt. Scopus.[15]

Even before the British military and administrative control of Palestine was formalized as a Mandate, Arabs and Jews began to clash in Jerusalem. In April, 1,920 riots broke out within the holy city in the course of which over 230 inhabitants were either killed or wounded. The clash was quickly suppressed by British military forces, but it served as a harbinger of things to come. The differences between the Arabs and the handful of oriental Jews who lived in Jerusalem before World War I were minimal. But now Arab-Jewish differences were assuming a cultural and intellectual character that would make their future coexistence virtually impossible. The Arabs, and to a considerable extent the oriental Jews of that time,[16] were steeped in the Eastern way of life. Their traditionalist outlook, their lack of familiarity with modern science, their emphasis on status—even their perceptions of space and time—set them off sharply from the immigrant Jews, more Western in outlook, more attuned to modern perceptions of reality, better organized and financed, and with invaluable political connections in London, Paris, and Washington, D.C. The British found themselves in the role of referee for this clash of two peoples. But the clash was not a matter of peoples divided by religion, for religious differences had existed in Jerusalem for centuries, between Christian Arab and Muslim Arab, as with these groups and

---

13. This point was made clear by the contents of a Zionist draft submitted to the British government on July 18, 1917 to be considered for future declaration as official British policy. The draft declaration states, *inter alia,* that the British regard "as essential . . . the grant of internal autonomy to the Jewish nationality in Palestine, freedom of immigration for Jews, and the establishment of a Jewish National Colonising Corporation for the resettlement and economic development of the country" (Hurewitz, *loc. cit.*). There is no mention made in the Zionist draft to either the civil or religious rights of the indigenous population.

14. Wilson's Twelfth Point of his 14-point address to Congress January 8, 1918, states in part, that ". . . nationalities which are now under Turkish rule should be assured . . . unmolested opportunity of autonomous development."

15. The university was moved to West Jerusalem following the 1948-49 Arab-Israeli war. Since the June, 1967, occupation of East Jerusalem, selected sections of the university have been returned to the Mt. Scopus site.

16. Particularly the *Nturei Karta* (Guardians of the City), who opposed Zionist aims in Palestine on the grounds only the Messiah can bring about the legitimate return of the Jew to Zion.

Jews; instead it was a clash between two political movements, Zionism and Arab nationalism. Both sides would use religion, the question of Holy Places, Jerusalem itself, as weapons in their struggle.

The British Mandate

On July 24, 1922, the League of Nations officially designated Great Britain as Mandatory Power in Palestine.[17] The Preamble to the Palestine Mandate specifically identified as one purpose of this Mandate "putting into effect . . . the establishment in Palestine of a National home for the Jewish people." Article 2 repeats this charge to Great Britain, while Article 4 recognizes the Zionist organization as the appropriate Jewish agency to advise the Mandatory Power. Furthermore, Article 6 calls upon the British to "facilitate Jewish immigration." To the Palestinian Arabs, all their fears seemed to be justified: the Mandate was to be merely a cover for the progressive transformation of an Arab Palestine into an essentially Jewish Palestine. Although Great Britain was made responsible for "Holy Places and religious buildings or sites in Palestine" (Article 13), it was obvious that the political struggle invited by the Mandate would, by the nature of the Zionist movement, involve these Holy Places, particularly in Jerusalem. If the site of the Holy Places, i.e., Jerusalem, represented the focal point of Zionist aspirations, then where else but in the holy city would the confrontation between Zionist and Arab take place? As noted above, such a confrontation had already taken place in Jerusalem even before the mandate was formally established.

The Wailing Wall Incident

By August, 1929, the demographic character of Palestine had been sufficiently altered so that an Arab-Jewish clash awaited only the appropriate incident. In the period 1920-29, alone, 99,805 Jews had been admitted into Palestine. Many of them had taken up residence in the New City, or West Jerusalem.[18] As might have been expected, the incident arose over one of the Holy Places in Jerusalem. Throughout 1928 and into the summer of 1929, the capacity of the Arab and the Zionist Jew to coexist peacefully in the holy city became increasingly more difficult to maintain. Emotions were becoming charged, as each group found the grounds of common discourse more difficult to discover. The bulk of the immigrant Jews were coming from Poland, Russia, and Lithuania—and they found little cultural relationship with the Arab community of Jerusalem. The exact point where the emotional fervor of the Zionist Jew and the Muslim Arab came into contact was the Wailing Wall or the Wall of al-Buraq. As early as 1925, one small incident had already occurred in connection with this Holy Place.[19] Under a Turkish decree (*firman*) of 1852 (reaffirming the position taken by the Sultan earlier, in 1757), the Holy Places of Jerusalem were subject to a rigorously-

17. For the text of the Palestine Mandate, see Cmd. 1785, *Parliamentary Papers, 1922* (London: H.M.S.O., 1923).

18. Cmd. 5479 *Palestine Royal Commission Report,* July, 1937 (London: H.M.S.O., 1937), p. 279 (Peel Report).

19. F. A. Andrews, *The Holy Land Under Mandate,* volume II (N.Y.: Houghton Mifflin Co., 1931), pp. 225-26.

enforced status quo, which Great Britain sought also to continue.[20] In 1925 the Jews sought to modify this status quo by bringing benches to the Wall to be used on the Jewish Day of Atonement. The Muslim Arabs protested immediately and these benches were removed. The Muslim Arab, however, was now suspicious of the Jewish community and its intentions with regard to the Wall—a site also holy to Muslims. The Wall was recognized Muslim property, to which Jews had customary rights, but only if used in accordance with the status quo.[21] No change could be made in this status quo without the consent of both Muslims and Jews. The implications of this point will be further drawn when the post-1967 actions of the Israeli government are analyzed in this connection.

A more serious incident occurred September 24, 1928, when Jews sought to set up a screen by the Wall to divide men and women. When ordered to remove the screen by the British, the Jews refused. The screen was eventually removed by force. The Jewish authorities protested vigorously, contending the screen was not designed "to menace the inviolability of the Muslim Holy Place." The Muslim Arabs, however, took the position that these recent efforts to break the long-established status quo governing the Wall represented "the Jews' aim . . . to take possession of the Mosque of al-Aqsa gradually." [22]

In the following months, this tension was further inflamed, as both Zionists and Arab nationalists made the Wall a political as well as religious issue.

The Zionist Jews were the first to trigger the new outbreak of violence. On August 15, 1929, the day of *Tisha B'Av,* a Jewish holy day in memory of the destruction of the Temple, a number of Zionist youths marched to the Wall, made political speeches, and sang the *Hatikvah,* or Jewish National Anthem. On the following day Arab nationalists put on a counterdemonstration. Rumor and fact, the trivial and the significant—all were fused into an inseparable pattern. To the Arabs the "provocative demonstration" [23] of the Zionist Jews confirmed their fears and dictated a violent response. A week later the "fire which had so long been kindling burst into flame." [24] From August 23-29 Arab-Jewish battles erupted throughout the Holy Land. By the time peace was restored, some 472 Jews and 348 Arabs had been killed or wounded.[25]

The Royal Commission of Inquiry (Shaw Report), which investigated this incident, succinctly summarized the basic reason why a conflict over the Wall could rapidly envelop all Palestine and involve Christian Arab, as well as Muslim Arab, in bloody conflict with the Jewish community:

> A National Home for the Jews, in the sense in which it was widely understood, was inconsistent with the demands of Arab nationalists while the claims of Arab nationalism, if admitted, would have rendered impossible the fulfillment of the pledge to the Jews.[26]

20. *Report of the Commission appointed by His Majesty's Government in the United Kingdom of Great Britain and Northern Ireland, with the approval of the Council of the League of Nations, to determine the rights and claims of Moslems and Jews in connection with the Western or Wailing Wall at Jerusalem,* December, 1930 (Hereafter referred to as Report, 1930) (London: H.M.S.O., 1931), p. 36.
21. Cmd. 5479, p. 66.
22. *Ibid.,* p. 67.
23. The phrase is that used by the Royal Commission, *loc. cit.*
24. *Loc. cit.*
25. *Ibid.,* p. 68.
26. As cited in *loc. cit.*

Two political movements were in conflict, and the focus of that conflict was the holy city itself.

The specific disputes arising out of the Wailing Wall incident led, after extensive British investigation, to the Mandatory Government of Palestine issuing detailed instructions in regard to the use of the Wall: Jews were to have access to the Wall at all times; no objects of a permanent character were to be placed by the Wall and nothing affixed to either the Wall or adjoining buildings; on specific Jewish holy days, a portable stand for use in prayer would be allowed, but this would have to be removed at the end of the holy day involved. It was further ordered that "no benches, chairs, or stools shall be brought to or placed on the pavement before the Wailing Wall" and that "no screen or curtain shall be placed on the Wall or on the pavement, for the purpose of separating men and women or for any other purpose." The maximum size of each portable object allowed was included in these instructions.[27]

The Wailing Wall incident could be resolved by such detailed instructions; the political question that led to this incident would prove to be far more impervious to administrative resolution.

The 1936 Riots

The Arabs of Palestine were concerned from the very beginning of the Mandate that British support of Jewish immigration, under the provisions of Article 6 of the Mandate, would eventually lead to Jewish community gaining demographic hegemony over the Holy Land. By the year 1936 this concern had assumed the character of panic because, with the rise of Nazi Germany in Europe, there followed a veritable quantum jump of Jewish immigration into Palestine. During the four-year period 1929-32, some 23,821 Jews had immigrated into Palestine. Between 1933 and 1936, however, Jewish immigration totaled 164,267.[28] One by-product of this rapid increase in Jewish immigration was that an Arab Jerusalem of 49,000 now faced a Jewish Jerusalem on the slopes rising westward from the walled city of more than 76,000, whose cultural and political orientation was alien to the Jerusalem across the Valley of Hinnom.

Although Jews constituted only 30 percent of the total population of 1936 Palestine, the danger of being overwhelmed by Jewish refugees from Europe now appeared real and immediate. The Royal Commission Report of 1937 (i.e., the Peel Report) suggested that Palestine could become predominantly Jewish in only a decade if the rate of immigration continued at its post-1933 rate.[29] It was this specter of Jewish inundation of Arab Palestine that brought forth in 1936 the most violent clash between Arab and Jew in the history of the Mandate up to that date.

The riots, which started in April, 1936, in Tel Aviv and Jaffa, soon spread across the Holy Land. A newly-formed Arab National Committee called for a general strike in Palestine on April 20 until "the British Government changes its

27. Report, 1930, op. cit., pp. 70-71.
28. Cmd. 5479, p. 279.
29. Ibid., p. 281. The total population of Palestine in 1936 numbered 1,336,518, of which 370,483 were Jewish. The Commission estimated that both Arab and Jewish populations would equal 1,210,000 by 1947, assuming an immigration rate of 60,000 per annum.

present policy . . . the beginning of which is the stoppage of Jewish immigration."[30] By May the strike brought the Arab part of the Palestinian economy to a virtual standstill. Sporadic attacks, indiscriminate sniping, and destruction of public property rapidly escalated the disturbance into incipient civil war. Throughout the summer Arab unrest continued its violent expression. By September the British had brought in more than 20,000 troops to contain the Arab community.

The 1936 riots were more than just another Arab-Jewish "disturbance"; they were a definite move on the part of the Arabs to challenge the legitimacy of British Mandatory rule. The conflict was directed as much against the British government of Palestine as against the Jewish community. This is reflected in the casualty figures for the 1936 riots: Arabs killed or wounded, over 1,000; Jews killed or wounded, 388; Mandatory Government casualties (including police), 243.[31]

As a result of the 1936 riots the Peel Report recommended that Palestine be partitioned into an Arab state that would include Trans-Jordan and a Jewish state in those areas of Palestine where the Jews already made up a clear majority of the population. In addition, it was recommended that, separate from both the proposed Jewish and Arab states, there would be a Jerusalem enclave which would include the holy city with its immediate hinterland and a corridor to the sea terminating at Jaffa.[32]

This partition scheme was never implemented, of course, although it did influence the subsequent United Nations partition plan. The justification cited in the Peel Report for proposing an enclave for Jerusalem was as follows:

> The partition of Palestine is subject to the overriding necessity of keeping the sanctity of Jerusalem and Bethlehem inviolate and of ensuring free and safe access to them for all the world. That, in the fullest sense of the mandatory phrase, is "a sacred trust of civilization"—a trust on behalf not merely of the peoples of Palestine but of multitudes in other lands to whom those places, one or both, are Holy Places.[33]

The 1936 riots posed a threat to the holy city, the fate of which was of concern to "multitudes in other lands." But the riots were only symptoms of a condition that made the whole Mandate system seem unworkable and partition inevitable: just as Jerusalem must be viewed as two cities, one Jewish and one Arab, so too was Palestine two countries, one Jewish and one Arab. The British Mandate for Palestine provided the juridical framework within the context of which this bi-national character of Palestine and its holiest site, Jerusalem, came into being. At the close of World War II, the clamor by Jewish refugees in Europe to emigrate to Palestine, coupled with a resurgence of Arab sentiment that Palestine should be freed of Mandatory rule, made continuation of such bi-nationalism in Palestine virtually intolerable. Could the inviolability of the holy city be preserved against this background? If the Mandate system were a failure, then what system could take its place which could at once satisfy both Jews and Arabs, yet still leave Jerusalem secure as "a sacred trust of civilization"? For the British only one thing was certain—they did not have the answer.

---

30. *Ibid.*, p. 97.
31. *Ibid.*, pp. 105-06.
32. *Ibid.*, pp. 380-93.
33. *Ibid.*, p. 381.

III. SEARCH FOR AN INTERNATIONAL FORMULA

With the dissolution of the League of Nations in 1946, Great Britain had no international authority to which it might report on Palestine pending the establishment of an appropriate organ by the newly-established United Nations. The creation on December 10, 1945 of the Anglo-American Inquiry Committee, however, clearly indicated that Great Britain was either unable, or did not wish, to assume sole responsibility for the problem of Palestine. When the Inquiry Committee recommended that Palestine be neither a Jewish nor an Arab state, but that "the Government of Palestine be continued as at present under mandate pending the execution of a Trusteeship Agreement under the United Nations," it did so because of what it considered "the depth of political antagonism beween Arab and Jew." [1]

Great Britain, however, did not want further responsibility for Palestine and on February 14, 1947, declared that it would refer the question of Palestine to the United Nations.[2] On April 28, 1947, the General Assembly convened in special session to consider this question. A United Nations Special Committee on Palestine (UNSCOP) was established to "report on the question of Palestine" [3] at the next regular session of the General Assembly. UNSCOP was further instructed "to give most careful consideration to the religious interests in Palestine of Islam, Judaism, and Christianity." [4]

In September, 1947, UNSCOP reported back with both a majority and minority report. In addition, the Committee submitted several recommendations approved unanimously. Among these it was recommended (V) that:

> The sacred character of the Holy Places shall be preserved and access to the Holy Places for purposes of worship and pilgrimage shall be ensured in accordance with existing rights, in recognition of the proper interest of millions of Christians, Jews and Moslems abroad as well as the residents of Palestine in the care of sites and buildings associated with the origin and history of their faiths.[5]

---

1. United Nations Special Committee on Palestine, *Report to the General Assembly*, Volume I, Doc. A/364, dated 1947, p. 27.
2. *Loc. cit.*
3. *Ibid.*, p. 2.
4. *Ibid.*, p. 36.
5. *Ibid.*, p. 44.

The Minority Report

The minority report called for a federal state with Jerusalem as its capital. It further recommended that the Holy Places in Jerusalem, Bethlehem, etc., be placed under the supervision and protection of the United Nations. Thus Jerusalem would remain an integral part of an all-Palestine political system, but there would be functional internationalization of the Holy Places.

The minority report also recommended that for purposes of local administration, Jerusalem would consist of two separate municipalities, one Arab (including "that part of the city within the walls") and one Jewish. These two municipalities would jointly provide for such common public services as sewage, fire protection, telephones, water supply, etc.[6]

While the minority report was never adopted by the General Assembly, it is instructive to note two points raised in this report. First, that the city of Jerusalem could not be considered as either a demographic or a political entity. At best, Jerusalem could be treated as an entity only for certain public services. Second, that sovereignty over Jerusalem was a separate problem from sovereignty over the Holy Places. The latter, by virtue of their international significance to members of all three monotheistic faiths, could only be properly dealt with when placed under international jurisdiction.

The Majority Report

The majority report recommended that Palestine be partitioned into an Arab state and a Jewish state, and that Jerusalem be placed under the international trusteeship system of the United Nations. It was recommended that:

> The city of Jerusalem . . . include the present municipality of Jerusalem plus the surrounding villages and towns, the most eastern of which to be Abu Dis; the most southern Bethlehem; the most Western Ein Karim and the most northern Shn'fat. . . .[7]

The report further recommended that Jerusalem be demilitarized, "its neutrality shall be declared and preserved, and no para-military formations, exercises or activities . . . be permitted within its borders." [8]

On November 29, 1947, the General Assembly recommended the partition of Palestine along the lines suggested by the majority report.[9] Under part III of the partition resolution it was stated that:

> The City of Jerusalem shall be established as a *corpus separatum* under a special international regime and shall be administered by the United Nations. The Trusteeship Council shall be designated to discharge the responsibilities of the Administering Authority on behalf of the United Nations.

The boundaries of the Jerusalem area were to be the same as recommended by UNSCOP except that the built-up area of Motsa was included along with Ein Karim.

6. *Ibid.*, p. 63.
7. *Ibid.*, p. 57.
8. *Loc. cit.*
9. United Nations General Assembly Resolution 181 (II), Doc. A/519 (1947).

In this same resolution, the General Assembly called upon the Trusteeship Council to draft a detailed Statute for Jerusalem designed, in part, "to protect and to preserve the unique spiritual and religious interest located in the city of the three great monotheistic faiths throughout the world" (section C1). The Statute was to come into force not later than October 1, 1948.

Finally, the resolution created the United Nations Palestine Commission and charged it with the task of implementing the partition of Palestine. Events in Palestine, however, soon made it impossible for the Commission even to begin operations in the Holy Land. First, Great Britain refused to transfer authority to the Commission until its mandate officially terminated (May 15, 1948); it even indicated it did not want the Commission on Palestinian soil before May 1, 1948.[10] Second, the partition resolution sparked what the Commission identified as "virtual civil war" in Palestine.[11] British forces could maintain, at best, only nominal control over Palestine. Within days after the partition resolution guerrilla warfare erupted throughout the Holy Land.

The Jewish community in Palestine was reluctantly prepared to accept the internationalization of Jerusalem as the price for obtaining an independent Jewish state under the partition resolution.[12] The Arabs, however, opposed both the partition of Palestine and the internationalization of Jerusalem. In the face of Arab resistance, the Jews armed themselves for the forthcoming struggle. Even before the mandate ended, Jewish military forces (i.e., the Haganah) seized the cities of Tiberias, Safed, Jaffa, and Haifa.[13] Within Jerusalem also battle lines were being drawn.

The Statute for Jerusalem

Seemingly unperturbed that the fate of Jerusalem was being determined by force of arms rather than international compact, the Trusteeship Council began sitting on February 18, 1948, for the purpose of drafting a Statute for an international regime in Jerusalem.[14] On April 21 this Statute was completed, but formal approval was postponed pending receipt of further advice from the General Assembly.

The Statute repeated the statement of the partition resolution that the City of Jerusalem be established as a *corpus separatum* under the United Nations. It also stated the general purposes of internationalization (protection of Holy Places, etc.).

Article 5 of the Statute, as in the partition resolution, states that Jerusalem shall be demilitarized and that no para-military formations shall be permitted

10. United Nations Palestine Commission, *Report to the General Assembly,* Doc. A/532 dated April 10, 1948, p. 3.

11. *Loc. cit.* The Commission reported (p. 12) that there were 6,187 casualties in Palestine between November 30, 1947 and April 3, 1948, including 430 British, 2,977 Arab, and 2,733 Jews, as well as 47 civilians of foreign nationality.

12. Government of Israel, Office of Information, *Jerusalem and the United Nations* (Washington, D.C., July, 1953), p. 1.

13. David Ben-Gurion, *Rebirth and Destiny of Israel* (N.Y.: Philosophical Library, 1954), pp. 530-31.

14. For the text of this Statute see Trusteeship Council, *Official Records (II), Annex,* Doc. T/118/Rn.2, dated April 21, 1948.

within its boundaries. The police force envisaged for Jerusalem (Article 14) would *not* be recruited from among either Jews or Arabs.

The governor of Jerusalem would be appointed by the Trusteeship Council to which he would be responsible. He could not be, however, a citizen of either Jerusalem, the Arab state, or the Jewish state (Article 10).

Under the governor, there was to be a unicameral Legislative Council made up of 40 members, 18 of whom would be Jews, 18 Arabs, and one or two representing groups neither Arab nor Jew (e.g., Armenian) and the remainder representatives-at-large (Article 20).

Under the provisions of Articles 36 and 37 of the Statute, the governor was made responsible for the Holy Places, not only within Jerusalem, but also within the Jewish and Arab states resulting from partition. He would therefore wield territorial authority over Jerusalem and functional authority over the Holy Places beyond the boundaries of the international regime.

Finally, an opportunity was included in the Statute (Article 44) for the residents of Jerusalem, after a period of ten years, to decide by referendum what modification of the international regime they might wish to have brought about. The Statute did not deny the principle of self-determination to the residents of the holy city; it merely deferred that right for ten years. Considering the previous (and subsequent) decades of deep, ofttimes violent, political antagonism between Jews and Arabs, stemming from fundamental religious, cultural, and ideological differences, the eventual partition of the holy city might have come about by the self-determination route, even had Jerusalem been made a separate city. As Lord MacDonald, speaking in behalf of the United Kingdom before the United Nations, contended in 1949, "if the people of Jerusalem were given normal democratic liberties, their first action would be to vote the international regime out of existence." [15] The factors that caused the partition of Palestine as a whole were present in the holy city as well.

The Partition of Jerusalem

The 1948-49 Arab-Israeli war led to a *de facto* partition of Jerusalem. At precisely 4:06 p.m. on May 14, 1948, the independent State of Israel was proclaimed. The Arab community, less organized and anticipating early destruction of the new Jewish polity by the several neighboring Arab states following the evacuation of British troops from Palestine, made no similar proclamation of independence until October 1, 1948.[16] By that date, the proclamation was of neither juridical nor political significance.[17]

On May 15 Egyptian troops entered Palestine and the first Arab-Israeli war began. For the Jews and Arabs in Jerusalem, however, this conflict was already over five months old. The fight for Jerusalem had broken out within days after the partition resolution was passed. With minor exceptions the battle line—and,

---

15. U.N. Doc. A/AC 38/SR75.

16. *Proclamation of the Independence of Palestine by the Higher Arab Committee and the Representatives of Palestine Meeting in Congress,* dated October 1, 1948. For text see Muhamma Khalil, comp. *The Arab States and the Arab League: A Documentary Record,* vol. II (Beirut: Khayates, 1962), p. 579.

17. See below page 28.

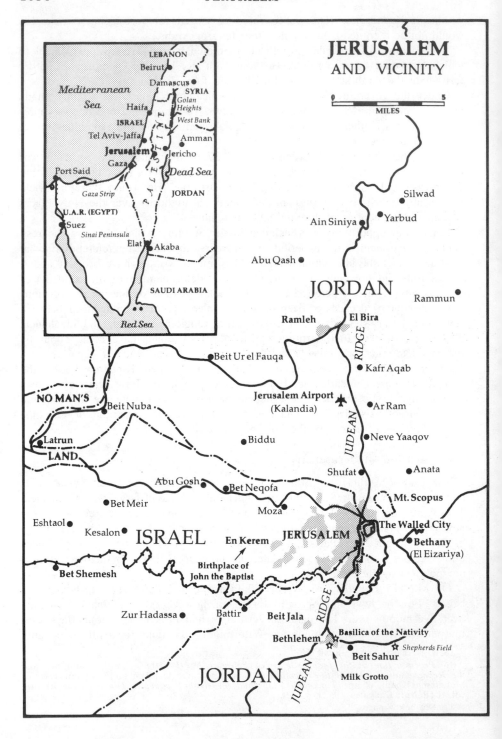

JERUSALEM
AND VICINITY

0   5
MILES

LEBANON
Beirut
Damascus
Mediterranean
Sea
Haifa
ISRAEL
Tel Aviv-Jaffa
Jerusalem
Gaza
Port Said
Gaza Strip
U.A.R. (EGYPT)
Suez
Sinai Peninsula
Elat
Akaba
SAUDI ARABIA
Red Sea
SYRIA
Golan
Heights
West Bank
Amman
Jericho
Dead Sea
JORDAN

Silwad
Ain Siniya
Yarbud
Abu Qash
JORDAN
Rammun
Ramleh
El Bira
Beit Ur el Fauqa
Kafr Aqab
NO MAN'S
Beit Nuba
Jerusalem Airport
(Kalandia)
Ar Ram
Latrun
Biddu
Neve Yaaqov
LAND
Abu Gosh
Bet Neqofa
Shufat
Anata
Bet Meir
Moza
Mt. Scopus
Eshtaol
Kesalon
ISRAEL
En Kerem
JERUSALEM
The Walled City
Bethany
(El Eizariya)
Birthplace of
John the Baptist
Bet Shemesh
Zur Hadassa
Battir
Beit Jala
Basilica of the Nativity
Bethlehem
Shepherds Field
Beit Sahur
JORDAN
Milk Grotto
JUDEAN RIDGE
JUDEAN RIDGE
JUDEAN RIDGE
PALESTINE

ultimately, the line of partition—within Jerusalem followed closely the communal division of the city.

According to the 1946 census there were 608,225 Jews in Palestine at that time.[18] Of these, some 99,320 were concentrated in the New City,[19] or what is now identified as West Jerusalem. With the bulk of the remaining Palestinian Jews clustered along the coast, the Jerusalem community was, as one Jewish writer has put it, "an outlying Jewish settlement." [20] With the exception of some 2,000 Jews living within the walled city, they constituted a compact Jewish island in an Arab sea.

From November 29, 1947, through May 14, 1948, the contest for Jerusalem focused on gaining control over the Tel Aviv-Jerusalem road. While Palestinian Arabs managed to blockade the road to Jewish convoys during the early months of 1948, large Jewish convoys did reach the New City in April.[21]

During this period the Jews of Jerusalem occupied several Arab quarters of the New City, including Talbiya, Bakaa, and Katamon. They also occupied most of Sheikh Jarrah, a large Arab quarter ranging north of Herod's Gate. The Arabs, in turn, attacked the Jewish quarter within the walled city.[22]

From May 14 to 18 the situation within Jerusalem was critical for the Arab community.[23] The Arabs already had been driven out of most of the New City. On May 14 and 15 Israeli forces occupied the Musrara quarter, a major Arab residential area north of the walled city. In the next two days the Arabs held little more than the walled city. On May 18 Trans-Jordan's Arab Legion entered the Jerusalem area, recapturing Sheikh Jarrah and reinforcing Arab irregulars within the walled city. On May 28, the Jewish quarter in the walled city surrendered to the Arabs.

The Legion also took over Lydda, Ramleh, and Latrun, thereby sealing off the road between Jerusalem and Tel Aviv. The Jews of the New City were then under siege. They retained their position, however, while Israeli forces from the coast succeeded in constructing a road to the New City that by-passed the Latrun Salient. This road was completed on June 9. On the following day the first truce went into effect. Resumption of hostilities in July and October threatened to alter the military situation in Jerusalem, but no major advances were made by either side. It was not until November 30, 1948, that a cease-fire in the Jerusalem area was reached. It was this cease-fire agreement that provided for regular convoy service to the Israeli enclave on Mount Scopus, behind the Arab-Israeli truce line in Jerusalem.

18. Doc. A/364, p. 11.

19. United Nations, Special Report of the Trusteeship Council, *Question of an International Regime for the Jerusalem Area and Protection of the Holy Places*, GAPR (v) Suppl. 9 Doc. A/1286, p. 17.

20. Rufus Learsi (Israel Goldberg), *Fulfillment: The Epic Story of Zionism* (N.Y.: World Publishing Company, 1951), p. 368.

21. *Ibid.*, p. 369; Ben Gurion, *op. cit.*, pp. 291-92.

22. Millar Burrows, *Palestine Is Our Business* (Philadelphia: Westminster Press, 1945), p. 107.

23. Exactly who was "holding out" against whom in Jerusalem at this time varies with the source cited. Two polar views on this period are Learsi, *op. cit.*, pp. 366-97, and Munib Al-Mahdi and Suleiman Musa, *Tarikh Al'Urdan fi Al-Qaran Al Ashrin* (Amman: Jamiya Al-Hakud, 1959), pp. 491 ff.

Peace Efforts at the United Nations

Even before the British mandate ended, violence and anarchy prevailing in Palestine led the United Nations to take steps to stop, or at least control, the Arab-Jewish conflict in that country. In February, March, and April the Security Council called several times for a truce in Palestine.[24] On April 23, the Security Council established a Palestine Truce Commission consisting of the Security Council members' consular officers in Jerusalem.[25] Three days later, the General Assembly passed a "Resolution for the Protection of the City of Jerusalem and Its Inhabitants" calling upon "the Trusteeship Council to study, with the Mandatory Power and the interested parties, suitable measures for the protection of the city and its inhabitants, and to submit within the shortest possible time proposals to the General Assembly to that effect." [26]

On May 14, with partition now being a product of warfare, the General Assembly adopted a resolution providing for a U.N. Mediator for Palestine.[27] Count Folke Bernadotte assumed this post May 20.

On September 16, just before he was assassinated, Count Bernadotte submitted a progress report on his work in Palestine.[28] The Mediator reported that "the City of Jerusalem, because of its religious and international significance and the complexity of interests involved, should be accorded special and separate treatment," and that, in view of this, Jerusalem should "be placed under effective United Nations control with maximum feasible local autonomy for its Arab and Jewish communities, with full safeguards for the protection of the Holy Places and sites and free access to them, and for religious freedom."

While Bernadotte was filing his report, Israel was moving toward making the part of Jerusalem under its control an integral part of the new Jewish state. In September the Israeli Supreme Court was established in the New City. A few months later, in February, 1949, the first meeting of the Israeli Knesset (parliament) convened in the New City and in that same month the first president of Israel, Dr. Chaim Weizmann, took his oath of office in Israeli Jerusalem. On January 23, 1950, the Knesset proclaimed Jerusalem (i.e., Israeli-held, or West Jerusalem) the capital of Israel. In the following year virtually all Israeli ministries were moved to West Jerusalem.

East Jerusalem, or that part of the city under military control of the Arab Legion, eventually was absorbed by Trans-Jordan, although the complexities and political machinations of inter-Arab politics delayed any move in this direction until late 1950. Even before the British withdrew from Palestine, it was tacitly understood by London that King Abdullah of Trans-Jordan would bring the Arab state proposed by the partition resolution under his wing.[29] In early 1948 negotiations were held on a new Anglo-Jordanian treaty and this assumption was necessary in order to spell out the precise juridical obligations Great Britain

24. United Nations Security Council, *Official Records* (III), pp. 295 ff.
25. United Nations Doc. S/727, dated April 23, 1948.
26. United Nations Doc. A/543, dated April 26, 1948.
27. United Nations General Assembly Resolution 187 (5-2).
28. United Nations General Assembly Official Records (III) suppl. 11. *Progress Report of the U.N. Mediator on Palestine.*
29. Benjamin Shwadran, *Jordan: A State of Tension* (New York: Council for Middle Eastern Affairs Press, 1959), p. 245.

would assume under a new treaty. To prevent either a Jewish occupation of Arab Palestine, or the rise of the Mufti of Jerusalem, Haj Amin al Husseini, as ruler over the proposed Arab state, Great Britain supported the idea of Arab Legion occupation of those areas contiguous to Trans-Jordan which had been allotted to the Arabs by the partition resolution. The British Foreign Secretary's only admonition in this regard was "do not go and invade the areas allotted to the Jews." [30] Since any discussion of formal annexation of the West Bank area occupied by Jordan during 1948 generated violent protest in other Arab states, King Abdullah moved slowly and cautiously in this direction. The Higher Arab Committee's proclamation of Palestine's independence on October 1, 1948, must be viewed as an attempt to block Trans-Jordanian annexation schemes, as much as a reaffirmation of opposition to the new Israeli state. [31] By the end of 1948, however, it was apparent that neither the rise of Israel as an independent state, nor Abdullah's annexation of the West Bank, could be reversed by the other Arab states.

In fact, the Bernadotte plan, although never adopted, did accord Trans-Jordan some juridical support for annexation by recommending that Arab Palestine be united with Trans-Jordan.[32]

In any case, Abdullah proceeded to alter his juridical position in the West Bank, including East Jerusalem. On October 1, 1948, the same day that the Higher Arab Committee was proclaiming the independence of Palestine from the Gaza Strip,[33] some 5,000 Palestinian notables met in Amman. They repudiated the Gaza proclamation and called on King Abdullah to take the West Bank under his protection. [34]

On December 1, 1948, a second meeting of this "Palestine Congress" was convened in Jericho. At this congress Abdullah was proclaimed "King of Trans-Jordan and All Palestine."[35] The Jericho Congress proclamation was subsequently approved by the Trans-Jordanian government. In April, 1949, Great Britain, with reservations over the future status of Jerusalem, approved the annexation more.[36] Formal annexation of the West Bank region, however, did not take place until December 30, 1949, [37] although military rule over the occupied areas of Arab Palestine included in the annexation scheme was ended March 17, 1949, and civil rule established.

While Abdullah was maneuvering to annex the West Bank, he also signed, on April 3, 1949, a General Armistice Agreement with Israel.[38] Under this armistice agreement, the demarcation line in Jerusalem was set as that defined by the November 30, 1948, cease-fire agreement (Article V 1 (b) of Armistice Agreement).

---

30. *Ibid.,* p. 246.
31. See *supra* n. 13.
32. But Jerusalem would still be given "separate treatment." See above p. 6.
33. See *supra* n. 13.
34. Shwadran, *op. cit.,* p. 280.
35. Esmond Wright, "Abdullah's Jordan: 1947-1951," *Middle East Journal,* V (Autumn, 1951), p. 456; *New York Times,* December 14, 1948.
36. *Ibid.,* p. 457.
37. *New York Times,* December 31, 1949.
38. U.N. Security Council. *Official Records,* special suppl. No. 1. U.N. Doc. S/1302/Rw. 1., dated April 3, 1949. One of the signatories was an Israeli Lt. Colonel by the name of Moshe Dayan.

The armistice also called for "free access to the Holy Places and the use of the cemetery on the Mount of Olives" (Article VIII 2). Under this armistice, it was also agreed (Annex II) that neither side would keep more than two battalions of infantry in the Jerusalem sector and no armored vehicles of any type would be allowed there.

Further Moves to Internationalize Jerusalem

While Jordan and Israel were taking steps to formalize their respective control over East and West Jerusalem, the United Nations continued to discuss the internationalization of the holy city. On December 11, 1948, the General Assembly asked the Palestine Conciliation Commission to present "detailed proposals for a permanent international regime for the Jerusalem area." [39] In the same resolution (194) the General Assembly again affirmed its position that the Holy Places "be under effective United Nations supervision."

The Commission under these instructions established a special Committee on Jerusalem and its Holy Places.[40] The Committee on Jerusalem considered acceptance by Israel and the several Arab states a prerequisite to formulating any proposal for the internationalization of the holy city. The government of Israel, however, "declared itself unable to accept the establishment of an international regime for the city of Jerusalem" but it was prepared to accept "without reservation an international regime for, or the international control of, the Holy Places in the City." [41] Almost all these places were under Jordanian control. Israel apparently was not prepared to give up the New City, but was ready to support an international regime over the Holy Places that were in Jordan.

The several Arab states, excepting Jordan, then reversed their previous opposition to internationalization and indicated to the Commission their support of such a plan. They too were generous in ceding what they did not control. In October, 1949, the Arab League Council even adopted a resolution in favor of internationalization of Jerusalem.[42] In the wake of this shift in Arab policy (again excepting Jordan), coupled with growing world support for internationalization of Jerusalem, Israel and Jordan found themselves strange allies in resisting territorial internationalization. Jordan stood alone in resisting a strictly functional internationalization of the Holy Places.

On September 1, 1949, the Commission approved a new arrangement for Jerusalem.[43] Under this plan Jerusalem would be divided into an Arab and a Jewish zone, each independent except in international matters, which would be under the jurisdiction of the United Nations Commissioner.

The U.N. Commissioner would have authority over the Holy Places, and would supervise the permanent demilitarization of Jerusalem. There would be

---

39. U.N. General Assembly, *Official Records (III)* pt. 2. U.N. Doc. A/810, dated December 11, 1948.

40. U.N. General Assembly, *Official Records (V) Suppl. 18.* U.N. Doc. A/1367/Rw. 1, p. 10.

41. *Loc. cit.*

42. Shwadran, *op. cit.,* p. 286.

43. U.N. General Assembly, *Official Records, Ad Hoc Political Committee Annex,* Vol. I. U.N. Doc. A/973.

a General Council composed of both Arab and Jewish representatives, and a mixed international tribunal to handle cases involving both Jews and Arabs.

In effect, this plan accepted the partition of Jerusalem as a *fait accompli* and restricted itself primarily to the internationalization of the Holy Places. As one writer has noted, this plan, which was submitted to the General Assembly in the fall of 1949, was "pigeonholed without even being accorded the honor of a debate." [44] Instead, the General Assembly passed resolution 303 (IV) charging the Trusteeship Council to revise its earlier Statute for Jerusalem and implement it immediately.[45] The Assembly emphatically instructed the Trusteeship Council not to "allow any actions taken by any interested Government or Governments to divert it from adopting and implementing the Statute of Jerusalem." [46] How this was to be done without coercive power was not indicated in the resolution.

At the same time, the General Assembly again affirmed its intention to establish an international regime for Jerusalem as a *corpus separatum*, rather than in the modified form proposed by the Committee on Jerusalem.

The Trusteeship Council, in response to the Assembly's instructions, convened in special session from December 8 to 20, 1949. It expressed concern that Israel's transfer of governmental ministries to West Jerusalem was "likely to render more difficult the implementation of the Statute" and requested Israel to "revoke the measures which it had taken." [47] Israel, on the contrary, proclaimed West Jerusalem its capital on January 23, 1950. As Prime Minister David Ben-Gurion himself admitted, "our rebuttal (to resolution 303 and the Statute of Jerusalem) . . . was unequivocal and resolute: the Government and Knesset at once moved their seat to Jerusalem." [48] Israel had made it clear from the start that she would resist any plan of territorial internationalization that would involve West Jerusalem, although "willing to accept the principle of direct United Nations responsibility for the Holy Places," which, as noted above, were virtually all in East Jerusalem. Jordan, for its part, "would not discuss any plan for the internationalization of Jerusalem." [49]

Roger Garreau, then President of the Trusteeship Council, sought to reach a compromise solution to the Jerusalem question by broadly interpreting that part of resolution 303 (IV) of December 9, 1949, allowing the Council to modify the Statute for Jerusalem drafted in 1948. Mr. Garreau's plan would have divided Jerusalem into three parts: an Israeli zone "under the authority and administration of the State of Israel"; a Jordanian zone "under the authority and administration of the Hashimite Kingdom of the Jordan"; and an "International City" under the collective sovereignty of the United Nations. Under this plan West Jerusalem would remain under the sovereignty of Israel. The International City would include all the Holy Places covered by the status quo of 1757, meaning,

44. P. De Azcarate, as cited in S. Shepard Jones, "The Status of Jerusalem: Some National and International Aspects," *Law and Contemporary Problems,* XXXIII (Winter, 1968), p. 179.

45. U.N. General Assembly, *Official Records V Suppl 4.* Doc. A/1306, dated December 7, 1949.

46. *Ibid.,* part I 2.

47. U.N. General Assembly, *Official Records, Suppl. 9. Question of an International Regime for the Jerusalem Area and Protection of the Holy Places.* Doc. A/1286, p. 1.

48. *Op. cit.,* p. 362.

49. Doc. A/1286, p. 2.

in effect, the walled city, minus the Haram esh-Sharif. The governor of the International City would exercise authority over Holy Places in any part of Palestine, in addition to governing the international zone.[50]

The plan of the Trusteeship Council's president, as so many others presented earlier, was rejected without further ado.

One year later the General Assembly tabled discussion of the Trusteeship Council's Statute of 1948, as amended, and, instead, took under consideration two draft resolutions. The first, submitted by Belgium, would have had the United Nations, "considering that, for lack of the necessary cooperation by the States concerned, the Trusteeship Council has been unable to give effect to the Statute (of Jerusalem)," set up a study group to investigate "the conditions of a settlement capable of ensuring the effective protection, under the supervision of the United Nations, of the Holy Places and of spiritual and religious interests in the Holy Land." [51] An alternative resolution, sponsored by Sweden, would have established a "United Nations Representative to represent the interests of the United Nations in the Holy City." [52] The Belgian draft resolution did not pass when submitted to a vote of the General Assembly December 15, 1950, while the Swedish Draft resolution never came up for a vote. For the next 17 years, the question of Jerusalem lay dormant, only to erupt again after June, 1967.

---

50. *Ibid.,* pp. 3-4.
51. U.N. Ad Hoc Political Committee Doc. A/AC 38/SR 73, dated December 7, 1950.
52. U.N. Ad Hoc Political Committee Doc. A/AC 38/L 73 Rw. 2, dated December 13, 1950.

IV. THE CONTINUING CRISIS

The *de facto* partition of Jerusalem lasted 19 years. The line of partition, although technically only a cease-fire line, was one solution to a complex political, economic, and sociological problem—it divided two peoples who never did constitute a single community. During the 19 years that Jerusalem was partitioned, the factors which divided these peoples initially became even more pronounced. No common municipal charter could bridge the cultural, economic, and ideological gap between the Israeli of West Jerusalem and the Arab of East Jerusalem.

Earlier this had not been so. For centuries, the Jew could coexist with his Muslim and Christian neighbors in Jerusalem because all three subscribed to the life styles of a single culture.[1] But the West Jerusalem of the twentieth century was made up largely of European Jews, whose culture was totally different from the Jerusalem Jew of yesteryear. The formalism of East Jerusalem culture contrasted sharply with the exaggerated informalism of West Jerusalem culture. In East Jerusalem political, economic, and social relationships were marked by face-to-face relationships that seldom suggested the impersonalism of Western culture. The daily behavior of the Israeli, despite the egalitarianism, by comparison reflected more of the bureaucratic style of the West. Whether it was a matter of selecting a bride or conducting a business transaction, East and West Jerusalem have not been culturally a single community since the Western, or Ashkenazi, Jew made his culture the dominant culture of Israel. The modernized Arab adhered to a version of Western culture that was not shared by the Israeli.

The partition of Jerusalem also reflected the diverse economic orientations of these two communities, West and East Jerusalem. The latter, linked to the agricultural communities of the West Bank, remained a typical Middle Eastern market town. Only that part of the economy associated with servicing the Holy Places distinguished East Jerusalem from dozens of similar market towns in the Middle East.

However, East Jerusalem remained the nexus linking the northern and southern parts of the West Bank. The commercial, communications, and transportation links of these two areas focused on East Jerusalem. In fact, Jerusalem remained

---

1. In fact, the Jew was even closer to the Muslim than was the Christian in that the Jew frequently secluded women, accepted polygamy, etc. Cf. Raphael Patai, *Golden River to Golden Road* (Philadelphia: University of Pennsylvania Press, 1962), *passim*.

at the apex of highways leading north to Ramallah, south to Hebron, and east to Jericho. Thus, East Jerusalem was a vital part of the economic structure of the West Bank, as was the West Bank to the economy of Jordan, itself. East Jerusalem, the district of Nablus, the district of Hebron, and Jordan east of the Jordan River constituted before 1967 an integrated economic unit.

By contrast, West Jerusalem was not in ecological relationship with its hinterland. It became an urban complex located without regard to ordinary economic facts of life. From the functional point of view, West Jerusalem could have been located in Galilee, the Negev, or as a suburb of Haifa. West Jerusalem was an extension of Israel into the Judean Hills, just as Israel had become an extension into the Holy Land of Diaspora Jewry. The administrative offices of the government of Israel, the Hebrew University,[2] or the various administrative branches of world Jewry were located in West Jerusalem by choice, not economic imperative.

Ideologically, the gap between West and East Jerusalem appeared irreconcilable. The Arab of East Jerusalem was precisely that—an Arab. His entire identity was derived from his "Arabism." The *umma al-arabiyyah,* or community of the Arabs, was his national referent. No matter how virulent may have been the character of inter-Arab squabbles, Arab nationalism was the source to which Arabs, whether in Amman, Beirut, or East Jerusalem, had to turn for a "definition of the situation." To the Arab of East Jerusalem, as to Arabs elsewhere, Israel was the expression of Zionism in the Middle East. The aims of Zionism were not compatible with the aims of Arab nationalism. For 19 years the Arab of East Jerusalem lived within the Arab world, not only geographically, but culturally and practically as well.

The Zionist Jew of West Jerusalem, on the other hand, was a part of a political movement that was more than just Israel; it was a movement that was in constant and significant relationship with all of world Jewry. The Jew of West Jerusalem looked westward; the Arab of East Jerusalem looked to the other parts of the Arab world. Ideologically, West and East Jerusalem stood back-to-back. The line of partition did not divide Jerusalem; it only affirmed a division that had characterized the holy city for half a century. It is against this backdrop that the events subsequent to June, 1967, must be viewed.

The Capture of East Jerusalem

Early on the morning of June 5, 1967, full-scale war broke out between Israel and four of her Arab neighbors, Egypt (i.e., the UAR), Jordan, Syria, and Iraq.[3] The Israelis' first move in the conflict was to mount air strikes against 18 Egyptian air bases. Within minutes of the Israeli attack on Egypt, Jordan's jets were attacking Israel. It had been hoped in West Jerusalem that King Hussein would limit his participation in this war to symbolic air and artillery attacks, which

2. The Hebrew University is a case in point. Originally located on Mt. Scopus, the campus was moved to Givat Ram in West Jerusalem following the Arab-Israeli war in 1948. The 12,000 students enrolled at the Hebrew University came from 50 different countries. The Honorary President of the American Friends of the Hebrew University is Arthur J. Goldberg, U.S. delegate to the Security Council when the critical debates on Israeli occupation of East Jerusalem were taking place, 1967-68. The Chairman of the Advisory Board is Senator Jacob K. Javits of New York.

3. Iraqi troops operated from Jordan.

could have been pictured as fulfilling his obligations to Nasser under the terms of the May 30 UAR-Jordan military alliance.[4]

In fact, Israel communicated with King Hussein through Lt. General Odd Bull, head of the U.N. Truce Supervision Organization on the morning the war started, promising not to attack Jordan if that country would stay out of the combat. This Jordan did not do and hostilities began at 10:30 a.m. all along the partition line separating West and East Jerusalem. The point to be stressed here is that Israel appeared prepared to leave East Jerusalem in the hands of Jordan as late as June 6, 1967. It was only *after* the capture of East Jerusalem that the ancient city assumed, retroactively, the status of *terra irredenta* for Israel.

The 1967 battle for Jerusalem lasted almost three days. According to Israeli military sources, the Jordanians fought tenaciously to hold East Jerusalem and Israeli forces succeeded in capturing this area only after suffering comparatively heavy casualties.[5] However, by June 7 East Jerusalem was firmly in the hands of the Israeli army. On that afternoon General Moshe Dayan and other Israeli military leaders passed through St. Stephen's Gate of the walled city and proceeded directly to the Wailing Wall where, as noted earlier, General Dayan and his party stopped to pray.[6]

Before leaving the Wailing Wall, General Dayan made a public statement marking him as the first Israeli leader to reopen the problem of Jerusalem. The General declared:

> The Israeli Defense Forces liberated Jerusalem. We have reunited the torn city, the capital of Israel. We have returned to this most sacred shrine, *never to part from it again.* (Emphasis added.)[7]

The Annexation of the Jordanian Sector

On the day the Jordanian sector of Jerusalem was brought under Israeli military control, Mayor Teddy Kollek of West Jerusalem put forward a plan to extend Israeli municipal services to the captured sector.[8]

On the following day, the Jerusalem Municipal Council (Israel) approved a $5,000,000 Jerusalem Fund for the restoration of the Wailing Wall and other religious sites in the Jordanian sector. Approval was also given by the Council that day for expansion of the Jerusalem Master Plan to include East Jerusalem. The water system of West Jerusalem was connected with that of East Jerusalem, also on June 8. Then quickly the Israelis united the sanitation, telephone, and electrical systems of the two sectors. The municipal bus service (Egged) extended its routes into East Jerusalem, street signs in both Arabic and Hebrew

---

4. Statement by Aluf (Brigadier General) Uzzi Narkis, Commander, Central Command at a press conference, Tel Aviv, June 13, 1967 in *Central Front,* Israeli Defense Force Spokesman's Office, July, 1967, P/R 111A.

5. See particularly the account of the battle for East Jerusalem given by Aluf Mishne (Colonel) Mordechai Gur, Commander of the paratroops that took East Jerusalem in *ibid.,* P/R 102.

6. It is to be noted, however, that this event would have been much less significant had Jordan permitted Israelis access to the Wailing Wall during the previous 19 years.

7. *Facts on File,* XXVII, June 7, 1967.

8. *Jerusalem Post,* June 8, 1967.

were posted, and the barriers once separating East from West Jerusalem were removed. Extensive plans were also prepared during these first few days to modernize the street lighting, to re-pave the roads, and to design future parks for the Jordanian sector.[9]

The pace of political unification was equally swift. On June 15 the Israeli Cabinet was called into session to study a bill that would enable Israel to annex East Jerusalem. On June 27 the Knesset approved a series of enabling laws for the "fusion" of East and West Jerusalem. Under the basic law, the Law and Administration Ordinance (Amendment No. 11) Law of June 27, 1967, the law, jurisdiction, and administration of the State of Israel could be extended to any area designated by the Israeli government by order.[10] On the following day, June 28, 1967, Israeli law and administration was applied to an expanded East Jerusalem that included the walled city, Sur Bahir, Sheikh Harrah, Kalandia Airport, Mount Scopus, and the vicinity of Shufat [11] (see map).

The "unified" Jerusalem then embraced over 100 square kilometers and included a population of at least 260,000, some 70,000 of whom, according to Israel, were Arabs.[12] In 1967 East Jerusalem had a population of 70,000 and the reconstituted Jerusalem encompassed several other Jordanian villages near Jerusalem. Apparently from 20,000 to 30,000 Arabs had left the Jerusalem area for eastern Jordan.

The 70,000 Arabs who remained in East Jerusalem posed an interesting problem for Israel. It was the Israeli Foreign Minister, Abba Eban, who had argued in 1950 that U.N. proposals for internationalizing Jerusalem, if implemented, would deprive 110,000 Jews of their right to belong to Israel and that, therefore, such action on the part of the U.N. would be morally incorrect, politically unwise, and a violation of U.N. principles.[13] This line of argument could also have been applied to the case of the 70,000 Arabs, who by Israeli action were deprived of their freedom to belong to the Arab community.

The actions taken by Israel with regard to East Jerusalem after its early annexation moves suggested that the problems of Arabs in East Jerusalem might only be viewed as a temporary situation by the Jewish state. Within a week after the capture of East Jerusalem by Israel some 100 homes near the Wailing Wall were razed.[14] A month later another 100 homes were destroyed in the same area.[15] Robert C. Toth of the *Washington Post* reported that according to local eyewitnesses several hundred Arab families were ousted from the Jewish Quarter in the early days after the capture of East Jerusalem. He wrote that there were "busses and trucks at the Damascus Gate waiting to take the displaced Arabs

9. U.N. Security Council, *Official Records, Supplement for July, August, and September, 1967.* Doc. S/8146.

10. *Ibid.*

11. *Ibid.*

12. *Ibid.*

13. Delegation of Israel to the United Nations, *Memorandum on the Question of Jerusalem Submitted to the Trusteeship Council of the United Nations,* Seventh Session, Lake Success, May, 1950.

14. *New York Times,* June 19, 1967.

15. *New Outlook* (Israel) September, 1968, p. 39.

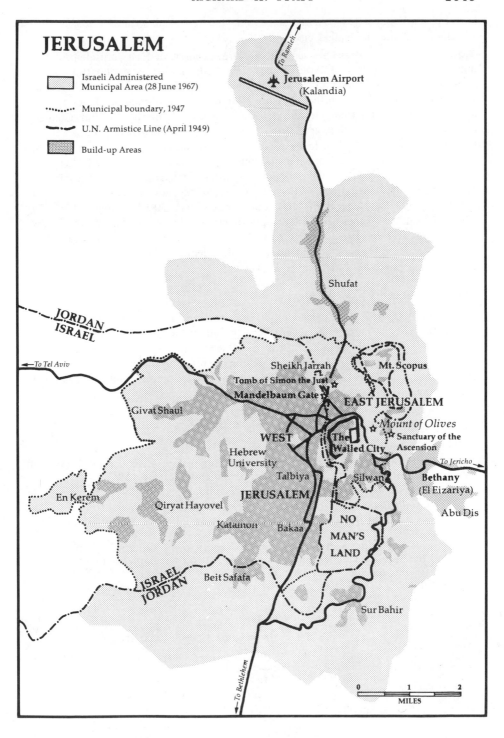

JERUSALEM

Israeli Administered
Municipal Area (28 June 1967)

Municipal boundary, 1947

U.N. Armistice Line (April 1949)

Build-up Areas

To Ramleh

✈ Jerusalem Airport
(Kalandia)

Shufat

JORDAN
ISRAEL

To Tel Aviv

Sheikh Jarrah
Tomb of Simon the Just
Mandelbaum Gate

Mt. Scopus

EAST JERUSALEM

Givat Shaul

WEST

Hebrew
University

Talbiya

The
Walled City

Mount of Olives
☆ Sanctuary of the
Ascension

To Jericho

Silwan

Bethany
(El Eizariya)

En Kerem

JERUSALEM

Qiryat Hayovel

Abu Dis

Katamon

Bakaa

NO
MAN'S
LAND

ISRAEL
JORDAN

Beit Safafa

Sur Bahir

To Bethlehem

0   1   2
MILES

to Jericho and beyond."[16] At the same time the *Jerusalem Post* was urging that Israelis move into the walled city.[17]

Since June, 1967, Israel has sequestered large sections of East Jerusalem, dynamited and razed scores of Arab homes, and "encouraged" the departure from Jerusalem of their inhabitants.[18] On November 23, 1967, the Israeli National Police confiscated the unfinished Muslim hospital on the Mount of Olives to use as their new headquarters, despite vigorous protests from the Muslim Council of East Jerusalem.[19] In January, 1968, the Israeli government expropriated some 838 acres of East Jerusalem to be used for Jewish settlers.[20] And in June, 1968, the expropriation by Israel of land and buildings within the walled city between the Haram esh-Sherif and the Armenian quarter, including part of the site of al-Buraq, resulted in a strong letter of protest by the government of Jordan to the U.N. Secretary-General. In this action, more than 700 buildings, about 50 acres of land, 437 shops, and 1,048 apartments housing more than 5,000 Arabs were taken over by Israel.[21] The Arabs of East Jerusalem were seriously disturbed that Israel might intend to alter the demographic character of East Jerusalem to make all Jerusalem a Jewish city.

Annexation—The U.N. Response

On June 13, 1967, the Soviet Union requested, under the provisions of Article 11 of the U.N. Charter, an emergency special session of the U.N. General Assembly to debate the Middle East crisis. Once again the question of Jerusalem was to come before the community of nations. This time the debate on the holy city was initiated by the USSR, the bastion of atheism and international communism.

The General Assembly convened on June 17, 1967, and, after extensive debate, approved resolution 2253 (ES-V) on July 4:

> The General Assembly
> *Deeply Concerned* at the situation prevailing in Jerusalem as a result of the measures taken by Israel to change the status of the City,
> 1. *Considers* that these measures are invalid;
> 2. *Calls upon* Israel to rescind all measures already taken and to desist forthwith from taking any action which would alter the status of Jerusalem;
> 3. *Requests* the Secretary-General to report to the General Assembly and the Security Council on the situation and on the implementation of the present resolution not later than one week from its adoption.[22]

16. *Washington Post,* June 20, 1967.
17. *Jerusalem Post,* June 19, 1967. See also the August 1, 1967, issue of this newspaper, wherein former Israeli prime minister Ben-Gurion argued that all of Jerusalem rehabilitate and settle as quickly as possible, with the resettling of 20,000 Jewish families in East Jerusalem, and the *New York Times* of June 18 and July 3, 1968, for a report on "settlement" plans to populate East Jerusalem with Israeli families.
18. See *New York Times,* January 16, 1968; March 8, 1968; September 19, 1968; *New Outlook II* (Israel) March-April, 1968; September, 1968.
19. *New York Times,* November 24, 1967.
20. *Ibid.,* January 16, 1968.
21. U.N. Doc. A/7107 (S/8634).
22. U.N. General Assembly, *Official Records, 5th Emer. Spec. Sess., Suppl. 1,* p. 4.

This resolution was adopted by a vote of 99 to 0 with 20 abstentions (including the United States).

Ten days later the General Assembly, "taking note with the deepest regret and concern of the non-compliance by Israel with resolution 2253," reiterated its call to Israel "to rescind all measures already taken and to desist forthwith from taking any action which would alter the status of Jerusalem." (Resolution 2254 (ES-V)).

These two resolutions (2253 and 2254) of the General Assembly reflected a widespread sentiment within the United Nations: territorial aggrandizement cannot be the product of conquest by force. Secretary-General U Thant, in discussing the operations of the United Nations during the period 1966-67, stated it this way:

> It is indispensable to an international community of states—if it is not to follow the law of the jungle—that the territorial integrity of every state be respected and the occupation of one state cannot be condoned.[23]

The territorial integrity of the State of Israel was recognized by the the United Nations when it became a member of that international organization. At the same time, the State of Israel accepted the territorial integrity of the other member states of the U.N. If the United Nations were to grant juridical validity to Israeli annexation of any Arab land, this would violate its charter.

The resolutions invalidating Israeli annexation of East Jerusalem evolved out of earlier proposals that Israel withdraw from *all* occupied areas. On June 28, 1967, a 17-power draft resolution was submitted by Yugoslavia calling upon Israel immediately to withdraw its forces behind the armistice lines established by the General Armistice Agreements.[24] This draft resolution, while it received a majority, failed to obtain the requisite two-thirds majority. In addition to Yugoslavia, this draft resolution was co-sponsored by Indonesia, Cambodia, Malaysia, India, Pakistan, Ceylon, Afghanistan, Cyprus, Somalia, Tanzania, Zambia, Congo (Brazzaville), Burundi, Mali, Guinea, and Senegal. These states, ranging from southeast Asia to West Africa, made up a significant part of the underdeveloped world, the so-called Third World.

Two days later, June 30, another draft resolution was submitted, this time by 20 other members of the Third World.[25] Formally presented by Trinidad and Tobago, the draft resolution was co-sponsored by Argentina, Barbados, Bolivia, Brazil, Chile, Colombia, Costa Rica, The Dominican Republic, Ecuador, El Salvador, Guatemala, Guyana, Honduras, Jamaica, Mexico, Nicaragua, Panama, Paraguay, and Venezuela—in brief, virtually all of Latin America. This draft resolution called upon Israel to "withdraw all its forces from all the territories occupied by it as a result of the recent conflict." This proposal, while it received a majority, also failed for lack of the requisite two-thirds majority.

If one combines the 37 states supporting these two resolutions, together with

---

23. U.N. General Assembly, *Official Records, Introduction to the Annual Report of the Secretary-General on the Work of the Organization*, June 16, 1966-June 15, 1967. Doc. A/6701/Add. 1, p. 6.
24. U.N. General Assembly, *Official Records, Suppl. 1, Annual Report of the Secretary-General on the Work of the Organization*, June 16, 1967-June 15, 1968. Doc. A/7201, p. 5.
25. *Loc. cit.*

the 14 Arab states, it becomes clear that the countries of the Third World are opposed to Israeli occupation of Arab territory. In terms of the Israeli occupation of East Jerusalem, the sentiment of the community of nations extended even beyond the Third World, because as noted above, resolution 2253 (ES-V) was adopted without dissenting vote.[26]

Even before the General Assembly convened its emergency special session, the Security Council had acted on the matter of Israeli occupation of Arab territory. On June 14, 1967, resolution 237 was adopted calling upon Israel to give scrupulous respect to the provisions of the Geneva Conventions of August 12, 1949, relative to the treatment of civilian persons in occupied areas. Although rejected by Israel, this resolution was "welcomed with great satisfaction by the General Assembly" (Resolution 2252 (ES-V), July 4, 1967).[27]

The Gussing Report

Under the provisions of the Security Council resolution, Mr. Nils-Göran Gussing was appointed on July 6 the Secretary-General's Special Representative in the Middle East. A few weeks later U Thant appointed Mr. Ernesto A. Thalmann of Switzerland as his Personal Representative in Jerusalem under the provisions of the General Assembly's resolutions 2253 and 2254. While Mr. Gussing did not include Jerusalem in his own report because of Mr. Thalmann's assignment, two aspects of the Gussing report bear upon the Jerusalem question.

First, the Special Representative noted that various kinds of pressure were exerted by Israel to get Arabs to leave their villages on the West Bank for unoccupied Jordan. While there was no evidence that physical force was used, in the words of the report, "there are persistent reports of acts of intimidation by Israel armed forces and of Israel attempts to suggest to the population, by loudspeakers mounted on cars, that they might be better off on the east bank." Moreover, continued the report, "there have also been reports that in several localities buses and trucks were put at the disposal of the population for travel to the east bank." [28]

Second, there was widespread destruction of homes in occupied Jordan. Much of this, of course, was the result of the war itself. However, a number of homes in several West Bank villages were destroyed by dynamite subsequent to the cease-fire. According to Israeli sources, the homes were destroyed by dynamite in the village of Qalqilya either because of "safety" or "sanitary" reasons. In the Latrun area the Israeli Minister of Defense told Gussing that the villages of Imwas, Yalu, and Beit Nuba were destroyed by dynamiting "for strategic and

---

26. Israel did not vote on this resolution on the grounds that the issue of Jerusalem was "outside the legal competence of the General Assembly," New York Times, July 5, 1967.

27. U.N. Security Council, Official Records, Supplement for October, November, and December, 1967, Doc. 3/8158, p. 81. Israel is also bound as a U.N. member by the obligations imposed under U.N. General Assembly resolutions 95(I) of December 11, 1946 which accepted as binding on the United Nations the Charter of Nuremburg, Article 6B of which proscribes looting and seizure of public property. See also U.N. General Assembly resolution 177(II) of November 21, 1947 and the Report of the International Law Commission to the General Assembly, dated December 12, 1950.

28. Ibid., p. 92.

security reasons." In the Hebron area several Arab villages were similarly destroyed or damaged by dynamite.[29]

Israel followed similar procedures in Jerusalem. The Gussing report thus is of value here in giving emphasis to a pattern of occupation administration that both alarmed the Arab with respect to the holy city and stiffened his resistance to making lasting peace with the Jewish state. The annexation of Jerusalem and the occupation policy of Israel in other Arab territories were perceived together by the Arab as evidence of Israeli expansionism. Israeli political leaders have on occasion advocated expansion of Israeli territory as a national goal.[30]

Thus, for example, in April, 1969, the former Israeli prime minister and one of that state's founding fathers, David Ben-Gurion, presented his formula for Arab-Israeli peace in an interview with Eric Rouleau of the French paper *Le Monde*.[31] He first said that "in exchange for peace . . . I would return all the territory conquered in June 1967." When asked if this would include East Jerusalem, Ben-Gurion answered, "certainly not." Moreover, he added, "after my recent visit to the region, I realize that we will also be obliged to keep the Golan Heights for strict security reasons."

The Thalmann Report

The report submitted by Ambassador Thalmann on East Jerusalem noted the changing landscape.[32] "To the destruction of the war" commented the Personal Representative, "new destruction had been added." Bulldozers had cleared the walls which had separated the firing lines, as well as many houses in the area of the former no man's land. Also in "the walled city one could see the debris of levelled houses." This destruction of homes within the walled city included the dynamiting and bulldozing of some 135 homes in the Maghrebi quarter and two mosques.[33] After noting the juridical and technical steps taken by Israel to "unify" East Jerusalem with West Jerusalem, Ambassador Thalmann records that:

> From the cultural standpoint, the fear was expressed that the Arab way of life, Arab traditions and the Arabic language would suffer permanent damage under the influence of the Israel majority. It was also pointed out in this connection that . . . the Israel community . . . might have an adverse effect on strict Arab morals.[34]

---

29. *Ibid.,* pp. 93-96.

30. In October, 1967, Israel renamed the occupied Nablus District of Jordan "Shomron" (Samaria) and the Hebron District "Yehuda" (Judea). See *Jerusalem Post*, October 2, 1967. On February 29, 1968, Israel issued a decree to the effect that occupied Arab territories were no longer to be regarded as "enemy territory." The decree established customs and civilian control points for official entry or exit from "Israel." Reference might also be given here to the rather broad guidelines used by Israeli authorities in expelling the political leadership of the Arab community from the occupied territories on the charge that they are guilty of "inciting subversion." See here *New York Times*, August 1, 1967; and on Israel, refusal to allow U.N. investigation of occupied areas in 1968, see U.N. Doc. S/8699, dated June 27, 1968.

31. *Le Monde, Weekly Selection*, April 23, 1969, p. 4.

32. U.N. Security Council, *Official Records, Supplement for July, August, and September, 1967*. Doc. S/8146.

33. *Ibid.,* p. 250.

34. *Ibid.,* p. 252.

Also, Ambassador Thalmann said, Muslims were shocked when the "Chief Rabbi of the Israeli Army, with others of his faith, conducted prayers in the area of the Haram esh-Sharif." [35] Muslim sensitivity to the treatment of their holy sites was also registered in their complaint to the Personal Representative that Israel was allowing visitors, "men and women, to enter the al-Aqsa Mosque while unsuitably dressed and in a manner which is inconsistent with religious belief and Arab and Islamic traditions." [36]

The Thalmann report also noted that East Jerusalem, as reconstituted within the expanded municipal area of unified Jerusalem, included almost 130,000 Arabs, all of whom are currently governed by a Municipal Council, "which is composed of twenty-one members all Israelis." [37]

Events of 1968 and 1969 confirmed the Thalmann report. The dynamiting and the bulldozing continued; further legal and administrative steps were taken to integrate East Jerusalem into the Jewish state; the Israelis continued to state "unequivocally that the process of integration [is] irreversible and not negotiable"; [38] and the differences between Israeli and Arab remained implacable. As the Israeli mayor of Jerusalem, Teddy Kollek, complained, in February, 1968, efforts to integrate the two sectors of Jerusalem "had been a total failure" because Israel had failed to recognize the cultural and psychological patterns of the Arabs and that the Israeli government ". . . cannot automatically impose on [the Arabs] the approach and procedures used in Tel Aviv." [39]

Israeli Foreign Minister Abba Eban continued to suggest that "where there has been hostile separation there is now harmonious union" and "where there has been constant threat of violence there is now civic peace." [40] But growing Arab resistance to Israeli occupation expressed in individual and group attacks on Israeli civilian and military targets (including a bomb explosion in a crowded Israeli market in Jerusalem on November 22, 1968) was difficult to reconcile with this claim.[41]

Security Council Resolution 242 (1967)

Although Israel moved rapidly to unify Jerusalem and refused to acknowledge the General Assembly's resolutions on the holy city, the United Nations has continued to express itself on the subject of Israeli occupation of any part of the Arab territories. On July 14, 1967, the United States refused to accept or recognize the steps taken by Israel on June 28 to alter the status of Jerusalem

35. *Ibid.,* p. 250.
36. *Ibid.,* p. 267.
37. *Ibid.,* p. 237.
38. *Ibid.,* p. 238.
39. As cited in *Facts on File,* XXVIII, p. 99.
40. Israeli Information Services, *Text of Mr. Eban's Letter to the U.N. Secretary-General on the holding of a parade in Jerusalem . . . ,* dated May 1, 1968.
41. *New York Times,* November 23, 1968. Some examples of Arab resistance would include the general strike in East Jerusalem protesting Israeli occupation (August, 1967), an East Jerusalem school strike (September, 1967), Arab riots protesting the first anniversary of the Israeli annexation move (June, 1968), a strike by shopkeepers in East Jerusalem (August, 1968), bomb explosions and riots in Jerusalem (August, 1968), a hunger strike by the Arab women of East Jerusalem protesting the Israeli annexation (January, 1969), a bombing incident in a Jerusalem bus station (February, 1969), and a bomb explosion in a Jerusalem cafeteria (March, 1969).

and took the position "that the measures taken cannot be considered as other than interim and provisional, and not as prejudicing the final and permanent status of Jerusalem." [42]

In accordance with this sentiment the United States, on November 7, 1967, submitted a draft resolution in the Security Council, Article 1 of which included as one provision of a "just and lasting peace in the Middle East" the "withdrawal of armed forces from occupied territories." Since the American draft resolution related this condition to the commitment of member states "to act in accordance with Article 2 of the Charter," it must be assumed that "occupied territories" included East Jerusalem. [43]

At that same meeting, India also submitted a draft resolution, co-sponsored by Mali and Nigeria, calling for Israeli withdrawal from the occupied territories. The Indian resolution was cast in stronger language than the American proposal. [44]

Neither the American nor the Indian resolution was accepted. Instead, on November 22, 1967, the Security Council accepted a draft resolution submitted by the British representative to the Council, Lord Caradon. This resolution 242 (1967) was adopted unanimously by the Council. In view of the fact that the vast majority of members in the General Assembly not represented on the Security Council had favored even stronger resolutions, resolution 242 (1967) constitutes the near unanimous position of the international community on the Arab-Israeli problem. The resolution, in full, reads as follows:

> *The Security Council,*
>
> *Expressing* its continuing concern with the grave situation in the Middle East,
>
> *Emphasizing* the inadmissibility of the acquisition of territory by war and the need to work for a just and lasting peace in which every State in the area can live in security,
>
> *Emphasizing further* that all Member States in their acceptance of the Charter of the United Nations have undertaken a commitment to act in accordance with Article 2 of the Charter.
>
> 1. *Affirms* that the fulfillment of Charter principles requires the establishment of a just and lasting peace in the Middle East which should include the application of both the following principles:
>
> (i) Withdrawal of Israel armed forces from territories occupied in the recent conflict;
>
> (ii) Termination of all claims or states of belligerency and respect for and acknowledgement of the sovereignty, territorial integrity and political independence of every State in the area and their right to live in peace within secure and recognized boundaries free from threats or acts of force;
>
> 2. *Affirms further* the necessity
>
> (a) For guaranteeing freedom of navigation through international waterways in the area;
>
> (b) For achieving a just settlement of the refugee problem;

---

42. U.N. Doc. A/PV. 1554, dated July 14, 1967.
43. See *supra,* note 9, Doc. S/8229.
44. U.N. General Assembly, *Official Records, 23rd Session, Suppl. 2,* p. 19, Doc. A/7202.

(c) For guaranteeing the territorial inviolability and political independence of every State in the area, through measures including the establishment of demilitarized zones;

3. *Requests* the Secretary-General to designate a Special Representative to proceed to the Middle East to establish and maintain contacts with the States concerned in order to promote agreement and assist efforts to achieve a peaceful and accepted settlement in accordance with the provisions and principles in this resolution;

4. *Requests* the Secretary-General to report to the Security Council on the progress of the efforts of the Special Representative as soon as possible.[45]

The day after this resolution was adopted, Secretary-General U Thant dispatched Dr. Gunnar Jarring of Sweden to the Middle East as the U.N.'s Special Envoy. Further Security Council resolutions,[46] as well as Dr. Jarring's peripatetic diplomacy, however, produced little result up to 1969.

On May 2, 1968, Israel held a military parade in the holy city.[47] For a number of years both Israel and Jordan had conducted military parades in their respective sectors, although such parades violated Article VII of the Jordanian-Israeli General Armistice Agreement of April 3, 1949. This time, however, Israel paraded her forces through the Arab, as well as through her own sector. Israel explained its decision to route this parade into the Jordanian sector with three points: (1) Jerusalem had become a unified city, (2) The General Armistice Agreement "was finally destroyed by Jordan on June 5, 1967," and (3) within the cease-fire area established after the June, 1967, war, the Israelis "are free to move, to act and to parade as they see fit." [48] Therefore the parade was held as planned, in the face of a specific request made by the Security Council of the United Nations in April, 1968, that Israel not route any military parade through the Arab sector of Jerusalem.[49]

The United Nations has been demonstrably unable to induce Israel to halt her annexation of East Jerusalem.

The United Nations' failure in this respect was ascribed by some observers to the absence of wholehearted support by the United States. In fact, Washington's policies toward Jerusalem was viewed by some critics as incompatible with its sponsorship of the principle of military withdrawal contained in the November, 1967, United Nations Resolution and as lacking sincerity and consistency.

---

45. See *supra,* note 6, Doc. S/8247.

46. Particularly U.N. Security Council resolution 252 (1968) of May 21, 1968, which "deplores the failure of Israel to comply" with G.A. resolutions 2253 (ES-V) and 2254 (ES-V) of July, 1967, Council resolution 258 (1968) of September 18, 1968, which "reaffirms" the position of the Council as expressed in resolution 242 (1967) of November 22, 1967, and Council resolution 259 (1968) of September 28, 1968, which "deplores the delay in the implementation" of resolution 237 (1967) of June 14, 1967, which called upon Israel to ensure the safety, welfare, and security of the inhabitants of the occupied areas. Resolution 252 (1968) was submitted by Pakistan and Senegal. The only two countries opposed to the resolution were Canada and the United States. *Cahiers de l'Orient Contemporain,* LXXII (October, 1968), p. 43.

47. *New York Times,* May 3, 1968.

48. Yosef Tekoah (Israeli Ambassador to the United Nations), *Barbed Wire Shall Not Return to Jerusalem* (N.Y.: Israel Information Services, n.d.), p. 42.

49. *New York Times,* April 28, 1968.

Care of the Holy Places

The Israelis have complained that Jewish cemeteries in East Jerusalem were desecrated, torn up, or destroyed. The Arabs, both Christians and Muslims, counter that the Holy Places at Ein Karim and the cemetery of Mamillah were subjected to similar desecration at the hands of the Israelis.

The Israelis also complain that they were denied access to the Wailing Wall for 19 years. While this grievance is based on fact and cannot be dismissed in considering alternatives for solution, it should be pointed out that the Wailing Wall was a casualty of a chain of events which began with the proclamation of the State of Israel and culminated, via the subsequent Arab-Jewish war of 1948, in the division of the city of Jerusalem, a division to which both parties have contributed through their military actions and their refusal to accept internationalization. On the other hand, under the post-1967 conditions, Muslim Arabs from the several Arab states have been denied access to their principal holy place, the Harem est-Sherif, which had been open to their pilgrimage and worship under Jordanian sovereignty. Similarly, with the present occupation of Jerusalem by Israel, Christian Arabs from most of the Arab countries have lost access to the Holy Sepulchure and other Christian shrines.

The Israelis contended that a slum area was permitted to grow adjacent to the Wailing Wall. The Arabs argued that the inhabitants of this area were Arab refugees from the Israeli section of Palestine and that, in any case, ousting poor Arab families and razing their homes would have been a dubious application of slum clearance.

The Israelis said that they would repair, restore, and maintain the Holy Places of all three faiths, as they did with the Wailing Wall. The Christian Arab, however, complained that reports of smoking, loud talk, improper dress, and dogs in the Church of the Holy Sepulchre were not compatible with the sacred character of this site; and the Muslim Arab complained that mini-skirts, embraces between the sexes, and holding a fashion show against the background of al-Aqsa Mosque were not in keeping with the character of their Holy Place.

Muslims safeguarded and respected the Holy Places of Christianity in Palestine for centuries without complaint. The controversy over the custodianship of the Holy Places centered, then, on the conflicting claims made by Israelis and Muslim Arabs on behalf of their respective religious supporters. As for the Christian community, one may note two alternate positions relative to the Holy Places.

The first position was that emanating from the Vatican: Jerusalem should be internationalized.[50] Since June 7, 1967, the Pope has continued to press for internationalization of the holy city. On June 26, 1967, Pope Paul contended "the holy city of Jerusalem must always remain that which it represents—the city of God, a free oasis of peace and prayer, a place of encounter, of elevation, of accord for all, with its own international status guaranteed." [51] In brief, the

50. The Vatican's position has been consistent since 1948, particularly as outlined in the encyclical letter (*In Multiplicibus*) of October 23 of that year. See *New York Times,* January 20, 1949.
51. As quoted in *Facts on File,* XXVII, June 29, 1967. See also the Pope's proposal for internationalizing Jerusalem, *New York Times,* June 19, 1967.

Vatican would like to see Jerusalem established as a *corpus separatum*, as originally envisaged under the 1947 U.N. partition resolution.

The second position was that advanced by the National Council of Churches. The Executive Committee of that organization adopted a resolution on July 7, 1967, which read, in part,

> We support the establishment of an international presence in the hitherto divided city of Jerusalem which will preserve the peace and integrity of the city, foster the welfare of its inhabitants, and protect its holy shrines with full rights of access to all. We encourage the earliest possible advancement of U.N. proposals to make such arrangement practicable.
>
> We cannot approve Israel's unilateral annexation of the Jordanian portions of Jerusalem. This historic city is sacred not only to Judaism but also to Christianity and Islam.[52]

Islamic conferences, whether held in Kuala Lumpur (Malaysia), Amman, or Mecca all voiced strong objections to the present status of East Jerusalem. The tone of the resolution on Jerusalem adopted by the World Muslim League at its October, 1967, meeting in Mecca was indicative of this attitude:

> The Muslims must realize that the problem of Jerusalem and the territory usurped in Palestine is a general Islamic problem, and a sacred problem, and that struggle (jihad) in the cause of God for the liberation of al-Masjid al-Aqsa and the occupied lands from the grasp of the aggressors is a sacred duty imposed upon all the Muslims, and not merely upon any one Muslim people.
>
> . . . no solution or settlement will be acceptable if it does not involve the restoration of Jerusalem to its previous status.[53]

The Muslims called for a return of East Jerusalem and the Holy Places located therein to Jordan; the National Council of Churches called for the return of East Jerusalem to Jordan and the establishment of an "international presence" in the holy city to "protect the holy shrines"; the Roman Catholic Church called for the internationalization of all Jerusalem. Most of the Jewish community around the world supported the proposition that Israel should be the custodian of the Holy Places of both Christianity and Islam.

But It's My House!

One theme recurrent in this study is that the inhabitants of Arab Jerusalem subscribe to a culture markedly different from that of West Jerusalem. This was apparent to casual visitors to the holy city. The culture of the Israelis reflected greater technological sophistication, organizational capacity, and know-how than the prevailing culture of the Arabs, Christian or Muslim. The culture of Arab

---

52. Although adopted July 7, 1967, and issued to the press, the resolution was not published in any newspaper within the greater New York area until it appeared one year later in the *New York Times,* January 14, 1968.

53. As quoted in *Islamic Review and Arab Affairs* (January, 1968), p. 11.

Jerusalem was not the culture of the Organization Man; it was the culture of a society steeped in tradition, spiritual in character.[54]

The impact of this Arab culture on East Jerusalem has been marked. East Jerusalem has been a city of open hospitality, rosary beads, and tranquility. The calls of the muezzin from the minaret of the Muslim mosque and the bells ringing out from the Christian church are constant reminders that East Jerusalem is a place of prayer. The social behavior of the East Jerusalem Arab expresses the timelessness of his culture, the depth of his religious feelings. Living conditions in East Jerusalem are almost Biblical; the life-style creates an atmosphere appropriate to the sacred character of the surrounding Holy Places.

All this was changing in 1969. Certain Arabs of East Jerusalem appeared to be better off in a material sense than they were two years before. Before 1967 East Jerusalem received water only three days a week; in 1969 fresh water was available daily.[55] The electrical system of the Jordanian sector was also being modernized and its capacity increased.[56] In short, the city was being modernized. To the Arab of East Jerusalem, however, this modernization was a shock. It meant not only better municipal services, health facilities, and public schools; it also meant neon lights, cabarets, Western music, and the end of a life-style he cherished.[57]

The development of East Jerusalem from 1967 to 1969 thus reflected a subordination of Arab culture to Israeli culture. The Arabs feared that this cultural interaction would lead to a decay in their moral standards. And after economic conditions in East Jerusalem were improved under Israeli tutelage,[58] the Arabs feared that they would be forced out. The Peel Report figuratively expressed the 1969 Arab attitude some 30 years earlier:

> You say we are better off: you say my house has been enriched by the strangers who have entered it. But it is *my* house, and I did not invite the strangers in, or ask them to enrich it, and I do not care how poor or bare it is if only I am master in it.[59]

54. A recent description of the contrast between West and East Jerusalem is presented in Ada L. Hustable's article "Jerusalem: Vista of Two Worlds," *New York Times,* May 12, 1969.

55. Israeli water lines were connected to the lines of East Jerusalem almost immediately after the sector was captured.

56. Suggestive of the pre-modern conditions prevailing in East Jerusalem prior to June, 1967 is the fact that the electrical plant capacity for this sector of the holy city was 3,000 KW. An American city of comparable size, Boulder, Colorado, has an electrical plant capacity of 120,000 KW.

57. One of the many examples of this culture change is the "modernization" of the 130-year-old Turkish Khan (rest house) located just outside the walled city. This old site was taken over by the Corporation for the Development of Eastern Jerusalem and made into a theater-cabaret, with most of the financing provided by Henry Gestetner of London. The site was formerly owned by the Greek Orthodox Church, *Jerusalem Post,* October 27, 1967.

58. It should be noted here, however, that the Arabs of East Jerusalem were enjoying a rate of economic growth even greater than Israel prior to June, 1967. Per capita agricultural production in Jordan, for example, reached an index of 193 (1957-59 = 100) just before the war, compared to only 146 for Israel. The overall rate of growth for Israel between 1958 and 1966 averaged 9.3 percent annually, while for Jordan it was almost 9.7 percent. Moreover, Israel has been the recipient since 1948 of almost $5,000,000,000 in outside financing, while capital inflow into Jordan was much more modest during this same period. George Lenczowski, ed., *United States Interests in the Middle East* (Washington: American Enterprise Institute, 1968), pp. 64 and 73.

59. Cmd. 5479 *Palestine Royal Commission Report,* July, 1937 (London: H.M.S.O., 1937), p. 131.

Others claim that, in time, no one will want to see Jerusalem divided again. Israeli Foreign Minister Abba Eban, in a press conference given September 6, 1967, mused:

> I think as more and more people come to compare the present unity of Jerusalem with its previous division, they will become convinced that the new unity is preferable to the old devision.[60]

These people, however, were not a majority in the United Nations, in the world Muslim community, or in the Christian churches, for they had resolved otherwise. The Arabs of East Jerusalem repeatedly protested the Israeli annexation of their sector and continued to resist this action.[61]

Former President Johnson remarked in a speech delivered on September 10, 1968, that "no one wishes to see the holy city again divided by barbed wire and by machine guns." [62] While the military methods of safeguarding the division might appear out of tune with the sacred character of the city, the principle of division itself has not been rejected as unanimously as Mr. Johnson tried to affirm. Invariably, that part of the population which is coerced by military means into subjection to an alien power would prefer the division to an enforced unity. This would seem to hold true of the Arab position in the post-1967 period; and it would undoubtedly apply to Israeli attitudes had the roles of victory and vanquished been reversed.

As a matter of historical record, it may be pointed out that Jerusalem is not the only place where division has been favored by the parties directly concerned over a wrong kind of unity. The United States and other Western powers have preferred partition of Germany, Korea, and Vietnam to their unification under Communist auspices. By the same token, for a quarter of a century Berlin has been a divided city; the Berlin airlift of 1948 proved the American determination to maintain the divided status quo rather than to accept unification under Soviet control.

Four-Power Talks

The question of Jerusalem is inextricably interwoven with the other issues of the Arab-Israeli conflict. This conflict has been a central feature of international relations for decades. Three times since Israel came into being full-scale war between the Jewish state and her Arab neighbors has taken place. Moreover, since June, 1967, there have been repeated violations of the cease-fire agreement by both sides; and the prospects for peace appeared less likely than a "fourth round" between Israel and the Arab states.

60. Consulate General of the State of Israel, Los Angeles, California, *Foreign Minister Abba Eban's Press Conference of September 6, 1967,* typescript, p. 16.
61. In August, 1967, Arabs staged a general strike in protest of Israeli occupation *(New York Times,* August 8, 1967); in September, 1967, there was a school strike in East Jerusalem *(New York Times,* September 19, 1967); in January of 1968 Arab women went on a hunger strike protesting Israeli annexation of East Jerusalem *(New York Times,* January 28, 1968); in November, 1968, Arab merchants in East Jerusalem went on strike protesting Israeli seizure of Arab shops *(New York Times,* November 24, 1968), and throughout 1968 and 1969 Arabs resorted to intermittent violence to underscore their hostility to Israeli occupation of East Jerusalem.
62. For the text of this speech see Lenczowski, *op. cit.,* pp. 122-26.

Both the Arab states and Israel agree that the Security Council resolution of November 22, 1967, formed the basis for an eventual peace treaty. The Israelis insisted, however, that the implementation of this resolution and the establishment of a just and lasting peace be the product of direct negotiations between the Jewish state and the Arab states.[63] Pending such direct negotiations, the Israelis were not prepared to withdraw from the occupied territories. As the late Israeli premier, Levi Eshkol, put it "our reply [to the Arabs] is that we are here." [64] The Arabs in turn, insisted that Israel first withdraw from the occupied territories before further moves toward peace could take place. Although the basis of a peace treaty existed in the form of the November 22, 1967, resolution, dispute over the procedure for implementing this resolution brought about a stalemate; a stalemate fraught with danger, not only for the parties to the dispute, but for the Great Powers too.

It was this recognition that the Arab-Israeli dispute could be a tinderbox for a more widespread conflagration which led the United States, France, Great Britain, and the Soviet Union in early 1969 to begin negotiations among themselves on the Arab-Israeli dispute. The talks were not designed to obviate Dr. Jarring's efforts to bring peace in the Middle East, but only to strengthen his hand by providing a framework within the context of which the Security Council resolution might be implemented.[65] Even before the talks began, Israel rejected this approach to reaching peace in the Middle East on the grounds that anything the Soviet Union and France agreed to would be "inimical to Israel's vital interests." [66]

Despite this, the talks between the four Great Powers opened on April 2, 1969. While the details of these talks are outside the scope of this study, certain developments concerning the city of Jerusalem are worth mentioning: At the beginning of the talks it was reported that the United States "indicated support for continued unification of the city, but with a statute providing Jordan with religious, economic and civic interests." [67] The American position, according to Ambassador Charles W. Yost, United States delegate to these talks, was that Israel should withdraw "to secure and recognized boundaries in the context of a peace settlement achieved by negotiation," with the implication that such "secure and recognized boundaries" need not be those existing prior to June 5, 1967.[68]

The general position of the United States toward the Arab-Israeli conflict has been stated on several occasions since 1967. On May 23, 1967, former President Johnson declared that "the United States is firmly committed to the support of the

---

63. On September 18, 1967, Israel rejected "foreign guarantees" of her security and reiterated her position that peace could only come about through direct negotiations with the Arab states. *Washington Post,* September 9, 1967. Israel has held to this demand for direct negotiations ever since.

64. *New York Times,* September 7, 1967.

65. *Ibid.,* April 1, 1969.

66. *Ibid.,* April 4, 1969, citing Yosef Tekoah, Israeli Ambassador to the United Nations. See also *New York Times,* April 1, 1969.

67. *New York Times,* April 3, 1969.

68. *Ibid.,* May 7, 1967.

political independence and territorial integrity of all nations of [the Middle East]." [69] The former President affirmed this position on June 19, 1967 (after the six-day war had ended) by saying "the crisis underlines the importance of respect for political independence and territorial integrity of all the states of the area." [70]

The American position in this regard was reaffirmed again on November 22, 1967, when the United States supported the Security Council resolution *"emphasizing* the inadmissibility of the acquisition of territory by war" and calling for the "withdrawal of Israeli armed forces from the territories occupied in the recent conflict." [71]

On September 10, 1968, addressing a Jewish audience in the United States, President Johnson stated with reference to the Arab-Israeli conflict that "boundaries cannot and should not reflect the weight of conquest." A few weeks later he repeated the American position that "the political independence and territorial integrity of all the states in the area must be assured." [72]

The election of a new President has not altered the American attitude relative to supporting the "political independence and territorial integrity" of the states of the Middle East. On March 27, 1969, Secretary of State Rogers, speaking before the Senate Foreign Relations Committee, outlined President Nixon's position: "a just and lasting peace will require . . . withdrawal of Israeli armed forces from territories occupied in the Arab-Israeli war of 1967." [73]

The United States' policy stand toward the Israeli annexation of East Jerusalem may be logically derived from the United States' general concern with the matter of territorial integrity of the state of Jordan. Washington has refused to recognize the validity of this annexation move by Israel [74] and has contended that "the measures taken [by Israel] cannot be considered as other than interim and provisional, and not as prejudging the final and permanent status of Jerusalem." [75]

Admittedly, our policy position on this issue has not always been clear cut. Two weeks after former President Johnson's speech of June 19, 1967, the United States refused to support a General Assembly resolution calling upon Israel to refrain from annexing East Jerusalem. [76] In explaining its abstention on the July 4, 1967, resolution on the status of Jerusalem, the United States delegation emphasized its preference for language that "no unilateral action should be taken that might prejudice the future of Jerusalem." The United States would have supported a resolution to that effect, a July 4 press release stated. [77] The resolution which passed

---

69. U.S. Senate, Committee on Foreign Relations, *A Select Chronology and Background Documents Relating to the Middle East* (Washington: Government Printing Office, 1967), p. 135.

70. United States Department of State *Bulletin,* July 10, 1967, p. 33.

71. Security Council resolution 242 (1967). See Section IV.

72. As cited in Lenczowski, *op. cit.,* p. 124.

73. As quoted in a speech delivered by Joseph J. Sisco, Assistant Secretary of State for Near East and South Asian Affairs, before the American Israel Public Affairs Committee at Washington, D.C., April 23, 1969.

74. No other nation has recognized this action by Israel either.

75. From a speech delivered by Ambassador Goldberg on July 14, 1967, before the U.N. General Assembly during its Fifth Emergency Special Session. Doc. A/PV. 1554, dated July 14, 1967, p. 48.

76. The United States abstained. This was resolution 2253 (ES-V), dated July 4, 1967. See section IV.

77. U.S., Department of State Bulletin, July 24, 1967, Vol. LVII, No. 1465, pp. 112, 113.

99-0, with 20 abstentions, singled out Israel for censure on grounds her moves to change the status of Jerusalem were invalid; it called upon Israel to rescind measures already taken and to desist from others planned. Almost two years later it was reported by a newsletter that "on one major and crucial issue, the Administration *appears to accept Israel's position:* Jerusalem should remain a unified city" [78] (emphasis added). Richard Scott, reporting from Washington to *The Guardian* (London), also noted this apparent deviation from United States established policy relative to "territorial integrity of all states." [79] Scott wrote that Jordan would "trade" East Jerusalem for some right of access to the Mediterranean through Israel. The Arab states, however, refused to modify their position calling for the complete withdrawal by Israel to her territorial possessions prior to the June, 1967, war; while Israel, in turn, refused to withdraw from the occupied areas prior to a peace settlement and appeared to consider her "unification" of Jerusalem an accomplished fact, and outside the framework of *any* negotiated peace.[80] Thus the stalemate continued.

On May 29, 1969, the four-power conference reconvened at United Nations headquarters in New York to draft a communiqué on their progress. They adjourned that same day, however, without issuing a communiqué, suggesting that the four-power conference had also reached a stalemate.

An Arab Proposal

On April 10, 1969, in a speech delivered before the National Press Club in Washington, D.C., King Hussein of Jordan outlined the Arab formula for peace in the Middle East.[81] He also stated that he was speaking on behalf of President Nasser of the UAR.

After referring to the Security Council resolution of November 22, 1967, King Hussein said that the Arabs would agree "to terminate the state of belligerency with Israel, to provide her with guaranteed access to Sharm al-Sheik and the Suez Canal, to recognize her right to live in peace and security, and to agree to provisions which would finally solve the refugee problem." The Jordanian king thus indicated that the Arabs would agree to virtually all the demands put forward by the State of Israel before June 5, 1967.

King Hussein further noted that if a peace settlement did not come "within the next very few months" then "no outside force, even with the best of intentions, will be able to divert the area from permanent conflict and eventual war."

Turning to the issue of Jerusalem, King Hussein remarked:

> Moreover, our plan for withdrawal must include our greatest city—our spiritual capital, the holy city of Jerusalem. To us—Christian and Muslim Arab alike—Jerusalem is as sacred as it is to the Jews. And we cannot envision any settlement that does not include the return of the Arab part of the city of Jerusalem to us with all our holy places.

---

78. *Near East Report,* May 14, 1969.
79. *The Guardian,* April 9, 1969.
80. *Ibid.,* May 8, 1969.
81. For the text of this speech see the article covering the king's visit to the United States in the *New York Times,* April 11, 1969.

In return for meeting all the Israeli demands of pre-June, 1967, King Hussein declared:

> Our sole demand upon Israel is the withdrawal of its armed forces from all territories occupied in the June, 1967 war, and the implementation of all the other provisions of the Security Council resolutions.
> The challenge that these principles present is that Israel may have either peace or territory—but she can never have both.

In a joint statement issued at the conclusion of King Hussein's visit to the United States, Washington reaffirmed its support of the territorial integrity of the Hashemite Kingdom of Jordan.[82]

Policy Alternatives

The number of juridical and administrative arrangements that could be applied to the holy city far exceed the limited number of available political options. For the United States, with multifarious interests in the Middle East,[83] which political option to favor is a matter of importance. United States policy toward Jerusalem should, of course, be designed to strengthen American interests in this part of the world. This means American policy on Jerusalem should contribute to general policies of maximizing peace and stability in the Middle East, facilitating peaceful economic growth of this area, and supporting moderate and democratic political elements where they exist. With these general objectives in mind, the following policy alternatives on Jerusalem [84] may be considered:

Alternative 1: Support the Israeli annexation of East Jerusalem. This gain for Israel might facilitate negotiation of Israeli withdrawals from Syria, the West Bank, Sinai, and Sharm El-sheik; and conceivably Israel might be prevailed upon to establish an administration in Jerusalem which would properly respect the shrines of Islam and Christianity. On the other hand, by supporting (or not opposing) annexation, the United States might jeopardize its military, political, and economic interests throughout the Arab world. It would strengthen the Soviet presence in the Arab world by weakening the countervailing influence of the United States in the more moderate Arab regimes. It could seriously undermine the authority of King Hussein of Jordan and encourage extremist trends in the Arab world. It could generate adverse political consequences in Pakistan, Nigeria, Indonesia, and other countries with significant Muslim populations. By defying the nearly unanimous Jerusalem resolution, it would deal a blow to the United Nations; and it would be a repudiation of the United States' position which supports the political independence and territorial integrity of all countries in the Middle East. Of greatest importance, this alternative might weaken, rather than strengthen, the hope for a "just and lasting peace" in this area.

Alternative 2: Support the Israeli annexation of East Jerusalem with some symbolic gesture made to Jordan to allow that Arab state to exercise a form of jurisdiction over the Muslim Holy Places in Jerusalem. To adopt this policy might

---

82. *Ibid.*
83. For a comprehensive analysis of United States interests in the Middle East, see Lenczowski, *op. cit.*
84. For another discussion of alternatives see Evan M. Wilson, "The Internationalization of Jerusalem," *The Middle East Journal,* Winter, 1969, Volume 23, No. 1.

induce the adverse effects to the United States position in the Middle East noted under Alternative 1. The principal advantage to this alternative is that the Muslim community might feel more at ease to have the Holy Places of Islam under Jordanian rather than Israeli control.

Alternative 3: Support the creation of an Arab Palestine from the West Bank and the Gaza Strip, but exclude Jerusalem. Under this plan, the Arabs of Jerusalem could be citizens of the Arab state while the city of Jerusalem would be Israeli. One modification of this plan would be to establish a federal political system for Palestine with Israel and Arab Palestine federal units of the system, with Jerusalem the capital of the combined federal state. Jewish residents of Jerusalem would be Israeli citizens and Arab residents would be citizens of the Arab state. This alternative would reduce Jordan to the territorial scope of pre-1948 Trans-Jordan. It could affect adversely the position of King Hussein of Jordan. Also the Arab state in Palestine might become a virtual client state of Israel. A degree of political cooperation between Arabs and Israelis appears to be implied here which would be inconsistent with the history of their relationships over the past several decades. Finally, the plan would only promote peace and stability in the Middle East if the Arabs could be induced to accept such a plan. Under present conditions, this possibility appears remote. The two advantages of this plan are (a) it would permit a greater degree of regional economic development than would be the case if the Arab sections of Palestine were returned to their pre-June, 1967, condition; and (b) Jerusalem would technically be unified, yet under neither Israeli nor Jordanian sovereignty.

Alternative 4: Support the internationalization of Jerusalem (including both the West and East sectors). This has been the position of the Roman Catholic Church. To support this alternative would generate less hostility within the Arab world than any of the previously mentioned alternatives. It appears difficult to achieve Israeli acceptance of this alternative, however. If such internationalization were made permanent, it would deny the principle of self-determination to the inhabitants of the city. If internationalization were made temporary as under the 1948 U.N. Statute of Jerusalem, it might invite subsequent partition of the city into its respective sectors at some later date. A plan of internationalization would also invite major economic problems, particularly with regard to West Jerusalem. The advantage of such territorial internationalization is that it would extricate, to a limited degree, the holy city from the arena of Arab-Israeli nationalist conflict.

Alternative 5: Support the internationalization of the Holy Places. This alternative is similar to Alternative 2, with the United Nations substituted for Jordan and all the Holy Places substituted for Muslim Holy Places. It would suffer from weaknesses similar to those in Alternative No. 2, primarily because the Arabs would feel resentful at leaving the general area of Jerusalem under Israeli sovereignty. However, this alternative would be preferable even from the Arab point of view to total annexation of Jerusalem by Israel.

Alternative 6: Support the internationalization of the walled city only. Depending upon the position taken by the United States with regard to the rest of Jerusalem, internationalization of only the walled city would probably not be disadvantageous in terms of the United States' general interests in the Middle East. It would bring under international jurisdiction the main Holy Places of the three monotheistic faiths. It would not, however, include the Holy Places that lie outside the walled city. It would still deny the inhabitants of the walled city the right of self-determination. Finally, it would necessitate an involved administrative arrangement with the state (or states) having sovereignty over the surrounding area. The great advantages of this plan are that it would establish a U.N. presence of some size in the holy city and would give assurance to members of all three faiths that access to the Holy Places within the walled city would be guaranteed by the United Nation..

Alternative 7: Support the return of East Jerusalem to Jordanian control. Given the United States' support of the November 22, 1967, resolution, as well as later official statements from Washington, it would appear that this is United States policy in principle. As noted earlier, however, there is sufficient ambiguity in the Washington position regarding Jerusalem to raise doubt as to whether the United States interprets Israeli withdrawal from occupied territories to include East Jerusalem or not. If the United States chose to pursue a policy designed to support the return of East Jerusalem to Jordan it would (1) reaffirm its position that political independence and territorial integrity are principles that are not tailored to fit each situation as a given administration may see fit; (2) strengthen the position of moderate pro-American Arab leaders; (3) strengthen the United States' political and economic position within the Arab world; (4) weaken any Soviet attempt to capitalize on anti-American feelings among Arab masses. Moreover, support of the return of East Jerusalem to Jordanian control would assure the Third World that the United States continues to reject any territorial aggrandizement by the use of force. Finally, such a policy would be compatible with the widespread feeling of the comity of nations as expressed in the several United Nations resolutions regarding Jerusalem.

The difficulties of taking this policy position are that (1) Israel is firmly committed to the retention of East Jerusalem and it would require much pressure (or persuasion) if the United States were to try to induce Israel to return this sector of the holy city to Jordan; (2) adoption of this policy position would generate domestic opposition, particularly among Zionist-influenced groups; (3) the Israelis would expect a guarantee in which they could have faith that they would have access to the Wailing Wall, one far stronger than a United Nations resolution; and (4) in all likelihood, some form of demilitarization of East and West Jerusalem would be necessary to provide a measure of security for the Israeli and Arab inhabitants of the city.

These difficulties, however, are not insurmountable. The principal merit of this alternative would be its conformity with the clearly articulated will of the overwhelming majority of nations, as expressed by the U.N. resolutions of July 4 and November 22, 1967, as well as with the basic American position that the peace settlement must not "reflect the weight of conquest."

The challenge for the United States is to adopt a policy on Jerusalem that would be compatible with the preservation of American interests in the Middle East within the larger context of Afro-Asia and that would prevent the City of Peace from becoming a source of a future war.

Contributors

Samir N. Anabtawi, Associate Professor of Political Science, Vanderbilt University.

M. Cherif Bassiouni, Professor of Law, De Paul University College of Law.

Henry Cattan, Barrister-at-law of the Middle Temple; formerly member of the Palestine Bar and the Palestine Law Council and Delegate of the Palestine Arabs at the United Nations.

Richard A. Falk, Milbank Professor of International Law and Practice, Princeton University.

Nathan Feinberg, Professor Emeritus of International Law and Relations, Hebrew University of Jerusalem.

Eugene M. Fisher, member of the Indiana Bar.

Leo Gross, Professor of International Law and Organization, The Fletcher School of Law and Diplomacy, Tufts University.

Benjamin Halpern, Professor, Department of Near Eastern & Judaic Studies, Brandeis University.

M. Burhan W. Hammad, Deputy Permanent Observer of the League of Arab States to the United Nations; formerly Senior Adviser to the Permanent Mission of the Hashemite Kingdom of Jordan to the United Nations.

Y. Harkabi, Lecturer in International Affairs, Hebrew University of Jerusalem; formerly Brigadier General and Head of the Strategic Research Department of the Ministry of Defense of Israel.

Louis Henkin, Hamilton Fish Professor of International Law and Diplomacy, Columbia University School of Law.

Louise W. Holborn, Professor of Government, Radcliffe Institute.

Thomas T. F. Huang, Deputy Assistant Legal Adviser, The United States Department of State.

Michael C. Hudson, Associate Professor of Political Science and Director of the Middle East Studies Program, The School of Advanced International Studies, The Johns Hopkins University.

D.H.N. Johnson, Professor of International and Air Law, The University of London.

S. SHEPARD JONES, Burton Craige Professor of Political Science, The University of North Carolina.

MAJID KHADDURI, Director of the Center for Middle East Studies and Professor, The School of Advanced International Studies, The Johns Hopkins University.

ELIHU LAUTERPACHT, Q. C., Fellow of Trinity College, Cambridge, and Lecturer in Law in the University of Cambridge.

W. T. MALLISON, JR., Professor of Law, George Washington University.

JOHN NORTON MOORE, Professor of Law and Director of the Graduate Program, The University of Virginia School of Law.

ISSA NAKHLEH, Permanent Representative of the Arab Higher Committee for Palestine in New York and Chairman of the Palestine Arab Delegation.

DON PERETZ, Professor of Political Science and Director of the Southwest Asian and North African Program, State University of New York at Binghamton.

RICHARD H. PFAFF, Associate Professor of Political Science, The University of Colorado.

CARL F. SALANS, Deputy Legal Adviser, United States Department of State.

CHARLES B. SELAK, JR., member of the bar of the District of Columbia.

JULIUS STONE, Challis Professor of International Law and Jurisprudence, The University of Sydney.

GEORGE J. TOMEH, Ambassador Extraordinary and Plenipotentiary, Permanent Representative of the Syrian Arab Republic to the United Nations.

Permissions*

RICHARD A. FALK, "Law, Lawyers, and the Conduct of American Foreign Relations," reprinted with the permission of the author and publisher, The Yale Law Journal Company and Fred B. Rothman & Company, from *The Yale Law Journal*, Vol. 78, 1969, pp. 919-34.

LOUIS HENKIN, "The Law Works: Suez (I)" and "The Law Fails But Is Vindicated: Suez (II)," reprinted with the permission of the author and Frederick A. Praeger, Inc., and the Pall Mall Press, Ltd., from LOUIS HENKIN, HOW NATIONS BEHAVE 186-205 (1968).

NATHAN FEINBERG, "The Recognition of the Jewish People in International Law," reprinted with the permission of the author and publisher from *Jewish Yearbook of International Law*, 1948, pp. 1-26.

W. T. MALLISON, JR., "The Zionist–Israel Juridical Claims to Constitute 'The Jewish People' Nationality Entity and to Confer Membership in It: Appraisal in Public International Law," reprinted with the permission of the author and publisher from *The George Washington Law Review*, Vol. 32, 1964, 983-1075.

BEN HALPERN, "The Anti-Zionist Phobia: Legal Style," reprinted with the permission of the author and publisher from *Midstream*, Vol. II, No. 2, 1965, pp. 74-85.

HENRY CATTAN, "Sovereignty over Palestine," reprinted with the permission of the author and publisher, The Longman Group Limited, from HENRY CATTAN, PALESTINE, THE ARABS & ISRAEL 242-75, Appendix XI (1969).

NATHAN FEINBERG, "The Question of Sovereignty over Palestine," reprinted with the permission of the author and publisher from NATHAN FEINBERG, ON AN ARAB JURIST'S APPROACH TO ZIONISM AND THE STATE OF ISRAEL 7-34 (1971).

SEMINAR OF ARAB JURISTS ON PALESTINE, ALGIERS, JULY 22-27, 1967, "The Palestine Question," reprinted with the permission of the publisher and the translator, Edward Rizk, from Monograph #18, The Institute for Palestine Studies, 1968, pp. 15-136, 183-96.

NATHAN FEINBERG, "The Arab-Israel Conflict in International Law," reprinted with the permission of the author and publisher from NATHAN FEINBERG, THE ARAB-ISRAEL CONFLICT IN INTERNATIONAL LAW 7-84, 96-120 (1970).

* Permissions are listed to correspond to the sequence of the materials included in this volume.

MICHAEL HUDSON, "The Palestinian Arab Resistance Movement: Its Significance in the Middle East Crisis," reprinted with the permission of the author and publisher from *The Middle East Journal*, Vol. 23, 1969, pp. 291-307.

SAMIR N. ANABTAWI, "The Palestinians as a Political Entity," reprinted with the permission of the author and publisher from HERBERT MASON (ED.), REFLECTIONS ON THE MIDDLE EAST CRISIS (1970). Copyright Mounton & Co., The Hague, Netherlands. The article is also reprinted in *The Muslim World*, Vol. 60, No. 1, 1970, pp. 47-58.

Y. HARKABI, "The Position of the Palestinians in the Israeli-Arab Conflict and Their National Covenant (1968)," reprinted with the permission of the author and publisher from *New York University Journal of International Law & Politics*, Vol. 3, 1970, pp. 209-44.

DON PERETZ, "Arab Palestine: Phoenix or Phantom?," reprinted with the permission of the author and publisher from *Foreign Affairs*, Vol. 48, 1970, pp. 322-33. Copyright by the Council on Foreign Relations, Inc., New York, New York.

ISSA NAKHLEH, "The Liberation of Palestine Is Supported by International Law and Justice," reprinted with the permission of the author and publisher from ISA NAKHLEH, THE LIBERATION OF PALESTINE IS SUPPORTED BY INTERNATIONAL LAW AND JUSTICE (pamphlet published by the Palestine Arab Delegation, 2nd edn., March 1969) 3-17.

JULIUS STONE, "Peace and the Palestinians," reprinted with the permission of the author and publisher from *New York University Journal of International Law & Politics*, Vol. 3, 1970, pp. 247-62. (A longer but less documented account is Julius Stone, "Self-Determination and the Palestinian Arabs," *The Bridge*, Dec. 1970, pp. 3-14.)

M. CHERIF BASSIOUNI AND EUGENE M. FISHER, "The Arab-Israeli Conflict—Real and Apparent Issues: An Insight into Its Future from the Lessons of the Past," reprinted with the permission of the authors and publisher from *St. John's Law Review*, Vol. 44, 1970, pp. 399-465.

LOUISE W. HOLBORN, "The Palestine Arab Refugee Problem," reprinted with the permission of the author and publisher from *International Journal*, Vol. 23, 1968, pp. 82-96.

GEORGE J. TOMEH, "Legal Status of Arab Refugees," reprinted with the permission of the author and publisher from *Law and Contemporary Problems*, Vol. 33, 1968, pp. 110-24.

CHARLES B. SELAK, JR., "A Consideration of the Legal Status of the Gulf of Aqaba," reprinted with the permission of the author and publisher from *The American Journal of International Law*, Vol. 52, 1958, pp. 660-98.

M. BURHAN W. HAMMAD, "The Right of Passage in the Gulf of Aqaba," reprinted with the permission of the author and publisher from *Revue Egyptienne De Droit International*, Vol. 15, 1959, pp. 118-51.

LEO GROSS, "The Geneva Conference on the Law of the Sea and the Right of Innocent Passage Through the Gulf of Aqaba," reprinted with the permission of the author and publisher from *The American Journal of International Law*, Vol. 53, 1959, pp. 564-94.

CARL F. SALANS, "Gulf of Aqaba and Strait of Tiran: Troubled Waters," reprinted with the permission of the author and publisher from UNITED STATES NAVAL INSTITUTE PROCEEDINGS, Vol. 94, No. 12, Dec. 1968, pp. 54-62. Copyright © 1968 by the United States Naval Institute.

D.H.N. JOHNSON, "Some Legal Problems of International Waterways, with Particular Reference to the Straits of Tiran and the Suez Canal," reprinted with the permission of the author and publisher from *The Modern Law Review*, Vol. 31, 1968, pp. 153-64.

THOMAS T. F. HUANG, "Some International and Legal Aspects of the Suez Canal Question," reprinted with the permission of the author and publisher from *The American Journal of International Law*, Vol. 51, 1957, pp. 277-307.

LEO GROSS, "Passage Through the Suez Canal of Israel-Bound Cargo and Israel Ships," reprinted with the permission of the author and publisher from *The American Journal of International Law*, Vol. 51, 1957, pp. 530-68.

MAJID KHADDURI, "Closure of the Suez Canal to Israeli Shipping," reprinted with the permission of the author and publisher from *Law and Contemporary Problems*, Vol. 33, 1968, pp. 147-57.

S. SHEPARD JONES, "The Status of Jerusalem: Some National and International Aspects," reprinted with the permission of the author and publisher from *Law and Contemporary Problems*, Vol. 33, 1968, pp. 169-82.

ELIHU LAUTERPACHT, "Jerusalem and the Holy Places," reprinted with the permission of the author and publisher from Anglo-Israel Association Pamphlet #19, 1968, pp. 5-85.

RICHARD H. PFAFF, "Jerusalem: Keystone of an Arab-Israeli Settlement," reprinted with the permission of the author and publisher from Analysis #13, American Enterprise Institute for Public Policy Research, 1969, pp. 1-54.